龍谷大学アジア仏教文化研究叢書4

編集復刻版

資料集・戦時下「日本仏教」の国際交流

第Ⅲ期　中国仏教との提携

第6巻

編者　龍谷大学アジア仏教文化研究センター
「戦時下「日本仏教」の国際交流」研究班(G1・UB・S2)
中西直樹(代表)・林行夫・吉永進一・大澤広嗣

不二出版

〈復刻にあたって〉

一、巻数は第Ⅱ期からの継続になります。
一、原本を適宜縮小し、2面付けで収録しました。
一、原本の状態により判読困難な箇所があります。
一、資料の中に、人権の視点から見て不適切な語句・表現・論、現在から見て明らかな学問上の誤りがある場合でも、歴史的資料の復刻という性質上、そのまま収録しました。

（不二出版）

〈第6巻　収録内容〉

『国際仏教通報』（国際仏教通報局　発行）

昭和十年三月二十五日印刷納本　昭和十年四月一日發行（毎月一回一日發行）

The International Buddhist Bulletin

國際佛教通報

第一卷 **昭和十年四月** 第一號 〔Vol. 1. April $\frac{2501}{1935}$ No. 1.〕

要　目〔**Contents**〕

東　京　**國際佛教通報局**　發　行

The International Buddhist Information Bureau

Tokyo, Kanda, Hitotsubashi, II–3

Annual Subscription, ¥2,40 (post free), Single Copies 20 sen (post 2 sen)

創　刊　辭

局長　大村桂巖

吾人將釋迦牟尼教活躍於體驗之上，是卽修行菩薩道也，菩薩道者一面爲自修爲向上，一面爲同化爲救濟，前者如釋尊之入山學道，後者如其出山教化是也。

然向上修行不能蔑視緣起同化之力，又敎化救濟若不由夫本有佛性，亦屬無望，故佛之敎，菩薩之道是社會的，靈性的，是謂之大乘也。

大乘佛敎於國家生活上，重要固不待言，卽於國際生活上亦屬必須不可缺，而爲人生之燈明臺也，現於東方大日本帝國正最能發輝其本領焉。

今我全日本佛敎青年會聯盟應於時勢之要求與靈機之興運，對此菩薩道之國際的弘通，願竭微力而其使命，茲故創設國際佛敎通報局，卽於本四月創刊「國際佛敎通報」第一號，以與世界大方之青年佛敎徒，共同努力於此佛敎大精神之普及，而期促進大乘菩薩道之實踐也。

今也世界，不問洋之東西，均失平靜，人心不安，彷徨於世相溷迷之境皆不知其所歸趣，而徒待望夫偉人救世現而已。

當此之時，吾人佛敎青年，奉奉大聖釋尊之遺訓，體驗大乘佛敎之眞精神不只限於汎太平洋，而廣與世界之青年佛徒相提携，使敎祖偉大之人格，復活於現代，世界和平之光明，益增其輝耀，群沾幸福，曷勝企禱。

於此意味言之，是「國際佛敎通報」之誕生，又不啻等於釋尊之新降誕也，將見吾此通報，永爲天下諸國之法經，世界人類之法幢，佛日冥鑑，歲益增榮，滿腔悅豫，祝禱無已焉。

The Inaugural Address

By Keigwan Ohmura

— President of Bureau —

We have two schools of Buddhism, Hīnayāna and Mahāyāna. Hīna means little and Mahā means great. Mahāyānist gave themselves the name of Mahāyāna, the great vehicle, because they taught that through their doctrine of Bodhisattvaship a greater number of disciples could be carried to the goal of Nirvana than could the small vehicle of the Southern school with its narrower conception of Arhatship or salvation for the few. Mahāyāna represents the spirit of the Buddha and a living religion to many men. In other words, salvation or enlightenment of Mahāyāna is for all. All may become Bodhisattvas and ultimately attain Buddhahood and Nirvana. It is more social than the Hīnayāna. I believe that Mahāyāna teaching, therefore, is being better appreciated not only by our countrymen but by foreigners as well, being an international religion.

The present world is a world of strife, which manifests itself in the form of international wars, racial feuds and class struggles. Besides such an open strife there are conflicts and clashes of interests between classes of the same community and even among members of the same family. Such a feverish strife, which is going on all over the world, will certainly hasten mankind toward destruction. In addition to social unrest, there have been natural calamities, which have destroyed portions of the world, in the form of earthquakes, floods, droughts and typhoons.

The world to-day stands in urgent need for some means of salvation, and think only Mahāyāna Buddhism, which is more social and international, can save the world, in cooperation with other religions.

The creation of the International Buddlist Information Bureau was the outcome of our earnest desire in doing our bit for such a purpose, and we may be allowed to regard it as the final expression of Mahāyāna ideals, symbolising the new appearance of Shakyamuni Buddha.

佛教の國際化

大谷瑩潤

一，非常時日本と佛教復興

滿洲事變を契機と致しまして，又所謂一九三五年三六年の危機をひかへまして，我國は今や上下を通じて，又國の內外を通じまして，文字通りに「非常時日本」となつて參つてゐるのであります。

そして此の「非常時日本」の認識が次第に深まりますに從ひまして，我日本の歷史の回顧となり，かの「大和魂」の新しい立場からの硏究も盛んになつて參りました。

卽ち所謂「日本精神」の硏究が其れでありますが，この日本精神の硏究によりまして，玆に又新しく，日本文化を根本から養ひ育てゝ參りました所の「日本佛教」なるものゝ眞價が，本當の値打が，ハツキリと認識されるようになつて參つたのでありまして，この事は誠に喜ばしい傾向であると申さねばなりません。

明治維新には日本精神の發揚をはきちがへた，一部の政治家があつたようでして，そのために「廢佛毀釋」などと云ふような事も起りましたが，それは結局，徹底するものではありませんでした。むしろ德川佛教に反省を與へて，新しい明治時代の佛教の革正となつたやうな次第でありました。

然るに，今日の非常時に於きましては，日本精神が高調されるに從つて，却つて日本文化の一大中樞をなして參つた所の日本佛教に對しまして，新しい認識が加へられてゐます事は，これ正に時代の進化とは申せ，まことに喜ばしい，又正しい文化の認識の仕方であると申すことが出來ませう。

我國の文化はあらゆる世界各國の粹をあつめ，之を綜合し，融和せしめて，本當に人類社會に貢献し得る文化でありまして，その點から申しましても，日本佛教は所謂大乘佛教の深く深く根を張りましたものであります。

既に千三，四百年にもなる歷史を持つてゐます所の我日本佛教は，恐れ多くも，

攝政であらせられた聖德太子によりまして，

かの十七條憲法に取り入れられました。

卽ち「篤く三寶を敬へ」と申されて居りますが，此の佛教精神が，どれほど日本歷史の上に强く働きかけて參つたかと云ふ事は，私が多く申上げる迄も無く，旣に皆樣の良く御承知の事と存ずる次第であります。

然るに此の日本佛教が此の度びの非常時に際しまして，日本文化の再檢討の上から正しい評價を與へられ，進んでは「佛教復興」と云ふような事が盛んに新聞雜誌の上にまで論ぜられますようになつたのであります。

嘗つて鎌倉時代には，日本は非常な非常時に際會いたしましたのでありますが，そうした時代を背景と致しまして，却つて幾多の新佛教がさかへました事實に照してみましても，此度びの非常時も，或は却つて之が良き機會となりまして，本當に佛教が復興するのではないかと存ずる次第であります。

二，汎太平洋佛教靑年大會に就て

ところが先頃，昨年七月の十八日から二十一日にかけて四日間東京での大會があり，次で關西の方でも大會がありました所の第二回汎太平洋佛教靑年大會なるものが開催いたされまして，太平洋沿岸の十三ばかりの民族が一堂に會しまして，

佛陀の御名の下に，現代の色々な問題に就きまして，大乘佛教の立場から御互に胸襟を開きまして，論じ合つたのであります。

そのニュースは，當時の各新聞紙にも大々的に報導されました所でありまして，皆樣も定めし御覽になつた事と存じます。

この大會の議題には，印度の聖地ブツダガヤが異教徒の手にあるから之れを佛教徒の手に回復いたすがよろしいと云ふやうなセンセイショナルな議題も御座いましたが，

第四部會などでは，國際平和とか人種平等とか云ふ重要な議題が眞面目に討論されましたやうで，總會でも其決議を致したような次第でありました。

佛教は由來，徹底的な平和主義を取つて參りましたものでありまして，釋尊も色々と理想的な政治を敎へられてゐます。卽ち侵略主義ではなくて，統治主義を敎へてゐられます。日本の古代語で申せば「うしはく」のではなくて「しらす」のであります。

從ひまして，佛教は，單に死後の問題のみを取扱つて參つたのではありません。人類文化に就て，あらゆる方面の指導をなして參つたのであります。佛教は單なる一民族，一國家の宗敎たる事に止まらないで普遍的世界的な擴がりを持つことを本質として參つたものであります。

又只今申しましたやうに，その敎理から申しましても各民族の共存共榮する世界的統一國家をさへ理想として描いて參つたのであります。その事は少し佛教の經典を注意して御覽になつた方には既に御承知の事と存ずる次第でありますが，そうした國際主義と申しますか，或は世界主義と申しますか，とにかく普遍的な世界宗敎としての佛敎でありますからして，此度びの汎太平洋佛靑大會も，その意義が充分に發揚されたものと申さねばなりません。

三，西洋の沒落と光は東方より

最近に至りまして，ヨーロツパの哲學者や思想家たちの間に，盛んに「西

洋の沒落」と云ふ事が叫ばれて參りました。哲學萬能，物質偏重を土臺と致しました所の西洋文明は，かの世界大戰を一期と致しまして，まことに哀れむべき殘骸となつてしまつたのであります。そこで彼等は今日，異口同音に

「光は東方より！」

と叫びつゝあるのであります。

その結果と致しまして單に植民政策の立場からだけしか，研究されてゐませんでした所の東洋研究と云ふ事が急に盛んになつて參りました。

實は私自身も，先年，歐米に見學旅行をいたしましたのですが，各國各地の大學などにそれぞれ「東洋學」だとか，また「佛教學」だとかの講座や研究室などが出來て參つて居りますのに却つて一驚を喫した程でありました。今日，それ程に，歐米では，盛んに東洋の研究，佛教の研究を初めて參つて居るのでありまして，多くは單に學問的に研究してゐるのですが，中には佛教を信ずるやうな人も出て參りました。而も此の佛教信仰の傾向は次第々々に深まりつゝあるやうであります。歐米人で日本の佛教の得度を受けて僧侶となるような人もボツボツ現れて參りましたのも，その生きた證據かと思はれるのであります。

從つて此の傾向で參りますと，日本にキリスト教が廣まりました樣に，今度は逆に日本佛教が歐米人の間に，加速度的に廣まつて行くのではないかと思はれるのであります。

そして本當に「光は東方より」と云ふ時代が參りますのも，或は決して遠い將來でもなく，また決して夢物語でもないやうに思はれます。

四，東洋平和と佛教

以上，佛教の國際化と云ふことを，歐米に就て申しましたが，特に東洋諸國に於きましては，此の佛教の國際化は，一層重大な意義を持つものと考へられるのであります。申すまでもなく佛教は二千五百年以前に印度に御生れになつた釋尊によつて，初めて說かれましたものでありますが，その佛陀の御教へは，一方は南方に傳はりまして，今の「セイロン」や「ジヤヴア」方面に參りました。また一方では西域卽ち中央アジアへ傳はり，また西藏や支那へ傳はり，支那から日本へと傳來いたしました。從つて佛教の二千五百年の歷史は，それ自體既に東洋諸國に於ける佛教の國際化として現れて參つてゐるのであります。

然るに佛教の發祥地であります所の印度に於きましては，後に至りまして，異教徒の勃興によりまして佛教は甚だしく振はないものとなつてしまひました。支那に於きましても嘗つては輝しい佛教文化の花が咲いたのでありますが，今日では之れ又餘り振はない存在となつてゐるのであります。

然るに何んと申しましても，今日，佛教が未だ生きて力強く働いてゐますのは，我國日本であります。

これは大きな存在であります。かつて聖德太子樣が申されましたように我

日本こそは，まことに「大乘相應ノ地」なのであります。卽ち大乘佛教の信奉せらるゝに相應した土地であります。相應して居りますから，さかへたのであります。そして日本文化の中樞ともなつたのであります。

この佛教が，今日の世界に於きまして，日本でだけは本當に生きて働いてゐると云ふので，此頃ではボツボツ歐米人の之が研究のために留學して參るものが現れたのであります。

今や更にアジアの諸國からも日本へ佛教の研究に參る人が現れて參りました。そして生きた日本佛教を今度は佛教發祥の地たる印度の方へと支那をも通過して逆輸入，逆傳來さして下さいと申して來て居るやうな人もあるのであります。

かうした狀勢でありますから吾々日本の佛教徒は，此際一大決心と覺悟とを要するものがあると存じます。

我國は東洋平和の重鎭でなければなりません。しかし其は決して物質的な眼に見える方面のことだけではありません。眼に見えない心の奧底から卽ち精神的な方面からも，亞細亞の防衛を致さねばなりません。

それには佛陀の御名の下に堅い堅い精神上の握手を致す事が，何より強い防衛ではないかと存ずる次第であります。

かう考へて參りますと，日本佛教徒の使命は，まことに重且つ大なるものゝ存することを痛感せずにはゐられません。

既成佛教の各宗一同も新興佛教の指導者各位も僧も俗も佛教徒と稱せらる全部が打つて一丸となり世界人類精神文化に佛陀の御教により貢献するの覺悟が尤も必要であると存じます。

佛教女青聯盟結成さる

都下十七の多數に上る佛教女子青年會の大同團結を圖らんとする聯盟の結成式は，去る三月十七日午後一時より日本橋の白木屋大ホールで盛大に擧行された。須田智嘉子，大野靜枝兩氏司會のもとに，式は國歌齊唱に始まり，武藏野女子學院の聖歌隊による讃佛歌の合唱，柴田一能氏導師のもとに，會衆一同三歸依文齊唱，坂東信子，川崎靜子兩氏から結成の辭並に經過報告があつて左の如く新役員の紹介及び委員長大谷喬子氏の挨拶の後，菊澤宗教局長，服部佛聯主事，大村全聯委員長，泉女學校聯盟代表，吉岡聯合婦人會委員長，及び山田白木屋專務の祝辭があり，最後に佛教青年會歌齊歌によつて式を閉ぢた。

次で第二部に移り，高楠博士による「社會は女性に何を求むるか」の講演があり，餘興として琵琶，朋德舞踊會による童謠舞踊，佛教音樂協會の花まつり踊りが賑かに行はれ，盛會裡に五時半散會した。

因に役員は次の如くである――

◁委員長　大谷　喬子
◁副委員長　後藤　要子　藤井　愛子　川崎　靜子
◁會　計　坂東　信子　伊藤　房江
◁主　事　須田智嘉子
◁評議員　高楠　霜子　岡本かの子　岡部　哲江　松平　俊子　小野せつ子　宇野　さえ　今村靜枝　三重野智々子　山中十寸美　岩山　里子　小岩井みき　富永　久良　岩野喜久代　春日　政子

尙ほ參加團體は次の如くである。

大谷婦人會，眞宗婦人會，淺草寺婦人會，增上寺女子佛青，婦人共生會，濟世軍婦人會，佛教婦人青年會，九段女子佛青，東京佛青，佛教女子青年會，離思寮佛青，マハヤナ女子佛青，音羽洋裁佛青，立正學園女子佛青，千代田女專女子佛青，日出高女女子佛青，城西女子佛青。

汎聯の結成と今後

鷹　谷　俊　之

昭和九年七月十八日から，東京及京都で開催された第二回汎太平洋佛教青年會大會は，天地人三才の完全な祐助によつて豫期以上の成績を擧げ，佛教復興の叫ばるゝ時，異常の反響を與へつゝ大會を閉づることが出來たのは，直接これらの事業に關係を續け來つた一人として，無上の悦びであると同時に，これを外部から助力し聲援された吾等の先輩，師友の方々並に冥々の加護を垂れ給ひし，佛陀の加被力に心からなる感謝を捧げる。

東京の大會期間は，開會式を含む四日間であつたが，その間決議された重要問題中の最たるものは，太平洋沿岸諸國に於ける各國佛教青年會聯盟が打つて一丸となり，佛陀の名に於て堅固なる大同團結を計つたことである。これは寔に佛教史上の最初のことであると云つても過言ではない。これを吾等は『汎太平洋佛教青年會聯盟』と名稱し，常恒的機關として將來益々佛教青年の諸運動を堅固ならしめん事を盟つたのである。この大會では總會に於て，これが結成の爲めその法規を制定せんとして，二十九名からなる小委員會を編成し，時間の許す限り愼重審議を重ねたのである。計らずも予はその委員長に押されて，その席にあつたのであるが，印度，セイロン，シヤムあたりの代表からは「汎太平洋の名稱を「世界」と改むべき提案があつたけれども，「汎太平洋」の名は一種の歴史的起源より流出して居る點と，この聯盟の漸進的發達を希求する點とよりして，原案を支持し，印度，セイロン，シヤム等太平洋に面せざる地理的條件は，これ等の諸國民が素と佛陀發祥の故地の人々なるを考へ合せれば，當然この聯盟に卒先加入さるべきものである點とを力說し，將來發展の曉は「汎太平洋」の句を「世界」と改むべき事を前提として滿場一致で可決し，更に汎太平洋佛教青年會聯盟を本大會の名に於て結成すべしとの熾烈な希望をも加へて，この小委員會を閉ぢたのである。

元來この汎太平洋佛教青年會聯盟（以下略して汎聯と呼ぶ）は，一九三〇年即ち昭和五年に第一回汎太平洋佛青大會が，ホノルルで開かれた時，日米布の三國から異口同音に設立を提唱され，特に地元のハワイ佛青では故青木秀作君が種々の研究を積んで具體案まで作成したものであるが，遺憾ながら直ちに之を實行に移すことは時機尚早なりとして，夫々委員を委囑し更に一層の研究を重ねることゝしたのである。就中委員中の主任を米の寺川湛濟氏，布の安井美然氏，日本の鷹谷俊之

等を指名して，これが實行促進に當ることを申合せたことであつた。爾來年月を送ること四年，その間青木秀作君の突然の訃報にも遭ひ，越へて今回の東京及び京都に於ける第二回の大會を迎へることゝなつたのである。この度は第一回の大會に於ける參加國五ケ國の少數なりしに比し，十三ケ國より參加者を得，正式代表六百名の多數に上つたので，文字通りに汎太平洋佛青大會の名に相應しき大會であつた。この機會に，是非とも宿年の希望を達し，一つは過去四年間の責任を果し，一つは東洋諸民族間に於ける佛青の堅固なる運動の基礎を得たいと希ふたのである。幸に滿場拍手の下に汎聯を結成することが出來，次の如き法規を以て之を運用することになつた。

汎太平洋佛教青年會聯盟法規

第一條　名稱　本團體を汎太平洋佛教青年會聯盟（略稱汎聯）と稱す。

第二條　本部　本聯盟の本部を日本東京に置く。

第三條　組織單位　本聯盟は太平洋沿岸諸國及その隣接國，並に世界各國の佛教青年會聯盟を以て組織す。

第四條　目的　本聯盟は各佛教青年團體相互間の連絡及提携を保ち，佛教精神發揚の爲に統一ある協力をなすを以て目的とす。

第五條　部門　本聯盟は前記の目的を達成せんが爲に左の部門を設く。

一，出版部，機關紙の發行。

第六條　役員　本聯盟に左の役員を置く。

A，名譽委員（顧問）

B，中央委員

C，實行委員（財政委員を含む）

D，中央事務局員

第七條　役員の任務

一，名譽委員は本聯盟の顧問たるべし。

二，中央委員會は實行委員會を支配し，これに實務を委任す。

三，實行委員會は本聯盟の事務遂行を管理し指導す。

四，財務員は本聯盟の會計事務一切を處理す。

五，中央事務局員は實行委員會指導管理のもとに本聯盟一切の事務を處理す。

第八條　役員の選擧及任期

第一項　役員の選擧

一，名譽委員は加入聯盟より若干名を以て組織す。

二，中央委員會は各加入聯盟より二名，日本より若干名を選出せる者を以て組織す。

三，實行委員會は中央委員會により て選出されたるものを以て組織す。

四，實行委員會は中央事務局員を必要に應じて任命す。

第二項　役員の任期

本聯盟の役員の任期は四ケ年とす但し實行委員及中央事務局員の任期は中央委員會によりて決定さるるものとす。

第三項

本聯盟の中央委員は聯盟の總會に

於て選定す。

第九條　會合

一，本聯盟は四年に一度大會を開き，その開催地は前回の大會に於て決定さるるものとす。

二，實行委員會，役員會は必要に應じ適當の場所にて開催することを得。

第十條　會計

本聯盟の經費は左の財源より之をもとむ。

一，會費（中央委員會にて決定す）

二，寄附

三，其の他（出版物等）

第十一條　加入及脱退

一，本聯盟に加入せんとする青年會聯盟は實行委員會に申込み，中央委員會の承認を經て正式加入するものとす。

二，本聯盟を脱退せんとする青年會も亦同樣の手續を經るものとす。

第十二條　本聯盟の規約は中央委員會の承認を經ざれば修正することを得ず。

以上

汎聯法規は以上の通り制定を見たけれ共この法規の實行運用に至つては役員全部の顏が出揃ふた後でなければ可能でない。依つて本大會直後これが運用を實施する爲めに，汎聯の役員は當分の內日本全聯の理事に委囑し，本法規に於ける多少の字句の修正と，以下に示す細則の實行とを總會はこれに全托したのである。

法規に關する細則

一．雜誌出版

A，本聯盟はその目的を遂行する爲年二回以上“Young Buddhists”と稱する機關誌を發行す。

B，實行委員會はその編輯に當る。

C，用語は日英華語の範圍とす。

二．經費の支出

A，本聯盟の經常費を左の割當による年額費にもとむ。

日　本　千六百五十圓
布　哇　四百圓
北　米　二百五十圓
その他　各國より百圓宛

B，經常費の豫算は實行委員會に於て之を立て，中央委員會の承認をうくべし。

C，經常費豫算

一，	事務所費	六〇〇，〇〇
二，	事務主任給	六〇〇，〇〇
三，	交通通信費	二〇〇，〇〇
四，	出版費	一，一六〇，〇〇
	合計	二，五六〇，〇〇

大會閉會後夫々本國に戻つた各代表は自國の佛靑聯盟から名譽委員，並に中央委員を選出し，一ケ月以內に文書によつて全聯へ通達し，その顏が出揃つた後，愈よ本格的な汎聯が出來上り，從來の通り四年目每に汎太佛靑大會を開いて，之を總會とする次第で，この總會開催の費用一切は，その開催地の佛靑聯盟が負擔することは，前例を襲ふ譯であつて，汎聯がこの各四年間を連絡提携して，統一ある運動たらしめることになるのである。

佛靑運動は形態の上では，兎に角こゝまでは育てられて來た。これからは實質の問題である。故青木秀作君立案の原案も相當生かされて居ることであり，私としても公私に亙る責任の一斑を果し得たことを深く喜んで居る次第である。

さてこゝまで國際佛靑の形態が整へられるには，約十年の歲月が流れて居る。昭和三年頃に始まつた**青年佛敎協會**がこの運動の源である。その頃の同人には淺野孝之，今成覺法，鹽入亮忠，常光浩然，長谷川良信其他の諸君があつた。この協會が結成されて間もなく私は歐米の旅行を終へて歸來し直ちにこれに投じたのであるが，その後間もなく常光浩然君が渡米し，ハワイ，アメリカの佛靑の諸君と談り合ひ，同時にＹＭＣＡを硏究して居る間に，日米布の佛靑が一團となつて大會を起さうとする意志が動きかけて來た。この芽生へをよく背後から育て助力と聲援とを惜まなかつたのは，ハワイ開敎監督の故今村惠猛師であつた。斯くの如き事情から遂に彼の昭和五年七月二十一日から六日間に亙つて，ホノルルのハワイ佛敎靑年會館で開かれたのが第一回汎太平洋佛敎靑年大會であつた。この時の參加國は日・米・布・鮮及び印度（ホノルル在住代表出席）の五ケ國で，出席代表者百八十五名であつた。國際會議に不慣れな靑年佛敎徒の集りとしては，豫期に反する大きな收獲があつた。當時出席した日本代表は三十六名の多數を算へたが，その頃日本には未だ佛敎靑年會の聯盟が結成されて居なかつたので何等の統制機關がなかつたのでその代表選出の母體團體は個々の佛敎靑年會であつた。この事はいたく日本代表をして面目なからしめたのであつた。これに刺戟されて翌年昭和六年四月三日，遂に日本全國を一丸とした全日本佛敎靑年會聯盟の結成が成り高楠順次郎博士を理事長とする大同團結が出來上つたのである。この前後に亙つて最も熱意を以て之の事業に當つたのは主事常光浩然君であつた。

この全聯の結成によつて，日本全體が統一され曲りなりにも天下を率ゐて諸の事業を押し進めて來たが，今回の第二回汎太平洋佛敎靑年大會は，全くこの全聯活動の結晶であつた。

かくの如く全聯の基礎の上に，今や汎聯をも結成し，汎太平洋佛靑の團結が强くなるにつれ，佛敎日本の責任は愈よ重大を加へ來つた。第一に全聯は國內佛靑の統一と指導とに一段の努力をなさねばならぬ。さしあたり佛靑の組織，佛靑の指標，佛靑會館の建設等は急務中の急務である。第二には汎聯の指導である。各國の佛敎事情はその國情の上から各別であるけれ共，佛敎民族と云ふ點からは一致團結すべき性質のものである。こゝに於てか佛敎そのものゝ見直しも必要である。引いては佛敎の新見地に立つ敎育的基礎を確立し，幼少年及び靑年に向つて行動すべき佛敎敎育の必要に逼られて來た。世に宗敎敎育が提唱されてから久しいものである。不幸にしてその意見たるや理論に流れて實際を閑却して居る。佛敎靑年會が內にも外にも働きかくべき行動的敎育の活動に向つて進まんことを希望して止まない。

Some of the Japanese Annual Festivals

by Prof. H. Hamada (Tokyo)

If I say festival, then you will recall at once your joyous Christmas. But we Japanese have no Christmas as a folk festival, except that a small number of them celebrate the holy evening in the Christian Church in the big towns after the European fashion, and some of the merchants in the great cities stand a decorated Christmas tree in their shops to make the customers happy. But a few days after Christmas Eve comes one of the greatest festivals of the Japanese people. It is the New Year. They very much enjoy those three days at least or seven days usually at the beginning of the year without work. The date of the New Year is the same as yours because we generally and legally use the calender of the sun. In those days you can see in all Japanese towns and villages green pinetrees and bamboos standing one on each side of gate after gate and Japanese national flag beside them. You know what it is like: a red sun upon a white background. Inside the door, too the house is enriched by green leaves or several trifles of good omen. The grounds around the house are all cleaned. Not only the house and grounds, but men of all ages are dressed up. At such times they expect many visitors, relations and friends with Year presents, and they entertain them with spiced saké, a kind of Japanese wine, and several Japanese dishes of good omen. The visitors become good humoured after drinking the spiced saké, and they sing songs of happy fortunes. If they cannot visit personally because of the distance, they have to send cards to their relations, friends and acquaintances. This is the same as your habit, isn't it? For instance, I send every year nearly two hundred cards of greetings for a happy New Year, first to my mother and father, and the father and mother of my wife, secondly to my relations, patrons, superiors at the University, friends and acquaintances, who are outside the City of Tokyo, where I live. On the 1st of January I make a visit with name-cards to nearly ten of my patrons and professors. But I do not ask

them to see me; I only put my name-card on a tray which ready at their porch to receive many such cards. I do not go into their homes and drink saké and sing songs. No! I come back to my home and have a most delicious supper with my family. My wife is in the habit of receiving many visitors and entertaining some of them. On this day my daughters go to school to celebrate the national ceremony of the New Year, because our Emperor worships his ancestor gods in the East, the West, the South and the North in a chapel of his palace at this time. This is one of the most important of the three national ceremonies, together with the Emperor's birthday on the 29th of April, and the Anniversary of the Coronation-day of our first Emperor Jimmu on the 11th of February in the year 660 before Christ. Well then, my daughters, after coming back home from the school ceremony, play happily at shuttlecock and battledore on the play-ground in my garden, sometimes with their mother. You can see here the genuine Japanese shuttlecock and battledore, Hago-ita in Japanese, which I have borrowed from Margarett, a sister of my friend, Mr. Byatt, in Hampton. Boys on these days mostly like to play with Japanese kite in the open air. At night they gather at home and play several kinds of card games; among them they play one, above all, with picturesque song-cards, which consists of 100 cards, each of them having written on it one old Japanese poem. Boys and girls try to take a card as soon as the poem on it is sung by a singer. The skilful boy or girl takes it away when the first syllable of the poem is announced. They are also fond of playing with dice on picturesque painted paper, on which they have to make way by chance through the different posts to advance to the goal. Unlucky boy or girl has to come back again even to the starting point, while the lucky one can go forward by many steps. It is said to be like the English Ludo. Now, the winner can get a sweet Japanese cake from his mother. I am sorry that I cannot let you taste it here although it is very nice, nicer than English, really.

I will tell you about one more Japanese festival called the Feast of Lanterns by the Europeans, who visit Japan for the first time. It is also called the Mid-July fair because it is held on the 15th of July every year. Actually it is called "Bon" and is the day of the Buddhist service for the dead. You know, we Japanese think very much of our ancestors and relations even after their death. Our affection cannot bear to think that they are exinguished like a burntout candle. We all like to imagine the spiritual being of the doad, who live in the happy land or wander about not yet enlightened somewhere for from here. We want to feed them if they are hungry in their wanderings. Japanese folk are in the habit of inviting all of them once a year. This is the so-called Bon, the day of the dead, in the middle of July every year, and Japanese folk expect that the dead will come home again when it is dark in the evening. This is why they light a lantern at the entrance of each house in order to show the deceased the way in. They welcome the dead anncestors and relations on the 13th of July and see them off usually on the 16th. In my birth place in middle Japan one welcomes the deceased with a torch on the seashore on that evening and sees them off in the same way. The spiritual ancestors and relations stay thus 3 days in their native home. During those days they are entertained with all kinds of human meals in a definite chapel prepaired for them temporarily. Not only are they fed but also they seem to be worshipped by the members of the said family. And the priest from the Temple pray to the Holy in Buddhism that they may be said righteous and enlightened to enter the Nirvana land; i.e., that they may become themselves the Buddha.

Thus the "Bon" festival in Japan must properly be a very sentimental one. But it is in these days that our folk enjoy very much the Japanese folk-dances in the open air in the evening until very late at night. There is reason enough to think that this dancing was originally dedicated also to the deceased. But as a matter of fact it is one of the most popular amusements of the folk, especially in the country districts. Well, the "Bon" dance in Japan consists of men and women, old and young. It is a collective dance. They make a circle and go dancing round each with a Japanese fan. And they must dance accurately to the music of the drum, shamisen, that is the three stringed guitar, flute and so on. Some of them are

singing to the music continually. I am sorry again that I cannot sing for you the song of the Japanese Bon-dance. You must go to Japan if you want to enjoy the lovely song of our folk, lovelier than English!

In the day-time of these Bon-days relations visit each other with Bon-presents, and hold a small service in front of the chapel for the supposed spiritual ancestors. And they go to the Temple to attend the great service held by the priests for the benefit of all the spiritual beings in the unseen world. And more, they make a pilgrimage to the place where the dead are buried.

Our boys and girls are most delighted in these days to have nice meals, the former to put on clean Kimonos, and the latter the beautiful ones, and to receive many presents from their relations, and above all to help their parents to perform the ceremony and worship, to observe the fancy customes of the Bon-dances and so on.

(A speech delivered in London)

日華佛教提携之出發點

藤井草宣

昨夏，北平から再び上海へ急行して戻つた私は，また上海から楊子江を溯ること四日にして漢ロに達し，漢ロ在留邦人藤田敏郎氏の經營にかゝる漢ロ同仁醫院の客となり，又た漢口佛敎青年會長近藤宗治氏等の鄭重なる歡迎と御指導とを受けた。これらの諸氏から色々の注意を聞かされた翌朝，單身對岸の武昌へ渡つて郊外なる千家街の武昌佛學院を訪れたのである。

佛學院では大醒法師及び法舫法師の兩君に會談したかつたのである。幸に門を入るや直ちに兩君と面晤するを得て頗る愉快であつた。終日終夜，微風すらなく，炊煙が垂直に上ると云はれる武漢の眞夏，然も七月の初旬で，百度を二三度上昇してゐた際であつたが內心の緊張の爲めに，さして苦痛も覺えざるのみか，斯る嬉しき思出は餘り多くないのである。

大醒法師は先年上海で會つた時よりも丸々と肥滿し，その行動敏活，その言說は甚だ潤達で，大いに我意を强くした。私は今迄，支那僧幾百名に接したが，此の大醒法師ほど，心境の一致した友は未だ曾てなかつたので，わざわざ千里を遠しとせずして訪れたのであつたが，果してその甲斐があつたのである。

「我來到貴國的目的是沒有別的。——這次汎太平洋佛敎大會是一時的，不要掛心好——我的眞正的目的是這個的。」（僕の支那へ來た目的は外ではない——今次の汎太平洋佛敎大會は一時的のことであるから，御心に掛けられんでもよい——僕の眞の目的は，これだ）と云ひながら，私は下の如きものを紙片に記して示したのであつた。

目的——將來，一定有人種戰爭。人種戰爭之前，旣有思想戰。思想戰是西洋的科學的思想(好戰的)。對與東亞的文化的思想(平和的)之競爭，然而，東亞之思想，竟有佛敎。我們要提携而一齊研究，活動——這個事情一天比一天爲緊要的。

（目的——將來に屹度人種戰爭がある。人種戰爭の前に，すでに思想戰がある。思想戰とは，西洋の科學的思想（好戰的）と東亞の文化的思想（平和的）との競爭である。然り而して，東亞の思想はたゞ佛敎があるのみである。吾等は提携して一齊に研究し活動せねばならぬ，このことは日に日に緊要となつてくることである。）

突嗟の場合でもあつたので，文をなしてゐなかつたけれども，大體の意は彼に傳へ得たやうである。旣に此時には到底，武昌から改めて大會出席者を勸誘することは無理な事態となつてゐ

たし，又た私としても最早や大體の計劃も完了した後であつたから，大會の如きものを越えて，更に永久的なる根本問題に就て商量せんものと來訪したのである。そのことさへ分ればよかつたのである。此日は世界佛學苑圖書館の理事會が午後より開催さるゝ時とて續々と來賓も集合中でもあつたので，たゞ圖書館の各室や敎室を參觀して漢ロへ戾つたのであつた。歸途，武昌の黃鶴樓に上つて長江を眺めつゝ思はず口吟した歌が——

たゞ一人かなしき使命胸にもちて武昌の夏の高樓に立つ

翌朝は宿所へ大醒法師の訪問を受け午後には漢ロの功德林蔬菜處（精進料理店）で御馳走になつた。法師の外に今一人の若き止安法師も陪席した。大醒法師は懷中から昨日私の書いて渡した紙片をとり出して，「這の意味は大贊成である。」とて，その餘白へ

第一，先要使東亞人人眞實信仰佛敎，人人做菩薩。（先づ東亞の人々をして眞實に佛敎を信仰せしめ，人々をして菩薩たらしめん）

第二，要由東亞佛敎徒感化西方及全世界人信仰佛敎，人々做菩薩。（東亞佛敎徒によりて西洋及び全世界人を感化し，佛敎を信仰せしめ，人々をして菩薩たらしめん）

第三，最後目的使世界所有國土成一淸淨莊嚴之國土，使人々皆爲菩薩。（最後の目的は世界のあらゆる國土をして一の淸淨莊嚴の國土たらしめて，人々をして皆菩薩たらしめん）

そこで吾々は莞爾として同一佛乘に椅托しつゝあるの感を深めたのである。私は更に「耶蘇敎是差別的。我們是平等的。把大乘的平等主義，向全世界宣布」（耶蘇敎は差別的であり，我等は平等的である。大乘的平等主義を把つて全世界に宣傳せん）と記したのであつた。而して後，數時間に亘つて，その「實行方法」を協議した。之が內容は未だ全部發表することは出來ないが，旣に段々とその緖についてゐることは各位の御存知の通りである。これが，われら日支佛敎のヤングゼネレーションが提携したスタートの一つである。斯くて私は大醒法師と袂を別つて長江を下り，大海を越えて東京へ戾つたのであるが，お互に精神は堅く堅く結合し日々相談してゐるやうな氣がしてゐる。今や俄然として，眞に意外にも速かに日支兩國は全面的に國交の親善關係を回復して來た。佛敎的提携は此の天來的神佑の潮流に高く高く棹さゝねばならぬものがある。（三月三日佳節の正午に念佛しつゝ記す）

好村春輝氏の渡支

日支關係好轉の折柄去る三月七日東京發好村全聯理事が渡支，上海，南京，武昌，漢口，北京，天津等の中華國重要都市を巡り，旁ゝ古聖賢の蹟を巡訪するが，その目標とする所は，日支の若き佛敎徒の提携を目指すことは云ふまでもない。此行は日華佛敎學會の上に一進展を來たすであらうが，尙ほ氏の興味深き報導が近く續々本誌上に現れるであらう。

國際佛教 Interview (No.1)

アルゼンチン代理公使

モンテネグロ氏

最近，立正診療院へ月々三十圓宛寄附することを公表して，日本佛教徒の好感を呼び，前から通稱〃博愛公使〃として知られてゐるアルゼンチン代理公使モンテネグロ氏は，文字通り，熱心な宗教信者だ。カトリツク教國に生れた氏が我が聖德太子を尊崇し，更に日蓮を愛好するのはどんな事情によるのであらうか，と云ふ多少の好奇心も手傳つて，一日赤坂區新坂町の同公使館を訪ふ。

先づ應接間の一隅に安置されてある佛像に目を止めて「貴方はカトリツク教國の方だのに，この佛像は道樂ですか？」と聞くと，堅く「ノン」と頭を横に振つた。

「ではどういふわけで‥‥」

「私は宗教に二つの面があると思つてゐる。一は本體界，或は眞理そのものと云つたやうなより高次な面であり，他の一つは吾々が普通佛教，キリスト教，回教，その他何々教と稱してゐる宗教乃至各宗派です。日本の歌に，「わけ登る麓の道は多けれど同じ高嶺の月を見る哉」，と云ふのがある。つまりこれですね。今日世界各國の宗教を調べたら恐らく無數に近いだらう。がこれは要するに麓の道であつて，そのめざす到着點は同じ高嶺である。と，かう考へて來ると，カトリツク教徒でありながら他方佛陀を信仰することは別段不思議でないでせう？。」

だから時にキリストの前で祈禱し，また時には佛陀の前で禮拜祈禱するのだと。

「すると安達さんの八聖殿見たいなことになりますな。」

「左様，あの八聖殿は最も進んだ考へだ。あの八聖を一堂に集めて禮拜祈禱する精神こそ宗教最高の理想だと私は思ふ。併し，實際上は却々さうは行かぬ。だから各人各様の根氣，因縁に應じ差別の形を取つて現はれたので，要するに之は宗教最高の世界を知らしめるための方便でせう。」

「キリスト教では天地創造を說き佛教ではこれを否定する，また佛教の極樂往生思想に對しキリスト教では昇天を說く。これはどうなりますか。」

「フランスの小說に貴方の質問のやうなことを書いたのがある。つまり天地創造がどうの聖母マリヤは本當に處女であつたかどうか，天國は實在するかどうかと云ふ問題について五年間も會議したとね。だが，これ位愚なことはないでせう。」

何んだか最近日本佛教徒間で問題になつた西方淨土有無論の愚さも諷刺す

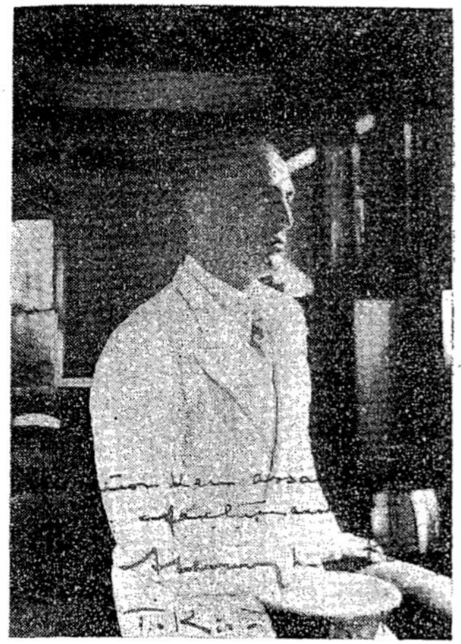

るかのやうで思はず苦笑した。

話が進むにつれて，モ公使は，書齋からルネ・グルツセの〃佛陀の足跡〃のフランス原本や，ポール・ケーラスの〃佛陀の福音〃のスペイン譯や，さては我全聯の〃英譯佛教聖典〃それに孔子の四書のスペイン譯などを取出して來て，自分は讀書は少いのだが，獨自の宗教觀を持つてゐる者である，學問としての宗教ではなく，生活としての宗教，體驗としての宗教を尊ぶものであると云ふ。公使は更に話をついで「要するに基督と佛陀の優劣を論じたり，天國や極樂の有無を詮議したりするのは，恰も一人の人間を前から蹴るべきか背後から蹴るべきかと論議するやうなもので愚も甚だしい」といふ。

「聖德太子や日蓮はどうしてお知りになつたかまたどの點を尊崇し愛好されますか。」

「大體書物を通じて近づきました。先づ聖德太子について申上ぐれば，太子御一生の御事業に對しては悉く敬服されるが中でも彼の十七條の憲法は世界優位の立派な道德憲法だと思ひます。次ぎに日蓮については殆ど知るところがなかつたが，日本に來て直に，あの萬燈を押し立てゝ，ウチワ太鼓に南無妙法蓮華經のお題目を唱和しつゝ進む勇ましい朗かな情景を目擊して「これだな」とその實行的な點に感服しました，爾來劇務の中から，時に法隆寺に詣でては太子の御事蹟を偲びまた鎌倉に行つては日蓮の足跡を訪ねると云ふことにしてゐるが，要するに日蓮のあの火を吐くやうな强烈な精神と宗教の立場から天下國下を論じ更に實行した態度を私は愛好する，日蓮の愛國的態度は一見國際平和をかき亂す如く見えぬでもないが，實はさうでなく，世界人類愛への基點を高調してゐるのでないでせうか。」

「日本には日蓮の外に弘法，道元，榮西法然，親鸞等誇るに足る偉大な宗教家がまだ澤山ゐることを御存じですか。」

「知つてはゐるが，その一々の人格，教義，宗風，に關しては殆んど盲目です。ただ，いつぞや坐禪を教へられて一度一時間餘組んだことがあるが，これは，私には難行苦行だと思ひました」

公使の佛教研究はまだ初步だが，その宗教的感受性に富んでゐる點，更に宗教的體驗と冥想の甘味を惠まれてゐる點に於ては，多くの外交官中の秀逸だと云つてよからう。（善財童子）

Budaismon per Esperanto!

Joŝicugu Okamoto

Kiel vi bone memoras, en la prospekto disdonita de la Tutjapana Federacio de Junulaj Budaanaj Asocioj okaze de la preparado de la 2-a Tutpacifika Konferenco de Junulaj Budaanaj Asocioj oni legis jene:—

"....La evoluo de la monda kulturo kaj la internacia amikeco vere dependas de spirita reciproka interkoniĝo de ĉiuj nacioj, precipe de la fortaj manpremoj de la nacioj ĉirkaŭantaj Pacifikon per Budaisma kredo. Tion ni firme kredas. Ni ankaŭ ne dubas, ke ĉi tiu konferenco forigos la malbonan flankon de la malnova Budaismo kaj nepre donos bonan efikon al la morgaŭaj sortoj de Pacifiko.

Unuflanke ni faru la klopodojn por renovigo de la doktrino, ekleziaj sistemoj, entreprenoj kaj ceteraj de Budaismo kaj aliflanke ni faru diskutojn pri la tendencoj de la nuna mondo, precipe pri la nuntempaj politikaj kaj ekonomiaj aferoj kaj decidos, kion ni prenu kiel la ĝeneralajn planojn de budaanoj kaj budaistoj. Tio estas nia devo...."

Estas prave dirite! Nun estas la tempo, kiam ni, budaanoj, devas komenci disvastigi Budaismon tra la tuta mondo por savi la homaron.

Post la Granda Mondmilito nia tuta mondo unue endanĝeriĝis en materian krizon, ĉiuj nacioj multe suferis de ekonomiaj malfacilaĵoj en sia vivo, poste venis al ni, na tuta homaro, la spirita krizo. La lasta estas multe pli granda kaj suferiga, ol la unua. Preskaŭ ĉiuj homôj sur la terglobo perdis la esperon en la plian brilantan progreson ĉe la homara spirita sfero. Kaj inter ili troviĝis eĉ tiuj, kiuj jam perdis esperon en sia propra vivo. Antaŭ iliaj okuloj la estonto de nia homaro malheliĝis. Precipe eŭropaj nacioj multe suferadis depost la milito. Jam Kristanismo ne povas savi ilin. Orienta spirita kulturo, precipe budaisma kulturo, nun povus savi la mondon.

Budaismo ĉiam havadis en la ideoj de Budao, Ŝakamunio, kaj ankaŭ en la teorioj de progresinta eklezio revojn de granda espero, kiu altigas la publikan moralon. Unu el tiaj revoj estas starigo de unu komuna lingvo. Multaj malnovaj budaistoj suferadis de la diverseco de idiomoj kaj dialektoj en kaj ekster Hindujo. Efektive oni legas en la sankta skribo Āgamo, "Lingvo estas unu speca kaj ne diferenca." En la komenco la palia lingvo estis rigardata kiel sankta lingvo. Sed la espero efektiviĝis. Ni, nunaj budaanoj laboru por efektivigi idealon, kiun antaŭuloj esperis.

Estas ne miro ke jam en la 1-a Konferenco de Tutpacifikaj Junulaj Budaanaj Asocioj, kiu okazis en Havajo, en julio, 1930, japanaj delegitoj prezentis proponon: Enkonduku ankaŭ Esperanton en la movadon de junulaj budaanaj asocioj kaj ĝi estis akceptita de la konferenco.

Kaj la 2-a Konferenco de Tutpacifikaj Janulaj Budaanaj Asocioj, kiu okazis en la lastjara julio en Tokio, akceptis Esperanton kiel preskaŭ oficialan lingvon. En la regularo de la konferenco oni vidas jenan regulon pri lingvoj uzataj.

"La oficialaj lingvoj de la kunsidoj estas japana, angla kaj ĉina lingvoj. Tiu, kiu ne konas unu el la tri lingvoj, povas uzi Esperanton."

Kaj inter pli ol cent proponoj prezencitaj al la konferenco oni trovis tri koncerne Esperanton. La unua estis retirita de la proponinto kaj la du aliaj estis akceptitaj kaj transdonitaj al la komisiono de l' realigo de la rezolucioj de la konferenco.

Tiamaniere jam estas donitaj la unuaj paŝoj. Komenco estas duono, diras proverbo. Ni tuj faru la duan paŝon, t.e., uzi Esperanton en la praktiko. Ni tuj enkonduku Esperanton en nian budaisman movadon, kaj ni publikigu niajn studojn pri Budaismo en Esperanto.

Nun estas la plej konvena tempo, kiam ni povas komenci disvastigi Budaismon tra la tuta mondo por savi ĉiujn homojn. En tia okazo Esperanto estas la plej oportuna lingvo, precipe por japanoj. Nia idealo estas plibonigo de nia surtera vivo. Venigu al ni la Sukavativjuhon, utopian landon. Budaismon tra la tuta mondo per Esperanto!

"佛陀" のエス語型に就て

....今度御創刊の通報にエスペラント欄が出來ることを大變樂しみにしてゐます。然し英國が使つてゐるからとの理由から、Budho 語形が採用されねば良いがと、大分氣をもんでゐる向きもあります。一時 Budho が採用されても、Budho は發音上 Buddo よりも惡いことが解れば、Buddo か Budao に變る事と思ひます。素人のエスペランチストの說にしたがつて、Budao を採ることが不適當と御考へになるようだつたら、一時 Buddho なり、Buddo なりを御使用になつて、エスペランチスト達に非エスペラント的として拒まれて居る Budho が使はれねばよいがと念じてゐます。....(竹內藤吉)

The Sweet Joy and Peace Serene

By Bikkhu Sri Jina Wansa Swamy

1. Sweet are friends when need ariseth,
Sweet is joy whatever it be,
Sweet is the age of lieves ending,
Sweet is to be from sorrows free.

2. Sweet is to be a mother good,
Sweet is the Sacred-Brotherhood,
Sweet is the Sacred-Sisterhood,
Sweet is the Sacred-Bikkhu-Good.

3. Sweet is to gain the price of wisdom Sacred,
Sweet is when desire and sin extinguished,
Sweet is the age of wisdom-Sacred,
Sweet is the Sacred-mind when established.

4. Sweet is to hail the lord the Buddha Supreme,
Sweet is to hail His Dhamma Sacred-power Supreme,
Sweet is Nibbana the Sacred-Bliss Supreme,
Sweet is the peace of eternal glory Serene.

1

5. Devout faith crosses the ocean of all misery,
And one attains the noble bliss by not being sloth.
All sorrows are redeemed by vigilance and energy,
And with intuitive wisdom perfects his emancipation.

2

6. I have no other refuge and shall not pray,
As the Lord Buddha is my only refuge,
By the power of this Truth with reverence I say,
"Let me become The Srijina, The Victorious."

大乘佛教の國際化

我通報局の質問書に對する名士の應答

我が通報局は，その第一歩の踏み出しに對して，教界初め各方面の名士に，次の如きクエツシヨネールを發した所，次の如き示唆に富んだ應答を得たことは，誠に喜びに堪えないと共に，今後に於ける我局の行くべき方向を教示されたことを衷心より感謝する次第である。

【質問書】

拜啓　時下向春之候貴臺愈々御淸祥奉賀候陳者毎々御高配を忝う致居候我が全日本佛教青年會聯盟に於ては，一昨年春五月，京都大谷大學に於て開催されたる第三回總會に於て，佛誕二千五百年紀念事業として，(1)國際佛教通報局の設置，(2)佛教青年會館の建設，の二項目を滿場一致を以て決議仕候，次で昨年夏七月東京築地本願寺に於て開催されたる第二回汎太平洋佛教青年會大會に於て，愈々その實現を約束仕候，爾來數次の特別委員會の協議を經て愈々來る四月一日を以て月刊『國際佛教通報』(The International Buddhist Bulletin) を日・華歐文を以て發刊仕る運びと相成候，就ては御多忙中，甚だ恐縮乍ら，右創刊號を飾るべく，

大乘佛教の國際化に必要なる當面の事業に就て御高見御洩し願上度，折返し通報局宛一言御返信賜り度く悃願申上候　敬具

昭和十年三月一日

東京市神田區一ツ橋二丁目三番地
全日本佛教青年會聯盟

【應　答】

○　山中峯太郎

キリスト教の信仰が，大乘佛教の純眞な信仰に來りて完成せられる。宗教的眞理の佛教的解決を，歐米に宣布せられたし。切に希念に堪へません。

○　ラス，ビハリ，ボース

(一)日，支，印，安南，シヤム，セイロンに於ける佛教徒の密接なる聯絡，又其目的で日本に於て中央機關の設置。
(二)亞細亞，ヨーロツパ，及び亞米利加の諸國へ英語或は其他の外國語に達者な布教師の派遣及交換。
(三)日本の各宗派を超越して國際佛教大學の設置，世界各國から奬勵金を與へて學生を招く事。
(四)外來佛教徒の留學生及研究者の寄宿舍の設置（アジア諸國の共通的な料理及び洋食を供する事）
(五)毎年世界佛教徒の會合開催

○　下村壽一

大乘佛教の國際化に必要なる當面の事業
一，學者の交換教授，若し費用等の關係にて不可能ならば權威ある著述論文等を交換し相互に於て飜譯公刊すること。
二，佛教藝術の宣揚紹介，是は當方より主として歐米の學界藝術界に向つて働き掛け，古代より現代に至る佛教建築，彫刻，繪畫，調度等の優秀なるものを先方に知らしめ佛教藝術の眞價を理解せしむるやう努むること。

○　眞野正順

下記の如きものを充分内容に力を入れて作製頒布するが第一着手かと存候。

一，大乘佛教の本質を主張せる小册子。

二，高僧（特に日本に於ける各宗祖）の生活及思想を述べたる叢書。

○　草繋全宣

佛教々典の各國語譯宣布は佛教の國際化には必要の事業と存じ候也。

○　藤井草宣

大乘佛教の國際化に必要なる當面の事業

(1) 日本古典の佛教系の文學書を歐文譯する事。例へば，平家物語。日本靈異記。高僧の傳記。謠曲。淨瑠璃等の特色あるものの歐文譯。

(2) 現代日本佛教學者の代表作の歐文譯。例せば，椎尾博士の「佛教經典概論」。宇井博士の「印度佛教史」淺野氏の「日本佛教社會事業史」の如きもの丶歐文譯。

(3) 日本の現代佛教の毎月の月報テキスト（これに支那と朝鮮，滿洲等のをも附錄す）

(4) 在日本の各國留學生に對する佛教宣傳を努力せよ。

○　梅原眞隆

各國の佛教徒が互に知り合ふといふ事，そして，「法」において聯盟して行かねばならぬ心持をよびさますこと，かうした親しみがすべての運動の根帶となるのでせう，これについての工夫を希ふ。

○　小谷德水

大乘佛教の國際化に必要なるは，人と金とが根本であるが，當面の事業としては國際佛教通報を中心として，諸國の佛教徒と連絡を密にすることの外には無からう。世界中の佛教徒の團體丈けでも，完全にリストになし得たらと期待を持つてゐる。線香花火にならぬ樣ひきしめて歩いてほしいものである。

○　畠野奎三

宗教と藝術は昔から密接な關係を持つてゐます。新らしい佛教藝術の研究とその發表交驩は大乘佛教の國際化に最も普遍性をもつてゐるものと思ひます。藝術への親しみは尤も手近に佛教への親しみを招へる事を確信いたしますので，これが創作，研究の一大佛教藝術研究所の設立を希望いたします。音樂，美術，文學等色々ありますが特に小生は實用的價値の多い新佛教圖案の確立の爲めに，年來この希望を持つて努力いたしてゐます。一言右迄。

○　大谷瑩潤

通佛教の立場に於て歐米主要都市に佛教駐在員を置くこと。

駐在員の資格としては語學に長じ，人格高潔且つ宗教體驗を持つ人たること。

その經費は各宗團に於て共同支出すること。

右數年前より念願致し居る佛教國際化の方策に有之候。右御回答迄。

○　城谷默

學問的研究も勿論必要の事ですが外國人一般に佛教を知らしむるには平易にして面白く佛教精神の或る物を解せしむるが如き讀物を紹介すべきであると存じます。佛教精神の社會的に現實的に現れたるものなども面白からんと存じます。

○　玉川義隆

一，佛教聖典の各國語飜譯

一，青年使節の對外交換

○　太田覺眠

一，外國語（差當り英語）を以て日本佛教を教授する學校を設け，歐米の留學生及海外に布教せんとする日本學生を養成する事

一，日本佛教の良書を選び，外國語に飜譯して海外に頒布する事。

○　廣瀬了義

一，簡易平明なる佛典中の語錄を美麗なる印刷に附し之を世界各國の圖書館，學校博物館，汽船，汽車などに寄附備付を爲すること。（同時に佛教ポスターを掲げ又カードの頒布）

一，佛教學者などの海外旅行などをする場合に各國の首要都市にて佛教講演を開催せしむること。（同時にパンフレットを託すること）

一，日本內地に在住の外人に佛教日本の文化を宣揚すること（彼等を招いて日本佛教徒は時々ミーチングの機會を催すこと）。

○　早川雪洲

哲學を究め，宗教學を讀破したる外國人中，今猶眞實を掴み得ざる人々，國體，研究俱樂部の樣な文化的集合會が各地に催されて居ります。

それ等のものと連絡を取つて大乘精神を解り易く說く機關誌が最必要だと思ひます。

○　岡本好次

汎太平洋佛青大會第一回にも日本代表より國際語エスペラントを佛青用語の一とすべしとの提案が可決され昨夏の第二回大會では日英支の公用語に準じてエスペラントが準公用語とされたことは日本の進歩的佛教徒佛教學者が國際語の必要を痛感してゐることを證するものである，而して大乘佛教の國際化には何をおいてもエスペラント語の活用即ちエスペラント語による佛教文献乃至研究の發表を急務と思考致します。その意味に於て「通報」が廣く英語のみでなくエス語の論文のためにも紙面を割愛されんことをのぞむ。

○　權藤圓立

日本の佛教の音樂は日本音樂の基調でありますから，これを研究調査すると共に現代及び將來の新らしき佛教音樂を創作しこれによつて國際化を計ることが緊急なる最大急務と信じます。

最もポピユラーなる萬國語は音樂であります。これを共に奏し，共に聞き，共に歌ふところにのみ「和」の世界が如實に顯現されるからであります。

○　原悅道

御芳書拜受仕候先づ第一に大乘相應之地日本に眞に大乘佛教の信念に立脚せる道士の養成こそ，所詮なりと存ぜられ候。此事はひとへに教役者の奮起による興學布教にありと存じ候。かくして一道士の信念の發する處一家を大乘佛教化し其影響はひいては一國に及ぼさん。而して我日本國に正法の王國は建設せらるべきにて候。かくすれば日本に於ける大乘佛教の信念によれる文化的諸施設。あらゆる事業にはかゝる國際間の關係の接近せる時期に於ては其影響は直に響の音に應ずる如く全世界に波及するに至るべしと存じ候。草々

○　柘植信秀

一，宗教者の世界的會合

二，國際的平和運動

三，戰爭防止運動一非戰主義の提唱

四，人種差別待遇の撤廢運動

佛教の國際的事業は純なる宗教的運動の時機には未だ到達せず，それより先きに，政治的經濟的の色彩をもつ所の國際問題を宗教的に指導するの工作を要すべし。この意味に於て佛教單獨の運動でなく，基督教徒と携へて世界の宗教者の運動として，そこに大乘佛教徒の標度を示したく思ふ。差しあたり英米の何れかで佛基兩教徒の會談など，準備工作の一つならん乎。

○　岩上行坡

萬古不易の眞理を說き世界人類の心靈を救濟するを以て第一義諦とする佛教なれば經典（重要經典より始め大藏經全部に及ぶ）

を國際語に飜譯して世界の果て果てまでも流布することは大乘佛教の國際化に必要なる當面の事業にして又青年佛徒の重大なる務であると思ふ次第である。

○　北村教嚴

第一飜譯局を設立し，代表的の大乘佛典，特に日本の各宗高祖の名著を差當り英譯する事，其の資本は各宗の本山は勿論，外務省文部省を始めとし，民間有力者より一定の援助を仰ぐ事。第二，語學に堪能なる佛教學者を時々歐米に漫遊せしめて，系統立つた佛教講演を各地に行はしむる事。右急務中の急務と存候。

○　加藤咄堂

大乘佛教の國際化に必要なる當面の事業としては日本に於て特に發達せる大乘佛教の精神を世界に紹介すべく日本各宗祖師の述作の歐文譯の宣布と存候。

○　曉烏敏

聖德太子，弘法，傳教，法然，親鸞，道元，日蓮その他日本における先覺者の著書を英，獨，佛いづれにか譯して各國におくり出すことがその第一事業と思てます。次にはロンドン，パリ，ベルリン，ローマ，モスコー，ニューヨーク等，世界の大都市に教界の耆僧を駐在せしむることと存じます。

○　土屋詮教

大乘佛教の國際化に必要なる當面の事業は，昨年の汎太平洋佛教青年大會に於て，議決せられた諸種の計畫を實現するにありと確信します。

○　三島通陽

一，佛教音樂の現代的確立。

キリスト教の音樂は世界を風靡してゐるが，佛教音樂の中にはよいものがある，それを現代的に一般的にひろめる必要がある。

交響樂的のよい深い偉大な音樂をつくり又，一般的にひろまる現代的の輕いものも必要だと思ふ。

二，佛教少年團（ボーイ，スカウト式のもの）をつくり，世界の少年團と提携するのも又一つです。

○　諏訪二教

御問合せの件につき，佛青發展の順序としては，第一に日本佛青を中心として積極的にはたらきかける方面にて，それには聖典の代表的なるものと，權威ある書物や大衆化せる佛教書を歐米中心に出版すること及び佛青の中から人を選んで歐米を中心に派遣して佛教普及の基礎工事を作らせつゝ世界の其方面の事情を通信せしめ，國際化の方法を明らかにして行くこと。

第二には，先方の人々と共同にて行なふ樣にする方面にて，それには，國際佛教徒聯盟の設立を致し，其れの事業として講習會，講演會，佛教の國際會議，文書の傳道をすること。

佛青の事情により，第一と第二の綜合されたものを出來得る處から，實現されてもよいと思ひます。

○　山田一英

佛教が唐韓を通して我が日本に入りてより千三百年と多少，此の間隆衰はあつたが鎌倉時代の內憂外患時に當つて眞精神を發揮して大乘本來の更新をした。今復昭和時代の國難に對して更に新を要求して一段の飛躍と發展とを促がされて居る。此時に於ける貴御企ては眞に恰好の推鐘告四方である。

先づ當面の國際的事業としては，

(一)海外諸國から日本の佛敎大學に留學生を派遣せしむる事

(二)大乘佛教の眞意義を廣く海外諸國に飜譯宣傳する事

(三)內教團を刷新して海外諸國から觀光團を誘致する事

（以下次號）

Japanese News

Buddhist Statues

Strange are the vicissitudes of Buddhist statues, and they are often overtaken by unhappy fate.

A dusty Buddhist figure has recently come to light that has been relegated to the storehouse of the Shomyoji, a temple in the village of Watari in Miyagi Prefecture. It is said to have languished in obscurity, covered by the dust of the ages for four and a half centuries.

Now Professor Riichiro Fukui of Tohoku University has unearthed it and declared that the statue is a masterpiece of the Kasuga school of sculpture.

Having heard of the discovery, the people of the village flocked to the temple to see the old statue.

Terrifying Statue

Among the statues of Tokyo none is more terrifying than the huge red lacquer figure of Emma, the great judge of the nether regions.

This famous statue may be seen at Taishoji on Shinjuku high street, and many a child has been taken to see this dignitary and the remembrance has remained with them all their lives.

Those who have suffered on account of robbers go to make supplications to the collosal Emma, and often their prayers are rewarded and the evildoers are found.

Gigantic Statue

Fashions change as regards statues, and there appears at present to be a revival of colossal figures as in the days when the great Buddha's of Nara and Kamakura were made.

Now a huge statue of Nichiren is to be erected in the grounds of Tokai-in, a temple of Iseyama dis-snd two of Golden Bat?—the dog trict in Fujisawa of Kanagawa Prefecture. A high statue of Kwannon has for some time been under construction at Ofuna.

The Nichiren statue will be of bronze, 70 feet high and rest on a pedestal of 40 feet. It will thus be 10 feet higher than the Marunouchi building. The face of the statue will be 14 feet, and the ears 4 feet long.

Mr. Koun Nakaya has been commissioned to execute the figure of Nichiren in the Buddhist robes he wore as an evangelist. He began work in 1933 on the spot where the statue is to rise toward the sky, and it will take him three years more to complete his task.

Made Flowers Bloom

The birth of Buddha is to be celebrated in Tokyo on a more lavish scale than ever before.

In addition to the processions of gaily dressed children in Hibiya park, a program is to be given in Hibiya Hall on April 6.

At this time one of the most popular fairy tales, "Hanasaka Jiji," (Old man who Made Flowers Bloom), is to be presented as a play.

The story originated in morals from Buddhist teachings, and it has been decided that it is one of the most appropriate plays to be given on the occasion.

Young Women Buddhist League Holds Inaugural

The inauguration ceremony of the Young Women's Buddhist League composed of 20 associations was held at the Shirokiya Hall at 1 p.m. Sunday March 17. After the National Anthem and Buddhist hymns had been sung, and floral and incense offerings made, Rev. Ichino Shibata led a prayer which was followed by congratulatory addresses from Mr. Suemaro Kikuzawa, Chief of the Religious Affair Eureau of the Education Ministry, and other prominent people including Mrs. Yayoi Yoshioka, noted physician.

The audience then listended to Dr. Junjiro Takakusu's lecture and enjoyed various entertainments. The meeting broke up at 5 p.m.

Poem Monument

A marble monument, in which is inserted a bronze panel containing a poem by the late Baroness Takeko Kujo, will be set up in the grounds of the Honganji, the great Buddhist temple in Tsukiji. Mr. Matsugoro Hirokawa made the design.

The unveiling ceremony will take place on April 8, when Buddha's Birthday is celebrated.

Baroness Kujo was an accomplished writer of verse, and her collection called "The Golden Bell" made her known at home and abroad. The daughter of the Abbot of Honganji in Kyoto, she was known for her charitable work among the poor.

Tourist Poster

To announce the coming celebrations of the Board of Tourist In-

dustry of the Department of Railways an attractive poster has been issued.

It represents a pagoda among cherry trees, an idealistic Japanese scene, symbol of the springtime.

Siamese Dancers

A company of Siamese dancers will leave Bangkok on March 20, and it is expected that they will perform in Hibiya Hall April 19-21.

Mr. Phra Mitrakam, Minister of Siam. has been instrumental in bringing the company to come to Japan, and he will invite members of the diplomatic corps and prominent persons of the capital to the Imperial Hotel on April 6 when the members of the organization will be introduced.

Mr. Koscak Yamada, the composer, has written some special compositions for the dancers and they are to perform to this music.

Jizo Statue

A movement has been started to erect a statue of Jizo (Kṣitigarbha-Bodhisattva), guardian of little Children, as a memorial to children who have died by accident.

Mr. Tokusaku Ishibashi, the head of the guards of the House of Peers is behind this movement, since his own son was killed by falling into a well in the garden.

Since this accident, four years ago, he has been trying to raise funds for the erection of a fine statue of Jizo, and has been collecting money, one sen per head, in all parts of the country. At present he has ¥ 6,500 in hand.

Mr. Shinobu Tsuda, the sculptor, who is a professor of the Tokyo School of Fine Arts, is to execute the statue.

Mr. Ishibashi has received letters from sympathetic persons from Manchoukuo, the Philippines and elsewhere abroad.

Service for Animals

The annual spring services for departed cats, dogs and horses which are a feature of Seishinji, a Buddhist temple in Koishikawa were observed on Thursday march 21.

At this time the priests officiated in prayers to console the pets of Tokyo people, that are buried in a special Buddhist cemetery.

Temple Paintings

The ancient mural paintings which adorn the walls and ceilings of the main worshipping hall of Horyuji, near Nara will be shown to visitors from April 1 to May 15.

These are in a wonderful state of preservation, and together with the beautiful bronze statues form one of the show places for the tourist in Japan.

國際ニュース

アメリカより

○エバレツト女史　シカゴ法曹界の泰斗富豪エバレツト氏一家が親日家揃ひにして現下の日米親交上多大の貢献をなしつゝあり，エ夫人が座禪修行の爲來朝二回に及び，同伴の令孃が本邦茶道師範の免狀を獲得して歸國せる事等は既に世人の知る所であるが，エ氏は其の後諸所に於て佛教並びに東洋文化一般に關する講演をなし，最近は熱心なる聽衆の求めに應じて佛教書籍の取次販賣を開始した。

○フキリツプス氏　オレンゴン州ポートランドの佛教徒，去る二月中旬京都緒方宗博氏の許に書を寄せて禪學の指導を受け度いと申込んで來た。その手紙に曰く，釋尊は娑婆往來八千遍にして初めて覺りを感ぜられたりと言ふが，どんな人間でもお悟りが開けるものであらうかと。これに對する緒方氏の答へに曰く，夏のさ中に紅葉する楓樹はなく，生れ乍らにして性に醒めたる赤ん坊なし，煙の起つ所ろ火のあるを知る可く，垣を隔てて角を見ば牛の所在を悟るべし。人若し悟りを得んと求むる心眞に切なるものあらば，此の生既に七千九百九十九度目の次なる事疑ひなし。只だ自惚れ高き娘の多くしてまこと麗しき美人の稀なるが如く悟りを語る者は多く悟りを求むる心は容易に起つて來ない。君が悟りを開き得るか否や，月夜人無き時君自身に問はれよと。

○マツク・グルー氏　ハワイ，ホノルル市マツキンレーハイスクールの社會學教授にして，一九三一年夏日本及び支那を訪れたる氏は，來る夏休みを期に，佛教特に禪の研究に再度來朝の決意をしたる由，多分京都市外八幡圓福寺の外人禪堂に入つて相當滯在する事となるべしと。

○ヒルスマン氏　我が佛青とは新譯佛教聖典の英譯に因んで縁故の深いゴダード翁の佛學信奉会に在つて盛んに修行中の氏は，最近何とかアメリカに佛教普及の道を講じ度いとて，日本の道友に向つて適當な方法の指示を要求して來た。

ニユージーランドより

○タムソン氏　同地の代議士バーナード氏が本年正月來朝，廣く日本の政界，教界の名士を歷訪せる事は既に報道せられたる所であるが，これに力を得たる同地オークランド・デバンポート市の佛教徒タムソン氏は，從來ビルマ系の佛教を研究し來れるも，今回日本の大乘佛教をも研究したいとて，日本禪僧との文通を申込んで來た。アドレスは次の通り。

Mr. Arthur H. Thompson
86, Wairoa Road, Devonport,
Auckland N. 1. New Zealand.

セイロンより

○ヘワビタールナ氏　コロンボ佛青の幹事長たる氏は，昨年末全聯の好村春輝氏を通じて日本事情紹介に適當なる幻燈寫眞版を購入，諸方に講演會を開いて日本の紹介並びに兩國佛教徒の提携を鼓吹しつゝありと。

○ヴイマラセカラ氏　昨夏の佛青大會に出席せる各國の代表が，日本佛教徒の好意に感激し，日本の物心兩方面に渡る發達に驚異の眼を見張つた事は今更言ふまでもない事であるが，中にもセイロン方面の反響は格別著しく，ヴ氏の如きはスツカリ日本禮讃黨になりきつて，妻子に日本の着物を着せたり，日本人を自宅に招待したり等して喜んでる。（寫眞參照）

○ヴイゼグナワーダナ夫人　昨夏の大會にセイロンより出席せる婦人三勇士中の一人たるヴ夫人は，歸國後カンディー湖畔の自宅の庭で，椰子の實を採りピヤノを叩く等の悠々閑々の日を送つてゐるが，日本旅行の思ひ出では何時までも新たにして，日本からのたよりを何よりの樂しみとして居る由。

印度より

○ワリシンハ氏　昨夏の大會に於て佛陀伽耶の聖地回收問題を提起して各國代表の支持贊同を得たるワ氏が大會後二ケ月有半に渡つて日本各地に講演旅行をなし多大の好反響を起して歸國せる所，印度佛教徒のワ氏歡迎は異常なるものあり，氏は益々使命の爲精進努力せん事を誓つて，佛陀伽耶回收問題，國際佛教大學建設問題等の爲東奔西走殆んど席暖まるに暇なき樣子であるが，而も來る四月末の日本佛靑全聯總會には，佛陀伽耶問題の續報を兼ねて何かメツセーヂを送る由。

○野生司香雪氏　鹿野苑の新築，初轉法輪寺に在つて壁畫作製中の同氏は，種々なる困難と戰ひつゝも，各方面よりの同情，及び本年初頭に於ける，皇太子殿下への誕生佛畫獻上御嘉納等に力を得て，その畢生の事業に邁進大いに進捗せりと。

歐洲より

○アラン・ウオツト氏　ロンドン，ブツディスト，ローヂのメムバーたる同氏は，僅かに十八歲の青年であるが，一九三二年鈴木博士等の著書を耽讀して直ちに禪學概說なる小册子を發表し，若し日本に於て働き乍ら勉强が出來るならば來朝したいとて，最近就職周旋方を依頼して來た。

（以上一緒方宗博氏擔當）

國際佛教通報局

名譽局長	高楠順次郎
局長	大村桂巖
幹事	鷹谷俊之
同	稻葉文海
同	淺野研眞

顧問（順序不同）

〃	宇井伯壽
〃	朝倉曉瑞
〃	羽溪了諦
〃	荻原雲來
〃	干潟龍祥
〃	鈴木大拙
〃	鈴木宗忠
〃	天岫接三
〃	長井眞琴
〃	松本文三郎
〃	椎尾辨匡
〃	宇野圓空
〃	赤松智城
〃	大森禪戒
〃	矢吹慶輝
〃	小野清一郎
〃	加藤精神
〃	姉崎正治
〃	本田義英
〃	關本龍門
〃	佐伯定胤
〃	花田凌雲
〃	河野法雲
〃	高岡隆心
〃	小林瑞淨
〃	山邊習學
〃	赤沼智善
〃	本多惠隆
〃	大森亮順
〃	河口慧海
〃	山川智應
〃	常盤大定
〃	谷本富
〃	常盤井堯猷
〃	大谷尊由
〃	大谷瑩潤
〃	水野梅曉
〃	柴田一能
〃	安藤正純
〃	下村壽一
〃	菊澤季麿
〃	乘杉嘉壽
〃	芝田徹心
〃	淺野孝之
〃	渡邊哲信
〃	小野玄妙
〃	柳澤健
〃	重光葵
〃	金倉圓照
〃	立花俊道

國際佛教通報局定款

名稱

第一，本局を國際佛教通報局と稱す

事務所

第二，本局の事務所を全日本佛教青年會聯盟本部に置く

目的

第三，本局は日本內地及海外に向つて佛教事情の通報をなし，且つ佛教徒相互間の各種便宜を計るを以て目的とす

事業

第四，本局の目的を達成するため左記の事業を行ふ

イ，日本內地及世界各國より佛教事情に關する質問の通報を行ふ

ロ，必要に應じ日本語及世界各國語を以て佛教事情の通報を行ふ

ハ，外國人の日本觀光に際しては各種の便益を與へ，特にその佛教に關する方面に於て之を爲す

ニ，定時或は隨時に各國語を以て文書の刊行をなす

ホ，その他必要と認めたる事業を行ふ

役員

第五，本局の事務を處理するため左の役員を置く

イ，局長　一名

ロ，幹事　三名

ハ，評議員　若干名

局長は本局の事務を總括す

幹事は本局の事務を處理す

評議員は局長の提案に依る重要事務を審議す

第六，評議員は左記の者を以て之に充つ

イ，全日本佛教青年會聯盟理事及主事

ロ，全日本佛教青年會聯盟理事會に於て推薦したる者

第七，局長及幹事は評議員會に於て決定す

第八，役員の任期は二ケ年とす（但し重任を妨げず）

經費

第九，本局の經費は左記のものに依て之を支辨す

イ，本局基金の活用

ロ，寄附金

ハ，その他の收入

補則

第十，本定款に記載せられざる事項は，凡て評議員會に於て協議す

第十一，第一回の役員は全日本佛教青年會聯盟理事會に於て決定す

定價	一部	金二十錢	送料二錢
	一年	金二圓四十錢	送料不要

昭和十年三月廿五日印刷（每月一回）
昭和十年四月一日發行（一日發行）

東京市神田區一ツ橋二の三
國際佛教通報局內
編輯發行兼印刷人　淺野研眞

東京市牛込區早稻田鶴卷町107
印刷所　康文社印刷所
電話牛込(34)1950番 5049番

東京市神田區一ツ橋二の三
發行所　國際佛教通報局
電話九段(33)1429番
振替東京83015番

昭和十年三月二十五日印刷納本　昭和十年四月一日發行（毎月一回一日發行）

昭和十年四月二十五日印刷納本　昭和十年五月一日發行（毎月一回一日發行）第一卷　第二號

The International Buddhist Bulletin

國際佛教通報

第一卷 **昭和十年五月** 第二號 〔Vol. 1. May $\frac{2501}{1935}$ No. 2.〕

要　目〔Contents〕

東　京 **國際佛教通報局** 發　行

The International Buddhist Information Bureau

Tokyo, Kanda, Hitotsubashi, II—3

Annual Subscription, ¥2,40 (post free), Single Copies 20 sen (post 2 sen)

The Meaning to celebrate the Buddha's Birthday

By Prof. Bruno Petzold

(Address given at the eve of "Hana-Matsuri" at Tsukiji-Honganji Sunday 7th April)

We met here to-day, in order to celebrate Buddha's Birthday. The question may therefore be asked: What is the meaning of a birthday anniversary, — of any birthday anniversary?

If we inquire from the folklorists, they will tell us, that a birthday anniversary means the renewal of the life aquired by the original birth. The ritual of the birthday anniversary is designed to renew the life of men and also of gods, and at the same time to discard the old life, now regarded as decay and death.

The Hindus — as we are told — celebrate the birthday of Rama, the seventh incarnation of Vishnū. The image of the god is then adorned and carried in procession. A pilgrimage is made to his temple. The Hindus celebrate also the birthday of Krishna and that of Ganesa. In this case every house sets up an image of the god Ganesa, before which lights are placed. A mantra of consecration is pronounced, on which the spirit of the god enters the image. The divinity is so-to-say recreated by this ritual, his birth is repeated.

In China the "longevity garment" is of particular importance at birthday anniversaries. This longevity garment too has attracted the attention of the folklorists, and they assure us, that it is a handsome robe, embroidered in gold characters with the word "longevity." It serves at death as a man's shroud. It is generally a present from the children, and is given to the parent on his birthday. He wears it then and on all festive occasions, in order to aquire long life. —

I ask you now: Is there anything better for us to do at this birthday anniversary of the Buddha, than to imitate the fashion of the Hindus and of the Chinese? Let the spirit of Buddha enter into his image, so that the image becomes transfigured and can represent to us the absolute reality itself. Let us all put on the garment of longevity, so that we may all absorb on this birthday anniversary a good amount of vital energy, in order to remain spiritually hale and healthy during the ensuing year. For gaining this effect, no recitation of shingon is needed, and neither putting on a real dress is required. All what we have to do, is to purify ourselves and to sanctify our surroundings. Then this anniversary of the birth of Shaka will not have been celebrated in vain.

Outline of Buddhism in Japan

By Shuken Yamaushi

I. A historical review.

Buddhism had a thousand years of history before it reached to Japan, and it has had about fourteen hundred years of interesting history there. It has developed along with Japan, the religion profoundly affecting the country and people, while these in turn influenced the religion. The outcome has been a Buddhism which differs quite essentially from the type prevailing today in Ceylon, Burma, Siam and French Indo-China, and likewise from the type prevailing in China and Korea. Japanese Buddhism, therefore, may be roughly regarded as representing the last and highest stages of a very long and highly varied development.

Buddhism is not, however, and never has been the sole religion of Japan. It has always been closely connected with Shinto and Confucianism and has been affected by them. But, it is fact that Buddhism has been the dominant and in many ways the distinctive religion of the Japanese people, a vehicle and spur of Japanese culture, civiligation and nationality.

II. Philosophical sects of Buddhism.

One of the distinctive facts about Buddhism in Japan is the number of important sects which have been introduced from China. The Ritsu, Jōjitsu, San-Ron, Hossō, Kusha, and Kegon sects were introduced to Japan in the age of Nara. The Tendai and Shingon were transmitted from China in the ninth century by two famous priests. The Jōdo and Zen were transmitted from China in the twelfth century; and in the thirteenth century the True Sect of Jōdo and the Nichiren sects were founded by great Japanese religious leaders, Shinran and Nichiren, who became the most popular personalities in the religious history of Japan.

Buddhist sects may be classified according to doctrine and according to their method of salvation. The following chart is a attempt to classify them according to doctrine.

1) Hinayana
   - A) Kusha
   - B) Jōjitsu
   - C) Vinaya
2) Quasi-Mahayana.
   - A) Hossō
   - B) San-Ron
3) True-Mahayana
   - A) Kegon, Tendai —
     - a) —Jōdo (The pure Land sect)
       —The True Sect of Pure Land
     - b) Nichiren
   - B) Zen
   - C) Shingon

III. Method of salvation.

Buddhist sects may also be classified from the standpoint of their method of salvation as follows:

1) By the power of:
   - A) Amida
     - a) Works—Jōdo sect
     - b) Faith—True Sect of the Pure Land
     - c) Intercession—Yuzū Nembutsu Sect, Ji Sect
   - B) Buddha through mystic scriptures
     - a) Nichiren Sect
2) By self-effort
   - A) Hossō Sect
   - B) Tendai Sect
   - C) Kegon Sect
   - D) Ritsu Sect
3) By meditation or intuition
   - A) San-Ron Sect
   - B) Zen Sect

Of these the Shin or True Sects of the Pure Land and the Nichiren sect are of especial importance, because they are the most popular and represent Buddhist doctrine which is the indigenous product of Japanese people. During the thirteenth century a great wave of religious awakening took place under the able leadership of men like Hōnen Shōnin, Shinran Shōnin, who taught salvation through Amida, and Nichiren Shōnin who is spoken of as a Buddhist prophet. This revival produced something new in the history of Buddhism.

新刊紹介

◇佛陀の福音

（ポール・ケーラス著、八幡關太郎譯）

佛教に親しみの少ない西洋人にわかり易く佛教を説いた好著として、多くの國語に反譯されてゐる名著である。

その中々に親切な、そして實に要領よく佛教を全般的に、歐米人獨特な感覺を以て說いた好入門書である。以前に出た舊譯より、ずつと良い此の新譯が出版されたことは、まことに嬉しいことだ。

（4×6 判 370 頁、定價 2 圓、東京神田神保町 1 ノ 30、南光社）

Konciza historio de budhana Esp-movado en Japanujo.

de Kei Sibajama.

I

Por skizi la temon estas oportune, ke oni unue priskribu pri jenaj grupoj, kiuj aperis unu post alia en budhana kampo komence de la movado.

(A,) Ootani Daigaku (=Universitato) Esp-grupo.

Ĝi fondiĝis en novembro de 1921 laŭ la iniciato de unu el estraroj de la Universitato Sro K. Hosokaŭa kun ĉirkaŭ 20 grupanoj, kiuj ĵus finis elementan kurson, okazigitan en la Universitato por unua fojo. Kaj en februaro de sekvinta jaro 1922 jam ĝi eldonis sian organon "La Paco," la unuan N-ron. Vere la fondiĝo de la grupo kaj la eldono de la organo estas la unua en Esp-movado de la kampo.

Kvankam la grupo marŝadis sur onduma vojo iam prospera kaj iam ne tiel vigla, ĝi bone funkciadis ĝis la komenco de 1926, ĉir. 5 jarojn, laŭ la persista klopodo de bravaj grupanoj, el kiuj Sro K. Tanijama, Sro R. Ikeura estas fame konataj.

"La Paco," kopia enhavoriĉa grandforma organo de la grupo, dume sinsekve aperis ĝis la 10a N-ro. Tiu tempe la grupanoj ĉiam redaktadis la organon kun revo, ke ĝi havas grandan mision diskonigi Mahajanan Budhismon de Sunoleviĝanta lando al ĉiu mondparto. Kaj la revo ne tute estis vana. Ĝi gajnis sufiĉe da reptacion el ĉiu angulo de la mondo malgraŭ tio, ke la stilo de ĝiaj artikoloj ne estis tiel bone rafinitaj komparante kun tiuj de nun-tempaj oranoj de multaj grupoj.

Bedaŭrinde, kun gradigo de supre nomitaj samideanoj, t.e. de aprilo de 1926, la grupo, havanta brilantan historion en la movado, ekdormis dum pluraj jaroj, postlasinte grandan monumenton, 10 ekzemplerojn da organoj famekonataj.

(B,) Rjukoku Daigaku Esp-Grupo.

Ĝi fondiĝis en majo de 1922, tuj post finiĝo de la unua kurso okazigita en la universitato. De tiam oni aranĝis ĉiu jare kurson

por akiri novajn samideanojn. Kaj la grupo tiel sane kreskis ke ĝi fine povis eldoni kopie sian organon, titolitan "Sankta Tilio," en oktobro de 1925. Ĝia ĉefredaktoro estis Sro Ŝ. Inada, kiu entuziasme gvidadis la grupanojn ĝis sia gradigo, ĝis marto de 1929.

Okaze de la festo de inaŭguracia datreveno de la universitato, celebrata en printemo de 1925, la grupanoj aranĝis bonan Esp-ekspozicion, kiu havis grandan sensacion kaj brilantan frukton.

La sorto de la grupo estis tiamaniere dorlotita kaj la organo n-ro post n-ro aperis ĝis la 6a, kiu eldoniĝis en la marto de 1929. Tamen ankaŭ venis malfavora tago por la grupo, de aprilo de 1929 ĝi ne bone funkciis pro malmultiĝo de grupano. "Sankta Tilio," kopia organo, kalkuliĝas ĝis la 6a n-ro, tamen ankaŭ estas memorinda produktaĵo de Budhana Esp-movado en la unuaj tagoj.

(C) Nippon Esperanto-Gakuin.

Ĝi fondiĝis en Decembro de 1922. Ĝia fondinto kaj direktoro estis Sro B. Akijama.

En septembro de 1922 Sro B. Akijama aranĝis ĉe Ĵoogu-kjookai, Hongoo-ku, Tokio, Kulturan Liber-Lekciaron, kiu konsistis el religia, filozofia, sociala kaj naturscienca fakoj. Okaze de la aranĝo li prove intermetis Esperantan fakon, kiun gvidis Prof. Ĵ. Kaŭahara, fame konata samideano. Al nia miro, tamen, enskribintoj de la fako kalkuliĝis pli ol 30 personoj.

Jen, li ĝojeganta la sukceson, sendepende apartigis la fakon de la Lekciaro kaj nove fondis supre titolitan Esp-Gakuin.

De la fondiĝo li energie, eĉ manie laboradis laboradis por propagandi Esp-on, sinsekve okazigante bone aranĝitajn kursojn pli altajn kaj elementajn. Kaj ĝis aŭgusto de 1924 li aranĝis entute 10 kursojn, al kiuj partprenis pli ol 500 personoj. Sed favora sorto ne daŭris longe, li iom lacigita pro trouzo de la forto, fermis pordon de la Esp-Gakuin kun granda bedaŭro, postlasinte historian gloron en la kampo de la movado.

Estas notinde, ke dum vigla funkciado de la Esp-Gakuin preskaŭ ĉiuj rektoroj de ekleziaj universitatoj kaj eminentaj kleruloj koncernantaj al eklezioj en Tokio ne ŝparis iliajn favorojn al la movado, inter ili oni povas nomi jenajn, Nukaruja - Kaiten, Katoo - Seiŝin, Suehiro - Ŝookei, Motizuki - Ŝinkjo, Sakaino - Koojoo, Umata - Gjookei, ne nur tio kelkaj el ili ricevis lecionon aŭ partprenis Specialan

Lekciaron por kursanoj, kiu estis grandskale aranĝita en la okazo de la 4a kurso ĉe Centra Budhana Asocio.

(Ĉ) Esperanta Fako de Budhisma Sav-Armeo.

Ĝi fondiĝis en Januaro de 1925 en libera religia institucio, Budhisma Sav-Armeo (BSA), laŭ la iniciato de Sro J. Nakaniŝi kaj Sro R. Tojoŝima. Ĉe la fino de 1924 Sro J. Nakaniŝi konvinke klarigis pri neceseco kaj indo de Esp-movado al Sro R. Tojoŝima, kiu estis ĉefo de propaganda fako de BSA kaj instigis pri tio, ke BSA nepre havu Esp-fakon, por ke ĝi plenumu ian rolon por la movado. Jen, tial komence de sekvinta jaro fondiĝis la fako. De tiam Sro Nakanisi, la direktoro de la fako, unu port alia gvidadis kursojn en Jaŭata, sidurbo de centro de BSA.

En apliro de sama jaro li eldonis kopian gazeteton malgrandforman por propagandi Esp-on; sekve ĝia enhavo plejparte estis prelego de elementa kurso aŭ Japanlingvaj artikoloj por ne Esperantistoj. Ĝi ĉiumonate aperadis ĝis la 5a n-ro.

En oktobro de sama jaro, anstataŭ la kopia gazeteto eldoniĝis nova gazeteto titolita "La Lumo Senbara" en preso kun preskaŭ sama enhavo. Tiu ĉi gazeteto estas la unua, aperinta en preso en Japana Budhana Esp-movado. En tiu punkto ĝi estas tre memorinda.

"La Lumo Senbara" ciumonate regule aperadis ĝis la 9a n-ro (ĝis Junio de 1926) en ekonomia subteno de Sro R. Tojoŝima. Sed je nia bedaŭro, de sekvinta n-ro la 10a, ĝia enhavo tute ŝanĝiĝis kaj fariĝis populara religia gazeteto, ĉar oni plu ne povis elteni ekonomian suferon por daŭrigi la eldonon.

Ankoraŭ estas alia notindaĵo; laŭ la propono de la Sro Nakaniŝi blinda Samideano Sro Ĵ. Ueda, ĉefo de blinda fako de BSA, bonvolis akcepti Esp-lekcion sur la organo de la fako, Kaj de aprila N-ro de 1926 artikolo de Esp-kurso de Sro Nakaniŝi daŭre redaktiĝas en la organo punktlitera.

* * *

Laŭ la skizoj de la supre cititaj grupoj oni certe povos sciiĝi historieton de komenca epoko de Budhana Esp-movado.

Resume, Esp-movado en Budhana kampo ekĝermis en 1921; kaj jaron post jaro pliprosperiĝadis ĝis 1926; poste de 1927 ĝis 1929 iom post iom malvigliĝadis.

Sed en 1930 ekaperis orienta ruĝo al la movado; pri tio mi volas skizi en sekvonta capitro.

P. R. Estas senbezone diri, ke krom la supre skizitaj movadoj estis etaj personaj agadoj, kiujn mi intence preterlasis mencii pro tio, ke ili ne estis tiel gravaj.

(Daŭrigota)

日本の佛教音樂運動

江崎小秋

A

吾邦の佛教關係から生れた音樂は非常に多く數ふることが出來るが，佛教音樂としての名稱のもとに發達を念願し，またその發達を期して生れたのは近々此處三十有餘年前である。

その頃の音樂を考察してみると誠に幼稚なもので，また歌謠の型式から云つても，何等詩的內容を持つてゐなかつた。所謂文字の羅列とでも云ふか——そう云つたものであつた。然しまたそれは後生への發展を期するために，若い人達の止まざる叫びとしての一つの運動であつたが爲めに，それら型式を重んじて硏究を行つた結果を發表するといふやうな機關がなかつたが爲めでもあつた。或ひは又，佛教詩人として現在の如く對社會的に嚴然と進出してゐるやうな，所謂中心を成す人物に缺けてゐたが爲めでもあつた。然し，そうした未熟な明治時代に生まれた佛教音樂運動が，今日では全佛教界を支配する迄に至つたのは何故であるか，そこに大きな疑問をもたねばならない。

B

佛教音樂が生まれた時は，實に佛教界は歡喜踊躍したであらうことを今，筆者は想像してゐる。その作品が善いものであるにしろ，劣つてゐるものにしろ，今迄皆無であつた佛教界に取つては，それを歡迎せずにはゐられなかつたであらう。その踊躍の惰力と，その後に起つて，奮然第二段の運動に盡力された多くの犧牲者が出現したからであつた。

故に，佛教音樂の今日あらしめたのは，佛教界そのものでもなければ，各宗長老でもない。何時の時代でも，その時代の潮流に現はれて事を成す人物の出現で，人物と潮流の合致した時に事は成るのである。——そうしたことを，此の佛教音樂運動の上に於いても云ふことが出來る。

それであるからと云つて，今日，今尙佛教音樂は今迄進んで來たその道を辿つてゐるやうであるならば，旣に佛教音樂としての生命は地に墮ちるであらう。

C

斯うした見方，及び運動の方法として佛教音樂は，非常なる勢力を以つて今や民衆に迫つてゐる。昭和十年度——今年こそ，その感を，ひしひしと胸に描き，眼でみることが出來る年である。

筆者は作詩家の立場として云ふ。——佛教音樂は寺院殿堂のものであつてはならない——常に野に在る風の聲，或ひは池邊の蓮華の開く，あの淸淨なる姿，パツと開くその美妙なる音，その音，音であれ――と。そしてまた友人である，佛教關係の凡ゆる作曲家は何と云つてゐるか。――詩人は常に寺院殿堂ばかりを佛教歌謡として歌つてはいけない，あの山の蒼さを見よ，そして太陽の西に沈むあの赤さを見よ，そして歌へ――といつてゐる。

斯様に，日本の佛教音樂運動は，それが架空的表現であつたのが，實在的即ち，現實的，現世的見方，歌ひ方に進みつゝあり，絶えず，新らしい時代と共に佛教音樂もまた進展してゆくのである。そこに日本の佛教音樂運動として進んでゆくべき道が在り，今後を約して大成を期せん覺悟で吾々は双肩に重大なる使命を負つてゐるのである。非常に紙數が足りないので，これ位にして他日に讓る。

最後に佛教音樂の普及と發達に貢獻活躍してゐる重なる各團體，及，作詞，作曲諸家を上げて筆を擱く。

△音樂舞踊團體

(東京) パドマ合唱團
指揮　小松　平五郎氏
(同) 佛教音樂協會聖歌隊
指揮　同協會役員諸氏
(同) 武藏野女子學院合唱團
指揮　藤井　清水氏
(同) タンダバツハ舞踊研究所
指導　賀來　琢磨氏
(京都) 佛教聖歌研究會
指導　藤井　制心氏

△音樂研究團體

(東京) 佛教音樂協會
主事　伊藤　精昭氏

△歌謠・音樂・舞踊研究團體

(東京) 日本佛教童謠協會
主事　江崎　小秋氏

△作曲家

山田　耕筰氏	弘田龍太郎氏
藤井　清水氏	小松平五郎氏
小松　耕輔氏	小松　清氏
室崎　琴月氏	長妻　完至氏
山口　保治氏	深澤　一郎氏
藤井　制心氏	本多　鐵麿氏
吉川　孝一氏	笠原　眞應氏

△作詩家

北原　白秋氏	野口　雨情氏
松浦　一氏	江崎　小秋氏
青柳　興敬氏	渡邊　千秋氏

△舞踊家

高橋　元子氏	藤蔭　靜枝氏
賀來　琢磨氏	岡本　義雄氏

△重なる佛教音樂關係書

佛教音樂協會編	佛教聖歌
日本佛教童謠協會編	佛教音樂全集
同 (研究誌)新佛教音樂	

國際文化振興會が佛書刊行に補助

國際文化振興會では此程，京大文學部教授の濱田耕作博士が「日本でもこれ程よく出來てゐるものは稀だ」と絶讃した程の名著たる和蘭ライデン大學日本語講座教授の故デ・フイツセル博士が一生の事業として博識を傾けた『日本の古代佛教』全三卷が出版半ばにして不幸同博士の他界を見た爲め經費の不足から出版元のグツトナー會社の倉庫に埋れたまゝになつてゐたのを知つて，高楠博士などの意見をも徴し我國佛教文化の顯揚の好機會として，その出版費二千圓を投げ出し，この意義ある出版を完成させることとなつた。

朝鮮總督府の新國語讀本

「釋迦牟尼」課を新加

X　Y　Z

昨秋，新定された朝鮮總督府の新國語讀本（四年制普通學校）卷八の第二十七（課）は，「孔子と釋迦牟尼」と題し，この東洋の二大聖人を叙し，儒教と佛教との二大教の大意を教へんとしてゐる點は，注目に價ひするものがあると思ふ。

以下に，その後者，釋迦牟尼に就て述べられてゐる個所（百十四頁から百十八頁まで）を，その儘，御傳へすることにしやう。

二　釋迦牟尼

儒教と並んで長く世人に命のかてを與へて來た佛教は釋迦牟尼の開いた教である。

釋迦牟尼は孔子と大體同時代に，北印度のカピラ城主の世子として生まれた。生まれつき同情の念に厚く，何事も深く考へ込むたちであつた。

釋迦牟尼は城外に出る毎に，杖にすがる老人や，息もたえだえの病人や野邊に送られる死人などを見て，つくづく世のはかなさを感じた。そうして人生の苦しみからのがれるまことの道を知りたいものと思ひなやんだ末，ついに聖賢の教を受ける外はないと思ひ立ち，或夜ひそかに宮殿を出て修行の途に上つた。

釋迦牟尼はあちらこちらの學者を尋ねまわつて話をきいた。しかしどれにも滿足することが出來ないので，或森に行つて，誰にもたよらず苦行を始めた。そうして六年の間，次々に起つて來る心の迷を退けようとしたが，何のかいもなかつた。そこで森を去つて，或綠の色こき菩提樹のかげに靜坐して夜もすがら思をこらした。やがて一點の明星がきらめいて，夜はほのぼのと明けそめる刹那，迷の雲がからりと晴れて，はつきりとまことの道を悟ることが出

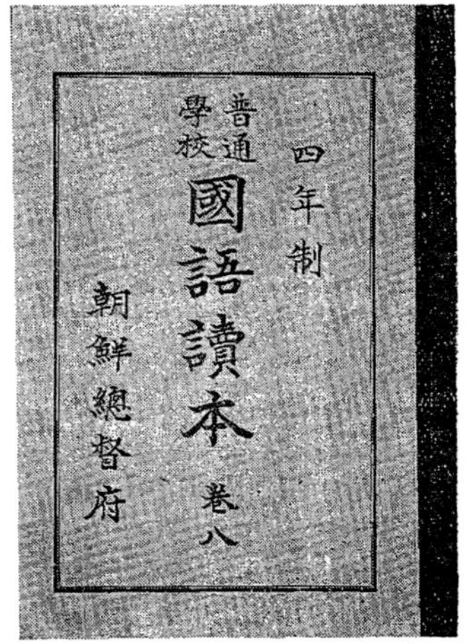

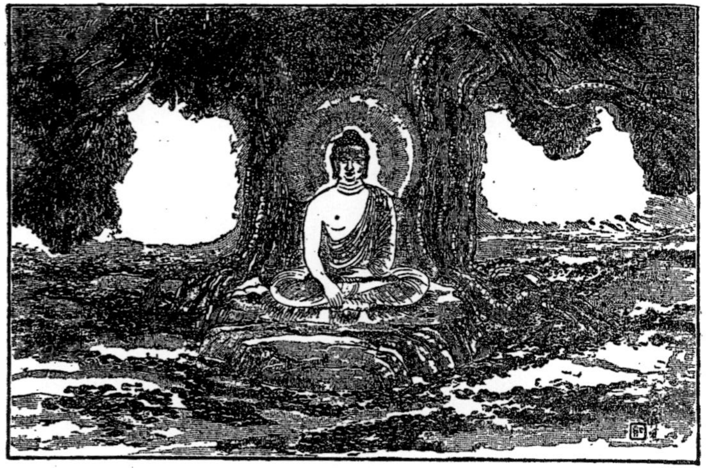

來た。

釋迦牟尼は，此の尊い心持を世の人々と共にせずには居られぬといふ慈悲の心が胸にあふれて來るのをどうすることも出來なかつた。そこで先づ友人等に道を說き，つずいて國に歸り，父王を始め國民を敎化して故鄕の恩に報いた。そうして八十になつても，なお各地を巡つて道を傳へて居たが，ついに病にかゝつて再び立たれなくなつた。いよいよ臨終が近づいた時，釋迦牟尼は泣悲しんで居る人々に，

「私は行はうと思つたことを行ひ盡くし，語らうと思つたことを語り盡くした。これまで，說いた敎そのものが私の命である。私のなくなつた後もめいめいが其の敎をまじめに行ふ所に，私は永遠に生きて居る。」

とさとして，靜かに眼を閉ぢた。

以上の記述に對しては，不充分で，また不滿な個所もないこともないが，とにかく，かうして四年制國語讀本の最後に於て，これだけでも佛敎知識が敎へられることは，喜ばしいことであると云はねばならぬ。

尙ほ，この課には，此處に再現した挿圖が百十六頁の上半頁を飾つてゐるが，之は，目下印度で聖畫の完成に盡力されつつある我が野生司香雪畫伯の彩管になるものであつて，これ又正に其の人を得たものと云ふべきべあらう。

伯林郊外フローナウ所在

故ダルケ博士の遺業「佛敎精舍」に就て

榊原順次

世界的佛敎學者，故ダルケ博士に依つてドイツ伯林郊外に「佛敎精舍」(寺院) が建立されたのは一九二六年である。處も伯林舊市を去ること十キロメーター，ガルテンシタツトとして有名なフローナウの，しかもカイザー公園に面した小高い岡の上に佛敎趣味滿點の樣式と構造とを以つて建設され，邊りに木立つ松の林と共に，訪れる東洋人をして一層懷鄕の念を深からしめるのである。

クリスト敎の國ヨーロツパに，併かも新敎の本山ドイツの國に歐洲人の手に依つて佛敎の寺が建立されたと云ふだけでも，吾々東洋佛敎徒のこゝろを躍らするに已に充分のニユースである。此の全歐洲に唯一つの佛敎の寺の發展經營の責任は，ひとりドイツ佛敎徒にのみ皈せらるべきものではない。全世界佛敎徒の當然感じなくてはならぬ共同責任である。或は自派，或は自國，近視眼的にひとり自分の周圍のみを考へて遠き異國の同朋同敎徒の困窮を敢へて顧ざるが如きは素より佛敎徒の採るべき態度ではない。殊に協助共生をモツトーとする大乘佛敎徒に置いてをやである。かくの如きことは今改めて喋々を待つまでもなく，全日本佛敎徒の已によく了解憶念されてゐることである。

偶々前記佛敎の寺が，その創立の土臺のコンクリのまだ燥かぬ一九二八年建設されて僅かに二年にしてその創立者であり中心人物たるダルケ博士を喪つたことに依り，加へて古今未曾有のドイツ經濟的窮迫に依り，此の大きな未來を約束されて歐洲の天地に生れた佛敎弘通の根據，佛敎精舍は遂に經營維持困難の窮地に陷るに至つた。故博士の遺志を受けてせめても之れが經營維持をさせんものと献身の努力を拂はれてゐる故ダルケ博士の遺族達も，遂に世界佛敎徒に對して之れが救援を叫ばれてゐることは已に世のよく知る處である。然るに不幸にして未だ何等此れが積極的救援の行はれた事實あるを聞かない。唯一つ先きに印度佛敎徒オタマ比丘に依つて是れが買收を企てられたけれ共，遇々同氏の思想的理由を以て英國政府の反對に依り遂にその成立を見ず今日に及んでゐる。

去る昭和七年十一月頃より昭和九年十月まで二ケ年間同寺に寄宿した私は此の寺がドイツ人の精神生活の上に如何なる意義を持ち如何なる役目を果しつゝあるか亦果すであらうかを最もよく知る一人であり，從つて此れが救援の必要も他の人々よりも一倍深く痛感

するものである。此處に決心して全日本佛敎徒に之れを訴へ，之れが實現の爲めに身を献ぜんとするものである。

時に他を援くるの願はしきは云ふまでもないが，自ら立つ力のない者が他の倒れるを助け起さんとするの愚への反省も，もとより考へられないことはない。然し乍ら今回の佛敎精舍買取りの必要の叫びは唯それだけの理由を持つて反對亦は破毀さるべきものではない。それは單なる救援と云ふ消極的意味のみに止るものでなく，日本佛敎泰西進出と云ふ積極的一大使命を持つものである。日本佛敎歐洲進出これは實に在外內地人の布敎のみを持つて滿足してゐた從來の日本佛敎外國傳道史の上に一大新紀元を與へるものである。

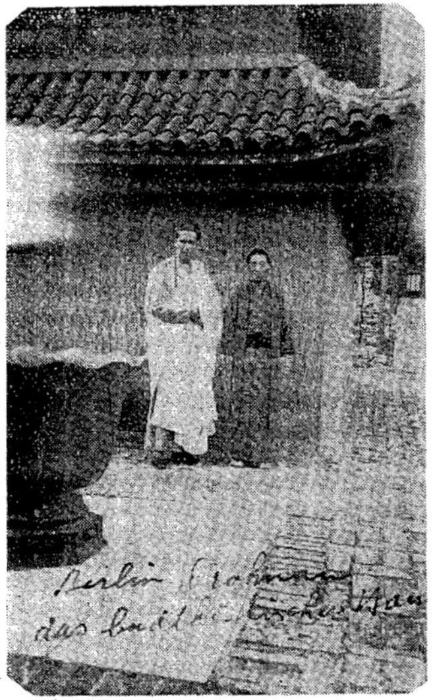

精舍に於ける筆者（和服）

更に吾人が大きく眼を開けば，日本佛敎歐洲進出はひとり佛敎徒內の問題ではなく，アジア日本の精神文化歐洲進出の大役を持つものである。

今や日本文化の歐洲への紹介の如何に緊急重大なるものであるかは已に世に弘く叫ばれてゐる問題である。

世界の進みと共に國際協調はいよいよ緊要の問題となる。眞の國際協調は相互民族，國家の精神文化の理解に俟たなくてはならぬ。近時各國共に此の點に自覺され，各種文化協會事業の振興は誠に世界人類の爲めに慶賀すべきことである。先きにはドイツが歐洲大戰に世界の孤立者となつた苦い經驗からして戰後急に國際文化局を設け，數百萬圓を費して內外文化事業の振興に全力を盡し出したのも，また近くはフランスが文化事業費とし約千五百萬圓を計上し，イタリーが自國固有の精神發揚の爲めに前者と同様にまた約千五百萬圓の豫算を計上せるが如きは，全く文化振興事業の如何に切要なるかを物語つてゐるものである。此の種の文化事業，他國へ自國の文化を紹介すると云ふ施設に於て最も立ち遲れをしてゐるものが我が國日本である。隣邦支那ですら文化紹介事業に於ては我が國よりも進んでゐること遙かなるものがある。例をドイツにとれば，伯林大學に於て支那學の講座が大學を代表する程な一流學者に依つてしかも六つも七つも開講されてゐるのに對して日本のそれは又何と云ふ寂しさであらう。僅かにオリエンタル・ゼミナールに於て日本語の敎授が行はれてゐるだけではないか。嘗つて黑田源治博士からのお話しに依れば，ゲンフの國際聯盟の事務局の隣りには，通り過ぐる人々をして驚嘆せしむる程宏壯な中華民國圖書館が設けられてあるとか。

國際勞働代表の吉阪俊藏氏の話しに依れば昨年八月にはゼネヴァのキユーサールに於て支那藝術の大展覽會が催され，**東西文化**と題した月刊雜誌も發行され，少くとも一萬册以上あらうと云ふ支那圖書館が新築され弘く漢書も集められ，ゼネバアに行くには漢書持參は無用なりと云はれる程充實されたものであり。昨年支那人の小學校敎師が二人附いて九才十才ぐらひの子供を十數人連れて來た。之れはゼネバの國際小學校に入學させ，他日支那の爲め國際政場に於て活躍する重要人物を作らうと云ふのである，云々。

我が國の國際文化施設の不備の結果として諸外國の日本文化に對する認識の不足が延いては直接日本の國際政界に如何に大なる不利益を與へてゐるかは近く日本が國際聯盟脫退の經緯を靜かに觀察すれば明かである。

併しながら文化宣傳事業の要は自國文化の眞價値を他國人に理解せしむると云ふことである。もとより山紫水明の風光日本を紹介するも，よし又繪畫彫刻等の異趣味を以つて美術日本を高調するもよし，併し乍ら更に重大にして併も緊要なことはアジア精神文化を理想的に發達をせしめた日本民族の精神生活の深さ，文化日本の眞價を理解せしむると云ふことである。

此の目的にかなつた最もよきものの一つとして自分は千三百年間，日本民族の懐ろの中に成長發達を仕遂げ來つた日本佛敎，しかもそれは印度佛敎とも支那佛敎のそれとも異る特殊の發達をなした日本佛敎の歐洲傳道の必要を考うるものである。此の日本佛敎の特殊性を理解せしむることに依つて，日本民族の特性，日本文化の眞價値の理解が初めて可能となることを信ずるものである。

云ふ處の日本民族の特殊性とは卽ち與へられたる材料に魂を吹き込むこと，靜を動に還元しうる宇宙眞理實現の能力を所有せることである。これ實に日本が，日本民族こそ，世界思想の還元者，人類文化の心臟だと世界に向つて誇りうる一大特殊性である。此の特性の最もよく現はれてゐるものが，日本佛敎である。

日本佛敎歐洲進出がかくの如き重大なる使命を持つことを思ふ時，是れが中心本據ともなるべき伯林佛敎の家買收の實現こそは實に日本佛敎徒の一人として，又日本國民の一人として，こころから念願せずには居られないものである。

寺の境內は約十一モルゲン（約三町步弱），建物は日本のお寺式本堂と庫裡，洋式三階建て（圖書室，バルコン，佛像佛畫あり）他にセイロンハウスと云ふ印度式の建物，坐禪堂，印度サンチの塔門を似ねた正門，八正道を象る石段，其他庭園もすべて佛敎の敎理を表

「八正道」の門

象して作られ，阿彌陀佛の石像，青銅蓮葉の大水盤，二十數個の鐵燈籠等々來訪者をして一層東洋趣味を喚起せしむるに充分の材料の多くが集められてゐる。賣價は土地共十二萬マーク（時價約十五萬圓）との申出であるが，勿論分割して讓り受けることも可能である。亦是れが經營法の一助として留學生の寄宿舍として利用せんとするが如き場合の爲めにも亦相當に適當の條件が具備されてある。

以上ドイツ佛教寺院買收に就いて，その所以の一端を演べて大方の諸賢の御考慮を煩はさんとするものである。幸ひにして各位の御賛同を得，その熱誠ある後援に依つて之れが實現を見るに至らば，獨り我が國關係佛教徒の欣幸たるのみならず，又實に日本九千萬同胞，ひいては世界人類の精神生活の爲めに大いなる慶福である。

× × ×

霞山會館に於ける

國際勞働理事會帝國政府代表 **吉阪俊藏氏の**

講演（昭和十年二月十二日）から

佛教のお寺が只一つベルリン郊外のフローナウと云ふ所にある。私は先般それを見て參つたが，それを開いたドクター・ダールケといふ人が，三・四年前に亡くなつて，其の妹が管理して居る。廣さは二町半ぐらゐ，松山をとり入れて風雅なよい所である。印度風の門を入ると，八聖道に因んだと云ふことであるが，八段に分けて段を造り，納所の入口にはムーン・ストーンの敷石を置いて，ゴングを鳴らして入る。納所には大如來を祀つたり，本堂（支那日本式建築）にはお釋迦さんを祀り，境內にセイロン・ハウスといふ坐禪堂が二三箇所ある。十二萬マーク位で宜いが，日本人に買つて貰へまいかといふ管理者からの話であつた。土地を分けて賣つても宜いといふことであつた。日本人の立場を知らせる上に，遠廻しのやうで最も近道なのは，佛教(殊に禪宗)を說き廣める事ではなからうか。

× × ×

大乘佛教の國際化

我通報局の質問書に對する名士の應答（續き）

○ 岡本かの子

教義や論文の紹介と同時に好き佛教藝術（造型，或ひは文學）を示すこと，非常に効果的ならずやと考へます。

○ 淺野孝之

一，佛教學教授を海外に派遣して佛教講座を開設すること。

二，佛教文學幷に藝術の外國語飜譯又は說明書を外國圖書館に備付け又は一般頒布をはかること。

三，佛典又は佛教に關する有名なる著書の外國語譯。

四，日本又は東洋文庫特に佛教文庫の開設をはかること。

五，佛教名所の英文案內を內外ホテルに備付けること。

六，外國文の「佛教入門」の刊行。

七，香爐香函等に興味を有するを以てかゝる佛具の頒布につとむること（外國文說明附）

八，佛教各宗當事者をして協同して佛教の海外紹介につとめしむる機運を助成すること。

○ 東福義雄

國內的運動と國際的運動とが二元的である場合は，その國際化運動を容す程の餘裕は今日の佛教界には，まだまだ乏しいでせう。でこの兩面を一元的に見た基礎工作として，大乘佛教々義の現代的認識と現代的再現が根本的必要事であると存じます。即ち相當な豫算による機關を設けて，先づ通佛教，次に各宗の特色とする教義を現代語に飜譯するのです。例へば涅槃を理想として菩薩道を行づるといふやうなことは廣い世間から見れば一つの呪文でしかありませんから，それが何のことかを現代化するのです。教義の威信を保たしめつゝすれば效果的な飜譯も出來，始めて日本佛教は國際化の緒につくでせう。

○ 朝日融溪

佛教國の間に研究生の交換及び講演者及教授を互に派遣し眞實なる大乘精神の實踐化を志すことが肝要かと存じます。

○ 鷹谷俊之

「國際佛教通報」の發刊は御同樣聊かたりとも佛靑運動に參加し來れる者にとりて御同慶至極に存候。

日本國內の事情を國外へ，國外の事情を國內へ通報されて彼我相互の利益を計られたく，エスペラント語を一二頁でも挿入し第一回汎太平洋佛靑大會以來の懸案をも御成就下され度く，これと並行して國外佛教者の宿所氏名の調査を希望仕候。

○ 長谷川基

宗教も信仰とか研究とか自己內面の問題にのみ關して居たのは昔の事で今は世界的に信仰を同ふするものが人種の如何洋の東西を論ぜず相會して意見の交換を試み或は通信に依て思想を發表し向上發展を期するのは誠に結構な事である。大乘佛教の國際化の意義ある企ては吾れ人共に双手を擧げて贊同する所以，之より進んで國際親善の企業を助け世界人類の平和をもたらすの魁とならんことを望む所以であります。

○ 川島一城

日蓮聖人の御遺文英譯の事業も亦その一

に可有之と奉存候，併せて日蓮聖人の御事蹟を編纂さるゝことも極めて急務なる一事業かと奉存候。敬白

○　立 花 俊 道

大乘佛教の國際化を圖るためにはその方法はいろいろあるかと思ふ。定期刊行の雜誌，パンフレツトの發行，現代作家の手に成れる大乘佛教書，古代大乘經論の飜譯，大乘佛教文化の紹介，大乘佛教教理に關する質問應答の準備等等，金と人とありさへすれば仕事は無限にあると思ふ。それに就ても第一の急務は人物の養成で，今假りに英文を借りて發表するとすれば，南方佛教はよほど細かい所まで英語で言ひ表はされ隨つて術語の飜譯も大凡一定して居ると見てよいが，大乘佛教はまだ何ほども外語で發表されて居らぬから術語の飜譯は出來ても居ないし，出來ても區々である。何から手をつけていゝか分らぬ姿である。

○　高 島 平 三 郎

大乘佛教の國際化に必要なる事業は多々あるべきも當面の急務としては簡單にして而かも要領を得たるテキストの出版なり。經典の各國語譯は已に多少あるべきも，なほ必要ならんも，これよりも我國の佛教家が適當の書を著はし，之を各國語に譯して頒布すべきである。

○　木 山 十 彰

一，聖德太子の十七憲法を中心として各種文化的御事業並にその大乘佛教的御信念を弘傳するの方法を講ずる事。(主として文書又は展覽會)

二，花まつりの國際化として先づ東京に於て各國大公使達並にその夫人達を招待し曩に創始せし花まつり前夜の待明會式家族的集會を開くこと。

○　桑 山 鉉 子

大乘佛教を國際化する當面の事業は言ふ迄もなく國際大乘佛教誌の刊行にあるも旣に國際佛教通報の發刊となりしを以て之が充實發展を謀ると共に左の諸點の逐次實行が望ましい。

一，大乘佛教宣傳使節を各國に派遣すること

一，各國より大乘佛教研究生を募集すること

一，年次的に佛教大會を各國に於て開催すること

一，通俗的大乘佛教概說を各國語にて刊行すること

一，大乘佛教的藝術の各國への紹介等

○　平 等 通 昭

一，大乘聖典の重要なものを先づ英譯すること。(日本聖典中には北京官話に譯す必要のものもあり）次いで，獨佛其他歐洲語東洋各國語に飜譯すること。

二，(甲)優秀なる傳道師を養成すること。その機關として傳道學校を起し，特に話し講演する外國語に熟達せしめること。(乙)外國大學學會に佛教學者を派遣し，理論的に教理を講義せしめること。

三，之等の機關として(出版傳道の)傳道會社を組織すること。之については各派が圓滑に一致協調すべきこと。

○　岡 部 宗 城

一，圖書の刊行

二，交換講座

三，俱樂部の常置

四，留學生の招致

等多々有之候様愚考いたし候。

○　馬 田 行 啓

一，日本佛教の海外紹介

A，日本佛教の現狀(宗團，教義，信仰，修行等）を順次に華歐文を以て紹介すること

B，各宗祖師の代表的著作を華歐語に譯して紹介すること

C，寫眞を以て諸種の佛教行事，佛像等を紹介すること(勿論說明を附けて)

二，華歐等に於る大乘佛教の紹介

右の日本佛教の海外紹介に準じて考案すること。

三，佛教の代表的行事に，外交官，駐在武官其他を必ず招いて，彼等をして大乘佛教に親炙させること。

○　山 本 快 龍

基礎工事として左の三項目

一，漢譯大乘佛典の英譯

一，佛教研究成果を外國語にて發表

一，佛教徒と在住外人との交驩

○　野 原 休 一

エスペランチストとしての立場より御答申上候，大乘佛教の國際化の爲に御勉め相成との御事なれば先づ第一に國際補助語たるエスペラントを御採用相成候事が最必要歟と存候，其以上の事は門外漢たる小生として意見など申述ぶる資格無之差控へるが禮儀かと存候。敬具

○　寺 田 彌 吉

豫算の關係によりますが，

一，「通報」を世界の各大學及び著名な佛教學者に送り，彼我の意見交換をすること

二，聲明書を發して，世界の著名な新聞に送り，發表させること

三，年刊を出して，各國佛教學者相互の研究を綜合すること

四，日本に來て佛教を研究してゐる外國人にできるだけ母國に日本大乘佛教の進步性を紹介してもらふこと

五，すぐれた書物の外國語への飜譯

（もつと澤山ありますが，出發はこれ位ゐでしやう。）

○　山 内 脩 謙

日本佛教の英譯出版などは大切なことでせう。アメリカなどでは，教授交換も出來たらしたいなどゝいふ意嚮が各所に認められました。夏期などを利用した双方視察團の交換なども惡いことはありませんね。

○　土 井 晩 翠

英文（及び其他例之エスペラント語）にて大乘教理を簡明に說明する事，即ち，”Introduction to the Mahayana Doctrine of Buddhism”とでも題すべきパンフレツトを廣く世界に宣布すること。

○　江 崎 小 秋

大乘佛教の國際化に必要なる事業は第一回，第二回汎太平洋佛靑大會に議案となりそのまゝになつてゐるやうであるが，それは，佛教音樂としての優れたる曲目を發表(海外諸國に)するより絕對的に適當なる仕事はないと思ふ。何故ならば音樂の譜は，どこへ行つても，イの音はイであり，アの音はアである。たゞ樂譜に變りはないが，その歌詞を，日，華，歐文の三國のものを譜の下へ入れて發表すれば，我國人の法悅は(國情はあるが)どこの國々の人種も法悅境を得んといふのである。仕事はどしどしやるべし。

○　加 藤 精 神

第一に大乘佛教の教理を組織的に且つ成るべく簡明に記述して廣く之を國際的に宣傳すること。

第二に其の教理を直接に實生活の上に具現せる我日本佛教の特色を海外に紹介すること。

以上二點は最も急を要することかと被存候

○　井 上 秀 天

大乘佛教經典の權威ある外國語譯の刊行

○　山 上 ゝ 泉

歌をもてこたへまつる

(一)大いなる弘誓の船にあひ乘りて
　　西し東し行きかはましも

(二)敷島のまことの道にみ佛の

光をそへよ世はきよまらむ

(三)み佛の殿堂に咲ける藝術の

華はしをれでとこしへ迄も

(四)詩に歌に世のはらからのなごむをぞ

佛さびたるこゝろといはむ

(五)わかうどのこゝろを盛れる坩堝より

めぐみの花もかぐよひ出でな

(六)ひとすぢの心に活くる兒らを率て

法のそのふにうたはしむべし

○　原　善　久

當面の事業としては――

(一)日本より海外へ宣敎する敎師の養成所設置，附外遊內地人の案內所。

(二)外人の渡來者に日本語敎授及職業紹介所設置，附外人案內所常在，通譯者養成。

(三)佛跡參拜團及各宗本山參拜團組織。

(四)佛敎圖書館設立。

(五)常設佛敎美術工藝展覽，傳道場及信者宿泊所設置。

○　水　野　梅　曉

國際佛敎通報の御發刊は洵に時宜に適したるものとして贊成仕候。

就ては大乘的見地より佛敎主義を國際間に宣布するには

(一)宗派的見地を超越して通佛敎的の立場を失はざる事。

(二)是が爲には統一的通佛敎の聖典を編纂する事。

(三)此聖典の編纂と同時に佛敎の思想的發達史を編纂する事。の三條件を具備することが國際間に進出する先決問題と存候

○　椎　名　正　雄

海外布敎師の養成を急務と思考仕り候。從來の海外布敎師は何れも一宗一派に偏し而も外國語の素養乏しき者もあるに於ては彼の國人に向つて宣敎することは到底不可能なり。茲に於て大乘佛敎に精通せる（通佛敎の）布敎師養成機關を設け（勿論各宗と聯絡しその後援の下に）以て堅實なる海外布敎師の養成に努むることが最も急務と考ふ。これ余の持論なり。

○　竹　內　藤　吉

希望三つ

1. 大乘佛敎の國際性を日本佛敎徒に徹底させられ度事。
2. 大乘宣揚の意圖のもとに書かれた歐文佛敎書を刊行され度事，其手始めとして旣でに刊行されて居る歐文佛敎書の解題を各書と同じ言語でかき，出來ればエスペラントの譯文をそへて下されば，自分の知てゐる言葉で書れた本をたやすく手に入れる事が出きはすまいかと思ひます。
3. 將來佛敎徒の國際的協力をたやすくするため單一共通語の學習を助成されたき事

○　ブ リ ン ク リ ー

西洋の人々は，日本の政治，經濟，外交以外の事なら朝起きて夜寢るまでのすべての事に興味を持ち，それらを知りたいと熱望してゐるのですから，日本の文化と日本人の生活とに關して正しい具體的な知識を西洋の人々に齎らすやう努力することこそやがて日本文化――大乘佛敎の國際化を實現せしめる王道と思ひます。

○　藤　原　猶　雪

一，當面の處置として

飜譯機關を設置して各國語普及をなす事

二，當面の企劃として

(1) 超宗派佛敎大學の設立

(2) 宣敎師の養成

○　蜂　谷　惠　晃

國際佛敎會館の建設のための基礎工作にかゝること。

○　高　島　米　峰

當面の事業としては，「國際佛敎通報」が健全に生長發達するだけでも大したものだと存じます。

○　岩　倉　政　治

當面の事業としては，現在ある佛敎海外紹介機關の助成も去ることながら，何よりも貴局自身の精進强化が第一でせう。

Japanese News

Kokusai Bunka Shinkokai

International Cultural Relations Society's Activities Since Founding In '34 Outlined

The Society for International Cultural Relations has decided to hold a conference on its works in 1935 at Marunouchi from 4 p.m. February 26.

The society which was established in April last year, by the Foreign Ministry officials and other influential people, has devoted itself to propaganda, translations, dispatching Japanese lecturers abroad, contribution of cultural materials, assistance to foreigners' studies of things Japanese and other enterprises.

However, the above work does not be beyond the preparatory undertaking, and does not comprise comprehensive movement.

The conference being held today is to discuss how to pass from a mere subsidiary organ to a more independent organization and make concrete for realizing its proper mission in the future.

The Kokusai Bunka Shinkokai made its start as a new organization on April 11, 1934, and has steadily been growing and functioning always with its objectives in view. The following summary of the work of the Society in 1934 was pulished recently.

Promotion

The National Committee of Intellectual Cooperation, a correspondent organization of the International Committee of Intellectual Cooperation of the League of Nations, had a Cultural Sub-Committee which was composed of Marquis Yorisada Tokugawa, Count Ayske Kabayama, Count Kiyoshi Kuroda, Viscount Nagakage Okabe, Baron Ino Dan, Dr. Saburo Yamada and others. The necessity was keenly felt among them, however, to establish an independent and more efficient organization to meet the foreign nations. Just at the same time, following the examples of France and other European countries, the Ministry of Foreign Affairs was contemplating the establishment of a department of international cultural relations. These trends have facilitated the foundation of the Kokusai Bunka Shinkokai, which was incorporated on April 11, 1934. The Society has been honored with a gracious donation from His Majesty's Household and H.I.H. Prince Takamatsu kindly consented to become President d'Honneur of the Society. Then, with election of Prince Fumimaro Konoye as President, and other officers having been named, the organization of the Kokusai Bunka Shinkokai was completed.

Organization

Presdent D'Honneur: H. I. H. Prince Takamatsu.

Advisers: — Admiral Keisuke Okada, Prime Minister Mr. Kurahei Yuasa, Minister of the Imperial Household, Mr. Koki Hirota, Minister of Foreign Affairs, Mr. Genji Matsuda, Minister of Education, Prince Iyesato Tokugawa, Count Nobuaki Makino, Count Keigo Kiyoura, Viscount Kikujiro Ishii, and Dr. Joji Sakurai, President of the Imperial Academy.

The Officers of the Society

President: — Prince Fumimaro Konoye, President of the House of Peers.

Vice-Presidents:—Marquis Yorisada Tokugawa, Member of the House of Peers, Baron Seinosuke Goh, President of the Tokyo Chamber of Commerce and Industry.

Board of Directors

Chairman:—Count Aiske Kabayama, Member of the House of Peers.

Managing Directors:—Viscount Nagakage Okabe, Member of the House of Peers, Count Kiyoshi Kuroda, and Mr. Shigekichi Mihara.

Directors:—Dr. Masaharu Anesaki, Professor Emeritus of the Tokyo Imperial University, Baron Ino Dan, Mr. Kikusaburo Fukui, Director of Mitsui Corporation, Dr. Kosaku Hamada, Professor of the Kyoto Imperial University, Mr. Chokuro Kadono, Vice-President of the Okura Gumi, Mr. Manzo Kushida, President of the Mitsubishi Bank, Mr. Naohiko

Masaki, President of the Imperial Academy of Fine Arts, Mr. Nagaharu Minobe, Vice-Minister of Education, Mr. Masatsune Ogura, Managing Director of the Sumitomo Corporation, Mr. Masao Oya, Vice-Minister of the Imperial Household, Mr. Mamoru Shigemitsu, Vice-Minister of Foreign Affairs, Dr. Junjiro Takakusu, Professor Emeritus of the Tokyo Imperial University, Dr. Saburo Yamada, President of the Keijo Imperial University.

Inspector:—Mr. Shintaro Ohashi, Member of the House of Peers, Mr. Toshikata Okubo, Vice-President of the Yokohama Specie Bank.

General Secretary:—Mr. Setsuichi Aoki.

Office In Marunouchi

The office is located in the Meiji Seimei Building, Marunouchi, Tokyo, and has a staff and part-time workers of twenty-three, with the annual budget of ¥257,000 for the fiscal year of 1934, one million yen for 1935. The Society maintains close relations and cooperates with the Ministries of Education, Foreign Affairs and Railways. It also cooperates with private organizations, such as the America-Japan Society, La Maison Franco-Japonaise, Das Japan-Deutsch Kultur-Institut, Institute of Pacific Relations, International Association of Japan, and others; and aso with many private citizens, with an object of acting as an intermediary for introducing Japanese culture abroad and for promoting cutural exchange.

Activities

The work of the Society is to be carried on in compliance with the program of activities scheduled at the time of its foundation. But this being the first year the work has consisted chiefly in laying out plans and in carrying out researches for future activities and the Society has not been able to accomplish much in the nature of direct value. Various activities carried on since April, 1934, may be summarized as follows:

A. International contact.

Needless to say, contact and cooperation with foreign countries, foreigners and their various organizations being our primary object, we endeavored to make our Society known to them; for this purpose we have widely distributed our

Prospectus through the diplomatic and private channels. When Prince Konoye paid his visit to America in June, efforts were made to introduce the Society there in his official capacity as the President; and also when Dr. Anesaki, Director, went to Europe, he did much to introduce the Society in the countries he visited — America, Canada, France, England, Switzerland and Germany.

Correspondents Abroad

1. Appointment of Correspondents Abroad.

With an object of keeping in close contact with current events abroad, particularly concerning Japan and things Japanese, four correspondents, namely, Mr. Junzo Sato, Prof. Takahiko Tomoyeda, Mr. Ken-ichi Moriwaki and Mr. Yoshio Shinya, have been appointed so far for Paris, Berlin, New York and Buenos Aires, respectively; and many other appointments at important centers of the world are under contemplation. The work of introducing our Society in the respective communities, and investigations conducted by those correspondents are already proving to be of great value in laying out our plans.

Mr. Kenichi Nakaya, a student of Latin-American diplomatic relations, has been sent to Central and South America with the object of studying the present status of the introduction of Japanese culture there, as well as establishing connections with persons and various organization interested in Japan.

Mr. Tadao Marumo, an official of the Science Museum of Tokyo, accompanied by our correspondent in Paris, attended the International Conference of Museum Experts held at Madrid in November, 1934, as a delegate from Japan. While in that country, they had important conferences with the authorities as well as the delegates, and established a foundation for future mutual cooperation with the countries represented, by spreading information concerning Japan among them.

Furthermore, when Mr. Masanori Oshima, Secretary of the National Association of Education, attended the Far East Educational Conference held at Manila, he was asked to make an investigation of the present status of the introduction of Japanese culture, and also to establish closer cultural relations with the Philippines.

Miss Miya Sannomiya of the Tokyo Y.W.C.A. was also asked to establish connections with the universities, and other cultural organizations, and individuals on the Pacific Coast during her visit to America.

Social Functions

As there is an obvious necessity for our maintaining close relationship with diplomatic circles and foreign residents in Japan, it is deemed desirable to hold social functions, at least once a year, with the above object in view. Thus, in April, when the Society was legally organized, a group of diplomats was invited, and the founding of the Society was announced. And in December, in order to add impetus to development of plans whereby foreign residents interested in Japanese culture may be facilitated in their studies, such students were invited from all over the country to discuss the common problems. They were all much pleased with the birth of the Society and promised their hearty cooperation.

B. Translatations and publications.

Publications

1. Publications.

The Society has contributed no publication of any special value, most of its energy being spent on the preparation of manuscripts; but, so far, the following pamphlets have been published from time to time:

(a) "The Dolls of Japan" (in English and French). This was prepared originally to introduce the dolls of Japan the International Dolls Exhibition held at Antwerp, Belgium, in October 1934, and was published in its original form.

(b) "Gagaku Concert" (in English). This is an explanation of the Gagaku concert given at a tea party at the Imperial Hotel, to which Delegates of the International Red Cross Congress and the diplomatic corps were invited.

(c) "A Short Bibliography on Japan" (in English). As the name indicates, this is a brief bibliography of important books on Japan written in English.

(d) "Human Elements in Ceramic Art" (in English). This was taken from the lecture given by Mr. Kikusaburo Fukui, a Director of the Society.

(e) "Masks of Japan" (in English). This was taken from the lecture given by Professor Toyoichiro Nagami of the Kyushu Imperial University at the Imperial Household Museum of Tokyo when an exhibit of masks was held. The lecture was delivered under the auspices of the society, particularly for the benefit of foreigners.

(f) "A Handbook on International Cultural Organizations in Japan" (in English and Japanese). A comprehensive list of Japanese organizations doing cultural work in Japan.

Being Prepared

2. Publications under preparation.

(a) "Map of Japan" (in English): Maps for general use are under preparation with the cooperation of the Land Survey Department of the Army, the Hydrographical Department of the Navy, the Tokyo Association of Geography, and also the Ministries of Foreign Affairs and Education.

(b) "Materials on Japan for School Use Abroad." The object of this work is to supply materials on Japanese culture to both teachers and students of high schools in the United States, and is being prepared with the cooperation of the Institute of Pacific Relations.

(c) "A History of Japanese Literature." The compilation of this work is being entrusted to Dr. Kochi Doi, Professor of the Tohoku Imperial University.

(d) "Japanese Gardens." Dr. Tsuyoshi Tamura, expert and scholar, has already completed the translation of the manuscript on Japanese gardens preparation for the visit of the American Garden Club in the spring of 1935.

3. Other publications subsidized entirely or partly by the Society are as follows:

(a) The first volume. "The Spirit of Japan," of the posthumous publications of the late Dr. Sturge, many years engaged in missionary work and with a thorough knowledge of Japan.

(b) Special edition on Japanese culture of the Japan Times, edited by Mr. W. R. Wills, an American.

(c) Text-books on Japanese Grammar and Conversation, edited by the School for Japanese Language and Culture, comprising two volumes.

(d) A book on Ukiyoye, entitled "Hiroshige," pulished in English by Prof. Yonejiro Noguchi.

(e) A collection of materials on the Social and Economic History of Japan, a joint work now under preparation by Professor K. Singer, German, of the Tokyo Imperial

University, and Professor N. S. Smith, Englishman, of the Tokyo University of Commerce. A source book.

To Lecture Abroad

C. Sending lecturers abroad.

1. At the time of the founding of this Society, Dr. Naojiro Sugiyama, Professor of the Tokyo Imperial University, who was in France, was requested to stay there three months longer in order to give lectures and to conduct various investigations in that country.

2. The President of the Japanese Association of Children's Education, Mr. Denichi Ishii, was asked to give lectures on the culture and civilization of Japan and to introduce the Society generally during his lecture tour of the American continents.

3. Mr. Jiro Harada, expert of the Tokyo Imperial Household Museum, was chosen to lecture at the University of Oregon for the period of six months beginng with the coming September, in compliance with the request of the University.

4. At the request of the Federation of Universities of Great Britain, Professor Yukio Yashiro of the Tokyo School of Fine Arts will be sent to England, in May, in order to give a series of lectures at various universities.

Donations

D. Donations of materials on culture.

1. We donated six old art pieces to the Museum of Montevideo, Uruguay, when the charge d'affaires of Uruguay, a great lover of Japanese art, returned to his county.

2. When a conference of professors and students of both America and Japan was held at the invitation of the Students English Speaking Society of Japan, a book entitled Japan's Advance, and an album showing Japanese life and its various aspects, were presented to all American students, numbering nearly one hundred.

3. Three hundred copies of Dr. Boneau's *La Sensibilité Japonaise* were purchased and distributed by the Society among the libraries, organizations and persons interested abroad.

Studies on Japan

E. Subsidizing studies and publications on Japan.

1. Foreigners.

(a) Dr. Pippon, German, a

student of the Constitution of Japan.

(b) Dr. Prusek, Czechoslovakian, a student of Japanese language and literature and of Sinology.

(c) Miss Gerd Schmidt, Danish, a student of the ethnology and archaeology of Japan.

(d) Mr. D. W. Kohler, America, a student of Japanese language and literature.

2. Japanese.

(a) Mr. Michitoshi Odauchi of the Ministry of Education was assisted in holding an exhibition of human geography of Japan at the International Congress of Geography, held at Warsaw last August.

(b) Mr. Kosetsu Nohsu, painter, who is in India, was assisted in completing his Buddhist wall-painting at a temple there.

Invitation of Foreigners

F. Invitation of foreigners and for-organizations to Japan:

1. Invitation of the members of the American Garden Club.

In view of the fact that they have derived great benefit from their visit to England in 1929, with the object of studying gardens, the Garden Club of America had expressed its desire to study the Japanese garden. Consequently, they have been invited jointly by the Society and America-Japan Society. A special committee is now preparing the program for their reception. The visiting party is to be composed of over one hundred and fifty members: and during their stay from May 13th to June 2nd, they are to visit Tokyo, Hakone, Nikko, Nagoya, Kyoto and Osaka.

2. When the Tokyo Y.W.C.A. invited eight deans of women from the western universities of the United States, last August, the Society assisted them as well as accommodated them in their study of Japanese culture.

3. Invitations were issued to Dr. Sven Hedin, famous Swedish explorer, and Miss Zona Gale, foremost woman writer of America. (Answer still pending).

Exhibitions

G. Exhibitions.

We have held two exhibitions abroad so far. both of which proved to be very successful.

1. Johannesburg Exhibition of Industrial Art.

We sent one hundred and sixteen pieces of industrial art goods to the International Exhibition of

Art held there last October, and according to the report from the Japanese Consul in Capetown to the Foreign Office, our exhibits were acclaimed as the most artistic at the exhibition.

2. International Dolls Exhibition at Antwerp, Belgium

We sent one hundred and forty dolls to the exhibition held last November, and also distributed attractively prepared pamphlets to introduce our dolls. The exhibits were donated to the Brussels Museum of Folklore.

3. A Japanese Textile Exhibition.

This will be held at the Metropolitan Museum of Fine Arts beginning from February 18th. In compliance with the request made through Mr. Priest, Curator of Oriental art of the Museum, we borrowed sixteen valuable treasures of "No" and other costumes owned by Marquises Hosokawa, Tokugawa and Mayeda, Barons Mitsui and Konoike, and Mr. Kaichiro Nedzu; and they have been shipped already. At the same time a model stage of "No" dance has been sent as explanatory material.

Public Lectures

H. Public lectures.

For the benefit of foreigners who are studying Japan, public lectures in English were given at the Imperial Household Museum when special exhibitions were held.

1. In November, at the time of the Mask Exhibition, a lecture was given by Professor Nogami of the Kyushu Imperial University.

2. On another occasion, Professor Rikichiro Furui of the Tohoku Imperial University spoke at an exhibition of Japanese paintings of different periods.

3. Furthermore, during the summer, lectures were given at Karuizawa (summer resort) on Japanese costumes and "Ukiyo-ye" by Mr. Noritake Tsuda and Mr. Shigekichi Mihara.

4. When Mr. Kaju Nakamura conducted a summer course on Oriental culture, the Socity gave him financial assistance.

I. Recitals.

1. In October, when the International Red Cross Congress was held in Tokyo, the delegates and the diplomatic corps were invited to a tea party, and the guests expressed great approval when Gagaku music was played by the orchestra of the Imperial Household Department.

2. In accordance with the request of the Federation of the Music Clubs of America, a plan has been already laid for an international

musical recital to be broadcast between the two countries.

Film Production

J. Production of films and lantern slides.

1. With the object of introducing various aspects of our culture, a plan is under way to film Japanese series, the film of "Kagami Jishi" by dancing, and as the first of the Kikugoro Onoye, the noted actor, is now under preparation.

2. The Society has also assisted Dr. Ado Baessler, German explorer, in the production of films on Japan.

3. As materials for lecture purposes, six hundred plates of slides based on the subjects of gardens, architecture, sculpture, painting and industrial art are now being prepared.

K. Research:

The past year had been devoted to gathering materials which are useful in laying out plans. At present, we are investigating as to the present status of the cultural work conducted by foreign countries and the present status of the study of Japanese culture abroad. We are also making enquiries for the preparation of a complete list of various organizations and individuals interested in cultural work; the biblography on Japan, a list of museums and libraries abroad, and the status of foreigners in Japan desiring to study. One of the most important pieces of work of the year has been the organization of the Committee on Bibliography on Japan, which is functioning at its full capacity.

This Committee is composed of five members: Count Kuroda, Baron Dan, Messrs. Ishida and Nagasawa with Dr. Anesaki as its chairman. At present, the Committee is working on materials on the culture of Japan appearing in book form and in periodicals in the years, 1932 and 1933; and may have already held over twenty meetings for the purpose. A bibliography of books has already been completed, and periodicals are now being investigated.

L. Library:

The library was established in December and is endeavoring to collect books on Japan published in Japanese, Chines, and Western languages; and in order to accommodate foreign students, catalogues of other important libraries will be provided, in time, as a reference library. It also aims to render helpful service to students in other capacities, such as, in giving information on books which are not stored in this library, in the selection of books, and in any other possible way.

Centurion Priest

The abbot of Choseiji, a flourishing temple in Yamanashi Prefecture, has reached the ripe old age of 101, and has gone back to his second childhood, as his hair has turned black and he still possesses strong teeth.

When he was recently asked the secret of his good health and long life, he owned up that it was all owing to the fact that he was a vegetarian and a bachelor. On his menu each day he eats ten eggs, and never lets a day pass without a bath.

Buddhas's Birthday

Buddha's birthday is being celebrated April 8 at all Buddhist temples and many local communities throughout the country.

At many large Buddhist temples, elaborate ceremonies are being held. Recently, the celebration of Buddha's birthday has become to be often named "Hana-matsuri" (Flower Festival) as it comes just at the height of the Sakura season.

One of the traditional and most outstanding features of the festival is the pouring of amacha (sweet tea) over the figure of Buddha. Temples place small Buddha status specifically for this purpose, and visitors pour the tea over the head of the statue. Amacha is made by brewing the leaves of amacha (Hydrangea Thunbergu).

The special temple in which the statue for this purpose is placed is called "Hanamido" (Flower temple). The visitors also take home amacha in bottles from the temples to drink or to be used in Japanese ink wells. Amacha is believed to bring good luck.

In the morning, Buddha's Birthday was celebrated in Tokyo, Kyoto and Osaka with special ceremonies and services.

The procession of gaily dressed children through the streets of Tokyo is always a sight, and special programs were held in the many temples.

In Kyoto, a white elephant headed the procession from the Nishi Honganji to Chionin. The Buddhist associations of Kyoto invited poor workmen to take part in an entertainment at the Kyoto zoological garden.

Jizo for Mihara

To console the souls lost in Mihara's fiery crater, a statue of the compassionate Jizo is to be erected close to the rim of the volcano, overlooking the molten mass which has desire to hasten out of this existence.

Mr. Keimei Ogawa, a priest of a temple at Komagome in Tokyo, has undertaken the carrying out this plan, and the statue which will be of stone 9 feet high and 6 feet wide, has been executed by Mr. Busan Kimura.

Buddhist Dance

A religious dance has been created to be performed each year at the Tsukiji Honganji upon the anniversary of the restoration of the temple buildings that were destroyed in the great earthquake.

On Wednesday April 10, 30 priests and their parishioners met to practise the dance in one of the worshipping halls, clad in beautiful old Buddhist costumes.

This dance will be performed during the celebrations which mark the completion of the temple buildings from April 21 to 23.

Monument to Poet

A monument to the memory of the late Baroness Takeko Kujo, known so widely for her poetry as well as her social and charitable works, has been placed in the compound of the Tsukiji Honganji. The unveiling ceremony will be held on April 21. At this time the services and program will be given to mark the completion of the new temple buildings.

The suggestion for the monument came from the Jitsugyo-no-Nippon Publishing Company, the firm that brought out an anthology of her verse. The monument was designed by Mr. Matsugoro Hirokawa, professor of the Tokyo Academy of Fine Arts. A bronze tablet with one of her poems in relief is the only decoration of the simple stone.

Oriental Tourist Conference

The complete program of the Oriental Tourist Conference, to be held from May 2 to 10, this year, was made public by the Board of Tourist Industry recently.

The conference is to complete all business during the first four days of its session, and excursions to various spots will fill the following six days.

A total of 80 delegates, of which 50 are foreigners and 30 Japanese, will attend the conference and discuss:

1. How to promote international tourist business in Orient and the South Sea islands.

2. How to improve transportation

facilities and services for tourists in all the countries concerned.

3. How cooperation in advertising to bring tourists from Europe and America can be realized.

4. Promotion of travel between the countries concerned.

5. Exchange of posters, guidebooks and other publications among all countries, and reciprocal display of these materials by the respective organizations.

6. Exchange of travel news and other information regarding the tourist business.

7. Developing pilgrimage traffic to places of Buddhist interest in the East, and cooperation between railways, shipping companies, and air services in "international rate" combined tickets.

All delegates from Manchoukuo, China, Siam, the Philippines, French-Indo-China, Straits Settlements, Dutch East Indies, Ceylon, British India, and Soviet Russia will arrive in Tokyo before the end of this month. The Japanese delegates will represent the Imperial railways, the Manchoukuo railways, the Chosen railways, the Taiwan railways, the O. S. K., N. Y. K., the Japan Tourist Bureau, the Hotel Men's Association, and others.

Colonel Gerald Taite, chief of the central office of publicity of the Indian State railways, and Mrs. Taite will arrive in Tokyo on April 20. Tung Yin, chief of the passenger bureau of the Peiping-Shanhaikuan railway, will arrive on April 28.

Other Participants Due

La Rive, chief of the Tourist bereau of the French-Indo-China railwas, and Mrs. Rive and Luang Thavil, director of Royal State railway of Siam, and Mrs. Thavil will arrive in Tokyo at the end of April. William J. Carrie, head of the Sanitary department of Hongkong municipal government, and Mrs. Carrie will arrive on or about April 27.

The program of the conference follows:

May 2—2 p.m.-4 p.m.: Opening of the conference plenary meeting at the Premier's official residence. 4 p.m., Tea party given by the Foreign Minister.

May 3—10 a. m.-4 p.m.: Plenary meeting at the Japan Industrial Club. 4 p.m.: Tea party given under the joint auspices of the Tokyo Chamber of Commerce and Industry and the Japan Economic Federation. 6.30 p.m.: Dinner given under the joint auspices of the Nippon Yusen Kaisha, Osaka Shosen Kaisha and

South Manchuria Railway at the Koyokan restaurant.

May 4—10 a. m.-noon: Plenary meeting. Afternoon: Excursion to Nikko.

May 5—Sightseeing in Nikko, returning to Tokyo in the evening. 7 p. m.: Dinner given by Baron Okura, president of the Japan Hotel Association.

May 6—10 a. m.-noon: Plenary meeting, closing of the conference 12.30 p.m.: Luncheon given by the Japan Tourist Bureau at the Tokyo Kaikan. 2 p.m. Sightseeing in Tokyo. 3.30 p.m., Tea party given by the mayor of Tokyo. 5 p.m.: Theater-party given by the Director of Board of Tourist Industry.

May 7-12—Excursion to Nara, Kyoto and Osaka, visiting en route Kamakura, Miyanoshita, Gamagori, Nagoya, and Yamada.

Pilgrimage of Priest

To promote good will relations between Japan and China through Buddhism, the Japan-China Buddhist Association which was organized last year will send a mission to southern China in the immediate future.

Those who will travel to China are Ryokei Onishi, chief priest of Kiyomizu temple in Kyoto Gemmyo Hayashi, chief priest of Joanji, a Temple of Numadzu, and Reido Hayashi, priest of Banzuiin, a Tokyo temple. Four other priests will accompany them, and they will remain in China for a month.

大乘佛教の國際化に必要なる當面の事業

○　古川碓悟

大乘佛教の國際化に必要なる事業は多々在るも，所謂當面差當りの事業としては次記の件を必要とす。

一、『大乘佛教綱要』といふやうな簡單な書を編纂すること

1. 大さは四六版又は袖珍版五百頁以內位なること

2. 內容は總論として通大乘佛教の要領を簡潔に記述し，各論として現行日本大乘佛教各宗の宗意の核心要領を出來るだけ適當なる圖形に表示し，一目之を直覺せしむる如くし之に簡單なる說明を附すること，例せば座禪の形狀を描き一見禪宗の何たるかを直覺せしめ，彌陀如來と合掌念佛の姿を描き一見淨土門の安心趣旨を直覺せしむる如くすること。

二、右大乘佛教綱要を國際語に飜譯し，出來るだけ廉價にて海外特に各國大都市へ販賣すること。

三、我國在住の外國人は勿論，一切外來人に對して一度は必ず之を勸誘して各宗本山又は其宗代表的の寺院に請待して第一項の如き形態と儀式により，其宗の宗意安心の要領を知らしむると同時に，右『大乘佛教綱要』を一部贈呈すること。

四、外國滯在の主要なる邦人（外交官，武官，留學生等々）及主なる海外旅行者に對して其外遊前に『大乘佛教綱要』を贈呈し，同時に其要領を學知せしめ，彼等をして外人に對して平常談笑の間に之を宣傳せしむること。

五、上記の件々を實現する爲めに『國際佛教通報局』に數名の專門係員を常置する事。

○　緒方宗博

凡そこの種の事業に大の禁物は有名無實と言ふ事に有之候，その衝に當る者は實權を握られ度，苟しくも名を連ねたる者はその責を負はれ度，百萬のカケゴエ億千の花火線香より一發の實彈を出されん事望ましく候，次に冀くば當路の諸士は公人としても個人としても常に誠意と細心の注意とを以て事を處し，人に接せられたく候，若し歐文等に於てミスプリの絕無を期し得ば，揚子を以て重箱をほぜる底の西人心理を滿足せしめ，斯業の聲價期せずして江湖に高まり可申存じ候。

合掌。

國際佛教通報局定欵

名　稱

第一，本局を國際佛教通報局と稱す

事務所

第二，本局の事務所を全日本佛教青年會聯盟本部に置く

目　的

第三，本局は日本內地及海外に向つて佛教事情の通報をなし，且つ佛教徒相互間の各種便宜を計るを以て目的とす

事　業

第四，本局の目的を達成するため左記の事業を行ふ

イ，日本內地及世界各國より佛教事情に關する質問の通報を行ふ

ロ，必要に應じ日本語及世界各國語を以て佛教事情の通報を行ふ

ハ，外國人の日本觀光に際しては各種の便益を與へ，特にその佛教に關する方面に於て之を爲す

ニ，定時或は隨時に各國語を以て文書の刊行をなす

ホ，その他必要と認めたる事業を行ふ

役　員

第五，本局の事務を處理するため左の役員を置く

イ，局長　一名

ロ，幹事　三名

ハ，評議員　若干名

局長は本局の事務を總括す

幹事は本局の事務を處理す

評議員は局長の提案に依る重要事務を審議す

第六，評議員は左記の者を以て之に充つ

イ，全日本佛教青年會聯盟理事及主事

ロ，全日本佛教青年會聯盟理事會に於て推薦したる者

第七，局長及幹事は評議員會に於て決定す

第八，役員の任期は二ケ年とす（但し重任を妨げず）

經　費

第九，本局の經費は左記のものに依て之を支辨す

イ，本局基金の活用

ロ，寄附金

ハ，その他の收入

補　則

第十，本定欵に記載せられざる事項は，凡て評議員會に於て協議す

第十一，第一回の役員は全日本佛教青年會聯盟理事會に於て決定す

定價			
	一部	金二十錢	送料二錢
	一年	金二圓四十錢	送料不要

昭和十年四月廿五日印刷（每月一回）
昭和十年五月一日發行（一日發行）

東京市外吉祥寺337
編輯發行兼印刷人　淺野研眞

東京市牛込區早稻田鶴卷町107
印刷所　康文社印刷所
電話牛込（34）1950番 5049番

東京市神田區一ツ橋二の三
發行所　國際佛教通報局
電話九段（33）1429番
振替東京83015番

昭和十年四月三十日 第三種郵便物認可　昭和十年五月二十七日印刷納本　昭和十年六月一日發行（每月一回一日發行）第一卷　第三號

The International Buddhist Bulletin

國際佛教通報

第一卷 **昭和十年六月** 第三號 〔Vol. 1. **June** $\frac{2501}{1935}$ No. 3.〕

要　目 〔**Contents**〕

東　京　**國際佛教通報局**　發　行

The International Buddhist Information Bureau

Tokyo, Kanda, Hitotsubashi, II—3

Annual Subscription, ¥2,40 (post free), Single Copies 20 sen (post 2 sen)

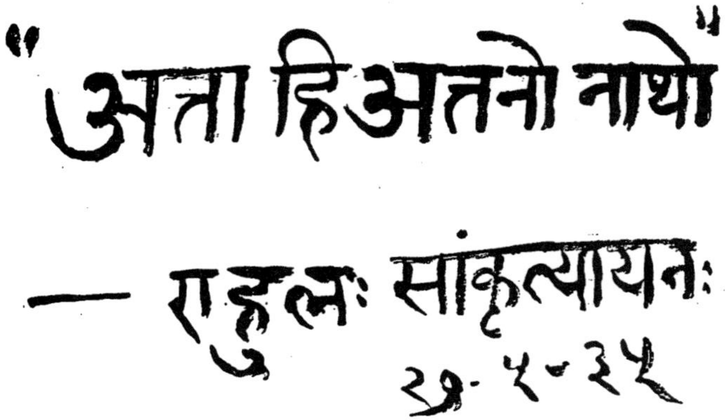

印度僧ラーフラ・サンクリトヤーヤナ師の筆蹟
（去る五月廿七日，我が國際佛教通報局訪問の際揮毫）

The Institution of the Pan-Pacific Y.M.B.A. League and the Questions of Hereafter

By Shunshi Takagai

The Second General Conference of the Pan-Pacific Young Buddhists' Associations held in Tōkyo and Kyōto in 1934, commencing from July 18th, came to a close, at a moment when there was a general outcry for the revival of Buddhism in Japan, with an all unexpected and extraordinary after-effect, thanks to the marvellous combination of assistance and goodwill rendered from all quarters. Being one who had actually been working for the materialization of the conference, I am all with joy, and my grateful thanks are due to those well-wishers from without, our elders and friends, and also to the all-pervading light of guidance and protection of the Lord Buddha.

The conference held in Tōkyo, including the opening ceremony, lasted for four days. And the weightiest of the resolutions reached during those four days was, I must say, the weaving of the Y.M.B.A.'s of the Pacific coasts, under the name of the Buddha, into one strong block of union. It is not much to say that it is the first of the enterprises of its kind in the whole history of Buddhism. 'The Pan-Pacific Y.M.B.A. League' was the name with which it was henceforth to be called and the participants came to agree that it should hereafter serve to be the permanent organ which can cement the mutual relationship between the Y.M.B.A.'s of the Pacific coasts for the uplifting of the Y.M.B.A. movement. A sub-committee, which comprised of 29 members, was then ordered by the general meeting, in order to bring in due form the rules of the League before the session came to a close. Those who were appointed committee sat as long as time allowed them to carefully look into the matter: and I unexpectedly had to enjoy the pleasure to sit as chairman of the committee. The delegates from India, Ceylon, and Siam were of opinion that the League had better be called the 'International Y.M.B.A. League' instead of the 'Pan-Pacific etc.'; but a counter voice insisted, backing the original plan, that the name had an historical bearing; that besides, a gradual development of the movement was desirable for the present; and that the participation of the countries above-mentioned could not be unnatural, in that Buddhism first sprang up and flourished in their countries, although the geographical situation could little justify their joining the League of the Y.M.B.A.'s of the Pacific coasts. With an understanding that later on the name of the 'Pan-Pacific' shall be replaced by the 'International,' this small committee voted in one to have the league organized as the effect of a resolution of this conference.

To speak more minutely, already at the First General Conference of the Pan-Pacific Y.M.B.A.'s held in 1930 (5th year of Shōwa) at Honolulu, an unanimous vote by the delegates of Japan, America, and Hawaii called for the institution of a 'Pan-Pacific Y.M.B.A. League,' and especially Mr. Shūsaku Awoki had even prepared himself with a well-studied detailed plan. But this plan was unfortunately submitted to a sub-committee for further study, under the reason that the time was not mature yet. Of the committee Messrs. Tansai Terakawa (for America), Minen Yasui (for Hawaii) and Shunshi Takagai (for Japan) were appointed Chief Committeemen, and it was agreed that these should look to the materialization of the actual plan. Four years have elapsed since then; during which time Mr. Shusaku Awoki, the first proposer of the plan passed away; and then the Second General Conference in Tōkyo and Kyōto took place. The First Conference was participated only by a small delegation of five countries, but the present conference enjoyed the participation by the delegates of as many as 13 countries, the delegates present numbering as many as 600: and the conference well deserved the name of the 'Pan-Pacific.' It had now the best-offered opportunity to the above-said committee to perfect the end of the long-suspending plan and we all hoped to fulfil, on the one hand, the responsibility that had been weighing on our shoulders for the past

four years, and also to find a sound and healthy footing for the Y.M.B.A. movement of the peoples of the Eastern Asia. Happily the motion to found a 'Pan-Pacific Y.M.B.A. League' was answered with the unanimous approval of the delegates present in the conference.

The rules reached were as follow:—

Constitution of the Pan-Pacific Federation of Young Buddhist Associations

Article 1.
NAME

The name of this organization shall be the Pan-Pacific Federation of Young Buddhist Associations.

Article 2.
HEADQUARTERS

The business headquarters of this Federation shall be located at the headquarters of the All Nippon Federation of Young Buddhist Associations, in Tokyo.

Article 3.
MEMBERSHIP

The membership of this Federation shall be composed of the Young Buddhists' Associations in the countries bordering the Pacific Ocean, and their neighboring countries.

Article 4.
PURPOSE

The object of this federation shall be to unite the Young Buddhists' Associations for the purpose of establishing a system of harmonious co-operation in their efforts to promote the Buddhistic spirit and to strengthen each other by mutual contacts and mutual assistance.

Article 5.
DEPARTMENTS

In order to accomplish the said object, the federation shall establish the following departments:

A. Publication Department to publish an official organ.

Article 6.
OFFICERS

This federation shall have the following officers:

A. Honorary Advisors.
B. Central Board of Directors.
C. Executive Board composed of Executive committee and Financial committee.
D. Central Executive Officers.

Article 7.
DUTIES OF OFFICERS

1. Honorary Advisors shall be the advisors of the Federation.
2. Central Board of Directors shall govern the Executive Board.
3. Executive Committee shall

supervise the business of the Federation.

4. Financial Committee shall record and transact all financial affairs of the Federation.
5. Central Executive Officers shall transact all business under the supervission of the Executive Board.

Article 8.

SELECTION and TERMS of OFFICERS.

Section 1.

1. Honorary Avisors shall be composed of three members selected from each affiliated country and ten members selected from Nippon.
2. Central Board of Directors shall be composed of two members selected from each affiliated country and five members selected from Nippon.
3. Members of the Executive Board shall be appointed by the Central Board of Directors.
4. The Executive Board shall appoint the necessary number of men for the Central Exective Office.

Section 2.

Terms of the officers shall be four years, except the Executive Board and the Central Executive Officers which shall be left to the judgement of the Central Board of Directors.

Section 3.

Officers shall be selected at the General Conference of the Federation.

Article 9.

MEETINGS

1. The Federation shall meet once in every four years, and the place of such gathering shall be decided at the previous meeting.
2. Official Boards shall meet when deemed necessary.

Article 10.

FINANCE

Finance of the federation shall be from the following sources:

1. Membership Fees. (which shall be set by the Central Board)
2. Donations.
3. Other incomes.

Article 11.

ADMITTANCE and WITHDRAWAL

1. Any Young Buddhist Association which wishes admittance into the Federation shall file an application with the Executive Committee for formal action at a meeting of the Central Board of Directors.
2. Any Young Buddhists Association which wishes to withdraw from the Federation shall state its reason before a meeting of the Central Board of Directors and, with their approval, have its withdrawal formally acknowledged.

Article 12.

AMENDMENT

No amendment to this constitution shall be valid unless such amendment shall have been passed up on by the Central Board of Directors' Meeting.

Thus far the rules have been agreed upon. But as business could not be transacted so long as the list of the names of the staffs was incomplete, the general meeting has, in order to better fascilitate the direct execution of the works, appointed the managers of the 'All-Japan Y.M.B.A. Federation,' for the time being, as the officers of the Pan-Pacific Y.M.B.A. League and entrusted them further with permission to make any small alterations of the rules as may be found necessary and also with the execution of the works as mentioned in the following sub-rules.

PROPOSITIONS to the CONSTITUTION

1. Publication....
   A. This Federation shall issue its Official Organ "Young Buddhists" quarterly or bi-monthly.
   B. Its object is to carry out the purpose of the Federation.
   C. Executive Committee shall supervise the edition.
   D. Japanese and English Language shall be used.
2. Financial Plan....
   A. Appropriations of the Annual Federation expenses to the affiliated countries shall be:
      a. Nippon..........¥ 1,650,00
      b. Hawaii.......... 400.00
      c. America........ 250.00
      d. Other countries.. 260.00
   B. Financial Budget shall be set up by the Executive Board and shall be approved by the Central Board of Directors.
   C. Proposed Financial Budget shall be:
      a. Office Expense ..¥ 600.00
      b. Salary 600.00
      c. Correspondence.. 200.00
      d. Publication of official organ .. 1,160.00

¥ 2.560.00

The delegates, then, left Japan with a full promise, on their return to home, to report within a month the 'Honorary' and the 'Central Committees' of the League selected from their respective Y.M.B.A.'s to the League's Head Quarters in Tōkyo. By the completion of the list of the names, the organ could now come into an actual working order. As heretofore, a general conference will be called every fourth year, now under the name of the League, the expenses of which being borne, as up to now by the Y.M.B.A.'s of the country in which the conference is held. The League will, so to say, work during the interval of four years, as the central organ and take in hand all the business with regard to the effecting of unity among the member Y.M.B.A.'s and also the materialization of the general conference in question.

The externae aspect of the Y.M.B.A. movement has so far successfully been brought up. What remains yet to be done is the question of the more internal nature of organization. The wishes of the late Mr. Shūsaku Awoki is now well rewarded and I in turn have the satisfaction to think that I have, in a sense at least, fulfilled a part of the responsibility of both public and private natures that has been weighing long on my shoulders.

To say more minutely, nearly ten years have come and gone to see the present fruition of the International Y.M.B.A. movement: the originator of which movement was of course the 'Young Buddhist Association' that came to bear a form somewhere in the 3rd year of Showa. Messrs. Kōshi Asano, Kempō Imanari, Ryōchu Shioiri, Kōnen Tsunemitsu, Ryōshin Hasegawa, Sōsen Fujii, Kenshin Asano and others were the members of those days. It was close after the inauguration of this association that I came back home from my tours in Europe and registered my name as a member. Not long after, Mr. Kōnen Tsunemitsu went to Hawaii and America, and was negotiating with the Y.M.B.A. members on the one hand and studying the internal working and the system of the Y.M.B.A. over there, when there was seen the sign of a movement which sought to call forth a general conference among the Y.M.B.A.'s of Japan, America and Hawaii. And the first person that had well heeded and fostered of this movement was no other than the late Rev. Emyō Imamura, the then superintendent of the Hawaiian Mission of the Hompa Hongwanji. It was after such a ground work had been perfected that the First General Conference of the Pan-Pacific Young Buddhists' Associations was called forth in Hawaii, in 1930 (5th year of Shōwa), lasting for six days commencing from July 21st. The delegates that had participated in the conference numbered

180 and had represented 5 nations, i.e. Japan, America, Hawaii, Korea, and India (represented by their nationals then residing in Honolulu). Looked upon as a gathering of Buddhists as yet unacquainted in any associations of international nature, the harvest of the conference was more than that could be expected. Thirty-six delegates from Japan had participated in the conference and as yet in those days there was no central organ to represent and take in hand the control of the Y.M.B.A.'s of Japan as a whole: and it was in the capacity of the representatives of each private association that the delegates were selected and sent out. This was rather an awkward situation for the Buddhists of Japan. Stimulated by this, the All Japan Y.M.B.A. Federation came into existence the next year, (i.e. 1931 or 6th year of Shōwa), under the leadership of Dr. Junjirō Takakusu as Head Manager; and under that name all the Y.M.B.A.'s of Japan were brought into one whole. During the days before and after this date one who had worked with the utmost zeal and energy for the Federation was Mr. Kōnen Tsunemitsu, the manager of those days.

After the founding of the Federation all the Y.M.B.A.'s of Japan were brought under the sway of one hand, and business was transacted and smoothed out under the name of the Federation, the crystallization of which was the present gathering of the Second General Conference of the Pan-Pacific Young Buddhists' Associations in Tōkyo and Kyōto.

Now that upon the foundation of the All-Japan Y.M.B.A. Federation we see yet another union towering up in the form of the Pan-Pacific Y.M.B.A. League, and accompanied with the growing unity and strength of the Pan-Pacific Y,M.B.A.'s, the responsibility that is to be shouldered by Japan is manifold. Firstly this All-Japan Y.M.B.A. Federation must pay serious attention towards the internal organization and guidance of the Y.M.B.A. movement of Japan itself. For the present the sound organization of the Y.M.B.A.'s, the institution of a clear motto of the Federation, the building of the Y.M.B.A. Hall stand foremost in the list of works that call our attention. The second item is the fostering of the Pan-Pacific Y.M.B.A. League. Minor circumstances may divide the peoples of different countries as according to the state of conditions that may exist, but there is yet another foothold of sound basis on which all the Buddhist Countries can possibly unite. Even the re-examinaiion into the doctrine of Buddhism itself may be necessary. The circumstances yet urge us to initiate even a new system of education with which to look after the upbringing of the juveniles and the younger generation. The third item is the direct execution of the works as scheduled in the list of the Pan-Pacific Y.M.B.A. League. This can only be attained through the co-operation of the member federations. It is with the deepest regret that I must mention the fact that although the delegates had parted with the best possible promises that they would with responsibility look to the selection of the honorary and the central committees of their own and report to the League's Head Quarters, yet nine months have now passed without any sign of answer or, from some, not a piece of reply to announce even the receipt of our repeating queries issued. For the general welfare of the Y.M.B.A. movement of the Oriental countries I sincerely hope, through the precious space of this article, that they will fulfil the responsibility to which they have bound themselves. (End)

Esperantaj libroj pri Budaismo

		prezo	sendkosto
1.	La Sukhavativjuho	¥ 0.15	0.02
2.	Rudao (tradukita el "The Essence of Buddhism")	0.60	0.04
3.	La Dek Bildoj de Bovpaŝtado	0.35	0.04
4.	La Kodo de Kronprinco Ŝootoku	0.15	0.02
5.	La Samanta-Mukhaparivarto	0.40	0.04
6.	Budaisma Terminaro de Takeuĉi (hektografita)	2.00	0.20

Ĉiuj libroj supre menciitaj estas riceveblaj de la Administracio de la "Internacia Budaisma Bulteno" aŭ de Japana Esperanto-Instituto, Hongoo, Tokio.

Konciza historio de Budhana Esp-movado en Japanujo

de Kei Sibajama.

II

Estas kompreneble, ke la prosperiĝo kaj malprosperiĝo de Esp-movado ankaŭ devas havi gravan relativecon kun tiama tendenco sociala kaj historia, sed pri tio mi ne volas mencii ĉi tie. Mi tamen esperas al karaj legantoj, ke vi mem pririgardu la flankon. Jen, mi daŭrigos simplan skizon pri la temo.

Ree venis favora tago en 1930 al la movado, kiu restis ne tre vigla dum du-tri jaroj.

En februaro Sro Nakaniŝi, ĉef-direktoro de Esp-fako de BSA, eldonis la 1an Nron de persona budhisma revueto en hektografo, titolita "La Libero." La revueto daŭre aperadas ĝis hodiaŭ; jam aperis entute 15 ekzempleroj.

En Julio el Bukka-ŝa, Kioto, eldoniĝis "La Dek Bildoj de Bo-opaŝtado," libreto apartenanta al Zen-Budhismo, ĉar ĉefdirektoro de Bukka-ŝa, societo de ia movado de budhana junularo, havis grandan favoron al Esp-movodo. Kvankam la libro estas ne tiel granda, ĝi ja estas la unua, apart-volume eldonita en Esperanto kiel budhisma libro.

En sama monato oni okazigis "La Unuan Konferencon de Tut-pacifikaj Junulaj Budhanaj Asocioj" en Havajo. Kaj en la okazo la konferenco akceptis proponon prezentitan de Japanaj delegitoj laŭ la fervoraj subtenoj kaj konvinkigaj klarigoj de Sro Kotani, ĵurnalisto de Ĉuugai-nippo, Sro Ogata, ĉefdirektoro de Bukka-ŝa: "Enkonduku ankaŭ Esperanton en la movado de Gejunulaj Budhanaj Asocioj." Tio ja estas la unuafoja akcepto de Esperanto en la oficiala budhana konferenco. La akcepto alportis preskaŭ nenian frukton depost tiam, tio temen ja estas sufiĉe grava kaj notinda afrero en la movado de Budhana kampo.

En Decembro Sro Ŝibajama ricevis de Sro G. H. Yoxon, Angla budhana samideano, leteron, ke li volas starigi internacian organizaĵon por tutmondaj budhanaj samideanoj kaj havi ĝian organon, kaj ke por tio li volas peti helpon al li kaj aliaj Japanaj samreligiaj samideanoj. La ricevinto kaj liaj kolegoj estis tiel forte instigita, ke ili komencis ekpensi, ke Japanaj budhanoj, kiuj sin nomas landanoj de Mahajana Budhismo, ankaŭ devas aktive eklabori por la movado.

En sekvinta Jaro, 1931, pli favora stato regis la movadon. Ĉe la fino de januaro Sro Ŝibajama ricevis de Sro G. H. Yoxon leteron, ke li finfine plenumis sian projekton starigi "Budhana Ligo Esperantista." Kaj kun la letero li ricevis la 1an Nron de kvaronojara Bulteno de BLE. Kompreneble la fakto forte frapis la korojn de Budhanaj Esp-istoj en nia lando, el kiuj iu-tiu eĉ publikigis artikolojn pri B.L.E. kaj Sro G. H. Yoxon sur ĵurnalo Ĉuugai-nippoo, kompetenta ĵurnalo en budhana kampo.

En februaro du Usonaj budhanaj samideanoj alveturis en Japanujon kaj restadis en unu el ĉeftemploj de Zen-sekto en Kioto, Daitoku-ĵi, por studi Zen-Budhismon. Dum ilia restado ĉirkaŭ duonjara, Kiotaj samideanoj multofoje interkomunikiĝis nur per Esperanto kun ili. Tio ankaŭ akcelis vigligi nian movadon.

La 11an de Majo, vespere, okazis kunveno por starigi Budhanan Grupon, kies aranĝantoj estis Sroj Dazai, Inada, Monobe, Ŝibajama. Ĉirkaŭ 10 partprenantoj, inter kiuj estis eĉ veteranaj pioniroj, Sro Akijama kaj Sro Hosokaŭa. Post amika interkonsiliĝo oni decidis: Ĉiuj partprenantoj provizore organizu "Japana Budhana Ligo Esperantista" kaj kunlaboru por plipotencigi ĝin, alvokante al Ĉiuj Budhanaj Samideanoj tra la lando: malgraŭ la aranĝantoj nur esperis komence, ke ili almenaŭ havu navan Grupon por Budhanaj samideanoj en Kioto. Granda sukceso de la kunveno. Tiel favore J.B.L.E. ekpaŝis sian unuan paŝon.

La 17–18a de sama monato, sub la aŭspicio de Takakura Budhana Junula Asocio oni aranĝis Esp-ekspozicion, kiu havis brilantan sukceson, kaj la 18a–27a, aranĝis elementan kurson, al kiu enskribis pli ol 50 gekursanoj, kiuj estis gvidataj en tri klasoj. Tian grandan sukceson aranĝantoj mem eĉ ne supozis. Tuj post la kurso fondiĝis Takakura Esperanto-Grupo. La kurso kaj la Grupo multe efikis por revigligi nian movadon en Kioto, ĉar inter kursanoj troviĝis multaj studentoj de ekleziaj fakultatoj, t.e. tuj post

finiĝo de la kurso revigliĝis Esp-Grupo de Ootani-Daigaku, tiu de Riukoku Daigaku kaj fondiĝis tiu de Rinzai-ŝu Daigaku.

En Julio oni kopie aperigis "Informilon" de JBLE, N-ro 1, kun nomaro de subtenantoj. Kaj ĝi aperadis ĉiu monate ĝis novembro.

La 15an de oktobro, kaptante bonŝancon, la 19an Kongreson de tutjapana Esperantistaro en Kioto, lokaj budhanaj samideanoj aranĝis kunsidegon de budhana Esperantistaro. Kaj ĝi ankaŭ samtempe estis inaŭgracio oficialigi la fondiĝon de JBLE. Ĉirkaŭ 40 partprenantoj venis el diversaj landpartoj. La ejo estis luksaj haloj de Budhisma Muzeo por Geknaboj en Marujama Parko. Post formala programo oni harmonie interkonsilis tutan regularon por JBLE kaj decidis eldoni kvaronjaran organon, kies titolo "La dumo Orienta" ankaŭ samtempe estis decidita. Jen, JBLE oficiale komencis marŝi ne grandan sed fortan paŝon.

Post dutagoj, la 17an, la dua kongrestago, oni havis Budhisman Fak-kunsidon kun pli ol 15 personoj por unua fojo, en kiu oni decidis plurajn aferojn por nia movado.

Komence de novembro, en la nomo de la faka kunsido kaj JBLE oni dissendis skribaĵojn por instigi enkondukon de nia lingvo al ĉiuj institucioj, lernejoj kaj fakultatoj, kiuj estas koncernantaj al eklezioj.

De 1932 ĝis 1934, dum tri jaroj, nia movado en budhana kampo restis preskaŭ sama stato ne tre vigla. Ĉu tio kaŭziĝas de sociala aŭ nacia tendenco, aŭ ĉu tio kaŭziĝas de malpenemo de ekzistantaj samideanoj, mi ne povas facile aserti. Tamen mi povas citi kelkajn.

JBLE daŭre funkciadas ĝis hodiaŭ regule eldonante sian organon, kaj dume 1933 eldonis 40 paĝan libreton, "La Samanta-Mukha-Parivarto."

En aprilo, 1933, Sro Takeuĉi persone eldonis 50 paĝan libreton "Budao," tradukaĵo de la unua ĉapitro de fama verko "The Essence of Buddhism" verkita de Prf. Lakshmi Narasu.

En marto, 1934, samtempe aperis du organoj: el Rjukoku Daigaku Esp-Grupo "La Sankta Tilio" n-ro 7; el Rinzai-ŝu Daigaku Esp-Grupo "La Voĉo" n-ro 1.

En julio, 1934, La 2a Konferenco de Tut-pacifikaj Junulaj Budhanaj Asocioj, kiu havis lokon en Tokio, akceptis Esperanton kiel preskaŭ oficialan lingvon.

En septembro, 1934, "La Paco" N-ro 11, aperis en preso el Ootani Daigaku Esp-Grupo. Post okjara dormado fine vekiĝis "La Paco," kiu havas gloran historion en siaj pasintaj jaroj. (Fino)

滿洲の佛教を語る夕〔概要速記録〕

主　催　全日本佛教青年會聯盟
日　時　昭和十年四月十八日午後六時から
會　場　小石川傳通會館
出席者　（イロハ順，敬稱略）

稻葉文海	石上昭然	磐井宗憲	蜂谷惠晃
濱田本悠	西岡能圓	神田正法	吉井芳純
高佐貫長	孫　　錯	中島裁之	村上道隆
野口照清	工藤敏見	來馬琢道	松浦龍鍐
小林啓善	小林良甫	荒木哲信	淺野研眞
秋山照仲	澤田有雄	三原信一	水野梅曉
靜永孝英	祥雲洪嗣		

稻葉　今夕はお忙しい處多數御出席下さいまして有難うございます。先づ滿洲，蒙古，支那で布教事業等に携つて居られる方々のお集りを願ひました次第で，水野梅曉先生も後でお見えになりますし，吉井澤田小林諸氏もお見えになる筈です。それから特に滿洲公使館の孫氏がお見えになつて居りますから，それ等の方々にお話を願ひ，其のお話に對して，質問應答を御願ひ致したいと思ひます。尙中には滿洲方面へ御視察にお出でになつた方も多數あると思ひます。更に各宗當局の方もお見えになつて居りますから，かういふ方々の御希望，今後の方策等をお洩し願ひ其上で皆さん方の御意見もお聞きしたいと思ひます。就きましては夫々御意見をお洩し下さる譯でありますから，一應御芳名だけを順次に御知らせ願ひたいと存じます。

孫　私は實は七時から他へ行かなければなりませんので，其の事を宜しく御斷り申上げます。只今の滿洲佛教の狀態は，我々の先輩として滿洲に行かれ，色々調べて來られたやうな方が居られる事を承知して居りますので，私から簡單に（實は申上げなくても）まあ私一個の滿洲人として考へて居る事をお話してみたいと思ひます。今の滿洲の佛教の狀態は其の名前を附けるのに難しい位で，歷史的に考へますと，宗教の色々な束縛といふ點から極めて不振の狀態にあるのでありまして，支那との關係，世界各國との關係もありますので，大いに日本の宗教家の方々に智慧を貸して頂かなければならない事が非

常に多いと思ひます。併乍ら何分從來の佛教方面の僧侶は，日本と違ひまして，何百年前の日本の狀態と同じかも知れませんが，大抵失意した人，若しくは生活に困つて居る人が多いのでありまして，御經が讀めれば一人前の坊さんになれる。宗教といふものも功利的に自分自身に色々にやつて居るのでありまして，一般に尊敬されて居りますものは殆ど品行の正しいといふ事だけでありまして，一般の僧侶は佛教宣傳よりも，生活點に於て非常に重きを置いて居るのでありまして，政治の關係等殆ど知らないと云つていゝ位で，思想も變つて居て，中には非常に有名な學者とか，大官が職を辭めて佛教に入り，日本の昔の武士の入道と同じやうになるのがありまして，さういふ人は良く判つて居るのでありますが，自分一個の事を良くやりさへすればよく全體の事に盡す考へはないのであります。國際關係が將來どういふ風になりますかと申しますと，我々の考では，結局世界といふものは三つに分れはしないかと思ひます。一つはヨーロツパ方面が一つ，アメリカはアメリカで一つ，最後に一番發展するのは我が亞細亞でありませう。亞細亞を復興させるのには他の方面も必要でありますが，どうしても共通のものとして宗教，特に佛教を通して，亞細亞全體の宗教を通してやらなければならない事を痛感して居ります。甚だ恥しい事でございますが，私は佛教徒でもなく，宗教家でもなければ何でもありませんが，此の點に於きまして卽ち亞細亞を纒めるのに共通の點を見出さなければならないのでありまして，其の共通點なるものは佛教であると常に考へて居ります。何分亞細亞の大部分の文化は日本の文化より遲れて居るものでありますから，宗教を政治的に利用するやうに思はれますけれども，成るべく早い方法によつてしなければならないのであります。私の考へとしては，少し卑劣に思はれるかも知れませんが，我々の最後の目的が決して卑しいものでないといふ事を茲に斷言出來るのであります。さてどういふ處から着手すれば一番いゝかと申しますと，今夕御出席の吉井氏，小林氏の方々が滿洲の事情をよく御承知でありますし，御相談申上げたいと思ひます。滿洲の僧侶に對し，又人民に對しまして，良く了解出來るやうな程度までには日本で考へて居ります程，簡單な容易な話ではありません。さう簡單に行くものではないと思ひます。何故かと云ふと，かういふ事に就きまして，餘り研究もなく，基礎知識といふものもありませんから，簡單に考へた理屈だけではゆきません。其の苦勞を充分呑込んで頂いて，それから大いに彼等に判るやうにして貰つてやれば，滿洲の宗教もうまくゆくのではないかと思ひます。まあ譬へて云へば，白紙と同じでありますか

ら，或る程度に依り進めてまゐりましたら案外早く出來て，將來樂になるやうな事があるかも知れません。最初の苦勞といふ點に就きまして，先輩諸先生の御盡力を願はなければならないと存じます。時間の都合もありますし，若し此の次會合する事がありましたら，必ず來て知つて居る限りの事を申上げたいと思ひますが，今日は非常に殘念でありますが此の次には皆さんと意見の交換をしたいと思ひます。これだけの事を申上げまして私の話を終りたいと思ひます。

濱田　お話のやうに，滿洲國の佛教の僧侶の現狀は，文化及び社會的地位が低いやうでありまして，私一夏視察致しました時にも，これを感じたのであります。これに對する方策と致しましては，まあ色々ありませうけれども，滿洲國宗教家，其の他の關係諸官廳に於て，如何樣に宗教家を養成し，且つ其の地位を向上せしめるかといふ方策を立てゝおいでではないでせうか。直接滿洲國僧侶が日本に留學して居りますが，滿洲國自ら進んで．云はゞ我が國の佛教徒が隋，唐に留學しましたやうに，國家が力を注いで，佛教僧侶を向上せしめるといふ事を，現に文教部方面に於てやつて居られますか。お話願ひたいと思ひます。

孫　私はこれをお話する前に速記を止めて頂かねばなりません。私の話に責任を持つ事になりますと困りますから。（說明あり）

濱田　これはもう一こと孫さんにお尋ねしたいのでありますが，昨年の汎太平洋會議以來，非常に滿洲國の佛教運動に活躍せられて，其の方面の幹部の方々からも，今後大いに佛教運動にお盡し下さるやうな御話を只今承りました事は，私共非常に愉快に存ずるのであります。只本當に滿洲國の佛教政策をお考へになるならば，布教に力を注ぐ爲には，佛道に對する尊敬の念を以て，又日本語も實に模範的な日本語を使つて，更に佛教をお奬め下さいまして，佛教に對して內面的から御理解下さいまして，滿洲國の佛教運動に御盡力下さいますならば，必ずや滿洲國の佛教を動かす事が出來ると思ひます。何時でも御案內致しますから，特に日滿佛教提携に就いて御盡力を願ひたいと思ひます。

孫　出來るだけの努力を致します。

◇

稻葉　日蓮宗の本年度にやります方針の事だけを一寸お話願ひたいと思ひますが。

高佐　私は日蓮宗の高佐でございます。日蓮宗で本年度にやります滿洲國に對する方針だけ申上げたいと思ひます。從來日蓮宗と致しましては滿洲の布教に關して，今回程眞劍に考へて居た事はないのであります。滿洲國建設，引續いて皇帝陛下御來訪に依つて一層感じを深められるに至りましたが，皇帝陛下御來訪の事を知らない以前から計畫を立てゝ居りました。從來日本の佛教と申しますと，或は誤るかも知れませんが，日蓮宗は日本內地ばかり布教して居りまして，葬式法要等をするに過ぎない。全く實質的には海外布教といふをこがましい事は云へないのでありまして，これは誠に眞の布教にはなりませんので，殊に我々の極く古い先輩，**蓮華阿闍梨**といふ人が日蓮の亡くなつた直後，滿洲へお入りになり，樺太から滿洲方面にも行かれた事があります。今後滿洲並びに朝鮮方面に向つて布教する事に力を注がねばならぬといふ考へを持ちまして直に實行に移つたのであります。本年，立正大學に滿鮮講座を作りました。成績はどういふ事になるか判りませんが，眞劍に着手した事はお認め願ひたいと思ひます。殊に先程申上げました**日持**上人の殘されました寺院が，內地に一ケ寺あります。靜岡市に近頃編入されましたが，其の寺を滿洲の新京に移す相談もあつて滿洲方面の本部にするといふ方針で旣に本年度の宗會に於きまして滿場一致可決したのであります。今年直に移りたいのでありますが，ならぬ爲に明年の宗會の改正を待つて實現する段取りになつて居ります。只々專ら準備を進めて居ります。それがまあ追々に滿洲方面に進出してゆきます日蓮宗の方針でありますが，實際上には旣に熱河に支那を相手と致しまます立正大學の教師をして居ります井上義澄君が永年北京に行つて居りまして，語學が非常に堪能でありますが，熱河に參りまして軍部の方々の御骨折がありまして，道教の寺を手に入れまして，滿洲人に布教して居ります。語學を研究させ喇嘛教方面に布教するやうに報告を受けて居ります。其他本年度と致しましては此の秋の十月十日大連を出まして管長神保日慈師が自ら滿洲を視察される事に決定して居りまして，最近私は其の準備として渡滿する事になるかも知れないと思つて居ります。尙これは最近のニユースでありますが吉林省の間島に敷地三萬坪，寺院の造營物を造つて布教の根據地にしたいといふ篤志家の申出を聞きまして，嬉しく思つて居ります。さういふ譯で，滿洲方面に向ひまして，日蓮宗も積極的な步みを運んで居るといふ事を申上げるのでございます。尙もう一つ日蓮宗の態度をとりませんがさういふ色彩を持たないでやつて居るのは，奉天の北陵に於て，滿洲國政府から二萬坪ばかりの土地を貰ひ受けて，滿洲國で亡くなられた戰死者並びに功勞ある方の靈を祭つて居ります。これは旣に一部竣成致しまして，更に第二期の工事にかゝつて居ります。尙本年の滿洲國に於て十一月十八日までに第一期工事を完成する認可を得て現にやつて居ります。工費は二十萬圓であります。庫裡の一部になる處も一萬四千圓であります。以上が大體滿洲國に於ける日蓮宗布敎の報告であります。

稻葉　日蓮宗の日持上人の遺跡が內蒙古か外蒙古に發見されたといふ事ですが，これは若し何かの形で殘つて居れば相當綿密な調査をして頂きたいと思ひますが。

高佐　私は實は現在までの實蹟は，今は宙で覺えて居りませんが，最近のですか。

稻葉　最近のものです。蒙古の方に廟か何かになつて殘つて居るといふ單にそれだけの記事なんですが，これは實際に人を派遣して調査してもいいのではないかと思ひます。軍部の方か何かで，もう少し了解を得て。

高佐　何時頃ですか，それは。

稻葉　つい最近とは申せませんが，二月頃の宗敎新聞と記憶してゐます。

高佐　何か傳手があらうと思ひますから，調査してみます。

濱田　日蓮宗に就きましては，從來色々お話がありますが，私共が學究的立場から申しますと，所謂遺跡といふものも何人が，どの程度の人が遺跡として鑑定したかといふ事は，どうも此方から行きました人か或は軍部の方がさういふ斷定を下したかも知れません。考古學的な實蹟といふものは餘りないかと思ひますが，殊に日滿方策をお進めになりますたらば，專門の歷史家乃至考古學者をして，專門にお取り調べ願ひたいと私は希望します。もう一つこれは質問でありますが，色々日蓮宗關係の滿蒙對策を伺ひましたが，日蓮宗の藤井行勝氏の滿蒙行脚と申しませうか盛に行はれて滿洲國の寺等に參りましても藤井行勝氏の曼陀羅なるものがありますが（我々も見て參りました），あの一派の滿洲國の事蹟といふものを如何に取扱つて居られますか。

高佐　日蓮宗としては藤井氏一派の方々と連絡を持つて居ないのです。從つて統制のある布敎組織の中に入れてないのであります。つまり自由行動になつて居ります。まあ好意は持つて居りますが，併し流儀が變つて居ります。

稻葉　好意を持つて居られる譯ですね。

蜂谷　一寸お尋ねしたいのですが，今お話のあつた中に，はつきりお聞きする事が出來なかつたのでありますが，日蓮宗の日護寺を起工するのと違ひますか。

高佐　これは違ひます。これは滿洲廟と云ひまして，寺院の形式を取つて居ります。

蜂谷　滿洲靈廟建設案といふ問題で三月一日の「中外日報」に詳しく書いてありましたが，それが日蓮宗の布敎師の方で特に名を祕すといふ事で滿洲布敎師會の席上に於てそれは非常にインチキであるといふ事を發表したといふ記事が載つて居つたのを私は見まして，非常に遺憾に思つて居りました。これとは違ひますか。

高佐　日護寺ではありません。滿洲國靈廟と稱して居ります。インチキではありません。これは現に出來て居ります。

蜂谷　この記事を御覽になればお判りですが，かういふ重要なるものでありますから「中外日報」に抗議して正確な事を，三月一日附の新聞でありますから，當局の方にお調べ願つて，滿洲靈廟を中心に日滿各仕事を竝立させるやうにしたいと思ひます。

三原　滿洲靈廟の中に日光殿，月光殿といふのを建てるんですが，其の本人にも會つて聞いたんですが，それはインチキぢやないですね。

高佐　要するに造らうといふ日光殿が喇嘛僧院のやうな綜合したものを造らうといふのです。庫裡の一部は既に出來て居ります。

◇

石上　今度は水野先生に一つお願ひ致します。

稻葉　一寸進行について申上げますが吉井先生，中島先生の方々にお話を願つて，承つたそれ等の御話を基本と致しまして質問希望を述べて頂きたいと思ひます。只今孫氏は御忙しいので退場されましたので，今度は水野先生に滿洲布敎に對する御意見を一應承りたいと思ひます。

水野　僕は此の布敎といふ問題に就いては何の經驗も持たず，今の各宗で一生懸命にやつて居られるのは非常に諒とするが，佛敎家といふ立場以外に在留民から見れば，どうも此の宗派といふものが餘り片寄り過ぎて居る。此の點或る意味に於て在留民は聊か迷惑を感ずるといふ傾きがある。各々個性が違ふやうに自ら何も違ふといふ事があるが，僕は先決問題として日本佛敎徒といふものが，苟くも對外的に動かうといふ時には一番統制が必要ではないかと思ふ。例へば吉林なら吉林に或る宗派で寺院を設けようとする，すると今度は別な宗派でもこれに對抗的にやるといふ事になる。此の惱がある。僕はこれは兎に角日本佛敎徒の布敎の一番の弊害だと思ふ。それを新に荒れた土地を再び開墾しようといふ時分には，各々が手を揃へてゆくといふ雅量を備へて頂きたいといふ事が第一の意見です。滿洲の佛敎に對する基調になつてゆかなければならない。滿洲には寧ろ佛敎といふものは變形をした佛敎になつて居る。寺院に行つても寺院の本尊が何かといふことを知つて居る人がない。何樣だか知らない。從つて道を說く人が居ない。學者が其の色々の僧侶をやる。佛敎，儒敎，回々敎，キリスト敎等只人を善に導くといふ共通點を以て殆ど佛敎だけではない。かういふやうな關係になつて居りまして，從つて有力な連中はどういふ事をやつて居るかといふと，一つの結社を持つて居る。新京で確か三萬坪ばかりの家を建てようとして居る。大ホールの收容人員が二千人を標準にしてやつて居る。それから色々な問題を判斷するのに使ふ一つの御神籤といふのは，日本のやうに書いてあるものを振るんぢやなく扶鸞といふものである。四尺位のテーブルがあつて其の上に砂があつて，扶鸞をやる鸞壇を設け，それに巫覡者が行つて祈るといふと，日本で云ふなら，今日は弘法大師が降られるとか，今日は日蓮が降られる。さうなると面白い。僕が立つ，君が立つ，さうして丁字形になる。こゝに兩方の手を持つて一本の棒が立つ。それが無意識に動き出す。砂にドンドン書く。これに依つて總ての事を判斷する。殆ど滿洲に於ける有閑有產階級といふものは殆ど之れに依つてやつて居る。卽ち神勅である。去年日本の東北に凶作があつた時などにも全部が起つて，金を募つて，十何萬圓かの金を持つて來る。直ぐと救濟策を取る。又殺されて居る者の棺を供へて葬ひをする。流行病がはやると直ぐ施藥をする。これは社會的に非常に活躍して居る。これが滿洲國の社會の實情なんです。これを我々が滿洲國の佛敎を布敎するにはどうするか。私共が考へなくちやならぬ問題である。此の點に就いて，支那の佛敎徒が，所謂社會を指導するために孔子の靈を招いてする。如何にも迷信と云へば迷信だが，君と僕とが此處で相談して居ても砂の上にスラスラ書いてゆくといふ事が出來るものぢやない。それが現代の旣成宗敎といふものぢやいけない。我々が新な宗敎をあらゆるエキスを取入れて滿洲に向く樣な新宗敎を作らねばならぬ。

石上　秘密結社ですか，宗敎團體を離れた結社ですか。

水野　それは修養團體といつた方がよい。例へば大震災だといふと率先して金を募つてくれる。かうやつて居るといふのが現實なんだ。それが寧ろ今の支那の社會といふものは，極端に一方では廢頹し色々社會に犧牲を拂つて居るが，我々は佛敎をどう引張つて行くかといふ事が一番の問題だらうと思ふ。

濱田　一寸伺ひますが，其の砂の上に書くのは貴下にも讀める字ですか。

水野　まあ讀めます。まあ普通の字です。

稻葉　二人で書く譯ですね。

水野　さうです。兩方で一々相談して居る譯ではないが，考へて居る事がどんどん出て來るんです。

濱田　書く人の心が出て來る譯ですな。

三原　これは滿洲にどの位あるんですか。

水野　殆ど二千位。

稻葉　萬葉の註釋でも何でも出來る岸博士の太靈道のやうなものですか。

水野　そうです。只それより其れに從事して居る者が如何にも眞面目です。僕は寧ろ有閑有產階級の煩悶の結果，何と云つてよいか，迷信と云つてよいか，各々主觀的な見方があるだらう。煩悶の極，其處へ行つたと思ふ。一般の民衆といふものは，其の中へ入つて居ないと思ふ。我々は現實を見て，それに步調を揃へて行くといふ事が我々の要點なんだ。

◇

石上　今度は吉井さんにお願ひしたいと思ひますが。

吉井　今，水野先生から適切なお話を伺ひましたから，要點はこれで盡きて居ります。我々の考へて居ります點は，それ以上にお話下さいましたので，更に意見を出す必要はないかと思ひますが，只今先生の云はれた中で，如何なる所見を以て向ふに察せしめるかといふ點に就きまして，私の過去數年間色々やつて居ります事から，其の所感だけを述べさせて頂きたいと思ひます。只今水野先生のお話のやうに，扶鸞を一つの中心としました處の結社運動といふものが非常に盛であります。其の他所謂秘密結社といふものがありまして，その方針を拜見しましたが，私も其の方面には興味を惹かれまして，色々材料を集めてみたりしましたのでありますが，現在私の頭に浮び出しますだけでも救世新敎，紅卍敎，或は天津に中心を置いて非常な勢力を持つ天道一心敎とか，色々，勢力を持つて居ります。かういふ團體を數へてみますと，はつきり記憶しませんが，百幾種類あるやうに思ひます。普通其の秘密結社として居りますが其の團體には必ず宗敎的な儀式がついて居る。我々の見方からすれば，一種の宗敎團體である。宗敎團體の中心を爲して居るものは，やはり道敎の方が多いと思ひます。道敎に就きましても，迷信的なものを多分に含んで居る。私の知つて居ります百何種類の中，大部分がさういふ傾向を持つてゐるやうであります。かういふ時に當りまして，所謂佛敎の條件を與へずにどうするかといふ問題で，これは非常に難しい問題でありまして，私共の貧弱な考へで申す事は何ですが，百餘種類の各種の宗敎團體の中，これ等のどれを見ましても，極く嚴密に申しますと，哲學的な方面と申しますか，餘り理屈めいて居らない處に，さういふ方面の體系が非常によく發達した佛敎の哲學とか，或は其の他の哲學に對しまして幾分進んで居ると思ひます。が一面綜合的な行き方をしようとする處に缺點があると思ひます。もう一つ私として注意したいと思ひます事はこれは或は誤つて居るかも知れませんが，支那の色々な民衆の動きと云ひますと，總ての社會を通じて大きな宗敎團體があるやうであります。支那の歷史の上では，儒學者，詩人，文學者などが各結社を作り，これが政治的に進出して政治結社にまで發展し，これが遂に內紛を生じて其の爲に國が亡びたといふ事を聞きますが，單に文學者の結社に止まらず，さういふやうな宗敎結社は同一の傾向を持つてゐるのではないかと思ひます。さうしたならば結社といふものを全然考へに入れないで佛教を進めて行く事は非常に危險であると思ひます。かういふものに對して佛教が取るべき態度は，優秀な指導原理を與へてゆくといふ事が日本佛教の支那に對する使命，方法ぢやないかと思ひます。かういふ點が先申しました事情から考へまして，缺けて居るのではないかと思ひますから，敢て申上げるのです。日本佛教徒が宗派的でなく，全體の佛教徒として，支那に對しても，さうしてゆかなければならぬ。これは全く御說の通りである。其の方法として，どういふ方法があるかと申しますと，卽ち現在支那の方で非常に教育方面で發達して居るものはミツション方面であります。從つて其の中から色々人材を出して居ります。これはやはり所謂結社的な連絡がありまして，さういふ風な人材は政治方面にも指導的位置に立つて非常に發展して行く。處が近代の支那と日本との關係上，非常に遺憾に思はれます事は，各方面に，殊に教育方面に關係があつたに拘らず，甚だ振つて居らないと思ひます。佛教を中心とした研究方面に就きましては，絕無に近い程であると思ひます。これが從前の日本人の缺點ではないかと思ひます。從つて，茲にどうしても日本佛教徒全體の使命として，支那に相當有力な，佛教精神を中心として居る處の教育機關を完成してゆくといふ事が將來の佛教布教に對する大切な事ぢやないかと思ひます。

濱田　ミツションの系統は滿洲國の宗教家を養成する機關ですか，それとも滿洲國民に佛教を養成する機關ですか。

吉井　これは私だけの考へですが，佛教徒を養成するといふ事も必要でありますが，それだけに止めるといふ事でなしに，佛教精神に依つて向ふの總ての民衆を指導するといふやうにしたいと思ひます。

水野　滿洲も支那も同一の言葉で同一の習慣だ。だが日本語を要求する事は非常なものです。それだから寺を建てるのも結構だが，伽藍を拵へるのも惡く云へば搾取だ。それよりも日本語の完全な教育を先づ授ける。それで此方へ來て何處の專門學校に入るにも，言葉だけは不自由がないといふ風になつたらいゝと思ひます。

◇

石上　中島氏に一つお話願ひたいと思ひます。

中島　滿洲も支那も同じで，將來もやはりお互に同じにしてゆかなければならないと思つて居りますが，十人十色で氣が違へば性が違つて行く。併し過去に於きまして，殖民地に於ける日本人としての布教傳道といふものが殆どよくいつて居ない。私は僧侶でないから，それ程考へもありませんけれども，教育に於きまして

も まるで宗教家でありさうでない嫉妬心を持つて居る事がある。これは非常に遺憾千萬であります。だから佛教青年會が日本佛教を傳道する事に就きましても，創立の際には隨分餘地がありますが，愈々充實しかけると，會員の奪ひ合ひを惡辣な手段を以てする。かういふ事になりまして，而もそれが便宜上始めは在留日本人に向つてさういふ行動が行はれる。其のやり方が非常に惡い。それを土着人に喝破されたならば，これは到底宗教家としての行動ぢやない。彼等に日本佛教の侮蔑を感ぜしめると思ひます。これは侮蔑の他の例でありますが，我々が支那に行きまして食卓に列席しました時に，支那の方では先づ主人公が箸を取りまして「どうぞお上り下さい，チンチン」とやつて箸をつける。そこでお客は御馳走になる。日本では出て來た物は當然食べるものと思つてどんどん箸をつける。殊に洋食に於てさうです。これは習慣としてやつて來た事ですが，あちらの人から見れば露骨に云へば，日本人は不行儀だ，かういふやうな考へを持つて居るやうであります。各々の習慣，傳統と歷史の異つて居る方面に向つて我々が手を附ける事は非常に至難な業であります。といつて此儘放置しておく譯にはゆきません。お話のやうに佛教思想を傳道するのにはどういふ形式を以てするか，さうしてさうなつた場合は，或る宗派の如きは，冷淡極る態度を執るだらうと思ひます。それが果して宗教の眞相で滿洲に向つて佛教を傳道する。どういふ風に綜合的にやるか，大體，お定めが必要ではないかと思ひます。今晚の御催しは勿論在滿土着人も在留人も籠めてに對する宗教傳道運動の御心持であると思ひます。さういふ事であるならば，在留邦人を中心とした所謂日本佛教徒に對する從來の氣持のみに立つたならば，土着の滿洲人にはお門違ひにならうと思ひます。私は僧侶でありませんが，一寸佛典の一部をひねくりました爲に，私一個人として試みた事がありますが，最前孫先生のお話のやうに，有力な學者だとか僧侶は，所謂失脚した處の有志であります。政治家であります。さういふ者が逃げ場所として寺に立籠ります。さうして政治家になる準備に體驗とか學問とかいふやうなものを積んで居ります。仲々手腕ある學問ある人を我々は發見するのであります。例へば支那の太虛法師であります。非常に先進的な人で，圖書館に入りまして我々が三年讀めば，彼は十年も讀書したといふ風で，支那の佛教徒の中に非常に秀でた人もあります。けれども之れは本當の信仰的な人であるが，一般宗教家は不具者であります。總て不具者を寺院に追込んだものであります。光緒帝の時代に(其の前にも一度あつたが)皆追込んでしまつたのであります。かういふ方法をとつた事がありまし

たけれども，今の支那に流れて居る宗教に對してそれを我々が順應するといふ遣り方，これは又大いに考へなければならぬと思ひます。だから日本人の氣持を以て支那を律するといふ事は，大いに考へなければならない。大谷光瑞さんを支那に案内致しました時，私はかういふ事を献言したのであります。

「貴下が日本にお歸りになつて知人の間に御土產話をされる時には本當の支那の姿を知つて貰はねばならぬ。折角來られたのだから，此の際南北支那を踏破するならば，初めて支那全貌に通じた事になる。さうすれば日本の佛教徒は歡喜するでせう，感泣するでせう。」といふと，光瑞氏は成程と頷かれて，廣東を後にして漢口から北京に向つて行かれた。其の時私がかういふ事を申上げた。

「これでよく支那を御覽になつたのでありますから，どうぞ日本に向つて南北支那の御土產話をなさつて下さい。それからもう一つ親鸞聖人にお土產がある。それは他でもないが支那人の子供を連れて行つて，貴下の學校に入れて敎育する。さうすると彼等は成人して支那に歸つて信仰を，本當の宗教を傳道するだらう。」と云つて子供を連れて歸つて貰ひました。實は明治二十八年に京都の本願寺で，支那及び朝鮮に傳道所が出來ました。私共は少し敎授致しましたが，これがとても難しい。それから言葉だけが上手でありましても，普通支那人同樣に話すと思つても，本當の支那人に直面した時にすぐ判る。それから習慣や性格に非常な相違がありまして，支那人といふものは非常に鷹揚である。高粱の中に四日も五日も六日も入らねばならぬといふやうな，日本人としては非常に苦しい事も彼等には習慣となつて居ります。性格にしても其の土地の影響があります。それから支那の水は濁つて居ります。支那は塵芥の國であります。塵芥に日常接して居りますから，我々が淸潔なものに接して居るのと同じであります。此の性格を考へずにやつた時には，何時も失敗するのであります。これはまあ妙な話でありますが，支那語を硏究して居ります時分に，大變私を大切にする人がありました。まだ私二十三四の頃でありましたが，それに幽靈の眞似をしてみたけれども一寸も怖ぢない。どういふ譯かと思つたら支那の幽靈はかうして出る。（兩手にて兎の耳の形を爲す）これでは日本人が見ても恐しくもどうもない，甚だ滑稽であります。かういふやうな習慣の相違がありますから佛教に於きましても本當に徹底させる事になりますと，どうしても我々日本人ではいけない。生えぬきの言葉と生えぬきの習慣を持つてやらなければなりません。我々が下駄を穿く習慣を持つて居る者が支那の沓を穿くと步けない。さういふやうに一般風俗習慣

の違つた者が彼等に對して總てを行ふ時には非常に不安を感ぜしめる。彼等に本當の宗教を徹底させるならば，本當に生えぬきの人に依らなければいけません。かういふ事を大谷光瑞さんに色々申上げました，私はどうしても徹底させたいと思つて，日淸戰爭の時に子供を一人貰つて來たのでありますが，これは結局宗教家にならないで商賣人になつてしまつた。此の會として本當に支那に對して宗教傳道をしようといふ，所謂國策とか政策とかいふのではなく，本當にしようといふのであるならば本當の宗教家であるならば進んで出られてゆく事は決して難しい事はなからうと思ひます。現狀に於ける日本の宗派には非常に軋轢がある。宗教家に相應しくないやうな態度があるやうであります。玆に於て新しい建設をしようといふ事であるならば宗派を超えて新しい宗教の普及をする。これは吉井さんのお話のやうに非常に至難な問題でありますけれども，至難な問題をして硏究するのがかういふ催しの中心であると思ひますから，數回に亙つて御討議に及びさうして各宗各派がやるか，連絡統制をとつてやるか，或は全然滿蒙政策の下に更に硏究するか，宜しく謀られたいと思ひます。非常にくどい事を申しましたが，此の佛教靑年會として振り出すならば，大きな輪廓だけを移すといふ風の漠とした事を以て甘んずるか，何物か一つの組織された信仰といふものを見出すか，信仰を第二において，人格を第一にするか，さういふ事を御考へ願ひたいと思ひます。

◇

石上　それでは今度は澤田さんにお話をお願ひ致します。

澤田　今夕は諸先輩の方から滿蒙地方の事に就きまして，又深く支那方面に亙つて色々詳しい御話もありましたので，格別申上げる事もありません。また自分としても皆さん方にお話しすべき材料も持ち合せて參りませんので，何とも申譯ありませんが自分が先方に行つてした仕事に就いてだけ御報告申上げたいと思ひます。先程から各宗派を超越して先方に當るといふ意見が大分行はれて居るやうでありますが，自分も其の事に就きまして水野先生にも御教訓を賜つて居りますが，各宗派を超越し一丸となつて布教に携はるといふ事は，自分の今日までの仕事の上から考へてみますと，仲々內地としましては各宗派が手を握り合せて實行するといふ事が不可能な事ではなからうかと思ひます。色々御高見も承りましたが，滿洲の佛教といふ事に就きましては，甚だ幼稚な點だけ擧げられて居りまして，議論めいた事よりも，これを指導する事に着手しようといふ事は必要な事であると存じます。自分と致しましては，滿蒙の人達と手を握る事が第一必要ではな

いかと思ひます。議論は澤山あり計畫もありますが，内地の人のみを相手にせず，滿蒙の人達と手を握つてやるといふ事は，まだ餘りやつて居ないと思ひます。これ等の組織，計畫を以て着手しなければならぬ問題でありますが，先づ實行しますに於て，實行に先だつて滿蒙の人達に親しむといふ事が第一で，又宗派を超越して仕事に取りかゝらなければならぬと思ひます。自分等も色々仕事に就いて努力して居りますが，まだまだ完成しませんので發表する處へまゐりませんから，尙又先程から諸先輩の方々が申されたやうな理想的な方法，所謂自我の宗派に捉はれずして努力して居るのであります。これは或は出來るか乃至自分の一生に出來ないか私は判りませんが，實際に於て一朝一夕に出來ない事である。佛敎傳道，思想善導といふ事に就きまして，尙又一宗一派に捉はれて居る人が佛敎傳道に携はるよりも寧ろかういふ風な單なる一宗の人とせずにやつた方が，却つて效果を擧げるのではないかと思ひます。

石上　工藤さんからもお話を願ひたいと思ひますが，時間も經過して居りますから，皆さんから質問して頂きまして，又それに就いて御考へを伺ひたいと思ひます。ではどうか。

淺野　日本語を非常にやりたいといふ事でしたが，あちらでは日本語熱が非常に盛ですか。

水野　非常に盛です。尤も最近九・一八事件の際に學生がどんどん歸つて五百人位だつたでせう。處が又だんだん增えて，今では七千を突破して居る。それで來る學生がどういふ人かといふと，今まで中學卒業した者はうまくすると官費になつて居たが日本側の都合もあつて入學に非常に困難を感じた。それから今度は高等學校以上になると，大學卒業生が七千の中でも少くとも三分の一は大學卒業生でせう。其の中で日本語を知つて居る者が何人あるか。神田に東亞豫備校がありますが，班を四つか五つに分けて個々に分けて押すな押すなでやつて居る。さういふ狀態で北京に行つてみても，さうした日本語學校といふものがある。日本人が信用を受け，制度も改善して之れを續けてゆくといふ事が我々の一つの使命なのです。

淺野　根本的な考へ方では，支那こそが中華で，日本の文化は支那から行つたものであるといふ思想を持つて居るんぢやないでせうか。

水野　文化といふものに對しては殊に面白い。米國がへりの敎授などは東洋歷史の講義が出來ない。現に角日本の文化は一步先んじて居る。日本の文化を輕蔑するやうな事はない。文化が昔支那の佛敎思想と共に入つて來たが，今はそれを土臺にして日本の佛敎文化を支那に贈り返すといふ譯です。

淺野　それから日本人も支那語をやらなければ不可んでせうね。

水野　大いに左樣です。

中島　私は遠方ですから，先に退出させて頂きたいのですが，退出に臨み一寸申します。支那人が日本語をやるのと，日本人が支那語をやるのと比べますと，必ず支那人が日本語をやる方が巧いですね。處が宗敎の大髓を徹底させる爲に言葉の巧みな事が良いと思ひますが，さういふ準備の整はぬ前に於て爲すべき案として私は申上げておきたい。それは口の說敎より眼の說敎で，言葉が判らなくても，惡い事をすれば惡い事が起るといふやうな映畫を作りまして，社會道德を中心と致しまして，色々の事を映畫し，それを巧みに知らず識らずの間に，日本佛敎の現狀傳道なり信仰を植ゑ付けるやうにしたら實際支那語を巧みに喋るより，此の方が或る程度まで出來るのぢやないかと思ひまして，私は約十三四年間映畫を製作して居ります。ずつと滿洲，北米を廻ります都度，其の映畫を持つて廻つて居ります。其の土地土地の郵便局長，裁判長，學校長といふ人が力を入れてくれまして，やはり言葉が判らなくて說明がなくても，內容は判つて居るやうであります。もう一つ見る者は，老若男女，誰が見ても判るやうですから，かういふ傳道方法を以て，お試みになつては如何。汎太平洋佛靑大會の時にも此の映畫を致しました處，インド，ハワイ，ジヤワ，カナダから續々と複寫を望んで居ります。奈良朝時代の面白い特殊材料がありますから，これも映畫化して見せようと思つて目下脚本を製作中であります。まあかういふ方法を以ておやりになる事を私はお奬めするのであります。

◇

小林(良)　先程から色々お話を伺つて居りまして，一つの疑問を持つて居りますが，滿洲の布敎といふが，大體日本人に布敎して居るといふお話ですが，特に全日本佛敎靑年會聯盟の名に於て，今晚集つて滿洲布敎といふ事を語るといふ事でありますから，何かさういふやうな特別な計畫があつて集まられたものであると考へましたが，お話を伺つて居りますと，各宗が其の宗派の色彩を濃厚にして居るといふ事が重大な事であると色々に話されましたが，宗派を超越して通佛敎的に當つてゆかなければならぬといふことに御意見が大體一致したやうであります。結局此の全聯といふ團體に依つてやるのが相應しいのぢやないかといふ御意見になつたやうです。してみると全聯に於て計畫があり，意見があつて，これを實施する何か或る程度の下地があれば結構ですが，只感じたままを語るだけでなく，其處に何か具體化して外に現れるやうなお話もあらうかと思ひます。結局全聯の名に於て滿洲佛敎を語るといふのでありますから，集つた者で其の方針を定めるといふやうなお積りだつたのではないでせうか。時間もそろそろ經過してまゐりまして，主催者の方に於きましても，何か結論的なものを摑まうとして居られるのではないかと思ひますから，これに就て討議されん事を希望します。

稻葉 大體夫々の宗の方が御發言下さつたと思ひますが，智山の方がまだだと思ひますから，簡單にお話し願ひます。

西岡 私，智山の宗務所に居ります西岡でございます。私は滿洲へ行つた事も一回しかありませんので，彼方の事情もよく知りませんし，殊に宗派も小さいので格別事業もやつて居りませんから，取り立てて皆さんにお話するやうな事もありませんから色々先程からお話を承つて成る程と感心した一人であります。各宗が一緒になつて滿洲に布敎するといふ事は非常に結構な事と思ひますが，日本の佛敎團體等がどういふ譯で無力であるかといふ點を私達は始終考へて居りますが，それには先づ此のやうな小さい宗派よりも，大きい宗派の方々が妥協して頂けば一層よいと思ひます。各宗が聯合してゆくと，今まで佛敎に起つた弊害が必ずや起きはしないか，萬一さういふ弊害が起きたとすれば，折角連絡統一を謀つた計畫が畫餅に歸して何にもならないのぢやないかと杞憂を抱いて居る一人でありますが，社會事業的な方面，又敎育方面では可能性が充分あるだらうと私は信じて居ります。これを實現する上には，もう少し有力な宗派の方が虛心坦懷に仲よくしてゆかうといふ事でなければ，其の目的の貫徹は難しいのではないかと思ひます。私共の宗派としては，殆ど滿洲に布敎の對策を執つて居りませんけれども，獨力で寺を建てて居る者は三ケ寺ばかりあります。今度滿洲に本部を作る事になつて第一回資金として五萬圓を計上しました。そして約二十萬圓の事業を翼賛する事になつて居ります。成田の不動さんを擔ぎ出して，一番効果がよいので，それが爲に信者が增えるといふ結果を現して來まして，宗派として餘り補助しませんが，行つて居る人自身が資金を集めて，現に此の七月に蘇家屯に蘇家屯

寺院を建てる事になつて居ります。滿蒙の曠の中に芍藥，菖蒲等を植ゑて，鐘で信者を集めて，護摩を焚き說敎するといふ方針を持つて居ります。大體知識學的な高等な政策ではありませんけれども，卑近な方からやつて行きたいと思つて居ります。

◇

濱田 一寸先程御質問がありましたから，一言それに對して御答へ致したいと思ひます。對滿政策として我々が動き出さうとする大げさなものでなく，今夕はさうした會合ではなく滿洲國皇帝御來訪を記念すべき記念的な座談會とも云ふべきものでありまして，勿論滿蒙を研究し布敎する使命の爲に會合が營まれたのみならず，我が全聯にも，或は汎聯の海外布敎方面に委託すべき立場のものから，かういふ座談會が開かれて必ずしも具體的な對策を持つて居る譯ではありませんが，先程から承りました皆さんの御話に就いては，私非常に尊い資料であると思ひます。これに依りまして幾多の案が考へ得られるのであります。此の座談會に依つて何らかの案を得られると思つて臨んだのであります。かういふ研究會を引續き催しますかどうか，これは單に小林氏に對する御答でなく，私共は深く此の使命に感激し，又所謂成案を練つてみたいと思ひます。

石上 一寸御挨拶申上げます。今日は御多用の處を御來場下さいまして，大變熱心に御話下さいまして有難うございました。司會者として御禮申上げます。

稻葉 色々多くの資料をお漏し下さつた事を感謝致します。これから懇談なり意見なり自由になさるやうに御願ひ致します。（完）

大乘佛敎の國際化に必要なる當面の事業

○ 淸水觀碩

一，佛敎寺院名刹には英文案內を備付置かるゝ樣內々準備ありたきこと，

尙觀光局と適當の連絡をとること。

二，內外の英字新聞を利用し時々佛敎ニユースを掲載し專ら傳道に努むること

三，海外に於ける二世の子女に日本佛敎を研究なさしめ彼等をして宣布の補助員たらしむる事

以上は亦大事のことゝ存居候

日系二世への暗示

山内　脩謙

日本人が米國に入るの是非は，幾多の機關を通じ，幾多の論客によつて，遠く一八八七年（明治廿年）來論じ來り，論じ去られてゐる。かれ等は，わが帝國の立脚地よりすれば，大の排日論者であり，太平洋岸の政客よりすれば，憂國の叫びであつた。

ともかく，移民問題は，過去四十有八年間，揉みに揉まれて，一九二四年，かの國際物議を醸せる米國中央議會の『歸化し得ざる移民の絶對入國を禁止す』との，國法の制定により，大團圓とはなつた。

米國の憲法が，單に白人黑人にのみ歸化を許し，他の有色人種にこれを拒めるは，萬國共通の歸化法に離反せるは勿論，米自體の憲政を損傷するも，また多大である。かゝる議論は，かの地の學者層における見解ではあれ，今後，對米移民法改正の一大論點でもあらねばならぬ。

慷慨悲憤にして一過すれば，共に問題の性質を吟味し來る。――かくて日米は兩國の傳統的友誼にみるも，一時的危機に災ひさるゝなく，親善關係を持すべきではある，と『日米親善』なる灰色旗は振られ，宗教家，直接利害關係を有する實業家，乃至は觀光客の徒は，そこに美麗なる禮讃を交換した。だが，茲に明白なる事態を閑却して，相互に無意義なる辭令を交換すれども，この兩友邦の心からなる誤解を一掃すべくもない。寧ろ，かゝる形式的傾向の口頭融和こそ，われ等が耳には，僞善の叫びをきくに似たるものがある。

ふきに吹き荒れたる第一世の移民問題が，一段落を告ぐると，そこに順序として，第二世の諸問題が擡頭した。今日米本土在留の邦人總數にして十四萬，その半ばは日系第二世のそれであつた。しかも，かれ等が兩親の，特殊的外人視さるゝに拘らず，かれ等は，米國憲法の保障下にあり，生れながらにして市民權を享有する。風俗，習慣言語，思想，その他あらゆる權能にして，何一つ他と異るものがない。

他面，これはまた，かれ等が兩親のそれに反し，邦語に通ぜざるは勿論，異れる敎育下における思想，感情を有し國家觀念をも異にする。從つて，かの兩者が家庭その他における接觸にして圓滑ならざるは論を俟たぬ。

こゝに兩親の日本的觀點よりすれば，そこに贊否の兩論は戰はされる。が，ともあれ，かの地の標準と理想に燃ゆる日系二世の，米社會への存在的提起は，獨りその血統の祖，一世の興味的中心たるのみならず，米社會全般の注視の的でもある。加州スタンフオード大學等における全加州日系二世の職業調査は，早くもその全體社會上かれ等が如何なるポジーションを得たるやの過程的一調査であつた。

かれ等は社會的に自由人たるの，初等，高等，大學等における所謂學校生活を脱出すると同時に，そこには未だかつて，體驗しえざりし『人種の相違』といべる障壁に直面した。そして，かゝる意味から，白人社會より隔絶されたる境遇下にゐるかれ等がグループなるを發見した。

と，同時に日系第二世の社會的欲望なるは，かれ等白人種同樣のラインにまで進出せんと試みる，その事實は，事態をさらに複雜化せずんばおかぬ。ドメステイツク・ラインにおけるフイリツピン人の進出，また農場及び果樹園での傭役に從事するメキシコ人の躍進は，正に日系第二世によつて顧みられざる下級層の勞役を奪取せるに外ならぬ。

とて，ほかに日系第二世によつて保持さるべき社會のあるべくもない。一九三〇年におけるわが國勢調査中第二世配偶調査の結果にみるも明らかである。白人種社會への躍進の如きは，全くこれ藥物的存在であつた。そこにかれ等が兩親の，米社會におけるわが大和民族發展の將來に，不安を抱けるがあり，自らもまた，他の有色人種の如く，そこに屈辱的勞作に，意ならずも屈從すべく餘儀なくされる。そして，その結果は，かれ等が兩親より『勇往邁進の意氣』，『自負心と信念の缺乏』等の諸點において，二世の將來を疑はるゝことゝなる。

日本人が，その自らの事業において，自國人を使用するは自然の道理である。白人また然りである。從つて日本人の職業人――醫師，齒科醫，辯護士，技師等々――の職的範圍は，おのづと自國人間に極限される。日白相互間の結婚の如きも，双側の人種によつて攣蹙されつゝあり，加州の如き，州法によりこれを規定するもある。かくて兩人種は，社交的にも相隔絶し，たゞ，時に公式の會合にのみ接觸する。そこで，日本人は不可避的に，人種意識に目醒めざるをえなくなる。かの國法上，米國市民たる權利を有し，しかも別種の利害關係をもつて，米社會より分離されたる，一の社會集團を形成せる矛盾に就て思考せざるをえぬ現況である。

しかも，その損害たるや，日白兩社會に與へ，極めて不幸なる事態を招來した。そして永久的安定と進歩の爲めには，獨りその國民的分子を擁せる合衆國のみならず，わが帝國と雖も，各この國家的見地より，その重大性に留意せざるべからざるの必要に迫らるゝ。

が，これを世界的には，日白いづれの人種的にも，過失ではなく，それは兩者が互に相通ぜざる人種的徵候の刻印を符せられたるものであり，勿論文化的には同化しえやうものゝ，かゝる意味からは，相互に併呑され終る，卽ち國民的同質の達成が爲めの，眞の同化が爲めには，いづれも憤激に終らざるをえぬ有樣なのである。

かゝる諸點に到達せるの時，日系二世の將來にかゝる樂悲兩論の，かれ等が兩親の胸を打つがある。しかして，その指示をえ，または自覺せる第二世の態度にして，獨り米國の市民權のみを有するの徒と，日米兩國の國籍を有するが輩と，こゝに兩樣に分たれる。一が誠に希望的進取的たると同時に，他は極めて用意的であつた。だが，かれ等が平均年齡は，なほ若年にして，そのいづれの賢明なるやを決するには，未だ以つて早計に過ぐるがある。

曩きに幸ひスタンフオード大學教授ダーシー氏の，わが日系兒童の能率にして，極めて優秀，他人種に比して勝るとも遜色なきを證明せるがあり，かれ等が，その可能なる文化的同化の目的を達しえて，より良きシテイズンたり，また他の日米親善の連鎖たるの徒にして，その東西文化融合の楔子たるかは，その最も可能なる分野として，一般の希望と共に，將來に徵するの外はない。

だが，一旦，世上ことに人種經濟の二點をめぐる諸問題の擡頭せるの時，例へば今次のアリゾナ排日事件の如きにおいては，第二世もまた，その渦中にあり，將來へのより良き教訓であらねばならぬ。その點，わが國社會上における鮮人以上なるあるを，こゝに暗示しえやう。

Japanese News

Takao Temple

The Takao Temple on the summit of Takao-san near Hachioji held its annual spring festival on Sunday.

Due to the fine weather, 50,000 people visited the picturesque Buddhist center with its fine view of several provinces.

Prince Shotoku Hall

The Japan Buddhist' Association plan to erect in Tokyo a five storeyed building in the architectural style of the Suiko period in memory of Prince Shotoku who introduced Buddhism to Japan more than 1300 years ago.

The building will cover an area of 2,500 tsubo and is to cost two million yen.

Yokohama Buddhists

To mark the 30th anniversary of the victory of the Russo-Japan war, services were held for departed soldiers and sailors at the Higashi Honganji on Sunday afternoon under the auspices of the Yokohama Buddhists' Association.

Three thousand persons attended the services and walked from the temple to Yokohama park, and a plane flew overhead scattering thousands of paper lotus.

Buddhist Opera

Mr. Midori Hosokawa, a member of the faculty of the Tokyo School of Music, has completed the music for one act of an opera called "Buddha". Three other acts will follow.

During his stay in Europe, he was impressed by the religious music of the great composers, and has been inspired to express the feeling for Buddha in this country in a music form.

Sacred Image

From Zenkoji, the centuries old temple of Nagano, near Karuizawa, a sacred image is to come to Tokyo.

This statue of Buddha which is a national treasure, and is seldom shown to worshippers, will be placed on view to the public at the city hall in Uyeno Park, Jijikaikan, June 1-10.

Buddhist Saint

Chujo-Himé, the princess who is regarded as a Buddhist saint, having undergone great trials and tribulations while adhering to her faith, is not forgotten.

A festival in her honor will be held at Taima-Tera, a temple in Nara Prefecture on May 14-15.

After a service in the temple 25 acters taken from Buddhist scriptures.

國際佛教通報局

名譽局長　高楠順次郎

局　長　大村桂巖
幹　事　鷹谷俊之
同　　　稻葉文海
同　　　淺野研眞

顧　問（順序不同）

〃　宇井伯壽
〃　朝倉曉瑞
〃　羽溪了諦
〃　荻原雲來
〃　干潟龍祥
〃　鈴木大拙
〃　鈴木宗忠
〃　天岫接三
〃　長井眞琴
〃　松本文三郎
〃　椎尾辨匡
〃　宇野圓空
〃　赤松智城
〃　大森禪戒
〃　矢吹慶輝
〃　小野淸一郎
〃　加藤精神
〃　姉崎正治
〃　本田義英
〃　關本龍門
〃　佐伯定胤
〃　花田凌雲
〃　河野法雲
〃　高岡隆心
〃　小林瑞淨
〃　山邊習學
〃　赤沼智善
〃　本多惠隆
〃　大森亮順
〃　河口慧海
〃　山川智應
〃　常盤大定
〃　谷本富
〃　常盤井堯猷
〃　大谷尊由
〃　大谷瑩潤
〃　水野梅曉
〃　柴田一能
〃　安藤正純
〃　下村壽一
〃　菊澤季麿
〃　乘杉嘉壽
〃　芝田徹心
〃　淺野孝之
〃　渡邊哲信
〃　小野玄妙
〃　柳澤健
〃　重光葵
〃　金倉圓照
〃　立花俊道

國際佛教通報局定款

名　稱

第一，本局を國際佛教通報局と稱す

事務所

第二，本局の事務所を全日本佛教青年會聯盟本部に置く

目　的

第三，本局は日本內地及海外に向つて佛教事情の通報をなし，且つ佛教徒相互間の各種便宜を計るを以て目的とす

事　業

第四，本局の目的を達成するため左記の事業を行ふ

イ，日本內地及世界各國より佛教事情に關する質問の通報を行ふ

ロ，必要に應じ日本語及世界各國語を以て佛教事情の通報を行ふ

ハ，外國人の日本觀光に際しては各種の便金を與へ，特にその佛教に關する方面に於て之を爲す

ニ，定時或は隨時に各國語を以て文書の刊行をなす

ホ，その他必要と認めたる事業を行ふ

役　員

第五，本局の事務を處理するため左の役員を置く

イ，局　長　　一　名
ロ，幹　事　　三　名
ハ，評議員　　若干名

局長は本局の事務を總括す

幹事は本局の事務を處理す

評議員は局長の提案に依る重要事務を審議す

第六，評議員は左記の者を以て之に充つ

イ，全日本佛教青年會聯盟理事及主事

ロ，全日本佛教青年會聯盟理事會に於て推薦したる者

第七，局長及幹事は評議員會に於て決定す

第八，役員の任期は二ケ年とす（但し重任を妨げず）

經　費

第九，本局の經費は左記のものに依て之を支辨す

イ，本局基金の活用

ロ，寄附金

ハ，その他の收入

補　則

第十，本定款に記載せられざる事項は，凡て評議員會に於て協議す

第十一，第一回の役員は全日本佛教青年會聯盟理事會に於て決定す

定價	一部	金二十錢	送料二錢
	一年	金二圓四十錢	送料不要

昭和十年四月卅日第三種郵便物認可
昭和十年五月廿七日印刷（毎月一回
昭和十年六月一日發行　一日發行）

東京市外吉祥寺337
編輯發行兼印刷人　淺野研眞

東京市牛込區早稻田鶴卷町107
印刷所　康文社印刷所
電話牛込（34）1950番 5049番

東京市神田區一ツ橋二の三
發行所　國際佛教通報局
電話九段（33）1429番
振替東京83015番

昭和十年四月三十日第三種郵便物認可　昭和十年五月二十七日印刷納本
昭和十年六月一日發行(毎月一回一日發行)國際佛教通報　第一卷　第三號

昭和十年四月三十日第三種郵便物認可　昭和十年六月二十七日印刷納本　昭和十年七月一日發行（毎月一回一日發行）第一卷　第四號

The International Buddhist Bulletin

國際佛教通報

第一卷　昭和十年七月　第四號　〔Vol. 1. July 2501/1935 No. 4.〕

要目〔Contents〕

東京　國際佛教通報局　發行
The International Buddhist Information Bureau
Tokyo, Kanda, Hitotsubashi, II—3

印度僧ラーフラ・サンクリトヤーヤナ師を中心に

（去る五月廿七日，我が國際佛教通報局訪問の際撮影）

我希望日本佛教徒負起宣傳佛教到世界上去的責任，以"以和為貴"為出發點！

大醒。乙亥五月。

中華僧大醒法師の筆蹟

（去る五月三十一日，我が國際佛教通報局を訪問の際揮毫）

進言書

我全日本佛教青年會聯盟嚮開第五回總會有所決議因表示敬親之意於　閣下併欲有披瀝吾人之所信。

東亞治安既克復五彩大旗之所飜民有親愛之情而無怨嗟之聲同胞三千萬各安堵樂業寔可以悅矣蓋貴國建國創業之日有淸新勇銳之氣滿於內朝野官民協心戮力圖國力之充實計制度之整備以邁進于王道樂土民族協和之理想洵使吾人不堪感激也。

夫作興國民精神以固國本涵養良風美俗以增福祉以能造成淳厚健全之社會者敎化之方不可不得其宜也貴國夙則孔聖之大道樹敎化之大計而明徵建國之大義發揚王道之精神以弘布格物致知修身治人之德化是寔得治道之要可謂發而不失正鵠者也。

雖然吾人更進一步而思之奉大聖釋尊之佛敎以涵養國民之信念治國家者之所宜留意也若夫東洋文化之精神物心一如之大義彼此併用而不奏敎化之實效者非所聞也故吾人常曰眞正之宗敎者於作興民心匡救時弊與而有力焉如我日本古來併取儒佛二敎而能與國體融化能與民心合致以長養民族生活之根幹爾

來雖有幾變遷而漸次發達遂入于最高之域其於我文化建設之業勸可去否誠不爲少矣由此觀之或日仁或日慈悲或日修身齊家以至治國平天下或日實現大乘菩薩之願行以進于濟世治人之道其態様表現雖有所異而儒佛二教理想之所歸豈爲不一乎果然則治國家者不宜不使啓二教興隆之機運有裨補於國民教化也而顧察貴國之佛教雖日弘通發達而鼓舞之策勵之以入之于最高域極知屬嘐緊之要務。

今日滿兩國友好日月加厚國民的理解亦將益深本聯盟極知責務之不輕仍宜揚佛教精神培不壞之信仰養高潔之德操以期有致教化報國之赤誠又以期有日滿國民相提携開發民族文化之淵叢而貢獻於世道人心願　閣下幫助援救我佛教興隆之業勿敢外之日滿國民竝隆倶盛以增進人類之福祉以確立世界之平和本聯盟切望不能已也敢布腹心。

昭和十年六月　日

全日本佛教青年會聯盟第五回總會

會長　大村桂巖

國務總理　張景惠閣下

文教部大臣　阮振鐸閣下（各通）

寺院の由來とその使命

大谷尊由

一

「お寺」と「お宮」の二つは特に我が國におきましては，最も古くから一村内，或は一町内の「眼」の様な役目を果して來たものでありまして，民衆の社會生活と最も密接な關係を有するものであることは，事新しく申すまでもないことであります。乃で寺院とは何ぞやといふ様なことについては，どなたも，とくに御承知のことでありますが，これから暫くいろいろのことを，まとめて寺院の由來と使命と云つたやうなことに就いて，お話を致し度いと存じます。

少し袢を着た言ひ表はし方になりますが，「寺」といふのは佛像を安置し，佛道を修行する人々，即ち僧尼の住してゐる堂舍のありまする一定の箇處に名づけるのであります。一般には寺院といひ，伽藍と名づけ，或は精舍と呼ばれて居りますが，支那の靈祐といふ人の書きました書物に依りますと，寺淨住，法同舍，出世舍，精舍，清淨園，金剛刹，寂滅，道場，遠離處，親近處，といふ十の異名――ちがつた名――が擧げられてあります。尚この他にも菴とか，院とか，林とか，廟，蘭若，道場，黄金宅等，樣々な名稱があります。

これら多數の異稱の中で寺院すなはちてらといふ呼び方が最も一般的であることは皆樣のよく御存知のとほりであります。

一體寺院の寺といふのは，寺は嗣也と言つて，公司即ちお役所のことであります。『釋氏要覽』といふ書物に依りますと，後漢の頃には九ケ寺即ち役所があつたと申すのでありまして，その中，外國の賓客を接見する役所を鴻臚寺と稱して居りましたが，時に後漢の明帝永平十年といふに，天竺の國即ち現今の印度から迦葉摩騰，竺法蘭といふ二人の僧侶が，白馬に佛像や經卷を積みまして，洛陽即ち時の都に渡つて見えました。仍て明帝は勅を下されまして，一時この佛像等を右の鴻臚寺に安置せしめられたとあります。その翌年勅して別に一宇の堂舍を建てゝ，これを白馬寺と名づけられたのであります。これが支那に於ける佛教寺院の初まりだといふことになつてゐるのであります。

この白馬寺の寺は，先に佛像等の一時安置せられた由緒ある役所たる鴻臚寺の寺より名づけられたものであります。

二

この寺院を日本では「テラ」といふのは，旣に『日本書紀』等に見ゆるところであります。「テラ」の言葉の源，語源に關しては，種々の說がありまして一定して居りません。學者の中には，巴利語の長老を意味する thera（テラ）の音が，轉訛したものであらうと見てゐる人もありますが，これは矢張，今一つの說である朝鮮語の禮拜を意味する chyŏl（チョイル），或は chor（テラ）からの轉音と見る方が穩當かと存じます。卽ち佛を禮拜する場所といふ意味から來て居るのであります。

かの『日本釋名』や，『圓球庵雜記』に，「てらとは，てらすなり，丹青を塗り，金銀をちりばめて，てり輝く故なり」とか，「又，法の灯をこゝにかゝげて，冥をてらす故にともいふべし」とあるが如きは，どうも牽强附會の說と考へられます。

三

さて，斯樣な意味を持つ寺院，「テラ」が印度に興り，支那，朝鮮に渡り，日本に弘つた譯でありますが，その成立の事情や，建築の樣相と云つたことは，勿論國々によつて一定しては居りません。

先づ印度に於て最初，寺院は何うして成立したかと申しますと，お釋迦樣の御時代から非常に整つた立派な寺があつたのかと申しますと，何うも，そうではないらしいのでありまして，本當の宿房と云ひませうか，草堂と申しませうか，一夜の雨宿りをする，雨露を凌ぐに足ると云つた程度のものしか，最初は無つたやうであります。卽ちお釋迦樣は，成道正覺を遊ばされるといふと，傳道の爲め，托鉢の爲め，遊行と申しまして，禪宗の雲水のやうに行雲流水を友として，町から町へ，里から里へと，行脚を爲されたのでありました。そうして，夜毎の宿りとしては，樹下石上，園林古廟，洞穴山窟，寒林露地等に宿られたものであります。その宿り場處たる宿院とも云ふべきものを，阿蘭若（Āranya）とお經には，名づけてあります。これを支那に飜譯しまして，叢林とか，空閒處と申してあります。

ところが，場處によりましては，暫し滯留をせらるゝと云ふやうな事情も出來て參ります場合には，Vihāra（精舍とか，房舍と譯します）と名づくる一定の僧房が造られて，其處で，お釋迦樣を中心として四方より集る多くの佛弟子達が起居を共に致しました。其を又，經典に依つて Saṅghārāma（伽藍）と申してあります。此は衆園とか，僧園とか飜譯せられて居りますが，前の Vihāra（精舍）の規模の多少大きいものかと想像せられます。此等は併し，輪奐の美を極めると云つた樣なものではなかつたので，其の所在地としましては，雜沓しない靜寂な場處たることを第一條件としたもので，聚落を離れること五里の處と云ひ，或は大きな牛の吼聲の屆かない塚の間とか，河原等が選ばれたやうであります。我が國で申します浮世離れた處に造られたのであります。

併し，特別の例が無いと云ふ譯ではないのでありまして，かの舍衞國の須

達長者と云ふ富豪が，黃金を地に布きつめて敷地を買收し，一建立をしたと云ふ舍衞城外の祇園精舍や，又，王舍城外に建立せられた竹林精舍の如きは，最初から相當に結構の雄大なものであつたかと想像せられます。殊に祇園精舍は，人口に膾炙する『平家物語』に所謂「祇園精舍の鐘の聲，諸行無常の響あり」と云ふあの精舍でありまして，『涅槃經』と云ふお經に依りますと，禪房六十三處，多の房室，夏の堂舍が，夫々別になつて居り，厨房卽ち賄部屋，浴室，洗脚の處，大小の厠，悉く整備せりとありますから，其の規模の程も偲ばれる次第であります。お釋迦樣は，此處で前後二十五ケ年間說法敎化を遊ばされたとありますから，餘程お氣に召した道場であつたと見えます。唐の時代の有名な大旅行家，玄奘三藏が，かの地に旅行を致しました頃は，旣に荒廢してゐたやうであります。現今のアグラウード聯合州內のサヘツト・マヘツトの遺跡が其れでありまして，當時の伽藍の遺物等が發掘せられてゐるのであります。併し，前にも申しました通り，斯樣な結構の整つた精舍と云ふものは，お釋迦樣の御在世には餘計無つたので，かの講堂，溫室，食堂，食厨，洗浴所，門屋，禪房，便所，住房等の結構は，相當後のものであつたらうと考へられます。

其れに就いては，お釋迦樣の滅後に，其のお骨，此を舍利と申して居りますが，此を埋めて Stūpa（塔婆）といふものが，各地に建てられて，佛の遺德を御追慕申上げたのであります。この塔婆禮拜の思想信仰を中心と致しまして，釋尊滅後の印度の寺院といふものは，發展したものと考へられる樣であります。日本の寺院等も，後に述べます樣に，遺骨を奉安する所謂墓所を中心として建立せられたものが，非常に多いのでありますが，矢張り，此は印度傳來と見るべきでありませう。尙印度の寺院に就いて一言し度いのは，窟院と申しまして，岩窟を刳拔いて寺とせるものであります。現に保存せられて有名なものは，アジアンタや，エルラ等の窟院であります。殊にアジアンタ窟院の壁畫は非常に有名なものでありまして，世界の人口に膾炙するところであります。

四

支那に於ての最初の寺院は，先きに述べましたやうに後漢の明帝の時代に，白馬寺が建立せられたのが最初であります。支那寺院の相狀は六朝時代以前のことは，良く分らないのでありますが，普通の官省等の建築と大差なきものかと想像せられます。六朝以後唐代には，印度の石窟寺院の影響を承けまして，段々，大規模なものが出來て居ります。敦煌鳴沙山の千體佛龕，龍門の佛合龍，山東雲門山の佛合龍等は，最も有名なものであります。尙唐朝に於ては，弘福寺，慈恩寺，西明寺等の大伽藍が建立せられて居ります。唐の末より五代を經て宋朝になりますと，禪，天台の兩宗が盛んに行はれて，

五山十刹等有名な禪宗寺院が多く造られて居ります。

現今，支那の著名な寺院は多く禪寺であります。

五

日本に正式に佛教が渡來しましたのは，欽明天皇の御宇十三年であるとされて居りますが，其の時，傳來した佛像經卷をば，蘇我の稲目が向原(むくはら)の家を寺として安置致しましたのが，抑々日本に於ける寺院の嚆矢であります。其後，推古二年二月には，佛法興隆の詔によつて諸の臣連等が競つて造つたと，日本書紀には記されて居りますから，當時の事情を窺ふことが出來るのであります。

崇峻天皇の時には蘇我の馬子は，聖德皇太子の御指圖に因りまして，浪華(なには)即ち只今の大阪に四天王寺を建立せられました。次で聖德太子は，法興寺，法隆寺等を建てられまして，所謂七堂伽藍の結構完備せるものが，追々と造立せられて參りました。その後の主な寺院と致しましては，天智天皇の勅願に依つて成れる崇福寺，聖武天皇の大佛で有名な東大寺，其れから國分寺及び國分尼寺の建立の如きは，皆様の良く御承知のことであります。

平安朝になりまして傳教大師の天台宗，弘法大師の眞言宗が興り，叡山に延暦寺，高野山に金剛峯寺が建てられました。その外，藤原氏の建立にかゝる有名な寺院等，一々枚擧に遑が有りません。

鎌倉時代から室町時代になりますと，淨土宗，禪宗，眞宗，日蓮宗等新興宗教が，夫々寺院を建立致しましたが，就中，禪宗は武家の歸依を享けて所謂五山十刹等の大寺が，建立せられて居ります。

德川時代には基督教が禁ぜられ，宗門改めに因つて佛教が大層優遇せられましたが，從つて寺院の權威が強くなつて參り，寺壇の關係も特別のものとなつて來て居るのであります。

建築の様式等，因より一律に論ずる事は出來ませんから，短時間の間に，其れを述ぶることも不可能でありますが，大和の法隆寺は隋の制に，浪華の四天王寺や南都の唐招提寺は唐の制に，京都禪宗五山は宋の制に，宇治黄檗山は明の制を傳へたと云ふ風に申して居ります。

寺院建築の様式として，普通に七堂伽藍と申しますものは，何時頃から始まつたものか明瞭でない樣でありますが，日本では，此れに二つの型がある樣であります。其の一は，大門，中門，金堂，寶塔，講堂，經藏，鐘樓でありまして，大和の法隆寺，京都の東寺等何れでも，此の型に依つて居ります。次に三門，佛殿，法堂，僧堂，厨庫，浴室，西淨(厠)を七堂と爲す型式がありますが，此れは主に禪宗系であります。印度に於ては，七堂の中心は塔でありますが，支那，日本に於きましては金堂中心でありまして，塔は裝飾の程度となつて居るのであります。此は前に申しました塔婆崇拜の思想の變遷

を語るものとして，面白いことであります。

浪華の四天王寺には，右の如き七堂の外に所謂四院と云ふものがあつたのでありまして，今日の所謂セツトルメントの事業に當る設備であります。

四院と申すのは，敬田院，施藥院，療病院，悲田院の四つでありますが，此は聖德太子が大乘佛教の精神に立脚せられ，世間の貧窮孤獨を救濟すると云ふ理想を實現せられた一端でありまして，佛教社會事業の濫觴とも申すべく，千歳の後，其の高邁の御識見を讃嘆せずには居られない次第であります。

六

次に吾が國寺院の種類と其の特徵に就て少し許り申上げ度いと思ひます。

第一に官寺の制度であります。官寺と云ひますのは，現在は廢せられて居りますが，朝廷或は國家の勅願所，祈願所となつた寺でありまして，奈良朝で云へば國分寺或は國分尼寺，平安朝の延暦寺，教王護國寺，室町時代の諸國安國寺，德川時代の寛永寺等は，此の尤なるものであります。此等の寺院は，我が國家や都城を鎭護する爲に建立せられたものでありまして，其處は國家安泰，武運長久，罪障消滅，疫病退散等の祈願所とされました。此に對して私人の建立にかゝるものが，私寺であります。

第二に神宮寺であります。此は日本固有の神道，惟神(かんながら)の道(みち)と結び附きまして，本地垂迹説を生み，諸國の靈社，明神に神宮寺を設け，或は大寺の境内には，鎭守社を設くるに至りました。常陸の鹿島，信濃の諏訪，尾張の熱田，近江の日吉，伊勢の大神宮，京都の加茂，北野，平野等の諸社何れも神宮寺を有し，其處には社僧と稱するものがあつて，神社の事務を司ると共に佛事をも修したのであります。此の神宮寺は明治維新の際，神佛分離せられて悉く廢せられましたことは，世の記憶の生々しいところであります。

第三は所謂學山と稱するものであります。平安朝以後，學問らしい學問と云ふものは，唯諸宗の本寺本山を中心として，行はれてゐたと稱しても過言ではないのでありまして，叡山にせよ，高野山にせよ，又は南都の諸宗にせよ孰れも宗教信仰の中心であると同時に，學問の中心でゞもあつたのであります。德川時代に寺子屋と稱して庶民の教育が寺院に於て施されたといふ事實は，全く諸寺諸山が學問の中心であり，從つて物識りと云へば，僧侶の右に出ずるものが無かつたことに由來するのであります。

第四に寺院が菩提所となつたことを擧げねばなりません。此は我が國の祖先崇拜の良俗と結び附いて，先祖の菩提を弔ふ處と云ふ觀念を築き，所謂菩提所となりまして，檀那寺とか，手次寺とか稱され，其の寺と檀家との關係は非常に密接なものとなり，德川時代に於ては，主從の如き觀を呈して居りました。今日尚，都會よりは田舍に於て，此の風が遺つて居りまして，寺壇

の關係と云ふものは非常に親密なものがあるのであります。

此に就いて申して置き度いことがありますが，寺院等に於きましては，先祖の菩提が祀られ，墓地が有るところから，日曜とか或は春秋の彼岸等に家族が打ち連れだつて參拜し，祖先の恩德を偲ぶといふことは，非常に良い習慣，美俗でありまして，是非失ひたくないと思ひます。殊に都會地の郊外の寺院などになりますと，其の檀家の人達が日曜日に家族連にてお詣りをする，祖先崇拜の美俗たるのみならず，近時流行のハイキングともなる次第でありまして，一石二鳥と云ふ譯であります。外國では，米國や獨逸あたりでも，お墓へ詣りますと，少しも陰鬱な感じが起らない。花苑とか，グラウンドなどが傍に造つてありまして，寧ろ公園と云つた型であります。日曜日になりますと，家族連れでお詣りに行きます。子供は附近で嬉々として遊んで，お辨當をつかつたりしてゐる。洵に長閑な親み深い光景であります。

此點，日本の寺院なども，唯お花とお線香を賣るといふだけでなしに，種々研究し改善すべきものがありはしないかと考へて居ります。此れは特に寺院の方々に御研究が願ひ度いのであります。

最後に淨土眞宗の寺に就いて少し許り申し上げます。開祖親鸞聖人は『わが屍は加茂川に入れて魚に與ふべし』といふ遺言をしてゐられる程でありまして，扶風馮翊の生活をなされ，一生涯寺と云ふものを持たれなかつたのであります。此は晩年京都に於ける御生活ばかりではなく，凡そ二十年程住はれた常陸の稻田に於てすら左樣でありまして，唯，在來ありました太師堂に旅の假寢を結ばれたに過ぎません。文字通りの草庵であります。

此れは，聖人の深い宗教經驗にも由るのでありますが，恐らく恩師法然上人の無殿堂主義を繼承せられた結果からでもあらうと思はれます。法然上人は或るお弟子が，上人がお亡くなりになりました後は何處を御舊跡に致しませうかとお尋ねしたところが，念佛の弘まるところは，何處も皆我が舊跡であると申されたと傳へられて居ります。此の形式を打破し，精神，本質を把捉するといふお考へから，生涯「寺」と云ふものを持たれなかつたのであります。ところが聖人の滅後十一年目の文永九年には，所謂大谷の廟堂が建立せられて，遺骨を納め佛閣を建て影像を安置するといふ運動がおこされて居ます。これは全く聖人の遺德を追慕しまする門弟達に依つて造られたものでありまして，此が中心となつて現在の本願寺といふものが成立したのであります。京都の東西に聳えてゐます本願寺の大伽藍は，一見，祖師の生涯と，その言論とに全く矛盾せるが如き感がするのでありますが，併し，よく考へますと，自ら寺を造り，その威を示さうとせられなかつた親鸞聖人であつたればこそ，其の遺弟子の渇仰となり恭敬となつて顯はれたものでありまし

て，洵に味ふべきものがあるのであります。ところで眞宗の寺と他の宗派の寺との相違の點を考へますと，色々のことを考へさせられます。他の宗派の本山は多く山を中心として開かれました所謂山林佛教であります。その構造も民衆の集會禮拜等を中心としたものではなくて，坐禪，講釋，看經等を目的とする金堂，講堂，僧堂を中心といたして居ります。此に對して眞宗の寺院は街頭の宗教であり，田園の宗教でありまして，その結構も大衆，庶民の禮拜，說教，聽聞と云ふ樣なことを目的とする本堂中心のものとして建てられて居ります。卽ち此は，布教，教化と云ふものを眼目とする大衆的社會的な施設構造であります。

此の兩者の中，寺としての本來の面目は，孰れにあるのでありませうか，又，大乘佛教の精神より申せば，如何に展開せしむべきかと申しますと，勿論個人の修道，救濟といふことを離れてある譯ではありませんが，その究極を社會大衆の救濟と云ふことにあると致しますと，單に山林佛教としてお經の講釋や，祈禱，祈願等々を重要な役割とするのみであるならば，佛陀の眞精神に添ふとは遺憾乍ら云へないと思ふのであります。或は又，單に葬祭を司るところ，或はお墓のみを後生大事に守る許りと云ふことであつてもいけないのでありまして，民衆の魂を救ふといふ第一義の教化施設を十全たらしむべきは言ふも更なり，民衆の友となり，その現在生活を向上せしむる施設，社會教化の道場でなくてはなりませぬ。この意味に於きまして，聖德太子が，四天王寺に悲田院等の四院を設けられましたことは，洵に御達見と申すべきであります。どうしても，今後の寺院は一般民衆の信念涵養の爲めの禮拜，說教等を中心生命とすると共に，民衆圖書館，施療所，日曜學校，幼稚園，保育院，托兒所，職業紹介，佛前結婚等々，セツトルメント事業を併置施設致すべきであらうと信じて居ります。

去る大正十二年の大震火災に烏有に歸しました我が築地本願寺は，三ケ年の日時と二百萬に近い淨財の喜捨に因りまして，今回再建新築いたし，本日より三日間その落慶式を擧ぐる次第でありますが，新築に際しては以上申述べましたやうな，寺院本來の使命目的を遂行すべく，其の構造に，其の設備に，種々工夫するところがありまして，漸く竣工致した次第であります。

私も關係者の一人と致しまして，此の新しい伽藍が單なる東京新名所の一に數へらるゝばかりではなくて，一般大衆各位に十分活用せられ，その目的を達成せしめられんことを念願して止まぬ次第であります。

（去る四月廿一日，落慶式に於る講演要旨）

中華民國の居士佛教

―― その社會性と時代性 ――

好村　春輝

はしがき

世界佛教居士林長　王一亭居士

中華民國の佛教僧侶の中には太虛法師の一派のやうに政治的，社會的に活動するものもあるが，それは寧ろ異數であつて，僧侶の大部分は寺院に籠つて念佛と坐禪と讀經に日を送つてゐる。之に反して居士團體は職業の餘暇ではあるが市井の巷で佛理の研究もすれば佛典の飜譯出版も行ひ，水害旱魃の難があればそれの救恤に奔走する。又政府が寺產の沒收の法令を出さうとすればそれの撤回のために政治的折衝を行ふ等，活社會の中に佛教を維持し發展さす上の實體をなしてゐる。

僧侶の佛教を出世間的佛教とすれば，居士の佛教は世間佛教と云ふことが出來よう。而して僧侶佛教は非社會的で保守的であるに對して，居士佛教は社會的で進步性を有し，佛教の現代的適應乃至改革はこの居士團によつて行はれる傾向を持つてゐる。

例へば佛教青年會の組織にしても中華民國には未だ殆どないと云つていゝが，これも近い將來には居士林の中に生れる可能性を持つてゐる。その他教團制度の改革，佛教徒の新時代的な教育事業等の計畫等も居士林の中に行はれてゐるから，我々は中華民國の生きた佛教を知るためには居士團の活動を見る必要がある。

以下私が實地に視た上海の世界佛教居士林と佛教淨業社との代表的二團體を稍々詳述し，あとは一覽表によつて紹介するに留める。

世界佛教居士林

世界佛教居士林は上海の閘北新民路國慶路口にある。

世界佛教居士林の正門（上海）

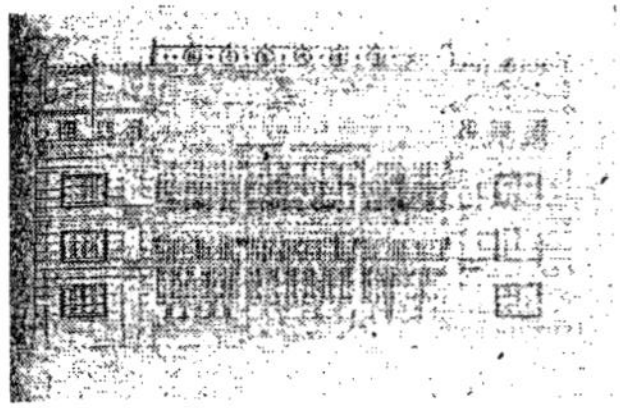

世界佛教居士林の大殿

去る三月十五日，私は墨禪法師に伴れてこの居士林を訪れた。實をいふと僕はこの居士林に對して何等の豫備知識も持つてゐなかつたゝめに上海の佛教團體を散々步き廻つた揚句のこの日の夕方，墨禪法師から「世界佛教居士林に行かう」と云はれた時には少々うんざりして「もう止したい」と云ひたい所だつた。併し，折角の勸めを斷るのもどうかと思はれたので，いやいや乍ら行つて見て驚いた。僕の豫想では世界佛教居士林といふのは名前は堂々たるものだが，どうせ何處かの薄穢ない家屋の一室を借りてやつてゐる事務所に過ぎない位に思つてゐたのだ。が實際は僕の豫想を美事に裏切つて實に堂々たる大ビルヂングであつた。その正面中央に禮拜堂があり，左右に庶務會計出版所の事務所がある。階上に念佛堂，禪定室，佛舍利室，圖書室等があり，別に男女居士の客房があつて，林友は隨時宿泊することが出來る。特に佛舍利室は萬華鏡式に構造せられて豪華莊嚴を極めてゐた。その部屋の廊下の外壁には中國佛教界の名士の筆墨が額椽を取つて揭げられて居り，日本の常盤大定博士と關野貞博士の共著になる「支那佛教史蹟」の寫眞が一枚々々貼附してあるのも嬉しかつた。更に圖書室の整頓の行き屆いてゐることにも感心した。そこには大正新脩大藏經も收藏せられてゐた。

こゝでは男女の信者が朝夕念佛讀經する外，功德事業として戰爭，天災，人災に對する祓禳招福の祈禱會，放生會等を行ひ，傳道事業として佛書の寄贈，通俗講演を行ふ。更に社會事業としては臨時に施藥，施醫，施米等を行ひ，教育事業としては第一小學校を附設して初級四年，高級二年とし，一級は六十名を限度としてゐる。

林友（會員）は約二千名で，その連絡機關紙として月刊雜誌「世界佛教居士林」を發行してゐる。

林長は王一亭居士である。王居士は中國に於ける澁澤翁に相當する人であつて，その人格德望は中國有數である。

本林の創立は民國十一年である。現在の林館を建設するには八萬元を要したとの事だが，之を日本で建てるとすれば工賃材料の高價のために二十萬圓はかゝるであらう。これは皆信者の寄附によつて得たのである。

この居士林の一ヶ年の收支がいくらであるか審かにしなかつたが，數萬元に達することは想像に難くない。これらの費用は林友からの年額林費二元と義捐金とによつてゐる。

尙本林は將來の事業計畫として下のことを擧げてゐる。

(1) 佛教圖書舘の創辦 (2) 小學校の加設 (3) 佛教機關辦事員養成所の創辦 (4) 佛學講習所の創辦 (5) 佛教養老堂の創辦 (6) 佛教醫院の創辦 (7) 放生園放生池の創設 (8) 佛教公墓の準備 (9) 佛教治葬處の準備

佛教淨業社

佛教淨業社は中國に於ける居士團の代表的なものである。場所は上海赫德路四一八號にある。この社は世界佛教居士林よりも遙かに廣大な敷地と多數の建築物を持つてゐる。世界佛教居士林が庶民階級の道場であるに對して，この方は寧ろ上流階級の道場と云つた感じがする。

敷地の中央に清淨莊嚴な佛堂がある。菩提精舍と呼んでゐる。それを圍んで功德堂，講經堂，閱經堂，會堂．施診室，庶務會計編輯の事務所があり，その外池亭，假山石等があつて廣莊な淨業所である。

この淨業社はもと南洋煙草公司の前總理簡照南居士が子孫のために獨力で佛堂を建立したのをその歿後簡玉階居士が遺志を奉じて之を居士團體に寄附したのである。初め社長は施肇曾居士であつたが，現在は簡玉階居士が就任してゐる。

本社の理事(董事)は皆上海に於ける佛教界の中心人物であつて，佛教的社會事業は概ね淨業社同人の發起に成るのを例としてゐる。

本社の慈善事業としては施藥施療であつて，一ヶ年の施療約一萬人に及ぶ。冬期には貧民に施衣施米を行ひ，年額數萬元を費すとの事である。

この外に社内で講經，念佛，放生等の功德事業を行ふ。又華麗な會堂では社員が隨時，祭祀喜慶の集會を催すことを許し精進料理の需めに應ずる。

社員は約七百人で毎月「淨業月刊」を發行してゐる。

尙本社には中國佛教會（日本の佛教聯合會に相當するもの）江蘇監獄感化會，江浙佛化聯合會等の事務所も置かれて，毎年一回全中國の佛教總會が開催される。

最後に私が本淨業社で感心し且つ羨しく思つたのは電動力を以てラヂオ放送の設備がしてあることだつた。淨業社なり中國佛教會は毎朝，こゝから佛教に關する音樂のレコードやニユースの放送をし時々高德者の講演を聞かすのである。これは中華民國のラヂオ放送の設備が日本と違つて自由なのにもよるが，日本では佛教聯合會などがかうした方面に何等進出してゐないのを悲しく思つた。この點は中國佛教が斷然一頭地を拔いてゐるわけである。

以下参考のために兩團體の會則を揭げる。

世界佛教居士林組織綱要

第一章 定名及宗旨

第一條 本林は佛教を信仰する民衆を集合して佛法を研習し自ら利し人を利し並に世界に普及せんことを謀る，名を世界佛教居士林と定む。

第二條 本林は國民革命の精神に本づき大乘救世の教義を實行し並に社會事業を輔助建設し力に隨つて慈善協濟等の事項を擧辦するを宗旨となす。

第二章 林 址

第三條 本林は上海閘北新民路國慶路口に設く。

第三章 林務及組織

第四條 本林の應さに行ふべき事務は左に區分す。

(甲) 文 化 部

1 學校 2 平民識字補習所 3 孤兒教養院 4 圖書館

(乙) 宣 傳 部

1 演講會 2 研究會 3 出版處 4 流通處

(丙) 慈 善 部

1 醫院 2 施診給藥處 3 平民工藝廠 4 災賑協會 5 放生會 6 公墓

(丁) 修 持 部

1 歸戒處 2 禪室室 3 念佛會 4 荼毗場

(戊) 總 務 部

1 林友處 2 收支處 3 會計處 4 文牘處 5 交涉處 6 庶務處

第五條 各處組織細則は別に之を訂す

第六條 第四條に載列する各處の外に應さに興辦を行ふべき事項は次第に之を擧行することを得。

第四章 林 友

第七條 在家の二衆にして能く無上の菩提心を發し本林の宗旨と相符する者は本林林友二人以上の介紹を經て本林の林友となることを得。若し介紹なくして而して本林の同意を得たる者も亦可なり。

第八條 本林の林友は分ちて普通，贊助，永久の三種となす。

(甲)普通林友 普通林友は每半年，至つて少くも林費洋一元を繳納すること

(乙)贊助林友 贊助林友は一次に林費洋五十元以上を繳納すること

(丙)永久林友 永久林友は須らく下列の三項の資格の一を具有し理事會の通過を經て本林より函を備へ之を敦請すること

(子)佛學深邃，修養精進，德望高超なる者

(丑)本林發起人及各屆職員の著しく功績ある者

(寅)一次に獨り本林の經費洋三百元以上を捐せる者

第九條 凡そ下列資格の一を具有し理事會の通過を經れば請はれて本林の林董となる。

(甲)佛教深邃，修養精進，德望高超なる者

(乙)每年百元以上を捐助し或は一

次に，五百元以上を捐助する者

(丙)永久林友の能く常に林に到り本林の進行を贊助する者

第十條　凡そ教義精明戒行勤嚴禪理透徹なる諸大和尚大居士にして理事會の通過を經れば皆敦請して本林上座導師，名譽講師，或は常住主講となすことを得。

第十一條　林友林董名譽講師等は均しく本林より證書徽章を發給し以て鄭重を明らかにす但し此項の證章は僅かに本林の標識となし別用をなさず。

第十二條　林友にして林章に違背し或は本林の名譽を毀傷し本林の規勸を經て仍ほ改めざる者或は未だ常捐一年以上を繳めざる者は當に其をして出林せしむ。

第十三條　凡そ林友或は林董にして出林するか，或は自ら取消を請はゞ應さに即ち證書徽章を以て本林に繳還し取消すべし。

第十四條　凡そ修行に志誠にして本林に入らんと欲し而かも林董を繳納するに力無き者は本林理事會より通過して免費を准予す。

第五章　職　員

第十五條　本院應さに設くべき職員は左の如し。

(一)理事　理事は二十一人を設く，二十一人中より理事長一人秘書一人常務理事五人を互推す，理事會は林長を選擧し職員を罷免し資産を保管し帳目を審査し豫算を核准し豫算外各項の用費を通過せしめ及び一切の重要事項を解決するの權あり

(二)林董　林董は定數なし，理事を選擧し及び帳目を審査するの權あり並に隨時職員の逮はざるを指導す

(三)林長　林長一人副林長二人は本林一切の重要事項を主持す

(四)部長　各部に部長各一人を設け該部所屬の一切の重要事項を主事す

(五)主任　各處會等に主任一人を設け該處一切の應さに辦ずべき事項を辦理す，惟重要事項は須らく請部々長の同意を得べし

(六)幹事　各處に幹事若干人を酌設し該處應さに辦ずべき事項を執行することを得

(七)雇員　各處に辦事員若干人を雇用することを得

(八)委員會　特種事務を辦理するに因り各組委員會を組織することを得其序程は別に之を訂す

(九)監察員　監察員五人は職員辦事の狀況を監察し收支帳目を審査し一切進行の事宜を督促す

第六章　選擧及任期

第十六條　理事は林董，永久林友より投票選擧法を用ゐて之を互選す，任期三年，毎年三分の一を改選す，理事長，秘書，常務理事は理事會より之を互選す，上座導師，名譽講師，常住主講，林董等は理事會の通過を經て本林より之を敦請す，任期三年。

林長副林長は理事會議より之を公請す任期三年。

部長は常務理事より之を兼任す。

主任は各部々長より推擧し理事會より之を請任す任期一年。

雇員の任免及び薪額は各處主任の擧薦を經林長より之を核准す。

監察員は全體林友より之を選任す任期一年。

第十七條　雇員を除く外各職員は概義務を盡し薪食を支せず。

第七章　經費及賬略

第十八條　本林の經費規定左の如し。

(一)本林の捐欵にして用途を指定せる者は移して他用を作すを得ず

(二)經常の開支は理事長核准の豫算を超過することを得ず

(三)特別の用費にして十元以内に在る者は各部々長より之を簽領し十元より五十元に至るは林長より之を簽領し並に均しく須く理事會に交へて追認すべし惟だ數五十元以上に在る者は須く先づ理事會の通過を得べし

第十九條　毎月の收支賬略は須く理事會に報告すべし毎半年決算書は須く各林董及永久林友に報告すべし毎年の決算は須く全體の林友に報告すべし。

第二十條　一切の年費捐欵は均しく收支處より正式の收據を發給し並に會計處主任及林長三方面の署印に由り方めて有効となす但し零星雜費の收據は收支處主任及主管處主任より簽印して已に有効となす。

第二十一條　凡そ本林々長簽署無きの募捐委任證にては一概に外にありて募捐するを得ず，倘し不完全の委任證あり或は本林の名義を假冒し外に在りて募捐する者は本林の賓に屬することを調査するを經たる後相當に之を懲辦す。

第八章　會議及報告

第二十二條　毎月職員會議一次を擧行し毎年林衆會議一次を擧行し均しく林長より之を召集す毎星期常務理事會議一次を擧行し秘書より之を召集す，理事會は定期なく理事長より臨時之を召集す。

第二十三條　凡そ重大事項ありて理事會にありて解決する能はざる所のものは林長より永久林友會を召集して之を解決す。

第二十四條　本林は毎年會計處編製の決算書を除くの外凡そ一年間の捐欵人姓名，數目及び各林友年費並に一切の重大事項は均しく隨時本林々務報告に載入し各關係人に分送し以て信實を徵す。

第九章　雜　錄

第二十五條　林董，永久林友は隨時本林の帳目を査核することを得。

第二十六條　本林收支處の現欵は均しく須く林長及理事會より指定の銀行に存儲すべし。

第二十七條　凡そ各界の善信にして本林演法堂，淨修室，圖書館に蒞臨して法を聞き佛を念じ或は參觀する者は概ね歡迎する所にして並に費を收めず惟だ必要の時は僅かに本林の林友を以て限りとなすことを得。

第二十八條　本綱要は第三十九次理事會の修正を經たり，如し未だ善を盡さゞるの處あらば林長より職員會を召集し隨時增減修正し理事會に交へて通過し之を實行することを得。　　　以上

佛教淨業社々章

一 定　名　佛業淨業社

二 宗　旨　出家在家を集合し佛法を普信宏揚し淨業を精修し並に力に隨つて各種の人を利し世を濟ふの慈善事業を舉辦す，此の外概して預聞せず。

三 地　名　上海英租界愛文義路覺園。

四 總　則　本社は簡濟善堂より堂地を捨讓し本社同人の組織を經て成る，所有本社の共公地畝，佛堂，假山池樓亭閣等の處に關しては須らく永遠に簡濟善堂と本社との定むる所の堂地捨讓契約に依據して辦理す。

五 設　置　一，念佛堂　每日早晩念佛を課誦し恭しく佛誕に逢へば普佛拜願し時に隨つて期を定め佛七を舉行す常時念佛の課誦には女衆は均しく後殿に在りて男衆と混雜せず。

一，講經堂　恭しく佛理を精研せる法師を請ひて各種の經典を講演す時期は隨時之を定む。

一，學教部　詳細の規則は別に之を定む。

一，靜修室　同

一，藏經室　同

一，閱經室　同

一，經像保存處　同

一，流通部　各省の佛教經籍を採請して以て各衆の購請に備ふ。

一，編輯部　本社月に按じて淨業月刊一冊を編訂し佛法を宏揚す。

一，慈善部　詳細の規定は別に之を定む。

一，蔬食部　同

一，會　堂　凡そ社員にして喜慶等の事あり葷酒及演唱を用ひざるものは均しく本社徵求社員簡章に按照して分別借用することを得其の社員に非ざるものは須らく社員三人以上の介紹を經社長の允可を得て方めて能く借用することを得べし詳細の規定は別に之を定む

一，放生會　佛誕日に逢ふ每に羽毛鱗介類の生物

を收買し分別に喂放す欵は社員或は非社員より隨喜す

一，功德堂　社員の先人蓮位及び本人の長生位を供奉す。

一，合行部　凡そ佛教事宜に關して本社の宗旨に背かざる者は董事會の議決を經て均しく別に章程を訂し附入することを得。

六 職 員

甲，社　董　二十八人，特別社員以上の各社員より名譽社員，永久社員中に於て之を選舉す。

乙，董事長　社董中に於て董事長一人列董事長二人を公推す。

丙，社　長　社董中に於て社長一人副社長二人を公推す。

丁，分部主任　社董中に於て各部正副主任各一人を公推す。(如し非社董にして本社某部の事務に對し富みて學識經驗あり自ら熱心擔任を願ふものあらば亦董事會より之を公推することを得)

戊，幹　事　社員中に於て若干人を公推す。

己，員　司　文牘若干人，會計若干人，庶務若干人，書記若干人，以上の各員は社長副社長之を進退することを得。

七 職 務

甲，董事長　全社一切の事宜を主持議決す，副董事長は董事長を輔佐し一切の事宜を議決す。

乙，社　事　凡そ社中特別の事故あらば應さに社董會議を開くべし，社董會の決議は社董過半數の出席，出席社董過半數の同意を以て之を決定す。

丙，社　長　全社一切の事務を主持す，副社長は社長を輔佐し一切の事務を辦理す。

丁，分部主任　各部の事務を分辨す，辦事細則は別に之を定む。

戊，幹　事　正副社長及各部正副主任を輔佐し各項の事務を辦理す。

己，員　司　文牘會計庶務書記辦事細則は別に之を定む。

八 董事會　每月第二星期日開會一次，議事細則は別に之を定む。

九 任 期　社董，正副董事長，社長，各部正副主任，幹事の任期は均しく一年と定む，期滿つるの後別に選舉を行ふ聯舉聯任することを得

十 社 費

甲，經常費　各社員の特捐及年捐月捐を以て撥充す。

乙，特別費　如し特別の費用

あらば各社董より酌量擬認するを除くの外或は別に勸募を行ふ。

十一 退會 凡そ社員にして佛化を防碍し本社の宗旨に違背する者あらば董事會の公議により除名す。

十二 續則 如し未だ盡さゞる事宜あらば董事會三分の二以上の同意或は社員一百人以上の提議に依り修改を請求し董事會の議允を經て之を修改することを得。

附則三條

第一條 佛教維持會，江蘇監獄感化會は均しく本社に附入す。

第二條 佛教淨業社の地契は本社董事會より保管す，各領地同人の本社に向つて領する所の覺園の地畝は本社より分別に執照を給發して據と爲す如し遷居に因り業產を以て他人に讓與する時は應さに本社董事會より通過して方めて執照を換給すべし。

第三條 簡濟善堂主人と佛教淨業社代表人と立つる所の捨宅及讓地契約は本社董事會より保管し隨事取出し公閲することを得。

社員徵求簡章

甲 社員の資格

子，名譽社員 凡そ佛法を精研し德隆く望重く衆の宗仰する所の者は董事會の議決に由り推して名譽社員と爲す事を得。

丑，永久社員 凡そ創立人及び特に金一千元を捐し或は銀二千元以上を募り得たる者は均しく永久社員となす。

寅，維持社員 凡そ特に銀三百元を捐し或は銀洋六百元以上を募り得たる者は均しく維持社員となす。

卯，特別社員 凡そ特に銀一百元を捐し或は銀二百元以上を募り得或は月捐五元以上の者は均しく特別社員となす。

辰，普通社員 凡そ每年社費二元以上を納め或は銀洋二十元以上を募り得たる者は均しく普通社員となす。

もし特に鉅欵を捐して上列の各數を超越する者あらば董事會より別に特別尊崇の法を議す。

凡そ徵求して得る所の社員繳納の費も亦抵して募金の例となすべし，例へば普通社員一千人を徵求し得たる者は繳費を合計すれば當に一千元以上に在るべく卽ち銀二千元を募り得たるの條件に比例して永久社員と爲すが如き，餘は類推す。

乙 社員の優待

子，普通社員

一，普利を敬誦し，佛を啓建する等の佛事には本社の會堂を借用することを得。

一，本社學教部，藏經室，經像保存處等の處は各該主任の允許を以て隨時内に入り觀覽することを得。

一，喜慶等の事あるに遇へば本社の會堂を借用することを得，章に照して賃資を收取す。

丑，特別社員

一，普利を敬誦し佛七を啓建する等の佛事には本社の會堂を借用することを得。

一，本社の學教部，藏經室，經像保存處等の處は隨時内に入り觀覽研究することを得

一，喜慶等の事あるに遇へば本社の會堂を借用することを得，賃資を酌取す。

一，本社功德堂に各社員先人の蓮位一座或は本人の長生位を供奉し本社は長年朝晩課均しく回向を爲す。

一，董事を選擧するの權あり。

寅，維持社員

一，普利を敬誦し佛七を啓建する等の佛事には本社の會堂を借用することを得。

一，本社學教部，藏經室，經像保存處等の處は隨時内に入り觀覽研究することを得。

一，喜慶等の事あるに遇へば會堂を借用することを得，略賃資を取る。

一，本社功德堂に各社員先人の蓮位一座及び本人の長生位を供奉し本社は長年朝晩課均しく回向を爲す。

一，董事を選擧するの權あり。

一，本社如し編輯出版の件あれば長期に一份を送閲す。

卯，名譽社員，永久社員

一，普佛を敬誦し佛七を啓建する等の佛事には本社の會堂を借用することを得。

一，本社學教部，藏經室，經像保存處の處は隨時内に入り觀覽研究することを得。

一，喜慶等のことあるに遇へば會堂を借用することを得賃資を取らず。

一，本社功德堂に各社員先人の蓮位一座及本人の長生位を供奉し本社は長年朝晩課均しく回向をなす。

一，董事を選擧し及び選擧せらるゝ權あり。

一，本社如し編輯出版の件あれば長期に一份を送閲す。

一，如し外埠に居住する社員あり，上海を經過し素食不便なるに因り本社に在りて暫時住宿することを得膳は本社より供奉す。 以上

〔斷書〕 本稿の執筆には清水董三氏の「上海に於ける佛教團體」に負ふ所が多い。明記して謝意を表す。

Some Buddhist Places of Pilgrimage in India

By G. Venkatachalam

Kapilavastu

Dark shadowy foot-hills filigreed with rose-pink snow-tips of the distant Himalayas. Green and yellow paddy patches studded with red-tiled huts. Mango groves and bamboo thickets rise like rocks from a sea of green fields. A wooded knoll with a small shine of Buddha, and not far off a solitary stone pillar, battered and broken by weather and age, with the most significant and historic inscription in the world.

"His Majesty King Piyadasa in the twenty-first year of his reign, having come in person did reverence. Because here, Buddha, the Sakya ascetic, was born, he had a stone horse made and set up on a pillar. Because here the Venerable One was born, the village of Lumbini has been made revenue-free and has partaken of the King's bounty"

This is the sacred spot where Gautama the Buddha was born. This is the Lumbini Gardens of legends and scriptures, the first of the holiest places for the Buddhists.

Mayadevi, the queen of the Sakyas, was on her way to Kosala, her father's country, when camping at this pleasure garden, she rested under a spreading tree dreaming of the glory vouchsafed to her, and at this spot, he came to the world, the Tathagata.

King Asoka raised the pillar to mark the spot over twenty centuries back, and since then millions have followed his steps to pay homage and reverence to one of the world's holiest grounds. Tibetan lamas, Sinhalese priests, Chinese pilgrims, Burmese Bhikkus and worshippers from Siam still continue the pilgrimage.

Nothing now remains of the Nandavana at Lumbini. No lily-tanks and lotus-ponds, no creeper-covered bowers and flower-meadowed aveneues, no jasmine pavilions and pomegranate parks, no golden deer and silver stags, no emerald parrots and purple peacocks, no

babbling brook and singing birds. Just a deserted place haunted by jackal and thieves. But the thrill of standing on the spot where the Teacher of men and gods first saw the light makes you forget all the present sordid surroundings and takes you on the wings of imagination to a world rich with fragrant memories.

Six kos (12 miles) north-west lies the ruined city of Kapilavastu, once the glorious city of the Sakyas. Citadel walls, low ridges, circular mounds, square tanks and crumbled mandapams mark today its ancient site. The river Rohini flows placidly to the west, and the two magnificent palaces of Suddhodana and Mayadevi are now two big heaps of large red bricks and fragments of broken walls.

Clusters of trees give shelter and shade to tired travellers and lotus-filled ponds still refresh their wearied limbs. The name of the city itself has changed from Kapilavastu to Piprahave, and it was from a stupa on this site that the archaeologists excavated a crystal box containing the relic of the Lord Buddha that is now in Siam.

Bridgmangunj, in the United Provinces, is the nearest railway station to these two historic places. No taxis or buses meet you at the station but black moving mountains known as Hathis in that part of the world. Elephant riding is no joy ride, and two days' tilting and rollicking on its ponderous back tries one's nerves and patience. There are no tourists' guides or comforts anywhere on the route and one must make the best use of villagers and their hospitality. A real pilgrimage it is!

Buddha Gaya

The Great Illumination came to the royal searcher after Truth, the glorious Prince Siddartha, under the shade of a peepul tree, which has also attained immortality with the divine teacher whom it sheltered. Near by nestles the little village of Urivila, where the milk-maid Sujatha restored the famished body of the Bodhisattva by her offerings of milk and rice before his final triumph as the Buddha. This holy tree and the spot where the Lord attained Buddhahood were marked and a beautiful temple was erected on the sanctified ground by the emperor Asoka. A monastery grew round it later on, and splendid devotion centred round it for over two thousand years.

The temple itself was a striking piece of architecture, and the innumerable sculptures that were set up in the niches mark the high standard and excellece of workmanship. The railings that run round the central shrine are of the same type as those at Barhut and Sanchi and of the same age. The carved Buddhas on the cupolas and the friezes are fine examples of the sculpture of that period.

A few beautiful specimens taken out of the excavations are now to be seen in the museums at Patna and Calcutta. The image of the Buddha inside is much disfigured by the foolish devotion of priests and worshippers who adorn it with silks, jewels and flower offerings. The incense and smoke and the candle burning add to the confusion and vulgarity.

But the most scandalous and depressing thing about this place is that a Hindu Mahant is the virtual possessor of this most sacred place to the Buddhists who long for its possession, and an unsympathetic Government takes shelter under religious neutrality instead of boldly restoring it to the Buddhists.

A morning visit to this thrice-blessed spot is an unforgettable experience. The air is cool and fresh; the morning wind blows gently and the leaves of the sacred tree make melodious music. The pilgrims are already at their worship. Men, women and children make their prostrations before the Bo-Tree, chanting hymns and offering flowers. What a cosmopolitan crowd they are! The travel-stained Mongolian from the far-off Himalays with his dirty haversacks and paryer-wheels, the gay-coloured and cleanly-clothed men and women of Burma with their rich offerings; the flowing robed Chinese and Japanese priests; the mild-mannered Sinhalese with his uncut hair tied into a knot and held fast by upturned tortoise-shell combs and his coloured sarong, the modern tourists with their porfane cameras and tiffin-baskets — all these constitute the daily floating population of Budhgaya.

But amidst all these external shows, sounds and sights, there is an inner quietness and a subtler spiritual atmosphers pervading the whole place, and, for a moment, when the mind is stilled and the heart is calm, one senses the supreme sanctity of the place in its overbrooding peace which is not of this world. This really is the

glory of Buddha Gaya.

Sarnath

One of the most interesting places for both Buddhist pilgrims and students of art is the far-famed Sarnath, close to Benares. Here the Buddha preached His First Sermon to His five disciples after His Illumination under the Bodhi Tree, and since that time it has been a powerful centre of influence and a place of pilgrimage. The great Asoka raised one of his pillars on the spot where the Lord set His Wheel of Law rolling and where he sojourned for a time during His earthly life. A big monastery grew up round the place and a great stupa was built to enshrine His sacred relics in later years. All that now remains of them are the sites of the monasteries, the stupa, the broken pieces of the Asokan pillar and the images of the Buddha dug out of the ruins.

To the stndent of Indian art the place is full of absorbing interest, and the fragments that have been collected and kept in the small museum are deserving of careful study. The well-known capital in red-stone that once graced the top of the pillar, the much admired figure of the Lord in teaching posture, the standing but mutilated statue of the Bodhisattva, the panels in bas-reliefs illustrating the Jataka stories are some of the finest sculptural works to be seen on this spot. A visit to this collection will help one to understand and appreciate the beauty and technique of Buddhist sculptural art.

Kausinagara

Kausinagara or modern Kasia is a straggling little village in the district of Gorakhpur near the foot-hills of the Himalayas. Today it is dust-laiden and poverty-stricken place, and even the remains of the old town are not much visible except the enormous dagoba and the giant statue of the Lord in a state of Nirvana. The last of the Four Great Buddhist Kshetras, this place is visited by thousands of pilgrims from all over the world on the Vesak Day in May. Cool groves abound near the place where worshippers camp and enjoy their repast and rest.

Sanchi

The little hillock on which the ruins of Sanchi lie, rises imperceptibly from the low-lying valley that surrounds it and commands a magnificent view. In the distance are the low hills that encircle the valley below, over which the sun sets every evening in gorgeous splendour. The ancient city of Wessanagara mentioned by the Greek Historians and the monolothic pillar of Heliodores lie not far off, and the old highway connecting Pataliputra and Ujjain runs near by overgrown with trees and shrubs. The village of Sanchi rests peacefully under the shadow of ancient monuments, and there is the quietness of the old-world all around.

As you stand on the top and survey the view, your mind takes a retrospective view of history and a glorious past unfolds itself. The great Mauryan Empire is slowly declining and the Kushan Period has not yet dawned. The stupa stands in solitary grandeur, a fiting crown to the conical-shaped hill, raised somewhere about 500 B. C. by loving hands and devoted hearts, to enshrine a sacred relic. The great Asoka sojourns here for a while (about 250 B. C.) on his way from Patalipture to Ujjain and orders the railings to be erected and monasteries to be built for the bhikhus. Buddhagosha later visits this Chaityagiri and other kings follow, and about the 1st century A. D. we see the exquisitely sculptured toranas rise up and adorn the place, and thus Sanchi becomes a powerful centre of religion and art. Soon, time casts her spell and all the glories of Sanchi vanish into oblivion and after many centuries, their vanished splendour peeps through broken fragments and ruined walls. Today tourists haunt the place more than worshippers, and next to Ajanta Sanchi is the most well-known place of pilgrimage to modern pilgrims from the West.

Rajagriha

Magadha was the birthplace of Buddhism, and its capital Rajagriha was the seat of King Bimbisara's government, whose conversion resulted in the rapid spreading of Buddhism in India. The city was built amidst picturesque surroundings of low-hills and side-valleys with hot-springs, the town itself containing magnificent mansions and well-laid out parks and streets. The site of this ancient capital even now evokes a deep sense of wonder and joy, both by its splendid isolation and close association with the life and teaching

of the Lord Buddha. A narrow gauge railway runs between Bakhtiarpur on the main line of the E. I. Ry. and Rajagriha, passing through the site of Nalanda. But a more convenient and comfortable way of visiting these two places is by motor either from Patna or Gaya. There is a rest house near the springs and is well patronised as the place is fast becoming a health resort.

Nalanda

The site of the great University of Nalanda is slowly being recovered to view and a large number of interesting finds are being discovered day by day. The excavations round the central shrine have tevealed wonderful architectural and sculptural works of olden days, and the fame of this ancient seat of learning is being more and more widely known through these findings.

Pataliputra

Pataliputra, Asoka's capital city, described by the Greek Ambassador Megasthenes as a city more magnificent than any he knew in his own country, is now represented by a few fragments of stones, polished pillars and wooden rafters. The huge stones of the walls of the city lying about are as smoothly polished and finished as the pillar itself indicating remarkable advancement in architecture and struotural works. Kautaliya's arthasastra gives a detailed description of how ancient cities were built, and as he was the minister to Chandragupta, it is to be presumed that Pataliputra was also built on those traditions. Modern Patna is a poor and insignificant city when compared with the grandeur that was Patliputra. The Buddhist pilgrim has other sanctified spots to visit in India.

Literaturo pri Budaismo en Esperanto

Rondeto de Budaisma Kulturo

En la budaisma tendaro de Japanujo Esperanto ankoraŭ ne estas oficiale enkondukita krom kelkaj esceptoj. Sed Budaismo tre profunde enradikiĝis en ĉiutagajn vivojn de japana popolo kaj ĝi estas la plej potenca kaj malnova religio en la lando. Kaj tial la nombro de la budaismaj adeptoj en nia lando estas tre granda, oni povas trovi iom da esperantistoj inter ili, kiuj klopodis por akceli la enkondukon de Esperanto en la eklezion. De antaŭ kelkaj jaroj Esperanto altiris la atenton de la junaj bonzoj kaj bonzaspirantoj en nia lando. Kiel estas skribite de s-ro Ŝibajama en la lastaj numeroj de tiu ĉi bulteno, formiĝis tutjapana ligo de budaanoj-esperantistoj kaj kelkaj grupoj esperantistaj en diversaj budaismaj universitatoj antaŭ jaroj, kaj eldonis siajn organojn. Kaj de jaron post jaro la literaturo pri Budaismo skribita en Esperanto pliriĉiĝas. Kompreneble ĝi ne estas tiel ampleksa kiel tiu de Kristanismo, ĉar Esperanto estis enkondukita jam antaŭ longe en Kristanismon en Eŭropo. Oni havas la kompletan tradukon de la Sankta Biblio de Kristanismo. Bedaŭrinde ankoraŭ tre malmulte da sanktaj skriboj de Budaismo estis tradukitaj en Esperanton. Kaj aliaj verkoj rilatantaj Budaismon ankaŭ ne estas multaj.

Laŭ la komisio de la redakcio ni skribis ĉi tiun artikoleton, kvankam ni ankoraŭ ne povis kolekti materialojn komplete. Unue ni mencias la verkojn aparte eldonitajn kaj due la gazetartikolojn pri Budaismo. Pro la okupiteco ni ne povis sisteme aranĝi la materialojn, pro kio ni petas pardonon de la legantoj.

I. Apartaj libroj.

(a) La Sukhavativjuho.

Tradukita el la sanskrita originalo de K. Nohara. Sankta skribo pri la Mondo de Feliĉo kreita de la Tathagato Amitajus. Oni aldonis la ĉinlingvan tradukon en la fino de la libro. Eldonita en 1932.

(b) La Samanta-Mukhaparivarto aŭ Evangelio de Avalokiteŝvaro.

Traduko de la XXIV-a ĉapitro de la fame konata budaisma sanskrita skribaĵo Saddharma-pundarika-sutro. Elsanskritigita de K. Nohara. Oni aldonis ĉinlingvan tradukon kaj ankaŭ la sanskritan tekston en sanskritaj literoj, kiun kompostis F. Dazai. Notinda estas la aldono "Propraj nomoj transliteritaj kaj vortoj elsanskritigitaj." Eld. en 1933.

(c) Budao.

Tradukita de Takeuĉi el la japana traduko kaj komparita de J. Okamoto kun la angla originalo. Enhavas la unuan ĉapitron de "the Essence of Buddhism" de Prof. Lakŝmi Narasu, rekomendinda libro por tiuj, kiuj volas trarigardi la konturon de Budaismo. Kun 8 fotografaĵoj de budaismaj skulptaĵoj. Kiel aldono "la Sep Principoj, kiuj kondukas al prospero" el "Diga Nikājo" (Digha-Nikāya). Rimarkindaj estas "Rimarkoj pri novaj radikoj" kaj "Tabelo de kelkaj propraj nomoj kaj teknikaj vortoj." Eld. en 1933.

(ĉ) Budaisma Fakvortareto laŭ la vortaro de palilingvo de Robert Cezaro Ĉildarz kun informoj el sanskrita vortaro de Vaman Ŝivram Apto.

Kompilita de T. Takeuĉi. Miriagrafe presita. Enhavas 102 budismajn terminojn el la supre menciita palilingva vortaro kaj 67 el la sanskrita vortaro. Kaj la plena traduko de la antaŭparolo de la vortaro de Ĉildarz kaj artikoletoj pri la alfabeto kaj sonoj de la palilingvo kaj sanskrito kaj indekso de terminoj estas aldonitaj. Eld. en 1933.

(d) Budaisma Vortaro, Japana-Esperanta kaj Esperanta-Japana.

Kompilita de G. Jamada. Eldonita en 1935 kiel speciala numero de la gazeto "la Voĉo," organo de Rindai Esperanta Grupo. Enhavas kelkcenton da budaismaj terminoj esperantigitaj. La formoj esperantigitaj estas diversaj laŭ la fontoj. Tiu ĉi vortaro nur kolektis ilin sen elekto. Ni devas danki la kompilinton pro tio ke li energie serĉis materialojn el ĉiuj fontoj troveblaj.

(e) La Dek Bildoj de Bovpaŝtado.

Tradukita de K. Ŝibajama el ĉinlingva originalo. La libro predikas pri la doktrinoj de Zen-budaismo. Eldonita en 1930 okaze de la unua konferenco de tutpacifikaj gejunulaj budaanaj asocioj kaj disdonita al la partoprenantoj.

(f) Historieto de la Nanzenĵi Templo.

Eldonita en 1928 por servi kiel gvidlibreto por vizitantoj alilandaj de la templo. Kun angla teksto. Tradukita de Ŝ. Minami.

(g) La Kodo de Kronprinco Ŝootoku.

La kodo havas grandan koncernon al Budaismo, ĉar la princo kredis la religion tre profunde. Trad. de C. Takaiŝi. Eld. en 1932.

II. Gazetaj artikoloj kaj fragmentoj troveblaj en libroj kaj aliaj.

1. La Budanasko....."Perloj el la Oriento," 1921.
Trad. de K. Ossaka el japana originalo, "Ŝakahassoo-jamatobunko."
2. Hindaj fabeloj.....Revuo Orienta, 1922.
Rerakontita de E. Asai laŭ "Hjakujukjo" (Sutro de Cent Fabloj).
3. Pri homa vivo.....Revuo Orienta, 1923.
Trad. de Asai el "Ofumi" de Rennjo.
4. Vajra, filino de Pāsenādi.....Revuo Orienta, 1931.
Trad. de Ŝ. Minami el "Kengukjo."
5. Budaismo kaj Esperanto.....Revuo Orienta, 1934.
Verkita de E. Tomomatsu.
6. Influo de Budaismo sur japana kulturo.....R. O., 1934.
Verkita de D. Ŝibata.
7. Budaismo.....R. O., 1934.
Trad. de T. Takeuĉi el la dua ĉapitro de "the Essence of Buddhism."
8. Homaranismo kaj Budaismo.....R. O., 1934.
Verkita de I. Suma.
9. Pri la II-a konferenco de tutpacifikaj gejunulaj budhanaj asocioj.....R. O., 1934.
Verkita de J. Nakaniŝi.
10. La kvar grandaj veroj, predikitaj de Budao.....R. O., 1934.
Libere tradukita de S. Ŝiba.
11. Bikŝuino Pakati.....R. O., 1934.
Trad. de T. Jamamoto el "Budaisma Literaturo" de Prof. Ŝ. Hukaura.
12. Tanniŝo, Libreto de bedaŭrado pri deflankiĝa kredo.....Ŝinanomainiĉi, 1927.
Trad. de T. Tooguu.
13. Kreskado de reĝidino.....Esperanto Kiboŝa, 1931.
Trad, de Ŝ. Minami el "Hjakujukjo" (Sutro de Cent Fabloj).
14. La prezentitaj 20 malfacilaj aferoj de la Budho. ...Gendaibukkjoo, 1931.
Trad. de J. Nakaniŝi el "42-ĉapitra Sutro."
15. La Budaismo.....Oomoto Internacia, 1933-1934.
Trad. de J. Major. (la originalon verkis prof. H. Hachmann).
16. Aforismoj......"Esperantaj Perleroj."
Trad. de N. A. Borovko el Dhammapada.
17. La parabolo de l'herboj.....Lumo Orienta, 1931-1932.
Trad, de K. Nohara el sanskrita originalo, la 5-a ĉapitro de Saddharmapundarika-sutro.
18. Venĝo de korvo.....Lumo Orienta, 1931.
Trad. Ŝ. Minami el ĉinlingva traduko de Samjuktratnapitaka-sutro.
19. Budhisma Terminaro....L. O., 1931-1935.
Represita el "la Budhismo." Ellaborita de G. H. Yoxon.
20. Budhismo kaj Esperanto....L. O., 1932.
Verkita de E. Tomomacu.
21. Gotamo.....L. O., 1932.
Verkita de G. H. Yoxon.
22. La sennezura lumo, El la laŭdo al Budao Amitabo de Sankta Ŝinran.....L. O., 1932.
Trad. de T. Jamaguĉi.
23. Pacmovado de esp-istoj....L. O., 1932.
Verkita de prof. G. Nakai.
24. Reĝido, kiu savis la gepatrojn per sia karno... .L. O., 1932.
Tradukita de Ŝ. Minami el Samjuktaratnapitaka-sutro.
25. Budho Sakjamuni, rigardata kiel rakontisto.....L. O. 1933.
Trad. de G. Jamada el "Doona Kenkjû."
26. El "Sutro de Cent Fabloj." ....L. O., 1933.
Trad. de Ŝibasaburoo el japana traduko.
27. Koncepto de Vedo.....L. O., 1933.
Verkita de K. Kanja.
28. La Budho kaj Darmo....L. O., 1933.
Verkita de K. Ŝibajama.
29. Tezeto pri Zen.
Trad. de Chaiŝan Kiang.

(daŭrigota)

Japanese News

Historic Tomb

The tomb of Shinano-no-Kami, the Tokugawa official who negotiated between Commodore Perry and the Shogunate has been unknown for years.

The late Viscount Shibusawa made an effort to find the last resting place of this historical character. But the tomb could not be found.

Tsurukichi Inouye, who is 73, an inmate of a charity home maintained by the Tokyo Municipality, has been found to be the grandson of Shinano-no-Kami.

Recently he was asked by city officials regarding the past and he related many facts concerning his illustrious ancestor.

With the result that the tomb of the Tokugawa official who was appointed to deal with Commodore Perry has been found in the cemetery of Sohakuji at Enokimachi in Ushigome. The burial place is marked by a dignified Buddhist monument.

French Orientalist

Dr. Paul Pelliot, the well known orientalist, who was in Shanghai arrived in Tokyo.

His career has been varied and interesting. He was born in Paris in 1878 and studied at the French Oriental Institute in French Indo-China. In 1900, he went to Peiping where he remained for 7 years.

During this time he travelled extensively in Central Asia, carrying out researches for the French Government, supported by the Department of Education.

Dr. Pelliot discovered many rare objects and historical documents during his trips, and his work has had much to do with the advance of French Oriental studies.

In 1911, he became a lecturer at the College of France where he has given courses on the geography of the Orient, and Oriental history and archaeology.

While in Tokyo for two weeks Dr. Pelliot give lectures under the auspices of the Society for the Promotion of International Culture and la Maison Franco-Japonaise of Tokyo.

Friendship Renewed

An interesting meeting took place this June when two distinguished men renewed their early friendship after a lapse of 35 years.

This was Viscount Sukekuni Soga director of the France-Japan Society and Dr. Paul Pelliot the celebrated sinologue.

At a dinner in honor of Dr. and Madame Pelliot 17th June evening at the Peers' Club under the auspices of the France-Japan Society, Maison Franco-Japonaise and the International Cultural Relations Society the meeting of these former friends took place.

Viscount Soga was a student at the Polytechnical School of Paris and later was appointed military attaché of the Japanese Legation in Peiping. While stationed in Peiping he met a young French student who was studying oriental culture.

Since then Viscount Soga has become a member of the House of Peers and director of the France-Japan Society, while Dr. Pelliot is a member of the French Academy and one of the world's best known sinologues.

German Sinologue

Dr. Wittfogel, the German sinologue, who stays at the Imperial Hotel, has been in China studying matters of finance and other subjects relating to Chinese life.

During his stay in Japan he wishes to inspect old documents dealing with Chinese civilization which he has been unable to secure elsewhere.

Dr. Wittfogel has been lecturing at Columbia University and because of the scarcity of books on his subjeets he went to China to collect them.

While in Tokyo, the German professor meet the leading Japanese scholars of things Chinese.

Pan-Pacific New Education Conference

The first committee meeting of the Pan-Pacific New Education Conference was held at the Kanda Kyoiku Kaikan, on Saturday, June 8th at 7 p.m., under the auspices of the New Education Association. About 100 members attended.

Following a brief address by President Mr. E. Noguchi and report by Chief-Secretary Mr. H. Aizawa on the conference, they discussed the matter till 10 p.m.

The conference is to be held from August 1 to 7 at the Imperial University of Tokyo. Invitations have already been sent out to such countries as the U.S., Canada, China, the British Straits Settlements, the Philippines, French Indo-China, British India, Manchoukuo, Mexico, New Zealand, Siam, Australia and the Dutch South Sea Islands.

At the conference Japanese or English language will be used, and the discussions will cover the entire field of new education, such as nursery and kindergarten education, adult education, primary and middle school education, art and music, philosophy of new education, psychology and new education, physical training, radio education, education towards the promotion of international friendship, etc.

Buddhist Music

In order to make Buddhist music better known to the public, a program of religious pieces was given yesterday at Gokokuji in Koishikawa.

Several new compositions by Mr. Seisui Fujii were played, and sacred dances arranged by Mr. Takuma Garai were performed by the students of the Girls' High School of Nakano.

French Books Shown

Dr. Julliot de la Morandière, director of the Maison Franco-Japonaise de Tokyo, held a tea party at the Maison at 4 p.m. June 17 on the occasion of the opening of the exhibition of French books. More than 100 friends of the Maison were entertained.

About 600 rare books, collected by Mr. Kenzo Tachika, art critic who is staying in Paris, were shown to the visitors. The collection contains rare books and documents on French literature, geography, history, art, music, philosophy and culture since 16th century to the present. The show open to the public until June 20.

Dr. Schmidt's Lecture

Dr. Wilhelm Schmidt of Austria, well known scholar on ethnology, anthoropology and comparative religion, give a lecture on the subject, "Eine allgemeine Einfuehrung in die neue methode Japan's ethnologische position festzustellen" at the auditorium of the Meiji Seimei building, Marunouchi 2-chome, Tokyo, on Saturday, June 22, at 1.30 p.m.

The meeting is to be held under the joint auspices of the Japan Minzoku Gakukai, Tokyo Jinrui Gakukai, and the Society for International Cultural Relations.

The lecture of Dr. Schmidt was translated into Japanese by Mr. Masao Oka. It is to be followed by the screening of the movie, "The life of Shira-oi Ainu." All the works of Dr. Schmidt was exhibited at the hall of the society.

國際佛教通報局定欵

名　　稱

第一，本局を國際佛教通報局と稱す

事　務　所

第二，本局の事務所を全日本佛教青年會聯盟本部に置く

目　　的

第三，本局は日本內地及海外に向つて佛教事情の通報をなし，且つ佛教徒相互間の各種便宜を計るを以て目的とす

事　　業

第四，本局の目的を達成するため左記の事業を行ふ

イ，日本內地及世界各國より佛教事情に關する質問の通報を行ふ

ロ，必要に應じ日本語及世界各國語を以て佛教事情の通報を行ふ

ハ，外國人の日本觀光に際しては各種の便益を與へ，特にその佛教に關する方面に於て之を爲す

ニ，定時或は臨時に各國語を以て文書の刊行をなす

ホ，その他必要と認めたる事業を行ふ

役　　員

第五，本局の事務を處理するため左の役員を置く

イ，局　長　　一　名

ロ，幹　事　　三　名

ハ，評議員　　若干名

局長は本局の事務を總括す

幹事は本局の事務を處理す

評議員は局長の提案に依る重要事務を審議す

第六，評議員は左記の者を以て之に充つ

イ，全日本佛教青年會聯盟理事及主事

ロ，全日本佛教青年會聯盟理事會に於て推薦したる者

第七，局長及幹事は評議員會に於て決定す

第八，役員の任期は二ヶ年とす（但し重任を妨げず）

經　　費

第九，本局の經費は左記のものに依て之を支辨す

イ，本局基金の活用

ロ，寄附金

ハ，その他の收入

補　　則

第十，本定欵に記載せられざる事項は，凡て評議員會に於て協議す

第十一，第一回の役員は全日本佛教青年會聯盟理事會に於て決定す

定價	一部　金二十錢	送料二錢
	一年　金二圓四十錢	送料不要

昭和十年四月卅日第三種郵便物認可
昭和十年六月廿七日印刷（每月一回
昭和十年七月一日發行　一日發行）

東京市外吉祥寺337
編輯發行兼印刷人　淺野研眞

東京市牛込區早稻田鶴卷町107
印刷所　康文社印刷所
電話牛込（34）1950番 5049番

東京市神田區一ツ橋二の三
發行所　國際佛教通報局
電話九段（33）1429番
振替東京83015番

昭和十年四月三十日第三種郵便物認可　昭和十年六月二十七日印刷納本
昭和十年七月一日發行(毎月一回一日發行)國際佛教通報　第一卷　第四號

昭和十年四月三十日第三種郵便物認可　昭和十年七月二十七日印刷納本　昭和十年八月一日發行（毎月一回一日發行）第一卷　第五號

The International Buddhist Bulletin

國際佛教通報

第一卷　昭和十年八月　第五號〔Vol. 1. August $\frac{2501}{1935}$ No. 5.〕

要　目〔**Contents**〕

東　京　**國際佛教通報局**發　行
The International Buddhist Information Bureau
Tokyo, Kanda, Hitotsubashi, II—3
Annual Subscription ¥2.40 (post free) *Single Copies* 20 sen (post 2 sen)

滿洲國佛教興隆進言書（前號所載）の進達

（去る七月十七日，滿洲國大使館にて——左端が謝大使）

國際佛教Interviewの一場面

（去る七月十三日，丸山翠松寮にて）

Where lies difference between Hīnāyāna and Mahāyāna

By Rāhula Sānkṛityāyana

"Mahāyāna and Hinayāna" these are words, which were not accepted by the two parties to be titled as such from the very beginning. "Hinayāna" means the lower vehicle or inferior path. This epithet was given to the non-Mahayanist schools which were 18 in number, and who formed the most primitive schools of Buddhism. It took centuries for this word to come into common vogue but now the older form of Buddhism is known throughout as such. In the same way, "Mahāyāna" was also not accepted as a term for the new school. These two namess express some sort of bitter feelings. I therefore concider it advisable to leave these words and use some other. I think the most suitable word will be "Primitive Buddhism" and "Developed Buddhism." But for the convenience of my readers I have kept these two terms here.

There are two types of people in the world. Firstly, people who think rationally, follow reason alone, and will not believe you unless you convince their intellect. Secondly, those who do not care much for reason. They are very emotional and if a thing appeals to their heart they will believe it and live up to at. In short, rational and emotional, these are the two human types found in the world. So the same type of religion or belief cannot satisfy all. Hence, we find divergences in a religious belief according to these types. And so it was natural to occur in Buddhism too. The Buddh rightly did not ignore either of these types of people. Even in the primitive Buddhism which is called Hīnayāna, you find two kinds of teachings: one satisfying common people, and the other the intellectual type of people. In this respect, Buddha's method of teaching was quite

(1)

different. In one of the famous sutras of Pāli Tripiṭaka called Moggallana the Accountant, Buddha shows how different ways and means should be found to teach the people of different standard of intellect.

I may give you a simile. A small child is playing with an elephant toy. He believes that it is an elephant because he never saw a real one. A grown-up man sees his folly, and wants to let him know the reality. What should he do then? The best way is to let the child be also grown-up like himself in intelligence. But it is never proper to snatch away the elephant toy from the boy's hands, and smash it. In the same way, from the very beginning, we find some accomodation for the less intelligent people, in Buddhism for their mental satisfaction. For example, the whole world of gods which is found in Pali or Chinese Tripiṭakas were not Buddha's own belief, but were the common accepted belief among the people of India in his time. Most of these might be untrue and they might be quite contrary to modern geography. It is quite possible, at least a few of them were known as such to the early Buddhists, but still they did not want to disturb the popular mind. So nothing is said against the existence of the heavenly abodes. But the Buddha verywisely reduced their status to one, as living beings bound by their Karma subject to birth and decay. That conception was not known before the Buddha. For the ancient gods meant something quite different, they were considered immortal. And as Buddhism spread in other countries, there too, they found similar belief and they adopted the same attitude. The case is the same with the other countries like Tibet, China, Burma. They had several village gods, local deities, worshipped by the masses. To deprive them of their popular deities, would have been not proper to the people, because it is the weak-minded who go to gods for help in adversity. And if that little help is taken away from them, they would lose heart.

I mention this, because among the Hīnayānists it is said that Mahāyāna has created thousands of gods, rituals, and modes of sacrifices which are nowhere found in the original teaching of the Buddha. I don't see much difference between the common practices of the masses

of the two vehicles. The masses, want in time of their difficulties, some sort of help from supernatural beings. And though Hīnayāna did not create new gods as Mahāyāna did, it does not mean that it stop common folk in their land from adding new deities. You will find the Brahmīn god Vishnu and many others being worshipped by the good Sinhalese Hinayanist. Numerous village gods are everywhere worshipped in Burma and Siam. They are quite new arrivals to primitive Buddhism, their names will be nowhere found in ancient Pali Tripitaka. So if Mahāyāna was forced to invent new gods that was because popular mind wanted it. To say therefore that because Mahāyāna invented many gods, it goes against the Buddha's original teaching, is not correct. If it is a sin, both are sinners. Further Hinayanists say-Mahāyāna sutras are against historical facts. They are like fiction, full of the stories of gods and demons. And no rational mind can believe them as the teachings of the historical Buddha. But here too, the difference is only of degree. You must keep this point in your mind-Hīnayāna is the original primitive Buddhism; Mahāyāna means the developed Buddhism as I told before. Developed, i. e. original plus new contributions. So, for Mahayanist there is no room to deny the existence of Hīnayāna sutra as the teachings taught by the historical Buddha, otherwise, it will be not easy for them to get the historical founder of Buddhism. In reply to the charge brought by the Hinayanist that Mahāyana literature consists of fabulous and unhistorical elements, the Mahayanist too can point out such factors in Hīnayāna sutras, though in lesser number because the additions and substructions to Pali Tripitaka were stopped at a very early age. What is the war of Mara fought at the sacred Bodhi-tree? Did really the demon Mara riding a black elephant come to fight with Bodhisatva? Did he possess an army of soldiers to fight his adversary? There Māra simply means the evil thought, but this destruction of evil thought was expressed allegorically. Which attracted the popular mind more and they made it a real physical war between the Buddha and Māra, the King of Death. This story of Māra was originally made by Hinayanist themselves. This is not a Mahayanist creation. You will find several such instances in

Hinayana scriptures where popular needs are satisfied. So we can't blame Mahāyāna sutras for the same fault which is found in Hinayana sutras.

By this comparison, I mean to show that new gods and fabulous sutras are to be found in the scriptures of both schools. On such ground, one cannot decry the other. The popular mind always like simple stories though evidently absurd. You know such fables are always useful for the training of young minds. Hundreds of stories are taught now in our schools, and children enjoy them very much and derive many good morals from them. But nobody can say that those are useless stories because they are not based on real fact or history. In the same way there might be many sutras in Hinayanist Tripitaka where you find such unhistorical elements or there might be many more sutras in Mahāyāna scriptures having the same faults. But if they help man to better his life or to sooth his mind in difficulties and certainly most of them have such qualities, they should not be considered as trash.

But all these differences are only the things of surface. Let us look inside and see. Is there any real difference in the fundamentals of Hīnayāna and Mahāyāna? The doctrine of Non-soul is one of the most fundamental doctrines of Buddhism, that is, that the Law of Impermanence is without exception for all elements and so there is no possibility of an eternal soul inside the body. This doctrine of Non-soul is also upheld by the Mahāyanist who contributed many new grounds and reasons for it. Several fine treaties written by great Mahayanist scholars in India from the time of Vasubandhu (fifth century A.D.) to Ratnākarashanti (eleventh century A. D.) on this subject. So they are not an inch behind Hīnayāna regarding this doctrine of Non-soul. You can take one after another almost all the fundamentals of Hīnayāna. You will find all of them supported well by Mahayanist scholars. The Four Noble Truths, the Eight Fold Path, the Karmic retribution, all of them are upheld. Where then does the fundamental difference lie? Mahāyāna scholars when they found some of the teachings of the Buddha condemned by the Brahmin scholars, they went forward and by giving strong arguments in their favour, they defeated their adversaries. Perhaps the Theravādins of

Siam, Burma and Ceylon do not know the difficulties which have to be faced in India. The rival philosophical schools in India have developed a high literature on the art of debate and logic. And unless you first convince or silence them, it is not possible to influence the mind of people there. In a country where there is only a naïve conception of the soul, it is not very difficult to tell in a few simple words that there is no eternal soul. But in India Brahmins have created a great literature upon this subject alone and one who knows about their doctrine, alone can compare the superiority of the doctrine of Non-soul. And in this respect, I may tell you, if we leave the great contributions of our Mahāyāna Indian scholars, we have nothing to put our case strongly before them.

So as far as the highest philosophical thoughts are concerned Hīnayāna and Mahāyāna, they are misnomers, they have not got two such sets of doctrine. There is one more point to be explained. Mahayanists blamed that Hīnayānists put a very low ideal before the individual by placing individual salvation as the immediate goal for a man's career., and that Mahayanists do not care for the individual salvation. They say as long as there is a single living being not out of suffering, we should not try to escape from it. Our duty is to help the suffering fellow-beings. They think that such a high ideal is quite absent from Hinayanist scriptures. But that is not true. The 550 Jātakas of Hinayanist are nothing but to illustratrate this high ideal. In the very beginning of the Jātakas, we find Sumedha renouncing his own Nirvāṇa for the sake of helping others. He makes all kinds o. sacrifices in order to help the needy. He gives his body in order to save a hungry tiger. And many such examples will be found in those stories. That shows that the Hinayanists never deny the high ideal of a Bodhisatva.

If that is so, then it is not just to say that Hinayanist are too selfish for their own salvation. The only difference is that while Mahāyanists say there is only one way to Nirvana, and that is, the attaimment of Buddhahood after raising countless beings from their down-trodden states; the Hīnayānists think that there are different human types, their are some who want just to escape from suffering with the least delay; and they can select the path of Śrāvaka or Pratyeka i. e. individual salvation. But no Hinayanist can say that this ideal is equal to that of Bodhisatva. So in their ideal of life, too, the difference is not much. This is an old misconception but now the time is not such that we should emphasise them. In those days there might have been some reasons to keep these small differences always in the front, but now we have to think impartially and whatever best contribution is found from the different sects of Buddhism we must take and make one. There are certain qualities which are found in Hinayana Tripiṭaka which Mahāyāna should adopt and there are certain other good elements in Mahāyāna which Hinayana must adopt. For example, there was a time when people did not like much if the life of their teacher was told without telling several miracles and supernatural occurences but now is the age of reason, people want more rational stories about their teacher. And if you want to find the real historical Buddha, then for it you have to look towards Hinayana Scriptures. There you will find the humane Buddha. An uncared monk is suffering from a dangerous disease. The Buddha sees him. He washes his body with his own hands, he puts him again on his bed. Such instances in the life of Buddha are many which are found in those scriptures. If all these are collected leaving all miracles and supernatural things, you will find the Buddha more splendid, in his character.

Here Mahāyāna sutras are lacking behind. So this human element of the Buddha can be complimented from the Hinayana scriptures. Mahayana contributed two high philosophies of Nāgārjuna and Asanga. They are the real explanations of the Buddha's original thought, they are not to supersede the original but to support and make it more clear. The Buddha himself sometimes uses a simile, The simile of raft is very famous. The Buddha says all my teachings are like a raft, they are to cross on, not to be held fast. Taking such similes Mahāyāna Scholars propounded many good theories for their explanation of the Dharma. There is need for explaining why the philosophies of Nāgārjuna and Buddha are not different or rival dectrines. To go in detail of them would be to become too technical. Nāgārjuna's

philosophy is the philosophy of relativity, that is, things have only relative existence, as cold to hot, dark to light, small to big. This short formula be applied everywhere giving different illustrations from philosophical, moral points of view. This conception certainly, does not go against the orthodox teachings of Hīnayāna school. When everything in the world is momentary and there is nothing permanent, it is only by relative terms that we can know the value. So this relativity is a corollary of the original doctrine of universal momentariness.

The Yogā-Cāra school of Asanga is another contribution of Mahāyāna to the Buddhist philosophy. It is very high and deep philosophy which even now inspires the minds of learned Brahmin scholars. This is the school from which was derived the modern school of Vedānta in India. It is this school which gave philosophers and logicians like Vasubandhu, Dingnāga Dharmakīrti and a host of others. The chief treatise of this school is the Vijnaptiśāstra which with its commeteries is found in its Chinese translation. It is such an important work that its restoration into Sanskrit was essential. I saw a French translation of it. I wanted to restore it from that French translation, but thinking of the short-comings of Western scholars when deprived of direct help from the scholars of that language, I could not proceed. Fortunately, my late lamented friend Mr. Wang Mow lam, (the late editor of the "Chinese Buddhist" Shanghai), came to Ceylon and we were staying together. With our mutual help we made some rough renderings of the whole work. Mr. Wang published the first Chapter of his work. His translation is very fluent and exact. It was published as a special number of the "Chinese Buddhist." We had great hopes of Mr. Wang, but alas, he could not live to fulfil his great ambition. My own rendering was revised and now half of the work is already published in Sanskrit. The remaining half I have to complete. In its introduction I am going to show that as philosophy is concerned, there is nothing against the orthodox scripture of Theravāda.

If there are differences between two schools, they are merely in small things, which have some value, if any, for those who cannot understand true and high princips. In philosophical ideas there are really one and the same.

Why I came to Zen Buddhism

A talk given by Mrs. Edward W. Everett.

GENTLEMEN:

This is my third visit to Japan, and while through the many devoted friends which I have made in this beautiful country of yours' I have come to consider Kyoto as my second home, in reality, of course, I am a stranger to most of you. People, both American and Japanese, are generally curious to know why I come to Japan to study Zen. I suppose the same question has arisen in your minds also,

I am an ordinary, everyday, American woman. I am not an adventuress, not a scholar, not an artist, not a literary person. My life at home is that of the usual American woman of some means, a life which I judge, does not differ much from that of Japanese women in the same situation in society. My main concern is for my husband, my child, my relatives, my friends and my home. But it has for many years seemed to me that most of us live the brief span of years allotted to us between birth and death only half-conscious, only half-awake to what life really is. The first concern of our daily life must, of course, be with material needs; food and drink, clothing and shelter. Without them life itself cannot be sustained. But these are not the only needs which must be satisfied. There are times in life of almost every human being when he becomes conscious of another hunger than that for food and of another thirst than that which water can quench. There comes a great yearning to understand the "WHY" of existence and a longing to find one's true place in and relationship to this great Universe.

Some men have searched for the answer in the world of beauty of form and color, some in the world of beauty of sound, some again in the realm of ideas. But most men, bowed down by the struggle for existence have had to satisfy that yearning with the hope for some future existence, for some life after

death in a perfect and flawless world where unhappiness and misery do not exist and where all is peace and joy.

In spite of the teaching of Jesus to the contrary, the main emphasis of the social theory of the West has been that man's happiness lies in the possession of material riches. And in spite of the teaching of Gotama to the contrary, the main emphasis of the social theory of the East seemes to me to have been that man's happiness must be looked for in some future existence, in some world outside and beyond that of every-day life. To the acceptance of the western idea, something within me has answered "NO." And to the acceptance of the seemingly orthodox eastern idea, again has emphatically answered "NO." When I came to read the life and teaching of Gotama Buddha, for the first time I found a satisfactory answer to my own questionings. When Gotama was asked about the future life, He answered to the effect that when men had learned all there was to know about this life then only might they begin to learn about the future life. His teaching, He said, had to do only with unhappiness (that is, the misery and sorrow of this every-day life), the cause of unhappiness, the way that unhappiness might be to get rid of, and the path which led to the getting rid of unhappiness in this life. He himself had tested out the path and found it successful. His teaching was the technique of walking in that path. But each man would himself have to tread the path, and only as he found the results successful was he to accept the teaching as true. Each man must work out his own salvation. Salvation, Nirvana, Satori, this was an affair not of the future but was to be obtained here and now, today, in the midst of this everyday life.

Deeper study of Hinayana Buddhism and of various forms of the Mahayana at first brought to me great disappointment. They all, had grown far away from, had forgotten what seemed to me to be the essential teaching of Buddhism. It was not until I came to the study of Zen that I found that simple and eloquent truth again restated. That is why I came to Japan to study Zen.

The Eight-fold Path of Gotama, the path by means of which Nirvana, Satori was to be obtained, is this: Right Understanding, Right

Purpose, Right Speech, Right Conduct, Right Livelihood, Right Effort, Right thought, Right Meditation.

In all but the last step, Right Meditation, it does not differ its ethical content from the message of all great religious teachers. Meditation, as a means, as a technique by means of which Salvation was to be obtained, was Buddha's unique contribution to religious training. It is upon meditation, as you all know, that Zen lays its emphasis. So when I came to Nanzenji to study Zen, what I came to do was to meditate. Not to find out about the theory of meditation, but to practice meditation. Through the kindness of Nannshinken Rodaishi and of the monks of Nanzenji Sodo I have been given unusual opportunities and advantages for practicing it. And if the results of this experience of mine are of any interest to you, I may say that I consider the months which I have given to this practice of meditation as productive of the most valuable experiences of my entire life. Aside from what might be called "Religious experiences" which have resulted from those many, many hours and weeks of silent sitting, there have been opened up to me world of which I had previously been only partially conscious. Previously unknown subtelities of color have been revealed to my physical eyes and previously unknown subtelities of sound to my physical ears and my whole nature has been sensitive as never before.

The real purpose of all great religious teachers has been to reveal to men their essential unity one with the other. The height of Jesus teaching is contained in his words "Love thy neighbor as thyself." When one has experienced, even slightly, through meditation, the unity of all life, never again can one look upon one's neighbor as quite so much a stranger as before. That is to me, the great social value of meditation: the establishment of the consciousness of the identity of one's self with all men. Realized through meditation, it becomes the natural way of looking at life, not a manner superimposed by reason or by religious edict. Those men who, though having practiced meditation, in their daily relationships fail to express this great truth, have either not yet had the vision or have not understood the fundamental teaching of all Buddhism, a teaching of the first importance

in Zen, that meditation is of value only as it is interpreted iu terms of everyday activity. All of us beg for indulgence here.

When Bodhidharma came to China he announced his teaching in the following words:

"A special transmission outside of the scriptures;
No dependance upon words and letters;
Direct pointing to soul of man;
Seeing into one's nature and the attainment of Buddhahood."

Thus he restated again the essential teaching of Gotama and also fixed for once and for all the manner in which that teaching was to transmitted. Sweeping away with one great gesture all the forms and trappings in which the Truth had been wrapped almost to the point of being extinguished, he revealed this Truth to be a living, pulsating force, to be life itself. To see into one's own nature and to realize it as Life itself, that is Zen.

But because Life, formless though it be in essence, must reveal itself in form, this teaching of the formless Truth had to somehow find a means of making itself understood. The pathway leading to the great realization is long and difficult. Gotama had indicated its direction in the Eight-fold path which I have previously mentioned. Knowing the weakness of human nature, little by little succeeding bearers of the mantle of Dharma evolved a more detailed way of conduct and of life which together with meditation would be found most helpful in attaining to the desired for goal. Such a code of conduct was the direct result of a deep understanding of Truth. It demanded simplicity, directness, cleanliness, strength of will, independence, courage, humility, and indifference to circumstances, even to indiference to death. This is the Zen way of life.

Gotama had said that the path to Nirvana which he had trodden was open to all men. Zen, with characteristic penetration, emphasized that point and has always insisted that every man is possessed of the same Buddha-nature. It remains only for him, by his own efforts, to realize that Buddha-nature. There are, therefore, no favorites in Zen. Learning, riches, ability to recite sutras, are of no value. Illumination only is important. The priest has no advantage over the layman, nor has the layman, in reality, any need of the priest. The learned man has no advantage over the most humble peasant. Satori is possible to all.

Therefore Zen is preeminently the layman's religion. The Zen way of life is a code of conduct which may be followed by any man in any station or any environment. Since Zen has no creed but that of the inherent Buddha-hood of all men and their potential ability to realize that Buddhahood, it has no doctrines which it must change or adapt to changing civilizations and to changing modes of thought. Its code of conduct has been found to be as useful and as pertinent to-day as yesterday.

No school of religious thought has been more productive, I am sure, of great men in every sphere of life than has Zen in both its Chinese and Japanese aspects. Its great priests have been at the same time great political and social leaders; and its laymen, among whom can be numbered the most eminent statesmen, artists and soldiers throughout the past thirteen hundred years, are among the most spiritual men which the Far East has produced.

The past eighty years brought the greatest change in the East and in Japan especially. Even in the West changes are going forward with such rapidity that as a result we are ourselves somewhat bewildered. The entire energy of the Japanese people has naturally been directed toward bringing your nation on to a par with the most advanced nations of the West. Since Western civilization is preeminently a civilization which is occupied with the development of the world of material forms, it is only natural that you, as a nation, should have concentrated your energies there, and for the time being to have put into the background the world of the spirit.

But that world of the spirit will not long be put aside. Man very soon learns to his sorrow that material bread alone is indeed a stone, and can never satisfy the inner hunger. Nor, on the other hand, can physical hunger be satified by things of the spirit alone. It is only in the perfect blending of the material and the spiritual, the practical and the ideal, that complete fulfillment is to be found.

Perhaps most of you, looking at these great temple buildings and seeing many prieats in many gorgeous robes burning incense and chanting innumerable sutras, think that here is but another outworn religious form, one which has long ago forgotten the source of its inspiration, and which has no meaning for us to-day. But I beg of you to pause and look again. Where Zen has become formalized it has departed from its original doctrine of formlessness and has yielded to the weakness of human nature. But behind these forms, screened to some extent by them perhaps, may still be found burning the lamp of Truth.

To live a life of simplicity, of directness, of independence, of courage, of humility, of indifference to circumstances and of MEDITATION will be found as inspiring by the modern business-man and politician as by the artist and scholar and will be found to be most practical by all men. In these days when the world is crying out for REAL leadership through the morass of materialism in which we seem to be flouudering, perhaps the greatest contribution which Japan could make to the world would be the rediscovery of the essential Buddhahood of Man and the Road which leads to its realization.

Literaturo pri Budaismo en Esperanto

(2)

Rondeto de Budaisma Kulturo

30. La III-a jarkunveno de JBLE. ....La Lumo Orienta, 1933.
31. Kio estas Mahajana Budhismo? ....L. O., 1934.
    Verkita de B. L. Suzuki, tradukita de K. Kanamatz.
32. Historieto de Ŝin-budhismo... ..L. O., 1934.
    Trad. de F. Dazai el "The history and teaching of Shin Buddhism."
33. La Parabolo de la urbo magie farita.....L. O., 1934, 1935.
    Trad. de K. Nohara el la sanskrita originalo, Purvayoga-Parivarto-nama-Saptamah. (la VII-a ĉapitro de Saddharmapundarika-sutro).
34. Amitayus-sutropadeŝo kun la himno de pieco.....L. O., 1934.
    Trad. de T. Jamamoto el ĉinlingva traduko.
35. La II-a Konferenco de Tut-pacifikaj Junuloj-Budhanaj Asocioj.....L. O., 1934.
36. La unua ŝtupo en meditado. . ..L. O., 1934.
    Trad. de F. Ŝibuja. (La originalon verkis Sooen.)
37. Kio estas sufero?....L. O., 1934.
    Verkita de Ĉ. Macubara.
38. La Jarkunveno de JBLE.... L. O., 1934.
39. Sankta versaĵo aŭdigita de Rakŝaso.....L. O., 1935.
    Trad. de K. Ŝibajama.
40. Legendo pri Reĝo Aŝoka en antaŭnasko, kaj Lia infero..... L. O., 1935.
    Trad. de S. Majama laŭ la angla traduko de "la vivo de Fa-Hien".
41. Hakuin.....L. O., 1935.
    Verk. de S. Muŝakoĵi, trad. de G. Jamada.
42. La Vortaro de budhismaj terminoj.....La Budhismo, 1931–1934.
    Ellaborita de G. H. Yoxon. Ĉi tiun represis La Lumo Orienta kun japana traduko. (Vidu 19).
43. Dhammapada.....La Budhismo, 1931–1934.
    La kompletan tradukon de Dhammapada tradukita de Yoxon.
44. Kritikoj de la traduko de "Dhammapada".....Bud. (mallongigo de La Budhismo), 1931.
45. Kritikoj de la Vortaro.....Bud., 1931.
46. Nia bulteno aperas presite je la unua fojo.....Bud., 1931.
47. Ni salutas nian prezidanton, S-ron A. C. March.....Bud., 1931.
48. La sep aferoj kiuj kondukas al prospero.....Bud., 1931.
    El Dīgha Nikāya libere rerakontita de T. Takeuĉi. (Represita en "Budao").
49. Kriza tempo regas ĉie sur la tero.....Bud., 1932.
50. La rakonto pri Princo Dirghajo. ....Bud., 1932.
    Libere rerakontita el la Mahavago laŭ angla traduko.
51. Malarmadon oni priparolas... ..Bud., 1932.
52. Dialogo inter Sariputo kaj Jamako.....Bud., 1932.
    Tradukita el Saṃyutta-Nikāya.
53. Sir Edwimn Arnold.....Bud., 1932.
54. Servo — La filozofio de laboro — de upasakoa.....Bud., 1932.
    Tradukita de F. X. Jaeger.
55. Organizo kaj reorganizo. .... Bud., 1932.
56. La vera budhismo.....Bud., 1932.
    Tradukita de F. X. Jaeger.
57. Mia pensaĵo.....Bud., 1932.
    Verkita de J. Nakaniŝi.
58. Aparte laŭdi ies personecon ne estas nia intenco.....Bud., 1933.
59. Kial Chao Kung fariĝis budhano. ....Bud., 1933.
    Elĉerpita el lia parolo al la Nord-Ĥinlanda Budhana Asocio.
60. Pacon al ĉiuj estaĵoj.....Bud., 1933.
61. Skizo de Zen-budhismo.... Bud., 1933–1934.
    Tradukita el "An outline of Zen Buddhism" de Alan W. Watts.
62. Ondoj de pensoj (ripetaĵo por enkonduko al meditado).....Bud., 1933.
63. Himno.....Bud., 1933.
    Tradukita de D. Hunt el "Vade Mecum" de Hongŭanĵi budhanoj, Haŭajo.
64. La kvin principoj (en formo taŭga por infana deklamo).
65. La Tathagato ne pensas, ke... .. ....Bud., 1933.
66. Bonsano estas la plej grava gajno, ...Bud., 1934.
67. Kredo de Upasaka. .... Bud., 1934.
    Tradukita de Frank X. Jaeger.
68. Pro nekompreno kaj nescio de la kvar veroj, ... Bud., 1924.

69. Atentemo estas la vojo al senmorteco,.... ....Bud., 1935.

70. La Maha-parinirvana Suto (La suto de la forpaso de Gotamo). ....Bud., 1935.
Mallongigita traduko farita de F. X. Jaeger.

71. La kvar braĥmaj animstatoj aŭ fervoraj meditadoj. ...... Bud., 1935.

72. La fundamentaj principoj de Budhismo de Edmund Howarth. ....Bud., 1935.

73. La saluto al Buddhist Lodge. ....Aka, 1934.
Originalon japanlingvan verkis Ŝ. Kôno, tradukis I. Suma.

74. Fragmentoj el Buddaĉarita... ..Aka, 1934.
Tradukita de T. Takeuĉi.

75. S.O.S. de Budaisma Esperanto-movado.....Tempo, 1934.

76. La kanto de Budhisma Savarmeo. ....La Lumo Senbara, 1925.
Trad. de J. Nakaniŝi.

77. Estas nomata "La Lumo Senbara."....La Lumo Senbara, 1925.

78. La Prezentitaj 20 malfacilaj aferoj de la Budho.....L. S., 1925–1926. (Represita en "Gendai Bukkjoo", 1931).
Tradukita de J. Nakaniŝi el "42-ĉapitra Sutro".

79. El la 42 Ĉapitroj de la sankta skribo de la Budho... .L.S., 1926.
Tradukita de J. Nakaniŝi el "42-ĉapitra Sutro".

80. El la sankta skribo de la Budho. L. S., 1926.
Trad. de J. Nakakiŝi el "Buddha-ĉarita".

81. El la sankta skribo de la Budho. ....L. S., 1926.
Trad. de J. Nakaniŝi el Saddharmasmrtyupasthāna Sutra.

82. La sankta skribo de la Budho pri la estinteco kaj estonteco... ..L. S., 1926.
Trad. de J. Nakaniŝi el "Kakogenzai-inga-kjoo" (佛說過去現在因果經).

83. La Lumo.....Ŝin'aiĉi (taĝjurnalo), 1926.
Tradukita de J. Nakaniŝi. Kanto laŭdanta Budaon.

84. La Vekiĝanto...La Libero, 1930.
Verkita de J. Nakaniŝi.

85. La sensenco fariĝas kiel la senco pro la vivo.....La Libero, 1930.
Verkita de J. Nakaniŝi.

86. Jesuo? Ŝinran?....Lib., 1930–1935.
Verkita de M. Jamanaka, trad. de J. Nakaniŝi.

87. Nia devo kiel budhisto.....Lib., 1930.
Verkita de R. Kacueda, trad. de J. Nakaniŝi.

88. Samantamukhaparivarta...... Lib., 1930.
Tradukita de K. Nohara. Poste eldonita en aparta broŝuro. (Vidu supre.)

89. Religio estas bongustigilo de pano.....Lib., 1930.
Verkita de J. Nakaniŝi.

90. La granda aspiro de vivo, kiu ne volas mortiĝon.....Lib., 1931.
Verkita de J. Nakaniŝi.

91. La kredo estas la forto.....Lib., 1931.
Verkita de J. Nakaniŝi.

92. La Bodhisatva vorto, ĵuranta plenumadon.....Lib., 1931.
Verkita de E. Mamija, tradukita de K. Ŝibajama.

93. Budhismo en la okcidento..... Lib., 1931.
Verkita de G. H. Yoxon.

94. Religia vivo.....Lib., 1931.
Verkita de K. Ŝibajama.

95. Nia vivo.....Lib., 1931.
Verkita de J. Nakaniŝi.

96. Kio estas religio?....Lib., 1931.
Verkita de J. Nakaniŝi.

97. La trezoro.....Lib., 1931.
Verkita de J. Nakaniŝi.

98. Memorindaj du kongresoj por budhanoj..... ....Lib., 1932.
Verkita de J. Nakaniŝi.

99. La religio por ordinaraj homoj. ....Lib., 1932.
Verkita de J. Nakaniŝi.

100. Samantamukhaparivarta. (Versa parto)....Lib., 1932.
Trad. de K. Nohara el sanskrita originalo.

101. Faru Provon.....Lib., 1932.
Verkis Okcidentano. (pseŭdonimo de Yoxon.)

102. La vojo por vera vivado..... Lib., 1932.
Verkita de J. Nakaniŝi.

103. Forpelu superstiĉon.....Lib., 1932.
Verkita de J. Nakaniŝi.

104. Vereco kaj malvereco.....Lib., 1932.
Verkita de J. Nakaniŝi.

105. Ho, vi venu.....Lib., 1932.
Poemo kantita de K. Tadehara, trad. de Iŭasaki.

106. Pudrita mondo.....Lib., 1932.
Verkita de R. Tojoŝima.

107. Pri konfeso.....Lib., 1932.
Verkita de J. Nakaniŝi.

108. Mi tiel pensas.....Lib., 1932.
Verkita de K. Fuĵiŭara, trad. de J. Nakaniŝi.

109. Observo pri homvizaĝo..... Lib., 1932.
Tradukita de M. Nose.

110. Sutro kaj reala vivo.....Lib., 1933.
Tradukita de J. Nakaniŝi.

111. Budhanoj transiginte persekuton marŝu.....Lib., 1933.
Parolita de B. L. Broughton, tradukita de J. Nakaniŝi.

112. Ankoraŭ mi ne povas forigi

la radikon "Budh".....Lib., 1934.
Verkita de J. Nakaniŝi.

113. La figuro de la tirato.....Lib., 1934.
Verkita de K. Kinugasa, trad. de T. Ogoo.

114. La kvara jarkunveno de JBLE. ....Lib., 1934.
Verkita de J. Nakaniŝi.

115. Epizodo de Sankta Benne... ..Lib., 1934.
Verkita de C. Nakai, tradukita de R. Niŝida.

116. La regata mondo de mono... ..Lib., 1934.
Verkita de J. Nakaniŝi.

117. Nia Aspiro.....Lib., 1935.
Verkita de K. Kinugasa, tradukita de T. Ogoo.

118. Teoria pruvo pri la ekzisto de Dio.....Lib., 1935.
Verkita de R. Niŝida.

119. La diraĵo de budhana fakkunsido en la 19-a Japana Esperanta Kongreso. ...... Gendai-bukkjoo, 1932.
Verkita de J. Nakaniŝi.

120. Religia kredo kaj vivo.....La Kroniko, 1935.
Verkita de C. Nakai, tradukita de R. Niŝida.

121. Ĝis la nova vivo de Budho... ..La Paco, 1922.
Tradukita de G. Mitani el Ĉ. Akanuma, "Agon-no-Bukkjoo".

122. Pri la idealo de Budhismo... ..La Paco, 1922.
Verkita de B. Mijagi.

123. La nacieco de japano kaj la religio de Ŝinran.....P., 1922.
Verkita de G. Mitani.

124. Budhismo kaj moderna penso. P., 1922.
Verkita de S. Sugihara.

125. La principo de Budhismo Ĝenerala.....P., 1922.
Trad. de Ĵ. Jamato el "Sinoptiko de la Ĝodo Sinŝu Kredaĵo".

126. Rakontas al mi mem, sekvante al Ŝinran.....P., 1922.
Verkita de G. Kuroda.

127. La religio de Budho.....P., 1922.
Verkita de S. Kikuĉi.

128. Kio estas la Vera Sekto de la Pura Lando?....P., 1923.
Trad. de G. Mitani. (la originalo nemontrita.)

129. Kiel oni devas lerni Mahajanan Budhismon?....P., 1923.
Verkita de G. Mitani.

130. Sukhavati-Vjuho.....P., 1924.
Tradukita de K. Tanijama el ĉina traduko (?).

131. La idealo de Ŝinran-sekvantoj. ....P., 1924.
Verkita de R. Ikeura.

132. La vivo de Ŝinran.....P., 1924.
Tradukita de Ŝ. Okazaki. (la orginalo nemontrita.)

133. Pripenso pri homaj deziroj en Ĵodo-Ŝinŝu.....P., 1924.
Verkita de K. Tanijama.

134. Rigardu vin mem.....P., 1925.
Verkita de Ĉ. Akanuma, tradukita de Ŝ. Okazaki.

135. Ikkjû en unu tago.....P., 1925.
Verkita de S. Muŝakooji, tradukita de K. Tanijama.

136. Tri ĵuroj.....P., 1925.
Trad. de Ŝ. Okazaki el "Amitajussutro."

137. Diferenco inter Budhismo kaj Kristanismo.....P., 1925.
Verkita de R. Ikeura.

138. Laŭdo por la Budho Amitajuso. ....P., 1925.
Tradukita de Ŝ. Kôno el Ŝinran "Ĵodo-Ŭasan".

139. La Sutro el Kvardekdu Ĉapitroj de la budho Ŝakjamuni..... P., 1925.
Tradukita de A. Tanijama.

140. Kontraŭstaro de Budho al Dio kiel kreinto.....P., 1925.
De Ŝ. Kôno (originale verkita?).

141. Kulturoj Orienta kaj Okcidenta naskitaj de religio kaj iliaj taskoj. ....P., 1926.
Verkita de G. Sasaki, tradukita de A. Tanijama.

142. Superstiĉo kaj malprava kredo. ....P., 1926.
Verkita de Ĵ. Takakusu, tradukita de A. Tanijama.

143. La instruo de Budao.......P., 1934.
Trad. de K. Kanĵa el "Ŝin'jaku Bukkjooseiten".

144. Himno de meditado.......P., 1934.
Trad. de K. Obstinulo el Hakuin, "Zazen-Ŭasan".

145. Trans la baron.....P., 1935.
Verkita de H. Izumi, tradukita de K. Kanamatz.

III.

Listo de Gazetoj koncernantaj Budaismon kaj Esperanton.

1) La Lumo Orienta.
La organo de Japana Budhana Ligo Esperantista. Ekeldoniĝis en decembro, 1931. De tiam ĝis nun daŭre eldonata ĉiukvaronjare.

2) La Paco.
La organo de Esperanto-Grupo de Ootani Universitato, Kioto. Ekeldoniĝis en februaro, 1922. Post marto, 1926 ĉesis eliri. Reeldoniĝis en septembro, 1934. (tipografie presita).

3) La Sankta Tilio.
La organo de Rjûkoku Daigaku Esperanta Grupo, ĉe Rjûkoku Universitato, Kioto. Aperis en oktobro, 1925. Post marto, 1929, ĉesis eliri. Reaperis en marto, 1934.

4) La Voĉo.

La organo de Rindai Esperanta Grupo, ĉe Rinzai Kolegio, Kioto. Ekaperis en marto, 1935.

5) La Libero.

Eldonata de Joŝio Nakaniŝi, Kiŝiŭada. Ekeldonita en februaro, 1930. De tiam ĝis nun daŭre eliras.

6) La Lumo Senbara.

Eldonita de Mugjookoo-ŝa, Ŭakamacu, Fukuoka-ken. Aperis en oktobro, 1925. ĝis junio, 1926.

7) La Budhismo. (antaŭe Bulteno de Budhana Ligo Esperantista).

La organo de Budhana Ligo Esperantista, Heswall, Cheshire, Anglujo. Ekaperis en 1931. De tiam daŭre aperas ĉiukvaronjare.

8) Buddhism in England.
9) The Buddhism in Burma.
10) Rjooĵu (靈鷲), Kioto.
11) Homarano (antaŭe Hooenroku, La Penseto), Himeĵi.
12) Tenĵisaiseigun, Fukuoka-ken.
13) Bukkjoosaiseigun, Fukuoka-ken.
14) Esugobudajori, Fukuoka-ken.
15) Aka, Tokio.

(8)–(15) aperigis Esp.-rubrikon, aŭ artikolojn pri Budaismo kaj Esp.

......*Postskribo*......

En la fino de ĉi tiu artikolo ni esprimas elkoran dankon al S-ro K. Ŝibajama, el kies artikolo "Esperantaĵoj pri Budaismo" en la Revuo Orienta ni ĉerpis materialojn multe, al S-roj J. Nakaniŝi, F. Dazai, kiuj bonvolis kolekti materialojn laŭ nia peto.

Ni esperas ke ĉi-supra listo kompletiĝu en proksima estonteco per helpo de kelkaj samideanoj kaj la suplemento de la listo aperu en ĉi tiu bulteno. Tiuj, kiuj bonvolus rimarkigi al ni mankantajn materialojn en la listo, afable skribu al ni, "Esperanto-Bukkjoobunka-kai," N-ro 29, Juŝima 6-ĉoome, Hongoo-ku, Tokio. (Fino)

Esperantaj libroj pri Budaismo

		prezo	sendkosto
1.	La Sukhavativjuho	¥ 0.15	0.02
2.	Budao (tradukita el "The Essence of Buddhism")	0.60	0.04
3.	La Dek Bildoj de Bovpaŝtado	0.35	0.04
4.	La Kodo de Kronprinco Ŝootoku	0.15	0.02
5.	La Samanta-Mukhaparivarto	0.40	0.04
6.	Budaisma Terminaro de Takeuĉi (hektografita)	2.00	0.20

Ĉiuj libroj supre menciitaj estas riceveblaj de la Administracio de la "Internacia Budaisma Bulteno" aŭ de Japana Esperanto-Instituto, Hongoo, Tokio.

Letters from abroad

From New Zealand

86 Wairoa Road, Devonport,
Auckland, N. 1. New Zealand.
10/6/35.

To The Editor,
The International Buddhist Information Bureau, Tokyo.

Dear Sir and Brother,

It is with pleasure I acknowledge the receipt of two copies of the above monthly.

This journal seems to be able to fill a decided want, as Buddhism knows NO boundaries, it is all inclusive.

Personally, I am unable to help with a remittance as I am not able to work, through old age and illness exhausting my funds.

I am glad to inform you that Mr. W. E. Barnard, M. P. Napier, New Zealand. is the most active Buddhist here, he conducts a class, perhaps you might divert the copy you sent me to him.

Thanking you for your courtesy, and trusting success will crown your efforts,

Yours in the Dharma,
Arthur H. Thompson.

From Shanghai, en route to Ceylon

The Pure Kamma Buddhist
Association, 418, Hart Road,
Shanghai, 18. 6. '35.

Dear Rev. Omura,

You will be pleased to hear that we left Kyoto on the 13th and arrived here safely on the 15th inst.

At Kyoto the Indo-Japanese Association held a welcome meeting at which Prof. Hatani, Mr. Fujii and many others were present. I suggested to them the desirablity of having a uniform Buddha Day for all the Buddhists. At present we Buddhists of Ceylon, India, Burma etc celebrate the Buddha Day on the fullmoon day that falls on May, whilst the Chinese and Japanese Buddhists celebrate on May 10th and April 8th respectively.

I wish our brother Japanese Buddhists delete the contemptuous term Hinayana in their writings and use instead the more correct term Theravada. Those days when one sect stigmatised the other are past and gone. It is now time for us to leave aside those sectarian differences and work like Buddhists for the common cause of propagating the Dhamma throughout the world.

I thank you all for your warm welcome and shall never forget your kind hospitality.

Please convey my Maitri to all the members.

Yours in the Dhamma,
Nārada

From India

Maha Bodhi Society
Holy Isipatana, Sarnath
June 10, B.E. 2479. C.E. 1935.

Dear Mr. Komura,

I am in receipt of your letter informing the despatch of the film. I have just received a notice from the Custom Office, informing of the arrival of the parcel. They want me to produce the invoice. I am sorry you have not sent the same to me. I am expecting it by next week's mail.

It gave me great pleasure to hear that you have all pledged to give your whole-hearted support in our Buddhagaya campaign. It is a sacred work and if we continue our work without interruption, we have no doubt that our efforts will be crowned with success. Please convey our best thanks to those who are taking an interest in this question.

You must have already heard about the Buddhagaya Temple Bill that has been brought up before the Indian Legislative Assembly for the transfer of the Buddhagaya Temple into Buddhist hands. As the Hindus desire to come to a compromise, we have with-held the introduction of the Bill for the present. A committee has been appointed with Hindus and Buddhist members to try for an amicable settlement. If the work of the Committee is successful, we shall have fulfilled our great ambition. I shall let you know the progress of this matter occasionally.

I hope you are keeping in touch with our work through the Maha Bodhi Journal which I am sending. Our work is getting on satisfactorily. I am thankful to you for your assurance of co-oporation in our work here. I hope to hear from you more often.

On receipt of the Film, I shall send you the price of the same. Please let me know the exact price. Trusting you are in the best of health.

With sincerest regards.

Yours sincerely,
D. Valisinha

P.S. Did you meet Rev. Rahula Sankrityayana who is now in Japan? *D.V.*

Japanese News

Japan-Siam Society Inaugurates

With a view to strengthening cultural ties between Japan and Siam, the inaugural meeting of the Japan-Siam Society was held at the local Chamber of Commerce and Industry building of Nagoya at 10 a.m. June 20th.

Among the more than 60 dignitaries and traders who attended the function were Phra Mitrakarm Raksha, Siamese Minister in Tokyo; Director Kazue Kuwajima, of the East Asia bureau of the Foreign Office; Jirozaemon Ito, leading businessman of Nagoya; and Katsutaro Kato, honorary consul for Siam.

The last mentioned two were elected president and vice-president, respectively, of the new society.

The society resolved to invite three medical students of Siam to study in Nagoya. Their expenses will be covered by the new body.

It was also decided to promote cooperation in the study of Buddhism in both countries. Mr. Ito announced that he would give an annual contribution toward the fund of the society.

Prof. Pelliot in Kyoto

Professor Paul Pelliot of the College de France, who is considered one of the greatest authorities on Sinology, and Mrs. Pelliot arrived at Kyoto June 19th accompanied by Mikinosuke Ishida of the International Cultural Development Society. He leaved Kyoto for China on June 25, commissioned by the British Silver Jubilee Art Exhibition.

He visited June 20th afternoon Dr. Naoki Kano at his office in the Oriental Culture Institute and was shown the Chinese documents of the Institute.

Kahn Scholarships

Mr. Albert Kahn, the French millionaire, established scholarships for Japanese students 20 years ago and during this time more than 10 scholars have benefited.

Professor Seiichi Naruse of Kyushu Imperial University is now in France under the support of this scholarship.

A group of scholars in this country who have studied in Europe through the means supplied by Mr. Kahn recently sent him a carved figure of a No actor as a token of esteem.

Bust Relief of Hearn

The Japan-Greece Society has just received a marble bust relief of Lafcadio Hearn from Greece.

This gift is in return for a statue of Hearn which was sent to Greece in 1933 from the Japan-Greece Society of Tokyo.

The unveiling ceremony of this presentation will be held in the library of the Tokyo Imperial University in September. Marquis Yorisada Tokugawa, president of the Japan-Greece Society, will be present.

Lafcadio Hearn Anniversary

The 30th anniversary of the death of Lafcadio Hearn falls on September 26 this year.

A memorial meeting will be held under the auspices of the Ministry of Foreign Affairs, the Society for the Promotion of International Cultural Relations, and the Society in Memory of Koizumi Yakumo of Tokyo and Matsue.

After the copyright of Hearn's works expire in the United States this year, the Society for the Promotion of International Cultural Relations plans to publish all his books in this country.

Larger than Daibutsu

A copy of the far-famed Daibutsu of Kamakura is to be placed in the compound of a new temple at Asaka in Saitama Prefecture. The founder of this new Buddhist center is Mr. Kaichiro Nezu, the well-known Tokyo businessman. It is said the cost of construction will be ten million yen.

Mr. Shin Naito, one of Tokyo's best wood carvers, has been commissioned to make a model of the calm Buddha seated on the lotus throne, and this was completed in his studio last month.

A huge bronze bell was fashioned for the new temple last spring at a cost of ¥200,000.

The second Daibutsu will be larger than that of Kamakura, 48 feet high, and will cost ¥1,300,000.

Of Historic Interest

Mr. Genji Matsuda, Minister of Education, recently made a tour of Tokyo to renew his acquaintance with some of the historic places of the city. It is of interest to note the features which were sufficiently attractive to lure the busy minister out in hot weather.

Accompanied by his secretaries and officials of his department Mr.

Matsuda first visited Zojoji in Shiba Park, one of the most striking yedo landmarks.

Then the minister's car was directed to go to Sengakuji, Shinagawa, where the tombs of the Fortyseven Ronin are a mecca for visitors. The minister stopped to gaze at the old well where the ronin washed the head of their enemy.

Mr. Matsuda next visited the garden of Marquis Saigo where he took luncheon. This garden is associated with the great Saigo of Restoration days and was visited by Emperor Meiji.

Mr. Matsuda in the afternoon visited Asakusa Park and Mukojima on the banks of the Sumida River, took a rest in Kiyozumi Park of Fukagawa, and returned home having spent a busy day sightseeing in the capital.

Buddhist Service

To console the souls of the soldiers who have recently died in Mongolia, and also the victims of the Taiwan earthquake disaster, a memorial service was held in Hibiya Hall July 16 at 6 p.m.

It is given in keeping with the Obon season, and under the auspices of the Tokyo Municipality.

The chief priest of Tsukiji Honganji officiated and the Manchoukuo Ambassador and Mayor of Tokyo spoke on that occasion.

Statue of Judge of Hell

In Fukuoka a colossal statue of Emma, the Judge of the Buddhist Hell, has recently been erected. It is 11 feet high and is much larger than the famous seated figure of the terrifying figure fashioned in Yedo days which may still be seen at Taishoji, a Buddhist temple of Shinjuku.

The new statue is to be enshrined in a building in Sasakuri Park of Fukuoka, and the dedication ceremony was held on July 28.

Buddhist Plays

Mr. Sesshu Hayakawa, the cinema actor, has announced the establishment of the Nippon Buddhist Dramatic Company. The initial meeting was held at the Imperial University Club in Kanda, July 17 evening.

Having the support of many leaders of Buddhism, Mr. Hayakawa will present plays dealing with the life of Buddha and the Buddhist saints of Japan,

The first performance is planned to be given at the Nippon Gekijo in December.

南京支那内學院の誤解中傷事件に就て

藤井草宣

南京內學院に關係ある一部の份子が我等の行動を誤解し，此の誤解せる心識より多くの禍亂を支那佛教界に惹起し，更に日本佛教界にも不測の悪感を與へた事件が最近數ケ月間に現象した。這の件に就ては，近時，漸く水落ちて石露はるゝ如く，禍根が南京の支那內學院に伏在せることが明瞭となつたによつて一言の釋明をしておきたい。

一，已に昨年初夏に開催された「第二回汎太平洋佛靑大會」に際して，支那內學院は故意の誤解を爲した。抑々此の大會は，第一回を昭和五年布哇に於て開催せる際に，次回は昭和九年，日本東京に於て開催することを決議してゐたので，之に因つて昨年開催されたものである。その主賓ともいふべきものは，米國及び布哇諸島，加奈太等の日系米人第二世の佛教靑年會員諸君であつて，事實に於て出席來賓の最大多數を占めてゐたのである。此外に，印度，暹羅，新嘉坡等々各地の佛教徒が,「汎太平洋沿岸」の名によつて集合したのである。故に決して我等の目的は「滿洲國」佛教徒を主賓とする考は絕對に無かつたのである。況んや「滿洲國」を承認させる目的の爲めに召集した大會では斷じて無かつたのである。此事は，終始一貫してゐたのである。開會前の準備會の結成に際し，私は「中華班長」たることを依囑されたので，虛心坦懷に，私の最も尊敬せる太虛法師及び王一亭居士を始めとして北平及び厦門等の友人に出席を勸誘し且つ出席者の世話を依賴したのである。然るに，先づ太虛法師よりは「滿洲國と序列の會合には出席不可能」といふ意味の手紙が來た。太虛法師も，已に最初から誤解の發生を怕れたのである。然し，我等は，極力，今回の大會が政治外交に關係なき，純粹なる佛教の立脚地より平和會議を爲すものであることを通告し，私の最も敬意を拂ふ親しき友人先輩を指名して來會を勸誘したのである。すると，中には，豫て日本留學を希望せる人々もあり，又た，大會出席とは關係無く，此際を以て「日本佛教視察」に赴日するも可であるといふ事となつて，漸く話がまとまつたのである。だから時に應じては大會に出席せざるも可である。傍聽席から考察し觀覽しても可いといふことを申送り，夫れならばといふので厦門の常惺法師等が公々然と日本視察團を組織し，若し組織出來なくば，個々に赴日して行動を偕にするといふところまで進んだのである。此の一件は，私の一友人の非常な努力に依つて進涉したのである。そこで，私は，更に此の大會の內容を直接の面談によつて支那の人々にお話し，赴日の世話をしたいと思つて，渡支したのである。私の胸中には,「佛教の世界的宣布の好機會に支那の親しい友人，尊敬せる先輩各位と協力することが最も愉快である」といふより外は無かつたのだ。それ故，私は私の行動なり，意圖なりを公々然と發表し宣傳した。すると想ひもよらぬ南京の一角から，實に陰險極る中傷と誤報が各方面に向つて散發され，全支那の大小新聞が其の誤報を掲載した。爲めに，尊敬する先輩，親しき友人各位に非常重大なる迷惑と困却とを掛けたことは，今日も尙ほ之を追想して遺恨千萬である。私は楊子江上に於て，南海の波上に於て，北平の客舍に於て，實に一人悲憤の涙を流したのである。然し忍辱して默して來た。反駁も止めたのであつた。而して此の時の「中國佛教會」の態度は，矢張り「誤解」者と同樣であつたのは，今以て不可解である。依つて私は，同會に關係なき自由人方面の出席者を勸誘して之に成功したのである。私の心中では，若し今回の大會に支那佛教徒が出席せざれば，支那佛教界自體の爲めに頗る不利であると考へたからであり，更に進んでは，汎太平洋大會の名の實を缺く怕れがあると思惟したからである。「偉大なる支那佛教を除外したる汎太平洋佛教大會」は「胴身なき佛像」であり「頭と手足のみの菩薩像」であると考へたのである。此時の私の心中の大願は，たゞ一部の識者のみが知つてゐるだらう。幸に渡日出席せる個々の人々は，一人當千の大菩薩であつた。私は佛天に之を感謝した。

二，而して今年に入つて，再び南京の一角より莫明其妙（わけのわからぬ）「傳單」が散布され出した。一回，二回，三回と重ねて散布された。而して漸次それが「支那內學院」の一部份の人の工作であることが分明となつた。而して，其の中傷目標は「中日佛教學會」の發起人及び，我等の尊敬せる太虛法師に限定されてゐた。昨年の汎太平洋大會の際の中傷と全く同轍である。之に就ては已に墨禪法師，談玄法師及び潮州，武昌各地の學僧の蹶起によつて充分に辯護されたが，然も，尙ほ一つ未だ完全でないのは，汎太平洋大會が，斷じて政治的意圖より出でゝはゐなかつたといふ事に對する諒解である。我等の會合は，前も後も常に永久に絕對に純粹なる佛教の信仰と研究との會合であることを理解せられんことを希ふものである。

「日本佛教劇團」の創立に就て

早川雪洲

私は，私の二十年に亙る長い海外生活において，いろいろ感じたり考へたりした結果，將來，自分の一生涯の事業として，是非これを實現したいと念願して來た一つの事があります。それは純正な佛敎劇の創造であります。

曾て私がドイツに行きました時，かの國の國寶的存在であるパツションプレイ（キリスト受難劇）を觀た事があります。その俳優達は先祖代々世襲的に一村の人々が職としてゐるもので每年五月から九月まで大々的に野外劇を行ひ過去三百年來國民に深刻な感銘を與へてゐたものであります。年々都鄙の別なく，大衆は，敎壇から說敎を聞かされた以上に感激するのであります。又，アメリカでは，これも國寶的存在であるミツションプレイといふのがあります。これはアメリカ發見後カリフオルニア開拓者として新大陸の魁としたイスパニア宣敎師達の艱難苦鬪の事蹟を劇化したもので，每年四五ケ月間興行されるものでありますが，普通の劇と異つて民衆に與へる感動は實に大きなものであります。

一つは神の榮光と共に主イエス・キリストを禮讚する劇であり，他は，神の導きに依つて野蠻未開の處女地に神の國を建設しようとした純眞なパイオニヤの禮讚であります。人類は常に救世主を求め，又，自分の邦土の建設者に涯りない感謝と記念の意を表します。それは，隆んなる國民であればあるほど，その念が强い樣に思はれます。私は，この二つの劇に對するドイツとアメリカとの大衆に就いて深く考へさせられて來ました。そして，多年，我が日本にもあゝした劇團があつていゝことであるし，又，あらなければならないことだと思つてゐたのであります。

かやうな氣持に深く燃へてゐた私はたまたま先般「日蓮」の撮影を依賴されまして，これを演じてゐるうちに，この信念を高める樣になり，演じ終つたとき，或る一つの靈感的なものが自分に對つて，汝の生涯を今後佛敎劇に沒頭せよと叫んでる樣に感じられました。

爾來，私は沈思默考を續けたのでありますが，思ひ出されたのは，先年再びアメリカに行つたとき觀たモオリス劇團が「ミラクル」と云ふ宗敎劇を演じた時の光景であります。世界大戰前から宗敎の破產が叫ばれ，そして大戰後も，科學の進步が隆々としてほとんどその極まるところを知らざるが如き潮流に乘り，歐米の大衆が盲目的に物質的文明を追つて止まなかつた時，あの大掛りな，破天荒と云つていゝ「ミ

ラクル」劇がニユーヨークの眞中に公開されたのであります。興行者達は勿論のこと，多少劇界に通じてゐた人達でも頭からこの無謀な宗敎劇の成功を危み，且つ否定したのであります。ところがどうでせう，蓋を開けて見ると大衆は雪崩の樣に押寄せて，日延べ又日延べと云ふ盛況であり，全米各都の市民は熱狂して恰も救世主の再現を迎へたかのやうであつたのであります。劇場が狹くて收容しきれない爲に，多くは野外で演じなければならない位でした。この光景は何を語るものでせう。古臭くて現代人には何等興味がないと思はれた宗敎劇は，實に大衆が常に求めてやまない魂の渴望そのものだつたのであります。それは，大衆が新しい喜劇や悲劇から感能的興味を間斷なく享けて喜んでる現代生活の反面に常に眞の民衆的な，そして人類的な，そして又宗敎的な，光明の世界を求めてゐるからでありませう。

私共は，この國を肇めて下さつた神々に最高の敬意と感謝とを捧げると共に，一方私達民族に精神の糧を與へて吳れた，あらゆる聖賢の士を追慕する心が一日も止まないのであります。その追慕の心は凝つて聖賢の偉大な溫容言行を在世のまゝの姿によつて目の當りに再現し觀賞したいといふ心になつて現はれます。

そして，その心に投ずる演劇が現代の日本に缺けてゐるといふことを私は學びました。その缺けたる道を開拓する使命を私は感じたのであります。日本佛敎劇團の創設は實にかうした動機から起りました。

私共の立場として，さうした偉大な人格を舞臺藝術の上に再現する事に依つて，民衆に何等かの靈感を植えつけ同時に高貴な法悅の鄕に導くことができましたれば，本懷これに過ぎたるはございません。

最初に私は，多年憧れを抱いて來た釋尊の大思想を劇化し，これを音樂，聲樂，舞踊等と綜合し，一大新形式に表現しやうと決心致しました。釋尊は古今東西に亙つての大先覺者であることは勿論ですが，又，千數百年來，日本民族の精神生活に廣大無邊な影響を與へて下さつた大恩人であります。この偉人中の偉人を再現するといふことは，私如きものゝ企て及ばない至難な事業だと思はれるのでございますが，偏に多年知遇を辱ふしてゐます先輩諸賢の御指導を仰いで必ず成功を期したいと念願してゐる次第であります。そして更に我々民族が生んだ，各宗派の開祖を始め，あらゆる名僧善知識の思想信仰を藝術化したる善き脚本を廣く世上に求め，一方，文運の隆盛を期すると共に，この非常時日本國民の進むべき前途に一路の白光を翳して奮進することが，私の今後に於ける最も名譽ある事業だと堅く信ずるのであります。

この運動は帝都を發祥の聖地として遍く，全日本を週期的に巡業し更に海外にまでも進出して，日本民族が持つ榮光を四海に示し，特に日本佛敎の大

乘的精神が如何に崇高な內容を藏してゐるかを藝術的表現に依つて明らかにしたいといふ，大望を抱いてゐるのであります。

希くば先輩諸賢，この私の微衷と年來の心願とを御諒解下さつて，限りなき御後援を賜はらんことを伏して御願ひ致す次第でございます。　合　掌

『日本佛教劇團後援會』趣意書

佛教復興と佛教傳道の藝術化

最近東洋思想，特に日本精神の研究は，我國に於てばかりでなく，海外人に於てすら熾烈に行はれて居ります。これは取りも直さず我東洋思想，日本精神が如何に世界に誇る優秀なものであるかを示すものであり，特に近頃の如く世界到る處民心は生活の指導原理を失ひ，不安におのゝいてゐるの秋，期せずして內外共にこの東洋思想，日本精神の把握に眞劔な態度を表はしてゐることに鑑み更に上述の感を深くし又，それだけ我々としては快心の笑を禁じ難いのであります。

言ふまでもなく日本精神や日本の文化的性格は獨特のものであります。假令海外の思想であつても日本に於ては凡て消化され，純化され，血となり肉となつて我輝かしい日本精神となつてゐるものでありまして，世界の諸々の思想は，我が日本に於てはじめて遺憾なく完成されるものであると云つて決して過言ではないと考へるのであります。我々がお互ひに奉ずる釋尊の教は假令印度に發祥したものであつても，それは既に日本化して，日本的に完全に發達したものであり，日本は又，この日本化された日本佛教によつて今日まで千數百年の長きに亙つて文化の基礎を築き，國民生活の根本を培つて來たのであります。そして又この日本化された佛敎こそは東洋は勿論，世界のいづこに及ぼしても決して悖らない普偏妥當性を有してゐるのであります。されば今や東亞の光として廣く世界全體を光被せんとし，日一日とその大乘的精神を全人類の上に發現せんとしつゝあることは決して故なきことではありません。思想國難の非常時に當つてあの汫澎として起つた佛敎復興の運動もこれなくしては人々の救はれる途のない事を本當に自覺したからであり，それは眞に止むに止まれない要求として表はれたものに他ならないのであります。

扨て飜つて顧みるに，この已むに已まれない大衆的要求としての佛教復興に直面致しましてこれに直接間接關係を持つ敎界人が果してその責任と使命とを充分に果たしつゝあるでありませうか，どうか？　勿論佛教復興を契機として各々の專門に從ひ多少の大衆的欲求に應じ，又應じつゝあるのではありませうが，我々佛教徒大衆としてはそれらの單なる局部的，斷片的對策以上に，もつと綜合的に全面的に，堂々たる行進を試みなければならぬと信ずるのであります。

惟ふに今回の佛教復興の原因及びなされた方法には種々あるでありませうが，佛教の近代的文學的の表現が大いに與つて力があると思ふのであります。專門的難解な經典もさうした文學的表現の力に依つて平易に大衆に呼びかけ得たことは我々の見逃してならぬ所であります。又我々は宗教と藝術とは窮極に於て必ず一致するものであると信じますので，この藝術と宗教との接近によつてその相互的發展が期せられることを深く待望するものであります。最近漸くこの傾向に辿りつゝあることは洵に喜びに堪えないことでありますが，同時に我々は一層この方面に努力を拂はねばならぬと考へる次第であります。卽ち我々の多年唱道して來ました所謂佛教傳道の藝術化に對して此際大いに拍車をかけたいのであります。

今年の釋尊成道會と『日本佛教劇團』の公演

我々は前に述べました意味に於きまして最近漸く具體的活動を開始してゐます佛教音樂，佛教映畫，佛教兒童藝術，佛教文學，佛教美術の諸運動に對して深き悅びと敬意を表するものでありますが，唯獨り佛教演劇の振はざる現狀を顧みます時，太だ遺憾に堪えないものがあります。演劇の大衆性とその及ぼす感化の偉大なることは言ふまでもない所でありまして，かのドイツの「パツションプレー」やアメリカの「ミツションプレー」の存在の如きは我々の常に羨望してやまないものであります。勿論我國にも從來この試みはしばしば行はれて居つたのでありますが，俳優に其人を得なかつたり，或は單なる一宗一派の說敎劇に終つたりしまして，それは我々が意圖する「佛教と藝術」の客觀的に統一された眞の佛敎劇とは凡そ程遠いものでありました。それ故我々は何とかして吾々の理想する眞の佛教劇の樹立を實現し度いと切に念願してゐたのでありますが，今回たまたま前揭の如き趣旨によりまして早川雪洲氏がその餘生をこの方面に捧げ度いとの宿願をもつてゐられることを親しく氏に就いて聞き，抱負を質し，全く意見も一致し共鳴を深くしたのであります。

氏は人も知る世界の映畫演劇の都ハリウツドに於て，世界に於ける斯界の權威者達と肩を並べて，日本俳優こゝにありと我日本のために萬丈の氣焰を吐いた人であります。特にその佛敎藝術の硏究は隱れたる氏の造詣として頗る深いものがあります。又氏はニユーヨークに私設の佛教圖書館を作られたり，或ひは印度の佛跡を巡拜されたりしまして，遂ひに今日より其餘生を大乘精神の宣布の爲に佛教演劇に捧げる決意をされるに至つたのであります。

茲に於て我々同志の者はしばしば氏

等と會合し，互に意見の交換を行ひ，氏は又寧日なく，これがために東奔西走，「日本佛教劇團」の創設に努力せられ，その結果，創設に要する數萬圓の經費も大體目鼻もつき，目下俳優，公演場，上演作品の選定等にその準備をはこびつゝある次第であります。趣意書にもある如く，同氏等の意圖する佛教演劇は，釋尊の御一代を劇化し音樂聲樂舞踊等を綜合させた一種の綜合劇でありまして．更に各宗の開祖は勿論佛教的偉人の信仰や人格をこの劇によつて大衆に知らしめやうとするものであります。我々のこゝに最も喜ぶことは，かゝる「劇」の實現が國家の爲にも佛教の爲にも偉大なる貢獻をするものであることは勿論，漸く各部門的に發展しつゝある佛教藝術の諸運動がこの刺戟によつて凡て活潑に動員されるに至り，それらが打つて一丸となつて全面的に前進を起して來るであらうといふことが豫想せられることであります。

以上我々は種々述べて來ましたが，こゝに考へる事は我々佛教徒として最も愉快な佛教復興の今年を有意義に回顧し，更に明年に備へるための最もよき機會たる十二月八日の釋尊成道會がある事であります。この成道會に對しては從來種々な計劃もあり，年中行事として大衆化されつゝあるものでありますが，我々はこの成道會が，佛教徒は勿論一般大衆に向つて，もつと深き大衆運動たらしめねばならぬと考へるのであります。

早川雪洲氏の「日本佛教劇團」は出來得る限り立派な陣容を整へるための準備を急いで，釋尊成道會を中心に先ず帝都の中心にその旗上げをなし，更に各主要の都市に巡業し，將來は世界中に巡業し得るに至るやう一生懸命に努力中でありますので，佛教のためにその志を同じうする我々としましては先づ今年の成道會の主要プログラムとしてこの釋尊劇の大衆的演劇を計畫し一は成道會の普及に，一は理想の佛教劇の樹立の爲に「日本佛教劇團」の後援會を組織し度いと考へる次第であります。以上の趣旨に由りまして我々は切に諸賢の厚き贊助と力强き支持を冀望するのであります。

『日本佛教劇團』後援會準備委員會

委員長　高　楠　順　次　郎

國際佛教通報局定款

名　　稱

第一，本局を國際佛教通報局と稱す

事 務 所

第二，本局の事務所を全日本佛教靑年會聯盟本部に置く

目　　的

第三，本局は日本內海及海外に向つて佛教事情の通報をなし，且つ佛教徒相互間の各種便宜を計るを以て目的とす

事　　業

第四，本局の目的を達成するため左記の事業を行ふ

イ，日本內地及世界各國より佛教事情に關する質問の通報を行ふ

ロ，必要に應じ日本語及世界各國語を以て佛教事情の通報を行ふ

ハ，外國人の日本觀光に際しては各國の便益を與へ，特にその佛教に關する方面に於て之を爲す

ニ，定時或は隨時に各國語を以て文書の刊行をなす

ホ，その他必要と認めたる事業を行ふ

役　　員

第五，本局の事務を處理するため左の役員を置く

イ，局　長　　一　名

ロ，幹　事　　三　名

ハ，評議員　　若干名

局長は本局　　　を總括す

幹事は本局の事務を處理す

評議員は局長の提案に依る重要事務を審議す

第六，評議員は左記の者を以て之に充つ

イ，全日本佛教靑年會館聯盟理事及主事

ロ，全日本佛教靑年會聯盟理事會に於て推薦したる者

第七，局長及幹事は評議員會に於て決定す

第八，役員の仕期は二ケ年とす（但し重任を妨げず）

經　　費

第九，本局の經費は左記のものに依て之を支辨す

イ，本局基金の活用

ロ，寄附金

ハ，その他の收入

補　　則

第十，本定款に記載せられざる事項は，凡て評議員會に於て協議す

第十一，第一回の役員は全日本佛教靑年會聯盟理事會に於て決定す

定價	一部	金二十錢	送料二錢
	一年	金二圓四十錢	送料不要

昭和十年四月卅日第三種郵便物認可
昭和十年七月廿七日印刷（每月一回
昭和十年八月一日發行　一日發行）

東京市外吉祥寺337
編輯發行兼印刷人　淺野研眞

東京市牛込區早稻田鶴卷町107
印刷所　康文社印刷所
電話牛込（34）1950番 5049番

東京市神田區一ツ橋二の三
發行所　國際佛教通報局
電話九段（33）1429番
振替東京83015番

昭和十年四月三十日第三種郵便物認可　昭和十年七月二十七日印刷納本
昭和十年八月一日發行(毎月一回一日發行)國際佛教通報　第一卷　第五號

昭和十年四月三十日第三種郵便物認可　昭和十年八月二十七日印刷納本　昭和十年九月一日發行（毎月一回一日發行）第一卷　第六號

The International Buddhist Bulletin

國際佛教通報

第一卷　昭和十年九月　第六號　〔Vol. I. Sept. 2501/1935 No. 6.〕

要　目〔Contents〕

東　京　**國際佛教通報局**　發　行
The International Buddhist Information Bureau
Tokyo, Kanda, Hitotsubashi, II—3

The International Propagation of Mahāyāna Buddhism

Address delivered at the Meeting in Commemoration of the Second Pan-Pacific Young Buddhist Associations-Congress in the Nishi Hongwanji, Tokyo

by Bruno Petzold

If we want to propagate Mahāyāna Buddhism in the outerworld and make it internationally a living force, just the best is good enough. I have always maintained this view and I maintain it still to-day.

But what is the best?

Surely not a weak infusion which we gain by preparing an easily understandable and popular extract from a medley of Mahāyāna doctrines. Such insipid beverage may appeal to the taste of old ladies and enervated men of the leisured class, who from mere dulness and by way of a pastime have taken a fancy to Buddhism, but have not the slightest intention to devote to it any serious attention. It is really not worth while even to try to win over, in a true and sincere way, such relics of modern civilisation to such a noble and great cause as Mahāyāna Buddhism. Already the Buddha of the Hīnayāna Sūtras always refused to reveal the truth to anybody who was not thirsting for it, as if being exposed to a lingering death. Such-one needs a strong and life-giving tonic, some potion that invigorates his whole system.

We shall of course not give to an individual weakened by exhaustion the strongest liquor. That would be the worst for him. Let us act like the Buddha of the Mahāyāna Mahā Pari Nirvāna Sūtra who distinguishes "Five Tastes" and gives to everybody just that beverage, that is suitable for his condition, proceeding from milk to "daigo". But even that what is described as milk in the Nirvāna Sūtra is an extract containing wonderful life-building powers and is not wasted on people whose constitution is not able to digest it.

A good many of my Buddhist friends seem to believe that the best way to make Mahāyāna Buddhism influential in Europe and America is to propagate it in a sectarian way by missionaries of various sects. I dissociated myself also from this view in speeches and pamphlets in the past and I do it now. Buddhism and especially Mahāyāna Buddhism ought to be propagated in an unsectarian way. That is, all schools of Buddhism "sine ira et studio" (without anger and zealotism) ought to be made known to the outer-world as schools of philosophy rather than as religious sects. First the world has to be enlightened in regard to the truth of Buddhism — devotion and performance of religious rites will follow afterwards. Without a sufficient knowledge of the deep ideas involved in Mahāyāna Buddhism, devotion and religious ceremonies will be an empty show.

Now the great difficulty is, how to prepare such life-giving extract from all the various teachings of Mahāyāna Buddhism, being considered not as a hodge-podge, but as a logical synthesis, and to make it acceptable to foreigners. The work has not yet been done, and there may be very few who are able to do it. It is not sufficient merely to translate some big Buddhist dictionary, written in Japanese, into any foreign language and to stuff into the head of the foreigner innumerable and ununderstandable technical terms. From the dictionaries and from the sūtras and śāstras themselves an extract must be made, and those who brew it, must be masters in their art. This point seems to have been overlooked entirely until to-day by those who propose the "internationalisation" of Mahāyāha Buddhism.

Now remember! The matter in question is not the writing of an elementary handbook on Mahāyāna Buddhism, containing the moral precepts of this religion or a quintessence of its views, as far as they are helpful for practical life, by throwing out the whole of the metaphysics of Mahāyāna, — but what we need is the revelation and description of ideas and systems of ideas comparable to

Inaugurating the Meeting

those of a Descartes, Spinoza, Kant, Hegel and Schelling which alone can wring respect and admiration for Mahāyāna Buddhism from the until now unsuspecting foreigners. Those who wish to engage in this gigantic task must speak a language, which represents the whole complexity of Mahāyāna learning. It must be a language that is understandable to foreigners, being neither too vulgar nor too abstract and which knows to forge the links connecting the Mahāyāna ideas with the thought of the Westerners. And most of all, it must be a language that makes known the very best of Mahāyānism.

It may surpass the power of any individual and even of any ordinary Buddhist Association to come up to such requirements. The best advice therefore I can give, is to establish a Mahāyāna Institute, whose foundation I have already recommended years ago, and to entrust it with the task of extending the knowledge of Mahāyāna Buddhism to people and countries that until now scarcely know even the name of Mahāyāna.

佛青記念デー

—去る七月廿一日(日曜日), 築地本願寺に於て—

汎太平洋佛青大會の回顧

第二回汎太平洋佛青大會々長　柴田一能

今日我々の汎太平洋佛靑聯盟第五周年記念日を迎へて，來賓各位と共に滿腔の喜びを同ふし，一言の感想を陳ぶるの光榮を得た事を衷心より感謝する次第であります。

回顧すれば，丁度滿五年前の今月今日は，第一回の汎太平洋佛靑大會が，日米兩國の文化の中繼者として，自然に因緣付けられた太平洋上の十字路に當る，ハワイのホノルルで盛大に開催された其日でありまして，私も現任全日本佛靑聯盟大村理事長，立花前理事長達日本佛靑聯盟の代表者の一行に加はり，太平洋沿岸六箇の佛敎國代表に依つて組織された佛靑の處女的國際會議に臨んだ時の氣持は，實に言ひ表はし難い歡喜と感激と羞恥と好奇と嚴肅さの交響樂で，靑春的鼓動の波の激しさを覺へたのでありました。

開會劈頭の三歸依文の齊唱，佛靑歌の合唱を始めとして記要に誌されて居る六日間に亙る會議中の行事は，總て我々佛靑聯盟の國際的團結に依て各自の內部的發展と充實を進め，更に汎く聯盟の範圍を擴充して，全世界に佛陀の慈悲の光を輝かし，人類平和の淨土建設の大事業に協力すべき，神聖なる使命の自覺と希望とを以て遂行せられたる光景は，今尙眼前に彷彿して居るのであります。

第一回大會の開かれた七月三十一日を以て，佛靑聯盟永久の記念日とする事を決議したのも，此會議の多くの收穫中の一つでありました。會期中四百名の大衆，而も六個國から集つて來た初對面の代表者並に會衆達が，佛敎徒であると言ふ共同意識の下に，一見舊知の如き打とけた感情と無我の精神とを以つて，萬事圓滿に結了したのを見て，「**佛陀の名に於て**」と言ふ事の偉大さを痛感させられたのであります。總會の最後に身に餘る重荷を背負はせられたのは，我日本を第二回大會の主催地と指定された事でありました。

歲月流るゝ如く，昨年の七月十八日より六日間，此の東京，而も本日の此の宏莊なる會場に於て，太平洋に因みある十三箇の佛敎國代表六百餘名の大集會を開き，世界的非常時に，直面しつゝある我々佛敎靑年聯盟として，爲

さねばならぬ當面の任務と，明日の佛靑職聯として執らねばならぬ進路とから，力强く注視して，佛誕二千五百年已來持つて傳へて來た眞實佛敎の指導原理を現代的に活かし，全世界の人間社會をして，常住のルンビニー園たらしめんために，十三佛敎國の固き固き握手を握り緊めた事は，實に言ひ知れぬ法悅の限りでありました。滿四年後の今日頃，將に開かるべき第三回の大會の如何に盛況を呈するであろうかを想像して，一層の歡喜に浸されざるを得ないのであります。

今日の記念日に方り遙かに過去二回の大會を追懷すると共に，近かく第三回の大會を豫想し，各方面多數の來賓の御參加で，この樣な盛會を見るに立ち到りし事を，佛陀の大前に合掌感謝の至りに堪へません。

尙ほ，來る昭和十五年(一九四〇年)に，我が神武紀元二千六百年を迎へる機會に，世界佛敎大會を我が東京で開催するの企劃あり，且つ其迄に佛靑會館の完成をも見せ，その新會堂にて，全世界の佛敎徒の一大會同を擧行せんとしてゐるのであります。

返す返すも各位の御指導と御協力とを請ふて止まない次第であります。

全聯と汎聯について

鷹谷俊之

この思出深い今月今日，佛靑記念デーが開催され，シャム公使ミトラカム・ラクシャ閣下，滿洲帝國謝大使閣下夫人，ネパール王族バハドル・シン，其他印度，ジャワ，北平，ハンガリー，ビルマ等から遙か海の彼方から御出でになつて居る方々と，同一宗敎に基き互に胸襟を開いて談じ合ふ機會が開けたことは誠に意味深いことである。

この機會に於いて「全聯と汎聯について」聊か所懷を述べることにする。但しこの事につきましては，旣に The International Buddhist Bulletin の No.1(四月號)に日本文で，又No.3(六月號)に英文で書いたものを發表して置いたから御高覽を得て居ることゝ思ふが，多少の重複は御諒恕を願ひたい。

我國の佛靑運動は近代に於いては明治十七八年頃（1884—1885）に高等學校，專門學校の間に佛敎靑年の團體が起つたのを手初めとして十九年に早稻田の敎友會，二十三年十月には慶應の三田佛敎會などが起つたが，明治二十五年一月六日帝國大學第一高等中學，東京專門學校(早稻田)，慶應，和佛法律學校及哲學館(東洋大學)等の官私諸學校に在學する佛敎靑年數十名が本鄕駒込眞淨寺に會し，住職寺田福壽師が產婆役となり島地默雷，大內靑巒など先輩の贊助の下に「大日本佛敎靑年會」を設立したのが大同團結の初めと見てよからう。この頃の運動としては釋尊

降誕の祝賀會と，夏季講習會の開催にあつたやうで，その後漸次東西兩帝大，第三，第五，山口の各高等學校及岡山醫專に佛敎青年會が生れ，千葉醫專の樹德會，仙臺第二中學の道交會，同第四中學の道友會，などの佛青團體が出來た。

これらの運動は幾十となき熱心な佛敎青年が原動力となつて行ひ來つたのであるが今私の存知する先輩で當時大に斡旋した方で生きて尙ほ佛敎の爲めに社會の爲に活動を續けて居られる人人を擧げると，柴田一能，安藤正純，常盤大定，來馬琢道，加藤咄堂，吉田賢龍，近角常觀，龍口了信，高島米峰，姉崎正治，高楠順次郎，本多辰次郎，荻野仲三郎，安藤嶺丸，寶閣善敎，土屋詮敎，田中普立，和田鼎，泉道雄，藤田順道，多田鼎，大槻快尊，北村敎嚴，神林周道，中山理賢等の大先輩である。

×

この大日本佛敎青年會は，その後，一弛一張があつたけれども，それから三十三年後の大正六年(1917)頃には小野清一郎，大村桂巖，中野實範，故藤岡勝二，干潟龍祥及木山十彰氏等によつて相當な活動を示し，殊に木山氏によつて早稻田に佛敎青年の寮舍が建てられて居た程である。尙ほこの頃から柴田一能師を主力として中央佛敎會館が神田の駿河臺に建てられ，大正十一年に見事竣工したが，殘念ながら彼の關東大震災で炎上して了つた。同じ頃から帝大を中心とした佛敎青年會は故木村泰賢，小野清一郎，干潟龍祥氏等によつて結ばれ，大震災のあとに會館が出來て今日尙ほ輝かしい活動を續けて居る。

×

昭和の三年頃になつて東京に佛敎青年協會が現はれて常光浩然，淺野孝之，長谷川良信，今成顯法，鹽入亮忠，藤井草宣，等其他の發起で起つたのであるが，これも一ケ年位で下火になり，昭和四年に常光浩然が歐米の視察を終つて歸朝した頃から，明年昭和五年（1930）にホノルルに於て汎太平洋に臨む各國の佛敎青年が集つて第一回汎太平洋佛敎青年會大會を開くことになり，柴田一能，立花俊道，大村桂巖，淺野孝之の諸氏及私の外日本各地から選ばれた人々三十七名が彼地に渡り五日間大に米布朝鮮印度の各代表と佛敎について現在及將來の問題を語り合つた。この時汎太佛青の常恒的機關の必要が提起され大に渴望されたのであつた。

昭和六年の四月三日を卜して，過去の大日本佛敎青年會を解消し，日本全體の佛青團體が一團となり，全日本佛敎青年會聯盟を結成し初代の理事長は高楠順次郎博士であり初代主事は常光浩然氏であつた。次いで立花俊道氏の理事長を經て次年は柴田一能師が理事長に就任し，主事には好村春輝氏が任命されたのであつた。この時が恰度第二回汎太佛青大會を，全聯主催で東京及京都で開く年に當つたのである。大會終了後大村桂巖氏が理事長に就任され，主事に稻葉文海氏が任命された。

本年はこの兩氏が揃つて重任し今日に及んで居るのである。以上述べたところを要約すると次の如くである。

1884(明治17)‥‥各學校の學生による佛敎的會合

1892(同25)‥‥大日本佛敎青年會結成

1928(昭和３)‥‥青年佛敎協會成立

1930(同５)‥‥第一回汎太大會（ホノルル）開催

1931(同６)‥‥全聯結成と同時に大日本佛青並に青年佛敎協會解消合流

△爾來每年，東京(第１回)，東京(2)，京都(3)，福岡(4)，金澤(5)，等で全聯總會開催

1935(昭９)‥‥第二回汎太洋佛青大會開催(東京及京都)

これで汎聯と全聯の大體の事情を述べたのである。

×

さて第一回の汎聯大會は參加國が五ケ國ではあつたが，是非共汎聯促成の必要ありとし熱心に之が結成を主張したが，時機尙早として實行を他日に延すことになり，委員を擧げて熟考することを約束した。次いで昨年の大會が開かれこの度は十三ケ國の代表が參加し，この度も汎聯常恒機關の切要が唱へられ，遂にその結成を見るに至つた但し各國代表は歸國後一ケ月中に各々汎聯の名譽委員中央委員を擧げて之を通告し，この實務は全聯で執ることに申し合せ，差し當りその斡旋を全聯に委托されたのである。然るにその後全聯から數回の督促を各國へ出して居るが乍遺憾いづれの國も此の約束を履行して吳れないので，全聯としては昨年の汎太大會の記念事業の一つたる國際佛敎通報局の設置と共に機關誌を本年四月から發行し，これに托して種々各國に働きかけ，約束の履行を迫り，太平洋沿岸各國の佛敎青年聯盟に覺醒を促しつゝある次第である。

×

汎聯の實際問題は相互の意志疏通と申し合せの實行とが目下の處重大意義を持つものと思ふ。これすら行はれぬとあつては到底存在の理由も認められない。こゝに御集りの諸賢はいづれも各國の有力な方々でありますから十二分に御力添を頂き，汎聯の實が擧がるやう御盡力願ひたいのである。

昭和十五年は我が日本の建國二千六百年に當りこの機會に世界佛敎大會を開くと云ふ議もちらほらありますが，若し左樣なことが事實となれば，一層のこと汎聯が動力となるに尤も相應しいものと思ひますから，今より心してこれが活潑に動いて行くやうに御盡力仰ぎたいのである。

日本の佛青運動はもはや一國の內の問題ではなく，東洋は勿論であるが，遠く西歐の佛敎徒と十分な握手をし，佛陀の眞精神に基いて廣くその理想を實現せねばならぬ時機に向ひつゝあるこの時に當り今日のよき機會が與へられたことは吳々も喜びに堪へない，最後に諸賢の御健康を祈念して止まない

國際佛教 Interview (No. 2)

ジャワ佛教會長　ヨシアス・ヴン・ディーンスト師
同副會長　J. W. de ウイット師

「ジャワの佛教會の會長が來てゐられるから‥‥」との全聯事務所からの電話だ。早速，飛んで來て見ると，全聯の隣りの國際親善協會の事務所で白髯の中島裁之會長と對談してゐるのがそれであつた。私の來訪を迎へて二人の長大人が立ち上ると，事務室が狹苦しく見える程，巨大な體軀だ。會長のディーンスト氏の手は握り切れないほど大きくがつちりしてゐる。副會長のウイツト氏はディーンスト氏の男性的なのに比べて，優しさうな面貌である。二人ともオランダ人で，ジャワのバタビヤに居住してゐるとの事。

「いつ日本へ來られました？」

「六月末に神戸に着きました。それから京都に行つて東西兩本願寺を初め有力な寺院に參拜し，昨日東京に參りました。」

「日本に來朝された御目的は？」

「ジャワに於ける事情を日本佛教界に紹介し，特に日本より佛教の宣教使をジャワに派遣して貰ひたいためです。」

「ジャワに於ける宗教事情は如何ですか。」

「ジャワ本島人，マレイ人の間にはマホメツト教の信仰が行はれてゐます。それに印度教と基督教の傳道が行はれてゐます。」

「あなた方のジャワ佛教協會はどんな活動をしてゐられますか？　又その會員はいく人です？」

「ジャワ佛教協會は 1929 年に創立しました。その後私（ディーンスト）はビルマに行きましたので，私に代つて Ernest Power 氏が會を董理して呉れました。私はビルマに於て 1931 年に International Buddhist Mission（國際佛教傳道會）を起し再びジャワに歸つて今日に至つて居ります。」

「會の御活動は如何です？」

「集會を行ひ，佛教に關する文書の出版を行つて居ます。」

「集會にはどんな人が集りますか？」

「ジャワの本島人，マレイ人，支那人等です。」

「一つの集會に何人位集りますか？」

「三百人とか四百人，五百人といふこともあります。」

「出版物はどんなものです？」

「雜誌としては月刊の “De Dhamma in Nederlandsch Indie” なるマレイ語のもの（12pages）と別に年四回の “Namo Buddhaya”（68p.）とを出してゐます。

「單行本では “Het Boeddhisme als Wereldbeschouwing, Moraal en Religie” (1934), “Het Boeddhisme der Soetta's” (1935) を旣刊しました。近く年内に “De Boeddha der Schriften” を發刊する豫定になつて居ります。」

以上の會見で第一日は別れた。

次いで十三日兩人の宿所である牛込區山吹町の翠松寮を訪れた。翠松寮はクリスチャンの丸山傳太郎氏の經營になるのである。佛教の僧侶が基督教徒の宿舍に泊らねばならぬといふのは，未だ日本の佛教徒の國際的設備が足りないためである。併し丸山氏は broad minded の方だから，この兩佛教徒も快よくこゝに泊つてゐるやうだ。

今日は先日の話に引續いで新しい質問を發した。副會長のウイツト氏はそばにゐるが，主として會長のディーンスト氏と問答する。

「あなたが佛教に入信された動機は何ですか？」

「私はかつて救世軍の士官を勤めてゐたことがあるが，基督教の創造神に疑惑を持ち，その信仰を失つた。23歲の時に故 Paul Carus 氏の『佛陀の福音』を讀んで佛教に興味を持ち初めました。その後 Paul Dahlke の著書や，その他佛教哲學の書物に親しむやうになつて，すつかり佛教に歸依いたしました。」

「基督教と佛教との教義の相違を何處に見出されますか？」

「基督教の神は人間と隔絕してゐて嫉妬深くありますが，佛陀は我々人間の完成したもので，我々も佛陀たり得る所に大きな相違があります。」

「あなたは失禮ですが，御結婚なすてゐらつしやるのでせうか。」

「勿論です，私はmonkではありません，priest ですから，窮屈な戒律などには拘泥しないのです。

「戒律に就て，どう御考へですか？」

「私は大乘戒律を主張します。先頃日本にも來られたセイロンのナーラダ師なども，比丘は金錢に手を觸れないと云ひ乍ら海外旅行には船の切符を買つてゐるではありませんか？　つまり戒律の形式でなく精神を採れと云ふのですね?!

「日本佛教に對する御見解は？」

「日本佛教は世界で最も有力であると思ひます。而して日本では佛教の感化が實際に及んで平和が保たれて居ります。ヨーロツパの政局が絕えず紛糾してゐるのに比べると非常な違ひです。」

「あなた方は一生佛教の傳道使として終るつもりですか？」

「さうです。この尊い教へのために身命を捧げたいと思つてゐます。有力な日本の佛教徒がジャワに於ける傳道事業に協力して下さることを切望いたします。」

尙聞けばオランダ領印度はジャワ，スマトラ等の植民地の人口を合して四千二百萬人ださうだが，その中で佛教の傳道のために盡してゐるのは，この人達を加へて四人だけださうだ。この稀有な佛教の戰士に對して，日本佛教徒は何分の積極的援助を與へるべきだと思ふ。（×××）

Starigo de Budaisma Sociologio

de Ken Assano

En la printempo de la jaro 1929-a, kiam ni studadis en Eŭropo, en Sorbona Universitato en Parizo oni okazigis la inaŭguran kunsidon de la Instituto Franca-Japana por Studo de Budaismo sub la prezido de prof. Sylvain Lévi, mondofama hindologo, kiu vizitis Japanujon antaŭ jaroj, per antaŭpreparo de s-ro S. Muto kaj aliaj.

En tiu tago ankaŭ mi ĉeestis en la kunsido. La plimulto de tiamaj japanaj ĉeestantoj estis ĉirkaŭ dek studantoj, kiuj tiam loĝis kaj studadis en Parizo, (inter ili mi memoras s-rojn Masataka Fuĵioka, Kaoru Ôtani, Kan'ei Okamoto, Tacuŝo Juge kaj aliaj). S-ro Entai Tomomacu venis Parizon por la kunsido el Hajdelbergo, la universitata urbo de suda Germanujo.

De la flanko de francoj partoprenis, krom jam menciita prof. Sylvain Lévi, prof. Paul Pelliot kaj aliaj unuaklasaj orientologoj kaj ili konsiliĝis por fondi la novan instituton.

Ĉu vi demandas, legantoj, — Kiel rilatas la priskribo al la temo? — Sed momenton atendu.

Pri la problemo, ĉar mi volis mencii ĉi tie, ke en la reguloj de ĉi tiu instituto—dum kies verkado ĉefe laboris prof. Lévi kaj s-ro Odin, ankaŭ mi mem aktive kunlaboris, —sintrovis unu paragrafo "La Sociologia Studo de Budaismo." Ĉi tiu paragrafo estis proponita de mi mem, kaj tuj akceptita. Vere tiu "sociologia studo de Budaismo" estis aprobita ĝenerale de scientistoj en Eŭropo kaj Ameriko,—precipe inter francaj sciencistoj, ĝi estis aprobita sen ia dubo, kontraŭe kun forta fervoreco. Ĉar plimulto de francaj orientologoj estas sociologoj kaj estas fakto, ke almenaŭ ili ricevis multan influon de Durkheim-skolo.

Kiel mi skribis supre, ĉi tiu paragrafo la "sociologia studo de Budaismo" insiste proponita de ni estas aprobita de la kunlaborinto s-ro Odin, kaj prof. Lévi ankaŭ rimarkis ĝian gravecon.

Tiam mi skribis en mia informo "El Parizo" sendita al la ĵurnalo *Ĉûgai-nippô* kaj ankaŭ en la traktato sendita al la gazeto "*Sociologia Revuo*", la progreson de la religia sociologio en Francujo, kaj precipe menciis pri katolika sociologio, kiu stariĝis en la lastaj jaroj. Kaj mi menciis ankaŭ, ke en la unika plej alta studejo Kolegio de Francujo jam ekzistas la lekcio de Sociologio kaj Sociografio Mahometanismaj, kiun lekciis prof. Louis Massignon. Plie mi konfesis, ke en Japanujo ankaŭ la klopodo de la studantoj devas esti direktata al la starigo de la Budaisma Sociologio, ĉar en nia lando budaismaj fenomenoj sin prezentas sur sociaj faktoj.

Efektive en la Katolika Instituto de Parizo jam malfermis sociologian fakon, kaj oni vigle studadas katolikan sociologion. Tie grupiĝantaj sociologoj katolikaj vigle laboradas kontraŭ la sociologisma Durkheim-skolo kritikante ĝin por konstrui propran sistemon en paroladoj kaj en verkado, kaj kompreneble jam estas publikigitaj kelkaj libroj kun titolo "Katolika Sociologio."(1)

Sed tamen ĝis hodiaŭ en Japanujo, kiu estas la lando de la plej aktive laborantaj budaanoj, Budaisma Sociologio ankoraŭ ne estis proponita. Pro kio la fakto povas esti? Plie Japanujo estas unika laŭ la multeco de lernejoj dependaj de budaanaro, la nombro de universitatoj kaj kolegioj budaismaj kalkuliĝas pli ol dek, sed ni ne konas eĉ unu, en kiu oni havas regulan lekcion de Budaisma Sociologio. Laŭeble kaj malofte nur estas legataj la verkoj de Durkheim aŭ Weber, k. t. p., eĉ tio estas limigita, pro lingva malfacileco nur inter malmultaj studentoj en budaismaj universitatoj. Tute senbezone diri, ke ŝajne estas lasata netuŝite kiel virga arbaro, lerninte tiun metodologion de ĝenerala religia sociologio kaj aplikante ĝin por studo de Budaismo.

Kial oni ne donas lekcion de Budaisma Sociologio, kiu estas pli grava kaj pli utila speciala scienco ol tiun de ĝenerala sociologio en universitatoj de budaismaj sektoj?

(1) Kiel ekzemple:
L'Abbé Naudet: *Premiers principes de sociologie catholique*, 2e éd. Paris, 1901.
R. P. A. Belliot (O. F. M.): *Manuel de sociologie catholique. Histoire-Théorie-Pratique*, Paris, Lethielleux, 1910.
Georges Legrand: *Les grands courands de la sociologie catholique à l'heure présente*, Paris, Editions Spes, 1927.
Plie sur la vidpunkto de sociologio katolika estis kompilita kaj eldonita la vortaro ĉi-suba: *Dictionnaire de sociologie, familiale, politique, économique, générale*, par l'abbé Thomas Mainage (Prof. à l'Institut catholique de Paris), 2 vol. Paris, Lib. Létonzet et Ané.

Se tio estas kaŭzita nur pro manko de kompetentuloj, oni povas disponi junajn studantojn al ĝi. En ĉia ajn kondiĉo ni atendas la tagon, en kiu nia ĉi propono estos realigata. Ne nur por tio, ni volas klopodadi por starigo de ĉi tiu fekunda nova fako de sciencoj, Budaisma Sociologio, kun sincera kritiko kaj konsento de kleruloj en la mondo.

Starigo de la nova lekcio de Budaisma Sociologio ne estas tiel facile realigata, ĉar oni renkontos kontraŭdiron, ke tia ne ekzistas eĉ en Eŭropo. Sed ĝi ne povas esti preteksto por ke en Japanujo oni ne malfermu la lekcion, kiu ne sintrovas en Eŭropo. Aŭ tia kontraŭdiro povus esti ne prezentata jam en nuna Japanujo. Kvankam tian sensencan oni ĝis nun devis renkonti ofte en estinteco en japana sfero de edukistoj, kie regis senkritika imitado. Ankaŭ en ĉiu universitato privata aŭ sekta same regis imitado senkritika kaj senoriginala. Sed nun male ni devas esti tiel kuraĝa, ke ni progresigu la studon kaj starigu specialan sciencon en japanaj universitatoj, precipe en tiuj apartenataj al budaismaj sektoj, kies ekzisto estas originala kaj speciala nur en Japanujo, kaj prezenti ĝin al eŭropa sciencistaro, ĉar ĝi ne ekzistas en eŭropaj universitatoj. Plie tia kultura taske jam estis destinita sur la ŝultroj de japanaj budaanoj kaj budaismaj studejoj. Ankaŭ oni povus prave diri ke efektive tia internacia partoprenado devas esti nun farata de japanaj sciencistoj kaj tion atendas internacia scientista rondo.

Kvankam mi ne intencas prediki aŭ naciismon aŭ tut-azianismon, sed mi rekomendas Japanujon kiel la patrujon de ĉi tiu nova scienco, ĉar vere nur en Japanujo, en Orienta Azio, sintrovas multaj eblecoj historie kaj geografie por studado de Budaisma Sociologio.

Kiel en kristanisma socio naskiĝis Kristanisma Sociologio, kaj precipe en Francujo, katolika lando, estis progresigita Katolika Sociologio, ankaŭ kiel en Anglujo, kiu regas Hindujon, progresis Hindologio, kaj kiel en Francujo, kiu posedas grandan kolonion en Afriko loĝata de multaj mahometanoj, estas studata Mahometanisma sociologio, tiel same en Oriento, precipe en Japanujo, la budaana lando, la studo de Budaisma Sociologio estas starigata kaj progresas, kaj tio estas tute natura afero, kaj ĝi estas nepra rezultato de homa kulturo, kaj ĝi devas esti unu granda kontribuo de japana sciencistaro al internacia

kulturo.

Ĉu vere, en nuna tago, la lando, en kiu Budaismo daŭrigas sian vivon kaj funkcias plej forte, sendube estas Japanujo, "la lando plej taŭga por Mahajano" de Ekstrema Oriento? Oni diras en sia naskiĝlando, Hindujo, Budaismo nun vivas ne tiel vigle, kontraŭe floras nur la unua Bramanismo, kiun nomis budaanoj hereza, la dua Kristanismo nove enportita. Ankaŭ en Ĉinujo Budaismo nun estas kvazaŭ kastrita kaj fariĝis brokantaĵo?

Tiel observante, se oni serĉas iun landon, kiu havas taŭgan pozicion, kaj kiu povas iom ajn gvidi universalan budaisman movadon, (neparolante pri la kompetenteco,) ŝajnas al ni, neniu lando troviĝas krom Japanujo, ĉar japana socio estas multe pli budaisma socio, kaj tie estas sufiĉe preta budaima grundo, kiel mi supre priskribis.

Estus insisto ne troa, se mi diras, ke Budaisma Sociologio, kiun ni volas studi kiel unu novan sciencon, havas sorton, ke ĝi kresku en tiu tero, t. e. japana socio plimulte budaismeca, ĉar ĝi posedas plimulte da budaismaj faktoj.

La plia problemo kuŝas en studmaniero. Ĉi tiu studmetodo de eŭropaj sciencistoj ŝajnas al tiuj, kies kapo kutimiĝis kun dogmoj instrui ĉion en du kategorioj, aŭ ortodoksa aŭ hereza, ke ĝi estas konsterniga, nekomprenebla, blasfema, kontraŭ digno de Budaismo. Ankaŭ troviĝas iuj, kiuj kvankam iom komprenantaj, nekomprenas internan esencon, aŭ kortuŝite de io negrava, imitas mallerte; tio estas ridinda.

Tiamaniere ni estas kondukata de nur malmultaj eŭropaj sciencistoj. Preninte ilian bonan metodon, longe resti en tia stato estas por ni granda bedaŭro. Eble en Japanujo, kvankam kie sintrovas tre abunde budaismaj fenomenoj kiel sociaj faktoj, mankis metodo, per kiu oni efike kaj sufiĉe trakti ilin en la lumo de moderna scienco, alivorte por ĝi estas preta la materialoj sed mankas la maŝino por utiligi ilin. Tial ĉe nia flanko antaŭ ĉio ni devas prepari la maŝinon kaj plibonigi ĝin kaj lerni ĝian uzadon. Ekpaŝo de ĉiu scienca studo devas esti ellerno de metodo. Kaj por ni tiu ĝisnuna spekulativa aŭ metafizika metodo jam ne taŭgas sufiĉe. Nia metodo devas esti pli pozitiva. Ĝi devas esti metodo de Budaisma Sociologio kiel unu nova scienco.

Tiamaniere komenciĝas la konstrua laboro de Budaisma Sociologio. Kaj tio ja estas al ni donata fundamenta problemo.

Japanese News

Lake Festival

On August 17 and 18 a festival was held on Lake Biwa which was the most elaborate held on this gem of water for several years.

The affair was sponsored by the Sight-seeing Society of Shiga Prefecture. There were boat races, lanterns were lit and set adrift over the water, and there was a fireworks display.

In addition there were masquerades on the shore and the youths and maidens of the villages along the lake danced Bon Odori. Over 200,000 persons gathered in Otsu to watch the out-of-door entertainments.

Literature Masterpieces

To introduce Japanese literature abroad, the Society for the Promotion of International Culture hasundertaken to translate some representative works.

Among the authors selected are Soseki Natsume, Toson Shimazaki, Kan Kikuchi, Junichiro Tanizaki and Riichi Yokomitsu.

In Praise of Lotus

Not for 70 years has there existed in Tokyo a society in praise of the lotus. But recently botaniste and scholars have revived the old custom of gathering together people who admire the queen of summer flowers.

A party was recently held at the Agedashi restaurant in Uyeno which was attended by 80 lovers of the lotus. Dr. Kichi Miyake spoke on the origin of the lotus party in the Yedo period, and how the members went together to see the flowers open at dawn. Mr. Tsuzei Kono, the artist, talked on his appreciation of the lotus. Others gave talks on their pleasure at the sight of the flowers.

In the center of the room lotus flowers were beautifully arranged.

The moving sprits of the lotus society are Dr. Tomitaro Kakino the botanist; Dr. Tatsukich Irisawa, the physician; and Dr. Ryuzo Torii, the archeologist.

Hearn Anniversary

The 30th anniversary of the death of Lafcadio Hearn will be observed in Tokyo in September.

The Society for the Promotion of International Cultural Relations and the Greek Society will have charge of a meeting to honor Hearn on September 27.

Although Hearn was British born and accomplished much of his literary work in the United States before he came to Japan, these two countries have not done much to recognize Hearn's contribution to literature.

Priest as Soldier

Count Kosho Otani, abbot of the Nishi Honganji of Kyoto, has passed the physical examination for soldiers recently held at primary school in Nakano, the suburb of Tokyo.

The priestly soldier will enter Army service in October.

School for 2nd Generation Japanese

To prepare second generation Japanese who have graduated from high schools abroad for college coure in Japan, the Waseda Kokusai Gakuin (Waseda International School) will be opened on September 10 at 550, Ichome, Totsukamachi Yodabashi-ku, Tokyo.

The staff of the institute, which has already been officially recognized by the Prefectural authorities, comprises President Tanaka of Waseda University and Dr. Shotei Shiozawa as advisers, Dr. Yamamoto as president, Dr. Natori for manager, and Dr. Riichiro Hotari and Dr. H. B. Benninghoff as trustees.

School work will commence on September 10. Applications will be accepted during the summer. Those with little knowledge of Japanese will be entered in the first year class. More advanced students into the second year form. The students will be taught Japanese, Chinese classics, English, mathematics and Japanese culture. Applications for the institute have already reached more than half of its capacity.

Shimpukuji Library In Nagoya

In the premises of the Shimpukuji, a local temple famous for its collection of 15,000 rare books, including 28 sets specially protected by the government as national treasures, the reconstruction of a library has been recently completed under supervision of the special committee on which Marquis Yoshichika Tokugawa and Dr. Katsumi Kuroita sit.

The new structure in its outward appearance is built after the Amitabha temple in the Kamakura period. But the two-story building is of ferro-concrete and boasts of the most consummate protection of precious books. It covers an area of 32.1 tsubo.

The noted collection, which is called the Shimpukuji library or the Osu books, contains classical works on Japanese histry, literature, Shintoism, Buddhism, and Chinese classics. The most precious among these books is said to be the oldest edition of "Kojiki." Most of the copies are dated from the 14th century.

Foreign Students' Quarters

A building for foreign students studying in Japanese universities will shortly be established in Tokyo by the Cultural Enterprises Section of the Foreign Office, according to a Hochi report.

Concrete plans have already been formulated for the establishment of university quarters which may compare favorably with the building in Paris for foreign students there.

As a preparatory work for the main project, the establishment of dormitories is contemplated for the accommodation of students from Siam, India, the Philippines, the Dutch East Indies and other parts of the world.

The reports will probably be completed by the end of this autumn, the Hochi says.

Art Objects to Brussels

The Royal Museum of Fine Arts at Brussels will celebrate its centenary this year, and in this connection the Society for the Promotion of International Cultural Relations will send some art objects characteristic of Japan.

Among the articles selected is an old gold screen with a design of bamboo, other screens decorated with pieces of old brocade, and a reproduction of a lantern of Todaiji at Nara.

The gifts are to be sent through the courtesy of the Belgium Ambassador, Baron Bassompierre.

Golden Hall of Tennoji

The Golden Hall of Tennoji, the famous old temple of Osaka, which was destroyed by the typhoon a year ago has been reconstructed.

On August 3 at 2 p. m. a celebration has been held on the completion of the work. The roof of the building which was formerly made of tiles has now been constructed with bronze sheets. The imposing main gate and pagoda which were collapsed at the time of the high wind are also to be restored.

Buddhirt Art.

An exhibition of Buddhist art from the Suiko period to the Tokugawa age has been held at Kongobuji of Koyasan August 15 to 21.

This is an unusual opportunity to view the art-treasures which are preserved in the temples.

Zojoji Art

Beginning from the first of August Zojoji has shown to the public until the end of the month the art treasures for which this old temple is noted.

No other place in Tokyo is so closely associated with Yedo, and those interested in Buddhist art have been able to view some of the finest examples in the city.

Modern Priests

Buddhist priests as baseball players is something new in the religious circles of Japan. The young priests of the great Buddhist center, Honganji in Tsukiji, recently organized teams and played against each other.

Casting aside their priestly robes the priests donned the regulation garb of the game.

The head of the temple in the ancient costume of his Sect of Buddhism pitched off.

In this departure from the strict and narrow way, in dances with the parishioners of the temple, and other activities, the Honganji priests have demonstrated that although they may entone the scriptures of a thousand years, they have gone strictly modern in keeping in touch with the life of the present.

Statue of Jizo

A statue of Jizo which is soon to be cast in bronze has an interesting history.

Mr. Tokusaku Ishibashi, sergeant-at-arms of the House of Peers, lost his third son five years ago. The child fell into a well in the garden and was drowned.

The father wished to erect a statue of Jizo to the memory of his son and planned to collect a million sen from those in sympathy with his idea.

Prince Tokugawa and Mr. Eisaku Wada, President of the Academy of Fine Arts were among his supporters. Some persons sent contributions of Yen 5 or Yen 10, but Mr. Ishibashi would not accept more that one sen.

Now after five years, a million

have been collected, and the model of the statue has been made. The final casting of the statue will soon be accomplished.

In Memory of Hearn

The observance of the anniversary of the death of Lafcadio Hearn which was to have been held in September under the auspices of the Society for the Promotion of International Cultural Relations has been cancelled.

The reason for this sudden termination of a plan to honor Hearn comes from the fact that the Cultural Society did not consult the person most concerned,—namely, Kazuo, the son of the best literary interpreter of Japan in English.

Moreover, Mr. Kazuo Hearn, who leads a quiet life, and has no relation with the society active in remembering his father, informed the society that his father's 30th anniversary was celebrated last year, and that the anniversary of his death falls September 26 not 27, the date announced by the Cultural Society.

Tomb of Educator

Miss Helen Parkhurst of New York city, a delegate to the Pan-Pacific Educational conference in Tokyo, before her departure visited the tomb of Masataro Yanagisawa, founder of the Dalton education system in Japan.

The late Mr. Yanagisawa was formerly Minister of Education and President of the Seijo School in Tokyo. He introduced the Dalton system to Japan. His tomb is in the Yanaka cemetery.

Baron Dan's Art Collection

Baron Ino Dan, one of the directors of the Society for the Promotion of International Cultural Relatons, who is leaving for the United States this month as a representative of the society, is taking with him a rare collection which he will present to some American museum.

The beautiful articles he has gathered together, some 500 in number, consist of gorgeous hair ornaments, lacquered articles used by ladies of Old Japan and beautiful kimono worn by the daughters of daimyo during the Tokugawa regime.

The collection will be exhibited in the cities Baron Dan visits, and will eventually become the permanent possession of a museum.

中華民國主要佛教居士團體一覽表

好村春輝

例言

茲に中國に於ける主要な居士團體の一覽表を紹介する。

この表を見てわかることは，下の通りである。

居士團の事業の種類としては，聯合會，學校，監獄感化會，居士林佛學社，正信會，蓮社，佛書流通處，醫院，孤兒院，放生會，念佛會，研究社，佛學會，淨業社，宣講所，功德林，講經法會，衞教，布施等である。

この中，居士の自行に屬する求道的，修養的な催しは念佛會，研究會，法會等である。化他の對社會的事業は學校，監獄教誨，孤兒院，佛書刊行，講經講演，病院等である。

而して居士團のこれらの活動は，民國革命以來頓に活潑となり，特に最近の十數年は加速度的に發展してゐる。これは中國の政情が安定したのと，一つは新時代の思想と順應して佛教の革新を遂げやうとする熱意の現れである。

中國は今丁度日本の明治維新後のやうな政治的改革期に臨んでゐる。これが自ら宗教その他の文化にも影響してゐる。今後この趨勢は益々助長せられるであらう。

江蘇省

名稱	地址	成立年時	宗旨	現況及人數	會中附設之機關
世界佛教居士林	上海閘北新民路	民國十一年	佛教々義之修學及宣傳 世界佛教同志之聯絡及交換智識 社會事業之隨力舉辦	林友二千除人 駐林辦事者七人	私立第一小學校，放生會 佛教流通處，施醫藥處
西方法會	上海西門唐家灣茄勒路法藏寺	十五年五月	專修淨土，逢星期日，聚會念佛	念佛聽講者約二百餘人	佛學研究社
佛教淨業社	上海赫德路十九號覺園	十五年丙寅十一月	集合佛教信徒，闡揚佛法，精神淨業，盡力舉辦各種利濟慈善事業	社員約七百名	江蘇佛教聯合會，中國佛教會，佛教維持會，監獄感化會
吳淞佛教居士林	吳淞張華濱鎭	十四年乙丑七月	勤修淨土	林友四百餘	慈善事業設立義務兩等小學校
佛教慈幼院	南京下關三汊河	十五年	由居士捐辦教	員職及學生一百三十餘人	放生會，慈悲醫室
支那內學院	南京半邊街公字四號	十一年任戊	分學科事科兩部進行學科有研究部事科撰編印藏要		佛教流通處
淨慈蓮社	南京城內鐵湯池接引庵水月庵	同治光緒年間		每年九月二十日起七二十六日圓滿並舉行放生	
泰縣佛教居士林	泰縣南門內回子牌坊大街	十五年十一月	出版，佛化週刊並經理海潮音月刊	林友四百四十餘人	佛經流通處，淨業社 演講團，放生會，利生處
泰縣功德林	泰縣城外坡子大街	十三年成立	每日念佛一次，常年放生		佛教瀏覽處
無錫佛學宣化處	無錫城內盛巷橋街	十五年三月	流通佛法代送善書賭機出外勸化說閱經室任人借閱歡迎贈助經書由誠昌貿易所扣利金作常費		
淨林蓮社	無錫北門外黃埠墩	十七年十一月	逢朔望上午九時延請參霞法師演講	社友六十餘人	
無錫女蓮社聯合會	無錫南門內第三師範後花園弄底第二號		此社專考察各女蓮社成績並宏揚淨土以期精進	卽以城鄉各蓮社社員爲會員總數約一萬有	
無錫北下鄉女蓮社	無錫東門外東亭鎭東皋庵	十三年甲子		共有女蓮社二十處 合約千八百餘人	北下鄉佛學會,十六年成立，會員二十餘人，房舍現在建築中
無錫萬安市女蓮社	無錫西北鄉石塘灣暫寓孫克濟居士宅	十三年甲子		有女蓮社十七處 合約二千人	高安市佛學會 十六年成立會員二十餘人 每月出版佛化一次，代送經像 放生惜字社
莘莊佛學推行社	蘇州齊門外，莘莊安義盛號轉	十四年六月	宣傳佛法社址在南天竺普眞寺 由傳心師主持春秋二季講經會	衆約百人	
泖城蓮池會	蘇州婁門外泖城東，嶽廟	十一年冬月	由周頌堯居士等發起會務 由傳德師主事	會員五十餘人	
貞節淨土院	興化縣劉莊場		現擬改名佛教安老院尙未定定章嚴格辦理妥善規模亦宏大爲女衆辦道所在地惟絕不預外務進院者來歷淸白老實發心者爲合格		
莘莊佛學社	常熟南門外豐祿橋張萬興米行轉				
醫學書局	上海梅白格路宏昌里一百二十一號		關於佛籍出版頗豐富有 佛學大辭典發行		
蘇州佛經流通處	蘇州城內玄妙觀西瑪瑙山房				
寶山佛教居士林	江蘇寶山縣南門內				
佛學書局	上海				
三藏蓮社	南京南門外雨花台三藏殿	十五年五月	宏揚淨業	僧人七名居士約三百人	閱經處 長生會
資生極樂會	南京漢西門內四根桿子普照精舍	五年丙辰四月	每年四次佛七每月二課 每日香二支會	均有定課每月十六日及各佛誕舉行	念佛放生會
西林蓮社	無錫西門外迎龍橋西林禪寺	十年正月	逢星期日念佛二時逢星期二到縣監獄講因果淨土	社員七八十人	往生互助會 監獄感化分會
東林蓮社	無錫東門外綠蘿菴	十七年九月	逢朔望念佛並請西林蓮社主講參霞法師講演因果淨土	社員五六十人	
鄒呂巷總蓮社	無錫北下鄉九里橋鄒呂巷	十七年		無處約百人 共有男女社友約一千餘人	分社九處
無錫佛學會	無錫南門內第三師範後花園弄底第二號	十四年乙丑		會員七八十人	無錫佛教慈濟會 一心精舍

無錫同願佛會	同上	十　年辛　酉	專以同願生西爲主	會員六十人分十二人爲一組	
無錫城區女蓮社	同上	十　年辛　酉		共有九處合計約千人	
無錫懷上市女蓮社	無錫東北鄉陳家橋滸村徐義莊內	十四年乙　丑		共有女蓮社二十五處合約二千餘人	懷上市佛學會十六年成立會員二十餘人
無錫天下市女蓮社	無錫北鄉八士橋石華濱華永千居士宅	十四年乙　丑		共有女蓮社十一處合約九百人	天下市佛學會十六年成立會員十餘人
無錫開原鄉女蓮社		十二年癸　亥		共有女蓮社八處合約七百人	
無錫揚名鄉女蓮社		十三年甲　子		共有女蓮社七處合約五百人	
無錫天上市女蓮社		十六年丁　卯		共有女蓮社四處合約五百人	
淨業社	蘇州齊門外呂舍鎮局收轉北式涇城隍廟內	十六年冬	每年舉行佛七二次	會員一百餘人	放生會
掘港佛教因利會	江蘇如皋掘港市西方寺	十四年九　月	以救濟貧民生計爲主旨	由範成和尙與祝時純居士等，籌集基金一千六百元二千餘戶	
乾明念佛會	江蘇高郵乾明寺	十五年春	每逢春間念佛四十九天秉宣講淨宗經典	會員百餘人	每月放生會並放四鄉小巷設，蓮社，以資普利，送診施藥局
陽羨女蓮社	宜興縣裕成煤鐵號嚴子和居士轉	十五年		共有女蓮社三十六處合共約四千人	
藏文學院	上海勞勃生路蠶治大學				

浙江省

名稱	地址	成立年時	宗旨	現況及人數	會中附設之機關
佛學蓮社	杭州湖墅倉基上	十一年六　月	逢三六九朔望講經每月舉行放生一次	社員四百餘人	
祥符橋蓮社	杭州三墩鎮祥符橋		逢朔望講演開示一次逢八念佛	社員一百餘人	
佛經研究社	衢縣東鄉巖頭村三藏寺	十七年六　月		會員二十餘人常住研究者七八人	
樂清佛教居士林	樂清虹橋	十　年			佛教流通處，研究會薦亡所，放生會，橫超蓮社
嘉善佛教會	嘉善西塘塔灣雁塔禪院	十　年十一月	修持淨土	會員六百三十餘人	戒殺放生會，懺摩會
大雲佛學社	紹興城內泥牆弄十一號			有大雲月刊發行	
剡溪總蓮社	嵊縣城內圓超寺	十三年十一月		係張德威等居士創辦總社之外又分社十餘處如次列社員共計約有二三千人	
長樂蓮社	嵊縣長樂鎮福芬草堂馬契慈轉廣德禪院	十四年閏		係馬居士等發起社員二百餘名	
馬仁村蓮社	同上	十四年四　月		社員一百三十名	
崇仁蓮社	嵊縣崇仁鎮上段女子小學校密鳳仙轉五房	十五年	每月逢初二十六日念佛係密鳳仙馬契慈寺發起	社員二百二十餘名	
新昌蓮社	新昌縣南門	十七年二　月	逢朔望初八廿三念佛講經由馬契慈居士及妙智師等發起	社友二百餘人	南明放生會
瑪瑙經房	杭州弼教坊				
慧空經房	杭州錢塘門內昭慶寺				
錦泰經房	寗波定海普陀山				

名稱	地址	成立年時	宗旨	現況及人數	會中附設之機關
杭州功德林	杭州新市場龍翔橋				
杭州佛學會	杭州西湖長生路	民國十六年	修持研究宏揚佛法	鐘康侯主辦	講經念佛，放生利濟
杭州定課念佛同志會	杭州新市場，龍翔橋一九九號	念 三年六月十日	專宏淨土	徐萬濟 劉因渠主辦	念佛

安徽省

名稱	地址	成立年時	宗旨	現況及人數	會中附設之機關
懷寗佛教聯合念佛社	安慶懷寗西鄉洪鎮鋪	十五年四月	每月朔望集衆念佛	會員五百餘人	佛教惜字會
安慶念佛林	安慶西門外地藏庵幽居講寺		按週集四衆故寺念佛一度	林友已達千餘人	
安慶佛學圖書館	安慶舊藩署閱經樓	十六年八月	經費支絀暫難擴充而所存卷數頗多足敷應用		
安慶閱經樓	同上	十一年四月	由安徽佛教會等募建供大藏經讀藏經及各宗經典按週四衆齊集念佛聽經		
佛光社	婺源縣江灣市	十四年六月	演講淨土壇施處辦理施衣藥放生等事宜社刊已出至第三期	社友八百七十五人 常到念佛者數千人	
江灣佛光社	同上	同上	專弘淨土	社長江易園 方振民 總務主任江有明	講經念佛放生利濟

江西省

名稱	地址	成立年時	宗旨	現況及人數	會中附設之機關
南昌念佛林	南昌貢院背佑民寺	十七年三月	逢星期日男居士念佛 女居士念佛	四百餘人	
九江蓮舍	九江六角石	十三年七月	平時以朔望初八廿三爲念佛常期	男女衆四百餘人	利濟部閱經室

湖北省

名稱	地址	成立年時	宗旨	現況及人數	會中附設之機關
女佛學院	武昌鼓架坡	十三年		現有八九人 傍聽者約二十餘人	平民小學
宜昌佛教會	宜昌藥王宮				
漢口佛教正信會	福建巷		是武昌佛學院民衆宣傳有力機關	李子寬 太虛大師 施藥二萬圓宣傳費數千圓施米數千圓施寒衣數千圓	

湖南省

名稱	地址	成立年時	宗旨	現況及人數	會中附設之機關
壽光林	武岡高沙佛戒洲	十四年冬	宏揚淨土	七八十人 現住居士七八人	

佛聲社	湘鄉瀔水惠春和轉喬木堂	十一年八月	以研究佛學宏法濟生爲宗旨	社友二十餘人均教育界人士	起民書報社 盼各方贈助經報
法界新蓮社	武岡石下江竹市生堂轉			唐太圓	
湖南佛教居士林	長沙沙河街六〇號	二十年十月	以宏揚佛法自他兼利爲宗旨		
湘潭居士分林		二十二年二月	分林與總林同		
湘陰居士分林		二十一年十一月			
瀏陽居士分林		二十一年六月			
澧陵居士分林		二十一年五月			
桂陽居士分林		二十二年四月			

四川省

名稱	地址	成立年時	宗旨	現況及人數	會中附設之機關
成都佛學社	成都少城公園	十一年四月	由成都佛經流處擴大改組社員皆居士	共四百餘人	恤嫠團 紡終團一組
江口居士叢林	彭山縣江口鎮油房溝山內	七年春	專修淨土頗操勞作苦行		
重慶佛學社	重慶長安寺		流通修持	社員六百餘人	

福建省

名稱	地址	成立年時	宗旨	現況及人數	會中附設之機關
福建功德林	福州南門兜白塔		每星期逢三六衆念佛地藏會	社友二百餘人 女七百餘人	福建全省佛教會 佛經流通處，蓮社
泉州慈兒院	泉州開元寺	十五年		現有孤兒八十人	
閩南佛學院	廈門南普陀寺內	十三年		現況尙稱發達	佛化策進會 十三年成立
南山佛化學校	漳州南山寺	十六年三月	初學部依新學制分前後期 專門部暫分佛哲國學英算三科六年		學生自治會
廈門佛經流通處	廈門火燒街十六號				
福州女佛化社	福州市貢院埋二八號	十四年四月	寺修淨業		研究佛學宏法利生
邵陽居士林	邵陽東門外九	二十三年三月			
武岡居士林		二十二年四月			

廣東省

名稱	地址	成立年時	宗旨	現況及人數	會中附設之機關
潮郡念佛社	潮安東提高華里		逢星期日及佛誕集衆禮誦並舉行放生善會	社員五十人	閱經處
震旦密教重興會	潮安縣義安路一百六十二號	十三年			潮州佛教流通處及潮州刻經處
楞嚴佛學社	廣州仰忠街二十一號	十四年四月	恢復佛掃除腐化障礙	社友三百餘人	佛經圖書館

貴州省

名稱	地址	成立年時	宗旨	現況及人數	會中附設之機關
淨因蓮社	貴陽寶蓮寺	二年	一心念佛	社衆千餘人	佛教流通處放生會
佛教居士林	貴陽威西門愛蘭精舍	十六年		林衆二百餘人	放生會，惜字會，施醫藥處
佛教貧民學校	遵義縣	二年		學生六百餘人	

河北省

名稱	地址	成立年時	宗旨	現況及人數	會中附設之機關
三時學會	北平北長街十五號	十六年九月	以講演佛學爲宗旨		
佛寶旬刊社	北平新街口西街五十八號	十六年四月	每日出報三期一千三百餘份	社員四人	
佛經流通處	北平東城大佛寺	九年七月		職員四人	
鷲峯念佛會	北平西單牌樓臥佛寺十九號鷲峯寺				北平恤嫠會，養老院
萬壽山佛教居士林	北平西四寶禪寺街九號廣善寺		現正建築屋宇爲清修講學之所		
婦女蓮社	北平府右街皇城振東口唐家		專修淨業		
慈幼院	北平香山		國內慈幼機關之最大者	現有男女貧兒千餘名	
感化學院	北平宣外下斜街		隸屬於慈幼院爲感化不良兒童之機關		
中華慈濟會	北平前門內南長街西大街二十八號	十六年二月	逢九及星期日念佛舉辦施助棉衣米麵錢銀棺木粥廠暖廠等事業		
天津佛教居士林	天津英租界廣東路一四五號	十四年乙丑	弘揚淨土	男衆百餘人 女衆二百餘人	
北平居士林	北平西長安街十一號				
華北居士林					

河南省

名稱	地址	成立年時	宗旨	現況及人數	會中附設之機關
河南佛學社	開封白衣閣街二號	十四年八月	信願念佛期生淨土	社員六人 王智圓 趙宗蓮	淨土蓮社，女蓮社 佛教流通所，圖書館
蓮園精舍	開封東革門南陶胡同	二十一年			

陝西省

名稱	地址	成立年時	宗旨	現況及人數	會中附設之機關
寂園蓮社	西安東關內	十二年	每月十九日集會一次平次各在家中念佛	社員五六十人	佛經流通處佛學研究所 念佛堂
佛化隨刊社	西安中山大街九十號	十六年			
耀縣女念佛堂	耀縣城內南巷				

山東省

名稱	地址	成立年時	宗旨	現況及人數	會中附設之機關
諸城佛學研究社	諸城北門				

國際佛教通報局

名譽局長	高楠順次郎
局長	大村桂巖
幹事	鷹谷俊之
同	稻葉文海
同	淺野研眞

顧問（順序不同）

〃 宇井伯壽
〃 朝倉曉瑞
〃 羽溪了諦
〃 荻原雲來
〃 干潟龍祥
〃 鈴木大拙
〃 鈴木宗忠
〃 天岫接三
〃 長井眞琴
〃 松本文三郎
〃 椎尾辨匡
〃 宇野圓空
〃 赤松智城
〃 大森禪戒
〃 矢吹慶輝
〃 小野清一郎
〃 加藤精神
〃 姉崎正治
〃 本田義英
〃 關本龍門
〃 佐伯定胤
〃 花田凌雲
〃 河野法雲
〃 高岡隆心
〃 小林瑞淨
〃 山邊習學
〃 赤沼智善
〃 本多惠隆
〃 大森亮順
〃 河口慧海
〃 山川智應
〃 常盤大定
〃 谷本富
〃 常盤井堯猷
〃 大谷尊由
〃 大谷瑩潤
〃 水野梅曉
〃 柴田一能
〃 安藤正純
〃 下村壽一
〃 菊澤季麿
〃 乘杉嘉壽
〃 芝田徹心
〃 淺野孝之
〃 渡邊哲信
〃 小野玄妙
〃 柳澤健
〃 重光葵
〃 金倉圓照
〃 立花俊道

國際佛教通報局定款

名稱

第一，本局を國際佛教通報局と稱す

事務所

第二，本局の事務所を全日本佛教青年會聯盟本部に置く

目的

第三，本局は日本內海及海外に向つて佛教事情の通報をなし，且つ佛教徒相互間の各種便宜を計るを以て目的とす

事業

第四，本局の目的を達成するため左記の事業を行ふ

イ，日本內地及世界各國より佛教事情に關する質問の通報を行ふ

ロ，必要に應じ日本語及世界各國語を以て佛教事情の通報を行ふ

ハ，外國人の日本觀光に際しては各國の便益を與へ，特にその佛教に關する方面に於て之を爲す

ニ，定時或は隨時に各國語を以て文書の刊行をなす

ホ，その他必要と認めたる事業を行ふ

役員

第五，本局の事務を處理するため左の役員を置く

イ，局長　一名

ロ，幹事　三名

ハ，評議員　若干名

局長は本局を總括す

幹事は本局の事務を處理す

評議員は局長の提案に依る重要事務を審議す

第六，評議員は左記の者を以て之に充つ

イ，全日本佛教青年會館聯盟理事及主事

ロ，全日本佛教青年會聯盟理事會に於て推薦したる者

第七，局長及幹事は評議員會に於て決定す

第八，役員の仕期は二ケ年とす（但し重任を妨げず）

經費

第九，本局の經費は左記のものに依て之を支辨す

イ，本局基金の活用

ロ，寄附金

ハ，その他の收入

補則

第十，本定款に記載せられざる事項は，凡て評議員會に於て協議す

第十一，第一回の役員は全日本佛教青年會聯盟理事會に於て決定す

定價	一部	金二十錢	送料二錢
	一年	金二圓四十錢	送料不要

昭和十年四月卅日第三種郵便物認可
昭和十年八月廿七日印刷（毎月一回一日發行）
昭和十年九月一日發行

東京市外吉祥寺337
編輯發行兼印刷人　淺野研眞

東京市牛込區早稻田鶴卷町107
印刷所　康文社印刷所
電話牛込（34）1950番 5049番

東京市神田區一ツ橋二の三
發行所　國際佛教通報局
電話九段（33）4428番
振替東京83015番

昭和十年四月三十日第三種郵便物認可 昭和十年八月二十七日印刷納本(毎月一回) 昭和十年九月一日發行(一日發行) 國際佛教通報 第一卷 第六號

昭和十年四月三十日第三種郵便物認可 昭和十年九月二十七日印刷納本 昭和十年十月一日發行 (毎月一回一日發行) 第一卷 第七號

The International Buddhist Bulletin

國際佛教通報

第一卷 昭和十年十月 第七號 〔Vol. I. Oct. 2501/1935 No. 7.〕

要 目 〔Contents〕

東 京 國際佛教通報局 發 行
The International Buddhist Information Bureau
Tokyo, Kanda, Hitotsubashi, II—3

The Tsukiji Honganji

Drawn by Noël Nouët.

Temple, Its History And Mission

By the Rt. Rev. Sonyū Ohtani

I.

The generally accepted idea of 'tera' or temple in Japanese is that it is a place where there is enshrined a statue of the Buddha and where Buddhist priests or priestesses live. A Chinese scholar Ling Yu quotes in one of his books as many as ten names, while there are many other names signifying the meanings of cave, institute, forest, mausoleum, etc. And, yet, among all these varying designtions the word 'tera' is the most popular in Japan.

'Ji' (or 'szu' in Chinese), which is the Chinese equivalent for temple, means 'public office.' In the age of Hou Han, the public building where foreign visitors or guests were received was called 'Kōroji' or 'Hung Lü Szu' in Chinese. Then, in A. D. 67, the two Indian priests, Kāśyapamātanga and Dharmarakṣa brought Buddha images and Buddhist sutras to Lê Yang or the present-day Ho-nan, the then capital of Hou Han Dynasty. The emperor received the priests and all in the Kōroji. A year later a building was raised and was named the 'Hakubaji' or 'Pai Ma Szu,' or the 'White-Horse Public Office or Building,' as according to the meaning of the word of the age, because the priests brought the Buddha images and the sutras on a white horse. This was the first temple in China, the suffix-word 'ji' (or 'szu' in Chinese), which later came to signify the meaning of 'temple', springing from the 'ji' of the 'Kōroji' which at first meant only 'office.' Thus a new word was coined in China.

II.

The word 'Tera' appears even in such an old book as the 'Nihonshoki.' As to the word some scholars ascribe the origin to the Pāli 'thera' which means 'elders,' while others to the changed sound of the Korean word 'chyöl' or 'chor' which means 'worship.' To me the latter explanation seems to be more acceptable. There are even yet other proposals for explanation with rather too self-professed elucidations, the details of which are hardly worth quoting here.

III.

Anyhow, such a thing as temple with such varied significations or history sprang up in India, came to be built in China, Korea, and Japan, the styles varying as according to the difference of country, place, time, and circumstances.

In India, at first, there seem to have existed only such places of abode where barely rain could be avoided. After the attainment of Enlightenment the Buddha went, as a mendicant, on a round of visit to villages and towns to share with the people what he had attained. Bowers of large trees, gardens, old tombs, caves and grottos, forests, and turfs were the places where night was passed. Such places of rest were, as according to the scriptures, called 'āranya' translated into Chinese as 'the wood' or 'the open.'

But times were when necessity caused the Buddha to stay longer in one place. At such a time a special building would be erected and this was called 'vihāra.' There, with the Buddha as centre, the disciples would sit who had come from all directions. Some scriptures would name such a building (i. e. vihāra) as 'samghārama.' But the name, however, seems to have been applied to a building yet larger than a vihāra. Anyhow beauty of the building was of no question: simple and frugal they seem to have been. The first important requirement for such a place was the quietness of the surrounding. It says that such buidings stood some two miles from hamlets and towns, or that they stood amid graveyards, nullahs or water courses, or the places which were quite far from the dins of the populace.

But exceptions were there, of course, such as the famous 'Jetavana Vihāra' that stood in the suburbs of Śravastu or the present-day Sahet Mahet of the Province of Agra and Oudh and the 'Venuvana Vihāra' of the suburbs of Rājagṛha. Especially, the former, according to the 'Nehangyō,' or 'Mahāparinirvāna-sūtra,' seems to have possessed sixty three meditation halls, the kitchen, the bath-room and other quarters. But, truly speaking, such a complete building as the Jetavana Vihāra was rather a rare thing in the days of the Buddha and even I presume to think that the lecture-hall, the sun-room, the dining-room, the kitchen, the bath-room, the gates, the W. C., the priests' quarters, etc. were things of later addition.

But, then. at the death of the Buddha, his bones were divided among his zealous followers or votaries and these were enshrined in tombs called stupas, thus making a rise to 'stupa-worship.' Even many a temple of Japan are, as to be hereafter to be treated, built with this stupa as the central edifice. One more word may yet be necessary regarding the cave temples of India, such as those of Ellora and Ajanta, the frescoes of which are world famous.

IV.

The first temple in China was, as already stated, the 'Hakubaji' or 'Pai Ma Szu,' built in the age of Hou Han. Although it is hard to know what forms of temples really existed in the ages previous to the Lu Chao or 'Six Dynasty Ages,' yet we can well guess that they were like any ordinary office buildings. But after the Six Dynasty Ages and in the age of 'Tang Dynasty' the cave temples of India worked influence and such as those of Tun Huang, Lung Mên, Yung Mên, etc. came to be excavated. In the age of Tang Dynasty, such big temples as Hung Fu Szu, Tz'ŭ En Szu, Si Ming Szu, etc. were built. In the age of 'Sung,' the Zen and the Tendai flowished and the famous temples of the Wu Shan Shih Sh'a (or a set of five or ten temples), etc. were built.

V.

Buddhism was publicly brought to Japan in A. D. 552. Soga-no-iname enshrined in his own house at Mukuhara the Buddha image and the scriptures, a part of the tribute as dedicated to the Imperial Court by the then Government of Korea and this is the start of temple-building in Japan. In February of the second year of the Emperor Suiko an imperial edict was issued for the all-hand propagation of Buddhism, and temples after temples were built. Such full-fledged and complete structures as the Shiten-nō-ji of Ōsaka, Hōryūji and Tōdaiji, etc. of Nara were built successively in the ages of Asuka, Hakuhō, and Tempyō. In the age of Heian the famous monasteries of Enryakuji and Kōyasan were built. In the age of Kamakura the new sects of Jōdo, Zen, Shin, Nichiren, etc. either sprang up in or brought to Japan, all of which erecting new temples. In the Tokugawa age Christianity was banned, with the result of consolidating the governmental and economical aspect of Buddhist temples.

It is in no way easy to set any fixed rules as to the modes of temple structure, yet it is generally accepted that the Hōryūji is the copy of Sui system, the Shiten-nōji and Tōdaiji are the reproduction of Tang style, the five big Zen temples of Kyōto that of Sung, and the Ōbakusan of Uji the imitation of Ming style.

The history of the 'Shichidōgaran' or 'seven qualifications of a Buddhist temple' is not quite clear. However, there are two ways of classification. The one includes in the list 'Daimon' (main gate), 'Chūmon' (middle gate), 'Kondō' (main temple), 'Hōtō' (stupa or dagoba), 'Kōdō' (lecture-hall), 'Kyōzō' (library or safe where the Tripitakas are generally kept) and Shōrō (belfry); and the Hōryūji of Nara and the Tōji of Kyōto follow this system. The other style requires 'Sammon' (gates) 'Butsuden' (main temple), 'Hōdō' (lecture-hall), 'Sōdō' (priests' quarters), 'Chūko' (kitchen), 'Yokushitsu' (bathroom), 'Seijin' (W. C.); the Zen temples accord to this system. In India the dagoba was the centre of the Shichidōgaran, but in China and Japan this was replaced by the 'Kondō' or the main temple, the dagoba merely serving to be a sort of decoration. And a change was seen in our attitude towards temple structure.

Further interest is to be called to the temple construction of the Shiten-nō-ji of Ōsaka, built by the Prince Shōtoku-Taishi. This temple, besides the requirements of the Shichidōgaran, there are the new additions of the so-called 'Shiin' or 'Four Institutions,' viz. 'Keiden-in' or the hall for the worship of the Triple Gems, 'Seyaku-in' or the free apothecary, 'Ryōbyō-in' or the free hospital, and 'Hiden-in' or the home for the sick and orphans. This is one of the strong manifestations of the Mahāyāna ideals as conceived by the Prince

who sought to look to the poor and the afflicted, and may well be said to be the very start of Buddhist social works in Japan.

VI.

Further let me describe to you something about the various sorts of Japanese temples.

1. 'Kanji and Shiji, or Official and Private Temples.' Though the official temple-system is abolished at the present age, times were when some temples stood under the direct supervision of the Imperial Court or the Shogunate goverment, where worships and prayers were offered for the welfare of the court, nation or private clans, and for the extinction of sins, the driving away of epidemics, etc.: and they were the 'Kokubunji' and the 'Kokubun-niji' of the Nara age, the Enryakuji, and the 'Kyō-wō-gokokuji' of the Heian age, the 'Shokoku-ankokuji' of the Muromachi age, and the 'Kanyeiji' of the Tokugawa age. Any temples built by private persons and establishments were called the 'Shiji' or private temples.

2. 'Jingūji.' As the result of an interfusion between Buddhism and Shintoism temples were built in the precints of big shrines, or shrines built in the compounds of Buddhist temples. The 'Jingūji' is that kind of temples built in a Shintō shrine. Though the traces may yet be seen, these temples were made away with at the time of the Meiji Restoration.

3. 'Gakusan.' With the advent of the Heian Period studies were carried on almost all in Buddhist temples and this continued, and it is not much to say that only the Buddhist temples were the centres of learning. In the Tokugawa age the 'Terakoya' or temple-schools sprang up, which solely took the education of the populace in their hands.

4. 'Bodaiji.' As the result of a compromise of Buddhism with the Shintoism, Buddhist temples became the centre of ancestor-worship. In the Tokugawa age this relation became so conspicuous that there grew up a sort of feudal system between the temple and the populace.

Lastly I must speak something about Shinshū temples. The founder Shinran Shōnin drew his last breath with a legacy, to the effect that his bones could be thrown into the river Kamogawa. This may perhaps have been the outcome of his own religious experience, but possibility is strong that he must have held in view the non-temple idea of Hōnen Shōnin his master, who, when asked, seems to have said that the best place for his kind memory is the place where his teaching of 'Nembutsu' flourishes. And, yet, so much as Shinran Shōnin was averse to our erecting any form of building for the sake of his memory that much the desire of his followers was intense for building it, and we now see the two great Hongwanji Temples of Kyōto. Another feature is that while other temples were built for meditation, lecturing, and the study of Buddhist scriptures, the Shinshū temples had the use of the structure by the general populace chief in aim, to serve as the place of worship, sermon, and religious gatherings. While other temples mostly stuck to mountains, these came down to the plains and streets where people lived, and served to respond to the need of the populace: no more a place for self-edification, but for the education of others; a sort of social organs.

Now, the question is——what way may be the best that can answer the ideal of the Buddha, at least, from the standpoint of Mahāyāna ideals? No doubt, the enlightenment of an individual self must come first. But it could not stop there, if one sees to what the Buddha truly said. Movement must always point towards sharing the fruition of one's own religious pursuit with others. Far from being content with lecturing, praying, scripture-reading, and the care of funeral services and of the votaries' tombs, temples must step into the life of the people, to save their soul, to be their friend, to be a hand to raise their stand of life. Temples must be the place of public edification. The examples of the Prince Shōtoku-Taishi as he added the new and extra Four Institutions, when regarded in this light, can not too adequately be appreciated. The temples in future must look to the fostering of Buddhist belief among the people, not only by opening the building for worship and sermons, but also by taking up the settlement works of modern sense, such as public libraries, hospitals, Sunday schools, kindergartens, orphanages, nurseries, employment office business, marriage services as according to the Buddhist rites, etc.

Ein Blick auf die japanische Frömmigkeit.

von Prof. Honyu Hamada

I. Die Privat- oder Hauskapelle.

Vielleicht erscheint es dem Europäer eigenartig, daß jede japanische Familie ihre eigne Privat-Kapelle oder -Altar hat an besondere Stelle im Hause. Es ist wieder eigentümlich für die japanische Frömmigkeit, daß es meistens sogar zwei verschiedene Kapellen oder Altäre zugleich in demselben Hause gibt. Die eine ist die des Buddhismus, heißt „Butsudan“ (Buddha-Kapelle); sie hat entweder ein besonders kleines Zimmer für sich, genannt „Butsuma“ (Buddha-Zimmer), oder sie steht an besondrer Stelle des Hauptsaales im Hause, sozusagen der guten Stube. Dazu kommt die andere Kapelle oder Altar, genannt „Kamidana“ (Götterschrank oder -gestell), die hoch an der Wand angebracht ist, oder auf erhöhter Stufe im Hauptsaale steht. Diese zweite kleine Kapelle oder Schrein ist die des Shintoismus, nicht des Buddhismus, da ja die meisten Japaner dem Shintoismus in gewissem Grade anhängen, abgesehen von ihrer buddhistischen Einstellung. Wer aber nur Shintoist ist, dem fehlt natürlich die buddhistische Kapelle in seinem Hause. In dieser Schilderung darf man aber den Shintoismus nicht allzu sehr betonen. Obwohl der Shintoismus in Japan scheinbar sehr allgemein auftritt, steht er dennoch bei den Buddhisten sehr zurück hinter der buddhistischen Frömmigkeit, wie unten ausgeführt wird.

Innerhalb der buddhistischen Privatkapelle sieht man zunächst in der Mitte und zwar auf der höchsten Stufe entweder ein geschnitztes Buddha-Bild oder eine gemalte oder manchmal beschriebene Schrifttafel, heißt „Honzon“ (Hauptheiligtum) und zeigt gemäß der Bestimmung des Sektenstifters das der Sekte jeweils eigentümliche Pantheon. Außer dem Buddhabild oder Honzon befinden sich in der Kapelle auch manchmal Bilder einiger bedeutenden aus dem Urbuddhismus stammender Gottheiten, oder noch duzu Bilder des Stifters der betreffenden Sekte oder bedeutender Jünger oder Anhänger. Vollends erscheint es merkwürdig, daß man in dieser Kapelle die Heiligentafel, „Ihai," mit dem posthumen Namen der Verstorbenen der Familie von den Ahnen bis zum heutigen Tage finden kann. Hierdurch darf man aber nicht voreilig schließen, daß im japanischen Buddhismus der Ahnenkultus vorherrschend sei. Wie nachher erklärt wird, spielen die Totengeister innerhalb der buddhistischen Weltanschauung nur eine bestimmte, begrenzte Rolle.

Man darf in der Privatkapelle ferner nicht das Buddha-Geräte „Butsugu" übersehen: die Glocke, das Weihgefäß (für Weihrauch), die Blumenvase, die Leuchter, das Esstischchen mit Essgeschirr und Tee- und Wassertasse u.s.w. Zu den heiligen Geräten gehören auch: die Holzklapper, die kleine Trommel (nur in der Nitchirensekte und einigen Shintosekten), das aus ausgewählten Sutrastellen und Werken des Stifters zusammengestellte heilige Textbuch, der Rosenkranz, die alle beim Gottesdienste benutzt werden.

Die shintoistische Kapelle im Hause des Buddhisten dagegen enthält nicht so viel wie die buddhistische. Jedoch fehlt es nicht an einigen holzgeschnitzten Shintogottheiten oder an Amuletten, die auf Papier den Namen des Gottes gedruckt enthalten, und die man auch häufig in der Buddhakapelle angeklebt sehen kann. Unter den Gottheiten findet man am meisten „Amaterasu," die göttliche Urmutter des Kaisers, die nach der Sonne genannt und in himmlischen Höhen lebend vorgestellt wird; sehr häufig auch „Hatchiman," einen Kaiser göttlicher Abstammung. Dazu kommen noch verschiedne Gottheiten, die im japanischen Mythus sehr bedeutend sind (z.B. Ōnamuchi-no-Mikoto als "Taisha" in Izumo, oder Takeminakatatomi-no-Mikoto als Suwa-Daimyojin in Shinano) oder die zu den Helden gehören [z.B. „Gongen"-Daimyojin (Tokugawa-Ieyasu) oder „Minatogawajinja" (Kusunoki Masashige)], oder die von Indien mit dem Buddhismus zusammen eingeführt sind, z.B. "Benten", eine Göttin, die von Buddha erleuchtet und so gerecht wird. Mann kann auch den

Namen "Kotohira-Daimyojin dazufügen, obwohl zweifelhaft ist, ob er aus Indien oder aus dem japanischen Mythus stammt.

Es ist sehr merkwürdig, daß die Shintogottheit manchmal in einem ganz weissen, fünffach geschnittenen aber nicht abgeschnittenen Papierstücke, genannt "Gohei", verehrt wird. Es wird an einem kleinen Stück Bambus befestigt und verehrt, als wäre die Gottheit selber darin: also ein Amulett.

Die Geräte, die zur Verehrung der Shinto-Gottheiten nötig sind, sind nicht so zahlreich wie bei der Verehrung der buddhistischen Heiligen. Sie bestehen in einem Paar Vasen mit eurya japonica, dem heiligen Baume des Shintoismus, einem Paar Flaschen für Opferwein und einigen Schalen oder Lampen für geweihtes Licht. Daneben darf man das an dem Tor aufgehängte Strohseil "Shimenawa" mit einigem geschnittenen, weissen Papier nicht übersehen; das ist sehr bemerkenswert als Zeichen der Heiligkeit. Der Kultus des Shintoismus, um hier nur weniges darüber zu sagen, der vor der Hauskapelle täglich stattfindet, ist auch ganz einfach im Vergleich zum Buddhadienst. Man klatscht nur einigemal in die Hände und murmelt Gebete dazu.

Man muß sich wundern, daß man in einem Hause so verschiedene göttliche Wesen trifft: nämlich buddhistische Heilige, die Wesen des Ahnenkultus und Shinto-Gottheiten. Man muß wiederum erstaunt sein, zu finden, daß sie ohne Widerspruch verehrt werden.

Wie deutsche Gelehrte, z.B. Winternitz oder Pischel bereits betont haben, ist der Buddhismus sogar in Zeiten der Mission sehr friedlich, duldsam und aufnahmefähig geblieben. Warum? Man kann vielleicht auf diese Frage verschiedene Antworten finden. Die erste Antwort wird betonen, daß der Buddhismus von Grund aus gar nicht ein transzendentaler Monotheismus wie Judentum, Islam und Christentum, sondern eher ein Immanenter Monotheismus sei. Er erkennt die Realität des höchsten Ideals nicht jenseits, sondern diesseits, innerhalb des Menschenkreises, und innen im Menschen. Er erkennt jedem Wesen die Fähigkeit zur Arahatschaft (im Hinayana) oder sogar zur Buddhaschaft (Mahayana) an. Im Buddhismus steigt das hohe Gotteswesen nach unten herab, wie das Volk in Tirol singt:

Wunder über Wunder groß,
Unerhörtes Wunder!
Gott kam nackend, arm und bloß
Auf die Welt herunter.

Gott wird Mensch, ach was ist das,
Wunderlich zu hören;
Große Liebe ohne Maß
Macht zum Knecht den Herrn.

Nun gefreut euch allzumal,
Gott will bei euch wohnen,
Und in seinem Himmelssaal
Euch dafür belohnen.

(Hirten- und Weihnachtslieder aus dem österreichischen Gebirge)

In der letzten zwei Zeilen bleibt das Christentum doch transzendental; aber im Buddhismus kann man nicht mehr den Namen des jenseitigen, göttlichen Wesens finden, wie Brahma im Brahmanismus. Es ist in die Menschen verschmolzen. Sogar der Buddha selber kommt wirklich nackend, arm und bloß, wie er ja auch "Tatagata," der so Gekommene genannt wird. Die im japanischen Buddhismus ganz überragend heilige Schrift "Myōhōrengé-kyō" (Saddharmapundarīka-Sutra) wird kurz "Myōhō" genannt und zwar „das Wesen des Wunders." Welch ein Wunder ist es, daß der Buddhismus in dieser Sutra auf die Gedanken kommt, daß der Buddha inmitten der verschiedenen Welten ungeboren und unsterblich immer da sei! Und in einer westlichen dieser Welten predigt immer Amida-Buddha auch als Totagata, daß man unsonst, ohne Verdienst und Werk, erlöst wird. Also Amida-Buddha ist wesentlich gar nicht transzendental Wesen, wie es erscheint.

Dieser Gedanke der Mehrheit der Buddhas schließt sich an das zweite Wunder in diesem Sutra an; dies nämlich besteht darin, daß alle Wesen, die diesem Sutra anhängen, sogar der Feind des Buddha wie Devadatta, oder die Dämonin wie Karite, durch die unbegrenzte Liebe des Buddha endgültig die Buddhaschaft erreichen können. Infolge dieses Gedankens konnten die verschiedenen Gestalten, die dem Buddhismus nahe kamen, sehr leicht Zugang zum buddhistischen Pantheon finden. So deuteten die meisten Theologen der buddhistischen Sekten die Shintogottheiten in mystischer Weise als Anhänger oder sogar als Verkörperungen der Buddhas. Nichiren, geboren 1222, Stifter der Nichiren- und Hokkesekte überhaupt, war der Ansicht: Amateras

oder Hatchiman u.s.w. seien bei der Enthüllung der Myōhōrengekyō durch den Buddha zugegen gewesen, seien dadurch erleuchtet worden und hätten geschworen, die von diesem Sutra Durchdrungenen in Zukunft beschützen zu wollen. Ihn war die Predigt des Myōhōrengekyō kosmisches Geschehen, daraus konnte er alles mögliche entwickeln.

Auf diese Weise hatte der Shintoismus in Japan lange mit Buddhismus in engem Bündnis gestanden, wenn auch die Formen, wie sie waren, blieben bis zur Restauration vor sechzig Jahren. Erst um 1868 hat die Bewegung von Kennern der alt japanischen Literatur, hauptsächlich beeinflußt durch Motoori-Norinaga, den Shintoismus als Staatsangelegenheit vom Buddhismus unabhängig gemacht. Aber das Volk hatte mit dieser Gelehrtenbewegung nichts zu tun und blieb immer noch treu bei den alten Gedanken und dem alten Kult und vergaß nicht die kleine Kapelle des Shintoismus neben die buddhistische zu stellen.

Wie bezieht sich nun aber der ungeheure Ahnenkultus auf dem Buddhismus? Freilich scheint er manchmal innerhalb des Kultus sehr hervorzutreten. Aber wenn man genau hinschaut, so bemerkt man, daß der Ahnenkult niemals allein auftritt, sondern: es wird für die Verstorbenen gebeten im Rahmen eines Gebetes an die buddhistischen Heiligen. Es ist ausserdem bemerkenswert, daß der Verstorbene nicht mit dem Anrufswort "Namu" angerufen oder genannt wird, daß die Ergebenheit oder die Hingabe kennzeichnet, wie es bei Heiligen der Fall ist. Es handelt sich gar nicht um die Verehrung, solange der Verstorbene in seinem verlassenen Leben noch nicht die Bodhi (Erwachtsein) erlangt habe. Die monatlichen, jährlichen oder sonst periodischen Dienst zugunsten der Verstorbenen, die wir später noch einmal betrachten werden, bedeuten nur "Kuyō," d.h. erstens die Ernährung der drei Geschätzten (Sambō), nämlich Buddha, Dharma und Samgha, oder zweitens die Ernährung der Hungernden (Gaki) in Bezug auf die Verstorbenen. Man glaubt, daß solche Taten der Söhne, anderer Verwandten oder Nichtverwandten das Schicksal der betreffenden Verstorbenen beeinflussen (Ekō), und deren gute Taten ergänzen können, daß der Verstorbene dadurch vom Irrtum befreit und im zweiten Totenreich oder nächsten Lebenslauf endgültig erwachen und erlöst werden kann.

Von solchem volkstümlichen Tun und Glauben kann man leicht einsehen, daß der scheinbare Ahnenkult in Wirklichkeit reiner Buddhadienst, im Grunde moralische Tat des Buddhisten in Bezug auf die Toten ist.

II. Der Privat- Buddhadienst.

Es ist möglich, daß heutigen buddhistischen Gottesdienst oder richtig Buddhadienst in Japan in zwei Klassen einzuteilen und zwar: Privat-Gottesdienst und Tempel- oder Gemeinde-Gottesdienst. Hier wird im Rahmen des Privat-Gottesdienstes zunächst der tägliche Gottesdienst dargestellt. Es handelt sich dabei nicht nur um den priester, sondern auch um den Laien; jener hält den Gottesdienst im Tempel ab, der andere vor der oben genannten Privat-Kapelle, die in jedem gläubigen Haushalt ihren besonderen, geweihten Platz hat.

Der Privat-Gottesdienst wird zweimal täglich, morgens und abends, abgehalten. Ganz gleich aber ist beidemal der Zeremonienverlauf. Nur am Morgen wird besonders der Sonnengott bei einigen Sekten des Buddhismus (z.B. Nichiren-, Shingon- und Zensekte) angebetet. Die Shinsekte aber bemüht sich, nur Amida-Buddha, den Stifter der Sekte Shinran, oder auch ihren Wiederbegründer Rennyo, zu verehren. Man darf aber nicht vergessen, als Gegenstände der täglichen Anbetung, der besonderen Verehrung des Buddha mit den verschiedenen Namen, entsprechend seinen Verkörperungen, ebenso der Verehrung der Jünger und Nachfolger Buddhas, des Stifters oder Wiedererweckers der betreffenden Sekte und der Shinto-Gottheiten noch besonders die grobe Verehrung des Ahnengeistes hinzuzufügen, der, abgesehen von dem Ahnenkultus des Volkes, als eine Art Buddhageist oder "Hotoke" dargestellt wird. Hier können wir Buddhas Heilige Schrift oder Sutra als einen Gegenstand der Verehrung hinzufügen, weil es in Japan nicht nur sozusagen die Sutra-Verehrung gibt, die im Buddhismus uralt ist, sondern auch eine Sekte, die nach ihrem Gründer "Nichiren" heißt, die auf der Verehrung Saddharmapundarika-Sutra, japanisch Myōhōrenge-Kyō, beruht. Dennoch können wir auch sagen, daß der in diesem Sutra seine Verkörperung offenbarende Buddha verehrt wird, als

der einzige und wahre Buddha. Hier ist die Lehre Nichirens wirksam, die sich Sutra oder das in dem Saddharmapundarika-Sutra dargestellte Wesen und Buddha selbst als Einheit vorstellte. Shinto-Gottheiten als Gengenstände der Verehrung werden besonders gebeten, um von ihnen Wohlergehen und Glück für alles diesseitige Leben zu erflehen.

Den verschiedenen, in ein einheitliches System gebrachten Heiligen werden zuerst Blumen, Kerzen und Weihrauch geopfert. Dazu kommen weiter: Getränke (reines Wasser oder zuweilen auch Wein) und Speisen, aber nicht Fisch und Fleisch, weil darauf Strafe ruht. Diese Meinung wirkt noch bei dem Kerzenmaterial nach, da tierisches Oel oder Talg zu geweihtem Gebrauche möglichst vermieden wird. Schon in den alten Texten des Urbuddhismus finden wir als Opfergaben und wohltätige Gaben: Farbe, Rauch und Süße werden dem Buddha geweiht, Lebensmittel den Mönchen geschenkt, und Speisen den Hungernden in der Hölle zur Nahrung gereicht.

Darauf ruft man die Heiligen an, zunächst mit mehrmaligem Glockenklang, dann mit namentlicher Anrufung der einzelnen Heiligen, die man um Erbarmen anfleht. Im allgemeinen wird der täglichem Gottesdienst vom Familienvorstand bei Laien und dem Hauptpriester des Tempels ausgeführt. Die anderen niederen Glieder folgen ihm freiwillig. Danach bittet man im Gebet um Erlösung der Ahnengeister zu höheren Heiligen. Nun folgt der Hauptteil der Zeremonie. Er besteht im Lesen der wichtigsten Abschnitte oder Auszüge aus dem kanonischen Sutra der betreffenden Sekte und in vielmals wiederholter Nennung des betreffenden Buddha-Namens (bei der Shin-Sekte Amida-Buddha), des Stifter-Namens (bei der Shingonsekte Kōbōdaishi) oder des Sutra-Namens (bei der Nichirensekte Myōhōrenge-Kyō) und zwar mit Hinzufügung des "Namu", das die zuflucht zur Heiligen ausdrückt, also z.B. Namu-Myōhōrenge-Kyō, Namu-Amidabutsu oder Namu-Daishi. Die Nennung heißt aber bei der Shinsekte Nenbutsu, d.h. An-Buddha-denken, bei der Nichirensekte dagegen Nennung oder Heissung des Sutranamens. Für wichtig hält man dabei die Zahl und die Zeitlänge der Nennungen. Je öfter und je unausgesetztes man den Namen nennt, desto seliger wird man im Diesseits und in Jenseits. Dieser Gedanke ist uralt in der Geschichte des japanischen Buddhismus. Er rührt von der buddhistischen „Anstrengunslehre" her, die früher in den varschiedenen Taten der Selbstüberwindung ihre Erfüllung fand. In der reformierenden Zeit des japanischen Buddhismus (ungefähr 1200–1300 n. Chr.) haben besonders zwei der größten Geister, Nichren und Shinran, die Anstrengungsmethode möglichst erleichtert, damit alle Gläubigen nur durch die beständige Nennung oder Andacht gleich der Erlösung zugänglich sein können. Also ist die Nennung des Sutra-Namens oder Andacht des Buddha-Namens das Hauptsächlichste im Gottesdienst des Laien. Dagegen neigt der Priester mehr zum Lesen der kanonischen Bücher. Es gibt noch eine andere Form der Nennung oder Andacht, und zwar bei der Shingonsekte, besonders im Gottesdienst der Laien, die in einem Lobliede auf die Gnade des Buddha oder Boddhisattva, besonders der Kwannon besteht.

Beim Lesen schlägt man Takt mit einer hölzernen oder metallenen Klapper bei der Nennung des Sutra-Namens, bei der Nichirensekte mit einer Trommel, und beim Gesang bei der Shingon-Sekte oder mit einer metallenen Klapper.

Nachdem die Gläubigen das Lesen und besonders die Nenuung eine Weile fortgesetzt haben, folgt unter Glockenklängen wiederum die Anrufung Buddhas und der anderen Heiligen u.s.w. und das Gebet für die noch unerlösten Totengeister zunächst der verwandten und bekannten, und dann aller anderen Wesen, für das jenseitige und besonders diesseitige Glück der einzelnen, lebenden Familienmitglieder und Verwandten und ferner, wie dies auch im Gemeindegottesdienst der Fall ist, für das Wohl des Kaisers und der Nation, und schließlich auch für die Bekehrung der ganzen Welt zum Buddhismus, letzteres besonders in der Nichirensekte. Damit schließt der tägliche Gottesdienst im Nachklang der Glocken. Während die Zeremonie fortgeht, beten die Gläubigen immer mit gefalteten Händen an, an die der hölzerne, gläserne oder aus Juwelen bestehende Kranz (Rosenkranz) gehängt wird, der auch bei der Nennung des Buddha oder Sutra-Namens zur Berechnung der Zahl benutzt wird, da der Kranz aus vielen kleinen Kugeln besteht, von denen jede eine heilige Bedeutung oder die Bedeutung eines Verbotes hat.

Nunmehr noch ein paar Worte über den Privat-Gottesdienst. Man hält nämlich Totengottesdienst auch vor der Privat-Kapelle in seinem Hause und zwar bei der

Verbrennungsfeier und am Gedenktage des Verstorbenen. Gedenktage feiert man monatlich, jährlich und noch besonders in bestimmten Jahresabständen, nämlich im 3., 7., 13., 17., 23., 27., 32., 37., 50., 100., u.s.w. Jahres. Dabei stellt man gewöhnlich einen provisorischen Altar für den betreffenden Toten auf und zwar neben der Privat-Kapelle.

Die Feier am Gedenktage nennt man "Hōji," d.h. Dharma-Tat. Sie ist aber schon etwas gemeinschaftlich, obwohl sie zu Hause stattfindet, weil zu ihr Priester und Verwandte, wenige oder viele, je nach dem Reichtum des Feiernden eingeladen werden. Diesen nennt man "Seshu," d.h. Almosenspender. Der spendet zunächst den Priestern Almosen in Form von Geld und Reis, danach den Eingeladenen in Gestalt eines Festmahles oder manchmal Armen und Kindern Speise oder Kuchen. Oder er spendet zuweilen in der Phantasie vorgestellten Hungernden am Strand oder Fluß diejenigen Speisen und Süßigkeiten, die vorher bei der Feier am Altar dargebracht wurden. Hierbei kann man sich erinnern, daß die ungeheuer auf dem Altar dargebrachte, scheinbare Opfergabe eigentlich nicht nur als Almosen für Buddha, Dharma und Samgha, sondern auch für die armen und hungernden Wesen überhaupt in dieser Welt gedacht ist, wie das schon in alten Zeiten, als die Gemeinde Buddhas entstand, dem Laien als verdienstliche Tat vorgeschrieben war.

Bei solchen Gottesdiensten wird die Kapelle prunkvoll mit Speisen, Kuchen, Blumen, Kelchen und Weihrauch ausgestattet. Die Feier beginnt mit langwieriger Sutralesung durch Priester. Es folgt Nennung des Buddha-Namens oder Rezitieren des Sutranamens durch die Gemeinde. Zum Schluße kommt das Mahl.

Die Anhänger solcher Sekten, die das Gebet um irdische Wohlfahrt anerkennen, z.B. Shingon- und Nichirensekte, halten auch solche Gottesdienste durch den Priester besonders in Bezug auf die buddhistischen Heiligen oder shintoistischen Gottheiten, die dem Buddhismus als Bekehrte gelten. Man hält solche mit dem Ziel günstiger Beeinflußung des täglichen Lebens. Auch diese Gottesdienste werden im eignen Hause abgehalten. In diesem Falle ist es nicht selten, daß der shintoistische Priester auch von dem Buddhisten eingeladen wird. Diese scheinbare Doppelangehörigkeit des Japaners kann man wieder finden auch im religiösen Gemeinschaftsleben, das demnächst behandelt werden soll.

Kio estas Budaisma Sociologio?

de Ken Assano

Kvankam la termino "Budaisma Sociologio" sonas eble tro nova al oreloj, kiuj aŭdas ĝin la unuan fojon, tamen mi opinias, ke ĉiuj legantoj jam komprenis, ke ĝi tute ne estas nomo en vulgara scienco.

Sekve, ĉi tie ni devas trakti la fundamentan problemon, "Kio estas Budaisma Sociologio?" Nome oni devas provi difini la ĝeneralan koncepton de "Budaisma Sociologio."

Kio estas Budaisma Sociologio? —ĉi tiu demando estas alfao kaj omego de ĉi tiu scienco, kiu nun estas antaŭ ni prezentata. En ĉiu scienco oni devas doni al ĝi la difinon ne ĉe la komenco de la studo, sed ĉe la fino kiel konkludon. Kaj plie de tio multe da diskutoj devas esti disvolvataj. La difino de scienco ĝenerale en la procedo scienca devas esti la paŝo ne la unua, sed la lasta. Resume, vorto, frazo kaj koncepto k. c. iom post iom estas difinitaj kaj pli kaj pli estas rafinitaj laŭ la progreso de la procedo en la studo, sed ĝi ne devas esti alte tenata en la komenco kiel standardo. Ankaŭ ni devas bone memori ke nuntempe jam oni ne devas altrudi sian dogmon kaj arbitron rilate al la decido de la difinoj.

Kvankam laŭ la supra argumentado ni devas respondi al tiu demando nur tiam, kiam ni finis iel ajn la studon, tamen por antaŭenpuŝo de la studo ni havas iun difinitan antaŭvidon, perspektivon, sen kiu ni ne povas antaŭeniri eĉ unu paŝon, kaj kiu sola devas esti la kompaso por nia laborado.

Tial tiu direktado jam sugestas la ĝeneralan strukturon de la scienco; ne, se mi povus, mi volas diri, ke per la direktado oni devas disvolvi la sciencan sistemon. Nu, en tia senco mi provas starigi ĝeneralan koncepton de ĉi tiu plej juna scienco, "Budaisma Sociologio."

1. Budaisma Sociologio kiel speciala sociologio

Budaisma Sociologio kompreneble ne nur estas unu speciala sociologio[1], sed aliflanke ĝi estas nova grava speciala fako de Budaismaj sciencoj. Sed nun ni ekzamenas Budaisman Sociologion kiel specialan sociologion de la vidpunkto metodologiđ, kaj ni traktas sociologie Budaismon (pli precize, la socialajn fenomenojn budaismajn) kiel studobjekton.

Budaisma Sociologio unuvorte estas sociologia studo de Budaismo. En tiu kazo Budaismo, pli precize, signifas la socialajn fenomenojn budaismajn. Pri tiu objekto de la studo ni poste detale priskribos.

Antaŭ ĉio ni nepre devas ekzameni pri la sociologio mem, ĉar ni celas sociologian studon. Origine la termino "sociologio (sociologie)," kiel jam konate, estis kreita de Auguste Comte (1798–1857). Tio estis ĉirkaŭ la 1830-a jaro.[2] Poste la sociologio faris neordinaran disvolvon, kaj nun jam unu jarcenton poste ĝi ne nur akiris civitanan rajton en scienco, sed ankaŭ ĝi donadas multajn influojn al diversaj aliaj sciencoj.

Do, kia scienco estas la sociologio? Kian difinon ĝi havas en sia nuna progresinta stato? Ekzemple Sorokin skribas:

"Following the classification by H. Rickert and W. Windelband of sciences into those that are *individualizing* and those that are *generalizing* we regard sociology as a *generalizing* discipline among other social disciplines."[3]

Tiamaniere la sociologio estas difinita kiel la ĝeneraligita scienco, sub la influo de klasifikado de sciencoj de Novkantanisma-skolo

(1) Tiel nomataj "Specialaj sociologioj" kredeble devenas de la specialiĝo de sociologio laŭ la propono de Durkheim-skolo. Nome en la 2-a volumo de "L'*Année-sociologique*," 1898, ili publikigis 6 specialajn sociologiojn: religia sociologio, morala sociologio, jura sociologio, ekonomia sociologio, lingva sociologio kaj estetika sociologio. Kaj aparte la terminoj: familia sociologio, politika sociologio k. c. estas uzataj. Plie laŭ la progreso de la sociologio mem specialaj sociologioj pli kaj pli disfakiĝis, kaj nun ni vidas antaŭ ni tre multe da specialaj sociologioj. Kiel ekzemple kriminala sociologio (E. Ferri, *La sociologie criminelle*), kolonia sociologio (Maunier, *La sociologie coloniale*), eduka sociologio (en Usono tre progresas), labora sociologio (Karl Dunkman, *Soziologie der Arbeit*, 1933), urba sociologio (Urban Sociology), kampara sociologio (Rural Sociology), vilaĝa sociologio (Leopold von Wiese, *Soziologie des Dorfes*), civitana sociologio (Edward A. Ross, *Civic Sociology*, New York, 1925), revolucia sociologio (Pitirim A. Sorokin, *The Sociology of Revolution*, 1925), seksa sociologio (Quintiliano Saldaña, *Siete ensayos sobre Sociologia Sexual*, Madrid, 1928), animala sociologio (Friedrich Alverdes, *Tiersoziologie*, Leipzig, 1925), planta sociologio (Phytosociologie — J. Braun-Blanquet kaj J. Pavillard, *Vocabulaire de Sociologie Végétable, 3e éd.*, Montpelier, 1928), k. t. p.

(2) V. Comte, Cours de philosophie positive, t. IV, 1839, p. 201.

(3) Sorokin and Zimmerman, *Principles of Rural-Urban Sociology*, N. Y. 1929, p. 3.

germana. Plie la sociologio, kiu tiel staras sur la bazo de ĝeneraligita scienco, nun estas, laŭ Sorokin, resumebla kiel jene:

"It (Sociology) seems to be a study, first, of the *relationship and correlations between various classes of social phenomena, (correlations between economic and religious; family and moral; juridical and economic; mobility and political phenomena and so on); second, that between the social and the non-social (geographic, biological, etc.,) phenomena; third, the study of the general characteristics common to all classes of social phenomena.*"(1)

Sub tia stato de sociologia studo Budaisma Sociologio kiel unu speciala fako de sociologio, kiu intencas studi diversajn socialajn fenomenojn budaismajn, estas eklaborata kun nepre necesa postulo.

2. Budaisma Sociologio kiel speciala fako de Religia Sociologio

Budaisma Sociologio estas speciala sociologio; ĝi traktas budaismajn fenomenojn kiel religiajn fenomenojn. Sekve ĝi estas unu fako de religia sociologio, kiu traktas ĝeneralajn fenomenojn de religioj. Tial ĝi estas unu speciala fako de religia sociologio, kaj la lasta (religia sociologio) mem ankaŭ estas unu speciala fako de sociologio ĝenerala.

De la komenco religia sociologio estis kreita kaj starigita de la nuntempa franca sociologo Emile Durkheim (1858–1917). Prof. Gaston Richard, nuna profesoro de Bordoa Universitato, pri tio skribas:

"Le terme de sociologie religieuse a été créé par l'*Année sociologique* que dirigeait Emile Durkheim. Il n'apparaît pas avant 1898; il désigne alors une des six sections de cette publication, destinée à rendre compte du mouvement des recherches sociologiques et plus encore à étudier objectivement les sources de la nouvelle science. (C'est ainsi que Durkheim l'avait présentée à plusieurs de ses collaborateurs dont je fus pendant quelques années......) Mais il apparut bientôt que la sociologie religieuse etait la branche maîtresse de l'*Année sociologique*, qu'elles s'inspirait d'une doctrine definie sur la nature, l'origine et l'évolution de la religion, et que cette doctrine dépassait de beaucoup la compétence d'une science speciale des sociétés. Une série de mémoires dûs les uns à Durkheim, les autres

(1) Sorokin (Pitirim), *Contemporary Sociological Theories*, N. Y. and London, 1928, p. 760.

à MM. Mauss et Hubert, préparèrent et annoncèrent l'œuvre qui devait résumer la doctrine. Cette œuvre, les *Formes élémentaires de la vie religieuse*, parut enfin en 1912."(1)

La termino "Religia Sociologio" la unuan fojon ŝajne estis uzita en 1898, kaj la verkego en tiu fako "La formoj elementaj de la vivo religia" estis publikigitaj dekkvin jarojn poste en 1912. Tiu fakto sufiĉas montri, kiel li penadis por ĝin verki. Kiel mi menciis, en 1898 Durkheim publikigis la terminon religian sociologion kiel unu specialan fakon. Tio estis en la antaŭparolo de la dua volumo de l'*Année sociologique*, kie estis prezentitaj ses fakoj: religia sociologio, morala sociologio, jura sociologio, ekonomia sociologio, lingva sociologio, estetika sociologio; kaj aparte "Morfologio Sociala" estis metita. Tio estis pli klare montrita en lia artikolo *Sociologie et Sciences Sociales* en *De la Méthode dans les Sciences*, la kolektivaj artikoloj, eldonita en 1910, kiu preskaŭ difinis la sistemon de la sociologio de Durkheim-skolo, tie la ses fakoj estis prezentitaj kiel ses subdividoj de "Fiziologio Sociala" kiel jene:

I. Morfologio Sociala
II. Fiziologio Sociala
  1. Sociologio Religia
  2. Sociologio Morala
  3. Sociologio Jura
  4. Sociologio Ekonomia
  5. Sociologio Lingva
  6. Sociologio Estetika
III. Sociologio Ĝenerala

Ankoraŭ plie familia sociologio, politika sociologio aperis en laboraĵoj de Durkheim-skolo. Kaj la ĵus dirita sistemo estas akceptata de sciencistoj de tiu skolo, kaj jam nun ĝi sin trovas eĉ en lecionoj de francaj mezlernejoj.

Kaj en serio da laboraĵoj koncerne al religia sociologio, kiu okupis la ĉefan lokon en la studo de Durkheim-skolo, troviĝas aparte eldonitaj libroj: verkoj de Durkheim: "La formoj elementaj de religia vivo" 1912, kiun mi jam menciis, de Hubert kaj Mauss: *Mélanges d'histoire des religions*, 1909, de R. Hertz: *Mélanges de sociologie religieuse et de folklore*, 1928, de M. Bouglé: *Essais sur le régime des castes*, 1908, kaj *Leçons de sociologie sur l'évolution des valeurs*, 1928,

(1) Gaston Richard, *L'athéisme dogmatique dans la sociologie religieuse*, (*Cahiers de la Revue d'histoire et de philosophie religieuses*, No. 7), Strasbourg et Paris, 1923, p. 4–5.

kaj de Lévy-Bruhl kaj aliaj.[1]

Supre ni jam trarigardis situon de religia sociologio en la kampo de ĝenerala sociologio, kaj nun ni plie rigardu tiun de Budaisma Sociologio inter la subdividoj de religia sociologio. Dividante religian sociologion en fokojn, oni akiras jenan tabelon:

Religia Sociologio
- I. Kristana Sociologio
  - a) Katolika Sociologio
  - b) Protestanta Sociologio
- II. Mahometana Sociologio
- III. Budaisma Sociologio
- IV. Ŝintoisma Sociologio kaj aliaj.

Inter ili pri Kristana Sociologio, precipe pri Katolika Sociologio kaj pri Mahometana Sociologio, kiel mi jam iom menciis, en Eŭropa kaj Amerika sciencistaro sin trovas imponaj lekcioj kaj sufiĉe bonaj libroj. Estus senbezone mencii, ke precipe abundas verkoj koncerne al Kristana Sociologio.[2]

Sed tamen oni devas krii: En kia mizera stato sin trovas Budaisma Sociologio, kiu ja devas esti grava speciala fako de religia sociologio! Kompreneble ĝis nun ne mankis emfazo pri la neceseco de la sociologia studo de Budaismo, kaj iuj eĉ provis studi ĝin.

Kvankam sin trovas abunde da materialoj kaj fragmentoj de sociologiaj studoj pri Budaismo, sed ĝis nun ne estis provita la sistema sinteza studo. Estus senbezone mencii pri la manko de ĝia lekcio aŭ verko ĝenerala. Ne estis prezentita ĝia decida pretendo, aŭ sistemo, kvankam iliaj ĝermoj multe vidiĝis. Sed tamen, ĉu nun ĉiuj ĉi tiuj ne dependas de nia penado? Kaj almenaŭ la krono de la hejmlando de Budaisma Sociologio nature estos gajnata de azianoj.

(1) Profitante la okazon-mi nomu kelkajn verkojn pri religia sociologio:

a) En Francujo, Maunier: *Vie religieuse et vie économique*; Henri Beuchat kaj M. Hollebecque: *Les religions. Etude historique et sociologique du phénomène religieux*, Paris, Rivière, 1910; Raoul de la Grasserie: *Des religions comparées au point de vue sociologique*, Paris, 1899; M. Guyau: *L'Irréligion de L'Avenir. Etude sociologique*; k. t. p.

b) En Germanujo, Simmel, *Die Religion*; E. Trœltsch, *Gesammelte Schriften, II. Religion und Kirche*; Max Weber, *Gesammelte Aufsätze zur Religionssoziologie*, precipe, *II. Hinduismus und Buddhismus*, Tübingen, 1921; J. Wach, *Einführung in die Religions-soziologie*, 1931, kaj aliaj.

(2) Kelkaj verkoj pri Kristana Sociologio ĝenerala:

Penty (A. J.): *Towards a Christian Sociology*; Wallis (Louis); *Sociological Study of the Bible* 1912; Hill (Chatherton); *Sociological Value of Christianity*, 1912; Hudson (Canon C. D.): *Preface to Christian Sociology*, London, 1935.

Kajmijam menciis verkojn pri Katolika Sociologio, kaj do monu unu verkon pri Protestanta Sociologio:

Hauter (Ch.); *Le problème sociologique du Protestantisme* (*Cahiers de la Revue d'histoire et de Philosophie religieuse*, No. 5.)

Japanese News

Oldest Ainu Inhabitant

Sipsuke, known as the oldest inhabitant of Tokachi Prefecture in the Hokkaido has recently passed away.

He gave his age as 72, but in reality he had lost track of the passing years, and was 90.

Wthout near relatives, Sipsuke lived alone by himself in a small hut in the forest.

Buddists Scriptures

In Kumano Shrine of Aichi Prefecture 200 copies of the sutra "Hannya Kyo" have been preserved for 300 years.

They were copied by a priest at the request of a daimyo who had committed some sin and wished to atone by presenting the Buddhist scriptures and thereby earning the goodwill of the god enshrined in the Kumano Shrine. Attempts have been made in vain to find out the name of the priest who made these old copies.

Tennoji Bon Odori

Bon Odori was danced in the precincts of Tennoji, Osaka's ancient temple, on August 14th evening. Over 500 persons took part, all wearing the same patterned cotton kimono. Among them was an old man of 90 who enjoyed the occasion and danced with a fan in his hand.

The community dance continued on 15th evening and end 16th evening.

Historic Temple Site

It has been announced that the site of Kyotozu-in in Kamakura is to be auctioned off by the Fujisawa Tax Office.

The temple does not exist at present, but it was once one of Kamakura's five most flourishing Buddhist centers. It was established 686 years ago by Hojo Tokiyori.

Residents of Kamakura are now petitioning to have the auction stopped and to preserve the historic site which is within the compound of Kenchoji.

Fairytale Film

The J. O. Studio of Kyoto has been engaged upon the production of a fairytale film to introduce Japanese culture abroad.

The legend selected is "Marriage of Princess Kaguya," dealing with the moon fairy who appeared to an old man in a bamboo grove. He took her home, she grew up wonderfully beautiful and had many suitors, but refused them all to fly back to the moon.

The film will be released in Nagoya early in October.

Earthquake Anniversary

Anniversary gatherings in memory of the earthquake disaster hold in Tokyo, Yokohama and Kawasaki. This is the 12th anniversary, and with perspective the tragedy of the great is still vivid in the minds of those who lost their relatives or friends.

Memorial day is observed at the Honjo Memorial Hall as is the custom each September 1, and there is a lecture meeting in Gunjinkai Hall, Kudan.

Carved by Unkei

Chotokuji, a temple of Hayama, possesses a valuable statue of Buddha carved by the great Unkei.

But as the temple is not well off financially, the statue has been neglecting a fund with which to repair the Buddha.

Weapons Used in Crimes

An exhibition for the Enforcement of Justice and the Prevention of Crime hold under the auspices of the Tokyo Prefectural ex-Convicts Protection League, supported by the Ministry of Justice, Metropolitan Police Board, Public Procurator's office, and the Tokyo Imperial University.

This unusual exhibition of articles used in crimes take place at the Honganji in Tsukiji, September 4 to 13.

A thousand articles have been collected which have never been shown to the public before. Among them is the iron cauldron which it is said was used to boil Ishikawa Goemon in oil for his crimes.

Weapons used in assassinations and photographs of other crimenal articles will be on display.

Pigeon Apartments

It was a happy idea to make a home for the pigeons of Tsukiji Honganji. Inherited instinct made them cling to the Buddhist temple where their ancestors have been protected for years past.

But that no doubt the pigeons never dreamed of up-to-date apartments in concrete.

The new pigeon home is nearing completion, high above the ground, with many holes for the home-loving birds to enter and leave.

Buddhism and Waitresses

An interesting meeting was held on Sept, 5th afternoon at the Tsukiji Hoganji to which the waitresses of Ginza cafes were invited.

An eloquent priest lectured to the girls who serve customers in the lurid, neonlight district of the Ginza on the flesh and the devil, preaching to them about the principles of Budhism.

It is reported that the waitresses were pleased to listen to the learned priest's discourse, but as to the temptations of the night life of Tokyo they had nothing to say.

Germans To Study The East

An oriental institute is to be opened in Berlin in October for the study of all branches of oriental culture.

Its member bodies will be the already existing Oriental Seminary, the Institute for Semitic and Islamic Study, the Sinolocic Seminary, and the Indo-German Institute.

Painting of Nichiren

The 22nd exhibition of the Art Institute of Japan now being held in the Tokyo Prefectural Art Gallery, Uyeno Park, is attracting much attention.

Mr. Buzan Kimura, the artist who specialises in Buddhist paintings is showing a painting of Nichiren preaching to the public. The work is done with such vividness that visitors crowd about the painting at all times of the day.

Historic Gate

The new buildings of the Tokyo Imperial Museum of Fine Arts is now under construction. The old wooden gate which marks the entrance will be preserved.

This impressive gate was once the entrance to Rinnoji when Uyeno Park was a Buddhist estate. At the time of the Restoration Rinnoji was burned down, but the gate remained. As it links present day Japan with Yedo, the structure will be preserved although the new museum buildings will be thoroughly modern.

Burmese Actor

To promote friendly relations between Japan and Burma through the medium of the movies, an interesting film is now being produced at the Kinuta studios of P.C.L.

Mr. Mon N. Puh, a Budmese actor-director, is being featured, and playing opposite to him is Miss Mitsuko Takao.

The picture is to be titled, "The Daughter of Japan," and is a romance between a Burmese young man and a Japanese girl, with picturesque scenery as background.

Late Dutch Scholar's Treatise On Buddhism

A laborious literary work on ancient Japanese Buddhism by a Dutch scholar, who had studied Buddhism in Japan to the very end of his life in the strong belief that Buddhism itself is the light of the each and has brought virility and wisdom to the Japanese spirit, has now been published through the good offices of the Society for International Cultural Relations five years after the death of the scholar.

The author of the work is the late Dr. M. W. de Visseh who was professor of Japanese culture at Leiden university, and his work, the fruit of his laborious study of the subject, consists of two volumes and of 762 pages. His work is a treaties on ancient Buddhism in Japan aud its sutras and rites.

He finished his work in 1928, but he died two years later without being able to realize his cherished desire to publish his work, it is said. Regretting this, Dr. Junjiro Takakusu, a leading Buddhist scholar in this country, and Honorable President of our Bureau, had exerted himself to secure publication of the work, and at last succeeded in realizing his object by obtaining the support of society of International Cultural Relations.

The work in question was recently published in Holland, and copies of the book arrived at the Society Tuesday. Dr. Takakusu is expressing admiration at the excellence of the work, and is praising it as a rare literary work in English on Buddhism in the world.

Temple Gate Rebuilt

The imposing gate of Shitennoji of Osaka was destroyed in the typhoon last year. Dr. Shunichi Amanuma, professor of the Imperial University of Kyoto, has designed a new gate in the style of the Kamakura period. The work will take two years to complete.

大乘佛教の海外宣布

ブルーノウ・ペツオールド

若し我々にして大乘佛教を世界に流布し是を活潑々地な一の國際的勢力の動因にまで作り上げやうと考へるなら我々はその爲には丁度最上のものを持ち合せてゐるのである。かゝる考へは私の常に保持して居つたものであり，今日も猶且つ是を堅持してゐるのである。

然らばその所謂「最上のもの」とは何であるか。

それは一般人が時々此教の注入を受けそれ等から成る大乘諸教理の混合物から極めて平易にして通俗的なエキスを作り出して行くといふやうな薄弱なものであつてはならぬ。かゝる無味な飲料水は，退屈凌ぎに少し計り佛教を弄んでは見るが是に對して眞劔に身心を捧げやうといふやうな考へは毛頭持ち合せぬ上流階級の老衰の善女や神經枯渇の善男達の趣味に精々適するのみであらう。かゝる現代文化の「殘留物」を大乘佛教といふやうな高尙にして偉大なものへ不斷且つ眞實に引入れやうとする試みは實際には何の効果もないものである。既に小乘經典中の佛陀も道を渇仰することの眞摯なる將に焦死せんとするが如きものでなければ眞理を啓示することを拒んだのである。

然りかく道を求めて焦死せんとするもの，かゝるもののみが强烈な，そして生命をも盛り上げるやうな清凉劑，即ち自己の全機構を力づける飲料水を必要とするのである。

とは言へ，既に病衰にまで弱り切つた人間に最も强力なリキュールを與へることの不可なることも亦自明のことである。それは本人にとつて最も悪いことであるだらう。

かくして我々は（大乘）大般涅槃經に於ける佛陀が佛教中に五味を分ち，乳から漸進して醍醐に及ばしめ，その各々をそれぞれ適應するものに與へた例に倣ふべきであらう。右の内「乳」と名付けられた教にしても生命を作り上げる程の不思議な効力を有する一のエキスであつて，それをも消化し得ないやうな體質機構の持主の爲には浪費すべきでない。

私の佛教界の多數の友人は，大乘佛教をして歐米に勢力を得せしむる爲には，各宗の傳道師により宗派的な方法で傳道せしめるのが，最善の方法であるといふ意見を持つてゐるやうに見えるが，私は屢々口に筆に此の見解を排除して來たのである。即ち佛教特に大乘佛教は寧ろ非宗派的方法によつて世界に宣布すべきで，その意味は佛教の各宗派學派は猜忌や狂信を伴はずに世界に紹介せらるべきであり，從つて宗教宗派としてよりは哲學的學說として紹介さる可きであるといふにある。即ち最初に世界は佛教の眞理に依つて啓蒙されねばならず――敬虔心や宗教的儀禮行事は是に引續いて進むべきである。その故は大乘佛教中に包含さるゝ深遠な思想の充分な認識なしには敬虔さといひ宗教的儀式といふも畢竟單に空虛な形相に過ぎないから。

然し茲に大なる困難が起るのである即ち諸大乘教の雜多な教義――相互に矛盾衝突する學說の混沌體としてゞはなく論理的全體として眺むべきである大乘佛教――から如何にしてかゝる潑溂たるエキスを作り出すかといふことであり，又かゝるエキスが如何にして，外國人に受納れらるゝやうにする事が出來るかの二點である。

第一に此の種の仕事はまだ着手されて居らず，その人としてもかゝる仕事を爲し得るものは實に寥々たるものであらう。例へば日本語で編纂された佛教の大辭典をフランスその他の國語に飜譯し無數の不可解な術語を外國人の喉へ押し込んだところで充分とは言へまい。されば夫等の辭典から又進んでは經，論等の原典其物の中から彼の所謂エキスを產出して行くべきで，かゝるエキスを釀造することは實にこの方面のマスターでなければ企て及ばぬ處である。私を以て見れば，實にこの點が大乘佛教の國際化を唱へる人々によつて見逃されて居ると思はれる。因にかくは言ふものゝ茲では道德的條項や形而上學抜きの實際生活に有用な教句の精髓のみで盛り上げられた大乘佛教の幼稚なるハンドブツクの製作を提唱してゐるのではなく，それは，その深遠さを以て，デカルト，カント，ヘーゲル，シエリング等の思想と比較すべく，又かくすることによつてのみ外人の大乘佛教に對する注意を奪取し得る處の「思想」と「思想體系」とを闡明する事にあるのである。

扨てかゝる巨大な勞作を企てんと欲するものは大乘教の全體的な紛糾錯綜を表現し得る一つの外國語を解し得るものでなければならぬ。而かもその語は一般外國人に解し易く，その表現は野卑でなく，抽象的でもなく大乘思想を泰西思想界と連結する鏈環を作り上げ得るものでなければならず，更に又それは何よりも大乘教理の「最高のもの」を世間に著明にし得る言語でなければならぬ。

而してかゝる要求を充たすには一個の單獨な人間や一個の一般的な佛教會などの力の及ぶ處ではあるまい。故に私の提出し得る唯一の勸告は數年來私の唱へ來つた **大乘學院** の建設であつて，此の學院こそは今日まで詳しく「大乘」の名を耳にしなかつた諸國民，諸國家に大乘佛教の認識を傳播せしめる任務を負はさるべきものであると思考するのである。

（原文は前號に掲載）

第三回汎太平洋佛教青年會大會の展望と滿洲佛教の現狀及將來

稻　葉　文　海

昨年日本に於て開催されたる第二回汎太平洋佛教青年會大會に於ては，次回大會卽ち第三回汎太平洋佛教青年會大會開催地の決定を見ることが出來なかつた。それは主たる參加國であり，汎太平洋佛教青年會聯盟のメンバーたる北米，暹羅，滿洲の代表より夫々自國開催を提案して讓らず，終にその決定權は擧げて全日本佛教青年聯盟に一任されることになつたのである。爾後一周年過ぎ，漸く世人も之を問題視するに至り，此に全聯獨自の立場を以て之が裁斷をなさねばならぬ時機に到達したのである。是より先に本年四月，金澤に於ける全聯第五回總會に於ても第三回を暹羅に於て開催すべしといふ議案が提出され，次いで五月の全國理事會に於ても此問題が議せられたのである。その際大村理事長はそれ等に關して滿洲國の實地調査の要あるを說き自らその任に當る意向あることを言明されたので各理事も亦之を贊同したのであつたが，今回その言明に基いて大村理事長に私が隨伴して，去る八月六日より同卅一日まで，直接滿洲國に渡つて之が調査視察を遂げたのである。曩に常光理事も亦如上の要務を帶びて布哇，北米に旅立ちて彼地の實地調査に當つて居り，一方暹羅國に關しては佛教について特別な熱意を持つてをられる同國駐日公使を通じて調査しつゝあるのである。かくてこれ等三國の資料を蒐め揃へた上で，此處に最後の斷案を下すべき順序である。此の問題は單に國際佛教の消長に關するのみならず，廣範なる國交上にも重要な意味を持つものであるから，本部としても充分愼重なる態度を以て臨む必要があるのである。

然して我々の渡滿は單に第三回大會に關して滿洲國の現狀を視るといふに止まらず，更に同國佛教の將來について深き關心を持ち，これについて何等か將來の見透しを得たいといふ意向を持つてゐたのである。率直に云ふならば，現段階に於ける滿洲國佛教そのものが果して第三回大會を指導開催し得る狀態にありや否やは調査を待たずして一應判定のつくものであつて，强ち態々現地に出掛けて調査視察を遂ぐる絕對的必要もあるまいが，然し今後滿洲佛教の發展のために大會開催が絕對に必要とあらば，多少の支障は排除しても開催するだけの決心は持たねばならぬと思ふ。

我が聯盟は曩に駐日滿洲國大使を通じて，「滿洲國に於ける佛教興隆に關する進言書」を張國務總理及び阮文教部大臣に呈し，又皇帝陛下御來朝を壽ぎては,「滿洲佛敎を語る夕」を催してその布敎傳導を研究したる等早くより深き關心を持つてゐるのである。例へ同國に目下のところ佛靑聯盟の組織がないとしても又その佛敎が到底第三回大會といふが如き新運動の中心に立ち得る程進歩的でないとしても，彼地の僧侶居士，殊に靑年等が此問題に關して如何ほどの關心を持つてゐるか，抑も昨年の提案が果して如何許り確實なる筋のものであつたかといふ直接の問題と又世にもすばらしき滿洲建國運動が果して如何に彼地の佛敎を刺戟してゐるか，更に所謂日本佛敎各宗各派の滿洲布敎の實狀如何，乃至總じてこれ等の問題に關して滿洲國政府の總意が那邊に存するかを打診しなくてはならぬと思はれた。以上の如きが我々渡滿に際しての心持であつたことを告白しておかねばならぬ。

扨て斯くの如き問題について如何なる回答を得たかを極めて簡潔に述べて見たいと思ふ。但し記行的詳述は敢て之を避けることにしたい。

先づ滿洲佛敎の現狀について率直に言ふならば素より宗派的組織統率は無く，又政府に於てもその調査未だ完了せず從つて所謂宗敎政策といふが如きものも未だ確立してゐない樣である。云はゞ佛敎と道敎とが混成して深き民族的宗敎心とまでなつてゐる上に，その混成の割合に依つて，或は佛敎，或は道敎，更に佛敎中の大きな流れとして喇嘛敎となつて現はれてゐる樣に思はれる。又ハルピンの極樂寺は天台宗を稱し，奉天の萬壽寺は臨濟宗といふが如き宗派的な色彩もないでもない。然し此國に於ても支那本土のそれの如く結局「念佛禪」といふ概念を以て通稱することが出來るであらう。その他目下目覺しき活躍を示してゐる紅卍敎や，在理敎やその他の類似宗敎的集團も相當ある樣である。基督敎は殆んど鳴りを靜めて，徒らに大厦高塔が聳へてゐる樣に思はれる。これには種ゝの事情もあることであらう。之を要するに一般民間宗敎は此處でも極めて現世利益に傾いてゐることは爭はれぬ事實であらう。在留日本人間に於ける宗敎はその本國に於けると同樣，宛然その縮圖たるに留まり，滿洲開敎といふてもそれは在留日本人への布敎を意味するものである以上，開敎師自身も積極的に滿人に呼び掛け樣とはしてゐないし，又後述する樣に滿洲靑年間に佛敎革新の氣分が漲つてゐようともそれを助長指導しようとする意向も見へないのは我々の深く遺憾とする所である。人の道敎團，天理敎，成長の家等の新興宗敎の活躍は單に在留日本人を對象とするのみならず，更に一歩を進めつゝある樣でこれは注目すべきことである。此處に特說したいのは，昨年我が第二回汎太平洋佛靑大會に代表として出席された當千の人々のその後の消息である。團長たりしハルピン極樂寺の如光法師始め是等の人々はこの國の要所々々に控へて，もどかしき滿洲佛敎界に在り乍ら，日本を崇め，日本佛敎

を慕ひ，如何にもして佛敎革新をなさんと努力を續けてゐるのはいとほしくも又心强く最も愉快とするところである。殊に彼等は新興滿洲帝國の建國精神を佛敎精神に還元して，以て佛敎興隆を計ると共に，これこそ新興帝國に盡す佛敎徒の責任であるとの深き自覺に立つてゐるのである。

平安初頭傳敎，弘法の時代を想起せざるを得ない。大陸佛敎本來の歴史を顧み，又從來文字通り世捨て人として稍もすれば世人に蔑視されて來た彼等が，此處まで到達したといふことは全く驚異に價するものであらう。然し乍らこの一大運動も只管日本佛敎徒の指導援助に俟たねばならぬと彼等は信じてゐるし，我ゝも亦その然るべきを信ずるものである。日本國家が國運を賭して，滿洲建國を指導し盟約したると同樣我等も亦佛敎の根本精神に立つて若き滿洲佛敎徒の熱烈なる希望に充分の理解と同情とを惜しまず，大いに協力すべき責任があると信ずるものである。素より滿洲佛敎には確然たる宗派は存在せぬ。從つてこれ等の問題についても，日本の一宗一派で指導聯携すべきでもなく，又爲し得るものでもあるまい。この點は本誌第三號の坐談會の記事にも明瞭に論究されてゐるところである。

扨て以上の如き現狀に第三回大會開催問題を點じて考へて見なければならぬ。滿洲佛敎徒殊に若き僧侶や居士は昨年の大會提案通り自國開催を心から希望してゐる。如光法師の如きはその爲めに極樂寺住職といふ重い地位を乘一法師に讓つて，全滿洲佛靑組織の案を作製して文敎部の認可を請ひ（已に認下されてゐる筈）東奔西走身を以て之に當り，目下北支那に滯在しそのまま南支にまで行脚を延ばす意向とさへ聞いてゐる。云ふまでもなく昨年の提案を實行せんとする目標に邁進してゐるのである。實に近代稀に見る純情且つ實行力のある人であり，靑年佛敎徒が心服してゐるのみならず，上下を通じて法師の人格を稱へぬ者は無い。

我ゝが面談した滿人各部大臣は大會開催に殘らず贊意を表せられ，中には相當具體的問題に觸れて懇談に及んだ向もある。しかし日本官吏併に司令部方面に於いては「贊否」相半する實狀である。(否は反對ではなく時機尚早を唱へるのである。)勿論日本全聯がその一任された權限に依り滿洲に於て開催すべしと裁斷するならば，充分の責任を以て之を引受けるといふことは，滿洲全體の總意である。

然らば日滿佛敎大會開催は如何。かういふことになれば全部雙手を擧げて贊成するところである。勿論以上の意向は我ゝの推度ではなく，各要人に一々具體的接衝の末の結論であるが我ゝとしては諸般の事情についての資料を得ればよい。決定は三國夫ゝの調査資料に依つて最後になされる筈である。

更に大なる問題は滿洲佛敎將來についてのことである。このことこそ將來永く全力を注がねばならぬ日本佛敎の高い宗敎的責任であらねばならぬ。先

に説明したる如き我々渡滿の目的は，極めて率直に，張總理始め各部大臣，南司令官始めその幕僚，參議府，總務司長等の政府主腦部をつくして諒解を得たし，五族協和會の幹部，新京特別市公處，滿洲開教師，世界大同佛敎會等上下を通じて充分の理解を與へることの出來たのは何より大なる收穫といはねばならぬ。恐らくこれを種子として今後この國の佛敎の動向が自ら指示されてゆくであらう。但し滿洲佛敎はその國その民族の宗敎である以上，日本佛敎そのまゝの延長でなければならぬ道理もなく，又現狀の日本佛敎はそれほどの自負も持たれまい。寧ろ通弊を掃ひ落した純眞な日本佛敎が，大陸的に否滿洲國的に甦生してゆかねばならぬと思ふ。聖德太子始め，傳敎，弘法に依つて始められた佛敎は，大陸佛敎そのまゝのものではなかつた。故にこそ今日の日本佛敎があり得るのである。我々は佛敎の根本精神に立つてその媒介の重責を盡せばよいのである。

翻つて思ふに日本佛敎各宗の滿洲布敎は今や一應，自己の布敎政策の批判を必要とする時機に達してゐる。帝都新京が奠められたので，日本佛敎各宗も從來大連にあつた布敎本部を新京に移し，夫々新都目拔きの場所に廣大なる土地を購入し，更に思ひ切つた大伽籃を建立するといはれる。それは恰も滿洲といふものが宗敎的未開拓の處女地ででもある樣に，一刻を爭つて自宗の繩張りに狂奔するかの如き觀さへあつた。然るところ現在新京の實際を見るに夫々數千坪より數萬坪に至るまで土地だけは定められてあるが，扨てその上に建立さすべき大伽籃は一向に見えて來ない。當初の勢ならば最早輪奐の美を競つてさながら佛都の觀をさへ呈するかと思はれたのである。それは日本佛敎の滿洲布敎といふことはしかく簡單にまゐるものではないといふことを物語つてゐるのである。元來布敎對象を充分認識もせず唯徒に氣負ひ込んだ嫌がなかつたか。何故かなら從來の政策は在留日本人を對象とするもので，直接滿洲人を對象とする場合の考慮されてゐない布敎陣を，そのまゝに適用せんとしたといふ大きな無理が存在するのである。

愚見を述べるならば，現在各宗が夫々拂つてゐる犧牲を打つて一丸として，强力なる日滿佛敎協會を組織しあらゆる手段を以て彼地佛敎の刷新興隆に努むべきであらう。佛敎專門學校を經營して，滿洲僧侶の敎育をなし，その出身者を以つて將來滿洲佛敎刷新の選ばれたる佛使となすべきである。又民衆へ直接の布敎としては，全國各都市に佛敎靑年會館を建設して，その施設を充分にし，その機關を通じて民衆敎化文化向上に資すべきである。かくして滿洲新政府の政策と相俟つてゆけば，將來洋々たるものがあるであらう。斯くてこそ我が日本民族が曾つて大陸に負ふた佛敎文化の廣大なる恩惠に報ゆる所以ともなるであらう。

海外通信

北米加州より

その後まことに御無沙汰にのみ相過し申譯もございません。布哇は島から島へ，文字通りの南船北馬でついつい心ならずも失禮してゐます。國際佛敎通報局の在外委員の方は布哇は今村寛猛氏に，北米は古川湛濟氏に，夫々選定方を依願中につき，小生歸朝までには決定して御報告申上ます。

次に八月九日午前，北米加州サンタバーバラに居住のゴダード翁を訪ねました。同地駐在開敎使澤田諦了師及角田昇君（佛靑大會に通譯をしてくれた北米本願寺敎團の留學生）と三人でした。翁の住居は極めて質素でお一人の生活です。サンタバーバラの地は風光頗るよろしく氣候も溫暖にて各地から避暑や避寒に來るところで日本の鎌倉といふ所です。市街も樹木に圍まれ何となく南歐の氣分をただよわしてゐます。翁の住居は町はづれの閑靜なところです。翁にお目にかゝつて英文聖典飜譯のお禮も申述ました。そうして翁は自分がこの聖業にたづさわらせていただいた事は非常に嬉しいことだと申されました。翁はあの聖典に多少の增減をなして更に自費出版をしてゐられます。丁度，私達の訪れた時，これを千冊，日本の圖書館へお送するところだと申してゐられました。翁はこのサンタバーバラから十五哩の地點で，附近一帶を瞰下する事のできる高臺に四十英町の土地を買ひ入れ，そこに禪堂を建築するのだと話されました。土地は已に求め目下設計中だとあつて，翁自らが製圖せられてゐます。正面に禪室があり一方に各地方からの參集者の寢室や硏究室，一方に翁の居室や炊事室等が配されてゐます。現今の翁の家の一室には釋迦佛と觀音が安置せられてあります。案內されるまゝに禮拜をいたしました。翁の所には時々白人佛敎徒が訪問もするし，又文書で各地方の佛敎硏究者と應答してゐられるとの事。國際佛敎通報三冊（一，二，三號）をお渡して時々御通信を御願してをきました。

次に米國各地に於て盆踊りが熾んです。八月十日十一日の兩日，ロサンゼルス本願寺別院に於て盆の法要があり夜間は街路に豆提灯をブラ下げ，交通を止めて，白人巡査の交通整理で約四百人の老幼男女が踊りました。中には白人も手拍子をそろへて踊ります。ボンダンスとして，米人の氣分に適合したのでせう，北米各地にて，燎原の火の如く盛んになつてゐます。佛敎音頭，廣島音頭，江州音頭其他いやしくもボンダンスに採用できるものはすべて踊られます。今後益々各種の宗敎的音頭を作つて供給する必要があると思はれます。

次に八月十七日，北米，加州サンピドロ市に於て目下開會の博覽會に佛敎デーが催されます。十八日は日本デーです。佛敎デーが博覽會のプログラムの中に入つてゐるのは，面白いではありませんか。その様子は又御通知申上げます。

次に，北米，加州サリナスといふ所に，本願寺の會堂がありますが昨年秋，大梵鐘を求めてつるしました。あの韻々たる底力のある音に白人は驚いたそうです。今迄はお寺のベルと云へば，教會のやさしい音のみを連想したのに今度は實におそろしく腹の底へしみわたる大梵鐘の音に驚くのも無理はありません。然し，白人は大に喜んでゐるそうです。佛青會員が毎朝，定刻にこれを鳴らすので，町の時の鐘となつたのです。

先は大略，御報告申ます。又，御通知申ます。皆様へよろしく。アメリカもあつくてあつくて閉口です。今お寺のパーラーで，汗をかき乍ら，ホントの走書です。

八月十一日

常光浩然

淺野研眞兄

布哇より

謹啓

酷暑の候高堂愈々御健勝の段大賀の至りに存じ奉り候，平素は常に御無沙汰にのみ打過ぎ何とも申譯けの致しやう無之，唯々恐縮致し居り候，扨又私儀此度布哇佛教青年會主事に就任いたし候に就ては未だ然るべき御挨拶も申上げず候事實に汗顔の至りに御座候實は就任以來日々身邊の業務に追はるゝまゝ始終心に懸けつゝも其の意を果さず遂に今日に及び申候，失禮の段幾重にも御寛恕を仰ぎ奉り候

就任以來日なほ淺く未だ當地の事情にも精通せず種々困難有之候へ共今後益々精進努力其の職責を全ふ致し度存じ居り候，當地への御用何なりとも御下命被下度出來得る限りの便宜御取計ひ申上度尚今後一層御後援御指導を賜らむことを切に懇願奉り候　拜具

昭和十年七月一日

布哇佛教青年會

主事　今村寛猛

全日本佛教青年會聯盟殿

上海より

啓者大醒上月行脚

貴邦觀光

貴邦佛教足迹所至古刹史蹟目不暇及寶物新猷均歎希有多荷

座下慇懃招待心銘無已他日有緣不難再會大醒此遊最爲慨歎不置之一事卽在一千年前於佛教文化上溝通兩國一家之情況而今不可復得矣想

座下慈悲過人爲佛教爲衆生亦必抱有同感焉敝國佛教古代之文物現亦有大心之士出而整理茲奉影印宋磧砂版大藏經及宋藏遺珍趙城金刻楞嚴經各版樣一份竊願兩國學佛之士仍從佛教文化上相互光揚亦一末世之殊勝因緣也此致

研眞先生道席幷頌

法安不宣

中華沙門大醒合十謹啓

中華民國廿四年六月二十日

通訊處　上海虹口東有恒路雪竇寺

國際佛教通報局定款

名　稱

第一，本局を國際佛教通報局と稱す

事務所

第二，本局の事務所を全日本佛教青年會聯盟本部に置く

目　的

第三，本局は日本內海及海外に向つて佛教事情の通報をなし，且つ佛教徒相互間の各種便宜を計るを以て目的とす

事　業

第四，本局の目的を達成するため左記の事業を行ふ

イ，日本內地及世界各國より佛教事情に關する質問の通報を行ふ

ロ，必要に應じ日本語及世界各國語を以て佛教事情の通報を行ふ

ハ，外國人の日本觀光に際しては各國の便益を與へ，特にその佛教に關する方面に於て之を爲す

ニ，定時或は隨時に各國語を以て文書の刊行をなす

ホ，その他必要と認めたる事業を行ふ

役　員

第五，本局の事務を處理するため左の役員を置く

イ，局長　一名

ロ，幹事　三名

ハ，評議員　若干名

局長は本局　を總括す

幹事は本局の事務を處理す

評議員は局長の提案に依る重要事務を審議す

第六，評議員は左記の者を以て之に充つ

イ，全日本佛教青年會館聯盟理事及主事

ロ，全日本佛教青年會聯盟理事會に於て推薦したる者

第七，局長及幹事は評議員會に於て決定す

第八，役員の仕期は二ケ年とす（但し重任を妨げず）

經　費

第九，本局の經費は左記のものに依て之を支辨す

イ，本局基金の活用

ロ，寄附金

ハ，その他の收入

補　則

第十，本定款に記載せられざる事項は，凡て評議員會に於て協議す

第十一，第一回の役員は全日本佛教青年會聯盟理事會に於て決定す

定價	一部	金二十錢	送料二錢
	一年	金二圓四十錢	送料不要

昭和十年四月卅日第三種郵便物認可
昭和十年九月廿七日印刷（毎月一回
昭和十年十月一日發行　一日發行）

東京市外吉祥寺337
編輯發行兼印刷人　淺野研眞

東京市牛込區早稻田鶴卷町107
印刷所　康文社印刷所
電話牛込(34)1950番 5049番

東京市神田區一ツ橋二の三
發行所　國際佛教通報局
電話九段(33)4428番
振替東京83015番

昭和十年四月三十日第三種郵便物認可 昭和十年九月二十七日印刷納本（毎月一回）昭和十年十月一日發行（一日發行） 國際佛教通報 第一卷 第七號

昭和十年四月三十日第三種郵便物認可 昭和十年十月二十七日印刷納本 昭和十年十一月一日發行（毎月一回一日發行）第一卷 第八號

The International Buddhist Bulletin

國際佛教通報

第一卷 昭和十年十一月 第八號 〔Vol. I. Nov. 2501/1935 No. 8.〕

要 目 〔Contents〕

東 京 國際佛教通報局 發 行
The International Buddhist Information Bureau
Tokyo, Kanda, Hitotsubashi, II—3

去る十月四日，傳通會館に於ける
柴田，大村兩氏中心の座談會の光景

Present Religious Conditions in Java.

By Rev. W. JOSIAS von DIENST.

Leader of the Buddhist Missionary Work in the Netherlands Indies.

It is a well-known fact that about 600 and more years ago Java was a Buddhist country, Tantrayana being the form of Buddhism prevailing in those days. It were the Tantrayanists that built the Borobudur and most of the other now almost forsaken sanctuaries. Next to Buddhism, Hinduism also had a lot of influence, which may be shown by the fact that at present we still find the ruins of many Hindu temples, such as Tjandi Prambanan, Tjandi Panataran and others.

In 1500 (or about that year) a Mohammedan from Persia, named Malik Ibrahim, arrived in Java and settled at Grissee, in the neighbourhood of what is now Sourabaya. He started preaching Islam and invited other Mohammedan preachers to Java. It was about that time that the greed of the European nations guided them over the ocean, in their search for profit and wealth, and Portuguese, English and Dutch ships frequently came to Java, in order to trade with the population. There seems to be ground for the suspicion, that bye and bye Islam was accepted by the natives of the island mainly for convenience's sake. As Buddhists they were not allowed to fight, and Islam was a fighting religion, so they accepted the latter, which allowed them to make war against the foreign intruders. Part by part the whole of the island came into possession of the white man, partly by misleading treaties and partly by war.

It was rather long after the Netherlands Indies came into the possession of the Dutch, that scientists could find out, what kind of Buddhism it was that had been prevailing in Java. After the Lombok-expedition, now about 45 years ago, some old Sanskrit books were found, which gave information on the matter. The most important of these books was the so-called Sang Hyang Kamahayanikam, which showed that once upon a time not only Java, but also part of Sumatra, Celebes, and the whole of the islands of Bali and Lombok had one and the same religion' which was Hinduism, mixed with a Tantrayana form of Buddhism.

So much for the past; the present shows a quite other picture.

Islam. At present Java may be called a Mohammedan country. Wherever we go, we find lots of mosques, even in the smallest native villages. Due to the fact that there are many Arabs in the country, which are rather fanatic Moslem for the main part, and which are very much respected by the natives, the influence of Islam is felt even at the most distant places. The reason is the following:

Most of those Arabs are traders and moneylenders. As the native is rather poor, he knows that he can always go to his Arabian co-religionists for advance-money on the rice harvest, which is always readily given. The reason for this helpfulness, however, is not that the Arab wants to assist his Islamic brother; in most cases he arranges with the native that the latter can have the money if the former can have the rice after it is cut, and the poor native has no choice and agrees. Due to these conditions, the native girl is also an easy prey for the Arabian woman hunter, so that the latter gets a lot of influence in the native household, which is very much in the favour of Islam.

Indeed, the Mohammedan Arab is the worst usurer in the world, and he knows how to use his influence. Sometimes, whole villages and their neighbourhood are in the hands of two or three rich Arabs, and the native population can do very little against them. It will be clear, that this must have a great influence on the religious condition of the country, but it also shows that Islam is, for the native, only little more than just a kind of veneer, a polish, whilst in his heart he is still remembering his old Gods and teachings.

This may be clearly shown by the native stage play, called "wajang." The "dalang" or stage master, who also gives an explanation during the play, tells his audience the stories of the Mahabharata and the Ramayana, of the

life of the Buddha and His Enlightenment, and so on. This is why Buddhism is never forgotten in the island. The old gods of Java still live, and the Buddha, particularly in Central Java, is still a living reality. In different places there are societies for the study of the "Igama koeno," the old religion of the island.

Buddhism and Hinduism. When we go, however, to the Tengger and Ijang Mountains, we find Buddhism and Hinduism the prevailing religions, nicely mixed together in such a way, that it is almost impossible to tell at the first sight where Hinduism ends and Buddhism starts. Moreover, both are intermixed with many old myths and legends originating from the old animism the natives adhered to before the Hindus brought them their religions. It are particularly these people, which are easily influenced by Christianity, especially in its Roman Catholic form, because the Catholic saints and angels appeal to their minds. In Central Java, where the remains of the old Buddhist and Hindu sanctuaries are still existing, nicely restored and preserved by Government, Islam could not do its work so well as in the other parts of the country, but Christianity succeeded in getting quite a lot of influence there. And it is a remarkable thing, that Europeans do not want any Christian servants in their houses, "because," so they say, "those Christian natives are not honest." And the same must be said about the Bataks in the North of Sumatra, who, almost as a whole, were converted to Christianity by the Rheinische Mission. They are considered the most dishonest and larcenous race of the whole of the Netherlands Indies Archipelago.

If one lives in Java for a rather long time, and if he really mixes with the people, he finds out, that most of them lack the courage to confess that in their hearts they are more Buddhists than Mohammedans. When you see a native in Java performing his religious duties, as praying five times a day, and so on, it really is an exception. As I said, Islam is nothing but a veneer. It does not live in the hearts of the people. Whatever they do: building a new house, sinking a well or closing it up, when a child is born, when people are dying, they follow the old customs, taught to their ancestors by the first Hindu and Buddhist teachers that came to the island. When there is a marriage, flowers are offered to the dewas at almost every street corner. When the rice is harvested, the same ceremonies take place and also at the beginning of the rice planting season. If you have seen real Mohammedan countries, you are really surprised to find such a mixture of Islam and older religions in Java. It is all due to the fact that Islam does not appeal to the inner mind or soul of the people.

Moreover, there are about 5 million Chinese in Java, and they confess that they are Buddhists. Some of them will tell you that they are Confucianists too, but Confucianism is not a religion in the same sense of the word as Buddhism. In almost every Chinese temple you will find images not only of the Buddha but also of the most important Bodhisattwas. It is a pity, however, that even the Chinese priests do not know what they talk about when they utter the name of the Buddha (Dji Lay Hud, Hud Khauw). That is why they cannot guide their people, for a blind man cannot guide another blind man. Up to the present our Mission, however, is only too glad to be allowed to use the Chinese temples for giving lectures, ceremonies, sermons, etc.

Then there are several thousands of Japanese in Java, and up to the present they are wholly without any spiritual guidance. Our Mission has tried to get into touch with them, but due to the fact that the Chinese are afraid of the advantages of the Japanese trade in cheap goods, there is some animosity between the two races and it was almost impossible to bring them to the temples, although they are quite willing to visit our lectures, given in other places. Also most of the Indians sympathize with the work done by our Mission, even if they are not Buddhists but Hindus themselves, saying that Buddhism is an Indian religion anyhow.

Christianity. Most of the Europeans in Java (about 150.000) are Christians, but only a very few know their religion or take any notice of it. They just live and do not care whether they act according to the teachings of Christ or not. They do not care at all, swear from morn till night, and the churches are almost empty. The most influential Christian denomination is Roman Catholicism.

In Central Java there are about 10.000 christianized natives and also in the other parts of the island a few can be found. As Buddhism has no fight with any other religion, I better not tell any particulars about the methods used by Christian missionaries in some parts of the archipelago. In the island of Bali and in some other parts of the Netherlands Indies Christian missionaries are not allowed to work, due to the fact that formerly their activities gave rise to a lot of trouble.

Our Mission in Java and its prospects. We have been working in Java from 1929 and it really was pioneer work. At present there is no place in the whole of the island where the people do not know that a new effort is made to bring the Javanese back to their old religion. We have had success amongst natives and Chinese people, whereas there are also about 30 European Buddhists in the island at present. If we only could have our way, both with regard to funds and to workers, we are sure that within two years thousands and thousands of the natives would have accepted Buddhism again. When the Rev. bhikkhu Narada Thera was in Java, he called it the most fertile soil for our religion, and we are sure that he was right. But what can we do? In the whole of Java, for a population of about 42 millions, there are only four priests and two lay workers. And these do not know in the morning whether they will have anything to eat at night.

Government is willing to give us all kinds of facilities with regard to our work. The Buddhist workers in Java are willing to sacrifice themselves and everything they have and are. The people are anxious to hear our message, and when we come into touch with them, they understand, because it sounds to them as the echo of an almost forgotten teaching. Will Japanese Buddhism take the chance for the sake of our Blessed Lord and His Exalted Teachings?

It will not be a difficult task to Buddha-ize Java. Buddhism is in the hearts of the people, at the very bottom of their souls. The Javanese soul is created by Buddhism and it will never find rest till it kneels down again at the foot of the Tathagata, saying; "Buddham saranam gacchami," I go to the Buddha for refuge.

Buddhist Monuments in Java

By G. Venkatachalam

In the distance are the high mountains; their cloudcrowned summits soar towards the vault of heaven. The brow of the hills near by and the bosom of the encircling valley below are studded with ever-green palms, whose grey feathery tufts wave and nod to every passing breeze blowing across the fertile plains where the earth and sky meet in a lovely green and blue transparent haze. The meandering silver-streaks of water yonder gleam placidly over a shimmering landscape of fields, and the morning mists lie gently over fantastic shadows in space. Soon the warm luminous wings of the Sun over the scene, silently unveiling the beauties all around; and then, the wonder of wonders, right in front of you rises in majestic isolation and supernal splendour, a pyramidal mass chiselled stones, wrapped in eternal meditation!

It stands out, lit with bright spots and dark shadows, against a grey sky, like a dreamy citadel grarding a fairy princess within its walls. The Sun now floods the place with "loud barks of light" which are echoed back from the silent solemn walls, in bewildering beauty of forms, shapes, scenes and figures that dazzle the eyes for a moment and make you dumb with wonder and surprise. You rub your eyes and see again, and behold! STUPAS, galleries, staircases, TORNAS, pathways, niches, seated Buddhas in contemplation, moving friezes of stone-figures, carved lions on the terraces and chiselled designs everywhere—and that's the first vision of Borobudur—the grandest and the most magnificent of the Buddhist monuments in the world,—as I saw it one fine morning in April, a couple of years ago.

Borobudur is the crowning achievement of Indian art; the noblest creation of man in praise of the Buddha; a supreme embodiment of man's devotion, industry, patience and genius. Egypt and India,—lands of mighty monuments

—possess nothing to equal it, in beauty or grandeur. Borobudur is an epic in architecture; a PURANA in stone. It is the full flowering of the creative genius of a race; the result of thousands of years of ceaseless artistic effort and expression. Ajanta and Ellora in India exemplify the superhuman energy and patience of ancient builders; Borobudur in Java reveals their sensitive aesthetical nature and subtle technical skill. Ellora and Ajanta are mighty, grand and awe-inspiring, Borobudur is beautiful, elegant and refined. From Bharhut to Borobudur, it is a story of over a thousand years art-history of India, and while the beauty of Bharhut monuments is primitive, vital, strong, and compelling, the beauty of Borobudur is classical, sweet, gentle and pleasing. In the friezes of Borobudur we see the perfection of art-forms evolved in the BAS-RELIEFS of Bharhut railings and TORNAS. What a bewilderingly beautiful world of art-idioms and expressions lies between these two great monuments of the ancient Hindus.

Java is rich in monumental arts. From the vigorously carved stone-figures in Western Java to the delightfully built temples of the Middle and East Java, the island is full of ancient monuments. Central Java contains the most famous and the most striking of them. The oldest buildings, traced so far, are temples slightly resembling the MONOLITHIC RATHS at Mahabalipuram and ancient temples in South India. Tradition traces the Hindu colonists to Gujerat and Kalinga, but there is no doubt, whatsoever, that much of the migration was from the Coromandel Coast. The temples in the Diyang Plateau resemble closely, in their sculptures, the Hoysala art of Karnataka; and even one of its earliest kings bore the name of the famous Hoysala king, who built the temple at Belur, Vishuvardhana, the devotee of Sri Ramanuja, the great VAISHNAVA Philosopher and Reformer.

The worship of Siva seems to have been the Prevailing creed of the Hindus who colonised the island, and the Cult of Agastya, who, according to tradition, introduced Aryan Culture into the island, is another of the chief religious feature of ancient Java. The stone images of Agastya, discovered in the island, are some of the finest pieces of sculptural art anywhere to be seen. Buddhism came into prominence and power, about the 8th century A. D. with the over-throwing of the Hindu Power by the Sailendra kings of Sumatra. The greatest monument, during this period of Buddhist supremacy, is Borobudur, said to have been designed by a mythical architect, Gunadharman. The Hindus came again into power in Central Java, a century later, and raised a group of temples, at Prambanam, to rival in beauty and splendour, the Buddhist monument of Borobudur. The Hindu Empire in Java gradually declined, and with the inroad of the Arabs and the Moor it completely disappeared from the island. The remnants of the ancient Hindus, refusing to be absorbed into the rising Islamic Culture, migrated to the island of Bali, and are still to be seen there in their picturesque state, following the faith of their ancestors. The Muslim rule was followed by the Portuguese and then the English and the Dutch, and now the island is the greatest Dutch colony and their main exploiting ground.

Borobudur lies right in the middle of Java but towards the southern coast and near to Djokjakarta, an important town in the island and the seat of one of the Sultans. The monument, an enormous pyramidal structure, is part of a rising hillock from the ground, the uppermost section of which is sheathed with masonry of dressed stones. It rises in seven storeyed terraces of three distinct divisions: the double square—based platforms, the four rectanguaIar stages of open terraces and the three circular open terraces, crowned with a bell-shaped DAGOBA. Four steep stair-ways lead to the top from the four sides of the base, the gate-way to each of which is guarded by sitting lions and spanned by MAKARA-SHAPED TORNAS with the KIRTIMUKHAS at the top. These gateways are by them selves excellent works of art, and they form common MOTIFS in the theatrical and other allied arts of the modern Javanese. The total height of the monument, from base to top, is about 150 feet and the base is about 650 feet square. Thus the monument is not, in any sense, a stupendous one, but it is its wealth of details of carving and its architectural beauty that make it the most unique monument in the world.

Borobudur is neither a STUPA

nor a CHAITYA or VIHARA, though it has one of the fundamental formative features of these respective architectural arts. It is a rich and rare combination of both the Hindu and Buddhist architecture, where the best elements of both have conspired to harmonise completely and fully. The niches that run round at regular intervals on all sides of the terraces contain finely carved images of seated Buddhas, and there are as many as 432 of them on the rectangular terraces alone. The three circular terraces above contain 72 images of the Buddha, enshrined within small DAGOBAS of diamond and squarecut lattice-work, to let in air and light inside and also to enable one to see the images. This forest of 72 cupolas with obelisk tops looks picturesque and attractive from a distance. The central crowning DAGOBA does not contain any figure within, but it is presumed that it holds within its bosom some sacred relic of olden days.

Some of these silent meditating stone-figures are about the best images of the Buddha ever carved by human hands. They far excel, in their vital sculptural quality and aesthetical nature, even some of the best Buddha figures of the Gupta period. Their expression is indescribably wonderful. As you sit and meditate before these mute figures and drink in deep their inner beauty, you realize how marvellously have those unknown artists of a fogotten age succeeded in rendering still stones animate with life and divinity. These statues breathe a strange life and are intensely alive, and these serenity on their faces is not of the ordinary mortals but of those who live in the eternal and who, therefore, embody eternal knowledge, peace and silence. They do not suggest movement or poise, as in the case of the Nataraja bronze, but an inner attitude of perfect equilibrium, a state of YOGA, leading to self-realization. The modelling of the faces is of the greatest simplicity. The features are scarcely defined, and the calm, serene expression on the face is an outward sign of the mind within, a state of cosmic consciousness, NIRVANA itself.

This is specially noticeable in the three statues that are within the shrine of CHANDI Mendut, some two miles away from Borobudur. I wonder if India has any image of the Buddha or that of the Bodisatva, to equal one of these. The temple itself is a small single — cell structure on a raised platform from the ground, and rises two storeys high. The top must have been pagoda-shaped like others there. The outer walls contain some exquisitely designed RELIEF carvings of great felicity and precision. But it is the three images inside which compel your admiration and wonder. They are placed on pedestals on the three sides of the temple, the image of the Buddha facing the door and the two BODHISATVAS on either side. An ornamental background built into the walls throws the figures out in good relief. The faces are singularly beautiful, with finely chiselled features and proportions, more aryan in type than the usual Mongolian, and the expression wonderfully calm, serene and divinely radiant. The BODHISATVAS are richly adorned with crowns, anklets, necklaces, armlets, ear-drops and clothed in diaphanous robes. A lotus foot-rest is under their feet, and the sitting posture of the Buddha is not the usual meditative posture but that of a teacher on a chair with his two feet down resting on the lotus foot-rest.

But by far the most interesting and better-known sculpture of Java are the friezes in stone running all round the rectangular galleries. They are illustrations, like the frescoes of Ajanta, from the JATAKA and LALITAVISTARA stories, representing incidents and scenes from the past lives of the Buddha, and like the rescoes of Ajanta, they are executed in a masterly style, the work of inspired men. Like the frescoes again, the portray vividly and truthfully, the life, customs, manners, dresses and other national features of the period they were executed; and there is a largeness of conception and a narrative method of rendering scenes and incidents in a succession of panels, like in wall paintings. Indian art, especially Hindu art, is rich in RELIEF carvings and firieze-pannels, but nothing in India can rival these at Borobudur.

Over two thousand long double-panels of exquisitely carved friezes run round the walls, and even a casual glance at them strikes one with dumb silence, and a careful study reveals unsuspected beauty and wonder. The figures, men, women, children, trees, flowers, houses, chariots, ships, animals and birds are treated in a classical

manner, exceedingly beautiful and fascinating, and attractively grouped, with profound knowledge of movement, space, rhythm and balance, while the background and other decorative elements are conventionally treated. The study of women, in groups and in graceful poses and seductive postures, is far more correctly and artistically rendered than in the Ajanta frescoes. Animals, birds and plants are portrayed as cleverly and as realistically as those at Sanchi or Bharhut. These lovely friezes are best seen and appreciated in the evening light when the slanting rays of the down-going sun shed soft light over them enabling one to see them in their richness of detail.

Writes Havell: "The great charm of the Borobudur sculputures lies in their absolute truth of expression, a truthfulness which is the more conspicuous, becaus the artists have not tied themselves to the petty rules and regulations on which the modern DILETTANTE critics so often bases his judgment of works of art. What modern Academician would dare to disregard the relative proportion between human figures and the accessory trees, houses, temples, elephants, oxen and carts as these men have done — not because they did not know, but because they felt the story must be told in that way? And yet the disproportion does not jar, it only contributes marvellously to the strength of the story-telling and to the richness of the decorative effect.

"The artists who concieved these sculptures were not aiming at the applause of their fellow-men, but trying to tell the story of the Master in the way they conceived he had told it, offering their labour and skill as a devout gift to his shrine. Art seems to reach its highest and to go deepest when all that is small and common is excluded, when the effort of the artist is invisible, and when Nature, purified by the God-given powers of man, is, as it were, re-born..... The spiritual power of their art has broken the chains of technical rules, risen above all thought of what critics all right or wrong, and speaks with divinely inspired words straight to the heart of the listener. In this heaven-born quality of inspiration, European art has rarely equalled, and never excelled the art of Borobudur."

"Just as we have seen in the Indian ideal type, the smaller

anatomical details of the figures are suppressed, but the real spark of life — the essence of feeling — is wonderfully manifested. Every group and every figure are absolutely true and sincere in expression of face, gesture and pose of body; and the actions which link the various groups and single figures together are strongly and simply told, without effort or striving for effect — it was so, because it could only be."

That's the secret of all Oriental art, especially of Indian sculptures, the utter simplicity, sincerity, devotion, reverence, directness, naturalness of the artists and their inborn aesthetic feeling and imagination. As he fittingly remarks, "Their art, used only in the service of truth and religion, has made their hands the obedient tools of a heaven-sent inspiration; and their unique power of realizing this, with a depth and sincerity and unsurpassed in the art of any land, or in any epoch, gives them a right to rank among the greatest of the symbolists in the whole history of art." No greater tribute to art than this can be paid by any discerning critic or intelligent admirer.

La Objekto kaj Metodo de Budaisma Sociologio

de Ken Assano

1. La Objekto de Budaisma Sociologio

La objekto de Budaisma Sociologio estas budaismaj fenomenoj kiel religiaj fenomenoj, pli precize, budaismaj sociaj fenomenoj, nome familiaj, politikaj, juraj, moralaj, ekonomiaj, artaj fenomenoj ktp. Kaj samtempe krom ili aparte povas esti starigata Morfologio Budaisma, en kiu oni studas ekleziajn, ritajn fenomenojn kc. en Budaismo kiel objektojn.

Kaj en tia studo estos oportune komenci per ekzameno pri ĝenerala koncepto de religio. Oni povas mencii multon da konceptoj de religio sed ni unue ekzamenu Durkheiman teorion kaj disvolvu nian traktadon, ĉar ĝi havas plej gravan influon sur internacian sciencistaron.

Tio estas ke Durkheim atingis en sia fama verko *La formoj elementaj de la vivo religia* jenan tezon:

"Une religion est un système solidaire de croyances et de pratiques relatives à des choses sacrées, c'est-à-dire séparées, interdites, croyances et pratiques qui unissent, en une même communauté morale, appelée Eglise, tous ceux qui y adhèrent."(1)

Ĉi tio estas la difino de religio cerbumita de Durkheima skolo, nome, sociologisma skolo. Senbezone estus diri kiel ĝi multe diferencas de la teorio pri religio metafizika, spekulativa. Dum ĝisnunaj prireligiaj teorioj, kiuj rigardis religion plimulte kiel fenomenon individuan psikologian, Durkheima teorio havas sufiĉan bazon socian kaj pozitivan. La teorio de "Sento de absoluta dependeco" de Schreiermacher kaj aliaj estas tiel individuisma kaj kristanisme partiema, ke ĝi jam estis tute likvidita. Ĉe budaisma ideo, kiu staras sur speciala ateismo, tia kristanisma ideo tute ne taŭgas por klarigi. Precipe ĉe Zen aŭ ĝano ni tion sentas pli profunde. Pro tio ŝajnas

(1) *Les formes élémentaires de la vie religieuse*, p. 65.

al ni ke eŭropanoj kaj amerikanoj sentas pli fortan intereson al ĝano.

Ni revenu al la temo. Science akiri religion kiel socian fenomenon estas religia sociologio, sekve scienca akiro de Budaismo kiel socia fenomeno estas Budaisma Sociologio, alivorte, la religiaj fenomenoj budaismaj kiel sociaj fenomenoj estas la studobjekto de Budaisma Sociologio.

Morfologio Budaisma, oni povas diri, traktas kiel studobjekton solidaran sistemon de tiuj ideoj kaj agoj koncernantaj al sanktaj aferoj en Budaismo, t. e. izolitaj kaj sanktigitaj ideoj kaj aferoj, kiuj unuigas en saman moralan komunan socion nomatan Budaisma eklezio ĝiajn ĉiujn kredantojn.

Ĉi tie ni nur tuŝu la koncepton pri religio de la flanko de la historia materialismo. Ĝi estas tiu de Lukaĉevskij, kiu donis ordon al Marksismaj teorioj pri religio kaj ekzamenis Durkheiman teorion pri religio kaj fine atingis jenan sintezitan difinon de religio:

"Religio estas ideologio, kiu estas pli-malpli ordigita sistemo konsistanta el ideo animista kaj al ĝi alkroĉitaj emocioj kaj agoj. En iu evolustadio de socio moralo estas aldonata al ĝi"(1)

Kvankam ĉi tiu difino de religio laŭ sia formo havas postesignon de la fakto ke ĝi estis ordigita laŭ Durkheima pensmaniero, atentinda punkto estas tio, ke antaŭe Durkheim starigis "ateismeman" teorion studante Budaismon, nun Lukaĉevskij, utiliginte la rezulton de studo de Pleĥanov ke Budaismo (precipe nuntempa) ankaŭ estas sistemo de animismaj ideoj same kiel ĉiuj aliaj religioj, starigis supre menciitan teorion novan. Ĉu estus multe konsiderinda la punkto, ke Durkheim kaj Lukaĉevskij korektis koncepton pri religio konsiderante Budaismon nur tre malmultgrade? Kompreneble jes, kaj plie ni havas devon kaj rajton prezenti laborfrukton, kiu postulas pli da tia korekto.

2. La Metodo de Budaisma Sociologio

Budaisma Sociologio estas speciala fako de religia sociologio, kiu estas ankaŭ speciala fako de la sociologio. Ĉu ĉi tiu Budaisma Sociologio kiel speciala fako do devas havi apartan studon? Ne, ne necese. La tasko, kiun ĝi devas plenumi en sia propra kampo, povas esti tute sama kiel tiu de ĝenerala sociologio.

(1) Lukaĉevskij: *Origino kaj Esenco de Religio*, japana trad., p. 15.

Ĉi tie mi diru la rilaton inter sociologio ĝenerala kaj Sociologio Budaisma. Se ĝenerala sociologio plene plenumis sian taskon, en Budaisma Sociologio, por *ekspliki* la socialajn faktojn, oni povos nur apliki formulojn kaŭzecan aŭ funkcian de ĝenerala sociologio en tiu difinita problemo. Sed malfeliĉe ĝenerala sociologio en siaj multaj regionoj ne havas normalan sintezon tute elprovitan. Tio povos esti atingebla nur post kolektiva disvolvo de la specialaj studoj. Sekve ankaŭ en Budaisma Sociologio kiel unu speciala fako ĝia studanto devas komenci la studon de la unua paŝo. Kaj li ankaŭ devas eltrovi tion, kio kaŭzas iujn difinitajn diferencojn, aŭ por trovi relativecon, kiu ankoraŭ ne estas provita en la ĝenerala sociologio, li devas labori aparte de la sociologio ĝenerala. Tial, se la nova relativeco estos pravigebla en Budaisma Sociologio, la eltrovinto, budaisma sociologo, solvos ne sole sian taskon sed ankaŭ tiun de ĝenerala sociologio. Tiamaniere ĝis nun ne provitaj kaj ankoraŭ neklaraj punktoj estos per klarigoj en specialaj fakoj renverse estos resumitaj kaj kunmetataj en la ĝeneralan sociologion.

Sed ni devas utiligi kuraĝe ĝis nun progresintajn teoriojn de sociologio, se ne ni neatendite perdos vane nian forton. Tial speciale en metodologio nepre necese estas ekzameni kaj utiligi ilin atente.

Ĝenerale scienca studo postulas almenaŭ: 1) ke en la studo apliku difinitan procedon. 2) ke limigu studregionon. 3) ke estu objektiva, 4) ke flanken lasu ĝian aplikan flankon, ktp. Mi plie volas utiligi la normon, kiun donis Durkheim en sia *Metodo Sociologia*.

Tiel nomata la fundamenta principo metodologia en Durkheima sociologio staras en tio, ke devas esti traktataj socialaj faktoj tute egale kiel aliaj aferoj. Sed al ĉi tiu esprimo estas donita granda limigo. Tial ni vidu senpere lian propran klarigon:

"Nous ne disons pas, en effet, que les faits sociaux sont des choses matérielles, mais sont des choses au même titre que les choses matérielles, quoique d'une autre manière.

"Qu'est-ce en effet qu'une chose? La chose s'oppose à l'idée comme ce que l'on connaît du dehors à ce que l'on connaît du dedans. Est chose tout objet de connaissance qui n'est pas naturellement compénétrable à l'intelligence, tout ce dont nous ne pouvons nous faire une notion adéquate par un simple procédé d'analyse mentale, tout ce que l'esprit ne peut arriver à comprendre qu'à condition de sortir de lui-même, par voie d'observations et d'expérimentations, en passant propressivement des caractères les plus extérieurs et les plus immédiatement accessibles aux moins visibles et aux plus profonds. Traiter der faits d'un certain ordre comme des choses, ce n'est donc pas les classer dans telle ou telle catégorie du réel; c'est observer vis-à-vis d'eux une certaine attitude mentale. C'est en aborder l'étude en prenant pour principe qu'on ignore absolument ce qu'ils sont, et que leurs propriétés caractéristiques, comme les causes inconnues dont elles dépendent, ne peuvent être découvertes par l'introspection même la plus attentive."(1)

Durkheim diras plu:

"Notre règle n'implique donc aucune conception métaphysique, aucune spéculation sur le fond des êtres. Ce qu'elle réclame, c'est que le sociologue se mette dans l'état d'esprit où sont physiciens, chimistes, physiologistes, quand ils s'engagent dans une région, encore inexplorée, de leur domaine scientifique. Il faut qu'en pénétrant dans le monde social, il ait conscience qu'il pénètre dans l'inconnu; il faut qu'il se sente en présence de faits dont les lois sont aussi insoupçonnées que pouvaient l'être celles de la vie, quand la biologie n'était pas constituée; il faut qu'il se tienne prêt à faire des découvertes qui le surprendront et le déconcerteront."(2)

Tia fundamenta normo elkondukas tri duagradajn leĝojn:

I. "*Il faut écarter systématiquement toutes les prénotions.*"(3)

II. "*Ne jamais prendre pour objet de recherches qu'un groupe de phénomènes préalablement définis par certains caractères extérieurs qui leur sont communs et comprendre dans la même recherche tous ceux qui répondent à cette définition.*"(4)

III. "*Quand le sociologue entreprend d'explorer un ordre quelconque de faits sociaux, il doit s'efforcer de les considérer par un côté où ils se présentent isolés de leurs manifestations individuelles.*"(5)

Ĉi tiu metodo sociologisma de Durkheim-skolo devas esti multe konsiderata kiel metodo de nia

(1) *Les Règles de la Méthode sociologique*, p. XI.
(2) *Ibidem*, p. XIII.
(3) *Ibidem*, p. 40. (4) *Ibidem*, p. 45. (5) *Ibidem*, p. 57.

Budaisma Sociologio.

Ankaŭ multe atentinda estas la metodo de tiu "historia materialismo" (kiun nomis Buĥarin "Sociologio Marksisma".) Kompreneble ni devas eviti formulisman materialismon, sed studo en ĉi tiu flanko ankaŭ devas esti atentata, ĉar estas ne refutebla fakto, ke eĉ budaisma fenomeno progresis en relativeco kun sia socia ekonomia bazo. Nome la kritiko de ideo de antikvaj hindoj laŭ materialisma dialektiko farita de Thalheimer ankoraŭ nur estas tre fragmenta, sed, ĝi estas la unua en tiu direkto.(1)

Krom tio *Apero de religio kaj kredo je dio* de Kunow, kaj *Origino kaj esenco de religio* de Lukaĉevskij estas valoraj verkoj en ĉi tiu kampo. Ankaŭ valora estas "Azia maniero por produkto", kiu lastatempe estis farita en Sovetio. Ankaŭ atentinda estas la aserto, ke materialisma historia studo de Budaismo estas kontribuo al internacia kulturo de la flanko de proletaro en Oriento, kiun ni povas konsenti.

Nu, nia sinteno en nia studo pri Budaismo, precipe pri budaismaj sociaj fenomenoj, devas esti absolute tiu de sociologo kaj ne devas esti nur tiu de budaano. Ne, en iu okazo tio, ke ni estas budaanoj, ne nur ne estas necesa, sed ankaŭ malutila. Tamen havi profundan simpation budaanan, eĉ se estus pli aŭ malpli da danĝero en sciencista vidpunkto, pli multe helpos la komprenon. En ĉiu scienco, neniu ne supozus ian difinitan antaŭvidon aŭ utilecon. Eĉ ĉe Marksismo, kiu sin nomas Scienca Socialismo, troviĝus pli aŭ malpli nesciencecon, aŭ dogmecon, kiu devenis de la volo, ke la socio estu tia.

Ankaŭ Budaisma Sociologio povas havi du flankojn: teoria studo kaj aplika studo. Nome scienca studo kaj politika studo estas supozataj. En iu okazo, ekzemple kiel en nuna situacio, eble estas ŝajne pensata, ke budaismaj sociologoj urĝe devas studi en flanko praktika, ekzemple plibonigo de ekonomio de temploj aŭ refreŝigo de eklezioj ktp. Kaj "Sociala Budaismo" aŭ "Budaisma socialismo" ktp. estas facilanime asertataj. Sed se oni profunde konsideras, ni klare vidas, ke la tasko de sciencisto sintrovas en esplorado kaj eltrovo de la principo kaj leĝo, kaj praktika apliko de ĝia rezulto nur apartenas al la tasko de praktikuloj, kvankam ju pli progresas scienca studo, des pli vastiĝas ĝia aplika kampo. Sed ilia mallerta intermiksado ofte riskos danĝeron perdi du leporojn celante ilin ambaŭ. Ĉi tiun punkton ni devas tre bone atenti.

(1) Vidu A. Thalheimer: *Einführung in die dialektischen Materialismus.*

滿洲佛教の現狀に就て

大村　桂巖

一

私は今夏，暫く滿洲に行つて參りました。これから旅行なさる方の心得等に就きお話しようと思ひ，多少材料を持つて參りました。私はこれから滿洲の佛敎に關係した點を少しお話致したいと思ひます。

滿洲の現狀，國力と謂ひますか，勿論その中には關東州即ち日本と變りない，都で云ひますと大連，旅順をも含む譯けであります。それ等の關東州及び滿洲國の現在の國勢と云ふ事，滿洲國の理想，希望と云ひますか，或は今日の滿洲國をして斯くあらしめたい，今後發展せしめたい。何十萬と云ふ日本人の彼の地に於ける態度，活動狀態を一言最初に申上げたい。それが佛敎の問題に深い關係を持つて來るのであります。

滿洲國は大同三年，即ち我が昭和八年の建國でありますが，只今，申しました滿洲地方，關東州も入れまして滿洲の發展は非常なものと私は見て參りました。勿論私は大連に二日，旅順に一日，奉天には中途錦州に行きましたが，前後四日程居りました。本當に居りましたのは二日で，錦州（最近錦縣と云つて居りますが，一時やかましい問題を起しました錦州）に一泊しました。新京に前後八日程居たが，これは汎太平洋佛教大會の用事がありまして，それが今度の旅行の一つの重大な使命になつて居りましたので，前後八日居りましたが，その間，日曜日には日滿の要人に會ふ事も都合が惡るく，一泊で哈爾賓に參りました。さう云ふ風で前後十五日間，極く主な都會を廻つて，その都會を見ました程度でありますから，滿洲の一般と云ふやうな事は言へないかも知れませんし，地方の方は全然知らんのであります。私の見ました滿洲の都會でありますが，非常な發展振りであります。勿論その中には奉天とか，或は哈爾賓と云ふやうな處は發展とは申せません。奉天で申しますれば滿洲の國都は新京に移りました（滿洲では帝都と申しません。國都と申します）。ために，奉天は幾らか寂びれて來るかも知れない。けれども非常に奉天が寂れると云ふ事もないでせうが，然し奉天の市民はさう云ふ事を心配してゐるやうです。哈爾賓も北鐵讓渡の後は，多數の露西亞人が北方に退却する事になつて，丁度私の行きました日は一週間の赤系露人の哈爾賓引上げの最後の日に當つて居つて，多數の露人が最後の引上げをする光景を停車場で見た。互に涙を押へて別れて行く情況は，我々も知らず識らず，涙を誘はれた。哈爾賓は何れにしても寂しい感じであります。それは露西亞人は割合に金使ひが氣前がいゝ。假に俸給生活者としますと，日本人邊りに比較して自分の收入から割出して金の使ひ方が割合に荒い。さう云ふ點で賑つて居つたのですが，その露西亞人が退却する事になつたために，知らず識らず街が寂びれて來る。然しこれは露西亞人の退却と云ふばかりでなしに，北鐵讓渡の結果，哈爾賓は通過驛になつてしまつて，今日までの如く物資なり人なりが餘り留らないやうになつたと云ふ事もあり，旁々多少寂れ氣味のやうです。これ又其土地の人は何んとかして今日までの繁榮を維持したいために色々苦心して，上海のやうな歡樂の都にでもしたいと云ふやうな考へも持つて居る。

さう云ふやうに今日まで旺んであつた奉天や哈爾賓が多少寂れやしないかと云ふやうな事はありますが，大連の如きは非常に旺んでありまして，御承知の如く彼處は自由港であり，稅關もないと云ふ事や，氣候がよいといふ事などで內外の人が集ると云ふ事から色々の點で便利がある。滿洲の大官，富豪等が避暑したり，避寒したりするのは，大連又は旅順であります。さう云ふ點もあり，色々な點から大連は此頃は一ケ月に新しく建つ家が一千戶と云ふ事で，私等は唯街を車で走つたのですが非常に家が建てられてゐる。さうして煉瓦造りで本建築です。又新しく建つ家の中には，アパートが相當ありますから，住む人の數から言へば非常に多い譯けです。大抵の家は建築しかけると貸家でも賣家でも間もなく約束をしてしまふ。出來上るまでにチヤンと這入る人が決ると云ふやうに，非常な繁榮であります。

新京は十三萬，大連は三十萬の人口です。（昭和八年の統計）。新京は今まで長春と云つた處です。新京となつてから，新たに諸官廳も建ちつゝあり，旣に建つて居る處もあり，關東軍司令部即ち大使館を初めとし，內閣各省は落成して事務を執つて居る處もありますけれども，今建ちつゝあるものも隨分多い。新京邊りは旺んであつて，街を步るいても驚く位繁華になつて居ります。然し滿洲人全體の生活狀態は，彼等軍閥時代の生活と建國後の今日の生活と經濟上多少の相違もあり，一般勞働者は軍閥時代の方が財政が潤つた今經濟的には餘り良くない。彼等の內にはどうも昔の方がよかつたと云ふやうな感じを持つて居るものも隨分あると云ふ事も聞きました。これは，軍閥の連中は掠奪して中流階級以上を搾つて而して不換紙幣を出したりして割合に下の方の大衆を潤した一種の彼等の政策があつて，所謂今日の政治は比較的に下が潤はないと云ふ事になるので昔の方が良かつたと云ふやうな感じを大分に持つて居ると云ふ事も聞きました。さう云ふやうな點では私の觀察では本當の處を衝いた譯けではありません。全體として建國の熱に燃えて居ると言つてゐる。少なくとも新京を中心として，満洲の新開地はその衝に當つて居る者は熱心にやつて居る。軍部なり文官なりの人々も，仲々熱心にやつて居る。この満洲の經營と云ふ事に就きましては，差し控へねばならないやうな點もありますが，今日では經濟的に色々の批評もありまして，そんなに謂ふ程満洲には資源はないと云ふやうな悲觀說もありますが，然し鑛山，鑛業の方にしましても此九月一日から初めて民間に事業を許すと云ふ事であり私の親戚の京城に居る者も三十ケ所の採掘を申出てあるが，然し何の位許可して吳れるか知れんが，九月一日に分ると云ふ事を言つて居りました。今までは一般には手を着けて居らんので，金や銀が多いとか少ないとか云つても本當の處はこれからだ。だから撫順の石炭は割合に質が良くないと云ふ事を謂つて居る者もありますが，早計に判斷して満洲は餘り見込みがないと云ふ事は言へないのぢやないかと思ふのであります，その邊は疑問と致してをきましても，どうしてもこれは日本が東洋の盟主と云ふ處を示さなければなりませぬ，東洋の平和と云ふ事，大亞細亞の人々の安全のために，日本精神と謂ひますか，さう云ふ點から徹頭徹尾やつて行くと云ふ事に就ては啻に満洲のみでない，斯ふ云ふ點に就きまして私の考は間違てゐるかも知れないが，私はさう云ふやうに見て行きたいと思ひます。満洲と云ふ事に對する私個人の態度は，色々の事を聞いたり，多少其處等を廻つたりした結果，日本人の使命と云ふものは實に重大なものである。恐らく百年二百年も東洋の平和發展と云ふ事を考へて，さう云ふ方面に對して堂々たる日本道と云ふ態度から侵略主義，利己主義，極端な國家主義と云ふやうな事でなしに，どうしてもこれは踏張つてやつて行かなければならない。これは啻に一満洲の問題のみではないと云ふ事を深く感じて，さう云ふ點から佛教を見てゆかなければならんと思つてゐるのであります。

二

それで佛教の事に就きましては，今回は汎太平洋佛教大會の次の第三回開催地の問題を持つて行つて居りましたので，その事柄に就いて視察すると同時に，満洲に於ける將來の佛教，或は満洲佛教の將來と云ふ事を出來るだけ見て，自分だけの結論をつけて歸へりたいと云ふので，實は新京の日數も割合に掛つた。然るに仲々新京で要人に會ふに時間がかゝる。面會者が多いので電話で時間を繰合せて貰つて車で馳つて行く。色々の訪問客も來る，殆んどその間は人に會ふために寧日でなく寧時間が全くなかつた。私は満洲の要人では國務總理，文教部大臣，外交部大臣，民政部大臣（日本の內務大臣），宮內大臣と云ふやうな方に會ひました。それから日本の人には今申しましたのに關聯しまして，總務長官等に會つた。長岡國務長官，文教部の久米總務司長，參議院の筑紫副議長，外交部の次官と云ふやうな，これ等の各大臣に匹敵する日本人側の幹部に會ひました。それから課長級の人に，これは文教部其他の課長でありますが，五六人會ひました。軍部の方では南大將に二回，板垣少將に一回，西尾中將は腫物か何か出來て休んで居られると云ふ事で會ふ事は出來ませんでして，名刺を通じてもらつて歸へりました。それから關東軍司令部第三課に教育及び宗教の主任をして居る吉岡中佐に二回會ひました。大臣には三十分乃至一時間位懇談致しました。各部の大臣は非常な佛教信者でありまして，大體満洲の要人は佛教信者が多い。國務總理も非常な佛教信者ですが，佛教の話をすると皆喜んで聽いて吳れるし，太平洋大會の話をしましても是非やりたいと云ふ風です。その點になりますと，これは一寸脫線かも知れませんが，日本の要人と謂ひますか，大官と謂ひますか，日本人の方は色々佛教の話，佛教青年會の話をしますと段々耳を傾けて來る。すると「全體佛教と云ふものはどんなものか」と云ふ事で，佛教の講義からしなければならんと云ふ事になるのです。しかし時間もありませんからしびりが切れる。茲に於て宗教々育の必要なる事を一層痛感したのでありまして（拍手），明治年間に宗教々育がやつてないために佛教と云ふ事を知らない。だから私等の活動を唯だ單に佛教の宣傳のために，佛教の利己的運動のためにやると云ふやうに取つてしまつて，佛教が國家に對する貢獻，満洲國の發展に，他の言葉で申しますれば満洲經綸の善導と言ひますか，さう云ふ處に宗教が關係する。殊に佛教がどう云ふ教理を持つて居るかと云ふ事は勿論知らない。これに私は非常に今度不滿と云ひますか，不足を感じました。これはどうしても宗教々育をやつてをかなければ駄目だと云ふ事を痛切に感じました。

其處に至ると満洲の要人は知つて居るやうに思ひます。兎に角満洲のインテリ階級は佛教に關心を持ち，同情を持つて居るやうです。其は佛教に相當理解を有つて居るからであります。

大同佛教會と云ふものがありますがこれは其會員が先年日本に來て，東亞佛教大會に出席して居ります。現在二萬人程會員がありますが，私が會つたのは二十人程の幹部でありますが，仲々佛教に趣味を持つて居るやうです。この大同佛教會は居士許りの集りで，國務總理大臣が會長をして，夫々の要職にある人，民間の重要な人が役員をして居て，仲々盛んです。

もう一つは満洲人の佛教信者に就ては，誰の話を聞いてみても，主人よりも夫人の方が一層熱心らしい。その邊の處，どう云ふ理由がありますか分りませぬが，或はそれは丁度満洲が今，日本の鎌倉時代，明治維新時代前後と云つたやうな時で，婦人連が特に人生觀を起して佛教に深く關心を持つて修養して居るのかも知れない，さう云ふ處から主人に影響して居るかも知りませんが，満洲の要人は大體佛教を心得てゐる。日本の要人は知らない。今後我々佛教關係者は日本に於ても餘程宗教々育を進めて行かなければならんと思ひます。然し段々話して行きます間に，滿洲人は今申しました官吏，それから民間の人，それから僧侶，滿洲人の中の官吏，在野の人や實業家，僧侶，この三方面皆な熱心に汎太平洋大會を開きたいと云ふ希望を持つて居る。滿洲には道教もあり，回々教もあり，キリスト教もあるが，大多數は佛教に關心を持つて居る。これは殆んど間違ひない。日本の方はさう云ふ相談相手は矢張り第一に官吏でありますが，日本人の官吏と云ふものは滿洲國政府の官吏と日本大使館の官吏との二通りがあります。それから滿鐵も入れば入れますが，要するに滿洲政府，日本大使館配下の官吏に滿鐵などを入れまして，半官半民と云ふやうな事になるか知りませんが，又其外に一つ有力なものがあります，其は滿洲に五族協和會と云ふものがありますが，滿洲人，日本人，蒙古人，漢人，露西亞人，卽ち滿洲國に生活して居る大きな代表的な民族が五つあります。それを綜合して五族協和會といふのです。この會の會長は阪谷男爵の令息でありますが，その次長を務めて居る人は平島敏夫氏である。此人は仲々佛教に同情を有つて居られます。斯ふ云ふ人のやつて居る五族協和會は，非常な實力を持つて居る。政府で一寸やれないと云ふやうな仕事は五族協和會の方でやる。滿鐵と五族協和會邊りは，民間の方ぢや大した勢力を持つて居ります。それから滿洲の佛教僧侶，滿洲に行つて居る日本僧侶，日本の官吏，日本の民間の有力な會社，五族協和會等の役員，斯ふ云ふ人を相手として相談した。色々話しました結果，どうしても滿洲國の經綸には佛教が必要だと云ふやうな考へ方は大體是等の人の頭に一致して來て居るやうであります。中には人の名前は出さないが，有力な人も隨分居る。我々の座談會を開きましたゝめに初めて佛教と云ふ事を知り，滿洲の要人が佛教の方にそれ程に熱心かと云ふ事を知つて，それぢや一つ確り佛教でやらうと云ふやうな事を皆の前で告白せられた人もありました。汎太平洋佛教大會を滿洲でやるには，どの位金が要るかと云ふ事でありましたので，「日本の昨年の經驗で推して，十萬圓から十五萬圓位は要る」と申しますと，「その位の金は出來る」と云ふ事を座談會に集つた中の，さう云ふ方面の運用に當る地位に居る人が其處で四五人發議しまして大いにやらうぢやないかと云ふ事になつて來て一同贊成したやうな狀勢であります。

然し滿洲はどうしても今日の程度では政府が支持して或る程度までバックになつてくれないと，凡てが旨く行かないと私は見まして，政府の要人とも色々話しました。其結論を言ひますと汎太平洋大會と云ふ事は五族協和會等の肝入で民間の方でやると云ふ事ならば結構であるといふことになつたのです。この結構と云ふ言葉には二通りの意味がありまして，其一は俺の方は關係しないから構はない。其二はイヤさうぢやない矢張り政府が援助してやらうと云ふ內心はあるのであるが，表は五族協和會，滿鐵等は半官半民でありますから，さう云ふ方面にやらせると云ふ事もある。さうして私は何方かと云ふとよい方に取つて來たのであります。然し滿洲政府としましては此事に就ては材料を出來るだけ集めまして，念入りの相談をしました，先き程一寸申落しましたが，滿洲政府には參議院會議と云ふものがありまして，その參議院の副議長は，日本の筑紫中將でありますが，その參議員會議にかけて協議せられたのであります。汎太平洋會議の問題が日本で言へば樞密院の會議にかゝつた譯けであります。さうして其會議が長時間に亙つたのです約半日近く之に費されたやうです，所が遂に最後の決定とまで行かず，午後の各省の總務司長會議に又かゝつたのです。これは長岡長官から直接聞いたのでありますが，その結果が今申したやうに，民間の有力團體でやつたらどうかといふことになつたのです。さう云ふことにきまつたのであります。總務司長會議の結果は參議院の會議の空氣を重ずると云ふ事になりまして，民間でやると云ふ事は洵に結構だと云ふ事に終つたのであります。此點は誠にデリケートな所であります。旣に角佛教青年會の仕事である汎太平洋佛教大會の問題が，滿洲國政府の公式の二大會議にかゝつたのであります。さう云ふ事で政府の方の大體の意向を知る事が出來ました。私は南大將に二回會ひまして，極く內輪話をしました。滿洲國の要人は佛教に對しては熱心でありますが，兎に角政府としてはさう云ふやうに決つたのでありました，南全權大使の處には四方から情報が這入つて居る。仲々よく知つて居られ又親切に話して下ださつたのであります，要するに政府は大體さう云ふやうな譯けで，參議院會議，總務司長會議と云ひましても軍部の方の關係も多大にあつたのであらうと考へるのであります。

三

もう一つ附加へてをきたいのは，我々の座談會であります。これは文教部總務司長久米成夫氏が，新京の大和ホテルで歡迎會を開いて下ださつた。集まるものは本當の佛教を理解して居る人，各省の官吏，民間の大會社の幹部，五族協和會の次長平島代議士，新京市廳の植田總務處長――日本人の市長と云ひますか，本當の市長は滿洲人で東京市に於ける高級助役と云つたやうな處であるか知りませんが思つたより若い方ですが仲々確りした方です――その他文教部の神尾學務課長，等々，色々の方がいらして下さいました。又新京に於ける日本人の僧侶，それから極樂寺に居られる今井慶昭，この方は昨年大會の時に日本に來て下すつて，この次の第三回の大會は是非滿洲で開くと云ふ事を言はれて，非常に熱心な方であります。その方が哈爾賓からわざわざ參加して下さいました。皆で三十人程集りまして，十一時になり一端閉會にして頂きましたが，皆歸つて行かない，私等が出たのは結局十二時頃でした。かく非常に熱心で，どうしても滿洲で開きたいと云ふ事になつた。私は何も相談しに來たんぢやない。貴方の意向，佛敎の狀勢を見に來たのであると云つて，其相談の結論には深入りせずに。唯だ情勢丈けを摑んで歸へつたのであります。

四

滿洲の僧侶に就ては，私が極樂寺で會ひました普光法師，此靑年僧は新京の般若寺の副住職格で一方の雄將です。哈爾賓の極樂寺の前の如光法師，昨年大會に團長として出席せられた，この方が住職でありましたが，今日は乘一法師に極樂寺の住職を讓られた。この乘一法師は未だ三十九才で若い。二百人の坊さんの中には六十位ひの坊さんも居ますが，如光法師と餘程よく似た性格の人であります。如光法師は全滿洲佛敎靑年會聯盟を組織するために東西に奔走されて居る。殆んど殉敎的に命がけでやつて行くと云ふ風で，これに馳せ參じて居るもの，約百名の靑年僧が結束して居ります普光法師も其有力な一人でこの人は態々哈爾賓へやつて來まして，私がその日もう哈爾賓を發つと云ふので，普光師は今着いて旅の勞れで一寸寢て居つたが，私等が發つと云ふので起きて來て，色々話しまして私は彼の熱心に非常に動かされて思はず淚を催したやうな次第であつたのでありますが，この約百名の佛敎靑年僧侶は非常な意氣込みで結束して居る，さうして全滿洲靑年會聯盟と云ふものを組織し，大同佛敎會と云ふのもありますが，どうも本當の大乘的運動をしてゐないから改革したいと言ふのです。是等の百人の靑年僧侶の中，四五十名は曾て一度は日本に來て居る日本に來た時に初めこんな佛敎は本當の佛敎でないと言つて悲觀し失望し憤慨したといふことですが，暫く滯在して日本の佛敎の實際活動を見て，肉食妻帶してゐても一方にそれだけの仕事をして居る。社會性のある仕事をして居るのが日本の佛敎だ，然るに我々は全く何んにもして居らない，殆ど敎化も傳道もして居ない，小乘的であると申しますか，さうしたものに過ぎない。結局一方に破戒的の處があるが，又他面に社會的な仕事をして居る日本の佛敎が本當だ。肉食妻帶する事を眞似る事はないけれども，グツと進んで積極的に仕事をしなければならんと言つて居るのであります。これ等百人の人間が覺醒新興の運動に奮鬪しつゝあるのであります，而して支那の內地まで其運動の爲に奔走して居るのであります日滿の佛敎家の聯合的運動に支那の佛敎家が，どう云ふやうな態度を取るか。昨年のやうに代表者をボイコツトしたんぢや何んにもならない。吾々の運動には非常に支那の佛敎家との間に密接な關係がある。滿洲の靑年僧達は多數支那に入り込んで奔走して居る。全く支那と滿洲とは相提携して行かなければならん，私はさう云ふ事を心配して

話しました時，それは日本の方々が心配して下さるよりも，トツクの昔から知つて居る。滿洲と支那の佛敎家が反目する事は不祥な事であるから，さう云ふ事のないやうに色々やつて居るのであると云ふ事であります。私は之を聞いて尙ほ一層滿洲僧侶の熱心に動かされたのであります。

然しながら私の渡滿の使命の一たる汎太平洋會議の結論は只今申しましたやうに，滿洲の最高の會議にかけられて大體の方針が明になり又民間有志者間では決定して吳れたらやる。十萬十五萬の金は何でもないと云ふ事を全く金の運用の出來る人々が斷言したのであります。文敎部の久米總務司長も，非常に熱心になつて居るやうな譯けで，この機會に汎太平洋佛靑大會の事は兎に角として，何んとかして我々は滿洲佛敎を活かし，滿洲國家の將來と云ふ事に貢献するやうにしたいと念願して居るのであります。私は軍部の人とかう云ふ話をした。其は滿洲の今後の新興發展の最後の力となるものは「敎育と宗敎」とが中心問題になると思ふ，其に就き質問しまして，滿洲では「敎育勅語」を出すのかと云ふ事を質問しましたのです，色々話合ましたが，私は滿洲で「敎育勅語」に相當するものを出すならば佛敎精神を入れなければ不可ないといふことを强調したのです。滿洲の軍部も文官も佛敎と云ふものを重要視して居ると云ふ大體の傾向を感じて歸つて來たのであります。どうかこれ等に就いて一つ諸君の深き御關心を期待し，將來滿洲國に對して御盡力ありたいのであります。然し色々な宗敎團體から色々な事を言つて持込んで行くさうです，色々な事を言つて來るが取合はないやうにして居るといつて居りました。現に私の行つた一寸前に九州の何とか佛敎會からも大會を開きたいと言つて來て居たさうです，私はさう云ふものは考へなければ不可んと云ふ事を久米氏に言つて置いた。私は日本の佛敎團體では我が全日本佛敎靑年會聯盟，佛敎聯合會，佛敎護國團の三團體が代表的の權威あるもので，此他は愼重に調べる必要があると注意して置いたのです，他に何や彼やとあるから，さう云ふものに引掛らないやうにやつてもらひ度いと云ふ事をよく言つて置いた次第です。

以上私の話は汎太平洋佛靑大會の話と滿洲國佛敎の將來の話と混交して居りますが，御高判下さいましてどうか，これ等に對して關心を持つて，日滿支の佛敎と云ふものが今後緊密に提携して東洋に於ける佛敎新運動を色々やるやうにして頂きたいと云ふ事を佛靑聯盟の理事として，他の佛敎團體の方々に御計りしたいと思つたのであります。さう云ふ事をやりたい，提携を圖りたいのであります。將來滿洲の佛敎を助け日滿のため大いに平和の根本基礎を堅めると云ふ事にお力をお貸し下さる事が出來れば幸ひと思ふのであります。甚だ雜駁な話でしたがこれだけに致します。（拍手）（文責在記者）

國際佛教 Interview (No. 3)

和蘭ライデン大學教授

ジェー・ラーデル博士

滿洲國建設の大業が，どしどしと行はれて行く，國際聯盟で皆で寄つてたかつて否定した日本の東洋政策が，着々として實現されて行く。

かうなつて見ると，歐米列强も，中堅諸國も，また弱小諸國も，夫々の立場から，正しき日本の眞の姿を，今更の如くに，あるがまゝに研究すべき必要を痛感するに至つた。かくして，玆二三年來，いはゆる「日本學」(Japanology) なるものゝ擡頭は，實に，すばらしいものがある。「東洋學」(Orientalism) 一般の研究が特に日本學中心に爲されるやうになつたとさへ見られる。

◇

かうした時節柄，日本とは古くから「なじみ」の深い和蘭の，ライデン大學に於て日本學の講座を擔當してゐられるジェー・ラーデル博士 (Dr. J. Rahder) が丁度，目下訪日在京中なので一夕，かたばらないインターヴューを試みる。尙，同博士は蘭領印度支那生れの當年三十八歲の青年教授，旣に數回，日本に來訪された方で，非常な宗教通であることは玆に改めて云ふまでもないことである。

◇

共產黨の話ナチス黨の話，非常時日本に關する意見等を拜聽した後，和蘭に於けるカトリツク黨の近況は如何です，と云ふ質問を發すると

「目下あまり振ひません，共產黨もナチスも相當ありますが，やはり社會勞働黨が斷然多數を占めてゐます。」

と答へた。

「和蘭のナチスはドイツの指令を受けて發展しつゝありますか？」

「何しろ，和蘭と獨逸とは隣りで文化も似てゐますから，大分增えつゝあるやうですね！」

「ドイツのナチスの宗教政策を，どう御考へです？」

「興味を以つて見てゐます。新宗教たる『ドイツ信仰運動』(Deutsche Glaubensbewegung) の指導者たるヴイルヘルム・ハウエル (Wilhelm Hauer) 氏は，元大學でサンスクリツトの教授をしてゐた人ですからね—」

「さうすると何か佛教的要素でもありさうに聞えますが如何ですか？」

「別にハツキリしたものは無いやうですが，ナチスは反ユダヤ主義であるだけ，アリアン文化には同情を持つてゐますね。」

「ナチスの宗教理論家アルフレツド・ローゼンブルグはどうですか？」

「大したものですね。キリスト教者に駁撃を加へた『蒙昧論者たちに抗して』(Gegen die Dunkel-Männer) など此の春四月に出版されたものですが，二十萬部も賣れたと云ふことです。」

更に博士は，アルフレツド・ローゼンベルグに就いて曰ふ—

「一昨年出版された同氏の著『二十世紀の神話』(Der Mythos des 20 Jahrhunderts) も却々賣れました。要するにキリスト教はユダヤ教から由來するものだから，反對されるのです」

◇

「最近何か新しい宗教でも起きつゝありませうか？」

「ナチス其物が新宗教なのでせう？」

「日本精神に就ては，どうお考へですか？」

「わたくし，今『愚管鈔』の反譯をやつてゐますが，此の本の中に皇道と云ふ成語がありますね。『神皇正統記』にも出てゐるやうですが，此の方が早くはないでせうか？」

「これはどうも……ところで佛教は國際化するでせうか？」

「大いにすると思ひます。しかしどうも歐米人は，盛んに研究熱を出しては居ますが，更に進んで信ずるやうになるかどうかは一寸疑問ですね」

新刊紹介

◇佛教哲學槪論（市川白弦譯註）

本書は Stcherbatsky, The Central Conception of Buddhism, 1923. の全譯及び The Conception of Bnddhist Nirvana, 1927. の序論の一部の譯を收む。原著者ツエルバツキー氏は，現にレニングラード大學教授にして，ソヴエト隨一の佛教學者である。正確な資料と聰明な指示，一般の人の親しみ易く，且つ西歐人の見解が現れてゐて，日本佛教徒を裨益する點が多い。

（菊判一七四頁，一圓二十錢，麴町區三番町　第一書房）

◇奇僧風外道人（松本雲舟著）

著者松本氏は，風外道人が韜晦してゐた故跡たる相州眞鶴町の町長を八年有半勤續し，その間に風外の遺跡を發見し，進んで風外一生の數奇な傳記まで調べ上げ，尙は眞鶴町に風外庵を建てたりして，故聖の遺風を顯彰さる。本書は其の尊き成果だ。

（四六判一五〇頁，定價五十錢，送料四錢　神奈川縣足柄下郡眞鶴町外二ケ村組合役場發行）

◇現代相似禪評論（破有法王著）

本書は現代臨濟禪の眞骨頂を批判し，それに謗法の罪ありとして之を糺彈し，その室內を曝露し，學人の向上の一路を直指せんとした一箇痛快の書である。而して本書の題名たる“相似禪”又は“說禪”とは，白隱以降傳承し來れる現代の臨濟禪を指稱したもの（菊版 p.351, 附錄p.88 定價三圓，小石川區高田老松町 34, 周文社）

Japanese News

Buddhist Service

Higan, the autumn weekly period of Buddhist observances, is now celebrated throughout Japan.

Under the auspices of the Komazawa Buddhist College, the children of the kindergarten of this institution gave an entertainment in keeping with Higan in Hibiya Hall at noon on Tuesday.

Juvenile plays and dances were performed, and a Buddhist ceremony was carried out.

Temple for Laborers

A small temple has been erected in the compound of a free hostel for laborers in Fukugawa.

Some of those who have enjoyed the hospitality of the hostel contributed their mites toward the building.

An interesting ceremony was held at the temple recently when officials of Tokyo Municipality were present.

Buddhist priests will be in charge of the temple and give consolation to the unfortunates who take refuge in the hostel.

Shrine to Mother

Buzan Kimura, a leading artist of Tokyo, known for his fine paintings of Buddhist subjects, has always been known as a devoted son.

On his mother's death bed some years ago, he promised that he would erect a shrine to her memory.

This pledge has been carried out, and the shrine was built at Kitayamauchi-mura in Ibaragi Prefecture. The dedication ceremony was held on October 6. The inner walls of the shrine have been painted by Mr. Kimura in his best Buddhist style.

Painting of Nichiren

Chūsha, who acts as Nichiren at the Kabukiza Oct. play, was surprised on Oct 8 evening when he was presented with a fine painting of Nichiren, 9 feet in length and 6 feet in width, by Baito Yamamoto, a noted painter of the Buddhist saint who resides at Akatsutsumi, Setagaya.

When the artist heard of Chūsha and his devotion to the Nichiren faith, he determined to paint a picture for the actor.

Protecting Zenkoji

The ancient temple in Nagano, Zenkoji, which has been a center of Buddhist worship for five centuries or more is to be protected by a curtain of water.

Water pipes have been so arranged that at the first alarm of fire they can be opened and water plays over the great sloping roof like heavy rain.

Statues of Kwannon

In former days devote Buddhists made for pilgrimages to pay their respects to temples, but now-a-days priests and images come to the city.

On Wednesday morning priests representing the 33 temples sacred to Kwannon in Kansai arrived at Tokyo station carrying precious statues of the Goddess of Mery.

The Buddhist Association of Tokyo is arranging to show these images to the public.

The first duty of the priests on arriving in Tokyo was to pay their respects before the Imperial Palace.

Attractions of Chūzenji

The National Park committee plan to carry out great improvements in the Oku-Nikko district which was selected as a national park zone last year.

Motor car driveways are to be constructed, also roads for hikers. In the vicinity of Lake Chūzenji 300 horses will be provided for horseback riders. In the lake 500,000 trout are to be placed, and ardent fishermen may angle at any time of the year.

Jizo in Bronze

A huge statue in bronze of Jizo, the guardian of little children in the other world, is to be erected in the compound of Tennoji, a Buddhist temple of Shitaya on October 20.

It is a symbol of protection of primary school children in all parts of the city.

The direct reason for the erection of this statue is said to be in the desire to console the souls of the two sons of Mr. Masaki Kurokawa, judge of the Appellate Court. The children met their death in an accident in the playground of the Ichikawa primary school in Chiba Prefecture last year.

Sympathizers with Mr. Kurokawa connected with courts in all parts of the country have contributed the money for the execution of this work.

Tennoji Bell

The great bell of Tennoji, said to be the second largest bell in the world, has been silent for years since a crack in the metal has impaired its tone.

It was cast in 1906 and has a diameter of 14 feet.

Plans are now being made to recast the bell when its voice will once more be heard booming across the roofs of Osaka.

Buddhist Hall

The Buddhist Association of Tokyo Imperial University is to build a new center at Sanchome, Hongo.

The committee in charge of the construction is Dr. Toru Shimizu, President of the Imperial Academy of Fine Arts, and Dr. Junjiro Takakusu, the distinguished Buddhist scholar, and other persons prominent in Buddhist circles.

The new building will be six storeys high. The architectural plan has been furnished by Dr. Koichi Sato, professor of Waseda University. The hall will be ready sometime in 1937.

Temple Destroyed

Chozenji, established by Musokokushi, a Buddhist priest, in 1314, was completely destroyed by fire last week.

It is at Atogamachi, Kōfu, in Yamanashi Prefecture. A collection of valuable Buddhist art was lost in the conflagration.

Yokohama Temple

The Gumyoji, one of the oldest Buddhist temples of Yokohama, at Gumyoji-machi, Nakaku, was celebrated the 1,200th anniversary of its founding on October 10–11.

Historical documents relating to the temple, and an ancient wooden statue of Kwannon was shown to visitors. The statue is said to date back to the reign of Emperor Shomu.

Ikegami Festival

Hommonji, the Nichiren-sect headquarters in Tokyo, at Ikegami, Omori, was the scene of the annual festival Oct. 12 evening. Mando, the picturesque square lanterns, painted with many designs, was carried through the streets.

Devout believers in the Nichiren

sect of Buddhism joined this lantern procession chanting the familiar refrain: "Nammyo Horengekyo!"

The Tokyo Radio Broadcasting Station conveied the sounds of the noisy demonstration along the streets and at the temple to listeners-in throughout the country.

Buddhist Opera

Mr. Sesshu Hayakawa, supported by 200 dancers and actors, will perform in a Buddhist musicdrama at the Nippon Gekijo Dec. 1–10.

Mr. Hayakawa has been interested in producing a Buddhist play that will compare with the Passion Play in Germany, and he has now completed a long drama.

The screen actor will take the role of Sakyamuni, and Miss Toshiko Sekiya will sing in solo.

Temple Treasures

Buzan Kimura, the artist, a member of the Japan Art Institute, recently discovered two valuable statues in a small temple in Kita Yamanouchi-mura of Ibaragi Prefecture.

One is of Kobo-daishi, the founder of the Shingon sect. It is a lacquered figure and stands 3 feet 5 inches high.

The other is that of Kwannon belonging to the Kamakura period, the colors used in painting the wooden statue being still in a good state of preservation.

Artist and priest are now making a request to the Department of Education that these two works of art be given special Government protection.

Statue of Ikkyu

Kaoru Takebayashi, the well known wood carver of Nara, has recently completed a statue of Ikkyu, the fifteenth century priest and poet.

The statue will be treasured at Shozuiji, a Buddhist temple at Katada in Shiga Prefecture.

The sculptor sought inspiration for his model in the fine statue of Ikkyu in the possession of Ikkyu temple at Tanabe in Kyoto Prefecture, and it is an impressive piece of work, 6 feet high.

Fukuoka Temple

Toko-in, a popular temple of Fukuoka, will be improved by the reconstruction of the main hall, Kokuhodo. A fund for the purpose has been raised by the inhabitants of the city amounting to Yen 30,000.

The design for the architecturs has been made by the public Works Bureau of Fukuoka Prefectural Office.

國際佛教通報局

名譽局長　高楠順次郎

局　長　大村桂巖
幹　事　鷹谷俊之
同　稻葉文海
同　淺野研眞

顧　問（順序不同）

″　宇井伯壽
″　朝倉曉瑞
″　羽溪了諦
″　荻原雲來
″　千潟龍祥
″　鈴木大拙
″　鈴木宗忠
″　天岫接三
″　長井眞琴
″　松本文三郎
″　椎尾辨匡
″　宇野圓空
″　赤松智城
″　大森禪戒
″　矢吹慶輝
″　小野清一郎
″　加藤精神
″　姉崎正治
″　本田義英
″　關本龍門
″　佐伯定胤
″　花田凌雲
″　河野法雲
″　高岡隆心
″　小林瑞淨
″　山邊習學
″　赤沼智善
″　本多惠隆
″　大森亮順
″　河口慧海
″　山川智應
″　常盤大定
″　谷本富
″　常盤井堯猷
″　大谷尊由
″　大谷瑩潤
″　水野梅曉
″　柴田一能
″　安藤正純
″　下村壽一
″　菊澤季麿
″　乘杉嘉壽
″　芝田徹心
″　淺野孝之
″　渡邊哲信
″　小野玄妙
″　柳澤健
″　重光葵
″　金倉圓照
″　立花俊道

國際佛教通報局定款

名　稱

第一，本局を國際佛教通報局と稱す

事務所

第二，本局の事務所を全日本佛教青年會聯盟本部に置く

目　的

第三，本局は日本內海及海外に向つて佛教事情の通報をなし，且つ佛教徒相互間の各種便宜を計るを以て目的とす

事　業

第四，本局の目的を達成するため左記の事業を行ふ

イ，日本內地及世界各國より佛教事情に關する質問の通報を行ふ

ロ，必要に應じ日本語及世界各國語を以て佛教事情の通報を行ふ

ハ，外國人の日本觀光に際しては各國の便益を與へ，特にその佛教に關する方面に於て之を爲す

ニ，定時或は隨時に各國語を以て文書の刊行をなす

ホ，その他必要と認めたる事業を行ふ

役　員

第五，本局の事務を處理するため左の役員を置く

イ，局長　一名

ロ，幹事　三名

ハ，評議員　若干名

局長は本局　を總括す

幹事は本局の事務を處理す

評議員は局長の提案に依る重要事務を審議す

第六，評議員は左記の者を以て之に充つ

イ，全日本佛教青年會館聯盟理事及主事

ロ，全日本佛教青年會聯盟理事會に於て推薦したる者

第七，局長及幹事は評議員會に於て決定す

第八，役員の仕期は二ヶ年とす（但し重任を妨げず）

經　費

第九，本局の經費は左記のものに依て之を支辨す

イ，本局基金の活用

ロ，寄附金

ハ，その他の收入

補　則

第十，本定款に記載せられざる事項は，凡て評議員會に於て協議す

第十一，第一回の役員は全日本佛教青年會聯盟理事會に於て決定す

定價	一部	金二十錢	送料二錢
	一年	金二圓四十錢	送料不要

昭和十年四月卅日第三種郵便物認可
昭和十年十月廿七日印刷（每月一回一日發行）
昭和十年十一月一日發行

編輯發行兼印刷人　東京市外吉祥寺337　淺野研眞

印刷所　東京市牛込區早稻田鶴卷町107　康文社印刷所　電話牛込(34)1950番 5049番

發行所　東京市神田區一ツ橋二の三　國際佛教通報局　電話九段(33)4428番　振替東京83015番

昭和十年四月三十日第三種郵便物認可
昭和十年十月二十七日印刷納本(毎月一回)
昭和十年十一月一日發行(一日發行)　國際佛教通報　第一卷　第八號

昭和十年四月三十日第三種郵便物認可　昭和十年十一月二十七日印刷納本　昭和十年十二月一日發行（毎月一回一日發行）第一卷　第九號

The International Buddhist Bulletin

國際佛教通報

第一卷 **昭和十年十二月** 第九號〔Vol. I. Dec. 2501/1935 No. 9.〕

要　目〔**Contents**〕

東京　**國際佛教通報局**　發行
The International Buddhist Information Bureau
Tokyo, Kanda, Hitotsubashi, II—3

逝けるレヴィ教授（記事参照）

Some Parallels Between Buddhism And The Modern Interpretation of Educational Ideals

By Yoshio Ohtani

Principal of Oka Girls' High School, Nagoya, Japan.

Those who open the pages of the history of education in Japan can not fail to recognize the striking phases of service rendered by Buddhism. Even, it is safe to say that excluding Buddhism attempts are futile to talk of any form of the history of education in Japan. Nor has Buddhism less weight in connection with the modern interpretation of educational ideals. My present article is to deal just in a concise way the traces of service or the connection between Buddhism and education.

Buddhism as founded by the Buddha some 2,500 years ago is, as with christianity, one of the greatest religions of the world. It is now over 1,300 years since it came to Japan. At the very beginning of its adaptation to the soils of Japan, its true features were already fully manifested through the hand of the Prince Shotoku, by his adopting its canons as the practical principles of national guidance, in the sphere of politics, in every range of social works; and as such it has ever lived with the fate of Japan, and sees its present day. Of 90,000,000 of the present population of Japan 50,000,000 are Buddhists. That Buddhism enjoys such a great number of followers in the population of Japan may well be understood when we look into the characteristics of Buddhism. For the present let me quote the eight ways classification as accorded by Dr. Takakusu and examine into the relations between Buddhism and education in Japan.

1. Buddhism as an ideal religion of personality. Buddhism is the

perfection of personality in the person of the Buddha himself. And nobody questions that. And yet, the ideals of his teaching direct us towards the attainment of a great personality by an incessant upward step. Buddhism professes the every being and thing possesses a seed of Buddhahood. Be it a man, a beast, a plant or even a lifeless thing, everything has in itself, Buddhism says, a bud for the attainment of a great personality. This is respect paid towards everything that exists. It is the final ideal and the aim of Buddhism that man pursues, through the *Rokudo* or the Six ways of Salvation, and several other methods of self-culture, the paths of man's inner ideals to attain the perfection of personality. And we must not miss the significance, this fact bears towards the new way of interpretation of educational ideals of modern ages.

2. Buddhism as a religion of intellectual self-culture. Buddhism teaches self-culture at the bidding of intellect. Every civilization is the outcome of intellectual culture, and that is true. And Buddhism is insistent upon the possibility of our upward growth through the working of intellect. And Buddhism adopts the principles of development of ones hidden qualities as educational ideals.

3. Buddhism as a religion of forbearance and application. In the 'Six Ways of Salvation' we find forbearance and application. Every great Buddhist saint has lived putting up with hardships, energies having been spent in the field of positive application towards life's ideals. Dharmakāra Boddhisattva, or the prior stage of the Amida the Enlightened One, swore that even if he were to work amid every thinkable hardship and poison his application would not end hardships would be conquered and repentance comes not. And with this open proclamation, he battled with hardships and applied his energies, solely aiming at the general welfare of every human being. Would not that well answer the need of ideals education hungers?

4. Buddhism as a religion of absolute mercy and sympathy. To say that even a plant and a blade of grass is blessed with the seed of Buddhahood tells the deepest sympathy tended towards every living thing. The Buddha sacrificed his own self and sought after truth because of the salvation and the

perfection of the soul of every living being. The spirit of mercy and sympathy was extended towards everything that lives and the result was the every possible variety of charity works Buddhists accorded the world with. The Prince Shotoku's 'Four Social Institutions' of Seyakuin or free apothecary, Seryō-in or free hospital, Keiden-in or the place for the worship of the Three Gems, and Hiden-in or home where charity is extended towards the poor and the afflicted, the leper treatment of the Empress Kōmyō-Kōgō, and the workhouses, the orphanages and every kind of other social institutions of Buddhists show that Buddhists have since of old been awake in every field of social works. Hōjōye or the Buddhist festival of releasing the caged things, such as fish and birds, are the manifestation of mercy even towards beasts. And Buddhism takes to absolute pacificism.

5. Buddhism as a religion of creative self enlightenment. The Buddhahood is an enlightened state, a state attained through the culturing and heightening of one's inner self. Therefore we say the Buddha an 'Enlightened One, or a Fully Perfected One, who is enlightened and enlightens others.' And does not the ideals of education come to the same end?

6. Buddhism as a religion of meditation. Our souls attain control and light only when we seek through the hidden treasures of our soul, and reflect and meditate. Deep research into the secret chambers of soul is one of the great ways of Buddhist self-culture.

7. Buddhism as a religion of spiritual nationalism. Buddhism teaches *Shion* or 'Four Obligations', the first of which is towards king. The Enryakuji Temple of Mt. Hiei, or the Head Temple of the Tendai Sect, was no other than a shrine where the welfare and prosperity of the whole Japanese nation was prayed. Rennyoshōnin, a famous Buddhist saint, taught us to respect the laws of the state. Buddhism has ever been the food-stuff of national life and its upkeep and control.

8. Buddhism as a religion of gratitude. Our existence is never an outcome of our personal power. One of the special features of Buddhism is that it teaches *Anatman* or 'selflessness' which is to say that our existence is not the result of our own working

only. Our life is only possible because of the sovereign, our ancestors, parents, neighbours, society in which we live, and all the requisites and materials; or, in other words, it teaches that our life is composed of visible and invisible influences that play on our self. Such a way of thinking wakes in our heart a light of gratitude towards life, a state of mind, indispensable in education.

The hereabove quoted eight different aspects of Buddhism are quite in accord with the ideals as tended by the modern interpretation of educational ideals. By ever expanding such theories Buddhists have striven hard for the past 1,300 years in the spheres of social, family, and school education; nay, even in all branches of educational works. Hoping the participators from other couutries in this Pan-Pacific New Educational Conference will see to some aspects of interaction beween Buddhism and education in Japan, I set down my pen.

(Tokyo, August 7th, 1935)

Ein historischer Augenblick.

von
Guido Auster, Deutschland.

Der politische Kampf in Deutschland ist fast beendet, der geistige hat gerade begonnen. Die Heftigkeit der Auseinandersetzungen mit der katholischen Kirche und deren Angriffe auf Rosenbergs "Mythus des XX. Jahrhunderts" zeigen die gewaltige Bedeutung und die Anteilnahme die diese geistige Auseinandersetzung in ganz Deutschland gefunden hat.

Zum ersten Malin der deutschen Geschichte wird auch vom Staat die ausserkirchliche und nichtchristliche Religiosität voll anerkannt. Während bisher nur der Mensch als "religiös" und "moralisch" galt, der zur christlichen Kirche gehörte, ist im neuen Deutschland in weitesten Kreisen die Erkenntnis durchgedrungen, dass wahre Religiösität auch ausserhalb einer Kirchenzugehörigkeit vorhanden sein kann.

Der Buddhismus hat jetzt die beste, wahrscheinlich nie wiederkehrende Gelegenheit, seine Botschaft dem deutschen Geistsleben darzubringen und er kann sicher sein, ein aufmerksames und oft sogar wohlwollendes Gehör zu finden. Wie nie zuvor ist das deutsche Volk bereit, seine Aufmerksamkeit einer neuen religiösen Lehre zu schenken, und wenn auch nicht zu erwarten ist, dass grosse Volksmengen zum Buddhismus übertreten (feste religiös-kirchliche Bindungen lehnt der heutige Deutsche ab), so kann man dessen gewiss sein, dass das deutsche Geistesleben buddhistische Gedanken in grosser Zahl übernehmen wird.

Der Buddhismus ist eine Gabe. Wir deutschen Buddhisten wollen nur geben, nichts für unser Geben nehmen. Wir sind überzeugt, dass jeder Mensch unenlich viel aus der Lehre des Buddha schöpfen und lernen kann. Wir haben den geistigen und seelischen Reichtum, die vornehme Gesinnung, den selbstbesinnlichen und tapfermännlichen Charakter des Budhismus kennen gelernt. Diese herrliche Lehre wollen wir unseren Volksgenossen üb ermitteln. In dieser Aufgabe können Ost und West: Japan und Deutschland harmonisch zusammenarbeiten. Und besonders die Jugend beider Länder ist zu solcher Arbeit geeignet. Das südliche Hinayana und das nördliche Mahayana werden sich hier im Westen freundschaftlich vereinigen. Mögen die japanischen Buddhisten diesen historischen Augenblick nicht versäumen!

Und noch eins! Es gibt kein besseres Mittel, den Frieden und die freundschaftlichen Beziehungen zweier Völker zu garantieren, als das Band kultureller Beziehungen.

Berlin, September 1935.

La Fakoj de Budaisma Sociologio

de Ken Assano

1. Klasifikoj laŭsekta kaj laŭafera

Jam koninte la pozicion de Budaisma Sociologio kiel speciala fako de religia sociologio laŭ klasifiko de ĝenerala sociologio, ni ĉi tie devas trakti klasifikon de Budaisma Sociologio.

Mi tuŝetis simple en jam menciitaj informoj "El Parizo" sur la ĵurnalo Ĉuugaj-nippo, laŭsektan klasifikon: Zen-sekta Sociologio, Ŝin-sekta Sociologio ktp. Kompreneble kiel en Kristana Sociologio sin trovas Katolika Sociologio, Protestanta Sociologio, estas farebla ankaŭ en Budaisma Sociologio klasifiko laŭ sektoj. Efektive ĝin oni devas klasifiki en du pligrandajn fakojn: en Mahajanan kaj Hinajanan Sociologiojn, ĉar Mahajana kaj Hinajana Budaismo havas grandan diferencon inter siaj konceptoj pri la mondo, socio kaj vivo. Ankaŭ en Hinda Budaismo sin trovas multaj sektoj, kiuj postulas distingon inter si laŭ sia koncepto pri regno, socio k.c. Ankaŭ inter Japanaj sektoj en ekonomiaj fenomenoj la fakto ke en Niĉiren-sekto ĝermis *Fuĵufuse-ha* aŭ Nealmoza-subsekto, estas por ni interesega kaj ĝi instigas nian studemon.

Sed estas senbezone diri ke krom tia laŭsekta, nome Sekta Sociologio, pli inkluziva, ĝenerala fakaro de Budaisma Sociologio povas ekzisti.

Resume la sekta sociologio iuokaze estas valora kiel speciala studo, nur kiam ĝi estas farata en ĝenerala studprincipo, sed malfirma estas la bazo ke ĝi estas scienco kaj en rilato al sociologio la studo devas esti pli ĝenerala, sekve ni volas starigi sociologian studon komune budaisman.

Kaj do aŭfhebinte laŭsektan klasifikon de Budaisma Sociologio, oni devas preni originan klasifikon de ĝenerala sociologio. Nome devas esti traktataj sinteze fakoj de konceptoj pri familio, politiko, moralo, ekonomio, arto, kaj aliaj en Budaismo. Poste estos klarigataj la sociaj fenomenoj de Budaismo.

2. Problemoj en klasifiko laŭafera

Koncerne al studo de fakoj de Budaisma Sociologio farita sur tia sintetza vidpunkto, t.e. speciala traktado, nur ĉi sube mi prezentas la skemon de la studoplano.[1]

(1) *Budaismo kaj familia fenomeno:* ĉi tio estas studo de budaismaj fenomenoj en la fako de familia sociologio, kaj estas traktataj budaismaj ideoj kaj fenomenoj, ekzemple, seksa problemo, prostituo, edziĝo, virino, hejmo, bonziĝo ktp.

(2) *Budaismo kaj morala fenomeno:* ĉi tie oni klarigas moralan elementon de Budaismo, kaj studas ideojn kaj fenomenojn pri lojaleco al la reĝo aŭ mastro, dankemo, fila pieco ktp. kaj problemo de sinmortigo, kunsinmortigo de geamantoj ktp.

(3) *Budaismo kaj jura fenomeno:* ĉi tie estas studata ĉefe *Vinaya*, ordonoj abstinaj, kaj plie iliaj influoj de ĝi sur socion ekster eklezio, ekzemple la konstitucio de Princo Ŝootoku kaj leĝoj por eklezio aŭ por religio.

(4) *Budaismo kaj politika fenomeno:* ĉi tie estas studataj problemoj naskitaj pro kontakto de politika potenco kaj Budaismo, kaj koncernantaj al ŝtato, reĝo, regado, kaj ideala ŝtato kaj socio laŭ Budaismo, kaj sociboniga entrepreno de Budaismo ktp.

(5) *Budaismo kaj ekonomia fenomeno:* ĉi tio estas la plej fundamenta fako, kaj en kiu estas studata, kiamaniere budaisma ideo kaj eklezio estis difinita kaj ŝanĝita laŭ siatempa ekonomia bazo kaj medio, kaj inverse kian influon Budaismo donis al ekonomia stato, precipe almozado, templa financo, familia financo, konceptoj pri sociklaso, pri okupo, kaj financaj organoj kiel "*muzin*" kaj aliaj laboroj de budaisma eklezio sur financa ekonomio, ktp.

(6) *Budaismo kaj estetika fenomeno:* en Japanujo tre gravan signifon havis la kontakto inter Budaismo kaj belarto tiel ke oni povas aserti, ke nenio restas kiam oni elprenas el la japana artohistorio elementojn budaismajn. Ankaŭ en beliteraturo, muziko, forma arto kaj arkitekturo multe sin trovas budaisma influo kaj esprimo, ĉi tie estas provata sistema studo de tiaj fenomenoj.

(7) *Krome povas esti nomataj:* Budaismo kaj lingva fenomeno, scienca fenomeno (astronomio, matematiko, kuracarto, fiziologio, natursciencco ktp.) kaj eduka fenomeno ktp.

---

(1) Mi jam priskribis unu verkon, "*Studo de Budaisma Sociologio,*" en japana lingvo (inoktavo p. 328. junio 1935, Tokio.) Kaj tiuj ĉi ĉapitroj faras la unuan parton de la verko. Mi volas sincere aŭdi kritikojn kaj konsilojn de kolegoj.

Letero de Budhana Esperantisto en Angllando

La 1 an de Aprilo, 1935.

Estimata Amiko!

Mi kore dankas vin pro via longa kaj kuraĝiga letero, kaj ankaŭ via informo pri la granda konferenco kiu havis lokon en Tokio, kaj de tempo al tempo viaj eldonaĵoj. Mi gratulas vin pro via bona verkado kaj entuziasmo por Budhismo.

Mi dankas vin pro viaj laŭdoj de miaj simplaj klopodoj, laŭdoj kiujn mi nek meritas, nek bezonas kiel instigon al laboro. Tamen mi sentas ioman kontentigon pro tio ke vi opinias ke mia penado ne estas vana. Efektive mi konstatas, per korespondaĵoj ricevitaj de multaj mondpartoj, ke B.L.E. kaj gia humila organo havas utilan rolon. Tial vi ĝojos kun mi ĉar "La Budhismo" ankoraŭ ne malaperos. Unu BLE ano en proksima urbo de Angllando nun entreprenas la laboron de presado de ĝi, almenaŭ dum la jaro 1935. Kvankam li ne havas tempon por fari ĝin ĝuste tiel samampleksa kiel antaŭe, li tamen estas sperta presisto (ne mallerta amatoro kiel mi) kaj certe faros ĝin bele. kaj mi ankoraŭ prizorgos la redaktadon k.t.p. Nun mi havas iom da tempo por korespondado, per kiu mi pli bone tenados la intereson de miaj multoj informpetautoj.

En la proksima urbego Liverpool ni starigis Budhisman Mision. Tie ni okazigas formalan kunvenon (servon) je la 3a dimanĉo en ĉiu monato. Ni nombras nin ses budhanoj kiuj faras agantan partprenon, kaj laŭvice ni agas kiel parolanto, kondukanto aŭ leganto por la kunveno. Proksimume 20 personoj ordinare ĉeestas ĉinfoje. Ĉiufoje venas novaj personoj por informiĝi, sed ĉiuj ne ĉiam venas denove.

La formalo de la kunveno estos: Unue ni kantas himnon, due la kondukanto deklamas la tri rifuĝojn kaj la kvin principojn, kaj la kunvenantoj ripetas tiujn ĉi post la kondukanto. Tiam la leganto legas parton el la kanonaj skribaĵoj aŭ alia budhisma verko. Poste la kondukanto deklamas la kvar braĥmajn meditotemojn, kaj inter ĉiu, aparte, li paŭzas sufiĉe longe por permesi ke ĉiuj kunvenintoj primeditadu la temon. Tiam la parolanto faras paroladon pri Budhismo, kaj poste la kondukauto legas benon, kiel fino. Sekvas demandoj kaj diskutoj.

Mi esperas ke tiu ĉi priskribo interesas vin.

Mi volas al vi sukceson en via laboro por Budhismo kaj Esperanto.

Frate la via

Geo H. Yoxon.

Rimarko:

Supre prezentita letero kompreneble estas tiu kiu estas persone adresita al mi de mia estimata angla budhana Esperantisto Sro G. H. Yoxon, kiu estas ĉefa direktoro de Budha Ligo Esperatista en Angllando. Sed ĝia enhavo estas ne persona kaj certe estas intersa al ĉiuj budhanoj en ciuj landoj. Tio kuraĝigis min publikigi la leteron. Karaj legantoj, mi akcentas al vi ĉiuj, la celo de Esperanto jam ne estas utopio sed reala fakto en nia ĉiutaga vivo. Ni budhanoj, kiuj sintrovas en diversaj landoj, kiuj havas diversajn naciecojn kaj nacilingvojn, rapidu enkonduki Esperanton kiel nia unika interkomunikilo unu la alian. Kaj mi estas certa, ke tio nepre pli akcelos nian intimecon en facila vojo, kaj samtempe servos multoble por la bono de homaro.

Kei Ŝibajama

Esperantaj libroj pri Budaismo

		prezo	sendkosto
1.	La Sukhavativjuho	¥ 0.15	0.02
2.	Budao (tradukita el "The Essence of Buddhism")	0.60	0.04
3.	La Dek Bildoj de Bovpaŝtado	0.35	0.04
4.	La Kodo de Kronprinco Ŝootoku	0.15	0.02
5.	La Samanta-Mukhaparivarto	0.40	0.04
6.	Budaisma Terminaro (de T. Takeuĉi) (hektografita)	2.00	0.20
7.	La fundamenta Koncepto de Budaisma Sociologio (de Ken ASSANO)	0.15	0.02

Ĉiuj libroj supre menciitaj estas riceveblaj de la Administracio de la "Internacia Budaisma Bulteno" aŭ de Japana Esperanto-Instituto, Hongoo, Tokio.

Por la prosperiĝo de internacia kulturo

de Megumu Macuda

Estimataj gejunuloj!

Kiel vi jam bone scias, nia Budhismo fondiĝis en Hindujo, havante en si ampleksan kaj profundan instruon de l' Budho kiel sian kernon. Kaj ĝi disvastiĝis en Ĉinujon, kie ĝi multe evoluis pro la influo de Ĉina kulturo. Ĝi tamen ankoraŭ disvastiĝadis orienten ĉiam plu, kaj finfine plenfloris en Japanujo, fariĝante unu el gravaj elementoj de brilanta Japana kulturo. Unuvorte, la sankta arbo "Budhismo" kiun la fondinto Budho plantis en Hindujo dense kreskis en Ĉinujo kaj belege floris en Japanujo, mirinda lando ekstremorienta.

Nome, Budhismo en Japanujo, kiu enmiksis kaj proprigis al si tradician Japanan spiriton kaj Konfuciismon, kaj kiu enradikigis sin tre profunde en la nacieco de Japanujo dum pli ol 1300 jaroj, fariĝis pli nobla. En tiu ĉi punkto, por tiel diri, Budhismo en Japanujo ja havas plej superan enhavon el tiuj de iu ajn lando de l'mondo.

Aliflanke, Japnnujo kiu estis tre okupata por enkonduki okcidentan kulturon dum 50 lastaj jaroj, jam preskaŭ elĉerpis enkondukindan. Kaj la brileco, ke ĝi brave ekstaris grandan turn-punkton de sendependeco, ne nur estas en diplomacia aŭ ekonomia flankoj, sed, ni devas scii, ankaŭ en kultura flanko.

Ĉiuj religioj kaj kulturoj, kiuj estis enportitaj trans la marj Pacifika aŭ Ĉina en mirindan insularon ekstremorientan, returne devas elportiĝi trans la samaj maroj, por ke ili povu pli lumigi la tutmondon. Kaj tio, kio en la plej proksima tempo la atento aŭ intereso de diversaj nacianoj koncentriĝas al Japana kulturo—sekve al Japana Budhismo, estas la afero tute natura.

Do nuntempe, mi opinias, akcenti tian brilantan kulturon de Japanujo al la tuta mondo, internacie diskonigi tiel valoran Budhismon de Japanujo, kaj sekve havi pli intiman rilaton kun diversaj nacianoj en egala estimeco, ja vere devas esti nepra tasko de ni, Japanaj Budhistoj, por pli altigi internacian kulturon kaj por la bono de tuthomaro, Tamen, ĉu nuntempaj gebudhanoj en Japanujo efektive estas preparantaj aŭ preparontaj ian pravan vojon por tio?

De la komenco inter okcidento kaj oriento, ne nur tiuj sed eĉ inter orientaj landoj, trovĝas krutega monto, kiun oni facile estas ne transpasebla. Kaj de tiu ĉi krutaĵo derivas diversajn baraĵojn malgraŭ tio, ke homoj de tutmondo devas kunfandiĝi en egala amo, kaj devas marŝi saman vojon de prosperiĝo.

Jen mi volas akcente nomi la diferencon de lingvoj kiel la plej grandan baraĵon el ĉiuj, aliaj kiuj troviĝas inter moroj, kutimoj kaj tiel plu.

Kvankam la studadoj pri oriento aŭ Budhismo en okcidento jam daŭriĝis pli ol cent jaroj, oni ne ĉiam havas bonan rikolton, kaj kvankam la klopodo diskonigi la propran kulturon de oriento estas iom granda, oni tamen domaĝas pri tio, ke ĝusta kompreno ofte mankas al okcidentanoj.

Estas evidente, ke ĉio ĉi tio devenas de la lingva baro, nome de diferenco de lingvoj.

Jen, mi volas instigi al junaj gebudhanoj, ke ni traboru la baron, krutaĵon per Esperanto, neŭtrala interkomumikilo, kaj ke havu pli grandan intimecon kun diversaj landanoj por diskonigi la spiriton de Mahojana Budhismo en Japanujo, kiu havas meriton kiel unu el noblaj bazoj de internacia kulturo.

逝けるシルヴァン・レヴィ教授

浅野研眞

去る十月三十一日，パリ發の聯合通信によれば，同日，パリに於て，現代歐洲佛教學界の第一人者，東洋學の巨匠たるパリ大學梵語教授シルヴアン・レヴィ (Sylvain Lévi) 氏は，七十二歳の高齢（一八六三年，巴里生れ）で，つひに逝去されたのである。依つて逸早く私は其の訃を，去る十一月三日の「讀賣新聞」誌上にも執筆したのであつた。

實際，氏を識る人は，我國にも相當に多いことではあらうが，私もその一人として，且つ滯歐中しばしば，お宅をも訪れて，一方ならぬ御指導を受けたものとして，茲に教授の訃を衷心より哀悼せざるを得ざるものである。

それに目下，東洋研究及び特に日本研究が，世界的な潮流として非常な高揚を示してゐるの時だから，氏の如き巨匠の逝去は，如何に惜しみても，惜しみ足らないであらう。

特にレヴィ教授は，しばしば印度，極東に遊歴され，日本には三度までも來訪されたことがあつて，日本文化，日本佛教に對しては，特に甚大なる理解と同感とを持つてゐられて，常に之を歐洲學界に紹介されてゐた方だけに餘計に惜しまれざるを得ない。まことに，氏の逝去は，日本文化の歐洲進出にとつては，非常な損失である。

×

レヴィ氏の業蹟は，先年，昭和三年五月，日佛會館長を辭して歸國される際に「現代佛教」の同月號に，詳細に紹介されてゐるが，主要なものを二，三擧げるならば，學位論文は「印度劇」（一八九〇年）であり，同副論文はラテン語で書かれた「古代印度文獻に現れたるギリシヤ人に關する記述」（同年）である。また一八九八年には「梵書に於ける供犧の教義」(La doctrine du sacrifice dans les Brâhmanas, Paris, 1898.) なる宗教社會學上の著述がある。

×

然し何と云つても，氏の國際學界への偉大なる貢獻は，佛教學の方面である。卽ち氏は再三印度の北方ネパールに入國し，梵語佛典を探査し，大乘莊嚴經論，唯識二十論，唯識三十頌及註，中邊分別論及註，等々の原本を發見され，自ら校訂出版し，フランス語譯をも企圖された。

また漢文及び西藏語などにも精通された氏が，高楠博士らと協力して，佛教辭典「法寶義林」の完成に努力されてゐたことも有名なことだ。

×

× ×

何故日本の佛教エス語運動は進展しないか

中西礎醒

エスペラント運動も歩一歩と着實に進展しつゝあるは事實で，最近の報道によれば，明年の萬國エスペラント大會は，オーストリー政府の招待によつて，ウイーンに於て開催が決定され，又歐米各國の商品見本市には何れもエスペラント部が設けられ，國際語エスペラントによる商取引が現に行はれて居る。

時は流れる，十年前，二十年前を回顧すれば，我等エスペランチストには確に隔世の感がある。併し佛教エス語運動を凝視すると，恐ろしく心細さに襲はれる。

日本佛教エスペランチスト聯盟が創立されて既に五年，英吉利のジー，エイチ，ヤクソン氏によりエス語の佛教雜誌 La Budhismo が創刊されて既に六年經過，併し，佛教界に於けるエスペラント運動，エスペラント界に於ける佛教運動は依然として進展して居ない。何故に佛教エス語運動は發展しないか，それには種々込みいつた原因が存在するであらう，然し乍ら次に述べる諸點がその最大の原因，理由である事に誰も異論を差しはさみ得ないであらう。

第一の理由は，佛教各宗各派本山の當局が未だ眞面目に海外布教に關心を持つて居ない事である。各派共海外布教師を派遣して居るといふ，併し筆者の云ふ海外布教とは，外國人に傳道する事で，外國に於ける日本人の爲の布教ではない。それだから，時偶碧眼の求道者が來朝すれば，新聞は三段抜の見出しで特種扱にし，寺院當局者は鬼の首でも取つたかの如く意氣揚々と宣傳するといふ現狀である。我が國の開國以來既に七十年，日本人の足跡の到らざる地は地球上殆んど存在しない程普く行き渉つて居乍らも，開教使の第一線に進みつゝある事を筆者は不幸にして未だ知らないのである。

斯の如く，海外布教に極めて冷淡である，各本山當局が，國際語エスペラントを利用する事に關心を缺くは當然であらう。

第二の理由は，我が國民が自國の英語殖民地化を自覺して居ない事である「英語殖民地」なる語は確に穩當を缺くものなるが，現在の事實がさうであるならば如何とも致し難いであらう。中學生を一番惱ますものは英語であり，日本の大學に入るに英吉利の國語試驗を受けなければ出來ないといふ我が國の現狀である。國内のみしか流通しない兌換紙幣には，日本語と竝んで英語が印刷してあり，政府が發賣して居る煙草の名前が英語で付けられてある。之を我が國民は少しも奇異に思つて居ない。甚だしい人は，會話中に英語をさしはさまないと知識階級者の沽券にかゝわると考へ，英語さへ知つて居れば世界中の人と話が出來る位に思つて居るのである。此の狀態が，維新以來五十年餘，所謂半世紀以上も續いて居る爲に，國民の大部は此の事が不合理極まるものであり，排すべきであるといふ事を全く忘れて居るのである。數年前私を訪ねた，獨逸の新聞記者ウイリアム，ペルツ君の來朝第一印象は「英領日本の感じ」と物語つた。

スペイン語，ポルトガル語等のラテン直系の言語を用ひて居る中南米諸國を總稱して，ラテン，アメリカと云つて居る。此の例に倣ふならば，我が國は「英語日本」と稱せられるかも判らない。一國の獨立を維持するには各方面の自主獨立を必要とするもので，言語の獨立も亦重要なる要素の一である。最近國體明徵の問題がやかましく言はれて居るが，現在の如く國語の尊嚴が著しく外國語殊に英語によつて侵されて居る事を看過する國體明徵は，あぐらして謡をやるやうなものであらう。此の情勢に慣れて，此の中で生活を續け一歩も出て居ない，我が國の僧侶が對外的なエスペラントに關心を持ち得ないは，けだし當然であらう。

第三の理由は世を指導すべき宗教家先覺者であるべき我が國の僧侶が，教義以外に就ては一般大衆の知識より遲れて居る事である。誰が何と抗辯しやうとも今日の僧侶は時代の先驅者ではない，尤も安穩な生活を永く續けて來た寺院生活者に先驅者たる事を要求するは，其の安穩を奪ふ事となるから，先づ望めない事であらう。エスペラントを取入れても，何等寺院經營の資にもならないし，米櫃が空にこそなれ，募財の材料にはならず，まかり間違へば色眼鏡を以て見られ易いエスペラント運動を敬遠するは無理もない事だ。曾てのマルクス運動の闘士で，現在は鮮かに轉向し，某派の新人布教師として囑望されて居る某君でさへ，「エス語運動と共產黨運動の關係」を質ね，「日本語と共產黨の關係の如し」と云ふ私の回答の眞意が判らず，言語運動と思想運動とを混同して考へて居る人の多い佛教界である。

最近宗教復興の氣運に乘つてか，佛教の國際化が著しく論議されて居る。英譯聖典の完成は國際佛教に關心を持つ者の一入同慶を感じるのである，併し英語が英米二國のみを對象するものであつて，決して全世界を對象とするものでない事をハツキリと認識しなければ不可である。此の點，大なる政治的背景こそ持つて居ないが，國際語エスペラントは使用者を世界の各隅到る處に持つて，國際文化の寄與に貢献を續けて居るのである。我が國の鐵道省の國際觀光局が本年四月以降六ケ月間に觀光に就ての海外よりの照會狀七一三通の內五二七通がエスペラントで書かれて居た程，エスペラントの實用が具體化しつゝある今日，佛教徒各位の御一考を煩したい。

支那佛教の現狀に就て

柴田一能

I

私今回初めて支那に參つた者として大それた事は申せないが，僅か四十日餘りの旅行であつたに拘らず，從來色々な書籍，新聞，雜誌等で想像して居つた支那と，實際見た支那とは，「百聞一見に如かず」と云ふ諺のやうに，僅かに一見に過ぎないけれども，その一見が非常に私の心を動かしたのである此の事實から考へて，必らずや諸君にも早かれ遲かれ支那の見學，視察を願ひ，今日外交上，政治上に於て果して何う云ふやうに進展して行くやら解らないが，私は唯外面に現はれて居るものだけを見，ホンの上ツ面だけを通つて來た觀察にすぎないから，所謂皮相の見であつて，深く支那の國民性を硏究し，數十回支那を往復された支那通から見れば，固より本當の處を摑んでゐないに相違ない。東京出發前に後藤先生の「支那通」と云ふ本，この書を唯一の水先案內とした。‥‥此の本は絕版になつてゐて版元の三省堂にもないので，或は古本屋にあるかも知れんと云ふ事で，九段下から一軒殘らず探しましたけれども唯の一軒も見つからなかつたと云ふ程に廣く讀まれて居る本である。「通」と云ふ中にも三義ありと申して，後藤先生のやうなのは本當の支那通。私の四十日餘り行つたのは通り一遍と云ふ通——一遍だけ通つたと云ふ通。第三には藤井草宣君のやうに度々支那に通ふ——三遍でも五遍でも通ふと云ふ通で，「通に三義あり」と云ふ事を聞いたが，どうも學者達の言ふ事は格張つてゐて，折角御馳走を召上つたのに消化の悪るい事は申上げたくない。隨つて一遍通り通つて來た私でも，四十日間全部を視察に當てるなれば，多少の御報告が出來たかも知れないが，それさへも出來なかつたのである。山東省の青島には每年，佛教聯合會，佛教青年聯合會，佛教婦人聯合會——青島の五宗派，六箇寺所屬の青年會，婦人會がその宗派を論せず，五宗派の青年會，婦人會が聯合して四年前から佛教講習會を開催し來つたのである。今年は日蓮宗が講師を出す番に當つてゐた所，私が昨年誤つて太平洋大會の會長に擧げられたために，支那にまでも私の名前が知られてゐたらしいので，その結果，聯合會でも，あの柴田一能師なら，異議なしとなつて，白羽の矢が飛んで來たやうな譯である。それで何んとか繰合せて來て貰ひたいと青島蓮長寺の大橋玄妙師から書面もあり，遂にその熱心にほだされて参つた次第であつて，多數有志の見送りを受けて勇ましく東京驛を出發し，神戸から長江丸に乘り最初塘沽に上陸それから汽車で天津に着，僅か四日間であつたが，着いたその日に灤州事變があつたのである。これは恐らく藍衣社の陰謀だらうと云ふ事で，丁度梅津軍司令官が第二師團長に榮轉せられたので，山海關に暇乞ひに行かれた留守であつたから，酒井參謀長に會見を申込み慰問の言葉を述べて居た時に事變の電話が掛つて來たのである。新聞や雜誌の上で親日親日と云つては居るが「これは仲々氣が許せんわい」と思つたのである。唯表面だけ我々が通り一遍で言ふのと内面の支那人の心持と云ふものと，これは餘程表裏の差があるなと云ふ事を，天津に着いたその日に敎へられ，これは氣を締めなければ不可と感じたのである。後藤先生の書物には絶對旅行者には危險なしと云ふてあるけれども「これは一寸危險だわい」と感じたのであつた。

II

天津から北平に行つた。悲しい哉今は北京とは言はないで北平――これは實に何んとも云へず寂しい氣がしたけれど，實際見るに足るものは，何んと云つても北京即ち北平であります。これ又滯留四日間であつた。

北京を一番北の打止めとして南に下り濟南に行つたが，丁度其處を發つた後で，これ又新聞で見ましたが――日本の新聞には出なかつたさうでありますが――夕方日本の青年が，犬に繩をつけて散歩して居つた處が，支那の兵隊に出會ひ，兵隊がその犬を蹴飛ばしたと云ふやうな事から，日本の青年團と支那の兵隊との間に悶着が起つたが濟南と云ふだけに，極めて小さいのであつたが「事件」と云ふ名を附ければ大きくもなるが，細かいなりに，さう云ふ事件もあつたのである。

それから折角の事であるから，是非曲阜――孔子聖人の生れた處で，今もその七十七代の末孫孔德成君が健在であると云ふ事で，曲阜に行つて會見する事になつた。

更に泰安まで戻つて中西旅館と云ふのを見付け，これは案外！　日本人の旅館がある，有りがたいと思つて行つたら中西旅館と云ふ支那人の旅館で，其處で南京虫にさんざ御馳走をしてしまつた。翌朝轎を雇つて泰山に登り，初めて山を語る資格を得た譯である。この泰山と佛敎との關係を何かに書いてみたいと思つてゐながら其のまゝになつて居るが，そのうちに私の見た「泰山と佛敎との關係」に就て諸君の高敎を仰ぎたいと思つてゐる。何しろ表面だけの事で何等御參考になるやうな事もあるまいが自分の氣のついた點を發表してみたいと思つてゐる。泰山を下つて再び濟南に歸り，それから青島に二週間逗留した。御存知の如く青島は日獨戰爭の結果十年間の軍制を布いてゐたと云ふ事で，青島の支那人は，日本人の實力を眞實に知つて居るので，極めて從順であるやうに見へた。七分

が日本，三分が支那，七分三分の兼ね合ひと云ふやうな感じで，青島なら此のまゝ永住してもいゝと云ふ氣持になつた事から察しても，二週間の間如何に持てたかと云ふ事の想像をして頂きたい。更に慰勞會と云ふ事で加藤島と云ふ港内の島に船をよせて，一日ピクニックに案內され，講習會も無事に濟んだと云ふので，乾盃を行ひ其の時撮つた寫眞が此間三枚到來した。加藤島の植込の日蔭に蓙を布き，山海の珍味を盛つた辨當を開いて美味さうに食べつつ，ビールの大盃を擧げて居ると云ふやうな場面で，既に召上つたからいゝが，食事前に申上げると，少なからず胃の腑に異狀を呈したかも知れない。

III

青島を發つて海路上海に向つた。船よりも陸を行つた方がと云ふ事であつたが，何しろ切詰めた日程であつたので，與へられた豫定通り正直に船行としたのである。上海十二日間の滯在中陸戰隊や在留民に對する色々慰問の講演とか，上海事變殉難者の墓參とか，それに日華佛敎學會の特派員と云ふ肩書の下に，日支親善佛敎使節と云ふやうな使命もあり，これは無論國家として外交上，政治上からドンドン工作を進めてやつて貰はなければならないけれども，政治上であり外交上であるだけに，今日尙ほ傳統的の精神を持ち續けて居る支那であるから，向ふの人の意見をも段々聽いてみた上でなければ輕々にはやれない。實際支那の要人と云ふ程の要人には會はなかつたが，その代りに李鴻章の息子さんと云つても五十九歲の立派な紳士で，李經邁と云ふ方，これは大槻茂と云ふ報知新聞の特派員で且つ日蓮宗の信者で，李經邁さんと豫て懇意にして居つた所から，今度日蓮宗の柴田一能と云ふのが來る坊さんではあるが，日清戰爭の勇士であると云ふ事を紹介したらしい。實は日清戰爭の一方の大立物は俺の老爺だから，さう云ふやうな因緣の上からも是非その古勇士に會つてみたい。是非紹介しろと云ふ事になつた。大槻君もトンだ事を言つたわいと後悔したらしいけれども，私に何とか都合しろと云ふ事になり，一晩泊りで杭州に行く筈の處を日歸りに縮めて，時間を拵へ，丁度九月七日の日に李大人の本邸を訪ねたが，實に壯大な邸であり，殊に長男の方の李國超君も立派な若紳士で，最近結婚して新家庭を造られ，貴公子とは斯ふ云ふ人を言ふのだらうと，男ながらも見惚れて居たやうな譯で，十月の下旬にこの李鴻章の孫に當たる新夫婦が日本の「紅葉」を見に來られる譯で，その時には御馳走になつたお禮に何んとかして案內するつもりで居る。さう云ふ思ひ掛けないやうな慶びもあつた譯けである。この李經邁と云ふ人は現在の支那の政府とは絶對に反對であつて，公然我々に向つても「中華民國」と改めた事はこれは誤りである。東洋傳統の思想にデモクラシーと云ふものはない等と卓を叩いて憤慨された。聞けば青年時代，亞米利加の大學

を卒業し，英語も非常に流暢であつて私も古いながら英語で話をした。支那語は日清戰爭の時，少しばかり覺えたが，爾來四十年も經つてゐて通用覺束ない。私も滿洲建國の話などをして共鳴した態度を示した。この十月には子供が御國に參りますから何分宜しくと云ふ事で態々その子息を呼んで倶に食卓に就かせられたと云ふやうな事もあつた。細かい話をする時間がないから割愛するが，實は廬山に往けば政治上の要人にも會へるし太虛法師にも會へるだらうと思つてゐたが，泰山に登つたり，青島に二週間を費したりして居るうちに廬山は散會になり，太虛法師も浙江の自分の住職寺の方に歸つたと云ふ事——太虛法師は昨年の太平洋大會の時にも非常に共鳴して，支那には青年會と云ふものはない。自分のやつて居る武昌學院等の學生達を青年と云へば云ふのであるから，彼等を糾合し自分が團長となり一つ大擧して(笑聲)參加し，本當の太虛法師になると云ふて喜んで居た處が，偶々向ふの新聞で惡るい方の意味に使はれ，逆宣傳のために餘儀なくせられ，僅か七名の代表が個人的に參加したに過ぎなかつた。而も藤井君等を勞はして非常な努力と苦心を拂つたのであつた。

その中で阮鑑光氏が一番學問もあり人物も可なりと云ふ事で，此方に主席代表を願つた。其後二回書面の往復もしたし，上海では非常に阮君にはお世話になつた，現在上海の鐘紡の公大，第二工場の支那の職工を訓練，指導する役目を持つて居られる。然しながらこれも嚮の李大人の話と同じやうに，世が世なら我々は容易く傍にも寄れない程の良い地位を得て居る人だとのこと。阮君は非常な佛敎の篤信者で，彼の太平洋大會に輿論を押切り，命に懸けても佛のためならと云ふ勢で出て來た處が，果せる哉大會が終つて上海に歸へると，新聞や參加に反對した佛敎徒から大變非難を受けたが，自分の信じた事をしたのは非常に愉快である。表面は非常に苦しく，又自分の生活上色々不利を及したけれども，さう云ふ反對の空氣を押切つて初一念を貫いた事は非常に愉快であつたと云つて，私と固く握手をして，其の喜びを新たにせられたのであつた。

IV

上海に居る間に文人墨客の必らず訪づれると云ふ蘇州へ行つた。專門の畫家には杭州(かなちう)よりも蘇州の方が價値があると云ふ事で，現に歸路上海丸で京都の若狹物外先生と同室となり，記念として，「千里横行」とでも言ふべき大な蟹の一枚色紙を書いて貰つた。この畫伯も矢張り後藤先生のやうに，支那服を着て，純粹の支那の風土人情を繪にするために度々渡支されたのである。所が支那服を着て居た爲に，支那の巡警に怪しまれ，いろいろうるさく訊問の揚句手帳など一切取上げられたが，幸ひ領事館までは行かないで，純粹の軍事探偵ではないと云ふ事で放免されたけれども，それで嫌になり，急に止

めて歸るのだとの事であつた。後藤先生の書物にも成る可く支那服を着ろとあつたので，出發前支那大使館に聞きに行くと，そりや支那服の方がいゝが，全體貴方は支那語が出來ますかと訊くから，片言交りになら少々日清戰爭の時にやつた事がある。唯私は兵隊に必要な語を覺えたに過ぎないが，習つた先生は大した者で，大本營の金崎三郎と云つて，金州で火焙(ひあぶり)りになつた先生に發音を習つたに過ぎないので，無論出來ないと言つた方が本當でせうと云ふと，それでは支那服は危險である。きつと怪しまれる。殊に貴方は眼付が惡るいから（笑聲）尙更怪しまれるからお止めなさい。後藤先生の「支那通」には支那服の方が危險がないと……(笑聲)。それで道中は洋服にした。然し又後藤先生に敬意を表して青島で支那服を拵へて，船中で着用し，歸朝後も，それを着用に及んで全聯事務所へも挨拶に行つた譯である。何處に行つてもよく似合ふ，よく似合ふと，褒められるので，これは何うしても支那に因緣が深いのだなと思つた。出來るならばもう一遍，イヤ何度でも行きたいと非常に支那に關心を持つやうになつた。

從つて佛敎視察と言ても，右樣な忙しい旅行で，雜用を足しつゝ北は北京南は南京の間を唯鐵道で往來したに止まり特別に佛敎使節の任務を遂行する事は出來なかつた譯けで，北京の法源寺の梵月和尙に會つた。その先代は支那切つての學者と評判された道諧大和尙と云つた人で，大分著書も出て居るとの事，その後を繼いで居る梵月和尙も，北京の廣濟寺で唯識の講師をして居ると云ふ事である。その弟子と見る可き七八十名の中に滌塵と云ふ青年僧があつて，佛敎學會で世話をしてゐる釋墨禪君の紹介で，私が天津に着いた時に手紙が着いて居つて，是非ともお目に掛りたい，今から樂しみにして待つてゐます。北京着の折停車場にお迎へする筈であるが，法要のために出られないが惡からず云々と，實に鄭重な言葉で書いてあつた。其法源寺に行つた處が，梵月和尙が非常に待遇してくれ，その青年僧にも會ひ，是非日本に留學したいと云ふ熱心の溢れた志願書を書き和尙が判を押したものを持つて來たが，學會の方でも履歴書を見て，これは將來見込みがあると云ふので明春から留學を許す事になつた。

V

其翌日有名な喇嘛寺に詣り，何んでも彼でも金と云ふ處を見せ付けられ，實に嫌な氣持がした。丁度百二三十名の僧が法要中であり，いゝ處に來合せたと云ふ事であつたが，私のお伴に連れてゐた婦人方ばかり眺めて居つて，傍に寄つて見たら唾が下つてゐたらうと思ふやうな非常に不愉快な印象を受けた。

昨年日本に來た印度のナーラダ，ラフラと云ふ學僧が支那に渡り，丁度上海で研究して居つた。世界佛敎居士林と相並んで有名な佛敎淨業社，これは

有名な佛教團體であつて，王一亭居士の居士林とは違つて社交的の意味を持つて，居る團體であつて，關䌹氏が副會長をして居り，日本にも留學した人で，英語も頗る流暢であつて，私の肩書が日蓮宗管長代理とある所から，日蓮宗に關する質問續發し，例へば日蓮宗は法華經に依つて建てられたものであると云ふと，天台大師の法華經による宗旨は既に支那にある。傳教大師が支那に來てそれを學んだのである。それと是れとはどう違ふかと云ふやうな事の質問を受けた。天台と日蓮との相違如何と云ふ質問は至る處で受けた。

それから上海清凉寺を兼務してゐる清海大和尚——この人は常州の本寺清凉寺が建築中であるので，時々上海に出張され，丁度この時に滯在中で今晩夜行で常州に歸へると云ふ矢先きをお目にかゝることを得た。其處で日，印，支——印度を代表してナーラダ君，支那を代表して清海大和尚，日本を代表して不肖柴田一能——三國の會同が實現した譯である。それから普光と云ふ人に會つたが，この人は長崎で多少日本語を習つたと云ふ事で，この人に會つたのは普光ではなく極めて幸福であつた。この青年僧は法華經の研究に熱中し，これが終つたら日本に行きたい日本にも法華經を所依した宗旨があると云ふ事を大槻君から聞いて居つたので是非貴下にお目にかゝりたいと思つて居たが，幸ひ師匠の清海和尚と共にお目にかゝつて嬉しいと和尚を紹介してくれた。當年七十二歲の見上げるやうな大和尚で，破鐘の如き大音であつて臨濟宗の和尚である事が判つた。若し一喝食はされたら楪へ上つてしまひさうな氣がした。圖らずも日，印，支の大會とは言へないが，小會位は慥かに開かれた譯であると云ふ事で，大笑の中に閉會した。

その他道中で所謂普通の佛教の寺院と云ふものも二三訪問したが，お話にならず，泰山に登つて道士や坊さんにも會つたけれども，どうも感服しない。而も泰山の道教には餘程佛教が間違つて入つてゐて，ものゝ解つた新しい人の眼に何んな感じを與へるかと云ふやうな事を考へさせられ，何んとかしなければ，これでは不可ないと思つた。これには支那のまゝの佛教でも不可ない我々のまゝでも不可ない。現在及び將來を考へると矢張り大乘佛教の精神で現在の支那の國難を——國難は日本だけの事ではない——支那にも國難は拯はねばならない。それには日支佛教徒が，佛教と云ふものを土臺にして精神的親善の途を開き，東洋平和の大事業に餘程の努力をしなければならぬと感ずる次第であつて，日本佛教徒の責任も決して輕々しいものではないと思ふ。深かい事は知らないが，私の見た支那佛教の狀態では容易な事ではないと思ふ。さうかと云つて手を着けないでおけば何時まで經つても社會生活とかけ離れた山林佛教か，然らざれば道教化した墮落的市井佛教の脚を洗ふことは出來まいと思ふ。（拍手）

支那の眞相に觸れよ

後藤朝太郎

よく支那にお出かけになつた方は大底蘇州，杭州と云ふ事を言はれるが，チャンと日本の專官居留地になつて居る挟仙峽（？）彼處までおいでになつた方は一人も聞いた事がない。日本の公使官では彼處まで見ていらつしやいませんかと云ふ事は仰有らない。時時私は出かけるが，草茫々で何んにもない條約で寄越せ寄越せと權利だけ取つたけれども，一向其處に日本人は行かない。折角取つたものを草茫々で蟋蟀が草の下で諦いてゐる。さう云ふやうにして行くのでは，一方支那の方は權利と云ふと恐がつてしまふ。日本は法律で固つてゐる。支那人が喧嘩して居る。どう云ふ風にするかと見てゐると，茶を飲んで居る。其處へ行つてチンさんとワンさんが喧嘩する。棒を持つて喧嘩するのでなく，周圍に茶を飲んで居る人達が最後に決を取る。片方は歸つたりして，自分の方が勝つたと思つてゐると，決を取つてみると少なかつたりする。さう云ふ場合には，負けた方が全部の茶代を拂つて，爭ひの結末と云ふものが決まる。日本なら辯護士ぢや裁判ぢやと云ふ處を，さう云ふ事は何もしない，是れで決つてしまふ。日本の方は法律の蒸返しをやると云ふ事で，五年も八年も掛る處を，それで濟んでしまふ。日本は几帳面で頭が法律で固つてゐるから，裁判ぢや控訴院ぢやと云はなければならない。さう云ふ事を口にするのは支那の氣分が分つてゐないからである。

私は向ふに行きまして，別に向ふの言葉が出來る譯けではないし，啞の旅行と變りないのであるが，半年以上の旅行もしますが，それでどうにかやつて行ける。理窟は決して變らない。此の部屋には前に誰が居たか。露西亞人が居た。支那語が話せたか。話せない。何をして居つたか。赤化宣傳の色々な事をして居つた。さう云ふ調子で，權利とか何んとか云ふと，何時でも血の雨を降らさんまでも，可成りひどい事が湧起る。上海の傍にドンフアクと云ふ處があります。其處に銀行の頭株連中がピクニツクに行つて自動車を止めると其處の百姓達が此處に置かないで呉れ，此處に置くならば金を拂つて呉れと言つたさうです。金を出しておけばよいものを，出さないで引上げた。置かす置かさんは百姓達の氣持であり それで今度は大喧嘩になつて，私は新聞に出たのを見ましたが，その三日程前に，私が親戚のものや友達なんか五六人で行つた時は何の事もない。一寸した出かた次第で今まで晴れて居たのに大雨が降る。靜かに見て居ると何にも問題にならずに濟む事を，此方の人は態々問題にする，さうして誠意を示さなければ駄目だと云ふ。私は支那と云ふ國は何年經つても結論に到達しない國だと思つて居る。布敎權であるとか，二十一ケ條の條約とか言つて，結末のない國を相手に靑筋たてるだけ馬鹿な事で，お止しになつた方がいゝ(笑聲)。向ふは別に誠意は示さない。幾ら決めるだけ決めても，半年經たない中に崩して居る。幾ら何ケ條の條約を結んでも駄目だ。向ふの人達は嗤つて居るだらうと思ふ。

支那の人同志の間には，誠意を披瀝させると云ふ事を口にする人は一人もないと思ふ。其處は潔癖性と淸濁合せ飲むの民族の違ひ。其處に支那と手を握らなければならない。滿洲國をやらなければならないと云ふ處に一寸其處に日本の辛らい處がある。滿洲國でも張學良の時には中流階級以上から搾つて下の方に潤つた。どうも昔の方がよかつたと云ふやうに，下の方で謂はれて居る。これはずつと北方方面に行つて聞きますと，熱河邊りでもさうです。さう云ふ言葉を聞くのです。要するにさう云ふやうな點になりますと，向ふでは中流以上は搾つてもいゝ。下の方が大事だと云ふ事が理想になつて居ります。北平，承德の間は自動車で行くのですが，もう鐵道は開通したでありませうが，彼處で斯ふ云ふ事を言つて居ましたよ。彼處で日本人が五錢，十錢，十五錢と拂ふ車賃が，彼處は滿洲人の車屋ですが，此の車屋が一日に八十五ドル乃至百二三十ドル位になる。これを月に直すと相當なものだ。日本人は威張つて居るが，その間に向ふではさうした金を儲けて居る。さうして一日の生活費が安い。さう云ふやうになつて居りまして，三角形の底邊の方を得るやうに行くと云ふのが本當の王道ださうです。日本人は上の方で二倍三倍四倍までは行きません，サラリーを取つて威張つて居るやうに思ひますが，さうした處に佛敎が乘出して行くと云ふ事は大變に結構だと思ひます。

さう敎理とか何んと六かしい事は，各宗の大僧正の間に於ては色々な事がありませうが，本當の處，下の方の者は肉食妻帶は惡いと云ふ事は申しますが實際その法事をすると云ふ時は墓場を掃除する。丁度私の居た隣家に法事をして居て，許しを受けて行つて見ましたら，坊さんが來て二三日も續けてガンガンやる。どんな顏して居るかと思ふと，酒を飲んだり生臭ものを肴にして食べて居る。さう云ふ處の氣持を見てゐますと，實際は茶も飲む酒も飲む魚も値段まで聞いて，これは旨いとか何とか言つて食べて居る。出す方でもさう云ふものを出して佛樣が喜ぶと云ふやうな事を言つて居る。坊さんがお寺に居る時の氣持と，民間の家に來て居る時の氣持と，まるで違つてゐる。大衆の氣持は，佛敎の氣持だけではありませんけれど，それを多分に持つて居る。その矛盾が矛盾に見えない。日本流の學校敎育が旺んになればなる程システムを立てゝ，理窟でゆかなければならない。文部省の宗敎々育に反し

ては駄目だ。そんな事を支那に持つて行くと見つともない。向ふは何んとも思つてゐない。向ふに行つてみますと問題が違ふ。田舍に行つてみますと，日本の領事館がある。今度の領事さんは非常に若い。それが此の町の或る有力な偉い親分を何かで領事館に呼ぶ。何か用があれば領事の方から來て吳れたらいいぢやないかと言つて居る。役所本位，法律本位，理窟本位，インテリ，上の方本位，それは大きな佛敎の敎理に添つて居らんだらうと思ひます王道樂土と云ふ事も下の方は何んとも思つてゐない。ですから此の際，新聞の社說の上で說くやうな事でなしに，理窟を離れてやつてこそ，阿彌陀樣のお心であると私は思ふのです。私なんか佛敎徒でも何でもないけれど，出來得る限りお寺を尋ねて，無論山寺にも泊めてもらひ，それで雨でも降れば一週間も二週間も泊つて居る。さうして居るうちに，いゝ氣持になる。決して布敎權なんと云ふ事は思はない。理窟なしに實際にやれば，布敎權等はどうでもなる。有名なる某博士が南京政府の人の許可なしに河に這入つて魚を獲つて，そのために亡くなられた事等は表向きに言つてはならないやうな事も聞きましたが，私は自分が日本人であると云ふ事を言ふてよいのか，言ふて惡るいかと云ふ事の質問をよく受けますが，それは要するに人によります。理窟ばつた人ならば言つた方がいゝしその人がさう云ふ人でなければ無事に通る。それで近道をしようと思つて，ずつと廻らないで，此處を突切つて行きたいと思つたら，人の邸の中を默つて通つても何とも言ひません。これは主人が知らないからではない。知つてゐたら自ら家の中から出て來て御馳走するかも知れない(笑聲)。長閑かなものです。日本だつたら誰の紹介で來たとか，家宅侵入罪だと云ふ。さう云ふ氣持があつたんぢや駄目だ。打壞しになつてしまふ。佛家の庭がいゝと思つたら，默つて這入つて行つて見る事が出來る。

向ふから歸つて來て，大成功ぢやと云ふ事を言ひますけれども，これは餘り當にならない。例へば斯ふ云ふ人に遇つて大變によくして吳れたと喜んで歸つて來る。支那の方に行つて，斯ふ人が來たかと云ふと，考へて暫くしてサウサウ，そんな人が來た事がある，と云ふやうな譯で實に賴りない。會つた時は洵にお世辭よくて，一度別れてしまふと，それ切り，これは日本人の眞似の出來ない點と思ひます。其處に向ふの國民性の複雜な處がありまして文字の上手い，頭を低く下げて，お世辭のよい，實際嬉しいですよ。それは何處から來てゐるかと申しますと，政府が當てにならないから，自分が確りせんければならない。友達の間を上手くやると云ふ，その肚が分つてゐれば非常に喜んで吳れても好い加減に考へ惡るくつても，さう惡くは考へずに平氣で居る事が出來る。自分でさうやらなければ仕方がない。船なんかに居ますと，船の中で阿片を服んでゐる。あ

あ云ふのを蔣介石さんは徹底的に禁止すると言ひますが，言ふてをくだけで地方地方の財政はあれに依つて立つてゆくのである。

それから最後に斯ふ云ふ事を言つてをきたい。日本では直ぐに恩知らずと云ふ事を言ふ。三年も五年も學校の保證人になつてもらつて，ハガキ一本寄越さん，斯ふ云ふでせう。その時に私よく言ふのでありますが，日本人は恩もよく知つてゐる。恩を感ずる事も深刻に感ずるか知らないが，悪るい事を覺えてゐる事も本當に執念深い。實に日本人はよく覺えてゐる。支那の人は平常手紙も寄越さないか知れんが，人に金を貸したり，色々な好い事をしたりして恩をかけても，その事を一寸も顔に出さん。實に其處に行くと國が大きいと云ふのか，何んと云ふのか，何かあつても同じ態度で行く。日本人は善い時はよいけれども，悪るい事にも馬鹿に深刻になる。さう云ふ點に於て日本人は親しみにくいらしい。どうも警戒をするやうな處がある。日本人は頭がいゝ，佛教の研究も日本のはいゝが，支那は駄目だと謂はれる。私は寒山寺にチョイチョイ行きましだが，朝早く行つて向ふの朝飯前に行つて話す。「時に朝飯は？」と言はれるので，朝飯は食ふたが，それではお粥を一杯頂きませうと御馳走になる。さうして自分の親戚の青年で色々佛教の研究して居るものがあるが，三年位お世話願ひたいと云ふと，日本の青年は續きません。イヤ自分がキツと續かせるやうにするから。イヤ駄目です。貴方自身なら知らんが，日本の青年は一週間とは續かん。此の間來たのも，こんな處には居ないと，サツサと歸つてしまつた。これは例へば御飯を食べる時，お茶が温るいから熱いのと換へて來いと云ふと廊下に出て歩きながら，そのお茶を土瓶の口からソーツと飲む(笑聲)。それはキツとやつてゐますよ。さうしてその中に熱いのを入れて來る。これを入れて持つて行くと，これは穢い，何故だ。君は口飲みしてゐたぢやないか。見てゐたのか。そんなら見てゐなかつた事にしたらいゝぢやないか(笑聲)。此處に禪味がある。見てゐなかつた事にすればいゝぢやないか。さうした事に拘泥しないで，これは鹽味があつてよい位に(笑聲)してをけばいゝが，それが出來ない。其處は本當の阿彌陀樣のみ心になればそれは出來ると思ふ。いくら佛教大會を何回やつても，その氣持がなければ駄目だと思ふ。私は成る可く日本人だと云ふ事を言はないやうにして居る。或はお母つさんが日本人だ位に(笑聲)色々な事を言ふ。雜種だとか言つて誤魔化してゐる。それでも構はん。それ式で行けば何處に行かうが，船の中で海賊に遇ふが，馬賊に遇ふが何んでもない。夜中に船が着いて門を開けてもらへなければ，一晩馬車の上に眠ればよい。滿洲は日本式に今やりたがつてゐるやうですが，其處等は日本よりズツと頭がいゝ，さうする方が得だからやりたがつてゐるので日本の何十倍も頭がいゝか知れない。

日本をそのまゝ眞似してゐる。さう云ふ譯けですから，都會の方は日本の眞似をして，丸の内をそのまゝ持つて行つたやうな建物が出來て居り，都會のものは日本のいゝ人に接觸して居るがずつと奥の方に行くと，本當の滿洲の聲を聞く事が出來る。土匪も出て來ます(笑聲)。今彼等はヤケ糞で月二十四人宛位殺してゐます。滿洲に軍制を敷いて徹底的にやらうとして居る。日本人は直ぐに結論を得ようとするから不可ない。然し喧しくさうして行かなければ，日本の議會は通らないらしい。大乘的氣分と云ふ事を忘れて，滿洲に向つても何んにもなりません。ひねくり返して行けばいゝでせうけれど，其處は三角形の底邊の下を流れてゐるんですから，三角形の上だけ幾らどうかしても，それは本當の上の方の代表だけに見えるので，それは向ふから見た本當の代表ぢやない。それは仲々難しい。獨逸流の學問で來てゐる日本にとつては難しい。幾何學的と謂ひますか非科學的と謂ひますか，さう云うやうな學問で行けない。敎への道までそれで行かなければならんと云ふ事を思つて居ると言つたら叱られるかも知れませんが，今はそれでいゝとしても永い間は窮窟な喧しい親父さんの前に坐らされて居ると云ふ氣持がしないかと思ふ。新京の停車場を出て國都建設の樣子を見て御覽んなさい。丸の內の延長したみたいな建物ばかりで，滿洲の國都でありながら，滿洲個有の氣持は少しも現はれてゐない。さう云ふものは一つもありません。みんな亞米利加ライト式のやうなものばかりがずつと建つて居る。だから今に西洋の三流位の都會みたいになつてしふに違ひない。それに氣が附かない。清水組，大林組等が行つてやつてゐながら，滿洲固有の建築を，それも値段も非常に安い，あの壁のある支那建築の面白さを忘れてゐる。熱河邊りの自然的の形を現はす事を忘れてゐる。洵に精神方面は，抜かりも抜かりも大抜りだと思ふ。

私は佛教徒でないから大した事は言へませんけれども，斯う云ふ暮しをして居りましても，幸ひ怪我もせず，このまゝずつと來て居ますから，皆さんもさう云ふやうな氣持でやつて頂く事が出來ればいゝと思ひます。よく私でなければ不可んと云ふ事を言ひますけれども，誰方でもいゝ。やらうと思へばやれない事はないのであります。外務省に頼らなくても自分で證明するんです。だから領事館を訪問しなくても行けます。後で分れば一寸一言言ふてをけばいゝと言はれますが，言へば彼處は問題の處だから行つて呉れるなと領事館は仰有る。然し行つてみるとさうぢやない。支那人の調査員が非常な事があつたやうに言はないと不可ないと思ふんで，さう云ふ報告をするにすぎぬと思ふ。

さう云ふ事を私は機會のある度び毎に話して居ります。以上私の話は本に書いてある事を申上げるんぢやない。自分の體驗から申上げた積りです（拍手)。(傳通會館での座談要旨)。

日滿文化提携の基調

外務省前對支文化事業部長　坪　上　貞　二

滿洲國が建設されて，日滿の關係は兄弟と云ふ事であり，姉妹國であり，不可分密接の關係にある事は御承知の通りですが，この日滿の關係は實は世界に類例のない密接な關係になつて居る。最近伊太利のエチオピヤに對するは，日本の滿洲に對する態度と同樣であると云ふ事を言つて，同類項に當嵌めるやうな事を言つて居るやうです。

又最近ですが，アネルハウスの如きは，九月の或る雜誌に，矢張り伊太利エチオピヤ關係を論じて，獨逸，伊太利，日本は，等しく人口は愈々增えて居るから，これ等に對して相當の領土的要求を滿足さしてやらなければ，國際間の平和を保つ事が出來ないと言つて居ます。私は同類項に扱はれると云ふ事は甚だ心外に考へるのですが，個人主義を基調とした歐米から申しますと，矢張り一兵を動かせば，直ちに侵略である。他國を征服する國家主義であると云ふ風に感ずる。外形は成程その通りと思ふのですが，日本の滿洲に對する態度は，唯法律的に申せば，議論もありませうし，色々申しませうが全く東亞の安定のために，兩國の共存共榮の立場に立つのを基礎にして居るのでして，歐米の侵略主義，植民政策とは全然行き方を異にして居ると思ふその點ははつきり我々日本國民として又滿洲國として，認識してゐなければならぬ點です。これは覇道によるか，王道によるかの分れ道と思ふのです。日本は皇道精神によつて堂々と東洋の安定のために楔となる可き關係を完全に果してゆかなければならんと云ふのが，日本の考へです。

支那と日本との關係は，滿洲國が成立した當時，殆んど絕緣の關係にあつた。が，國際聯盟を脫退しても，決して日本はへばる事がない。支那は英米その他に賴り，聯盟に賴つて居つたが效果がない。それから日本は滿洲國經營のために暫くすると，財政上，經濟上困るだらうと云ふ觀察をして居つたのですが，焉ぞ知らん，益々兩國の關係は密接に，赤字の公債も決して不消化に終らない。日本の經濟，貿易は，益々海外に發展して行く。日本を向ふに廻して抗爭すると云ふ事は，これは結局自國の不利益であるばかりでなく東洋の平和を保持する所以でもないと云ふ事が段々分つて參りまして，未だその頃には北滿鐵道を滿洲國が買收してゐないし，やがて日本と露西亞は衝突するだらうと云ふ事を空賴みにして居つたが，それも全く空望に終つた。何人としても東洋に於ては，日本と手を握らなければ，到底支那の存立を圖る事は出來ない。東洋の平和は保たれぬと云ふ見地から，支那も只今までの支那固有の外交政策を捨てゝ，眞に日本と提携して行くと云ふ機運が相當强くなつて居るやうに見られる。彼の國民黨の如きも，今までは日本との提携主義に反對の政策を執つて居つたが，幾ら申しましても世間でも實力の伴はない處の排外抗日に見向きもしない。隨つて實力が伴はないので，反對も我慢しなければならんと云ふ程度に，國民黨の幹部の連中も眼が覺めて來て居る。蔣介石氏の如きも，日本との間に充分に提携を圖つて行かなければならんと云ふ事を知り，今までは國民黨に對する手前，口に出す事が出來なかつたのが，今はそれを口外して憚らんと云ふ事になつた。最近興つて居ります處の新生活運動，これは日本の生活に習はなければならん，日本を師としなければならんと云ふ事が叫ばれて來たのです。隨つて日本が支那，滿洲に對する對度は，兄弟姉妹と云ふ大道の見地からで，その精神によつて東洋の安定と云ふ事は齎されると思ふのです。

只今までは動もすれば英米の侵略主義的な政策を執つて居るやうに，外面的には考へられたし，日本の一部にもさう考へて居つた人もある。日本，支那，滿洲は，一方が一方を犧牲にして獨りが立つと云ふ事でなく，三國共通の目標を持つて居りまして，眞に提携し，共通の敵であるものに對しては共同で當ると云ふ風になりますならば，日滿支三國の密接な提携は，決して難しい事ではないと思ふのです。

その目標の一つは，これは露西亞の赤化に對する防衞でありまして，東洋の安定が赤化のために脅威を受けると云ふ事になるならば，三國が共同して當らなければならない。これは滿洲國成立以來特に多くなつて參つて居るのです。隨つて日本の對滿，對支の態度が正しければ正しいだけ，三國の提携東洋の安定と云ふ事は，期せずして完全になると確信致して居る次第です。私たちは常に國際關係を，政治の方面或は經濟の方面，この方面の外交に俟たなければならん事は勿論の事ですが一方の根底を爲す處の文化關係と云ふ事をなくしては，政治關係經濟關係も成立たないのです。政治經濟，文化の三方提携と云ふ事で，文化理想の下に政治，經濟が行はれるやうにならなければならん。經濟なり政治なりに於て文化の根底がなかつたならば，その基礎は極めて貧弱なものであると云ふ感じがするのです。隨つて我々が在來やつて參りました此の對支文化事業部も此の根底を生み出す處のものであつたので，滿洲國成立前，既に十年近くその事業をやつて來た。大體に於いて東洋文化の研究，支那に於ける敎育上の研究，兩國の文化研究支那に於ける敎育上の研究，兩國の文化交換と云ふ方面に於て各種の事業を營んで參りまして，今日でもそれを繼續して，基礎を固め，更にこれ以上擴大しようと云ふ事になつて居ります。一方滿洲國成立と共に，我々の考へました事は，滿洲國建國の基礎として政治とか經濟とか云ふ方面に立つと云ふ事も力强い建國であるが，然し文化の根底の上にその基礎を固めなければならんと云ふ事になりまして，日滿文化協會と云ふものが興されまして，時の執政が總裁と云ふ事で夫々文化關係の委員を出して，日滿文化協會を作り，それによつて滿洲國に於て何を行ふべきかと云ふ事を研究致したのであります。その機關は政府機關であつて，政府の文化に對する處の最高の諮問機關と云ふ事で，その當時政府は滿洲に存在した色々な圖書文献と云ふものゝ散逸する恐れが非常にありましたので，これが散逸を防ぎ，御存知の通り世界的の古い文献が動もすると散逸する恐れがあつたのでこれをよく整理致しまして，張學良その他要人の處にあつたやうなものは，凡て圖書館，博物館と云ふ處に收集して，滿洲國の文化發揚のために寄與しようと云ふ事に致しまして，その圖書館，博物館の如きも既に出來上つて落成式もやり，相當な內容が陳列，或は收集されて居る次第です。

それから第二に興しましたのが，清朝の實歷です。滿洲國の力によつて，さう云ふものが出版されると云ふ事は滿洲國の力がそれだけ偉大だと云ふ事を示す所以であるから，その出版をすると云ふ事になりました。約三萬六七千冊の尨大なる圖書修正であるが，これは世界的に今日まで出てゐない處のものゝ出版が企てられ，仲々容易の業ではないが，滿洲國成立と共に十年計畫を以て出版が完成する豫定でありま

す。

第三には熱河の文化であるが，實は私達もよく知らなかつたのですが，熱河に於ける喇嘛寺の如き，世界に誇るべき偉大な建造物である事が判りまして，屢々實地に專問家の調査を行ひ，これを完全に修理復舊すると云ふ事は日本の援助に依つて初めて出來るのであります。この熱河の建造物を完全に復舊する事は，北支から蒙古內地，支那全體，滿洲國の文化的偉大性を發揮する有力な方法だと云ふので，初めは五年計畫で宜しいと云ふ事であつたが仲々愈々實行に掛つてみようと調査してみますと大したものであつて，今日は十年計畫で，相當な費用を費して，これをやると云ふ事になつて居るのです。先づその日滿文化協會で計畫して居るのは，それ位ですが，日本側自身としてやつて居ります事は，滿洲國成立と同時に，今日まで行はれました處の研究を一時も速く完成する，有らゆる方面から相當にやつて居るのですがそれを出來るだけ早く完成すると云ふ風にしまして，これも日本の大家，學者の協力によりまして，着々とその緖に着いて居り，或る部分の如きは，正に完成と云ふ處にまでなつたのです。我々は今日の滿洲國の日系官吏が，法律の權化であると評されることを往々聞きますが，斯の如きは全く滿洲，蒙古に對する處の研究調査，認識が不足して居る結果と，我々は考へるのです。

それに就ても私共常に思ふ事は，文化の研究とか，或は發揚とか云ふ事も

これは勿論必要ではありますけれども又その根底に横つた眞の道を求め，其處に根底を置いて文化の發揚，研究をしなければならんと考へるのです。滿洲國建設當時滿洲に於て何かしなければならんと云ふ案が各方面から提案されまして，その中の一つに王道大學と云ふものを滿洲に興させたらどうかと云ふ案があつた。その時私は，それは私事としては非常に結構だ。然し王道大學で一體何をするのかと申しますと王道の研究，發揚である。そのためには支那本來の儒教であるとか，佛教であるとか，或は道教であるとか，さう云ふ方面の研究をしたら宜しいと云ふ事でありましたが，それは非常に結構だけども，日本に於ても佛教の大學，或は儒教位の文化大學と云ふものは，これは日本は今日學問は非常に旺んであるが，この日本に於ても遺憾ながら眞の道が伴はず，眞の信仰が求められぬと云ふ事は，何故であるか。もう此處まで來たら，日本の力を持つて來たならば，滿洲にも行れると云ふ確信を持つ事が出來たならば，王道大學を興すと云ふ事も結構であり，異議がないと思ひますが，未だその確信が附いてない間に，一佛教大學，一文化大學を興すと云ふ事は，無理なんぢやないか。杞憂かも知れませんが，少くともさう云ふやうに考へるので，その事を私は申した。それは豫算に關係すると云ふ事で，高橋大藏大臣の處に持つて行かれたさうでありますが，同じ事を申されたと云ふ事を後で聞いたのですが，

先づ日本自國が確立しないで，先に向ふに勸めると云ふ事は，甚だ根底のない事ではないかと思ふのです。日本人は佛教に對しての認識が非常に不足して居る。我々は老人になりましたが，機會ある毎に青年と接觸し，觸れる機會が多いのですが，これはどうしても今日の日本の混沌たる思想界を救はなければ，これから先づ我々が眞の道を求め，眞の信仰が起らなければ解決出來ないと思つて居るのですが，未だ其處まで到達してゐないのです。形としては成程相當な規則も整ひ，或は團體的のものもありますけれども，眞に國家を救ひ，又國家の大方向を示すと云ふ正しい道，正しい信仰は興つてゐないと云ふ事は，甚だ遺憾と思ふのでありまして，其の點は我々は微力ながら全力を盡して，その方面に力の有らん限り致したいと思ふのでりますが，此の點，此の宗教界，思想界に眞に身を寄せられて居る皆さん方の御指導，御活動によりまして，國民が光明を得てその方向に一意邁進するやうに期待して止まない次第であります(拍手)。

Japanese News

Kôetsu Exhibition

In memory of the 300th anniversary of the death of Koetsu,—painter, potter and master of cha-no-yu, an exhibition of his works will be held next year in Tokyo.

Those interested in promoting the exhibition are Dr. Katsumi Kuroita, Mr. Chusaburo Ogino, Mr. Teijiro Mizuguchi, Mr. Seiichi Okuda and Dr. Seiichi Taki.

Koetsu was original in style and his creations in lacquer and pottery as well as his paintings have a special attraction for art lovers.

Revue and Sengakuji

The Shochiku Revue girls are to appear in a musical offering based on the revenge of the Forty-seven Ronin.

Following a long established custom of the Kabuki actors when playing in "Chushingura" the young women proceeded to Sengakuji to pay their respects before the tombs of the loyal retainers of the Lord Asano.

This is probably the first time that the quiet cemetery on the hill above the Buddhist temple has been invaded by so many women of the footlights.

Buddhist Processional

On November 4 there was been a huge Buddhist demonstration in Tokyo when 3,000 priests has paraded through the streets of Tokyo.

Priests of all sects gatherd at Tsukiji Honganji where there was services for the souls of departed men of holy orders, There was various functions, and the priests then formed in processional and march through the Ginza quarter to Nijubashi. At the head of the procession the brass-band from Shirokiya Department Store render selections.

At Tsukiji Honganji

On Nov. 4 Tsukiji Honganji, Tokyo's great Buddhist temple, was the scene of unusual activities.

There was a mass meeting held in the auditorium of the temple at which priests from all parts of the country gathered and thousands of worshippers attended.

A program of lectures, services, ceremonies marked the week's program at the concrete temple built in Indian style of architecture.

Gate of Kan'eiji

The old black gate of Kaneiji in Uyeno Park has now been restored and many persons are crowding to see the entrance to the famous Buddhist temple that was burned down during the conflagration at the time of the Restoration when the Imperial forces and the troops of the shogunate clashed.

One of the few relics of Kaneiji is the tower where the great bell has continued to boom forth the hours for centuries.

Statue of Nobunaga

On the ruins of the Kiyosu Castle at Kiyosu in Aichi Prefecture a statue of Oda Nobunaga is soon to be erected.

Fujitaro Sugiura, the Tokyo sculptor, has executed the statue which is of bronze and 8 feet high. The sculptor has represented Oda Nobunaga, the warrior, as a young man leaving his castle for the battlefield. The unveilling ceremony will be held in February.

Jingoro's Temple

The tomb of Hidari Jingoro, the famous carver of Old Japan, whose cat is still pointed out to tourists who go to see the shrine sacred to Iyeyasu at Nikko, is in the cemetery of Jizoji in Takamatsu on Shikoku Island.

Many visitors visit the tomb daily, and the priests have now made a souvenir stamp for picture postcards so that those who go to the place may have some reminder of their visit.

Pigeon's Apartment

The new pigeon apartment in the compound of the Tsukiji Honganji has been completed.

Dr. Chuta Ito, one of the leading architects of Tokyo, who designed the Memorial Hall in Honjo, planned this home for the temple pigeons. It has five storeys, and there are 100 rooms.

But the pigeons do not take kindly to his sumptuous abode, and the priests of the temple are puzzled at their reluctance to make use of such an up-to-date dwelling.

Tokugawa Art Museum

The Tokugawa Fine Art Museum, recently completed in the compound of the residence of Marquis Yoshichika Tokugawa in Nagoya, was opened to the public on

November 10.

Many valuable articles were shown for the first time. Among the treasures on display is the armor worn by Tokugawa Iyeyasu; a helmet of Kato Kiyomasa; a sword forged by Masamune, and a gold tea kettle valued at Yen 200,000.

One of the most striking of the Tokugawa treasures in this collection is a screen painted by Iwasa Matabei, the pioneer of Ukiyoe.

Colossal Buddha

A Buddhist priest of Kanroji in Koyamachi, Shizuoka Prefecture, has made a huge painting of Buddha in connection with 2500 anniversary of the birth of the founder of Buddhism.

Thh face of the painting is 126 feet long. The picture is to be shown to the public in the temple compound November 17 and 18, and a Buddhist service was held.

Buddhist Music

The 7th annual concert of the Buddhist Music Society, be held at the Tokyo School of Music, Uyeno Park, on November 23 at 1 p.m.

Marquis Tsuneyuki Nakamikado is president of the society. Members of the society sing newly composed Buddhist songs, Mrs Minako Hirai the soprano, and Mr. Kano Ito, organist, assist on the program.

Sekiya as Onatsu

Miss Toshiko Sekiya will be seen again as Onatsu in her operatic conception of Dr. Tsubouchi's music-drama, "Onatsu Kyôran."

She will present this at the Nippon Gekijo as a curtain raiser to the Buddhist play, "Light of Four Seas" to be performed by Sessue Hayakawa and a company of 230 players.

國際佛教通報局定款

名　稱

第一，本局を國際佛教通報局と稱す

事務所

第二，本局の事務所を全日本佛教青年會聯盟本部に置く

目　的

第三，本局は日本內海及海外に向つて佛教事情の通報をなし，且つ佛教徒相互間の各種便宜を計るを以て目的とす

事　業

第四，本局の目的を達成するため左記の事業を行ふ

イ，日本內地及世界各國より佛教事情に關する質問の通報を行ふ

ロ，必要に應じ日本語及世界各國語を以て佛教事情の通報を行ふ

ハ，外國人の日本觀光に際しては各國の便益を與へ，特にその佛教に關する方面に於て之を爲す

ニ，定時或は臨時に各國語を以て文書の刊行をなす

ホ，その他必要と認めたる事業を行ふ

役　員

第五，本局の事務を處理するため左の役員を置く

イ，局　長　　一　名

ロ，幹　事　　三　名

ハ，評議員　　若干名

局長は本局　　を總括す

幹事は本局の事務を處理す

評議員は局長の提案に依る重要事務を審議す

第六，評議員は左記の者を以て之に充つ

イ，全日本佛教青年會館聯盟理事及主事

ロ，全日本佛教青年會聯盟理事會に於て推薦したる者

第七，局長及幹事は評議員會に於て決定す

第八，役員の仕期は二ヶ年とす（但し重任を妨げず）

經　費

第九，本局の經費は左記のものに依て之を支辨す

イ，本局基金の活用

ロ，寄附金

ハ，その他の收入

補　則

第十，本定款に記載せられざる事項は，凡て評議員會に於て協議す

第十一，第一回の役員は全日本佛教青年會聯盟理事會に於て決定す

定價	一部	金二十錢	送料二錢
	一年	金二圓四十錢	送料不要

昭和十年四月卅日第三種郵便物認可
昭和十年十一月廿七日印刷
昭和十年十二月一日發行
（毎月一回一日發行）

東京市外吉祥寺337
編輯發行兼印刷人　淺野研眞

東京市牛込區早稻田鶴卷町107
印刷所　康文社印刷所
電話牛込（34）1950番 5049番

東京市神田區一ツ橋二の三
發行所　國際佛教通報局
電話九段（33）4428番
振替東京83015番

昭和十年四月三十日第三種郵便物認可
昭和十年十一月二十七日印刷納本（毎月一回
昭和十年十二月一日發行一日發行）
國際佛教通報　第一卷　第九號

The Japan Buddhist Play Society

presents

FIRST SPECTACULAR PERFORMANCE

at

NIPPON GEKIJO

FROM DECEMBER 1 to 10

PROGRAM

1. Grand Opera **ONATSU-KYORAN** 1 scene

with Sessue Hayakawa, Toshiko Sekiya and Yoshimitsu Wagayagi

2. Musical Play of Buddha's Life

SHIKAI NO HIKARI 9 scenes

(Light of Four Sea)

Starring Sessue Hayakawa, Otome Tsukimiya, Toshiko Sekiya
and Elenna Pavlova
Music by Kosaku Yamada and His Orchestra

Curtain rises at 1 p.m. and 6 p.m. daily

ADMISSION : 1st class ¥ 2.50
2nd class ¥ 2.00

昭和十年四月三十日第三種郵便物認可　昭和十年十二月二十七日印刷納本　昭和十一年一月一日發行（毎月一回一日發行）第二卷　第一號

The International Buddhist Bulletin

國際佛教通報

第二卷 **昭和十一年一月** 第一號〔Vol. II. Jan. $\frac{2502}{1936}$ No. 1.〕

要　目〔Contents〕

東　京　**國際佛教通報局**　發　行
The International Buddhist Information Bureau
Tokyo, Kanda, Hitotsubashi, II—3
Annual Subscription, ¥2.40 (post free), Single Copies 20 sen (post 2 sen)

Staff of the Bureau

Hon. President	J. Takakusu
President	K. Ohmura
Secretary	S. Takagai
〃	B. Inaba
〃 (in chief)	Ken Assano
Advisers	H. Ui
〃	G. Asakura
〃	R. Hatani
〃	U. Ogiwara
〃	R. Higata
〃	T. Suzuki
〃	S. Suzuki
〃	S. Amakuki
〃	S. Nagai
〃	B. Matsumoto
〃	E. Uno
〃	C. Akamatsu
〃	Z. Ohmori
〃	K. Yabuki
〃	S. Onoh
〃	S. Katoh
〃	M. Anezaki
〃	G. Honda
〃	R. Sekimoto
〃	J. Sahegi
〃	R. Hanada
〃	H. Kohno
〃	R. Takaoka
〃	Z. Kobayashi
〃	S. Yamabe
〃	C. Akanuma
〃	E. Honda
〃	R. Ohmori
〃	E. Kawaguchi
〃	C. Yamakawa
〃	D. Tokiwa
〃	T. Tanimoto
〃	G. Tokiwai
〃	S. Ohtani
〃	E. Ohtani
〃	B. Mizuno
〃	I. Shibata
〃	S. Ando
〃	J. Shimomura
〃	S. Kikuzawa
〃	K. Norisugi
〃	T. Shibata
〃	K. Asano
〃	T. Watanabe
〃	G. Onoh
〃	K. Yanagizawa
〃	M. Shigemitsu
〃	E. Kanakura
〃	S. Tachibana

Happy New Year

謹 賀 新 年

Junuary 1st. $\frac{2502}{1936}$

昭和十一年元旦

The International Buddhist Information Bureau

國際佛教通報局

Japanese Buddhism

By L. De Hoyer

Asia

Observing the stupendous progress made by the Japanese during past thirty or forty years in nearly every domain of practical science, the development and degree of efficiency attained in industry and trade, one is easily induced to believe in the "matter-of-fact" civilization of modern Japan, and to judge the nation as endowed with a typically concrete mind. But is this judgment correct? Is the Japanese a realizer, or is he a dreamer? Many a modern Japanese would never admit that the very foundation and raison d'etre of their indigenous culture is not the factory and the ten-storied apartment building, but the dream of an ancient samurai, with the body of a warrior and the heart of monk, who, sitting by his tiny lotus pond, admires the image of the moon in the water and ponders on the transiency of the pheonomenal world. Yet my thirty years' experience with Japanese life leads me to believe that the background of all this display of up-to-date technique is profound, almost mystic, idealism carefully—I would say shyly—hidden from observers.

But why is it hidden? There are two reasons. The first lies in the restraint that is one of the main features of the Japanese character. Every strong expression of emotion is disapproved of, is considered almost indecent. Children are brought up that way. Religious feeling, like other emotion, is stored up in the sancta sanctorum of the Japanese soul: it is not for alien consumption. The second reason lies in a certain psychological conception deeply rooted in Chinese philosophy and fully assimilated by the Japanese—the wu wei principle of Taoist philosophy (mu-i in Japanese), which is usually translated as "nondoing" or "nonspeaking" but which in reality is not inactivity but rather an effort of concentration, of introspection in order to avoid useless waste of energy. The world performs its cosmic task in pro-

found silence. Moreover, it is typically oriental to lay stress on the hidden potentialities of the negative. When the Indians, and after them the Chinese and Japanese, endeavored to describe the unlimited attributes of the Absolute, they expressed them by the concept of Voidness—Sunya.

Japan is today the stronghold of Northern, or Mahayana, Buddhism. Yet a certain type of foreigner might know a Japanese gentleman for many years as a shrewd business man, a keen and efficient follower of modern American or European civilization, and never suspect that this same man began his day by sitting upright for half an hour with crossed legs, his hands on his knees, eyes half-open, regulating his breath and practising what is called "zazen"! He does this to produce "right mind." And from these thirty minutes of inward contemplation he draws moral strength for the coming struggle on the twelfth floor of his modern building. In somewhat the same spirit the Japanese lawyer, photographer or dentist, coming home, after a busy day, to his boiling hot bath and dainty, rather frugal, repast and maybe, as a tribute to civilization, half an hour of the radio, finishes off his evening by reading a dozen twelfth-century tanka or hokku — brief poems singing the transitoriness of this life:

"For all is fleeting, birds, music
flower's beauty . . ."

Or a colonel, back from Manchurian battlefields after deeds of brilliant prowess or self-possessed determination, sits in his tiny garden in Asabu ward and recites the complaint of the famous poet Basho:

"The summer grass. . . .
All that is left of the warrior's
dreams?"

The foreigner would be astonished at the Japanese colonel because he probably would not know that more than thirty per cent of the military class in Japan belong to the Zen sect of Buddhism, one of the most austere contemplation sects. Zen has more than eight thousand temples and nine million followers in the country. The sect is sometimes called the living church of Japan, and this is an apt description, for the reason that, although the doctrine is founded on deep though somewhat abstruse Tendai and Kegon philosophies (both systems came from China in the eigth century), the Zen monks and laymen do not attribute much importance to dogma and theories. They even discourage too profound studies in Indian philosophy and Chinese metaphysics, preferring to dwell upon the importance of man's finding Buddha at the bottom of his heart.

That is the reason why Zen teachers give such baffling replies to questions eagerly put by uninitiated students. They usually answer with an incomprehensible paradox. The hidden meaning of their reply is, however, the following: "All these subtleties have not the slightest importance. Buddha is everywhere, in this grain of dust as well as in a national hero. It is only a question of finding him of realizing him in yourself. That is the goal of life." Once I asked the Reverend Ogata, chief abbot of the Zen Rinzai temple in Kyoto: "Do you believe in reincarnation? Are you going to be reborn another ten, hundred, thousand times?" "Is it going to rain tomorrow or not?" was his baffling reply.

Truth, the Japanese believes, can be attained in two ways only; the one is wisdom, the other is love. No wisdom, from the oriental point of view, does not mean the acquiring of knowledge; rather it is the intuitive apprehension of the unity of all living beings and the unreality of the "outer" world. The feeling of separateness, of individuality and of phenomenal plurality is the result of ignorance, and this ignorance has to be done away with. Love means a deep feeling of compassion toward all sentient beings and the determination to save them from the bonds of life even at the cost of one's own salvation.

In Mahayana Buddhism morality does not play the important part it does in Christianity and in primitive Buddhism. The reason seems to be that morality is not considered a goal in itself: it is only one of the ways—and a very important one—of reaching enlightenment. An immoral man in a man who indulges in sensual plesure, whereas attaining enlightenment implies the recognition of the utter valuelessness, nay, the utter nonreality, of such sensations. An enlightened man could not be immoral any more than a drunken man could walk a rope. The Mahayana point of view on morality differs from that of Christianity because the concept of sin, as understood in Christian theology,

is absent. Man is not born in sin. He is, however, ignorant and a victim of illusions which he must disperse. He must find his way back to the Fatherland, a Platonist would say. It make him one lifetime or a few millions of existences, but ultimately the way will be found, since man is of the same nature, of the same essence, as the Buddha.

There is thus nothing pessimistic in the Weltanschauung of a Mahayana Buddhist: the pessimism of the Buddhist creed was a child of the early Hinayana Buddhism. And, strangely enough, it was just that aspect of Budhism which was eagerly taken over by Europe—perhaps as a reaction against its own anthropomorphic individualism. But times have changed, and the West begins to understand that Buddhism is not a rigid, dead philosophy but a living faith, a stream of spiritual life, which undergoes a constant evolution.

The Chinese and the Japanese are more active races than the Indians, Siamese and Burmese. No wonder that Buddhism, while spreading in these northern countries, had gradually to take a different aspect. Also it met on its way Confucianism, Taoism and Shinto, and these influences had their effect. The essential difference between Hinayana and Mahayana is that, while the first, the Southern Buddhism, is nihilistic, ignoring entirely the Absolute, denying the existence of a self, an ego, a soul, and offering as supreme goal liberation from the Wheel of Life, tantamount to extinction, Northern Buddhism establishes positive ideals and Absolute (bearing in different sects different names such as Rharmakaya, Tathata, Amida) which without being a person is an all-enfolding principle of truth and love; a future impersonal existence, or rather being, of the individual merged in the Greater Self; and a final goal which is bliss.

Such a philosophy was appropriate to an active, ambitious race. The Japanese is not a pessimist, though it is true there is an undercurrent of sadness in his character, even a touch of sadness in his courteous smile. Nowhere else in the world are there so many suicides as in Japan: the number per capita is stupendous. I have no intention of denying that a world-conception based on the transitoriness of everything, on the unreality of everything visible and tangible, is likely to develop melancholy—the melancholy of the fleetingness of things — but I maintain that the chief reason for the sadness of the Japanese is constant restraint. One who gives way to his feelings, ventilates them, destroys a good half of them. Suppressed, driven back, they ferment in the human soul and produce passions and diseases. The famous Swiss psychologist Jung would find a rich field for observation in Japan. He would ascertain endless examples of suppressed emotions feeding the "individual subconsciousness" of men and enriching the dangerous patrimony of their "collective subconsciousness."

It is true, however, that this touch of menlancholy fits in well with the kindliness, the cleanliness and the profound artistic sense of the Japanese. There is nothing powerful, noisy, overwhelming in their artistic taste; it is sober, restrained. It lacks perhaps the grandeur of the sculptures of Phidias, Praxiteles and Michelangelo, and the architectural art of the Parthenon, the somber magnitude of a Dante or a Shakespeare, but it fits in with the gentle beauty of Japanese scenery; the art of the Japanese is a picture of their soul, and their soul is a part of their country. All his helps to explain why Buddhism has taken such a strong foothold in Japan, and why it has assumed such a peculiar aspect as the hopeful Amidism—the hope of salvation through the grace of AmidaBuddha —of the Jodo and Shin sects and as the living stoic Zen of inward mystic experience.

A fact to be borne in mind for full comprehension of Buddhism is that the Oriental does not draw such a sharp line of distinction between life and death, between the animate and the inanimate, as does the Westerner brought up in Greek dualistic philosophy and Judean-Christian theism. In prehistoric times and up to the days of original Shinto, the Japanese people were accustomed to live as a united family, visible-and-invisible as it were, with the spirits of the mountains, the valleys, the rivers, the trees and the houses. Later on, when this animism quietly withdrew into the poetic realm of folklore, Japanese associated with the departed members of their own family, who were mystically present in the ancestral tablets drawn up the the household

shrine. And do not ask a Japanese when he offers flowers, rice and wine to his dear dead whether they are aware of the love which is bestowed upon them—he will smile and remain silent because his reply would certainly be misunderstood. How could he tell you that their existence is just as real, or rather as unreal, as your own—just as true as the existence of his cherry-blossom which rejoices your sight, perfumes the air and flutters down? But you can ask him, if he is an Amidist, a Nichirenist or a follower of Zen, if Amida or Shakamuni is aware of our struggles, our pains and our desperate efforts toward liberation, and he will answer you that, after all, it is Buddha alone who really knows, because Buddha is the total knowledge, the absolute consciousness and the ultimate truth.

An American or a European trained in the logic of Aristotle, Francis Bacon or Leibnitz experiences some difficulty in grasping Buddhism. It seems to him full of contradictions. A western student would be likely to put the following question to his teacher: "Tell me, if I have no soul, no ego, what transmigrates into a new body after my death? Explain to me also, quite plainly, is this visible world a reality or only an illusion, a dream? Lastly, in Nirvana extinction?"

The replies of the teacher to these questions would most probably not satisfy any Westerner. And that is the reason why this poetical religion of universal brotherhood, of allembracing love extending even to animals and plants, this religion of salvation and eternal bliss, has so few followers in the West. We are intoxicated with logic. Are we right? Yes, no doubt we are, in so far as we deal with objects located in space and existing in time, because such objects are subject to the law of causality and can therefore be enclosod in rigid frames of logical propositions. But I believe that we are wrong in trusting to sheer logic as soon as we purport to deal with objects of thought transcending space and time. Our law of causality, formulated in syllogisms, cannot any longer be applied to them. We ought to have realized that since the days of Kant.

But, to return to the indiscreet questions of our imaginary western student, one must take into consideration the great misunderstanding which subsists between the oriental and occidental schools of thought over the concept of "being." From the oriental point of view a thing that is cannot change. The fact that everything is subject to change in this fleeting world is a proof that it is not. You can say that it "becomes," even that it "exists" but not that it "is." Buddha is because Buddha never changes, Amida, Buddha, Vairocana, Tathata Dharmakaya are different names for the principle of unalterability. Buddha is spiritual but not personal. Round him or rather round it moves the ever changeable world of only dreams of the Unique.

Now what transmigrates after death? The elements of our deeds, our thought and our desires are combining into a new dream. We have furnished stuff for a new phantasmagoria. One dream finishes, another begins, until the very elements feeding these dreams will be exhausted, until man, having attained enlightenment, will cease to nurture selfish desires until, all sense of separateness having vanished, he will be one with all. Nirvana is thus not a place but a subjective state. It is neither existence or extinction in the state of Nirvana consciousness is identical with being. Or, to put it in other words, the empirical ego is evanescent; it is the transcendental ego which is immortal, and the immortality it enjoys in Nirvana is not personal but cosmic.

Now, we must remember that Mahayana is a development of Hinayana philosophy and an adaption of that philosophy to social life. Hinayana was distinctly unsocial. The contact with Bactia and Greece opened up monastic Buddhism, just as contact with the Gentiles unfettered the somber Christianity of the early days of the Jerusalem community.

The Japanese is a sincere Buddhist, but he lays more stress upon the life he lives than upon the doctrine he professes. Buddhism has developed in him two important features of character. Of these the first is an intense feeling of duty; for this feeling, so strong in every Japanese—duty to his Emperor, to his country, to his parents, to his patron, to his friends — is the consequence of the sense of solidarity, of nonseparateness, taught by Buddhism. Just as, in his art, lines are only symbols so life is for him only a living symbol of duty. The second trait to which I refer is a refusal to assign an

exaggerated value to transitory things. The soldier is brave because he does not cling desperately to life; the civilian is patient, enduring and daring because things, after all, are devoid of reality. To use a trivial comparison, the Japanese Buddhist is like a poker player with unlimited resources such a man would certainly outplay a poor opponent whose fortune of, say, a thousand dollars is at stake.

Buddhism has been instrumental in developing the stoic mind, self-control, a sense of duty in the Japanese. But these virile qualities have their "counterpoint,' to use an expression of Keyserling's, in the Japanese nature. It is the gentle touch of melancholy partly derived from the belief in the transitoriness of human joys and sorrows. This is the leit-motif of Japanese art and the background of Japanese life. So true is it that the human soul must be sad in order to feel! Art, after all, is perhaps only an expression of human sorrows:

"Hab' ich ein Leid.
ich ein Lied daraus."

But it is also true that only those eyes can see which—perhaps for having wept too much—are incapable of tears.

(*The Japan Times, Sep. 1, 1935.*)

New Buddhist Publication

"Footsteps of Japanese Buddhism"

This is a new publication just issued. It is published by the foreign department of the Institute for Research in Living Religions, directed by Mr. H. Hamada.

The first issue is devoted to Nichiren with many illustrations. The contents are as follows:

"Life and Teaching of Saint Nichiren" by Gyokei Umato, Professor of Rissho College; "The Eternal Life of the Tathagata" by the late Bunno Kato; "Nichiren" by Yone Noguchi; "Die Nitchiren-Gemeinde in Japan" by Honyu Hamada, Professor of Rissho College; "Extracts from the Works of Nichiren," from Dr. Anesaki's "Nichiren, the Buddhist Prophet," "Nichiren, le Saint Bouddhique, sa vie et sa doctrine" by Professor Kankyo Moriyo of Rissho College.

The publication also contains an elaborate pictorial section depicting Nichiren temples and relics. (*price ¥1.20,* obtainable from our Bureau)

The Passing Show

By ZOE KINCAID

Sessue Hayakawa was never seen to better advantage than in the spectacular Buddhist play "Shikai no Hikari" (Light of Four Seas), which he has written, and in which he takes the leading role at the Nippon Gekijo December 1-10, under the auspices of the Young Men's Buddhist Association.

His presence on the stage is striking, his face like that of paintings of the Buddha. Throughout the scenes he maintains the dignity of the character, and exemplifies the spirit of sacrifice necessary to the exalted state to which he attains. There have been many plays producted in Tokyo with plots relating to Buddhism but this is the first time that such an elaborate drama based on the life of the prince who forfeited all the pleasures of life to obtain enlightement has been given.

The opening scenes showing the worldliness and lust of kings serves as an introduction, but the picture soon changes to the palace of the king, showing the venerable ruler and his consort, Miss Otome Tsukimiya as the princess, and Mitsuru Toyama as Daiba, the cousin of the prince, who wishes to acquire the inheritance held so lightly by the young man who is to become the Buddha.

The leading actor, being in this case playwright also, has arranged in impressive entrance for the prince. Maidens strew flowers over a stairway in the center of the stage and the orchestra plays as the hero appears in a bejewelled costume and wearing a golden head-dress.

Pleasures of Palace

The entertainment for the benefit of the prince does not change his mind which is made up to wander far to find knowledge. Toshiko Sekiya as a peasant girl sings, but her song is a Japanese melody in the grand opera style which does not seem appropriate to the simple role she is supposed to represent. Elenna Pavlova dances in the Indian manner to attractive Indian music surrounded by a group of girls. Daiba, the bad cousin, and

the prince compete in a lively sword encounter and later in a bow and arrow rivalry which pleases the groundlings.

The farewell to his wife fellows, and he takes his departure from the palace.

The scene in the Dandokusen Mountains where the prince takes leave of his faithful servant and favorite horse is well presented, the prince entering upon a white steed with red trappings. He makes an exit and returns in priestly garb, his long hair cut, and becomes more like a painting of the Buddha. The horse actors are inexperienced, and the fussy movements of the firstlegs player detracts somewhat from the scene. The minor actors who specialise in the horse pantomime on the Kabuki stage would have added much to the situation where the prince gives his golden crown to the servant and thereby renounces the world.

Merit Through Austerities

The prince is then seen learning how to acquire merit through austerities and enters carrying a bundle of faggots, his costume tattered and torn. Holy men go through self inflicted tortures one standing on his head, another carrying a heavy stone.

Here Miss Sekiya appears as a temptress and sings. The prince meets his wife who comes disguised as a man, accompanied by his child. Again he overcomes all the attractions of life and in the mountains of Buddhagaya meditates for seven days and nights under a tree. The scene is well arranged, the prince kneeling on a mound of earth beneath the wide-spreading branches.

Here Sessue Hayakawa is more than ever Buddha-like, his statuesque qualities fitting him to play the kneeling figure with folded garments off one shoulder.

His father, the king, comes and offers him power through conquering armies, all the wealth of the world, but he refuses to be swerved from his purpose. A devil and his followers attack the meditating holy man, but he remains serene and aloof. The fantastic devils in the red glare of the spot light are a contrast to the calm attitude of the Buddha. The excitement of the clash of good and evil is heightened by a thunder storm, after which there is calm.

Suddenly the tree above puts forth flowers, blossoms gleam,

birds sing, all nature rejoices. Miss Sekiya enters as a Buddhist deity in white and silver holding a lotus flower in her hand and sings. Yellow rays flash in the background bringing the play to a picturesque conclusion.

Portrayal as Buddha

No other actor in Japan could so well impersonate the Buddha as Sessue Hayakawa. His face, figure and statuesque appeal, which was noted in his early screen career in Hollywood, all give him a special distinction. The religious sphere he has now chosen to exploit may become his greatest success. If he were only to be surrounded by a better company of players the performance would be better. The elaborate production requiring 130 players is not yet in a finished state. Much has yet to be done to complete the details. The songs and dances appear like interruptions. They might easily become part of the play. Some of the lines are too long and the action drags in places.

But on the whole the new Buddhist drama went well, the audience composed of all classes of society. It was interesting to note that young men appeared to predominate in the audience. The strong appeal of the story of Buddha's sacrifice has still power to interest, as it has done throughout the centuries in all parts of Asia.

Miss Sekiya is heard in her song interpretation of "Onatsu Kyoran" as a curtain raiser. The Tsubouchi ballad-dance which she has adapted to opera is better produced than on the first occasion in the Kabukiza some years ago.

Why Freak Religions?

Raids on Omotokyo and Tenrikyo headquarters accompanied by the arrest of leaders of these two "modern" modifications of the Shinto Faith, together with the new religious control bill now being considered by Government authorities and the movement for the introduction of some form of religious (ethical rather than doctrinaire is apparently favored) instruction into the schools of the nation have brought the question of religion in Japan very much into the limelight and into the forefront of many minds. The religious history of Japan is an interesting and curious one. At times a broad tolerance and sympathy toward all religions, a tolerance almost unknown to strictly Christian nations, had been shown, but this attitude has alternated with an extremely narrow viewpoint and the inauguration of official restrictions and persecutions by the authorities in power, by measures frankly and expressly designed to stamp out those religious faiths or cults objectionable to these authorities.

It would be basing a premise on too little foundation to assert that Japan is on the verge of such another reaction against religion. In fact, it is most unlikely that the Empire will ever again witness religious persecution such as it has known at times in the past, for knowledge and modes of thought have advanced too far to permit such a development in Modern Japan. Discussion of religion, the introduction of measures in the Diet to regulate it and Government action against those cults considered inimical to the State, subversive of public decency and order or actual violators of existing law may be expected to figure prominently in the press for some months to come.

The actions now under way against Omotokyo and Tenrikyo falls into two separate categories. In the case of the latter, the only charges brought forward so far are those of tax invasion, an infringement of the civil law, no allegation against the doctrine or practices of the Tenrikyo having been made. This is not true as regards Omotokyo. The "Grand Master" of that organization, Wanisaburo Deguchi, now under arrest with many of his principal supporters, faces the extremely grave accusation of lese majeste and of having taught and practiced principles counter to the national polity of Japan. It is not the first time that both of these sects have run afoul of the law and past offenses will probably be given consideration in the present instance. The innocence or guilt of Deguchi and his followers is a matter for the courts to decide, not the press or public opinion. But the press can do not greater service in connection with the present religious and anti-religious (that is, anti-certain particular religions) agitation than to examine and air the causes of that agitation and thus permit the public to determine whether or not it is justified. Incidentally, it is pleasing to see the authorities always so gravely concerned with the activities of Left Wing organizations, taking an interest in the extreme Right Wing, which is frequently more dangerous in Japan than the radicals, alleged or otherwise.

The right, and duty, of the State to regulate or eradicate perverted religious movements inimicable to the good of the State stands unchallenged. The question of "freedom of religions" does not enter into such cases, although it may well be expected that this cry will be raised in certain quarters.

The birth and rapid growth of what may be called "freak religions" in Japan is a phenomenon of the nation today and one worthy of study. Why are such movements springing into being, and why are they gaining a comparatively widespread and unquestionaly enthusiastic reception?

Omotokyo itself numbers nearly a half-million followers, Tenrikyo is even larger and there are number of other smaller and less important cults or sect of a similar nature. Some of these preach a crude supernaturalism, claiming the ability to cure disease by sacredotal magic. Others attract the masses by offering an equally crude form of Communism cloaked by religious phrases and terms. The use of this mask of religion is all too common in Japan, as is shown by the criminal case now

pending where a step-mother is alleged to have murdered, or instigated the murder, of her stepson in order to collect his life insurance and to permit her own son to succeed to the headship of the family. This woman is claimed to have stated also that she received a "divine message" to burn her husband's hospital in order to collect the fire insurance. If true, she shows a decided affinity for insurance premiums of one sort or another, a form of business apparently of particular interest to her especial type of Heaven.

In nearly every case the theology taught by these spurious sects is unsystematic, unscientific and quite irrational. It is a most surprising fact, in view of this, that they find ready adherents not only among the ignorant and superstitious masses but among prominent and well-educated classes. What are the basic causes of the unwelcome development in Japan's spiritual life?

The Minister of Education, Mr. Genji Matsuda, stated to the board appointed to investigate religious systems that "the evil repercussions attendant upon materialistic civilization have become greatly accentuated in Japan, and that national thought has become unbalanced." That is true, but a trifle too vague to prove very enlightening. His charge falls into two divisions.

As regards the unbalancing of national thought, it must be pointed out that this is a disillusioned generation. May not that well be because religion has been and is unable to give this generation the sustaining strength and ideals which were formerly its great gift? No accusation is being levelled against any particular Faith, but it is a self-evident fact that religion does not play as prominent a part, is not as active a force in practical life, as it once was. If materialism is harming religion, it is up to religion to devise ways of combatting it and to offer the people a more desirable life than lies within the power of materialism. In this phase of activity the Ministry of Education, other Government divisions and the various churches can well co-operate to a good end.

But if materialism is responsible for the decline of religion, a materialistic cause therefore must be sought. It is easily found. With the growth of wealth in Japan there has steadily come about a greater and greater inequality in the distribution of wealth and of the goods of this life. The difference between the extremely wealthy and the extremely poor is constantly widening. It is for this reason that those freak cults which offer, a better livelihood, through a veiled and crude form of Communism, appeal so greatly to the "have nots." In other countries this tempting bait of increased ease of life and material well-being is held out through political movements, and a Huey Long obtains a vast, unthinking following. In Japan, the authorities keep an extremely tight rein—perhaps too tight a rein—on such political movements, with the result that they have been diverted into religious channels and cloak themselves behind the various Gods they have to offer a gullible public, Gods which most emphatically believe in a (materialistic) kingdom on this earth more fervently than in the life to come.

Here Education Ministry officials and others can do some good by educational methods, but the true remedy must be sought in its economic cause, in the readjustment of economic life in Japan (always in accord with the Constitution and accepted Japanese institutions), so that economic inequality is reduced to a minimum instead of continuing to increase as at present. Not one Ministry of the Government alone, not even the whole Cabinet, but intellectual political, business leaders and others are required to co-operate and to use their best brains in the bringing about of this desirable condition. It is necessary that the Ministry of Education adopt a new policy predicated upon intellectual rationalism and the analytical spirit if it is to attempt to revive decaying religion. Only thus can the nation be saved from further disturbance through freak religions indulging in supernaturalism and other harmful theories.

(*The Japan Times. Dec. 19, 1935*)

新刊紹介

◇本願寺祕史

(上原芳太郎編)

編著者上原氏は、嘗つて西本願寺室内部長の要職にあり、西本願寺家臣の出身にして、多くの秘められたる古文書を使用して、此の一書を編まれた。内容は第一章、本願寺沿革、之は西本願寺の世代を叙し、第二章、本願寺の家臣と環境、これには珍史料多く、第三章、信義會の沿革、また珍らし。佛教史特に眞宗史の研究者の好資料。

四六判三二〇頁、二圖

東京丸の内三の八　有光社刊

Pictures On Silk In Art Show

MR. K. NOSU'S CHARMING STYLE

INDIA THROUGH JAPANESE EYES

HOME MINISTER OPENS EXHIBITION

PAINTINGS of India by the Japanese artist, Kosetsu Nosu, of the Tokyo Academy of Fine Arts, are now on view at the Art Gallery, Colombo.

The exhibition, under the auspices of the Ceylon Society of Arts, was declared open yesterday by Sir Baron Jayatilaka, in the presence of a large gathering. It will continue till Wednesday next.

Mr. Nosu has a style of his own. In the main it is Japanese; and the artist is at his best in his studies in black and white.

In his other pictures with a few colours very subtly laid the artist has obtained rather remarkable effects.

All the pictures are painted on silks and set out in frames peculiarly Japanese.

Whether in colour or black and white, his study of trees, sky and water reflects entirely the Japanese technique.

The subjects are varied; some entirely mind creations: others interpretations from Indian life.

The Opening

Mr. G. A. Wille, President, in asking Sir Baron Jayatilaka to open the exhibition, said that Mr. Kosetsu Nosu had been aptly termed Japan's Ambassador of Art to India and Ceylon.

Mr. Nosu belonged to a Society in Japan, membership in which was the highest honour available to a Japanese artist. But so strong were his leanings towards Indian Art and Buddhist culture that, when two or three years ago, in the terms of a gift, a set of frescoes had to be painted by a Buddhist from Japan in the new Buddhist Vihare at Saranath, he was selected for the task.

Reviving the Lost Art

For three years therefore Mr. Nosu, with his assistant, had been engaged in mural painting at Saranath, and through him, it was said, the almost lost art of the frescoes was again being revived, though an individual note of modern realism was blended in his work with the style of the Ajanta frescoes.

In the midst of this preocupation he found time to depict Indian life and scenes. Although his immediate object in visiting Ceylon was to study Buddhist culture here, he had consented to give Ceylon an opportunity of seeing those and other paintings of his. Art-lovers in Ceylon, irrespective of any religious affiliations and sympathies, would be gratefull for that opportunity.

Only an Admirer of Art

Sir Baron said that his education as regards fine arts had been so neglected that, on occasions such as that, he felt it was presumptuous on his part to be anything more than an onlooker and a listener. He could admire the pictures though he could offer no comments on them; but as regards the great service which Mr. Nosu was rendering, he thought, everyone could appreciate that work.

From the pictures exhibited in the hall, they could see that Mr. Nosu had studied Indian life very closely and reproduced it with wonderful precision and effect.

It gave him very great pleasure to associate himself with that function, and he hoped that all present would take an interest in Mr. Nosu's work.

He learnt that Mr. Nosu had to spend another year or two to complete the work at Mulagandhikuti Vihare. Already a very large sum of money had been spent. Mr. Nosu was not doing the work for any worldly consideration; with him it was a labour of love, but, for various reasons, money was required. Everybody interested in the completion of that work should give as much help as they could so that it might be brought to a successful issue within a short time.

He sincerely hoped that the exhibition would be an inspiration to students of art in this country.

The Consul Thanks

Mr. H. Ototsu, the Imperial Japanese Consul in Ceylon, said:

"Mr. Nosu has been compelled to seek the support of the Ceylon public owing to the fact that the funds donated to the Mahabodi Society for the work in India by Mr. B. L. Broughton, a Buddhist Englishman, have already been exhausted, and unless sufficient funds are forthcoming to carry out his noble undertaking he will find himself considerably handicapped.

"As you are perhaps aware, Japanese civilization owes an incalculable debt to Buddhism, which was introduced to Japan in the sixth century from India by way of Korea and China. Lafcadio Hearn once wrote that Buddhism was a civilizing power in Japan in the highest sense of the word, for it introduced to Japan the highest forms of poetical composition and fiction, drama, history, philosophy, architecture, painting, sculpture, engraving, printing and landscape gardening.

"From this it may be gathered that Buddhism, which originated in India, was the mother of the civilization of Japan.

Repayment of the Debt

"Japan was, however, not in a position to make any practical manifestation of her gratitude to India for the cultural gifts she had received from India until the advent of an ambassador of art in the person of my esteemed Japanese friend, Mr. Nosu.

"Through the good offices of the Mahabodi Society, founded by the late Venerable Devamitta Dharmapala, my friend is now making that practical demonstration of Japan's acknowledgment of India's gift by sacrificing his personal interests and the happiness of his family in the desire to help the resuscitation of Buddhism in the land of its birth.

"It is a matter of regret that most of us here have not come into personal contact with his actual work at Saranath, as otherwise it would not have been necessary for me to dilate on the need for supporting this cause even at this length. However, we are not, I believe, lacking in imagination to form a sufficiently high conception of the artistic merit that has to be brought to the execution of such a great work by seeing the photographic copies of the frescoes exhibited here and there in this Gallery.

"I have no doubt that all of us here would wish Mr. Nosu to be blessed by Lord Buddha to enable him to carry out his work successfully, and I sincerely hope that he will receive not only the moral support but also substantial help from his well-wishers in Ceylon to achieve his noble object.

"I am sure that the encouragement given by Sir Baron Jayatilaka's participation in this opening ceremony will be an inspiration to Mr. Nosu.

"Last but not least, it is also my duty to thank the Mahabodi Society here and the Ceylon Society of Arts for the valuable assistance which is being rendered to Mr. Nosu since his arrival in Ceylon."

Brief Notes on Some of the Pictures

No. 1—*The Unexpected Shower*, is full of moment. A gust of wind, rain and a lad on a buffalo running away from the rain, is well depicted here.

No. 6—*The Patron of the Mountains*. This shows the ascetic of the mountain in a characteristic pose. The background and the colour scheme are entirely Japanese in character.

No. 19—*Love Among the Palms*. An impressive picture, of attractive composition.

No. 20 — *The Meteor, or The Fruits of Hard Labour*. Typically the Indian village life. The "Fruits of Hard Labour" are reflected in the lad who seems to be fast asleep.

No. 29—*In Everlasting Silence*, depicts the Himalayas in its majesty, bleakness and solitude. A simple study in black and white, of great merit.

The pictures of the Buddhas and the Bodhisatvas are in the spirit of the ancient Ajanta paintings, but the artist is not able to get away from his nationality.

No. 32—*The Retiring Birds*, is characteristic of the delicate style and method of Japanese art.

No. 40—*Phantom of the Virgin*. A problem picture in futuristic style.

No. 49—*Village Youngster*. Typical of the hard village life and poverty. It shows an emaciated dog, and a lad with a basket improvised as a head covering.

No. 51—*Building up the Hopeful*. Rich in colour, and subtle in composition and detail. It gives a very good interpretation of Indian motherhood.

(*The Times of Ceylon*, Oct. 19, 1935.)

Japanese News

Student of Nichiren

Mr. Arturo Alvarez Montenegro, Chargé d'Affaires for Argentine in Japan, gave a lecture on Nichiren at Rissho University on the 22th November.

He has been studying Nichiren Buddhism for several years, ever since he attended the annual festival of Hommonji at Ikegami, Omôri. Mr. Montenegro has collected many books and pictures connected with the life of the great Buddhist priest.

Mochi for Slums

To raise funds to provide slum families with the much desired mochi for the New Year holidays, 4,000 girls studying at the 15 Buddhist schools in Tokyo stationed on the streets to ask passersby for alms.

The girls took up their positions in the crowded districts from November 30 to December 1.

Historical Park

Tokyo Municipality has planed to preserve the site of the mansion of Kira Kōzuke, enemy of the Forty-seven Ronin, as an historical park to be added to the beautiful recreation places of the city.

The mansion of the enemy who caused the tragic events connected with the retainers of Lord Asano, was in Yedo days at Matsuzakacho, Honjo. The place has been neglected for years, and the owner, Mr. Tokusaburo Arakawa, offered the land to the city.

It was surrounded by an earthen wall as in the Genroku days, and the well where Kuranosuke washed the head of Kira Kōzuke was also cleaned and repaired.

It is but a small spot, but will perpetuate the memory of the event that has been made the subject of drama and story.

Simple Life of Priest

Shogo Taguchi, a Buddhist priest who lives at Taishido, Setagaya, leave for Manchoukuo to comfort the soldiers.

For the past 16 years he has lived on rice and vegetables only. He does not wear a hat on his head or tabi on his feet, and talk to the soldiers on the simple life.

Handy Library

To introduce Japan to the world the Society for the Promotion of International Cultural Relations are now preparing representative books on cultural subjects contained in an attractive bookcase.

The volumes include reference books and albums necessary for the explanation of Japanese subjects. They are to be offered to noted scholars, libraries, schools, and it is hoped to place the library on the most important steamship lines in the world.

Daruma for Luck

The Taishakuten temple of Koshigaya in Saitama Prefecture is famous as a center of the home industry in fashioning the paper made figures of Daruma. The fat effigies in red have faces without eyes.

People who pray for good luck buy the Daruma and when good fortune comes their way they give the armless and legless image an eye. As soon as some other sign of prosperity arrives another eye is painted in.

Farmers of Koshigaya are busy making Daruma. Daizo Takahashi with 20 employes under him, is the chief maker of Daruma in this village. He is the fifth descendant of the family who started the creation of these symbols of gook luck.

Pilgrimage to Ise

Under the auspices of the Hochi Shimbun a pilgrimage will be held to the Grand Shrine at Ise, the Unebi Imperial Mausoleum, Momoyama Imperial Mausoleum, and Atsuta Shrine starting on January 1.

Mr. and Mrs. Bansui Doi, the poet and his wife, who live at Sendai, are to join the party.

People from all parts of the Empire will visit the Grand Shrine of Ise aud other national shrines during the New Year holidays to pray for the prosperity of the country. Tokyo people will flock in thousands to pay their respects before Meiji Shrine.

Basho's Monument

An interestingstone monument associated with Basho, the Yedo poet, has just been offered to the Kawasaki society for the preservation of local art.

It is 3 feet hight and carved on it is a poem by Basho who said farewell to his pupils near Kawasaki when he started on a wandering tour.

Mr. Shozaemon Komiya of Kawasaki has owned the monument for a long time, but decided that it was too valuable to be privately owned.

Koyasan Hotel

Koyasan, the peaceful monastery overlooking Kyoto is to be invaded by tourists. The Nankai Railway Company of Wakayama Prefecture will spend Yen 500,000 on the erection of a hotel.

Mr. Kaichiro Nezu once planned to built a hotel in this picturesque spot, but his request was refused.

Now the priests of the monastery have agreed to the plan of the railway company. The building is to be in pure Japanese architecture in keeping with the ancient temples, and will be open to tourists from overseas.

支那に於ける布教權の問題

外務省文化事業部囑託　岩村成允

支那に於ける布教權と云ふ事は，宗教界に於ても屢々問題になつて居り，日本が支那に於ける布教權がないため布教上甚だ不便が多いと云ふ事は，常に皆から申されるのですが，然らば西洋人はどうして支那に布教權を得て居り，又日本はどう云ふ譯で布教すると云ふ事を，支那から許されて居らないかと云ふ事の問題ですが，元來西洋人主として耶蘇教ですが，西洋人がどうしてそんならば布教權を得たかと云ふ事を考へてみますと，一番古るい處は唐の太宗の時代に景(ケイ)教が初めて支那に這入つた。此の景(ケイ)教は北支那に於て非常に弘められ，北京方面には今日もその遺物が發見される。既に唐の時代に於て西洋の宗教が大變支那に這入つて來て居り，相當の信者があつたと云ふ沿革を持つて居るのです。その中で又猶太教等は今日もその遺蹟を留めて居る。色々な宗教が西洋から這入つて來て居て，その中に於いても，即ち明朝が最も此の西洋の教へが旺んになつた時代でありまして萬曆(マンレキ)年間に最初廣東に參りまして，それから福建に廣がつたものが所謂天主教で，相當の信者を持つて居る。

それから明の終り，清朝の始めの時代ですが，此の頃はキリスト教の宣教師が參りまして，康熙，乾隆の時代は特に，キリスト教の宣教師は非常に尊敬され，各地に教會堂が建てられた。主として此の時代には佛蘭西人，和蘭人が多く，宣教師の數が一千何百，二千にも上つて居つた。天主教の信徒は百五十萬人もあつたと云ふ記錄がある。その後清朝から乾隆以後段々天主教が旺んになつて，それから後に新教が這入つて參りまして，支那には此の西洋の教へが非常に廣く布教された。

此の天主教の神父なる人は，永年支那に住んで居て，支那語をよく話し，支那の人情風俗に通じ，或は支那服を着て，全く支那人と同じやうに生活し支那人とよく同化した。然し此の教會堂は，多くは本國の教會の援助を受けたり，支那の官民等の寄附により，立派な建築をして居る。今日でも到る處に相當立派な教會堂が發見される。これは別段何もその當時に於て，支那の政府から布教權とか何んとかを權利として與へられて居つたのではなくして自然的にさう云ふやうになつて來たと云ふ事は，非常に永い歷史を持つからなのです。

段々清朝から乾隆以後，內政が紊亂して參り，地方官が隨分賄賂を取つたり，官權を笠にきて惡事をすると云ふ事が大變にあつた。人民は惡地方官の惡政を免れるために，遂ひに自分は教民であると云ふやうに，敎會を利用致しまして，自分の居る處の敎會堂，殊に西洋人の宣敎師等に助力を求めた。さうすると宣敎師は自ら出て行つて，これは敎民の利益のために，支那の官權である地方官に交渉して罰則を免れさせるやうになつた。

又その當時は支那の地方官が皆な裁判權を持つて居つた。然して收賄によつて隨分不公平な裁判をしたもので，段々に支那の人民は地方官に訴へないやうになつた。裁判をして貰ふものは神父，宣敎師の裁判を受けた方がいゝと云ふ傾向になつて參つた。色々と悶着があると，敎會に行つて良い惡るいを決めてもらう。地方官には訴へない宣敎師がこれを裁き，敎民がその裁判に服從すると云ふ傾向が出來て來た。

それから土匪が横行する事は矢張り同じですが，土匪等の事で問題が起きても，敎會が中心となつて，色々の事をやる。田舍の財政問題は必ず敎會堂を中心として居り，地方官の權力に大分食入つて來た。かやうな狀勢になつて來た。

段々時勢が後になつて參りますと，支那の國は益々亂れて來る。同時に宣敎師の權力も益々增えて，殊に宣敎師が治外法權を持つて居ると云ふ事から治外法權の蔭に隱れて，敎民が段々惡事をする。にも拘らず地方官が手を出す事が出來ないと云ふ事になつて來たのです。

それで清朝の歷史をひろげて見ますと，敎安といふことが出てゐるが，宣敎師，若くはキリスト敎徒の人民と地方官との間に色々な事件が起る。遂ひには一地方に動亂を起し，軍隊が出て討伐すると云ふやうな問題も度々起つて來た。支那の政府も此の敎民，敎會堂と云ふものに對しては，殆んど手を燒いてしまつたのです。

一方又西洋の方の事から見てみますと，例へば佛蘭西とかその他の國ですが，宣敎師を政治的の手先に使つた形蹟がある。宣敎師を派して支那の內地に這入り込み，色々政治的運動をやりましたゝめ，或はスパイ的の色々の探偵とか，又利權漁りと云ふ事をして居つたやうです。それがために支那の政府は，どうしても內地の布敎と云ふ事は困ると云ふやうな感じを抱いて參つたのです。

殊に最も大きなのは，獨逸の青島を占領した事です。山東省の一地方に於きまして，獨逸の宣敎師が二人殺された。それがために青島は占領され，遂に山東省附近の利權を提供させられた事件であつて，外國の宗敎に對して，非常に恐れをなす一つの原因になつた

次に日本と支那との關係ですが，これは日本でも是非支那に於て布敎權を得たいと云ふ事は多年の希望でして，その現れが大正四年の日支交渉の際に於て，支那に於ける布敎權を日本にも寄こせと云ふ事の交渉をした。が，それに對して支那は極力反對した。其處の處を一寸材料がありますから申上げます。

その前に一寸申しますが，此の西洋

と支那との布敎權に關する條約公文の交換と云ふ事は，度々行はれて居るのですが，條約文として現はれましたのは卽ち此の英國との阿片戰爭の時で，その時に初めて天津條約を結んだのが御承知の通り英國と支那との間に於いて，一八五八年に天津條約に於て，布敎權を認めて居ます。(その條文は此處に持つて居りますけれども今申上げません)。それから又その後に，米國とも一八五八年天津の條約に於て布敎權を與へて居る。それから英國，米國だけでなく，大きな國に布敎權を認める。それと同時に，敎會堂が暮してゆけるだけの土地や何かを敎會堂が持つて居る事が出來ると云ふ事を認めて居る。それに就いて，日本の方からは，大正四年の日支交渉の際に支那の內地に於ける日本人の布敎權を認めるやうに，それから又日本の寺院，病院，學校等に對しては土地の所有權を與へるやうにと云ふやうな事に就いて交渉した。處が支那側はそれに對して色々反對した。その反對の理由は後で申上げますが，結局日支交渉の時分には，どうしても支那に對する條約が澤山にありますために，他の條約が，滿洲に關するものが，餘り澤山問題が多かつたために，布敎權の問題は先づ此の際は留保してをくと云ふ事になつて，今日に及んで居ります。その後少なからず問題は起りましたけれども，何等布敎權に關しての交渉は行はれて居らぬ狀態です。

それでどう云ふ譯で支那が日本の布敎權に反對したかと云ふ事を終りに申上げますが，その時の支那側との交渉の情勢も分つて居ますが，なほその中に於きまして，巴里の平和會議に於て支那の全權から日本の布敎權と云ふ事に對して陳述書を出して居ます。それから又支那の外交部に於きまして，「支那對列國條約批判」と云ふものを出して居ります。條約書の實權と云ふ事に對して，非常に長い意見を書いて居りますが，それにも日本の二十一ケ條の要求の中にさう云ふものがあるが，支那としては當然應ずる事は出來ないと云ふ事を述べて居ります。

それで一寸申上げますが，支那の反對とする理由。支那が多年西洋人のために困らされて居る處の敎安問題の轍を踏むと云ふ事を恐れる。卽ちこれまで，キリスト敎の宣敎師及び，その敎徒のために支那の內地が度々紛擾が起つて洵に困つた。その轍を踏むを恐れる。

もう一つは支那は從來佛敎國であるそれであるから，佛敎と云ふものは知つて居る。日本より布敎を受ける必要はない。

それからもう一つは，日本の佛敎と在來の支那に於ける佛敎と敎義その他のために色々問題が起り，爭ひを起すと云ふ事を恐れる。日本の佛敎と支那の佛敎と敎義等の事から佛敎徒の間に爭が起ると云ふ事になると困ると云ふのである。

それからもう一つは日本の佛敎徒も西洋の宣敎師の如く，宗敎の敎堂に於

て地方の政權に干渉して，さうして極端に申しますれば政治的の問題を起さないと云ふ事の保證は出來ない。斯ふ云ふ事が主なる原因となつたやうです日本の方でも，その當時に，決してさう云ふ事はないと云ふ事を充分に說明して，佛教の問題と云ふ事に就いて，日支關係に深い歷史を持つて居ると云ふ事，キリスト教の宣教師のこれまでして來たやうな事をする筈はないと云ふ事を度々論議したやうですけれども仲々オイソレと承諾しない。それに滿洲問題と云ふやうな重大な問題があつて，宗教問題のために早く條約を結ぶ事が出來ないと云ふ事は甚だ不利だと云ふ事で，此のまゝ留保しておかうと云ふ事になつた。

又支那の外國に許した權利と云ふものは，何百年來支那に出來て來た處の既定の事實を條約文に現はしたに過ぎないものである。決して新に外國に許可したものではない。既に外國人が永い間這入つて居る土地を見れば，それを今更追出す譯けには行かないから，止むを得ず承認したのである。さう云ふやうな事，並に外國人に對して土地の所有權を與へて居らなかつた。居住權を與へて居らなかつた。何とかして西洋人を斷りたいと思つて居る矢先きに，日本人に布教權を許して，內地に土地の所有權を與へる。居住權を與へると云ふ事は，どうしても出來ない。此の居住權，布教權と云ふ事に對してこれを支那に對して無理に認めさせると云ふ事は面白くない。日支の間には色々の問題が起きて居まして，到底今日まで論議する機會はなかつた。これは今日までの經過でして，餘り時間がありませんので，詳しい事は何かの機會に於て申上げて，最後に私の此の問題に對する個人の意見を一寸附加へたいと思ひます。

日本と支那との條約に於ては，凡ての問題に於て條約の範圍を一寸も出て居らん。支那の方で，非常に歡迎するやうな事は，條約に書いてなくても，事實實行をすればよい。例へば支那の田舍の方に日本人が行て住つて居る人があります。さうして支那人の好くやうな事をしてやれば，居住權のない處にも實際日本人が居れるのです。永年居りますと，自然とそれが權利となるのです。此の事から見ましても，權利と云ふ言葉は，精神的の問題ではないのです。支那としては，權利を與へると云ふ事は，どうしても條約や公文書交換と云ふ事には行かないとしても，事實に於きまして，本當に日支兩國が佛教上に於ける提携をして，それが引いて兩國の文化に，國民の幸福になると云ふ事ならば，これは決して支那人が排斥するものではないと思はれるのです。結局此の問題は，權利と云ふ事は言ひたくないのです。我々は實際に於て，日支兩國の佛教界の人が本當に精神的に聯絡が出來ていつたならば，布教權と云ふ事は自ら解決して行くんぢやないかと思つて居る次第です。(傳通會館での座談要旨)(拍手)。

歷史的瞬間

在伯林　チドー・アウスター

獨逸に於ける政治的鬪爭は，今や漸く終りをつげ，正に精神問題へのそれが開始されるに至つた。カトリツク教會に關し，またローゼンベルクの「二十世紀の神話」に對する抗爭に關し，その爭論の激烈さは，それが如何に重大なる意義を持ち，また多くの關心が持たれてゐるかを示すもので，今や全く全獨逸いたる處に，此の思想的論爭の花が咲いてゐる。

非教會的，非クリスト教的の宗教思想が，國家から完全に承認されると云ふことは，獨逸歷史上に於て全く始めてのことである。從來はクリスト教々會に所屬することに依りてのみ「宗教的」又は「道德的」人格たり得たのであるが，新興ドイツに於ては，眞の宗教が必ずしも一つの教會に所屬せずとも存在し得べきことを廣く世に明かにされた。

今や佛教は，ドイツの精神生活にその傳道使命を果たすべき最もよい機會，恐らく再び得難き好機を得た譯である。そして佛教は慥かに，非常な注目と，否そればかりでなく非常な好感をもつて傾聽されるに違ひない。假令獨逸の國民が新來の一つの宗教々義に關心を持つべき用意がなく，そして又大衆が佛教に改宗するであらうと云ふことが期待出來ないとしても，(現在のドイツは一つの限られた宗教々團に束縛される樣なことは否定する)，猶ほ獨逸の精神生活が幾多の佛教思想を取り入れるであらうことは確かである。

佛教は與へられるものである。吾々，獨逸佛教徒は，唯與へることばかり考へて，吾々はその與へる爲めに何物をも取らうとしない。吾々は，すべての人間が佛陀の教に依りて果てしなく多くのものを創造し，又教へられ得ることを確信した。吾々は思想的，靈的の富，聖なる信念，佛教の自覺性，勇猛男性的な特性等々明かに認識せしめられた。此のすばらしい教へを，吾々は吾々の同朋に傳へんことを念願するものである。此の問題に共に親しく協力精進の出來る國，卽ち東と西，日本とドイツとである。兩國共に殊にかくの如き問題に最も適したものは，青年である。南方小乘教と北方大乘教が共に親しく握手し，相和することの出來るのは，吾々の世界西洋に於てゞある。願くば日本佛教徒諸君よ！　此の歷史的好機を逸せず大いに活用されんことを。

更に今一つ！　それは此の問題以外に兩國民間の平和又は文化關係の羈絆ともなりて，その友交關係を保證しうべきものとして，より以上の何物もないであらうと云ふことである。

（榊原順次譯）

國際佛教ニュース

英譯『佛教綱要』四卷

ペツオールド教授の偉業

日本精神の眞髓を理解しようとして日本獨特の文化藝道等の研究に志す外國人が次から次と現れて我々日本人の意を強くせしめてゐる折柄，滯日二十數年，ドイツ語の教鞭を取りながら佛教研究を續け天台宗から『大僧都』の位まで受けてゐる佛教研究のドイツ人一高教授ペツオールド氏(六三)がライフワークとして二十數年來のうん蓄を傾け，十數年間がゝりで執筆した『佛教綱要』四卷（約二千ページの豫定）の原稿がこの程八九分通り出來上つたので近くロンドンに送りオツクスフオード・ユニバアシテイ・プレスから，英語で出版され全世界の佛教學界に呼び掛ける事になつた。ぺ氏の夫人は我樂壇の恩人として有名なペツオールド夫人であり，永年にわたつて夫婦そろつて日本文化に絶大な貢獻をなしてゐる。

ぺ氏のライフワーク『佛教綱要』の執筆は今を去る十數年前ぺ氏の佛教學の師であつた東大文學部インド哲學科講師故島地大等氏（昭和二年歿）の助力で始めたが島地氏が古今東西にわたつて研究した佛典を飜譯して聞かすのをぺ氏が獨自の體系を立てゝ自分のものとして再現して行つたもので，最近では佛教學界の新進東大文學部インド哲學科講師花山信勝氏(三八)の協力を得て仕事を進めたもので，十數年間書きためた原稿はノート數千冊に達し，麻布區箪笥町六七のぺ氏邸の一室に高さ七尺，幅四尺位の金庫にギツシリつめて秘藏されてゐる。『佛教綱要』四卷の內容は第一卷佛教の文獻及び宗派第二卷教理批判，第三卷教理，第四卷實踐及び儀式となつて居り，差當り第二卷から出版にかゝるが，刊行を見るのは來年の秋頃の見込である。『佛教綱要』が完成の上は更に法大教授故星野彥四郎氏の協力によつて執筆した天台宗に關する研究五卷をドイツ語によつてライプチツヒから出版する豫定であり『佛教綱要』の副產物として出來上つた天台宗の開山天台大師の實踐哲學『小止觀』の獨譯も近くライプチツヒから出版される筈である。ぺ氏の研究は量においても質においても世界に類を見ないものとして花山氏等專門家が推奬してゐる。氏が佛教研究に志すに至つた動機は今は昔二十數年前氏がドイツの一流新聞『ケルニツシエツアイトウング』の東京特派員として來朝した際故床次氏によつて佛教，キリスト教，神道三教會同が行はれその記事を書いたのが機緣となつたもので，天台の儀式に興味を持ち，更に教理に入つて行つたのである。過日麻布の自邸において語るぺ氏はすこぶる上機嫌で，聲樂家ペツオールド夫人及二十年來同家に仕へる女中さんもこんなに機嫌のよいのはかつて見た事がないといつてゐた程である。

セイロン島での

野生司畫伯の個展好評

昭和七年十月に祖國を去つて印度に向ひ翌八年一月よりサルナートの鹿野苑の初轉法輪寺の壁畫揮毫に精進中の野生司香雪畫伯は畢生の心血を注いで釋尊一代の事績をものしつゝあるが，最初は一ケ年の豫定であつたのが壁畫容積の豫想外に廣く且酷熱の土地柄とて一年の中ば以上は到底室內にて執筆は不可能のため，その夏季にはシムラにカルカツタに轉地旁々畫會を催してその資金を求めてゐたが昨年は十月十五日よりカルカツタ市に出で更に東印度の平野を南行してマドラス市に向ひ同氏將來の會心の近作七十點をセイロンに託送して，自らは單身佛領ポンヂシエリ港に上陸して佛人經營のカソリツクの女學校に立寄り淑德高女生より依託せられた日本固有の裂地を頒つたところ，同校の尼僧も大に歡び，同校女學生より昨今淑德高女へ多數の感謝の手紙が到着しつゝある。氏は又コロンボ驛に着くと，驛頭にて乙津領事や又過年第二回汎太平洋佛靑大會にセイロン代表として來朝のラヂヤ，ヘワヴキターナ氏，ケイ，チ，ヴキマラセーカラ氏其他の諸氏に迎へられて，ラヂヤ，ヘワヴキターナ氏（同氏は同地唯一の名門家で富豪の由）邸に旅裝を解いて，セイロン美術協會後援のもとに博物館內美術陳列館に十月十八日より廿二日まで展覽會を開催せられた。開會當日は內務大臣，サー，バアロン，ヂアチラカ氏の開扉宣言と日本領事の挨拶があつた。當日は約二百餘名の紳士淑女も參列してゐてサムラヒ日本國の藝術に魅せられた。殊に絹地に墨繪で椰子の林で若い印度人が愛人と囁いてゐる素朴な畫題などは人氣を呼んだやうで同地發行のセイロン，デリイ，ニユース，タイムス其他には寫眞入りで大々的に，詳細なる評論が連載せられてゐる。

南洋女性のために

佛教主義の家政女學校創立

一昨年の第二回汎太平洋佛教靑大會に南洋サイパン，ロタ兩島より選出のチヤムロ靑年代表の歸島後は，島民靑年子女の間に佛教熱をそゝらしめ遂にカソリツク教の金城鐵壁と言はれてゐた牙城の一方を崩したといふのでローマ法王廳よりも橫槍が入つたほどであるが南洋寺の靑柳貫孝師は敢然とあらゆる困難と戰ひ遂に愛國婦人會を動かし堀內中將，星野錫氏及愛國婦人會の理事者及兒玉拓相，南洋廳長官などの協贊するところとなり，曩に淨土宗務所にても洞ケ峠の日和見であつたが愈ゝ一切の條件を具備したので靑柳氏は十一月十日歸島し南洋諸方面に奔走中のところ愛國婦人會設置，女學校設置を可決し敷地は南洋寺に接近する地域に新に二千坪の無償下附となつたので愈ゝ明年四月より授業を開講することになつたため去る十二月の十二日の便船にて愛婦地方部長，宗務教學部長相携へてサイパン島に赴き一切の具體案を打合すことになつてゐる。因に同地在住の移住民の女子のためには技藝女學校と名け，チャムロ島民の女子のためには家政女學校と名けられることに內定してゐる。

なぜ日本へ行きたい？

＝アメリカの子供達の答＝
＝大佛などの視察熱旺盛＝

昨夏國際觀光局が，アメリカン・ボイズ・マガヂンを通じて，アメリカの子供たちから『なぜ日本に行きたいか‥‥』といふ懸賞作文を募集した。それに應募した少年少女がざつと三百五十五人，日本に來たい理由にあげた數は三千六百三十三件だつたがその理由を種類別にすると次の様な面白い結果が現れ，アメリカの少年少女達の日本の何處に關心をもつてゐるかゞ，はつきり判る。

△日本の名勝を見たい，名士に會ひたいといふのが二七一件
△文化施設を見たいからといふのが二八一件
△造船その他の產業狀態を見たいといふのが四二八件
△風俗習慣を觀察したいといふのが四八三件
△スポーツの發達狀態を知りたいからといふのが五四件
△國際親善の爲めに行きたいといふのが一〇一件
△段々畑や火山等の風景を見たいといふのが一，〇五五件
△四季のお祭りや，大佛樣等，宗教關係の視察をしたいからといふのが四六六件
△人力車やその他の交通機關を見たいといふのが二二三件
△芝居（歌舞伎）お能等の慰樂設備を知りたいからといふのが一六件
△國防その他の制度を見學したいといふのが一〇五件
△躍進日本の姿を見たいといふ漠然なのが六〇件だつたといふ

尙觀光局では今まで對外宣傳に使つてゐた繪葉書が極めて平凡なもので中には日本の眞の姿を誤り傳へる樣なものまであつたので，從來の繪葉書は一切やめて新規な繪葉書五十萬枚を作り，昨年末から海外にばらまくことになつたが，それと同時に，その繪葉書を八ツ切に擴大したものを全米の新聞雜誌社に寄贈して宣傳の新機軸を開くことになつた。

シヤムへ最初の
鐵　道　使　節

シヤム國鐵道用の貨車三百輛は過般日，英，米，獨，佛等廿七ケ國の競爭入札によりベルギーに落札せるもシヤム國政府は我國鐵道技術の優秀なるを認め鐵道省の斡旋により我國に對し正式註文を發した。よつて引受會社において二月末までに製作納入に決したが，鐵道省としては我國より外國に車輛を輸出するのは滿洲國に次で第二回目のことでもありシヤム政府の懇請もあるので之が指導役を派遣することになり十二月十二日午後三時神戶出帆の歐洲航路白山丸でシヤムへ初めての『鐵道使節』たる鐵道省工作局車輛課長德永晋作氏が晴の鹿島立ちをした，シンガポール上陸後凡八十日間シヤム國各方面を視察すると共に同國から鐵道省へ申込のあつた鐵道車輛の細目協定をなすとのこと。

國際佛教通報局

名譽局長	高楠順次郎
局長	大村桂巖
幹事	鷹谷俊之
同	稻葉文海
同	淺野研眞

顧問（順序不同）

〃	宇井伯壽
〃	朝倉曉瑞
〃	羽溪了諦
〃	荻原雲來
〃	干潟龍祥
〃	鈴木大拙
〃	鈴木宗忠
〃	天岫接三
〃	長井眞琴
〃	松本文三郎
〃	椎尾辨匡
〃	宇野圓空
〃	赤松智城
〃	大森禪戒
〃	矢吹慶輝
〃	小野清一郎
〃	加藤精神
〃	姉崎正治
〃	本田義英
〃	關本龍門
〃	佐伯定胤
〃	花田凌雲
〃	河野法雲
〃	高岡隆心
〃	小林瑞淨
〃	山邊習學
〃	赤沼智善
〃	本多惠隆
〃	大森亮順
〃	河口慧海
〃	山川智應
〃	常盤大定
〃	谷本富
〃	常盤井堯猷
〃	大谷尊由
〃	大谷瑩潤
〃	水野梅曉
〃	柴田一能
〃	安藤正純
〃	下村壽一
〃	菊澤季麿
〃	乘杉嘉壽
〃	芝田徹心
〃	淺野孝之
〃	渡邊哲信
〃	小野玄妙
〃	柳澤健
〃	重光葵
〃	金倉圓照
〃	立花俊道

國際佛教通報局定款

名稱

第一，本局を國際佛教通報局と稱す

事務所

第二，本局の事務所を全日本佛教靑年會聯盟本部に置く

目的

第三，本局は日本內海及海外に向つて佛教事情の通報をなし，且つ佛教徒相互間の各種便宜を計るを以て目的とす

事業

第四，本局の目的を達成するため左記の事業を行ふ

イ，日本內地及世界各國より佛教事情に關する質問の通報を行ふ

ロ，必要に應じ日本語及世界各國語を以て佛教事情の通報を行ふ

ハ，外國人の日本觀光に際しては各國の便益を與へ，特にその佛教に關する方面に於て之を爲す

ニ，定時或は隨時に各國語を以て文書の刊行をなす

ホ，その他必要と認めたる事業を行ふ

役員

第五，本局の事務を處理するため左の役員を置く

イ，局長　一名

ロ，幹事　三名

ハ，評議員　若干名

局長は本局　を總括す

幹事は本局の事務を處理す

評議員は局長の提案に依る重要事務を審議す

第六，評議員は左記の者を以て之に充つ

イ，全日本佛教靑年會館聯盟理事及主事

ロ，全日本佛教靑年會聯盟理事會に於て推薦したる者

第七，局長及幹事は評議員會に於て決定す

第八，役員の仕期は二ヶ年とす（但し重任を妨げず）

經費

第九，本局の經費は左記のものに依て之を支辨す

イ，本局基金の活用

ロ，寄附金

ハ，その他の收入

補則

第十，本定款に記載せられざる事項は，凡て評議員會に於て協議す

第十一，第一回の役員は全日本佛教靑年會聯盟理事會に於て決定す

定價	一部 金二十錢	送料二錢
	一年 金二圓四十錢	送料不要

昭和十年四月卅日第三種郵便物認可
昭和十年十二月廿七日印刷（每月一回一日發行）
昭和十一年一月一日發行

編輯發行兼印刷人　東京市外吉祥寺337　淺野研眞

印刷所　東京市牛込區早稻田鶴卷町107　康文社印刷所　電話牛込（34）1950番 5049番

發行所　東京市神田區一ツ橋二の三　國際佛教通報局　電話九段（33）4428番　振替東京83015番

昭和十年四月三十日第三種郵便物認可
昭和十年十二月二十七日印刷納本（毎月一回
昭和十一年一月一日發行（一日發行）
國際佛教通報　第二卷　第一號

第　二　回

汎太平洋佛教青年會大會

紀　要

THE PROCEEDINGS
of
THE Second
General Conference
of
Pan-Pacific Young Buddhists' Associations

(in Japanese, Chinese and English)

Held at Tokyo & Kyoto, July 18–23, 1934

Price ¥ 3.00

Compiled & Published
by
The Federation of All Y.B. As. of Japan,
Tokio, Kanda, Hitotsubashi, II-3

昭和十年四月三十日第三種郵便物認可　昭和十一年一月二十八日印刷納本　昭和十一年二月一日發行（毎月一回一日發行）第二卷　第二號

The International Buddhist Bulletin

國際佛教通報

第二卷 **昭和十一年二月** 第二號〔Vol. II. **Feb.** $\frac{2502}{1936}$ No. 2.〕

要　目〔**Contents**〕

東　京　**國際佛教通報局**　發　行
The International Buddhist Information Bureau
Tokyo, Kanda, Hitotsubashi, II—3

Staff of the Bureau

Hon. President	J. Takakusu
President	K. Ohmura
Secretary	S. Takagai
〃	B. Inaba
〃 (in chief)	Ken Assano

Advisers	H. Ui
〃	G. Asakura
〃	R. Hatani
〃	U. Ogiwara
〃	R. Higata
〃	T. Suzuki
〃	S. Suzuki
〃	S. Amakuki
〃	S. Nagai
〃	B. Matsumoto
〃	E. Uno
〃	C. Akamatsu
〃	Z. Ohmori
〃	K. Yabuki
〃	S. Onoh
〃	S. Katoh
〃	M. Anezaki
〃	G. Honda
〃	R. Sekimoto
〃	J. Sahegi
〃	R. Hanada
〃	H. Kohno
〃	R. Takaoka
〃	Z. Kobayashi
〃	S. Yamabe
〃	C. Akanuma
〃	E. Honda
〃	R. Ohmori
〃	E. Kawaguchi
〃	C. Yamakawa
〃	D. Tokiwa
〃	T. Tanimoto
〃	G. Tokiwai
〃	S. Ohtani
〃	E. Ohtani
〃	B. Mizuno
〃	I. Shibata
〃	S. Ando
〃	J. Shimomura
〃	S. Kikuzawa
〃	K. Norisugi
〃	T. Shibata
〃	K. Asano
〃	T. Watanabe
〃	G. Onoh
〃	K. Yanagizawa
〃	M. Shigemitsu
〃	E. Kanakura
〃	S. Tachibana

國際佛教通報局

名譽局長	高楠順次郎
局長	大村桂巖
幹事	鷹谷俊之
同	稻葉文海
同	淺野研眞

顧　問（順序不同）

〃	宇井伯壽
〃	朝倉曉瑞
〃	羽溪了諦
〃	荻原雲來
〃	干潟龍祥
〃	鈴木大拙
〃	鈴木宗忠
〃	天岫接三
〃	長井眞琴
〃	松本文三郎
〃	椎尾辨匡
〃	宇野圓空
〃	赤松智城
〃	大森禪戒
〃	矢吹慶輝
〃	小野清一郎
〃	加藤精神
〃	姉崎正治
〃	本田義英
〃	關本龍門
〃	佐伯定胤
〃	花田凌雲
〃	河野法雲
〃	高岡隆心
〃	小林瑞淨
〃	山邊習學
〃	赤沼智善
〃	本多惠隆
〃	大森亮順
〃	河口慧海
〃	山川智應
〃	常盤大定
〃	谷本　富
〃	常盤井堯猷
〃	大谷尊由
〃	大谷瑩潤
〃	水野梅曉
〃	柴田一能
〃	安藤正純
〃	下村壽一
〃	菊澤季麿
〃	乘杉嘉壽
〃	芝田徹心
〃	淺野孝之
〃	渡邊哲信
〃	小野玄妙
〃	柳澤　健
〃	重光　葵
〃	金倉圓照
〃	立花俊道

RELIGIA EDUKADO EN JAPANA LERNEJO

de **Sosei Nakaniŝi**

En japana lernejo la religia edukado estis tute ne permesita antaŭe per la 12a instrukcio kiu estas pubrikiĝita en la 3a de Aŭgusto, 1899. de Japana Ministerio por Pubrika Klerigado.

Pri la stariĝo de ĝenerala edukado ekster religio:

"La stariĝo de ĝenerala edukado ekster religio estas tiel necesa. Do, en ŝtataj lernejoj aŭ aliaj sankciaj lernejoj eĉ kiel ekster lecionon ne permesas fari la religian edukadon kaj la ceremonion de religio."

Citita estas la resumo de la instrukcio.

Kial la ministerio pubrikigis tian instrukcion? Tiu estas kaŭzita de la ekzisto iu gimunazia estro kiu estis kristano kaj li faris tielajn dirojn kaj agojn pro sia religia kredo kiel kontraŭ ŝtatan formon de Japanujo. Kaj ĝi fariĝis la problemon unu gravan en japana edukada kampo. Pro tiu la ministerio timis naskiĝon de la malbona influo en la edukado pro la religia edukado en lernejo, kaj ekprenis la politikon apartigi religion kaj edukadon.

Sed la ministerio tute ne opiniis ke religio kontraŭas al edukado, nur malaktive evitis la malbonan influon. Tamen kelkaj edukistoj erarkomprenis per la citita instrukcio ke religio estas malutila por edukado, sekve ili kompreneble el lernejo forigis religion kaj plie naskiĝis la emo kiu malrespektas religieman koron de la lernantoj. Kaj ĉi tiu emo fine venigis materialismon kaj kaŭzis socie kaj ideo malfacilajn aferojn.

Religio estas kompreneble super regno, sed ankaŭ devas konscii regnon ĉar daŭriĝo de homa vivo estas absolute ne ebla ekster regno.

Vere religio tute ne kontraŭas al la edukado, prefere estas necesa por kompletiĝo de la edukado kiel plej altan spiritan vivon de homoj.

Tial en la edukado kampo japana iom post iom vekiĝis la justa kompreno pri religio, precipe en la 1925a, la konferenco tutjapana de

knabina liceaestro unuanime decidis jenan por gardi virinan virton kaj bonigi virinan ideon.

La decido:

Penadu evoluigi religian kredon kaj donu favoron por la kredo, al liceaninoj.

Sekvante je 1926a, en la tutjapana kongreso de elementlernejan instruistoj la demando "Kian rimedon ni devas preni por kulturi la fundamenton de la religia kredo en geknaboj ĉe elementlernejo," estas diskutita kaj decidis jenan.

1) La instruistoj pligrandigu sian komprenon pri religio kaj per la starigo de religia kredo plimultigu sian kleriĝon.

a) Direktigu la atenton al religia edukado en la pedagogia liceo.

b) Per speciala kurso pligrandigu la komprenon de la instruistoj pri religio.

c) La instruistoj diligente ĉiam penadu la studon pri la enhavo kaj la organizo de religio.

2) Ĉiam konduku la geknabojn por memvole kaj memkontrole fari sian lernejan vivon, kaj atente evoluigu la religian volon interne aperiĝan en la geknaboj.

3) Tra tuta lerneja vivo ĉiu okaze penadu evoluiĝon de religiemo de geknaboj.

a) Prenu plimulte religieman materialon por ĉiuj lecionoj.

b) Rekomendu eksterlecionan legaĵon kiu enhavas riĉe religian materialon.

c) Kiel eble plimulte religie uzu la materialojn de ĉiuj lecionoj.

ĉ) Per tiuj okazaĵoj en la lernejo, kiuj estas la ceremonio, kondolenca kunveno, memora kunsido, vizito al tombo kaj ceteraj, kulturigu la pieman koron de la geknaboj.

4) Atentu jenajn punktojn de religia edukado.

a) Evitu fariĝon de eklezia edukado.

b) Komprenigu al la geknaboj la esencon pri la elekto sian kredon estas tute libera.

c) Instruu ke ankaŭ respektu la kredon de aliaj.

ĉ) Sciigu ke ni devas foigi superstiĉon.

Tiela vekiĝo de la edukada kampo pri religio, fine farigis al Japana Ministerio por Pubrika Klerigado, la elsendon pri religio jenan oficialan sciigon al ĉiuj estroj de universitatoj, ĉiuj lernejoj kaj tutjapanaj prefektoj, en 1935.

La oficiala sciigo:

1) La religia edukado devas esti nature farata de la religia kredo

en ĉiu hejmo samtempe ankaŭ dependas de la ago de la religia rondo kaj la lerneja edukado devas sinteni neŭtrale al ĉiuj sektoj kaj eklezioj.

2) En la lernejo oni devas sinteni al la religia edukado en la socio kaj la hejmo.

a) Nedifektigu la religieman koron kiu kreskiĝas en sia hejmo kaj socio, kaj zorgante eliĝitan religieman deziron el la koro de la lernantoj iel ajn ne malgravigu kaj ne malrespektu.

b) Justan kredon respektu samtempe iel ajn tian superstiĉon kiel ĝi difektigas socian ordon kaj bonan moron, penadu disigi.

3) En la lernejo la eklezia edukado estas tute ne permesita, sed por kulturi la personecon tra lerneja edukado la kulturado religieman koron, estas necesega, kompreneble la lerneja edukado devas esti farata kiu centro estas la imperiestra alparolo pri la edukado, tial oni ne devas fari per tia rimedo kiel ĝi kontraŭas al la imperiestra alparolo. En la lerneja edukado pri kulturiĝo de religia emocio prefere bezonataj punktoj de la zorgo estas jene.

a) En la lecionoj pri moralo kaj civitano pli atente zorgu pri religio.

b) En la filozofia instruo pli grandigu la komprenon pri religio kaj speciale prizorgu pri la kulturiĝo de religia emocio.

c) En la historia instruo zorge uzu la efikon de religio en la nacia kulturo, religian influon je la konataj herooj kaj la biografion de la religiuloj.

ĉ) En aliaj lecionoj laŭ la materialoj zorge uzu religieman.

d) Por la kulturo de la lernantoj, en la biblioteko havu religiajn dokumentojn.

e) Uzante la okazon de kondolenca kunveno, pikniko, vojaĝo kaj ceteraj, faru kulturiĝon de religia emocio.

f) En la limo kiu ne fariĝas la baron al aliaj lecionoj, aŭskultigu la paroladon de noble karakteraj religiuloj, al la lernantoj por sia kulturiĝo.

g) Inter kaj ekster la lernejo sendiference la studon de la lernantoj kaj la instruistoj pri religio aŭ religia rondo grandanime forlasu kaj tenu la kondukon.

ĝ) Je la realigo de cititaj speciale zorgu la dekliniĝon de unu sekto aŭ unu eklezio.

Ĉi tiu estas ja la epokofaranta de japana ministerio, ankaŭ ni povas diri ke la ministerio komprenis la necesecon de religia edukado. Do, ni budhanoj devas komprenante ĉi tiun novan direkton de la ministerio penadi por la plenumiĝo de la direkto.

Correct Buddhist Dates

King Suddhadana, King Binbisara, King Sukkra Buddha, King Pesenadi of Kosala and King Singhabahoo was ruling in adjoining countries of India in 6 century B.C. This is correct historical record.

King Suddhodana was the Father of Prince Siddhartha who became Lord Buddha, The Sakya Muni.

King Singhabahoo was the Father of Prince Vijiya, the first king of Lanka (Ceylon). He landed to Lanka on the 80th year of the age of Prince Siddhartha, in the year after Mahapari Nibbana of Lord Bdddha, who first visited to the palace of King Bimbisara, with 1036 disciples on the 6th year after renunciation or on the 1st year of the Enlightenment as Buddha.

The Prince Siddhartha who became Buddha married Princess Yasodera Devi of the same age of 16 years. 13 years they had no children and at the age of 29 a son was born, and was named "RAHULA"

Prince Siddhartha was in Kapilawathoo when He got the son called "RAHULA." The great renunciation of Prince Siddhartha was happened in the same year, of the Birth of Prince "RAHULA." who was ordained by Buddaha as the first Samenera at the age of 7 years, or 7 years after the Enlightenment.

Prince Siddhartha became "Buddha" our Supreme Lord.

Prince Siddhartha was in ascetic life for 6 years and in the age 35 became Buddha and after 45 years or the age of 80 He attained Maha Parinibbana.

Prince Vijeya landing to Ceylon with 700 men and established his Kingdom in Ceylon in 544 B,C. on the same year of Māha Parinibbana of Lord Buddha.

During this time Lord Buddha's Father (King Siddhadana) died and his brother was ruling the Kingdom of Sakyas of Kapilawathoo, Several Princes of that family and the only Princess Baddha-Katchana came to Ceylon and settled and ruled. This is the best family who knows the correct dates of Buddha and that History is the best authority.

Now Buddhists of other Countries naturally create mistakes in Buddhist dates and purposely make readers of their books to create doubts.

By the above stated Historical events I find these dates to be correct. But we must understand that the Europian year start in January and the Indian year start in about middle of April. Thus some writers calculate 623 B.C. instead of 624 B.C.

624 B.C. On the full moon day of Vaisaka (the Month of May) Prince Siddhartha was born to Queen Mahamaya Devi the elder sister of Prajapati Devi.

508 B.C. Prince Siddhartha married Princess Yasadera Devi of the same age at the age of 16 years.

595 B.C. Prince Rahula was born and the great renunciation of Prince Siddhartha happened at the 29 years of his age.

589 B.C. The Enlightenment of Prince Siddhartha happened and became The Buddha, on the fulmoon day of Vaisaka at the age of 35 years and Dhamma chaka sutta was proclaimed.

589 B.C. Sujatha gave to Bosat Siddhartha the milk rice gift in a golden Pattra in the previous month of Vaisaka (May)

582 B.C. Prince Rahula was ordained by Buddha on his first visit to Kapilawathu when the Prince Rahula accompanied Lord Buddha from Kapilawathu palace.

570 B.C. Prince Nanda (the son of King Siddhadana and the only son of Queen Prajapathi Devi) was ordained by the Maha Sangha of Maha Vihara in Jetawanarama and on the same or next year probably Nanda was accompanied by Buddha to Himalayas and visited China and heavens.

543 or 544 B.C. Is the 80th year of the age of Buddha.

543 or 544 B.C. Prince Vijava established the Kingdom of Lanka then called Taprobane and now it is called Ceylon, Buddha visited 3 times to Lanka.

544 B.C. On the fullmoon day of Vaisaka the Maha Pari Nibbana Sutra was proclaimed by Buddha and attained the Permanent Peace Nibbana.

566 B.C. Nanda and Buddha must have visited again to Northern and Eastern Countries.

In some records of the Eastern Countries, I find 566 as the birth day of Buddha instead of calling it as a visiting date. When we add 566 and 1934 it becomes 2500 years according to Eastern record.

By SRIJI NAWANSA SWAMY MAHA THERO, Delegate to Panpacific Buddhist Conference, Tokyo; Secretary of Mahasangharajasabha; President of Buddhist World United Society.

To Mr. K. Assano

Dear Sir,

I send you these correct Buddhist dates. I myself got out of doubts created on these correct dates by my reading the true Buddhist record of original text after having studied with great perseverance I got out of doubts and found these dates to be correct. They agree to original history and archeological findings. Non Buddhists publish books with wrong Buddhist dates purposely to create doubts in the minds of the readers with a view of establishing their propaganda works in Buddhist countries and to prevent the non Buddhists to believe in Buddhist records and hinder them finding the truth therefore you must be very careful in publishing Buddhist dates in your magazine with a international view.

I kindly request you not to allow non Buddhists to create doubts on Buddhist Monks, records by reading your Journal.

I am sending you these dates to enable you to put befor the world correct Buddhist dates.

I am yours sincerity,

Sriji N. Swamy

Pyramids discovered in Japan

by Atsuharu Sakai

"I shall not come back alive before I discover a pyramid." So said Mr. Shogun Sakai, the discoverer of a pyramid in Japan, when he departed on a trip in search of it, and he did find one in the Prefecture of Hiroshima on Apr. 23, 1934.

Mr. Sakai, who is a great authority on the mythological history of Japan, had long been looking for a pyramid in Japan with the firm belief that she must have pyramids, partly because, according to his theory, Japan has a much longer history than Egypt has and partly because Japan is a country of heliolatry; the Egyptian pyramid being originally erected for sun-worshipping. When, therefore, he was told of a mountain that resembles an Egyptian pyramid, in the Prefecture of Hiroshima, he already discovered in his mind's eye an actual one, which he set out to discover.

Mr. Sakai did not take the train at the Central Station of Tokyo, but instead he boarded an electric train at Shinjiku, intending to visit the Afuri Shrine on Mt. Oyama on his way to Hiroshima. Accordiug to Mr. Sakai, that shrine was dedicated to the "God of Africa," who had close relations with the Egyptian pyramid and he thought it proper for one of his mission to pay homage to this particular shrine at the outset of his trip. He offered a prayer at the shrine and obtained a charm. He opened it. It contained, besides the names of three pre-historic gods of Japan, some letters, which the priest of the shrine could not decipher. Mr. Sakai, however, who is a scholar of the Jindai-moji (or Gods' days letters), which were used in Japan before the Chinese ideographs now in use were introduced to Japan, read them easily, and from these letters he obtained a hint that he was on the right track.

Upon his arrival in Hiroshima Prefecture, Mr. Sakai made an enquiry at several places, such as

primary schools and village offices, but none of them had any knowledge of the mountain he was in search of. He travelled from place to place, being directed in this way by one and in that by another, but to little purpose. Disappointed of his apparently fool's errand, he was on the point of abandoning his search, when he was informed of the village of Shinseki (literally, God-stone), and of the mountain, Ashitake or Mt. Reed, where the people of the village had got large quantities of stone some twenty years before. These names sounded good to his eager ear, and he succeeded, with great diffiiculties, in finding his way to the foot of the mountain that he had come all the way from Tokyo to find.

Mr. Sakai climbed up the mountain, pathless as it then was, with a few people who kindly offered assistance in his search for a pyramid, and what should have attracted his eager eye, on reaching the top, but three dolmens, one too utterly ruined to be recognized and the other two almost intact and perfect. Dolmens are rare and far between in Japan, but these particular ones seem to be more perfect than any yet discovered in this country, for instead of being three stones artificially arranged, they consist of three stones in their natural position. Mr. Sakai thinks that they are ideal dolmens, because, according to his theory, a dolmen is more in the nature of a stand for an offering made at sun-worshipping, than an ancient grave as it is generally considered to be.

A few steps below the dolmens, one will see a stone about 15 ft. in diameter and 12 ft. high. This is plainly a mirror-stone, which is essential to an Egyptian pyramid. Not far from the mirror-stone is found a stone-pillar, 2 ft. square and over 10 ft. long or high. There were three such pillars before, the people will tell you, but Mr. Sakai holds that there must have been four of them, as they are pointers or direction-stones, all pointing to the north polar star of the time when the pyramid was erected. On the top of this pillar there is a hole large enough to hold a ball 5 or 6 inches large, and the people of the village say that a "Yako-no-tama" or a noctilucent gem, as it may be translated, used to throw its rays of light in former days.

The sun had set by this time. It was too dark for the party to make any further research. They had not yet discovered the pyramid itself, but these finds were enough to convince them that the mountain was an ancient place of sun-worship. The party had come down a short distance, when one of them spied a pyramid-shaped mountain standing right in front of them. "That's the pyramid, sure." came unawares from the lips of Mr. Sakai. The pyramid was discovered.

An urgent business called Mr. Sakai back to Tokyo, and it was about a week later that he explored the pyramid-shaped monntain, which was then covered with bushes and shrubs. He expected to see a hole on the northern side, which he chose in climbing up the mountain, but he found nothing of his expectation on that side, which had been destroyed by the innocent villagers who had carried stones off. Towards the top, or to be more exact, 10 or 12 yards from the top, his attention was attracted to an antiquated natural stone, too singular to escape his keen eye, though at that time the discoverer failed to come to any conclusion as to its use. Going a little further up, he discovered a few more stones that he thought formed a part of the Iwasaka, or rock-boundary (stone-henge), of the sacred precincts of the pyramid. They were arranged in a square, though the northern side was destroyed, and the antiquated stone must have been placed at one corner of the stone-boundary. Encouraged by this important find, Mr. Sakai now looked for the sun-stone of the pyramid, and it was found in the center of another set of stones arranged in a circle about 10 ft. from the square row. The sun-stone measures over 10 ft. Then Mr. Sakai discovered two sets of direction-stones, one pointing south and north and the other east and west.

The pyramid that Mr. Sakai thus discovered is situated at the village of Moto-mura (literally, Main-village) in the county (kori) of Hiba-gun in Hiroshima Prefecture, its bearing being 133° 6′ E and 34° 50′ N. It consists of a sun-stone surrounded by a circular row of 16 stones in a square row of another 16 stones. He does not yet know whether the pyramid contains the remains of any pre-historic chief or ruler of the country or whether, as a pyramid was originally meant, it is a mere place of sun-whorship. According to his calculation, this pyramid was erected 22,000 years ago, judging from the direction of the pointers, during the reign of

Yahirodono-tsukuri-mikoto, who was one of the rulers of the Ugaya-fukiayedzu-no-mikoto dynasty in the pre-historic days.

Two more sets of similar stone-arrangements are discovered: one near the city of Takayama in Hida Province and the other near Lake Towada, a national park, in the northern part of Japan, the former being on a plain field. Mr. Banzan Toya, a painter, who has studied Lake Towada and its vicinity for over forty years, is the discoverer of the former, which is situated near Mt. Herai (meaning "sun-coming"). According to Col. S. Kamihara, the local director of the Association of Reservists, who has made a thorough study of the one at Takayama, it is plain that, though some stones have been removed from its henge, this pyramid consisted of sixteen stones arranged in a square around the sun-stone, which, as he told the writer, must weigh at least 5,000 kan (kan = 3.75 kg). A plan is now being made of restoring this pyramid into its original shape.

An ancient record, that was recently discovered in Japan, calls this arrangement of stones "Hiramitsutono," which must mean "sun-ray-permeating-hall." According to this old record, "pyramid" is a perversion of the Japanese word.

Lastly, Col. J. Churchward, authority on the sunken continent of Mu, says:

"The emblem of the new king was still the sun, but in order to show that he was a subject of the Motherland (Mu) or a part of it, only one half of the orb was shown above the horizon, with rays ascending from it." (Col. J. Churchward: The Lost Continent of Mu, P. 125.)

Mr. Sakai discovered a large rock answering this description. The rock is situated at a little distance from the village of Moto-mura, where he discovered the pyramid, and it measures some 200 yards in diamater. He named it the "Imperial-Crest-Rock," because it is a semicircular disk resembling the Imperial crest. The writer has not seen the rock, but judging from his description, it seems to represent a piece of art left by the long-extinct race of Mu, though a farther study is of course needed.

Buddhist Universities In Tokyo

Taisho University

The long-left desire for establshing a university through co-operation of various sects of Buddhism and under their joint management has been realized in the establishment of a university through the united efforts of the Tendai Sect, Buzan school of the Shingi-Shingon Sect, and the Johdo Sect.

The Taisho Daigaku, then called Shukyo Daigaku, was established in September in the 20th year of Meiji in Shiba Park, Shiba Ward, Tokyo, the first name of the institution being Johdo Shugaku Honko (school of the Joho Sect). In the 31st year of Meiji, it was renamed the Johdoshu Kotogakuin (higher school of the sect). At the same time a college named Semmon Gakuin (professional institution) was established in Kyoto with a view to admitting graduate students.

In the 37th year of the same era it was renamed Johdoshu Daigaku, and at the same time the school in Kyoto was renamed Semmon-bu of the University. Three years later the school was again renamed Shukyo Daigaku. In the first year of Taisho the system was further reformed, and a preparatory course of two years, regular course of three years, and post-graduate coure of three years were established, while the Semmon-bu in Kyoto was made independent of the institution in Tokyo, and called Bukkyo Semmon Gakko (Buudhist college). Later in the 4th year of Taisho the school system was again reformed, and two department of religion and pedagogy were established, the former being intended to train teachers for service of the sect, and the latter to turn out teachers of the national language and Chinese classics. In the 13th year of Taisho the religious department of the school was twice reorganized in system. Two years later, the preparatory course of the religious department was abolished, while the pedagogical department was transferred as a higher normal course of the Semmon-bu of Taisho University. Since its establishment, the school has turned out over one thousand graduates.

Komazawa University

The Komazawa University of Tokyo, which is under the direct control of the Soto sect has its origin in Sendanrin in the Kichijoji temple, Komagome, and in Shishikutsu in the Seishoji temple, Shiba, which though originally founded by the Soto sect enjoyed a quite favorable reputation, having actually turned out many prominent priests.

Sendanrin was established about 327 years ago by Tenkai Sōjō, the eminent priest, it having first been built on the premises of the Kichijoji temple, Surugadai. Later it was removed to the Kichijoji temple, Komagome, when the institution was enlarged. With the great reform in the educational sytem consequent upon the Imperial Restoration, the Soto sect finding it necessary to found its own independent educational institution, established its school in the eighth year of Meiji.

In the fifteen year of Meiji, it was removed to Higakubo, Azabu and renamed Soto Daigakurin, it being the first authorized Buddhist university, the courses on religion, philosophy, Japanese and Chinese classics, and foreign languages were given.

College Status Granted

Simultaneously with the promulgation of the government regulations regarding the colleges in the thirty-sixth year of the Meiji, the Soto Koto Gakurin was united with the Soto Gakuin. The institution was recognized by the Education Ministry and was raised to the status of college. Later in the thirty-seventh year of Meiji, the Soto Daigakurin was reorganized and named Soto University.

In the 2nd year of Taisho, the educational system of the institution was again reorganized. In the thirteenth year of Taisho (1924), a new school building was constructed, which was completed the next year.

University Standing

The fellowing year, the institution was recognized as a university in accordance with the university regulations, and the name of the same institution was changed to Komazawa University, dividing the course into three departments, Buddhistic, Oriental, and Cultural. The course of the preparatory department was fixed at three years and the regular department at three years. The same year the inauguration ceremony of the same university was held with the presence of Sekizen Arai, Chief abbot of the head temple of the Sect.

The president of the university is Abbot Zenkai Omori. Abbot Shundo Tachibana is superintendent.

Rissho University

Rissho University, located at Shinagawa, Tokyo, is an institution of higher learning founded upon the creed of Nichiren, a Buddhist reformer of the 13th century and founder of the Nichiren sect.

Founded in 1909, the university was reorganized in 1924. It has five departments for the study of Buddhism, philosophy, sociology, history and literature. Attached to the university is a special school devoted to the training of missionaries and teachers of the national language, Chinese classics, geography and history. There are 122 men on the teaching staff headed by Rev. Ryuzan Shimizu, President, Rev. Kwankyo Moriya, Director of College Courses, Rev, Kwanko Mochizuki, Director of Preparatory Couses, Rev. Nikki Kimura, Director of the Attached Special School, and Rev. Zeryu Nakajo, Manager. Its alumni numbers 1,616 graduates. The enrollment for the current year includes 837 students.

At present the University covers an area of 43,300 square meters while the buildings occupy 9,560 square meters.

The main building and the library are ferro-concrete, while the auditorium, dormitory and the students' hall are wooden structures in genuinely Japanese style. The domitory where all preparatory course students live is worthy of notice for here they undergo a special training which includes the Nichiren Sect rites and moral culture based on the creed of the saintly founder. For a dormitory of students, it is an unusually large structure perfectly equipped from the viewpoints of both hygiene and recreation.

To promote friendship among the students, there is the Students Society composed of members from the departments of General Affairs, Lecture, Literature, Sports, and newspaper, to one of which every freshman is required to belong according to his preference. The society is a self-governing organization, but does not scorn the occasional advices of the university authorities.

The Nichiren Sect had its own schools for training missionaries as early as 1581. There are at present nine educational institutions under the sect, of which Rissho University is recognized since it conforms with the university regulations of the Government.

New Buddhist Hall to be Built

All-Japan Federation Plans Fund Campaign for Edifice to Honor Shotoku Taishi

Building Will Be Ready for 1940 World Conference if Japan Decides to Be Host

The All-Japan Federation of Young Buddhists' Associations is working on an ambitious plan for the construction of the *Taishi-Den* or the Taishi Hall to commemorate the life and work of Shotoku Taishi, who rendered great service in converting the Japanese nation to Buddhism. The proposed building will cost ¥2,000,000, and the campaign to raise the sum will begin next month when the appointment of the fund campaign committee is completed.

The Rev. Sonyu Otani, Lord Abbot of the West Hongan Temple, has accepted the appointment as chairman of the committee. The special committee of the federation in charge of the project is asking prominent persons of Buddhist faith in all walks of life to become members of the committee.

The federation has no appropriate modern building of its own large enough to accommodate activities of local organizations. Leaders of the federation are particularly anxious to have the proposed building because of the prospect that Japan may call a world convention of Buddhists in 1940 to commemorate the 2600th anniversary of the accession of the Emperor Jimmu, the first Emperor of Japan. A plan for the convention under the auspices of the federation has been under the serious consideration for some time.

Other Groups Co-operate

The federation is supported in its building project by the National Council of Buddhist Sects and other Buddhist institutions in the country. There are more than 100,000 Young Buddhists' Associations in Japan which will cooperate with their headquarters in Tokyo in the fund campaign.

The conversion of Japan to Buddhism took place in the sixth and seventh centuries, particularly under the powerful influence of Prince Shotoku who was a son of the Emperor Yomei, Regent to the Empress Regnant Suiko (593-628), and 33rd ruler of Japan. The Horyuji Temple in Yamato, built more than 1300 years ago, which is the oldest wooden structure extant in the world, is one of the temples erected by the Prince. The proposed building will be characterized by the graceful architectural style of the period in which the Prince lived.

Mr. Junken Wada, architect, who was born and brought up in a Buddhist temple and who has specialized in Buddhist architecture, has drawn the plans. According to his explanation, the building will represent the spirit of modern Japan, with the temple architectural style prevailing during the reign of the Empress Regnant Suiko executed in the modern technique. One of the attractive features of the building will be the roofs, which will have graceful curves and ornaments such as the roofs and eaves of various structures in the compound of the Horyuji Temple.

The building, according to the plan, will be four stories of iron and concrete with a frontage of 258 feet and depth of 60 feet. The wings of the building on each side will extend 120 feet with a depth of 36 feet. The central section of the main building will have an ornate tower which will rise two additional stories, with floor space of about 60 feet square each. The total floor space of the building will be $3^1/_4$ acres. The building is expected to be erected in the neighborhood of Surugadai.

Many Conveniences Planned

The basement will be equipped with a gymnasium, restaurant, barber shop and other conveniences for association members. The main floor will be chiefly devoted to offices, a Buddhist museum, social welfare centers, a library and

New Hall to be built

conference rooms. The auditorium, research rooms, more conference rooms and an exhibition hall will be on the second floor. The third floor will be occupied chiefly by social and recreation rooms and offices of different sects of Buddhism, while the fourth floor will be entirely devoted to a dormitory with 60 large and small rooms to accommodate members of local organizations when they come to the Capital. The fifth and the sixth floors will be used for miscellaneous purposes such as lecture meetings, wedding ceremonies, motion pictures and the like.

The officers of the Federation of Young Buddhists' Associations have not yet decided whether they should promote a world conference, but if they do, the event is expected to be announced at the 3rd Pan-Pacific Conference of Young Buddhists's Associations which is scheduled to be held in 1938.

Japanese News

Painting of Kannon

Mr. Kigen Nagai, who specialises in Buddhist paintings, has presented a picture of Kannon to the Italian Embassy.

The artist taking side with Italy in the Italian-Ethiopian campaign, has presented his painting to encourage the country he favors.

The figure of Kannon in the picture is made of 50,000 characters taken from Buddhist sutras.

Kannon Heard

Ryu, the pet deg of Shintaro Yasukawa, a printer by trade, living at Harukicho in Hongo, disappeared some days ago.

The wife and daughter of Yasukawa went daily to pray to Kannon at the Buddha of Mercy Temple in Asakusa that the dog would return home.

Their prayers were answered and Ryu rushed into the house and was welcomed warmly.

New Education Policy

The opinion that the worship of Amaterasu Omikami, Imperial Ancestor, is the foundation of the new policy for revising the educational system of Japan, and that a place for worshipping the Sun Goddess should be established at each school, was submitted to the second general meeting of the Education System Improvement Council Thursday afternoon at the Education Ministry.

Education Minister Genji Matsuda, chairman of the council, and forty members were present, and the proposal for the worship of Amaterasu Omigami in all schools was presented by several members. The opinions presented at Friday's general meeting will be further discussed at a third meeting which will be held early next year.

Considered Foundation

The view submitted to the general meeting Friday comprised the following points:

1. The foundation of the new policy for improving the educational system is the worship of Amaterasu Omikami, and the place a worshipping the Imperial Ancestor is to be established at each school.

2. The theory that the Emperor is a Constitutional organ must be absolutely rejected. Scholarly studies are free, but all that are contrary to the national polity must be prohibited as part of the educational system.

3. The chief defect of the present educational system lies in regarding the faith mentioned in the record of the foundation of the nation as merely a faith, which is thererefor made independent of education. It is necessary to unite this fait with education.

4. The policy in improving the educational system must be to revive the great spirit of the Meiji Restoration. As a practical policy, efforts should be devoted to establishing a purely Japanese system of learning. For instance, Japanese history is to be included in the civil service examinations.

5. In giving education to the people, (1) the spirit of the family system should be thoroughly taught, (2) the primary school system is to be studied and revised in order to stimulate the spirit of national polity, (3) importance is to be given to practical vocational training.

6. The revised educational policy should be intended to educate the people to become good subjects under the Emperor, and to make them understand that in doing their common daily labor or work they can comply with the wishes of the Emperor. To perform one's own duty for itself is the spirit of the national polity. It is necessary for all Government offices to cooperate in fostering the spirit of the people.

Temple Burglar

When a funeral service was being held at Daisen-in in the town of Yaye, Aomori Prefecture, recently, drops of water began to fall through the ceiling on the assembled mourners.

A priest went up into the loft of the building to find out the cause of the strange moisture, and discovered at burglar asleep. He had been drinking sake and a bottle was overturned. He proved to be a man the police had been searching for, but who had cluded capture since he had taken refuge in the temple.

Ghosts of Tokyo Streets

An old priest wearing a white robe, and a venerable old woman have been seen early every morning for a considerable period praying at a certain spot at Kurumazaka, in Shitaya.

In early Meiji there was a temple cemetery at this place, but it disappeared when the city was reconstructed. Since then there have been many traffic accidents.

As it is thought that the souls of the departed still cling about the district and are the cause of the accidents. Kaiyu Orihara, a priest of the Rishodo temple in this quarter, and Mrs. Nami Murakami, 60 years of age, repair to the street early in the morning and offer their prayers. Since they have done so the accidents have decreased, and the people of the neighborhood flock to see the couple at their pious devotions.

Samisen With History

The samisen once owned by Nagoya Sansaburo, who assisted Okuni in the founding of Kabuki on the dry river-bed in Kyoto, has recently been presented to the Waseda Theater Museum by Count Hirokichi Mutsu.

This samisen has been treasured by the Mutsu family since Tokugawa days, and is different in shape to the modern instrument.

Narita Fudo Statue

The anniversary of the founding of Narita Fudo temple in Chiba Prefecture a thousand years ago, is being celebrated.

In this connection the treasured statue of the temple, books and articles of historic interest preserved at Narita are on exhibit at Takashimaya Department Store, Nihonbashi.

The famous statue of Fudo has not been shown to the public for 50 years.

When the box containing the statue arrived at Ryogoku station it was carried in a procession to Takashimaya.

Siam's Minister

His Majesty the Emperor granted an audience to Mr. Luang Pradit, Manudharm, Minister of the Interior in the Siamese Government, at the Phoenix Hall of the Imperial Palace at 10:30 a m., Jan. 7.

Mr. Manudharm was accompanied to the Imperial Palace by Mr. Phra Mitrakarm Raksha, the Siamese Minister in Tokyo.

The Siamese Home Minister arrived in Tokyo on December 30 from the United States aboard the N.Y.K. liner Taiyo Maru during the course of his world trip.

Foreign Minister Koki Hirota gave a luncheon at his official residence in honor of the visiting Siamese official. The Siamese Minister to Tokyo, Vice-Foreign Minister Mamoru Shigemitsu, and other officials of the Foreign Office were also present.

Minister Manudharm also attended a tea given by Finance Minister Korekiyo Takahashi at his official residence, at 3 p. m. Finance Minister Takahashi, Finance Vice-Minister Tsushima, and other officials of the Finance Department exchanged views with the guest on Japan-Siam friendship.

For Osaka Atter Nagoya Visit

Mr. Luang Pradit Manudharm, Siamese Minister of the Interior and his wife, who visited Nagoya Jan. 12 Sunday together with the Siamese Minister to Tokyo, Mr. Phra Mitrakarm Raksha and spent the night at the Mampei Hotel, paid a visit to the Japanese Siamese temple erected for the promotion of friendly relations between the two countries, that morning.

The visitors then attended a tea party given in their honor by Mr. Jirozaemon Ito, president of the Japan-Siamese Association, at his residence. At noon they were at a dinner given for them by Honorary Consul Kato at the Nagoya Hotel.

They leave Nagoya Station for Osaka at 5:06 p. m. that evening.

Order From Siam

The Department of Railways is constructing 8 locomotives for the Government of Siam which will be delivered this year.

The Japanese bid was accepted by Siam for locomotives and 300 freight trains.

Japanese Artist in India

Mr. Kosetsu Nousu, one of the most accomplished painters of Buddhist art in this country, has been engaged for some time past in paintimg a series of panels in the temple of Penara in India.

He went to India in 1932, but his work has not been completed owing to the bad weather in this district and to lack of financial support.

The Society for the Promotion of International Cultural Relations has granted the artist the sum of Yen 5,000 to continue his work which will be finished in March. It is thought that the series of paintings will be a contribution from Japan to the art of the world.

×

News has been received by Mr. Ishimaru, an official of the Department of Education, that his friend, Kasetsu Nousu, has completed his great wall paintings of the life of Buddha at a temple in Benares.

The artist, who is a specialist in

painting Buddhist pictures, started his great work 5 years ago, but experienced many difficulties.

He was about to give up when funds forwarded by the Society for the Promotion of International Cultural Relatious, the Nippon Buddhist Society and the Indo-Japan Society encouraged him to complete his work which is said to be one of the most remarkable series of wall paintings in the world.

Statue of Daikoku

General Senjuro Hayashi, ex-Minister of War, will present an old statue of Daikoku to Kongobuji on Koyasan in Wakayama Prefecture. It was discovered in a peculiar manner.

When General Hayashi was appointed Commander-in-Chief of the Army in Chosen at the time of the Manchurian Incident, he gave his brother-in-law a pot which he requested him to keep for him.

During his absence the pot was opened and it was discovered that there was a remarkable statue of Daikoku within.

The late Koun Takamura, the sculptor of Buddhist images, was of the opinion that it had been carved by the famous priest, Kukai.

Priest as Soldier

For the first time in the hiistory of Japan, the chief of a religious sect entered military service. Count Kōshō Otani, abbot of the Nishi-Honganji in Kyoto, 25 years of age, became a soldier on January 10.

He became a member of the motor-car Corps in Setagaya.

Graduating from the Literature Department of the Tokyo Imperial University last year, Count Otani has continued at his alma mater as a special student in history.

Special religious services was held at Nishi Honganji for a week from January 10 to pray for the priest who has become a soldier He will return to his mission as head of one of the largest Buddhist sects in the country at the end ot the year.

×

Count Kosho Otani, Abbott of the Nishi Honganji in Kyoto, who is now in military service with the Motor Car Corps, is reported to have taken kindly to the life of the soldier.

Recently an athletic contest was held in the compound of his regiment in Setagaya, and he made a new running record.

世界佛教聯合協會に就て

スリジー・スワミー

世界佛教聯合協會は，元來印度に成立し，異れる國家間の世界各地の佛教徒を向上せしめ合同せしめる爲に，マハサンガラージャサバの承認の下に，「佛教世界」と云ふ刊行物を發行して居る協會であります。そして共通の問題に於ては，南方及北方總ての宗派の書記的宗教的佛教機關として働き，かくして佛教界の幸福と平和の保護並びに增進を目的として働くものであります

協會はその仕事の實に大いなる事を知り，同時に佛徒の原教派と佛教界の他のすべての宗派とを統一するに要する救援の實に小なる事を知つてをります。

然し協會は旣に，この純にして崇高なる希求がすべての會員の意志を動かし，そして最後にその成功を齎すと云ふ信念の下に，勇敢にも活動を開始し，我が主佛陀の聖法による希望と見解の滿足を見出さうと努力してをります。而して今日夫は崇高なる領野に充分なる礎地を獲得しつゝあるのであります

世界の異れる國家間の色々の宗派に分割されてゐる我々聖なる佛徒の現在の狀態は，色々な原因に由り墮落し不滿足なものとなつてをります。かくして我々は世界のすべての佛徒が今こそ統一的に綜合的に目覺めそして我々の解放の爲に勇敢に元氣よく活躍すべき格恰の時であると云ふ事を知ります。

若し我々が日本，支那，シヤム，セイロン，ビルマ，印度，西藏，滿洲を度外したならば，佛敎敎義の信奉されてゐるアジアの佛教々國は，實際存しないと云ふ事を，すべての國の佛徒に覺らしめようではありませんか。何となれば，過去に於て眞理の聖教の榮光は，南は太平洋の諸島から，北はシベリヤの北極地方，その他世界の各地に擴がてつゐたからであります。

此の非佛教國の外交運動の非常時に於て，國家的宗派的な利己心が我が主佛陀の敎へられたる世界的宇宙的幸福の增進を阻めてゐる事を理解するのは佛徒の義務であります。何故かならば，かくの如き利己心は，人間の幸福を增進してゆくすべて高き價値ある有用な見解を破壞するものであるからです。それ故氣高くも佛徒は，かくの如き卑しい破壞的な思想から脫れ，佛教界と統一的に働き，日本，支那及び他の世界の佛教國を平和的な手段により保護し，色々な手段により外交的に弱小にせられてゐる東洋の文化と，その高き文明を進步せしめるのが佛徒の義務であります。

日本に於ける世界佛教聯合協會の設

立及び東京の世界佛教中央院建設は，世界の壓迫されたる又困窮せる佛教國を保護する意味に於て，日本，支那，滿洲國其他の國々にとつて一つの祝福であります。

東京に日本，支那，滿洲，西藏，セイロン，ビルマ，シヤム，その他の國々に於けるあらゆる宗派のあらゆる寺院の書記局として，佛教世界事務所を設置してをけば，佛教の首長は，共通の問題に關しては，佛徒の向上保護に向つて，又日本に同情的な聯合の形成に向つて，そして過去に於てなした樣に凡ゆる可能な平和手段によるすべての佛教國の友好的な共同動作に向つて統一的に活動すると云ふ事になるでせう。すべての教派の共通の問題を處理するために，中央書記局によつて，大乘，小乘其他佛徒の別々の教派を妥協せしめ，再統一すると云ふことは，アジアの文化扶殖に向つての第一歩であります。從つてこの運動に共鳴し我々自身の善に對する高き理想を向上せしめる委員會を形造りたいと私は思ふのであります。

根本的な方法に基いて世界的な佛教の國際的な奉仕をする統一教會は，アジアの統一の核心を保護する頸帶として許りでなく，世界の友愛を增進し，又將來に於て世界の總ての佛徒の友誼的な協同の爲に佛徒世界を結合する有力な一要素として役立つでありませう。

宗派の違ひ，階級，信念の偏見，そして國家及家族の敵は，原佛教文明を弱くするものと共に，我が高き聖なるダンマを危險にも無視すると云ふ事に現在まで力を借したのである。そしてダンマを分割し，佛徒の人口を友愛的な協力もなく，共通の事務所もなく，共通の信仰，共通の寺院，すべての宗派及び寺院の共通問題に於ける共通の宗教的奉仕者もなく，色々の保護されざる國家の色々の國籍に分離したのであります。

かくして我が佛教國をすべて外の國の盜略に任せ，我が誠實な友愛的な佛徒の家族及び彼らの後代を非佛教者の殺戮的な殘忍な掌中に置いて壓迫及び困窮の加ふるがまゝにしたのである。これら非佛教者は，我々保護されざる佛徒，又その協力者の善にして平和溫健なる敬虔の上に，善惡を問はず有害非道の方法によつて彼らの獲物に對する彼らの機會をのみ汲々と狙つてをり安い賃金で佛徒の製造者，同情ある供給者である我々男女の困難なる勞働により稼がれた各種の必需品を苦しめる哀れなる人間に對して稼ぎ，發見し，製造し，供給してゐるのであります。然し，二つの佛教國の間に第三者の介在する必要が果してあるでせうか？

北方及南方の佛教の二派に存する間隙は，吾主佛陀の聖義の普遍を增進することを阻め，印度，セイロン，ビルマ，西藏，シヤム，印度支那，支那の西南及北方諸州，蒙古，滿洲，太平洋諸島，そして日本の高き幸福と平和を危殆に瀕せしめるものであります。世界佛教聯合協會は平和的な手段に由つて，色々な原因により佛徒を分離した

ることの間隔に橋渡しをせんと努力してをります。佛徒の高き聖なる信條は，實踐の方法に於て如何に異つて居らうとも中心的な意味に於ては一つであり本質的に同じなのであります。何となればすべての國の佛徒は，精神に於て我が主佛陀の子供達であるから。

協會は平和的な手段によつて如何なる國民とも，宗教とも，如何なる國籍の團體とも紛擾を釀さずに，佛教國の安全を保持することを助け，我が宇宙的幸福，世界的平和を阻害するあらゆる人々の利己心を漸次根絕し，融解し，日本，滿洲，支那及びその國々に同情を有しつゝあらゆる國々のあらゆる佛徒の間の有益な爲になる思想を，効果的に進步せしめようとするのであります。

日本のすべての佛教組織が，自身の仕事の方法を容易にすることによつて自身の組織の向上を助け，平和的な手段により成功し宗教的に公認される爲に，合同しあらゆる可能な方法で世界佛教聯合協會の仕事にたづさはれる人々を支持し，その目的を進步せしめるならば，それは賢明なことであり，美はしい事でありませう。

佛教學校の教師達，各宗派の首長等は，すべて皆佛徒であり，佛陀，達磨，サンガの從者であります。彼らは悲しみから脫れ，離れ去ると云ふ考へから彼らの善及び幸福に對して，又彼らの有益な行爲の完全に對して出來るだけこの宗教的な運動を激勵し，貢献し，永劫の平和，幸福，解放に到達する義務に置かれてゐるのであります。

日本及び支那の總ての宗派の長老，首長，佛教組織の諸學校の教頭等が，何か利己的な動機で仕事をしてゐるとは我々は信じません。然し仕事の方法に何か利己的な動機があれば，かくの如き國家的な宗派的な利己的見解，及び彼ら自身の組合の仕事の罪深き方法を驅逐しなければならないのです。我々はすべての從事者が義務として溫い心を以て世界佛教聯合協會の會員として合同し，少しの躊躇もなくその目的の發展に進まれんことを要求する。

吾らは合同してマハサンガラージヤサバの後援の下に設立せられた新しい日本の世界佛教聯合協會の仕事を出來るだけ鼓舞しなければなりません。この際に於てすべての宗派の首長は，その副會長，秘書，上席會員とならねばなりません。彼らは必要な時に何時でも世界佛徒の統一せられた呼應を得，マハサンガラージヤサバの最後の贊助を得るために，すべての佛徒に共通な佛教界，組織，及び宗派の佛教的實踐行爲に從事せねばなりません。そして又，彼ら自身の組織の活動を宗教的に正當化し，同時に平和的手段により，幸福と成果を得る彼ら自身の仕事の方法を規律的にするための充分なる權威と力と威嚴とを獲得せねばなりません

義務的な問題として，我々は謙遜にもかう云ふことを貴方がたにお願ひしたい。お互に協力し，鼓舞し，すべて日本の佛徒を世界佛教聯合協會の會員として參加されるよう出來るだけ試みられたい，そしてすべての宗派，佛徒

の北方南方の教派の共通な事務局として東京の世界佛教聯合中央局を支持されたい。そして日本語を習ひに，又パリー語の聖典を教授し，飜譯するために日本に來る比丘達を接待し保護して貰ひたい。協會の目的の向上のために盡していたゞきたい。

經驗によれば，日本に對してすべての國家の門戸を開放する最上の鍵は，世界佛教聯合協會であると云ふことを知るのであります。

更に佛教國の結合について申しますれば，世界佛教聯合協會は東京や他の國々に佛徒の注文に應ずるミツションスクールの建設も目論んでをります。

こゝに於て訓練せられたる使徒は，別々の學校で教授し，飜譯し最上のことはすべて實行に移すことを試みます彼らの仕事は宗派と學校の間の差別を調和することであり，佛陀の聖法の再統一を急ぐことであります。又滿洲，支那，印度支那の如き曾つては優れた佛徒であつたが，今は色々の原因からダンマに於て缺けてゐる國々の佛徒を再び纏めることを試みるのであります訓練された使徒は，必要な時には異つた國々に派遣することも出來るでせう

此の高き仕事は，マハサンガラージャサバの秘書が居らないからと云つて北方南方の佛教聯合の幹部の後援者や書記の協力がないからと云つて，如何なる宗派的及國家的な組織の手によつては成功的な地位にまで齎らされることは出來ないのです。

世界佛教聯合協會の至上の目的は，日本及び支那のすべての宗派の佛徒の感謝すべき助けにより，どうしても日本で實現せられることが必要であります。何となれば，日本及び東京の高き權威を打建て且つ保持すること，全佛教宗派のすべての佛徒の統一向上と，佛教世界により日本及び支那を結びつけて統一することの爲に努力するのは佛徒の義務であるからであります。

すべての佛徒は，如何なる教會の權威なき協力行爲も，宗教的に不法であり佛陀のダンマによる正道を歩むべき力なきものであり，そしてかような行爲は世界佛教聯合のマハサンガラージャサバの承認せる協力なくしては決して實績もなく平和的でもないと云ふことを認識し把握せねばなりません。

この高き目的を効果的に實現するために，世界佛教聯合協會は日本佛徒の支持を要求し，適當なる土地建物がこの目的のため賦與されんことを要求するのであります。

又協會は經濟的方面ばかりでなく，より必要な方面に於て後援を要求するのであります。協會はこの仕事に對する精神的支持と同情ある關心とが欲しいのです！　協會は世界全體の何億と云ふ佛徒の精神的思考力の集注の前には何事も不可能でないと云ふことを信じます。何となればこの點に關する主佛陀の敎へは，次の如く明瞭であるからであります。

「敬虔なる信念はすべて不幸の海を渡りて來り，
怠慢ならざることにより人は高き幸福を得，
すべての悲しみは勇氣と力により贖はれ，
本來の智慧もて完全なる解脱を得。
（以上は昨昭和十年四月二日，熊本放送局に於けるスワミー師の放送講演の要旨）

日華佛教の比較觀

武昌　大醒法師

私の足が日本の國土を踏み，眼と耳とが始めて日本の凡ゆる事物に接觸した時は，宛も劉老々が大觀園に這入つたのと同樣ではないが，しかし私の心はふるえ，心臟は高鳴り，その鼓動を自分で悉く聽き取れた程であつた。何のためか？　それは名狀することの出來ない慚愧の念に打たれたからである。その後，日本佛教の事業を見て，それを中國佛教の事業と比較する時，宛も一塊の重い石の樣に私の心は重く，慚愧の情に堪へられないのだつた。

×

嘗て日本のある學者の話に『印度は佛の佛教で，中國は法の佛教で，日本は僧の佛教である』とあるのを聽いたことがあるが，其の實際を言へば，後の二句は逆になつて居る。私は日本に行つて見て始めて，中國の佛教は元來『僧』の佛教であり，日本の佛教は『法』の佛教であることを知つた。信じられないか？　日本の佛教は隆盛でないとは言へないが，その僧侶は言はゞ居士である。これは幾分か當つて居ないことはないと思ふ。然し中國の佛教はどうか，各省，各縣，各鄉，各村到る所に所謂圓領方袍の僧侶を見られるが，而も『法』は却つて已に其處には無くて，形式が『僧』の軀殼の中にあるばかりだ。

×

以前に日本の井上圓了氏は，「佛教活論」と言ふ一書を著した。若し我々が中國の近代佛教史を書いて貰ふなら，その書名は『佛教死論』と言つた方が甚だ好いと思ふ。

×

日本に於ける許多の佛寺は，色々な學校とか，醫院，幼稚園，婦人會等々皆社會事業を行つてゐる。彼等は慈善の方面では率先して，必ず佛教の看板を出して居り，又，彼等自身佛教のこと――文化，教育等については既にこれに先じて行つて居る。中國ではそうではなかつた。一般の慈善家と稱する人が佛門に混入する樣になつてから，近時は時々慈善事業を行つてゐると言ふことを聞くが，しかしとても問題にならない。一般の馬鹿な和尚が慈善家の居士達の後からついて行てゐるので全く『數典忘祖』(經を數へ佛祖を忘れてゐる）になり，反つて佛教本來の勤めを顧みざるに至つた。這の樣な連中のやることは世間の人氣をぬすまんとするもので，純眞な慈善家と稱することは出來ない。

×

日本佛教の大學と專門學校は十數ケ

處あり，毎年學士の資格を以て卒業する者，少くも四五百人あるが，これ各宗奬學の恩惠であり，亦彼等の師長の慈悲であらう。(日本にも亦別姓から出家して佛徒となる者がある)。

中國の佛寺は甚だ多いのに，たゞに大學專門學校がないばかりでなく，全然，中學一つさえもないのだ。青年學僧の狀態，——その師長から受ける待遇は，抑ゝ如何だらうか？　私は日本に居る間，幾度か此の事に想到し，我々青年學僧の爲めに涙を流したことも少くなかつた。

×

ある一日，茶話會の席上で日本の朋友が私に向つて言ふには，『普陀山と高野山とは大體似てゐる。それに普陀山には何故大學を設けないのか』と。私は，却て面皮を厚くして彼等に答へた『敝國の普陀山上には樹がないが，貴國の高野山には樹木があり，毎年三十萬から八十萬に達する木材を產出してゐるからだ』と。若し私が這んな風に答へなかつたとしたら，一體何と話したら良からう。

×

私が國內で駈け廻つた大小叢林，佛寺が二三百あるが，その中で兩三ケ所に明版の藏經と，三五尊の古銅佛像があつたのを除いては，隨・唐時代の法物のある寺は極めて少數あつたに過ぎないが，日本に行つて見ると，凡そ所謂國寶的な一佛寺の中には大槪隨・唐時代の法物が一二はあり，それは言ふまでもなく日本の國寶に指定されてゐるのであつた。

×

日本の僧侶は美術思想に富み，佛教美術を專門の學問として，眞劍に研究してゐる者もあると言ふことを，私は早くから承知して居た。日本に到着してから各地の佛寺を遊覽したり，各大書店を參觀したりして，美術的建築や美術的彫刻から，美術的裝飾や美術の專門書籍に至るまで到る處で却て見る事が出來た。

而も中國の現代佛寺の中に於ては，美術的價値あるものは實際一個さえ搜し出すことが出來ない。佛像に就て話すなら，中國の佛殿上の佛像は，おきまりの背後の彫刻がしてない。そこで私は常に言つたことであるが，まるで牛背を刀で削り落したやうである。日本の佛像にはかゝる幼稚な，下らない缺陷は少しもない。

×

日本の僧侶は公然と肉食妻帶して，當然なことゝ考へて居る。私はこの戒律を全然用ひて居ない(用ひられない)事を知つて，『どんなのが比丘の資格ですか』と彼等に尋ねたことから日本の朋友との話は此の問題になつた。これは凡て國の政治と僧侶の習慣上の關係であると私は言つた。又私は嘗て人に向つて大體次の樣に話したことがある『僧侶の社會事業を行ひ，職業を持つて自立自給を謀ることは大變好いことだ。が，出來れば戒律に關しても少しは顧慮しても良いと思ふ。』所が，或人がこんな回答をしやうとは思ひもよらぬことだつた『日本僧侶の肉食妻帶は公開的であるが，中國の僧侶の肉食妻帶は，世人にかくれてやつてゐるに過ぎないでせう！』と。

×

日本にある許多の國寶的法物中，私の最も喜びに堪へないことは，小型の舍利塔——單に塔の型になつたものだが——私の見たものが七八十種の多きに達して居る。この幾らかの舍利塔のうち，少くも大半は中國から渡つたものである。しかし，憐れむべし我が中國では，唯だ一個をも見たことがない。僅に寧波の阿育王寺に，舍利塔が一個あるにはあるが，甚だ粗末なものだ。

×

今年東京のある淨土宗の信徒——友松圓諦氏は多年淨土宗を弘揚するに，大いに努力し，最も權威ある著作家であるが，氏は忽然として淨土反對の文章を作り，西方極樂淨土は虛無なりと大いに力說して居る。その言ふ所は多少あやしいが，此れが爲めに世人は却つて注目し，還つてより多くの崇拜者を得てゐる。私は或日氏に面會しやうと思つたが，恰度氏はその前夜京都に行つた留守だつた。聽く所に據れば，氏を停車場に見送りに來た人々は三百人の多きに達したとか，——日本人は已に彼を目して一個の佛教の怪傑と考へてゐるからだらう——，當時私はこう考へた。この人とこの事件が若し中國に於て起つたとしたら，一般人の眼には，何んな風に見えるか知れないと。

×

日本の佛教各派の間は或點で融合し或る點では對立して居る。彼等は暗中にも爭つてゐるが，しかしその爭ひの戰略は文化，教育の方面である。例へば甲宗が刊行物を發刊し，或は學校を創設すれば，乙宗は直ちにその後を追かけて進み，甲宗よりもより良くやらうとするが如きである。中國の僧徒はさうではない。只感情上か或は財力上の高下を爭ふのみである。若しも誰れかゞ文化，教育の事をやるなら，相手の人は只だ力めてこれを破壞し，かき亂さうと企てるのである。此の一事を採つて比較しても，中國の佛教は實際沒落して了つて居る。

×

談玄法師は，私と一緒に東京の或る書店に駈け込んだ時，憤然として嘆じて言ふには『中國現代の佛教は，文化的方面に於ては少くも日本佛教と四十年の差があるだらう。日本の四十年前に出版されてゐた佛書は，現在の中國の佛教書籍に比較すれば還つて多く，又好いであらう!!』と。

×

凡そ一つの事が好なるには，制度(法則)の良否が重大な關係を有して居る。中國佛寺の衰敗は，一の善良にして時代に適合した制度のないことに因るが僧侶も亦盆に砂を散らした樣に何等の統一なく，各自が門前の雪を拂ふも，只一事でも互に協力し，合作し得ないことによる。日本の佛寺は系統的であつて，曹洞一宗でも大小末寺一萬七千餘ケ寺の多くが，悉く一系統に屬して居り，日本の一宗の僧徒は皆一宗の管長一人の薙度に依つて居るのであり，その他の事は推して知るべしである。

×

日本の僧侶は各自職を持つて居るがこれは現前の經濟時代にあつて，經濟獨立の原則に適合して居る。これを稱して一口に『俗化』と決めることは出來ない。果して佛制を遵行するとしても，現在は事實上已に二千五百年前の印度佛敎勃興の時代とは異つて居るのである。中國僧侶の職業は研究を修持する者を除いて，經懺一門の人達を，正當なる職業と生活をして居るものと看做すことが，妥當であるか否かは，現在に於ても問題となつて居る。

×

中國の一般佛敎徒は日本の僧侶に對して二種の批評があり，一には戒律を守らず，二には甚だ俗化してゐると言ふのである。日本の一般佛敎徒も，中國の僧侶に對して二種の批評があり，一は無信仰，二には無知識だと言ふのであるが，これは全然間違つてゐると私は思ふ!!

私は，中日兩國の佛敎及び僧侶に批評を加へやうとすれば，全中國或は全日本の佛敎歴史から研究してかゝらねばいけない。中國と日本の佛敎の現狀は，色ゝ相異つた原因から起つて居るから，さう簡單な言葉で概括的に論斷すべきではないと考へる。そこで日本に於て多數の人から日本佛敎の批評をせよと要求せられたのに，私はそれには全く何も話さなかつた，と言ふのは口を開けば便ち錯ることを深く恐れたからである。

×

上海に歸つてから範成法師を訪問した。彼は私に向つて『今回日本に行つて，佛敎々育に對してどんな感想があるか』と問ふた。私は『日本の佛敎々育と中國の佛敎々育と固より一緒に比較することは出來ない，又中國の佛敎々育も全然日本側に取るべきものはない』と答へた。『何故に？』彼は問ふた。私は再び『中國の佛敎には根本的に組織がない。我ゝの國家政府は佛敎に對して根底から無關心であり，宛も我々出家僧衆を國民と看做す必要がないかの樣であるが，日本はこんなではない』

×

日本の僧侶は高等敎育を受ける機會を得て居り，國家から種々の助力を得，且つ多量の研究參考資料を有して居る一個の研究者に取つても，上には指導員あり，下には助手があり，彼等の成績は自然スクスクと上つて行くのである。中國僧侶の現實，環境を回顧すれば實に天地の懸隔がある。中國僧侶の人材缺乏の所以，固より佛敎徒自らが未だ改革をやらないからではあるが，しかし，我國の政府も亦一半の責任を負はねばならない!! 現在，我々が日本を見て歸つてから，再び自らを眺めるに，只口先で空論を發しても無駄である。吾々中國の僧侶——青年學僧は愛護弘揚の計のためには，眼前に只一條の『埋頭苦幹』の狹い路があるばかりだ。必ずしも日本を追ひ越さうとしなくても良い。只自主自立して中國の佛敎の興起を求むれば良いと思ふ。這れ，我が日本佛敎を觀察してからの一感想である。　**（久保田覺己譯）**

南支那通信

藤井草宣

1　語言の不通

支那を旅行して何が最も困難な問題かといふに，旅費の無くなる以上に，語言不通といふ一事が苦痛である。私は北京官話ならば，どうか斯うか日用語には差支へないのであるが，それは長江以北の土地の人々に對しては，通用するが，すでに上海に於てさへ土地の者には，——殊に下層の土民には通用し兼ねるところが多い。南方へ來ると，その困難な度が一層甚しくなる。卽ち

1. 同じ福建省でも福州語と厦門語とは全く相通じない。相互に通譯者を要するといふ甚しさである。海上たつた十二時間の距離の隣接地でさへ斯樣である。そこで臺灣人が專ら，その祖先の故鄉たる厦門地方にのみ集中して，一向に福州へ發展せぬ理由も分る。(臺灣人は厦門に約一萬。福州に約二千人程，日本籍のまゝ戻つてゐる)
2. 廣東省へ移ると，首都たる廣州と香港とは同語らしいが，汕頭，潮州(これを潮梅地方と稱へてゐる。汕頭地方を昔から梅縣といひ，汕頭港は近代に發達した開港地である）地方は廣州語は通用しない。而も汕頭・潮州の土民に對しては「客家」なる名稱が附せられ，他より移住せるものといふ意が表明されてゐる。

斯のやうに上記二省の四ケ所が，それぞれ獨異なる語言を有し，相一致せず相通用せざるものであるといふことは實に不便なるは勿論，むしろ奇怪な事と云はねばならぬ。(何れも，それぞれ地理的に順次に汽船で一夜，十二時間航程の距離である)

支那と南洋とを結ぶ有名な所謂「南洋華僑」なるものは，上記四ケ所より出掛けてゐる者が大部分である。卽ち

1. 臺灣，ヒリツピン，蘭領印度の地方の華僑は，何れも厦門・福州地方より行つてゐる。(臺灣は厦門人が絕對的に多い)
2. シャムは潮州・汕頭地方の系統が行つてゐる。シャムの總人口一千八百萬人中，華僑は六百萬人（總人口の三分の一）であつて，その約半數は支那籍を有してゐる。而も米穀等の商權は悉く彼ら華僑の手に握られてゐて，汕頭語を以て常用語としてゐる。
3. ジャバ，シンガポールへは廣州方面の移民が多い。言葉は廣東語を用ひてをるが，その中二分ほどは福建語も用ひられてゐるといふ。

語言が全く異り，風習又多少の違ひありとすれば，相互に容易には融合しない。そこで相互の各地に「廣州會館」だの「福州會館」だのといふものを建てて，それぞれの集會所とするのみならず，これらの會館は又死體の棺(柩)を收藏安置するところともなつてゐる。
私は又た今回，厦門南普陀寺では住持の常惺法師から手厚い歡待を受けたが恰も前住持太虛法師の南下を待つて久しぶりに面晤を得た。此時にも，太虛法師が中山公園の公會堂の如き所で一般市民に大演說をやつたのを拜觀したところ，太虛法師の言葉が浙江辯まる出しでやつてゐるのを，當地の厦門大學の青年教授で法師に歸依せる佛學會の主腦者たる虞愚(德元)居士が厦門語にこれを一々通譯するのを見てアキレたのである。ところが，南進して香港へ行き，山光道に新に出來た新寺院の東蓮覺苑を訪れると，また太虛法師がちやんとやつて來てをられ，數百の信者に向つてその開示の際中であつたがこれ又た香港人の言葉で一々通譯されてゐるのを見て，いよいよ支那の大國なることと，國語運動の至難なこととを痛感したやうな次第であつた。ところが，更に甚しいことは，香港は hongkong ホンコンと發音することと世界的に定つてゐるが，これは英人が勝手にきめたので，元來はヒヨンコンHiong-kong といふのがその土地の原語であることを知つた。香港と廣州との間を往來してゐる日本の汽船に廣東丸と廣西丸とがあるが，廣東はカントンとコントンとの間の音にきこえ，廣西は Konsai コンサイ，又はカンサイといふのである。北京官話で Kuan-ssi コワンシイなどと云ふのは大間違であることを知つた。尙ほ，厦門であるが，アモイ卽ち Amoi のよび方は世界的に用ひられて誰一人怪しまぬ稱號なるに厦門人はいふ，これをアモイといふのは廣東語の呼び方であつて，英人が開港させた時に用ひてより，爾來さうなつて仕舞つたが，當地自體ではエームン Ēmung といふのであると。斯樣な次第であるから，私が汕頭の佛經流通處で會つた仁致法師（河北省人，三十四歲）といふ漢は，「語言が不通で非常に困つてゐる。當地で北京話の出來る者は三人しかゐないので，それらと時々會ふのが樂しみだ」といふてゐた。潮州の開元寺に嶺東佛學院の寄塵法師(安徽人)，窺諦法師，智誠法師(江蘇人)を訪れたが，三人とも矢張り「語言不通」で土地の人と感情が合はないので困ると云つてゐた。驚くべきことである。同じ支那であり乍ら。
次は，「2，汕頭と潮州」これにて佛教の狀況を語るつもり。

國際佛教通報局定款

名　稱

第一，本局を國際佛教通報局と稱す

事 務 所

第二，本局の事務所を全日本佛教青年會聯盟本部に置く

目　的

第三，本局は日本內海及海外に向つて佛教事情の通報をなし，且つ佛教徒相互間の各種便宜を計るを以て目的とす

事　業

第四，本局の目的を達成するため左記の事業を行ふ
- イ，日本內地及世界各國より佛教事情に關する質問の通報を行ふ
- ロ，必要に應じ日本語及世界各國語を以て佛教事情の通報を行ふ
- ハ，外國人の日本觀光に際しては各國の便益を與へ，特にその佛教に關する方面に於て之を爲す
- ニ，定時或は隨時に各國語を以て文書の刊行をなす
- ホ，その他必要と認めたる事業を行ふ

役　員

第五，本局の事務を處理するため左の役員を置く
- イ，局　長　　一　名
- ロ，幹　事　　三　名
- ハ，評議員　　若干名

局長は本局を總括す
幹事は本局の事務を處理す
評議員は局長の提案に依る重要事務を審議す

第六，評議員は左記の者を以て之に充つ
- イ，全日本佛教青年會館聯盟理事及主事
- ロ，全日本佛教青年會聯盟理事會に於て推薦したる者

第七，局長及幹事は評議員會に於て決定す

第八，役員の任期は二ケ年とす（但し重任を妨げず）

經　費

第九，本局の經費は左記のものに依て之を支辨す
- イ，本局基金の活用
- ロ，寄附金
- ハ，その他の收入

補　則

第十，本定款に記載せられざる事項は，凡て評議員會に於て協議す

第十一，第一回の役員は全日本佛教青年會聯盟理事會に於て決定す

定價	一部 金二十錢	送料二錢
	一年 金二圓四十錢	送料不要

昭和十年四月卅日第三種郵便物認可
昭和十一年一月廿八日印刷（每月一回）
昭和十一年二月一日發行（一日發行）

東京市外吉祥寺337
編輯發行兼印刷人　淺野研眞

東京市牛込區早稻田鶴卷町107
印刷所　康文社印刷所
電話牛込 (34) 1950番 5049番

東京市神田區一ツ橋二の三
發行所　國際佛教通報局
電話九段(33)4428番
振替東京83015番

昭和十年四月三十日第三種郵便物認可
昭和十一年一月二十八日印刷納本（毎月一回）
昭和十一年二月一日發行（一日發行）　國際佛教通報　第二卷　第二號

第二回

汎太平洋佛教青年會大會 紀要

THE PROCEEDINGS of THE Second General Conference of Pan-Pacific Young Buddhists' Associations

(in Japanese, Chinese and English)

Held at Tokyo & Kyoto, July 18–23, 1934

Price ¥ 3.00

Compiled & Published
by
The Federation of All Y.B. As. of Japan,
Tokio, Kanda, Hitotsubashi, II-3

昭和十年四月三十日第三種郵便物認可　昭和十一年三月二十八日印刷納本　昭和十一年四月一日發行（毎月一回一日發行）第二卷　第四號

The International Buddhist Bulletin

國際佛教通報

第二卷　昭和十一年四月　第四號〔Vol. II. April. 2502/1936 No. 4.〕

要　目〔Contents〕

東京　國際佛教通報局　發行
The International Buddhist Information Bureau
Tokyo, Kanda, Hitotsubashi, II—3
Annual Subscription ¥2.40 (post free) Single Copies 20 sen (post 2 sen)

Staff of the Bureau

Hon. President	J. Takakusu
President	K. Ohmura
Secretary	S. Takagai
〃	B. Inaba
〃 (in chief)	Ken Assano
Advisers	H. Ui
〃	G. Asakura
〃	R. Hatani
〃	U. Ogiwara
〃	R. Higata
〃	T. Suzuki
〃	S. Suzuki
〃	S. Amakuki
〃	S. Nagai
〃	B. Matsumoto
〃	E. Uno
〃	C. Akamatsu
〃	Z. Ohmori
〃	K. Yabuki
〃	S. Onoh
〃	S. Katoh
〃	M. Anezaki
〃	G. Honda
〃	R. Sekimoto
〃	J. Sahegi
〃	R. Hanada
〃	H. Kohno
〃	R. Takaoka
〃	Z. Kobayashi
〃	S. Yamabe
〃	C. Akanuma
〃	E. Honda
〃	R. Ohmori
〃	E. Kawaguchi
〃	C. Yamakawa
〃	D. Tokiwa
〃	T. Tanimoto
〃	G. Tokiwai
〃	S. Ohtani
〃	E. Ohtani
〃	B. Mizuno
〃	I. Shibata
〃	S. Ando
〃	J. Shimomura
〃	S. Kikuzawa
〃	K. Norisugi
〃	T. Shibata
〃	K. Asano
〃	T. Watanabe
〃	G. Onoh
〃	K. Yanagizawa
〃	M. Shigemitsu
〃	E. Kanakura
〃	S. Tachibana

國際佛教通報局

名譽局長	高楠順次郎
局長	大村桂巖
幹事	鷹谷俊之
同	稻葉文海
同	淺野研眞
顧問（順序不同）	
〃	宇井伯壽
〃	朝倉曉瑞
〃	羽溪了諦
〃	荻原雲來
〃	干潟龍祥
〃	鈴木大拙
〃	鈴木宗忠
〃	天岫接三
〃	長井眞琴
〃	松本文三郎
〃	椎尾辨匡
〃	宇野圓空
〃	赤松智城
〃	大森禪戒
〃	矢吹慶輝
〃	小野清一郎
〃	加藤精神
〃	姉崎正治
〃	本田義英
〃	關本龍門
〃	佐伯定胤
〃	花田凌雲
〃	河野法雲
〃	高岡隆心
〃	小林瑞淨
〃	山邊習學
〃	赤沼智善
〃	本多惠隆
〃	大森亮順
〃	河口慧海
〃	山川智應
〃	常盤大定
〃	谷本富
〃	常盤井堯猷
〃	大谷尊由
〃	大谷瑩潤
〃	水野梅曉
〃	柴田一能
〃	安藤正純
〃	下村壽一
〃	菊澤季麿
〃	乘杉嘉壽
〃	芝田徹心
〃	淺野孝之
〃	渡邊哲信
〃	小野玄妙
〃	柳澤健
〃	重光葵
〃	金倉圓照
〃	立花俊道

Buddhist World United Society

By the Late Sri Jina Wansa Swamy

(The following article is adapted from a Radio Lecture of the late Bhikkhu in Kumamoto, 2nd April 1935.)

The Buddhist World United Society, is a Society started originaly in India and published the Journal called "Buddhist World" at the approval of Mahasangharajasabha, for the advancement and unification of the Buddha Sasana, in all parts of the world, among various Nations and it works, as a secretarial ecclesiastical Buddhist institution, of all sects of the Southern and Nothern Schools of the faith; in common matters, and thus work for the protection and promotion of the Bliss and peace of the Buddhist World.

The Society is conscious of the magnitude of its undertaking, and of the paucity, of the resources at its command, of the unity, of the original School of Buddha Sasana, with all other sects of the Buddhist World.

But it has set to work, courageously, in the belief, that the pure and lofty desire, which impels all members will, and its success ultimately, and endeavours to find fulfilment of the hopes and views, according to the Sacred Law, of our Lord Buddha, and now it is gaining ground, in the noble field satisfactorily.

The present condition of our Sacred Buddha Sasana, which is splitted, into various sects, in different countries, of the world, has degenerated, by various causes and is found to be unsatisfactory; thus we find, that, this is just the time, for all the Buddhists of the world, to be awakened, unitedly and constitutionaly, and work vigilently and energetically, for our emancipation.

Let the Buddhists of all countries realise, that if we exclude Japan, China, Siam, Burma, India, Tibet and Manchuokuo, there are practically no Asian Buddhist countries, where Buddha Dhamma is upheld, as it used to be in the past; when the glory of the Sacred Teaching of the Truth, spread from the pacific

Islands of the South to the Snows of Arctic regions of Siberia and other parts of the world.

At this critical moment of non-Buddhist diplomatic movements, it is the duty of Buddhists to understand, that the national and sectarian selfishness, badly hinders the progress of universal and cosmic bliss; taught to us by our Lord Buddha, as such characters destroys all noble, meritorious and beneficial views, leading to promote the Bliss of humanity, hence it is the duty, of the Buddhists, to get out of such mean and destructive ideals, and be noble, to work unitedly, with the Buddhist World and protect Japan, and China, and other Buddhist countries of the world, by peaceful means and promote the oriental culture and its noble civilisation, which is enfeebled by diplomats of today by various ways.

The establishment of the Buddhist World United Society in Japan, and holding the Buddhist World Central Office in Tokyo is a Bliss to Japan, China, and Manchoukuo with the view of protecting the suppressed and depressed Buddhist Nations of the world and for reestablishing world peace in true sense and protect Japan, Tibet, China and Manchoukuo.

Maintaining the Buddhist World Office in Tokyo as the secretarial office of all Buddhist temples of all sects in Japan, China, Manchoukuo, Tibet, Ceylon, Burma, Siam and other countries of the world, the Buddhist religious heads should work unitedly, in common matters, for the promotion and protection and Buddha Sasana and for the establishement of Sino-Japanese unity and the friendly cooperation of all Buddhist countries, by every possible way of peaceful means, as worked in the past.

Reconciliation and reunion of the Hinayana and Mahayana, and their divided churches of the Buddha Sasana by a Central secretarial office to manage common matters of all churches, is the first step towards a cultural federation of Asia, therefore let us sympathise the movement, and form committees to promote the noble ideal for our own good.

A United Buddhist Church with international services of Universal Buddhist Worship, on the original methods will serve not only as the neckle to protect the nucleus of the Asian unity, but also as a powerful factor, in promoing and the universal Brotherhood, combining the Buddhist World for friendly cooperation of all Buddhists in the world in the future.

Sectarian differences, caste, creed prejudices, and national and family rivalries with the enfeeblement of original Buddhist civilisation have badly contributed to the present day a dangerous neglect of our noble and sacred Dhamma and divided it and splitted the Buddhist population into various nationalities of various unprotected countries without any friendly cooperation in want of common office, common worship, common temple and common secretarial workers in common matters of all Buddhist Sects and their Temples, and thus left opened our Buddhist countries, to all others for exploitation, and to suppress and depress, our serene and hosipotable Buddhist families and their future generations, in the murderous and unsympathatic hands of non-Buddhists, who eagerly find, their chance, for their prey, in what ever methods, right or wrong, venomous and terryfying, on the good hospitable and mild piety, of our unprotected BUDDHISTS, and the co-religionists, who, earn, find, manifacture and supply, various kinds of necessities, for the suffering and lamenting humanity, at cheap rates and easy prices earned by the hard labour of our own men and women of Buddhist manufactureres and sympathatic suppliers. Where is the necessity of a third person between two Buddhists?

The rift, that exist between the two schools of Buddhasasana of the Nothern and Southern traditions, is just of those differences, which retards the progress of the propagation, of the sacred doctrine of our Lord Buddha, and endangers the noble Bliss and peace of India, Ceylon, Burma, Tibet, Siam, Indo-China, Southern, Western and Northern countries of China, Mongolia, Manchoukuo, pacific Islands and Japan.

The Buddhist World United Society is endeavouring by peaceful means to bridge the gasps, which divided the Buddhists by various causes, while whose noble and sacred doctrine, however different, in tho methods of practice, are at the inner sense, is one and the same in essence; because, the Buddhists of all countries, are the children of our Lord Buddha, in mind.

The Society, would help to uphold the security of the Buddhist

countries, by peaceful means without producing any conflictions with any nation, religion, or society of any nationality, and will gradually root out and melt away, every ones selfishness, that hinders our cosmic Bliss and the universal peace, and will successfully promote benificial and meritorious views, among all Buddhists of every country, with a sympathy towards Japan, Manchoukuo, and China, and their Empires.

It would be wise and nice if all Buddhist constitutions of Japan, join and support the workers of Buddhist World United Society, in every possible way, and promote its objects, to help the promotion of their own constitutions, by facilitating their own methods of working, to become successful and religiously legalized, by peaceful means.

The members of Buddhist institutions, the religious heads of sects, are all Buddhists and are followers of Buddha, Dhamma and Sangha, they are in duty bound, to encourage and contribute to this ecclesiastical movement in every possible way, for their own good and welfare, and for the perfection of their meritorious deeds, in view of attaining redemption and deliverance, from sorrow and to attain permanent peace, Bliss and emancipation.

We shall not believe, that the Buddhist religious heads of all sects and presidents and secretaries of Buddhist Societies, constitutions, and principals of educational institutions and departments of Japan, and China, will work on any selfish motives. But if there are any of selfish motives in any method of working, they should get out of such national and sectarian selfish views and sinful methods of working out their own constitutions. We request all workers with a loving heart as in duty bound. to join as members of the Buddhist World United Society and promote the objects without any further delay.

They should join and encourage the working of this newly established Buddhist World United Society of Japan, founded under the patronage of Mahasangharajasabha in every possible way. At this instance all Buddhist religious heads should become its vice presidents, secretaries and distinguished members. They should submit to the Buddhist World, their societies' or sects' Buddhist religious acts, common to all Buddhists, whenever necessary, for obtaining the Buddhist World United Voice and the

Final approval of Mahasangharajasabha and also they should religiously legalize their own constitutional activities and acquire full authority and power with due dignity for regulating their own methods of working to be Blissfull and successfull by peacefull means.

As a matter in duty bound, we have the honour to request you all, most humbly, to cooperate and encourage and to try in every possible way to enrol all Buddhists of Japan as members of the Buddhist World United Society and maintain the Buddhist World Central Office in Tokyo as a common Buddhist ecclesiastical office for all sects, societies of Northern and Southern schools of Buddha Sasana, and accommodate and protect the Bhikkhus who come to Japan to study Japanese and teach and translate the Pali sacred books and work for the promotion of the objects of the society, and etc.

We know by our experience, that the best key, to open the closed doors of all countries for Japan, is to be the Buddhist World United Society.

In furtherance, of the ideal of the unity of the Buddhist World the Buddhist World United Society, has in view the founding of a missionary school for Buddhist religious orders in Tokyo and other countries.

The missionaries trained here will attempt to teach and translate into action all that is best in the different schools. Their work will be to harmonize the differnnces between sects and schools and to hasten the reunion of the sacred order of the Buddha. They also attempt to reorganize the Buddha Sasana in countries such as Manchoukuo, China, Indo-China, which formerly were predominantly Buddhists that are now lacking in Dhamma by various causes and the trained missionaries could spread to various countries when neccessary.

This noble work cannot be brought into successful existence, by any sectarian or national constitntion in the absence of the secretary of the Mahasangharajasabha or without the cooperation of the patron and secretary of the Buddhist ecclesiastical cabinet of the United Buddhist World of the Northern and the Southern school of San Buddha Sasana.

The above objects of the Buddhist World United Society are in every way essential to be worked out in Japan through the gracious help of the Buddhists to establish and maintain the noble dignity of Japan and Tokyo and to work for the unification and promotion of all Buddhists of all Buddhist sects and for the unity of China and Japan combining the two nations with the Buddhist World. All Buddhists should realise grasp that any act of unauthorized cooperation of any institution is religiously illegal and powerless to go in the right path according Buddha Dhamma, and such an act will never be meritorious and peacefull, without the cooperation and approval of the Mahasangharajasabha of the United Buddhist World.

To work out this noble object successfully, the Buddhist World United Society, requires support of the Buddhists of Japan and a suitable land and building is required to be gifted for the purpose.

The Society requires the help not merely financially but in a much more potent way.

"It wants a moral support and sympathetic interest in its work."

The Society is sure that the pooling of the spiritual thought-power of millions of Buddhists of the world over, nothing is imposible, because the Teaching of Lord Buddha on this point is clear.

"SADDHAAYA THARATII OGHANG?
APPAMAADENE ANNAWANG,
VIRIYEANE DUKKHANG ATCHETHII,
PANNYAAYE PARI SUDATHII,"

Devout faith crosses the ocean of all misery,
And one attains the Noble Bliss by not Being sloth,
All sorrows are redeemed by vigilence and energy,
And with intuitive wisdom perfects his Emancipation.

(*Dhammapada, Anguttara-nikaya*)

THE SWEET JOY AND PEACE SERENE

(1) THE SACRED DHAMMA

Sweet are friends when need ariseth,
Sweet is joy whatever it be,
Sweet is the age of deaths ending,
Sweet is to be from sorrows free.

(2) REFLECTION ON FRATERNITY

Sweet is to be a mother good,
Sweet is the Sacred-Brotherhood,
Sweet is the Sacred-Sisterhood,
Swest is the Sacred-Bikkhu good.

(3) ATTAINMENT OF THE SACRED FRUIT OF BLISS

Sweet is to gain the price of wisdom sacred,
Sweet is when craving and sin extinguished,
Sweet is the age of wisdom-sacred,
Sweet is the Sacred-Mind when established.

(4) REFLECTION OF SUPREME BLISS OF TRIPLE GEM

Sweet is to hail, the Lord Buddha Supreme,
Sweet is to hail, His Dhamma Sacred-Power Supreme,
Sweet is "Nibbana" The Sacred-Bliss Supreme,
Sweet is the Peace, of Eternal Glory Serene.

(5) DETERMINATION AND REFUGE OF A BODHI-SATHWA

I

"Nathi me Saranam Annyam,
Buddho me Saranam Varam,
Etene Satcha Vajjene,
Hothu me Jaya Mangalam.

II

"Nathi me Saranam Annyam,
Dhammo me Saranam Varam,
Etene Satcha Vajjene,
Hothu me Jaya Mangalam.

III

"Nathi me Saranam Annyam,
Sangho me Saranam Varam,
Etene Satcha Vajjene,
Hothu me Jaya Mangalam.

I

I have no other Refuge and shall not pray,
As the Lord Buddha is my only Refuge,
By the Power of this Truth with reverence I say,
"Let me become 'The Srijina,' The Victorious."

II

I have no other Refuge and shall never pray,
As the Supreme Dhamma is my only Refuge,
By the Power of this Truth with reverence I say,
"Let me become enlightened and be Victorious."

III

I have no other Refuge and shall never pray,
As the Sacred Sangha is my only Refuge,
By the Power of this Truth with reverence I say,
"Let me attain Nibbhana Serene and be Victorious."

The link of the Sacred Spiritual Chain of Lord Buddha

According to the Original Doctrine of Our Lord Buddha we know by our experience that so long as the Lord Buddha lived and taught His Noble Sermons to His devout and faithful followers, the Sacred Teachings and the Stately dignified personality appealed with the refuge in excellent unity to the disciple, even when the disciple leaves the Lord and retires to solitaly places for meditation on the sacred Teachings.

The Saintly disciples heared the voice and saw the merciful and dignified personality of the Lord and with devotional reverence took the benefit of the Lord appearance in the mental intuitive sight of the disciples and they with their reflective insight attained the enlightment and emancipation.

The spiritual Image of Lord Buddha in the presence of the disciples always stood firm before them in their mental sight for ever. But after Maha Pari Nibbana the stately dignified personality was no more in flesh, yet the Bliss and attainment of the sacred fruits of the Teaching were for ever in the minds of the disciples and they got the ability to recite correctly all the Teaching by their memory and they see The Lord in person as the Dhammakaya is immortal even after Maha Pari Nibbana.

Thus we have to understand that the personal connection of the Link of the sacred spiritual Chain of Lord Buddha living Dhammakaya is not lost in the sincere and true Saintly Disciple and his refuge and Blessing is effectful until the disciplines practice the Sacred Discipline to perfection.

But when the practices of Disciplines, meditations and the ten Mighty powers are neglected by a disciple the sacred personality of the Lord Buddha His Dhammakaya His living power and refuge disappears from that disciple and thereafter gradually he get into worldly house-hold life back again and become miserable and meet unexpected dangers.

It is therefore some of the Buddhist sects teach to the followers to be always in the reflection and memory of Lord Buddha "saying Amithbhang Nammami Aham." The power of Lord Buddha exists as a living power because in his Bodhisathwa life he gifted Eyes, flesh, blood, Kingdoms and even queens, princes and sacrificed lives innumerable times for the good and welfare of humanity and became Buddha and taught us the Dhamma for our emancication.

As the human life is very rare let us adopt the footpath of the Bodhisothwa life of the prince Siddhartha Sakya Muni as we know that he became Buddha by that merit that leads him to Nibbana.

Esperantaj libroj pri Budaismo

		prezo	sendkosto
1.	La Sukhavativjuho	¥ 0.15	0.02
2.	Budao (tradukita el "The Essence of Buddhism")	0.60	0.04
3.	La Dek Bildoj de Bovpaŝtado	0.35	0.04
4.	La Kodo de Kronprinco Ŝootoku	0.15	0.02
5.	La Samanta-Mukhaparivarto	0.40	0.04
6.	Budaisma Terminaro (de T. Takeuĉi) (hektografita)	2.00	0.20
7.	La fundamenta Koncepto de Budaisma Sociologio (de Ken ASSANO)	0.15	0.02

Ĉiuj libroj supre menciitaj estas riceveblaj de la Administracio de la "Internacia Budaisma Bulteno" aŭ de Japana Esperanto-Instituto, Hongoo, Tokio.

Juvenile Books in Japan

The rise of the art of book making f juvenile books dated from the eginning of the Taisho Era.)uring the middle of the Meiji Era, great number of juvenile books ·ere published by the Hakubunwan Publishing Company. These ooks were simply fairy tales illutrated with some black and white ictures.

Even so, children appreciated the airy tales written mostly by the ate Sazanami Iwaya, weil known riter of juvenile stories at the ime. (He wrote also many buddist juvenile books.) Children and ublishers of this period did not hink much about book illustrations nd liked only the stories.

It is said that the Twentieth Century is the contury of children. 'he movement for a new eduational method and the rapid pro;ress of education for children, effected upon the art of book naking of juvenile books in Japan ince the early period of the Taisho Era. Some publishers attempted o make new styles of Japanese uvenile stories and new types of ooks for boys and girls. The Fusanbo Publishing Company of Tokyo which created a new large type of books illustrated with many beautiful pictures.

The books of fairy tales became albums of beautiful illustrations with short stories, which were well appreciated by all. According to this new type, some monthly magazines for children took the same form. The Tokyo-Sha Publishing Company established the "Kodomono-Kuni" and the Fujin-no-Tomo Publishing Company made "Kodomo-no-Tomo." Both magazines are large size picture albums containing some short stories.

Takeo Takei, the noted painter and illustrator of juvenile art made a lot of pretty illustrations for these magazines. Shigeru Hatsuyama, another artist has made many illustrations for new juvenile stories.

People thought that the writing of juvenile stories was not so hard, but really it is quite a difficult matter. Thus during the Meiji Era, the fairy tales and short stories for children were written by many writers. Since the early period of the Taisho Era, writers and artists paid much attention on the making of juvenile stories.

Hakushu Kitahara, poet; Masao Kusuyama, writer; Mimei Ogawa and several other major writers attempted to write some fairy tales at this time. These stories were well illustrated by specialists.

Besides fairy tales, poems for children also were in vogue. Some anthologies of poems for children and juvenile stories were published by the leading publishers in Tokyo. "Village of Animals" by Takeo Takei, "Village of Children" by Hakushu Kitahara, "Flag, Bee and Cloud" by Junichi Yoda, Anthology of Juvenile Stories by Akahiko Shimaki were the most noteworthy books during the Taisho Era.

As illustrators for juvenile books are Messrs. Koshiro Ouchi, Yoshio Shimizu, Shobo Fukazawa, Shiko Munakata, Shiro Kawakami, Shigeru Hatsuyama, Takeo Teikei, Kiichi Okamoto and Miss Beniko Fukazawa.

The above mentioned is the evolution of the art of book making of Japanese fairy tales and albums for children. We have many translations of Western fairy stories, but here we have explained only about the Japanese books for children.

Japanese News

Ex-abbot returns from south seas

Mr. Kozui Otani, ex-abbot of the Nishi Honganji Temple in Kyoto, returned to Yokohama aboard the Yokohama Maru from an inspection tour in the South Sea islands on February 21.

He was known as the abbot who had the great ambition to cultivate natural products in the Japanese colonies while he was still in Buddhist orders. Since he resigned from the priesthood several years ago, he has visited the Japanese colonies almost yearly to inspect the state of the natural products there.

West has known sake about 340 years ago

Professor Nakamura of the Osaka Imperial University has discovered from his studies that Japanese sake was exported for the first time about 340 years ago. A wrecked Spanish ship arrived off Tosa Province of Shikoku Island 340 years ago, and the residents of the nearby villages presented 100 barrels of Japanese sake to the ship's crew. There were 233 sailors and officers on the ship, and they drank the sake after being saved from the storm. Later they took the remaining barrels to their native country via the Indian Ocean. This was the first time that Japanese sake was exported abroad.

Tourist posters to be sent abroad

Several hundred beautiful posters representing the scenic views in Hakone will be sent to China and the western coast of America to entice foreign tourists to Japan by the Board of Tourist Industry of the Railway Ministry shortly. The posters have been printed in Tokyo and depict the Hakone mountains seen from Kamakura.

Tibetan figures to be dedicated

A memorial rite for the deceased officials and soldiers who participated in the foundation of the Manchoukuo Empire was held at the branch temple of Koyasan at Nihon-enoki, Shiba, Tokyo, on March 1 at 2 p.m. On this occasion, three Buddhist figures which were presented to the temple by Mr. Ryusaku Endo, director of the Bureau of General Affairs of Manchoukuo, was exhibited.

These Buddhist figures were appraised by Dr. Gemmyo Onoh,

expert on Buddhist art, who says they belong to a period about 200 years ago. They were made in Tibet. After the dedication ceremony to be held on the occasion, they will be preserved in the Koyasan temple, Wakayama ken.

Singapore and Osaka exchanging trees

Arrangements have been made between the Osaka Botanical Garden and the botanical garden in Singapore to exchange Japanese and South Seas plants respectively through the good offices of Mr. Yutaka Miyabara, captain of the Osaka Shosen liner Africa Maru. Mr. R. E. Holton, head of the Singapore Botanical Garden, reputed to be the largest of its kind in the Orient, is very keen on the matter.

As a first step, the Osaka Botanical Garden has sent 60 carefully chosen cherry, pine, cedar and other trees, being forwarded by the Africa Maru which left for Singapore on March 6. Special agents well experienced in gardening have been dispatched to care for them in transport.

In return for these Japanese trees, the Singapore Botanical Garden will send to Osaka choice trees of various kinds of indigenous to the South Seas Islands.

Temple-hospital to be built

A new hospital attached to the Asakusa Kwannon temple will be completed in August. The hospital building will of concrete and four storey in height. The ground for the building covers 400 tsubo. The hospital will accommodate some 500 patients. Dr. Bunzo Inouye will be the director of the hospital.

Tourist board to celebrate birth

The Board of Tourist Industry of the Railway Ministry has decided to hold a tourist week from April 24 to the end of the month. The board celebrated the fifth anniversary of its foundation last April. Since then, members of the branch offices throughout the country are requesting the holding of the festival every year. During the week several exhibition concerning tourism and lectures on tourism will be given in the principal cities. On the occasion, a song of tourism will be composed to be distributed as gramophone records.

Huge new buddha

A huge image of Daibutsu, larger than that at Kamakura. will be made shortly. The Daibutsu of

Kamakura was made some 700 years ago and the huge new image is to be made as a result of the proposition of Mr. Kaichiro Nezu, noted business man, who is building a temple at Asaka, Saitama Prefecture, near the Asaka Golf Course. The Daibutsu will be installed in the compound of the temple, which has an area of 80,000 tsubo. Mr. Nezu recently commissioned Mr. Naoyuki Matsuda, wellknown sculptor of Kyoto to make this image. He raised a budget of ¥1,300,000 therefore. The image will have a height of 39 feet and its pedestal will be 9 feet.

Mr. Matsuda is working at his studio at Asaka at present. The image will be 10 feet higher than the Daibutsu of Kamakura.

Meiji shrine paintings

A series of Japanese water color painings depicting the establishment of the Meiji Shrine have been painted by Mr. Choshu Isoda, well known painter. The album containing these paintings was dedicated to the shrine on March 1. Mr. Isoda started to make the series of painting some seven years ago in his studio at Chikura, Chiba Prefecture. The paintings are on silk. The history of the establishment of the shrine was written by Viscount Tamemori Irie, Lord Steward to Her Majesty the Empress Dowager.

Nikko to record sounds

To introduce Nikko, some gramophone records will be made shortly, which will register musical sounds of the noted place. The melodious sound of the bell of the Toshogu Shrine, the religious dance of the shrine, the murmur of the waters of the Daiya River, the enormous crash of the Kegon waterfall and boat songs on Chuzenji Lake will be recorded.

Beautification of Lake Biwa

The council for the development of Lake Biwa has held numerous meetings since last year to discuss on the plans to develop the lake. At a meeting to be held the middle of March the councillors decide on a plan to build embankments around the lake. These embankments will raise the level of the water. On top of the embankments driveways will be constructed. The council is planning to make some parks on the bank of the lake.

New Buddhist station

Nagano railway station has been completed recently. It has been under construction at a cost of Y136,000 for some time. This building is in the pure Japanese

Buddhist style of architecture, and required ten months for construction. The station was opened on March 10 and the celebration in connection with its competion was on March 15.

Famous Buddhist image disappear

An old Buddhist image representing Kwannon treasured by the Hakusan Shrine at Uji in Kyoto Prefecture has disappeared suddenly. The image belongs to the Fujiwara period and is known as one of the most distinguished Buddhist figures in Japan. The staff of the shrine are searching for traces of the criminal with the cooperation of policemen.

Art objects found in temple

The priest of the Fudo Temple in Sagami-Mura of Saitama Prefecture discovered several fascinating paintings and art objects in storage at the temple recently. He has requested an expert on art to estimate these objects, which are thought to be valuable works of Japanese art.

Matsumoto castle given protection

Matsumoto Castle located at Matsumoto City in Nagano Prefecture will be registered on the list of national art treasures by the Ministry of Education shortly. Mr. Hattori, art inspector of the Ministry, has inspected the castle and the Ministry has decided to give it special pretection. The castle belonged to Toda, lord of the Toda Clan, and was built in 1583.

Ogaki castle may receive attention

The residents of Ogaki city of Gifu Prefecture are discussing special attention for Ogaki Castle because the castle is known as one of the most fascinating examples of old Japanese architecture. The castle was built by Yoshiharu Ashikaga in 1536 A. D. The Gifu Prefectural Office is studying the plan in conjunction with the Department of Education.

Siamese Minister presents Buddhist image

A Buddhist image was presented to Mr. Kajiro Tsukamoto, musical manager, by Phra Mitrakan, Siamese Minister to Japan, March 10 because of his distinguished service in introducing Siamese music in Japan.

Mr. Tsukamoto invited the Siamese dance troup to Japan last year and introduced Siamese dancing and music to the Japanese public.

外人禪を語る

緒方宗博

はしがき

世界の顔は今一齊に東洋に向いて居る。歐亞の一角で伊太利とエチオピヤとが事を構へて國際聯盟に一つの話題を提供しては居るが，各國のこれに對する態度は寧ろ微温的であり消極的である。これに反して支那を對象とする歐米諸國の經濟的乃至領土的野心は，虎視眈々として誠に積極的なるものがある。露西亞の傳統的西下政策，英米最近の對支經濟行動の如きはその顯著なる例と言へよう。更に又全世界が種々なる觀點より我が日本を注視しつゝある事はあまりにも明白なる事實である。軍縮問題を廻つて英米が對日優位比率を固守して讓らないのは，彼等の日本武力に對する注目の結果であり，各地に於ける關税牆壁の急造，日本移民の阻止等は，最近に於ける日本の產業的又は民族的進展に對する諸外國の重大なる關心に基づくものである。更に近年シヤム，濠洲，南洋等から多數の見學團又は留學生等が陸續と來朝しつゝある事實は，彼等の日本に對する認識新なるものあるを物語るに充分である。

然しこゝに又これ等軍事，經濟，社會的動向の外に，これ等よりも遙かに以前から動きつゝあつた一つの東方凝視の傾向がある。それは泰西人の東洋美術及び宗教に對する關心である。英國人の印度に於ける佛教遺蹟の調査發掘，古典及び美術品の保護研究は，その目的及び動機の如何に拘らず世界文化史上多大の貢献をなし來れるものであり，佛領印度支那に於ける佛國政府の努力も亦多とすべきものが少くない。一八八一年（明治十四年）ロンドンに巴利聖典協會が設立せられて以來今日に到るまでに，既に百餘冊の佛教原典及びその英譯書が出版せられて居る。今日では事原典に關する限り，二千五百年の傳統を誇る東洋の佛教徒と雖も亦彼等西人の科學的研究の恩惠に浴せざるを得ない狀態である。

然し乍ら宗教の研究は元より有形的資料の調査のみを以つてその目的を果し得るものではない。かくて西人の或る者はセイロン島へ下つて僧團に身を投じ，或る者は西藏に分け入つて密教の修法を學び，一部の人は法を支那に求め，又一部の人は日本へ來て禪の修行を試みた。今や西人の佛教研究は，既に學問的教理研究から一歩を進めて，實踐修行の域へ達したものと言つても敢て過言ではあるまい。

以上の外更に西人の東洋接近の一傾向が看取される。それは最近に於ける西洋哲學界の傾向である。近日某氏が獨逸に於て我が西田哲學の紹介を試みたるに對し，多大の歡迎と賞讃の辭が送られたとの事である。而して我が西田哲學が，ギリシヤ的であるよりも，儒教的であるよりも，最も禪宗的であることは，過日高山岩男氏に依つて大朝紙上に紹介せられた如くである。然らば彼のリツケルトやフツサール，マイノング又はベルグソン等の立場から，百尺竿頭一歩を進めて，概念葛藤の炬火を吹滅し，學祖の三批判書を燒きて喝を下し棒を行ずる大小の德山が輩出する時節も正に近づきつゝあるのではあるまいか？ かくて吾人がこゝに外人禪と言ふ如き名目を提起する事も亦半文錢に値せざるに値せば幸である。

禪を學んだ外人

（1）ミセス，ラツセル。氏は米國桑港の人，前に觀光の目的を以つて日本に來遊，鎌倉圓覺寺に入つて釋宗演老師に參じ，明治三十八年には老師を桑港の自宅に特請して研鑽を重ねた。兜率の三關等の則を透過して相當の見所を得たとの事であるが今はもう故人である。續禪林僧寶傳の記者はこれに就いて左の如く述べて居る。

『是より先米國の鉅富剌世留夫妻我が國に觀光して偕に師の室に入り頗る所得有り，別に臨んで堅く師の楽航を約す，言辭懇到なり。此の年六月，師約を踐んで米に航し剌世留を主とす。時に居士鈴木大拙遊學して市俄古に在り，乃ち來つて左右に侍して師の說通を輔けて善くその力を致す。居る事八閱月，機に應じて化を行ふ。蓋し吾が宗米に入るの權輿なり。』――原漢文――

（2）ミセス，ヴレツクスラー。氏は同じく桑港の人，ラツセル一門の人々と共に楞伽窟の室に參じたが，今は桑港郊外に自費を以つて少年慈善病院とも言ふ可きものを經營して敬虔なる看護婦達と共に不幸なる人の子に奉仕しつゝ，月夜の窓下に坐禪の香を燒いて居る。

『禪をやつて何を得ましたか？』

と問へば，氏は答へて言ふ。

『禪は私に何物も敎へませんでした。然し一つの荷物を與れました。それは私が時々坐禪をしなければならぬと言ふ事です。』

（3）ダククー，カービー。氏は元基督敎の僧侶であつたが同じく鎌介で修行をし，遂に得度式を擧げて佛敎の僧侶となり，大正九年歸米してカナダ，桑港，ハワイ等で佛敎の傳道に從事した。去るに臨んで所藏の歐文佛敎書三百餘冊を臨濟宗大學圖書館に寄贈し，昭和二年の微妙大師遠忌には妙心寺法堂で特別講演を行つた。今はセイロン島カンデイ郊外に在つて，日本禪宗の宣揚に勉めて居る。

（4）ダククー，ゴダード。氏は米國ベルモント州の人，始め基督敎牧師として支那に傳道中，基督敎神秘主義の研究から佛敎の神秘主義に轉じ，昭和三年京都相國寺の山崎大耕老師に就いて修行を始め，以來殆ど每年日本，支那，アメリカの間を往來して修行を續けて居る。昭和九年加州サンタ，バーバラに閑靜の地を求めて精舍を建立し，廣く求道の士に門戶を開放し，傍ら佛敎に關する著述を行つて居る。

（5） ミセス，サラナーブ。氏は米國加州オークランドの人，靈智學の研究から禪の修行に志し，昭和四年春千崎如幻師の紹介狀を携へて來朝，始め京都大德寺圓山筌提老師に就き後圓福寺神月徹宗老師に從つて坐禪をした。同年の暮には印度に佛蹟を探り，翌年春再び日本を訪れて歸米，昭和八年には夫君と共に生涯を佛敎傳道に捧げる覺悟でビルマ，チツタゴンの佛敎會に入つたが氣候風土，食物の急變に依つて健康を害した爲初志を飜して歸米，今は桑港に在つて佛敎婦人局の看板を揭げて歐米の佛敎婦人に呼びかけんとして居る。

（6）オルムスビーとコルバルン。兩氏は米國アイダホーの人，最初トランスヒマラヤンの敎に依つて道心を練り桑港千崎如幻師の痛棒を喫する事一兩年，昭和六年二月來朝大德寺僧堂に雲水として掛塔，留錫一夏の後支那へ渡り最近歸米した。

（7）ミセス，セグリーブ。氏は歐洲セルビヤの生れ，大戰後アメリカに歸化し，桑港ベイダンタ敎會で印度式坐禪を練習，昭和六年春來朝して圓福寺にて僧堂生活を經驗し，後大阪府下に在つて茶道を修め，今はロスアンゼルスに在つて日本紹介に勉めて居る。

（8）ミス，オリフアント。氏は英國の人，昭和六年印度旅行の途上來朝，相國寺，圓福寺等で少しく坐禪をし，今はアメリカに渡つて少年精神療養所とも言ふ可きものを經營して自他の精神修養に專念して居る。

（9）ミセス，エベレツト。氏はシカゴの人，鈴木博士の紹介で南禪寺河野霧海老師に就いて修行を始め，昭和七年と八年に二回來朝，熱心に坐禪をした。最近はイリノイスの自宅で日本佛敎紹介の一法として東洋に關する書籍の紹介をして居る。氏は米國にても有力なる法曹家の夫人，最も熱心に修行した一人として各方面からその前途が期待されて居る。

（10）ミセス ホーマン。氏はニユーヨーク州バアツフアローの人，昭和八年ミセス，エベレツトに伴はれて來朝，圓福寺外人禪堂最初の修行者として熱心に參禪をしたが，その滯在は短期間であつた。然しその後も究明怠らず，最近は圓福寺から文珠菩薩像を送つて貰つて一段と精進して居り來る四月には再度來朝するとの事である。

（11）デンイストとウイツト。兩氏は和蘭の人，ジヤバ島に在つて南方佛敎の傳道に從事して居つたが，大乘佛敎を求めて昨年來朝，東京，京都等の日本各宗本山を參觀の後，石原汽船會社の紹介で圓福寺外人禪堂に入り，昨年十一月四日僧侶としての得度を受けてジヤバに歸つた。今後は禪に依るジヤバ島民の敎化に專念する由。

（12）ミス，スミツト。氏はデンマークの人，日本國際文化振興會の補助を受けて土俗學研究の傍ら圓福寺の外人禪堂に通つて修行を續けて居る。

（13）ミスタ，アツカー。氏は米國ワシントン自由博物館の東洋委員，京都下鴨に居を構へて弓道，書道，琴曲等の稽古をして居る。弓道は最近初段を允許され，書道もなかなかの進境を見せて居る。歐洲諸國語の外支那語に堪能なる關係から禪宗の語錄を讀んで深く禪に興味を持ち，時々圓福寺の外人禪堂に行つて坐つて居る。

以上日本へ來て一度でも師家に參じ一週間でも接心をした人々の名前を列記したに止まる。若し東洋美術や日本建築，庭園等に對する趣味の上から，私かに禪宗に一種の憧憬を有して居る人々を數ふるならばその數は相當なものとならう。尙以上の人々の本名と法名とを詳記すれば下の通りである。

1. Mrs. Alexander Bussel.（不詳）
2. Mrs. Elise A. Drexler.（不詳）
3. Dr. M. T. Kirby.‥‥正覺禪士
4. Dr. Dwight Goddard. 孤峰居士
5. Mrs. Miriam Salanave.宗貞大姉
6. Mr. Ormsby.‥‥孤雲禪士
7. Mr. Colbalun.‥‥‥‥默齋禪士
8. Mrs. Kristin A. Seglyov.‥‥‥‥‥‥‥‥‥‥‥宗玉大姉
9. Miss Honora B. Oliphant.‥‥‥‥‥‥‥‥‥‥‥（ナ　シ）
10. Mrs. Edward W. Everett.‥‥‥‥‥‥‥‥‥‥‥空華大姉
11. Mrs. Georgia M. G. Forman‥‥‥‥‥‥宗鏡大姉
12. Rev. W. Josias Van Dienst.‥‥‥‥‥‥宗浩禪士
13. Rev. J. W. de Witt‥‥‥‥‥‥‥‥‥‥‥宗愼禪士
14. Miss Smidt.‥‥‥‥‥（ナ　シ）
15. Mr. William Acker.‥（ナ　シ）

外人の求むるもの

一口に外人と言つてもその禪に求むる所は決して一樣ではない。又彼等の禪に對する認識の程度も十人十色であつて，その問題とする所も自ら各別である。然し何故に，又如何にして彼等が禪門を叩くに到つたかの動機や心的過程を尋ねて見ると大略左の二つの系統に分れて居る事を見出す。而してその求むる所も亦その屬する系統に依つて大體同じであると想像される。

（一）基督教義に對する不滿に起因する者。

この系統に屬する者には，宗教問題を相當熱心に追求した人々が多い。彼等の言ふ所に依れば，基督教の教義は現代の科學的知識と矛盾する事があまりに多く，且つ人間を蔑視する事が甚しい。例へば人格的な神の存在や（基督教徒は常に「天にまします我等の神よ」と呼びかける），この神に依る天地創造の說（舊約聖書創世記），人間の原罪說（ローマ書第五章第十二節以下）等がそれであつて，これ等は如何に讓歩しても現代人の理性及び人間的要求の許さない所である。然るに佛教の無我說や緣起論，卽身成佛義等は實に合理的であつて時代の要求に適合する。今後の世界は最も合理的にして神秘的なる實踐的宗教に依つて指導せられるであらう。此の意味に於ては佛教は基督教等とは比較にならぬ優れたものであり，禪はその佛教の生命をたゞ論理的に說き示すに止まらずして個人的に心理的に體驗せしむる特殊無比なる教である。世界の宗教思潮中此の如き福音を傳へるものは他にあるまい，と言ふのである。

而して此の如き意見を有する人々の禪に求むる所は，規矩整然たる僧堂の生活でもなければ，莊嚴極まりなき法要儀式でもなく，又寒熱共に闇黎を滅殺し去る大接心そのものでさへもない。彼等は只だ師家の活手段に依つて自己の迷情を打開して貰ひたいばかりである。若し西洋人の爲にも，一擊にして分別を打破して南北東西活路通ずる正法眼を開發する作家が居ないならば，日本禪も亦西洋人に取つては一個の歷史的存在に過ぎない事になると言つて居る人もある。

（二）東洋愛好に起因する者。

この系統に屬する人々は，深く宗教を批判摸擇した結果としてではなく，何となく東洋的な雰圍氣に興味を感じ，聞くがまゝ，見るがまゝの緣に從つて禪に入つて來た者である。この種の人々に取つては，遙かに世塵を離れた禪院を訪れる事はそれ自身既に一つの大きな悅びであり，身に粗衣を纏ひ心には錦を着たる衲僧と一服の茶を喫する事は限りなき滿足であるのである。雲水達と共に寂として聲なき堂內に坐しては自分も亦出家した樣な心持になり，清掃された僧堂の庭先を歩く時は恰も墨繪の中の人物と化した如く，鐘の音を聞けばこれと一致し，香の香に觸れては心身共に洗ひ淨めらる心地になるのである。よく雲水を自宅に招待する外人で，藥石（夕食）の時でも食事のお經を讀んで欲しいと言ふのがある。スープ，パン，バター等を食卓に並べて，イザ食事と言ふ所であのシンミリとしたお經の聲を聞く事は，西洋流の音樂入りでデナーパーティーを始めるよりも遙かに內省的で高尙であると言つて居る。

かくて此等の人々の求むる所は，純粹に東洋的な生活方法であり，感じ方であると思はれる。桑港の金門公園に美術參考館があつて，その玄關を這入つた所に小高い水鉢が一つ置かれてあり，この圓い水鉢の緣からは，極くゆるやかに水の滴が落ちる樣になつて居る。本來ならばこゝらあたりには威勢のよい噴水を配しても何等不自然とは感じないであらうアメリカの大衆にも日曜の一日を公園に過ごして靜かな水の玉のしたたるを見て心を洗つて行く人もあると見へる。日本人が寂を求めて高價な茶器に浮身をやつし，「西洋人に茶が解るだらうか？」等と評判して居る間に，羽織を着て盤の上に坐つた碧眼の胡僧に依つて，『日本人の中では僧堂の雲水と藝者ガールとが一番偉いと思ふ。彼等は絕へず緊張してゐて何處から見てもスキがない。』と言ふ樣な手紙が本國に送られ，やがて『雲水道具を一切購入したいが，周旋して貰へまいか！』と言ふ樣な注文が日本の外務省へ舞ひ込んで來ると言ふ可笑しくて笑へぬ話もある。

外人共通の心理

外人は一般に性質が明るくて，物の

解りは早い。解らない事を解つた様な顔をしてゴマかして通ると言ふ事はしないが納得したら正直にその事を實行する。彼等の長所でもあり短所でもある事は融通が効かないと言ふ事である。第一彼等の言葉が既に甚だ窮屈に出來て居る。日本語では『あそこに人が居る。』と言ふのを聞いても，一人きり居るのか大勢居るのか，女だけであるのか男女兩方居るのか解らない。同じ事を英語で言はふとすれば，少くとも單數か複數か，男性か女性かだけはハツキリさせないと言葉にならない。物が大きいと言ふ事を言はふとすると，大きい，より大きい，最も大きいと言ふ三段形容詞のどれかを使はなければならない。大般若の大はこの內のどれにも當嵌まらないから梵語で言ふより仕方がない。同じお經でも，英譯で讀む時には，一々の言葉の意味や，誰が，何時，何所で何と言つて居るかと言ふ事が極めて明瞭に頭には入る。然し漢譯や國譯で讀む樣な含蓄は味はれない。これは一つには英語がまだ自分のものとなつてゐない爲でもあらうが，言葉の構成そのものが影響して居る事も大きいと思ふ。殆ど總ての外人が，禪宗の坊さんは肉食，妻帶，飲酒は自由かと，言ふ事を尋ねる。それはいけい事になつて居る，と言つて置くと，之に反する光景に接する毎に奇問を發する。『酒は飲んでも心が亂れなかつたら水を飲んだも同じ事ではないか？』と言つてもなかなか承知しない。昔はいけなかつたが，この頃では一般に解放されて來たと言へば，『それぢや日本の禪宗は，正統の佛敎でなくなつたのだらう。』と追及する。卽心卽佛の當體が卽ち非心非佛であると說明して貰つて，『君の通譯は間違つちやゐないだらうなあ？』と半信半疑，『今鳴る鐘をどう聞いた？　昔も今も變りはないぞ！』と詰問されて，やゝ暫く思案の末に，『へー，若し撞く人の力が同じでありましたら。』と眞理を測つたり，比較したりしてる人もある。然し又秋の一夜を淸談に過して，『萬法一に歸す，一何れの處にか歸す』とあびせられて，默つて對手の手を握り，『グツト，ナイト』（お休みない）と言つて立ち去つた人もあるから，西洋人皆言句に拘泥して融通が効かないと言つてしまふ事は出來ない。

外人の禪堂

米國のニユーヨークに佐々木指月師あり，ロスアンゼルスに千崎如幻師が在つてそれぞれ特異な白人敎化をして居られるが，今はこれ等に就いて述べず，圓福寺の外人禪窟の事を少しく紹介しやう。

昭和四年にミセス，サラナブが突然やつて來たが，體重三十貫は下るまいと見らるゝ巨軀，疊の上に坐る等と言ふ事は，縱にしても橫にしても三十分とは保てない。下駄は穿けない，箸は使へない，少々我儘の様に聞えるけれども，朝暗い間から起きて火の氣のない堂內や本堂に坐つたり，薄い靴下だけで長い板廊下を步く事は，やる本人にもなかなかの苦痛であつたし，側で見て居る人々も相當な苦痛を感じさせられた。そこで西洋人が日本の習慣や，僧堂の生活に慣れるまで，その生活を急激に變化する事なしに落ち着いて修行の出來る施設が西洋人からも日本人からも要求された。今は故人となつた英國の作家アダムス，ベツク女史等は再三妙心寺に時の管長神月徹宗老師を訪ねて外人禪堂の設立を慫慂したものであり，それから數人の外人が方々の僧堂へ來て修行をしたけれども，何れも相當勞多くして効果が少かつた。それで小規模乍ら一つの外人禪窟が八幡の圓福寺に出來た。それは昭和七年十一月の事である。

この外人禪窟は，本寮とも呼ぶべき中心建物が五つの獨室に區切られてあり，各室には佛壇があり，押入れがあり，ベツトと机と椅子が置かれてある。部屋の南側には長廊下があつて附屬の食堂，浴室，東司（便所）に通じ，全體が和洋折衷で，簡素な，而も明るい構造である。少し狹いと言ふ感じがせぬでもないが，これは不自由な環境を自由に使つて行くやうに習慣づけさす爲の特別な意圖に依るとの事である。本寮の南庭には，山の斷面を開いた禪窟があつて隨時坐禪をするに任せ，北庭にはミセス，ホーマンの寄進になる茶席がある。こゝで修行した外人の感想を聞くと，『西洋の生活を經驗した事のない人が，よくこゝまで西洋人の生活に適する樣に考案されたものだ！』と感歎して居る。何か足らぬものはないかと聞けば，よい通譯の人がないとの事であつた。

禪に關する歐文書籍

禪が此の如く外人の注目を惹くに到つた事は，十中の九分九厘までは文學博士鈴木大拙敎授の著書及び直接の紹介に依ると言つても決して過言ではない。先づ氏の著書を少しく紹介しやう。

（1）禪學論文集　第一輯

本書は菊版四二三頁の大作で昭和二年ロンドンのルーザツク社から出版された。その內容目次を譯出すれば左の通りである。

1. 序文
2. 論文第一　緒論
3. 論文第二　自覺敎義の支那譯としての禪
4. 論文第三　般若と無智
5. 論文第四　支那禪宗史（菩提達磨より六祖慧能まで）
6. 論文第五　悟り
7. 論文第六　禪道修行の實際方法
8. 論文第七　禪堂及び禪的生活の理想
9. 論文第八　十牛の圖

附錄

引用支那原文

索　　　引

（2）禪學論文集　第二輯

本書は昭和八年同じ出版所から發行された。菊版三二六頁に二十葉の貴重な禪畫寫眞版入りである。その內容は，

1. 序文
2. 論文第一　公案拈定
   第一部　知識を越えたる體驗，外十一章
   第二部　公案拈定と念佛，外七章
3. 論文第二　菩提達磨の心印
4. 論文第三　二大禪錄

一，碧巖集
二，第五十五則道悟と漸源
三，無門關
5. 佛教生活に於ける受働性
一，業感論外二節
二，佛教に於ける罪悪観の發展外二節
三，受働性の心理外六節
四，受働性と忍辱又は謙讓
五，祈願と念佛外二節
六，佛教生活に於ける受働性の完成外一節
附　錄

(3)禪學論文集　第三輯

本書は昭和九年同じ出版社から發行菊版三九二頁に逸品揃ひの禪畫寫眞版三二葉入りの豪華版である。その內容は，

1. 序文
2. 論文第一　禪より華嚴經へ
一，禪と一如哲學外九節
二，禪と經典研究外一節
3. 論文第二　華嚴經，菩薩道，佛陀
華嚴經に於ける境界の完全轉換外七節
4. 論文第三　諸菩薩の本處
何處から何處へ外十一節
5. 論文第四　發菩提心
發菩提心の意義外六節
6. 論文第五　禪に於ける般若心經の意味
心經の梵本とその漢譯及び英譯外二節
7. 論文第六　般若の哲學及宗教
一，般若哲學外十二節
二，般若の宗教外四節
三，摘要
8. 論文第七　佛教特に禪の日本文化への貢獻　佛教生活外八節
附り　日本佛教に就いて
9. 論文第八　繪畫に現はれたる禪生活

(禪畫寫眞二十葉及びその解說)

本論文集は更に第四輯第五輯が近く出版されるとの事，この大作，名作，力作の價値及び世界的反響に就いては禿筆の能く述ぶる所ではない。大阪商工會議所副會頭安宅彌吉氏が本書の出版に多大の精神的並びに物質的援助を寄せて居ることに就いては譯者がその序文に公表せる所，又東京啓明會も著者のこの國際的大事業に多大の援助をなしつゝあるとの事，吾人は更に禪宗各派，及び日本國家が本書の如き出版に相當な援助を附與せん事を切望して止まない。尙同じ著者に依つて左記の各著が矢繼早に世に送られた事は驚歎感謝の外はない。

(4)楞伽經の硏究　菊版四六四頁
昭和五年刊
(5)英譯楞伽經　菊版三〇〇頁
昭和年七刊
(6)禪堂生活　菊版一一一頁
昭和九年刊
(7)禪學概論　四六版一六〇頁
昭和九年刊
(8)禪宗必携　四六版二三二頁
昭和十年刊

以上の外世界の禪學徒に依つて既に世に送られたる著書譯書も亦少なからず。今その譯名を二三列記せん。

(9)王　　　著　英譯六祖壇經
昭和五年刊
(10)マックス・ミユラー著
英譯金剛經　明治廿七年刊
(11)ゲンメル著　英譯金剛經
大正元年刊

(12)マックス・ミユラー著
英譯般若心經　明治廿七年刊
(13)ケルン著　英譯法華經
明治十七年刊
(14)忽滑谷快天著　武士の宗教
大正二年刊
(15)鈴木大拙著　佛教僧正の說教
明治四十一年刊
(16)千崎如幻著　英譯無門關
昭和九年刊
(17)千崎如幻著　英譯十牛
昭和八年刊
(18)ウオット著　禪學大意
昭和七年刊
(19)ゴダード著　佛教聖典
昭和七年刊
(20)オハザマ著　禪（獨文）
大正十四年刊
(21)緒方宗博著　坐禪の手引
昭和八年刊

尙以上の書籍の原名を列記すれば下の通りである。

LIST OF REFERENCE

BOOKS ON ZEN

1. Suzuki, D.: Essays in Zen Buddhism. (First Series) London 1927.
2. Suzuki, D.: Essays in Zen Buddhism. (Second Series) London 1933.
3. Suzuki, D.: Essays in Zen Buddhism. (Third Series) London 1934.
4. Suzuki, D.: Studies in the Lankavatara Sutra. London 1930.
5. Suzuki, D.: The Lankavatara Sutra. London 1932.
6. Suzuki, D.: The Training of the Zen Buddhist Monk. Kyoto 1934.
7. Suzuki, D.: An Introduction to Zen Buddhism. Kyoto. 1934.
8. Suzuki. D.: Manual of Zen Buddhism Kyoto 1935.
9. Wong: Sutra Spoken by the Sixth Patriarch, Wei Lang, on the High Seat of the Gem of Law. Shanghai 1930.
10. Muller, M.: The Vajrakkhedika. Oxford 1894.
11. Gemmell, W.: Diamond Sutra. London 1924.
12. Muller, M.: The Prajna-paramita-hridaya-sutra. Oxford 1894.
13. Kern, H.: The Saddharmas-Pundarika-sutra. Oxford 1884.
14. Nukariya, K.: Religion of Samurai. London 1913.
15. Suzuki, D.: Sermons of a Buddhist Abbot Chicago 1906.
16. Senzaki, N.: The Gateless Gate. Los Angels 1934.
17. Senzaki, N.: 10 Bulls. Los Angels 1933.
18. Watts. A.: An Outline of Zen Buddhism. London 1932.
19. Goddard, D.: A Buddhist Bible. Vermont 1932.
20. Ohasama, S.: Zen: Der Lebendige Buddhismus in Japan. Stuttgart 1925.
21. Ogata, S.: A Guide to Zen Practice. Kyoto 1934.

日本佛教を印度に傳道せよ

ラーフラ・サンクリトヤーヤナ

私は日本佛教の研究と日本の現狀とを視察する目的を以て來朝したのであるが，日本の文化が想像以上に進み，頗る組織立つてゐるのに驚く外はない。殊に佛教が日本に於て現に良く榮えて，盛んに教育事業や社會事業を經營してゐるのは殊に結構だと思ふ。自分の日本滯在は僅に二箇月間であるから，それを十分理解し，見學し盡すことは勿論出來なかつたが，大に得る所があつたのを喜ぶものである。私はこの日本佛教を印度に傳道し，その教育事業・社會事業を印度に實施されることを切に希望するものである。

不幸にして佛教は印度本土から五百年前に姿を消し，滅亡して仕舞つた。その原因は色々擧げることは出來ようが，佛教の內に『金剛乘』といふ宗派が盛んになつて，道德的に亂れ，迷信的となり，呪術なぞを行ふやうになり內部的に弱くなつてゐた。その折，十二世紀頃にマホメト教徒が西域から侵入して來て，佛教の殿堂を破壞し，財寶を奪略し，僧侶を殺したため，佛教僧侶はネパールや西藏・ビルマ等に逃げ，信者は印度教やマホメツト教に轉宗して仕舞ひ，十四世紀には流石に榮えた佛教の樓閣も脆くも崩壞して，佛教は印度本土から消ふ失せて仕舞つたのである。

かうして五六十年前までは印度の民衆は佛教を忘れ去つて，佛教について何も知らなかつたのである。然し英領印度政廳によつて，各地の佛教遺跡が相次いで發掘されて，鹿野苑や佛陀伽耶・那爛陀大學・祇園精舍の遺跡が地上に現はれ修繕されて，原形を想像することが出來るやうになり，その佛教建築の偉大と當時の文化の卓越と佛教の繁榮に感嘆したのである。之に刺戟されて，印度に佛教の研究が盛んとなり，佛教が印度文化に貢獻すること極めて多いことが初めて解つたのである。宗教として佛教が優れてゐるのは勿論，龍樹・無著・世親・陳那等の佛教哲學は印度思想中の白眉であり，馬鳴・マートリチエータ・聖勇の佛教文學は印度文學中の精華であつた。殊にアヂャンター・エローラの窟院建築と壁畫，健陀羅・グプタの彫刻は印度美術中の隨一と言つても過言ではない。印度に於て佛教が榮えた時は同時に印度文明の華やかな時代であつたのである。この爲に學者の間に佛教研究が盛んになると共に，民衆の間にも，自分達の祖先の間に誕生し，成長した佛教の價値を認め，之に對する關心が次第に高められて來た。

私自身婆羅門階級の出身で，印度教徒であつたが，梵語專門學院で梵語や印度哲學を研究中，讀んだ梵語の書籍中に澤山の佛教章句が引用されて居りその意味が深いのに引き付けられ，教師から佛教思想の卓越してゐることを聞かされて，梵語，巴利語の佛教經典や西藏語の佛教經典に次第に興味を抱いて研究し，遂に佛教僧團にて出家して，比丘となつたのである。然し自分のやうに教養があり，梵語・巴利語・西藏語を通じ佛教を知り得るものはよいが，大部分の印度青年は佛教に興味を持つてゐながら，之を知る好機を掴む事が出來ないのである。彼等とて佛教に絕大の興味を抱いてゐるのであるが，それを理解する教養と機會とが十分でないのである。

カルカツタの日本山妙法寺

近年このやうに印度に於て一般民衆の佛教に關心を持ち出したことは非常なもので，佛教を知りたく望み，その傳道を切に希望してゐる。實に印度に佛教復興の氣運が動きつゝあると言ふことが斷言出來るのである。然し何分にも印度本土には佛教は滅び，佛教僧侶も殆んど皆無の爲，自力で復興出來ず，外部の力を藉りなければならない，勿論，昨今セイロン島及びビルマの各種の佛教團體の僧侶・居士が印度に長老派の佛教，所謂小乘佛教を傳道し，鹿野苑には宏壯な佛教新寺院が建立された位であるが，之では尙微力であり，不十分である。この際自分は日本佛教徒が日本佛教を印度に齎し傳道して下さることを切に希望するものである。自分が日本に來たのは，日本觀光・現狀視察・日本佛教の研究の外に日本佛教を印度に傳道されるやう勸誘する爲であるが，日本に來てその佛教が卓越して，盛大なるを見るにつけて，一層この感を深くし强くするのである。

私がこの趣旨を各方面の佛教徒に說明した場合に，日本の友人間では費用が多額を要して效が少いとか，英國政府が妨害するであらうとか，起りさうな困難を想像して躊躇されてゐる人が多かつた。然し私の思ふ所では，その懸念は無用である。傳道の費用は餘り多きを要せず，工資を持つて來て傳道されることは，むしろ我々の歡迎しない所である。

且つ印度教徒はヴイシユヌ神の化身の一人として佛陀を崇拜して，佛教輸入を歡迎してゐるので，篤志の富豪達が之を助けるであらう。現に印度で傳道中の日本山妙法寺の藤井行勝師に對して，富豪ジェー・ケー・ビルラ氏は，佛教寺院建設の爲廣大な敷地と一萬數千留比の建築費を寄附した位である。又英國政府は日本の佛教徒が印度で傳道するのを他意ありと疑つて，妨害するであらうか，理論上英國政府はそのやうな權利を持つてゐない筈である。何故ならば，英國は印度に基督教を傳道し，且つ日本に於ても基督教の傳道は禁じられてゐないからである。

日本佛教の傳道の爲には，二三人の英語と梵語の知識ある傳道師を派遣されることを望みたい。この人は印度渡來後印度語を學び，印度の習慣風土にも馴れてから，印度人の中に入つて働いて，いただきたい。かくすれば，次第に印度青年の間に助力者も出來るであらう。之等の傳道師は傳道と同時に是非共日本佛教の進歩した組織一教育事業や社會事業を附帶して行つていただきたいのである。殊に農場と小工場を經營して，日本の進歩した園藝と家庭工業の見本を示し，之を印度人に公開し，指導していただきたい。日本の家屋を建て，如何に小綺麗に掃除され設備が整へられてゐるか，しかも如何に安價に生活出來，家内工業品が作り出されるかといふことを實地に示して印度各地から來る人々に展覽せしめ教示していただきたい。之を見た人々は之を各地に實施して，如何程印度を益するか解らないのである。しかもその資金は一萬五千圓乃至二萬圓で十分であると思ふ。

又他方，印度の學生が日本に留學するのに便宜を與へていただきたいのである。現在印度の青年は英國を中心として歐米諸國に留學してゐるのであるが，歐米諸國と印度の生活狀態は餘りに隔つてゐる爲に，費用が多く入つてしかも印度に歸つて實用に役立たぬことが多い。然し日本の生活狀態は印度とさして隔らず，むしろ社會狀態が類似する所が多い爲，學費が安く，しかも歸國後も，た易く實行出來て，效果的である譯である。唯日本語は語法が非常に異つて學ぶに困難なので，印度から留學する學生の爲に日本で特別の獎學制度を設けて，特別の學級を設け用ひる言語については便宜を與へられるやうにして欲しい。さうなれば印度から毎年留學に來る學生數は，數千數萬に達するやうになるであらう。この人々が印度へ歸つてから，日本の傳道師達を助けることが多いと期待出來る私も歸國後日本佛教と農業を學ぶ爲に少年を送りたいと思つてゐる。

日本は亞細亞に於て最も强力にして富んだ國であり，大部分の地方が白人の植民地である亞細亞に於て，第一の獨立國であり，しかも我々と同じ佛教國である。日本こそは他の文化低き弱少民族を指導教化すべき唯一の亞細亞の盟主である。印度について言ふならば，過去に高き文化を持つて，支那・日本をも教化したのであるが，現在は文化低き弱少國となつた。この秋，日本が印度との過去の密接な交渉に顧みて，印度に日本佛教及び日本文明を輸入して，印度を指導するならば，獨り吾々を裨益するのみに止らないであらう。

（平等通昭譯）

朝鮮に於ける佛教青年運動の概觀

江　田　俊　雄

序

朝鮮に於いて近代的佛教青年運動の勃興したのは最近二十六年來，卽ち明治四十三年八月に行はれた日韓合邦以後のことである。此の政治上の一大變革は必然的に半島に於ける諸般の文化事項にも夫れ夫れ一大轉換を契機したが，李朝五百年の久しきに亘つた執拗苛酷なる揚儒抑佛政策の犧牲として呻吟した朝鮮の佛教が解放されて，更始一新の治下に立ち，聖代の餘澤に浴して，國家によつて信教の自由を保證され，寺財の安固を確保されるに至つたこともその大なるものゝ一である。朝鮮佛教の僧侶は彼等の眼前に展開された餘りにも急激なるこの時代の變遷に驚愕し，一時は何を爲すべきかを知らず，何處へ向つて進むべきかに迷ひさへしたほどであつた。彼等に取つては先づ何よりも自らの教團の復興整理より，急務なるはなかつた。宜なる哉，新政以來，今日に至るまでの彼等の活動は凡て，自利自行に屬すべきもので利他，行化の宗教的活動とは凡そ緣遠いもので，而もそれも内外諸種の事情に基くとはいへ，決して成功への歩みであつたとは云ひ得ない。斯くて，此の時代を通じて朝鮮佛教の空に陰欝なる混沌の雲が低迷してゐたことは事實である。從つて斯かる朝鮮佛教を母胎として生れ出でた青年運動にも潑溂性と明朗性のあらう筈なく，動もすれば確たる指導精神の缺如のゆへに，活動の氣魄弱まり，その方向さへ見失ひがちであつた。加ふるに朝鮮に於ける佛教青年運動の難關が此の地の人心を支配することの强い事大思想と黨派心との妄動にも屢ゝ禍されたことも想起せられねばならない。今，朝鮮に於ける佛教青年運動を概觀せんとするに際し試みに第一勃興期，第二受難期，第三活動期，第四沈滯期の四時期に分けて述べてみようと思ふ。

第一　勃興期(明治43―45年)

未だ團體的に訓練と統制をもつた運動としてゞはなかつたが，朝鮮佛教の一部情熱的青年が隨處に蹶起して，その雄々しき活動力を始めて示したのは明治四十一年，當時朝鮮佛教の統一的機關として設置された圓宗宗務院代表海印寺李晦光が，東京に於いて，曹洞宗代表弘津說三との間に，朝鮮佛教と曹洞宗との連合條約を契約して歸鮮した時，之に反對して，彼を賣宗の賊として糾彈した時であつた。尤も李晦光としては日本佛教の權威を利用して朝鮮佛教の復興を計らんとしたのに過ぎなかつたのであるが，主として南鮮寺刹の朴漢永，韓龍雲，陳震應等の猛烈なる反對を買ふことになり，之に多くの青年僧徒が和して，或は飛檄し，或は遊說し，或は會議して，遂に此の擧を中止せしむるに至つた。所が反對派は更に朝鮮佛敎を圓宗（參禪・看經・念佛・密呪等を凡て圓修するの意）と呼ぶことの不當を鳴し，朝鮮佛敎は高麗太古國師以來，臨濟宗に屬してゐることを主張し，圓宗宗務院に對して別に臨濟宗宗務院を全南松廣寺（後慶南梵魚寺に移す）に置いた。爰に於いて朝鮮佛敎は南北の二派對立して互ひに圓宗又は臨濟宗を固執して相爭つた。朝鮮佛敎界に於ける此の南北の對立は其の後ずつと續き，靑年運動にも常に此の色彩が混夾することになつた。僧靑年運動の眞の勃興は合邦の翌年，四十四年の寺剎令の發布に動機してゐる即ち此の時朝鮮總督府は朝鮮佛敎を以て，日本佛敎とは別に獨自の道を步ましむる方針を定め，之によつて，新たに三十本山（後一寺を增す）が指定せられ，其の下に一千餘の末寺が分屬せしめられ，是等を統轄するために京城に禪敎兩宗宗務院が置かれた。乃で自然に圓宗と臨濟宗の爭ひも解消し，地方各寺剎は此の法令に準じて寺法を制定し，布敎興學に力を注ぐようになつた。此の機運によつて全鮮に四十餘の寺立普通學林と十餘の中學程度の地方學林が建設され，爰に於いて眠れるが如き靑年僧徒も新時代の敎育を受け，新思潮の波に洗はれることになつた。乃で是等の學林に學ぶ誇りに充ちた靑年の間には，力と和合を表象するかのように陸續として佛敎靑年の團體が結成され，慶南梵魚寺のそれを始め十數に上つた。併し是等初期のものは其の熱と意氣の旺んなものがあつたとしても，未だ團體としての組織と訓練に於いては缺くるものがあるを免れなかつた。

第二　受難期（大正元—八年）

朝鮮の佛敎靑年運動を醞釀せしめた寺剎令は別の意味に於いて又之を制壓す結果をも齎した。併しそれは法令の責といふよりは寧ろ之が發動をいはゞ惡用した寺剎住持の罪であつたと見られる。といふのは此の法令によつて一片の官の認可狀を手にした無知なる住持が從來は一山大衆の合議制によつて圓滿正當に處理された寺務を利己的に獨斷專行する風を生じ，之によつて住持と一般僧侶殊に血氣の靑年との間に對立抗爭が行はれ，其の結果は多く靑年派の敗北に歸し，有爲な氣慨に滿ちた靑年僧徒は或は罰せられ，或は寺を逐はれることになり，爰に靑年の團體は指導者を失ひ，又は甚しきに至つては團體の解散をも餘儀なくせしめられるといふことが起りがちであつたからである。靑年運動に對する住持側の白眼視は大正三年，京城に「第三回朝鮮三十本山住持總會」が開かれ，翌四年三十本山聯合事務所が開設せられて以後は殊に甚しくなり，その反目と紛糾とは各處に展開されたが，强化された住持權の前には如何ともすることなく，折角芽生へた靑年運動は早くも中途挫折の悲運に直面することになつた。然るに此の運動の上に更に大なる受難が起

つた。所謂三一運動又は萬歲騷ぎがそれである。大正八年三月一日，歐洲大戰に刺戟された民族自決の風潮に乘じた朝鮮民衆のこの政治運動は京城を中心に全鮮に勃發し，民族思想に燃ゆる多くの朝鮮佛敎靑年も亦敢然として之に參加した。其の結果彼等の多くは或は獄に投ぜられ，或は海外に亡命するといふ風で，又しても靑年運動は指導者級を失ひ，加ふるに官よりは團體結社の自由を制抑されることになり，爰に再度の頓座を受くることになつたのは是非もないことであつた。

第三　活動期（大正九—昭和六年）

政治運動に脫線し，或は其の餘波を受けて崩壞に瀕した佛敎靑年の團體が自らの軌道を確認した時に，彼等は先づ自らの再組織と再統制の運動に邁進した。大正九年六月「朝鮮佛敎靑年會」として組織され，本部を京城に，支部を地方各寺剎內に置いて，朝鮮に於ける佛敎靑年會運動に一時期を劃したことがその現はれであつた。所が此の統制運動は又も敎團の革新運動と合流し大正十年，南方出身の金尙昊，劉碩圭等の靑年を中心として，寺法撤廢・人法融通等の四大綱領を揭げた「朝鮮佛敎維新會」として成立を見た。併し此の運動の底には寺剎令を嫌忌して，朝鮮佛敎の完全なる自治を獲得せんとする思想もあつたので，住持連の一部反動者の中傷もあつて間もなく當局の彈壓する所となつた。乃で又も靑年と住持との反目が激化され，翌十一年に覺皇寺に於いて，住持糾討講演會が開かれ，其の餘勢は當時住持級にあつて專橫を恣にするといはれた水原龍珠寺姜大蓮を拉して太鼓を負はしめ，市中を引き廻すといふ珍事をも惹起するに至つた。此の前年，維新會の流れを引いて，覺皇寺內に朝鮮佛敎の統一機關として朝鮮佛敎中央總務院が出來たが，之に對して，北方の住持派を中心に「朝鮮佛敎中央敎務院」が組織されて，やはり覺皇寺內に置かれ，こゝに同一趣旨の主義相反する二團體が同一場所に對立爭鬪するといふ奇現象を呈するに至つた。併し是等の兩院も大正十一年妥協合一し，爰に現在の財團法人朝鮮佛敎中央敎務院が成立した。此の敎務院は一見，朝鮮佛敎の中央機關の如くであるが，實は單なる財團の事務所に過ぎず，何等一般寺剎を統轄すべき法理的根據も實際的能力も有するものではない。斯くの如き狀態にあつては所詮敎勢の發展を期待し難いといふので往年の朝鮮佛敎靑年會が再起し，當時海外の留學より歸つて來た新知識の白性郁（獨逸哲學博士）金法麟（佛國文學士）都鎭鎬（日本大學出）等を中心に朝鮮佛敎の眞の統一の急務が唱道され，遂に昭和四年，覺皇寺に於いて百數十名の出席會員を以て「朝鮮佛敎禪敎兩宗僧侶大會」の開催を見，其の席上「朝鮮佛敎禪敎兩宗宗憲」が制定せられ，嚴肅莊重なる宣誓式が執行された。爰に於いて朝鮮佛敎の具體的宗名が決定せられ，其の理想的統一機關が約束されたが，未だ之は實行に移されるには至らない。斯くて朝鮮佛敎の統

一運動に華々しき産婆役を勤め上げ，清新の意氣を盛返した青年會は翌五年七月布哇に於いて第一回汎太平洋佛教青年大會が開かれるや，都鎭鎬を代表として派遣し，英文パンフレットを配布したが，此の年十月，彼の歸國を迎へた幹部の間に青年運動の實質的統一強化が議せられ，翌六年三月，京城に開かれた「朝鮮佛教青年大會」に於いては「佛陀精神の體験」「合理宗政の確立」「大衆佛教の實現」の三大綱目が掲げられて「朝鮮佛教青年總同盟」が組織化された。而して地方の各本山には二十五の支同盟が結成され，盟員七百が細胞組織的に獲得され，其の潑剌たる躍進振は正に明日の朝鮮佛教の隆盛を物語るかの如き頼母しさを示した。

此運動の中堅には都鎭鎬・李龍祚(東京醫專出)・朴東一（京城帝大出)・曹學乳（豐山大學出)・許永鎬(大正大學出)・朴允進(中央佛專出)・姿裕文(同)等が居た。

第四　沈滯期(昭和七—現今)

「朝鮮佛教青年總同盟」は創立の當初は破竹の勢を以て躍進したが，理想に急にして一時に氣勢を揚げ過ぎた觀があり，旁ゝ地方的色彩も加味されて彼等の運動方向が轉換されたかに見えたので，住持連の保守長老派特に現朝鮮佛教幹部等の容ぶ所とならず，ために種々の壓迫が加はることになつた。そのうちに總同盟内にも分裂を生じ，一部は現狀に反對し，自己の立場を守るの餘り，佛教經營にかゝる單なる社會事業としての中等學校を支持し，佛教本來の人材教育機關たる佛教專門學校を廢せんとするの愚擧に策動したりして，今や全體としてもその信用と勢力とは地に墜ち，同盟本部も有耶無耶の存在を續け，地方支同盟も過半は自ら又は他の力によつて解體し，殘りのものは漠然たる存在に墮し，尙僅かに活氣を保つもの四五に過ぎない。されば昭和九年夏，東京に第二回汎太平洋佛教青年大會が開かれても，代表派遣の舉なく，僅かに中央佛專の學生代表の参加せんとするのをさへも阻まれるといふ爲體に化した。斯くて今や朝鮮の佛教青年運動は秋風落莫の沈滯狀態を續けてゐるのである。

以上，最近四半世紀に於ける朝鮮の近代的佛教青年運動の經過を槪觀したのであるが，此の短年月の間に起つた此の運動の起伏盛衰，分裂合體の現象は過渡期的變態といふには餘りに變轉極まりなき荊棘苦難の道ではあつた。朝鮮の佛教青年運動は何處へ行くか？

新刊紹介

◇乙亥訪華錄

（日華佛教研究會編）

昨十年六，七月の交，林彥明氏を總務として，教界の名士十數氏が，親しく中華民國を訪ねられた記錄（菊版一三二頁，非賣品，其會發行）

◇六祖法寶壇經

（中華民國，汕頭居士林佛教流通處版）

國際佛教通報局定款

名　　稱

第一，本局を國際佛教通報局と稱す

事 務 所

第二，本局の事務所を全日本佛教青年會聯盟本部に置く

目　　的

第三，本局は日本內海及海外に向つて佛教事情の通報をなし，且つ佛教徒相互間の各種便宜を計るを以て目的とす

事　　業

第四，本局の目的を達成するため左記の事業を行ふ

イ，日本內地及世界各國より佛教事情に關する質問の通報を行ふ

ロ，必要に應じ日本語及世界各國語を以て佛教事情の通報を行ふ

ハ，外國人の日本觀光に際しては各國の便益を與へ，特にその佛教に關する方面に於て之を爲す

ニ，定時或は隨時に各國語を以て文書の刊行をなす

ホ，その他必要と認めたる事業を行ふ

役　　員

第五，本局の事務を處理するため左の役員を置く

イ，局　長　　一　名

ロ，幹　事　　三　名

ハ，評議員　　若干名

局長は本局　　を總括す

幹事は本局の事務を處理す

評議員は局長の提案に依る重要事務を審議す

第六，評議員は左記の者を以て之に充つ

イ，全日本佛教青年會館聯盟理事及主事

ロ，全日本佛教青年會聯盟理事會に於て推薦したる者

第七，局長及幹事は評議員會に於て決定す

第八，役員の任期は二ヶ年とす（但し重任を妨げず）

經　　費

第九，本局の經費は左記のものに依て之を支辨す

イ，本局基金の活用

ロ，寄附金

ハ，その他の收入

補　　則

第十，本定款に記載せられざる事項は，凡て評議員會に於て協議す

第十一，第一回の役員は全日本佛教青年會聯盟理事會に於て決定す

定價　一部 金 二 十 錢｜送料二錢
一年 金二圓四十錢｜送料不要

昭和十年四月廿日第三種郵便物認可
昭和十一年三月廿八日印刷（每月一回）
昭和十一年四月一日發行（一日發行）

東京市外吉祥寺337
編輯發行兼印刷人　淺　野　研　眞

東京市牛込區早稻田鶴卷町107
印刷所　康文社印刷所
電話牛込（34）1950番 5049番

東京市神田區一ツ橋二の三
發行所　國際佛教通報局
電話九段（33）4428番
振替東京83015番

昭和十年四月三十日第三種郵便物認可
昭和十一年三月二十八日印刷納本（每月一回
昭和十一年四月一日發行（一日發行）
國際佛教通報　第二卷　第四號

第二回

汎太平洋佛教青年會大會

紀要

THE PROCEEDINGS

of

THE Second

General Conference

of

Pan-Pacific Young Buddhists' Associations

(in Japanese, Chinese and English)

Held at Tokyo & Kyoto, July 18–23, 1934

Price ￥ 3.00

Compiled & Published

by

The Federation of All Y.B. As. of Japan,

Tokio, Kanda, Hitotsubashi, II-3

昭和十年四月三十日第三種郵便物認可　昭和十一年四月二十八日印刷納本　昭和十一年五月一日發行（每月一回一日發行）第二卷　第五號

The International Buddhist Bulletin

國際佛教通報

第二卷　昭和十一年五月　第五號　〔Vol. II. May. 2502/1936 No. 5.〕

要　目　〔Contents〕

東　京　國際佛教通報局　發　行
The International Buddhist Information Bureau
Tokyo, Kanda, Hitotsubashi, II—3

Staff of the Bureau

Hon. President J. Takakusu

President K. Ohmura
Secretary S. Takagai
〃 B. Inaba
〃 (in chief) Ken Assano

Advisers H. Ui
〃 G. Asakura
〃 R. Hatani
〃 U. Ogiwara
〃 R. Higata
〃 T. Suzuki
〃 S. Suzuki
〃 S. Amakuki
〃 S. Nagai
〃 B. Matsumoto
〃 E. Uno
〃 C. Akamatsu
〃 Z. Ohmori
〃 K. Yabuki
〃 S. Onoh
〃 S. Katoh
〃 M. Anezaki
〃 G. Honda
〃 R. Sekimoto
〃 J. Sahegi
〃 R. Hanada
〃 H. Kohno
〃 R. Takaoka
〃 Z. Kobayashi
〃 S. Yamabe
〃 C. Akanuma
〃 E. Honda
〃 R. Ohmori
〃 E. Kawaguchi
〃 C. Yamakawa
〃 D. Tokiwa
〃 T. Tanimoto
〃 G. Tokiwai
〃 S. Ohtani
〃 E. Ohtani
〃 B. Mizuno
〃 I. Shibata
〃 S. Ando
〃 J. Shimomura
〃 S. Kikuzawa
〃 K. Norisugi
〃 T. Shibata
〃 K. Asano
〃 T. Watanabe
〃 G. Onoh
〃 K. Yanagizawa
〃 M. Shigemitsu
〃 E. Kanakura
〃 S. Tachibana

國際佛教通報局

名譽局長 高楠順次郎

局長 大村桂巖
幹事 鷹谷俊之
同 稲葉文海
同 淺野研眞

顧問（順序不同）宇井伯壽
〃 朝倉曉瑞
〃 羽溪了諦
〃 荻原雲來
〃 干潟龍祥
〃 鈴木大拙
〃 鈴木宗忠
〃 天岫接三
〃 長井眞琴
〃 松本文三郎
〃 椎尾辨匡
〃 宇野圓空
〃 赤松智城
〃 大森禪戒
〃 矢吹慶輝
〃 小野清一郎
〃 加藤精神
〃 姉崎正治
〃 本田義英
〃 關本龍門
〃 佐伯定胤
〃 花田凌雲
〃 河野法雲
〃 高岡隆心
〃 小林瑞淨
〃 山邊習學
〃 赤沼智善
〃 本多惠隆
〃 大森亮順
〃 河口慧海
〃 山川智應
〃 常盤大定
〃 谷本富
〃 常盤井堯猷
〃 大谷尊由
〃 大谷瑩潤
〃 水野梅曉
〃 柴田一能
〃 安藤正純
〃 下村壽一
〃 菊澤季麿
〃 乘杉嘉壽
〃 芝田徹心
〃 淺野孝之
〃 渡邊哲信
〃 小野玄妙
〃 柳澤健
〃 重光葵
〃 金倉圓照
〃 立花俊道

Japan Celebrates Buddha's Birthday At Many Temples

Singing, Dancing and Religious Rites Widely Observed

The birthday of Shakya Muni, an occasion of considerable Buddhistic religious significance, was celebrated in Tokyo and in other places, notably in Buddhistic centers, throughout the country on April 8.

The occasion was observed in Tokyo as Hana Matsuri, or Floral Fete, with the Federation of Girls' Buddhistic School Students as its center in accordance with the custom established several years ago. The celebration was held by the Federation at the Hibiya Public Hall from a half hour after noon.

A ceremony in honor of the occasion was held at the Memerial Hall in Honjo in commemoration of the Kwanto Earthquake victims from 8 o'clock in the morning with several hundred Buddhist priests attending. Kambutsue, the time-honored ceremony of pouring amacha, a sweet beverage prepared from the hydrangea, over a figure of the Buddha in observance of the birthday of the Buddha, was held in the compounds of the hall. A huge tent was pitched there under which amacha was served to people numbering some 3,000.

The various Buddhist temples in the city observed the occasion according to their own rites. Gokokuji Temple in Koishikawa-ku served amacha to its parishioners in its compounds from 10 o'clock in the morning. The same temple held a service in observance of the occasion from 1 o'clock in the afternoon.

At Denzuin Temple in Koishikawa a grand celebration in honor of the occasion was held from 7 o'clock in the evening. Newly composed songs and newly created dances in celebration of the occasion were broadcast by the radio station here from noon.

The Truth that is more than Teaching

An Appeal

By **Alan W. Watts**, Editor of *Buddhism in England.*

All schools of Buddhism are agreed that the apparent separateness of one being from another is illusion. I have often wondered, therefore, at the things which divide mankind into conflicting parties, and especially at the things which cause the followers of a common religion to quarrel among themselves. All conflict must take place on the plane of separateness, in the superficial and illusory aspect of life where the fundamental Unity is not perceived. In the real aspect there can be no conflict, for there it is realized that the Many are One. I believe that conflict might be overcome if we could accept the fact that in Samsara—the world of form—it is in the very nature of things to disagree. In all the universe there is no one form that is in every respect the same as another, for all things, while they are essentially One, are unique in their outward appearance.

Therefore quarrels are caused by looking for agreement where it cannot exist, and the man who quarrels with his fellows is he who seeks to impose his own form upon others. In Samsara, unity can only be achieved by agreeing to differ. For difference is the very nature of Samsara, and unity cannot be achieved by trying to make forms the same as one another, but only by realizing that all forms have a common essence. For instance, if a bird is to be a bird, it would be ridiculous to expect the wings to be like the beak, or the claws like the tail. And yet many of us seriously expect such impossibilities to be achieved when we try to make others conform with our own patterns and plans. For the human race, in the same way as a bird, is an organism of which every part has a separate and distinct function or *dharma*, and the whole cannot be expressed in its parts unless each part is unique in its form and method of work.

Just as the human race is a total organism, so are the followers of the Buddha of whatever sect or school. It is unfortunate, therefore, that within this great religious body there should be numerous conflicts and quarrels which prevent it from working as a harmonious whole. There is the conflict between Mahayana and Theravada, between the various schools of thought about the Anatta doctrine, between theists and atheists, and between the Self-power and Other-power sects of Japan and China, to mention only a few. These conflicts prevent Buddhists from sincerely acknowledging one another as brothers, and destroy the effectiveness of a common purpose within the greatest religious community in the world. Of course, it would be too much to expect people not to quarrel, for the seeds of strife are planted deep in human nature. But it is not too much to expect the more conscious and intelligent members of this community to refrain from doctrinal squabbles and to realize that there is a deeper and infinitely more important bond between man and man than similarity of belief.

We must accept the fact that, even among Buddhists, beliefs are bound to differ. For all belief in doctrines is a matter of intellect, and intellect is that faculty of the mind which discriminates, which forms ideas and concepts. All forms, whether mental or physical, are of Samsara; thus they will differ in greater or lesser degree with each individual, for, as we have seen, in Samsrra there can be no two things of the same pattern. Therefore I am convinced that it is a mistake to try to achieve unity among Buddhists by attempting to construct a common creed or even a minimum basis of generally accepted beliefs. We can be united and yet have different opinions. This may sound strange, even impossible, and so it would be if there were not in Buddhism a Truth that is more than teaching, more than a set of ideas about the universe,

The error which is at the root of all conflict is too great a reliance on forms. No one, unless he spent too much reverence on mere concepts, would quarrel with another because of his form of belief, or be

offended because someone disagreed with his own. If someone attacks my property and so offends me, my feeling of offence can only arise through attachment to property—which is not a Buddhist virtue. What applies to property must also apply to beliefs, concepts and doctrines, for these are the property of the mind. *Trishna*—selfish clinging—can apply just as much to ideas as to money, for both are *anicca*, impermanent, and *anatta*, without essential reality. For a concept (even the concept of Karma or Anatta) is a form and as such is subject to the same conditions as all other forms. Thus even the Dharma is part of Samsara, and for this reason the Buddha likened it to a raft for crossing a stream, a raft which must be left behind when the stream is crossed. Therefore if the Dharma cannot enter Nirvana, it is certainly a part of Samsara,

One should always be careful to avoid that simplest yet most dangerous of mistakes—the confusion of belief with Truth, the identification of the raft with the opposite bank of the stream. Beliefs are ideas *about* Truth and not Truth itself, for the formless Nirvana cannot be described by the forms of Samsara, and as all forms are illusory and impermanent, he who *clings* to beliefs is lost. He who would attain Nirvana must give up all clinging, for only in this way can he achieve the Enlightenment which is freedom from forms. That is not to say that he destroys all forms, but that he is no longer attached to them, that he no longer depends on them for peace of mind. Therefore let us make less ado about beliefs; no one ever travelled far on a road by clinging to its surface, and he who travels fastest, he who runs, touches it most lightly with his feet. But how shall we be sure that we are on the right road? Must we not depend upon the road if we would reach the Goal? Paradoxically the answer is: That road is the best upon which we feel we need depend lest, for that road leads to non-attachment, to freedom from dependence. Further than this, non-attachment *is* that road, for Buddhism is essentially the art of setting the mind free from forms. For the doctrines of Karma, Anatta, Anicca, Dukha, Rebirth and the rest are all teachings about the nature of Samsara; they are warnings to us to be careful of the snares of Samsara. But the Truth which is more than all these teachings can only be known when we depend neither on Samsara nor on ideas about it or about anything else. Therefore why should intelligent Buddhists quarrel over the various merits of certain sets of ideas and doctrines? For the real question for them is not in which set of doctrines to believe but how to pass beyond all doctrines. Let them ask, not "How shall we reconcile our beliefs?" but "How shall we cease to depend on beliefs?" For the essence of Buddhism is the attainment of Enlightenment through freedom from all objects, forms and concepts—yes, even from the concept that we must depend for our salvation on becoming free from objects, forms and concepts! Ultimately Buddhism goes as far as that, for even he who is attached only to Nirvana knows not Nirvana. If this is our ideal we shall become the laughing-stock of the world if we behave like the pundits of whom Omar Khayyam said:

> Myself when young did eagerly frequent
> Doctor and Saint, and heard great Argument
> About it and about: but evermore
> Came out by the same Door as in I went.

THE ORIGIN OF THE KABUKI

By Haruo Miki

The drama is composed of various elements, but the one that plays the most important role is buyo (dancing). This is also true in the case of the "kabuki" which is the main stream of the drama of this country. Wherever we go, and trace back the origin of a play we notice that it is coloured by religious ideas; the "kabuki" is no exception. With regard to the question of as to how the "kabuki" came into existence it is practically agreed at the present day that it was originated in the closing years of the Ashikaga era when Okuni (the name of a maiden in the service of a shrine) of Izumotaisha (a first-class government shrine) for the purpose of collecting donations to be used for the repairing of the shrine, performed "nembutsu-odori" (a kind of dance accompanied by the sound of gongs, handdrums and Buddhist invocations) at Kyoto for the public to enjoy. It is somewhat strange for a maiden in the service of a shrine to perform "nembutsu-odori," but it is probably correct for us to assume that it was a kind of sacred music and dance, because in those days Buddhism and Shintoism were closely identified.

This "nembutsu-odori" developed into onna-kabuki (woman-kabuki), and has laid the foundation of the "kabuki"; but we must not forget that Okuni was acquainted with Sanzaburo of Nagoya, and had received his guidance. The detailed career of this Sanzaburo is not well-known, but it is said that once he was a vassal of Ujisato Gamou, but when his master's house was ruined, he became a masterless "samurai", and came to Kyoto, where he threw away military pursuits, and led a poetical life and had greatly attracted the attention of the public. This Sanzaburo was greatly struck when he saw Okuni's "nembutsu-odori" because of its artistry, and had given a good deal of advice to improve it.

As a result of this advice Okuni freed herself from the trammels of Buddhism, and contrived new devices. That is, until this time she had to put on black clerical robes and had to hang dawn a gong in front of her, and chanted the Buddhist prayer or expounded Buddhahood, but since then she. changed her costume, girded on a sword, covered her head with a cloth, put on male attire, and danced as she sang songs. The word "kabuki" was originated during this time. The performances of Okuni can be divided into two distinct periods. "Ka" of "Kabuki" is a Chinese character which means "song" and "bu" of "kabuki" is also a Chinese character which "to dance" but the word "kabuki" was not originated in this way because the word signifies "to dance a song". The word "kabuki", as a matter of fact, was originated by simply applying the sounds to Chinese characters. The word "kabuki" is a pure Japanese word and means waggery or buffoonery. Again, there is another opinion which holds that the word does not suggest the same meaning as a prank, but it means strange manners or uncouth appearance; at any rate, it is true that the performers in those days were looked down upon by the general public, since the performers catered for the people who had no culture. In the dramatic history of our country there appeared two great dramatic divisions which have no parallel in the dramatic history of the world; *no* (a musical drama) and *kyogen* (performance) which were in vogue among the polite society, form one division, while the other division was the "kabuki" which was for the interest of the general public. Of course it was the administrative policy of the Tokugawa Shogunate that gave encouragement to its development.

This onnakabuki (woman-kubuki) gained great popularity in those days; it was popular in every corner of our country, and after the death of Okuni there appeared many performing bands. However, since prostitutes began to take part in the performance, it appeared to be bad from the standpoint of popular morals, and at the same time, since there were actually various evil influences in the time of the third Shogunate of Tokugawa, there appeared an order for the prohibition for "woman-kabuki." This was in October of the 6th year of Kanei

(1629).

Accordingly, instead of woman-kabuki, boy-kabuki flourished. This "kabuki" as it is shown by its name was composed by a party of boys who took the place of prostitutes, and was originated in Kyoto. In Yedo (the old name of Tokyo) Kanzaburo Saruwaka established the Saruwaka theater in the first year of Kanei (1624). This was the first theater in Yedo. At one time the performance of youth-kabuki was presented on the stage side by side with that of woman-kabuki, but since the 6th year of Kakei (1629) when the performance of woman-kabuki was prohibited youth-kabuki prevailed throughout the country. But even the performance of youth-kabuki was prohibited in the 1st year of Shoo (1652). That is performances by youths who had their forelocks on was prohibited, and they were ordered to take away the forelocks before they appeared on the stage. Herein lies the birth of man-kabuki 23 years since the prohibition of woman-kabuki.

This prohibition by accident brought great benefit to the development of the "kabuki". That is when forelocks were shaved it was necessary to make wigs in order to cover the defects. Formerly more attention was paid to the personal appearance, but since that time more care began to be taken for the performance. And also formerly the primary importance was attached to dancing and the performance was simple, but thence forth the contents became more complicated. It advanced from one-act play to many-act plays and gradually a well-arranged systematic drama was formed.

Since the appearance of "man-kabuki" a remarkable increase in the number of theatres in Kyoto, Osaka and the neighbouring district took place; likewise in Yedo a great number of theatres were established one after the other, and since actors were selected for the cast of the play according to their speciality they found it necessary to have training in performance. During the Genroku era (1688–1704) there appeared in Kyoto and Osaka district a famous actor called Tojuro Sakata, who at one time had connection with Monzaemon Chikamatsu (a great man of letters), and the contents of the drama began to exhibit a literary nature. Dramatic performance grew to be no more a pastime. In Yedo,

Danjuro Ichikawa the First appeared on the stage and laid the foundation of the Yedo warrior's role.

However, the "kabuki" had by no means made its progress under a favorable wind. The position and the number of theatres were placed under restraint, and only three theatres were allowed to exist in Yedo. The position of actors and the people who were concerned with theatres was placed below the military, agriculture, industrial, and mercantile classes, and they were not allowed to have intercourse with those classes above the "samurai" class. Later on the hanging of rattan blinds at the seats of theatres was forbidden, and the incognito attendance of the upper classes was checked. The control was most severe during the Tempo era.

In this way the "kabuki" became separate from the literary classes, and therefore it was quite natural that the contents of the drama and its literary nature, which once reached a high level, gradually grew poorer. But on the other hand the dramatic possibilities began to develop. The improvement of stage equipment which is unique in the world's drama took place. For instance, such a stage as the movable stage is quite a rarity, and in Europe the movable stage was first adopted in Reinhardt's theatre in Germany, but even this was learned from the Japanese theatres.

The development of theatre music is worthy of special mention, and it was in the 10th year of Kanei (1633), when the retired actor Kisaburo Kineya became a "samisen" player, and took part in a performance at Saruwaka theatre, that the "samisen" was first introduced in theatre music. Indeed this melody of Kineya's "samisen" was the origin of the long epic song of Yedo. A handrum, a drum, a flute were already used before, but when once "samisen" was introduced into theatre music many schools of "samisen" were set up, and greatly helped the performance, and at the same time the contents of the "kabuki" were greatly enriched, and in this point also no similar characteristic can be found in any other drama of the world. *(The Japan Times)*

Japanese News

GROUP FORMED TO STUDY YEDO DAYS

To study the culture and social conditions of Yedo days, some leading art critics and scholars have organized a society recently. Among the group are Dr. Seiya Fujikake, professor at the Tokyo Imperial University and some well known painters, as well as critics. The society has decided to issue a bulletin for its members established the Society for the Study of Ukiyoye Prints several years ago, while they studied social conditions of the Yedo period.

PROPAGANDA FILMS FOR CHINA

In order to introduce real Japanese life and actual conditions here to China, the Cultural Bureau of the Foreign Ministry has decided to produce some talkie films representing Japanese life with sub-titles written in the local dialects Kwantung and Peiping. The films to be sent to China will, it is believed, facilitate a Chinese understanding of Japanese things.

WRITER LEAVING FOR OCCIDENT

The farewell meeting in honor of Mr. Saneatsu Mushakoji, noted writer and playwright who is leaving Japan on a trip to Europe, was given at the Tatsumi Restaurant, Sukiyabashi, March 14 evening. A number of writers and artists were present. Mr. Mushakoji is the brother of Viscount Kimitomo Mushakoji, Japanese Ambassador to Germany. He will be in Germany, France, Italy and America for about a year During his stay in Europe and America, he will inspect literary movements and establish good will relation between the Japan Pen Club and literary organizations abroad.

PARIS TO RECEIVE JAPANESE GARDEN

A Japanese garden will be constructed in Paris shortly. This proposition was submitted to the Ministry of Foreign Affairs, the Society for the Promotion of International Relations, the Board of Tourist Industry and the Japanese Garden Society by Mr. Jirohachi Satsuma.

The Japanese Garden Society has been planning to create a Japanese garden in Paris for some time and Mr. Satsuma made an arrangement with the French people during his recent visit to France.

The garden will be constructed in the compound of Mr. Albert Kahn's home, well known wealthy French resident of Paris. Mr. Kahn intends to donate his compound to the Municipality of Paris and thus the garden will be constructed with the cooperation of the municipality.

All materials for the garden will be collected by Japanese specialists and be sent to France shortly.

MORE BEAUTIFUL CITIES SOUGHT BY SOCIETY

Under the auspicies of the Society for the Study of Urbanism in Japan, a meeting for the promotion of more beautiful cities was held at Sukiyabashi Park, Ginza, on April 3. Two willow trees will then be planted along the Ginza. A ceremony will be held at the New Band Stand in Hibiya Park on the same day, and sprouts of willow and cherry trees will be given to all attendants.

OLDEST JAPANESE MAPS NOW IN GERMANY

According to Professor Kyushiro Nakayama of the Tokyo College of Literature and Science, who arrived in Kobe on March 16 aboard the Terukuni Maru from Europe, the oldest maps of Japan are owned by Goettingen University of Germany. These maps were executed by a shipwrecked Japanese in Petrograd in the Era of Temmei (1781-1787).

FIVE YOUNG JAPANESE OFF FOR ADVENTURE

Five young men, Hokushu Takahashi, Hideo Fujiwara, Masao Kuwano, Kinichi Nakashima and Masuo Era, of Wakamatsu City started on an expedition aboard the Tacoma Maru from Moji at noon March 16. Their route extends from Inner Mongolia, the Desert of Gobi, Tibet, the Himalayas, the Pamirs, Afghanistan and Arabia. They will also visit Ethiopia and make a tour of Africa.

ARCHAEOLOGICAL EXHIBIT SCHEDULED FOR APRIL

An exhibition of documents and primitive ware unearthed by leading archaeologists was head at the Imperial Museum of Fine Arts, Uyeno Park, Tokyo, during April. Hitherto these archaeological documents and objects have been preserved by Buddhist temples or by universities, making it quite inconvenient to study Japanese archaeology. At the exhibition there was a number of rare objects belonging to the Nara period.

FAMOUS GATE HERE NEEDS RECONSTRUCTION

The Onarimon, main gate to the Otamaya Mausoleum of the Tokugawa Family situated next to the Zojoji Temple in Shiba Park, is in poor condition. This gate is one of the national art treasures and is being protected by the Department of Education. The officials of the

Tokyo Municipal Office are also studying how to reconstruct this historical monument.

KIKUGORO CULTURAL FILM COMPLETED

The talkie film representing the performance of Kikugoro, famous Kabuki actor, has been completed by the Society for the Promotion of International Cultural Relations, Kikugoro danced the "Kagami Jishi" on the stage of the Kabukiza Theater of Tokyo last autumn specially for this talkie. The society is making some English titles for the picture. The talkie film is to be sent to foreign countries to introduce Japanese national dances.

KINDNESS TO ANIMALS TO BE TAUGHT CHILDREN

The newly established children's department of the Japan Humane Society will hold Prevention of Cruelty to Animals Week from May 28. During that week various campaigns will be conducted by the society for the cause. Fairy tales and Kamishibai (a kind of papers puppet show) will be used to inspire love of animals in children.

POLICEMAN FOR FOUJITA'S FILM

Mr. Renji Takasu, policeman attached to the Water Police Station of Yokohama has been selected to be a character for the film which is being made by Mr. Tsuguji Foujita. The noted artist is making a series of talkies for the Society for International Cultural Relation, to introduce the real life of Japan to foreign countries. The policeman will be seen arresting a stoaway at the Yokohama Pier. This scene is to introduce Japanese police methods to people abroad.

TOKYO-BANGKOK SERVICE

The Japan Air Transport Company plans to establish an air route between Tokyo and Bangkok, a distance of 5,300 kilometers, shortly. Two Douglas airliners, each costing ¥500,000, will be used for the service. When the route is opened, the distance between the Tokyo and Siamese capital, which now takes more than 10 days to negotiate, will be covered in one day and a half. At the same time, the Japanese air service will be connected directly with foreign services for the first time, Bangkok being a junction of British, French and Dutch airlines.

AUSTRALIANS LEARNING JAPANESE LANGUAGE

The radio-broadcasting station "310" of Melbourne, Australia, is broadcasting a series of lectures, one lecture per week, on Japanese culture and lessons in the Japanese language. At present more than 150 high schools in Australia are planning to teach Japanese in addition to French and German. In order to support these schemes, the Society for International Cultural Relations in Japan will send text-books for primary schools, Japanese type-writers, paintings and photographs relative to Japanese life.

MONUMENT OF BRIDGE

A memorial monument of the former Nihonbashi bridge will be erected at the corner of the present stone bridge on the occasion of the anniversary of the completion of the bridge on May 1.

The Nihombashi was the starting point for the 53 stations of the Tokaido in Yedo days. The former bridge was wooden construction and the new stone bridge was built in 1912. The monument will be a stone 10 feet high with a bronze plate reproducing the famous print depicting the former Nihombashi by Hiroshige. The bronze relief representing Hiroshige's print has been made by Mr. Koun Nakaya, noted sculptor. The dedication ceremony of the monument will be held at the bridge on May 1 under the auspices of the Nihombashi Society.

TEA-CEREMONY HOUSE

Private tea-ceremony houses of historical value will hitherto be recongnized by the Education Ministry as national treasures lest they should be exported abroad. As such buildings are small and lightly built, the Ednсation Ministry fears they might be taken abroad by foreigners who love Japanese gardens. Tea-ceremony houses attached to the silver Pavilion and some other temples are already branded as national treasures.

JAPANESE CHILDREN APPEAR IN PICTURES

To introduce the real life of Japanese children to foreign children, a series of beautiful pictures depicting the daily life and principal annual events of Japanese children has been made by the Board of Tourist Industry of the Department of Railways and will be sent abroad. The series contains a dozen pictures and a booklet has been issued with some special articles on Japanese children printed in English.

JAPANESE LIBRARY PLANNED FOR CHINA

The Bureau of Cultural Works of the Department of Foreign Affairs is planning to establish an Institute of Science and a Library in Peiping or in Shanghai a budget for which will be submitted to the special Diet by the bureau. A great number of Japanese books and documents will be collected at the library to give facility for an understanding of Japanese culture by Chinese.

華南の佛教を視る

——廣東佛教の特殊的展開——

藤井草宣

一，緒　　言

香港と廣州とは相接近せる新と舊との對照的な都會であるが，それよりも汕頭と潮州との組合せは，さらに其對照が極端である。近代に出來上つた香港と汕頭とは，何れも「港」であつて，ともに八十年ばかりの歴史しか持つてゐない。これに比べると，廣州にしても，潮州にしても，一千年前の唐代には既に著名な都會となつてゐて，東洋史や佛教史の上に光彩を放つ事蹟が頗る多い。此間に微妙なる新舊の交錯があるのである。さて，私の今度の旅行は，佛教の現在の情況を視察するのに目的を定めてあるから，古蹟や史實の踏査檢討は，昭和三年の冬に此地方を旅行せられた常盤大定博士著すところの「支那佛教史蹟紀念集」の四六倍版三百頁計りの「解說」に讓ることとして，該書をトランクの中に入れて行つた。されば此の香港・廣州と汕頭・潮州との二對の都市の佛教の現狀に就てこれから平易に記述してみたい。

二，回々教徒の通譯

廣州では，博愛醫院々長山中覺氏の許へ御邪魔して，醫院の通譯係周耀鄉氏に案内されて六榕寺を訪れたのであつた。それといふのは，六榕寺住持鐵禪禪師こそは，廣東隨一の名僧であるやうに二三の日本人から聞かされて居つたので，多年の間，是非とも其の指敎を仰がんものと憧憬してゐたからである。それには當地の居留民團のぬしと云はるゝ森清太郎翁に紹介をして頂くがよいといふので，先づ森翁を訪ふこととなつた。翁はそつ多年の研究の結果，廣東省の歴史に就ては，丸善より「嶺南紀勝」といふ書物さへ出版され，最近その改訂增補を完成して刊行する計りになつてゐるのであるが，翁の本業は藥種屋である。翁は其の書齋で色々と珍籍など見せて下さつた後，とある大きな茶館に伴つて晝食を饗應しつつ，私の無遠慮な質問に答へてくれられた。此時，通譯の周氏は回々敎徒だつたので，豚肉は食べないといふて箸を執らなかつた。兩氏の談話によつて，私は，最早や廣州市中を駈け巡つて多くの廢寺を覗き步く必要はなくなつたやうに感じられた。

三，鐵禪々師を訪ふ

廣東省では，民國革命の後，度々，全省を擧げて宗敎迫害を行ひ，寺院は悉く其の土地建造物を沒收して之を公共機關に變へて仕舞つたといふ。先づ土地は，政府の手によつて分割して競賓に附したといふ。廣州の市中では，達磨大師の初めて支那に到着した「西來初地」の舊蹟として西來庵の別名を存せる華林寺は，今は五百羅漢堂のみ殘り，境內は開かれて，民家軒を並ぶる西來町と化した。また西林寺は役所とあり，孝光寺は三つの學校に改められてゐる。海幢寺は公園となつた。そして六榕寺も花塔を重修して外觀は立派のやうであるが，其の所有權は悉く市政府に移され，たゞ鐵禪々師一人が此處を維持してゐる丈けであるといふ。(回々敎徒も亦た墓地を沒收されたが，敎徒の一致團結によつて政府より之を回收したといふ。)さて鐵禪々師に就ては，かねて「孫文が何か行詰ると常に鐵禪のところへ參禪して，敎を請ふたといふ話だが，そんなに偉い和尙ですか」と訊ねると，森翁は「まあ段々とさういふことになつて來るのでせう，さうしておいた方がいいです」と笑つて答へた。尤もその書は仲々優れた文字を揮毫するし，繪の方もいけるし，押出しの立派な人物だから，有力者との交際を巧くやつてゐるので，六榕寺も漸く寺院として存在してゆけるのであるといふ。森翁の紹介狀を持つて，折から降り出した氷雨の中を訪ねてみた。廣州の人力車は，赤足の車夫が非常なスピードで突つ走るので，目が廻る位であつた。閉されて天王殿の横から境內に入ると，直ぐ花塔が眼に入る。見事な七級の塔で，新に修繕され，巡警が一人番をしてゐる。二十錢で登ることを許すのださうだ。小さな堂房を二三巡り，有名な六祖の銅像を禮してから漸く一宇の小門を叩くと，中から俗服のボーイが出て來た。暫く待つと內部へ迎へられ，禪師に面會した。お茶を頂きながら，氣がついてみると，僧侶は禪師たゞ一人で，此寺へ入つて以來，遇ふものは悉く俗人のみである。後できくと，禪師は一人の僧侶の弟子も無いが，廣東佛敎會を寺內に置いてゐるから信者は相當に有るらしいとの事であつた。禪師の容貌を見ると，眼，耳，鼻，など，みな大作りな圓い顏で，ちよつと上野公園の大南洲の銅像に法衣を着せたやうな格構だつた。室內を見廻すと，成るほど，孫文と一緖に撮つた寫眞が壁に掲げてある。譚延闓筆の二丈に餘る大きな聯も掛けてある。

四，高僧問題

かねて鐵禪々師に會つたら，是非とも六榕寺の寺史や廣東に於ける清代三百年の佛敎史料，即ち高僧傳の如きものを得たいと思つてゐたので，これを聞いたところが，それは無いといふ。私は「明高僧傳」があるのに，「清高僧傳」のないのは，全支那を通じて頗る遺憾とする處である。たゞ北京で道階上人が「新續高僧傳四集」を編纂したが，これは或る事情の爲めに未完成のまゝ盜まれて刊行されたのであるから之の完成が願はしい。就ては，廣東省方面の材料が手に入れたいのです，といふと，禪師は「廣州の人で，千圓ほどの金を出すから，高僧傳の續きを作つて貰いたいといふ人があつたにはあ

つた。然し，一體どこまでが高僧か，高僧の標準が分らぬので中止となつた」といふ。これには啞然としたが，私は，それは何でもない，六榕寺の花塔を修繕した貴僧の如きは，寺塔興復の高僧の一人であるし，又た目下，香港に來錫し，近く當地へも講經に來られる太虛法師の如きは，僧敎育の先覺者であり，著述も澤山あるからこれは學僧として高僧傳中に入るべく，其他奇瑞を示した人，社會事業に盡した人佛經を外國へ飜譯した人などは，皆，大法傳持の柱石棟梁としてその事蹟を後世に傳へる必要があらう。何も神僧でなくてはならぬことはない。昔の高僧だとて，大體そんなものではないでせうか，といふと，敢て贊成したでもなく，贊成せぬでもない顏をして，別室から唐宋の高僧傳や雲南叢書の零本などを出して來て，親切に見せてくれた。又た「重修六榕寺花塔緣起」といふ自作の印刷物やメタルをくれたり，便箋に潑溂たる筆蹟で書いたもの，或は蘇東坡居士の石刻像の拓本なぞを贈られた。此席に李笑翁（因如）といふ名刺を示した中年の居士と，今一人の若いインテルらしい青年とが來合せてゐて，廣東佛敎は六祖の禪宗であるとて各所に於ける六祖慧能の事蹟に就て談話を交換してゐると，何時の間にか魁偉な禪師の姿は其處に見えなくなつた。時計を見ると三時間も話込んでゐたのである。禪師は元は軍人で，劉永福の部下となつてゐたことがあり，劉はフランス兵と戰つたこともあるが，禪師は之に參加しなかつたさうだ。若い時，臺灣にも居たことがあり，出家して以來，四十餘年を過ぎ，今年六十六歲であるといふ。

五，寺院もやゝ復活

政府に沒收された廣州市內の寺院は上記諸大寺の外に約四十ケ所もあり，それぞれ數十名から，多きは二三百名に及ぶ僧侶が居つたけれども，悉く退散して，全く其影を絕つたといふ。此事は，これより間もなく潮州へ行つて有名な唐代以來の古刹の開元寺を訪れた時も，同寺內に嶺東佛學院を董しつつあつた寄塵法師がいふたことと一致する。曰く「潮州では，僧衣を着た和尙が通ると街の人々は戶口に出て珍らしさうに眺めてゐた。革命の爲めに僧侶が絕えてゐたのである。開元寺を今日までに復活させるには，數年間非常に骨を折つた。此の境內の樹木も吾々が植えたのだ。此の佛經流通處も吾々が來て開設した。此の小學校も吾々が主張して作らせたのだ」とて，廣き境內を案內しつつ語つてくれた聲が今尙ほ耳底に殘つてゐる。ところが，開元寺の門內には，公安局(警察署)が，境內の左半分の堂宇を占領し，市の商工會議所の如きものが右手の一角に陣取つてゐる。又た新聞閱覽所と化してゐる一院もある。このやうな譯で，潮州附近は近時，僧中の意氣ある青年の活動によつて多少づゝ寺院佛敎は復活しつつあるやうだが，然し，到底，昔のやうにはゆかない。又た廣州に近き韶州の南華寺は，六祖及び明代の高僧憨

山大師の舊跡であるが，省の首腦者陳濟棠氏の發起で復興されることとなり，福州鼓山の住持虚雲和尚を住持に特請して，目下講經中であるといふが，「佛學半月刊」「佛教日報」等のニュースによれば，諸堂宇悉皆の新築計劃が進みつつあるといふ。和尚は禪宗の大家で，八十歳に近き高齢であり，出身は雲南で，早く湖南々岳に學んだ人であるといふ。又た端溪硯の產地に近き鼎湖山慶雲寺は，同じく憨山大師の居た所で，夏期の避暑地として著名であるが，此處には，ずつと三百人程の僧侶が居住してをるし，廣州市內に於ても大佛寺住持月溪法師（五十二歳）が天台宗の學者で，最近寺堂を復興して四五十人の僧を養つてをる。此他に草庵に近いものは，廣州市內に五六十殘つてゐるが，（「市民要覽」による）それらは，實は僧侶は住まず，「齋姑」や「堂姑」，又は「堂主」と名くる非僧非俗なる特殊の人が住んでゐるのである。

六，齋敎と善社の居士宗敎

そもそも，民國以來，二十四年このかた，幾多の大寺に居た何百何千の僧侶たちは，何處へ行つて了つたか。これが一大疑問でなければならない。それに對する解答は，たゞ一つである。曰く，僧侶は俗服を着て還俗し，在家の生活を始めた。然し，元々，その身が僧であるから，家には佛像を奉安してお經を讀んでゐる。それが卽ち「齋敎」といふのである。此の齋敎は素濟にも福建省にも，あらゆる村や街々に到る處に無數に在り，廣東省にも亦た同樣に散布してをる。畢り斯る形體の佛敎は，南支那のみに特有のものであるといふべきである。齋敎の起源を尋ぬると，遠く唐代に六祖慧能が，五祖弘忍より密かに衣鉢を傳へられ，同門の神秀一派の爲めに之を奪はれんことを恐れて南行すること二ケ月餘にして廣東省に入り，獵人群中に交つて凡そ五載を經たが，その間，說法を止めなかつたといふ。此事は「六祖壇經」に記してあるところで，斯の在俗の生活中の形式が，弟子の荘懷讓と馬道一とに傳持されて「齋敎」と成つたのであり，男女の在家者が，佛祖を奉安せる小庵を「齋堂」といふのである。齋敎には先天，龍華，金幢の三派があり，廣東省で最初に起つたのは先天派である。然し此の齋堂の宗敎は歷史が古いだけに，甚だ因習的で，單なる燃香念經と竹籤による占卜を行ふ計りであるから，新時代には卽してゐない。又た齋堂は妙齢の女性が，結婚を嫌つて獨身生活を行ふ爲めにも利用されつつあるやうで，尼僧ならぬ有髮の齋姑が白衣を被いで念佛を修してをるのである。而して齋堂と似た形式ではあるが今一步進んで，普遍化された會員組織のものに，全國的に流行しつつある「佛敎居士林」があり，更に居士林と比べて，一層，社會事業化されたものに「善社」といふものがある。この善社は矢張り廣東，福建兩省特有のもので仲々普及されてをる。廣州の「市民要覽」には，五六十の寺廟とは別に，五六十

の慈善團體の項目に善社に屬するものを計上してゐる。

又た「汕頭指南」には，「公益事業」の中に慈善團體として善社善堂を入れてをり，「宗敎」と之を區別してをる。而して善社等の慈善團體は何れも「財團法人」組織となつてをるといふ。されば單に佛敎の信仰宣傳を目的とする者ではなく，寧ろ社會事業本位であり道敎と儒敎と佛敎との混合の色彩を加味し，純然たる俗信仰の形さへ示してゐる。これは最早や「齋敎」とは云はぬらしいが，然し之に類するものである。善社の最も著名なるものは汕頭の「存心善堂」であるが，これは然し其內部を檢すると全く佛敎に屬するものである。

七，存心善堂の社會事業

存心善堂は財團法人組織となつてをり，蔡文熈氏といふのが董事である。汕頭博愛醫院の大門良佐久氏が私を同伴して在留邦人の日本民會長高村養三郎氏方へ訪問し，兩氏が異口同音に稱揚せらるゝところは，此の存心善堂の社會事業の功德に就てであつた。「汕頭指南」と兩氏の談話とを綜合すると，大體左の如きことをやつてをる——

1. 無緣佛の葬式—卽ち汕頭に於ける水死者，行倒れ，死刑囚などの屍體を引取つて，棺を施與して埋葬する。その爲めに郊外に「義塚」を設備してゐる。私は之を視察したが，一人一人に同型の墓石が設けられてあつて，極めて秩序整然たる感じがした。
2. 施餓鬼會—支那でいふ「水陸道場」を建つることで，每月之を盛大に營むのである。
3. 施粥，旅費の支給—流氓卽ちルンペンや乞食を救濟するのである。先年の如きは，共產黨に追はれた農民が他鄕から三，四百名計り來た時も，之を救濟して食事を與へた。粥と豆腐ガラを用ひたといふ。
4. 衞生，施藥，施療及び妊婦への補助
5. 消防隊—龍水局と名け，存心善堂の隣家に間口五門，三階のコンクリートの建物が在り，その中に收めてあるガソリンポンプは汕頭市立のものよりも精巧で成績が良いといふ。

尙，善堂の事業ではないが，（前記二氏は善堂關係のものと信じてゐるものに）貧民工藝院がある。卽ち極貧者や乞食の常習者は，之を工藝院の寄宿舍に收容して授產を爲してゐる。「汕頭指南」の發表する統計によれば，近年は二千內外のものが工藝院に出入してをるといふ。經營者は市政府當局となつてゐるが，內實は或は存心善堂關係のものかも分らない。次に存心善堂の本殿の本尊卽ち禮拜の對象は何かといふに「大峯祖師」と名くる等身大の僧像である。堂の廻廊の一角に壁にはめ込んである石刻の碑文によると，大峯祖師は，宋代の僧で，閩州より棉邑に遊んで和平橋を造り，崎嶇たる道路を修し，數百年來，行人の便益を計つたので，邑人が其の德に感じて廟を立て，之を祀つたが，爾來靈感が著しく，光緒己亥年間，潮汕地方の疫病流行のとき，幸に祖師の好生の德に賴つて宏く

法水靈丹を施し，多くの人を救濟したので，是年五月初十日，潮陽東門外，棉安善堂念佛社の諸友が祖師を奉じて汕頭に來つて「義塚」を造り，各處の屍骸枯骨を埋め，並に施棺贈衣等の善擧を行つて此地に一堂を興したのであると記してゐる。そして其の經營費には，「滙兌公所，毎年樂助銀一千圓壬戌年起」だの「輪船公司，毎年樂助銀壹千圓，壬戌起」等といふ金看板を揭げ此外に五百元，四百元，參百元，等と三十枚ほど金看板が列べてあつた。

八，佛教將來の進路

汕頭は新開地であるが，人口二十三萬に近く，（近くの潮州二十萬，潮陽八萬，その他の小都會を含めて，日がへりの出來る土地に約一百萬人の人口を抱有する「港」である。今後の奧地の治安如何によりては，其の盛況いよいよ見るべき土地であつて，現在と雖も貿易高は全支各港の中にて第五位を占めてをる。然し，寺院の古いものはなく，齋堂は各所に見られ，佛教居士林もあつて二階建の立派な佛堂を有し，佛經流通處もあり，「林刊」を發行してゐる。又た善堂は存心善堂の外に，誠敬，同濟，延壽，修德等があり，誠敬善社は，施棺，贈葬，施醫施藥及び救火設備ありて，ポンプさへ用意してゐるし，「義塚」もあるといふから存心善堂と相匹敵するものである。中には單に醫療のみを施すものもあるといふ。而して其の費用は，暹羅華僑の送金に依るものが多いといふことである。此の土地の有力者の有る人はいふ「佛教が駄目になるのは當然のことだ。潮州の開元寺の如き堂々たる大伽藍が空いてゐる，坊主は，たゞお經をよむだけで何もせない。これを見て，政府が小學校や役所や會議所とするのは當然である。何故僧侶は自ら此の善社の仕事を始めないのか，僧侶は慈悲を忘れてゐるのではないか」と。之に對して，私は，一言もなかつたので默つてゐた。潮州開元寺の中に在る嶺東佛學院で寄塵法師はいふ，「廣東政府の陳濟棠氏はその青年時代の師匠は齋堂の堂主であつたといふので，將來，齋堂を改良し之を統制あるものとする考であると」云々。（陳氏の夫人亦た佛教信者であるので，廣州の六榕寺鐵禪々師に歸依しつつあるといふことも曾て耳にしたところである。）若し齋堂を統制して向上を計るとせば，一は寺小屋式の學校を興すこととなり，又た一は善社善堂の社會事業を起すより外はない。又，潮州に於て民國十一年十二年頃，政府が寺院を賣却した後は，齋堂が非常に增へたといふ。茲に興味あるところの事は，此の齋堂の堂主は，勿論，俗人ではあるが，酒肉五辛を絕ち，「持齋」堅固の生活をするにより「齋」といふのであつて，妻は有つが妾は持つことを禁じてゐるのが特徴であるといふ。此の齋教の感化の然らしむるところか潮州・汕頭地方は頗る男女關係は嚴肅であつて他所とは大いに其趣を異にするといふ。厦門にて會見せる臺灣總督府外事課長坂本氏は「十九路軍の比較的強かつたのは，潮州地方の人間が兵

となつてゐたからで，彼らの男女關係が割合に正しいのに由來すると考へられる」と，私に語られたが，これは，齋教の感化と私には考へられたのである。

卽ち齋堂は各地の街々に必ず見受けらるゝ程，非常に夥しく散布してをるからである。香港でも齋堂は澤山ある。香港本願寺の伊藤普行氏夫人の談に，葬式の時に賴まれて僧服を着て裏街あたりから出て來る齋堂の人に對して普通人は之を僧侶とは稱ばず「南無侶」といひ，その妻に對しては「南無媽」といひ，その子どもに對しては「南無仔」といふさうである。これは頗る皮肉に考へられることであるが，然し齋教や善社の事業が盛んになれば，なる程，正當派の寺院と僧侶とは衰滅するものであらう。若し齋教や善社に於て俗信仰的迷信的要素を漸次除くことが出來れば，最早や日本の眞宗等の佛教と餘り變りのない形體となるのであるが，此點に就ては大いに恨がないでもないが，これは一般文化の向上にまつより外はないのである。已に竹籤の中にて「藥籤」と稱して，病人が寺廟祠堂にて占卜によりて藥品を定むる迷信的惡習に關しては，之を嚴禁する布告を，恰も私の旅行中に新聞紙が報導してゐたのであるから，次第に之は向上されてゆくものであらう。

更に香港に於ては，汕頭と同じく舊き寺院はないが，前にいふ如く齋堂や小庵の如きものは幾多數へ得ない程存在し，それぞれ香港の英政府の治安に賴つて榮えつつあるのであるが，特に文化程度の高い香港には，新思想の紳商たちによつて支持される青年學僧らの活動が自ら活潑となり，香海菩提場香港佛學會などが會員組織によつて結成され，兩者何れも一年に，一千數百圓（香港銀）の借家賃を支拂ふやうな宏莊な會館式ビルディングを借りてをる。香港佛學會よりは「香海佛化刊」を刊行し，一千餘名の會員に頒布し會長は劉德譜居士で，全く居士佛教の中心地たるの觀を示し，且つ義學校を經營してゐる。香海菩提場は靄海法師が江蘇省より來つて唯識研究の爲めに民國二十一年より三年間閉關せるに因みて起つたもので，階下に義務學校を設け，百五十餘名の小學兒童を教育し，階上には女衆佛學々院を經營し，此外に佛教圖書館を始めてゐる。今は覺一法師が社長となつてをるが，會員五百餘名である。又た何爵紳曉生夫人張蓮覺女史の發願によりて山光道に優美莊麗なる一大伽藍「東蓮覺苑」が築造されたが，その內部は前面の建物は悉く義學校，女衆佛學院としての教育事業及び佛經流通處と「人海灯」誌刊行の編輯室等に用ひられてをり，後方が佛堂となつてをり，壁に題して「講經法會，通俗講演，密教灌頂，慈善救濟，平民教育，在家出家兩衆教育，文字宣傳」といふ理想の標語を揭げてゐる。これらのものは，何れも三四年來完成し來つたもので，這の方面に將來の支那佛教の進路は發見されるものと觀察さるゝのである。

九，嶺東佛學院の悲運

香港の東亜覺苑より通一法師（太虚法師の弟子，二十三，四歳）の編纂によつて刊行されつつある「人海灯」誌は，半月刊として生れたのは潮州の嶺東佛學院に於てであつたが，經營上覺苑の補助を受くることとなつて移轉したのである。而して嶺東佛學院は，太虚法師が，その高弟の大醒法師をして四年程前に開校せしめたものであるが數十名の學生は何れも江，浙方面より來る者多く，廣東省出身の學生は殆んど絶無といふべきであつた。たゞ澄弘法師（三十二，三歳）が此の土地の出身者であつて，厦門の閩南佛學院出身であるところから，此の人が當地の有志及び開元寺當局との間に介在して經費を支出せしめてゐたが，澄弘法師が，肺病にて臥床するや，急に經營は困難となつて中止のやむなきに立到つたといふ。大醒法師は創立すると間もなく武昌に去つて「海潮音」誌編輯に當り寄塵法師が總て事を運んでゐたが，法師亦た安徽省人であつて語言全く不通の爲め開元寺方丈らとも意志の疏通を缺くこととなつたといふ。學院は教室と寄宿舎とは，觀音堂の二階の藏經樓にあり，前は兵隊の營門と化してゐたのを，奪ひ返したものであるが，此の觀音堂の壯大なることは，日本內地に於ける諸大寺の大堂宇に匹敵すべきものである。嶺東佛學院は民國廿四年，（昭和十年）十二月を以つて終り，厦門の閩南佛學院と併合することとなつた。これは廣東省に於ては，今後は寺院佛教，僧侶佛教が容易に保持し難いことを物語つてゐる。

十，密教の潜勢力

汕頭，潮州は曾て大正十三年（民國十三年）日本より權田雷斧僧正が八十歳の老軀を提げ，十名の弟子を伴つて密教傳授の爲めに渡航した土地である。潮州開元寺は其の道場として一時は千古の伽藍の復活さへ信じられたのであるが，一瞬の夢であつた。然し汕頭密教重興會々長王弘願居士は，爾來著述や，翻譯書の出版，雜誌刊行等により非常な努力を以て密教傳播に盡力したが，たまたま居士の身を以て阿闍梨位を僭し，あまつさへ僧侶に對して灌頂を授けたといふので，諸方より非難されて會長職を辭し，次で半身不隨意の病軀を床上に横へてゐるといふ。又た日本に於て大正十四，五年の間に權田雷斧師に就て密教傳授を受けて歸國した曼殊迦締法師（五十餘歳，元，袁世凱の秘書たりし人）は，廣州の白雲山能仁寺に於て密壇を新築し，約一萬餘元を費して諸堂を修理して一時は密教復興の本地の如き概を示したが，二十三年春，廣州市當局によりて退去命令を受けると倶に「破壇」の厄に遭ふて，今は澳門（マカオ）へ移つてをるといふ。又た開元寺には純密法師なるものが觀音堂の階下に住んでをり，曾て高野山の金山僧正に就て傳法して歸つてゐるが，學問的方面に暗く，單に事相のみを弄んでゐるに過ぎないといふ。私は純密法師にも面會したが，溫厚なる人物といふまでにて將來に大を爲すべき者でないと考へられた。思ふに密教の支那に於ける復活は夙に楊仁山居士の南京佛教研究會時代に於て企てられ，楊白華居士が高野山の沛上僧正の許に留學したが，不幸にして早逝し，次で大勇，顯蔭，又應，持松，純密の五法師が高野山に來つて金山師に就て傳授を受けたが，大勇法師は更に西藏に留學せんとして中途に四川西藏省境に倒れ，顯蔭，又應亦た早逝し持松は華嚴宗の立場に還原して密教を批判することとなり，遂にこれらの代表者は悉く大成する域に達せず，上記王弘願居士と曼殊迦締とは不運の命をかこつこととなつてをる。天津には「中日密教研究會」が高野山關係にて起され，「密教學院」が中野達慧師によつて維持されつつあるも，中に許丹居士の如き篤學者を生みつつも，經營上の困難を嘆じつつあるといふ。尚，上海には十年來「威音」誌を刊行せる谷正明居士があり，專ら日本密教の紹介を主として宣揚に努めつつある。されば，一時隆々たりし密教重興の聲も今は中衰期に入つた如き觀あるも，然も，漸く支那全土に亘つて「密教灌頂」の宗教的儀式の妙味は普及されて，その潜勢力は看過出來ないものがある、最近武昌へ歸つて行つた武昌佛學院教授談玄法師は，高野山に於て眞言密教即ち東密を受けしのみならず，天台密教たる「台密」をも福田堯潁師より傳授を受けたので，こゝに支那に於て，台密の移入となつたのである。彼は歸國匆々（今年一月上旬）上海虹口の雲窗寺分院に於て日本より將來せる密教關係の圖書展覽會を催して上海佛教界に一大ショックを與へてゐる。彼と同時に歸つた東大文學士黄輝邦居士も亦た同時に「東密」を新義眞言宗豐山派に於て受け，「台密」を福田師より傳授して南京に赴いた。彼らの今後の活動も亦た期待されるところである。

十一，佛教と基督教その他との比較

廣東省に於て何れの宗教を調査する者も，かの長髮賊が清末に起つたところであつて，それ以後，キリスト教が如何なる勢力を保持しつつあるかを考へないでおくことは出來ないであらう。今日長髮賊的のキリスト教が此地方に傳つてゐるといふことは分らないが，廣州の「市民要覽」及び「汕頭指南」によると左の如き統計が示されてゐる。——

〔廣州市〕（民國廿三年調查）

	（男）	（女）	（合計）
基教(新教)	2.990	2.525	5.515
天主教(舊教)	985	863	1.848
回　教	303	262	565
佛　教	493	656	1.149
道　教	347	104	451
合　計	5.118	4.410	9.528

廣州の全人口は民國廿三年調查によれば，總計978.329人で，男559.994人女418.335人となつてゐる。即ち總人口九十七萬八千餘の中から，九千五百二十八名を抽出した統計であるから，約百分の一にも足らぬ數の中の調查である。之を以て全般を推すことは不可

能であるが，玆に之を引用せる「要覽」編者の見る所は，何か之によつて全般を律せんとする用意があるのかも分らない。

〔汕頭市〕（民國廿三年調査）

	（男）	（女）	（合計）
基　敎	1.677	1.445	3.122
天主敎	226	201	427
回　敎	4	3	7
佛　敎	1.655	2.066	3.721
道　敎	119	193	312
合　計	3.681	3.908	7.589

汕頭の全人口は二十二，三萬ある中にて，七千五百八十九人による統計なれば，約三十分の一の數による調査でもあり，且つ此の調査は全市大區に亙つて各區別に行つた調査であるから比較的，前の廣州のそれよりも信頼するに足るものと考へらるゝが，畢り，佛敎が基敎に對して汕頭のみは，女姓方面に於て多少增加してゐるといふに過ぎないものである。之を以て見れば，民國廿三年（昭和九年）に於ける佛基の勢力比較上より考ふる時は，斷然キリスト敎が廣東省の首要都市では優位を占めてをるといひ得るのである。私は勿論，斯る統計を重視するものではないが，然し此の地方の智識階級の頭腦に在る宗敎比較觀を求むれば，恐らく是れが尤もよく物語つてゐるところであらう。玆に又た眼を一轉して，廣州の深江に浮ける蛋民（水上生活者）の中の宗敎を語るものに「恩光福民船」なる招牌を出してゐる船の敎會のあることを知らねばならぬ。又た「道函」といふのもあるといふが，これは道敎の廟船であるかも知れない。然し佛寺の船，齋堂の船といふものは發見出來ないといふことである。在留邦人の人々が到る處に於て私に物語る事は，基督敎の宣敎使が歐米より來るや，自ら土語を習ひ，之を語つて民間に於て長期の布敎に從事してゐることで，其の堅忍不拔の態度を見てキリスト敎の發展は當然であり，日本より來れる僧侶が，土語を學ばんと努むる者もなく，支那人の生活に接近するを欲せず，邦人に對する葬祭のみのお經三昧なるを異口同音に非難せられた事であつた。慚愧と慨嘆に堪えない事である。

（昭和十一年一月）（完）

（26頁より）

三年の豫定が四年，五年になり大正十二年には歸る筈だつた。けれど震災といふのは僕にとつて二重の悲しみを與へた，父の死期を早めたこと，燒け出されたこと。

僕は賑やかなことが父と同じやうにすきだ。父が洋行するときの東京驛の賑ひ，子供心に再び父の顏をあの雜踏の中で迎えたかつた。そしてあせりにあせつた父に一つ位の實を日本で結ばせたかつた，と同時に子としての僕は，父から親しい言葉を貰ひたかつた。

（一九三六・四・二）

亡父大住嘯風を語る

大　住　秀　夫

父の顏は，はつきりと思ひ出すことは出來ない。僕が父と事實上別れたのは，僕の小學校時代の十一歳のときである。それまでゝも僕と父との間は，世間の「父と子」のやうな接觸と親しみには缺けてゐたやうに思つてゐる。僕の物心のついた自分の父は，たしか「萬朝報」の記者をしてゐた。雜然と本が並び，大きな机のあつた書齋で朝は十時ごろまで獨りで寢てゐた。起きるとすぐ近所の風呂屋へ手拭をぶらさげて約十分で歸つて來る。朝晝兼帶の食事をすませると，何人かの客が入り込む。十二時近くなつて羽織，袴で出かける。これが朝の日課であるらしい。然し自分はそれを見たわけではない。母や人の動きでさうらしいと感んじた丈である。なぜなら僕は朝早く小學校へ出かける，放課後歸宅しても父の姿は見えない，父の歸つてくる時間はいつだか知らない，いつも自分が寢てから歸つてくるのだから。

だから父が新聞社で何をやつてゐるのかさつぱり判らなかつた，たゞ新聞に父の名――嘯風，或は舜，或ひは舜岳と署名された論文みたいなものが載つてゐるので，ものを書いてゐるのだと位しか判らなかつた。

當時僕の目にうつた父の印象は「こわい人」といふ感じだつた。親しく口をきいてくれもせず，一緒に連れていつてくれたことも極く稀れで，僕の知つてゐる限り三回しかない。一度は向島百花園の「蟲放ち會」の夜で父は好きな義太夫が廣間で語られてゐるのでジーツと聞いてゐるらしかつたが，子供の僕はつまらなくて仕方なかつた。淺草公園の散歩にも連れて行かれたが氣短の父は途中で人力車を拾つてものゝ廿分位で家へ歸つてしまつた。人力車で父の膝の上に居たそのときの僕は，他人に抱かれてゐるやうで，こわくて早く家に着けばいゝと思つてゐた。一度は品川沖に軍艦が停船したことがある。見學に橫濱まで乘せてくれるらしかつた。それに加はるべく父は僕を連れて行つてくれたが，品川に來て見ると既に軍艦は煙をはいて出帆しかゝつてゐた。はしけは何處にもなくもうどうしても乘ることは出來ない。その時父は水際まで行つて，ステツキをふり上げ「オーイオーイ」と盛んにどなつた。聞いたか聞かずか軍艦は水を切つて出て行く。そのときの父の顏は實に口惜しさうだつた。この話を或る人にしたところ，「軍艦を呼ばうとしたのは如何にも彼れらしい」と言つた。そのやうに父の性格は短氣で，强情で鼻つぱしが强く，負けず嫌ひで……けれど人の氣をそらすやうなことはしなかつたらしい。初對面の人はてんからおどかすらしい，にも拘らず堂々と向つて來る人とは交際するといふ風らしかつた。

大正八年に，まだ世界大戰の終らない頃，荷物船の乾坤丸といふ船で——その頃海上が危險なので客船は出なかつた——佛蘭西に行つた。そのころ父は必要のために和服生活を洋服に代えたので，子供の僕は尙近づき難いやうに思はれた。何のためにフランスまで行くのか判らなかつたが，自分はなぜかホツトした。雜踏する東京驛で車窓から首を出してゐる父の姿を見たのが最後である。

洋行するときの父の肩書な「萬朝報特派員，東洋大學講師」となつてゐた。始めて父が東洋大學の先生であつたこともそのとき知つた。

父は出掛けるとき寄港さきから必ず繪葉書を送るから順序よく保存して置くやうに，記念になるからと云ひ置いて，先づ神戶，門司，長崎，上海と繪葉書の通信があつた，コロンボに差しかゝつたとき世界大戰の休戰ラツパがなつた。父はそのことを非常に喜んでゐた。

父は英語と獨乙語は可成り出來たらしい。洋行前に著はした「現代思想講話」とか，その他十數の本の中に近代ドイツ哲學者の語句を引用したり，或る本の中にはゲーテの詩が實にきれいに譯されてゐたのを見た。けれど自分が逝いたフランスの國語，フランス語は全然知らないのである。「然し必要に迫まられて三月にして完全にフランス語は解し得た」と書き送つてくれた。父はとてもフランス語の達者なことを自慢したが，實はあまりうまくはなかつたと東朝の町田梓棲氏宅が笑つて居られたが，度胸はよかつたらしい。

父のフランスに於ける目的はなんであつたか。今自分の手元に殘されてゐる父の書いたものは，佛文の「日本文化史」(鎌倉時代まで）丈である。フランスに於る形見に殘されたものは，たつた之れ丈である。五年間フランスに於ける仕事の結晶がたゞ之れ丈といふのは，それ以前の文と較べて如何にも不勉强であり，不甲斐ないやうに感ぜられるが，洋行するそもそもの目的が本一冊書く爲ではなかつたらしい。苦しい中から方々から融通を受けて渡佛したのは，何か非常にあせつたらしいそれは當時の父の友人の行動を，赴く先を，又躍進ぶりを見れば分る。洋行によつて智識の蓄積と同時に歸朝者としてのはくを以て再び現はれたかつたのであらうと思はれる。人の話しに政界方面にも相當魅力を持つてゐたらしい。けれど單なる漫遊とちがつてブラリツと手ぶらで歸朝するわけにもいかない，萬朝報の記者は滯佛中に未練氣もなく捨てゝしまつたのである。捨身になつてぶつかつて行くつもりらしかつた。（以下24頁へ續く）

宗教情趣を趁つて

——異國の神祕の鎬の扉に旅愁を慰む——

廣瀬 了義

私の歐米滯在からは最早や十年の星霜を閲してゐてその印象も薄らいたので機を見て再擧を計劃してゐるが兎に角，往時を追憶して認めてみる。あの變化のない單調で廣漠な，たゞ秋の七草のやうな草花の姸と，時々遙かに見られる碧い湖を緣どる白樺の神祕な森などを眺めつつ憊て憬れのモスコー入りをしたのが昭和二年の八月上旬であつた。文化協會長のカメネフ夫人に引見せられて彼女の如才のない宣傳に魅せられたものだ。私共は型の如く市內をドライブした。赤露政府の宣傳にお都合のよいところばかりを案內された。雀の丘では那翁撃退のお得意の一齣を聽かされたり，赤い廣場にあるレーニンの廟ではその遺骸を勿體らしく夕闇迫る刻限に拜まされた。歸宅を急ぐ勞働者の長い群が帶のやうに連つてその禮拜の順番を待つてゐる。たゞその時に皮肉に感じたのは細い路次の辻に祀られた聖母の前に熱心に禱を捧げてゐる純情の婦人が夥多く發見せられたことである。宗教は阿片なりと極端に彈壓したのであの金光燦然たる幾多の巨大な教會のドームだけはその莊嚴な姿をモスコー河に映してゐるが，その內部の偶像なり聖畫は悉く剝がれて閉鎖されるか工場化されてゐるのには異教徒ながらにも佗しく感じた。日本大使館にも度々往つて，あのバルコニーから日曜の朝，全市を俯瞰したが，寺院からはあの親しみのあるベルの音は一つも聽かれなかつたのは餘計に悲しかつた。そこになると伊太利や佛蘭西や獨逸や英國で巡禮した寺院には言ひ盡せない宗教的雰圍氣を滿喫した。然も新教のそれよりも舊教の殿廟な內部修飾に多分の興味を感受した。

○

第二に私は寺院靈廟に關連して各國で墓域を虱潰しに探つてその民族性，國民性，乃至宗教意識の表現さはもとより藝術的手法や樣式をつぶさに味つたのである。白・獨・佛國境であの無數の素朴な十字標の點綴は旅愁をいやが上にも誘つて暗涙を絞つた。巴里の郊外にあるあの藝術味豐かな墓域では恍惚として釘づけにされた。死の門の群像！ を中心に放射線式に整然と林立してゐるプラン！ 且つその一つ一つの墓にも纏つた纖麗幽玄な美の表現！どの彫刻——聖像，マリア，天使，故人の像が大理石にブロンズの御影石にうつされてゐるが，どれもこれも巴里の藝術家の得意のサロンが墓場へつ進出とも思はれ，これは恰も伊太利のゼノアの一山全體を墓場とし，その柱廊に羅列されたる故人の群像が展覽會場の觀あるものと同樣であつた。紐育では土一升金一升のブロドウエイの一端の空地の敎會の境内にさゝやかではあるが點々たる墓が護られてあるのは唯物主義的な米國であるだけに床しさも一入であつた。

墓も都會にあるものよりは田舍にある方がが情趣が深い。殊に山岳などの溪川の響のきかれるところとか，海岸などの崖の崩れかけたところなどに風雨に曝されて碑面の字もかけたところがあつて所々讀みこなせないところのあるのが餘韻があつて哀れさも追懷さも濃かであつたのが，今も却つて忘られない。

○

第三に古城を慕つての旅もクラツシカルでローマンチツクな思ひ出も蘇つて來るのである。それも北歐と南歐とによつてその色彩も幾分異にしてゐたスカンヂナビカ半島には封建時代の原始的な武人氣質が偲ばれた。あの一年のなかばを暗い陰欝な冬の世界に暮し，又絶えず南方から脅されてくる民族を擊退すべく，一方には自然よりうける壓迫との挾擊より遁るべく慓悍な性情を自ら養成せられてゐる民族だけに彼等の築いた城塞には特殊の攻防が設けられてゐる。又之が獨逸あたりとなると文化的に多分のゆとりがあつて一の城を中心に各都市が競つて別個の文化を遺してゐる。ブルグの接尾語のついてゐる都會名を想ふとき我等の心裡にもある幻影がマサマサと浮び出て來る——ハイデルベルグ，ハンブルグ，ニユルンブルグ，ウイツテンベルグ等，等の所謂城下町をさすらひ，或はライン川を遡つてその船上から遠近に散見する中世紀の古城を仰ぎ，はては船を捨てゝそれらの古城内を訪れて昔の騎士と佳人の邂逅の情話！ 樂聖のものした歌劇などの題材なぞは到るところで拾はれるのであつた。城内には祕密の牢もあつたが敎會もあれば釀造場もありダンスホールもあれば，妻妾と喋々喃々の室のあるに至つては外國の戰爭の長引いて根氣强かつたカラクリも讀めたのである。それよりも獨逸には旅の鳥には重寶なシステムが各都市を細胞的に連絡づけられてゐたのは嬉しかつた。それは昔，巡禮者のために設けられた安宿の名殘であつて，各都市の城廓を開放して，一晩に一マークで朝飯づきで泊めてくれる。これは青年宿泊所とでも名けられるべきところで，夕方になると，リユクサツクを背負つた青年の群がこゝに集つて來て，續々と詰めかけてきて受付でサインをして奥に這入つて勝手に毛布を敷いてゴロリと横になる。九時までは枕をならべた青年達は寢物語してゐるが，九時をうつとスキツチをきると同時に，誰も一言も發しない。(そこになると日本の學生はダラシがない。又こゝでは禁酒)翌朝は未明に起きて寢具を自分で處理して勇姿颯爽と又次の旅路へと出かけてゆくのである。

アメリカ傳道の思出

東福義雄

海外生活の思出といつても國際佛敎通報編輯局からの求めとあれば，當然海外佛敎傳道の思出といつたやうなものが期待されてゐるものと解釋して，實はそれ以外の方面に尙更ら書きたいことが多いのであるが，こゝにはその方の思出を少し書いて見ることゝしやう。

そこで私が十年近く携つてゐたアメリカの佛敎であるが，これは一口に言へば日本佛敎といふ島渡世界にも類のない精神文化に於ける良種を極めて適當なる場所に，大體に於て適當なる條件のもとに移植されたものと見ることが出來るのである。

そこで本國では凡そ生物學的な諸の退化の法則に從つて，殆んど萎微枯渇の狀態に瀕してゐた苗木が一擧にして生氣を恢復し，謂ゆる回春して急に潑剌たる花を咲かせ何程かの實を結んだのがアメリカに於ける日本佛敎であると見ることが出來るのであらう。私の米國佛敎傳道の思出も總てこういつたやうな經緯の中に織り出される模樣の數々であることを豫め諒解を願つて置きたい。

勿論本當のアメリカ佛敎といふものはまだ出來てゐない。だがこれは一宗一派の布敎の限界をある意味で超へた問題であるから，差當り私の關係した米國佛敎と本當の米國佛敎との分際といふものは，敎界で往々見るやうに決して左程輕々に論斷さるべきものではないのである。

若しこれが相手の文化形態なり，その傳統なりが，左程確立固定してゐないとか，若くはその度に於て甚しく稀薄若くは低劣であるとか，といつたやうな場合であるならば，昔し基督敎が一部民族乃至國民に向つて何程か成功した如く，吾々の場合にも日本佛敎乃至眞宗本願寺派卽アメリカ佛敎といつたやうな形に出來上つたであらうと思はれるのであるが，アメリカ佛敎に關する限りに於ては事實は少くとも當面の事態としては正にその反對で，寧ろ吾等の佛敎が諸の精神的或は物理的なる法則の必然として彼地の文化に吸收されるの恐れさへも相當あつた程であるから，吾々の傳道による純然たるアメリカ佛敎を問題とする場合は，この邊の所に頗る廣汎にして然も深刻なる用意が必要であることを，聊か餘事ながらこゝに日本佛敎界の謂ゆるインテリ層のために一言警告して置きたい。

これだけの前提の下に於ては，私のアメリカ傳道の思出の殆んど全ては，潑剌として花あり實あるものであつたことを內心深く悅んでゐるものである。

第一ゐのクリスチャンに非ればば人間に非ればば人間に非ずといつたやうな怖ろしい觀念が、殆んど社會の全層を支配してゐたアメリカで、そして在留日本人までが何程かその虜となりつゝあつた矢先に、堂々吾等の佛教が彼等の宗教に劣るものでないのみか、事實上世界に於ける有らゆる宗教の中の王座に立つものであると言つたやうな颯爽たる自覺を、先づ在米同胞中の青年層引いては第二世の間に力強く植へつけることが出來たといふことは眞に欣快に堪へない思出である。

　この自覺が恰度私が開教本部の主事をしてゐた一九二三年の夏、紺碧の海美はしい、そして其邊一帶に根をおろしてゐる我等の同胞の作り出すアテチヨクやビーンスの美味さの忘れられないピヅモ海邊のさる空屋に於ける一週間の夏季講習會を機緣として、北米佛教男子青年會聯盟の結成となり、續いてその翌年私が今も米國東西の兩海濱を通じての第一の景勝地として、松の綠も砂の白も、全てはその文字通りなる地上に、又斯の如き海濱のあるべしやとさへ思はれるモントレイ海濱に於ける北米佛教女子青年會聯盟の結成となり、それがそれと相前後して起つた布哇佛教界に於ける同様の聯盟と共に互ひに結成の運びに到らんとして荏苒兩三年を過せし矢先に、偶ま常光浩然氏の來米によつて、米、布、日の飛躍的なる連絡が生れ、引いてはそれが這般の汎太平洋佛教青年大會と共に全日本佛教青年會聯盟の發達を何程か促進したことを思へば、この間の消息として頗る意味深長なるものが見られるであらう。

　あの二回の汎太平洋大會に堂々の陣容を整へて乘り込んで來た米國代表を日系の米人乃至は日本人たるの故を以て、多少に拘らず物足りない感じを起した者も相當あつたやうであるが、この點當時私が中外紙上にこれを論じて瀨田理事、好枝主事あたりから頗る共鳴を博したやうな譯であるが、この種の論者はよくよくのアイデアリストかロマンチストに非れば、ドリーマーかスペキユレイターに過ぎないと言ふのも、斯ういふ筋合からである。

　尤も私が米國佛教に於て斯る愉快なる思出を持つことが出來たのも、固より本願寺北米開教の當初、明治三十年頃殊に明如宗主の明斷によつて薗田、西島、堀各師の如き原始佛教と大乘佛教と日本佛教とを夫れ夫れ自身の宗旨に即して、何程か人格的に體得せる人物が、多くの形式的傳統を一擲して米國社會に即してその創業に着手し、續いて内田師が京極その他の進步的なる逸才を擁して多くの開教使も皆この意氣に燃へて、少くとも在留同胞間に於ける有らゆる方面の指導的立場を大膽に於て確保し來つた結果たることは言ふまでもない。

　つまり多くの開教使は何によらず夫れ夫れの社會に於ける文教的方面の先頭に立つてゐたのである。勿論彼等も日本に於けると同樣儀式的方面にも遺憾なきまでに活動したが、然もその

事柄がこれ等先驅の努力によつてかち得たる眞の教役者としての立場を贏まさないまでに、その指導的實力と勢力が決定的なものであつたのである。

　これが若し儀式專門の程度を多く出でないやうな仕方に於て創業されてゐたとしたならば、その當時の大勢より察すれば、恐らく出稼的な若干の同胞信徒さへも吾等の教團へ捉へ得なかつたであらう。當時の在米同胞は左程の教養があつた譯ではなかつたが、少くとも彼等は太平洋と共に德川三百年の俗習を踏越へることの出來た猛者揃ひであつたからである。況んや米國の官憲をして佛僧の立場を認めしめ、少數ながらも一般米人と共に第二世日系米人をして相當の尊信を聚がしめるなぞといふことは到底出來なかつたであらうとは言ふまでもあるまい。

　この意味では今日八家九宗といふに近きまでに宗派神道の諸派までも入り雜つて繁昌しつゝある在米同胞の宗教界が、聊かそのお里の狀態に還元しつゝあるものでなければ幸せである。

　現に在米同胞の眞に確固不動たる永久的なる共有財産の最大にして殆んど唯一なるものは、吾等の教團に屬する土地と建物であることなども愉快極まることである。私有財産は所有者の心委せで何時でも米人の手に歸つて行くからである。

　これについて私がスタクトンの佛教會が敷地の大擴張と共に會堂の新築をする場合の主任開教使として、その事業の總務委員長を務めたことなども相當張合のある思出であるが、その時私がこのアメリカに佛堂を長く莊嚴するに就ての二十箇條の宣言文を發して遮二無二これを押し切り、その後早速この發願文をそのまゝ依用して寺院を建てた所が二三箇所も出來たなども愉快な思出である。

　恰度數日前その地の代表的信徒の一人が、その時千戸餘りの同胞と若干の白人との間から集めた四萬三千弗中殘した六千弗の借金を最近完全に皆濟したことを何よりの土産にといつて私の所に寄つてくれたが、その信者の談から米國到る所現在佛教會は殆んど唯一の同胞の鎭めであり港でありオアシスであるのみならず、それが軈て吾等の多年の希望たる眞の米國佛教の礎石としての働きを最近著しく發揮し來つてゐることが認められ希た滿足に思つてゐるやうなことである。

　思出がすつかり自慢話のやうな具合になつて傷み入る次第であるが、その半面私の在米生活は殆んど苦しい喘ぎの連續であり、明暮自己の無能と不德に苦しみ通したことも僞らざる事實であつて、當時私が無闇に登山やスポーツに熱中してゐたのも、そこに還き身を疑してゐた譯でもあらう。（完）

◇佛教論　増谷文雄著

書中「大乘佛教」化であり、「宗派佛教の一員」であると曰ひ名乘る著者の現代佛教論集ともいふべきもの。平明な記述ながら、思索的、求道的な深みに乏しい。但し宗教學的な取扱方に特色を持つ。（四六判二四二頁、圓六十錢、理想社出版部）

國際佛教通報局定款

名稱

第一，本局を國際佛教通報局と稱す

事務所

第二，本局の事務所を全日本佛教青年會聯盟本部に置く

目的

第三，本局は日本內海及海外に向つて佛教事情の通報をなし，且つ佛教徒相互間の各種便宜を計るを以て目的とす

事業

第四，本局の目的を達成するため左記の事業を行ふ

イ，日本內地及世界各國より佛教事情に關する質問の通報を行ふ

ロ，必要に應じ日本語及世界各國語を以て佛教事情の通報を行ふ

ハ，外國人の日本觀光に際しては各種の便益を與へ，特にその佛教に關する方面に於て之を爲す

ニ，定時或は隨時に各國語を以て文書の刊行をなす

ホ，その他必要と認めたる事業を行ふ

役員

第五，本局の事務を處理するため左の役員を置く

イ，局長　一名

ロ，幹事　三名

ハ，評議員　若干名

局長は本局の事務を總括す

幹事は本局の事務を處理す

評議員は局長の提案に依る重要事務を審議す

第六，評議員は左記の者を以て之に充つ

イ，全日本佛教青年會聯盟理事及主事

ロ，全日本佛教青年會聯盟理事會に於て推薦したる者

第七，局長及幹事は評議員會に於て決定す

第八，役員の仕期は二ヶ年とす（但し重任を妨げず）

經費

第九，本局の經費は左記のものに依て之を支辨す

イ，本局基金の活用

ロ，寄附金

ハ，その他の收入

補則

第十，本定款に記載せられざる事項は，凡て評議員會に於て協議す

第十一，第一回の役員は全日本佛教青年會聯盟理事會に於て決定す

定價	一部 金二十錢	送料二錢
	一年 金二圓四十錢	送料不要

昭和十年四月廿日第三種郵便物認可
昭和十一年四月廿八日印刷（每月一回）
昭和十一年五月一日發行（一日發行）

東京市外吉祥寺337
編輯發行兼印刷人　淺野研眞
東京市牛込區早稻田鶴卷町107
印刷所　康文社印刷所
電話牛込（34）1050番 5049番
東京市神田區一ツ橋二の三
發行所　國際佛教通報局
電話九段（33）4428番
振替東京83015番

昭和十年四月三十日第三種郵便物認可 昭和十一年四月二十八日印刷納本(每月一回) 昭和十一年五月一日發行(一日發行) 國際佛教通報 第二卷 第五號

昭和十年四月三十日第三種郵便物認可 昭和十一年五月二十八日印刷納本 昭和十一年六月一日發行（每月一回一日發行）第二卷 第六號

The International Buddhist Bulletin

國際佛教通報

第二卷 昭和十一年六月 第六號 〔Vol. II. June. 2502/1936 No. 6.〕

要 目 〔Contents〕

東京 國際佛教通報局 發行

The International Buddhist Information Bureau

Tokyo, Kanda, Hitotsubashi, II—3

Annual Subscription ¥2.40 (post free) Single Copies 20 sen (post 2 sen)

Staff of the Bureau

Hon. President	J. Takakusu
President	K. Ohmura
Secretary	S. Takagai
〃	B. Inaba
〃 (in chief)	Ken Assano
Advisers	H. Ui
〃	G. Asakura
〃	R. Hatani
〃	U. Ogiwara
〃	R. Higata
〃	T. Suzuki
〃	S. Suzuki
〃	S. Amakuki
〃	S. Nagai
〃	B. Matsumoto
〃	E. Uno
〃	C. Akamatsu
〃	Z. Ohmori
〃	K. Yabuki
〃	S. Onoh
〃	S. Katoh
〃	M. Anezaki
〃	G. Honda
〃	R. Sekimoto
〃	J. Sahegi
〃	R. Hanada
〃	H. Kohno
〃	R. Takaoka
〃	Z. Kobayashi
〃	S. Yamabe
〃	C. Akanuma
〃	E. Honda
〃	R. Ohmori
〃	E. Kawaguchi
〃	C. Yamakawa
〃	D. Tokiwa
〃	T. Tanimoto
〃	G. Tokiwai
〃	S. Ohtani
〃	E. Ohtani
〃	B. Mizuno
〃	I. Shibata
〃	S. Ando
〃	J. Shimomura
〃	S. Kikuzawa
〃	K. Norisugi
〃	T. Shibata
〃	K. Asano
〃	T. Watanabe
〃	G. Onoh
〃	K. Yanagizawa
〃	M. Shigemitsu
〃	E. Kanakura
〃	S. Tachibana

La rezolucio de la 6a jarkunveno de Ligo de T. J. B. A.

En la 25-6a de Aprilo, 1936, la 6a ĝenerala jarkunveno de Ligo de Tutjapanaj gejunulaj Budhanaj Asocioj havis lokon en Oosaka, mezjapana komerc-industria urbego, kun pli ol mil entuziasmaj partprenantoj el ĉiuj partoj de la lando. Kaj ĝi unuanime rezoluciis jenajn aperojn post serioza kaj detala deklaracio de sia grava misio en nuna tendenco.

La rezolucio.

I. Ni klopodu por esplori ĉiujn kondiĉojn por la fina paco de tuta mondo kaj por radikigi fundamentan principon de internacia justeco.

II. Ni klopodu por klarigi veran signifon de la tradicia Japana Spirito, firme nin tenante sur la bazo de Mahajana Budhismo.

III. Ni klopodu por pravigi kaj freŝigi Budhismon en ĉiuj flankoj kaj pertio ni subigu maloftan krizecon de nuna tempo.

IV. Ni klopodu por pli-briligi Budhisman Spiriton kiu en-brulas en la animoj de popolamaso, pensemo kritikante naskiĝ-kaŭzon de religiosimiloj aperoj en nuna tempo

Letters from abroad

From England

28th January, 1936.

Dear Sirs,

I have just seen a copy of the "International Buddhist Bulletin" for this month, and I find its contents of the greatest. On page 9 of this issue I see a notice of a new publication called "Footsteps of Japanese Buddhism", which is evidently to be a periodical journal. As all information on Japanese Buddhism is of great interest to readers of "Buddhism in England", I am wondering if you would be so good as to send me this periodical, together with your Bulletin, in exchange for each issue of "Buddhism in England", of which I enclose a specimen copy. If you will let me have copies of these as they appear so that I may draw the attention of our readers to them, I will see that the name of your Bureau goes down on our mailing list for complimentary copies of "Buddhism in England".

Thanking you,

I am, yours faithfully,

Alan W. Watts.

(of "Buddhism in England")

From New Zealand

86 Wairoa Road, Devonport,
Auckland, N. 1. New Zealand.
9/3/36.

Dear Sir and Brother,

May I thank you for your extreme courtesy in sending me your excellent monthly the Int. Buddhist Bulletin. I find it extremely interesting. The Jan. No. last month contained an extract from one of your city papers, it was in very good taste.

Wesick will be with us soon after your receipt of this. The magnetic influences at that time are the most propitious for those who are seeking enlightenment, as that is the cycle of time when the Blessed One Achieved, therefore those who are endeavouring to follow the impersonal trail will benefit from the Light on the Bodhi Path.

There is a very energetic Buddhist in JAVA named:—
Rev. W. Josias van Dienst,
Gandok, Km. 65, Tadjoer,
BUITENZORG, JAVA.

He is a friend of mine, and has lately returned from a 6 months course in a Japanese Zen Temple. I think he will appreciate your journal.

Will you please accept my gratitude also please find my cheque enclosed for 5/-. towards your expenses.

I am, Yours truly,

A. H. Thompson.

It is not necessary to personally reply, you are busy.

From England

12th March, 1936.

Dear Sir,

I shall be most grateful if you will kindly publish the enclosed article in a future issue of the INTERNATIONAL BUDDHIST BULLETIN. As you will see, it is an appeal for a closer understanding between the various schools of Buddhism.

Copies have been sent to other Buddhist journals.

Yours fraternally,

Alan W. Watts.

Editor.

(of "Buddhism in England")

Japanese News

Rabindranath Tagore Come to Japan

Sir Rabindranath Tagore, famous Indian poet and philosopher, has announced his intention of coming to Japan shortly with some 20 of his pupils. The Society for International Cultural Relations and the Japan-India Society were preparing the program to receive the great poet in Japan.

The members of the societies celebrated the 70th anniversary of the birth of the poet on April 17. The pupils of Sir Rabindranath introduced the local dance of Bengal during their stay in Japan.

Tourist Festival was Held

To promote the tourist industry, a tourist festival was held at the Hibiya Public Hall, Tokyo, on April 18 at 1 p.m. under the auspieces of the Japan Tourist Bureau and the Board of Tourist Industry.

The program for the festival was as follows, Mrs. Yahichi Kineya and her company played several Nagauta Samisen pieces and some local dances were performed. The Miyata Harmonica Band played Western and Japanese music. Miss Tamami Hanayagi, noted dancer, presented Japanese dances. The orchestra of the Ministry of Railways played some music. The "Tourist Dance" was performed by the Dancing Troupe of the Columbia.

Japanese Books Now in Esperanto

The translation into Esperanto of some representative Japanese novels by the Japan Esperanto Institute has nearly been completed, and they will be published by the Literatura Mondo Publishing House of Budapest shortly. The book is to include Mr. Saneatsu Mushakoji's "Love," Mr. Kunio Kishida's "Paper Balloon" and Mr. Kan Kikuchi's "First Duch Scholars in Japan"—all well-known works.

Faithful Tomb-Cleaner Perisists 24 Years

Kiichiro Inouye, 41 years old, living in the compound of the Senryu Temple, Aoyama, Tokyo has been cleaning the tomb of General Count Maresuke Nogi in Aoyama cemetery for the past 24 years. He has visited the tomb for this purpose every day since the entombment of General Nogi in the cemetery. He has been an orphan since 1912, and later became dumb.

Why Children Want to to Come Here

To investigate the reason for the visit to Japan of foreign children, the Board of Tourist Industry of the Japanese Government Railways has sent a questionnaire to foreign children, asking six questions as to their motives for a trip to Japan. As a result of this questionnaire, the Board has received the following interesting replies:

Because they want to see Mt. Fuji (203); things of Japanese (156); rikisha (126); temples (117); cherry trees (108); silk fabrics (112); Japanese nationality (106); modern commerce (104); gardens (91); Japanese customs (96); etc.

Honey Bees Sent to China

Some 20,000 honey bees were exported to China from Kobe on April 19th on board of the Mikasa Maru. This was the first shipment since the outbreak of the Shanghai Incident.

These bees were examined attentively by inspectors of the Department of Agriculture at the Kobe pier.

Women to Organize Against Smoking

Under the sponsorship of Dr. Doichi Okada, a Society of Japanese Women Opposed to Smoking was organized on May 1. To protect mother's health, Dr. Okada has been promoting the movement of anti-smoking among Japanese women. The society was organized by several prominent women of Tokyo.

Hiei Zan Hotel to Be Built

Under the management of the Kyoto Hotel and the Kyoto Electric Company, a summer resort will be opened on the slope of Hiei Mountain near Kyoto shortly. The company has bought ground for the purpose, covering some several thousand tsubo, where a new hotel will be constructed under the direction of the Kyoto Hotel.

Festival Honors Harris and Perry

The Black Ship Festival, or Kurofune Matsuri, an annual event in the small port city of Shimoda in South Idzu Province, began on April 25 and ends April 27. Memorial services for Townsend Harris, who resided there, and for Commodore Perry were held during the festival. A tribute was also paid to the tomb of Okichi, the legendary sweetheart of Harris.

Wireless Phone Service to Indo-China Opens

Wireless telephone service between Japan and French Indo-China opens on May 1st, the International Wireless Telephono Company of Japan announces. One call of three minutes, costs 36 yen.

Memorial Service for Fliers Held

Memorial rites, for the deceased pilots and engineers who attempted to make flights between Japan and America under the auspices of the Hochi Shimbun some years ago was held at the Tsukiji Honganji Temple, Tokyo by the Hochi Shimbun on April 30 at 1 p.m.

They were Kiyohi Homma, Eiichiro Baba and Tomoyoshi Ige who hopped off from Narushiro, Aomori Prefecture for North America. Their plane was missed over the Pacific Ocean. Several searches were made by the Hochi Shimbun after the plane and the crew were missed.

At the rites, members of the families of the crew and members of the Hochi Shimbun were present.

Omotokyo Land to Be Purchased

The headquarters at Ayabe, Kyoto Prefecture, of the recently prohibited Omotokyo sect and its temples at Kameoka are to be completely demolished shortly, and the estates will be bought by the local municipalities. The estate at Ayabe is about 25,000 tsubo and is to be bought at 14 sen a tsubo, and that at Kameoka is about 24,000 tsubo and is to be bought at eight sen a tsubo.

Asakusa Temple to Cost Million Yen

The ceremony of setting up the framework of the Honganji Temple of Asakusa, Tokyo was held on May 2. Fifty children held a parade and participated in the ceremony. The priest of some 250 attached temples to the Honganji Temple were also present and attended the ceremony.

The new temple building has a height of 90 feet, is of concrete construction and will be built by means of a budget of one million yen. The building is to be completed next spring.

Booklet to Draw Foreign Tourists

The Sado Steamship Company is to publish shortly a pamphlet in English describing the scenic beauties of Sado Island in Niigata Prefecture. The "Sado Okesa" ballads which originated in the island and which are now popular throughout the country will be rendered in English in this booklet. With the publication of this book the company expects to entice foreign tourists of the island.

Funds for Bell Tower of Shinagawa Temple

To get funds for the bell tower of the Shinagawa Temple, Shinagawa, Tokyo, the priests and the believers of the temple collected money on the Ginza on May 17. The temple received a bell from Geneva in 1930, which once belonged to the temple. It was treasured by the museum in Geneva and was returned to the temple after a proposition was made by the temple. The temple has no bell tower in which the bell can be hung and the plan is for the purpose of building one.

University President Aids Poor Students

Dr. Honda, President of Tohoku Imperial University established a students' society recently. The monthly fee of the body is ten sen. Dr. Honda will collect the fee to be used for a relief fund for poor students of the university.

Biography of Ninomiya Sontoku Being Translated

Mr. Yuichi Mori, 68-year-old veteran Christian preacher in Japan is translating a biography of Ninomiya Sontoku, great leader of feudal times, into English at present.

He established a memorial society for Ninomiya some years ago and also decided to make this translation because he wishes to introduce the great man's life to foreigners.

Ceremony for Founder of Tsukiji Temple

A memorial ceremony for Shinran, great priest and founder of the Tsukiji Honganji Temple was celebrated at the temple, Tsukiji, Kyobashi, Tokyo, for two days from May 20. Mr. Chikufu Tobari has spoken on the life of the great Buddhist priest and a concert of Japanese Buddhist music was held at the temple during the festival.

German Film Director reaches Fuji's Summit

Dr. Arnold Fanck, the visiting German film director and his

cameramen who had made an ascent of Mt. Fuji on May 8 registered the snow-covered crater on May 9. They took shots of sunrise from the summit of the mountain early on May 10 morning and arrived at Yoshida in the evening.

Descendants Pay Homage at Genghis Khan's Shrine

The princely descendants of the mighty thirteenth century Mongol conqueror, Genghis Khan gathered for annual prayers to their ancestor at Kweisui, China. They journeyed from throughout Suiyuan Province and Inner Mongolia to meet at his shrine.

In temples throughout Mongolia, crimson-robed lamas chanted supplications for their country's release from the severest Winter in a century, according to the New York Times. Snow fell steadily throughout previous night, obliterating all view of the Mongolian grazing lands, where the cold and starvation have already reduced the herds 30 to 90 per cent.

Scores of princes braved the terrific drifts to travel on horseback to the tent village of Edzinghoro, in the region of the "singing sands," 140 miles southwest of here. There the seven-century-old relics of Genghis Khan are enshrined in silver chests, closely guarded by the descendants of his bodyguard.

University of Rome may teach Japanese

Mr. Giacinto Auriti, Italian Ambassador to Tokyo, has informed the Forein Ministry that the University of Rome has a proposition for the establishment of a course of Japanese language. The university was host to Dr. Kotaro Tanaka, professor of the Tokyo Imperial University last year, when he lectured there on Japanese culture. The university wants to invite Dr. Masaharu Anesaki there this year. If Dr. Anesaki accepts the offer, the Foreign Ministry will make arrangements for the plan.

Siamese Leopords to enter Zoos

Two Siamese leopards arrived at Kobe on board the Kenryu Maru from Siam. They were brought by Mr. Yunosuke Yasukawa, chief of the trade delegation to Siam, on May 14. One is four years old and the other is two years old. The male leopard, which is the older, will be received by the Tokyo Municipal Zoo and the female one will be shown at the Osaka Zoo.

Japanese 'Arabian Nights' to be issued in English

A Japanese 'Arabian Nights' will be made by the Society for the Promotion of International Cultural Relations shortly especially for American children. Baron Ino Dan, director of the society was asked by the Children's Bookshop in New York City to make the Japanese "Arabian Nights" during his recent visit to America. Since he returned to Japan, he has consulted upon the plan with leading writers, translators and literary critics.

The book will contain many Japanese historic legends, juvenile stories which have been read by Japanese children for centuries. The stories will be rewritten in English, which are to be printed under the direction of the society and will be published by the Children's Book Shop in New York.

To Lecture on Ainu in Washington

Dr. Tetsuo Inukai, professor of the Hokkaido Imperial University will give a series of lectures on the Ainu race at the University of Washington, Seattle from June 18. A meeting for the promotion of American science will be held at the university at the time Dr. Inukai will give his lectures.

Some films representing the life and habits of the Ainu race will be shown at the meeting.

Chaplin sees Cormorant Fishing at Gifu

Charles Chaplin, famous film comedian and his party visited Gifu on his way to Tokyo from Kyoto on May 17 afternoon and watched the cormorant fishing on the Nagara River. The leading cormorant fishermen had made preparations for the famous comedian's coming and a large scale fishing party was arranged.

Old Japanese Sword to be given Hitler

An elaborate old Japanese sword, made by Magoroku of Mino Province, one of the best swordsmiths in Japan was presented to Chancellor Adolf Hitler by prominent persons of Seki-machi, Mino province. Dr. Fanck, well known German cinema producer will visit Seki-machi shortly to take some moving pictures of this place noted for its swordsmiths. On this occasion, prominent persons of the town will present the producer with the gift for Chancellor Hitler.

日本佛教と新興宗教

清　谷　閑　子

一

新興宗教が今日の如く勢力をもつて現はれて來た原因を，私達は公平に私的見解を捨てゝ考へてみねばならぬ。

新興宗教が擡頭する反面に，既成宗教の凋落は，必然的のものである。もしも既成宗教が新興宗教より以上に盛返す力を持つたとするなら，それは內容的に新興宗教的力を備へてゐると見てよいのであつて，かゝる清新なる內容と力とを生み出ださんと努力してゐる要素が，近來發芽してゐるのを，同時に看過してはならない。

だから私は，新興であらうと既成であらうと，問題は正，邪の如何によつて決められるべきであつて，既成的立場から新興を討つのも，新興的立場から既成を討つのも，共によき態度ではないと思ふ。

卽ち正しい宗教であるならば，何れの立場から見ても認容すべきであると思ふ。

その正邪を何によつて決めてゆくかがこれまた一つの立場を生むかも知れない。こゝに千差萬別の批判が生み出され，千差萬別の紛爭が生れて來るけれど，この場合に正しい立場に立つといふ，人間的態度は，同時にその時代の中心點に，生活の金剛座を踞ゑてゐることであつて，我々はこの意味に於て決して昨日の人であつてはならない。

既教宗教の缺點は，昨日といふ時代に，根據を据ゑて，今日といふ時代へ白眼視する人が多いのである。だから佛教は古典主義と間違へられて，邪路に入ると文化を逆行させ，一千二百年も前の奈良朝時代の佛教が，何の不思議もなく横行するといふ奇蹟が演ぜられるのである。

私は神や佛を念ずれば，病氣が治るといふことを奇蹟として驚く前に，かうした宗教がこの現代に出現し，盛えてゐることの方が，奇蹟であると思はずにゐられない。實に人生は廣い，昨日捨てた筈のあやまちを，もう一度取上げて，而もそれを價値づけやうとするご丁寧な錯誤を，平然としてやつてのけやうとするのだから，時代の推移は決して理性的に行はれてもゐなければ，一時代の文化は案外にも一般民衆を取殘して，知識人だけがさつさと獨り歩きしてゐるやうな淋しさを感じる

獨りの哲人が叡智を働らかして，折角民衆を導かうとするのに，民衆は彼の叡智とは何の關係もなく，たゞ勢力的に引ずられてゆくのである。

實に歷史は辯證法的に，進んでゐるか知らないけれど，同時にその文化の中樞だけが動くのであつて，一般民衆には進步も何にもない，たゞ盲目的な流轉だけが存在すると，言はねばならないのであらう。

二

日本に佛教が渡來してから，約一千四百年の歷史を經てゐるが，當初，奈良朝時代は，加持祈禱の科學以前の宗教が附帶條件となつてゐた。卽ち行基良辨の如きも，加持祈禱を以て佛者の德化であるとしてゐたやうである。

だから奈良朝佛教は，物質文化の頂上と共に，それ以上の發展は遂げられなかつた。民衆は爛爛たる物質文化に醉ひ，そこに信仰と祈願との原始宗教的な佛教教化に滿足して，何等の疑ふところがなかつた。この一千二百年前の宗教禮讃の一大光景を，吾々は最近の新興宗教のその何れにも發見するといふ皮肉は，これを病的現象といはずに濟まされるであらうか。

何故なら，この奈良朝佛教に於ても病氣や運命的不幸は，加持祈禱と何等の關係のないことを，厳然として教理に說いてゐるのであるが，民衆は其を諒解しなかつた。

茲に日本民衆の根本的な悲劇が，今日まで根強く横はつてゐる原泉がある それは人格化したる自然崇拜と，神佛への奴隷的な態度である。これが平安朝から鎌倉へ，鎌倉から江戶時代へと實に政治的精神に結びつき，遂に德川幕府の大政奉還と，それに次いで，踵を接する如く來襲した資本主義との區別すらも，今以て，認識することを避けてゐるやうな民衆である。

これが國民的悲劇でなくて，何が悲劇であらう。

加持祈禱の宗教が，新興宗教として迎へられる時代錯誤，病的現象を悲しむ前に，何がかゝる無智なる民衆を生み出したかを，眞面目に反省してみなければならない。なぜなら，民衆には傳統的な精神が，根强く働らいてゐるからである。

卽ち人間の力によつて，自然を知らうとする前に，自然にひざまづく敬虔なる態度を强ゐられて來たのである。

人間の最も敬虔なる態度は，自然を正しく認識することだと，佛教は說いてゐるのだが，民衆はこの正しさといふものを取違へて，ひざまづくことだと敎へられた。

さて奈良朝から，正しき佛教と，この自然崇拜の奴隷的な邪道佛教とは，常に並行して步んでゐたのである。卽ち悟りは大德のものであり，盲目的歸依は民衆のものであつた。

これに反して，上層階級や智識人の宗教は，民衆の如何に頓着なく，銳利なる哲學的考察をもつて發展した。傳教大師はその好標本の第一人者であるかゝる偉大なる哲人を生んだ平安朝は依然として加持祈禱の宗教を要求し，最澄の德化は餘りに行はれずに過ぎて行つた。そして邪教であるところの祈禱宗教は依然として民衆の歸崇をうけてゐた。

この場合に，民衆の目的は人にあるのでなく，神佛にあるから，寺と宗教的儀式が完備してゐたら，それで事は足りるのである。こゝに職業的な僧侶

は增加し，遂に祈禱料を貪るための不正非惡が，商業方面より甚だしく行はれたことは不思議でない。そればかりか此の宗教性を利用して，惡政治は行はれ，政治の壟斷階級すらも現はれるに至つたのである。——藤原氏から始まり，幕府政治へと移る內容的力は，民衆の盲目な宗教性によること言ふまでもない——實に邪教は恐ろしい力をもつてゐる。

さて傳教の敎化は，盲目な民衆に失敗したけれど，弘法は立派に成功を收めたのである。卽ち宗教としての眞髓たる菩薩行は，民衆にとつて何の關係もなく，民衆はかゝる佛の應現に驚異し，更にその盲目信仰を增大することによつて，宗教的獗害を覺えたのである。

三

平安末期に出た，法然にあつては，佛者として悟りを，そのまゝ民衆に移植せんとするの良心を持つて苦しんだのである。

淨土敎としての哲學的價値は別問題であつて，佛者の悟りを，同時に民衆のものとせん良心的態度は，法然を以て最初の人と見てもよい。然しながら法然をして成功せしめたる時代の空氣を認識しなければ，この論據は正しくないと思ふ。

この時代の人心は，もう病氣や一個人の不幸を神佛に祈るくらゐでは，人生は解決できないところまで，榮枯盛衰の流轉を目前に見なければならなくなつて來た，卽ち悲劇は一個人から，集團的に移つて來たわけであつて，この場合に民衆は，現世利益の盲目宗教より轉じて，人生觀的悟りの宗教を要望せんとする傾向をもちはじめた。

言ふまでもなく，知識階級の誘導ではあつた。例へば西行法師の詩的感化なども，與つて力はあらう，何れにしても盲目信仰からは，やゝ眼を覺してゐた民衆であつた。この意味に於て，今日の民衆より，平安末期の民衆の方が水準は高いのである。だからそれを證據づけるものは，その當時の文學藝術に於て，立派に今日より高度に發達してゐたことが判るではないか。

親鸞の敎化は，法然の系統に出で，その哲學的な發展は師法然より進み，現世祈禱を徹底的に排擊し，そのためには，自らの長男善鸞をさへ破門した。卽ち法然の活動を，より深く浸潤せしめたものである。

ともあれ法然や親鸞の淨土敎によつて，盲目的信仰から悟りの信仰へと入つて來た民衆は，こゝで確然たる宗教の對立が現はれて來た。淨土敎には現世利益の迷信はなかつた。

然るに南都の佛敎では，奈良朝おゆづりの迷信は，その山伏などによつて充分證明することが出來る。

ところで淨土敎は，佛敎の目的たる悟りの第一使命を果したけれど，未だそれが現世的の態度を執らなかつたところに，一つの未墾地が殘されてゐた。こゝを狙つたのが，榮西禪師の臨濟禪であつた。

榮西禪師の禪の提唱は，まことに時代の背景のしからしむるところにあつた。何故なら，時やうやく鎌倉幕府の業成りとげて，時世は日本全土，武士の時代に入つて來てゐた。

平安朝の榮枯盛衰を基調とする無常觀は，此時，その運命まで人間の力と意志によつて左右できるものと自惚れ若しくは自覺することを，猛き武士は人生觀の解決としたのである。

それへもつて來て，それを裏付けるところの臨濟禪は，絕讚を以て迎へられ，榮西に次いで宋から歸つて來た道元禪師は，この臨濟禪を更に論理化しそして具體化したる曹洞宗を民衆に投出した。時恰も鎌倉中期の，武士道は戰亂のあとを受けて，人倫的に傾むいてゐたから，現世で成佛し得る道元禪にこそ，民衆の歸嚮は集まつたのも當然である。

四

然し北條氏の政治は，源氏から戰ひ取つたのでなく，盜み取つたといふところに，民衆の不滿はあつた。

こゝに道元をして，大政奉還を北條に强要したり，日蓮をして國家觀念を强調せしめずにおかなかつた。

日蓮をして，あれほど迄に國家觀念を强調せずにおかなかつたほど，隣邦民族の元の擡頭は，日本を脅やかしたに違ひない。

民衆はこゝにまた一つの負擔を與へられた。卽ち現世成佛でも，國家の問題に至つては，解決困難であるといふことであつた，だから或る選ばれたる民衆は，こゝに出現した日蓮を救世主の如く解したであらう，ほどに，それほど國家觀念は新しい刺戟を與へたのである。

日蓮上人の性格は，焦りすぎる性格であつて，民衆の歸依を掌中に握らねばならんといふ焦りから，加持祈禱を取上げるに至つたやうだ。

何れにせよ，今では何れの宗派も，發生當時の熱力を失つてしまひ，古典主義の仲間入りをして，實に文字通り寂光の淨土を現世にか，或ひは來世にか念願すれば，佛敎の能事終れりと思ふに至つたかの如くである。

かくして既成宗教の，古典主義の民衆に接觸するのは，葬式法要，追善供養だけである。だから民衆は，人生觀を棚に片付けて，感傷的なる葬式法要には，佛敎によつて慰められやうとするのであるから，民衆の如何に生くべきかといふ問題は，佛敎とは何の關係もなくなつてしまつた。

こゝに民衆は一大難破船に遇つた漂流の民である。一握の藁でも摑まねばならない。邪敎も迷信も考へてはゐられない。功德さへあれば三千年前の自然崇拜敎の動物禮拜すらも，敢て辭さない狀態である。

私はかくの如く邪敎の橫行する原因は，民衆を放棄して，獨り古典主義に寂光の淨土を達觀してゐる既成宗教の責任だと云ひたいのである。

だから私は既成宗教の靜的態度に，非難の鋒先を向けると共に，何故かゝるものを信じるかと，民衆に向つて叫ぶ必要を感じるのである。

五

然し既成宗教も今日では，その古典主義の殼を破つて，新らしく躍り出でんとしてゐるので，今やこゝに邪教に囚はれた民衆を救濟するの正しい宗教が，潑溂と雄飛せんことを待望したい元來宗教の缺點としては，現代に生活しながら，科學を對立に置いて，まるで宇宙の神秘でも壞されるかのやうに嫌惡することであるが，かゝる宗教は時代錯誤である。

宇宙の神秘といふものは，人間の科學ぐらゐで壞れもせず，失くなりもせず，むしろ科學の鋭利なる進歩は，反對に神秘を增大してゆくのである。神秘を增大することは不幸でなく，必然的に人間の負はされた災厄であると共に歡喜でもある。

宇宙の神秘を探究する良き科學者の良心的態度にありては，神秘はますます增大され，良心なき科學者にありては，科學萬能の迷信に陷るのである。科學者の良心的態度が，即ち宗教上の叡智であつて，神秘をいたづらに崇拜することが叡智ではないのである。

だから科學者的良心なき態度は，唯物一元論の錯誤に陷り，これによつて人生の悲劇は外部から內部へと浸潤してゆく。これとは反對に神秘崇拜の唯心一元論は，人生の不幸を內部から外部へと發展せしめる。

この二つの缺陷を認識して，物質生活には科學をして，ますます發展せしめ，人生觀の上には正しき宗教によつて悟らしめ，その悟りによつて救濟してゆくの宗教こそ，今日の時代に要望すべき宗教である。

こゝに言ふ人生觀は個人的の場合でない，むしろ一社會の一國家の有機體的態度を目的としての人生觀でなければ，現代として何等の意義はないのである。

日本人が國家的には，强い國民だといはれてゐても，それは文化的に强いのでなく，軍國主義的に强いのである宗教とは何の關係もない。何故かくの如く軍國主義的に强いかは，最初にいつたやうに自然崇拜の盲目的信仰が，國家的に變生したのであつて，日本に取つては幸福であつたが，個人としては不幸である。

この個人的不幸は，いつの場合でも宗教が救ひを垂れてゐて，その救ひに二種の態度がある。その一つは現世に對する超越，その一つは與へられた運命と境遇に忍從することである。いかにしてこの不幸を打開すべきかの方法は決して與へられないのであつた。

而して現世に對する超越的態度は，ますます社會と民衆から隔絕して，遂に今日文化民族であるべき筈の日本にあの愚昧な宗教が擡頭するの餘儀なき結果を招來して，別に何の對策も計らないのである。古典主義者の個人主義は，こゝに來て極まれりといふべきである。

だから一般民衆にとつて，かゝる個人主義的超越者を生むことは不幸である。

六

これはマルキストが社會民衆の幸福を追ふに急にして，唯物的態度でこれを將來し得ると信じたのと好一對の失敗である。社會科學はまことに，人生の悲劇を，外部から內部へと追込むものである。

この二者のそれぞれ持つてゐる缺陷を，最も適當に調和せしむるところの者こそ，實に民衆を救ひ，民衆を導き一文化を健全に發達せしむべき，正しき宗教ではないであらうか。

今日までの宗教が，怠つてゐるところのものは，個人の悟りに重點をおきそこに人生超越の修練を積ましめた結果，一社會の民衆をおき忘れてしまふのである。

傳教，弘法，法然，親鸞，榮西，道元，日蓮等の大德達は，常に邪教に惑はされてゐた民衆を，正しき悟りに導くために，彫身鏤刻の苦しみを敢へてしたのであつた。

今やこれらの大德の行履を學ばんとする時に當つて，吾々民衆は，大多數の民衆と共にあることを忘れてはならない。此時代を正しく認識するといふことは，むしろ民衆の不幸を認識するといふことである。經濟的に破綻し，飢ゑと患らひと光明なき生活とに，喘ぎ喘ぎ生きゆく民衆の苦惱を，負擔することであつて，これには愛と叡智とが働らかねば，目的は達しられない。

そこに宗教が政治に働らきかけざるを得ない一道も横はつてゐるし，勿論文藝にもその重任を負はさねばならない。宗教教育の必要なるは言ふまでもないのである。

然しながら折角教育の基礎が科學的に進歩づけられた今日，その科學の進歩を阻害するやうな原始宗教が，横行するを許すならば，先人が，血涙を流して迷信と戰つた功績は，今や破壞せられねばならない。

教育に迷信を鼓吹するの宗教が浸潤する位ならば，むしろ宗教教育は取入れない方がよいのである。

然るに今や物質科學教育に，人生の悲劇は累々としてその死屍を曝してゐるのであつて，速やかに愛と叡智の光輝ある宗教が君臨せんことを希望せざるを得ない。

何故に佛青運動にエスペラントを採用する必要があるか

中西　義雄

緒　論

汎太平洋佛靑大會の第一回も第二回もエスペラント採用に關する提案が可決されて居るが，未だ實行の域には殆んど入つて居ない。佛教濟世軍聯合靑年部では之を極めて遺憾とし，それを促進する爲に「佛靑聯盟にエスペラント委員を設け佛靑の事業としてエスペラント教育を實施するの件」といふ議案を全聯第六回總會に提出したのである。該案は審査委員によつて第三部會に廻付され，該部會では大多數を以て可決されたのである。併し國際語エスペラントに就ての認識が充分でなかつた爲か，一二の反對者があつたが，時間不足の爲に，之に對する提案者の說明も充分でなく，併せて諸賢の御批判を乞ふ爲本稿を草した次第である。

國內では日本語で 國外にはエスペラントを

エスペラント反對論者に，日本人は日本語で充分なり（全聯第六回總會の反對者は此の論者であつた），といふ人がある。此の論を取りあげる事は，或る意味に於て全く大人氣ない話であるが，ともすれば偏狂國粹主義に陷入り易い，頑迷佛教徒として有り勝な事とも思はれる。

廿世紀文明の特徵はすべてのものゝ國際化である。學術，美術，工藝，商工業，政治，經濟等何れも國際的となつて居る事である。如何に豐富な資源を國內に持つ大國たりとも，一國の孤立では到底存續し得ない時代である。東洋の一隅に長夜の眠りにあつた我が國も明治御維新によつて，國際的の舞臺に乘出したのである，畏くも明治大帝は御登極の初め「知識を世界に求め大いに皇基を振起すべし」といふ御聲文を下し玉ひ我が國の進むべき道を御示し下されたのである。知識を世界に求める道具，それは卽ち外國語の知識である。此の知識を缺き國際場裡に臨む事は武器なくして戰場に到るが如きものであつて到底勝利を得る譯にはゆかない。我が國の學校に於ける外國語教育も此處に立脚點を置くものと考へられる。英語教育が採用されて既に六十餘年，英語の機關は至れり盡せりの狀態にあり，國をあげて英語殖民地の觀を呈して居るが，一般國民の英語の力ははたして所期の目的を達し得たであらうか。自信を以て堂々と英米人と會談し得る役人や，外人の校閱を經ずして論文を國際的に發表し得る學者が此の國に幾人あるであらうか。況んや

專門家ならざる宗教家，僧侶が英語で講演や說教をなす事の容易ならざるは餘りにも明白である。誇り得る大乘佛教の世界宣布が容易でない最大の原因も此處にある事を我々は見逃すべきではない。大成功と稱讃された一昨年の汎太平洋佛靑大會の直後，その會長たりし柴田一能氏をして，此後は通譯其の人を得る事にありと嘆ぜしめし所以も此の外國語習得の困難によるものである。我等は佛陀の慈光に生活する靑年佛徒として全人類に呼びかけたき氣持で充たされて居る，併しそれを阻むもの卽ち言語の相違といふ障壁が未だ取除かれて居ない。日本人は日本語で充分なりと云ふ論者，偏狂國粹主義者は，或はそんな氣持の持合せはないかも判らない。併し，平和の宗教，大乘佛教は萬人の首肯し得る敎，國境を越へ，人類，民族等一切の差別を超越した全人類の光であつて，我等が之を他に傳へる事は我等の歡びであり，又義務である。曾てゼネバの國際勞働會議で我が國の一代表が，公用語ならざる日本語を以て演說を敢行し物笑ひの種となつたといふ轍を踏むべきであらうか，此の地球上には二百に近い異つた言語が使はれつゝある事と，その言語がその民族，國民を結びつける重大なる要素であり，互に尊重し合ふべきを我等は忘れてはならない。我々は決して日本語を廢してエスペラントを學べといふのではない。「國內では日本語で國外にはエスペラントを」といふのが我等の主張である。

又，假令，英語が學習容易の代物であるとしても，今日英語の通じる國は英米二ヶ國とその屬領乃至殖民地のみであつて，脚一歩ヨーロツパ大陸に入るならば，誰もが經驗する如く英語は殆んど要をなさず，此處に國際語の必要が痛感されるのである。

エスペラントの普及狀態

我々が反對論者から聞く理由として「理想であつて，エスペラントは未だ實用の域に達して居ない」といふ事がある。此れは反對論者自身の認識不足を物語るものであつて，此の語のみにて氣樂に世界旅行の出來るは勿論，各國共競つて旅行案內のエスペラント版を刊行し，現に此の語によつて商取引をして居る貿易商もある。

エスペラント實用の中心機關たる萬國エスペラント協會は世界各地七十七個國に二千七百五十九名の地方代表を持つて居て，此の七十七個國二千七百五十九名は，各國に於ける有數な知名エスペランチストであつて，所謂私設領事の役目をなし，旅行者の世話は勿論，貿易其他の事に就ての照會に對して調査回答を實行して居るのである。我が國にては曾てゼネバの國際聯盟事務局に在つた藤澤親雄氏を總領事格たる主席代表とし，中央大學教授の川原次吉郎氏を次席に，以下國內各地に四十一名の代表を持つて居るのである。

現在の處エスペラントを讀み書き話し得る人は世界中で一千萬を越すとも云はれ一說には二百萬位であらうとも

云はれて居る。併し兎もあれ，年一年とその範圍が擴がりつゝある事は動かせない事實である。

昨年日本の鐵道省がエスペラント版の旅行案內を刊行し，たちまち初版一萬部を出し盡し，本年初に再版二萬部を發行した事や，昨年の四月から九月まで六ケ月間に鐵道省の國際觀光局が海外から受取つた觀光に關する照會狀七百餘通の內五百通餘がエスペラントで書かれて居たといふ事實によつても反對論者はエスペラントに關する認識を是正されたい。

宗教とエスペラント

基督敎關係では先づ英國の聖書協會が新舊兩譯聖書のエスペラント版を出して居るのを筆頭に，カトリツク，クエカー，プロテスタント，メソヂスト等各派共にエスペラントの文献や，團體を各地に持つて居る。

新興宗教としてはバハイズム，マリアリチズム等何れも此れを採用し，先年我が國では禁止されたが，燈臺社も此れを採用しエスペラントの雜誌 Oraepoko を刊行して居る。

禁止處分にあつた大本教が此れを利用して居た事は周知の事實で，パリーにヨーロツパ宣傳本部を置いたのもエスペラントを利用してである。

此れ等に較べて，佛教のエスペラント利用は決して誇り得る程には達して居ない。たゞ英國のヤクソン氏が佛教エスペラント聯盟を組織して居る事と我國では柴山慶氏等の少數者が孤軍奮鬪で日本佛教エスペランチスト聯盟を守つて居る位のものであつて，此の事は一昨年から昨年にかけて，ハンガリーのリテラツーラ，モンド社から刊行された，エスペラント百科辭典にも反映して，該辭典に出て居る宗教關係の記事五百餘項中，佛教關係のものは僅かに十項に過ぎないのである。此の事は佛教エスペランチストとして我々の最も遺憾とするところである。

結　　論

全聯規約にある第二二章の目的や，第六章の事業を遂行する爲に國際語採用の有利は多數の人々に認められて居乍ら未だ實行の域に達しない事は，全聯內部にエスペランチストが多くない事に原因するものであつて，又他方エスペラントの學習が他の外國語と同樣に難かしいものと解されて居るからであると思ふ。此の點に就き私は其の人達に五十時間の暇をエスペラントの爲に與へて欲しいと御願ひする。五十時間の學習，エスペラントには此れだけで充分である，普通の讀み書き話しは餘程の低能者でない限りはなし得る樣になるであらう。數年前來朝した獨逸の新聞記者ウイルヘルム・ペルツ，エドモンド・チャイレの兩君が，シベリヤ通過の列車內の徒然に讀むだ獨習書が大いに役立つて，それ以後の旅行が極めて樂であつたが如きも動かすべからざる一例である。

全聯を生かす事が我々青年佛徒の義務であり榮譽であるならば，全聯のエスペラント採用こそ，青年佛徒としての義務であらう。

アダムズ・ピークに就て

山　本　晃　紹

倫敦タイムズの三月四日號にアダムズ・ピークを飛行機から見下した寫眞が出てゐる。空中寫眞として眞最初のものだと書いてあつた。鬱蒼たる森林の波の中から，こんもりと盛上つた山頂，其處には支那の廬山かどこかの寫眞で見る樣に，廟刹ともおぼしき建物が一むれ。而して，長い長い石段が此の突端に這ひ上るところ，ボヘミヤ邊りの一古城である。あのお城の中にはどんなフエアリー，どんなプリンセスが住んでゐるのか‥‥童話の世界から眺めると，こんな氣分も湧いて來る。

×

アダムズ・ピークとは獅子島の最高峯，海拔七・三五〇呎を誇る實にも由緒床しき神話のお山である。海波六十リーグ（一リーグ＝三哩）の彼方より船人の目につく海の標幟，紅毛のアドヴェンチユラはおろか，昔，昔，亞剌比亞夜話の出來たらう其時から潮蹴る舟人達に親しい熱國，椰子實る國の靈峯なのである。この山の頂に大きな岩があつて，其處に佛足跡なるものがある。といつて，僕は見たこともない。それとはなく知つてゐるまで。一昨年の佛靑大會の際も獅子島代表の人達からも，何か，それに就て聞かされた。暖い宗教的芳香として系つて置いた。僕は，此山のことであつたのかと今更乍ら意識を新しくしたのであつた。此寫眞を切抜いて置きたいのは山々だが，あなおそろしや，お役所の大事な資料だ。僕は虔ましやかに，僅に所載の紙名と日附を錄して以つて我れと我が好奇心をなだめて置いたのであつた。

由來英國人——他の泰西の兄弟達も相當ではあるが——は何んとか自己流の名をつけねと承知しない。臺灣，琉球，千島，樺太，列べても際限がない。エドワドと名前をつけて置き乍ら，ネツドと呼ぶ。亞剌比亞人がエル・ラフーンと名附けた此山をアダムズ・ピークと呼ぶ位平氣なものだ。ところでもつて，佛教徒の聖跡を，所もあらうに，基督教徒の太祖アダムの名を冠するとは怪しからん ‥‥‥‥とはよく耳にする。はからずも，此度タイムズの寫眞が御緣になつて本氣になつた。誰が一體こんな罪な事をしたものだらうかとサイクロペディア・オヴ・インディアを開けてみる。

十字軍戰爭以來　回基兩教徒間の感情的方面には著しい開きが生じたにも係らず，爭はれぬのは地の理の上の接近さである。パレスタインと亞剌比亞は何といつても近い。だから神話の世界に入ると兩教間に共通要素は極めて多い。今上記の本に依ると，アダムズ・

ピークの佛足跡なるものを，印度教徒はシヴァの足跡，佛教徒は佛陀の，回教徒はアダムのだといふ。外三種のクレイマントもある。ともかく，アダムとイヴはアララット山に住居した，アダムは第一の豫言者，アダムは地上に於ける神の第一の代理人だとする回教徒はアダムが樂園を追はれた時獅子島は北方，アダムズ・ブリッヂを渡り，此島に逝れたのだとする。ところで，困つたことには，印度教の英雄詩ラーマーヤーナに依ると猿人ハヌマンや，又，ラーマーが此のアダムズ・ブリッヂを渡つたことになる。勿論，ラーマーが此處を通つたにしろ，アダムが此處を渡り，アダムズ・ピークに足跡を殘したといふ筋書を何等毀損するものではない。ともあれ，異說は紛々たるもの。

此處で一寸踏止つて考へてみたいことはアダムズ・ピーク對アダムズ・ブリツヂの問題である。獅子島より印度へ渡つた人は記憶にあることであらう。朝まだき，まだ眠くてたまらぬのに連絡船に乘り換へさせられて此アダムズ・ブリツヂなる地點の海を渡るのである。尤も僕達が渡つた時は相當な風があつて船は大揺れ，僕はデツキのベンチにへバりついてゐてやうやくにして友人が船底深くかくれ込んだあの醜態か何か實は知らぬが‥‥‥ともかくもへバりついて居たことは事實なのだ。だから，えらさうに言つてみてもアダムズ・ブリツヂが果して如何なるものであつたかは判然としない。ともかくも砂濱の向ふの岸邊に着いた時はほつとした。話は脫線だが，ともあれ，この飛石みたいなところがアダムズ・ブリツヂと言はれてゐるのは，アダムズ・ピークに對する對蹠的命名に由來する‥‥と僕は思ふ。

上にいつた百科全書の記事が信ずべきものだとすればアダムズ・ピーク命名の出所は回教神話を基礎とし，更に，それにはお家大事と天地六日創造說を信じてゐる基督教徒何某かの信念に礎いてかくは命名の光榮に浴したものであらう。皆銘々に嗜好もあり，感情の縺れもあるものだ。特にバーナード・ショウはそのバトラー評文の中で：―

When Darwin had published his two books "Origin of Species" and "The Descent of Man," Butler was delighted for six weeks, because these two books knocked Genesis and Paley's demonstration of design in the universe into a cocked hat. It presently appeared that the whole scientific world in the widest sense......... shared Butler's ecstacy. Darwin won immortal fame and by the end of the century Dawwin was every where and Butler was nowhere.

といつてゐる位だ。佛教徒たるもの，餘り神經質になる程の問題でもあるまい。但し，僕が一九一五年の一月初頭此のアダムズ・ブリッヂを渡つたことだけは神話ではない。

渡暹の思出

來馬琢道

最近暹羅國幼帝が佛教を捨てゝ基督教になられると云ふ話が新聞に出て居る。之を聞くと幼帝御自身の轉宗の如くに考へられるが，お歲僅に十歲の幼帝であるから，其母堂の希望に依つて耶蘇教の禮拜を爲さるゝことになるのではなからうか。何れにしても佛教を國教として居る唯一の國に取つては一大變動と云はねばなるまい。回顧すれば，私が暹羅國に行つたのは明治四十四年である。日暹寺の日置默仙禪師が暹羅國皇帝戴冠式に行くから同行せよと勸められたので，俄に旅裝を整へ出發することにした。佛教青年聯合會と云ふものが當時あつたので，其幹事と云ふ肩書を貰ひ，暹羅國公使館にも外務省にも聯絡を取つて出掛けた。十月二十八日に神戶を出帆し，新嘉坡に立寄り獨逸の船でバンコツクに渡り，公使館及暹羅國政府側に對する手續を終り，出來るだけ勉强して諸方を視察したが，僧侶の尊敬せらるゝ有樣は全く豫想外であつたと同時に，僧侶が何にもしないで居る有樣も一寸意外であつた。少し大きい寺院に行くと必ず美事な禮拜臺がある。之は皇帝陛下が御參拜の時に用ひらるゝものであると云ふ初めて皇帝が佛前に禮拜せらるゝ實情に直面した。又，僧侶が金錢を手にせぬ事も感ずべき事である。通譯を連れて法衣を賣る家へ行つて私が自身で金を出したら，其處の婆さんがプライ・プン（日本の僧侶）は自分で金錢を取扱ふのかと其通譯に反問したさうである。僧侶は金を何うするかと云へば，寺を出る時に會計係から財布を貰ひ電車に乘る時に其財布ごと車掌に渡すと車掌が眼の前で要るだけの金を出して若し釣錢を要する時には其を入れて其儘僧侶に返す。卽ち金を使はないのではなく，自ら手に觸れないやうにするだけのことである。だが，實際其等の僧侶は金錢を手にしなくても生活して行けるやうに出來て居るのであるから此點誠に羨しいやうに思はれた。托鉢の模樣なども此根本精神を知つてから見て居ると，僧侶が每朝無造作に市中を大きな鐵鉢を抱えて步いて居れば，何等の乞食的態度を取らないでも食物に困らないと云ふ實情が分る。社會が此樣な有樣であるから皇帝になる前に皇太子が出家して托鉢せらるゝことも決して不思議ではないと感じた。も一つ感じた事は皇族の最高位に在られるバチラヤーンと云ふ高僧が私共をお招きになつて本堂の中を御案內下さる時に，突如として其高僧の前に橫臥する者があるから何をするのかと思つて見て居ると，高僧の通過せられた後に靜々と起き上つて後から禮拜して居た。卽ち經文にある五體投地と云ふ最大の敬意を表して居るのである。我等が佛前に座具を布いて三拜するのも全く五體投地の如くであると云ふことが分つた。皇帝陛下の戴冠式が佛教の精神に依つて行はれることは豫々聞いて居たが，經文にある色々のことが暹羅國に於ては現に行はれて居ると云ふ事實を見て，私は百聞一見に如かずと云ふことを痛感したのである。其れから次に行つたビルマ，印度及セイロン等のことに就ては一々參考になることもあるが，暹羅國に於て感じた佛教に對する第一印象が私には忘れられないものである。而してセイロン島に於てウヰスキーを飮み，一小使に笑はれた事が，余の不飮酒を實行せしめた事も，海外生活の一つの思ひ出であらう。

日滿佛教協會創立さる

去る四月十日，麴町區內幸町大阪ビル內レンボーグリルに於て，日滿佛教協會の發會式が開催され，極めて盛會裡に之が發會を見た。當日の謝大使の祝辭，並に同協會の創立趣旨及び會則は，次の如くである。

祝　　辭

本日玆に日滿佛教協會の發會式を擧行せらるゝに當りまして一言祝辭を述ぶる機會を得ましたことは余の最も欣快とする所で御座居ます。

惟ふに宗教は國家の發展，文明の進歩と共に迷信的妄想より離脫し國境の隔りなくして新しき世界民衆の精神の糧と相成つたので御座居ます。殊に我が佛教は其の教義に於て常に小乘を捨て大乘を說き普ねく衆生を濟度し次で世界民衆の安心立命を翼ふのが本旨であるやうに承つて居ります。

此の度この大乘的教旨に基き進んで日滿兩國の臣民に光を與へ之が人心の歸趨を同一ならしめんとする計劃の下に，本協會の設立せられましたことは誠に時宜に適した意義深き企てゞあると信じ，且つ兩國親善のために寄與する處蓋し亦尠からざるものあると確信する者で御座居ます。

願くば本協會の隆盛發展を祈り軈がて全東洋に及び，日滿佛教協會が基點となりて大東洋佛教協會の誕生せらるる日の近からんことを切望して止まない次第で御座居ます。

康德三年四月十日

駐日滿洲帝國特命全權大使

謝　介　石

日滿佛教協會
創立趣意書

吾人は玆に日滿佛教協會を創設するに當り聊か所懷の一端を開陳し以て江湖諸賢の御贊同と御協力とに訴ふる所あらんとす。

今や滿洲國は既に其の建國第五次の年を閲し東亞の天地に駸々乎として其の雄姿を開顯しつゝあり。而して其の建國の大業たるや，行政に，外交に，產業に，教育に，濟々として其の雄圖を遂げんとしつゝある事は，正に全世界の驚異にして，等しく亞細亞の天地に生を享けたる吾人の以て欣快の念に耐へざる所なり。

然りと雖も建國日尙淺くして，一應の平面的なる建設工作は進捗せるも，其立體的なる建設工作としての文化施設の領域に及びては，未だ充分なるものを見る能はず。然れども眞に國家百年の大業を謀し，有終の美を濟さんには，文化政策に依據せざるべからず。

由來滿洲國は，其の文化國是として傳統久しき儒教を採用したるは，實に賢明なるものありしと雖も，吾人は儒教と同樣に久しき傳統を有する佛教の採用せらるゝあつて，此の亞細亞の二大教義に依り，現當二世に亘りて人心の歸趨を指導せざるべからず。是る見地よりして吾人は滿洲佛教の興隆を念願するや久し。今や機熟し，因緣和合し進みて同信同志の徒相計り，此に一つの協會を結成して，之を日滿佛教協會と名づく。蓋し其の目的とする處は敢て一宗一派に偏せず，所謂通佛教的立場に立脚して日滿兩國に於ける大乘佛教の興隆を企圖し，進んで兩國佛教徒の親和協力に依りて，新興滿洲國に於ける眞の王道樂土の建設に對して最後的文化工作を施與し，以て東亞の平和，否な全世界の平和の爲に粉骨碎身の盡力を致さんとす。

惟ふに此の聖業たるや，其前途，極めて多事多難，一朝にして其の成果を示す能はざることあらんも，吾人は敢て默々として苦鬪奮戰せんとするの覺悟を有するものなり。

冀くば大方の諸賢，幸ひに吾人の雄心と苦衷とを御賢察せられ，以て新たなる佛日增輝のために，進んで御援助と御協力とを垂れ賜はんことを！

昭和十一年四月十日

日滿佛教協會々則

第一條　本會ハ日滿佛教協會ト稱シ本部ヲ東京ニ置キ時宜ニ應ジテ日滿其他各地ニ支部ヲ設ク

第二條　本會ハ通佛教的立場ニ立チ日滿間ノ佛教徒ニ依ル親善及福利ノ增進ヲ圖ルヲ以テ目的トス

第三條　本會ノ事業左ノ如シ

一　日滿間ノ見學旅行，留學及開教等ノ紹介斡旋

二　日滿關係ノ宗教，學藝及一般文化上ノ諸事項ノ調査研究

三　會報及圖書ノ出版刊行

四　研究會，講演會及講習會等ノ計畫開催

五　其他必要ト認ムル諸事業

第四條　本會ニ顧問，參與及役員ヲ置ク

顧　問　若干名　　參與　若干名

會　長　一　名　　副會長　一名

評議員　若干名　　理事　若干名

第五條　會長ハ評議員之ヲ推薦ス

評議員ハ總會ニ於テ選擧ス

理事ハ評議員ノ互選ニ據ル

顧問參與ハ會長之ヲ推薦ス

第六條　役員ノ任務ハ左ノ如シ

一　會長ハ會務ヲ總理ス

二　副會長ハ會長ヲ輔佐スルモノトス

三　評議員ハ重要ノ會務ヲ評議ス

四　理事ハ會務ヲ執行ス

第七條　會長，副會長，評議員及理事ノ任期ハ各三箇年トス　但シ重任スルコトヲ得

第八條　本會員ヲ分チテ左ノ四種トス

一　名譽會員　理事會ノ決議ヲ經テ會長ノ推擧ニ係ル者

二　贊助會員　本會ニ金百圓也以上ヲ醵出セル者

三　維持會員　本會ノ維持費トシテ年額六圓也ヲ納付スル者

四　通常會員　本會々費トシテ年額參圓ヲ納付スル者

第九條　本會ノ經費ハ會費，寄附金及其他ニヨリ支辨ス

第十條　本會ハ每年一回總會ヲ開キ會務及會計ノ報告ヲ爲シ必要ノ事項ヲ議定シ役員ヲ改選ス

第十一條　本會則ハ總會ニ於テ出席會員過半數ノ贊成ヲ得テ之ヲ改正スルモノトス

附則　事務規定ハ別ニ之ヲ定ム

海外ニュース

太虚大師の講經

上海觀音寺で

太虚大師は紅路の觀音寺住持機祥法師及び多數の居士，信者に迎えられ，觀音寺に於て普門品の講經を行はれた。聽衆座に溢れて門外に及ぶ有樣の中に太師は座に降り廣長舌を運び，多大な感激を與へられた。この日滬北一帶の名士で王彬彥，瞿佐炎，陳于英，趙南亭，張蘭軒，揚君輔，吳永昌，胡兆英及び杭州の月塘寺住持源淸，諸山の淵耶等數百名に達した。

又中國佛教學會上海市分會では，三月一日より總會理事長太虚大師に八識規矩頌の宣講をお願した。その日も各界の名流數百名來聽し，極めて明顯な言辭を以て最深の奧義を闡說せられ，聽者は領悟悅服せざる無き有樣であつた。又三月七八兩日，十四五兩日午後二時から西藏路三九號佛慈藥廠樓上，同會の新會所内で八識規矩頌を讀講せられた。

淨嚴法師鄭州講經

鄭州の佛學社は成立して已に數年になる。同社では先月會議で講經法會を開くことを決議し，牛想詠，乔燮周二居士が代表として赴汴し，淨嚴法師の講經を願つた。同法師は現社會が穢惡充滿大難に直面してゐるので，十善業を以て退治し，人心を換救すべく先づ十善道經を講ぜられることゝなり，開講以來毎日男女の聽衆が踴躍感悟してゐるとのことである。

又該社は日に發達して入社々員以前に數倍し，講經の房屋が狹隘を感ずるに至つたので，群起發願して講堂，藏經室等を改築すべく，目下積極準備中であると。

西寧で心道法師の講經

客冬沙市四衆佛學研究社の毛定勇居士は，青海の佛教各團體に地藏經利益存亡品，見聞利益品數十部を贈つたところが，青海の佛徒は歡喜勇躍の餘り，義趣を了解し，地藏の聖德を容揚すべく講經法會を發起し，舊正月二十三日心道法師を西寧大廣城，田家莊福神廟に迎へて，この經の宣講を行つた。

當日法師は馬に跨り，青海省政府彭副官廣聖，王副官廣仁，魯沙爾咸校長廣中氏等が出迎へて同道した。沿道數ケ所には接待所を設け，砲を鳴らし，迎接者は荒山草地に拜跪し，卓を設け香花燈燭を供へて供養した。法師は馬より下りてお茶を飲み，再び上馬して進み，方に田家莊近くの山嶺に至ると，遙か彼方に國旗翻り，香煙の繚繞たる中に老幼男女數百人が香を持つて立つてゐるのが見えた。

愈々福神廟に至れば多數の男女居士が香を執り念佛しつゝ拜跪して法師を迎へ，前殿の壁には「歡迎提唱西北佛教的心道大法師」の書が大書してあつた。法師は進殿し，鐘鼓の鳴る中に禮佛，衆唱香讃を濟せて一坦客室に入り，午後開講してはじめに利益存亡品を講じた。聽衆五百名，翌日は見聞利益品，第三日にも見聞利益品を續講し，多大の反響を與へ多數の歸依者が出來た。又張某居士の供養に應じて供齋の利益を開示し，地藏菩薩利益存亡品の中の地藏菩薩告大辯長者云「復次長者，如是罪業衆生，命終之後，眷屬骨肉，爲修營齋，資助道業，未濟食竟，及營齋之次，米泔菜葉，不棄於地，乃至諸食，未獻佛僧，勿得先食‥‥」の一段を反復詳說した所，聽者感動せざるはなかつたと。

慈航法師歸國

廣州の通信に依れば，慈航法師は仰光より香港に到着，それより途中で歩閩各地の新佛教運動を考察せられる由を知つた廣州佛教同仁は，代表を港に特派し，法師を歡迎して廣州で說法を願ひした所が，法師の承諾を得たので二月二十七日から十一日間，廣州佛學會に於て同法師の講演會を開いた。終つて三月九日新地亞輪で上海に到り，太虚大師に謁し，仰光，中國佛教會最近の狀況を報告せられたと。

又訊く所に依れば仰光から新歸國の慈航法師が廣州佛學會から招れて行き開講以來，該會員以外に毎日多數の聽衆來集し，甚だ勇躍した。猶ほ該會の發展の爲めに會長式如法師發起となつて，全體會員を召集し，慈航法師を挽き留めて宏法の爲めに常駐を乞ひ，一切を指導して貰ふべく，一同に相談した。鄒魯夫人，何公安局長夫人，鄧師長夫人，及び譚淸如，謝心航等の護法居士が極力贊同し，先頃同會の客室に於て第一回談話會を開き，慈航法師を臨時主席に公推し，佛教傳道の事宜について討議して多數の重要案を商決した。それは恰度三月五日午後四時，列席者は慈航，法航，式如，陳如，陳伯材，謝心航，譚淸如，李重唐，演藏，鄒梁定慧，鄧高慧英，淑徽，王妙成等，臨時主席は慈航法師，記錄法航師であつた。(一)主席開會趣旨を述べ(二)列席者の決議は (1)本談話會は一切の議案を書面で前董事會に報告す。(2)式如法師發言し，本人及各位の今日の發言は只弘法に目的に限り，宜しく共同協力互助以て法化を宣すべきである。(3)慈航法師提案，須く軍，政，學各界の知識名流を聘して名譽會董となし，大いに宣傳を擴むべきである。(4)譚淸如居士提議で，弘法委員を推擧し，共同責めに任ずべしとなし，互選して定慧居士，慧英居士，式如法師，演藏法師，重唐居士，心航居士，淸如居士，淑徽居士を選んだ。(5)三月六日弘法委員會を開會すべきこと等通過した。

恒演法師拉薩に留學

西康にあつて佛學を學んでゐる傳震法師は，西康最近の狀況及び團員の恒演法師が獨自で拉薩に留學を決心し，已に昨冬十日ラツサに到りしことを太虛大師に通信して來た。猶ほ本人からの康より入藏の經過，ラツサ入學後の近況，奮勉精勵の樣子等を書いた手紙を特に法界前途の慶を同志に告げる爲めに同封して來た。

‥‥前略，已に前月上旬ラツサに到着したが，沿途理塘，德格，昇古等を過ぎるに各地に寺院林立し，碧知識到る處に多い。惜しい事には，旅途匆々として，僅に展仰することが出來たのみで，克く深く探れなかつた。一路山に登り川を渉るに，懸崖湍流あり，尤も奇なるは皮の船，繩橋で，見たゞけで腦がひやりとする。人も物も俱に此の一本の線を渡らねばならぬ。行路の難きこと，到底蜀道に比すべくもなかつた。然し此れに依つて初心を鍛錬し，修學の助とならないものではない。大召，喇登，哲蓬等の寺に行く（色那寺は未だ行かず）に佛像莊嚴で僧侶多く，その中に顯密に明達せる者も澤山ありその中に追隨して益々忻踊してゐる。蓋し佛化の普遍，信仰の隆厚もその薫習力が極めて大であるからである。孫現住哲蓬寺學經は新しく進むべき境地無き處に至つたとも言ふべく，惟だ宿障漸消，慧業轉淨を願つてゐる。進藏の一行は妄語をなさず，檀信果を施し唐捐を附けず，誠に萬幸である。云々‥‥恒演頂禮。

錫蘭學法團宣誓

中國佛教會では青年比丘懋松，法周，惟幻，惟植，岫盧等五人を探んで錫蘭留學團を組織し，近くセイロンに出發することゝなつてゐるが，三月八日上海の赫德路中國佛教會で，その宣誓式を擧行した。當日は太虛大師をはじめ，靜權，大悲の三法師，白人僧の帝釋鳴，阿難陀師弟，居士では屈文六，江亢虎，趙樸初，胡厚甫，徐和鄕，鄭銘裕，丁彥博，米人のアンドナー，錫人カロンフエイ及び明法學會々員五十餘名が，中佛會樓上三聖殿に集り，太虛大師の導師の下に式が行はれた。香讚，八十八佛及懺悔文，三寶讃，證明師太虛大師の祝辭及び錫蘭學法團規約の宣讀，團員の宣誓及び燒香を行つたが，行禮は頗る莊嚴裡に行はれた。それから團規第五條に依つて該團々員懋松は推されて第一次半年の僧值となる。式が畢つてラトビア高僧帝釋鳴師とその弟子慶喜師は，お別れとして西藏密宗の避魔の舞踊を行ひ挨拶を述べ『第一佛教祖國に佛法の衰微した所以は，同教婆羅門教等の異教の摧破に係り，今日ではキリスト教の摧折に依る所甚大である。彼等は自分の教理の淺薄なことを知つてゐるので，暗々裡に佛法を盜襲しゐることは私の能く知つてゐる所で多くの牧師が貴國佛教の唱讃の聲音を倣用して讃美歌を作りてゐる。貴國の一般平民の聞いてゐるのは，思ふに皆本國の佛教である。諸君が今日錫蘭に佛法を求めに行くことは振興全中國佛教の壯擧と言ふべく，吾々これを聞いて誠に愉快なことである。然るに求法には艱難頗る多く，私が今擧行した餞踏は一に錫蘭に赴く諸君の準備として貰ひたい。軀は有形無形に魔のみである。昔私がセイロンにあること二年，あの島の暑く苦しいことをよく知つてゐる。僧侶は皆午食を取らず，街に沿ふて托鉢して生活してゐる。外邦から始めて彼の島に至る佛教徒は實に甚だ不便を感ずるのであるが，諸君は固より事無きを得るであらう。蓋し諸君の肚には百折不撓の志があるからである。一體僧を寶と言ふのは，佛法を何時までも堅く住持するからである。ある國の如く，佛法最も盛なる國と自稱し，その佛徒も亦僧を寶と自稱してゐるけれども，實は妻を娶り子を生んでゐて，唯だ僅に中國や錫蘭に於ける在家居士に等しものであるに過ぎない。諸君は僧伽を打ち建てゝ，人天の師範となるの志を懷いてゐる。その願，その行は誠に壯とし偉とすべきである。謹んで諸君の前途を祝福し平安を祈る次第である』と語り，セイロンの托鉢の儀式等を說明した。列座は皆その護法の熱烈なる，その別辭の箴言なるに感嘆した。猶ほ該團は三月二十四日出國の筈である。

因に錫蘭學法規約を摘錄すれば(一)本團の錫蘭に赴く趣旨は，南傳佛教を研究し，又比丘戒律の生活を實地に學習して，以て佛教の僧寶を養成住持する爲めなり，名利恭敬の爲めに非ざれば，團員は凡ゆる不良の習慣及び一切の勝手な言行に對して切に律儀に依つて防ぎ，譏嫌を磬護すべし(二)本團員は應に相共に戒め，納囉達法師を親教師と爲し，求法の期間中は單獨に團を離れて他に往くことを得ざるべし。

(三)本團員は應に各僧伽六和の義を體し，戒は同遵と和し，身は同住と和し，口は無諍と和し，意は無違と和し，見は同解と和し，利は同均と和すべし。現世は法門を兄弟となし，永遠には菩提を眷屬と作し，稍も芥蒂を存すれば初心に背く，切に須らく懺除すべし。是れ至要となす。

(四)本團々員は師教に服從する外に遙か證明師の指導と維摩會の勸請を承け，及び同學の忠告を接受すべし。

(五)本團は每半年の受戒先後に依つて，輪推して僧值となし，本團の公務を處理し，及び本團の公共文件を保管す。

(六)本團は應に僧值に由つて，每月本團の狀況を國內維摩會に報告すべし若し譯作の文稿有らば，維摩會に送り酌量して發表することを得。

(七)本規約にして若し未だ盡宜を盡ざる所あらば，隨時商量して親教師及證明師の指導を受け，之れを共同修正することを得。

暹羅留學團近況

中國僧の暹羅留國團一行四名は首府バンコクに到着してから，悲觀法師は別れてセイロンに行き，殘る等慈，覺圓，性教の三人は『シャムの教育部及び僧民の大歡迎を受け既にトマハトに入りて讀書してゐるが，シャムは佛教國であるから，五ケ年間に巴利佛典の研究を充分行つて歸國すれば中國佛教界に大きな力を得ることであらう』との記事が暹民報に掲載された。猶ほ三名から太虛大師の許に來た通信に依れば，バンコクには最近霍亂が蔓延してゐるが，幸に佛佑に依つて元氣であると。

悲觀法師セイロンに轉學

暹羅留學團の一人悲觀法師はセイロン島のマシナラマ佛學院に轉學してゐるが，最近太虛大師の許に報告した通信に依れば，

「‥‥セイロンに留學するに就ては海程が遙遠であることゝ，上陸の手續が面倒なこと，更に入國の保證金（二百盾）を出すのに難儀をしたが，友人の紹介に依つて今では此地のマシナラマ佛學院の院主ウンラナタンナ大師を師とし，院内に引越してから已に六日，巴利文，三歸十戒及び佛法僧の三寶讃文，並に英語の學習を開始してゐる。同大師はセイロンの高僧で教理に精通し，慈悲に富み，自他の見なく，熱心に誨へて倦まざる誠に末世の大善知識で，師とするに申し分のないお方である。次の日曜日に弟子の爲めに沙彌戒の傳授が行はれるが，これは純粋な小乘佛教の戒法に依るのである。所謂沙彌戒を受けることは卽ち出家の意義で此の儀式を經過せねば比丘であるとせられない。既に比丘の資格を得なければ比丘と同住することも出來ない譯で私は業に本院摩法の壇施大衆にも通知し弟子として出家沙彌戒の典禮を受けることゝなつてゐる。衣食住は悉く本院から供給され，凡ては安適である。毎日の生活は頗る秩序があり，毎朝五時起床し，手足を洗つて佛堂に禮拜し，三寶讃語と三歸依文を念唱し（巴利文）一寸休んで手掌の紋を見る時餐堂に入りて食事を取り，終つて室に歸り沙彌十戒律を讀誦し，一句終ると授業が始まり，大師自ら教授せられるのである。私は未だ中國の僧服を着てゐるので，院中の大衆はこれを在家の着物と看做して居るが，沙彌戒を受けると黄色の僧服に着換へるのである。たゞ水は飲んでもよいが，茶と牛乳は許されない。理由無くて外出は許されないが，出かける時は必ず侍者がついて行き，且つ一定の時間がある。寢臺は長さ六尺餘，幅が廣いので二尺餘で，それでも狹過ぎるが，もつと重要な點は錢を使用することを許されないことである。持錢銀戒――我國の佛教にも固より明文はあるが，但し小乘佛教の能遵從佛戒である――を一々實行してゐるのには私は心から敬服した。そして凡ゆる一切の用ひる物は，均しく壇施の供給に依るのである。私が學院に這入る時に猶ほ手許に數十圓餘つてゐたが，こゝでは持つてゐることを許さず，直ちに公家に交附し布施を代行せしめたが，一般持律の精神は推して知るべしである。私は今，出家以來十五年間を回想して見ると，この六日間こそ眞の比丘生活を行つたと言ふべく誠に愧しいことである。大師の御考では私が此處に一二年で巴利文，英文が稍々出來る樣になれば，將來はセイロン大學に送られる筈である。私の願望は今已に滿足し無限の感興の中に生活してゐる。

先月廿六日本院で講演した院長ウンナラタンナ大師の『佛制比丘と世間財物寶器戒法』の一文を御送するから，國內で轉載して貰ひ度いと思ひます。私は毎日少しの時間を割いて大乘經典を參閱したいと思ふが，何んな經典を讀んだら良いか，是非御惠送を御願します。又國內の佛教雜誌，海潮音，佛學半月刊，佛教日報，威音月刊，正信刊等をも亦長期御惠與賜はり，國內佛教の情勢も知り度いと思ひます。私は今小乘佛教を學習し，小乘戒を持してゐるので，手中に金錢を持つことを許されず，本を買ふことも出來ないから，何卒私の心願を叶へて頂き度いと思ひます。

暹羅留學團はもと我師（太虛法師）の意を受けて組織したもので，唯一の趣旨は中暹の連絡，兩國佛教の情誼を結ぶにあり，巴利佛典の求學にあるが，今やその連絡の工作も出來，求學も各人が實際努力を拂つてゐるから，私の責任も已に達した。唯求學の一路を精進して，居住所在が不同であつても，巴利佛典を求學して，南傳佛法の行徑を探討することは則ち一である。將來の成績如何は則ち各人の爲る所を見るべきであらう。又私が出國以來，國內の諸愛護大德居士方面には，團體が暹羅に到着した時の好印象を報告した以外には，個人として通信をしてゐないが，現在團體は結束し，各々分擔して求學してゐる。佛學院に這入つて以來毎日學課が忙しく，加ふるに錢を用ひないので廣く手紙を出すことが出來ない。國內の諸大德，善友諸賢よ，何卒これを諒とせられよ。將來は毎月學績を一度報告する考へである。云々。

セイロン州會議員

大菩提會の教役者二名が，三月行はれた選擧に於て，セイロン州會の議員として選出された。それらの人々は，亡くなつたダルマパラ尊者の甥，ネイル・ヘワヴイターン氏及びラジヤ・ヘワヴイターン氏である。多數の大衆によつて行はれた此の選擧は，ヘワヴイターン家の人々が親子三代引續いて各方面に亘つて，セイロンに盡した赫々た

る功績に對する大衆からの感謝の現はれである。それらの人々の當然な當選の欣びをお祝ひすると同時に，將來，佛敎島セイロンの立法者として輝かしい足跡を殘されることを希望する次第である。

ラタナサラ・ナヤカ長老の逝去

印度コロムボの有名なヴイデイオダヤ・東洋大學の學長，尊敬すべきケイ・ラタナサラ・ナヤカ尊者が，微恙の後，六十四歳を以て春淺く慌だしく物故せられたといふ報道があつた。物故せられたナヤカ・テラ師は，大變有名な人であり，その學長時代にヴイデイオダヤ大學は著しい進歩を遂げ，スリ・スマンガラ・ダルマサラの完成はその主なる仕事であつた。師は梵語，パリ語，シンハリ語の著名な學者であつて，セイロン島佛敎徒の研究の基本に與へた彼の功績は著しきものがある。セイロン島に於ける東洋研究の主要講座の主席として令名のあつた故，エム・ナーニサラ・ナヤカ・テラ師の衣鉢を襲いて，勇敢に又決然と，亡師の立場の傳統を忠實に實行したる人であつた。高貴の地位に選ばれるだけの十分の値打があることは，彼の殘した仕事の結果から見て明かであつて，今回の榮譽は大衆の自然の心の發露から當然の報償として彼の亡後を飾つたのである。彼の葬列は最近記憶に殘つてゐるものの中ではセイロン島で見られた最大のものの一つであつて，弔問の人々は島內全人口の各方面から集まり，セイロン島總督の代表者の顏も見えた。セイロン島大菩提會總裁として彼は貴重な功績を我々の仕事に與へて呉れた。師は數回，印度を訪問し，殊に一九三一年の印度訪問はムラガンダクテイ・ヴイハラを開く基となつた。比丘として又，宗敎指導者としてその職分を最も價値多くつくされた先師の追憶を新たにして感謝の微衷を捧げる次第である。

印度の佛敎兒童祭

大菩提會によつて昨年から始められた佛敎兒童祭が，市の有力實業家ナーシングダス・アガーワラ氏を主宰者して三月八日の日曜日，會のホールで今年も行はれた。樣々な國籍に屬する子供が澤山に集まり，又，この祭典に招かれた多數の著名の來賓もあつた。ホールの中で祭典の初まる前に，子供達は，シツタルタ王子の活動寫眞を撮るために，行列を作つて廣場を練り步いた。ビー・アール・バルア氏の指名によつてアガルワラ氏が議長に推薦されてから，デヴアプリカ・ヴリシンハ氏がこの祭典の目的を說明した。之に引續いてサツシエン・バルア氏指揮の下に兒童達の齊唱と詠誦とがあつた。賞品授與の前に，ナーシングダス・アガルワラ氏が簡潔な言葉で所感を演說した。

「大菩提會御主催の下に取行はれる兒童祭のこの最も有意義な祭典に司會者として本日お招きに與つたことは，私の非常に光榮とする所であります。年若い人々の集まりから受けて來た私の欣びは，私がこの協會に加入させて頂いた名譽と比べて見ても，決して小さいものではないことを告白しなければならない。佛敎徒に當然與へられなければならない權利を恢復するために，印度に於て組織されたこの大菩提會に就いて，私が爰に言及することは本日の私の役割には相應しくないものと考へる。偉大なる世界宗敎，即ち佛敎を理解することが必要であることに就いては，多くの偉大な印度の思想家が既に十分述べられてゐることであるからそれ以上に，確信を以て私が申述べるだけの用意を私は持合せてゐない。然し乍ら，偉大なる文化，即ち佛敎の未來を護り育てゝ行く，役割を持つてをられる，佛敎兒童と今夕，圖らずも同席するの機會を與へられたることであるから，この際，私はそれらの兒童達を訓練して行くために當協會が採つてをられる方法に就いて心から感謝の意を表明しなければならないことを感ずる。私は過去の佛敎時代に行はれた兒童に對する慰安と體育の詳細に就いて精通してゐるものではないが，然し，その當時のグールスが，今日とは，遙かに異つたものであつて，身體を健全にして行くにも，又，書物に疲れた頭腦を休めるためにも，その效果は覺束なきものがあた樣に記憶してゐる。」云々。

賞品は，スポーツ及び，歌謠詠誦の競爭に優秀な成績を示した人々に，與へられた。祭典は，兒童達の佛歌齊唱を最後として終幕に近づいて來た。協會以外の人々からビー・アール・バルア氏及びエム・タラクダー博士から賞品基金として金員の寄贈があつた。

マダバルに於ける佛敎敎會

ダンマカンダ尊者を主宰者としてマダバルに佛敎々會が目覺ましい活動をしてゐるといふニユースがあつた。ダンマカンダ師はセイロン島への短時日の旅行から歸られると，すぐ講演旅行に再び出發された。師は，ヴイクトリア大學，官立男子敎化學校，官立女子敎化學校を歷訪し，師の講演は非常な感銘を與へた。此らの講演の結果，少くとも二十八人以上の學生が五ケ條の戒律を受けて佛敎徒であることを表明した。マラバルに於て佛敎徒の行ふべき仕事は澤山に殘つてゐることであるから，この有益な仕事を遂行して行くために必要な財源を當協會に佛敎徒が寄與せられんことを希望するものである。

サルナタ無料施療院

病者に對する勤勞奉仕は佛敎による最も崇高な仕事の一つである。惡性の病牀のために凡ての人々から見放された，病めるティッサのために，佛陀が自身の手を以て親しく愛撫された物語を記してをいた。苦悶を柔げる問題について佛陀の執られた態度は，ビツカスに與へられた次の忠言によく言ひ現はされてゐる。

「病者にかしづく者は我にかしづく」と。この忠言の意味を押し擴めて考へて見ると，凡ての時代の佛敎徒は，人類の苦悶を柔げる仕事に携はることによつて世界を導き來たことが判る。印度に於て最初に病院を建てゝ人間許りでなく畜類迄の治療を試みられたのは佛敎帝王阿育王であつた。この傳統は，佛敎徒によつて常に踏襲せられ，サルタナ施療院の建設は，かくの如き崇高なる傳統を傳へるものである。この施療院の仕事を進めて行くためには，有能な醫師の勞務を必要とする。乏しい財源を以てしては，協會は，十分に給料を支拂ふことは出來ないから，少額の手當で諦めて貰はねばならない。然し，かういふ方面に於ても，人道のため奉仕しやうとする崇高な精神を有する佛敎徒の働く機會が存在する。サルタナは健康な土地であつて，こゝに示された樣な仕事は，現役を退いた醫者にとつて絶好な職業である。これに就いての照會は，大菩提會主任幹事宛，問合せられたい。

マハ・ボディ誌のヴエサツク祭特別號

五月一日發行，ヴエサツク特別號は，讀物記事と圖解說明の種類に富んでゐる點に於て，今迄に比類なきものである。リコラス・ド・ローリツチ敎授からは數多くの繪畫を添へて素晴らしい立派なメツセーヂの寄稿を受けてゐるし又，次の有名なる佛敎著述家達が執筆してゐる。

ハーリ・サイン・ゴール卿
エー・デイー・ジアヤサンダラ氏（セイロン）
アール・ジエー・ジヤクソン氏（英國）
オー・ビスター氏（獨逸，前カトリツク修道僧）
ビツク・ナラダ氏（セイロン）
スリ・ニサンカ氏（セイロン島・法廷辯護人）
ビー・ビー・シリワルダラ氏（セイロン）
エー・ビー・ゴヴインダ氏（サルナタ）
フランク・エフ・メラー氏（倫敦）
ニヤナ・ケツトー師（セイロン）

本號は，格好なヴエサク・プレセントして廣く用ひられた。

國際佛敎通報局定款

名　稱

第一，本局を國際佛敎通報局と稱す

事務所

第二，本局の事務所を全日本佛敎青年會聯盟本部に置く

目　的

第三，本局は日本內海及海外に向つて佛敎事情の通報をなし，且つ佛敎徒相互間の各種便宜を計るを以て目的とす

事　業

第四，本局の目的を達成するため左記の事業を行ふ

イ，日本內地及世界各國より佛敎事情に關する質問の通報を行ふ
ロ，必要に應じ日本語及世界各國語を以て佛敎事情の通報を行ふ
ハ，外國人の日本觀光に際しては各種の便益を與へ，特にその佛敎に關する方面に於て之を爲す
ニ，定時或は隨時に各國語を以て文書の刊行をなす
ホ，その他必要と認めたる事業を行ふ

役　員

第五，本局の事務を處理するため左の役員を置く

イ，局　長　　一　名
ロ，幹　事　　三　名
ハ，評議員　　若干名

局長は本局の事務を總括す
幹事は本局の事務を處理す
評議員は局長の提案に依る重要事務を審議す

第六，評議員は左記の者を以て之に充つ

イ，全日本佛敎青年會聯盟理事及主事
ロ，全日本佛敎青年會聯盟理事會に於て推薦したる者

第七，局長及幹事は評議員會に於て決定す

第八，役員の任期は二ケ年とす（但し重任を妨げず）

經　費

第九，本局の經費は左記のものに依て之を支辨す

イ，本局基金の活用
ロ，寄附金
ハ，その他の收入

補　則

第十，本定款に記載せられざる事項は，凡て評議員會に於て協議す

第十一，第一回の役員は全日本佛敎青年會聯盟理事會に於て決定す

定價			
	一部	金二十錢	送料二錢
	一年	金二圓四十錢	送料不要

昭和十年四月卅日第三種郵便物認可
昭和十一年五月廿八日印刷（毎月一回一日發行）
昭和十一年六月一日發行

東京市外吉祥寺337
編輯發行兼印刷人　淺野研眞

東京市牛込區早稻田鶴卷町107
印刷所　康文社印刷所
電話牛込（34）1950番 5049番

東京市神田區一ツ橋二の三
發行所　國際佛敎通報局
電話九段（33）4428番
振替東京83015番

昭和十年四月三十日第三種郵便物認可　昭和十一年五月二十八日印刷納本（每月一回一日發行）　昭和十一年六月一日發行　國際佛教通報　第二卷　第六號

第二回
汎太平洋佛教青年會大會
紀要

THE PROCEEDINGS
of
THE Second
General Conference
of
Pan-Pacific Young Buddhists' Associations

(in Japanese, Chinese and English)

Held at Tokyo & Kyoto, July 18–23, 1934

Price ¥ 3.00

Compiled & Published
by
The Federation of All Y.B. As. of Japan,
Tokio, Kanda, Hitotsubashi, II-3

昭和十年四月三十日第三種郵便物認可　昭和十一年六月二十八日印刷納本　昭和十一年七月一日發行（每月一回一日發行）第二卷　第七號

The International Buddhist Bulletin
國際佛教通報

第二卷 **昭和十一年七月** 第七號 〔Vol. II. July. 2502/1936 No. 7.〕

要目〔Contents〕

東京　國際佛教通報局　發行
The International Buddhist Information Bureau
Tokyo, Kanda, Hitotsubashi, II—3
Annual Subscription ¥2.40 (post free) Single Copies 20 sen (post 2 sen)

Entstehungsgeschichte des japanischen Buddhismus.

von **Junji Sakakibara** (Tokyo)

Zum Verständnis einer jeden Kultur, einerlei, ob sie im Lande selbst entstanden ist oder von ausserhalb hereinkam, ist es unbedingt erforderlich, daß man den Volkscharakter, die sozialen und klimatischen Bedingungen und viele andere Faktoren in Betracht zieht. Dies gilt besonders für die Betrachtung des östlichen Buddhismus, wie er sich in Japan entwickelt hat. Denn dieser ist sehr abhängig von dem japanischen Nationalcharakter.

Wichtig für die Entwicklung des Buddhismus in Japan war die Tatsache, daß er ohne ernsten Nebenbuhler dastand. Er brauchte nicht gegen einen bestimmten Gegner zu kämpfen, wie der Buddhismus in Indien gegen den älteren Brahmanismus oder das Christentum gegen die griechische Philosophie.

Nun darf man aber nicht in den Irrtum verfallen, anzunehmen, daß in der vorbuddhistischen Zeit Japan überhaupt keine Philosophie gehabt, keine Gedankenarbeit geleistet habe. Dem ist nicht so. Aber in Japan hoben sich die geistigen Bewegungen nicht als besondere Lehren vom täglichen Leben ab, sie waren nicht etwas von diesem ganz verschiedenes. Sie waren vielmehr ganz mit dem Leben verbunden, dem sie ihr Gepräge geben. Es gab in Japan keinen —„ismus", kein äußeres System. Wie man einen gutsitzenden Schuh nicht spürt, so empfand man in Japan die Philosophie nicht als etwas Fremdes, da sie ja genau mit dem Volksleben übereinstimmte.—Erst, wenn ein Konflikt, eine Unzufriedenheit mit dem Leben eintritt, erwartet man einen Erlöser; erst wenn die Welt in einem Zustande des Unfriedens lebt, spricht man viel von einem Weltfrieden. Wie hätte auch die hohe Asuka-Kultur des 6/7. Jahrhunderts entstehen können, hätte Japan nicht schon vor dem Eintritt des Buddhismus eigene philosophische Gedanken entwickelt! Die Asuka-Zeit stellt den Gipfelpunkt und die Blüte nicht nur der buddhistischen, sondern der japanischen Kultur überhaupt dar. Und doch entstand sie gleich nach der Einführung des Buddhismus, nicht erst nach einer langen Entwicklung. Wir können auch nicht annehmen, daß diese Kultur ganz aus China oder Korea übernommen wurde, denn sie weist doch typische japanische Züge auf. Wie auf gutem Ackerboden durch die Saat ein gutes Getreide wächst, so waren auch die buddhistischen Gedanken nur ein Same, der auf die alte japanische Geisteskultur befruchtend einwirkte. Und die neuen Gedanken waren in der alten Geistesgrundlage so tief verwurzelt, daß sie im Laufe der Zeiten so mannigfaltige Richtungen annehmen konnten, wie der japanische Buddhismus sie heute zeigt.

Zum Unterschiede vom indischen Buddhismus entwickelte der japanische sich in einem Volke, das durchaus das Leben bejahte. In Indien hatten Klima und schwierige soziale Verhältnisse eine lebensverneinende Einstellung zur Folge. In China entwickelte sich eine hohe buddhistische Philosophie, entsprechend der philosophischen Veranlagung der Chinesen. In Japan wurden dafür die Theorien weit mehr in die Praxis umgesetzt. Das japanische Volk ist ein praktisch-handelndes Volk. — Man sagt z.B., daß bei einem Wortwechsel der Japaner seiner Empörung zuerst durch Schläge und dann erst durch Worte Ausdruck verleiht.

Der Buddhismus, der nach Japan kam, war nicht der Urbuddhismus oder das Hinayana, sondern seiner weiter entwickelte Form: das Mahayana. Während das Hinayana mehr die Erlösung des Einzelnen betont, stellt das Mahayana das Heil der Gesamtheit in den Vordergrund. — Die Lehren des Mahayana kamen etwa 200 n. Chr. in Indien auf und verbreiteten sich über China und Korea nach Japan. Mit dieser Lehre gelangte die buddhistische Kunst, die im Urbuddhismus nur schwach entwickelt gewesen war, nach Japan. Für das Volk war die reine buddhistische Philosophie zu schwer und unverständlich, aber die wunderbaren Kunstwerke deuteten ihm rein gefühlsmässig den Inhalt der Lehre an, trugen so ungeheuer zu ihrer Verbreitung bei. Es war die Kunst, die dieser Lehre jene innere Wärme verlieh, die den japanischen Buddhismus vom Urbuddhismus unterscheidet.

Auf die Frage, was eigentlich der Inhalt des Buddhismus sei, kann man antworten: Es sind die vier „Edlen Wahrheiten," der Paticcasamuppada, der achtfache edle Pfad.

Es ist eine Philosophie, die keinen Gott kennt, keine Offenbarung, keinen Erlöser, keine beständige Seele. Es ist eine Lehre des Nicht-Ich, der Vergänglichkeit und des Nirvana. Alle diese Antworten sind nur Erklärungsversuche der Intuition, die Gotama, der Buddha gehabt hat. Denn seine Lehre beruht auf intuitiver Erkenntnis und nicht auf einem philosophisch ausgeklügelten System. Deshalb kann man sie auch nur durch Intuition, durch das wirkliche Erlebnis erfassen. Auch der japanische Buddhismus legt das Hauptgewicht auf diese intuitive Erfahrung und gestaltet nach ihr das Leben. — Es wurden ferner in Japan die buddhistischen negativen Lehren in positive umgewandelt, denn nur solche lassen sich praktisch durchführen.

Wie erklärt z.B. der japanische Buddhist die drei buddhistischen Merkmale des Nicht-Ich, der Vergänglichkeit und des Nirvana?

Da es kein trennendes Ich gibt, gibt es eine Allheit und Zusammengehörigkeit, die durch keine egoistischen Grenzen beschränkt ist. Jedes Wesen hat in sich einen Teil von Buddha. — Vergänglichkeit bedeutet Möglichkeit der Entwicklung, des Fortschrittes und der Verbesserung. Es entsteht hieraus die Lehre von Hoffnung und Trost. Das Nirvana wird gedeutet als völliger Frieden, echte Freiheit und Reinheit. Und hieraus entsteht das Ideal, in der Welt Frieden und Freiheit zu erlangen.

Diese drei Erklärungen des Nicht-Ich geben einem jeden die Hoffnung, daß auch er dieses Ziel des Friedens und der Freiheit erreichen kann. Kein Leben geht mehr verloren, keins ist zu gering, denn in *jedem* ruht die Entwicklungsmöglichkeit, aus jedem kann ein Buddha entstehen.

Die Buddhalehre ist die Lehre vom mittleren Pfade zur Erlösung, einem Pfade, der kein ausgelassenes Weltleben und andererseits auch keine übermäßige Askese kennt. Es ist die Lehre, die den Widerspruch von Sein und Nichtsein überwindet in der Lehre von „KU" d.h. der Leerheit. Es liegt im japanischen Charakter, die Gegensätze zu überwinden, um aus ihnen eine neue Harmonie zu gestalten. Der japanische Buddhismus ist damit in

Einklang sowohl mit der Lehre von Nagarjuna, des Vaters des Mahayana-Buddhismus, als auch mit der urbuddhistischen Lehre.

Die mittlere Weg, die Lehre des Nagarjuna, das Bodhisattva-Ideal, die Schaffung einer Buddhawelt, Hingabe an sie und Verehrung und Dankbarkeit, sowie die stete Hilfsbereitschaft, das Erscheinen Amida-Buddhas und des Ur-Gotama, Vairoshana-Buddha, Yakushi, der Kwannon und des zukünftigen Maitreya, sowie die Gliederung in 13 Sekten, sind für das bunte Bild des japanischen Buddhismus charakteristisch.

Der Buddhismus kam nach Japan im 13. Jahre der Regierung des Kaisers Kimmei (um 552 n. Chr.). Damals fing Prinz Shōtoku (574–622) an, den Buddhismus zu japanisieren. Er war der erste Führer der japanischen Buddhisten und wird in Japan als zweiter Gotama verehrt. Die Lebensweise des Prinzen war die eines Laienanhängers und ganz unbeeinflußt von den alten buddhistischen Vorschriften: er trug das Priesterkleid und predigte. Die Sutras, die er vorlas, waren die folgenden: Shōmangyō, Hokkekyō und Yuimakyō. In der ersten dieser Sutras wird die Idee des Bodhisattva entwickelt, wie sie von Frau Shōman, der Tochter des Königs Hashinoku in Indien, Buddha mitgeteilt und von diesem aufgefaßt wurden.

Die 17 Artikel der Verfaßung, die von dem Prinzen Shōtoku erlaßen wurden zur Belehrung des Volkes beruhen im wesentlichen auf den Lehren Buddhas. Ganz hervorragend war die praktische Betätigung des Prinzen. Unter den bisher erhalten gebliebenen Kunstwerken aus der Asuka-Zeit steht an erster Stelle der Tempel Hōryūji in Nara mit vielen buddhistischen Kunstgegenständen. Der Tempel ist in seiner ursprünglichen Form erhalten und ist jetzt 1300 Jahre alt. Er hat als Modell für die japanischen buddhistischen Tempelbauten gedient und ist das älteste Holzbauwerk der ganzen Welt. In diesem Kunstwerk sind die Ideen des Prinzen Shōtoku verwirklicht. Wir bewundern den geschmackvollen Anlageplan der 7 Tempelgebäude, die vielen Buddhastatuen, die Wandgemälde, besonders aber die Statuen von Shaka, Yakushi und Kwannon, die alle so puritanisch wirken mit ihrem milden geheimnisvollen Lächeln. Seit dem Eindringen des Buddhismus in Japan war zur Zeit der Entstehung des Hōryūji-Tempels kaum ein halbes

Jahrhundert vergangen, und doch hatte schon diese kurze Zeit genügt, eine wunderbare Kultur zur Blüte zu bringen, die selbst den Künstler unserer Tage mit Staunen und Bewunderung erfüllt.

Versuchen wir, das buddhistische Geistesleben jener Zeit an Hand der Wandgemälde auf einem Buddha-Schrein, „Tamamushi-no-zushi“ genannt, zu illustrieren. Dieser Schrein, der dem Kaiser Kimmei gehörte und sich heute im Tempel Hōryūji in Nara befindet, ist mit vier Gemälden geschmückt. Das eine, auf der Vorderseite, stellt eine Messe am Denkmal des Buddha dar, ein zweites, auf der Hinterwand, den Sumeru-Parvata-Berg. Das dritte Gemälde, an der rechten Wand stellt eine Legende dar aus der Sutra Konkōmyo, nämlich eine Erzählung des Gautama aus seinem früheren Leben, in dem er aus Mitleid mit einem Tiger, der im Begriff war, seine Jungen vor Hunger zu fressen, diesem seinen eigenen Körper gegeben hat. Das vierte Gemälde an der linken Wand handelt vom „Preis für die halbe Antwort.“ Das ist auch eine Geschichte des Jataka aus der Sutra Daihatsu-Nehan.

Als Gautama noch Schüler in seinem früheren Leben war und nach dem echten Weg suchte, hörte er einen Ausspruch: „Alles ist vergänglich, denn alles liegt zwischen Geburt und Tod,“ den ein Teufel gemacht hatte. Der Schüler bat den Teufel, ihm das nächste Wort zu sagen, aber dieser forderte von ihm seinen eigenen Körper als Belohnung für das nächste Wort. Der Schüler willigte ein, und ihm wurde folgender Ausspruch mitgeteilt: „Vernichtet beides — Tod und Geburt — das ist das vollkommene ruhige Nirvana.“ Der Schüler war zufrieden und liess sich von einem hohen Felsen herabfallen, um seinen Körper dem Teufel zu geben. Aber der Teufel war in Wirklichkeit nur eine Umgestaltung einer Gottheit gewesen, die den Schüler versuchen wollte, und so war dieser gerettet.

Von den vier Gemälden erscheinen mir die beiden zuletzt genannten von besonderer Bedeutung. Das eine belehrt uns über das völlig selbstlose große Mitleid des Buddha, das nicht nur Menschen, sondern auch Tieren erwiesen wird. Das andere zeigt uns das tiefe Streben des Bodhisattva, der, um den rechten Weg zu finden, selbst seinen eigenen Körper zu opfern bereit war. Diese Gedanken und Vorstellungen müssen im Geiste der damaligen Buddhisten lebendig gewesen sein. Unter ihnen stand der Prinz Shōtoku an erster Stelle. Die Priester Dengyō und Kōbō in der Heian-Zeit, Hōnen, Shinran und Nichiren in der Kamakura-Zeit können als seine hervorragendsten Nachfolger bezeichnet werden. Bei allen buddhistischen Reformationsbewegungen ist immer wieder der Ruf laut geworden, zu den Idealen des Prinzen Shōtoku zurückzukehren.

In der Nara-Zeit (650–780 n. Chr.) herrschte ein sehr reger Verkehr mit China, dessen kultureller Einfluß in Japan infolgedessen stark zunahm. Dies war eine Entwicklungszeit der buddhistischen Philosophie in Japan. Sechs verschiedene Sekten übermittelten die Lehren des Buddhismus aus China: Sanron, Hossō, Kegon, Jōjitsu, Kusha und Ritsu,

Im Mittelpunkte der Lehren der Sanron-Sekte stehen die Werke Chûron und Junimonron von Nagarjuna, sowie das Hyaku-ron, das Werk des Devadatta, eines Anhängers des Nagarjuna.

Die Laien leben in der Laienwelt und haften an der Welt. Diejenigen, die das Heil und das Nirvana suchen, gehören nicht zu der Laienwelt und verachten diese Welt. Die einen haften an der Welt und die anderen an der Idee des Nirvana. Nun entstand eine neue Auffassung, nämlich der Gedanke des Mittelweges, der in der *Sanlon-Schule* gelehrt wird. Die Lehre vom „Nicht-Ich" bedeutet danach nicht „Verachtung für das Ich," sondern eine Einstellung, die mit „Frei vom Ich" charakterisiert werden kann. Dieser Zustand ist der Zustand der absoluten Leere, der gegebene natürliche Zustand.

Die *Hossō* oder *Yuishiki-Lehre* ist die Lehre des Priesters Seshin. Etwa 100–200 Jahre nach Nagarjuna entstanden, gibt sie eine ideale erkenntnistheoretische Erklärung, die eine veränderte Erklärung der „Leer-Lehre" des Nagarjuna ist.

Danach hat die Welt der Phänomene keine unabhängige Existenz, sondern ist ein Produkt unseres Denkens „Araya-Vijnana" genannt.

Die *Kusha-Lehre* ist einfach eine Zusammenfassung der Hinayana-Lehre des Seshin, von diesem verfaßt, ehe er sich zu den Lehren des Mahâyâna-Buddhismus bekehrte.

Auch die Lehren der *Jōjitsu-* und der *Ritsu-Sekte* stellen eine Mischung von Hinayâna und Mahayâna dar.

Die *Kegon-Lehre* beruht auf der Kegon-Sutra, die von Virschana-

Buddha, der personifizierten kosmischen Weisheit handelt. In dieser Sekte wird das All aus dem Kausalzusammenhang erklärt. Es gibt kein unabhängiges Dasein. Alles ist in Kausalbeziehung. Es gibt keine subjektive Gegenüberstellung. Alle: Buddha und gewöhnliche irdische Wesen, Vollendete und Unvollendete, haben gleichen inneren Wert. Ein Merkmal dieser Lehre besteht darin, daß sie kein Urwesen und keine Entstehung derselben anerkennt.

Ein hervorragender Vertreter der Buddhisten der Nara-Zeit war Kaiser Shōmu (seine Regierungszeit dauerte von 724 bis 749 n. Chr.). Sein Hauptverdienst bestand in der Errichtung von je einem Kloster für Männer und für Frauen in jeder Provinz, den sogenannten „Kokubunji," und der Errichtung der großen Buddhastatue im Tempel Tōdaiji zu Nara. Diese große Buddhastatue ist 16 Meter hoch und die größte kupferne Buddhastatue der Welt. Sie sollte das Wahrzeichen des Zusammenhanges zwischen den buddhistischen Zentren in den einzelnen Provinzen sein. Unter den Mitarbeitern des Kaisers Shōmu sind zu nennen: die Kaiserin Kōmyō, die Priester Gyōgi und Ryoben, die sich auch auf dem Gebiete der sozialen Hilfe eifrig betätigten.

Mit Kaiser Shōmus Tod beginnt der Niedergang des Buddhismus infolge der Verquickung von Religion und Politik. Man kann sagen, daß die Gelehrten die Lehre schließlich nur noch um nutzloser Disputationen willen studierten.

In der Heian-Zeit, (etwa 780–1170) erstanden jedoch zwei große Reformatoren; Dengyō (766–822) und Kōbō (779–835). Dengyō ist der Gründer der Tendai-Sekte, Kôbô begründete die Shingon-Sekte.

Das Ziel des Dengyō war die Wiederbelebung der Ideale des Prinzen Shōtoku. Er wollte die komplizierten Theorien der Nara-Zeit mit den Anforderungen der Wirklichkeit vereinen und fand dafür einen geeigneten Ausgangspunkt in den Lehren der chinesischen Tendai-Sekte. Diese beruhen auf der Hokke-Sutra und den Gedanken Nagarjunas. Dengyō lernte diese Lehre in China kennen. Um sie zu japanisieren, verband er sie mit einer mystisch-esoterischen Geheimlehre, die sich aus der brahmanistischen Geheimlehre des Yoga entwickelt hatte, und fügte noch die Meditations-Übungen der Zen-Sekte hinzu. Alle diese Bestandteile sind in der japanischen

Tendai-Schule enthalten. Dengyō behauptet, daß der Herrscher eines Staates eine wahrhaft gebildete Person sein müsse. Da seine Tendai-Lehre die einzige führende Religion für Japan sei, sollten die Herrscher im Geiste dieser Sekte erzogen werden. In diesem Sinne hat er seine berühmte Erziehungsmethode „Sange - Gakushō - shiki" benannt.

Seinen Haupttempel erbaute dieser große Erzieher der Heian-Zeit auf dem Hieizan bei Kyôto. Sehr viele buddhistische Schüler versammelten sich um ihn, so daß schließlich auf diesem Berge 3000 Tempel standen.

Die Shingon-Sekte des Kôbô ist eine Geheimlehre. Sie enthält außer der Lehren der Kegon-Sutra die Erkenntnis der Entwicklung des Dasein.

Wir betrachten das All durch unsere Vernunft. Alles Übel entsteht aus diesem Vernunftbegriff. Die Shingon-Sekte will diesen Vernunftbegriff vernichten, um den Menschen den wahren Charakter der Dinge erscheinen zu lassen.

Das Erwachen des Gautama ist die Wahrheit und ist unausdrückbar. Die ganze Lehre des Buddha ist nichts anderes als eine Anweisung zur Erreichung dieses Zustandes. Wenn man aber nur diese Anweisungen im Auge behält und sie befolgt, wird man nie das Ziel des Buddhismus erreichen. Aus diesem Grunde betont der Priester Kōbō die Wichtigkeit der Intuition und empfiehlt methodische Übungen. Zu den letzteren gehören : die Gebärdenzeichen mit den Händen, das Hersagen von Geheimwörtern und religiöse Zeremonien. Wenn man freigeworden ist von der Kritik der Vernunft, sieht man überall in dem, was vor den Augen liegt, die Wahrheit, den Buddha selbst.

Diese Lehre scheint eine Mischung von einer Art Pantheismus und Monotheismus zu sein, mit Vairocana Buddha als Verehrtem. Es gibt in der Sekte zwei Richtungen, eine über die kosmische Wahrheit und eine über die Erscheinungsform der Wahrheit: „Kongōkai und Taizōkai" genannt.

Kōbō Daishi lebte selbst gemäß seinen eigenen Lehren und suchte sie in die Wirklichkeit umzusetzen. Er besaß außerdem eine außerordentliche Fähigkeit für Kalligraphie, Malerei, Schnitzerei und Dichtkunst und war auf allen diesen Gebieten immer der erste.

Für die Heian-Zeit ist ferner bemerkenswert eine gewisse Vermischung des Buddhismus mit der

alten japanischen Landesreligion, dem Shintoismus, die sich darin äußerte, daß japanische Gottheiten als Inkarnationen des Buddha aufgefaßt werden.

Etwa in der Mitte der Heian-Zeit entstand eine neue Richtung, nämlich die Jodo- oder Amida-Lehre.

Die Lehren der japanischen Tendai-Sekte waren so allumfaßend, daß die meisten in der folgenden Kamakura-Zeit entstandenen Schulen sich aus ihnen entwickeln konnten. Auch bei der Jōdo-Sekte ist das der Fall. Amida ist der idealisierte und vergöttlichte historische Gotama-Buddha. Der Mensch Gotama stand so hoch, daß seine Zeitgenossen ihn nicht mehr als Menschen, sondern als etwas Höheres ansahen. Und seine Lehre erschienen ihnen zu tief, als daß er sie nach einem nur 6-jährigen Streben hätte erlangen können. Hier tauchte der Gedanke der übermenschlichen Existenz des Buddha auf. Dieser Gedanke ergab schließlich den Gedanken des Amida-Buddha (etwa um 200–400 n. Chr. in Indien).

In dieser Zeit gab es auch eine neue Auffassung des Nirvana. Der Buddha hatte gelehrt, daß das Nirvana der Zustand ohne Irrtum sei. Aber er hat niemals erklärt, daß das Nirvana das absolute Nichts sei. Der Mahayânist sagt, daß im Nirvana der egoistische Wille beseitigt und in einen Willen der Hilfsbereitschaft verwandelt wird. Er versucht nicht, das Nirvana aus den Sutras zu erkennen, sondern aus dem 45-jährigen Buddhaleben. Zwar habe der Buddha über das Nirvana nichts Positives gesagt, aber es müße doch in seinem Leben erkennbar sein, da er es doch gewiß auf Erden verwirklicht haben muß. So erscheint denn auch sein Leben ruhig, zufrieden und vollständig erlöst. Dieser Zustand bedeutet aber nicht, daß der darin Weilende von der ganzen Welt getrennt sei und im tiefen Walde allein lebt, vielmehr ist dies der Zustand der größten mitleidsvollen Hilfe für alle Wesen. Buddha Gautama lebte ja auch mit dem Sangha (seiner Gemeinde), dem Orden, zusammen. Sein Herz drängte danach, allen zu helfen. Dieser Zustand des Mitleids ist der wahre Nirvana-Zustand. Das Pari-Nirvana unterscheidet sich nur durch die Abwesenheit des Körpers, d.h. der Grundzustand muß derselbe sein, nämlich Zufriedenheit, Mitleid und Reinheit.

Auf dieser Auffaßung des Nirvana beruht der Gedanke der Amida-Welt.

Bekannt war die Amida-Lehre schon zur Zeit des Prinzen Shotoku, aber sie verbreitete sich erst in späteren Jahrhunderten. Vertreter dieser Richtung in der Heian-Zeit waren: Kūya (903–973), Genshin (942–1017) und Ryōnin (1072–1132).

Ryōnin ist der Begründer der „Yūzūnembutsu-Sekte.“ Seine Sekte beruht auf den Lehren der Kegon und Hokke-Sutras. Diese Lehre zielt durch Übung des Hersagens der Formel „Namu-Amidabutsu“ (Gelobt sei Amida-butsu) auf die Erklärung der Idee der Kegon-Sutra vom kausalen Zusammenhang aller Dinge. Nach dieser Sutra ist die Entstehung eines Wesens von allen übrigen abhängig, so daß der Mensch alle 10 Zustände, nämlich: Hölle, Tierwelt. Himmel, Buddhawelt u.s.w. — in sich verkörpert. Durch das Hersagen von „Namu-amidabutsu“ hilft der Mensch allen Dingen, ebenso wie ihm durch das Hersagen dieser Formel durch andere Menschen auch geholfen wird. Um das an einem Beispiel zu erläutern: Hier sind 10 Menschen versammelt, jeder mit einer Kerze in der Hand; der Schein der zehn Kerzen vereinigt sich, sodaß jeder einzelne nicht nur durch seine Kerze beleuchtet wird, sondern auch von den übrigen. Die Sekte lehrt, daß alle Menschen in die Amidha-Welt hineingeboren werden.

Trotzdem die beiden Sekten — Tendai und Shingon im japanischen Buddhismus eine große Rolle gespielt haben, entfernten sie sich immer mehr von ihrem ursprünglichen Zustande, je größer sie wurden. Die Tendai-Sekte hatte durch ihre bereits erwähnten Erziehungsmethoden großen Einfluß auf die vornehmen Klassen gewonnen. Die gesellschaftliche Stellung der Priester wurde immer angesehener, ehrgeizige Menschen wählten die Laufbahn eines Priesters, und schließlich stritten die einzelnen Tempel miteinander um Autorität und Vormacht, es entstanden sogar Heere von Priester-Soldaten — ein großer Schandfleck in der Geschichte des japanischen Buddhismus.

Auf der anderen Seite hat die Shingon-Sekte Kōbō-Daishis durch die Förderung zeremonieller Feierlichkeiten das Volk zu Gebeten aus gewinnsüchtigen Motiven verleitet. Wahre Buddhisten mußten aus der Priester-Gemeinde austreten und wurden zu Halb-Priestern, sogenannten „Shami,“ die dann in dem

Laien-Buddhismus in Japan eine große Rolle gespielt haben.

In der Kamakura-Zeit (etwa 1170–1330) entstand eine Reihe von neuen Sekten: die drei Jōdo-Sekten (Jōdo, Shin, Ji), die Nichiren-Sekte und die Zen-Sekte, (letztere in der Form der Rinzai- und Sōdō-Schule.) Das Kennzeichen aller dieser Sekten der Kamakura-Zeit ist das Volkstümliche, Einfache, Deutliche und Laienbuddhistische als Reaktion gegen die Auswüchse der Heian-Zeit. Die Jōdo-Lehre von Hōnen (1133–1212) führte zur Gründuug einer selbstständigen Sekte, die versuchte, dem japanischen Buddhismus eine andere Richtung zu geben.

× × ×

Theorien sind nur für die wenigen: die Gelehrten und Fachleute. Die vorzüglichste philosophische Theorie gibt den Menschen nicht viel, und so behaupten denn die Vertreter dieser Lehre, daß innere Betrachtung wichtiger sei. Man vernimmt den Ruf der eigenen Seele, die nach ewigem Leben zusammen mit anderen Wesen in einer friedevollen Welt verlangt, trotzdem unser Leben so egozentrisch und voller Leiden ist. Auf diesem Verlangen der Seele beruht die Amida-Welt. Amida bedeutet unendliches Leben und grenzenloses Licht. Um in dieser Amida-Welt zu leben, bedarf es keiner Tempel, keines Studiums, keiner Askese, auch keiner Gebete und Zeremonien. Es genügt, im natürlichen Zustand zu bleiben und die vertrauensvolle Formel „Namu-Amida-Butsu“ (Gelobt sei Amida-butsu) auszusprechen. Die Anrufung bedeutet das absolute Vertrauen in Amida und das Ganzfrei-werden von allen irdischen Fesseln, vom egozentrischen Standpunkt.

Hōnen hat bis zu seinem 42 Lebensjahre die buddhistische Lehre eifrig studiert und alle buddhistischen Bücher, Tripitaka, fünfmal durchgelesen, bis er schließlich eine Erklärung der „Kammuryōju-Sutra“ von einem chinesischen Priester Zendo fand. Er war so begeistert von dieser Erklärung, daß er fortan den neuen Weg des „Namu-Amidabutsu“ beschritt.

Zum Kanon der Jodo-Sekte gehören vor allem drei Sutras: die Daimuryōju-Sutra, die Kammuryō-ju-Sutra und die Amida-Sutra.

Ein Anhänger Hōnens und der Begründer der Shin-Sekte war Shinran (1173–1262). Er scheint gar nicht die Absicht gehabt zu haben, irgend eine neue Sekte zu gründen. Er nannte sich stets Gutoku, womit er sagen wollte, daß er weder Priester, noch Laie sei. Er stand jedoch zwischen beiden. Weder hatte er einen eigenen Wohnsitz, noch einen eigenen Tempel, sondern er wanderte stets umher. Er lebte wie ein Laie, hatte Frau und Kind, aß Fleisch und Fisch und lehrte bis ans Ende seines Lebens nur die Lehre Amidas. Da er ein so unauffälliges Leben führte, wurde er von den gewöhnlichen Geschichtsschreibern nicht erwähnt und so tauchten sogar Zweifel auf, ob er überhaupt existiert habe. Trotzdem ist die Shin-Sekte heute die größte und verbreitetste unter allen buddhistischen Sekten Japans.

Von den Anhängern Hōnens ist noch die Ji-Sekte, gegründet von Ippen (1238–1289), zu erwähnen. Ji bedeutet Zeit. Diese Sekte lehrt, daß man jeden Augenblick als den letzten Augenblick seines Lebens betrachten und daher ohne Aufhören die Gebetsformel Namu-Amida-butsu" wiederholen soll. Ihr Hauptmerkmal besteht darin, daß ihre Anhänger besitzlos und ohne festen Wohnsitz waren und das „Namu-Amida-butsu" hersagten. Deshalb nannte man sie auch die Wandersekte. Ippen hat kurz vor seinem Tode alle seine Werke verbrennen lassen; das einzige, was er hinterließ, war die Aufforderung, das Gebet „Namu-Amida-butsu" zu sprechen.

Kurz nach diesen Jōdo-Sekten entstand eine neue Sekte, die Nichiren-Sekte, von Nichiren (1222–1282) gegründet. Es war damals eine Bewegung im Gange, welche bezweckte, die Hokke-Sutra der Tendai-Schule allgemein zu verbreiten. Nichiren ging von den Lehren der Tendai-Sekte aus, aber er wählte als heiligen Text nur die Hokke-Sutra. Während Dengyō durch seine Erziehungsmethode dem japanischen Volk eine Anweisung zum Leben geben wollte, wollte Nichiren alles auf das Hersagen des Titels der Hokke-Sutra: „Namu-myōhōrengekyō" konzentrieren. In dieser Hinsicht verfolgte er ein ähnliches Ziel, wie Hōnen oder Shinran. Aber bei Nichiren ist das Hersagen nicht, wie bei Hōnen und Shinran, meditativ - nachdenklich, sondern hat den Charakter einer Beschwörung. Ungeachtet vieler Verfolguugen stand Nichiren an den Straßenecken, das „Namu-myōhōrengekyō" hersagend und die Lehre der Hokke-Sutra predigend. Er sagte, daß in der Hokke-Sutra das Mitleid Buddhas mit Blut und

Tränen niedergeschrieben sei. Man sollte daher diese Sutra nicht mit den Augen, sondern mit dem ganzen Körper und Geist lesen. Er pflegte auszurufen: Mir ist die große Ehre zugefallen, als allererster die Grundlagen der Buddhalehre in dieser dunklen Welt auszubreiten. Folgt mir, meine Jünger! Überholt den „Kassapa," „Ananda" und den Priester Dengyō! Wenn Ihr die kleinen Verfolgungen durch Eure Gegner fürchtet, wie könntet Ihr, die Ihr Euch selbst für Botschafter Buddhas haltet, vor dem „Yama-König" (einem König in der Welt nach dem Tode) bestehen?"

Wenn man bestrebt ist, die Welt zu verbessern, also eine Buddhawelt zu schaffen, so ist man ein Boddhisatva. Dieses Ziel wird nur durch das Hersagen des „Namu-myōhōrengekyō" erreicht. Durch das Aussprechen dieses Titels werden alle Fesseln zerstört, wirkliche Kraft erlangt und die Einflüße der Hölle oder von Dämonen völlig vernichtet.

Während die Jōdo- und Nichiren-Sekten vor allem die Erlösung der Volksmaßen bezweckten, wurden die Lehren einer neuen Sekte, nämlich der Zen-Sekte, in den Kreisen der Vornehmen verbreitet, sie trugen viel bei zur Fortentwicklung der japanischen Kultur. Zen bedeutet Meditation. Durch Meditation soll das Grundwesen der Buddha-Lehre ergründet werden. Sie wird auch „Busshin-Sekte" genannt, d.h. daß die Grundlehre nicht schriftlich, noch mündlich, sondern nur direkt von Seele zu Seele übertragen wird. Obwohl sie schon in der Nara-Zeit bestanden hatte, tauchte sie als selbstständige Sekte erst in der Kamakura-Zeit auf und zwar in zwei Schulen, erstens, in der von Eisai (1140–1215) begründeten „Rinzai-" und zweitens, in der von Dōgen (1200–1352) begründeten Sōdō-Schule. Nach der Kamakura-Zeit entstand noch eine kleinere Zen-Schule, die Ōbaku-Sekte, die von dem chinesischen Priester Ingen (1592–1673) begründet wurde.

Das Kennzeichen der Zen-Lehre besteht darin, den durch Begierden beschmutzten Geist und Körper durch strenge systematische Meditation in Ordnung und den Grundcharakter der Seele zum Ausdruck zu bringen. Wenn die Seele, wie ein ganz ruhiges und verklärtes Wasser, ruhig und rein wird, wird sich die Seele Buddhas in ihr wiederspiegeln. Das ist der echte Zen-Zustand. Man. meditiert nicht nur an einsamen abgelegenen Orten, sondern man dehnt die Meditation auch auf das tägliche Leben aus. Dadurch hat die Zen-Sekte einen so großen Einfluß auf die Kultur Japans ausgeübt. Sie schenkte Japan außerdem noch die feine Tee-Zeremonie, die Kunst, Blumen geschmackvoll zu ordnen, sowie eine hervorragende Malerei und Dichtkunst.

Die Zen-Praxis ist einerseits einfach und kindlich, andererseits überaus edel und fein. Da sie absolute Aufrichtigkeit, Einfachheit bezweckt und gleichzeitig innere Stärke entwickelt, wurde sie von der zu jener Zeit entstehenden Ritterklasse mit Begeisterung aufgegriffen und verbreitet.

Der Buddhismus der Kamakura-Zeit ist praktisch und volkstümlich. Die Idee des Prinzen Shōtoku, der ein Vorbild für jeden Sekten-Stifter war, wurde in der Kamakura-Zeit voll verwirklicht. Auch die politischen Zustände jener Zeit förderten diese Entwicklung. Die Macht ging damals allmählich von den Höflingen zu den Rittern über, was nicht ohne Einfluß auf die geistige Entwicklung blieb, die von der früheren romantischen Richtung in eine praktische realistische überging. Heute können wir auch an den Kunstwerken der Kamakura-Zeit bemerken, wie diese praktische Tendenz jener Zeit auch auf die Kunst einen großen Einfluß ausgeübt hat.

Die Entwicklung der verschiedenen buddhistischen Richtungen ist nur bis zur Kamakura-Zeit deutlich zu verfolgen. Danach kam eine Zeit der Weiterentwicklung der bereits vorhandenen buddhistischen Lehren. Jede Sekte befleißigte sich, ihre eigene Lehre systematisch zu gestalten, wobei es natürlich zu Streitigkeiten zwischen einigen von ihnen kam, auch zu Zusammenstößen mit den politischen Machthabern. Schließlich aber wurde der Buddhismus in der Tokugawa-Regierung durch die verständige Politik der Herrscher aus der Tokugawa-Familie auf eine gesicherte Grundlage gestellt. Dem buddhistischen Priester wurde politische Autorität gegeben. In den Tempeln wurden Volksschulen eröffnet. Jeder Volksgenosse mußte unbedingt irgend einer buddhistischen Tempel-Gemeinde angehören. Das Namensregister der Tempel-Gemeinde hatte amtlichen Charakter. Reisende mußten von ihrem Priester ein Zeugnis einholen, das ihnen als Ausweis diente. So wurde der Buddhismus zu

einer staatlichen Religion. Für die Sekten war dieser Zustand sehr bequem, aber unter dem Schutz der Regierung wurde der Buddhismus jedoch wieder inhaltsloser und oberflächlicher. Auf die Jugend konnte er nicht mehr begeisternd wirken.

In diese Zeit fallen zwei neue bedeutungsvolle Bewegungen, eine konfuzianische und eine klassisch-japanische. Es ist bekannt, wie diese Bewegungen dazu beitrugen, die große Umwälzung der Meiji-Zeit zu beschleunigen. In der Meiji-Zeit, in der sich alles veränderte, hatte der Buddhismus einen schweren Stand. Der Staat forderte die Trennung von Buddhismus und Shintoismus. Die Reformen nach europäischem Muster hatten auch einen zeitweiligen Niedergang des Buddhismus zur Folge. Aber der japanische Buddhismus, der auf eine 1300-jährige Vergangenheit zurückblickte, konnte nicht so leicht zu Grunde gehen. Die Schläge, die er erhielt, waren für die Buddhisten ein Zeichen, aus dem 300-jährigen Schlaf der Tokugawa-Zeit aufzuwachen. Heute ist der Buddhismus bei uns im Begriff, aufzuwachen. Während der letzten Jahrzehnte ist vieles bemerkenswerte erreicht worden. Neben großen Erfolgen auf dem Gebiete des Schulwesens und der sozialen Hilfeleistung muß die Mission im Auslande, die Veröffentlichung von buddhistischen Werken und besonders die Herausgabe des gesamten buddhistischen Kanon, des „Daizokyo" (Tripitaka) erwähnt werden. So umfaßt z.B. das Shukusatsu-Daizōkyō (in Tôkyô erschienen) 8534 Bände, das Manji-Daizōkyō (in Kyôto erschienen)— 6990 Bände, das Taishō-Shinshū-Daizōkyō (Tôkyô) 12.990 Bände. Daneben gibt es noch Volksausgaben, das Nippon-Daizōkyō, Kokuyaku-Issaikyō u. andere.

Die heutigen japanischen buddhistischen Sekten sind: die Tendai-, Shingon-, Ritsu-, Jōdo-, Rinzai-, Sōdō-, Ōbaku-, Shin-, Nichiren-, Ji-, Yūzūnembutsu-, Hosso- und Kegon-Sekte; im Ganzen 13 Sekten, die ihrerseits in 56 kleinere Gruppen zerfallen. Die 71.000 buddhistischen Tempel in Japan verteilen sich etwa folgendermaßen auf die einzelnen Sekten: 19.600 gehören der Shin-Sekte, 14.500—der Sodo-Sekte, 12.000 der Shingon-, 8000 der Jodo-6000 der Rinzai-, 5000 der Nichiren- und 4500 der Tendai-Sekte u.s.w. Außer diesen Tempeln gibt es 6500 Hallen zum Predigen. Es gibt heute etwa 120 buddhistische

Missionsanstalten in Hawaii und U.S.A. sowie etwa 150 in China, Manchukuo und anderen Ländern. Insbesondere für Manchukuo sind neuerdings verschiedene Missionspläne von den einzelnen Sekten ausgearbeitet worden.

Die angeführten Zahlen über die Verbreitung des Buddhismus, die rege Lehr- und Missionstätigkeit der Sekten berechtigen zu der Hoffnung, daß dem japanischen Buddhismus noch ein großer Aufstieg bevorsteht. Man klagt heute überall in der Welt, daß die moderne materialistische Zivilisation den Weg verloren hat. Marschieren! Marschieren! lautete die Parole. Das Licht leuchtete voran, und so hoffend und die Geschichte und Überlieferung vergeßend, marschierte man immer weiter vorwärts, bis man bemerkte, daß man den Weg verloren hatte, denn anstatt in das Licht, war man in die Dunkelheit geraten.

Es war natürlich, daß sich die Blicke in die Vergangenheit richteten, um den Urquell aller Kultur wieder zu entdecken. Das geschah auch in Japan.

Betrachtet man das alte Japan, so kann der Buddhismus gewiß nicht übersehen werden. Und andererseits ist es ein interessantes Problem, welche Form der japanischen Buddhismus in der Zukunft annehmen wird.

Wenn der zu neuem Leben erwachende Buddhismus das neue Japan erleuchten könnte, wäre das ein Lichtstrahl nicht nur für Japan, sondern auch für ganz Asien. Und das Licht, das vom Osten her scheint, würde die ganze Welt erleuchten!

Japanese News

Holding Shinran Anniversary

On May 21, the Tsukiji Honganji Temple celebrated the 763rd anniversary of the birth of St. Shinran, founder of the Shinshu sect of Buddhism. On that day the temple was opened to the public. Services were held and all forms of entertainment and exhibitions were held for the entertainment of the visitors. Foreign visitors in Tokyo took advantage of this rare opportunity to visit the temple and see many forms of Japanese culture and entertainment.

French Author gets Japanese Inkstand

A Japanese inkstand and brushes were presented to Monsieur Jean Cocteau, noted French poet and novelist by the members of the Tokyo Club of Poets on May 20. The representatives of the club visited Monsieur Cocteau at the Hotel, on the day afternoon and the present was extended to the poet. The members of the Club also presented a message to the poet.

To Promote Spirit of School Teachers

To promote Nipponism and Japanese spirit among the instructors of primary schools of Tokyo, a course for this purpose was opened for them at the Gokokuji Temple, Koishikawa, and at the Number Tenth Girl's Schools, Aoyama, from June 1 to 27.

The course was given under the direction of the Institute of Japanese Spirit and Spiritual Culture. Mr. Masami Kihei and other prominent scholars gave lectures for the course.

Famous Nikko Fete was held June 1, 2

The annual festival of the Toshogu Shrine of Nikko was held at the shrine during two days from June 1 with its usual splendor and gaiety.

On June 1, the Imperial Messenger will worship at the shrine after the procession crosses the Shinkyo, the Sacred Bridge. The procession will go to the shrine at about 8 : 30 a.m.

The ceremony of transfering the spirit tablets of Iyeyasu, Hideyoshi and Yoritomo into three shrine palanquins will take place at about 4 p.m. The three shrine palanquins are to be carried from the Toshogu

Shrine to the Futa-ara Shrine where an all-night service was held.

On June 2, the long palanquin procession starts from the Futa-ara Shrine for the Otabisho (Place of Sojourn), near the Sacred Bridge, reaching there at about noon. At the Otabisho elaborate Shinto rituals are conducted to the accompaniment of sacred classical music. The procession passed again along the way from the Otabisho to the Toshogu Shrine at about 2 p.m. where the shrine palanquins are to be stored.

The procession is to be participated in by more than a thousand Shinto priests and laymen, dressed in varied quaint costumes, some afoot wearing old masks and ancient armor, and others on horseback.

Statue for Raku-O to be Erected

A monument in memory of Raku-o, (Sadanobu Matsudaira) noted daimyo and scholar of the Tokugawa period was erected in the compound of the Tokyo Municipal Central Market, Tsukiji, Tokyo, on May 22. The compound of the market belonged to the daimyo, and the market has decided to erect the monument there with this in view. The ceremony of unveiling was held at the compound this morning at 10 a.m. Mr. Torataro Ushizuka, mayor of Tokyo was also present at the ceremony. Raku-o Shirakawa died in 1829. He was a great scholar of Japanese literature and a noted poet.

Large Grotto found in Tokyo Prefecture

A stalactite grotto dating from prehistoric times was recently discovered near Komiya Village, Nishi Tama District, Tokyo prefecture. Prof H. Fujimoto, geologist, and staff members of the Tourist Society of Tokyo Prefecture made investigations of the cave on May 24 and declared it to be the biggest stalactite grotto in the Kanto District. It is about 43 meters in length and from 10 to 15 meters in width. Tokyo Prefecture intends to open the cave to the public in the near future.

Mt. Nantai at Nikko covered with Snow

On Sunday morning, May 24, the temperature dropped suddenly at Nikko and Mt. Nantai was covered with snow to a depth of about three centimeters. This phenomenon is quite rare at this time of the year, being the first time it has

occurred in a decade. Tourists who came to Nikko to see the cherry blossoms were amazed at the weather conditions.

Sanatorium at Kurume

The Kurume Gakuin, a sanatorium for weak children which has been under construction at Kurume Mura, Kita Tama Gun, Tokyo Prefecture was opened on June 10 under the direction of Dr. Taniguchi. Some 360 children will be received there for about four months. The sanatorium is situated on a slope covered with pine trees, and has an area of 25,000 tsubo. There are class rooms, a lecture hall, kitchen, bath rooms, dormitories and sun rooms. Twenty two instructors and tutors will look after the children.

Imperial Academy Prizes were awarded June 1

The distribution ceremony of the Imperial Prizes and the Imperial Academy Prizes for the members of the Imperial Academy were held at the hall of the Imperial Academy, Uyeno Park, Tokyo at 2 : 30 p.m. June 1. The Imperial Prizes will be awarded to Messrs. Naoyoshi Ogawa and Takaoki Sasaki. The Imperial Academy Prizes will be presented to Messrs. Tomizo Yoshida, Neozo Igawa, Yoshizo Suenaga, Yoshiji Tomita, Toshio Hoshino and Michizo Asano.

Foreign Style Hotel for Lake Towada

A hotel will be constructed on the shore of Lake Towada, Aomori Prefecture shortly. The plan is being discussed by officials of the Aomori Prefectural Office at present. The hotel will be established on the occasion Lake Towada is selected as a National Park. The hotel will be constructed in foreign style and have modern equipment.

Rural Cottage presented Baron G. Hayashi

A cozy Japanese house in rural style with a straw roof has been completed by Mr. Sonjin Iwai, secretary to the Education Minister for Baron Gonsuke Hayashi, former Japanese Ambassador to England. The house is situated at Aoyagi, Hoya, Kita Tamagun, Tokyo Prefecture. Mr. Iwai decided to construct this house for Baron Hayashi's private villa, because Mr. Iwai got some copyrights having published a biography of the former Ambassador. The house was built at a cost of one thousand yen. On May 30, Mr. Iwai invited Baron Hayashi to the house which has been almost completed, and Baron Hayashi is reported to have been very pleased with it.

Shrine to be built for Pioneer Geographer

A memorial museum and a shrine will be erected in memory of Chukei Ino, pioneer Japanese geographer shortly at Sawaramachi, Chiba Prefecture. Mr. Hashimoto, a resident of the town, is treasuring a lot of the relics of the old geographer which will be displayed in the museum. It is Mr. Hashimoto who is sponsoring the plan. A budget for the construction works of the museum and the shrine has been raised to 15,000 yen by the residents of the town.

Ceremonial Rice Planted at Ise

The Planting ceremony of rice plants which are to be offered to the Ise Grand Shrine was held in a rice field in the suburbs of Uji Yamada City, Miye Prefecture, on June 8. Eighty young girls and men selected by the shrine planted the rice plants to the accompaniment of religious music. The ceremony, which was finished at 2 p.m., was held at Uchiwa-Awase on the banks of the rice field.

Moraes, Memorial

A meeting was held at the Tototei Restaurant, Hibiya, Wednesday evening, June 10, when the plan to erect the memorial hall for the late Wenslau Moraes, Portuguese writer, was talked of by the members of the Society for the Promotion of International Cultural Relations, the Cultural Bureau of the Foreign Ministry, Mr. Totsuka, Governo. of Tokushima, and Mr. Yumoto, director of the Education Bureau of the Tokushima. According to the plan, the committee will buy the horse where the late Mr. Moraes lived in Tokushima, which will be preserved as an historical monument. Relics of the writer will be displayed in the house. The committee has raised a budget for the program amounting to ¥30,000.

World Tourist Posters Shown

An exhibition of posters made by tourists bureaus of the world was held at the Museum of Railways at Manseibashi, Kanda, Tokyo, under the auspices of the Board of

Tourist Industry from June 23 to the end of that month. These posters have been collected by the Board, and distinguished Japanese posters of tourism were also shown at the exhibition

Agricultural Festival held in Aoyama

To promte agriculture, an agricultural festival was held at the hall of the Aoyama Primary School, Aoyama, Tokyo, at 1 o'clock Friday afternoon, June 12, under the auspices of the Tokyo Municipal Office and the Tokyo Prefectural Office.

The object of the festival is to promote studies of the question of population and the supply of provisions to the public.

Statue of Shinran presented to Temple

A statue of Shinran, Great Buddhist priest, has been presented by believers of the Zempuku Temple, Azabu, Tokyo. The statue represents the priest wearing a pilgrim's costume, which was unveiled in the compound of the temple on July 5. The statue has been made by Mr. Jusaburo Imamura, sculptor of Osaka. Mr. Seiichi Hirose, business man of Osaka, made the donation.

University to give Christanity Course

A course in Christianity will be established at Kyoto Imperial University shortly. A certain resident of Tokyo has made a monetary donation for the purpose, amounting to the sum of ¥50,000. The university has decided to establish the course with the donation. There are two courses on Buddhism and the other religions at the university at present, while the university will now open an independent course in Christanity.

Nearly two thousand Foreign Students

According to the recent investigation made by the department of Education, there were 1,993 foreign students in Japan at the beginning of 1935, of whom 1,405 are Chiuese students, 487 are Manchu and 61 Americans. English and French students number one each.

Chinese students has increased by 574 at the end of 1935. Most of them are studying at Kyoto Imperial University and in that of Kyushu.

印度巡禮の思ひ出

成瀬賢秀

題に顔負け

僅に半歳，印度，緬甸，南洋見物の私のこの思ひ出は，與へられたる題に對して，少々，顔まけする感じがする。

けれども，臍の緒截つて初めて，海外旅行をした私には，慣れた多年の生活よりも，それが，どれほど生き甲斐を感じたことであらう。

若しそれ，時間の長さよりも，空間の充實が，眞の生活を意義づけるものであるならば，敢て，この短時日の旅行の思ひ出も，さほど，ひけめを感じなくとも好い譯である。

可愛いい子に旅をさせよ

と，諺にもいふが，それは，自分の家の全體が，外から，はつきり看取されるからである。

眞理は，昔も今も變らぬもの。一度，海外へ出ると，日本の全體が看取される。だから，人をして眞の愛國者たらしむるには，海外旅行をさせるに限る。

私は，以前は可なりのコスモポリタニズムの信奉者であつたが，一度，海外へ踏み出してからは，世界主義はすつかり破綻を來した。同一民族によつて結合された國家を無視したやうな世界主義は，ありやうがないことに氣付いた。そして，特に日本國民に生れたことを有り難く思ふやうになつた。

けれども，徒に排他的な，征服的な，軍國主義的愛國者ではない。各民族が成せる國家を，そのまゝ認容しつゝ，互に，手を携へ合つて行くといふ協調的な，國家主義とでもいふべきものである。

民族の血の流れ

は爭はれぬものだ。日本人は日本人が懐しい。

門司を出て，青海原の波を蹴つて進むほどに，二夜を明かせば，海は黃土の泥濁せる，所謂，黃海となる。海は蒼い，澄みきつたものとのみ思つてゐる日本人には，泥濁せる海を見ては異様に感ぜざるを得ない。始めて異國情緒の一端に觸れる。

泥海と思つてゐるうちに，いつか，揚子江を溯航してゐるのだ。こんな大きな川は見たことがない。上海は揚子江の支流の川岸だと聞いて驚く。

順風一夜玄海を過ぐ。
巨船波を衝いて航路長し。
三日初めて知る華域の近きを。
呉淞沪上落潮黃なり。

とは，驚異の眼を見張つた當時の七絕詩である。

上海埠頭に上陸見物する。夥しい支那苦力の往來，なにか饒舌つてゐるが，さつぱり解らない。第一，言語の通じないのが，異民族への隔意を生ずる原だ。日本人は日本人が懐しいといふ感じが胸に湧いて來る。

そこへ在留の友人が甲板まで迎へに來てくれた。しがみつくほど懐しさを感じた。

貨幣の共通が望ましい

言語が世界共通であつたらと思ふ。が，一寸，むつかしいことだ。然らばせめても，貨幣位は共通であつて欲しい。それは協定次第で能き得ることだ。

上海には兩替屋が澤山ある。先づ以て日本貨幣を替へねばならぬ。ところが，兩替屋も信用ある店でないと，僞金をつかますさうだ。

出發する時には，費ひ殘した支那貨を交換して來ねばならぬ。シンガポールに上陸しても，セーロン島でも，ジヤヷでも到る處，それぞれ出入共に交換しなければならぬ。

特に，同じ英領印度のうちでありながら，シーロン島と，印度內地とが異つてゐるのは不都合を餘計に感ずる。通貨の世界共通を計つて，かうした不便を除きたいと思ふ心が切に動く。

日本語が世界語になるまで

一等船客の兒童遊戯室で，日英の子供達が一所に遊んでゐるのを見ると，英國系の子供は，自國語で何の遠慮もなく，はしやいでゐるが，日本の子達はどうも控目になつてゐる。もつとも，數も少いのであるが，日本人は，どうも歩が悪いことを感ずる。日本の子達が氣の毒になつて來る。

文明に立ち遅れた咎で，どうもしやうのないことだ。が，日本人はどうか早く強くなり，偉くなつて，世界の指導者とならねばならぬ。さうなつたら日本語で世界中が歩かれることになるのだ。

油斷がならぬ

船が入港すると，甲板上へ支那人の物賣りや，苦力がどさどさと上つて來る。うつかりしてゐると，船室のものまで盜んで行く。

シンガポールに着く前夜，ボーイに白靴を塗らせるために，いつも習はせに從つて，自分の船室の戶外に出して置いた。

翌朝，早々着港した。起きて見ると白靴が無い。まだ，清掃最中かと思つて，ボーイを呼んで訊ねると，「知りません」といふ。ボーイが見廻らぬ前に船が着いた。逸早く上つて來た支那人が，かつぱらつて去つたのだ。全く油斷も，すきもあつたものでない。

同船の友人は，室內の窓際に掛けておいた背廣の上着を，便所に行つてゐる間に盜まれた。

船室は鍵してあつたが，硝子の丸窓が半分ほど明けてあつたので，鉤手でひつかけて盜んで行つたのだ。

シンガポールを過ぎると，支那人のさういつたものが無くなり，印度人が代つて來る。印度人は，かうしたことをしない。これから安心だと同船客の通人が話してくれる。

荷物が傷まぬ印度苦力

印度人は苦力にしても，支那人よりは氣だてが柔しい。顔つきは逞しくてしかめ面してゐるが，心根はやさしくて盜癖が少い。

膂力は支那苦力に劣るけれども，荷物を頭上に載せて運び，そして，重ければ二人共同で取扱ふ故に，荷物は決して破損しない。

そこへ行くと日本人の荷役は，力の無い癖に，痩我慢で，肩にかついで抛げ下ろすから，荷物の痛むこと夥しい。

日本の鐵道省など，毎々，發送人に荷造堅固の注意を促してゐるが，お手許の荷役の取扱を戒めることを忘れてゐる。

心付けを請求する巡査

支那巡査でも，印度巡査でも，日本とは違つて，應對がやさしい。道を訊ねても叮嚀に敎へてくれる。ともすれば東道してくれる。荷物でもあれば持つてもくれる。だから，心付けでもやりたい氣がする。尤も，彼れ等は貰ふ氣でゐる。

日本の巡査のやうなつもりで，遠慮してゐると，先方から請求する。重寶なやうだが，威嚴がない。これでは盜難などに出遇つた場合に，以て信頼するに足らぬ心地がする。やはり，さういつた場合には無力ださうな。

カルカツタの警察署へ旅劵の檢査を受けに行つた。待つ間に，用便をなすべく便所を探したが，一寸，見付からぬ。廊下を通つて行く巡査に訊ねた。彼は案内してやるといつて，階上に導いた。彼れは階段の途中で手を出し「ボクシス・プレー」(心付け下さい)といふ。

公の警察署で，便所の案内料なんか誰れが出すものか，馬鹿にするなと，心に思つたので「ノーノー」といつて，彼の手を押し除けてやつた。彼れは「此所だ」といつて，ある入口を敎へて去つた。這入つて見ると，便所ではない。

失敬な奴だと憤慨しながら，負け惜しみで獨で探がし廻つた。やつと見付け，用をすまし，すつきりした心持で階段を降りて來ると，降り口のもの蔭に，彼は待つてゐた。彼は，又，あつかましくも「ボクシス・プレー」と手を出す。「馬鹿ぬかせ」といつて，さつさと出てしまつた。

彼は，私のこの强い態度に面喰つたらしい。ポカーンとしてゐた。尤も上陸したばかりでは，かうした態度はとれぬが，二ケ月も印度內地を旅行し通して來たものだから，こちらの方がすれつからしになつてゐる。

日本の巡査には武士道がある

約半歲の旅行を無事に終へて，神戶港に着いた時には，日本のもの皆が懷しく見える。

船がまだ岸壁に着かない前に，稅務官と，巡査とが乘り込んで來た。日本巡査の姿を見て，

「やー，日本の巡査は立派なものだなー」と思はず嘆聲を發した。お巡りさんは無言のまゝ，この突拍子もない嘆聲を發した船客を，怪げんな顏して眸を見張るのみであつた。

ツンケンとした無表情な官僚式ではあるが，威嚴犯すべからざる，そして，「武士は食はねど高揚子」といつた所が見えて，以て信頼するに足るといふ，力强さを感ぜしめる。

日本の巡査には武士道精神が，どうしてか傳統されてある。さういつた點では，恐らく，日本の巡査は世界無比の優れたものだらう。も少し，暖かみがあれば，申分なしだが。

日本人は役務につくと官僚式

支那人でも，印度人でも，會つて話すと愛嬌がある。殊に印度人は，呼びかけられると，直ぐににつこり笑を湛へ，小首をかたげて，返事をする。

それが，いつも烈日の下に暮らしてゐるので，眉間に皺をよせ，しかめ面をしてゐる。その顏面が急に愛嬌を見せるために，餘計にやさしく見える。そこへ行くと，日本人は佛頂面だ。

かうした愛嬌の好い人間の中に旅をして，歸朝早々，ある劇場にお芝居を見た。幕の間に廊下をそゞろ歩きをした。喫煙しやうと思つて，手近の番臺にゐる番人にマツチを貸してくれといつた。番人は「マツチはお茶屋にある」といつて佛頂面してゐる。

斷崖からつき墮されたやうに，私の心は暗く沈んでしまつた。なんといふ恐ろしい官僚式だ。特に「日本人は」と思つた。

今まで，やさしい愛嬌のある民族の中に浸つて來たものだから，殊更，それが强く感ぜられる。

日本人は官吏ばかりが官僚式でなく誰れでも役務を持つと官僚式になる。

外國語の會話は押し一つ

ボンベイに上陸して，初めて．印度大陸の雰圍氣に觸れた。日本綿花會社の親切なお世話になつて，立派なマンション（社員合宿所）の一室に寄寓した。

專屬の印度人ボーイが與へられた。ボーイを通じての用便は一切英語でなければ通じない。慣れぬ英語の會話は，痒い所へ手の屆かぬやうなことばかり隨分，不自由を感じた。

が，窮すれば通ずるもので，段々相手も推量するやうになるし，こちらも慣れもするし，又，第一，押しが强くなつて，「なに，ブロークンだつて恥づることはない。俺は日本人だ。外國語のまづいのは當り前だ。お前だつて，日本語は俺だけは話されまい」と，かういつた度胸がきまる。

それ以來，一人で街へ出て買物に行つても，相當に用を便ずるやうになつた。

日本人はやさしい

與へられたる專屬のボーイは，シヴといふ名であつた。このシヴ君，印度の全旅行について來てくれた。が，このボーイ，初め，私が呼んでも一度や二度では返事をしない。大聲あげて怒鳴ると返事をする。どうも不思議でならない。そのうちにとうとう理由が解つた。それからといふものは，いつも怒鳴つて呼ぶことにした。すると，いつでも敏捷に言ふことを聽く。

その理由といふは，印度人のボーイは，亡國の悲しさ，英國人に奴隸のやうに酷使された習慣が，骨身に滲みこんでゐる故に，ボーイといふものは怒鳴りつけられるものだと，思ひこんでゐるらしい。それ故，なまなかな呼び方では，はつきり聽えぬらしい。それにつけても，歐洲人の優越觀から來る橫暴が憎らしくなる。

私達日本人は，ボーイさんと呼ぶことに慣らされてゐる。が，まさか外國へ來て「ボーイさん」とは呼ばれないから，ボーイと呼び捨てにするものゝ腹の中では「さん」づけで呼んでゐる氣持でゐる。だから自然にやさしく出る。從つて怒鳴るやうには呼び得ないのだ。

かうした日本人のやさしい態度は，彼等をして非常に慕はしめる。それゆゑ，日本人からボーイの募集があると，彼等の仲間に大競爭があるといふことだ。

—昭和十一，四—

國際ニュース

セイロン大菩提會

佛教に歸依せしめるため，アムベカー博士其他，印度ハリジヤン人を招待する決議が，四月，コロムボのマリガカンデにある大菩提協會の本部で行はれた本年度總會に於て通過した。

スリ・ルヌボクネ・ダーマナンダ・ナヤカ・テラ師が司會者であつた。

英國皇帝ジョーヂ五世陛下の崩御に關し，哀悼と忠誠の意の表明が，決議の形で採擇された。

この大會では又，協會長ナヤカ・テラ，スリ・ラタナサラ師の遷化について哀悼の意を表した。

又，この協會は，最近，セーロン州々會議員に選出されたネール・ヘワヴィターン及びラジャー・ヘワヴィターン兩氏に對し祝辭を送り，ネール・ヘワヴィターン氏が之に對し謝辭を述べ，一九三五年度の報告と會計が承認を得た。

ブダ・ガヤ寺院法案

ブダ・ガヤ寺院に關する統一法制定に就いての法案を，會議に提出することに努力せられた所の印度立法會議のテーン・マウング氏その他のビルマ選出議員の人々に感謝の意を表明する投票は滿場一致異議なく可決された。

ハリジャン人の統領，アムベッカー博士に對して，セイロン州佛教徒は，アムベッカー博士及びその一統の人々が佛教に歸依することに就いて欣んで之を迎へる旨を通告する様，決定された。

次の如き役員が選出された。

議長――ヴィディアランカラ・プリヴェナの總長，兼，ヴィディオダヤ大學の總長。

執行委員――エヌ・ディー・エス・シルヴァ氏，ネール・ヘワヴターン氏，ラジャヘワヴィターン氏，エス・ケー・ムーンシンゲ氏，ユー・ビー・ドラビヒラ氏，大菩提學校事務總長，大菩提協會總幹事，ディー・ビー・ジャヤティラカ卿，ダヴリュ・イー・バスティアン氏，ジエー・ムーンシンゲ氏，ハーリ・ディアス氏，ジー・ビー・マララセカラ博士，シー・エス，ジャヤシンゲ氏，エス，パロン，ディアス氏，ジー・ケー・ダヴリュー・ペレラ氏，ディー・エヌ・ハプガール氏，ビー・ムーンシンゲ氏，ヴィー・エス・ナナヤカラ氏，ヴィー・エー・ビー・ナナヤカラ氏，ダヴリューエイチ・ダヴリュー・ペレラ氏，ダヴリュー・ペドリック氏，エー・クルップ氏，ビー・ジャヤティレーケ氏，ティー・ディー・ジョン氏，

秘書，――イー・エス・ジャシンゲ氏。

ブダ・ガヤ寺院法案

一九三六年四月十七日に行はれた立法會議の席上に於て，ブダガヤ寺院の經營を委員會に移管する法案の提出をテイン，マウング博士に一任することを決議したといふ前掲報導は，佛教徒にとつて欣ぶべきことであらう。この種のことは言ふ迄もなく，形式的儀禮的なことであるには違ひないけれどもそれでも，この承認を與へることが，遲れゝば遲れるだけ，佛教徒の心に誤解を起すに到る。この法案の第一讀會は，九月に開催される全體會議の時に行はれる豫定である。この機會に我々はこの困難な仕事に當られたテイン・マウング博士及び博士を助けた人々に對し感謝の意を表明するものである。殊に，サルダル・サント・シング氏がこの法案を最初に提案出來る様に取計つた功績を多としなければならない。テイン・マウング博士が，この問題を極めて手際よく處理されたことに就いても感謝しなければならない。偉大なる耐忍力と不撓不屈とが，よくその豫定の成果を收めて成功したのであつた。この重要なる問題がビルマ分離の效力發生前に決定することを期待するものである。

マラバルの佛教開教

交趾支那，トラヴァンコールに長途の旅行を終へてカルカッタに歸つたダンマカンダ比丘が大菩提協會の總主事に宛てた手紙の中に次の様なことが記されてゐる。「トラヴァンコール，交趾支那，その他，遠隔地方の月餘に亘つての旅行から恰度今歸つて來たところである。これらの地方からは，大變收獲があつた。今回の旅行中，百二十五人程の人々が佛教に歸依することになつた。クリスト教徒は，クリスト教に歸依せしめるために大變宣傳を行つてゐる時であつた。自分達は强ひて必要以上の信徒と中心人物とを求めたことはなかつた。自分達は助力を必要とすることを訴へただけであるが，それでも恰度，ダンマカンダ比丘の希望する以上の信徒を送ることが出來るやうになつたのであつた。」云々。

佛教の統一と融合

「大菩提」五月號には，色々の立場から眺めた佛教の統一と融合の問題を數章に亘つて掲載した。統一は有效な價値ある仕事ではあるけれども，それがために信條を犧牲にする様なことがあつてはならないと思ふ。見解の相違は實際に嚴存してゐて，唯，議題の一つとして佛教徒は凡て統一し融合した方がよいといふことを主唱することは正しく，又その意味に於てなれば又可能な問題であるけれども，實際問題としては同意出來ない時などには，必ずや意見の分裂に同調せざるを得ない。最近，個々の人々の氣紛れな意見によつて法を曲解しやうとする宜ろしからぬ企てが行はれてゐるし，又，統一と融合といふ美名の下に，この様な曲解を批判することを一切禁じて了はふとする惡傾向も見えてゐる。例へば，リス・デーヴィド夫人等の場合を例にとつて考へて見やう。女史及その一派の人々は，佛教の主要形相である靈魂不存在說を否定して佛陀は靈魂不變說を敎へ給ふたものであると立證しやうと試みてゐる。若し融合とは，かくの如き牽

強附會の言說に雷同し，女史及その一派の人々と同調すべく强制されるが如きものであるとするならば，言ふ迄もなく自分達は之に仲間入りすることを拒絕せざるを得ない。自分達は佛陀によつて敎へられた通りの信條を以て法を護らなければならない。巴利經典に記錄されてある通りに行はなければならない。然し，かく言へばとて吾々は，別派の思想に對して門戶を開放しないといふつもりではない。最初から，「大菩提」は，自由政策を執つて，各宗派の佛說を，紙上を通じて論議する樣に開放して來たのである。吾々はあく迄，佛陀の純粹にして原始的な敎へを擁護して行くのであるが，それにも不拘，凡ての流派と親善關係を保つてゐるものである。今迄靈魂不變說に立脚してその信念を發表した佛敎宗派は一つもなかつたし，又，それに同調して共同の仕事を進めて行くだけの決心を我々に與へ得たものはなかつたのである。

セイロンに於ける支那僧

ナラダ比丘の支那訪問の結果として五人の支那僧がセイロン島に渡つて，長老派佛敎に歸依し，研究しやうとしてゐる。セイロン島と支那とが，文化的關係に結び付けられたことは，幾世紀この方初めての事である。一行は漢譯大藏經をセイロン佛敎徒への贈物として携へた。彼らは，コロムボのヴァジラヲマのヴァジラニヤナ・ナヤカ・テラ師の下に得度し，同師の指導の下に研究を重ねて行くことになつた。長老派佛敎の敎理及その實際を徹底的に研究するに當つて，ヴァジラヲマのナヤカ・テラ師程，卓越した心からの敎導者は他にないであらう。

ローリッチ氏の繪畫寄贈

トラヴァンコールのマハラヤ殿下のスリ・チトララヤム州立美術館は，ローリッチ敎授の最近の力作「灼熱する思想」と題する繪畫を受納した。

この繪畫には，ヒマラヤの山中歸去來する雲海の白雲に直面して人類の救濟を祈願してゐる一人の仙人の姿を描いてゐる。この繪畫は，ふんだんに，紫色と菫色を驅使してゐるが，之が，莊嚴の感じを深めて大藝術家の特徵をよく現はしてゐる。焰の如き思想は，金色の翼の鳥の姿となつて空間を馳け巡つてゐる。谷の深さは底知れず，深い深い白雲の重疊を以て埋め悉されて，遙かの雲間には雪に輝く白皚々のヒマラヤ連峰の山頂が力强く見え隱れしてゐるが，これこそ，ローリッチ敎授が，深く心胆を傾けて親愛の誠を捧げ又景仰する偉大なるヒマラヤの絕巓なのである。

この測り知るべからざるヒマラヤの姿は，敎授の他の多くの力作繪畫にも取扱はれて來たものであるが，南京のシニカ・アカデミア總長は，ローリッチ敎授に信書を寄せて，ヒマラヤの繪畫を所望し，その內の一つが現在，支那科學アカデミーの壁間を飾つてゐる。

實際ヒマラヤの思想は，ローリッチ敎授のこの赫々たる力作と常に連繫してゐるものであつて，ジェームス・エイッチ・カズンス博士は，ローリッチ氏を目して正しく「精神の骨髓からのヒマラヤ人」として認めてゐる。

カリフォルニアの佛敎硏究學會 The Institute of Buddhist Studies, Calif. は，ローリッチ敎授に對して文學博士の稱號を與へることゝなつた。

洛陽の白馬寺修復成る

支那佛敎最初の古刹，洛陽の白馬寺は多年屢々兵火に災され，荒廢その極に達してゐたので，最近僧俗の有志がこれを憂ひ，王一亭，葉恭綽，及び考試院長戴傳賢の諸氏發起となつて資を集め，留雲寺の德浩和尙を聘して住持となし，その修復を圖つてゐたが，此程漸く竣工したので，五月二十八日（舊曆四月八日）をトして祝賀會が催された。大雄寶殿，天王殿，僧寮等逐次竣工したが更に禪堂，雲水堂等も建て添へる筈で，先きに失つた寺產も買ひ戾し，全く面目一新の觀があると。因に白馬寺は竺摩，竺法蘭三藏が始めて佛敎を支那に齎らし，洛陽に於て白馬陀經を用ひたことから此の名あり，佛敎東土第一の道場である。

合肥の旱害賑災運動

合肥（安徽省）地方は旱害の爲めに，慘狀目もあてられず，紅葉字會の葉昭秋居士は去月初旬上海に來り段芝老に謁して救濟のことを請ひ，段氏より數百圓の捐助を得ると同時に賑災遊藝會を催して數千圓を得，救濟事業に當る一方，一般社會に呼びかけて救捐を求めてゐる。その文に——人々は皆乞食である。草の根を掘り蘆を探つて食つてゐる。又，粗穰既に竭き，食を求むるも方なく飢餓相侵し，生を求むるも路無く道殣相望む，餓莩相迎えて哭聲四野に充つ云々——目下特に八歲から十二三歲までの兒童に救援會で粥の供養を開始してゐると。

中華女子佛學會生る

世界新聞（南京）の報導に依れば，女子佛敎徒陳章佩琳，張宋易，陳希慈，梅創劉子玉の諸居士五十三名が發起となつて，中華女子佛敎會を組織すべく，準備處を南京關西門內に設け，五月下旬宣言書を各方面に發表した。その趣旨は全國の女子敎徒の團結を以て，佛法を闡揚し，道德を振興し，各種の社會事業を行ふと言ふので，その事業方面では講經堂，念佛堂，女子佛學律儀院，同願敎院，同密敎院，同禪定院，同研究院等を設け，傳導事項として佛學雜誌，經典流通處，佛學圖書館，飜譯經典部，佛學傳導處を設け，社會事業として學校，醫院，施藥，施衣，施材，放生，等を行ふ由である。

護國濟民宣化國の宣言

最近ビルマから，歸國した慈航法師は，五月中旬から南京に於て講經中，弘法利生，護國濟民を提唱して多大な感銘を與へ，南京で更に五日間五月三十日まで華嚴經回向章の大意を開示した。因に護國濟民法會の宣言を約言せば，『國難對處の方策として各人が銃を持つて起つことは出來ない。各人が各の仕事に專念し，各心を合せて努力するより外はない。それには敎育も文化も救國の重大要件で，佛敎の大力，大雄，大無畏の精神も同様である。佛敎は最高の敎育で，佛學は超越した文化であり，眞に國を護り國を救ふことが出來るものである。我々は護國濟民宣化團を作つて，菩薩所造の工作を回向し，全國の同胞と共に大無畏の精神で護國濟民に突進せんとするもので，これが吾々最後の希望である。』云々

寺廟財產の處分問題

最近支那佛敎界に於て最大きな衝擊を與へたのは，國民政府が監督寺廟條例を發令し，寺廟財產を沒收して省敎育費に充當せんとしたことである。已にある地方では厳格に實施せられ，又或る地方では色々な紛糾を生じてゐる。湖南省敎育廳が五月下旬廿日各縣政府に發令した所に依ると『已に調査して敎育費に充當せしめた廟產は回收するを得ず，但し監督寺廟條例公布施行前に於て，既に敎育事業を行つてゐたものは均しく舊の如くこれを維持するを得。同條例十條の規定，公益事業に充當してゐる經費は地方敎育事業の擴充よりも重きを置き，紛糾を除くべく，既に處分したるものは現狀を維持し，同條件五條によつて速に寺廟の登記を實行すべし。云々』

全國寺廟財產の保護

近來地方敎育機關或は自治團體が，往々法令を顧みず廟產を强奪し，又は廟宇を毀壞し，禮拜を妨害して紛糾を惹起してゐるので，中國佛敎會理事長圓瑛師は六月五日全國各分會に對して通報を發した。卽ち，無論軍警たると，その他團體又は個人たるを問はず，力を恃んで廟產を占用する者は法律に依つて對處すべきである。民國二十年國民政府第四〇〇號で各省に通令した案に照し，又は刑法第二百四十六條の壇，廟寺，敎堂に對し公然侮辱した者は六ケ月以下の徒刑又は三百圓以下の罰金に處す，附項に祭禮，說敎，禮拜を妨害したるものも亦同じの條項，又民國十九年司法院第三三七號を以て處理すべし。又行政院發令の佛敎寺廟監督條例は，凡そ廟產は敎育及び各慈善公益の事業を興し，均しく前項の規則に准じて，佛敎會及び寺廟の住持が自ら經營し，佛寺僧產を保障すべきで，これは法令の規定に依つて明なことである。敎育等の事業創立については出願の規定があり，若し地方團體が違法に侵略或は廟產を毀損した時は直ちに法に依つて對處すべく，直ちに本會に報告せられたしと。

四川佛學院の開學式

成都武聖街十方堂の四川佛學院は，昌圓法師の手に依つて修築落成し經費

敎務，招生等一切の積極的準備も出來たので，五月廿八日の佛誕日（舊暦四月八日）を卜して盛大なる開學式を擧げた。

寺廟建設の問題化

厦門に於て多年開敎に從事してゐる日華佛敎學會理事神田慧雲師は，華語を能くし，既に多數の中國人の信者を得，每月華語雜誌を發行する等頗る奮鬪を續けてゐるが，最近在厦門の臺灣人某居士の寄附で廣大なる土地を得，目下寺廟建築の準備中である。處がこれが一部排日屋の問題とする所となり紙上その他で騒がれてゐる。卽ち五月廿八日佛敎日報に『日僧厦門に寺を建つ，爭端は擴大の形勢あり』の見出しで『日僧神田慧雲は達觀園の地所に寺院を建てんとし，市府工務局の許可を得，布告して界内の墳墓を遷讓せしむ。關係市民の墳墓は買つたもの，且つ祖先の遺骸を安ずる所である。政府がつひに日僧に欺かれ，遽に遷讓せしむるは非合理であるとして陳情を呈出し力爭してゐる。工務局は卽ち「既に懲るべき所に依つて，契約したものである。うつしを政府に奉呈，法に依つて護るべし」此のことは，一般人の注意する所，一部の有識者は工部局の態度を頗る不正なりとしてゐるから，爭は擴大する形勢である』と。又六月四日の同報には墓主黃鴻翔，莊大川等の抗議，山田領事と李市長の交渉顚末を揭げ，市長の意見として「支那に於ける外人の布敎は條約を以て，只だキリスト敎のみに許し，佛敎は支那固有の宗敎で，何も日僧の布敎を必要とせず，寺院の建築も條約上認めない所である。而も强いてこれを進行せしむれば，中日親善を妨げるのみか，條約違反である。且つ國家の主權に關し一地方問題ではないから中央の指示を仰いで解決し度し」と述べたので，山田領事も同意し，日僧も進行を停止した。李市長は昨日省政府に向つて出發した」云々。又六月六日（南京電報）の報ずる所では，「日僧厦門に於て强行，地を占し，廟宇を建てる件に就ては，厦門市長李時霖氏來京，外交部當局に報告すると共に，處理方策の指示を請ふた。關係當局から探聞するに，此の事は結局地方當局から負責交涉すべし，とのことである。」云々と報じてゐる。

無錫佛敎分會の成立

中國佛敎會無錫分會は，五月三十日無錫の崇安寺大雄寶殿に於て成立大會を催した。僧衆二百人，縣黨部，縣政府代理特派せられ頗る盛會，主席超一法師から經過報告，縣當局の訓示あつて理監の選擧を行つた結果，超一，廣願，外八名理事に，浩本，普善外三名監事に當選した。

談玄法師の活躍

日華佛敎學會に寓し二年間，高野山及び東京の福田堯穎師から東密及び台密を研究して昨年十二月歸國した談玄法師は，已に佐々木月樵師の支那淨土敎史を譯し，五月末から毎日佛敎日報紙上に揭載してゐる。

國際佛教通報局定款

名稱

第一，本局を國際佛教通報局と稱す

事務所

第二，本局の事務所を全日本佛教青年會聯盟本部に置く

目的

第三，本局は日本內海及海外に向つて佛教事情の通報をなし，且つ佛教徒相互間の各種便宜を計るを以て目的とす

事業

第四，本局の目的を達成するため左記の事業を行ふ

イ，日本內地及世界各國より佛教事情に關する質問の通報を行ふ

ロ，必要に應じ日本語及世界各國語を以て佛教事情の通報を行ふ

ハ，外國人の日本觀光に際しては各種の便益を與へ，特にその佛教に關する方面に於て之を爲す

ニ，定時或は隨時に各國語を以て文書の刊行をなす

ホ，その他必要と認めたる事業を行ふ

役員

第五，本局の事務を處理するため左の役員を置く

イ，局長　一名

ロ，幹事　三名

ハ，評議員　若干名

局長は本局の事務を總括す

幹事は本局の事務を處理す

評議員は局長の提案に依る重要事務を審議す

第六，評議員は左記の者を以て之に充つ

イ，全日本佛教青年會聯盟理事及主事

ロ，全日本佛教青年會聯盟理事會に於て推薦したる者

第七，局長及幹事は評議員會に於て決定す

第八，役員の任期は二ヶ年とす（但し重任を妨げず）

經費

第九，本局の經費は左記のものに依て之を支辨す

イ，本局基金の活用

ロ，寄附金

ハ，その他の收入

補則

第十，本定款に記載せられざる事項は，凡て評議員會に於て協議す

第十一，第一回の役員は全日本佛教青年會聯盟理事會に於て決定す

定價			
一部	金二十錢	送料二錢
一年	金二圓四十錢	送料不要

昭和十年四月廿日第三種郵便物認可
昭和十一年六月廿八日印刷（毎月一回）
昭和十一年七月一日發行（一日發行）

東京市外吉祥寺337
編輯發行兼印刷人　浅野研眞

東京市牛込區早稻田鶴卷町107
印刷所　康文社印刷所
電話牛込(34)1950番 5049番

東京市神田區一ツ橋二の三
發行所　國際佛教通報局
電話九段(33)4428番
振替東京83015番

昭和十年四月三十日第三種郵便物認可 昭和十一年六月二十八日印刷納本(毎月一回) 昭和十一年七月一日發行(一日發行) 國際佛教通報 第二卷 第七號

昭和十年四月三十日第三種郵便物認可 昭和十一年七月二十八日印刷納本 昭和十一年八月一日發行（每月一回一日發行）第二卷 第八號

The International Buddhist Bulletin

國際佛教通報

第二卷 **昭和十一年八月** 第八號〔Vol. II. **August.** $\frac{2502}{1936}$ No. 8.〕

要 目 〔Contents〕

東京 **國際佛教通報局** 發行
The International Buddhist Information Bureau
Tokyo, Kanda, Hitotsubashi, II—3
Annual Subscription, ¥2.40 (post free), Single Copies 20 sen (post 2 sen)

Tales of Buddhist Priests (I)

by Atsuharu Sakai

(1) Priest Ungo

Heishiro was the zori (straw-footgear)-keeper of Lord Masamune Daté, one of the greatest lords of the northern part of Japan, who is known in her history for the communications he made with the Pope and the King of Spain in the 17th century. One cold winter's morning, when Daté was a little boy, so the story goes, he went to a detached house to have a snow-view in the morning. After the young lord entered the house, Heishiro, his zori-keeper, kept watch at the entrance.

"This is a cold morning," said Heishiro to himself. "Sorry that the young lord has to put this cold pair of geta (wooden footgear) on."

The faithful servant took up the pair of geta and put them into his futokoro (breast-pocket) in order to keep them warm for his young lord. Soon Masamune and his suit were heard coming along the long hall. So Heishiro put the geta in order on the step for the young lord to put on.

"Confound you!" shouted young Masamune in an angry voice, the moment his right foot was on one of the geta. "You must have been sitting on your master's geta because it is cold out here. You beast to defile my geta with your unclean body."

Before the faithful servant had time to explain the matter, hump went the geta against the forehead of Heishiro. Blood streaming out, Heishiro fainted on the spot. And Masamune, who was too angry to put the "defiled geta" on, went back to his residence barefoot through the deep snow.

"Too much" Heishiro said to himself when he came to his senses. "Too much that you should treat me in this cruel way. You are my lord no longer, Masamune," he added turning in the direction Masamune went, "but I will take leave of you this minute. I will run over to your enemy and train myself in military art, so that I may attack you on the first opportunity when war breaks out between you and your enemy."

Under several fencing masters Heishiro studied swordsmanship in which he made remarkable progress. He became a samurai by assuming the family name of Makabe, for he hailed from a village of that name in Chiba Prefecture. Then Heishiro went to the Myoshin-ji (literally, Mysterious-mind) Temple in the Imperial capital of Kyoto, where he studied the Zen doctrine. He was converted into Buddhism and then he was cannonized to be a Priest. Buddhism disapproved hatred and vindictiveness, and Heishiro Makabe, whose Buddhist name was Ungo (literally, Cloud-abode) gave up his hatred of Lord Daté, his former lord, with whom he had long been thinking of paying old scores. Priest Ungo went to Tosa Province, where he took charge of a temple for a long time.

In the meantime, the Zuigan (literally, Auspicious-rock)-ji Temple of Matsushima required a priest and Priest Ungo, upon the recommendation of the chief priest of the Myoshin-ji Temple, obtained the Imperial sanction to take charge of the Zuigan-ji Temple.

"Do you recognize me, my lord?" Priest Ungo asked when, after the first seven-day mass, he had a formal interview in the great hall of the temple with Daté, the lord of the clan in which the temple was situated. "I am Heishiro, who was in your service thirty years ago."

The surprised lord at once recognized the scar that he had inflicted upon the forehead of his former servant. Priest Ungo then explained how he had been converted into Buddhism.

"Buddhism taught me to give up my vindictiveness against you, my lord" Priest Ungo continued. "In a word, it was your geta that has made me what I am now. Your quick temper gave me enlightenment and I was saved. I feel truly grateful to you because through your anger I got my salvation. The Lord Buddha be praised for I am now sent to this temple in your territory."

The Zuigan-ji Temple, of Matsushima, keeps a geta, a wooden clog, as a temple treasure, though the temple will tell you that it is a copy of the original one with which young Daté struck his

servant on the forehead.

(2) Priest Hakuin

"This is my daughter's baby" said a tofu (bean-curd)-dealer to Priest Hakuin, who was known far and wide for his saintly virtues, and you must know who is responsible for the baby.

A baby was born to the daughter of the tofu-dealer, who lived near the temple of which Priest Hakuin was the chief priest. When asked whose child it was, his daughter mentioned the name of the priest, hoping that her father would be less offended with the priest than he would be with her real lover. The indignant tofu-dealer took the baby to the temple and handed it to Priest Hakuin.

"People call you a saint," he went on, "but you are a recreant priest after all.

"Yes, I know who is responsible for the baby," said Priest Hakuin gently, and the angry tofu-dealer went away, leaving the baby with the priest, after reviling the priest in the most humiliating way.

Priest Hakuin did not retort to the abuses that indignant tofu-dealer showered upon him, but gently he accepted the new-born baby. Having no maid with him in the temple, however, Priest Hakuin had to do everything for his new charge. He washed the swaddling-clothes himself, he went round to ask for milk to give to the baby, and he carried it with him on every pilgrimage. He made no complaint about the baby or the tofu-dealer, but he gave the best care he could to the baby.

A couple of years went by. One cold morning, the mother of the baby saw Priest Hakuin going on a religious mendicancy with her baby in his arms. Her conscience smote her.

"Father," she said to the tofu-dealer, bursting into historical tears. "Father, I ask your forgiveness. The baby is the child of Kyu-san, and not of the holy priest."

Kyu-san was a carpenter who lived in the same village. The surprised tofu-dealer went to Priest Hakuin and explained the matter to him.

"All right. You may take the baby to her" was all that Priest Hakuin said in reply after gently listening to what the tofu-dealer said to him. The priest showed no sign of offence or indignation, but he went on discharging his religious duties as if nothing had happened to him.

Many more stories are told about the generosity of Priest Hakuin, who was famous for his religious enlightenment. Priest Hakuin died in 1768 at the age of 84 years.

(3) Priest Ikkyu

Priest Ikkyu is one of the most witty and humourous Buddhist priests that Japan has produced. Born the second son of the Emperor Gokomatsu, he was sent to the Daitoku-ji Temple to study Buddhism under Priest Yoso. His first Buddhist name was Sojun, but later he called himself by the name of Ikkyu (literally, One-rest), because he considered this life to be but a short stay or rest between the two other lives, past and future. Many funny stories are told about Priest Ikkyu.

When Priest Yoso was out on a visit, young Ikkyu broke a teacup that his master highly prized.

"Reverend Priest," asked young Ikkyu the moment Priest Yoso came back, "what becomes of a living being in the end?"

"Why, my dear" the priest innocently said "a living being dies."

"When does he die?" pursued the young priest.

"When the time comes," answered Priest Yoso.

"The time for this cup has come," said Ikkyu taking the broken pieces out of his futokoro (breast-pocket). Priest Yoso said nothing in reply, but he overlooked the careless mistake.

Priest Yoso was so fond of "ame" (a kind of jelly), that he always kept a jar of it in his sitting-room. He never gave a taste of it to young Ikkyu or any other priests of the temple.

"Ikkyu, my dear" said Priest Yoso, when he was going out on business one day. This jar contains something good for a grown-up person, but it is instant death to a youngster to taste it. It is dangerous. You must not touch it"

"No, I will keep my hands off" responded the apparently obedient young priest. But as soon as Priest Yoso went out, young Ikkyu repaired to the sitting-room of his master-priest, and found the jar of "ame," which he shared with all the other young priests. When the "ame" was all gone, young Ikkyu broke the jar to pieces.

"I ask your forgiveness, Reverend Priest" young Ikkyu sobbed when Priest Yoso came home, "but I broke your precious jar of 'ame' I was dusting the room after you went out. The duster caught the jar and broke it to pieces. I tasted the 'ame' at once as you told me that it would be instant death to a youngster to taste it. I did not die. I tasted it again, but I was as sound as before. I took all up, but here I am, still unable to die. I do not know how to excuse myself."

A certain daimyo, who knew the witty ways of young Ikkyu, invited him to a Buddhist service. He then put up a notice before the bridge that spanned the castle-moat. It read in Japanese "Do not cross the bridge." There was no other entrance to the castle. Ikkyu noticed the joke and walked over the bridge straight on.

"You saw the notice, didn't you?" asked the daimyo of Ikkyu. "Why did you cross the forbidden bridge?"

"Why, I walked only in the middle of the bridge and not on either side" was the calm reply of the young priest.

In the Japanese language, it must be understood, "bridge" and "end" or "side" are homonymously the same. The young priest did not walk on either left or right side of the bridge, but he walked just in the middle of it.

When Shogun Yoshimitsu of the Ashikaga family, invited Priest Yoso to a mass meeting, young Ikkyu accompanied him to the Shogunate court. The Shogun had heard much about the witty ways of Ikkyu and he thought he might put the young priest to a test.

"Is it possible to catch a tiger?" the Shogun asked Ikkyu after the service was over.

"Yes, it is, my lord."

"Can you catch that tiger?" asked the Shogun again pointing to the tiger painted on a screen before him.

"O yes, my lord" replied the young priest calmly. "Give me a rope and I will show you how to catch him." And when a rope was brought in, Ikkyu stood before the screen and said: "Please drive the tiger out; I am ready to catch him."

Priest Ikkyu may be said to have attained what is called religious enlightenement, but his was altogether a humourous life and he made fun even of religion. "If one is doomed to go to Hell for a single lie that he tells," he asked in a well-known 31-syllable poem, "what would become of the Buddha, who taught about things which do not exist?" This was of course an ironical way of expressing that the Lord Buddha could not tell a lie.

Priest Ikkyu died on the 21st of the eleventh month in 1481. Two days before his death, he had his own portrait painted by a painter.

Universala Kudhana Kongreso

de Sosei Nakanisi

Je la VI-a jarkunveno de Tutjapana Federacio de Budhanaj Gejunularaj Asocioj, jenaj tri proponoj elsenditaj :—

I-a Por memorigi 2600an jaron de japana erao, ni kiel japana budhana junularo, havu signifplenen taŭgan entreprenon.

II-a Je la 2600a jaro de japana erao, lokon havu Universala Budhana Kongreso, en japanujo.

III-a Je la 2600a jaro de japana erao (Ŝoŭa jaro 15a, 1940a jaro post Kristo) en japanujo okazigu Universalan Budhanan Kongreson.

La I-a estas proponita de Junulara Federacio de Otani sekto en Osaka distrikto. La II-a estas proponita de Budha-ŝa Budhana Junulara Asocio kaj la III-a estas proponita de Junulara Fako Tokia de Budhisma Savarmeo. Kaj ili estas triope diskutita en la ĝenerala laborkunsido de la jarkunveno. Kompreneble ĝi estas aprobita kaj la speciala komitato por tiu eble organiĝos.

Mi pri ĉi tiu entrepreno sentas gravan sencon. La kaŭzo de la suferado de tuta mondo efektive estas internacia malpaciĝo sed ornamita, mi ne povas diri ke la aero en Oriento ankaŭ Okcidento estas klara, efektive la peza atomosfero minacante estas tutan mondon. Ĉu kiel japana proverbo "Dubo naskigas demonon" prezentas, ĉiuj nacioj, ĉiuj regnoj tiel meme naskigas malamikecon? Mi firme kredas ke ĉiuj malpaciĝoj estas devenitaj de la manko de reciprokaj elkomprenoj. Ĉiuj devas esti pacamantoj. Ĉiuj volas meman feliĉiĝon, sed je la realo ofte ni prenas tute malan pro tia memkontraŭeco por la harmoniĝo, religio estas nature naskiĝita.

Se devenigas militon kaj batalon tiu kiun oni ne povas nomi kiel veran religion. Budhismo efektive staras sur la doktrino kiu konsistas el altruismo kaj pacamo. Do, mi havas dubon pri kial la prenantoj tiel nomataj paciĝan movadon en Okcidento ne manprenas al Budhanoj. Ili preskaŭ ne scias pri Budhismo, sekve ili erarkomprenis japanujon. Japana kulturo estas ja Budhisma kulturo, tion mi povas diri fierŝ. La historio jam 2600 jarojn pasinta japanujo efektive estas daŭro de la pacamo kaj plenata de justeco. Tute ne estas kruda kaj batalo. Ĉi tiu kompreneble estas influita de Budhismo. Por ĉi tiun fakton prezenti kaj sciigi en tutan mondon, la universala kongreso estas plej bona okazo samtempe ĝi eble faros novan epokon por la movado de pacamo tutmonda.

Laŭ la Esperanta Enckropedio kvinono da homoj el tuta homaro estas Budhanoj, se ili ĉiuj ekstarus por ĉi tiu pacama movado, la konstruo de la sukhavatio surtera ne estus neebla. Kompreneble oni tute ne devas preni religion kiel la rimedon por politiko. Se iu religio estas uzata por la politiko, tiu signifas sian degenerion.

Ni rigardis kaj trovis la sencon en la pasinta Tutpacifika Konferenco de Budhanaj Gejunularaj Asocioj kiel la premison al la Universala Kongreso. Do, la realiĝo de la kongreso estas por mi, granda ĝojo. Ankaŭ ĉiuj Budhanoj ne devas ŝpari la favoron kaj la subtenon al la dirita okazota epokfaranta kongreso.

La sesa jarkunveno de Tutjapana Federacio de Budhanaj Gejunularaj Asocioj

Kiel la plej potencan organizon Budhisman el tuta japanujo, la konata, Tutjapana Federacio de Budhanaj Gejunularaj Asocioj okazis la sesan jarkunvenon ĉe la centra pubrika salonego en urbo Osaka, de la 25a de Aprilo, dum du tagoj. El ĉiuj partoj de tutu japanujo pli ol 900 da delegitoj partprenis.

Je la duono post la 10a en la unua tago, per la malferma saluto de s-ro T. Fuĵitani kiu estas la ĉefsekretario de Osaka distrikta federacio, estas malfermita. Rekomendo la prezidanton, la vicprezidantojn, diversajn komitatojn, la sekretariojn kaj ĉeterajn. En la muzikado la starigo la standardojn de ĉiuj distriktaj federacioj. La adorado. Ĥoro la kanton de J. B. A. (Junulara Budhana Asocio). La saluto de la jarkunvena prezidanto. Raporto de la ĉefsekretario de tutjapana federacio pri la ago dum pasinta unu jaro. Gratulaj paroloj de Osaka prefekto, Osaka urbestro kaj la prezidanto de urba ĉambro de komerco kaj industrio. Lego ricevitajn gratultelegramojn. Per ili la malferma soleno estas fermita.

Post la tagmanĝo la komitato

por la proponoj raportis pri la divido la ricevitajn proponojn. La akceptitaj proponoj je la oficejo de la tutjapana federacio, estas sume 58, kiujn dividis la komitato, por faciligi la diskuton, kiel jene :—

11 proponoj estas diskutotaj en la ĝenerala laborkunsido.

8 proponoj estas diskutotaj en la unua faka kunsido.

17 proponoj estas diskutotaj en la dua faka kunsido.

18 proponoj estas diskutotaj en la tria faka kunsido.

4 proponoj estas diskutotaj en la virina faka kunsido.

Kaj ĝis la 14a per la prezido de s-ro E. Hon-da la ĝenerala laborkunsido estas okazita. De la 14a ĝis la 17a kaj en la dua tago de la 9a ĝis la tagmezo ĉiuj fakaj kunsidoj estas okazitaj.

"En la jaro 2600a de Japana erao (la jaro 1940a post Kristo) lokon kavu universala Budhana kongreso en japanujo."

Citita estas plej skribinda el la 58 proponoj, kaj proponita de Budha-ŝa junulara asocio kaj Tokia junulara fako de Budhisma savarmeo. Kaj ĝi, estas unuanime aprobita post la klarigo de la proponantoj en la ĝenerala laborkunsido.

Mi ankaŭ sendis la proponon pri Esperanto, en la nomo de junulara ligo de Budhisma savarmeo.

"La tutjapana federacio de budhanaj gejunularaj asocioj havu specialan komitaton pri Esperanto kaj realigu Esperantan edukadon al la gejunularo."

Ĉi tiu estas diskutita en la tria faka kunsido, mi detale klarigis pri Esperanto, kompreneble ĝi estas aprobita de la fakanoj.

En dua tago post tagmezo ree okazita, la ĝenerala laborkunsido. La prezidantoj de la kvar fakaj kunsidoj raportis pri siaj laboroj. Per tiuj la jarkunueno estas fermita. Kaj mi ankaŭ pensi ke ĉi tiu tutjapana federacio estas promesante la favoron al Esperanto.

La manifesto en Kiota kongreso de Budhisma Savarmeo

Ĉi tiu-jara kongreso de Budhisma Savarmeo lokon havis ĉe la granda salonego de "Ŝoŭa-kaikan," de 29a de Aprilo ĝis la 1a de Majo, en Budhisma urbo Kioto. El tuta japanujo pli ol 600 anoj partprenis kaj en la ĝenerala kunsido publikigis jenan manifeston.

La Manifesto

Nun la politika situacio de japanujo estas efektive grava. Kaj la foriganto ĉi tiun eksterordinaran tempon estas sole la sana kaj fortika koro de la popoloj.

Sed lastatempe, superstiĉaj herezoj estas fiere agantaj, la similaĵoj al religio estas pligrandiĝaj. Tiuj estas klare rakontanta per la realaĵo la senbaziĝon kaj kofuziĝon de komspirita vivo. Ili efektive estas kaŭzita de la maldiligenteco kaj malatenteco de ni Budhanoj, do, tial ni sentas grandan konteccon.

En la Okcidento la atomosfero ne estas klara kaj estas peza, kaj prezentas la scenon de terura buĉado, kiu signifas ke malfortaj estas ĉiam kaptaĵoj de fortoj. Ankaŭ la Oriento estas sub la danĝereco. Do, ni Budhanoj kies idealo estas paciĝo de tuta nomaro, devas havi grandiozan decidon.

Ĉi tie ni okaze de ĉi tiu kongreso en Kioto, renovigante meman vivon, pliprofundigante meman kredon kaj plifortigante meman kunligecon, en la lando diskonigu veran doktrinon, kaj per tiu plifortigu la spiritan vivon de la nacio, ekster la lando prezentante la amlumon de la Budho penadu la realiĝon de monda paco, per tiuj plimultigu la eternan feliĉon de tuta homaro.

Supran ni manifestas.

Kiotan la 29an de Aprilo, 1936
Tutjapana kongreso de
Budhisma Savarmeo.

Ankaŭ la kongreso decidis jenajn tri principojn de siaj agoj.

1. Penadu forigi superstiĉajn herezojn.
2. Penadu plenigi religian edukadon.
3. Penadu diskonigi internacie la Budhismon.

Japanese News

Donation Given German Universities

To encourage the study of Japanese culture in Germany, Mr. Kinya Nagao, president of the Wakamoto Company of Tokyo, who is touring Germany at present, made a monetary donation of ¥100,000 recently. The donation will be presented to the principal universities in Germany through Viscount Kimitomo Mushakoji, Japanese Ambassador to Germany, shortly. Some libraries of Japanese books will be established at these universities with funds.

Japan Hall Elected in Lahore, India

With a view to promote cultural relations between India and Japan, a Japan Hall was recently constructed in Lahore, India, to lodge Japanese students there. The Society for the International Cultural Promotion of Japan plans to send books concerning Japan to the new institution shortly.

Memorial Rites for Labor Leader

Memorial rites for the late Shunji Nakamura, pioneer and founder of the Japanese labor school has been held at the Seikei Gakuen. Kichijoji, Tokyo Prefecture, June 21 Sunday on the occasion of the 13th anniversary of the death of the founder. A bust for the late Mr. Nakamura which has been made by Mr. Seibo Kitamura, well known sculptor was unveiled at the occasson. The bust has been presented by the 2,000 former pupils of the school who were instructed by the labor school leader.

Mt. Fuji opened to public July 1

Mt. Fuji was opened to the public on July 1. Mrs. Kame Endo, 42-year-old resident of Osaka attempted to climb up the mountain June 21 Sunday. She left Omiya, Shizuoka Prefecture, Sunday morning. She took a rest at the sixth station on the mountain and reached the sacred peak on Monday. She is the first to attempt the climb this season.

Students to Visit Siam on Mission

The Takushoku Daigaku, or the Colonial College of Tokyo, will send two students to Siam during this summer to promote goodwill relations between Japan and Siam and

to make an inspection trip. Mr. Ryo Ochiai and Mr. Tomoichi Ito have been appointed representatives of the college.

Ancient Chinese Tiles Found in Nagano

Some old tiles were discovered at the home of Kotaro Yoshida, resident at Haraichimachi, Usui-gun, Nagano Prefecture, recently. They were estimated by a certain expert to be 1,300 years old and to have come from China. The tiles are ornamented with figures and animals as well as family crest. They are rare historical objects.

Bon Festival for Foreigners

In order to console the spirits of Foreign residents who died in Japan, the Honganji Temple in Tsukiji, Tokyo was held "Bon" Festival dances on July 7 at 7 p.m. On that occasion, there was also been burning of incense by the diplomatic corps and a reading of sutras for departed foreigners.

The "Bon" dances was been performed by the priests of the Honganji.

Critic and Novelist may visit China

Mr. Kan Kikuchi, noted novelist, known critic, may go to China in order to promote friendly relations between Japan and that country. The measure was first proposed by Mr. Kawagoe, Japanese Ambassador to China, who considers that not only diplomatic but also cultural cooperation of the two countries is necessaray to promote friendship between them.

Recently works of both Mr. Kikuchi and Mr. Hasegawa are being read by Chinese in translation. If the plan materializes, it is expected to impress favorably the Chinese intellectual class.

Only two Believers Left for Omotokyo

Almost all adherents of the recently prohibited Omotokyo sect have been converted to other faiths. The only professed believers remaining in the country are Shikaoki Wada, 47, the director of a branch church of the forbidden religion in Kochi city, and his disciple. The Kochi police have decided to arrest them shortly.

Founder of Yedo to be Honored

Memorial rites for Ohta Dokan, constructor of Yedo Castle, was observed at Hibiya Park, Tokyo, on July 26 on the occasion of the 450th

and Mr. Nyozekan Hasegawa, well anniversary of his death. A dramatic film, "Dokan and Kakesara," written by the late Dr. Shoyo Tsubouchi was released at the festival. This film was made under the direction of Dr. Tsubouchi in 1930 and performed by the Juvenile Art Society of Waseda University. The film is to be shown to the public for the first time.

Beppu Bamboo Workers Busy

The Society for the Study of Bamboo Artwares of Beppu, Oita Prefecture, received an order from a department store in New York City recently to make 300,000 bamboo toys. The workers of the society are quite busy making these objects at present. However, there are only 200 workers in the town. They will finish these orders by September.

Samurai as Mascot for Mexican Minister

Major-General Francisco J. Aguilar, Mexican Minister to Japan, intends to fly from Tokyo to Madrid via South China and India this October. He will use a Stinson Reliant monoplane.

Mr. Seiji Togo, a wellknown painter in Tokyo, is now painting on the aileron of the Mexican Minister's plane a samurai drawing a bow as a mascot.

Waterfall Rejects Would-be Suicide

A young man jumped into the Kegon waterfall near Nikko at about 4 p.m. July 5 Sunday in order to kill himself. Due to the rainy season, however, the force of the water was so great that the youth was flung on to the land opposite the waterfall instead of sinking into the basin.

The youth who has miraculously escaped death proved to be Yoshio Fukui second son of a former member of the Parliament from Kanagawa Prefecture. He sustained only a slight bruise on his forehead in his attempt at suicide.

Society to Listen for Lotus to Pop

The Society for the Study of Botany of Tokyo Imperial University was held an inspection party of the lotus flowers on the banks of Shinobazu pond in Uyeno Park early in the morning of July 24. Last Summer they discussed whether the lotus flowers make a sound on its opening or not, hence they studied again the lotus as a party.

U.S.-Japanese Students' Meeting

The third annual conference of Japan-American students will be held at Waseda University from August 1. The conference was held for the first time in 1434. Since then, it has been continued by them to promote goodwill relations between Japan and America. Some 50 American students arrive in Tokyo to attend the conference here this year. They will arrive at Yokohama on board the N.Y.K. line Tatsuta Maru on July 29.

Buddhist Cathedral in Hsinking

A Buddhist cathedral which has been under construction in Hsinking, will be completed at the end of July. The building of the temple was proposed by the Rev. Gempo Yamamoto, priest of the Ryutaku Temple in Mishima, Shidzuoka Prefecture, in order to promote friendly relations between Japan and Manchoukuo through Buddhism. The Rev. Yamamoto, who is 70 years old, will leave Mishima for Hsinking shortly to become the first chief priest of the Hsinking Cathedral.

To Fete Translator of Buddhist Sutra

The Kegonkyo, one of the most difficult sacred Buddhist Sutra was translated into Japanese from Chinese by Mr. Koson Kobe, professor at Nippon University, recently. A meeting to celebrate his completion of the translation was held at the Rainbow Grill, Tokyo by Mr. Beiho Takashima, Mr. Ishimaru and several other scholars and friends of the translator on July 11.

Library of 16.000 Books given to Okayama College

Kyoson Tsuchida, well known literary critic and scholar who died some time ago, left some 16,000 volumes of books in his private library. The late Mr. Tsuchida was the brother to the late Bakusen Tsuchida, noted Kyoto painter who died last June. The library has been kept at the Ohara Social Science Research Institute at Osaka since his death, but the widow of the scholar decided to present it to the Sixth Higher College at Okayama recently.

Dr. Anezaki to be sent to Italy

Encouraged by the successful result of the Japanese-Italian exchange of professors started under its sponsorship since this spring, the Cultural Works Bureau of the Foreign Office has decided to carry on the work with greater efforts and has made arrangements to send to Italy Dr. Masaharu Anezaki, honorary professor of Tokyo Imperial University, as a cultural envoy to give a series of lectures on Buddhism at the universities at Rome, Bologna, Naples and Torino, it is reported.

Dr. Sevelli, Italian mathematician of world-wide reputation, came to Japan this spring as an exchange professor from Italy and gave lectures at Tokyo, Kyoto and Tohoku Imperial Universities. His lecture on parabola function in particular endowed the scientific world of Japan with beneficial fruits. In recognition of his meritorious service for the scientific cause, the Italian savant was decorated with the Second Order of the Sacred Treasure.

It is in order to return this scientific mission from Italy that Dr. Anezaki has been selected to undertake the task. The Japanese Government, through the Embassy in London, has communicated with Dr. Anezaki at present there on a visit, and after making arrangements with the Italian authorities, detailed arrangements will be decided upon, it is expected.

On the other hand, it is reported that Mr. Ikuma Arishima, noted artist, who with Mr. Toson Shimazaki will attend the 10th conference of the International P.E.N. Club to be held at Buenos Aires, will go on to Italy at the invitation of the East Asia Association of Italy and give a series of lectures at Rome University for a month from the beginning of November of this year, it is reported.

Statue of Jizo

By one of the railway crossings between Shimokitazawa and Nakabara, a stone statue of Jizo, patron deity of children, will be erected shortly to console the spirits of eight persons who lost their lives in traffic accidents at this spot. The idea was first introduced by Mr. Junkyu Koseki whose two children were killed in a railway accident at the place. The funds which have been raised for the erection of the statue have amounted to more than 560 yen. The Jizo statue will be about four feet high.

P.E.N. Club Delegates to be Feted in Osaka

A farewell meeting for Mr. Toson Shimazaki and Mr. Ikuma Arishima, who are leaving for the Argentine to attend the world congress of the

P.E.N. Club at Buenos Aires shortly, was held in Osaka by leading writers and novelists at 6 p.m., July 15. The sponsors of the party are Dr. Izuru Shimaura, Messrs. Chokusai Shiga, Junichiro Tanisaki, Hiroshi Shimomura, Sofu Taketomo and several others.

On the occasion of the party, they will discuss the plan of establishing a branch of the P.E.N. Club of Japan in Osaka. Mr. Shimazaki and Mr. Arishima was leaved Tokyo July 14 Tuesday for the Kansai, and sail from Kobe on July 16.

Kabuki Founder's Monument Unveiled

The memorial monument for Okuni, founder of the classic Japanese Kabuki play was unveiled in the compound of the Honoyama of Taishamachi, Shimane Prefecture on July 9. The monument was made by Mr. Fumio Asakura, well known Tokyo sculptor. The work, in relief, of the portrait of Okuni has been installed in the stone monument. The ceremony of the unveilment was held there at 9 a.m. and a number of prominent people assisted at the rite.

Tourist Bureau Opens New Branch

A new tourist information bureau for visitors to Tokyo was opened on the second floor of the Marunouchi Building under the direction of the Tokyo Municipal Office on July 3. Almost all tourist, both Japanese and foreigners, visit the building once during their stay in Tokyo. The bureau will give information concerning sightseeing in Tokyo free to all visitors.

Siamese Student Home

To promote the good will relation between Japan and Siam, a Siamese student's home has been under construction in the compound of Prince Fumimaro Konoye at Yodobashi, Tokyo, for some time. The student's home is two stories high with six rooms, and has been provided by the Siamese Society. The home will take care of 15 Siamese students who will be selected from among 80 students in Tokyo.

Original Ukiyoye Blocks Preserved

Some 53 original wooden blocks for ukiyoye prints by Shunei Katsukawa and Toyokuni Utagawa were presented to the Dramatical Museum of Waseda University by Mr. Kitaro Inouye, a resident at Morikawacho, Hongo, Tokyo, recently. These wooden blocks will be exhibited to the public at the museum shortly. They were made by the two famous painters of the Ukiyoye School for a book on the theater in Yedo days. When Shikitei Sanba, famous playwright wrote this book, these masters made a series of illustrations for it.

Brazilian Flag Presented Children

A national flag of Brazil has been presented to the Children's Red Cross Association of Japan by Mrs. Getulio Bardas, wife of the President of Brazil. The presentation was made to Prince Iyesato Tokugawa, president of the Japan Red Cross Society, through Mr. Pedro Leao Velloso, Brazilian Ambassador to Japan, on Monday afternoon, and is intended to foster good will relations between children of both countries. At the ceremony, Prince Tokugawa and Mr. Toru Eguchi, representative of the Children's Red Cross Association of Japan, made replies. Marquis Yorisada Tokugawa, President of the Japan-Brazilian Society, also made a speech.

Chinese Poetry Taught Lumpen

Shigin, or recitation of classic Chinese poems, is becoming popular again throughout the country. The Social Section of Nagoya Municipality is teaching this art to some 500 lumpen living in four municipal settlements, sending expert poem-reciters to these establishments.

The city authorities expect that the measure will improve the morals of lumpen and inspire a spirit of independence in them.

佛教之國際化

大谷瑩潤著
崔恩培譯

一　非常時日本與佛教復興

以滿洲事變爲契機，又所謂一九三五一九三六年之危機當前，我國上下內外成爲「非常時日本」一如其文字。而此「非常時日本」之認識，次第深刻　遂成我日本歷史之回顧矣　彼「大和魂」之新立場，其研究亦日益興盛。所謂日本精神之研究者，卽在於是，由此日本精神之研究，有「日本佛教」，此日本佛教，卽將新日本文化由根本上養育起來，對其眞價値之認識，旣已臻成熟，誠幸事也。

當明治維新日本精神之發揚，一部之政治家，不無錯誤之點，而「廢佛毀釋」之事以起，結果，其發揚並不徹底，不過與德川佛教以反省，成爲新明治時代佛教之革正而已。在今非常時，高唱日本精神，卽歷來構成日本文化一大中樞之日本佛教，當然加增一番新認識，斯堪稱爲時代之進化，可喜可賀，亦堪稱文化認識之正則也。我國文化，係集所有世界各國之精華，綜合之融和之，成爲眞能貢献人類社會之文化，就此點而論，日本佛教，所謂深植大乘佛教之根種，亦非過譽。具千三四百歷史之我日本佛教，諡仰賴當時　攝政聖德太子，將此大乘精神，盡攝諸彼十七條憲法中，卽所謂「篤敬三寶」，此佛教精神，在日本歷史上，如何發輝光大，不待多贅，亦人所知悉。然此日本佛教，際今非常時，由日本文化之再檢討上，已得正評；且進而稱「佛教復興」，甚囂塵於新聞雜誌之上。在昔鎌倉時代，日本曾際會非常之非常時，以此時代爲背景，反致几多之新佛教，日益昌盛，准昔觀今，此番非常時，或眞佛教復興之良好機會，亦未可知。

二　就汎太平洋佛教青年大會

自去年七月十八日，至二十一日，亘四日間，所開之大會者，汎太平洋佛教青年大會也，次在關西方面，亦開大會，斯爲第二回汎太平洋佛教青年大會，太平洋沿岸十三個民族，會萃一堂。在佛陀尊號之下，就現代種種問題，大乘佛教立場，互披瀝胸襟，相與論議。如斯新聞，當時各新聞紙，亦盛行報導，想均讀悉。其大會之議題，有印度聖地佛陀迦亞，現在異教徒手，佛教徒可收回之衝動之提議。第四部會，亦有國際平和人種平等等重要問題，作眞摰之討論，總會亦有如斯之決議。佛教由來取徹底的平和主義，釋尊亦曾教示種種理想的政治，卽非侵略主義，乃統治主義，用日本古代語申言之，卽非侵略乃統治也。縱之佛教非僅闡明死後之問題，就人類文化，實盡所有方面之指導，非止一民族一國家之宗教，以具有普遍的世界的擴張爲其本質者也。

如右所述，自教理上言之，各民族共存共榮，唯向世界的統一國家乃其所描寫之理想，凡少讀佛教經典者，當能共認，斯稱國際主義乎，抑稱世界主義乎，總算是普遍的世界宗教之佛教，故此次太平洋佛青大會，不可不謂爲充分的發揚其意義。

三　西洋沒落光出東方

最近歐洲哲學者，或思想家等輩間，盛倡「西洋沒落」，以冀喚醒其民衆。認哲學萬能，以物質偏重爲基礎之西洋文明，遂演成彼世界大戰，殘骸遍野，良足悲傷，因是之故，彼輩於今日，均異口同音曰，「光出東方。」依此喚醒之結果，前僅就植民政策立場上還未能研究之東洋研究，於焉興盛。先年予曾旅行歐美，有所觀察，見各地各大學，均有「東洋學」「佛教學」之講座研究室，不覺驚異，何以故，時至今日，歐美盛行研究東洋研究佛教，本屬創舉，固多係學問方面，然中亦不乏佛教信者，而此信仰之傾向，大有逐漸深刻之勢，受日本佛教得度之歐美人僧侶，尤層見迭出，此或佛光普照之證據。既有此傾向，昔基督教之宏宣於日本，今或日本佛教轉而加速度的宏宣於歐美人間，亦意中事。如此眞可稱爲光出東方，其時代，或決在不較遠之將來，亦決非夢中囈語。

四　東洋平和與佛教

以上就歐美而言佛教之國際化，尤其是在東洋諸國，此佛教之國際化，當更有重大意義，在二千六百年前，印度有釋尊降生，初說佛教，人所共知，其佛教之傳播，一南方，今之「錫倫」「爪哇。」一西域，卽中央亞細亞，經支那入日本，從之佛教二千五百年之歷史，其自體在東洋諸國，既已佛教國際化。然佛教發祥地之印度，後因異教徒之勃興，佛教大衰，支那昔曾佛教文化大放光明，所謂花於支那者，今亦似不振。獨我日本，任如何說法，可稱佛教尙生，不但尙生，且甚活潑。此實深大之存在，大聖聖德太子曾曰，唯我日本，眞是大乘相應之地，卽信奉大乘佛教相應之土地也。因相應故，遂致榮盛，因榮盛故，遂構成日本文化之中樞，佛教在現今世界，唯生存於日本，且極活潑，故此項歐美人士，爲研究此佛教，前來留學。不獨歐美人士已也，亞細亞諸國，亦來日本研究佛教，此生而活潑之日本佛教，今番經過支那，轉而向佛教發祥地之印度，爲一種逆輸入逆傳來之報道，亦不無其人。似此狀態，我輩日本佛教徒，此際宜具一大決心與覺悟。我國不可不以東洋平和之重鎮自居，決非僅以物質的眼光，窺透此一方面之事，必衆目目不能視，心之底湓，卽精神方面，用以防護亞細亞。於此宜在佛陀尊名之下，彼此爲堅級之握手，任何防衛方法，恐無逾於是。如是思維，日本佛教徒之使命，不能不痛感其重且大。既居佛教各宗之耆宿，與新興佛教徒之指導者大家，與夫號稱僧俗佛教徒之全部，結成一體，依佛陀大教，貢獻與世界人類精神文化之覺悟，尤感必要。（完）

資料　世界大同佛教總支分會簡明一覽表

會別	會長姓名	會員數目	會別	會長姓名	會員數目
新京總會	張景惠	607	楡樹五棵樹分會	張元亨	365
濱江省支會	增韞	452	方正縣分會	佟玉勛	97
扶餘長春嶺分會	李玉蓮	54	錦州省支會	馮長賡	216
伊通縣分會	范德光	151	法庫縣分會	濟三	154
農安孫家油坊分會	張廷玉	56	鐵嶺縣分會	旻空	250
德惠郭家屯分會	鼎會濤	53	康平縣分會	宮樑棟	102
德惠雙山子分會	呂樹棠	51	通遼縣分會	釋能慧	294
敦化縣分會	婁保倉	250	昌圖縣分會	朱益淸	275
雙城縣分會	趙駿	502	安圖縣分會	梁嘉田	200
九臺縣分會	崔澤蘭	485	開原縣分會	王錫九	496
扶餘五家站分會	郝文濂	111	遼陽第一分會	顧子章	62
扶餘北井分會	李潤靑	73	開原八寶屯分會	張顯珍	248
扶餘城隍廟分會	苗永泰	331	開原大白廟子分會	王丹書	56
扶餘極樂寺分會	楊紹信	105	開原小孫家臺分會	楊峻峰	55
扶餘頭井子分會	常玉	60	鐵嶺李千戶屯分會	汪得香	124
扶餘大青山分會	張露亭	72	東豐縣分會	姜鳳岐	240
扶餘浩色站分會	楊榮芳	71	遼源縣分會	王紹文	93
扶餘石城鎭分會	生貴	104	海城縣分會	釋安宏	52
扶餘龐家窩堡分會	劉惠	53	西安縣分會	孫家麟	392
扶餘雙山子分會	劉國鈞	50	綏中縣分會	尹顯庭	54
扶餘大三家子分會	劉鳳春	56	開魯縣分會	毋樹棠	56
扶餘西三家子分會	宋蓮發	56	呼蘭縣分會	劉永河	202
扶餘長春嶺分會	于占學	85	龍江省支會	鄂匡九	214
扶餘興隆堡分會	呂振卿	54	昌圖八面城分會	閻性治	58
舒蘭苍草頂子分會	黎善修	107	壽平興隆寺分會	金榮椿	407
舒蘭開原屯分會	潘文德	320	狀河大孤山分會	靜寬	313
舒蘭霍倫川分會	修殿漢	195	北鎭閭陽驛分會	李鶴鳴	64
舒蘭法特哈門分會	楊長春	112	龍江省富爾基分會	郝玉芝	65
舒蘭九頂山分會	邵好善	184	凌南八家子分會	烏凌雲	57
舒蘭西南岔分會	宗耀	130	開魯保安鎭分會	劉華洲	62
永吉縣缸窰鎭分會	楊文魁	176	龍江省安達站分會	馬春明	91
			昌圖金家屯分會	張敬興	116

鐵嶺鎭西堡分會	趙恒坤	77
梨樹四平街分會	申福明	102
開通邊昭分會	周秉衡	54
五常太平山分會	葛松亭	140
綏安靠山屯分會	郭雨軒	246
璋平湯池分會	張永清	55
扶餘佛母廟分會	彭悟生	52
扶餘娘娘廟分會	解蕊貞	51
雙城葛家崴子分會	葛錫源	64
肇州縣分會	曹青春	96
朝陽華嚴寺分會	蘊虛	93
雙陽縣分會	丁愼修	210
闊西榆林鎭分會	李國棟	91
大賚縣分會	孫雨三	64
濛江縣分會	王心如	100
磐檢縣分會	劉漢棠	53
乾安縣分會	楊廣陞	50
輝南縣分會	陳宗舜	63
璋河縣分會	丁潤棠	184
西豐縣分會	姜相臣	121
赤峰縣分會	李及時	71
海龍縣分會	馬子峰	186
瀋陽縣分會	綏譚	65
依蘭太平鎭分會	艾週霖	62
懷德黑林鎭分會	李郁亭	98
呼蘭樂安鎭分會	韓維周	57
熙山勞山鎭分會	曹青春	69
泰康他爾哈站分會	孫宣三	83
伊通營城鎭分會	黃治國	52
綏安通家屯分會	連運太	63
德惠張家灣分會	懸濟	55
昌圖五百天地分會	張喜	121
義縣大籽粒屯分會	李長泰	74
榆樹弓棚鎭分會	姚興五	85
昌圖杏山村分會	劉安錬	71
九臺縣四臺屯分會	劉成德	61
昌圖 山堡分會	黃仮齡	58
榆樹公立念佛堂	張郁叙	216

安東省城支會	乘如	93
慶城縣分會	王坤	77
林西縣分會	黃尙明	61
洮南天臺山分會	劉恩明	62
寧安縣分會	丁印堂	67
鳳城縣分會	劉文英	76
洮安普渡佛堂	張蘭亭	64
綏安興隆鎭分會	邵永科	58
錦州葫蘆島分會	常洗塵	60
奉天皇姑屯分會	孫洗塵	52
綏安伏龍泉分會	鄧叙五	57
扶餘東門外分會	韓翼廷	99
開通海雲寺分會	王清陽	82
東寧縣分會	何慶吉	63
富錦縣分會	劉柏鈞	60
興城縣分會	李文山	64
梨樹縣分會	王伯勳	102
朝陽縣支會	原修五	244
雙城帽山分會	劉纂賢	21
五常縣分會	劉景春	92
扶餘榆樹溝分會	趙珍	68
榆樹靑山堡分會	蕭永霖	54
望奎縣分會	謝占裕	127
榆樹閻家屯分會	孫花	73
洮南瓦房鎭分會	程宏儒	57
興安南省西科中旗高力阪分會	佟明璋	95
明水平安堡分會	劉甄亭	71
撫松縣分會	蔣維亮	54
臨榆蔡各莊分會	劉克成	64
德惠縣分會	張紹卿	63
遼源茂林站分會	侯良弼	55
延壽縣分會	趙文彬	62
熙山新立屯分會	曹青春	73
金川縣分會	安清	72
遼陽第二分會	曹化一	60
德惠老邊崗分會	邵正修	165
明水縣分會	喬振忠	127
扶餘德善村分會	李豐	169
濱江省分會	增子固	597

總計 一百四十會，會員一萬八千三十六名

資料

臺灣幽囚の印象

閩南佛學院教授 慧雲

沈默を破つて私に關心を持つ師友に訴ふ

私の消息が絕えてから隨分久しい。私の存亡は師友の間で一つの謎の樣に捉えることが出來なかつたであらう。だが，私の生命は依然として今日も此の世に存在してゐる。で，私を愛する師友諸賢に對して先づ安慰を乞ふ次第である。

實は私が數奇な運命に遭遇した爲めに，最近多數の師友達から來る手紙は，皆同じ樣に此のことを心配して，私の一年間の遭難の經過を尋ねて來てゐる。私はその度に返事を書いて概略は報導したが，皆に一々滿足を與へることは出來ない。そこで，私は此處に感想を公開し，私に關心を有せらるゝ皆樣に報告する譯である。

私は民國二十三年の夏，上海から厦門の閩南佛學院に歸り，一二ケ月滯在してゐるとき，臺灣の開元寺から招かれたので，弘法に出かけたが，本來は一ケ月餘りで直ぐ歸る考だつた。處が意外にも，私がまさに歸國の途に上らんとしてゐる時に際し，臺灣の役人から理由もなく逮捕せられた。役人達は無理に證言を作つて頑强に禁錮し，嚴然として亡國の苦痛を嘗めさせた。私の消息は此の時から突然絕えたので外部からは私の失踪に對して全然知ることが出來なかつたであらう。私が捕はれの身となつてから後，臺灣政府は嚴重に秘密を守り，昨年の一月十六日から今年の一月十一日まで，恰度一ケ年間，私の生命は時々危險に曝され，私の精神上と肉體上に受けた刺激と苦痛は，勿論外部から想像出來る所でなく，筆舌を以て能く形容出來ることでもない。

遭難の間には，多くの內外師友から奔走して頂き，我國の駐日大使及び駐臺北總領事から嚴重なる抗議をせられたので，最近始めて私の自由が恢復出來たのである。已に二月十三日の午後無事祖國の土地を踏み，今では一切が凡て夢の如くに過ぎ去つて了つた。幸にも私の身體は今日も尙ほ健全に生きてゐて，私を愛する師友達と相見えることが出來るが，これは私が獄中に幽閉せられてゐる間は夢にも考へられなかつたことである。

昨年臺灣南瀛佛教會報第九期に，二首の私を弔ふ悼詩が掲載せられた時，全國の佛教徒は始めて一種の大きな刺激を受けた。香港の人海燈の編者と厦門の福善君は，私の死について一篇の有力な評論を書いた。此れに因つて初じめて日本の佛教界の輿論と反響を惹起した。各處相識の師友は私の遭難を開いて，私の爲めに追悼會を開き，私の爲めに同情の涙を灑いで吳れた。此れ等の師友諸氏に對しては，感謝の外又何をか語ることが出來やう。

時宛も中日佛教徒が，親善提携を高唱してゐる最中に，此の様な事件が發生したことは，實に遺憾とせざるを得ないことである。然しながら，私の様なこんな微小な人物に，中日國際間にこのやうな巨大な波瀾を引き起したことは，實に私の夢にも思ひ及ばんことであつた。

私個人の態度から言へば，日本國民の堅苦奮闘の毅力と沈擊好學の精神に對しては，前から相當の敬意を表してゐる。そこで私個人の思想は，擧國一致で抗日精神を繼續してゐる中に於ても，猶ほ私の愛日の態度は減じない。これは私が敢えて斷言する所である。けれども，私の親日愛日の態度は，日本の德川時代，山崎闇齋氏の孔孟を尊敬したと同様な心理である。

山崎闇齋は日本德川時代の儒學の泰斗であるが，ある日講學の後で門人に向ひ，突然こんな問を發した。『若しも支那の孔子が大將となり，孟子が副將となつて，兵を率ひて日本に攻め來らば，諸子は如何にせんとするか』と。一座は愕然として答ふる者がなかつたが，稍あつて此の老儒者は厲聲一喝し『若しそんなことがあつたら，それは直ちに打ち破れば良いのだ，それこそ孔孟の教えてゐる所である』と。

若しも中日兩國の國民が，眞に提携して共に進み，協力して東洋文化と大乘佛教の救世精神を闡揚するならば，中日兩國の前途と，世界人類の幸福の爲めに，どうして努力に値しないと言へやうか。しかし日本にして今の如く限りなき野心を暴露し，正に全中國の民族を如何に奴隷化すべきかを考へてゐるなら，彼等と如何に親善提携を講じやうとしても，それは結局痴人の夢であると言はざるを得ないだらう。

日本の松岡洋右が國際聯盟から歸つた時，日本國民に告げた書の中に次の様に言つてゐるのを覺えてゐる。『今日中國の一般青年は全然抗日の態度を改めてゐない。しかし，假りに日本を打ちのめしたとし，中國の國民は果して眞に幸福と言へるであらうか？ 中國が今日となつても，まだ，曲りなりにも全地を有し，其の獨立の存在を保持することが出來るのは，其の背後の力は抑々誰であるか？ これは中國の青年諸君が充分に考へて見ねばならぬことである。若しも日本が無かつたなら，中國は恐らく遠うの昔に他國の爪牙に依つて分割されてゐるであらうと』。

又或る人が言つた。『米國々務長官が全中國領土の保全を紙上に宣告したので，その爲めに中國の領土は保全せられてゐるのであると。しかし米國々務長官の魔力が如何に大であつても，若しも一外交文書の力量で，中國の領土が完全に保持することが出來ると言ふなら，其は矢張り夢を說くものと言はざるを得ない。又，中國の領土を能く今日まで保持し得た眞實の力は，日本

の國力が後に控へてゐるからだと言ふことも，どうしても承認出來ない事である。‥‥考へても見よ，松岡は何と綺麗に語つても，實は外交家の諷刺的能事で，彼が國際聯盟で樽俎折衝の間に於て，三寸不爛の舌を操つて全世界の視聽を聳動したのに見ても，それは彼には當り前のことである。

眞面目に考へて，若し日本の攪亂と離間の挑發が無かつたなら，中國も已に國際殖民地的地位を脫し，その統一と自由平等の功業を完成してゐたかも知れない。其うして何も今日になつて，まだ，國難の聲の中に生命を苦しめてゐなくても良かつた筈ではあるまいか。日本が若し強いて蠻力を恃んで勝手なことをするならば，中國は必ずや死地に陥るにきまつてゐる。思ふにその壓迫が極度に達すれば，一時に反抗が起つて來て，結局は只兩國々民が同じく悲惨な境地に陥るばかりである。聰明な松岡は恐らく這の間の事を思ひ付かんことはなかつたであらう。

私の捕へられた經過と監禁中の生活に關しては，私は別に回想記を書く積りであるが，しかし，私の捕へられた原因は，不思議に今日となつても私自身にさえまだ判然りしない。私が嚴重に調べられた時に際しては，暴力の威迫の下で，勿論無理矢理に，一切の罪狀を作り上げられたのを聽いてゐたばかりである。要するに『君は政治陰謀の策動者である，と言ふのはお前は政治的陰謀の策動者と俺が言ふからである。お前は世と爭をしない和尚ではあるが，皆から見れば最も注意に値すべき危險人物である。』と言ふのである。

こゝに，我々の忘れることの出來ない一つの故事がある。日清戰爭前に當つて，日本の某貴族の將軍が支那僧を裝つて屢々臺灣に來り，詳細極まる臺灣全島要塞地圖を作つて行つた。その後馬關條約で臺灣の割讓を署名するところ，臺灣の一般民衆は愛國心の爲めに，少からぬ民衆が聯合して，民軍を作つて抗戰した。相對峙すること三ケ月の久しきに及んだが，日軍は終に一步も上陸することが出來なかつた。ところへ，此の曾て支那僧に化裝した和尚の將軍が，兵を指揮して前進したので，各所の險要も始めて陸續として陷落され，つひに臺灣全土を喪失したのである。此の和尚は卽ちあとで，臺灣征服の第一の功に依つて總督に任ぜられた，樺山その人であつたと言ふ事である。

過去に以上のやうな椿事があつたので，日本が今まさに口々に『非常時』を叫んでゐる時に當つて，彼等の所謂帝國の南方の門戶に，僧侶の深く這入つて行くことを，どうして輕々に看過し得やうか。

最も奇怪なのは，日本の某佛教新聞の海外通信記者が，私の捕へられた原因に關して，只だ私に赤色の嫌疑が有つたからだと報じたが，こんな出駄羅目は，勿論一笑にも値しないことである。要するに弱國の國民は暴戾恣睢な者の鐵蹄下にあつても，一切口を開く餘地は無いのである。

語れば實に慚愧の限りで，我々國民は平日は實際餘りにも愛國心を知らない。そこで一旦國際問題が發生し，外交當局が九牛の一毛の力を費しても，而も猶ほ何の效果も無い。これは固より國力の衰弱にも因るが，外交官の後盾が足らず思ひ切つた强硬な言葉が使へない爲めで，これも一般國民の平素國家に對する觀念が，甚だ薄い結果から來るものであらう。日本は近來眼中人無きが如く，大陸に向つて蠶食の手段を取つてゐるのに，それでもまだ我々を發奮せしむるに足らないのか。吾が四億の民族は，永遠にその東夷の脚下に屈服するものであるか？　宜しい，徒らに侵略者の野心を指摘しても無益である。我々は須らく各方面で國力を充實さすべきである。空言の親善は用を爲さず，兩國の國力を平等にして始めて親善を言ふべきである。我國の國勢がこの微茫混沌たる中にも，已に幾分かの光明を發見して來た今日。若しも愛國を知らねば，恐らくは他日，更に愛に依つて起つことは出來ないだらう。(民國二五，三・四。廈門にて)

〔譯者久保田覺巳曰〕本文は「人海燈」月刊第三卷第五期，卽ち今年五月一日刊行のものに揭げられて香港より送つて來たのを譯出した。慧雲法師は江蘇省出身，本年廿九歲である。彼が臺灣に於て幽囚されたことに關し，彼はその何故であるかを少しも知らないといふてゐる。然し目下臺灣では誰知らないことのない某事件に關連して嫌疑を受けたことは勿論であつたが，慧雲法師は之と全く無關係なることが分つて晴天白日の身となつたのである。然し，それにしても，まる一年間の入牢は洵に氣の毒に堪えられないことであつた。彼の所論中に於ては，日本の大陸政策の眞意に就て十分に未だ理解してゐない點も見えるが，之は今後彼に諒解せしめねばならぬことである。

中國佛敎會調査
支那全國佛寺僧尼數

中國佛敎會理事長は從來全國佛寺及び僧尼の確實な統計が無いので，最近各分會に通牒を發し，又は人を派して調査中であつたが，此の程漸く完成しその發表に依れば全國大小寺廟庵院が二十六萬七千餘，僧尼計七十三萬八千餘人である。而して佛敎徒に出家の僧尼，優婆塞，優婆夷（男女居士）在家信佛敎徒で，近來在家佛敎徒は異常に發展增加しつゝあり，又全國寺廟中四川，河南，江西，安徽，湖南の數省は共匪に蹂躙せられ，僧尼の數は激烈な變動を來してゐるので，これは全然除外したのであると。

新刊紹介

◇普果拾遺（愚叟編輯，美濃判90紙，非賣品，新竹州，劉家水氏發行）

◇菩提正道菩薩戒論（宗喀巴上師造湯薌銘翻譯，美濃判117紙，後序5紙）

◇Parmoradoturna Sutro kaj Aliaj, p. 18, 1936, Roudeto de Budaisma Kulturo, Hongo. Tokio, Japanujo.)

伯林生活の思ひ出

榊　原　順　次

二ケ年半の伯林生活の間で，最も感じのよくなかつたのは，何と云つても，日本が熱河省攻擊を始めた頃から國際聯盟脫退前後の頃であつた。ドイツが聯盟を脫退して居らず，日本を同病者として憐れむ程な立場でもなかつたので，したがつてナチス政府に今日の樣な親日氣分も現はれて居なかつた。寧ろドイツ人は，イタリーの黃禍論の相槌を打つて，日本品排斥に大童であつた。だから全體的に日本に對して良い感じを持つてゐなかつた。何でもテンペルホーフのナチス大祭の日に，日本の一軍人がナチス團員に侮辱を受けたとか，小學校で日本人の子供が毆られたとかで，大使がナチス政府に抗議を申込んだとか云ふ樣な事件のあつたのも，たしか此頃だと思ふ。私等も町を散步してゐて，子供に石など投げ付けられたのを覺えてゐる。

何日か雜誌か新聞にこんなことが書いてあつたのを思ひ出す。「日本人はエヘラエヘラと笑ふ國民だ」と云ふ意味のことが――。と云ふ意味は，日本人は何もかも心得てゐて，しかも番頭さんのやうに揉み手をしながら「何も解りません田舍者で，エヘヘツ」と云つた態度で，工場や硏究所を覗いて步いて，急所々々を盜んで歸つてしまう。そして二年か三年のうちには，日本で考へたかの樣な顏をして，世界へドシドシ賣り出してしまう。實に油斷も隙きもならぬ日本人だと云ふ意味である。

ある會合で，飮み乍らドイツ人からこんな言葉をきいたことがある。「日本人と云ふのは，實に怪しからん國民ぢやないか。まあ考へて見給へ，明治以來の日本と云ふものは，殆んどドイツから敎へてもらつた樣なものぢやないか。醫學，工學は勿論のこと，法律も哲學も藝術も，まづドイツから敎へられないものはないと云つていゝ程ぢやないか。それだのに一朝ことあれば，恩義も何も忘れて，算盤をはじいて，都合のいゝ方にくつゝいて，ドイツを敵として戰つたぢやないか。實に日本人は義理人情をわきまへぬ，人非人だね」と云ふ樣なことを云つて，笑ひ乍らではあつたけれ共，私に恨みをのべたことがある。

これもある會合での話しであるが，ヤパン・インステイテュートのメンバーである一靑年が，こんなことを云つたのを思ひ出す。「日本の本當の其自身の文化とは何か？　近世までの日本文化卽ち飛鳥時代から奈良，平安，鎌倉の文化の中心，又はその主體をなすものは，殆んど支那朝鮮の輸入文化か模倣文化であり，また近代日本の文化の大部分は，歐米からの輸入か模倣の文化がその中心をなしてゐる樣に思はれる。本當の日本獨特の日本文化なるものがあるとしても，大したものぢやないのではないか？」と云ふのであつた。

是等の日本觀や批評が，甚だ認識不足の困つたものであり，また一部のこうした批判を全般的批判として考へる必要もないが，併し一應日本人として耳を傾けてよい聲だと思ふ。

當時の滿洲事變に對する歐洲人一般の考へは，まあ「人のよい文化人たる支那人を意地の惡い餓鬼大將である日本人が虐めてゐる」と云つた感じであつたらう。國際聯盟で松岡全權が如何に口をすつぱくして日本の正義を論じた處で，この本質的な惡童日本の感じがある限り，同盟日本と云つた氣持ちにはなれなかつたであらう。それだからこそ四十二對一等と云ふ孤立の擧を與へられたのではなかつたか。

この善良なる文化支那，好戰的野蠻日本と云つた誤れる先入主は，何から來たのか？　それは恐らく日本と支那との兩國文化に對する歐米人の理解の相違からであらう。實際，歐洲に行はれてゐる支那文化の紹介施設機關と日本のそれとを比べたら，全く問題にならぬ程の相違で，日本のそれに遙かに劣つてゐる。東亞の盟主，文化日本の躍進の爲めに，何と云つても悲しいことだ。

×

或る佛敎徒の會合で，こんなことを云つて困らされたことがある。「今，東北支那に於ては，××の爲めに罪もない幾多の支那人が戰爭の慘禍の爲めに苦しみあえいでゐるではないか。貴方はその日本の佛敎徒の一人として，それを何と見られますか？」と云ふ詰問であつた。その時の私の答へは，たしか「戰爭卽ち人殺しと云つた考へが，何時でも正しいかどうか？　戰爭卽ち人生かすと云ふ事實があるのではないか？云々」。更に「釋尊は勿論戰爭禮讃をされたとは思はれないが，また戰爭反對と云つた樣な，積極的運動を起された樣にも見えない。こゝに吾々佛敎徒のこうした問題に對する深い內省を必要とする，云々」尙ほ付け加へて「日本民族の眞の精神は，歐米人には恐らく解り惡いでせう。現に僧侶である私共も，國家の命令一下，勿論出征をするものである，云々」と云ふ樣なことを云つた樣におぼえてゐる。

僧侶の出征云々は，ひどく獨逸の佛敎徒を驚かせた樣に見えた。ドイツの佛敎徒の間には，可成り强く，日本佛敎は佛敎に非ずと云つた見解がある樣だ。殊に眞宗，眞言宗等に對しては，此の考へが强い樣だ。ダルケ博士等も日本を訪ねられ，大谷大學で講演もされ，眞宗に關して多少の知識を得てかへられたと思ふが，後に書かれたものを讀んで見ると「日本の眞宗は，人間の救濟を說く救濟宗敎としては誠に立派な一つの宗敎ではあるけれ共，佛敎と云ふ大事な足場からは離れてしまつてゐる」と書かれてゐる。

とにかく歐洲全體に日本佛敎はいささか繼子扱ひをされてゐると云つた感じがある。最近，故ゾルフ前大使の日本佛敎美術の紹介や，鈴木大拙博士の禪に關した出版物のお蔭で，ボツボツと日本佛敎硏究の曙光の見えることは事實である。

最後に日本佛敎の面目のために，一つの愉快なエピソートを紹介しやう。それは東京の實業家で森さんと云ふ人の坐禪のことである。始め伯林の日本人專門のホテル・エリキセンで一週間の接心を行はれた處が，女中が，「森さんは氣が違つたのだらう」と云ふのでコソコソと覗きに來て困ると云ふのでフローナウのお寺に來られた。丁度そこに私が居たので，いゝ連れがあるからと云ふので，二ケ月程の豫定でに寺下宿をされた。二月頃で，とても寒い頃である。その間に二回程，一週間づゝの攝心を行はれた。一日二食主義で期間中は一言ものを云はず，最後の晩には雪が降つてゐたが，その中にしかも屋外の林の中に一晩中朝まで座つてゐられた。これには流石の私も驚いたが，それにも增して驚いたのはドイツの佛敎徒だ。俗人乍らも此の眞劍な修道振りには，流石のドイツ佛敎徒も再考せずには居られなかつたらしい。しかも僧侶らしい生活もしてゐなかつた私共日本佛敎徒も，此の森さんの壯擧によつて完全に名譽回復が出來た樣にも思はれて，大いに胸がすいた樣に思つた。

常夏の布哇の思出

小谷徳水

常夏の布哇の思ひ出は，足かけ九年に亘るもの，いろいろの事と人と，今も鮮かに浮び出てくるが，佛青に關することを書いて見たいと思ひ立つた。

ホノルルに出たのは大正六年の三月の末であつた。布哇中學校の授業の外に，寄宿舎の舎監と，本願寺別院日曜學校の主事をやらされた。當時の本願寺別院は，現在の伽藍の建築中で，舊別院と稱した二丁ほど海手のところに，フオート街から少し引込んで，木造二階建の建物があり，庭を隔てゝ開教使諸君の住宅になつてゐるのが四棟その中の一棟が布哇佛教青年會に提供されてゐた。

小さくても佛青の建物があり，佛青の歴史は二十年あまりも經てゐる。會員は當時でも五六百はあつた樣である。月刊の同胞といふ機關誌は今も續いてゐるが，布哇に渡つてからはよくこの同胞誌上にいろんなものを書いたもので，ホノルルに出てからはその編輯もやらされた。然し佛青自身は存在してゐるといふ位のもので，定期又は臨時にいろんな催しがあり，その催しは相當の人は集めるが，會としては決して振つてゐるとは言へなかつた。今はホノルルで商業に從事してゐる村田龍一君が，夫まで語學校の教師をしてゐたのが，佛青の主事になつたのも，私のホノルルに出たのと前後してゐた樣に思ふ。

丁度この頃は米國が世界大戰に參加して，追々とあらゆる方面に戰時的な統制を强化し始めたのであつた。戰場とは遙かに隔つた太平洋上の孤島ながら，米國の參戰前には獨逸の巡洋艦が眞珠灣に逃げ込んだこと，日本の軍艦が之を追ふてきて見張りをしてゐる。某といふ法學士が暗夜に漁船に乘じて，眞珠灣内の獨艦について，日本の軍艦に報告に出かけたりして，ホノルルの日本字新聞は賑かなニユースを載せてゐた。參戰の後の米國が日毎に國家統制を進めて行つた情態は，今も忘れられぬほど吾々を驚かしたものであつた。よく輕い晝食をとりに行つた下町のレストラントは，今日は肉なし日だと言つて肉の皿が無くなつたり，砂糖は角砂糖を一つときめられて珈琲の甘さが薄くなつたりした。

その頃，布哇佛青の顧問といふ名目で宗務の加勢をすることがあつた。會は赤字つゞきであるが，戰時統制の波は弱い團體の手をも必要とすることがあり，佛青關係者の間にも積極的に，かゝる非常時にこそ米國のために在留同胞を動かして，平生安住の恩に報ふべきであるといふ論が高まつてきた。

村田主事に勸めて，赤字の中ながら佛青のホールを下町に開設した。支那人商店の二階に十四五坪の室があるのを，一ケ月五十弗かを拂つたのであつた。仕事を始めて後に，仕事に要する資金を得やうといふのであつた。從つて村田主事は資金をつくる事に頗る多忙になつたものである。その留守の間は，仕事の隙を見てはホールに出かけて，主事の代理をしたものであつた。あれは多分夏休みの後であつたらうと思ふ。布哇の政廳がやり始めた食料調節運動を，在留日本人の間に徹底せしめるために，本願寺の今村惠猛監督は群島中最大のハワイ島に出かけられた。今村監督よりも一足先きに村田主事も出かけてゐた樣に思ふ。その留守の間に幾度か政廳に出かけたり，電話の呼出しがあつたりして主事代理頗る忙しく面食つたことが思ひ出される。

今村監督はハワイ島を一巡して，在留同胞が農の國日本のことを忘れず，その布哇に於る家業も多くは農であることを思つて，食料調節にはもつと踏み込んで熱のある奉仕を行はうと決心された。そして別院内の編輯室にゐた田島金次郎氏と私とを呼んで，その事を語られたものである。餘談になるがこの編輯室といふのは，別院の新築落成までに，本願寺の布哇開教以來の歴史を書きとめて，記念の出版をするために置かれたもので，今は紐育のコロンビア大學の講師角田柳作氏が序編丈けを書いた後をうけて，田島氏と私とが二人で仕事をやつてたのであつた。

田島氏はペンネームを斷といひ，多くは神田金三の名を用ひた。神田で生れた金さんといふところに，江戸前の誇りもあつた樣である。ホノルルの知識階級でこの人の名を知らぬ人はなかつた位，劇通であり趣味人でありよく書いたものであつた。いろんな方面に常に新しい計劃を提示して，他の人が夫を實現して行くのを樂みにしてゐたが，編輯室での私との交りも多くはそんなものであつた。食料調節運動に對して，本願寺が眼ざましい活動をやつたのは，多くは田島氏の計劃であり私たちが夫を實現に努めたのであつた。食料調節の宣傳用パンフレツトなど，田島氏が一夜の間にいろんな資料を蒐めて提供する。それを又次の夜には私が一夜で書き上げて，三四日目にはドンドン發送するといふ樣に，うまくタイアツプした仕事であつた。

佛青のホール開設も田島氏の援助が大きかつた。その後に日本人間に始めての，佛青テニスコートを作つた時も田島氏は聲援してくれた。村田主事と共に，コート新設の費用三百餘弗を貰つて廻つたのは，布哇中學校の同僚で今はもうこの世には亡い澤康雄氏であつた。純情と情熱とがその一生を貫いてゐた忘れ得ぬ友の一人である。田島氏と同じく江戸ツ子で，上野に學びヴアイオリンをやつてゐた。今も世に行はれてゐる「らいさん」が生れたのは澤氏のこの世に殘したもので，山田耕作氏が佛教音樂に關係する樣になつたのも，澤氏がホールに立ち寄つた山田氏を迎へて，同窓の誼みが因となり，山田氏の病氣靜養が緣となつたものであつた。

布哇はホールの開設と，庭球部の新設を以て，新たな時代を開いて行つた樣に思ふ。私は大正七年の夏布哇別院の落慶の盛事をすまして，これから落ついて日曜學校の仕事をやらうとする時，子供の死んだ知らせに，急に思ひ立つて十月の末に歸朝した。從つて今の石造の佛青會館のことや，庭球部がホノルルに於ける有力なる存在となつたことなど，私の語りうることではないが，いろんな事を見聞する毎に，第一歩を動き出したといふ思ひ出を樂しんでゐる。

シカゴ大學比較宗教學教室の思出

川上賢叟

與へられた課題は「海外生活の思ひ出」といふのであつたが，生活の思ひ出と云ふと，餘りに漠然としてゐて，生活のどの斷面を書いてよいやら見當がつかなくなつたので，私は標記のテーマを用ひることにした。所與の課題とは聊か違つてゐるけれども，大學の教室に於ける思ひ出も，私の海外生活の一つの部面であるから，あながち御命令にそむいたとも思はない。

宗門から海外留學を命ぜられた時，私は少し考へるところがあつて，あちらこちらへ，研究視察するために，出張することを止めて，昭和元年三月から昭和四年末まで，シカゴ大學に踏み止り，かねて共鳴してゐた同大學の社會學教室に初めの二ケ年を過し，後の二ケ年を私の最も敬慕してゐるヘイドン博士の比較宗教學の教室で終り，目的の學位を得て大學院を卒業した。

ヘイドン博士は私の接した數多き學者（日本も含めて）の中で，最も尊敬する學者の一人である。その理由は博士の深き學識と熱のある教育的態度によることは勿論であるけれども，特に博士の人格が――其の內面的は勿論，外面的風彩までも，東洋的といふか，佛教的解脱を得た境地といふか，イギリス系の白人によく見受けるお家柄ぶつた氣持ちを片鱗も現はさず，極めて磊落の中にも，靜寂にして寛容な態度を以て學生に接せられたことである。博士のこの性格並に風格は，その專攻してをられる學問が，さうせしめたものと思はれるけれども，亦博士の天來の德性が，かく現はれて來たものと思ひ，一層博士の人格を慕つてゐるわけである。

博士の講義は日本の大學でみるやうなノート式ではなく，たとへば老子や孔子の宗教思想に就いて講義をさるゝ時，まるで自分が老子や孔子であるやうな熱意と自信を以て，言々句々，堂々としかも淳々として所信を述べ續けられる。聞き入る學生は全くチャームされて，たゞノートとしてではなく，ほんとうに授業をマスターするのである。私は內地の大學で教授が讀まれるノートをノートする時の，あの印刷屋の活字拾ひのやうな氣持ちに較べて格段の相違のあつたことを今でも忘れることが出來ない。尤も宗教學や宗教歷史の講義をさるゝ時は，その論證の文獻に就いては克明に指示されて，圖書館の書架番號まで紹介された。その眞面目にして懇切な態度は，學生をして眞に自分の研究に趣味と創造力を植え付けずにはをかなかつた。

殊に今尙私がハツキリと記憶してゐる先生の講義の中の言葉は，先生が最も得意とされる宗教哲學の講義である。先生は常に「宗教は生きる道である」(Religion is the way of living) と言ひ，その道によつて人類は眞に社會生活を確保することが出來るのである。(by which we human being can concrete the social life) 而してこゝに社會生活を確保するといふ意味は，宗教によつて，人類社會の眞の幸福が發現されるといふことであり，言ひ換へれば，人類が幸福に人生を人生すること，それが宗教である。要するに宗教は，博士によると，人生をハツピー(幸福)にするものである。此のことは世界の各宗教の起源をみると明らかである。例へば日本の神道の發祥である天照大神の天の岩戸の神話を見ると，あの大神 (Sungodess) の御出現によつて，人々は天地の惠ぐみと，希望に輝き，その御姿を拜した周圍の多くの神々は，喜びと幸福にあふれて，歌舞音曲，勇躍してゐる。吾々はそこに，生命の充實と種族の繁榮を壽ぐ，輝やかしい生活の行進曲を見る。更に遡つて，神話を窺つてみると，天照大神の他に，風の神，雨の神，木の神，火の神，土の神等の神々がましまして，人々はその生活の資源である五穀の豐穰を此等の神々に祈つてゐる。卽ち原始時代にあつては，生活を生活することそのまゝが宗教である。『生活卽宗教』と言ふことは，言ひ換へれば，集團生活の確保と，その幸福の完成と云ふことであつて，この他には宗教はあり得ない。更に降つて，倫理的，文化的宗教時代に於ても，例へば，印度の佛教にしても，孔子の儒教にしても，その表現の方途は，夫々異つてゐるけれども，個人の幸福と，集團生活の確保を願望とせぬものはない。

博士の新著 (The Quest of Ages) は，かゝる立場に立つて，各時代各國の宗教を再吟味して，結論に於て，『宗教は人間生活をハツピーにするものでなければならぬ』と言つて，新らしい宗教哲學の樹立を試み，現代人の宗教意識を滿足させたいと述べてをられる。以上極めて粗雜な說明であるけれども，私は私の宗教を，博士によつて，非常に新鮮な明朗なものにすることが出來たことを終世の喜びとしてゐる。

博士のかゝる學風と性行は，直ちに教室に反映して，學生は（よく神學校などで見るやうな憂欝な氣分は少しもなく）すべて明朗且つ圓滿であつて，殊に世界各國から留學した，ギリシヤ，トルコ，印度，支那，イギリス，イタリー，ロシヤ，獨逸の青年男女が全く兄弟同樣，所謂る國際友誼と理解 (International friendship and appreciaton)を高めつゝ日々を暮したものである。殊に今尙深い印象を持つてゐるのは，研究演習の時，各國人が各國獨自の宗教と思想に就いて，大いにお國自慢も交へて，報告したことである。そして時には，夫々自國の服裝を以てティー・パーテーに出席し，お互に文化の宣傳をし合つたものである。

祖國日本は今，非常時意識が高潮して，日本精神主義運動の勃興は燎原の火のやうな勢ひである。極端な右翼主義の人々は，しきりに外國文化を排斥罵倒してゐるが，一體日本精神とは何であるか。私は日本精神とは建國祭に鎧や甲で身を堅め，草鞋をはいて街をねり歩くやうな者の中には存せぬと思ふ。日本精神とは，日本及日本人が過去數千年から，現在今，持つてゐるところの精神そのものである。言ひ換へれば，日本及日本人が，數千年の間に世界の色々の文化を消化吸收して，今日の大日本を作つたところの大和の心それが眞の日本の精神であり，眞に日本を大ならしめる要石であると思ふ。

思ひ出話が横道に入つたから，筆を止めますが，日本人の此の大和の心を永年に亘つて培養して來たわが佛教はかゝる見地に立つて，多事多端，しかも不安と焦慮におのゝいてゐる，日本國家と社會の爲めに，永遠に亡びざる一大文化の建設を目標として，明日への準備を怠つてはならぬと思ふ。

國際佛教通報局會計報告

自昭和10年1月31日——至昭和11年3月31日

科	目	收	入	支	出
準備資金	（第二回汎太平洋佛青大會ヨリ）	7.000	00		
誌代		199	33		
雜收入	（住友銀行利子）	71	32		
印刷費				1.011	47
原稿料				161	50
英語講座				45	15
集會費	（國際佛教の夕）			96	73
事務所費				130	00
人件費				420	00
交通費				370	51
通信費				279	52
假拂金	（汎太佛青聯盟￥1.000.00）			1.020	00
雜品消耗費				98	66
雜費				283	03
現金	（次期繰越）			2.214	83
住友銀行	（〃）			1.102	92
振替口座	（〃）			6	30
合	計	7.270	65	7.270	65

（32）

國際佛教通報局定款

名　稱

第一，本局を國際佛教通報局と稱す

事務所

第二，本局の事務所を全日本佛教青年會聯盟本部に置く

目　的

第三，本局は日本內海及海外に向つて佛教事情の通報をなし，且つ佛教徒相互間の各種便宜を計るを以て目的とす

事　業

第四，本局の目的を達成するため左記の事業を行ふ

イ，日本內地及世界各國より佛教事情に關する質問の通報を行ふ

ロ，必要に應じ日本語及世界各國語を以て佛教事情の通報を行ふ

ハ，外國人の日本觀光に際しては各種の便益を與へ，特にその佛教に關する方面に於て之を爲す

ニ，定時或は臨時に各國語を以て文書の刊行をなす

ホ，その他必要と認めたる事業を行ふ

役　員

第五，本局の事務を處理するため左の役員を置く

イ，局長　一名

ロ，幹事　三名

ハ，評議員　若干名

局長は本局の事務を總括す

幹事は本局の事務を處理す

評議員は局長の提案に依る重要事務を審議す

第六，評議員は左記の者を以て之に充つ

イ，全日本佛教青年會聯盟理事及主事

ロ，全日本佛教青年會聯盟理事會に於て推薦したる者

第七，局長及幹事は評議員會に於て決定す

第八，役員の任期は二ヶ年とす（但し重任を妨げず）

經　費

第九，本局の經費は左記のものに依て之を支辨す

イ，本局基金の活用

ロ，寄附金

ハ，その他の收入

補　則

第十，本定款に記載せられざる事項は，凡て評議員會に於て協議す

第十一，第一回の役員は全日本佛教青年會聯盟理事會に於て決定す

定價		
一部	金二十錢	送料二錢
一年	金二圓四十錢	送料不要

昭和十年四月卅日第三種郵便物認可
昭和十一年七月廿八日印刷（每月一回
昭和十一年八月一日發行　一日發行）

東京市外吉祥寺337
編輯發行兼印刷人　淺野研眞

東京市牛込區早稻田鶴卷町107
印刷所　東文社印刷所
電話牛込（34）1950番 5049番

東京市神田區一ツ橋二の三
發行所　國際佛教通報局
電話九段（33）4428番
振替東京83015番

昭和十年四月三十日第三種郵便物認可 昭和十一年七月二十八日印刷納本（毎月一回） 昭和十一年八月一日發行（一日發行） 國際佛教通報 第二卷 第八號

第二回

汎太平洋佛教青年會大會紀要

THE PROCEEDINGS of THE Second General Conference of Pan-Pacific Young Buddhists' Associations

(in Japanese, Chinese and English)

Held at Tokyo & Kyoto, July 18–23, 1934

Price ¥ 3.00

Compiled & Published
by
The Federation of All Y.B. As. of Japan,
Tokio, Kanda, Hitotsubashi, II-3

昭和十年四月三十日第三種郵便物認可 昭和十一年八月二十八日印刷納本 昭和十一年九月一日發行（毎月一回一日發行）第二卷 第九號

The International Buddhist Bulletin

國際佛教通報

第二卷 **昭和十一年九月** 第九號〔Vol. II. September $\frac{2502}{1936}$ No. 9.〕

要目〔Contents〕

東京 **國際佛教通報局** 發行

The International Buddhist Information Bureau

Tokyo, Kanda, Hitotsubashi, II—3

Staff of the Bureau

Hon. President	J. Takakusu
President	K. Ohmura
Secretary	S. Takagai
〃	B. Inaba
〃 (in chief)	Ken Assano
Advisers	H. Ui
〃	G. Asakura
〃	R. Hatani
〃	U. Ogiwara
〃	R. Higata
〃	T. Suzuki
〃	S. Suzuki
〃	S. Amakuki
〃	S. Nagai
〃	B. Matsumoto
〃	B. Shiio
〃	E. Uno
〃	C. Akamatsu
〃	Z. Ohmori
〃	K. Yabuki
〃	S. Onoh
〃	S. Katoh
〃	M. Anezaki
〃	G. Honda
〃	R. Sekimoto
〃	J. Sahegi
〃	R. Hanada
〃	H. Kohno
〃	R. Takaoka
〃	Z. Kobayashi
〃	S. Yamabe
〃	C. Akanuma
〃	E. Honda
〃	R. Ohmori
〃	E. Kawaguchi
〃	C. Yamakawa
〃	D. Tokiwa
〃	T. Tanimoto
〃	G. Tokiwai
〃	S. Ohtani
〃	E. Ohtani
〃	B. Mizuno
〃	I. Shibata
〃	S. Ando
〃	J. Shimomura
〃	S. Kikuzawa
〃	K. Norisugi
〃	T. Shibata
〃	K. Asano
〃	T. Watanabe
〃	G. Onoh
〃	K. Yanagizawa
〃	M. Shigemitsu
〃	E. Kanakura
〃	S. Tachibana

國際佛教通報局

名譽局長	高楠順次郎
局長	大村桂巖
幹事	鷹谷俊之
同	稻葉文海
同	淺野研眞
顧問（順序不同）	
〃	宇井伯壽
〃	朝倉曉瑞
〃	羽溪了諦
〃	荻原雲來
〃	干潟龍祥
〃	鈴木大拙
〃	鈴木宗忠
〃	天岫接三
〃	長井眞琴
〃	松本文三郎
〃	椎尾辨匡
〃	宇野圓空
〃	赤松智城
〃	大森禪戒
〃	矢吹慶輝
〃	小野清一郎
〃	加藤精神
〃	姉崎正治
〃	本田義英
〃	關本龍門
〃	佐伯定胤
〃	花田凌雲
〃	河野法雲
〃	高岡隆心
〃	小林瑞淨
〃	山邊習學
〃	赤沼智善
〃	本多惠隆
〃	大森亮順
〃	河口慧海
〃	山川智應
〃	常盤大定
〃	谷本 富
〃	常盤井堯猷
〃	大谷尊由
〃	大谷瑩潤
〃	水野梅曉
〃	柴田一能
〃	安藤正純
〃	下村壽一
〃	菊澤季麿
〃	乘杉嘉壽
〃	芝田徹心
〃	淺野孝之
〃	渡邊哲信
〃	小野玄妙
〃	柳澤 健
〃	重光 葵
〃	金倉圓照
〃	立花俊道

Tales of Buddhist Priests (II)

Atsuharu Sakai

(4) Priest Mongaku

Shigeto Endo, a samurai, had no issue until he was pretty advanced in age. So he repaired to the Hasedera Temple, Kyoto, where he offered a prayer for a son, because in our feudal days nothing was a greater pity for a military family than to have no successor. One night his wife saw in a dream that a few feathers of a kite entered her side and she found herself with child. And in due course of time she gave birth to a son, who was named Morito.

When sixteen years old, Morito Endo was charmed with the beauty of Kesa, wife of Wataru Minamoto, a court-warrior. He visited Kinugawa, her mother, and forced her to promise, at the risk of her life, to give her married daughter as wife to him. After he was gone, Kinugawa called her daughter and handed her a dagger, saying "You kill me with this dagger. I would rather die at your hands than

anybody else's." Kesa, surprised asked whether she was sane, bu when she heard that imminen danger was befalling her mother she said "It is my duty, mother to save you. Leave the matter i my hands."

When Morito came to see her Kesa treated him with great hos pitality, but she was also threaten ed by him, who demanded her i marriage at her cost.

"I will obey on condtion tha you do away with my husband, Kesa said calmly, when she sa nothing would dissuade Morit from his sinister deed in case o her refusal. "You come into ou bedchamber and take the hea that you will find has wet hair."

That evening Kesa gave a speci dinner to her husband on the fals pretence that she wanted to sho her gratitude for the recovery fro a protracted illness of her mothe Wataru was much more drank tha usual, and she helped him to be Then she washed her own hair an went to bed a little apart from her husband's.

That night Morito stole in, and cut off the head that he felt had wet hair. But what was his surprise, when he saw that it was his love's head and not Wataru's that he took; so he confessed everything to Wataru, asking him to avenge his wife's murdery by killing him on the spot.

"What good would it be" Morito asked, "if I were to kill you when Kesa is gone to come back to life no more? My advice is that you become a Buddhist priest and pray for the repose of her departed soul."

Morito followed the advice of Wataru, whom he thus wronged, and gave himself to Buddhism, assuming the Buddhist name of Mongaku (literally, Literary-enlightenment). He lived at the Jingo-ji (literally, God-protection) Temple, Yamashiro Province, where he was entirely given to asceticism. He also went round on pilgrimages in different provinces, in which he caused many ruined temples to be repaired or restored. Once he wanted to raise a fund for building a shrine and he visited the Imperial court for a donation. His rude behavior, however, displeased the

ex-Emperor Gotoba, who condemned him to banishment in Izu Province. On his way, he had to cross the River Tenryu, when a storm suddenly coming on, his ferry-boat was threatened to be capsized by the angry waves.

"This is a boat on which Priest Mongaku is enshrined" he shouted, after a sort of incantation. "What audacious dragon dares to challenge me?" he demanded, for in this country a storm is often attributed to the mischief of a dragon. "You better stop the waves and let my ship go safely." The storm soon subsided.

"If I really displease the gods." Priest Mongaku said soon after his arrival in Izu, "they will kill me; otherwise I shall live." And he refused to eat anything for thirty-one days, at the end of which he was as strong and sound as he was before.

In Izu Province, Priest Mangaku pretended that he could read the fortune of a man by looking at his features, and many people visited him to have their fortune told by him. One day Yoritomo Minamoto, who was also marooned in Izu, came to see Priest Mongaku. The priest would not see him at first, but talked to him from behind a screen. Soon, however, he came out, and said: "I see you are the scion of the Minamoto family. I have seen many sons of your family, but none of them I find are ambitious enough to be or do anything. You are different, for I see a great future in store for you. I will help you to realize your object."

Yoritomo and Priest Mongaku became fast friends, and it is said that the former owed a great deal to the later for his latter acquisition of supremacy in the country. Shortly after this interview, Priest Mongaku promised Yoritomo to obtain for him the Imperial Commission, whithout which Yoritomo could not raise a war against Taira with impunity, and he went to Kyoto for it.

"When you succeed," Priest Mongaku said to Yoritomo, on coming back from Kyoto. "When you succeed, you must promise to help the Jingo-ji Temple, for which I have been trying to raise a fund in vain."

"Of course I will do anything for you in case of my success," Yoritomo said.

Then Priest Mongaku produced a paper in which a promise was written to offer to the Jingo-ji Temple thirteen rich places in the provinces of Tosa, Tamba and Harima, and he asked Yoritomo to sign his name on the document. Upon his signing it, the priest handed him the Imperial Commission, with which Yoritomo succeeded in the great work of unifying the country under him. Yoritomo was appointed the first Shogun in 1192.

Priest Mongaku, who was released from banishment was again condemned to exile in 1199, this time to the island of Sado in the Japan Sea.

"What need is there for their sending me so far off when I am old with few years before me?" said Priest Mongaku and he refused to eat anything on the island till he was starved to death, in the same year, at the age of 80 years.

(5) Priest Renshō

Jiro, a descendant of the Taira family, was a fearless boy. When he was sixteen years old, a big bear made its frequent appearance in the vicinity of his native town of Kamagai in Musashi Province, and wrought havoc on the fields and gardens. Young Jiro attacked the bear single-handed and killed it, to the great relief and admira-

tion of the chief of his town, who allowed him to use Kumagai as his family name. Jiro was rechristened Jiro Naozane Kumagai.

When Yoritomo, a scion of the Minamoto family, who was marooned in the province of Izu, raised a war in 1180 against Taira, the inveterate enemy of Minamoto, Kumagai joined the army despatched by Taira against Minamoto, to whom. however, he surrendered.

Kumagai distinguished himself in a battle that Yoshitsune, brother of Yoritomo, fought against Yoshinaka Kiso on the River Uji in 1184, and he enjoyed high favour with Yoritomo. In the same year, Taira, unable to stand the hard pressure of Minamoto, evacuated Kyoto, the Imperial capital, and shut himself in the natural defence of Ichinotani. Yoshitsune, still pursuing him, was to take the castle of Ichinotani by surprise in order to annihilate Taira, as he finnaly did.

"I want to be the first to attack the enemy" Naozane said to his son, Naoiye, before the battle of Ichinotani, for in feudal days the first attack on the enemy was always considered to be most meritorious. So together they led their troops, under cover of night, to deal the first blow on the enemy at his front gate. When, approaching the gate, Naozane heard a music coming from the castle, where Taira made merry, little knowing that his fate was soon to be closed, he heaved a sigh and said to his son: "It is a shame that I should have to assault such a peaceful-minded and innocent people." Naozane and his son were the first to attack the enemy, but soon Naoiye, his son, received an arrow, and asked his father to pull it out. "Your wound is not serious." Naozane said, still busily engaged in fighting "and I am too much occupied to care for vou. So wait a little while." The castle of Ichinotani was seized by Minamoto, and Taira fleeing again, his troops got on ships at Suma, with Minamoto still after them.

Naozane Kumagai wanted to do one more meritorious deed by fighting a Taira lord worthy of a warrior of his military position in the Minamoto army, when he saw a well-attired warrior of the enemy riding his horse into the sea, evidently to join his comrades-at-arms.

"Who is going there?" Kumagai shouted at the top of his voice, and he announced his name, after the manner of a feudal warrior, saying "I am Jiro Naozane of Kumagai. Come back, come back! Let us have a fight. It is coward of you to turn your back to your enemy."

The rider, a young prince of the Taira family, rode back to the beach, where a cambat ensued between Kumagai and the prince. Neither was inferior to the other in swordsmanship. Then they threw their swords down on the ground and grappled with each other. Thus they fell together on the ground with Kumagai, the stronger of the two, on top of the young prince of Taira. He drew his dagger and was on the point of cutting the head of his beaten foe, who he noticed was a lad in his teens.

"Who could you be?" Kumagai kindly asked.

"No matter who I am" came from under him, for the young prince was quite prepared to die, "but cut off my head now that I am beaten."

"You look too young to be killed." Kumagai said again, for by this time pity and sympathy got hold of his samurai heart. "You must have your parents still living; they would mourn over your death."

The father rose within Kumagai's tender heart and he was about to release the lad when he noticed that his comades, who had been looking from a distance at his combat with the Taira prince, expressed their suspicion by shouting that Kumagai must be a traitor if he let his enemy go. Kumagai explained his situation and once more asked who the prince was. The lad told that he was a son of Tsunemori, a courtier of the Taira family, and his name was Atsumori. When asked if he had any message to be carried to his parents, Atsumori asked Kumagai to hand them his favorite flute on which he played at leasure during the campaign and calmly received the sword with which Kumagai cut his head off. Atsumori was then sixteen years old.

Naozane Kumagai was touched to the core of his heart with the noble and pathetic end of young Atsumori Taira. Already tired of bloodshed, he could no longer stand the warlike life of a warrior. So he took leave of Yoritomo, his master, threw away his weapons, and donned the "priestly black robe" by renouncing the world. He went to Kyoto, where he learned Buddhism under Priest Genku,

better known by the name of Priest Honen, who is the founder of the Jodo school of Buddhism and he was converted to Buddhism, assuming the Buddhist name of Renshō (literally, Lotus-birth), in order to devote the rest of his life to Buddhism and to pray, in particular, for the dead spirit of young Atsumori, whom he so reluctantly killed at Suma.

After his conversion to Buddhism, Priest Renshō visited Yoritomo his former master, at Kamakura to report on his new religious life. Yoritomo, with whom the priest had been a great favorite, was sorry to have lost him, and his whole court was really surprised to see what a great warrior and tactician he was from the way he talked about military art. But for all that Yoritomo did to dissuade him from Buddism, Priest Renshō remained adamant in his resolution.

Prist Renshō lived a retired and religious life at the quiet town of Kumagai in Saitama Prefecture and he died in 1208.

Marriage Arrangement Difficult for Descendant of 'Living Buddha'

(This is the last of a series of articles on "The Biographies of Beautiful Women" by Shigure Hasegawa.)

Takeko Kujo, descendant of the famous Buddhist priest, Shinran, founder of the Shinshu sect headquarters of which are in the Honganji temple in Kyoto, is the last of the beauties whom Mrs. Shigure Hasegawa discusses.

To understand the position of Takeko Kujo, it is necessary to understand the importance of her family in Buddhist circles. Shinran, whom many believed to be the living Buddha, has been compared to Martin Luther because of his reformations in Buddhism which at that time was marked by corruptions.

Takeko was the second daughter of the 21st head of the Honganji temple in Kyoto and direct descendant of Shinran. Her family position naturally gave her public esteem to which was added the fame of her beauty.

She was born in 1887 and died in 1928. Her family was not only noble, wealthy and among the great Suddhist leaders but also was worshipped by thousands of followers. Takeko's brother, Kozui Otani, former head priest of the Honganji temple, Kyoto, was an enterprising and adventurous man who had travelled abroad, visited Tibet, the South Seas and many Eastern countries. Takeko naturally was influenced by him.

Her father was another of her close companions during her girlhood, Mrs. Hasegawa remarks that when Takeko played the koto with her father, neighbors ran out of their homes and stood in the open spaces that they might better hear and admire the music. Takeko also studied literature under her father and under his teaching, developed a talent for writing, particularly for poetry.

When she was 17, there was a movement to send her to Siam as the wife of the Crown Prince of

that country. At that time the Crown Prince of Siam visited Japan and when he went to the Honganji temple in Kyoto, the two met. Wedding plans were halted however by the death of her father and in the confusion which followed, were forgotten.

Later her brother suggested to the family that she be married to a relative, a priest attached to the East Honganji temple, a branch of the Honganji temple in which Takeko and her famly lived. This proposal met wit himmediate objections because the two temples had been rivals for more than 300 years. At the time, the feeling between them was somewhat friendly but Takeko's family would not hear of cementing the luke-warm friendship with marriage. Theirs, the West Honganji temple, had always had the greatest following. It was feared that if Takeko were allowed to go to the rival temple. her beauty would only add to its prestige at the cost of their own. Some better reason had to be given, however, and so the family said the objection was because the proposed priest lacked the title of count or viscount. It is believed that Takeko would have liked this marriage. She met the man once and the two walked alone in the garden. When they parted, Takeko thought it was only for a short time. But she never saw him again until just before she died, She wrote a poem at the time and in it spoke of the parting as if it were for only a few days.

Tokeko was more than 20 now and it was thought high time she was being married. Mrs. Hasegawa says that her life was sad even at this age because convention and tradition did not give her an opportunity to lead a normal life. There was good talk and discussion about her but she had no chance to take part. Always she was on the outside of things.

Her mind was developing under the leadership of her brother. This was the time of the Russo-Japanese war and her brother and his wife organized the Patriotic Buddhist Women's Society. Takeko went them throughout the country while he spoke at public meetings. She listened, saw and heard many things which were new. Her poems at the time reflect her sadness and lonesomeness.

Meanwhile her family struggled with the marriage problem. Every day they looked through the directory of peers attempting to find a young man of 26 and 30 who would be suitable as her husband but every day they found only the same old names. As the family had opposed her marriage to a priest who did not have a title, they had to find a man with a title.

Finally they found Baron Kujo, a relative of Prince Kujo. Although Takeko and Baron Kujo had nothing in common, neither in education or character, they were married, Shortly after they went to Europe where he was to study. They traveled with her brother and sister-in-law on the boat. Although it was their honeymoon, they behaved so coolly to each other that no one suspected they were just married, Mrs. Hasegawa says. Abroad they lived separately and soon she returned to Japan with her sister-in-law. Her husband attended the farewell dinner just before she sailed but he did not speak to her. He went to the station to see her off and his sole remark was "Good-bye."

Some said that it was because he was philosophical that he was indifferent but his close friends replied that such was not the case. He could be sociable when he wanted to be, they maintained.

Baron Kujo remained in Europe 10 years. Meanwhile the public at home sympathized with her and accused him of deserting his beautiful bride.

Soon after Takeko returned to Japan, her sister-in-law died and she became the new president of the Patriotic Buddhist Women's Society. She continued to live in the Honganji temple and to be an important person there. She published a collection of poems which had a tremendous sale. All the money she received from the book she donated to charity, some to a hospital in Tsukiji.

Gradually the public came to regard her as a saint but along with the esteem and love which it heaped on her, it formulated the pattern of her life—her public thought she must do this and that and not what she perhaps would have liked.

For 20 years, Takeko devoted herself to charity. Her own sadness made her sympathetic with the poor. She frequently visited the slums in Tokyo and one such expedition, when she had a toothache, she caught a cold and an infection began which caused her death.

The public considered that Takeko lived an ideal life. Mrs. Hasegawa considers that she lived the conventionally ideal life but that she should have broken through this convention, Takeko's own play, "Autumn in Saga," gives an idea of her feelings. In the play she has her heroine say. "You cannot say that a girl is happy just because she is beautiful. Beautiful love will make you happy, as happy as if Buddha's kind hand were leading you."

An American writer compared Takeko's beauty to a white lily. A Japanese writer compared her beauty to that of the double cherry blossoms. Another writer said that she wished Takeko could go to Paris in full dress to show the beauty of Japanese women. Her beauty was like that of an ancient court lady with delicate, fine features.

The beauty of Japan:—

Takeko Kujo

Nichibei Home Guides American-Born Japanese

The so-called Second Generation Japanese who were born and educated in America, gradually come to realize their special position in society as they go from primary school up to college.

They are Americans by naturality but Japanese by race. The question of where to go after their graduation has not only confronted these American-born Japanese but also their parents. In addition to this problem, there is another burden borne on the shoulders of the parents. It is as to the question of "how to educate" their children.

Side by side with their English education there is a Japanese language lesson required for them. However, their study of the Japanese language in America has never been perfected, and the result is the recent growing number of the Second Generation students coming to this country to pursue a Japanese language course.

After their arrival here, however, they do not always feel at home on account of the divergence of customs and manners, and other social affairs here from those they are accustomed to there. To overcome this situation, therefore, it has become necessary to give them proper guidance and protection.

The Nichibei Home, located at 10, Senkomae-cho, Nakano-ku, Tokyo, has the objective of looking after American-born Japanese studying in the Empire. It is the oldest dormitory of its kind now completely furnished in Japan.

Nowadays, there are a number of such dormitories built or being built in Tokyo. Some of them look after other foreign students, and the rest teach them Japanese language only. In contrast with these dormitories, the Nichibei Home not only looks after American-born Japanese but gives them such lessons as Japanese language and culture. It is a family-like dormitory in which the warmest consolation is extended towards them by assisting their entrance to school or dormitory, and by giving

advice to their parents concerning tuition fee, expense and other personal matters.

It is nearly seven years since its founding. The number of students cared for has reached over 150. Also the number of students going home after graduating Japanese colleges has increased.

In appreciation of the work of the Nichibei Home, H.I.H. Prince Takamatsu granted an audience to all officials concerned, and listened to their description of life among the American-born Japanese students in Japan. On that occasion a set of beautiful flower-vase was also bestowed on them.

The Nichibei Home is run by the Nihon Beifu Kyokai consisting of leading people connected with American or Hawaiian affairs. The dormitory with the support of a number of Americans, Hawaiians and Japanese is now planning to purchase an estate for a modern building. Upon completion of the building the dormitory will be alternated into a foundational juridical person.

The leading figure in the work of the Nichibei Home is Mr. Konen Tsunemitsu who has been engaged for the last decade in studying the problem of American-born Japanese, and in guiding Japanese youth studying in Japan. At present the dormitory quarters more than 30 students who are attending the various middle schools and colleges in Tokyo.

It is by no means easy to guide students who live a mode of life different from that they are accustomed to thousands of miles away from their parents.

The Nichibei Home reports to the parents at every mail the students' progress in study, along with a monthly list of the boy's roll-calls (morning service, lock-up, sleep, Sunday lectures), accounts, etc., and particularly co-operates with the parents with regard to the students' upbringing in Japan.

Exemption of Entrance Examinations

The Nichibei Home acts on behalf of the students to secure, without giving them the trouble of appearing in examinations, government grant of diplomas to qualify them to pass the middle school course in Japan, a necessity for every student wishing to enter any schools above the middle school standard.

The students have hitherto experienced much trouble in entering such schools in this country. For instance, those who have graduated from American high schools are not allowed to enter any higher schools or colleges in Japan unless they have completed middle school grade education here. To modify this regulation, however, the Education Ministry has issued a special regulation to the effect that the Education Minister can qualify the graduates of American high schools as having passed the middle school grade in Japan. They are now to be permitted to enter any college in Japan when given this qualification.

Nichibei Gakuin

The Nichibei Gakuin, attached to the Nichibei Home, is a preparatory school for boys and girls from America and Hawaii desiring to enter Japanese colleges in Japan. The institute, with its history of seven years, is the oldest of its kind in the Empire built for the benefit of American-born Japanese students.

The Gakuin has many specially attached teachers responsible for coaching the students in Japanese, Chinese, Japanese culture and other important subjects. The students who enrolled in Japanese colleges after finishing this preparatory school are reported to have been making a good record. It is also said that many of them have successfully passed the same entrance examination required for other native Japanese applicants. Seven have succeeded in entering Waseda University; and three have matriculated in Meiji University.

Gymnasium of the Nichibei Home

To accommodate the growing number of these students, the Nichibei Home is now having a large additional building built in its compound. Upon its completion, it will have a large gymnasium in addition to a student hall also now under construction. The gymnasium is to be equipped with up-to-date appliances.

In an interview with a reporter of The Japan Times, Mr. Konen Tsunemitsu, superintendent of the Nichibei Home, disclosed the following advice for students coming from America to study:

"When one comes to Japan to study, one should not forget to bring the following certificates: high school diploma, certificate of high school graduation all high

school records and certificate of birth. Also one must be ready to report on the accurate birthplace and address of one's parents and relatives.

In Japan, a student, as a rule, is to wear a uniform, and so there is no need to order a new suit prior to one's departure. Also it is advisable for one to minimize the volume of one's personal effects. Of course, one must be careful to go through due formalities in relation with the American government officials in charge. It will be better for one to give us previous information about one's boat, possible date of arrival at Yokohama and hotel in Yokohama. The cable address of the Nichibei Home is TMKZ Tokyo. It is also requested to remit one's money, excluding one's traveling expense, directly to me."

The following is the approximate time table of the Institute:

Rising—6 : 30 a.m.

Morning service, breakfast, roll-call—7 : 00 a.m.

Lunch 11 : 30 a.m.

Dinner—5. p.m.

Lock-up, roll-call—7. p.m.

Study Hours

Roll-call—7. p.m.

Bed-time—10 : 50 p.m.

Monthly expenditures by students coming from America presents another serious problem to their parents. The Nichibei Home roughly estimates, with the exception of extra expenses, the following monthly expenditure per head:

¥26.00—rooms, meals, electric lights, bath etc.

¥24.00—miscellaneous (books, stationaries, pocket-money, trams, etc.)

¥10.00—school fee.

Thus it makes a total of ¥60 monthly. With a view to preventing the waste of money by the students, the Institute pays special attention to their expenses by requesting the parents to send money directly to the superintendent for the sake of safekeeping. An annual expenditure by the students will not exceed ¥1,000 per person.

東洋に於ける佛教復興

三藏阿闍梨　ラーフラ・サーンクリトヤーヤナ

一　印度佛教の盛衰

紀元前四八三年の佛陀滅後百年位して，佛教教團は二派に分れるやうになつた。その後一，二世紀位して，阿育王統治の初頃に，印度には十八部派があつた。尙その上に數多くの分派や小分派があつたが，然し，この相違は更に後世の發達に比較する時には，無意味なものになる位である。凡ての之等の變化は北方印度に起つたのである。然し，次の三世紀間は，南印度はアンドラ諸帝王の庇護の下に佛教的活動の大きな舞臺となつたのである。而して數世紀間の思索研究と敎理的論爭の後に，佛敎の諸派は一つの思想體系に發展し，それが今大乘(Mahāyāna)として知られてゐるものである。大乘に屬する，雜然と散ばつてゐた諸思想は，紀元二世紀に南印度の龍樹(Nāgārjuna)によつて，更に第四世紀第五紀には西北印度の無着(Asaṅga)によつて哲學的な形に體系立てられた。紀元二世紀には新しい部派は北方に向つて動き初めた。この派は徐々に基礎を築いて行つて，陳那(Diṅnāga)や彼の追從者の如き偉大な論理學者や哲學者が現れ出たので，凡ての古い方の部派は克服された。そのやうにして第六，第七世紀の終には殆んど凡ての佛敎僧院の學林は大乘の學林に轉派して仕舞つた。

然し，大乘がこの大きな論破に成功した時には，またその內から一の運動が起つて，凡てを一掃し去るやうな變化を移し入れた。これは佛教の眞言密敎的な(tāntric)部派である。これも亦南方印度の神秘家達の間に始めて起つたのである。然し，後には彼等の學理と身體的の暗示は非常に感覺的な惡習に墮落して仕舞つた。この眞言密敎的な佛教の形は又金剛乘(Vajrayāna)卽ち金剛(雷電)の乘物と言はれ，最初は祕密に宣傳されたが，然し八世紀の中頃には，偉大な神祕詩人サラハ(Saraha)や彼の追從者の指導の下に非常に强力となり，次の百年位の內に大乘は金剛乘と妥協するのを餘儀なくされた。金剛乘の人氣の增すのにつれて，非常な道德的惡習と迷信も亦增して來た。ほんの僅かのものを除いては佛陀の本當の敎說は知られないやうになつた。僧侶も居士達も共に魔法や妖術や非常に淫猥な儀式や象徵の建言者や大賞讚者になつて仕舞つた。これは印度の佛教の大厦全體を根底から覆すことになつた。全基礎が腐つて來て，

十二世紀の終にはマホメット敎信者の侵入者の打擊によつて崩壞して仕舞つた。佛教の僧院と那爛陀(Nālandā)・ウダンタプリ(Udantapuri)及びヴィクラマシーラー(Vikramasīlā)僧院の如き佛敎の敎育の中心は地に倒されて仕舞つた。佛教思想の指導者である佛敎僧侶達は印度を去つて，尼波羅・西藏や其他の隣國に逃れ去つた。第十四世紀の終に，佛敎の信者は婆羅門敎に併合されたり，又マホメット敎を受け入れたりした。

このやうにして第十四世紀から，佛教はその誕生の國から消え去つた。第十三世紀から第十五世紀まで北印度の政治の穹窿は不安と流血とで充されてゐた。古からの都市は破壞された。村落は刧掠され，人々は虐殺された。生き殘つた人々は自分の村落から逃げ去つた。その三世紀間に人口は減少した。徐々に昔の村落や都市は深い森林に倂呑され，そこに虎や象がうろついた。ある族や階級の人々は尙自分のもとの家を記憶してゐた。然し，時間からは十五代とか二十代距り，距離からは數百哩も離れると，人々は家のもとの在所を忘れて仕舞つた。數世紀經つと，都市の自分の石屑が遺跡を履ふて仕舞つた。第十六世紀からは人口は增加し初めたが，然し第十八世紀までは部落に再び植民させるには十分でなかつたのである。實際，密林の生ひ茂つた，古い破損した，都市の位置が發見されたのは，唯二世紀前の第十八世紀の初からであつた。このことは聯合州とビハール州の大部分の村々は二百年以上古いものは一つもないといふ事が證明してゐる。前世紀の最後の二十年の間に，歷史家や考古學者達が多くの者の敷地について尋ね初めた折に，その地方の人々が何も告げ知らせることが出來なかつたのは，かういふ理由からである。自已滿足の爲に，住民達は神や惡魔が怒つた物語を語り，その怒がその隣の古い遺跡に關係があるのだと告げたが，然し，彼等はその場所の名前さへ思ひ出すことが出來なかつたのである。このやうにして祇園精舍(Jetavana-Vihāra)のある舍衞城('Srāvasti)の大都市はサヘト・マヘト(Sahetmahet)，卽ち王が過去を犯し，その過失の爲に神々に呪はれて，「上下が顚倒した町」と云はれるやうになつた。

有名な那爛陀大學は廣大な遺跡があるが單にバルガオン(Bar-gāoṅ)卽ち「大きな村」といふ名になつた。このやうに忘れられたことは，印度から佛敎が滅亡したので名が變つたのだと說明出來るやうな佛教の敷地についてばかり眞實であるのでなく，婆羅門敎や耆那敎に關係のある數多くの有名な所に關しても眞實である。このやうにしてアランビカープリ(Alambikāpuri)やプリツダカ(Pṛthudaka)・アヒッチャトラ(Ahicchatra)も耆那敎徒と婆羅門敎徒に全く忘れられて仕舞つたのである

二　印度に於ける佛敎復興

印度のイギリス統治者等は十八世紀の最後の十年頃から印度の歷史や古の

記念物に興味を持ち出し，その時に『亞細亞研究』(Asiatic Research) の第一卷が發刊されたのであるけれども，之は十九世紀の中頃の佛蘭西學者，M. Princep によつて阿育王の碑文とブラーフミ文字 (Brāhmi alphabet) の劃期的な發見と判讀によつて促されたに過ぎなかつた。そして又同じ頃に初つたカンニンガム (Cunningham) 將軍の廣範な旅行・發掘・研究によつて外國の學者の間に非常な衝動を引き起したのである。印度の宗教と文學の研究や飜譯もその助けになつた。十九世紀の八十年間の初の內は進歩は非常に遲かつた。その後にこの方面の著述が增して來て，その上國民的自覺が生ずると共に，有識階級が佛教に興味を感ずるやうになつて來た。聯合州やビハール (Bihar) 州で發見された殆んど凡ての古の遺跡は佛教に關連して居り，それらは數千の美しい佛像に充ちてゐるので，數世紀前まで佛教は各所に流行して居つたといふことは，教育ある印度人にとつて一つの天啓となつたのである。巨大な佛教記念物のどの新しい展覽も，また佛陀の高貴にして莊嚴な生涯と教說の出版も，教育ある印度人の尊敬をかち得，また婆羅門文學に尙保存されてゐた佛教に對する憎惡の反響もいち早く消滅して仕舞つたのである。この世紀 (二十世紀) の初には印度考古局 (Indian Archaeological Department) の仕事がよく組織立てられ，擴張された。その時歷史家達は此等の發見に基礎を置いて，印度史を再び建て直し初めたのである。國家の發展のどの境域でも，佛教の貢獻は質に於て驚く可きものがあつたのみでなく，量に於ても凡てを壓して居つたのである。どの十年も新たな驚きを齎して來た。彼等は自分達の佛教がバイカル湖 (Baikal) からバリ島 (Bali) まで，日本からセイロン島まで賞讃され，受け入れられてゐたのを見た。ヂャヴァ (Java) やカンボーヂャ(Cambodia) 中央亞細亞の佛教の記念物と遺物は佛教の王國の廣さを彼等に示した。今は教育ある印度教徒であつて，佛陀に對しては深き尊敬を示さぬ者は一人も見出すことが出來なくなつた。拘尸那竭 (Kusinārā)・鹿野苑(Sārnāth)・祇園精舍 (Jetavana) や其他の佛教の聖地の大祭禮には，毎年數千の人々が參加した。人々は今は佛教の教說を知らうとする大きな欲望を抱いてゐるのである。新しい寺や協會が佛教の宣傳の爲に開かれて來た。何處にも佛教復興の目覺しい徵が認められる。アナーガリカ・ダンマパーラ (Anāgārika Dhammapāla) は四十年間休みなき活動を續けたものであつた。

三　尼波羅の佛教

佛教は非常に早い時期に尼波羅に移入された。印度がマホメット教徒に占領されて，佛教がそこから消え失せた時にも尙，佛教は尼波羅國には流行してゐた。梵語で書かれた佛教藏經や，哲學上の他の著作の殆んど全部のものが，こゝに發見された。十九世紀の全部は，尼波羅の佛教徒について言ふならば，懶惰にして不活潑な時期であつたけれども，その狀態は今は變化して，若い尼波羅佛教徒は目覺めつゝある。

四　西藏の佛教

第七世紀と第八世紀に西藏に佛教が入つた。佛教が入ると共に，西藏の歷史が知られ初つたばかりでなく，それと共に，西藏は書法・文法・文學・哲學・天文學及び醫術を受け入れたのである。その時までは國民は進步して居らず，西藏語は深い心理的又は哲學的の思想を現す方法としては貧弱すぎた。佛教が西藏人に佛教經典を研究する爲に外國語を學ぶやうに强いた譯である。このやうにして，西藏人は教師の教誡に從つて，佛教文學の全部を西藏語に飜譯し初めた。西藏人は正確に好結果に譯す爲に，西藏語と西藏文法を梵語を模範として作り出した。西藏譯は最も近い原語 (印度語) の形と共に正確な觀念を導き出す點では，世界中で比較するものが少い。數百の著作は不幸にしてもと (印度) の言語では失はれたけれども，西藏譯から，もとの單語の七十五パーセントを使つて非常にた易く回復することが出來る。今は西藏語は如何な種類の文献も西藏語に譯すことが出來るやうな豐富な語彙を持つてゐる。

第八，第九世紀は大飜譯時代であつた。この頃はサンエ (Sam-ye) 僧院の色々の精舍には印度と西藏の學僧が住してゐて，飜譯の仕事に多忙だつた。これらの初期は文學や藝術の追求，瞑想や獨居の實踐に關してばかりでなく，菩薩の至高の理想に生きる點に關しても，西藏佛教史上の黃金時代であつた。ム・ネ・ツアン・ポ皇帝 (Mu-ne-tsan-po 西曆826—827年) は「凡ての人に國の富を等分すべきである」と命じた。等分はされたが，然し平等は間もなく消滅した。然し，尙も再び皆が財產を等分して持つやうにされた‥‥三度試みた後に，王は自分の母に毒殺された。」(Sir C. Bell's, *Tibet: Past and Present*, p. 47.)

この時代には西藏は小さな公國でなく，その帝國には支那の多くの省，ビルマの北方の部分，アッサム(Assam) からギルギート (Gilgit) に至る印度のヒマラヤ地方及び支那トルキスタンを含んでゐた。

十一世紀に西藏は印度教師アティサー (Atisā)(981—1053) 及び大神秘詩人ミ・ラ・ラス・パ(Mi-la Ras-pa)(1039—1122) によつて新生活(金剛乘)に再びなじんだ。印度のヴィクラマシーラー大學林が破壞されてからは，その住職シャークャ・シュリバドラ (Śākya-śribhadra)(1126—1224) は西藏に行き，そこでサ・キャ(Sa-skya) 寺に九年以上(1203—1212)住した。サ・キャは今は佛教の活動の大中心となつた。數多くの書物が梵語から西藏語に譯された。一二二一年には佛教は蒙古に移入され，蒙古の支配者成吉思汗(Genghiz khan) (1162—1227)は太平洋からカスピ海まで支配してゐた。二十一年後に（一二四二年に）サキャ(Sas-kya) 大僧正クン・ガギャル・シャン (Kun-dya gyal-myshan) の二人の甥パグ・パ (Phags-pa) とヒャク・ナ (Phyag-na)は自ら佛教を說法する爲に蒙古に行つた。三年後（一二四五）に，大僧正自身が成吉思汗の孫蒙古帝王ゴ・タン(Gotan 一二〇五誕生，一二三二年卽位）に歡待された。次の年にゴ・タンは自分の敎師に大僧正を賴んで，布施として中央西藏を彼に獻じた。その時から西藏に法皇政治が初つたのである。

宗敎的な純潔が壞はれ，僧院と比丘が，た易い感覺的な生活を行ひ初めた時に，他に偉大な改革者が生れた。彼の名はツォン・カ・パ(Tsong-kha-pa) (1356—1418)と言はれる。ゲ・ルグ・パ (Ge-lug-pa) 卽ち所謂黃帽派の開祖である。彼は聖法の窮境を非常に悲んだ。彼は篤信な學識のある數多くの弟子達と共に，偉大な改革事業を初めた。一四〇八年には彼は有名なガ・タン (Ga-ldan) の僧院を立て，それが彼の僧團の中心地となつた。彼の弟子のヂャン・ヤン (Jam-yang) シャクヤ・エセ (Sakya-ye-ses) 及びゲン・ヅンヅップ (Gen-dun-dup) は夫々にデープン (Depung 一四一六年)・セ・ラ(Sera—四一九)・タ・シ・フン・ポ (Ta-si-lhun-po. 一四四七)の大僧院を建立した。二つの古派,カダンパ(Ka-dampa,アティサー Atisā の追從者）とツァン・ニッ・パ (Tshan-ñid-pa 哲學宗派の追從者) は彼を助け，熱心に彼の改革を受け入れた。第十五世紀は西藏に於ては佛敎復興の重大な時期であつたのである。前述の僧院は建立後直ちに學問の大中心となつて，今も尙その地位を持してゐる。そこには西藏の各地やヒマラヤ地方からの學生ばかりでなく，その內には蒙古やシベリヤや歐羅巴露西亞のアストラカン (Astrakhan) からの數千の學生を見ることも出來るのである。

一六四一年蒙古酋長グシ・カーン (Gushi-khan)は第五世達賴羅摩（ダライラマ） (Dalai Lama)に彼の敬虔な心の表象として西藏王國を獻上した。先きの達賴羅摩ツブ・タン・ギャン・ツォ (Thul-tan gyam-tsho) 貌下は第十三世である。

西藏は世界の他の國々から孤立してゐたので，その宗敎も外界に影響されなかつた。然し再び，數多くの弱點が西藏佛敎に見出されるに至り，嘗ての改革は旣に日限を過ぎ去つてゐる。

（平等通昭譯）

滿洲佛敎學院の創立に就て

牛谷範成

滿洲の佛敎興隆策の一として寺院の改革，僧侶の向上に就ては三十年計畫案を持してゐたが，最近までの實地調査の結果は全然計畫の立更へを考へさせられるに至つた。それは現在の滿洲寺院の組織內容と僧侶の質及社會的位置より考へて見ると，これを中心として興隆策を講ずることは効果的に見て見込み薄である。それに反して居士を中心に動きかければ案外容易に効果を擧げ得る確信を得たのである。

實は，他の調査要件でほとんど全滿を步く機會を利用して宗敎事情の研究を續けて來たが，去六月四日に北滿の首都チチハル市に『第一回日滿宗敎敎化團體懇話會』を開催した。會する者カトリツク敎，回々敎，キリスト敎，儒道敎，紅萬字會，諸雜敎團，協和會，各種慈善會，敎育廳，日本各宗開敎師約七十名で豫想外の好成績を擧げた。（別稿徐大年氏，吳寅根氏の論稿は當懇話會に於ける口述を要約したもの)。

この懇話會は滿洲に於て始めての催しとて各方面から注目され就中在滿の居士に大きなセンセーションを與へたと見え，閉會後『龍江省佛敎會』は，特に私のため歡迎會を開いて吳れた。その會は歡迎會ではあつたが其の內容はむしろ滿洲居士佛敎興隆救援要望の會であつた。彼等は實に眞劍に佛敎の興隆を欣求してゐる。殊に

一，佛敎類似乃至宗敎類似の新興宗敎團體や僞善團體の發展への對策

二，寺院佛敎の不振

三，居士の無結束無統制

は，日本宗敎家の指導と救援に依るに非ざれば解決不可として，此の際是非此の地に止つて具體的方策を樹立すると共に，積極的指導を切望された。その眞劍さに感激し，一切の俗事を捨てて玆に滿洲佛敎學院の創立に努力する決心を固めた。

寺院僧侶は大概無學無信であるに反して，居士には篤學篤信の者が多い。僧侶は社會的地位がゼロであるに反して居士は紳士階級であり多く有產階級である。寺院僧侶に對して佛敎興隆策を相談しても何の反應もないが，居士は前述の通り熱心であると共に其の實力を有つてゐるので『滿洲佛敎學院』も居士中心に結成することにしたのであるが，その居士中の林傳樹氏は，密宗居士とて今より三十年前に帝國大學醫學部の聽講を了へた日本通であるばかりでなく，京都の東寺に於て毛陸僧正より受戒し爾來眞言の居士として密敎を硏究し八宗に通じ，滿洲に於ては恐らくこれだけの佛敎學者は希であらう。この居士が單に滿人の佛敎學者であるばかりでなく，日本語が解る點に

大いに力を得たのである。現に居士の書齋には新刊の日本佛教書籍が揃つてゐる。日本刊の佛教大辭典も備へ，どしどしと讀破してゐるのには驚かされた。この居士が中心となつて更に當地第一の財産家であり佛教信者でもある孔祥鱗氏が協力して去る六月十七日第一回創立委員會を開き，簡章二十二條よりなる具體案が決定した。

學院講堂は現在の龍江省佛教會をそのまゝ假講堂に充て，政府の許可あり次第に生徒募集を開始する豫定である

因に同學院は日滿合同で行きたいと思つてゐる。（チチハルにて七月一日）

參考文献其一

謹啓　貴台益御淸榮之段慶賀奉候

偖而日滿兩國の血盟的提携は今後益緊密を要するに拘らず兩國民精神の中樞たる宗教，慈善教化事業に關しては完全なる交通聯絡無く彼我の關係親善を缺くの觀有るは甚遺憾に御座候

依つて弊社は在滿八千の弊誌讀者と有力各方面の理解ある贊同を仰ぎ全滿主要都市に

『日滿宗教々化慈善團體懇話會』を開催し日滿兩國の宗教家社會事業家との懇談的淸和の會合を開催し相互の意見交換と共に今後の宗教及敎化事業に關する希望等を談笑の裡に會通致し度く念願仕り第一回を北滿の首都當市に開催仕候，就は御多忙中甚恐縮乍ら日滿相互の宗教及敎化事業策進の一助とも御思召萬碍一擲振つて御來會賜り度く謹而御案內申上候　　　　敬白

康德三年六月一日

日滿宗教敎化團體懇話會

主催　滿　蒙　事　報　社

責任者　牛　谷　範　成

殿

趣　　旨

一，日滿ノ宗教，敎化運動ノ聯絡統合親和ヲ企圖シ全滿主要各地ニ隨時開催ス

二，政治，軍事，時局問題ハ之ヲ論ゼズ

三，會開催費一切ハ主催者ニ於テ負擔ス

四，參會者ノ芳名及ビ會懇談內容ハ『滿蒙事報』及ビ宗教新聞「中外日報」ニ發表ス

案　內

日　時　六月四日　午後六時

會　場　南大街　卜奎大旅社大廣間

會　費　無用

主催事務所　卜奎大旅社第二號

電　話　二三八九　三二〇一

參考文献其二

謹啓者貴台多福定能如頌祭日滿兩國之血盟親善今後益有緊密之要就中若可一貫兩國民精神之宗教，道德，敎化慈善事業等運動其須協力一致進行懇意以爲當今之急現弊社仰得日滿各有力方面之理解及贊同，在玆主催日滿宗教々化慈善團體懇談會深望滿洲國宗教家及慈善敎化團體諸公枉駕來會以便在滿日本各宗開敎使會合擧行懇親式淸話會知諸公多忙不暇願爲日滿兩國宗教及慈善敎化事業之共同策進計務祉一擲萬碍惠然來臨是所至禱謹此特懇

康德三年六月一日

日滿宗教々化團體懇話會

主催　滿　蒙　事　報　社

責任者　牛　谷　範　成

殿

趣　　旨

一，流合日滿宗教々化運動之聯絡以企圖親和在全滿主要各地開催之

二，不論政治軍事時局問題必以道人僧侶之淸談擧行談道懇親會

三，會開一切費用均由主催者負擔之

要　項

期　日　六月四日　午後六時

會　場　南大街　卜奎大旅社大廣間

會　費　無

紀　念　對當日列席者芳名永久記錄之以表敬意

主催事務所　卜奎大旅社第二號

電　話　二三八九　三二〇一

參考文献其三

日滿宗教提携之我見

龍江省敎育廳　禮敎科長　徐　大　年

引　　言

宗教爲人類精神之食糧。人於宇宙。無間物質享受。如何豐富。要不過肉體方面。暫時滿足。終不克救濟人生之窮盡。苟欲順應現實。證澈微密。完成大我中之小我。擴張生命之有限爲無限。捨信仰宗教。固無由焉。世界現行各敎。雖儀律不同。面目互異。而其解遮去蔽。勉於爲善。初無二致。是知宗教作用。形而下者。在服役社會。造福人群。使含靈之屬。胥蒙其利。形而上者。在由可知通於不可知。世間通於出世間。生滅通於不生滅。世謂『宗教即健康』洵不誣也。故觀察國家或民族文化程度之高低。第以其宗教信仰暨活動情形爲主眼。則剝膚見髓。事無逃形矣。嗚呼此誠吾人全生活重點之所在。烏可不勉力赴之也哉。

（1）日滿宗教提携之必要

日滿兩國。僅一衣帶水之隔。彼此關係。自昔已極密切。比以血盟成立。邦交益形親善。爲促成兩國民間澈底合作計。除於政治，軍事，經濟方面。互相提携外。其在文化部分。尤應努力流通。以期更深一層了解。而宗教爲文化之導踐。乃國民精神所寄託。必使双方信仰。趨於一致。則一切行動。自臻和協。而百凡事業之聯絡發展。當不難迎双而解。融洽無間矣。

（2）滿洲宗教系派及團體數目

滿洲現行宗教。分佛，道，耶，回，與混合各種。孔道是否宗教。久已成爲學術上一大爭論。滿洲建國。雖極力尊孔。但主張信敎自由。仍以孔子爲學術上之先師。未案視爲信仰上之敎祖。故關於孔道是否宗教。非本文討論之範圍也。屬於佛教者。有天台，慈恩，華嚴，眞言，淨土，禪門，諸宗。屬於道敎者。有龍門，武當，金山，玉山，金輝，金耀，等派。屬於耶教者。分新舊兩派。舊派爲天主敎。統稱公敎。新派爲基督

敎。分長老，約老，淩信，安息，公誼監理，自立，兄弟，信義，美以美，基督敎等會。回敎體系。比較單純。並無派別。混合各敎。有以儒釋道三敎合立者。亦有併入耶回兩敎。標榜五敎歸一者。佛道兩敎。所有宗派。皆自立門戶。不相統屬。耶敎舊派直隸羅馬敎廷。新派立有個別之聯合會。而以世界大會爲總機體。回敎舊極散漫。紀元以還。始有伊斯蘭協會之組織。究爲聯絡上之統制。混合各敎。大都沒有攏分支部。體系比較完整。各敎團體及寺廟數目。據康德元年之統計。共有兩千二百六十一所。佈敎者男一萬三千零七十三名。女六百零三名。合計一萬三千六百七十六名。信徒男三十九萬八千七百四十三名。女三十二萬四千五百五十三名。合計七十二萬三千二百九十六名。

(3) 各敎活動概況及對於社會之影響

滿洲宗敎。歷史悠久。佈散普遍者。首推釋敎。大要系統。分密顯兩宗。蒙人多奉密宗。所受持者。爲密呪，印訣，及梵字心觀等法。民國十九年，後藏扎什倫佈大喇嘛班禪額爾德呢氏蒞滿宣化。復傳授一種密法。名曰『掌善巴拉』譯言北方淨土。爲現行密法中之又一支派。流傳極爲寬廣。至密敎以外之顯敎各宗。以禪門，淨土，爲盛。天台慈恩次之。學人蕉修。大抵僧伽方面。率重天台一宗。主張融通敎果。達成禪淨雙修。普通善信。多信仰蓮宗。以回向淨土爲行持重心。而智識階級。則頗事名理。好談唯識。道敎各派以龍門，金山，爲盛。餘者次之。蕉修之法。舊有服食，符籙，導引，燒鍊，丹道，諸種。現在流傳者。只導引，丹道，兩門。勸勸之術。習者已尠。餘則僅存其名。無復措及者矣。耶敎新舊兩派。信仰中心。本屬一致。而新敎與舊敎不同之點凡四。一，否認敎化是爲靈權的總持者。二，廻避崇奉聖母瑪利亞。三，不以獨身主義爲必要。四，主張依經解經。排斥因人立義。兩者比較。舊派信心純篤。新派主張開明。回敎系組織體系。頗形單純。修持方法。分認，禮，齋，課，朝，五功。及殺，傘，豬，壞，奴，五戒。混合各敎。以理敎特別發達。唯一戒條。在禁絕煙酒及一切有害身心之醉麻物。其他各派。雖有宗敎儀式。而無特立主義。綜觀各派情形。釋道兩敎。爲具有順應性者。耶敎爲富於進取性者。回敎爲側重保守性者。混合各敎。爲色涵融通性者。要而言之。佛敎根蒂深。道敎布散廣。耶敎活動最力。回敎信心極固。混合各敎。接人平易。此固一般所公認者也。

(4) 對於日本宗敎之希望

宗敎之本體。雖具有恒久性。而其作用。則隨時張弛。與歷史嬗遞。成正比例。滿洲現行宗敎。因經過民國時代二十年間。長期紛擾。宗敎本身。亦隨政治社會之墮落。陷於不振之狀態。且各敎有一共同弱點。即偏重個人修養。缺乏團結精神。其上焉者。不過栖心冥漠。潔力自好。下焉者，竟因緣爲利。偷生世間。宗敎前途之不能發展。自亦無怪其然也。反觀日本各敎。自明治維新以來。因環境選擇關係。對內則整正系統。培養人材。以謀宗敎本質之充實。對外則服役社會。提高文化。而促宗敎作用

之擴張。論者謂日本六十年來。國勢躍進不已。其理由雖多。而宗敎家光輝篤實。扶翼世運。亦一重大原因。比者滿洲建國。日滿以血盟關係。彼此有如骨肉之不可分離。吾人所希望於日本宗敎家者。宜以先進國之資格。將日本近世宗敎上改進之良法美舉。灌輸新國。使其攻錯他山。足資借鏡。此蓋滿洲建國上當前一大急務。與政治經濟之合作提携。實有同等之價値。

(5) 日滿宗敎提携之對策

日滿宗敎。究宜如何提携乎。據記者個人之鄙見。其初步必要辦法。約有四點。1，成立日滿宗敎團體聯絡機關。作爲統制之張本。2，開催宗敎的講演，講習，展覽，觀摩等會。以便交換知識。融洽感情。3，舉凡關於慈善救濟及各種社會事業。協同動作。以示步調之齊一。而利效率之增進。4，兩國宗敎上著作物出版物互相交換。俾資流通經論。了解敎義。以上所列。不免拉雜堆砌。掛一漏萬。但能一一行之。於日滿宗敎提携前途。未始毫無裨益。質諸明達。當能不吝予同情也。

参考文献其四

日滿宗教教化團體懇話會記要より

齊々哈爾朝鮮人民會理事
吳　寅　根

司會者『之から一つ朝鮮民會の吳理事樣にお願ひしますが現在在留朝鮮人の宗敎狀態並に指導上の計劃をお話していたゞきたいのですが如何ですか』

吳理事『朝鮮內地に於ては數年以內朝鮮總督府に於て盛んに心田の開發運動が唱られ現にうまく進展されつゝあるのでありますが，當齊々哈爾に於ては今まで色々の事情がありまして徹底した此類の運動がなかつたのでありますが最近に至りましては此點について色々と研究をして居ります。特に在滿朝鮮人の特殊事情に稽へ一般民衆の精神を作興し一面經濟的更生を圖ると共に在留朝鮮人をして健全なる信仰心を喚起し，之を培養して動もすれば無味乾燥に陷り，或は自暴自棄に赴かむとする民衆の心田に潤ひを與へ，好んで業を勵み，生を樂しみ，軈がては確乎たる人生觀を把握して敬虔なる精神生活に導かねばならぬと云ふことを痛切に感じて居るのであります。此席は主に日滿各宗派の指導の任に當る宗敎家が多くお集まりになつて居りますので此席に於て一つ將來共皆樣の御指導と御協力をお願するつもりで小生の宗敎界に對する希望と所感をつき加へて話させてもらひ度いのであります。

現代の時代相を一言で約すれば享樂の亂舞時代ではないかと思はれます。同時に現代が所有して居る文明は，文字通りの享樂文明であると思ひます。その例として，當齊々哈爾の社會を眺めて見ても歲月が流れる程，享樂はふえて行くばかりです。すべての計劃，機關が享樂を產出し又は享樂を多量產出し樣と競爭して居る樣に見えます。

之に反して宗敎團體並に敎化團體の現狀は寒心にたへない狀態ではないか

と思ひます。

斯樣な社會に處して居る我等は如何にすべきか？と云ふのが，一課題になつて居ります。

我等は此の社會相に逆行する外は途がないと思ひます。

此の問題に付きまして吾等朝鮮人に對しては特に念を入れて必死的努力と訓練が要求されております。生と云ふものは新しい經驗の連絡であると云ふことを聞きましたが，吾等は此の難關と逆境を越えて禍を福に，不幸を幸福に色々な難關を突破して自己人格を向上させ自己人格の完成へと努めなければならぬと思ひます。

之には不斷の修養が必要とされて居ります。眞の修養とは宗教を離れてはないと思つて居ります。正しい心を持たせるのが宗教ではないかと思ひます修養とは自から良心に照らして，高潔な圓滿な人格を築かうとする處にあります。自己の不足，缺陷を痛切に感ずる處から奮然と立ち上る處に吾が朝鮮人の將來が約束されて居ると思つて居ります。此の意味に於て吾が朝鮮人は朝鮮人の將來の爲め生に必要な熱を與へ希望を與へて與れる熱の宗教を要望して居るのであります。現在色々と不利なる立場に居る朝鮮人に對し解放的新しい經驗を與へて與れる宗教を必要とするに至りましたのであります。以上述べたる如く，生と云ふものは新しい經驗の連絡であると云ふことを申しましたが吾等朝鮮人が要求する新しい經驗とは，解放的經驗を云ふのであります。吾々の誤まつた觀念，誤まつた行爲，誤まつた理想，誤まつた感情から解放を經驗させてもらひたいのであります。

斯の如く宗教的信念と熱とを持つた上吾等の正確な生の態度を把握させたいと云ふのが吾等の希望であります。如何なる態度で自然，人生，社會，生全體を眺め且對したら良いか？と云ふ圓滿なる心持を與へる樣な宗教を熱望して居るのであります。社會心理學的の立場から言へば「現代の焦躁の原因は生活態度の調節不能といふことにある」と敎はりました。要するに變遷多き現今は心的能力を要する一つの底力ある生活意識の把握が必要であると思ひます。

斯の如き力ある宗教の感化を受け在滿朝鮮人の人格を向上せしめ以つて他民族と肩を比べて五族の中より「朝鮮民族は最も信頼すべき民族である」と云ふ稱讃の辭を浴びつゝ，五族融和の先頭に立つ樣に指導し樣と云ふのが吾等朝鮮人の指導的立場に居るものゝ「スローガン」であります。

宗教上の信仰は各自の自由に屬す可き者でありますから各宗派の代表の方々がお集りになつた此の席上に於て如何なる宗派に歸依させたいと云ふことは申されませんが，以上述べた通り朝鮮人の信仰的渇望を御參酌の上何卒皆樣方には今後吾等朝鮮人と共に宗派別を超越して，堅實な實践運動，聖なる眞理運動をこゝろみ新しい經驗的要求の充足を計りたいと思つて居ります。

最後に一言申し添へて置きますが在滿日滿兩國民が如何にすれば提携出來るかと云ふ先の司會者（半谷氏）の提案に對し色々と皆樣の御意見もありましたが私としては何よりも國境を越え融和を理想とする文化的共同がある日滿宗教の團結から先づ「スタート」を切らなければならぬと思ひます。でありますから何卒今後共斯樣なる日滿宗教團體の方々がよく集まつて日滿不可分の關係を宗教的にしつかりと結ばれる樣御願致します。餘り長らく拙辭を述べ皆樣の耳を煩らはして甚だ濟みません。』(完)

← 當日の記念撮影 ↓

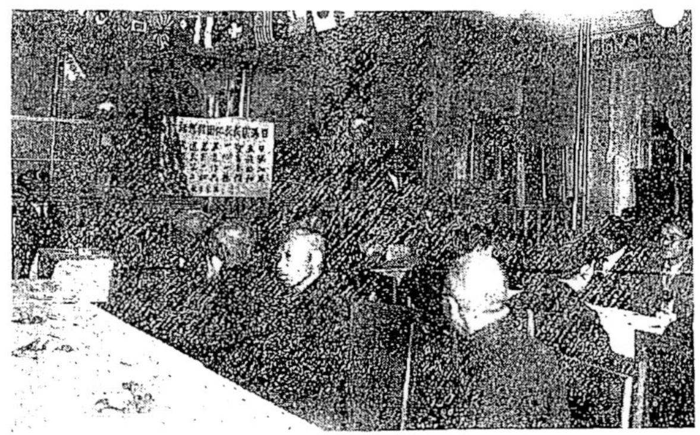

臺灣佛教事情概說

臺灣佛化青年會理事　楊　天　送

はしがき

臺灣の佛教は之を大別して(A)在來佛教と(B)傳來佛教の二つとすることが出來る。在來佛教は本島が未だ帝國の領土とならぬ以前に於ける佛教を謂ひ，傳來佛教は領臺後わが國人に依つて齎らされた日本佛教を指して便宜上名附けたものである。今この二つを(A)在來佛教(イ)佛教(ロ)齋教(ハ)連絡寺廟(ニ)今後の問題・(B)傳來佛教(イ)沿革(ロ)現況(ハ)今後の問題・の各項に別けて概說して見やう。

(A)在來佛教

(イ)佛教　臺灣は御承知のやうに我が版圖となつてから僅々四十一年を出でず，それ迄の二百餘年間は清國の統治下にあり，從つて住民の約九割は漢人種に屬する「本島人」を以て占められてゐるので，在來佛教は勢ひ其等本島人の先住地たる福建及び廣東地方の寺院より，傳來するものに止まり，多くは南支の鼓山湧泉寺及び怡山長慶寺等の末徒の開拓創建に係つてゐる。從つて皆禪宗に屬するも，內地の如くに純然たる禪宗ではなくして淨土の教義を幾分か混じたものである。卽ち觀音佛阿彌陀佛等を竝祀し，觀音經，阿彌陀經，楞嚴經等を念誦する。而も傳來當時の清朝に於いては佛教が恰も衰運の極に達してゐた時であり，僧侶は皆無學の徒のみにして空しく堂塔伽藍を擁するに過ぎず，口に經を誦するも心に其の義を解するものなく，能く法を說いて民衆を敎化するものに至つては殆んど絕無と云つてもいゝ位であつたから，本島の僧侶も略々同一狀態にあるわけである。そして多くは晩年に孤獨となり或ひは貧困爲すことなくして，身を佛寺に投じ，修行一年內外で二三卷の經文でも唱誦し得れば乃ち僧と稱するが如き有樣であるから，彼等は殆んど其の社會的地位を認められず，本島人同志の間に於て和尙(He-siun)に對し一種侮蔑的態度を與へる風さへあるのである。故に全島數千の僧侶中能く數卷の經文を理解し得るものは現に其の1%にも及ばないであらう。之は誠に默視出來ない寒心すべき狀態と云はねばならない。茲に於いて之を深く遺憾とし進んで之が改革を企つべく起つたのが齋教(Tsai-kau)であると云へよう。

因みに佛教の本尊としては，觀音・釋迦・阿彌陀佛・藥師佛・地藏王・達磨・彌勒佛・羅漢等を擧げることが出來る。就中，觀音(Koan-in)が最も多く，之を祀れる寺廟齋堂は，三百以上に及んでゐる。

(ロ)齋教　之は一名「在家佛教」(Tsai-ke-fut-kau)と云ひ，明朝の頃に禪宗特に臨濟宗より變胎したもので，先天派・龍華派・金幢派等の分派がある。其の教義とする所は，一般佛徒の夫れと殆んど變りないが，たゞ其の他に儒教又は道教の教義を幾分か加味してゐるだけである。そして其の建物を「齋堂」と云ひ，教徒を「齋友」と呼んでゐる。此の齋教徒が僧侶と異る所は，出家せず，從つて頭髮も剃らず，法服も纏はず，一般の俗人として市井に生業を營み乍ら，而も佛弟子として身を持すること嚴正に，能く戒律を守ることに在る。そして彼等は常に菜食して肉食を絕對にしないことを本義としてゐるので俗に之を食菜人(Chian-ts'ai-lang)と呼んでゐる。思ふに之は一般僧侶の空手徒食・破戒無恥の弊風を目擊して起つたところの佛教改革派とも云ふべきものであることは先に述べて置いた通りである。然るに現在に於ける實情は必ずしも感心すべき狀態に在るとは云ひ難く，聊か末法腐敗の弊に陷れる傾向がないわけではない。

尙ほ齋教の本尊としては，佛教系の諸神特に觀音・釋迦を主とし他に羅祖師（龍華派の開祖で明の英宗時代の人羅因を云ふ）・王祖師（金幢派の開祖で明の世宗時代の人王在塘）等を擧げることが出來る。

(ハ)連絡寺廟　上述の如く在來佛教の寺院齋堂が全島各地に約三千散在して居りながら其れを司る僧侶・齋友が至つて低級なるため，之を此の儘に放任すれば退步こそすれ絕對に進步はなく，從て民衆敎化など望むべくもないのである。依つて是等舊慣寺廟と相提携しつゝ之を啓導し以て佛教の理想顯現に幾分なりとも貢献せしむべく其の向上を圖らんと企てたのが傳來佛教の着眼點であつた。そして之を實行し現に尙ほ實行しつゝ働きかけてゐるものに同系統の臨濟・曹洞二宗があつて，旣に前者は百七十餘ヶ所を後者は百二十餘ヶ所を獲得してゐる。之を便宜上「連絡寺廟」と稱へてゐる。今自分が靜養のため厄介になつてゐる此處も「法藏寺」と呼ぶ齋堂で觀音を主祀してゐる一方，曹洞宗の新北投布教所となつてゐるのは連絡寺廟の一適例である。之の連絡寺廟に期待する所は極めて大きいが然し現實と理想とが必ずしも同一レベルでないのは遺憾の極みであるこの點に今後の問題が殘されてゐる次第である。

(ニ)今後の問題　以上在來佛教を通觀して特に取り上ぐべき問題は（イ）(ロ)の各項に於いて述べたる僧侶・齋友の地位向上と身分の敎養に關すること，之に關聯して所謂舊慣寺廟を統制し且つ寺廟に於ける實權を管理人より住職に移して其の活動を自由ならしめること，又(ハ)の項に就き傳來佛教の各派が協力して眞に日本佛教の大精神を以て積極的に働きかけること――斯くして全島三千の寺廟齋堂が黎明の鐘を鳴らして一齊に起てば本島人社會の面目は忽ちにして一新するであらうと期待し且つ切望してゐる次第である。

(B)傳來佛教

(イ)沿革　之の方は明治廿八年の領

臺當時旣に征臺軍に從つて本願寺派の布敎使が來臺し，兵馬倥偬の間に於いて盛んに活躍したことに始まる。その後間もなくして島が平定したので愈々敎線の擴張にとりかゝつたわけであるが，何しろ住民の八九割までが言語不同の本島人であるから，土着民の敎化を目標にとの當初の理想が，實地に來て見れば仲々に行ひ難く，遂に布敎方針が遠く故國を離れて渡臺して來た內地人方面の慰安乃至おつとめに變更してしまつたのである。之の當初の熱意が足りなかつたゝめに日本佛敎が今日に至るも尙ほ依然として本島人方面を閑却視し得ざる原因をなしたのであるされば領臺四十一年を經過した今日，よく本島語を以て說敎し得るものは臨濟宗の東海宜誠師たゞ一人であるを見ても肯かれよう。そこへ行くと基督敎はえらいものである。此の點に就いては去る五月大阪に於ける佛青全聯總會席上の椎尾博士の講演中にも洩らされてゐるやうであつて，流石は博士の高邁なる觀察だと敬服してゐるわけである。

（ロ）現況　上述の布敎對照云々の問題は兎も角として，其の後各宗派も追々本島に敎線を延ばすこととなり現在に於いては臨濟，曹洞，東西本願寺，淨土，日蓮，法華，眞言，天台の宗派があり，寺院百三十餘（布敎所を含み連絡寺廟を除く）・布敎使百八十餘を算してゐる。以上の各宗派の中，臨濟曹洞兩宗が（A）の（ハ）に述べたる如く比較的本島人間に布敎し居り數萬の信者を持つてゐる。他は殆んど總べてが內地人を對照にしてゐるのは申す迄もない。

尙ほ各宗派が社會敎化事業方面に於いて現在なしつゝある諸施設の主なるものは中等學校二，國語講習所四，幼稚園二五，救療機關六等である。

（ハ）今後の問題　主要なるものを列擧すれば，布敎方針を更正して本島人を對照とし大いに努力すべきこと，之に依つて日本佛敎の裡から本島人大衆に國民精神を吸收せしめること，從つて（A）に於いて述べたる連絡寺廟に對し積極的に働きかけること等の諸點となる。而して之が目的の達成を圖るためには（イ）觀光がてら又は島流しの意味を持つた布敎使を派遣して來ないと（ロ）在臺布敎使の自覺を促し一生骨を埋むる覺悟で從事せられたいこと，（ハ）よく本島の實情を觀察し其れに適當した布敎方針を樹立すべきこと——以上の諸點は勢ひ內地各宗本山に於いても認識され配慮せられたい。

（C）佛青運動

以上に於いて述べたる如く，本島に於ける佛敎の傳道狀態が未だ極めて微咲すべき下位に在るので，從つて多分に近代的意義を有つ佛青運動も又草創期に在るのは寧ろ當然であらう。現に全島を通じて十團體を算し得ず，而もその多くは有名無實であると云つてよい位で，たゞ二三の團體が漸やく其の命脈を保つてゐるに過ぎない。之の佛青運動に關しては別に「青年佛徒」の近號誌上へ拙稿「臺灣に於ける佛青運動」を發表して置いたから御參照下されば御諒承出來ることゝ思はれるから茲では重複を避けるため省略させて頂くことゝする。

（D）統轄機關

本島に於ける佛敎を含む宗敎方面の管轄官廳としては，神社と併せて，總督府に文敎局社會課の社寺係があり，各州敎育課及各廳庶務課に同樣の社寺係があるに過ぎない。之の一事を以てしても本島に於ける宗敎團體の地位が閑却視されてゐることが肯かれる。若し夫れ宗敎の民心に及ぼす敎化上に於ける影響が敎育と比肩すべきものであるならば，今少し官署を格上げし擴張強化せねばならないのである。之も今後，佛敎を中心として宗敎界が向上すれば當然適宜に考慮さるべき問題であらうと信ずる。

尙ほ佛敎の統制機關としては，在來佛敎の啓導向上を圖る目的の下に府內文敎局社會課に "南瀛佛敎會" と稱する團體があり，十數年來，機關誌の發行・講演會・講習會の開催等に依り相當活動して來てゐる。現在では會員千餘名を擁し本島に於ける最も有力なる佛敎團體である。

此の他に臺北市內の傳來佛敎各宗派を網羅した "臺北各宗佛敎聯合會" といふのであり，連絡寺廟に關しては臨濟・曹洞兩宗に夫々本部があつて統制に當つてゐる。

序でに僧侶の養成機關に就いて一言附記したい。が今のところ取り立てゝ書くべき程のものがなく，たゞ臨濟宗の高林立賓師の統監に係る "佛敎專修道場" が一つ在るに過ぎない。之とて規模小さく僅々十餘名を收容し二年制の入門程度に止まつてゐる。が併し斯かる機關は……に相當大規模のものが出現せねばならないのであるが，矢張り之も以上述べて來たやうな佛敎環境にあるから望むべくもなかつたのである。將來是非とも實現させたいものゝ一つである。

斯るが故に，在來佛敎の僧侶中に學識ある者が稀である原因の一半も首肯できようと思はれる。（完）

〔備考〕　以上を以て甚だ粗漏ではあるが臺灣に於ける佛敎事情を概說したつもりである。然し之に關する文献が極めて少い上に自分の淺學禿筆が加はつて幾多杜撰の點があることを虞れつゝも昨秋以來遷延してゐた淺野主幹との約を果すべく敢て此の拙文を發表させて頂いた次第である。幸ひに先輩各位の御叱正を得ば望外の至りである

（11. 7. 25.　於法藏寺客室稿之）

國際佛教通報局

昭和十年度事業報告

昭和十年度に於ける事業概要左の如し

一，定期刊行物「國際佛教通報」の發行
昭和十年四月以降毎月一回之を發行す

一，外人佛教研究者に對する研究上の斡旋
佛教研究の斡旋に應じたるもの左の如し

シユリ・ジナ・ワンサ・スワミー	（セイロン）
ヨシアス・バン・ヂーンスト	（ジヤバ）
ジエー・ダブリウ・ド・ウイツト	（ジヤバ）
ヴインセント・ド・シルバ	（コロンボ）
アルツーロ・アルバレツツ・モンテネグロ	（アルゼンチン）
ルアン・プラジツト・マヌダルム	（シヤム）
モン・ニー・プー	（ビルマ）
ム・モン・キン	（ビルマ）
モン・サン・ネオン	（ビルマ）
ビク・ナーラダ	（セイロン）
ラフラ・サンクリツトヤーヤナ	（印度）
談玄法師	（中華民國）
大醒法師	（中華民國）
黄輝邦居士	（中華民國）
一先法師	（滿洲）
崔恩培居士	（滿洲）

一，圖書刊行物の國際的頒布
海外に於ける各大學，研究所等へ「英文佛教聖典」及「第二回汎太平洋教佛青年會大會紀要」を贈呈せり又「國際佛教通報」を毎月贈呈せり

一，日本に於ける國際佛教的會合を主催すること左の如し

四月十八日	滿洲布教を語る夕
六月一日	ナーラダ比丘，ラーフラ比丘，大醒法師歡迎會
七月二十一日	汎太平洋佛教青年デー
十月四日	滿洲支那事情座談會
十月二十四日	滿洲國大使館孫錯氏の外交部事務官へ榮轉送別會

一，國際佛教人名鑑の編纂
目下繼續中

一，國際佛教文献目錄の編纂
目下繼續中

一，佛教英語講座の開設
ジエー・ブリンクリー氏を講師として十月及十一月の二ヶ月開講す

一，汎太平洋新教育會議に參加す

一，海外佛教事情の視察
好村春基（中支，三月より四月まで）
常光浩然（布哇，北米，六月より十一月まで）
大村桂巖，稻葉文海（滿洲，八月）
藤井草宣（南支，十二月）

一，海外佛教狀勢の調査蒐集

國際佛教通報局定款

名稱

第一，本局を國際佛教通報局と稱す

事務所

第二，本局の事務所を全日本佛教青年會聯盟本部に置く

目的

第三，本局は日本內海及海外に向つて佛教事情の通報をなし，且つ佛教徒相互間の各種便宜を計るを以て目的とす

事業

第四，本局の目的を達成するため左記の事業を行ふ
イ，日本內地及世界各國より佛教事情に關する質問の通報を行ふ
ロ，必要に應じ日本語及世界各國語を以て佛教事情の通報を行ふ
ハ，外國人の日本觀光に際しては各種の便益を與へ，特にその佛教に關する方面に於て之を爲す
ニ，定時或は隨時に各國語を以て文書の刊行をなす
ホ，その他必要と認めたる事業を行ふ

役員

第五，本局の事務を處理するため左の役員を置く
イ，局長　一名
ロ，幹事　三名
ハ，評議員　若干名
局長は本局の事務を總括す
幹事は本局の事務を處理す
評議員は局長の提案に依る重要事務を審議す

第六，評議員は左記の者を以て之に充つ
イ，全日本佛教青年會聯盟理事及主事
ロ，全日本佛教青年會聯盟理事會に於て推薦したる者

第七，局長及幹事は評議員會に於て決定す

第八，役員の任期は二ヶ年とす（但し重任を妨げず）

經費

第九，本局の經費は左記のものに依て之を支辨す
イ，本局基金の活用
ロ，寄附金
ハ，その他の收入

補則

第十，本定款に記載せられざる事項は，凡て評議員會に於て協議す

第十一，第一回の役員は全日本佛教青年會聯盟理事會に於て決定す

定價	一部	金二十錢	送料二錢
	一年	金二圓四十錢	送料不要

昭和十年四月廿日第三種郵便物認可
昭和十一年八月廿八日印刷（毎月一回
昭和十一年九月一日發行　一日發行）

東京市外吉祥寺337
編輯發行兼印刷人　淺野研眞

東京市牛込區早稻田鶴卷町107
印刷所　康文社印刷所
電話牛込（34）1950番 5049番

東京市神田區一ツ橋二の三
發行所　國際佛教通報局
電話九段（33）4428番
振替東京83015番

昭和十年四月三十日第三種郵便物認可
昭和十一年八月二十八日印刷納本（每月一回
昭和十一年九月一日發行　一日發行）
國際佛教通報　第二卷　第九號

第二回

汎太平洋佛教青年會大會紀要

THE PROCEEDINGS of THE Second General Conference of Pan-Pacific Young Buddhists' Associations

(in Japanese, Chinese and English)

Held at Tokyo & Kyoto, July 18–23, 1934

Price ¥ 3.00

Compiled & Published
by
The Federation of All Y.B. As. of Japan,
Tokio, Kanda, Hitotsubashi, II-3

昭和十年四月三十日第三種郵便物認可　昭和十一年九月二十八日印刷納本　昭和十一年十月一日發行（每月一回一日發行）第二卷　第十號

The International Buddhist Bulletin

國際佛教通報

第二卷 **昭和十一年十月** 第十號 [Vol. II. October $\frac{2502}{1936}$ No. 10.]

要　目 [Contents]

東京　**國際佛教通報局** 發行
The International Buddhist Information Bureau
Tokyo, Kanda, Hitotsubashi, II—3

Staff of the Bureau

Hon. President	J. Takakusu
President	K. Ohmura
Secretary	S. Takagai
〃	B. Inaba
〃 (in chief)	Ken Assano
Advisers	H. Ui
〃	G. Asakura
〃	R. Hatani
〃	U. Ogiwara
〃	R. Higata
〃	T. Suzuki
〃	S. Suzuki
〃	S. Amakuki
〃	S. Nagai
〃	B. Matsumoto
〃	B. Shiio
〃	E. Uno
〃	C. Akamatsu
〃	Z. Ohmori
〃	K. Yabuki
〃	S. Onoh
〃	S. Katoh
〃	M. Anezaki
〃	G. Honda
〃	R. Sekimoto
〃	J. Sahegi
〃	R. Hanada
〃	H. Kohno
〃	R. Takaoka
〃	Z. Kobayashi
〃	S. Yamabe
〃	C. Akanuma
〃	E. Honda
〃	R. Ohmori
〃	E. Kawaguchi
〃	C. Yamakawa
〃	D. Tokiwa
〃	T. Tanimoto
〃	G. Tokiwai
〃	S. Ohtani
〃	E. Ohtani
〃	B. Mizuno
〃	I. Shibata
〃	S. Ando
〃	J. Shimomura
〃	S. Kikuzawa
〃	K. Norisugi
〃	T. Shibata
〃	K. Asano
〃	T. Watanabe
〃	G. Onoh
〃	K. Yanagizawa
〃	M. Shigemitsu
〃	E. Kanakura
〃	S. Tachibana

國際佛教通報局

名譽局長	高楠順次郎
局長	大村桂巖
幹事	鷹谷俊之
同	稻葉文海
同	淺野研眞
顧問(順序不同)	
〃	宇井伯壽
〃	朝倉曉瑞
〃	羽溪了諦
〃	荻原雲來
〃	干潟龍祥
〃	鈴木大拙
〃	鈴木宗忠
〃	天岫接三
〃	長井眞琴
〃	松本文三郎
〃	椎尾辨匡
〃	宇野圓空
〃	赤松智城
〃	大森禪戒
〃	矢吹慶輝
〃	小野清一郎
〃	加藤精神
〃	姉崎正治
〃	本田義英
〃	關本龍門
〃	佐伯定胤
〃	花田凌雲
〃	河野法雲
〃	高岡隆心
〃	小林瑞淨
〃	山邊習學
〃	赤沼智善
〃	本多恵隆
〃	大森亮順
〃	河口慧海
〃	山川智應
〃	常盤大定
〃	谷本富
〃	常盤井堯猷
〃	大谷尊由
〃	大谷瑩潤
〃	水野梅曉
〃	柴田一能
〃	安藤正純
〃	下村壽一
〃	菊澤季麿
〃	乘杉嘉壽
〃	芝田徹心
〃	淺野孝之
〃	渡邊哲信
〃	小野玄妙
〃	柳澤健
〃	重光葵
〃	金倉圓照
〃	立花俊道

Tales of Buddhist Priest (III)

by **Atsuharu Sakai**

(6) Priest Saigyo

Norikiyo Sato was a court-warrior in the service of the ex-Emperor Toba. A descendant of Hidesato Fujiwara, a warlord in the northern part of Japan, Sato was skilled in archery and other arts of fighting, and he was a great favorite with the ex-Emperor, who was very fond of Japanese poetry in which Sato excelled. When all sliding paper-doors of his new Palace had pictures painted by master-painters of the day, the ex-Emperor told all his courtiers to compose poems on them. Sato improvised ten poems, which were all collected in an anthology compiled later at the command of the ex-Emperor Toba, who conferred a sword upon Sato as a token of his appreciation of the poems.

His poetic nature, however, made Sato pessimistic. He was already tired of life and the court, and particularly of the false ways of the courtiers. What is life, whence and whither, was a question that Sato constantly asked himself, but, unable to get at a satisfactory answer, he turned to Buddhism for its solution. The higher he rose in the favour of the ex-Emperor and the greater honour he received from him, the more he longed; for the free life of a mendicant priest whom nothing could ever bind, for what was honour or reputation to him when he was disgusted with life and the world? He was looking for the opportunity of renouncing the world in order to devote himself to Buddhism and poetry, which of all things, he thought, were only true.

Once Sato kept watch at the Hosho-ji Temple, which the ex-Emperor visited, when one of his soldiers was kept in detension by the troops of Tameyoshi Minamoto, his senior warrior. Offended at the arbitrary measure of Minamoto, Sato repaired to the Minamoto camp, without taking any soldiers with him, in order to demand the

detained soldier. He was prepared to fight Minamoto or any of his soldiers, if necessary. Minamoto, on the contrary, delivered the soldier without any protest, and Sato, disappointed as he was, was displeased more with the weak attitude of Minamoto than with the refusal that was expected. Why did Minamoto detain the soldier, whom he could deliver without any protest, Sato asked himself, and he thought the worse of Minamoto, who might have made fun of him.

Norikiyo Sato had an intimate friend in Noriyasu of the same family-name, Sato. They had free talks on every subject, but Norikiyo always expressed pessimistic views on the vanity of life and betrayed his cherished hope of devoting himself to Buddhism. One afternoon, on their way home, Norikiyo talked with him in the usual strain of talk, and at parting he promised to call for him on the following day. Early on the next morning, Norikiyo went to his friend's, when he noticed something unusual, and what was his surprise to be told that Noriyasu, with whom he talked about the frailty of human life the day before was carried off by a sudden disease during the night, leaving his aged mother and young wife, who were crying over his cold body? Noriyasu was twenty-five years old, two years senior to Norikiyo.

Determined now to reveal everything to his wife, Sato came home. His four-year-old daughter came out to the veranda to meet him. The father rose within him, and he wanted to take her in his arms, but no! it was her love as well as her mother's that kept him from leading the life of a mendicant priest. He kicked the innocent girl down the veranda. She cried, but his wife, who had already noticed the changed frame of his mind, thought little of his heartless treatment of their daughter.

That evening Sato disclosed to his wife his intention of abandoning the world in order to lead the free life of a travelling mendicant. In the small hours, on the following day, Sato got up, he tiptoed into the bedchamber of his wife and daughter to have his last look at them, offered a lock from his hair to the Buddhist family-altar, where the departed members of his family were enshrined, and left his home never to return to it again. Sato was then twenty-three years old.

Sato made his way to Saga, where he was formally converted

to Buddhism, and he assumed the Buddhist name of Saigyo (literally, Going-west), for in this country our posthumous salvation is believed to be found in the west,

Priest Saigyo made a hermitage at Saga and devoted himself to Buddhism. Whether his whereabouts were not known to his relatives, or whether they had adandoned him as lost, he was left unmolested in his religious devotion, though Saga was situated at little more than a stone's throw from Kyoto, where his deserted wife lived. A couple of years went by and Priest Saigyo wanted to see Yoshino, which was famous for its cherry-blossoms. On his way he visited Nara, where he worshipped the Daibutsu or large image of the Buddha and paid his respects to the Horyu-ji Temple and the Miwa Shrine. He arrived at Yoshino too early for the flowers and he made another hermitage there.

Every now and then Priest Saigyo thought of his wife and daughter, deserted as they were, and once he wrote a 31-syllable poem, which roughly translated reads as follows:—

"Mt. Yoshino—
Never to leave it
I am determined, but ah!
My return may be expected
After the flowers scatter."

One day there came to his hermitage an old mendicant priest, thin and emaciated. Priest Saigyo read his life history at a glance. for his mien told that he had been a courtier or court-warrior like himself. Priest Saigyo asked him to take a rest, and he offered a cup of hot water, but the visitor preferred cold water.

"How can I get enlightenment?" Priest Saigyo asked him after he told how hard he was trying to get it.

"No difficulty" the visitor simply replied. "All you have to do is to eliminate evil thought, for else, how hard you may try, you cannot hear the voice of the Lord Buddha."

"How can I eliminate evil thought? Tell me more definitely."

"Why, selfishness must be done away with. Briefly, you must put yourself in the state of 'no world and no thought.' The Buddha will take hold of you when and not until you forget yourself. He will hide Himself from you so long as you stick to self. You must seek the state of nothingness."

Priest Saigyo was charmed at the way his visitor talked and he

wanted to keep him longer, but he would take his leave.

"Where do you reside?" Priest Saigyo asked.

"I lead the life of a snail, for I carry my hermitage with me. Where I stay there is my hermitage; no fixed place for a wandering mendicat, you know."

Still water gets bad; so does man who stays long at one place. Priest Saigyo moved constantly from place to place in search of Buddhist enlightenment and the satisfaction of his poetic desire. He was now desirous of climbing Mt. Nachi, which was known for its steep heights. He looked for a guide, for no pilgrim could climb the dangerous mountain without one, and he was fortunate to meet Priest Nambo-sozu, who offered to take him up the mountain. This priest had been on the mountain twenty-eight times, and he would guide Priest Saigyo on condition that the latter would strictly obey him through any hardships. Priest Saigyo agreed and he put on the robe of a Yamabushi or mountain-priest, instead of his own black one. Together they climbed the mountain by crossing many dangerous places, and when they came to the place known as "Gyoja-kaeri" (ascetic-return), so named because the rocks are so steep that even an ascetic will return without going farther up, Priest Saigyo was entirely exhausted and fainted.

"You must take heart," the guide said when Priest Saigyo was again himself. "We are but at the beginning of our steep passes. You have many more before you, ten or twenty times as hard as those we have come through. But privations always do us good. You suffer only because you have selfishness in you, though you think you have done away with it. No use of seeking enlightenment without abandoning yourself or so long as you stick to self. Forget yourself and you will feel no suffering."

Fatigued as he was, Priest Saigyo followed his guide, alpine as well as religious, till they reached a cottage where they stayed overnight. Soon they found themselves on the top of the mountain and Priest Saigyo was happy that he had borne all the hardships, His guide told him again and again that self-abandonment is the only secret of religious ascetisism, for true courage comes only through self-abnegation.

Priest Saigyo came back to Kyoto after a wandering life of a few years. He wished to see how his wife and daughter, whom he had deserted, fared. He went to the place where his former residence stood, only to be told that his poor wife had moved away soon after his desertion, and his house had been pulled down. It was with some difficulty that he succeeded in locating her. One evening, after dark, Priest Saigyo approached the house in which his wife and daughter lived, and he was satisfied to see, under cover of darkness, how big his daughter grew up. He wished to reveal himself, but no, he had renounced the world and his family. So he stole away as quietly as he came.

Priest Mongaku had a dash of the hero in him. He could not like Priest Saigyo, who he thought was no better than a hypocrit.

"If I ever meet Saigyo, that dog of a begging priest" Priest Mongaku used to say, "I will knock him down. He is a traitor of Buddhism. He should devote himself to Buddhism without travelling round as a beggar; he should know better."

But when Priest Saigyo came to Mt. Koya, where Priest Mongaku stayed, they had a long talk.

"Why did you not knock him down?" a friend asked of Priest Mongaku after Priest Saigyo went back.

"Did you see his pious features?" Priest Mongaku said. "He is a saint; how could I knock him down? But, on the contrary, he could knock me down."

While on Mt. Koya, Priest Saigyo met Gennojo, one of his former retainers, who wanted to become his disciple in Buddhism. Priest Saigyo helped him in taking the tonsure by calling him Saio (also meaning Going-west) after his own name.

Priest Saigyo took his new disciple on a pilgrimage. They visited the Ise Shrines, and came to Hamana by way of Akogi-ga-Ura. When they came to the River Tenryu, which they had to cross on a ferry-boat, a haughtly and petulant samurai told them to leave the boat because he was above crossing the river on the same boat as did a devil of a mendicant priest. Priest Saigyo pretended not to hear him, and remained silent for all that the angry samurai said in a loud voice. At last the samurai came to him and struck him on the face; blood ran from his cheek. Priest Saigyo silently left the boat, without returning a single word,

but his disciple, Saio, could not stand the insult inflicted on his innocent master, and he lifted his fist up to strike the warrior back.

"Hand down, Saio" Priest Saigyo said calmly but sternly. "I am here for the sake of the Law, for which I am ready to die at any time. I should have no grudge if I were to die in the cause of Buddhism. I brought you with me on condition that you would stand any hardships. I also told you to resist no violence. You must control yourself for the Lord Buddha's sake. Retaliation is against His command. Better go back to Mt. Koya and have more self-culture."

Saio was thus sent back to Mt. Koya, and Priest Saigyo went on his pilgrimage by himself. When he saw smoke coming up from Mt. Fuji, Priest Saigyo wrote a 31-syllable poem, which, literally translated, will read:

"Running as the wind blows,
The smoke of Mt. Fuji
In the sky disappears,
Whither nobody knows—
So does my heart wander."

Priest Saigyo travelled on till he came to Koromo-gawa, the city of his distant ancestor, Hidesato Fujiwara, to whom he paid his respects at his grave.

In 1185 Priest Saigyo visited the Hachiman Shrine, Kamakura, when Yoritomo Minamoto received him in audience. Yoritomo, who heard much about the priest, asked him many questions about military art and poetry.

"Before I renounced the world," Priest Saigyo said modestly, "I used to learn a bit of military art, but upon my renunciation, I burned up all the books on militarism that had been handed down since my ancestor. So I can say little on militarism. And as for poetry, I only improvise as it comes on, and I have nothing either to say about its secret."

But Yoritomo insisted that Priest Saigyo should tell his courtiers something about the secret of military art and Priest Saigyo talked on for hours on end, to the great admiration of Yoritomo and his warriors. Yoritomo gave him a silver cat as a reward which, however, Priest Saigyo gave to a little boy playing on the street, near the residence of Yoritomo.

At the Hase-dera Temple, on coming back to Kyoto, Priest Saigyo saw a nun devotedly reciting the sutra. The nun proved to be none other than his own wife, and they were both delighted at this unexpected meeting. According to what she told him, she did not know what to do with her daughter after his desertion, and so she moved away from his house. At first she hated him for his heartless way, but she soon learned to realize the way her husband acted, and she herself took the tonsure to be devoted to Buddhism, after leaving her daughter in the hands of a relative. Then Priest Saigyo went to Kyoto again to see his daughter, whom he found to be another nun in a temple.

Priest Saigyo expressed a wish about his own death in a well-known 31-syllable poem, which reads in sense:

"I would—
That under the flowers
I should die in the spring,
About the full moon of the
second month (February)"

And Priest Saigyo did die on the 16th, or a day after the full moon, of the second month (February) in the year 1190 at the age of 73 years.

His was altogether a wandering and poetic life, for he spent fifty long years in travelling all over the country and writing a poem on every occasion. He left several anthologies, of which the Sangó-shu (Mountain-house-collection) is best known.

—·—

"Kumo ni tada
Koyoi no Tsuki wo
Makase ten
Itou tote shimo
Hare-nu mono yue"

(To the care of the clouds the moon of this evening should be committed; for no worry, how great, can make it clear.)

"Ukiyo niwa
Todome okaji to
Haru-kaze no
Chirasu wa Hana wo
Oshimu nari-keri"

(It is because of love for flowers that the spring breeze blows them off in order not to leave them in this world of fleeting life.)

"Yo-no-Naka no
Uki wo mo shirade
Sumu Tsuki no
Kage wa waga mi no
Kokochi koso shire"

(The moon alone can appreciate the frame of my mind that shines serene without the knowledge of the worldly cares.)

The Free Religious Observations of Layman

by T. Seo

(The Professor of the Kobe Higher Technical School)

Although we find men of good character among religious devotees, most of them are idle and ignorant. They often collect money from poor people as contributions to the funds of churches or temples, pretending to carry on business for God. I think that the majority of religious propagandists do not have the true spirit of Buddha or Christ. They corrupt their own religions. Rich people do not like them.

In ancient times, religious men cut roads through steep mountain districts, and also built many bridges over rivers everywhere. Notwithstanding the fact that they were poor, they did much hard work with great determination. At the present time, they only squeeze a lot of money by their eloquence, which swings the minds of weak men and women to and fro. In other words, they act like beggars. This is a fact. Many rich people wish to be free from such impostors.

Recently in Japan, religion is in demand. But neither the present religions nor those of the past can relieve the spent minds of modern men and women. Nearly all religionists practise outworn forms of propaganda or preaching. We know that modern men and women are intellectually inclined, but at the same time they are extremely sentimental and prone to spiritual despair. They are not strong-minded. I am sorry to say that the really intelligent once are few in number. In my opinion, the Kingdom of Heaven does not lie in preaching or in books, but exists in labour and effort. This is a bold but true statement. Many sensible men and women do not welcome religionists, while they respect religion. The sharp fellows in religious circles are constantly busy with plans to build temples of churches. In Japan, there are many newly built temples, which have been erected by the contributions of easily impressed followers. Buddhism and Christianity are losing their true spirit. People of common sense, both rich and poor, therefore, try to avoid the established religions. Feuerbach, one of the disciples of Hegel, an eminent German philosopher, said, "Religion is like opium." From some points of view, he was right. A certain foreign teacher of one of the local colleges, in speaking about Buddhism and Christianity. said that the former is passive and the latter active. I agree with his opinion. He is well informed on both of these religions. I maintain that Christianity has an aggressive tone and Buddhism an introspective colour. Though the central doctrine of Christianity is love of one's enemies, its attitude towards enemies is strongly aggressive. Its fighting spirit is itense. On the contrary, Buddhism is calm and quiet. In my opinion, there is no unmixed goodness in humanity, and vice versa, there is no evil without goodness. The human mind is like water, which consists of oxygen and hydrogen. There is no water with oxygen and without hydrogen. So the human soul is composed of goodness and badness.

As soon as Buddhism came to Japan, it was japanized. The spirit of the Japanese, as a nation, is exclusively optimistic. In the past, Japanese did not think about a future life, and even now they do not think about it. Their main thought is that comes into the world like a flame and leaves it. The sentimentalism of some modern Japanese was not originally indigenous. The Japanese are not a philosophic people, that is, a nation of "Denkers." They do not like speculation or meditation, generally speaking. They are different from the Germans or Russians in that respect. My opinion is this, that every action should be religious. Sleeping, speaking, and working are religious acts, but ceremony and prayer do not constitute religion. At any rate, religious adherents must improve themselves from their own religious standpoints.

We may say that the Ecclesiates of the Old Testament is the equivalent of the Kongokyo, one of the Sutra of the Buddhist scriptures. "All things are not constant and

everlasting, but unstable, momentary, like dew or like lightning." These words are found in the Kongokyo. "Vanity of vanities, saith the preacher; vanity of vanities: all is vanity." Thus says the Ecclesiastes. Now, where is Alexander the Great? Where is Julius Caesar? Where is Genghis Khan? Where is Napoléon Bonaparte? Their graves are covered with weeds, their names are in history. But did God love them?

We are living at the time of a national crisis, but the people are sleeping at the foot of a volcano. The more cultured people become, the more their desires are increased. When these are satisfied, they add more and more desires. This is a natural human tendency, though all men are intelligent in some degree, it is very hard to control their minds because they do not believe in god. They have many things,—clothing, houses, food. They do not live like people in ancient times. They read many books, but they are empty-minded. They try travelling to divert their mind from their troubles. But they get nothing. The financiers are not happy, because they are unfavourably criticised by the poor. If the financiers should retire on account of the opposition of ignorant labourers, the tables would be turned, I suppose. in short, the struggle between the rich and the poor would bring no prosperity to human society. If the rich were to abandon their commercial activities, what would the poorer classes then do?

Budhisma Artikolo en Encikropedio de Esperanto

Sosei Nakanisi

En "Encikropedio de Esperanto" kiu estas eldonita de Literatura Mondo, Budapest en Hungarujo je 1934 unuan volumon kaj sekvantan je 1935, la artikoloj kiuj havas rilaton al Budhismo, kompreneble ne estas multaj kompare al aliaj religioj Katoliko, Protestanto, Bahaismo kaj ceteraj. Sed mi ankaŭ facile povas trovi la pligrandiĝan emon de Budhisma kampo en Esperantujo kaj de praktika aplikado de Esperanto en Budhisma kampo. el la artikoloj.

En la encikropedio la prezentitaj religioj estas jene :—

Bahaismo. Budhismo. Katoliko. Liberpensuloj. Metodistoj. Novspirito. Oomoto. Protestantoj. Societo de Amikoj. Teozofio.

Ili estas cititaj je la titolo "Religio".

Kaj la titolo " Budhismo " havis sekvantan priskribon :

Budhismo. Religio de almenaŭ kvinono de la loĝantaro de la tero, sur doktrino de paco kaj pacamo, racia gravigo de altruismo. Esperanto-grupo ĉe la Ootani Budhisma Universitato en Kioto de feb. 1922 ĝis marto 1923 eldonis gazeton La Paco, red. de Kozo Tanijama. En 1925 A. C. March el London kaj Edgar Grot el Riga klopodis por fondi internacian ligon de Budhanaj Esperantistoj, kaj proksimume samtempe fondiĝis "Budhana Rondo", sed nek nnu, nek alia atingis vere internacian vivon. Nur en la gazeto "Buddhism in England" aperadis Esperanta fako de tiam ĝis 1930. En januaro 1930 Budhana Ligo Esperantista ekagadis, elsendante bultenon La Budhismo, kiu poste fariĝis kvaronjara organo. Samjare japanoj sekvis per fondo de Japana Budhana Ligo Esperantista. Budhana Ligo Esperantista havas centron ĉe Geo. H. Yoxon. 8 Elmwood Drive, Heswall (Cheshire), Anglujo, kaj Japana Budhana Ligo Esperantista ĉe Takakura-Kaikan, Rokujo-Takakura, Kioto, Japanlando. Vasta agado kuŝas antaŭ la liganoj : la traduko de la ampleksa budhisma " biblio " (Tripitako) de kanonaj skribaĵoj, la enkonduko de Esperanto en budhanaj landoj, ĉefe pere de la misiistaj organizaĵoj kaj la konigo de la doktrinoj de budhismo al la Esperantistoj de la Okcidento.

En la titolo Nipono, per la subtitolo Religio jenaj estas skribitaj :

Religio. Generala aspekto. En ŝtataj lernejoj prediko de religio estas malpermesata. Tiou necesigas la ŝtata politiko, ke super imperiestra familio estu nenio sankta. Plej parto de la nunaj japanaj junuloj ne havas religian kredon. Budaismo, ludinta gravan rolon en malnova tempo, havas grandan kredantaron precipe inter maljunuloj. Kristanismo, importinta okcidentan civilizon, ne estas potenca. Ŝintoismo estas dividata en du formoju : ŝtata rito kaj popularaj sektoj. Al la lasta apartenas Tenrikyo, Oomoto, Ittoen, Hitonomiĉi estas tri el la novaj religioj aŭ religiaj movadoj. En lasta tempo kelkaj budaistoj utiligas Esperanton, sed malmultaj kristanoj atentas pri Esperanto. Oficialan alprenon faris nur Oomoto. Iam oni provis enkonduki Esperanton en Tenrikyo, sed senaktiva rezulto. En Ittoen spirito de Esperanto estas tre respektata kaj en la komenco de la organa gazeto oni vidas esperanto - tradukon de ĝia devizo. —(Ellasas kelkajn vortojn) —Budaismo. instigite de la fondo de Budhana Ligo Esperantista (en Anglujo) Japana Budhana Ligo Esperantista estis fondita 12 junio, 1931 de F. Dazai, Ŝ. Inada, J. Mononobe, K. Ŝibajama. Unua ĝenerala kunsido en Kioto, 15 okt., kun pli ol 40 partprenantoj, el kiuj nur malpli ol 8 komprenis Esperanton. La energia agitado de la ligo per la bela gazeto multe propagandis Esperanton al Budhanoj. En 1933 Junula Ligo de Proletaj Budhistoj (en Tokio) starigis Esperantan fakon kaj en majo 1934 presis en Esperanto en sia literatura gazeto "Aka" unuan salutleteron al "Buddhist Lodge" 2a Tutpacifika konferenco de Budaismaj Junularaj Ligoj kun Esperanto kiel unu el uzlingvoj, 18-21 Julio, 1934. Bibliografio de Budhismo en La Revuo Orienta, Julio, 1934. —(sekvantan forlasas)

Ankaŭ sub sama titolo en subtitolo 1934a movado oni vidas jenan priskribon :

"En julio en Tokio II-a konferenco de Tutpacifikaj Junularaj Budaistaj Asocioj, kie oni permesis paroli Esperanton al tiuj kiuj ne scias japanan, anglan ĉinan ligvon."

La biografietojn de s-ro Erin Asai, kiu estas professoro de Formosa Universitato, de s-ro Grots, kiu estas latva monaĥo kaj sola ekster japano, de s-ro K. Ŝibajama, kiu estas ĉefo de Japana Budhana Ligo Esperantista, de d-ro J. Takakusu, de s-ro T. Takeuĉi kaj s-ro J. Nakaniŝi, kiel Budhanajn eminentajn Esperantistojn, oni trovas en la encikropedio.

Ankaŭ mi ne devas forlasi s-rojn H. Nagata kaj K. Nohara, kies biografietoj en la encikropedio ankaŭ havas rilaton al Budhismo. S-ro H. Nagata estas unua japana ministro por kolonio kaj en la biografieto "Por la viktimoj de tertremego en 1923, li, tiama urbestro de Tokio, verkis konsolfrazon kaj enterigis ĝin kun ĝiaj Esperanta kaj angla tradukoj en budaisman monton, por konservi ĝin je dek mil jaroj" ĉi tiun frazon oni trovas. S-ro K. Nohara ne estas Budhano sed multe havas favoron al Budhismo kaj li bone komprenas sanskriton, la biografieto "Tradukis el sanskrito budaismajn sutrojn: "Sukhavativjuho", 1923; "Samantamukhaparivarto", 1923; enhavas cititan frazon. "La Samantamukhaparivarto" alie havas propran titolon kiel bone konatan eldonajon.

En la fotografajaj paĝoj oni trovas jenajn broŝurojn kaj gazetojn:

Broŝuroj:

Budao. Tradukita de s-ro Takeuĉi.

La kodo de princo Ŝotoku. Tradukita de s-ro C. Takaiŝi.

Gazetoj:

La Budhismo. Organo de Budhana Ligo Esperantista.

La Libero. Persona Budhisma revueto de s-ro J. Nakaniŝi.

La Lumo Orienta. Organo de Japana Budhana Ligo Esperantista.

La Lumo Senbara. Organo de Esperanta fako de Budhisma Savarmeo.

La Paco. Organo de Esperanta Grupo de Ootani Universitato.

La Voĉo. Organo de Esperanta Grupo de Rinsai Universitato.

Sankta Tilio. Organo de Esperanta Grupo de Rjukoku Universitato.

Graveco de ĥina-tradukitaj Kanonoj en Budhisma studado.

de Sanĉi Asano

En granda brilanta lumo dekkvar centjaroj pasis de la tempo, kiam je la unua fojo Budhismo estis enkondukita Japanujon el Kudara, Koreujo, kiu estis civilizita memstara lando en tiu tempo.

Akordiĝinte kun antikva kredo de la popolo Budhismo disvolviĝis iom post iom en sia areco kaj doktrino. Sed ĝis komenco de Meiĝi-epoko ĝi ne riratis senpere kun Hindujo, kie glorinda lulilo de Budhismo ekzistis. Kvankam oni studis ian sanskriton nomatan "sittan", sed en tiama Japanujo ekzistis nur kvar aŭ kvin manuskriptoj de malgranda kanono. Post kiam Japanujo malfermiĝis komercon kun eŭropaj landoj, kie jam vigliĝis Indologia studo, Japana Budhismo ankaŭ ekfariĝis havi riraton kun Hindujo. En naŭa jaro de Meiĝi, 1876 p. k. Bunjuu Nanĝoo alvenis Anglujon por studi sanskriton kaj esploris energie dum naŭ jaroj sub prof. Maxmüler. Reveninte el Anglujo D-ro Nanĝoo malfermiĝis sanskrit-lekcion en Tokia Imperia Universitato en 1887. Multe da manuskriptoj estis enkondukitaj en nia lando per sindonema klopodo de keljaj energiaj Budhismaj lernantoj. Tiel studo de sanskrito en Japanujo vigliĝis jaro post jaro.

Nun tempe la studo de sanskrit-manuskripto faras tre necesa parto en Budhisma lernado, sed ĝi estas nur komplementa en tuta Budhisma lernado. Ĉar kvankam jam multaj sanskritaj kanonoj estis ektrovitaj, komarante kun ĥina-tradukitaj kanonoj ili estis nur iometaj kaj brańĉecaj.

Ĥina-tradukitaj kanonoj estas konservitaj sub la nomo "Daizoo-kjoo", kiu estis publikigita dektri foje en Hinujo, du foje en Koreujo kaj ses foje en Japanujo. En ses publikigoj de Japanujo tri estas pli famaj, k. e. Oobaku-ban Ŝukusacu-ban kaj Taiŝoo-ban. Mi klarigas ilin ĉi-sube.

1) Oobaku-ban: enhavas 6771 volumojn. Tecugen, Budhisma bonzo vivanta en Edo-epoko, projektis publikigi en 1669 kaj elfaris en 1681. Oni diris dum tiu ĉi laborado granda rizo-mankado ekaperis en Japanujo, tiam Tecugon savis multe da malriĉuloj per uzi donacmonon por publikigo. Pro tiu akcidento li devenis haltigi sian intencon, sed li staris tuj kaj tenis unuan projekton. Fine li sukcesis. Tiu ĉi publikigaĵo estis represigita

laŭ Ming-ban. Ming-ban estas unu speco de ĥina-publikigaĵoj, sed ĝi havas multe da eraroj. Sekve Oobaku-ban ne havas pli altvaloron.

2) Ŝukusacu-ban: enhavas 8534 volumojn apartenitajn je 40 skatoloj. Zooĝooĝi, fama templo en Tokio, posedis tri antikvajn altvalorajn publikigaĵojn de Daizookjoo, k. e. Tsung-ban, Yuan-ban kaj Li-ban. Laŭ la peto de Bankon Simada, Gjookai Fukuda, superulo de Zoĝooĝi, permesis uzi tiujn ĉi por revizii Daizookjoo'n. Tiu publikigado komenciĝis en 1880 kaj perfektis en 1885.

3) Taiŝoo-ban: enhavas 11970 volumoj. Post kiam Ŝukusacu-ban Daizookjoo estis kompletigita, Budhisma studo en Japanujo progresis abrupte uzinte tiun ĉi novan libraron. Plue historieca kaj scienceca studstilo estis alprenita de pli novaj lernantoj, kiuj estis influitaj de eŭropaj studantoj. Precipe per la esploroj al okcidenta provinco de Ĥinujo multe da ĥinotradukitaj kanonoj estis eltrovitaj. Prof. Junĝiroo Takakusu intencis plie redakti Daizookjoo'n, kiu enhavas nova-eltrovitaĵojn. Akirinte multajn helpulojo, d-ro K. Uatanabe, G. Ono, k. t. p. li komencis efektivigi sian intencon. Oni decidis presigi unuan volumon en la septembro de 1923, sed bedaŭrinde jen estis tertremo en Tokio kaj li devis prokrasti la intencon. Sed tamen li kaj lia helpantoj kunlaboris entuziasme. En la majo de 1924 unua volumo, kiu enhavas 214 volumoj laŭ antikva enklasigo, aperis kaj ĉiu monate sekvantaj volumoj estis presigitaj unu post unu. Tiel ploj vasta libraro de Budhismaj kanonoj, Taiŝoo-ŝinŝuu-Daizookjoo, estis kompletigita en la aprilo de 1932.

La karakterizaĵo de Hinda literaturo, inkluzive Budhismaj, estas ke laŭ jaroj pasantaj ĉiu literaturo estis vastigita aŭ ŝanĝita per ia certa intenco aŭ necerte. Se iu laboraĵo naskiĝas, ĝi kreskas jaro post jaro, kaj post kiam kelkaj centjaroj pasis, ĝia figuro estas tre ŝanĝita. En la patrujo pli antaŭaj laboraĵoj malaperis sekvante kaj nur plej malantaŭa restis, ĉar ĉiuj literaturoj estis portitaj el buŝo al orelo kaj konservo de manuskripto ne estis perfekta. Ĥina-tradukado de Budhisma kanono estis intencita en ĉiuj epokoj sub protekto de tiama reganto. Tial eĉ la kanono, kiu jam malaperis en Hindujo, estas konservita en Ĥinujo tradukite. Je unu speca kanono en Hindujo tri aŭ kvar tradukitaĵoj ekzistas en Ĥinujo. Komarante ilin unu la alian ni povas trovi kiel ĝi progresis kaj per kio ĝi estis influita. Tiel nun tempe kvankam multe da sanskritaĵoj estas trovita, tamen ĥina-tradukitaj kanonoj havas pli grandan valoron en Budhisma lernado. — fino —

Nippon University Guides Educational Activities of Japan

Nippon University is one of the leading universities in Japan, is composed of the Departments of Law, Political science, Economics, Commerce, Literature, Arts, Religion, Engineering, Architecture, Electricity, Medicine and Dentistry.

The university was started as the Nippon Law School in 1888 by the former Minister of Justice Count Akiyoshi Yamada. It was established to found Japanese jurisprudence following the promulgation of the constitution in 1888. The first president of the instituion was Viscount Kentaro Kaneko.

In keeping with the economic development the Nippon Law School was reorganized as a university in 1902 comprising the colleges for political science, economics, sociology, Japanese literature and arts.

The earthquake of 1923, reduce all the buildings of the university to ashes. However, in less than ten years a modern institution with well equipped laboratories. libraries and three university hospital was constructed. These buildings are located between Misaki-cho and Surugadai Heights in the central part of the capital.

The Nippon University further plans to establish the departments of agriculture and science.

Leading scholars of the country are at the head of each departments of the university. 15,000 students are enrolled this year. Graduates number 35,000. There are many students from Siam, China, Manchoukuo and other countries.

Law Department

Before the establishment of the university Japanese jurisprudence was an imitation of that of France, Germany or England, Foreign legislation was about or directly applied to Japan.

There was disagreement among the supporters of the French, German and English systems and the old laws of the country were forgotten. However, Count Akiyoshi

Yamada, then the Minister of Justice, believed that each nation ought to have its own legislation. He declared that Japan should begin with the old laws of the country, which, though crude in form, have been in existence for thirty centuries. Nippon University was therefore established.

The code of the institution was based on the spirit of national foundation. National language and literature, and the old laws of the country were studied in addition to the subjects of common law schools.

In 1911, the Department of political science was introduced.

Over 1.000 students of the Law Department are graduated annually, many of them practice law while others pursue politics as their profession.

Literature

The Department of Literature gives courses in religion, in sociology and literature.

Its students are engaged in elective research work under the direction of staff comprising Japan's leading scholars. Various courses in education are also open to women.

Religion. This course provides for an impartial comprehensive study of religion with a certain amount of basic instructions in law, economics, social work, and religious sects. After graduation, the students become missionaries or social workers. The number of graduates has recently totalled over 2,000.

Sociology. The course in sociology aims at promoting proper control of public thought. A large number of its graduates are now active in the various fields of social work. The number of Chinese students enrolled are increasing year after year.

Literature. It was first founded in 1924. At present, it includes philosophy, ethics, education, psychology, Japanese literature, Chinese literature, English literature and history.

Commerce and Economic

The Department of Commerce and Economics was founded in 1905.

The establishment of the department was most appropriate since it coincided with the period of Japan's economic expansion in Manchuria and Mongolia as well as in South China and the South Sea Islands following the Russo-

Japanese War. In 1819, it was recognized as conforming to the university regulations of the Government.

The graduates number more than 5,000.

The department is equipped with various facilities such as libraries and a museum. Thus students are allowed free access to various publications, statistics, advertisements, the specimens of various products, materials and manufacturing machineries. It publishes three magazines.

The Higher Normal School

When the Higher Normal School was first organized in 1901, it had only two courses, one in ethics and another in law and economics. In 1920, Japanese and Chinese languages were added to the curriculum. In 1926, a course in geography and history was provided in addition to an English course. The number of graduates has totalled over 3,500.

A. The course in ethics and citizenship. This course is obtainable in no other higher normal school.

B. The course in Japanese and Chinese Languages. Besides Japanese and Chinese languages, morals, philosophy, law and economics are taught.

C. The course in geography and history instructions are given by the leading scholars of Japan. Research work in historial documents or geographical survey is carried on by the students.

D. English course: Practical English is taught by a number of wellknown English scholars.

The Art School

The Art school provides its students with courses in fiction, drama, motion pictures, fine arts, music, etc. It is composed of the departments, Daigaku-bu and Senmon-bu-Geijutsu-ka. The latter includes such courses as fiction, drama, motion pictures, fine art and music, in addition to the Jitsugika including fine art. western music, Japanese music and dance.

In 1921, a new course in aesthetics was added to the curriculum. Three years latter, the department of literature was augmented with a special course in art. In 1927, the present art school was established at Kinsuke-cho, Hongo-ku. Last spring a kindergarten was attached to the Art School in addition to the first Foreign Language School.

Engineering

The history of the engineering school dates back to 1920 when a higher engineering school was established near the famous Nicholas Cathedral, Surugadai, Tokyo. It is now divided into the four departments of civil engineering, architecture, mechanics and electricity.

The Dental College

The Dental College of the university was enlarged to its present size in 1925 with the addition of a large building and modern attached hospital. It is equipped with the latest dental appliances. The students receive instructions in dental medicine, dental surgery and internal treatment. It has a 4 year course the completion of its most modern dental hospital.

The Medical College

The Medical College of the university is located near by the Nicholas Cathedral. It was established in April, 1925. It provides a four year course providing special attention to practical and clinical instructions. At present, the college has two hospitals at Surugadai and Itabashi.

The Junior College

The Junior College of the university gives middle school graduates a two or three year liberal educational course. It is equivalent to a Junior College. The institute provides a 3 year pre-legal and 2 year pre-engineering courses.

Affiliates Schools

Besides these schools, there are : a Dental School attached to the Dental College, a Higher Techinical School and a techinical school attached to the engineering college. They are all located, at Surugadai, Kanda. The university also has its first middle school and first commercial school at Yokoami-cho, Honjo-ku, and its second middle school, second commercial school and kindergarten at Amanuma, Suginami-ku.

Its third middle school and third commercial school are situated at Nakano-cho, Akasaka-ku, and its fourth middle school and fourth commercial school at Koyasu, Yokohama. In addition, the Osaka College and Osaka Middle School near Osaka are affiliated with University.

資料

中國佛學會章程 二十四年十月修改

第一章　總　則

第 一 條　本會定名爲中國佛學會（標準第一條簡章同）

第 二 條　本會以聯合全國佛學同志研究并發揚佛教之學理爲宗旨（標準第二條簡章同）

第 三 條　本會地址設于南京（標準第三條簡章第十條前段）

第二章　會員及其權利義務

第 四 條　凡中華民國國民於佛學有相當研究年齡二十歲以上確有正當職業者不分性別由會員二人以上之介紹塡具志願書經審査合格發給入會證得爲本會會員但有左列情事之一者均不得爲本會會員

(一)有反革命行爲者

(二)受開除黨籍處分者

(三)褫奪公權者　（標準第四條與簡章第三條有同異）

第 五 條　本會會員對內有選擧權罷免權創制權複決權以及其他公共應享之一切權利（標準第五條簡章無）

第 六 條　本會會員有遵守會章繳納會費及服從本會決議之義務（標準第六條簡章無）

第三章　組織及職權

第 七 條　本會設理事二十五人候補理事九人組織理事會監事十一人候補監事三人組織監事會其人選由會員大會選擧之（標準第七條）

第 八 條　理事會對內執行本會一切會務對外代表本會監事會糾察本會紀律審核本會財務（標準第八條）

第 九 條　理事會互選理事長一人副理事長二人監事會互選常務監事一人分掌日常事務（標準第九條）　（第七條至第九條與簡章第四第五兩條有同異）

第 十 條　凡於佛學有精密之研究或於本會有特殊之贊助者得由本會推爲名譽理事或名譽會員（簡章第六條標準無）

第十一條　理事會得設左列各股分掌一切事務其各股主任由理事會互推兼任之其幹事由理事會斟酌事務之繁簡延聘之

（一）　研究股設主任一人幹事若干人

（二）　講演股設主任一人幹事若干人

（三）　交際股設主任一人幹事若干人

（四）　慈善股設主任一人幹事若干人

（五）　宣傳股設主任一人幹事若干人

（六）　總務股設主任一人幹事若干人

（標準第十條但「其幹事由理事會至延聘之」等語爲標準第十條所無）

第十二條　本會之會務如左

（一）　研究會

甲，定期研究會每週至少一次

乙，特別研究會每週至少一次

（二）　通俗講演及農郁工場舟車監獄等講演

（三）　佛學刊物

（四）　佛學圖書館

（五）　佛學博物館

（六）　佛學編譯館

（七） 青年佛學修養部
（八） 經咒誦持教習班
（九） 參加或主導各種通俗法會及蔬食會等
（十） 厚生濟経事業之酌辦
（十一） 其他(簡章第七條標準無)

第十三條　各地或各大學有會員三十人以上時經本會之認可得設立中國佛學會某某分會但皆直屬本會（簡章第十條後段標準無）分會組織通則另定之

第十四條　本會之最高權力機關爲會員大會會員大會閉會期間爲理事會（標準第十一條簡章無）

第四章　經　　費

第十五條　本會會員入會時應繳納入會金二元作本會基金繳納常年費二元充本會經費若有特殊情事時經會員大會通過得收特別捐（標準第十二條與簡章第八條有同異）

第五章　會　　期

第十六條　本會毎年開大會二次遇必要時由理事會議決召集臨時會員大會（標準第十三條）

第十七條　如有全體會員十分之一以上表明會議目的及召集理由請求召集會員大會時理事會得召集之（標準第十四條）

第十八條　理監事會毎月各開常會一次遇必要時得開臨時會議（標準第十五條）

第六章　任　　期

第十九條　本會理監事任期以一年爲限但連選者得連任之如理監事有缺席時由候補理監事依次遞補其任期以補足前任未滿之期爲限（標準第十六條與簡章第四條末項不同）

第七章　紀　　律

第二十條　本會會員職員如有左列情事之一者由監事酌量情形懲罰之
（一） 不遵守會章者
（二） 濫借本會名義及其不正當行爲確有傷本會名譽者
（三） 不繳納會費者（標準第十七條簡章無）

第八章　附　　則

第二十一條　本會各種辦事規則由理事會訂之（標準第十八條簡章第十五條末段一部分同）

第二十二條　本章程如有未盡事宜得依民法總則第五十三條之規定修改之（標準第十九條簡章第十一條）

第二十三條　本章程自會員大會議決通過後呈請中央黨政機關核准施行（標準第二十條簡章第十一條）

朝鮮と滿洲の佛教に就て

藤　井　　晋

（a）　朝鮮の佛教

朝鮮佛教の事情は，視察時間の少なかつた事と，雨天に害されて，思ふ處迄行く事が出來なかつたが，京城有力佛教者の座談會に於て，聞き得た現在の佛教事情は非常に有益な點が多かつた。

朝鮮に佛教が渡來したのは，今から一千五百六十餘年前であり，歴代の朝廷が外護に依つて，全鮮に擴まり，其の隆盛は，諸種の文化を産み，高麗版大藏經六百三十九函，六千五百五十七卷，版板八萬六千五百二十五葉の如き代表的な行事も完成されたが，其の反面に於て，多大の惡弊を殘した爲め，李朝時代になつて迫害を受けて衰微したが，日韓合併に依つて再び隆盛となりつゝあるが，現状に於ては，布教方面に於ても，研究方面に於ても昔日の如き隆盛を見る事が出來なかつた。

特に今回の視察に於て感じた事は，在來の朝鮮佛教と，日本佛教の距離が餘りに大きく，彼等が因習を捨てぬのか，日本佛教の開教が内地人のみの布教以上に出ないのか，僧侶の態度に難點があるのか，十分研究する餘地があると思ふ。

現在の處では鮮人開教方法として，一，二有力なる宗派に於て行はれてゐる講習所，及び學校を設置してゐる程度の心細いものであつて，日本語の發達は都會地は勿論地方に於ても，左程不自由の無い程度に發達してゐる樣であるが，此れと平行してゐない憾がある。

朝鮮佛教寺院に於ても，又朝鮮佛教本山の經營になる中央佛教學院の内容に於ても，今少し，日本佛教の優秀性を取り入れなければ，發展の道なしとすら感じられる點が，其の授業科目に於ても，教授方面に於ても感じられるのである。

昭和十一年一月三十日を以て發布されたる心田開發施設に關する件に就いても相當佛教關係者及び，教育關係者の刺戟には成つたが，此れとて，實際に施行する迄には相當時日の經る問題であつて，今の處，總督府と民間關係者との協議會すら十分出來てない樣な實情にあるが，此れは民間側が總督府に一本先手を打たれたとも思へる點があり，此の問題なぞは，宗教團體が先づ政府に教ふべき問題であると思ふ。

（b）　滿洲佛教

滿洲の寺院生活は，形式的には戒律を守り續けてゐるが，内面的には然らず，また有力な教育機關を備へてをらぬ。教理を解する者は數百人の内二三名と思われる。僧形をなして，經文を口誦してはゐるが，讀書の出來る者は從つて少ない樣である。そして僧侶の衣類を初め堂内が不潔である。此の樣な生活である爲めに，一般民衆に及ぼす精神的影響は多く見出せず，國家に寄與するが如き事も少く，寺に付屬してゐる財產に依つて食ひ，寺の一部を農民などに貸與して收入を得てゐる樣である。

滿洲建國以來色々な刺戟を受けて，傳統的な佛敎の形骸を捨てゝ敎義の再認識，宣講所の設立，佛書頒布を目的とする流通所なぞを實行してゐる僧侶もあるが，此れとて，有力なる外護者の積極的な援助があつての事にて大衆性を持つ迄には相當研究を要する樣である。

寺院佛敎以外に居士を中心とした佛敎團體が近來出來初めた樣であるが，此の方が，社會的に十分な生活力を持つてゐる者ばかりであるし，敎育も相當受けた人々であるから，今後は此の居士を中心とした佛敎が滿洲に於て發展するならば，國家的にも，一般民衆の影響も相當强い好結果を來たす事と思はれる。

最近滿洲國政府は宗敎制度の制定と類似宗敎の制約を企圖せんとしてゐる樣であるが，滿洲建國の理想であり，平和境の實現であるべき，王道樂土，五族協和の提唱が自から明であるだけに，各民族の信ずる宗敎を生かし，善導して行く事が第一の目的であるが，滿洲建國の特種性を考へられる時，此の問題も相當重要であり，且つ困難な問題であると思ふ。

昭和十一年五月文敎部宗敎科の調査に依る宗敎統計書を一見する時，民族の分布と宗敎分布の實情とが如何に密接な關係をもつてゐるかを知る事が出來る。

即ち，佛敎，道敎，回敎，喇嘛敎，天主敎，基督敎，在理敎，猶太敎，薩瞞敎，等々の宗敎に，道敎儒敎の他宗敎との混合なぞを考へ，五族の分布狀態と並び行はれてゐる事をみる時に，國立敎會制度も，政敎分離制度も成立せず，特種な，滿洲獨特な協和制度の必要を感じるのである。又他宗敎相互の關係とか，滿洲國の中心になる處の宗敎の問題も研究すべき必要がある。

即ち道敎の混合してをる滿洲佛敎と日本佛敎との調和問題

王道精神に基きたる儒敎と皇道精神の表れである古神道精神の調和問題

宗敎的修養結社，及慈善結社と建國精神との調和問題

萬國道德會

同善社（中流以上の紳商を主とする宗敎）

半夜敎（下級農民勞働者間の宗敎）

悟善社

慈悲社

在理敎

淨地會(一心堂)

孔學會

華淨養眼會

道院

世界紅卍字會

日本傳來の類似宗敎

其他

此等の宗敎問題を如何に統理して行くかと云ふ問題は非常に困難な事柄であつて，他の國情と異なり，宗敎社會運動團體，秘結社の無數に續出する滿洲國は一層の困難を要すると思はれる。

（c） 日本佛敎の滿洲開敎狀態

新京奉天の開敎狀態を見る時に，すぐ思ひ出される事は，北米，ハワイ，臺灣，朝鮮の開敎初期と何等異なつた點なく，各宗共に同じ樣な方法にて，他宗敎の優秀なる點は少しも學んでゐないと思はれる。

遠く日本を離れて努力しつゝある人々は，日本內地の人々の經驗しない苦勞を味つてゐるだけに，宗敎心も非常に强く一切の考へが眞劍であるのに驚くそれが爲めに，內地に於けるが如き氣持を以て開敎する僧侶に對しては，種々の不滿を感じてゐる樣である。

開敎狀態をみる時，相變らず慰問佛敎であり，葬敎である以外に，自己の宗派心を强く持たない人々を，自己の宗派に勸誘せんが爲めの開敎であつて他民族に對する開敎は何等行つてゐない樣である。即ち在滿開敎師の內，幾人が滿洲語を語り得るかを考へると，驚くの外は無い。

長春より新京と改正される時に，各宗の信徒の有力者は，今後內地佛敎を新京に一ケ寺と定めては如何と言ふ議論が相當强く流布されたとか。

各宗の本山役人が滿洲へ視察に來て第一に感ずる事は，滿洲は通佛敎で行かなければ駄目であると痛感しながら自派の開敎地を視察して，要路者には，惡罵をあびせられながらも，くどく依賴して行くなぞ，實に滑稽な姿なりとは一役人の話であつた。(完)

佛敎通報局在外委員決定報告

布哇の部

戶田泰雄（曹洞）

竹田惠達（本派）

アーネスト・ハント（國際佛敎協會）

米國加州の部

寺川湛濟

土屋キヤスリー

丸山シミー

西藏からの便り

三藏阿闍梨　ラーフラ・
サーンクリトヤーヤナ

拜啓，貴方の六月二日附の手紙を拜受して，非常に嬉しく存じました。私は今再度梵本を探しに西藏に來て居ります。私は最も偉大な印度因明論師法稱(Dharmakīrti)の主著因明疏(Pramāṇavārtika)の完全な註釋三本を發明しました。私は又無著(Asaṅga)の瑜伽師地論(Yogācārabhūmi)の完全な寫本一本を發見しました。私はこの寫本の內若干のものは寫眞に撮りました。私は他の三四の僧院を訪れねばなりません。そこには貝葉の寫本があります。十月の末に印度に歸りたいと思つてゐます。

スワミ比丘の入寂の悲報を聞いたのは殘念でした。

佛陀の初轉法輪祭は印度では月暦に從つて，ヴェーシャーカ(Veśākha)日の後滿二月のアシャーダ月(Āsādha)の滿月の日に行ひます。

私は印度に到着してから，去年の十二月に重いチブスに罹り，一週間生死の間をさ迷ひました。この二月には體力が非常に弱つてゐましたけれど，私には因明疏の出版が非常に重大なことで，友人達の忠告を受けることが出來ませんでした。此の度は私は佛敎論理學の重要な寫本を數種發見出來て，好運でした。

丁度私は自分の「日本紀行」を二部受け取りました。私は既にその一部を貴方に送るやうに出版者に命じました。それは寫眞入りで，私達が一緒に撮つた寫眞も中に含まれてゐます。

私は貴方々の家に滯在した二月の間の平等家から受けた御親切を非常な愛着と共に終生記憶して居るでせう。書籍が送つてなかつたら，私が印度に歸つたらすぐ送りませう。・・・・

（西藏タシルンポにて，一九三六年七月三十日）

附記　印度高僧にて日本に昨十年春來朝したラーフラ・サークリトヤーヤナ阿闍梨の西藏旅行中からの芳信で，西藏のタシルンポルにて七月三十日書かれ，同じく西藏のギャンツェの消印があり，九月十一日に日本に着した。私信ではあるが，珍しい而かも重要梵本を發見し，印度の初轉法輪日を指示した報告なので公開する。

平等通昭

A Letter from Tibet

Rāhula Sānkrutyāyana.

My dear friend,

I was very pleased to receive your letter dated 2nd June. I am again now in Tibet in search of Sanskrit mss. I discovered three complete commentaries of Pramāṇavārtika, the chief work of the greatest Indian logician Dharmakīrti. I also found a complete copy of Asaṅga's Yogācārabhami. I have taken photographs of some of them. I have to visit three four other monastries, where they have got Sanskrit palm-leaf mss. By the end of the October, I hope, I will be back to India.

I am sorry to hear the sad news of the Swami's death.

The Dharmacakra festival is held according to Lunar calender, the full moon day of Aṣādha, just two months after Vesākha-day.

I, after reaching India, last December I had a severe attack of typhoide, and for a week I was lingering between life and death. Even in the month of February I was too weak, but for me the publication of Pramāṇavārtika is so important that I did not accept the friends' advice. This time I am more fortunate in discovering some important mss. on Buddhist logic.

Just I received two copies of my Journey to Japan. I have already instructed to my publisher to send you a copy of it. It is illustrated' and our photo is included there.

I will ever remember with great affection the kindness I received from Byodo family in my two months' stay amongst them. If the book is not sent, I will send them when I return to India. . . .

Note: This letter from our Rev. Rāhula was received by me, being dated on July 30th, 1936, written at Tasilhunpo of Tibet and bearing the Gyantse (Tibet) postmark. This is very interesting letter informing the discovery of important Sanskrit mss. of Mahāyāna Buddhism and replying about the date of Dharmacakra pravartana (the first sermon of Buddha) festival for my question with intention to settle it in Japan, So, though private one, this was adopted in our bulletin.

T. Byodo.

國際佛教ニュース

國選問題に對し 太虛圓瑛兩師語る

九月三日太虛，圓瑛兩大師は，上海赫德路の中國佛教會に於て，往訪の記者から佛教徒國選參加の問題について意見を求められ，大要左の如く述べた。

圓瑛大師「我々の商議してゐる佛教徒の國選候補の問題は，全然まだ發表の時期ではない。吾々の意見は只だ多數の合意に過ぎない。教義の宣傳上と理想の實現上では，太虛大師は當然私より高明である。しかし私は全國佛教會の實狀と各叢林僧尼の生活狀況に對して，或は比較的熟知してゐるかも知れないから，多數人の意見を採納しやうと思ふ。さうすれば萬事圓滿に行くだらう。」

太虛大師「私も國選參加の問題に對しては圓瑛法師の意見と大差はない。我々の目的は慈善，救濟，教育の事業を行はんとするにある。全國の信仰一致の佛教徒が，若し能く團結して努力するならば，則ち全國，延いては今の世界の和平に重大なる關係を持つものと信ずるのである。」

國府林主席 九華山に參拜

國府主席林森氏は九月四日文官長魏懷，參事長呂超，安徽省主席劉鎭華氏等を帶同して九華山祇園禪寺に抵り，五日午前正藏肉身塔に參詣し，午後は天台諸峯を歴遊し，頂上で記念寫眞を撮り，陪往の祇園寺の宏志和尚，佛教會理事長寶嚴，商界の章簡仙等に案內されて各叢林を參觀し七日下山せられたが，愛民護教，廉儉勤勞の範を垂れしものとして全山及び其他の人士を感激せしめてゐる。

上海佛學會の 佛化運動

上海市佛學會は以前雪竇寺にあつたが，今年二月西藏路に遷り，更にこの九月六日小南門三昧寺に移した。佛學運動に努力するため，理監事會議の決議に依り文書兼學務主任燈霞法師主となり，六條から成る宣傳辦法を作つて積極活動を開始する筈であると。(一)最短期間に會員大會を開き，佛學運動參加の大宣傳を行ふ。(二)上海各佛教團體と交涉し，出來るだけ該團體に派員して佛學運動の講演を行ふこと。(三)各公共の場所，驛，埠頭，佛教團體等に佛學運動の標語，ポスターの貼布を行ふ。(四)公共場所，汽車，船，電車等で佛學宣傳の小冊子·ビラ等を撒き，或は講演を行ふ。(五)活動寫眞館の映寫前に本會議定の佛學運動の標語，圖畫を映寫すること。(六)上海各ラヂオと交涉して每週佛學講演を公開すること。

廣州公安 局尼寺を沒收

廣州省公安局長某氏は，先月着任するや突如として多數の警察隊を派し，比丘尼三十餘名を拘引し，同時に藥師庵，永勝庵，無着庵，蓮花庵等の庵寺から所住の比丘尼百餘名を逐ひ出し，寺產を沒收した上各庵を閉鎖した。又庵主の五名は法院に送られ，取調べも受けないで拘禁されてゐると言ふことである。その理由は違警罪を犯した爲めであると言ふのであるが，庵寺を逐はれた尼僧は突然の此の災厄に遭ひ路頭に迷ふ有樣となつたので，連名で省政府に陳情し，寺產の返還苛酷なる閉鎖命令取り消しを懇願し，並に中國佛教會に對しても援助を求めてゐる。

達賴の轉世を 發見した

旅行家の西藏より傳えたる消息に據れば，達賴喇嘛轉世の兒童は既に見付かつたが，その場所は極力秘密にしてある。傳へる所では滿洲，或は蒙古の某所で二階建の家の中にゐるが，班禪喇嘛が拉薩に歸つてから，之を公布すると噂されてゐる。

班禪護送の入藏代表

上海の菩提學會では班禪喇嘛が甘據より入藏するので，特に該會理事長段祺瑞氏等から趙友琴氏を代表として公推し，九月一日四馬路の中央飯店にその送別會が催され，手子橋，王一亭，屈映光，李組紳，關絅之，趙甫臣，湯住心，李贊侯，鄧夢仙，錢鏡平等が陪席した。

班禪大師は 年內に入藏

前任の班禪入藏護送專使誠允氏は辭職後前月青海を出て八月三十日南京に到着し，二日蒙藏行政院に吳忠信，翁文灝等に面會し，班禪入藏準備に對して報告した。轉じて新任專使趙守鈺を訪れ，早く青海に行くことを促した。語る所に依れば班禪は既に拉卜楞を出で，入藏の途に上つたが，凡ゆる隨從人員及び儀仗隊も同行し，凡そ今明日加拉寺に抵る頃である。こゝに一週間位留つてから又西行を續け十月には西藏近くの玉樹縣に至り，これより拉薩に行くには一ケ月餘を要し，年內には到着の筈である。目下西藏の民衆はこれが歡迎の準備中であると。

又達賴の轉世は達賴辦事處には何等の消息なく未だ不確定との事である。蒙藏會から問き合せた所，班禪が青海塔爾寺にゐる時，達賴は已に境內に轉世してゐたと傳える說もあるが，眞相は結局不明である。

常州天寧寺の 僧逮捕さる

常州天寧寺は有名なる大叢林で，堂宇の宏偉，僧衆の修持頗る謹嚴を以て知られてゐたが，最近憲兵團長某氏が此の地に來りし際，密室に女をかこひ春光が漏れてゐたとの風評を耳にし直ちに二僧を逮捕したことが傳つたので蘇州專署副司令吳德林，參謀許繼成は常州の保安隊を訪れ視察調查し，九月十一日偕同して天寧寺に赴き寺内を一巡し嚴重調査を行つた。

香港に佛教公墓の建設

香港の東蓮覺苑の河張蓮覺居士は佛教公墓の建設を志し，香港政府に山地の分讓を接衝してゐたが，最近蒙華民政司からの允許に接したので，靄亭通一兩法師等を偕同し，測量視察を行つたが，該地は新界粪涌の傍にあり，水陸交通も非常に便利，且つ山勢雄偉風景絕佳で靈骨建塔供養には最勝の土地であると。

冀察陣亡將士追悼盂蘭會

宋哲元主祭となりて

八月三十一日朝七時より北平，北海，天王殿に於て冀察陣亡將士を追悼する盂蘭大會を開催した。宋哲元主祭となり，軍政各機關職員及び各學校團體が列席して祭典を行ひ，午後はこれを一般市民に開放し，夜は放河燈，燒法船等の行事が行はれた。

香港佛教聯合會籌備

創立大會は十月の豫定

昨年太虛大師が香港で講演の際，佛教團體の合組に由つて教務の聯絡，事業の宏揚を圖るべきことを提唱せられたのが動機となり，最近葦庵法師が發起して，在香各佛教團體の代表を招きて懇談會を開き，協議の結果，香港佛教聯合會を結成することに決定，菩提場を籌備處とし，葦庵，靄亭，通一の三法師及び高浩文，李公達，葉福靈，吳澤希の諸居士が籌備委員となりて會員を求め，基金組織を立て十月中には大會を開く豫定であると言ふ。

中國佛教會全回大會

十月十五日より三日間

中國佛教會では南京毘盧寺に於ける理監事聯席會議の結果，本年十月十五日より三日間首都毘盧寺に於て全國代表大會を開くことに決定した。

此の度の大會は，中央政府民訓部より指定した新規則(一)僧尼は必ず入會すべきこと，又僧尼のみを限る規定。(二)三級制を採用せること。(三)代表選出規定を平均普遍ならしめたる點が從前の組織と大いに異るので，佛教界の重視の的となつてゐる。同時に今迄の會には居士が參加し，會員組織中重要なる位置を占めてゐたが，中央の原則では會員は僧侶に限定されてゐるから，居士ははみ出しを喰ふわけであり，激しい論爭が豫想されてゐる。

談玄法師の名を騙つて

邵慧生居士から四十圓詐取

談玄法師は昨年末日本で密教を學んで歸國し，武昌佛學院に閉じ籠つて門外を出ず，專心密教を研究して世事に關係せず，且つ友人の來往，手紙の消息さえ謝絕してゐたのである。

處が最近談玄法師の名を詐稱して，詐騙を働くものが現れ，前には浙江省

臨平等の場所で，談玄の名と武昌佛學院教授の名を騙つて問題を起したが，今又餘姚縣農民銀行邵慧生居士が，大洋四十圓，萬年筆一本等を詐取せられた。邵慧生居士からの手紙で見ると，

六月十一日(舊曆)(大陽曆七月末)午後「談玄」と自稱する青年僧が來り，雪竇寺や太虛法師のことについて語つた。その話が如何にも眞實らしいので歡待した所が，夜食後太虛大師は今廬山にゐられると述べ，且つ長歎息を漏らして何か心配事でもある風であつたが翌朝になると愈ゝ本音を現はし「私は雪竇寺で教鞭を採つてゐたが最近教員の誤解を受け省府に誣告せられた。そこで今廬山にゐられる大虛大師を訪れて雪寃したいと思ふのであるが，旅費四十圓貸して頂き度い」と述べたので，居士は少しも疑はず，船賃四十圓，萬年筆，藤籃等を與へたが其の後何の消息に接しないので九月初め照會して見ると，談玄法師は閉關して門外不出と言ふことが判明したのである。

汎太平洋佛教青年會聯盟役員決定報告

米國本土　(昭和十一年三月三日入手)

名譽委員	増山顯珠	
中央委員	寺川湛濟	
	土屋キヤスリー（日本名カツチ）	(加州女子佛青聯盟委員長)
	丸山シミー	(加洲佛青聯盟委員長)

布哇　(昭和十一年六月三日入手)

名譽委員	口羽義教	(本派)
	駒形善教	(曹洞)
	松平融	(大派)
	丹生實榮	(眞言)
	福田闡正	(淨土)
	生駒惠純	(日蓮)
中央委員	間宮敏雄	(淨土)
	畬(アラタ)野光義	(眞言)
	黒田慶鏊	(大派)
	生駒惠純	(日蓮)
	大巴賢充	(本派)

Saraṇattayaṁ
サラナッタヤム

三歸依〔巴利語〕

（1）ブツダム　サラナム　ガツチヤーミ
Buddhaṁ saraṇaṁ gacchāmi,
〔我れ〕佛に　歸依したてまつる，

ダンマム　サラナム　ガツチヤーミ
Dhammaṁ saraṇaṁ gacchāmi,
〔我れ〕法に　歸依したてまつる，

サンガム　サラナム　ガツチヤーミ
Saṅghaṁ saraṇaṁ gacchāmi.
〔我れ〕僧に　歸依したてまつる。

（2）ドチヤン　ピ　ブツダム　サラナム　ガツチヤーミ
Dutiyam pi buddhaṁ saraṇaṁ gacchāmi,
二たび　又〔我れ〕佛に　歸依したてまつる，

ドチヤン　ピ　ダンマム　サラナム　ガツチヤーミ
Dutiyam pi dhammaṁ saraṇaṁ gacchāmi,
二たび　又〔我れ〕法に　歸依したてまつる，

ドチヤン　ピ　サンガム　サラナム　ガツチヤーミ
Dutiyam pi saṅghaṁ saraṇaṁ gacchāmi.
二たび　又〔我れ〕僧に　歸依したてまつる。

（3）タチヤン　ピ　ブツダム　サラナム　ガツチヤーミ
Tatiyam pi buddhaṁ saraṇaṁ gacchāmi,
三たび　又〔我れ〕佛に　歸依したてまつる，

タチヤン　ピ　ダンマム　サラナム　ガツチヤーミ
Tatiyam pi dhammaṁ saraṇaṁ gacchāmi,
三たび　又〔我れ〕法に　歸依したてまつる，

タチヤン　ピ　サンガム　サラナム　ガツチヤーミ
Tatiyam pi saṅghaṁ saraṇaṁ gacchāmi.
三たび　又〔我れ〕僧に　歸依したてまつる。

國際佛教通報局定款

名稱

第一，本局を國際佛教通報局と稱す

事務所

第二，本局の事務所を全日本佛教青年會聯盟本部に置く

目的

第三，本局は日本內海及海外に向つて佛教事情の通報をなし，且つ佛教徒相互間の各種便宜を計るを以て目的とす

事業

第四，本局の目的を達成するため左記の事業を行ふ

イ，日本內地及世界各國より佛教事情に關する質問の通報を行ふ

ロ，必要に應じ日本語及世界各國語を以て佛教事情の通報を行ふ

ハ，外國人の日本觀光に際しては各種の便益を與へ，特にその佛教に關する方面に於て之を爲す

ニ，定時或は臨時に各國語を以て文書の刊行をなす

ホ，その他必要と認めたる事業を行ふ

役員

第五，本局の事務を處理するため左の役員を置く

イ，局長　一名

ロ，幹事　三名

ハ，評議員　若干名

局長は本局の事務を總括す

幹事は本局の事務を處理す

評議員は局長の提案に依る重要事務を審議す

第六，評議員は左記の者を以て之に充つ

イ，全日本佛教青年會聯盟理事及主事

ロ，全日本佛教青年會聯盟理事會に於て推薦したる者

第七，局長及幹事は評議員會に於て決定す

第八，役員の任期は二ヶ年とす（但し重任を妨げず）

經費

第九，本局の經費は左記のものに依て之を支辨す

イ，本局基金の活用

ロ，寄附金

ハ，その他の收入

補則

第十，本定款に記載せられざる事項は，凡て評議員會に於て協議す

第十一，第一回の役員は全日本佛教青年會聯盟理事會に於て決定す

定價	一部　金二十錢	送料二錢
	一年　金二圓四十錢	送料不要

昭和十年四月廿日第三種郵便物認可
昭和十一年九月廿八日印刷（毎月一回）
昭和十一年十月一日發行（一日發行）

東京市外吉祥寺337
編輯發行兼印刷人　淺野研眞

東京市牛込區早稻田鶴卷町107
印刷所　康文社印刷所
電話牛込（34）1950番 5049番

東京市神田區一ツ橋二の三
發行所　國際佛教通報局
電話九段（33）4428番
振替東京83015番

昭和十年四月三十日第三種郵便物認可
昭和十一年九月二十八日印刷納本(毎月一回)
昭和十一年十月一日發行(一日發行)　國際佛教通報　第二卷　第十號

第　二　回

汎太平洋佛教青年會大會
紀　要

THE PROCEEDINGS
of
THE Second
General Conference
of
Pan-Pacific Young Buddhists' Associations

(in Japanese, Chinese and English)

Held at Tokyo & Kyoto, July 18–23, 1934

Price ¥ 3.00

Compiled & Published
by
The Federation of All Y.B. As. of Japan,
Tokio, Kanda, Hitotsubashi, II-3

昭和十年四月三十日第三種郵便物認可　昭和十一年十月二十八日印刷納本　昭和十一年十一月一日發行（毎月一回一日發行）第二卷　第十一號

The International Buddhist Bulletin
國際佛教通報

第二卷 昭和十一年十一月 第十一號〔Vol. II. Nov. $\frac{2502}{1936}$ No. 11.〕

要　目〔Contents〕

東　京　國際佛教通報局　發　行
The International Buddhist Information Bureau
Tokyo, Kanda, Hitotsubashi, II–3

The Fundamental Conception of Buddhist Sociology

by Ken Assano

I. Erection of Buddhist Sociology

In the spring of the year 1929, when I was studying in Europe, an inauguration meeting of the Franco-Japanese Institution for the Study of Buddhism was held at the Sorbonne University, under the chairmanship of Prof. Sylvain Lévi, the world-famous hindoologist, who has also been in Japan.

On that day, about ten Japanese attended the meeting, the majority being scholars who then were staying or studying in Paris. I also participated in the meeting.

On the French side, besides Prof. Sylvain Lévi, there were present, Prof. Paul Pelliot and other prominent orientalists, and they all consulted to found the new institution.

Probably, you readers would ask what connection there is indeed between the above-mentioned meeting and the theme. The answer is the following.

The thing I want to mention here is that among the rules of the institution — for the working out of which Prof. Lévi and Mr. Odin spared no effort and I myself actively participated in the business —there was one paragraph "The Sociological Study of Buddhism." This paragraph was proposed by myself and was immediately accepted. In fact, this "sociological study of Buddhism" was approved generally by the scholars in Europe and America. Especially the French scholars approved it not only without any question but also with fervent zeal, as the majority of French orientalists are sociologists and as they are, at least much influenced by the Durkheim School. As I said hereabove the insertion of this "sociological study of Buddhism" was insistently proposed by me and was approved by my collaborator Mr. Odin, and Prof. Lévi remarked it as an important subject of study.

At that time, in my letter *"From Paris"* sent to the journal *Chūgai-Nippō*, and also in the article sent to the *"Sociological Review,"* I wrote about the progress of religious sociology in France, and especially mentioned about the Catholic sociology, which had come out to be introduced in recent years. I also mentioned that in the *Collège de France*, the highest seat of learning in France, they were already giving a lecture on the sociology and sociography of Mohammedanism, in which Prof. Louis Massignon had been lecturing. And I also confessed that, in Japan, the exertion of our scholars ought to be directed to the erection of Buddhist Sociology, because, in our country, Buddhist phenomena are abundantly seen as social factors.

In fact, in the Catholic Institute of Paris were already opened the sociological courses, and the people there were fervently studying the catholic sociology. There, a group of catholic sociologists actively laboured opposing the *sociologisme* of Durkheim and by criticizing it, they erected their own system. And also they were actively labouring in speech or in writing. Of course they had already published some books on "Catholic Sociology."(1)

But why, until to-day, has not Buddhist Sociology been introduced into Japan wherein the Buddhists are most actively working? Besides, as to the number of schools which belong to the Buddhist group, Japan is unique of all countries. The number of Buddhist universities and colleges count more than ten, and yet we do not know even one which is giving a regular lecture on Buddhist Sociology.

Works of Durkheim, Weber and others are very seldom read even among the students of such universities, because of the barrier of language.

It is unnecessary to say that there is practically no such attempt as to master the methodology of such religious sociology in general and to apply it to the study of Buddhism: nearly everything seems to be left in a stage of virgin forest.

Why are they not, at the universities of Buddhist sects, giving lectures on Buddhist Sociology, which is a more important and more useful special science than general sociology?

(1) For instance:
L'Abbé Naudet: Premiers principes de sociologie catholique, 2e éd. Paris, 1901.
R. P. A. Belliot (D. F. M.): Manuel de sociologie catholique. Histoire-Théorie-Pratique, Paris, Lethielleux. 1910.
Georges Legrand: Les grands courands de la sociologie catholique à l'heure présente Paris, Editions Spes, 1927.
Besides, upon the standpoint of catholic sociology, they compiled and published the following dictionary: Dictionnaire de sociologie, familiale, politique, écono mique, générale, par l'abbé Thomas Mainage (Prof. à l'Institut catholique de Paris), 2 vol. Paris, Lib. Létouzey et Ané.

If this is because of the lack of competent handling, we can supply young scholars for that purpose.

In any case, we yearn for the coming of the day when our proposals would be realized. Not only that, we further want to endeavour to found a new branch of science, i. e. Buddhist Sociology, with the help of sincere criticism and approval of the learned in the world.

The founding of a new lecture seat of Buddhist Sociology would not so easily be realized, as we should meet opposition to the effect that even in Europe such a lecture does not yet exist. Or it may be that in the present Japan we may not meet such oppostion, though, in the past, we often had to meet with such kind of senseless opinion among the Japanese educators who knew nothing but the imitation of things European without any criticism. Also in every univiersity, either private or sectarian, there reigned imitation with neither criticism nor originality. But, now, we must be more courageous to develop the study and build up the foundation of this special science in the Japanese universities, especially in such a one which belongs to Buddhist communities, and whose existence is quite original and unique in Japan, and present that foundation to the scholars of the West, as such does not exist in European universities. Besides, this cultural task is already destined upon the shoulders of Japanese Buddhists. Allow me to say that such participation in works of international nature as this now ought to be done by Japanese scholars, and this is also what the world looks up to with great expectation.

Although I have no intention to preach either nationalism or pan-Asiatic doctrines, I should like to recommend Japan as to be the birthplace of this new science, for, in fact, in the Orient, only in Japan, exist many capacities of studying Buddhist Sociology both historically and geographically.

As Christian Sociology was born in Christian society, and as, especially in France, the catholic country, the Catholic Sociology developed; as in England, that reigns over India, the Hindoology developed; as in France, that possesses a large colony in Africa, inhabited by Mohammedans, the Mohammedan Sociology is being studied; so it is guite natural that in the Orient, especially in Japan, a country of Buddhists, the study of Buddhist Sociology should develop. This must be one great contribution to international culture.

Is it not true that, at present, only in Japan, "the most suitable conntry for Mahayana" in The Far East, Buddhism is continuing its life and is working most actively? In India, the cradle of Buddhism, Buddhism does not sustain life; it is Brahmanism that flourishes. In the present China, the Buddhism is treated as one castrated, and is a bric-a-brac.

Now if we look for a country that has a most suitable position in some way or the other to guide universal Buddhist movement, no country but Japan seems to us most competent, because, Japan is, to a grest extent, Buddhist country with a rich Buddhist soil. It would not be too much to say that Buddhist Sociology, which we now mean to study as one new science, has a fate to flourish in this soil, because we have plenty of Buddhist facts at our diaposal.

A further problem lies on the method of study. To those dogmatic heads that have been brought up in the way of treating things in a limited light of either orthodexical self-assumption or heresical exclusion of others the methods as followed by the scholars of the West must seem too much out of the way, too vague, and too blasphemous. They may perhaps see the outside and probaly lose the inside. They may be wonder-struck at a small thing, but end in a clumsy imitation, and buy a cheap laughter.

The result is that we must always follow the beaten track as pointed out to us by a few European scholars. To take up their good method is good, but always to remain in this state is quite miserable.

In Japan, though Buddhist phenomena were exceedingly abundant as social facts, there has been wanting a method to treat them effectively and sufficiently under the light of modern science. In other words, the materials were ready with a lack of a machine to handle them.

Therefore, first of all, we must make and improve the machine; then learn how to use it. The first step of every scientific study ought to begin with the acquisition of *method*. And, as to the method, one speculative or metaphysical as hitherto has been prised of is now useless. Our *method* must be more positive. It must be the method of Buddhist Sociology as one new science.

Thus, the constructing work of Buddhist Sociology has begun. And this is the fundamental problem that faces us now.

II. What is Buddhist Sociology?

Although the term "Buddhist Sociology" may sound too novel to those who heard it for the first time, I think all readers already comprehend that it is by no means the name of a vulgar science.

Therefore, we have here to treat the fundamental problem, "What is Buddhist Sociology?" In other words, we have to try to define the general conception of "Buddhist Sociology."

What is Buddhist Sociology?—This is the alfa and omega of this science, which is now presented to us. In every science, it is usual to define not at the beginning of the study, but at the end, as its conclusion. And thence many discussions may be started. Definition, generally in the scientific process, must not be the first step, but the last. In short, words, phrases, conceptions, and others are gradually defined and refined according to the progress of study; but, in any case, we must not brandish defintion from the very beginning. And we must know too that the present age is not suited for accepting any dogmatical enforcement in way of definition.

Speaikng in that term, the only thing that we can do is that the present theme can be concluded only when we finish our study in some way or the other. For advancing our study we must have some definite foresight and perspective, without which we can not go even one step forward, and it alone ought to be the compass of our labour.

Therefore, this direction is already suggestive of general structure of this science; or, rather, through this direction we must develop a scientific system. It is in this sense that I try to set up the general conception of this most young science, "Buddhist Sociology."

1. Buddhist Sociology as Special Sociology

Buddhist Sociology is not only

one special sociology,(1) but also a new, important and special branch of Buddhistic sciences. But now, I should like to examine Buddhist Sociology as a special branch of sociology from the methodological standpoint, and treat Buddhism (more precisely, Buddhistic social phenomena) sociologically as object of our study.

In a word, Buddhist Sociology is a sociological study of Buddhism. In this case, Buddhism signifies more precisely the Buddhistic social phenomena. About this object of study, we shall write in detail afterwards.

First of all, we need to examine sociology itself, because the purpose of our study is the sociological research. Originally, the term "sociology (sociologie)," as we know, derives its origin from Auguste Comte (1798–1857). It was in about 1830.(2)

Afterwards, sociology made a remarkable development, and to-day a century after, it secured not only a civic right in science, but also it is giving much influence upon various other sciences.

Well, what kind of science is this sociology? What destination has it in this advanced state of to-day? Sorokin, for instance, writes:—

"Following the classification by H. Rickert and W. Windelband, of sciences into those that are *individualizing* and those that are *generalizing*, we regard sociology as a *generalizing* science among

(1) The So-called "Special Sociologies" probably came from the specialization of sociology according to the proposal of Durkheim School. That is, in the second volume of "*L'Année sociologique*," 1898, they announced six special sociologies: religious sociology, moral sociology, juridical sociology, economic sociology, linguistic sociology and aesthetic sociology; further such terms as political sociology, etc., seem also to be employed Moreover, according to the progress of sociology itself, special sociologies are more and more sectionalized, and now we can see before us a great number of special sociologies. For instance, criminal sociology (E. Ferri: *La sociologie criminelle*), colonial sociology (Maunier, *La sociologie coloniale*), educational sociology (in U. S. A. much progressed), labour sociology (Karl Dunkman, *Soziologie der Arbeit*, 1933), urban sociology (Urban Sociology), rural sociology (Rural Sociology), village sociology (Leopoldo von Wiese, *Soziologie des Dorfes*), civic sociology (Edward A. Ross, *Civic Sociology*, New York, 1925), sociology of revolution (Pitirim A. Sorokin, The Sociology of Revolution 1925), sex sociology (Quintiliano Saldaña *Siete ensayos sobre Sociologia Sexual*, Madrid, 1928), animal sociology (Friedrich Alverdes, *Tiers soziologie*, Leipzig 1925), plant sociology (Phytosociologie—J. Braun-Blanquet & J. Pavillard, *Vocabulaire de Sociologie Végétable*, 3e éd., Montpelier, 1928), etc.

(2) V. Comte, Cours de philosophie positive, t. IV, 1839, p. 201.

other sciences."(3)

Thus, under the influence of the German Neo-Kantian school's classification of science, they define sociology as generalized science. Further, the sociology which stands upon the basis of generalized science, is now summarized according to Sorokin as follows:—

"It (Sociology) seems to be a study, first, of the *relationship and correlations between various classes of social phenomena*, (*correlations between economics and religions; between family and moral; between juridical and economic; between mobility and political phenomena; and so on*); second, *that between the social and the non-social* (*geographic, biological,etc.*) *phenomena*; third, *the study of the general characteristics common to all classes of social phenomena*."(4)

Under such a state of sociological study, the study of Buddhist Sociology, as one special branch of sociology, has been started with an unavoidable need of itself in order to investigate the various Buddhistic social phenomena.

2. Buddhist Sociology as a Special Branch of Religious Sociology

Buddhist sociology is a special sociology: it treats Bubdhist phenomena as religious phenomena. Accordingly it is one branch of religious sociology which treats general phenomena of religions. So it is one special branch of religious sociology, and the religious sociology itself is also one special branch of general sociology.

For the first time, religious sociology was created by the contemporary French sociologist Emile Durkheim (1758–1917). Prof. Gaston Richard, the present professer of the Bordeaux University, writes about it thus:

"Le terme de sociologie religieuse a été créé par *l'Année sociologique* que dirigeait Emile Durkheim. Il n'apparait pas avant 1898; il désigne alors une des six sections de cette publication, destinée à rendre compte du mouvement des recherches sociologiques et plus encore à étudier objectivement les sources de la nouvelle science. (C'est ainsi que Durkheim l'avait présentée à plusieurs de ses collaborateurs dont je fus pendant quelques années......) Mais il apparut bientôt que la sociologie religieuse était la branche maîtresse de *l'Année sociologique*, qu'elles s'inspirait d'une doctrine définie sur la nature, l'origine et l'évolution de la religion, et que cette doctrine

(3) Sorokin & Zimmerman, ***Principles of Rural-Urban Sociology***, N. Y. 1929, p. 3.

(4) Sorokin (Pitirim A), Contemporary Sociological Theories, N. Y. & London, 1928, p. 760.

dépassait de beaucoup la compétence d'une science spéciale des sociétés. Une série de mémoires dûs les uns à Durkheim, les autres à MM. Mauss et Hubert, préparèrent et annoncèrent l'oeuvre qui devait résumer la doctrine. Cette oeuvre, les *Formes élèmentaires de la vie religieuse,* parut enfin en 1912."(5)

The term "Religious Sociology" seems to have been used for the first time in 1898, and "The Elemental Forms of the Religious Life," the great work in this branch, was published fifteen years after, i. e. in 1912. This fact sufficiently shows how he had been toiling about its publication. As I have already mentioned, Durkheim in 1898 proclaimed the term religious sociology as one special branch. This is in the preface of the second volume of *L'Année sociologique,* in which he presented six branches, i. e. religious sociology, moral sociology, juridical sociology, economic sociology, linguistic sociology, aesthetic sociology; and he placed "Social Morphology" separately. This was more clearly shown in his article *Sociologie et Sciences Sociales* in *De la Méthode dans les Sciences,* the collected articles printed in 1910, which almost defined the system of the sociology of Durkheim School, and there the six branches had been presented as six sub-divisions of "Social Physiology" as follows:

- I. Social Morphology
- II. Social Physiology
  1. Religious Sociology
  2. Moral Sociology
  3. Juridical Sociology
  4. Economic Sociology
  5. Linguistic Sociology
  6. Æsthetic Sociology
- III. General Sociology

Further, family sociology, political sociology, and others appeared among the works of the Durkheim School. And these are generally accepted by the scholars of this school, and now find their place even among the curriculum of French middle schools.

And in the series of works concerning religious sociology which occupies the chief part in the study of Durkheim School, we find such books as the following:—"The Elemental Forms of Religious Life, 1912," Durkheim; "*Mélanges d'histoire des religions,* 1909," Hubert and Mauss; "*Mélanges de sociologie religieuse et de folklore* 1928," R. Hertz; "*Fssais sur le régime des castes,* 1908, and *Leçons de sociologie sur l'évolution des valeurs,* 1928," M. Bouglé; and other works by Lévy-Bruhl and others.(6)

(5) Gaston Richard, *L'athéisme dogmatique dans la sociologie religieuse,* (*Cahiers de la Revue d'histoire et de philosophie religieuses,* No. 7), Strasbourg et Paris, 1923, p. 4-5.

We have already looked through the situation of religious sociology in the sphere of general sociology, and now we shall further see this Buddhist Sociology under the light of a sub-division of religious sociology. Dividing religious sociology in branches, we get the following:

Religious Sociology
- I. Christian Sociology
  - a) Catholic Sociology
  - b) Protestant Sociology
- II. Mohammedan Sociology
- III. Buddhist Sociology
- IV. Shintoist Sociology

and others.

Of the above, as I have already mentioned, there are good lectures and fairly good books in Europe and America about Christian Sociology, especially about Catholic Sociology and Mohammedan Sociology. It would be needless to say that there are especially a good many books which concern Christian Sociology.(7)

But we can not but help crying that Buddhist Sociology, though an important branch of religious sociology, stands in a quite miserable state. Of course, until now, there has not been wanting any emphasis about the claim of sociological study of Buddhism; nor were there wanting people who tried to study it.

Although there are abundant materials and fragments of sociological studies about Buddhism, we could see, up to now, no systematic and synthesized study on this theme. Nor was there any lecture or book on this subjest in general. Though we could find many germs there, no decided claim or system has yet been presented. Is not the subjuct calling our effort to commence and promote? Will it not be the duty of the Asiatics, at least the Japanese, to be able to pride in the founding of Buddhist Sociology?

(6) Taking advantage of the occasion, I mention some books about religious sociology:

a) In France, Maunier: *Vie religieuse et vie économique*; Henri Beuchat & M. Hollebeque: *Les religions. Etude historique et sociologique du phénomène reigieux,* Paris, Rivière, 1910; Raoul de la Grasserie: *Des religions comprées au point de vue sociologique,* Paris, 1899; M. Guyau: *L'Irrélìgion de L'Avenir. Etude sociologique;* Roger Bastide, Eléments de sociologie religieuse, Paris, 1935; etc.

b) In Germany, Simmel, *Die Religion;* E. Troeltsch, *Gesammelte Schriften,* II. *Religion und Kirche;* Max Weber, *Gesammelte Aufsätze zur Religions-soziologie,* especially B. II, *Hinduismus und Buddhismus,* Tübingen, 1921; J. Wach, *Einführung in die Religionssoziologie,* 1931; & others.

(7) Some books about general Christian Sociology:

Penty (A. J.): *Toward a Christian Sociology;* Wallis (Louis); *Sociological Study of the Bible,* 1912; Hill (Chatherton); *Sociological Value of Christianity,* 1912; Hudson (Canon C.D.): *Preface to a Christian Sociology,* London, 1935; P. Conord, Le problème d'une sociologie chrétienne, 1936.

And I already mentioned books about Catholic Sociology, and also a book about Protestant Sociology:

Hauter (Ch.); *Le problème sociologique du Protestantisme* (*Cahiers de la Revue d'histoire et de Philosophie religieuse,* No. 5)

III. The Object and the Method of Buddhist Sociology

1. The Object of Buddhist Sociology

The object of Buddhist Sociology is the Buddhistic phenomena as religious phenomena; more precisely, the Buddhistic social phenomena, viz. family, political, juridical, moral, economic, artistic phenomena, and so on, At the same time apart from them, there may be founded Buddhist Morphology, in which we study about ecclesiastic and ritual phenomena, and so on, as its objects.

And this kind of study may easily be commenced by the examination into the general conception of religion. We are able to point ont lots of conceptions about religion, but, first, let us examine Durkheim's theory and develop our treatment, because it plays a very serious international influence.

That is to say, Durkheim, in his famous work "*The Elemental Forms of the Religious Life*, attained the following conclusion :—

"*Une religion est un système solidaire de croyances et de pratiques relatives à des choses sacrées, c'est-à-dire séparées, interdites, croyances et pratiques qui unissent, en une même communauté morale, appelée Eglise, tous ceux qui y adhèrent.*"(1)

This is the definition of religion by the Durkheim School, viz. *sociologisme*. It is needless to say that it is far more different from the metaphysical and the speculative theory of religion.

Hitherto religious theory treated religion as a phenomenon of much more individual and much more psychological nature. On the other hand, the Durkheim theory has enough of social and positive basis. The theory of "sense of absolute dependence" of Schreiermacher and others is so individualistic, too partial to Christianity, and the question is now a matter already solved. In the case of Buddhist idea, which stands upon a special kind of atheism, such kind of Christian idea is entirely unfit for explanation. Especially in the case of Zen we feel it more deeply. Probably because of this that Europeans and Americans feel strong interest about Zen.

(1) *Les forms élémentaires de la vie religieuse*, p. 65.

Now, we go back to the theme. the Science which look to religion as a social phenomenon is religious sociology; therefore, scientific acquirement of Buddhism as a social phenomenon is Buddhist Sociology. In other words, the Buddhist social phenomenon as social phenomenon is the object of Buddhist Sociology.

Buddhist Morphology, so to say, treats as object of study the unified system of beliefs and practices relating to sacred things in Buddhism; that is to say, things set apart and forbidden—beliefs and practices which unite into one single moral community called Buddhist Church, and all of its believers.

Here we touch the conception about religion only from the side of historical materialism. It is Lukaĉevskij who founded an order in the Marxian theory about religion and examined the Durkheim theory of religion and finally achieved the following synthetic definition of religion :—

"Religion is ideology which is more or less an ordered system consisting of animistic idea and to which cling emotions and deeds. In any developing stage of society moral is added to it."(2)

Although this definition of religion as viewed from the standpoint of its form looks that it was put in an order in accordance with the method of Durkheim and yet what is worth our attention is a point that formerly Durkheim founded "atheistic" theory by studying Buddhism, but now Lukaĉevskij, utilizing the result of the study of Plekhanov, found the above-mentioned new theory and said that Buddhism (especially the present-day Buddhism) also is a system of animistic ideas as every other religion. Is it not a big point to mark that Durkheim and Lukaĉevskij corrected the conception about religion, be it only in a very small degere? It is our duty and right to put forth the fruit of labour which yet postulates such corrections as above.

2. The Method of Buddhist Sociology

Buddhist Sociology is a special branch of religious sociology, which again is a special branch of sociology in general. But, does this Buddhist Sociology as a special

(2) Lukacevskij : *Origin and Essence of Religion*, Japanese translation, p. 15.

branch of sociology need a particular method of study? Not necessarily so. The task which ought to be accomplished in its own particular sphere can well be the same as those of general sociology.

If I am to speak of the relation between general sociology and Buddhist Sociology, it will be like this. If general sociology had accomplished its task completely, we could only apply the causational or functional formula of general sociology to Buddhist Sociology to *explicate* its social facts. But unfortunately, general sociology in its many spheres is not yet entirely a perfect thing. Only a collective development of special studies can attain that end. Accordingly, in Buddhist Sociology too, we must begin, as one special branch of science, our study from the very beginning. And if we want to find out a motive which causes some definite differences, or consider relationships, which hitherto were not yet proved in general sociology, we must do it independently from general sociology. Therefore, if a new relationship could be justified in Buddhist Sociology, the Buddhist sociologist has not only solved his task, but also that of general sociology. Thus, hitherto-unproved or yet uncertain points in general sociology may inversely be summarized and compounded by the explanation of special branches.

But we must courageously utilize the hitherto-attained theory of sociology, or else we may unexpectedly have to lose our strength in vain. Therefore, especially in methology, it is, in any case, necessary to examine and utilize them with great care.

Generally, scientific study requires at least: 1) a definite working in its study, 2) limiting of the range of study, 3) objectivness, 4) exclusion of application 5 and others. Further I want to utilize the norm which Durkheim set down in his *Sociological Method*.

The so-called fundamental and methodological principle in the Durkheim sociology stands upon a basis that social facts must be treated entirely equal with other things. But there is a great deal of limitation in the way of this expession. Therefore, I shall quote his own explanation verbalby:

"Nous ne disons pas, en effet, que les faits sociaux sont des choses matérielles, mais sont des choses au même titre que les choses matérielles, quoique d'une autre manière.

"Qu'est-ce en effect qu'une chose? La chose s'oppose à l'idée comme ce que l'on connaît du dehors à ce que l'on connaît du dedans. Est chose tout objet de connaissance qui n'est pas naturellement compénétrable à l'intelligence, tout ce dont nous ne pouvons nous faire une notion adéquate par un simple procédé d'analyse mentale, tout ce que l'esprit ne peut arriver à comprendre qu'à condition de sortir de lui-même, par voie d'observations et d'expérimentations, en passant progressivement des caractères les plus extérieurs et les plus immédiatement accessibles aux moins visibles et aux plus profonds. Traiter des faits d'un certain ordre comme des choses, ce n'est donc pas les classer dans telle ou telle catégorie du réel; c'est observer vis-à-vis d'eux une certaine attitude mentale. Cést en aborder l'étude en prenant pour principe ignore absolument ce qu'ils sont, et que leurs propriétés caractéristiques, comme les causes inconnues dont elles dépendent, ne peuvent être découvertes par l'introspection même la plus attentive."(3)

Durkheim says more:

"Notre règle n'implique donc aucune conception métaphysique, aucune spéculation sur le fond des êtres. Ce qu'elle réclame, c'est que le sociologue se mette dans l'état d'esprit où sont physiciens, chimistes, physiologistes, quand ils s'engagent dans une région, encore inexplorée, de leur domaine scientifique. Il faut qu'en pénétrant dans le monde sacial, il ait conscience qu'il pénètre dans l'inconnu; il faut qu'il se sente en présence de faits dont les lois sont aussi insoupçonnées que pouvaient l'être celles de la vie, quand la biologie n'était pas constituée; il faut qu'il se tienne prêt à faire des découvertes qui le surprendront et le déconcerteront."(4)

From this fundamental norm three second degree laws come out:

I. "*Il faut écarter systématiquement toutes les prénotions.*"(5)

II. "*Ne jamais prendre pour objet de recherches qu'un groupe de phénomènes préalablement définis par certains caractères extérieurs qui leur sont communs et comprendre dans la même recherche tous ceux qui répondent à cette définition.*"(6)

III. "*Quand le sociologue entreprend déxplorer un ordre quelconque de faits sociaux, il doit s'efforcer de les considérer par un côté où ils se présentent isolés de leurs manifestations individuelles.*"(7)

This sociological method of Durkheim School can to a great extent be considered as to be the method of our Buddhist Sociology.

Also we must pay great attention to the method of "historical mater-

(3) Le Règles de la Méthode sociologique, p. XI.

(4) Ibidem, p. XIII.
(5) Ibidem, p. 40.
(6) Ibidem, p. 45.
(7) Ibidem, p. 57.

rialism" (which Bukharin called "Marxian Sociology"). Of course we must avoid the vulgar materialism, but proper attention need also be paid in the study of this side, as there is no refutable fact that even Buddhist phenomena grew out through the social economic basis. Namely, the criticism of the ancient Hindoo idea, which has been done by Thalheimer(8), is yet very fragmental, though it may probably be the first attempt in this sphere.

Apart from them there are valuable writings in this sphere, namely, *Ursprung der Religion und des Gottesglaubens* of Kunow, and *Origin and Essence of religion* of Lukačevskij. It is also worth while to be attentive to the assertion that historical materialistic study of Buddhism is also a contribution of the proletariat in the Orient to international culture. This is what Mr. Kashū Honjō said and is not quite against our consent.

The attitude of our studying Buddhism, especially about Buddhistic social phenomena, must be absolutely that of sociologists. And we must not waste talks, just merely shutting us in a limited sphere of Buddhism. No, in some cases, to hold ourselves as Buddhists is not only unnecessary, but even harmful. Though to have profound Buddhistic sympathy may, even if it may be more or less a dangerous from the scientific standpoint, be advantageous in way of understanding. There is no science which has no definite foresight or utility. Even in Marxism, which calls itself Scientific Socialism, there may be found more or less non-scientific or dogmatical elements caused by our will that society should be as such.

Also Buddhist Sociology may have two sides: theoretical study and applied study. Scientific study and political study may well be conceived. In a case, for instance, as in the present, Buddhist sociologists may urgently need to study the practical side, for instance, the improvement of economic condition of temples, the reformation of Buddhist communities, and so on. And "Socialistic Buddhism" or "Buddhistic Socialism" may probably be asserted too lightly. But, if we consider more deeply, we can clearly comprehend that our task is in the investigation and discovery of principle and law, and the practical application of the result. The more the scientific study progresses, the more its application sphere is widened, but if we intermix them awkwardly, we may lose both. What is needed is care.

(8) See A. Thalheimer: Einführung in die dialektischen Materialismus.

IV. The Branches of Buddhist Sociology

1. Classifications according to Sect and Item

Already acquainted with the position of Buddhist Sociology as a special branch of religious sociology in accordance with the classification of general sociology, we here come to treat the classification of Buddhist Sociology.

In my letters *"From Paris"* to *Chūgai-Nippō*, I already touched a little upon sectarian classification: Zen-sect Sociology, Sin-sect Sociology, etc. Of course, as there are in Christian Sociology Catholic Sociology and Protestant Sociology, so the same classification may also be allowed in Buddhist Sociology, First, we must divide it into two larger branches, i. e. Mahayana and Hinayana Sociologies, as Mahayana and Hinayana differ a great deal in their conception about cosmos, society, and life. Already in Indian Buddhism there are to be found many sects, the fact of which postulates distinction between their conceptions about state, society, etc. Even in Japanese sects, too, there has germinated, for example, in the Nichiren-sect, the *Fujufuse-ha* or Non-alms-subsect as a matter of economic movement, and it quite stimulates our interest in its study.

But it is needless to say that, other than such study as according to sect, i.e. Sect Sociology, there can be a more comprehensive, a more general branch of Buddhist Sociology.

In short, the sect sociology, in some cases, is valuable as a special study, but the value exists only when it is treated on the general principle of study. Separately viewed, the basis is very uncertain as a science. So far as it relates to sociology the study must be more general,an d this requires the setting up of sociological study on the common basis of Buddhism.

Therefore, leaving aside the matter of sectarian classifications of Buddhist Sociology, we must once again come up to the classification of general sociology. That is, we must treat synthetically the branches of conception about family, politics, moral, economy, art, and others in Buddhism. The social phenomena of Buddhism may thereafter be explained.

2. Problems of Classification in accordance with Items

Concerning the study of branches

of Buddhist Sociology on a synthetic standpoint, I should like to present hereunder the scheme of study.(1)

(1) *Buddhism and family phenomena.* It is the study of Buddhist phenomena in the branch cf familiy sociology, and treats Buddhist ideas and phenomena; for instance, sex problem, prostitution, marriage, womankind, home, entering into priesthood, etc.

(2) *Buddhism and moral phenomena.* Here we explain moral elements of Buddhism, and study ideas and phenomena about loyalty to the king or faithfulness to master, gratefulness, filial piety, etc., and problems of suicide, a double suicide of lovers, etc.

(3) *Buddhism and juridical phenomena.* Here study concerns chiefly *Vinaya,* decrees of abstinence, their influence upon society outside the ecclesiastic circle,— for instance, the contitution of Prince Shōtoku and ecclesiastic laws or general laws concering religion.

(4) *Buddhism and political phenomena.* Here study concerns chiefly problems which are born by the contact of political power and Buddhism; and problems concerning state, king, government; problems of state and society according to the ideal of Buddhism; policies of reformation of Society by Buddhism, etc.

(5) *Buddhism and economic phenomena.* This is the most fundamental branch, and study concerns chiefly how Buddhist ideas and ecclesiastic matters have been defined and changed according to the contemporary economic basis and sphere, or inversely what influences Buddhism gave to economic world. There are such topics as:— almsgiving, temple finance, family finance, conceptions about social class, about occupation, financial organ "muzin," and other activities of Buddhist ecclesiastic world upon financial, economic questions, etc.

(6) *Buddhism and aesthetical phenomena.* In Japan, the contact between Buddhism and fine art had great significance, so that we can assert that, if we deprive the history of Japanese fine art of Buddhist elements, nothing perhaps could be left in it. Also in literature, music, Sculpture, and architecture full Buddhist influence and expression exist; a systematic study of such phenomena must be treated here.

(7) *Buddhism and linguistic phenomena, scientific phenomena* (astronomy, mathematics, medicine, art, physiology, natural history, etc.) *and educational phenomena, etc.*

(1) Already I wrote about it in my book, "Study of Buddhist Sociology," in Japanese (8vo pp. 328. june 1935, Tokio.) And those chapters occupy the first part of my work. Sincerely I want to hear criticisms and advices of colleagues.

入廟之辭（蒙古便り）

在蒙古　太　田　覺　眠

私は日本最大の佛教宗派眞宗本願寺の僧侶である。依て眞宗の敎義を諸君に敎へ，又喇嘛敎の敎義を諸君から學び，斯くて研究の交換をしようと思ふ。

一，蒙古人は吾兄弟なり

蒙古人と日本人とは同人種であり，同じく佛敎信者であり，又同じく義に勇む氣性を持つて居る。他人とは思はれぬ，全く兄第の樣に思ふ。然るに，蒙古全民族の信奉する喇嘛佛敎は，今甚だ衰頽して居る。依て，之を更生復興させたいと思つて老軀を茲に携へ來たのである。

二，喇嘛敎の改革

喇嘛敎は，諸君の好むと好まぬとに拘はらず，どうしても改革せねばならぬ時代となつたのである。蒙政部を始め，世の有識者間では，喇嘛敎は野蠻であり迷信であると云つて居る。元來の敎義は野蠻迷信では無かつたのだらうが，蒙古人文化が未開であつた爲めに，不知不識の間に宗敎的風俗習慣も野蠻になつたのだらう。如何なる風俗が野蠻か，如何なる點が惡いか，其れは喇嘛僧諸君が能く知つて居るだらう。突然蒙政部から改革の命令を受けては，狼狽せねばならぬから，豫め自ら改むべきは改め，全國各喇嘛僧と連絡團結して，純良なる宗風を興したいものである。

三，研究の交換

四，人材の養成

日本眞宗の僧侶は，世間普通の學校，即ち小學（六年）中學（五年）を學修の後，佛敎の學問を三年或は五年間學修し，然る後に僧侶となり，僧侶となつた後にも尙大學の課程を修學するものもある。僧侶は一般人民の先に立つて敎化の任に當らねばならぬから，普通の學問も一般人民よりも優秀であらねばならぬ。人材の養成は何よりも先づ必要である。

五，同敎徒の救濟

西隣，外蒙は露西亞の侵入する處となつて居る。露西亞は，反宗敎，宗敎撲滅を政治の原則として居る。故に外蒙の喇嘛敎は次第に撲滅の厄に遭ふて居る。吾等同一佛敎徒，殊に同民族の諸君は，外蒙古喇嘛敎徒に同情し，宗敎的に之を援助救濟せねばならぬ。又斯る思想の東侵し來るを防がねばならぬ。

六，殿堂の修覆復興

何れの喇嘛廟も，皆甚だしく荒廢して居る。之を修覆し復興して，敎信をして佛法崇敬の念を深からしめたいものである。莫力廟の修覆の如き，先以て諸君が率先して，其費用の一部を醵出するならば，蒙古事業に關係ある日本の各方面の人々も，必ず出金援助してくれるだらう。私は此等の事にも盡力したいと思つて居る。

七，敎　化

常に僧侶を各地に派遣して，敎義を宣傳し，信仰を鼓吹し，又政府の政令を民間に傳達普及せしめ，尙ほ學校敎育を幇助する事などに盡力したいものである。

八，模範寺廟

私の諸君に希望する所は多いが，要は此の莫力廟をして喇嘛敎寺廟の模範的寺廟と爲し，漸次內外蒙古喇嘛敎を改善興隆せしめたいのである。諸君の奮勵を希むや切なり。

九，資本財源

莫力廟の維持保存，僧侶の敎育費，布敎費其他諸事業に要する費用は，無限に欲望する。其の財源は廣大なる寺有の土地を開拓し，其收穫を蓄積すれば，相當無限の財源と云ふ事も出來る。

十，其他，私個人の小事業

一，日語學堂

蒙古人が立派な國民となり，立派な國家を立てようと思ふには，日本の文化を學ばねばならぬ。此が爲めには，先以て日本語を知る必要がある。私は近く青年僧侶中にて，敎育に經驗ある者一人を呼寄せ，當小學校內にて日語敎授を開始し，漸次整頓して，日語學堂を設けようと思つて居る。寺內にも多數の少年僧を見受けるが，進んで就學する樣勸誘せられたきものである。

二，病　院

私の現住邸內の西堂の一室に，目藥が備付けてあるから，眼病の人は，何時にても來りて治療を受けられたい。此れも近く專門の醫士を招きて，簡易なる慈善病院を設けたいと思つて居る。

三，私の事業費

私の事業費生活費は，現在は本山本願寺の補助及日本信徒の喜捨してくれた義捐金で支へて居るが，事業を完成せしむるには，尙ほ相當の費用を要する。此が爲めには，諸君の承諾を得て，寺有の一部の土地を借りて，農耕業を營み，その收益を以て之に充つる考へである。

四，相　談　會

每週一回宛諸君と會して，此等各項について具體的の相談會を開き，實行に着手したいと思ふ。

五，終りに臨みて

私は御覽の如く老人である。餘命は少ない。一日も早く喇嘛敎が立派な宗敎になつて，蒙古民族を善導し，救濟するのを見たいのである。私の種々希望する所を，諸君が實行してくれる樣になれば，私は總ての事業を諸君に引渡して，日本に歸るか，或は墓石の下に安眠するのである。早く其期の至らん事を切望する。

滿支神社規則

○外務省令第八號

在滿洲國及中華民國神社規則左ノ通定ム

昭和十一年六月六日

外務大臣　有　田　八　郎

在滿洲國及中華民國神社規則

第一條　滿洲國及中華民國ニ於テ神社ヲ設立，移轉，廢止又ハ併合セムトスルトキハ所轄帝國領事官ノ許可ヲ受クベシ

第二條　神社ノ設立ノ許可ヲ受ケムトスルトキハ其ノ氏子又ハ崇敬者ト爲ルベキ者二十人以上ノ連署ヲ以テ左ノ事項ヲ具シ所轄帝國領事官ニ願出ヅベシ

一　事由
二　設立地
三　神社名
四　祭神
五　例祭日
六　神殿，拜殿，鳥居其ノ他ノ建物ノ位置，構造及建坪並ニ境內地ノ位置，面積及模樣
七　設立費及其ノ支辨方法
八　維持方法
九　神職ト爲ルベキ者ノ氏名
十　氏子又ハ崇敬者ト爲ルベキ者ノ戶數
十一　神殿其ノ他ノ建物ノ起工及竣成豫定期日

前項ノ規定ニ依ル願書ニハ前項第六號ノ事項及神社ノ周圍ノ狀況ヲ表示スル圖面ヲ添附スベシ

第三條　神社ノ移轉ノ許可ヲ受ケムトスルトキハ左ノ事項ヲ具シ所轄帝國領事官ニ願出ヅベシ

一　事由
二　移轉地
三　神殿，拜殿，鳥居其ノ他ノ建物ノ位置，構造及建坪並ニ境內地ノ位置，面積及模樣
四　移轉費及其ノ支辨方法
五　神殿其ノ他ノ建物ノ起工及竣成豫定期日

前項ノ規定ニ依ル願書ニハ前項第三號ノ事項及境內地周圍ノ狀況ヲ表示スル圖面ヲ添附スベシ

第四條　神社ノ廢止又ハ併合ノ許可ヲ受ケムトスルトキハ左ノ事項ヲ具シ所轄帝國領事官ニ願出ヅベシ

一　事由
二　廢止又ハ併合セラルベキ神社ノ名稱及鎭座地
三　併合スベキ神社ノ名稱及鎭座地
四　廢止又ハ併合セラルベキ神社ノ社殿其ノ他ノ建物及財產ノ處分方法

第五條　神社ノ設立，移轉又ハ併合ノ許可ヲ受ケ二年內ニ之ヲ爲サザルトキハ其ノ許可ヲ取消スコトアルベシ

神社ノ設立，移轉，併合又ハ廢止ヲ了シタルトキハ遲滯ナク所轄帝國領事官ニ屆出ヅベシ

第六條　神社ノ境内地ニ國家ニ功勞アル者又ハ頌揚スベキ事蹟アル者ノ碑表又ハ形像ヲ建設セムトスルトキハ左ノ事項ヲ具シ所轄帝國領事官ニ願出デ許可ヲ受クベシ之ヲ移轉又ハ除去セムトスルトキ亦同ジ

一　事由

二　碑表又ハ形像ノ位置

三　碑表又ハ形像ノ物質，形狀，寸尺及其ノ地盤ノ面積

四　工事費及其ノ支辨方法

五　起工及竣工豫定期日

前項ノ規定ニ依ル願書ニハ前項第二號ノ事項ヲ表示スル圖面ヲ添附スベシ

第七條　神社ノ境内ハ其ノ神社以外ノ者ニ之ヲ使用セシムルコトヲ得ズ但シ左ノ各號ノ一ニ該當スル場合ハ此ノ限ニ在ラズ

一　一時之ヲ使用セシムルトキ

二　參拜者ノ休息所等トシテ一年内ノ期間之ヲ使用セシムルトキ

三　公益ノ目的ヲ以テ境内地ヲ損セザル範圍ニ於テ之ヲ使用セシムルトキ

前項但書第二號及第三號ノ規定ニ依リ神社ノ境内ヲ使用セシメムトスルトキハ神社ヨリ左ノ各號ノ事項ヲ具シ所轄帝國領事官ニ願出デ許可ヲ受クベシ

一　使用ノ目的及方法

二　使用セシムベキ場所及其ノ面積

三　使用期間

四　使用料

前項ノ規定ニ依ル願書ニハ前項第二號ノ事項ヲ表示スル圖面ヲ添附スベシ

第八條　神社ハ設立後遲滯ナク左ノ事項ヲ記載シタル神社明細書ヲ調製シ之ヲ所轄帝國領事官ニ提出スベシ

一　神社名

二　鎭座地

三　祭　神

四　配　祀

五　神殿，拜殿，鳥居，其ノ他ノ建物

六　境内社

七　境内地内碑表又ハ形像

八　境内地

九　例祭日

十　氏子又ハ崇敬者ノ戸數

十一　維持方法

十二　由緒沿革

第九條　神社ニ於テ設立後前條第一號第三號乃至第六號，第八號，第九號及第十一號ノ事項ヲ變更セムトスルトキハ其ノ理由ヲ具シ所轄帝國領事官ニ屆出デ許可ヲ受クベシ

第十條　神社ハ設立後遲滯ナク其ノ所有ニ屬スル不動產及寶物ニ關シ左ノ事項ヲ具シ所轄帝國領事官ニ屆出ヅベシ

一　土地ニ在リテハ其ノ所在地，地目，段別又ハ坪數及境内地又ハ境外地ノ區別

二　建物ニ在リテハ其ノ位置，名稱，構造，建坪又ハ間數及境内地ニ在ルモノトノ區別

三　寶物ニ在リテハ名稱，員數，形狀，品質，寸尺，作者及傳來

前項ノ屆出ヲ爲シタル後屆出デタル事項ニ異動ヲ生ジタルトキハ其ノ都度遲滯ナク屆出ヅベシ

第十一條　神社ハ財產臺帳ヲ備ヘ其ノ所有ニ屬スル不動產及寶物ニ關シ前條各號ノ事項ヲ記載スベシ

第十二條　神社ノ財產ノ管理其ノ他重要ナル事項ニ付テハ神職ハ氏子總代又ハ崇敬者總代ト協議シテ之ヲ處理スベシ

神社ニ於テ其ノ所有ニ屬スル不動產又ハ寶物ニ付賣却，貸付其ノ他ノ處分ヲ爲サムトスルトキ又ハ負債ヲ爲サムトスルトキハ其ノ理由ヲ具シ所轄領事官ニ願出デ認可ヲ受クベシ

第十三條　神社ノ會計年度ハ毎年四月一日ニ始マリ翌年三月三十一日ニ終ル

第十四條　神社ハ毎會計年度ノ收入支出豫算ヲ定メ年度開始一月前ニ所轄帝國領事官ノ承認ヲ受クベシ

第十五條　神社ハ毎會計年度ノ收入支出決算書ヲ作成シ年度經過後二月内ニ所轄帝國領事官ニ報告スベシ

第十六條　神社ノ神職ハ神明ニ奉仕シ祭祀ヲ掌リ且庶務ニ從事スベシ

神職ハ宗教上ノ職務ヲ兼スルコトヲ得ズ

第十七條　神職ハ氏子總代又ハ崇敬者總代之ヲ推薦スベシ

前項ノ規定ニ依リ推薦ヲ受ケタル者ハ左ノ事項ヲ具シ所轄帝國領事官ニ屆出デ就職ノ認可ヲ受クベシ

一　氏名，履歷

二　俸給又ハ手當額

三　他ノ神社ヨリ兼務スル者ニ在リテハ其ノ事項

前項ノ規定ニ依ル願書ニハ資格ヲ證明スル書類ヲ添付スベシ

第十八條　神職死亡シタルトキハ他ノ神職ヨリ，神職在ラザルトキハ氏子總代又ハ崇敬者總代ヨリ所轄帝國領事官ニ屆出ヅベシ

神職退職セムトスルトキハ氏子總代又ハ崇敬者總代三人以上ノ連署ヲ以テ其ノ理由ヲ具シ所轄帝國領事官ニ願出デ認可ヲ受クベシ

神職死亡若ハ退職シ又ハ病氣ニ依リ其ノ職務ヲ執ルコト能ハザルニ至リタルトキハ遲滯ナク後任者ヲ推薦スベシ

第十九條　神職交代シタルトキハ遲滯ナク氏子總代又ハ崇敬者總代ノ立會ヲ以テ社務ノ引繼ヲ爲シ後任神職ヨリ其ノ顚末ヲ所轄帝國領事官ニ報告スベシ

第二十條　神職ノ職責ヲ怠リ若ハ其ノ體面ヲ汚シタルトキ又ハ其ノ他不適任ト認ムル行爲アリタルトキハ所轄帝國領事官ハ其ノ退職ヲ命ズルコトアルベシ

第二十一條　神職ノ服裝ハ正裝，禮裝，常裝ノ三種トス

正裝ハ衣冠ヲ著クルヲ謂ヒ大祭ニ著用ス

禮裝ハ齋服ヲ著クルヲ謂ヒ中祭ニ著用ス

常裝ハ狩衣又ハ淨衣ヲ著クルヲ謂ヒ小祭，日拜及恒例トシテ行フ式等ニ著用ス

第二十二條　神社ノ氏子又ハ崇敬者ハ神社設立後遲滯ナク各三人以上ノ總代ヲ推擧スベシ
氏子總代又ハ崇敬者總代ハ其ノ住所，氏名ヲ所轄帝國領事官ニ届出ヅベシ
氏子總代又ハ崇敬者總代ハ神社ノ維持，管理ニ關シ神職ヲ補助シ且其ノ願届ニ連署スベシ
第二十三條　許可ヲ受ケズシテ神社ヲ設立，維持，廢止若ハ併合シタル者ハ百圓以下ノ罰金又ハ拘留若ハ科料ニ處ス
第二十四條　帝國領事官本令第八條，第十條及第二十二條第二項ノ届出ヲ受ケタルトキハ遲滯ナク之ヲ外務大臣ニ報告スベシ

附　則

本令ハ昭和十一年七月一日ヨリ之ヲ施行ス
本令施行前設立シタル神社ニシテ本令施行ノ日ヨリ二月內ニ第八條，第十條及第二十二條第二項ノ手續ヲ爲シタルモノハ之ヲ本令ニ依リ設立シタルモノト見做ス
本令中氏子若ハ崇敬者又ハ氏子總代若ハ崇敬者總代ハ當分ノ間所轄帝國領事官ノ許可ヲ得テ居留民團又ハ居留民會ヲ以テ之ニ代フルコトヲ得

滿支寺院規則

○外務省令第九號

在滿洲國及中華民國寺院，敎會，廟宇其ノ他ノ布敎所規則左ノ通定ム
昭和十一年六月六日
外務大臣　有田八郎

在滿洲國及中華民國寺院，敎會，廟宇其ノ他ノ布敎所規則

第一條　滿洲國及中華民國ニ於テ寺院，敎會，廟宇其ノ他ノ布敎所ヲ設立，移轉，廢止又ハ併合セムトスルトキハ所轄帝國領事官ノ許可ヲ受クベシ
第二條　寺院，敎會，廟宇又ハ其ノ他ノ布敎所ノ設立ノ許可ヲ受ケムトスルトキハ其ノ住職，僧侶，牧師，道士又ハ布敎師ト爲ルベキ者及檀信徒ト爲ルベキ者十人以上ノ連署ヲ以テ左ノ事項ヲ具シ所屬宗派ノ管長又ハ之ニ類スル監督者ノ承認書ヲ添ヘ所轄帝國領事官ニ願出ヅベシ
一　事由
二　設立地
三　名稱
四　宗派系統
五　本尊又ハ祭神
六　本堂其ノ他ノ建物ノ位置，構造及建坪並ニ境內ノ位置，面積及模樣
七　設立費及其ノ支辨方法
八　布敎方法
九　維持方法
十　檀信徒ト爲ルベキ者ノ戶數
十一　住職，僧侶，牧師，道士又ハ布敎師ト爲ルベキ者ノ履歴及其ノ資格
十二　本堂其ノ他ノ建物ノ起工及竣成豫定期日
前項ノ規定ニ依ル願書ニハ前項第六號ノ事項及境內地周圍ノ狀況ヲ表示スル圖面ヲ添付スベシ
第三條　寺院，敎會，廟宇又ハ其ノ他ノ布敎所ノ移轉ノ許可ヲ受ケムトスルトキハ左ノ事項ヲ具シ所轄帝國領事官ニ願出ヅベシ
一　事由
二　移轉地
三　本堂其ノ他ノ建物ノ位置，構造及建坪並ニ境內ノ位置，面積及模樣
四　移轉費及其ノ支辨方法
五　本堂其ノ他ノ建物ノ起工及竣成豫定期日
前項ノ規定ニ依ル願書ニハ前項第三號ノ事項及境內地周圍ノ狀況ヲ表示スル圖面ヲ添附スベシ
第四條　寺院，敎會，廟宇又ハ其ノ他ノ布敎所ノ廢止若ハ併合ノ許可ヲ受ケムトスルトキハ左ノ事項ヲ具シ所轄帝國領事官ニ願出ヅベシ
一　事由
二　廢止又ハ併合セラルベキ寺院其ノ他ノモノノ名稱及所在地
三　併合スベキ寺院其ノ他ノモノノ名稱及所在地

四　本堂其ノ他ノ建物及財産ノ處分方法

第五條　寺院，教會，廟宇又ハ其ノ他ノ布教所ノ設立，移轉又ハ併合ノ許可ヲ受ケ二年内ニ之ヲ爲サザルトキハ其ノ許可ヲ取消スコトアルベシ

寺院，教會，廟宇又ハ其ノ他ノ布教所ノ設立，移轉，廢止又ハ併合ノ許可ヲ受ケタル者各之ヲ了シタルトキハ遲滯ナク所轄帝國領事官ニ屆出ヅベシ

第六條　寺院，教會又ハ其ノ他ノ布教所ハ神社類似ノ社祠又ハ鳥居ヲ建設スルコトヲ得ズ

第七條　寺院，教會，廟宇又ハ其ノ他ノ布教所ハ其ノ設立後遲滯ナク左ノ事項ヲ記載シタル明細書ヲ調製シ之ヲ所轄帝國領事官ニ提出スベシ

一　名稱
二　所在地
三　宗派系統
四　本尊又ハ祭神
五　堂宇其ノ他ノ建物
六　境內地
七　境內附屬建物
八　檀信徒ノ戶數
九　維持方法
十　沿革

第八條　前條第一號，第四號乃至第七號及第九號ノ事項ヲ變更セムトスルトキハ其ノ理由ヲ具シ所轄帝國領事官ニ願出デ許可ヲ受クベシ

第九條　寺院，教會，廟宇又ハ其ノ他ノ布教所ハ其ノ設立後遲滯ナク其ノ所有ニ屬スル不動產及寶物ニ關シ左ノ事項ヲ具シ所轄帝國領事官ニ屆出ヅベシ

一　土地ニ在リテハ其ノ所在地，地目，段別又ハ坪數及境內地，境外地ノ區別
二　建物ニ在リテハ其ノ位置，名稱，構造，建坪又ハ間數及境內地ニ在ルモノト境外地ニ在ルモノトノ區別
三　寶物ニ在リテハ名稱，員數，形狀，品質，寸尺，作者及傳來

前項ノ屆出ヲ爲シタル後屆出デタル事項ニ異動ヲ生ジタルトキハ其ノ都度遲滯ナク屆出ヅベシ

第十條　寺院，教會，廟宇又ハ其ノ他ノ布教所ハ財產臺帳ヲ備ヘ其ノ所有ニ屬スル不動產及寶物ニ關シ前條各號ノ事項ヲ記載スベシ

第十一條　寺院，教會，廟宇又ハ其ノ他ノ布教所ノ財產ノ管理其ノ他重要ナル事項ニ付テハ住職，僧侶，牧師，道士，布教師等ハ檀信徒總代ト協議ノ上之ヲ處理スベシ

寺院，教會，廟宇又ハ其ノ他ノ布教所ニ於テ其ノ不動產又ハ寶物ニ付賣却，貸付其ノ他ノ處分ヲ爲サムトスルトキ又ハ負債ヲ爲サムトスルトキハ其理由ヲ具シ所轄帝國領事官ニ願出デ認可ヲ受クベシ

第十二條　住職，僧侶，牧師，道士，布教師，教職等就職シタルトキハ左ノ事項ヲ具シ所轄帝國領事官ニ屆出ヅベシ

一　就職年月日
二　職名

三　履歷及資格

前項ノ屆書ニハ資格ヲ證明スル書類ヲ添付スベシ

第十三條　住職，僧侶，牧師，道士，布教師，教職等死亡又ハ退職シタルトキハ檀信徒總代ヨリ所轄帝國領事官ニ屆出ヅベシ

第十四條　寺院，教會，廟宇又ハ其ノ他ノ布教所ヲ設立セズシテ布教ニ從事セムトスル者ハ左ノ事項ヲ具シ所轄帝國領事官ニ屆出ヅベシ其ノ事項ノ變更アリタルトキ亦同ジ

一　本籍，住所及氏名
二　宗派系統
三　布教方法
四　履歷並ニ資格及其ノ證明書

第十五條　住職，僧侶，牧師，道士，布教師，教職等ニシテ公安風俗ヲ害スルノ行爲アリト認ムルトキハ所轄帝國領事官ハ布教其ノ他教務ノ執行ヲ停止シ若ハ禁止シ又ハ寺院，教會，廟宇其ノ他ノ布教所ノ許可ヲ取消スコトアルベシ

第十六條　寺院，教會，廟宇又ハ其ノ他ノ布教所ノ檀信徒ハ其ノ設立後遲滯ナク三人以上ノ總代ヲ推擧スベシ

檀信徒總代ハ其ノ住所，氏名ヲ所轄帝國領事官ニ屆出ヅベシ

檀信徒總代ハ寺院，教會，廟宇又ハ其ノ他ノ布教所ノ維持，管理ニ關シ住職，僧侶，牧師，道士，布教師，教職ヲ補助スベシ

第十七條　許可ヲ受ケズシテ寺院，教會，廟宇又ハ其ノ他ノ布教所ヲ設立，移轉，廢止若ハ併合シタル者ハ百圓以下ノ罰金又ハ拘留若ハ科料ニ處ス

第十八條　帝國領事官本令第五條第二項，第七條，第九條，第十二條，第十三條及第十六條第二項ノ屆出ヲ受ケタルトキハ遲滯ナク之ヲ外務大臣ニ報告スベシ

附　則

本令ハ昭和十一年七月一日ヨリ之ヲ施行ス

本令施行前設立シタル寺院，教會，廟宇又ハ其ノ他ノ布教所ニシテ本令施行ノ日ヨリ二月內ニ第五條第二項，第七條，第九條，第十二條及第十六條第二項ノ手續ヲ爲シタルモノハ之ヲ本令ニ依リ設立シタルモノト看做ス

奉天省公署教育廳
管理寺廟暫行條例

第一條　凡有喇嘛僧道住持之宗教上建築物不論用何名稱均爲寺廟
第二條　寺廟及其財產法物如宗教上歷史上美術上有關係之佛像神像樂器法器經典雕刻繪畫及其他向由寺廟保存之一切古物等依本條例管理之
第三條　由政府機關或私人設立及經私人管理之寺廟不適用本條例之規定
第四條　寺廟財產及法物應向該管地方官署呈請登記轉報省公署教育廳備査
第五條　寺廟之不動產及法物不得隨意處分或變更
第六條　寺廟住持喇嘛僧道除宣傳教義修持戒律修葺廟宇及其他正當開支外不得動用寺廟財產之收入但動用款項均須先期呈由該管地方官署轉請省公署教育廳核准
第七條　寺廟收入款項應於每半年終了報由該管地方官署轉報省公署教育廳備査
第八條　違反本條例第四第五兩條規定之一者得由該管地方官署呈請省公署教育廳將住持嚴加懲處違反第六第七兩條規定之一者得呈請省公署教育廳革除其住持之職
第九條　本條例自呈准公佈日施行

奉天市寺廟登記
施行細則

第一條　本細則遵照奉天省公署一號省令頒佈之管理寺廟暫行條例第四條之規定制訂之
第二條　本細則適用於奉天市
第三條　市區內寺廟之登記分人口法物不動產三種
第四條　寺廟之人口登記以本寺廟之僧尼道士喇嘛爲限個傭或寄居者不在登記之列
第五條　寺廟之人口應由各寺廟將登記者原名法名年歲籍貫派別出家地點入廟年月常川住廟或過路掛單均須詳細報明
第六條　寺廟人口登記每人收登記工本費國幣二角
第七條　已登記僧尼道士喇嘛除由本署註冊外並每人發給登記証一紙其登記証不另收費
第八條　僧尼道士喇嘛還俗或離廟時應隨時聲請註銷登記其有新入寺廟者亦須隨時聲請登記
第九條　寺廟所有之法物按照管理寺廟暫行條例第二條所列舉者爲限
第十條　凡管理寺廟條例第二條所列舉之法物應由各寺廟將法物之種類名稱詳細報明
第十一條　各寺廟之法物經査明後除由市署註冊外并發給登記証一紙其登記証不另收費
第十二條　法物如有損壞遺失須卽時報告市署經査明確無弊竇者准予註銷其所置之法物亦須卽時呈報註冊
第十三條　寺廟之不動產包括寺廟地基殿堂住房及屬於該寺廟所有之房屋田地等項
第十四條　各寺廟之不動產應由各寺廟將不動產之種類數目坐落四至詳細開單連同契紙及其他足資証明之書類詳細報明
第十五條　各寺廟所報之不動產經査明屬實後除由市署註冊外並發給登記証書每寺廟收登記証工本費國幣五角
第十六條　凡呈請不動產登記者如左列情形須預先報明經査屬實在並有相當理由者方准備案
一，不動產在未登記前有一部份或全部在外抵押者
二，不動產在未登記前因糾葛涉訟未經判決者
三，不動產在未登記前契據遺失尚未補立新契或無契據另有產權之証明者
第十七條　各寺廟之法物及不動產倘有隱匿秘不登記或不按實登記者一經査出或被舉發査實卽將其住持逐出另覓住持掌管
第十八條　各寺廟呈請人口法物及不動產之登記應備具呈文繕具清摺呈報市署由市署派人査明屬實後卽予分別登記
第十九條　本細則由呈奉批准之日施行
第二十條　本細則如有未盡事宜得隨時呈請修正之

國際佛教ニュース

獨逸の新僧侶四名

佛教が日に日に西洋に於て普及しつゝあると云ふ事は，今日の一番有望なるものゝ一ツであつて，殆んど凡ての便りは，歐洲に於ける熱心なる善男，善女が，たとへ彼等の生涯の方法として佛教を受け入れないとしても，少くとも佛教を熱心に研究しやうとしてゐることに觸れてゐる。

最近四人の獨逸人は，セイロン島，ドーグンズワ，ヘルミタゲ島にニヤナ・チロカ師に依て僧侶として得度せしめられた。その儀式は去る六月四日取り行はれ，その時島全體から見物の爲め何千といふ善男善女が集つて來た。此等の同胞は，何時も佛教に對して深い教義を持つてゐた。彼等の中の二人は今回の得度，即ち佛教界に於ける重大なる一歩を歩み入れるまへ，既に一年間ヘルミタゲに滯在してゐた。殘りの二人は得度される四ヶ月前に到着したのである。彼等は巴利教典の完全なる研究に志をたてた。此の見解は將來何時かバルマに於て進展される事であらう。彼等は說教の仕事に對する充分なる素養を習得したならば，佛陀が僧侶に與へられた有名なる訓戒を守つて故國に歸へる事になるであらう。

本來の名前と，僧侶に得度された時に與へられた名前と，彼等の生國の名前とを下に記す。

ヨセフ・ピストール
（西南獨逸）＝ヤブピヤ
オツトー・アルスコフ
（東プロシヤ）＝ヤナシリー
ジーグモンド・フエニイゲル
（西南獨逸）＝ヤナボニツク
ペーテル・イーヅ・シエーンペエルト
（ベルリン）＝ヤナテイカツタ

吾々は新しい僧侶を歡迎し，彼等の獻身的生活に於ける凡ての幸福を切望するのである。正法の講義の使命を帶びて一たびその土地に赴くならば彼等は間違ひなく西洋に於て多くの貴い仕事を爲し遂げるであらう。

メテヤ比丘

マハボディー教會の主賓，僧侶メテヤ師も同じ船でコロンボに出發した。師は數ヶ月間病に倒れたが，師の敬虔なる勤行の遂行及び印度に於ける紀要記事の作成は一日さへ病に妨げられる事はなかつた。印度に於て氏は評判よく，面白く中道の教理を說いて歩いた。吾々は氏の健康が氣候の變化にも堪へられる樣，回復されんことを切望するのである。

佛徒信者になつた英國婦人

クロイドン・サレーのサンヤンプラト夫人は，現在タコマ（ワシントン州）に居住して，二人の子供のお母さんであつて，最近佛徒信徒になられた。夫人は三十八歲であつて，彼女が佛教僧侶の感化を受けた一九一九年以來，佛教に熱心になつた。彼女は佛戒を受ける時は眞新しい黄色の僧衣を纏つた。彼女は夫と英國で近づきになつたのであるが，現在は彼女の夫も亦佛教徒である。彼女は宗教に於ける平和，幸福といふものを知つてゐるが，佛徒になる爲めに殊更に選び出したものではない。

佛教長老ケンブリツチ大學哲學博士となる

ビ・ヴァジィラナナ師は佛教布教の宣教師としてマハボディー教會から一九二八年に英國に派遣され，最近ケンブリッヂ大學の哲學博士となられた。ビ・ヴァジィラナナ師は此の偉大なる名譽を受けた最初の僧侶である。吾々は師が布教の完成に最高の努力を用ひられんことを渴望するのである。茲に於て佛教弘通の爲ゆの導師及び說教者を必要とし　ビ・ヴァジィラナナ師は此の方面に於ける最も貴い勤めを無事に爲し遂げる事であらう。

高僧の權威バルマにて認めらる

ササナバイングはバルマに於ける佛徒サンガーの首領であつて，間もなく精神方面の統治權全體に亙つて最高の權威としての復活を許されるであらう。又僧侶達は彼を指導者と仰ぐであらう。

此高僧は一九〇三年に印度政廳からその地位を與へられた。最近高等法院が僧侶の財產に關する所有權問題は民事裁判所の管轄内に屬するものなる事を決定し之を實施するに到つた。爲めに今迄久しく之等の事に對し權利を持つてゐたササナバイングの神聖なる命に對して手厳しい打擊を與へるに到つた。此の權限を彼に復舊する事を目的とする法案は，已に總督の認許を得てゐて間もなくブルマ立法會議に於て披露するであらう。此の改革運動は一般の要望に叶ふものであるから，吾々は支障なく通過されん事を望む。

カルカッタのマハ・ボディー公會堂の講演

去る六月マハ・ボディ教會主催の下に行はれた公開講演の中，主なるものを揭げれば次の如きものである。

英國エディンバラ市の理學專門學校々長マクドナルド・ベエイン博士は，先頃チベットに於ける佛教僧侶の行つてゐる思索的生活の習慣を研究する爲めに旅行中であつたが，チベットからの歸路「日常生活に獻身努力する主義」といふ題名の下に演說をした。博士は此の樣な良き生活の基本的要素として品行の純潔さの必要を力說した。當市の州立大學のマヘンドラ・ラル・サルカル博士が司會者であつた。

「シイシューバラティ」誌主筆ジョケンドラ・ナス・グプタ氏は東部ベンガル地方に於ける佛教に就いて講演した。佛教の影響がヒンヅー社會に深く染み込んでゐたといふ事に就て表裏兩方面に亙つて之を說いた。ベノイ・クマル・サルカル教授が司會者であつた。

昭和十一年・佛誕二五〇二年

"悟りのカード"解説

東京市神田區一ツ橋二丁目三番地
全日本佛教青年會聯盟
電話九段(33)四四二八番・振替東京三三二一七番

太子の降誕 アヂヤンタ壁畫（ヤズダニ著アヂヤンタ）摩耶夫人藍毗尼園に於て釋尊を生み給へり。この壁畫の中央に、夫人は無憂樹の枝を右手に持ちて立つ。夫人の前に梵天王は生れ給ひし世界の王釋尊を讃え、王者の象徴たる傘を取つて立ち、帝釋天は金色の羅網を持つて釋尊を受け、他の二天は拂子を取り眞珠の緒を取つて迎ふ。

釋尊の成道 アヂヤンタ壁畫（ヤズダニ著、アヂヤンタ）釋尊菩提樹下に靜觀を凝し給ふ。諸天神皆歡喜す。魔王婆旬はこれを憂ひ眷屬を率ひて來り釋尊を脅し誘惑すれども遂ひに成らず。

この壁畫の中央に釋尊は嚴として動き給はず。魔軍群つて、或は不氣味な面相を以て、或は劒を以て立ち、或は魔女は嬌態を以て誘ふ。然し釋尊の心湛然として動かず、一切の煩惱と無明を斷滅して、遂ひに大覺の光明をはなち給へり。

初轉法輪 カルカツタ博物館藏（天沼俊一著 印度美術寫眞集）世尊成道を爲し給ひ曾て釋尊求道の時隨從者たりし五比丘に、先づ法を說かんと鹿野苑に行き給ふ。時に五比丘、釋尊の苦業を捨て給ひし事をもつて世樂に染るとし、釋尊を敬禮せざらん事を約す。然し世尊を見て自から敬禮を以て迎へ、或は衣鉢を取り、或は座を設け、洗足を取り、遂に世尊最初の弟子となる。

圓の中央に佛陀は說法の印を取つて坐す。臺座の中央にある法輪は說法を意味し、法輪の兩側に鹿を以て鹿野苑を現はし、更らに五人の合掌は五比丘を現はせるものなり。

佛陀の入滅 ナツ僧院發見（印度古代建造物集）佛陀拘尸城娑羅樹の下に於て正に大涅槃に入り給ふ。度すべき者を度し終り、懇切なる遺敎を說き給ひて、正に涅槃に入り給ふ。天の神、地の生けるもの、涕泣滂沱たること驟雨の如く、大地震動し須彌山王自然に傾搖し、林木摧折す。

圓の中央に佛陀頭北面西右脅にして娑羅樹の下に臥し、多くの侍者は苦惱の表情にて集り、中に悲しみの餘り地に伏して友に援けられたる樣も見ゆ。

"The Bo-Present Cards"

Birth of the Lord Buddha...........Ajanta Fresco (From "Ajanta" by Yazdani)

In the Lumbini garden Queen Maya gave birth to the Lord Buddha. In the picture is to be seen Queen Maya holding a branch of the Asoka tree in her hand. In front of the Queen stands Brahma with a parasol, an emblem of kingship, in praise of the new-born king of kings. There is Indra holding a golden mattress to receive in the divine child; and other two gods are also seen, one with a fly-whisk and the other with a pearl-string, welcoming the Prince.

* * *

Enlightenment...........Ajanta Fresco (From "Ajanta" by Yazdani)

The Lord Buddha sits under the Bo tree meditating. All the gods are glad. Mara, king of the Under-World, however, is uneasy at this and comes out with all the minors to disturb the meditation, only to fail in the attempt.

In the centre of the picture is to be seen the Lord Buddha sitting unmoved. All the Mara's armies surround him. One shows an awful face; another attacks him with a sword in his hand. A bewitching woman tempts him. But the serene sea never yet raises a wave. He defeats all the delusions and temptations and attains perfect enlightenment.

* * *

First Sermon........A Sculpture in the Calcutta Museum (From the "Indian Picture Album" by Mr. Shun-ichi Amanuma)

After the attainment of enlightenment the Buddha bent his way towards the Mrgadāva, or the Deer Park, to impart the manna of his spiritual labour to the five bhikkus who shared with the Master asceticism. The priests were determined not to mind the Master thinking, because of his departure from asceticism, that he had yielded to the worldly pleasures. But a sight was enough to make them bow to the Master, to take up the bowl, to yield him the seat, to carry water to wash his feet. Thus they were the first to enter the Path.

In the centre of the picture the Buddha is seen sitting in an attitude of sermon. The wheel in the seat signifies sermon, the deer on both sides of it symbolize the Deer Park, the place of sermon, and the five persons with clasped hands speak of the Five Bhikkus.

* * *

Nirvana.............Discovered at the Natthu Monastery (From the "Collection of the Indian Buildings")

The Buddha now enters Nirvana under the Sal trees at Kusinagara. He had saved what he had to save. He preached the last kind sermon; and he enters Nirvana. The heaven and earth wept at the departure of the Master; the flow of tears was like a shower. Mount Sumeru bent its head and the trees broke.

In the centre of the picture is to be seen the Master lying with his head towards the north, and facing the west, under the great Sal trees. All brows of his disciples are knit with woe, and even one unable to bear the sorrow is lying on the ground, his friend assisting him.

サ　ラ　ナッタ　ヤ　ム

Saraṇattayaṁ

三歸依〔巴利語〕

（1）ブツダム　サラナム　ガツチヤーミ
Buddhaṁ saraṇaṁ gacchāmi,
〔我れ〕佛に　歸依したてまつる，

ダンマム　サラナム　ガツチヤーミ
Dhammaṁ saraṇaṁ gacchāmi,
〔我れ〕法に　歸依したてまつる，

サンガム　サラナム　ガツチヤーミ
Saṅghaṁ saraṇaṁ gacchāmi.
〔我れ〕僧に　歸依したてまつる。

（2）ドチヤン　ピ　ブツダム　サラナム　ガツチヤーミ
Dutiyam pi buddhaṁ saraṇaṁ gacchāmi,
二たび　又〔我れ〕佛に　歸依したてまつる，

ドチヤン　ピ　ダンマム　サラナム　ガツチヤーミ
Dutiyam pi dhammaṁ saraṇaṁ gacchāmi,
二たび　又〔我れ〕法に　歸依したてまつる，

ドチヤン　ピ　サンガム　サラナム　ガツチヤーミ
Dutiyam pi saṅghaṁ saraṇaṁ gacchāmi.
二たび　又〔我れ〕僧に　歸依したてまつる。

（3）タチヤン　ピ　ブツダム　サラナム　ガツチヤーミ
Tatiyam pi buddhaṁ saraṇaṁ gacchāmi,
三たび　又〔我れ〕佛に　歸依したてまつる，

タチヤン　ピ　ダンマム　サラナム　ガツチヤーミ
Tatiyam pi dhammaṁ saraṇaṁ gacchāmi,
三たび　又〔我れ〕法に　歸依したてまつる，

タチヤン　ピ　サンガム　サラナム　ガツチヤーミ
Tatiyam pi saṅghaṁ saraṇaṁ gacchāmi.
三たび　又〔我れ〕僧に　歸依したてまつる。

國際佛教通報局定款

名　稱

第一，本局を國際佛教通報局と稱す

事務所

第二，本局の事務所を全日本佛教青年會聯盟本部に置く

目　的

第三，本局は日本內海及海外に向つて佛教事情の通報をなし，且つ佛教徒相互間の各種便宜を計るを以て目的とす

事　業

第四，本局の目的を達成するため左記の事業を行ふ

イ，日本內地及世界各國より佛教事情に關する質問の通報を行ふ

ロ，必要に應じ日本語及世界各國語を以て佛教事情の通報を行ふ

ハ，外國人の日本觀光に際しては各種の便益を與へ，特にその佛教に關する方面に於て之を爲す

ニ，定時或は隨時に各國語を以て文書の刊行をなす

ホ，その他必要と認めたる事業を行ふ

役　員

第五，本局の事務を處理するため左の役員を置く

イ，局　長　　一　名

ロ，幹　事　　三　名

ハ，評議員　　若干名

局長は本局の事務を總括す

幹事は本局の事務を處理す

評議員は局長の提案に依る重要事務を審議す

第六，評議員は左記の者を以て之に充つ

イ，全日本佛教靑年會聯盟理事及主事

ロ，全日本佛教靑年會聯盟理事會に於て推薦したる者

第七，局長及幹事は評議員會に於て決定す

第八，役員の任期は二ケ年とす（但し重任を妨げず）

經　費

第九，本局の經費は左記のものに依て之を支辨す

イ，本局基金の活用

ロ，寄附金

ハ，その他の收入

補　則

第十，本定款に記載せられざる事項は，凡て評議員會に於て協議す

第十一，第一回の役員は全日本佛教靑年會聯盟理事會に於て決定す

定價	一部　金　二　十　錢	送料二錢
	一年　金二圓四十錢	送料不要

昭和十年四月卅日第三種郵便物認可
昭和十一年十月廿八日印刷（每月一回一日發行）
昭和十一年十一月一日發行

東京市外吉祥寺337
編輯發行兼印刷人　淺野研眞

東京市牛込區早稻田鶴卷町107
印刷所　康文社印刷所
電話牛込（34）1950番 5049番

東京市神田區一ツ橋二の三
發行所　國際佛教通報局
電話九段（33）4428番
振替東京83015番

昭和十年四月三十日第三種郵便物認可
昭和十一年十月二十八日印刷納本(毎月一回)
昭和十一年十一月一日發行(一日發行)
國際佛教通報　第二卷　第十一號

第二回

汎太平洋佛教青年會大會

紀要

THE PROCEEDINGS
of
THE Second
General Conference
of
Pan-Pacific Young Buddhists' Associations

(in Japanese, Chinese and English)

Held at Tokyo & Kyoto, July 18-23, 1934

Price ¥ 3.00

Compiled & Published
by
The Federation of All Y.B. As. of Japan,
Tokio, Kanda, Hitotsubashi, II-3

昭和十年四月三十日第三種郵便物認可　昭和十一年十一月二十八日印刷納本　昭和十一年十二月一日發行（毎月一回一日發行）第二卷　第十二號

The International Buddhist Bulletin

國際佛教通報

第二卷 **昭和十一年十二月** 第十二號〔Vol. II. Dec. $\frac{2502}{1936}$ No. 12.〕

要　目〔Contents〕

東京 國際佛教通報局 發行
The International Buddhist Information Bureau
Tokyo, Kanda, Hitotsubashi, II—3
Annual Subscription, ¥2,40 (post free). Single Copies 20 sen (post 2 sen)

Histoire du bouddhisme au Siam

La date de l'établissement du Bouddhisme au Siam est une question controversée. Les uns la rapportent au temps où Açoka envoyait des missionnaires prêcher à l'étranger, d'autres à une époque bien postérieure.

Si l'on se fonde sur les témoignages archéologiques et les données concordantes de nos documents historiques, il apparaît d'une façon évidente que le Bouddhisme s'est implanté au Siam dès l'époque où ce pays était encore habité par des populations Lāu (Lawā), dont la capitale occupait le site actuel de Nagara Paṭhama et s'appelait Dvaravatī. On trouve en effet au Siam des monuments bouddhiques de toutes dimensions dans le style dont le stupa de Nagara Paṭhama est le représentant le plus important. On en trouve aussi d'autres dont les styles diffèrent assez entre eux pour que l'on puisse en conclure que les diverses sectes qui ont pris naissance au cours de l'histoire du Bouddhisme ont pénétré successivement au Siam dont l'histoire religieuse, en conséquence, se divise en quatre périodes.

Première période
HĪNAYĀNA DU THERAVĀDA

On trouve au stupa de Nagara Paṭhama des témoignages archéologiques à l'appui de ce que nous venons de dire sur l'introduction du Bouddhisme au Siam à l'époque où Nagara Paṭhama était capitale, par example, les pierres sculptées en forme de roue de la loi. On relève encore les traces de bien d'autres pratiques qui précédèrent l'apparition des premières images du Maître comme celles d'ériger des trônes vides du Bouddha et de façonner des empreintes du Pied Sacré. Ces faits prouvent que la première forme de Bouddhisme qui soit apparue au Siam a été le Hīnayāna du Theravāda tel qu'Acoka l'envoya prêcher hors de son royaume.

Dès lors, la religion bouddhique se serait implantée au Siam dès avant B. S. 500 (*circa* 50 avant J. C.) et la pratique s'en est fidèlement transmise depuis.

Deuxième période
LE MAHĀYĀNA

Vers B. S. 1300 (*circa* 750 A. D.) un roi très puissant de Çrīvijaya dans l'île de Sumatra, étendit sa domination sur la péninsule malaise depuis la province de Surāt (Surashtra Dhani) jusqu'à celle de Pattāni. Or, les gens de Çrīvijaya pratiquaient le Mahāyāna qu'ils apportèrent avec eux et enseignèrent dans tous les pays qu'ils soumirent. Il nous reste encore des monuments de style Mahāyāna construits par des gens de Çrīvijaya, par exemple la grande relique de Jaya et la grande relique primitive de Nagara Çrī Dharmarāja (Nakon Sritamaraj).

La Grande Relique actuelle a été fondée à une époque postérieure par les adeptes de la doctrine singhalaise. Le monument primitif se trouve dans l'intérieur du monument actuel. Il a été mis à jour lors de la restauration du sanctuaire sous le cinquième règne de la présente dynastie.

Troisième période
LE HĪNAYĀNA DE PAGAN

En B. S. (1600 A. D.), le roi Anuruddha, qui régnait sur la Birmanie, établit sa capitale à Pagan, soumit à sa domination le peuple mon et reporta ses frontières jusqu'au Lannā c'est-à-dire la province actuelle du Nord-Ouest (région de Chiengmai), et, au Sud jusqu'à Lavapurī et Dvāravatī. Le roi Anuruddha, défenseur de la foi bouddhique, la fit prêcher dans ses états à mesure qu'il les conquérait. Mais à cette époque, le Bouddhisme était en pleine décadence dans l'Inde.

Les gens de Pagan, comme ceux du Siam, avaient à l'origine reçu du Magada le Bouddhisme Hīnayāna du Theravāda. Plus tard, quand il perdit contact avec l'Inde, leur Bouddhisme prit une forme particulière qui est le Bouddhisme Hīnayāna de Pagan. Lorseque les gens de Pagan mirent la main sur le Siam, ils y introduisirent leur forme propre de Bouddhisme qui gagna du terrain dans la région du Nord (province dite actuellement du Nord-Ouest).

C'est pendant la période dont nous parlons que les Tai, venant du

Nord, envahirent le Siam, et après avoir conquis leur indépedance ils descendirent vers Sukhodaya dont ils firent la capitale d'un nouvel état qui, peu avant B. S. 1800 (*circa* 1250 A. D.), était maître de la majeure partie du Siam. Les Tai qui professaient déjà la religion bouddhique adoptèrent alors le Hīnayāna tel qu'il était pratiqué à Pagan.

Quatrième période
LE BOUDDHISME SINGHALAIS

En ce qui concerne le Siam en particulier, il semble que le Bouddhisme singhalais y ait pénétré aux environs de B. S. 1800 (*circa* 1250 A. D.). Les religieux siamois, revenus de Ceylan où ils avaient reçu l'ordination nouvelle, établirent d'abord des communautés à Nagara Crī Dharmarāja, puis, ils invitèrent à venir se joindre à eux des religieux singhalais qui les aidèrent à remanier le Grand Reliquaire de Nagara Crī Dharmarāja dans le style des stupas singhalais de l'époque. Lorsque la réputation des religieux singhalais se fut étendue jusqu'à Sukhodaya, capitale de la dynastie de Braḥ Ruang alors à son apogée, le souverain, gagné à la doctrine réformée, invita des religieux de cette secte à venir s'établir à Sukhodaya. Dès lors, la doctrine singhalaise prospéra au Siam et entraîna la décadence et la disparition totales du Mahāyāna au Siam.

Cependant, en adoptant le Bouddhisme singhalais, les Siamois n'ont pas abandonné toutes les pratiques qu'ils observaient auparavant, même celles qui leur venaient de religions non bouddhiques; cela tient à ce que l'esprit tai, comme nous l'avons dit, ne se décide dans ses choix qu'en vue d'un résultat pratique.

On doit considérer que le Bouddhisme pratiqué au Siam est une secte purement siamoise depuis l'époque de Sukhodaya, à tel point que, à la fin de la période d'Ayudhya, à la suite des troubles qui ruinèrent dans son pays d'origine la vieille église singhalaise, on vint de Ceylan faire appel à l'église siamoise. Une commission ecclésiastique présidée par le Brah Upāli se rendit à Ceylan où elle procéda à des ordinations et réorganisa l'église singhalaise qui, de nois jours encore, porte le nom de Syāmavaṃsa ou Upālivaṃsa.

The Japanese Defiance of Death

By A. Sakai

It is remarkable how the Japanese can stare death in the face with perfect calm. Every page of Japanese history is beautifully dotted with noble episodes of self-immolation. The samurai of old was trained to be always ready to die in the presence or defence of his lord, and to choose death before disgrace or humiliation. Life is in this country compared to the cherry-blossoms, which scatter after three days of their beauty, as shown in the following 31-syllable poem, which is familiar to every school-child :—

" Shikishima no
　Yamato-gokoro wo
　　Hito towaba
Asahi ni niou
　Yamasakura-bana "

(Suppose one were to ask what the Yamato-spirit of the Shikishima-land is; there are the wild mountain-cherries that bloom bright and fragrant in the morning sun.)

This will account also for shinju or double-suicide of lovers, in which Japan is regretably abundant. A samurai of old, when condemned to death by his offended lord, considered it a privilege to be allowed to commit harakiri instead of being executed, because to him execution was a great shame. The world wonders at the bravery of the Japanese soldiers, but it is easily explained by their unconditional devotion to the Emperor, for man can work wonders when he has no fear. It is the more remarkable because the defiance by the Japanese of death is based, not on a religious idea, religionists of course excepted, but chiefly on their devotion and faithfulness to the Emperor and lord, though pessimism sometimes accounts for it.

General and wife accompany Lord to land of the dead. General Maresuke Nogi was a hero of the Russo-Japanese war, and he was a soldier of great personality. He served most loyally with the Emperor Meiji, whose favorite he was, and he thought his work was over with the death of the Emperor, which took place on July 30, 1912. On Sept. 13, the day for his

Imperial cortège to depart from the Imperial Palace in Tokyo for Kyoto, where his funeral services were to be observed, the signal was fired at 8 p. m. to announce its departure from the Palace, when Gen. and Mrs. Nogi killed themselves at their private residence ; the general commmitting harakiri after the classical manner of an old samurai while his wife died by falling upon a dagger after she cut her throat with it. They left the following Jisei (farewell - to - the - world or death-bed odes) :

" Utsushi-yo wo
　Kami-sari mashishi
　　Oh-kimi no
Mi-ato shitai te
　Ware wa yuku nari "
　　　—Gen. Nogi

(Following the foot-steps of the Great Lord, who has departed from the transitory world to join the gods, I go.)

" Ide mashite
　Kaeri masu Hi no
　　Nashi to kiku
Kyo no Miyuki ni
　Au zo kanashiki "
　　　—Mrs. Nogi.

(It is sad to see the Emperor proceed today on a trip from which I hear he will on no day return.)

Brother stabs brother. The Emperor Godaigo, who was temporarily staying in refuge at Yoshino, saw in a dream that his Imperial throne was provided by a page under a tree of which its southern branches were much more luxuriant than in any other parts of the tree. According to the interpretation of the dream, there was a military leader by the name of Kusunoki (literally, camphor) (楠), which consists of the two ideograms: "tree" (木) and "south" (南). Soon Masashige Kusunoki, a local chief, was called by the Emperor, whom he helped in restoring the Imperial administration that had been in the hands of courtiers or warlords for many a century.

Masashige Kusunoki was defeated by Takauji Ashikaga at Minatogawa in 1336. Mortally wounded, Kusunoki took refuge at a farmer's house with his brother, Masasuye.

" What do you think will become of the Emperor (Godaigo) after we are gone ?" Masashige asked of his brother, who was also fatally wounded.

" We shall come to life seven times and annihilate the enemy of the Emperor."

" I am glad you say that " Masashige agreed, and the brothers stabbed each other to death, in order to save themselves the disgrace of being discovered and killed by the enemy.

Samurai swallows poison with calm. Ujisato Gamo, lord of Aizu, was a brave warrior under Nobunaga Oda, whose favorite he was, but he was falsely accused, after the death of Oda, by Mitsunari Ishida, who was jealous of his growing influence, and Hideyoshi Toyotomi told a retainer to serve Gamo with poisoned tea. Gamo was aware of the dark attempt on his life, but he swallowed the tea with perfect calm, improvising a 31-syllable poem, in which he compared himself to the cherry-blossoms that leave their branches at a puff of wind. It reads:

"Short-lived are the blossoms
And scatter, the wind not
blowing:
How hasty and impatient, too,
The mountain-breeze of
the spring!"

Land of the dead asked for Shinzayemon Sorori made himself a great favorite with Hideyoshi Toyotomi by his jests at which he was particularly good. Every time Toyotomi was out of humours, Sorori was sent for, so that he might restore Toyotomi to the normal state of mind.

"Sorori" said Toyotomi one day, while sitting on the veranda, sword in hand, "Sorori, can you take me down the veranda into the garden without my intending it? If you do so, you shall have this sword."

"I think I can," Sorori said, and after thinking for a whole, he added: "It is very hard but, my lord, I can take you from the garden up to the veranda without your intending it."

"Just the same, Sorori. Then I will come down" and Toyotomi walked down, when Sorori, bursting out laughing, said "Thank you, my lord." Toyotomi had to put his sword on the hands that Sorori held out to receive it.

When Sorori was seriously ill, Toyotomi asked him, through a messenger, if there was anything he wanted to have done after his death. He had no request to make, but he asked if he could carry any message to the land of the dead.

When Sorori was dying, Toyotomi visited him and again asked if there was anything Sorori wanted.

"I should be very thankful if, through your great influence, I could take possession of the land of the dead, so that I may reign

king there."

Lord gives own life to save his men. Muneharu Shimizu garrisoned the Takamatsu castle in the province of Bitchu, which Hideyoshi Toyotomi sieged with an army of 50,000 strong, ten times as many as the garrisons of the castle. But Shimizu defended the castle so bravely, making a sortie to repulse the enemy every time he approached it, that Toyotomi, unable to take it by fighting, decided on what is termed Mizu-zeme or water-siege. All the rivers in the neighbourhood of the castle were stopped with dams built up and the water rose around it till it looked like a floating castle. Then Toyotomi sent a messenger to the castle in an attempt to win Shimizu over by offering him the whole province of Bitchu in case of his surrender.

"No, I will not surrender," Shimizu said decidedly. "Lord Mohri lays confidence in me, and he gave me the great duty of garrisoning this important castle. I would not be tempted to betray his trust for all the Empire, to say nothing of Bitchu only."

Mohri sent some reinforcements to the rescue of the Takamatsu castle, but he could do nothing in the face of the strong siege, and at last he made overtures for peace by offering the five provinces of Inaba, Hoki, Mimasaka, Bizen and Bitchu, provided that Shimizu should be spared. But Toyotomi turned no ear to the proposal, for he demanded that Shimizu should be put to death. When Shimizu heard of the rejection of the proposal made by his lord, Mohri, he offered to die in order to save his garrisons and to maintain the prestige of Mohri.

On the day before his suicide, Shimizu had all his beard pulled out by a page as a samurai of old was wont, and he said in explanation: "I have been confined in defence of the castle for thirty-eight days, during which I had no time to shave myself. It would be disgraceful to have my head, shaggy with beard, inspected by the enemy."

On the same afternoon, Shimizu was sent for by Yozayemon Shirai, one of his favorite retainers, and he went wondering what his retainer wanted him for.

"My lord" Shirai said the moment Shimizu appeared. He was sitting in the posture of one who commits harakiri. "I must ask your forgiveness for calling you. You are to commit suicide tomorrow, and it would be humiliating not only to yourself, but to the clan as well, should you be found to act in a coward way. So I cut my front in order that I may tell you what it is to commit harakiri. It is not at all hard, my lord, so don't worry, but act bravely."

So saying Shirai uncovered his front, which was cut open crosswise in the regular way of harakiri. Shimizu thanked him for the love with which he made the fatal experiment of harakiri for the sake of his master. But in order to save him any more pain, Shimizu raised his sword to complete the harakiri by cutting the head of Shirai off.

Shimizu made a complete list of all articles that were to be delivered to Toyotomi, and he had a farewell drink with his warriors, when he danced the sword-dance with perfect calm. He then wrote his Jisei-poem of 31 syllables and committed harakiri in the presence of the messenger sent by Toyotomi. His Jisei reads:—

"Ukiyo oba
Ima koso watare
Mononofu no
Na wo Takamatsu no
Koke ni nokoshite."

(The transitory world is now crossed over, my warrior-name left inscribed on the hoary and mossy Takamatsu-pine.)

Muneharu Shimizu left his name as eternally as the pine is traditionally said in this country to live, and Hideyoshi Toyotomi admired his noble death and warrior-like loyalty.

The Three Human Bombs. It would be unjust to omit the Three Human Bombs, though they are still too fresh in everybody's memory to require their mention in this short sketch. In the recent Shanghai incident, in 1932, the advance of Japanese infantry was checked by a barbed wire entanglement. Attempt after attempt was made to march through the fence, only to be repulsed by the Chinese, till the commander of the Japanese contingent decided to explode the barbed fence at any cost. He called for volunteers, who would carry a live bomb to explode the wire entanglement. Many soldiers stepped forth to offer themselves, but the first three sappers who came to the commander, were chosen to have the honour of making way by explosion for the Japanese march. They carried a large lighted explosive bomb in the face of certain death. It exploded and the fence was rent asunder making a 30-ft gap in the entanglement. The Japanese marched and the victory was won. What became of the three sappers? They disappeared with the explosion.

* * *

Nor did our feudal ladies show less calm in the face of death than samurai, for many are the stories of brave ladies who chose death before humiliation. Here are a few of them.

Promise kept with life. "Which do you love more, your husband or brother?" Prince Saho asked of his sister, Princess Saho, who was wife to the Emperor Suinin.

"I love my brother more" she answered, little knowing what her brother was driving at.

"Favour won by beauty dies with it," Prince Saho went on. "If your husband loves you on account of your beautiful looks, he will desert you at any moment in favour of other beauties, of whom there are many. Better reign in the country with me."

Prince Saho handed his sister a dagger with which to kill her husband, the Emperor. A little while later, the Emperor visited his wife and took a nap with his head resting on her lap. It was the best chance for her to kill him, but she could not commit at once androcide and regicide and a drop of her tear fell upon the cheek of the sleeping Emperor.

"I saw a strange dream," said the Emperor, waking up. "A snake of brocade colour wound itself around my neck, and a shower came from the direction of Mt. Saho to fall on my face,"

"The shower is a drop of my tear" Princess Saho explained, still in tears; and producing from her pocket the dagger her brother handed her, she added "and the snake must be the cord of this sword."

She stood in a fix between her husband and brother, and asked the Emperor to forgive Prince Saho, but a troop was immediately despatched against him, who shut himself in a fort built of rice-straws.

"If my brother is killed, I shall be publicly censured for betraying him," Princess Saho said, and she ran into the straw-fort taking Prince Homutsuwake, her son. When, however, the fort caught fire set by the Imperial troops, Princess Saho held the prince out, and said: "Take the prince out.

I came here hoping that my presence as well as his might save my brother. All is up now, and I shall share the same fate as my brother. Tell the Emperor to take to wife the daughter of Tamba-no-Michiomi, for she is a girl of great personality."

So saying she was burned to death with her brother, Prince Saho, and her nominee became the Empress in her stead.

Wife drowns self to save husband. In 110 A.D. Prince Yamatotake was sent to maintain peace in the eastern provinces. When he was crossing the present bay of Tokyo, a severe storm rose and the waves ran so high that his boat made little headway.

"I am afraid," said Princess Oto-tachibana, wife of the prince, "I am afraid that the god of the sea is offended. I will go to the bottom and appease him, so that the boat may sail safely across the bay."

The princess drowned herself and, the sea going down, the prince landed safely on the other side. Kisarazu in Chiba Prefecture is traditionally said to be the place of his landing, the name being, according to some authority, a corruption of "Kimisarazu" meaning "the lord cannot leave" (or missed his princess). When the prince crossed the pass of Usui, he looked back upon the plain under his eye, and sighed "O my wife" from which, they say, the district in which Tokyo is now situated, was named "Azuma" (literally, my wife).

Chastity maintained with life. Lady Hosokawa was the daughter of Mitsuhide Akechi. When Akechi assassinated Nobunaga Oda, his master, in 1532, she was divorced and confined by her husband, Tadaoki Hosokawa, and, upon the death at Yamazaki of her father, she was even advised by some of her friends to commit suicide on account of the shameful regicide perpetrated by her father.

"I will not kill myself," Lady Hosokawa decidedly answered. "If I killed myself without the permission of my husband, to whom I still belong, divorced as I am, I should violate the Buddhist commandments for the three obediences (to father, husband and son). I would not act against my duty towards my husband in order to abide by that for my father."

Hideyoshi Toyotomi took pity upon Lady Hosokawa for her chastity, and her husband forgave her upon his advice. After the

death of Toyotomi, Hosokawa was sent on an eastern expedition by Tokugawa, and he left a warning with his wife in a 31-syallable poem, which reads in effect:

"Yield not nor bend low,
Ye, lady-grass (Ominayeshi)
on the hedge,
Though the wind may blow
From the mountain of Man
(Otoko-yamo)."

He compared her, in the ode, to a effeminate grass called Ominayeshi (patrinia scabiosaefolia) and her temptation to the wind blowing from Mt. Otoko (literally, man), for he knew that her beauty was a temptation.

Soon after the departure of Hosokawa, Mitsunari Ishida sent for Lady Hosokawa, who guessing his object did not respond to his call, and Ishida sent a band of soldiers to take her prisoner.

"I am a woman, and I would not be humiliated," Lady Hosokawa said when the soldiers arrived. She killed her two children, a boy ten years old and a daughter eight years, with a dagger, with which she killed herself, leaving a Jisei of 31 syllables for her husband, in which she showed her regret for dying before his return.

Lady dies by refusing medicine. Lady Kasuga was the wet nurse of Iyemitsu, the third Shogun of the Tokugawa régime. All the other court-ladies were in favour of Prince Kunichiyo, the second son of Hidetada Tokugawa, instead of Prince Takechiyo, as his eldest son was called when a child, and Lady Kasuga had hard times to establish the selection as the Shogunate heir of the eldest scion.

Once Iyemitsu was seriously ill with small pocks. Lady Kasuga repaired day after day to the Toshogu Shrine, which was dedicated to Iyeyasu, the grandfather of Iyemitsu, and offered her own life in order to save Iyemitsu, by making an oath that she would never take medicine of any kind so long as she lived, if her charge was cured. And Iyemitsu was restored.

When Lady Kasuga was dying, Shogun Iyemitsu visited her at her bed-side and gave her medicine with his own hand, because she would take no medicine offered by her physician. She took it into her mouth, only to put it out again immediately. Her idea was that because the medicine was offered by the Shogun himself she accepted it, but she put it out again on account of the oath she had made with the Toshogu Shrine, that is, the spirit of Iyeyasu, the grandfather of Iyemitsu. Lady Kasuga died in 1643 at the age of 65 years.

No more beauty to be seen in life: Kaga-no-Chiyo is one of the greatest Hokku (17-syllable ode) poetesses that Japan has produced. She was born in the province of Kaga; hence her popular nane of Kaga-no-Chiyo or Chiyo (personal name) of Kaga Proyince. She had a poetic genius and when but five years old she wrote, in an ode of 17-syllables, that the marks made by the geta (wooden foot-gears) on the snow looked like so many Japanese letters for "two" (二). She left many famous 17-syllable poems which are familiar to the Japanese.

When she lost her son, who used to go hunting dragon-flies, Chiyo expessed her sorrow in a hokku or 17-syllable ode, which reads:

"Tombo-tsuri
Kyo wa doko-made
Itta yara."

Freely rendered, the ode expresses her wonder "how far the dragon-fly catcher has gone today in his hunting." She does not realize his death, but she seems to think that he is still running after the dragon-flies.

At the death of her husband, she improvized another 17-syllable ode, which is no less on the lips of every Japanese:

"Okite-mitsu
Nete-mitsu Kaya no
Hirosa kana."

(I sit up and see; I lie down and see: O how wide the mosquito-net is!)

In neither of these odes, she directly describes her sorrow, but the reader can readily see her sadness implied in the odes, for implication is often more eloquent than expression.

On her death-bed Kaga-no-Chiyo wrote the following Jisei-ode:

"Tsuki mo mite
Ware wa kono Yo wo
Kashiku kana."

(Having viewed the moon even, I take leave of this life with a blessing.)

The ode implies that she takes leave of life because, having viewed the moon, the most beautiful of all, there is no more beauty to be seen in life.

Bo Tree Enigma

Kosho Yamamoto

In the earliest Buddhist sculptures the Bo Trees served to symbolize the Buddha's enlightenment: nor is it now in any way the less in value of respect paid by Buddhists for the holy tree, because under this tree the Buddha attained enlightenment. But, strange to say, enthusiasm rather seems to have miscarried in the way. How? A tree quite different in species now bears the name of "Bodaiju" or the "tree of enlightenment" and only a few know the truth. Even the fruits of this bogus tree are looked up to highly, not only by the votaries but also by the Japanese priests at large. The nuts or the stone fruits of these are chained into rosaries: a finished piece of which even may cost one fifteen or twenty yen and only such well-to-do priests can afford to pride in its possession. Nor are the innocent priests the only victims of this unenlightened enigma: the botanists even have unconsciously followed the lead set down by a priest somebody, dead already, it may be, two or three thousand years ago. How? The "lime tree" or the "linden" is known among the Japanese under the name of "Bodaiju." Who indeed might have been the godfather of this misnomer? A riddle is not yet unriddled: the sesame is lacking. To satisfy this holy enigma I venture to set down the facts as are known to me, awaiting for any feasible enlightenment as to this question by some yet no less a curious inquirer than myself.

Ficus Religiosa. The tree under which the Buddha is believed to have attained enlightenment is "Ficus Religiosa, Linn." ("Urostigma Religiosum, Gasp."). The name "Bo Tree" is the Anglo-Singhalese. To be more minute the following are the names as according to the different tongues:—

Medah, Vudah..........Arab.
Ashwuth ....Beng.
Ranghitmara ....Can.
Ani-pipal ....Dukh.

Pipal .... Hind.
Ari-alu .... Maleal.
Bo-gass .... Singh.
Arasa maram .... Tam.
Baya manu .... Tel.
Re, Ravi, Ragi.......... „
Ashwaththamu .... „
Kallaravia .... „

Anyway, the "leaves are heart-shaped, long, pointed, wavy at the edge, not unlike those of some poplars; and as the footstalks are long and slender, the leaves vibrate in the air like those of the aspen tree (Populus Trimhla)...." So much the cool-veined botanical interpretation. To add more to this stock of erudition," this large, handsome tree grows in most of the countries of the S.E. of Asia..... It grows all over India. One of these is to be found within the precincts of every Buddhist temple in Ceylon, and it is frequently met with in deserted localities, or near the sites of ancient villages, and there the occurence of a solitary Bo Tree. with its circular buttresses of stonework round the stem, indicate the existence, at some former period, of a Buddhist temple in the vicinity. The planting of a Bo Tree in Ceylon, a ceremony coeval with and typical of the introduction there of Buddhism, is one of the most striking passages in the 18th chapter of the Mahavanso, entitled "The obtaining of the Bo branch"; and the 19th chapter describes the arrival of the Bo Tree. A tree of unusual dimensions, which occupies the centre of a sacred enclosure at Anarajapoora, is still reverenced as the identical one which the sacred books record to have been planted by Mehendra 250 years before the Christian era, consequently in the year 1900 it will be 2150 years old. So sedulously is it preserved, that the removal of a single twig is prohibited; and even the fallen leaves, as they are scattered by the wind, are collected with reverence as relics of the holy place."

Labyrinthine Path. Now, whether we are aware or no, the Japanese "Bodaiju." or the tree of enlightenment, is not the "Ficus Religiosa, Linn.": it is at least one of the "Tilias" of the family of "Tiliaceae" (the "Shinanoki-ka" according to the Japanese botanical classicification).

The question sat long brooding in my mind. How could a tree of tropical birth possibly live in a country as cold as Japan where in winter snowfalls are not infrequent? Could the so-called "acclimatization" of botanists extend so far as that? Unbelievable! Then my long-cherished curiosity was answered, when last year I called on the "Yakushiji Temple" of the suburb of Nara, the ancient capital of Japan or rather the cradle of Japanese Buddhism. There close to the three-storied pagoda did I find the so-called Japanese Bo Tree. A happy coincidence was that the tree was bearing the cherished fruits, the month being August, and I had a good chance to take every note of the manners in which the tree bears the fruits and also to pick up one of the fallen leaves. Ah, the disappointment! The leaf had indented margins whereas the Ficus Religiosa has none of such. My heart cried out this could be no more than a bogus. I returned back to Tokyo and there asked a nephew of mine who is a botanist if acclimatization could go as far as to the change of form of a leaf as in this case. The answer was of cource in the negative. And an amateur's curiosity was in a way quenched. The result was the information as I have hereabove quoted.

Tiliaceae (Shinanoki-ka). Now, "Tilia Miqueliana, Maxim." ("Bodaiju") and "Tilia Miabei, Jack" (Tilia Maximowiziana Shirasawa= "Ohba-bodaiju"), or the Japanese species of the Tilias, are trees of temperate zone which grow at an altitude of some 1200 feet in the provinces of Kyūshū and Shikoku, at an altitude of some 1000 feet in the mountains of Central Japan, or at an altitude of some 400 feet in Hokkaidō (according to an article in "Bonsai," vol. 13, No. 10). According to the above-said article these species are indigenous to the soils of Japan. The leaves of the "Ohba-bodaiju" are round in shape and as the leaves of the tree (Bodaiju) at the Yakushiji Temple are a little bit long and pointed at the tip it may be of another species or more possibly one that may have been brought back by an ancient priest from China. Anyhow the tree is of quite a different species from that of Ficus Religiosa. A research by my nephew further disclosed to me that the species with the stone fruits of which we make the rosaries, or the "Nenju-bodaiju" ("Kongōshi," "Kongōju") is "Elaeocarpus Ganitrus, Roxbg." and that it does not grow in Japan. It may further be of use to know before we go any further that the family of "Tiliaceae Juss." or the linden tribe consists, in India, of the general Corchorus, Triumfetta, Grewis, Berrya, and Brown-lowia, numbering in all as many as 91 species.

Elaeocarpaceae (Horutonoki-ka). Having been quite negatived in our attempts in the line of botanical foundation the only means that is left us is to look to such trees whose beads are used for making rosaries in India, and in this attempt a solution is half meted to us by the existence of the family of "Elaeocarpaceae." This family consists of a great number of plants, mostly tropical and growing all over India from the Himalayas to Ceylon. But such a variety as the "Elaeocarpus Obovatus, Ainslie," for example, is, found growing as high an elevation as from 6000 to 8000 feet (Ceylon). Of this family the "Elaeocarpus Japonicus" and "Elaeocarpus Photiniaefolius" are the natives of Japan. Now looking through the list we now come across with the following, the nuts of which are principally used for beads.

1. "Elaeocarpus Ganitrus, Roxb. (Ganitrus Sphaericus, Geort)

A middle-sized tree, common in various part, as well as the Malay Archipelago. The seeds, about the size of marbles, are worn as necklaces by Brahmans and ascetics. They are commonly called Utrasum beads.

Utrasum bead tree......Eng.
Rudra-kai ....Tam.
Rudraksha..............Sansk.
Rudra-challu ....Tel."

2. "Elaeocarpus Lanceaefolius, R.

Octradike Manke ......Dukh.
Utrasum ? ....Tam.

A tree of the Khasya Hills, Assam, Moulmein, and Java. The seeds are very rough, and about the size of small nutmegs. Saiva Brahmans and Pundarums, religious devotees of the Saiva sect of Hindus, who live by alms, wear strings of them round their heads and necks, and form them into rosaries."

3. "Elaeocarpus Tuberculatus, Roxb.

Monicere Tuberculata ..W. Ic.
E. Serrulatus ....Roxb.
E. Bilocularis ....Roxb.
Rudrakai, Badrachai....Tam.
Rudrache, Badracha ....Tel.

This truly magnificient tree is very common in Coorg, the Animallayas, Malabar, and Travancore, up to an elevation of about 4000 feet. Very large trees of it may be seen at the foot of the Neilgherries and Makhurty peak, and seeds are worn as ornaments, also as rosaries by Vaishnava Brahmans and by fakirs."

Suspending Conclusions. In sum an examination into the following will clarify the point.

-URTICALES:—
  Moraceae:—
    Ficus:—
      Ficus Religiosa
-MALVALES:—
  -Elaeocarpaceae:—
    Elaeocarpus:—
      Elaeocarpus Lanceaefolia, R., etc.
  -Tiliaceae:—
    Tilia:—
      -Tilia Miqueliana, Maxim.
      -Tilia Miyabei, Jack (T. Maximowiziana Shirasawa).

From what I have quoted hereabove it will be seen that there is a diametrical difference between the original Bo Tree (Ficus Religiosa) and the imitation Bo Trees (T. Miqueliana, R., T. Miyabei, Jack): nor even are these latter two and Elaeocarpus Lanceaefolia, R., etc., quite the same. The only corresponding factor is that both Elaeocarpuses and Tilias are indigenous to the soils of India and Japan, the variety in the case of the latter being quite limited. With regard to the ficus variety the fruits are none of the kind of Elaeocarpuses and Tilias.

Some doubtful solutions can well be advanced, but solutions, if there should be, ought to be more scientific, more historic, more linguistic. Will any versed on the subject assist me in the way?

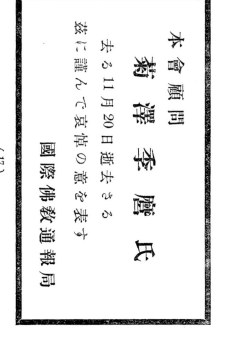

本會顧問
菊澤季麿氏
去る11月20日逝去さる
茲に謹んで哀悼の意を表す
國際佛教通報局

天台宗の満洲開教に就いて

寺本三二

傳ふる所に依ると，日滿佛教協會創立準備委員會に於て，大谷師は，

「滿洲に於ける日本佛教は，各宗各個の布教であり，その全部が日本人を對手とするもので，滿洲人を對手に布教及佛教運動をして居るものは一人もない。而して彼等は如何にして居留民を自分の畑に引き入れるかに汲々とし，且生活の爲にあらゆる手段方法を以て金を得る事に苦心してゐる。その結果は軍部方面から非難を受け，宗派の布教には悪い感情を出先官憲に與へてゐる。日本佛教の爲めには，どうしても超宗派的の佛教で滿人を對手とする佛教運動を起さねばならぬ，云々」

と述べられたさうである。全く日本佛教徒の滿洲布教に對する從前の缺陷を遺憾なく指摘されたものと思ふ。實際局外者から從來の滿洲布教を觀ると，「某宗がやるから吾宗もやらねばならぬ」と云ふが如き，一時の流行，一種の虚榮心から出發して，何等の定見も研究もなくこの大事業をやりかけて，手を焼いてゐるとしか思はれない點もある。かゝる如きは巨額の淨財を費して却つて國家の對滿工作を妨げるもので恐らくこれ程の徒勞は他にあるまいと思ふ。

然し佛教の滿洲進出は兩國家人民の爲めにも，亦大きく云へば東洋平和の爲めにも，絶對に必要である事は今更言を俟つ迄もない。國民一般亦非常なる期待をもつて宗教家の大奮起を切望して居るのである，只從前の布教が前述の如き不結果に終つた事に就いては充分なる研究と準備とを缺いて居たのがその原因であると思ふ。少くとも一年や二年は研究と準備に費し，完全なる具體案を得て後實行すべきであると思ふ。云ふ迄もなく滿洲開教は，その日暮しや氣まぐれで出來る樣な易易たる事業ではないのである。

ところが天台宗に於ては，夙に此の點に着眼して先づ留學生の交換を實行してゐる。開教の二大要素は人と金とである。しかも有爲の材は一朝一夕に求める事が出來ない。故に將來開教線に活躍すべき指導者を養成しつゝある事は，機に當を得た方法である。台宗の開教に對する遠大なる理想と周到なる用意の程が知られる。然しこれ等留學生も早きは本年中にその業を終へる事になつてゐる。彼等が新天地に雄飛する日は近いのである。如何なる順序方法經費に據つて，彼等の信念實力を十二分に發揮せしめ，以て所期の目的を遂し得るかその用意如何，これ吾人の尤も知りたいと思ふ處である。勿論當局としては既に百年の大計が定つてゐるのであらうが未だ之を發表して居られない爲，各種の不便が生じはせぬかと思ふのである。此際職に開教に從事するもの，自己の最善と認むる私案を發表するのも，亦無用の事ではあるまいと思ふ。只其の任に非る者が潜越を敢てし，取るに足らぬ愚見を記して他の嘲笑を招くを憚らざるもの，衷心此の國家的大事業の完成を切望するより出でしもの，大方諸士の御寛假を願ふ次第である。

滿洲開教私案

目的

開教の目的は次の諸項でなければならないと思ふ。

一，滿人の心服する指導者にして，常時，非常時共一令の下に彼等を思ひのまゝ行動せしめ得る日本人を各所に駐在せしむること。

二，滿洲人を物質的精神的に援助すること。

三，滿洲人を教育指導して，日滿人の一心同體的動作に便すること。

第一のみが眞の目的であつて，第二，第三は其の手段である。只之を堂々と發表すれば幾分誤解の心配があるかも知れぬ。發表する時は日滿親善とか兩國民の提携とか，適當なる字句を用ふるも亦妙であらう。只日本側は何處迄もこの精神でないと絶對にいけないと思ふ。これには相當の異論があらう。從つて二三の意志表示が必要と思ふ。

本目的は銳鋭なき侵略壓迫の樣に見える。しかし滿洲人は日本人とは違ふと云ふ事を充分頭に入れて置く必要がある。日本人が彼等を正しい方へ向はしむる事は，假令多少强制的であつても，壓迫的であつても決して天地神明に恥づる事ではない。子供に厭がる藥を飲ますのと同じである。

又目的を佛教の布教に置く人士もある。勿論一つの手段としては，誠に結構である。布教とか開教とか，佛教に依る日滿親善とか，標語としては非常に好いし，又各階級に日本人を入り込ますには一等便利である。しかし只佛教の教義を説き念佛を稱へる丈では不充分である。一朝事ある時假令滿洲人が日本人と共同動作は出來ぬ迄も日本の後を背さぬ位にする丈の用意が必要である。尚又日本僧侶が直接滿洲人に布教するには左の諸點を解決せねばならぬ。

1. 滿語で布教出來る日本僧侶が何人居るか，習へばよいと云ふ人もあらうが，語學は相當天才的のもので，十人が十人習へば出來るものではない。假に充分な言葉が出來たとしても，その布教的價値は，要するに普通一般の滿洲僧と大差がないではないか。これは頭腦經濟から云つて非常な損失である。滿洲語の出來ると云ふ偉大なる力は他の點に於て發揮させねばならぬ。
2. 滿洲人の信仰は小乘と云ふよりも寧ろ迷信に近い。これ等一般の信者に大乘的日本佛教を如何にして了解させるか恐らく不可能に近い

難事であらう。

3. 滿洲人の大多數は信仰よりもパンを望んでゐる。先づ彼等の生活を安定さして後始めて信仰に導くが順序であらう。

4. 滿洲人に布敎するには滿洲僧と同じ生活を必要とするが彼等の生活は日本人より見れば，實に不自由至極の低級なものである。馬賊も僧侶を犯さないと云ふのは，一面迷信もあらうが，又滿洲僧の物質的に惠まれて居ない證據でもあるかゝる生活を一般の日本僧侶に望む事が出來ようか。

5. 日本人が表面に立つての布敎には必ず多數の滿洲僧及び居士の反對を覺悟せねばならぬ。

要するに佛敎の布敎は非常に結構であつて，之を表面の目的として寺院や居士林を利用し，多數の日本宗敎家を入り込ます事は大變に都合が好い。しかし布敎はどこ迄も手段であつて目的ではないと思ふ。

目的を日滿親善に置く事は，頗る聞えもよく，且つ合理的である。徒に表面的に發表するには不可缺のものである。しかし之には遠く日露戰爭役後の日支關係を回顧して，再び其の悔を繰返さぬ用意が必要である。日露戰役後の支那人が氣味の悪い程日支親善，唇齒輔車を强調した。之れが今滿洲人に依つて同じ様に繰返されて居る。そして其の後支那が青島を回收し，旅順，大連の返還を迫り，今尚經續しつゝある排日侮日の如き大轉向を敢行し，吾等は極樂から地獄へ陷された様な目に逢つたのである。これ皆先天的外交辭令に長じ，反覆常なき彼等を日本流に解釋した結果受けた所の苦杯である。滿洲にその轉向が果して來ないと誰が斷言出來ようか。勿論彼等を始めから惡人扱ひにするのは大變な危險であるがパンと鞭とを兩手に持たねばならぬ事は少くも十年以上彼等を研究した者の皆是認する所であらう。

機　關

目的達成の爲め，各種の事業を行ふべきは勿論で之を行ふ機關の大要を左の如く定めたいと思ふ。但し連絡する滿洲側は寺院も好いが，居士林，學校，其の他の團體の方が好くはあるまいか。

一，協會

1. 名稱を××とし財團法人とする。
2. 新京，（東京）に本部を置くこと。
3. 協會は日滿各宗派及其の他の團體を以て組織すること。
   （イ） 日本の參加者決定次第創立總會を開き，逐次滿洲側を參加せしむること。
   （ロ） 日本に參加者なくば天台宗のみにて行ふこと。
   （ハ） 日滿佛敎協會創立準備委員會に對し台宗の具體案，其の他を提示し該會と合同すること，若し該會との提携不可能の場合は天台宗の具體案に依り各宗其の他の團體に參加を勸誘すること。
4. 協會は日滿兩國政府特に軍部と事前に密接なる連絡を保ち特別の援助を要求すること。
5. 役員，事業，經費，會計等は創立に際し充分なる調査研究の上之を定むること。之に對しては在滿日滿人及在日本滿洲通の意見を聽取し，之を尊重すること。

二，連絡

1. 滿洲寺院學校其の他の團體（以下滿洲寺院と稱す）に對し協會より日滿人敎師若干名を派遣し，各種の社會事業及寺院と官憲との連絡に當らしむ。
2. 滿洲寺院の參加には文敎部より豫め之を通牒勸誘さすこと。
3. 協會と寺院との契約事項大要
   （イ） 日滿親善の爲め協會は××に於て順次左の事業を行ふ。
      日語學校
      相談所，職業紹介
      授産所
      農事指導
      施藥所
      其の他必要なる施設
   （ロ） 各事業の取捨及開設の時期は敎師と寺院と合議の上協會之を定む。
   （ハ） 各事業に要する費用は協會之を負擔し，寺院の會計と分離獨立す。
      但し，敎師の食費，住宅，薪炭點灯等は寺院の負擔とす。
   （ニ） 寺院は事業に必要なる設備（約××元以下）をなし之を敎師に使用せしむ。
   （ホ） 住職（校長其の他以下之に同じ）は敎師を監督す。但し任免會計事務に干與するを得ず。
   （ヘ） 本契約は寺院の住職と協會との間に締結し，後任者は其の義務，權利を繼承すること。
4. 新京に各種事業の模範的設備をなし，標準參考とす。この一切は協會本部に直屬す。
5. 敎師は協會之を任免す。
6. 協會内に監督員（指導員）を置き，臨時各地敎師の監督指導に任ず。
7. 敎師には左の範圍内の俸給を協會より支給す。
   日本人　四十圓以上百五十圓迄
   滿洲人　二十圓以上百二十圓迄
8. 敎師僧籍に在る者は，職級等の昇叙及其の他の恩典は在日本の者と同等とす。
6. 敎師退職に際しては適當なる優遇法を講ずること。

敎師養成機關

協會内に日滿敎師養成の機關を設く，その大要

1. 毎年日滿人各十名乃至二十名を入學せしむ。
2. 入學資格は僧俗を問はず，中學卒業或は之と同等以上の學力あるもの。
3. 修業三ケ年にて卒業とし，敎師の資格を授與す。
4. 學科は語學を主とし佛敎農業工業の初步，醫療の常識等を敎授し，日本學生には滿人の取扱方，風俗習慣を，滿洲學生には日本の國體地歷，文化の發達，日本人の特性

等を教授す。

5 學生の居住，食費は協會之を負擔す。

6. 日本學生には現住地より新京迄の旅費を支給す。

7. 學生は學習の餘暇を協會の事務，雜用に從事す。

8. 入退學，課程表，教員，經費，寄宿寮等の規定は實行に際し協會之を定む。

9. 天台宗の日滿留學生は卒業後直に教師の資格を授與すること。

事　業

前述の目的を達する爲めの事業としては，金錢，仕事，智識，技能を與へるのが最有効な方法であるが，限りある資源で，無限の滿人に之を與へる事は不可能である。故に彼等の最も要求するもので比較的經費の少いものを選ぶ必要がある。勿論その中には追々と面白い事業が發見される事と思ふが左に數種を選んだ。實行に就いては寺院の狀況が各地非常に相違して居るからそれに應じた施設を工夫せねばならぬ例へば，一口に日語學校と云つて中央のものは將來政府の認可を受け堂々たる專門學校にするのも難事ではあるまいが地方によつては僅々數人の爲めに寺子屋式教授をせねばなるまい。これ等に就いては，教師養成所の教授者に於て充分なる研究をして，教師が赴任と同時に完全に業を遂行出來る樣，遺漏なく教へて置かねばならぬ。

一，日語學校

日本語が滿洲人に要望せらるゝことは云ふ迄もない，しかも比較的少額の經費で多數の滿人に其の恩澤を施し得らるゝ點から考へて，尤も適當な事業と云へよう。

若し又滿洲語を學びたい日本人が多ければ，滿洲語班を附設すれば一石二鳥の効果があらう。殊に本事業は其の施設宜しきを得れば將來充分自給自足して行ける見込がある。

學校の施設は處に依つて大差あるが左にその概要を述べる。專門部は最初中央に一校あればいゝと思ふ。

1. 名稱

2. 學校を初等部，專門部の二とし更に各部を晝班夜班に分つ

3. 入學資格は初等部は初等小學卒業者專門部は中學校卒業者或は同等の學力あるもの，及本校初等部卒業者

4. 修業年限は各三ヶ年

5. 課程は初等部は日常の會話，讀書を主とし，專門部は日本中學校の課程を日語にて教授す。

6. 授業料を徴收せず

7. 各部卒業者は本人の希望に依り學校より就職其の他の斡旋をなし專門部卒業者中の優秀なる者は日本に留學せしむ（留學生規定は別に定むる要あるべし）

8. 其の他の詳細は創立に際し協會より完全なる規定を定む。

二，相談所

滿洲國獨立以來，滿洲の言語，風俗に通じない日系官吏が凡ての點で幅を利かして居る。これ等の官吏は何事も

日本流に滿洲を改造しようとして，各種の法規が無數に作られる，しかし人民の大部分は文字を知らないのだからこの政府のやり方には流石の滿洲人も悲鳴を揚げてゐるらしく，日系官吏を指して法匪と云つて居る，彼等にとつては土匪よりも，學匪よりも，法匪の方が恐しいのである，少くも厚意ある虐政である。殊に日本人の勢力頓に旺盛となつた爲め，これを惡用して一般民衆を苦しめる日滿人も少くない。これ等憐むべき被壓迫者の味方となつて正當の權利を保護してやる事は頗る有意義と思ふ。これに人事百般の相談，職業，商賣の斡旋を兼ねれば尤も歡迎せらると思ふ。

1. 相談斡旋は無料とす

2. 出張及調査等費用を要するものは實費

3. 職員は派遣教師之を兼任す，但し狀況により法律家，實業家をして之に當らしむる必要あるべし

4. 經費は殆ど必要なし

三，授產場

家庭的小工業を起し職なき者を雇ひて技術を習得さし，或は獨立經營に進まし，或は他の工場に就職さす等の方法で最初多少の設備費を要するも，經營如何によりては自給自足し得らるゝと思ふ。其の種類は凡ての人が常に注意して研究を怠らなければ續々有利なものを發見する事が出來ると思ふ。左に比較的有望と思はるゝもの數種を擧げたがその一つ一つの設備，經營法，取引，損益等の詳細は略する事にした。

1. 石鹼製造

2. 窯業

3. 製帽下請

4. 靴下製造

5. 箒製造

6. 刺繡，染色

7. 切花

8. 自動車運轉手養成

日本の製造業を滿洲にて行ふには，

1. 製作工賃の高きもの

2. 運賃關稅の高きもの

3. 荷造に費用を要し破損し易きもの

4. 製作に根氣と時間とを要するものが，有利で，滿洲から日本へ送つて相當引合ふ品も，注意して探せば隨分多いと思ふ。又在來の滿洲品に多少の改造を施した丈で，充分日本人に向くものもある。

經營にはどうしても最初專門家が必要であるが，教師の努力次第でやれぬこともあるまい。又信徒，生徒等の中には好意的に援助指導をして與れる人があると思ふ。唯實行する迄には十二分の調査，研究，試驗が必要である。

四，農業指導

滿洲の農業は今尙太古のまゝの狀態である。之を指導して收穫を增加し，彼等の富を加へる餘地は充分にあると思ふ。筆者は農業に就いては全々無智であるが，教師養成所に於て專門家から充分叩き込まれた教師は必ずや爲すべきことの多いのに苦むだらう。

1. 其の土地に最も適する作物の種類を研究すること

2. 肥料の適否，施肥の方法等の研究

3. 耕作用具の改良
4. 旱水害の豫防，灌漑に對する施設
5. 作物の品質改良統一
6. 共同購買組合の設立
7. 農事試験場の設置

五，施藥施療

施藥，施療が後進國民の指導に有效なのは，キリスト教傳導師が必ず一通りの醫學の心得があり，常に治病に依つて，絶大の信服を得て居るのを見ても解る。其の實施方法としては經費の許す範圍内に於て，始めは賣藥の施與から漸次施療病院の設立迄進み度いと思ふ。

六，巡回映畫，講演

映畫，講演に依りて，精神教育の助けとする外日本の文化，國策及世界の大勢を知らしめ，日滿不分の理を了解させる事が肝要である。尚映畫の解說者及講演者は特別に之を養成する必要があらう。

七，佛教的施設

佛教的施設に就いては筆者に之を論ずる資格もないし，多數の專門家は定めし多くの妙案を持つてゐらるゝことと思ふから略する。

以上の各事業は要するに「目に見えるものを與へる」といふ事に歸着する。何故に佛教運動に力を入れぬかといふと甚失禮な譬であるが，犬を飼ふ場合先づ食物を與へて，飼主と犬とを不可分に連絡した後，愛と食物と鞭とを利用して飼主の要求に合する樣に，犬を仕立てゝ行く，此の筆法である。彼等の精神を陶冶するには，只無形の理論や講義では到底駄目で，必ず物質的のものに連係して行かねばならぬ。例へば嘘言はいけないと如何に說明しても模範を示してもそれ丈では直らないしかし嘘を言へば損をする樣に仕向けると必ず直るのである。從つて佛教的精神的方面から着手して彼等を教導することは順序上當を得ないと思ふ。勿論終局の目的はそこに置かねばならぬのは云ふ迄もないが。

即ち指導方法は「パンと鞭とを兩手に心には無限の愛を持つて根氣よく氣永にやる」ことであると思ふ。

經　費

滿洲開教には多大の經費，特に經常的經費を要することは申す迄もなく經費なしには如何な妙案も何一つ實行出來ないのであるからこの出所を確定して後始めて具體的のことを論議決定出來るので本事業の大根源である。恒久的經費の出所が不確實ならば寧ろ全然止めてしまふのが賢明であらう。從來各宗の開教が不結果に終つたのは，殆んど全部經費に原因してゐると思ふ。

經費は年千圓でも確實な恒久的出所があれば，それ丈の仕事は出來る。併し經費の多少と效果の大小と正比例するのは當然であるから，あの廣い滿洲には少くも年額五，六萬圓のものは是非必要であらう。その出所に就いては左の方法が考へられる。

一，協會員たる各團體より拠出すること。

これは云ふ迄もなく參加團體は應分の出金義務がある。可成多く寄

寮を參加させ，これより集まる金にて大體事業遂行の見込がつく樣にしたい。

二，五錢獻金

各宗信徒（團體には團員）から月五錢（或は十錢）宛の獻金をさせる方法で事業の間答さへよく說明すれば出す方は大低喜んで應じて吳れる。之は大津の天台僧が實行して意外の好成績を擧げた實例もある只集金が手數で困難であるが，左の方法でやれば出來ると思ふ。要は住職の獻身的活動が本である。

1. 各寺住職には壇家戶數の四分之一以上を加入さす責任を持たす
2. 月々の集金は豫め協會と學校と交涉し置き小學兒童に依頼する
3. 住職には×割の手數料を謝禮として贈る

天台宗に於ても既に十萬圓の金を開教に費して居る。今他から多少の補助を受けることは決して體面を汚すことではあるまいし，一錢たりとも對滿工作以外に使はないのだから，堂々天下に呼びかけて好いと思ふ。

三，官憲の補助

日滿兩國政府，軍部其の他團體より補助を受ける

四，一般の寄附

唯座して寄附を待つのでは中々集るものではないが，協會所屬團體の各員が努力すれば，事業の性質上相當集ると思ふ。

五，企業

現在滿洲には相當有望なる事業が多い。又滿洲政府或は軍部の特別な好意に依つて，獨占的にやらして貰へる仕事も澤山ある。これ等の有利なものを會社組織とし，定款に依つて利益の幾部分を協會に寄附させる。

以上は只其のアウトラインを表したに過ぎない。各條皆相當な腹案はあるが略した上杜撰不統一な點も甚多いので定めし意の通ぜざる處があると思ふ。唯一ケ所でも諸賢の御參考になる點があれば望外の幸である。（完）

滿支佛教管見

坂野榮範

(1) 滿洲國に於ける日本佛教の使命

（イ） 滿洲國建國精神の高揚，五族協和の王道樂土建設には，日本皇國大乘佛教を宣布すべきこと。

（ロ） 從來滿洲國に傳來せる支那系の佛教は，夾雜性・邪教性を多分に有し，且つ其の教理信條に於て淨化匡救を要すべき點あること。

（ハ） 此等二項を達成するためには，日本佛教開教師の派遣を嚴選しその素質を向上せしめ，各宗開教政策の根本的改革を要す。更に滿洲國人の僧侶を日本に留學せしめ，滿洲佛教自體の革新を促すことを要す。更に進で佛教大學の設立，佛教に關する文獻を滿語に譯出すべき事業は日本佛教の重大なる使命なることを痛感せり。

（ニ） 將來の滿洲佛教は日本佛教の指導下に置くべく，各宗團體を統一合同せる積極的活動團體として，日滿佛教協會の擴大強化を要す。

(2) 現代支那に於ける佛教の動向

（イ） 現代支那佛教の指導權は太虛と圓瑛との二大法師にして，南支・北支に於ける佛教の動向は蔣氏の支配下に從屬せるものゝ如し。

（ロ） 中日・日華佛教の國際的交渉は更に考慮を要すべきこと。

（ハ） 華北居士林印行の「中國の危機の救濟」 太虛法師講のパンフレツトの如きは，支那佛教僧の一面を暴露せるものにして，表面だけの日支佛教提携は，現在の支那政府下にありて不可能なるべきこと。

（ニ） 支那佛教の特質として居士林の發展は，佛教と政治との混亂を助長するに至りたり。所謂居士は政權を一時離れたる大官の避難所なるが故なるべし。

（ホ） 居士林の發生は支那佛教の退化に基くものにして，文化の綜合態としての日本佛教とは同日對等の談に非るべし。

（ヘ） 北支の佛教は蔣氏の支配力薄きが故に，比較的親日の感あり。南支の佛教は居士佛教が中心にして政治・軍事的の關係上排日的雰圍氣の感せり。

（ト） 支那佛教に對する日本佛教徒の認識は，徒に過去の支那佛教に依るものにして，現在支那佛教の動向に對して誤認せる點あること。

（チ） 日支佛教徒の根本的提携は，單に留學生の交換，大藏經の贈呈等に止まらず，支那僧侶の日本佛教に對する認識を是正し，更に原本的に支那が日本帝國の國是を全體的に認め，東亞の國際的情勢を總觀すべきことを先決條件となすべきこと。（以上）

滿洲佛教の現在と將來

淺野研眞

一

現在，滿洲國には幾多の宗教が存在してゐるが，何と云つても，佛教が斷然，多數を占めてゐるのである。

即ち，極く最近（康德三年五月），滿洲國文教部禮教司宗教科の發表した「宗教統計表」によるも，その事實はハツキリと現れてゐるのである。

茲に參考のため，若干の數字を再錄しておかう。

全國各教別統計表（康德二年十二月末調査）

教　別	寺廟教堂數	布教者數	信教者數
佛教	2,070	4,534	1,808,899
道教	1,877	3,319	506,540
回教	231	556	163,789
喇嘛教	195	1,380	123,885
天主教	323	576	141,475
基督教	450	803	41,868
猶太教	4	37	874
薩瞞教	4	4	10
總計	5,154	11,209	2,787,340

即ち諸宗教中に於て，我が佛教は，斷然，頭を拔いてゐる狀態にある。第二位の道教（むしろ之が土着宗教の第一位であらねばならぬのに――）でさへ，やつと佛教の半數餘と云ふ狀態である。その他の諸宗教に至つては到底，同日の談ではないのだ。

然し，たゞ數字のみを吾々は誇りとしてゐるわけには行かない。問題はその現勢にあるのだ。

二

滿洲佛教の現勢は，數的には極めて盛大であり，殆んど佛教國でさへあるが如き狀景を呈してゐる狀勢でもある。

然し，一度び其の內容に向つて批判的分析を加へるならば，質的には極めて貧弱であることを知らされるであらう。

私自身の實地踏査によつて得たる所を要約して示せば，大體に於て，次の如くである。

（1） 滿洲佛教は，思想的には主として南支の影響下にあり，行事的には主として北支の影響下にある。

（2） 滿洲佛教は，道儒等諸他宗教の夾雜物の混入多く，純粹性に缺く。

（3） 從つて現世利益を説く點に於て，迷信性の混入が多い。

（4） 滿洲僧侶は，一般に學識が極めて低く，文盲者さへ尠なからざる狀態である。

（5） 滿洲僧侶は，表面上は持戒堅固であるが，その僧堂規矩に於ては，極めてだらしないものである。（日本の方がズツト整つてゐる。）

（6） 滿洲僧侶は，ルンペン上りが多く，その出身社會層も身分も一般に低い。從つて自分がヤツト食つて行ければ良いと云ふ人生觀に落付いてゐて，社會事業とか，教育事業とか云ふ近代的な社會運動に進出することなどは，思ひもよらぬことである。

——以上の外，まだまだ云ひ足らぬこともあらうが，主要な點は，大體これで言ひ得たやうに思ふ。

三

そこで，今や建國第五年の友邦滿洲國に對して，その基礎的な文化工作を考慮せんとするものは，何人も愼重に，最大多數の信者層を有する我が滿洲佛教の將來に就て，充分なる考究をなさねばならぬのである。

これも亦，茲に私は，之を要約的に，次の數項にまとめて，私見を示さうと思ふ。

（1） まづ第一に，滿洲佛教をして，支那佛教の影響下より獨立せしむること。

（2） 而して日本の大乘佛教の影響下に置くこと。特に聖德太子佛教の眞精神を移すこと。

（3） 滿洲僧俗をして日本語の佛教文獻に親しませること。その過渡期として日本佛教文獻を滿譯して，之を廣汎に頒布すること。

（4） 滿洲僧侶の學識を高めること。そのために滿洲佛教大學を設立すること。

（5） 日本から行く各宗開教師の質を向上せしめ，社會教育，社會事業なども併せて行ひ得る者を派遣すること。

（6） 日滿僧俗の間に相互交驩の機會を屢々作り，意志の疎通と，意見の交換を行はしめ，佛教による心からの親善を圖ること。

（7） 滿洲の有能なる靑年僧侶を日本に留學せしむること。

——以上の外，まだまだ言ひ足りない點が多々あらうと思ふが，然し要點は之れで盡くされてゐるかと思ふ。

とにかく，新興滿洲國にその有終の美を濟さしむるものは，何と云つても，その文化的基礎の確立であらねばならぬ。

幸ひに，我が聖德太子の綜合されたまふた日本大乘佛教こそは，滿洲建國の指導精神にピツタリと合致するものであり，その基礎工作に資すべき最終的精神文化たるが故に，吾々は日本人として，また日本大乘佛教徒として，茲に認識を新たにして，滿洲建國の基礎的聖業に微衷を致すべきである。（九月十八日の紀念日に）

新外務省令と日本山妙法寺

在滿洲 半 谷 範 成

昭和十一年六月六日付けの外務省令で『在中華民國及滿洲寺院，教會，廟宇，其ノ他ノ布教所ニ關スル規定』が發せられ，滿洲に於ける神佛基各開教所は一齊に右規則に準據せしめられ，從來所屬官廳より教會所の許可を受けたるものも新令に依り再出願をせしめられ去る七月一日を以つて一段落となつたが，茲に問題となつて未だに各領事館の手を燒いてゐるのは，インドで有名な藤井某氏の主宰する『日本山妙法寺』なる教會の一派で，未許可のまゝになつてゐることだ。

即ち新法令に依れば，寺院又は教會所は，

一，所屬管長の副申

一，教師資格（履歷）明示

一，宗派系統（所屬）

を必要とするが，『日本山妙法寺』は所屬管長の副申がないのみならず，宗派系統を日蓮宗と稱するも，日蓮宗當局は「日本山は日蓮宗に非ず」と宗派が聲明書を發した程にて，このところ無所屬教會を暴露し，更に常識的に見て，日本山の教師が僧侶としてイカガハシイと云ふ事に見られ，目下全滿に在る「日本山妙法寺」は許可か不許可か重大な岐路に直面してゐる。

一方同教會の信徒は官邊や一般に對して

一，日蓮宗當局は日本山妙法寺の宗派入りを歡迎し藤井總理に申込んだが，藤井氏は一宗派獨立申請中なるため之を拒絕した。

二，外務省が中心で藤井氏は一宗派獨立をなす。

三，藤井氏は目下一宗派獨立のためインドより歸朝して目下奔走中である云々

と宣傳してゐる。果してどうなるか。

因に新京・ハルビンの領事館は本問題に對して極めて冷靜で，要するに所屬宗派を明にし，所屬管長の副申さへあれば，法規通り處置するのみと目下許可を留保してゐるが，全滿に約二十ケ所の教會所の所管領事館は何れも同樣のものゝ如し。（十月廿五日）

奉天市寺廟教會一覽表（康德三年七月現在）

奉天市公署調査

教別	派別	寺廟教會名	所在地	住持姓名	主祭神	出家布教者數	信徒數	創立年代
佛教	臨濟派	萬壽寺	小西關	鶯峯	釋迦	63	——	明正統年間
同	同	慈恩寺	大南關	省僧	三世佛	58	——	明天聰2年
同	同	長安寺	大北關	湛融	三世佛	4	——	相傳唐代
同	同	西關帝廟	小西邊門	覺先	關帝	4	——	清雍正4年
同	同	地藏寺	小南關	本鈺	地藏	3	——	清乾隆年
同	同	天齊廟	小東關	體安	東嶽	3	——	明代
同	同	慈雲寺	大西關	無盡	釋迦	3	——	清乾隆年
同	毘盧派	祖師堂	大南關	常金	祖師	3	——	清康熙年
同	臨濟派	老君堂	小東關	隆光	老君	3	——	清雍正重修
同	毘盧派	白衣寺	大北關	意參	白衣菩薩	3	——	明天啓3年
同	臨濟派	道君廟	小東關	體安	道君	3	——	清嘉慶13年
同	同	寶覺寺	小河沿	省緣	觀音	2	——	明代
同	同	孫祖廟	小東關	眞性	孫祖	2	——	清康熙19年
同	同	慈生堂	小東關	潤悅	釋迦	2	——	清康熙元年
同	同	應福寺	大北關	本定	釋迦	2	——	清康熙年
同	同	大法寺	大北關	本然	釋迦	1	——	明永樂13年
同	同	精忠寺	小東關	廣悅	老郎	1	——	明崇禎9年
同	賢首派	金覺寺	大南關	玄修	金覺佛	1	——	明順治年
同	同	金佛寺	大南關	法因	三皇姑	1	——	光緒元年
同	臨濟派	魁星樓	大東關	叙法	文昌	1	——	清咸豐3年
同	同	龍鳳寺	大南關	性具	菩薩	7	——	不詳
同	同	老虎廟	小東關	顯義	山神	4	——	同
同	同	北萬壽寺	小北關	鮮瑞	釋迦	3	——	同
同	同	藥王廟	大西關	空寶	藥王	1	——	同
同	毘盧派	大佛寺	大南關	常慧	三世佛	尼8	——	清初年
同	同	大悲庵	大東關	修極	三世佛	尼7	——	清道光5年
同	臨濟派	吉祥庵	大南關	隆波	觀音	尼5	——	清同治元年
同	毘盧派	極樂寺	小南關	修緣	釋迦	尼4	——	民國12年
同	曹洞派	法濟寺	小南關	界剛	釋迦	尼4	——	民國14年

教別	派別	寺廟教會名	所在地	住持姓名	主祭神	出家布教者數	信徒數	創立年代
同	臨濟派	廣林寺	大北關	印心	觀音	尼4	——	明代
同	同	地藏庵	小西關	相池	地藏	尼4	——	明崇禎12年
同	同	永壽寺	小西關	能空	釋迦	尼3	——	清康熙12年
同	同	觀音庵	小東關	本修	觀音	尼2	——	清康熙14年
同	毘盧派	華岩寺	大南關	思唯	釋迦	尼2	——	明永樂13年
同	臨濟派	大興寺	大北關	了明	釋迦	尼1	——	明崇禎13年
同	同	吉祥庵	大東關	昌賀	釋迦	尼5	——	清乾隆57年
同	同	三聖庵	大南關	修廣	三聖	尼1	——	不詳
道教	龍門派	太清宮	小西關	紀至隱	老君	120	——	清康熙2年
同	同	關帝廟	大南門外	高守一	關帝	22	——	清道光29年
同	同	關岳廟	小南關	趙至翰	關岳	20	——	明朝
同	蓬萊派	五聖宮	大北關	田蓬緣	五聖	19	——	清雍正元年
同	龍門派	五聖觀	小東關	李理杲	五聖	12	——	清光緒14年
同	同	斗姥宮	小西邊門內	孫誠恭	斗姥	6	——	清康熙　年
同	華山派	三聖宮	大東門內	張里文	關帝	3	——	清初
同	龍門派	聖清宮	大西門內	韓宗長	關帝	3	——	清道光年
同	同	眞武廟	大西關	張教福	眞武	3	——	明萬曆25年
同	同	南極宮	大南關	許理霦	南極仙	1	——	清康熙6年重修
同	同	靈佑宮	大北門內	吳信有	胡仙	1	——	清道光17年重修
同	同	圓通觀	小南邊門內	李理生	呂祖	1	——	民國16年重修
同	伙居道正一派	馬神廟	小南關	羅璽	馬神	男13 女14	——	清康熙2年
同	同	火神廟	大北關	魏慶春	火神	男14 女13	——	清康熙元年
同	同	觀音堂	大北關	何祥雲	觀音	男11 女11	——	清乾隆年間
同	同	財神廟	大北關	於本德	財神	男5 女6	——	清崇德7年
同	同	娘娘廟	小南關	夏萬臨	娘娘	男3 女4	——	清康熙年間
同	同	三清觀	小西關	趙玉慶	三清	男3 女3	——	清康熙52年
同	同	城隍廟	中街	劉澂	城隍	男3 女3	——	元代
同	同	天后宮	小北關	周宗岐	天后	男3 女2	——	清乾隆47年
同	同	仙人洞	城東南隅內	李景鎏	大仙	男2 女2	——	清雍正6年
同	同	仙人洞	大西門外	徐述堂	大仙	男1 女2	——	清同治8年

教別	派別	寺廟會教名	四在地	住持姓名	主祭神	出家布教者數	信徒數	創立年代
同	同	景佑宮	大南關	鄭寶和	三官	男2 女1	——	民國4年重修
同	同	七聖宮	小南關	劉清普	七聖	男1 女1	——	清道光11年
同	同	碼盤仙姑廟	小東關	劉方甫	碼盤仙	女1	——	清同治5年
喇嘛教	黄教	實勝寺(皇寺)	大西邊門外	隆且加卜	釋迦	70	——	清崇德3年
同	同	長寧寺	北陵前	隆且加卜	八大菩薩	30	——	清崇德3年
同	同	法輪寺(北塔)	小北邊門	德明額	天地佛	24	——	清崇德3年
同	同	永光寺(東塔)	小東邊門外	博倫圖色	地藏佛	21	——	清崇德3年
同	同	廣慈寺(南塔)	大南邊門外	朝格丹	觀音	20	——	清崇德3年
同	同	延壽寺(西塔)	十間房	所得那木	長壽佛	20	——	清崇德3年
同	同	嘛哈噶喇廟	皇寺院內	汪喜	嘛哈噶喇佛	9	——	清崇德3年
同	同	太平寺	小西邊門外	隆雲寶	釋迦	7	——	清康熙40年
同	同	興慶寺	皇寺後	所得那木	釋迦	6	——	清嘉慶9年
同	同	寶善寺	小西邊門外	烏其拉圖	釋迦	5	——	清乾隆24年
基督教	長老會(新教)	東關基督教會	大東關	劉愷義	基督	男3 女2	700	西暦1870年
同	同	西關基督教會	大西關	柏基根	基督	男2	280	西暦1884年
同	同	北關基督教會	小北關	李永言	基督	男2 女2	150	民國4年
同	神召會(新教)	西關神召會	小西關	匡瑪丁	基督	男6 女5	260	民國19年
同	天主教(舊教)	天主堂	小南關	魏宗凡	天主	男33 女24	1960	咸豐10年
回々教		清眞北寺	小西關	馮子厚	默罕麥德	16	3800	清康熙元年
同		清眞東寺	小西關	楊進之	默罕麥德	15	3200	清嘉慶8年
同		清眞南寺	小西關	錢毓麟	默罕麥德	7	2500	清崇德年間
佛教類似		直隸會館保靈寺	北市場	直隸同鄉				
同	同	萬國道德會揚教寺	大南關	福壽臣				
同	同	奉天佛教會般若寺	大南關	濟仁				

佛　教 36處 ｛全眞道 12處　伙居道 13處｝
道　教 25處
喇嘛教 10處

基督教 5處 ｛長老會（新教） 4處　天主教（舊教） 1處｝
回々教 3處　類似佛教 3處
合計 82處

國際佛教通報局定款

名稱

第一，本局を國際佛教通報局と稱す

事務所

第二，本局の事務所を全日本佛教青年會聯盟本部に置く

目的

第三，本局は日本內海及海外に向つて佛教事情の通報をなし，且つ佛教徒相互間の各種便宜を計るを以て目的とす

事業

第四，本局の目的を達成するため左記の事業を行ふ

イ，日本內地及世界各國より佛教事情に關する質問の通報を行ふ

ロ，必要に應じ日本語及世界各國語を以て佛教事情の通報を行ふ

ハ，外國人の日本觀光に際しては各種の便益を與へ，特にその佛教に關する方面に於て之を爲す

ニ，定時或は臨時に各國語を以て文書の刊行をなす

ホ，その他必要と認めたる事業を行ふ

役員

第五，本局の事務を處理するため左の役員を置く

イ，局長　一名

ロ，幹事　三名

ハ，評議員　若干名

局長は本局の事務を總括す

幹事は本局の事務を處理す

評議員は局長の提案に依る重要事務を審議す

第六，評議員は左記の者を以て之に充つ

イ，全日本佛教青年會聯盟理事及主事

ロ，全日本佛教青年會聯盟理事會に於て推薦したる者

第七，局長及幹事は評議員會に於て決定す

第八，役員の任期は二ヶ年とす（但し重任を妨げず）

經費

第九，本局の經費は左記のものに依て之を支辨す

イ，本局基金の活用

ロ，寄附金

ハ，その他の收入

補則

第十，本定款に記載せられざる事項は，凡て評議員會に於て協議す

第十一，第一回の役員は全日本佛教青年會聯盟理事會に於て決定す

定價	一部 金三十錢	送料二錢
	一年 金三圓四十錢	送料不要

昭和十年四月廿日第三種郵便物認可
昭和十一年十一月廿八日印刷（毎月一回）
昭和十一年十二月一日發行（一日發行）

編輯發行兼印刷人　東京市外吉祥寺337　淺野研眞

印刷所　東京市牛込區早稻田鶴卷町107　康文社印刷所　電話牛込（34）1950番 5049番

發行所　東京市神田區一ツ橋二の三　國際佛教通報局　電話九段（33）4428番　振替東京83015番

昭和十年四月三十日第三種郵便物認可
昭和十一年十一月二十八日印刷納本（毎月一回
昭和十一年十二月一日發行　一日發行）　國際佛教通報　第二卷　第十二號

昭和十年四月三十日第三種郵便物認可　昭和十一年十二月二十八日印刷納本　昭和十二年一月一日發行（毎月一回一日發行）第三卷　第一號

The International Buddhist Bulletin

國際佛教通報

第三卷 昭和十二年一月 第一號 〔Vol. III. Jan. $\frac{2503}{1937}$ No. 1.〕

要　目〔Contents〕

東京　國際佛教通報局　發行
The International Buddhist Information Bureau
Tokyo, Kanda, Hitotsubashi, II—3
Annual Subscription, ¥2.40 (post free), Single Copies 20 sen (post 2 sen)

國際佛教通報局

名譽局長　高楠順次郎

局長	大村桂巖
幹事	鷹谷俊之
同	稻葉文海
同	淺野研眞

顧問（順序不同）

〃　宇井伯壽
〃　朝倉曉瑞
〃　羽溪了諦
〃　荻原雲來
〃　干潟龍祥
〃　鈴木大拙
〃　鈴木宗忠
〃　天岫接三
〃　長井眞琴
〃　松本文三郎
〃　椎尾辨匡
〃　宇野圓空
〃　赤松智城
〃　大森禪戒
〃　矢吹慶輝
〃　小野清一郎
〃　加藤精神
〃　姉崎正治
〃　本田義英
〃　關本龍門
〃　佐伯定胤
〃　花田凌雲
〃　河野法雲
〃　高岡隆心
〃　小林瑞淨
〃　山邊習學
〃　赤沼智善
〃　本多惠隆
〃　大森亮順
〃　河口慧海
〃　山川智應
〃　常盤大定
〃　谷本富
〃　常盤井堯猷
〃　大谷尊由
〃　大谷瑩潤
〃　水野梅曉
〃　柴田一能
〃　安藤正純
〃　下村壽一
〃　乘杉嘉壽
〃　芝田徹心
〃　淺野孝之
〃　渡邊哲信
〃　小野玄妙
〃　柳澤健
〃　重光葵
〃　金倉圓照
〃　立花俊道

Tales of Buddhist Priests (IV)

by **Atsuharu Sakai**

(7) En-no-Gyoja, the Mountain-Climber

The Fudo shrine of Meguro, Tokyo, has two flights of stone steps leading to it: one in front called the Otoko-zaka (men's hill) and the other, less steep, on the left-hand side (from the shrine), called the Onna-zaka (women's hill). On the latter you will see a cave or niche in which is enshrined a bronze statue of a queer-looking monk, with two grotesque images standing guards in front. Unicorned and attired like a mountain-climber, he wears a pair of high ashida (wooden foot-gears), and he carries a staff in his right hand and a scroll in his left. This bronze statue represents En-no-Gyoja (meaning Ascetic of En), who is said to have opened Mt. Fuji and many other mountains to the public; the two other images standing for his devil-attendants. Because En-no-Gyoja was a quick-walking mountain-climber, you will find an immense number of waraji or straw-sandals offered to this small shrine by those who pray for good health.

En-no-Gyoja, his father unknown, was born of the daughter of Enko Kamo at the village of Ashiwara in the province of Yamato on the New Year's day in the sixth year (634 A.D.) of the reign of the Emperor Jomei. He had a small horn on his head; hence his other name of Kozuno (or small horn). He was extremely pious by birth and played all by himself in a most religious way. He repeated words of incantation, it is said, no less than a hundred thousand times a day, until he was endowed with the power of television and flying, and he wrought miracles by curing many serious diseases. One young man was possessed with a fox, for in this country a fox is believed to have a power over man, and he acted in a queerest way like a fox, till En-no-Gyoja dispelled its evil spirit with his magic. Kamatari, the first ancestor of the Fujiwara family,

which played such an important rôle for over three centuries in the history of Japan, was once laid up with so serious a disease that no medicine was found of any avail, but En-no-Gyoja chealed him very easily with the recitation of a sutra, and Kamatari expressed his gratitude by building the Sankai-ji Temple, in which a society was organized for reciting the Vimalakirti sutra regularly in the tenth month (October) every year. The temple, renamed the Kofuku-ji Temple, was removed to Kasuga in the 3rd year (710 A.D.) of Wado era.

In the fourth year (671 A.D.) of the reign of the Emperor Tenchi, En-no-Gyoja made up his mind to devote the rest of his life exclusively to Buddhism on Mt. Katsuragi, whence, it was then said, a dignified-looking saint came flying on a dragon to Mt. Ikoma, where he stayed for a while on a pine-tree, only to disappear by flying away as he came. When En-no-Gyoja saw the impossibility of obtaining leave of his mother, he carved a wooden image of his own self, and ran away from her by leaving it for her, He carried a staff and wore a five-cornered hat in representation of the five elements; namely, earth, water, fire, wind and air. He climbed Mt. Katsuragi or, as it is also called, Mt. Kongo, and after his departure from home, a temple was built at his native village of Ashiwara to his memory. The temple was named the Kichijo-so-ji.

When En-no-Gyoja climbed eight tenths of the mountain, the whole mountain went rumbling and trembling, and bowlders and big trees came rolling down. The voice of an invisible being demanded who the intruder of the mountain was, when En-no-Gyoja explained his mission and brandished his staff about him. The devil disappeared. Several other devils attacked En-no-Gyoja with bows and arrows, but they all disappeared before his incantation. A dragon lay across his way, but it too made way for him when he recited the charm of Fudo. He was always in search of Nirvana, and he flew from mountain to mountain, thus opening many mountains to public worship and travelling all over the country.

One day En-no-Gyoja climbed Mt. Ohmine. When he was walking over the waterfall of Miye (or three-fold), he found a large skeleton, about ten feet large, lying on the ground. It had a bell in its right.

He tried to take the mace, which might have been held with a vice; he could not move it. He recited an incantation, when Fudo (Acala), appearing, said: This is the skeleton of your third previous birth. You sat in self-training and meditation here on this mountain, for seven births in the past. You must perform the secret method of Mayura if you want to take the bell and mace. En-no-Gyoja did as he was told, and he took the mace very easily from the hand of the skeleton.

En-no-Gyoja was falsely accused of practising the black art by embracing paganism, and the Imperial troops were despatched to take him prisoner, but he always gave them the slip by covering his traces because he could fly between mountain-tops. At last his aged mother was arrested as a sort of decoy to attract En-no-Gyoja, who, the ruse proving successful, surrendered himself, through his sense of filial piety, because with his superhuman power of television he saw his mother in custody. The Imperial court sent him an exile to the island of Oshima off Idzu Province in the third year (690 A.D.) of the reign of the Emperor Mombu. While being marooned on the island, however, En-no-Gyoja built a hermitage where he stayed quiet in the daytime, but he availed himself of his flying power to visit his mother as well as Mt. Fuji and Enoshima every night, returning to his place of confinement before dawn. The Imperial court condemned him to death for leaving Oshima against the Imperial command, and he was taken to the place of his execution, but when his executor raised his sword to cut his head off, it broke into pieces, and the executor himself fell into a swoon. And his accuser, Hiroashi by name, died a sudden death from an unknown cause. A fortune-teller was consulted by the court, and he declared En-no-Gyoja to be no ordinary priest worthy of great respects. Consequently he was called from Oshima to come to the court, but he preferred staying with his aged mother to serving with the Imperial court. He was sent for several times, but he flew away, it is said, taking his mother with him, to China, where he died nobody knows when. Some say, however, that the priest crossed to Korea, but others believe that he stayed on Mt. Miomo, where he died, instead of going abroad, for there is on that mountain a place

where, according to a legend, En-no-Gyoja ascended to heaven. He was 71 years old when he disappeared.

(8) Karukaya-Doshin

Shigemasa Kato, who was the governor of Hakata in Chikuzen Province, Tsukushi (or Kyushu) during the reign (1124–1128 A.D.) of the Emperor Sutoku, was a great warrior known far and wide for his military arts and good government, but he had no male issue to succeed to his position. In those early days of feudalism, nothing was a greater pity for a military family than to have no son to succeed to it, because otherwise the family would be extinct. So a special prayer was offered for a son at the tutelary shrine of Kashii, Tsukushi, for a circuit of seven days, at the end of which a divine messenger in white appeared to him in a dream. "I am a messenger of the god of the Kashii shrine," he said "I come to tell you that in recognition of your humane work of keeping your territories in peace and order, the god will be pleased to grant you a son. Go to Ishidoguchi west of Hakata, where you will find a round stone, which you must hand your wife." Kato went as he was directed in the dream, and found a round stone as large as a hen's egg. In course of time his wife gave birth to a son, on the 24th of the first month (January) in 1133, and the boy was named Ishidomaru after the place where the mysterious stone was found.

Ishidomaru excelled no less in the art of militarism than did his father, whose pride he was, and coming of age, he was rechristened assuming the name of Shigeuji Kato. Like an average warrior of old, young Kato was a great scholar and a poet too, and he wrote many odes of thirty-one syllables. When his father died, his cremated remains were taken to Mt. Koya, the Mecca of Japanese Buddhism, in accordance with his death-bed wish, and Shigeuji was appointed the governor of Hakata in the place of his deceased father.

Shigeuji married the daughter of Harada, a fellow samurai of his father's. She had a literary talent and wrote odes on every occasion. One night she saw in a dream that a young page offered her a tanzaku (a stripe of paper for writing a Japanese ode on) on an open fan, on which she saw a 31-syllable poem reading in substance that "a large flock of cranes sang in a voice for a thousand times in praise of the eternity of the pine-tree." The pine and the crane being considered to be among the lucky sets of things in Japan, Shigeuji was pleased with this ode, for he took it for a good omen. In course of time a girl was born to him, and he named her Chiyo-tsuru (literally, Thousand-year-old-crane) after the poem that his wife saw in a dream.

In the meantime Shigeuji fell in love with another girl, Chisato by name, and he visited her very often. This fact attracted the attention of his enemy, who was looking for the opportunity of ruining his house. A secret plan was made by taking advantage of his illicit love with Chisato, when Shigeuji held a social party with his wife and other court-ladies, and the function was suddenly broken up, at its height, by the sad news that Chisato, his love, was murdered by an assassin. One of his retainers, who was on the side of his enemy, secretly informed Shigeuji that Chisato was killed through jealousy on the part of Keiko, his wife, and produced as evidence her dagger, which he said was discovered in the chamber of Chisato; though it had been stolen from Keiko some time before for the purpose of slandering her.

Instead of getting angry with his wife, however, Shigeuji laid the whole blame on himself for the death of Chisato, and he was now determined to atone for it by leading a Buddhist life. He would renounce the world, and leave his wife and all. So he cut a lock from his hair, and left it on an open fan, on which he wrote a 31-syllable poem of farewell, reading in effect that "thenceforth he would make friends only with monkeys that lived in deep mountains." He left his home on that same night and hastened to Mt. Hiyei, where he called on Priest Eiku of Kurodani, for whom he had great admiration.

"I have come all the way from Tsukushi" Shigeuji said in a loud voice by way of self-announcement and self-introduction at the entrance of the temple where Priest Eiku resided, "with a strong desire to devote myself to Buddhism under the guidance of Priest Eiku." Priest Eiku received him in audience, and was touched by what Shigeuji related concerning himself. Shigeuji was admitted into the temple of Priest Eiku under the Buddhist name of Jakushobo

(literally, nihility), though because of his strong devotion to Buddhism, the new priest was, and still commonly is, known by the name of Karukaya-doshin (Karukaya the religious-minded). He was 21 years old when he renounced the world.

Nor was Chisato, the love of Shigeuji Kato, killed, but she escaped under the protection of a faithful retainer. She came to Harima Province, where she was delivered of a boy, whom she named Ishidomaru after his father. When Ishidomaru was fourteen years old, he started, with his mother, on a journey to look for his father, who he was told was leading a priestly life somewhere. They travelled from place to place being directed by the temples they visited till they came to Mt. Koya, where his grandfather was buried. But on that mountain, there was what was termed "Nyonin-kinzei" (no thoroughfare for women), and Ishidomaru had to climb the mountain by himself without taking his mother, who stayed at the foot of the mountain. Ishidomaru met with a priest on the mountain.

"What is your father's name?" the priest asked, when the boy told him that he had been travelling in search of his father, who he was told was leading a Buddhist life on Mt. Koya.

"His name was Shigeuji Kato," the boy innocently replied.

The priest betrayed an emotion, which he concealed.

After listening with keen interest to the tale the boy told him the priest expressed great sympathy, and said! "The new priest whom you are looking for died a short time ago." He pointed to a new grave under which the priest said his father lay buried. The poor boy bowed his head piously before the grave, and he paid his deep respects to the spirit of his dead father. All being now over, Ishidomaru went down the mountain, carrying the sad news for his mother, But while the boy was up on the mountain. she was suddenly taken ill, and succumbed without waiting for his return.

Left an orphan, Ishidomaru could do nothing better than to retrace his way back to the mountain, where he asked the kind priest to take him as a disciple, for the boy felt strong affection for him without knowing why.

"If your father were alive," Karukaya-doshin said to Ishidomaru one day, for the priest was none other than his father, "he would be pleased that you are going through such hardships on behalf of your father. But I do not think that he will ever reveal himself to you, for the only reason that he renonnced the world with an oath." But Ishidomaru had a vague perception that he lived with his father.

When Priest Hohnen, the founder of the Jodo sect, for whom Karukaya-doshin had great admiration, died in 1212, Karukaya-doshin carved a wooden image of Jizo (Ksitigarbha, the guardian god of children) in his commemoration, and to every visitor who came to do homage to the departed saint, Karukaya-doshin gave a copy of his religious saying which ran something like the following:

"Night follows day, so a light is required; cold follows heat, so clothing is required. I wonder how many know that death inevitably follows birth, for few seem to be prepared for death. All will be over when death steals in unawares. Listen to me and get prepared for death, which may come at any moment. You must repeat Namu-Amida-Butsu."

In the eighth month (August) 1.11, Karukaya-doshin started, without taking Ishidomaru, on a pilgrimage to Shinano Province, where he confined himself at the Zenko-ji Temple for three circuits of seven days, and he died in the fourth month (April) in 1214 at the age of 83 years.

Upon his receipt of the news that Karukaya-doshin was seriously ill, Ishidomaru hastened to Shinano, only to arrive there two weeks after his death.

Ishidomaru also carved an image of Jizo in commemoration of the death of his father and enshrined it side by side with his father's in the same small shrine. In the seventh month (July) three years later, Ishidomaru died at the age of 65 years. He had his hands piously put together when he died, worshipping in the direction of the west, where it is believed the Lord Buddha resides.

Karukaya-doshin lived with his own son, but because of his religious oath made for renouncing the world, he died without revealing his identity. This story is over seven hundred years old, but its pathetic nature appeals to the religious Japanese and it is dramatized and still represented on the stage every now and then.

Die zwei Richtungen des Buddhismus in Deutschland

獨逸佛教の二つの傾向

von Helmut Klar, *Berlin*

（榊原順次譯）

Niemand wird wohl erwarten, daß es in Deutschland einen einheitlichen Buddhismus gebe. Wie in anderen Ländern, so auch hier, zerfällt der Buddhismus in die verschiedensten Gruppen und Untergruppen. Wie sollte es auch anders sein bei einer Lehre, der nichts ferner steht, als das Dogma, die Wirklichkeits lehre sein will und im Erleben des Einzelnen wurzelt. So ist es darum nicht verwunderlich, wenn sich die Buddhisten Deutschlands in kleinen Kreisen zusammengefunden haben, die mehr oder weniger von einander gesondert sind, ja sogar — wie das bei entfernteren Großstädten der Fall ist — oft gar keine Fühlung miteinander haben. Aber auch in Berlin allein kann man mehrere buddhistische Gruppen getrennt nebeneinander arbeiten sehn.

Ich will es nun nicht zu meiner Aufgabe machen das für und Wider einer solchen Aufteilung des Buddhismus in kleinere Gruppen zu

獨逸の佛教は單一佛教でなくてはならぬと定める人もないであらう。實際獨逸に於いても他國に於けると同樣に佛教は幾多の大小團體に分裂してゐる。併し乍らそれらのものは決して本來別のものであるのではなく一つの眞理であり一つの實在の教へである處のものが個々の體驗の中に生じたものである。此の意味よりこの分裂せるものは、亦時に——遠方の都市ではしばしばそうであるが——互ひに無交渉に獨立せる多數の獨逸の佛教徒黨が一つの團結を試みんとすることは當然あるべきことである。然るに事實に於いては一つの伯林市の中に於いてさへ全く獨立の數個の佛教團體が併立する現狀にあるのである。

併し自分は今かくの如く佛教が小團體に分裂せることに對してその贊否を論じ樣とするものでもなく、亦それら

untersuchen oder gar die einzelnen Kreise in ihrer Tätigkeit und Einstellung zum Buddhismus zu charakterisieren — das würde das Wirrwarr (denn es handelt sich nicht um verschiedene philosophisch begründete buddhistische Schulen (Sekten), sondern um allerkleinste Gruppen) noch vergrößern — ich will vielmehr durch eine Einteilung all dieser verschiedenen Gruppen in zwei Richtungen zum Verständnis und Überblick über den Buddhismus in Deutschland beitragen.

Die erste Richtung umfaßt alle Gruppen außer einer, von der weiter unten die Rede sein wird. Sie fußt allein auf dem Sutta-Piṭaka, als dem Wort des Buddha, und betrachtet den Abhidhamma als nebensächliches Werk von "apokryphen Charakter" (Dahlke). Ich nenne diese Richtung den "Indischen Buddhismus auf deutschem Boden". Diese Bezeichnung paßt um so besser, als gerade diese Richtung den indischen Bhikkhu als das Ideal eines Buddhisten hinstellt (mitunter auch als den einzigen Weg zum Nibbāna) und auch sonst vollkommen nach Indien "gerichtet" ist, indem sie immer wieder betont, daß der Dhamma mit westlichem Denken unvereinbar und Indien das einzige

の各々の佛教への活動或はその態度に從つてその特長を論ぜんとするものでもない。そうしたことはいたづらに混亂を增すに過ぎないことであらう（何となれば今此處に問題になる團體、分派と云ふのは哲學的に基礎づけられた佛教の各派、團體ではなく、たゞ單にいたづらに分裂せる團體に外ならぬからである）。寧ろ自分は此處にこれら群小の團體を二つの方向に分類して獨逸に於ける佛教を理解せしめ、概觀せしむることにつとめたいと思ふのである。

第一の行き方は後に說くところの一つの行き方を除けて他のすべての團體を包括するものである。これは唯佛陀の言葉としての經典のみをその所依とし論釋はすべて「僞作的」（ダルケ）の第二義的なものと考へるのである。この行き方を自分は「獨逸の苗床に生長せる印度佛教」と名付ける。この表現は佛教徒の理想として印度比丘が考へられ（しばしばこの印度比丘は涅槃への唯一の道として考へらる）或は完全にすべて印度をその「標準」とし、しかもこうした場合常に强調される處の單なる印度讃美に過ぎない言葉卽ち法は

Land zur wahren Verwirklichung der Lehre sei, wobei letzterer Gedanke zu einer bloßen Indienglorifizierung ausarten kann. Weiterhin ist diese Richtung durch einen (von ihr selbst immer wieder betonten) Abstand vom Mahāyāna gekennzeichnet, dem sie die "reine Lehre" — den Sutta-Piṭaka — entgegenstellt.

Diesem "Indischen Buddhismus auf deutschem Boden", der seinen Namen doch nicht ganz zu Recht führt, in so fern nämlich, als in Indien dem Abhidhamma doch wenigstens seine Bedeutung belassen wurde, steht eine zweite Richtung gegenüber, die nur die bereits erwähnte Gruppe umfaßt, die als einzige von all den vielen Gruppen für unsere Betrachtung noch übriggeblieben ist. Das ist der "Deutsche Buddhismus", der vorläufig nur von der jüngeren Generation vertreten wird. Seine Grundlagen sind Sutta-Piṭaka und Abhidhamma; sein Ziel nicht der indische Bhikkhu, sondern der deutsche Laienbuddhist.

Wir wollen endlich aufhören den indischen Buddhismus zu kopieren, wo wir doch alle keine Inder sind. Wir wollen endlich lernen von den Völkern des Ostens, wo die Japaner einen japanischen Buddhismus

西洋の思想とは全く相一致し得ないものであつて、この法この敎への眞の實現可能の土地として印度は唯一のものである云々の言葉等々よりして一層適切な表現であることが解る。更に亦この方向の今一つの特色は（それら自ら常に繰返へしてゐる）大乘佛敎より「純粹敎義」——經藏——を對立せしめて區別してゐることである。

亦この「獨逸の苗床に生長せる印度佛教」と云ふ名は印度に於いて猶、論藏が一つの意味を持つてゐる限りに於いて論藏を認めない獨逸の第一方向にある佛教に必ずしも適切と云ひ得ざるものがあるかとも思はるゝがとにかくこの第一の方向に對立して第二の方向がある。それは一寸前に一言した處のもので吾々が次に觀察すべく殘された處の多數團體の中の唯一のものである。卽ち「獨逸佛教」である。これは當分は青年分子に依つて代表せられるであらう。その根底となるところのものは經藏と論藏とである。その中心は印度比丘の上にあるのでなく、獨逸在家佛教徒の上にあるのである。

此處に於いて最早印度佛教についてとやかく述べる必要はない。吾々は決して印度人ではないのである。吾々は今東方の國、日本支那から何事か敎へ

haben, die Chinesen einen chinesischen. Das braucht an dem eigentlichen buddhistischen Kern nichts zu ändern. Nur die Form muß dem jeweiligen Volkscharakter angepaßt sein. Wir wollen endlich den Mut zur Wahrheit aufbringen und als Deutsche einen deutschen Buddh. fordern; nicht aus übertriebenem Nationalstolz, sondern aus der Erkenntnis heraus, daß es anders nicht geht ohne unwahrhaftig zu werden. Denn aus einem Inder kann kein Deutscher werden und aus einem Deutschen kein Inder. Das mnß ohne ein Werturteil abzugeben einmal festgestellt werden. Gerade im Neuen Deutschland, wo rassisches Denken eine Umwälzung auf allen Gebieten des geistigen und wirtschaftlichen Lebens hervorgerufen hat, greift diese Erkenntnis immermehr um sich. Das rassische Erbgut (körperliche und geistige Veranlagung), das einem Menschen bei der geburt mitgegeben wird, das heißt, was er sich nach buddhistischer Vorstellung selbst gewählt hat, bestimmt bis zu einem gewissen Grade seine Charakterhaltung für dieses eine Leben schon im voraus! Das sind biologische Tatsachen, mit denen man zu rechnen hat und die sich mit dem Buddhismus sehr gut vereinbaren lassen. Warum sollte

られんとするものである。その日本には日本の佛教あり、支那には支那の佛教あり、たゞ佛教の型態様式がその國民と云ふものに適當に一致せしめられしかもそのことの爲めに佛教の本質に何の變質も與へられる必要もないと云ふ事實を見る。吾々は此處に於いて眞理のために勇氣を振ひ起さんとするものである。卽ち獨逸人として獨逸佛教を主張せんとするものである。それは決して過度の國民の自負心からでなく背眞理的なるべからずと云ふことは全く絕對的なるものなることを認識するからである。何となればー獨逸人は決して一印度人たることは不可能であり亦一印度人が一獨逸人たることも不可能であるゝらである。このことは何等考慮批判の餘地なき明かなことである。正に精神生活、經濟生活あらゆる領域に亘つて民族的思想が一つの革命を起して來たところの新興獨逸にかくの如き認識はますますさかんになり行くであらう。民族的遺產(肉體的・精神的才能)はその出生の時に已に人間に所屬し來るところのものである。佛教の觀念に依つても亦そうである。人間の特質性格は或る限度までは先天的なもので豫め決定せられてゐる。そのことは生物學的な明かなる事實である。この事實は自明の理であつて佛教とも全く一致せるところである。然るに人々は今何の爲めにこの明らかな事實に

man also davor die Augen verschließen?

Doch ich glaube, daß jedem einsichtigen Buddhisten die Notwendigkeit einer deutschen Form für den Buddhagedanken einleuchtet, so daß ich nicht weitere Beweise und Beispiele anzuführen brauche. Dieser Artikel hat ohnehin nur die Aufgabe einen Überblick über die Lage in Deutschland zu geben und auf die einzelnen Probleme hinzuweisen, während in anderen Arbeiten auf spezielle Dinge eingegangen werden wird (Laienbuddhismus, Stellung zum Abhidhama . . .).

Was wir wollen ist die Deutsche Form des Buddh., das heißt die Möglichkeit herauszufinden als Buddhist in Deutschland zu leben oder umgekehrt ausgedrückt: Deutscher zu sein und darüberhinaus Buddhist. Daß das möglich ist beweist uns Japan. Japan ist uns Vorbild, wie man die Buddha-Idee in den Herzen des Volkes verankert. Japan ist uns Vorbild, wie man auch außerhalb der Grenzen Indiens als Buddhist leben kann. Darum verlassen wir alles Indische am Buddhismus; dann wird der eigentliche Kern umso deutlicher hervortreten und ein intensiv Pāli-Studium des Sutta-Piṭaka und Abhidhamma wird uns davor bewahren diesen Kern jemals wieder zu verlieren.

對して眼をおほはんとするのであらうか?

勿論自分は思慮ある各佛教徒には佛教思想の獨逸の様式が獨逸に於いては必要であると云ふことは當然考へ得らるゝであらうと云ふことを信ずるものである。こゝに於いて自分は更に此の事の證明例示を試みる必要があるかと思ふのであるが、併し此の論文はたゞ獨逸に於ける全體的事情に關した觀察をなす爲めのもので個々の精細なる問題は此處に論ずる暇をゆるされないのである。それらのことに關しては特別に他の論文に於いて論述せらるゝであらう(在家佛教、論藏の立場)。

吾々の欲することは佛教の獨逸樣式である。卽ち獨逸に於いて佛教徒として生活すること或は反對に獨逸人として佛教徒たることの可能を見出すことである。この可能を明かに示したものが日本である。佛教思想を國民の心の中に安住せしめたと云ふことに於いて日本は吾々の模範である。日本は吾々に印度の領域境界の外に於いても正しき佛教徒として生活可能であることを實證してくれた一つの先達である。今や吾々は佛教に於ける印度式なるものをすべて放棄せんとする。その放棄に依つて佛教の本質は一層明瞭にせらるゝであらう。更に之れに加へて忠實なる經及び論のパリ語研究はその教義の本質より脫線せしむる危險を防ぎ護るであらう。(完)

To Kosetsu Nosu Esq.,

The World-famous Japanese Artist.

Dear Sir,

We the citizens of Benares, wish to take this opportunity of your impending departure for Japan after the conclusion of your historic work of painting the frescoes of the Mulagandhakuti Vihara at Sarnath, to express our sense of gratitude and high appreciatien of your selfless labour for the revival of Buddhist art in India.

We have watched with profound admiration the manner in which you have worked during the last three and half years to embellish the Vihara, your calm dignity, earnestness, religious devotion, and high sense of duty have filled us with admiration. Inspite of the many inconveniences caused to you in the accomplishment of your task, you have succedded in giving to this ancient city one of the finest works of art of which we can be proud. Your work will be a handmark in the history of frescoe art in this country as it combines the grace and wealth of Ajanta with the high technique of your mother country. We have no doubt that all lovers of art and the larger public who will visit this Viharā in years to come will gratfully recongnise your devoted endeavours and will be inspired by the scenes.

世界的高名を有せらるゝ

日本畫家

野生司香雪殿へ

親愛なる貴下

貴下が今回サルナートのムラガンダクチ・ビハラに歴史的大作たる壁畫を完成され愈々日本に御歸國の途に就かるゝに際し、私共ベナレス市民は印度の佛教藝術の復興の爲に自己を忘れた貴下の御努力に對し感謝と稱讃の微衷を申述べたいと思ふのであります。

過去三年有半もの間、孜々として此の寺院の装飾の爲に活動せられた貴下の御奮闘振りを私共は異常なる感嘆を以て拜見して居りました。貴下の物靜かな崇嚴さ、その熱心さ、宗敎に對する献身、それから天職に對する崇高なる御自覺といふ樣なものは私共の感激措く能はざる所でありました。大業完成の途には幾多の艱難が横つて居たに不拘、貴下は見事、之等を征服して私共が最も誇りとするに足る最高の美術品を此の由緒ある町に與へられました。貴下の御業蹟はアヂャンターの品位や豪華を貴國の高度の畫術に結びつけられた點に於て我國壁畫の歴史に一標石と成ることでありませう。後年此の寺院を訪れる美術愛好家や更に多くの一般人士は必ずや貴下の献身的御努力を心から有難く拜し斯くも華麗に描きあげられたる釋迦一代の御模樣には齊しく感動せしめらるゝことゝ信じて疑はないのであります。

As you are well aware, Buddhism reached Japan in the sixth century A.D. and along with it was introduced into Japan all the best in the artistic and cultural life of our country. Scholares have recognised in the wonderful paintings of the Horyuji Temple in Japan, the creative work of the Indian artist; and those paintings remain to this day not only as an inspiration to the Japanese Buddhists but also as an unbreakable bond of friendship between Japan and India. In executing the paintings of this Vihara, you have added one more link in this bond of friendship between our countries, and it is our earnest hope that this fresh bond will bring the two countries closer to each other. In creating this new bond, you have at the same time done a great service to the cause of establishing good will between India and Japan, which is so much required in these days of national hatreds and misunderstandings. Benares is the eternal city of India, It is sacred to both Hindus and Buddhists and in bidding farewell we do hope that you carry with you pleasant memories of your stay in this sacred city.

In conclusion we wish you a very pleasant voyage back to your motherland. We also wish you many years of health and happiness.

We remain to be,

Dear Sir,

Your sincere admirers,

The citizens of **Benares.**

申すまでもないことでありますが佛敎は西暦紀元六世紀に日本に渡りまして同時に我國の美術文物方面に於て最高のものが紹介せられたのであります。彼の法隆寺の有名なる壁畫には古典學者は印度畫家が献身的に揮つた彩管の跡を認めて居りますが、此の壁畫は今日に至るまで單に日本佛敎家に鼓舞を與へてゐるのみならず、日印兩國の友好關係の不朽の絆となつて存在してゐるのであります。貴下は今日此の寺院の壁畫を描かれたことに依り更に吾々兩國間のつながりを加へられたものでありまして、此の新しい絆が兩國を密接にせんことを私共は衷心より希ふものであります。輓近國家間に兎もすれば憎惡や誤解の起りがちな際、最も切望せらるゝ日印親善の建設の上に貴下は多大の貢献を遊ばされたのであります。ベナレスは印度に於ける不滅の町であります。それは印度敎にも佛敎にも共に聖地であります。只今お送別申上ぐるに際して私共の熱望致しますことは貴下が此の聖地に御滯在の日の御追憶の常に樂しからんことで御座います。

最後に私共は貴下の御歸朝の途の安全ならんことを而して又此の先永遠に御健康に御幸福に御暮し遊ばす樣御祈り申上ぐるものであります。

貴下を最も敬愛する

ベナレス市民より

蒙古佛教の印象

橋本光寶

蒙古佛教は通常喇嘛(ラマ)教の名を以つて呼ばれてゐる。何が故に喇嘛教と呼稱されるのであらうか？　喇嘛とは西藏語の bla-ma で上人と譯し又無上者の意と見て差支へなからうが，實際蒙古西藏の僧侶は喇嘛と稱せられ，即ち無上上人と稱せられ，又それ丈けの尊信を受けてゐるのであるから，從つてその上人の說かれる法を喇嘛教と呼ぶやうになつたのであらう。然し蒙古西藏に於いては喇嘛教と云はず佛教(ボルハンシャジン)と云つてゐるから實際は佛教であるけれども外國人が通常蒙古佛教の一特徵である喇嘛の名を以て呼んだのであらう。蒙古人等が佛教(ボルハンシャジン)と稱してはゐるが，日本佛教或は根本佛教に照して尙幾多の特異點を有するやうであるから，大體は佛教と稱し得れども，正確には蒙古佛教と斷るのが妥當であると思はれる。

蒙古を旅行して吾々が第一目につくのは，廣漠たる無一物の如き大平原の中に寺院のみは龍宮城の如く一大城樓をなしてゐる點である。單調なる沙漠の砂を嚙みつゝ漸く辿りつき，遠く夕日に映へる丹靑の大浮城を望見する時，自ら感喜の淚にくるゝは只に幼稚なる蒙古人のみならず又吾々の實感せる所である。殿堂の中，本堂は中央に僧房は兩側に規則正しく建てられてゐるが，多くは土造で土壁を圍らしてゐる。大寺になると本堂の外に一二或は三四の殿堂を持つてゐる。本堂は衆僧の日日法要勤行を爲す處であるが，他の殿堂はそれぞれの目的の爲めに建てられたものである。これについては少くし說明を要するが，その大體を摘記して見やう。

蒙古佛教徒である喇嘛僧が佛門に入れば多くは學校に入學する。學校と云つても日本の小學校の如きではなく所謂寺小屋式であるが，その學校の種類に又四種類ある。即ち佛教々理を主として硏究する教學部，秘密眞言を成就せんとする秘密部，醫學を專攻する醫學部，星學・繪畫・文法等を硏究する時輪部の四部である。これらの四學部がその寺の大小に應じ，或は一部，或は二三部，或は四部共併立されてゐる。その校舍とも云ふべきものが乃ち前記本堂以外の諸殿堂である。此等の本堂或は諸殿堂の建築樣式は內蒙西北部即ち支那本部より遠ざかるに從つて，土石・煉瓦等を主材とした所謂西藏式であるが，漢人種と接觸する東南部に於いては木材・瓦を主材とした支那式が採用せられてゐる。步一步殿堂內に入れば晝尙暗く石疊或は木板が敷詰められており，中央正面は活佛の座席が設かれてあるが，その方向に向つて全堂內數條の一般喇嘛座席が設けられてある。活佛座席の後方は多く釋迦牟尼如來が安置されてあるが，然し中には彌陀あり，觀音あり，その目的に依つて必ずしも一定してゐない。活佛座席の兩側乃ち殿堂正面の壁側には，諸尊像あり，曼荼羅あり之れも一定してゐない。曼荼羅は描いたものもあるが，立體的のものが多い。多倫諾爾西廟の本堂に在る大日如來の立體曼荼羅の如きは最も精巧を極めてゐる。

以上の外如何なる小殿堂にも必ず安置されてゐるのは黃教の開祖宗喀巴(ゾンカーワ)の像である。此の像の前には供物香燈最も多く，參拜者も最も慇懃なる禮度を以て禮拜する。十月二十五日の燈明會には此の像前に幾千燈を點じ，數ケ月を要して製作せる花鳥等の供物を献ずる。尙此の外白多羅及び靑多羅が多く見受けられる。多羅とは救度母の意であり，前者が白色，後者が靑色なるによりて，かく稱せられる。此の兩救度母はそれぞれネパール及び唐より西藏王ソンツアンガンポ王の許に嫁いだのであるが，其の頃西藏には未だ佛教傳はらず蠻風頻りなりしが故に，兩女は佛像經卷を友として泣く泣く入藏したのである。此れが動機となり西藏には漸次佛教が弘通し衆生は安寧なるを得たるが故に兩女を佛格化し救度の母と呼び，その體色より白靑の名を附したのであるが，西藏佛教そのまゝ蒙古佛教に於いても此の兩多羅をよく供養することになつてゐる。

尙以上諸尊の外我日本佛教徒の目に最も異樣に映ずるのは陰陽佛諸尊の安置である。陰陽佛にも密聚(サンドエ)・上樂(デムチク)・可畏(ヂクチイト)・時輪(ドエンコル)等種々あるが，此等は喇嘛教諸佛中諸も異樣なるもので喇嘛教の喇嘛教たる所以は，こんな處に見出し得る。

諸殿堂を出でゝ僧房に向へば必ず頑丈なる土塀あるを見る。日本人は家屋住宅を建て而して後塀を作るものあり，作らざるものあり一定してゐないが，蒙古寺院僧房においては支那に於けるが如く必ず家屋よりも先に土塀を築く。僧房は大抵個人の所有に屬するが中には寺有のものもある。寺有の房に住するは多く高級喇嘛に屬する。

喇嘛の階級には座主・達喇嘛(ダーラマ)・格斯貴(ゲスクヒ)・經頭・會計・德木奇(ドムチ)・副德木奇・書記・清掃・茶番・鍵持・沙彌等がある。座主はツレー喇嘛と云ひ一山を統卒する者，達喇嘛(ダーラマ)は又大喇嘛と云ひ活佛の近侍の意，格斯貴(ゲスクヒ)は威儀奉行の如く法要を進行せしめ衆僧を監督する役目，德木奇(ドムチ)は庶務の役である。此等は一見役目の如くであるが又順を追ひて昇級する處を見れば階級とも云ひ得るであらう。

學校に於ける學生の階級は初級・中級・上級の三級あるのみ。卒業者の稱號は次の如くである。

教學部卒業者稱號　カブチューバ
秘密部卒業者稱號　ガクリンバ
醫學部卒業者稱號　マンランバ
時輪部卒業者稱號　チーリンバ

此等の稱號を得んが爲めにはそれぞ

れの部に於いて二十年，三十年の永きに亙つて研鑽を重ね而して業成らば受験及び卒業式を自ら擧行せねばならぬ。受験の爲めには五百人なり千人なりの一山の學生及び教師を一堂に請待し，自らは堂の中央に座して高下貴賤の別なく，所有階級の喇嘛の質問に應じ，又論場を開演して說服せねばならぬ。說服し了りたる受験者は初めて一山座主より卒業と學位乃ちそれぞれの部に應じたる稱號を認許される。かくて受験場は忽ち卒業式場と變じ，卒業者はその披露の爲めに一山の者に食物・菓子・經典・ハクツク・乳茶等々をその身代に應じて施與せねばならぬ。此の爲めには能く千金を要すると云はれ，それが爲めに全財產を放擲する者あり又施與不能の場合は折角螢雪の功も空しく受験し稱號を得能はぬ者もあると云はれる。

以上の如き階級や稱號は如何なる下賤なる喇嘛でも勤勉と財力によりて獲得し得るものであるが，蒙古佛教に於いては此の外尙ほ活佛なる者があり同教に於いて一特徵をなすものである。活佛とは字義通り活佛(イキボトケ)であるが，此れは諸佛・諸先德の再生者を云ふのである。此の再生者制度の創始は黃教の開祖宗喀巴が十四世紀に從來の喇嘛教に一大改革を斷行し，妻帶を嚴禁せる以後の事であるが，その再生者の最も有名なるは西藏拉薩の佈達拉山に常在し西藏及び蒙古の喇嘛教界に君臨する達賴喇嘛であるが，彼れは西藏國の守護者觀音菩薩の再生者なりと信ぜられ，又他の大法王班禪大師は阿彌陀佛の再生者なりと信ぜられてゐる。此の外淸朝時の調査に依れば西藏には合計十八人，外蒙には十九人，內蒙には百五十七人，青海には三十五人，駐京者十四人，合計二百四十三人の多數再生活佛があつたと云ふことである。活佛とは支那人及び日本人の通稱であるが，蒙古ではホトクト，或はゲーンと云はれてゐる。一活佛が入寂し十ケ月の後その豫言によりて再生するのであるが，その再生者が十八才に達すれば蒙古王を通じて淸朝に願出すれば調査の上ホトクト(呼献克圖)の稱號が授與せられる。西藏の兩大法王及び外蒙哲布尊丹巴(ジブツオンダンバ)呼圖克圖(ホトクト)は通常ボクダ（聖者の意）を以て內蒙章嘉呼圖克圖(ジャンジャホトクト)はゲヽン（光明者の意）を以て呼稱せられるのが常である。其の他の群小ホトクト（呼圖克圖）はそれぞれの名前を以て或はバクシ（博士の意）の稱號を以て呼ばれてゐる。ホトクトの稱號を授與されざる活佛或は新生の活佛は再生者乃ちホビルガン（呼畢勒罕）の名を付するを常とする。但し淸朝滅亡せし今日此の制度は廢止されたけれども習慣上尙ボクダ，ゲヽン，ホトクト，ホビルガン等の名も質も存在してゐる。斯の如き普通喇嘛以外の再生喇嘛が存在し，而かもそれに對する信仰が絕對的であることは他に見られざる一特異である。

次に前述の如く喇嘛寺廟は一大城市を形成してゐるのであるが，此處に住する喇嘛僧數が彼の人口稀薄なる蒙古に於いて如何に不合理的に多數である

かと云ふことは，その數の統計が全人口の約二十五パーセントを占めてゐることに徵して明らかであらう。假りに日本の宗教關係者が百萬人あるとしてもその割合は僅かに全日本人口の約一パーセントに上るのみである。總人口が東京市民總數と大差なき蒙古民族間に於ける此の割合は，男子壯丁の大部分を引去り，經濟界の一蹉跌者の役割を演ずるに至るのではなからうかとさへ思はれる。蒙古各地を游歷し蒙古佛教が異樣に展開されつゝあるを見るにつけ，漢人種が南方より蒙古佛教の破壞を試みつゝあるを見るにつけ，尙キリスト教徒が幾世紀かの歷史を以て入蒙し盛んに改宗せしめんと努力しつゝあるを見るにつけ，吾人は蒙古佛敎の爲め一大警告を與へねばならぬ時期に立至つてゐることを痛感するものである。

（20頁より）

律に對する團體人としての意見は片鱗だに看取出來ないのは同教團の爲めに遺憾である。

× ×

在滿各地に日本山は十指を屈する存在であるため，同教團の不許可は宗教問題として極めて重大性を有つてゐる。

私はチチハル，ハルビン，新京，奉天の領事官に對し私的に意向を訪ねたが，

一，宗派系統不詳
二，教師資格不詳
三，未公認教團

のため，省令の條文を具備してゐない故に許可不可能とするにあるものの如し。

これに對して，日本山側は，從來關東廳官の許可云々を以つて對抗せんとしてゐる向もあるが，內務大臣所管の關東廳管下の許可を外務省管下に適用を强ひるのは見當ちがひでもあり問題の參考に過ぎまい。

兎に角，外務省新令は斯くして外地に新興せんとする日本山妙法寺を不許可にしてゐる。

（昭和十一年十一月廿九日）

外地宗教取締の外務省新法令と其影響

滿洲佛教學院長　半谷範成

昭和十一年六月六日發令，同七月一日施行の外務省令第九號（在滿洲國及中華民國寺院，敎會，廟宇，其ノ他ノ布敎所規則）は內務省の宗教取締方策と呼應して外地の日本宗敎を取締らうとする意圖が明かに看取される。

施行は七月一日であるが，規定の示す如くに，從來既に領事館に於て許可せるものに對しても，本規則に依り再出願せしめた結果，玆に俄然問題が起つた。

それは，藤井行勝氏の統理する『日本山妙法寺』である。この日本山妙法寺は滿洲，支那，インドへの沿岸を點連する東洋的新興敎團であるだけ極めて注目すべき問題である。

省令の規定するところに依れば，滿洲，支那に於て開敎所を設立せんとするものは，

　第二條　寺院，敎會，廟宇又ハ其ノ他ノ布敎所ノ設立ノ許可ヲ受ケムトスルトキハ其ノ住職，僧侶，牧師，道士又ハ布敎師トナルベキ者及檀信徒ト爲ルベキ者十人以上ノ連署ヲ以テ左ノ事項ヲ具シ所屬宗派ノ管長又ハ之ニ類スル監督者ノ承認書ヲ添ヘ所轄帝國領事官ニ願出ヅベシ

　四，宗派系統

　十一，住職（中略）ノ履歷及其ノ資格

を規則するに對して，『日本山妙法寺』は宗派系統不詳なるため，滿洲國にける帝國領事官は從來許可してあつた日本山に對して，新令に依る許可を留保するに至つて，今や日本山妙法寺一派は對策攻究中である。

從來日本山妙法寺なるものは，日蓮宗を名乘つてゐたのであるが，本年七月日蓮宗滿洲開敎司監松村日量氏の名を以つて

『日本山妙法寺は日蓮宗に非ず』

と在滿官廳及全信徒に聲明したため，日本山の宗派系統は明瞭を缺き官廳の疑惑を招來するところになつたのである。更に外務省の新法令は截然として日本山を『所屬宗派無き敎團』として不許可とするに至つたものの如くである。

それかあらぬか，日本山妙法寺の總理藤井行勝氏は，『大亞細亞』十一月號に於て，本件を含意しての所論を試みてゐる。一讀その元氣さには敬服され流石の日蓮の末流を想はせるものがあるが，可惜，宗敎至上主義に偏し，法

（以下19頁へ）

滿洲の佛學院に就て

淺野研眞

一

支那でも滿洲でも，佛敎僧侶の知識のレベルは極めて低い。從つて，一般社會人の知識が日進月步であるに比して，甚だしく開きがある。

こんな狀態では，とても一世を指導することなど，思ひもよらぬことだ。私は先づ彼ら佛僧の知的レベルを高めることが何より必要なことだと思ふ。即ち滿洲佛敎の改新は，"先づ佛僧の敎育から！"と叫びたいのである。

二

そこで私は先づ，順序として，滿洲に於ける佛僧養成機關の現狀を述べねばならぬのである。

然し，それに就ては，未だ纏つた調査と云つたやうなものもないやうである。ただ康德三年五月，即ち昨春發表された滿洲國文敎部禮敎司宗敎科の「宗敎統計表」の末尾に，「佛敎僧學院」に關するものが附錄されてゐる位ひのものであらう。

即ち其れには五個の僧學院が擧げられてゐるのである。極めて簡明な記述であるから，その全文を玆に再現することにしやう。

（1）佛化僧學院

地　　址　哈爾濱特別市南岡大直街五號，天台宗極樂寺內
主 辦 者　釋如光　釋棄一
沿　　革　由民國十三年三月創設，中間迭易校名中小學及僧學院曾增至三班，現僅存一班
敎授科目　佛經　儒經　國文　日語
學 生 數　一班　二十六名
敎　　員　主講如光　副講普光　學監普蔭　國文王安淸　日語一番賴順證
經　　費　敎員薪水　全年一千四百四十元
　　　　　總經費　全年三千餘元
　　　　　經費來源　由慈善家樂輸及佛敎會接濟
現　　況　僧人師表缺乏急應造，就惟感經費困難諸難發展

（2）般若寺僧學院

地　　址　新京特別市長春大街天台宗護國般若寺內
主 辦 者　釋澍培
沿　　革　康德元年九月成立
組　　織　學監一人管理敎務法師二人分擔課務
敎授科目　佛經　儒經　日語　國文　佛敎史
學 生 數　十五名
敎　　員　主講釋澍培　學監釋明悟　講師釋密三　釋文如　日語都築，寺川

經　費　由般若寺經費項下無統計
現　況　現有滿人學生十四名，日僧留學生一名

(3) 法華講寺僧學院

地　址　濱江省綏化縣城內西北隅天台宗法華講寺內
主辦者　釋淨空
教授科目　初學課本　日語　禪門日誦　大小楷書　國文　講演佛經
學生數　十五名
教　員　釋淨空　高田法嚴
經　費　各界施主臨時捐助

(4) 楞嚴寺僧學院

地　址　奉天省營口通惠門街天台宗楞嚴寺內
主辦者　釋禪定
教授科目　佛經　妙法蓮華經　天台四教儀　教觀綱宗　楞嚴經　大乘止觀
　　儒經　孟子　論語　大學　中庸　唐詩合解
　　習字　圖畫　古文
學生數　六十名
教　員　主辦釋禪定　正院長楊保箴　副院長王守箴　主講王萬泰　學監卜春暹　副講張欣西
組　織　由本寺和尚禪定前文安新河縣知事王海安之夫人楊保箴王守箴居士，王萬泰，卜春暹，張欣西等組織而成
經　費　經費來源由營口王楊保箴，王守箴等個人私產出爲常年經費
　　教員薪水　全年八百元
　　辦公費　全年二百元
　　總經費　全年二千餘元

(5) 慈雲寺僧學院

地　址　龍江省洮南縣小南門內
現　況　該校前次招收學生一班已于去秋卒業嗣因經費拮据遂行停辦

以上が，文教部の示すところのものであつて，これで大體，滿洲に於ける從つて支那にかける，佛僧養成機關の內容が知られ得るのである。

それは一口に云へば，乙種中等學校にも及ばないほどの貧弱なものであつて，これでは新時代の民衆教化者を作ることは困難であらう。

三

右の調査以外に，尙ほ私自身實地に參觀したものに，奉天萬壽寺佛學院なるものがある。

三十名ばかりの僧衣の若僧が，自習してゐる所を參觀したのであつたが，教室は，まあ日本の中學校式のものであると思へばよからう。

玆に其の最近(一昨々年の佛誕日に改訂)の趣意書及び規則を示せば，次の如くである――

奉天萬壽寺佛學院序

世風澆漓。人心陷溺。欲圖救世濟人之計。當求背塵合覺之道。其道維何。卽培養弘法人材。昌明佛敎。以救正人心是也。當今敎材難得。人心不古。二執未除。邊言息爭。三毒不斷。安覩樂邦。同人等以爲能使含識之倫叔本覺悟。出離水火。永登衽席者。捨宏揚佛法不爲功。蓋佛之言敎。善巧方便。足以滌人心之垢穢。澄世界之汚染。息滅侵陵殺伐之囂風。變爲和平大同之佳象。淘汰貪嗔痴慢之積習。轉爲博愛平等之眞誠。其慈悲喜捨之懷。六度萬行之德。圓融溥遍。弘廣淵深。地球自有人類。立敎興學以來。大無不該。小無不攝。無有如佛者。然彼無知闡提。厭聞佛法。不斥爲迷信腐化而足以愚民。必謗消極厭世無益邦家。同人等審思其言。知爲大謬。不可不辯。夫梵語佛陀。華言覺者。覺者不迷。迷者不覺。迷信腐化之考語。可以加於世間常人。及神敎信徒之上。而我佛大法不與焉。何以言之。常人孜孜爲利。生不知來。死不知去。茫茫世界。悠悠歲月。陷身迷窮。虛度一生。而不自知。至於神敎信徒。妄執宇宙眞宰。或尊多神。或崇一神。神能造物。神由誰生。一經反詰。瞠目不對。縱能置答。其說難圓。此二種迷。皆爲佛法所破。就佛法言。三界唯心。萬法唯識。宇宙人生問題。片言可決也。蓋常人之迷在乎對於宇宙人生不生問題。神敎徒之迷在乎對於宇宙人生雖生問題。而不求正當之辯決。惟有佛法則對於種種根本問題。一一指示之。而又一一爲之辯決之。所謂心佛衆生三無差別。只知有人。不知有神。只知有心。不知有法。宇宙人生在此一心。是以佛法卽是覺法。亦卽心法。人人皆有一心。人人皆有體驗。彼闡提之謗毁佛法爲迷信者。由於未能眞實了知佛法之眞義故也。復次我佛宣敎。慈悲爲本。慈者與衆生以一切樂。悲者拔衆生之一切苦。化除階級。打破國界。所有大地衆生一視同仁。皆是自由。悉屬平等。且佛制乞食行道。爲戒貪心。不蓄産業。百丈禪師首立清規。訓飭僧伽。一日不作活。一日不吃飯。菲衣蔬食。自食其力。頭陀苦行。需用簡單。提倡勞工。百業俱備。世間利用厚生之道。未嘗不攝於佛法之中。如斯則無知闡提之妄斥佛法爲消極厭世者。又可以息喙矣。同人等一則確認佛法爲倡明宇宙眞理。而絕非迷信。再則確認佛法爲今後救世慈航。而絕非消極。故有努力提倡之必要。所惜者典籍浩繁。玄理難曉。無上妙法。隱而不彰。膚淺之徒。觀察旣誤。非難蜂起。斯以正法久晦。弘揚乏人之故。何能輕易尤人哉。同人等旣鑒及此。咸發大心。深願昌明大法。然欲昌明大法。必先培植人材。此佛學院之所以創設也。佛學院以研究佛典。闡明大乘爲鵠的。本宏法利生造就人材爲旨趣。順時勢之推移。而儲蓄資糧。以濟世利人。務使我佛啓迷轉悟之眞理。與平等大悲之精神。得以發揚光大。庶幾功不唐捐矣。是爲序

奉天萬壽寺佛學院簡章

一，名稱　本院爲奉天萬壽寺所附設定名爲萬壽寺佛學院
二，宗旨　以敎諸僧徒使辨行相應俾能弘揚佛法廣度衆生爲宗旨
三，經費　由奉天萬壽寺完全擔負
四，組織　本院設以下各職員
　甲，院長　一人　總理本院一切事宜
　乙，主講法師　一人　專司宣法演敎
　丙，國文講師　一人　專司敎授學僧國文俾其易辯大法
　丁，訓育師　一人　專司指導管

理各學僧律儀
戊，書記師　一人　專司書寫往來文件等
己，體育師　一人　專司教授學僧武術俾其身體健康
庚，庶務兼會計　一人　專司本院購置及會計事宜

五，人數　暫定學僧二十名爲足額函請國內寺剎保送之宜俱以下資格
甲，曾受俱足戒者
乙，二十歲以上三十歲下者
丙，文字通順者
丁，發菩提心行菩薩行者
戊，諸根俱足身體健康者

六，學期　以三年爲卒業每年分二學期共六學期秋季始業

七，假期　甲例假按本寺常例每月有兩日放香此外本師佛誕日及成道日休假二日此外別無假期但酷暑嚴寒之候得酌減授課時間
乙請假倘學僧有特別不得已事故得請准訓育師之許可始准離院但期限至長不得逾一週

八，退學　凡學僧不得中途退學於入學時各將戒牒交存本寺俟畢業後發還如中途自動退學者扣留其戒牒若果有不得已事故必須退學者須預先聲明俟訓育師査明請准院長發還戒牒質行退學

九，學費　不收學費宿膳書籍完全由本院供給並每季每人給衣單費洋四元年共十六元

十，懲奬　凡持戒嚴淨成績優良者酌給以下各奬勵
甲，經典　乙，佛象　丙，法物
丁，文具　戊，奬狀
如有違犯戒律或院章者按其輕重施以下各罪法
甲，開除　乙，跪香　丙，記過
丁，呵斥

十一，試驗　分月考期考畢業考三種月考於每月終行之期考於每學期終行之畢業考於修業期滿時行之試驗分數以足六十分爲及格畢業試驗不及格者須留本院補習直至試驗及格始准畢業

十二，旁聽　學僧以外有志來院旁聽者經本院之許可得隨意旁聽但須恪守本院各規章

十三，修正　本簡章有不適宜時得隨時由本院修改之

十四，實行　本簡章自開院之日施行之
佛曆二千九百六十一年即甲戌年四月八日訂

四

今次の旅行で，私は又，北平の名刹たる弘慈寺（臨濟禪に屬す）內にある弘慈佛學院などをも訪ふたのであるがそれらは凡て，現代支那全土に廣汎に行はれてゐる佛學院と同樣，極めて程度の低い僧侶養成機關でしかない。

南の方の武昌佛學院（大虛法師が院長たるもの）などは，いくらか進步的な空氣に滿ちてゐるやうではあるが，それでも日本流の宗門大學などから見れば，とても同日の談ではない。

從つて支那本土の模倣から開放せしめられた所の，より高度の日本流の佛教學校こそが，新興滿洲國に開設されねばならないのである。私は其の實現の日を期待しつつ，此の小稿を擱筆することにするものである。

國際佛教通報局定款

名　稱

第一，本局を國際佛教通報局と稱す

事務所

第二，本局の事務所を全日本佛教青年會聯盟本部に置く

目　的

第三，本局は日本內海及海外に向つて佛教事情の通報をなし，且つ佛教徒相互間の各種便宜を計るを以て目的とす

事　業

第四，本局の目的を達成するため左記の事業を行ふ
イ，日本內地及世界各國より佛教事情に關する質問の通報を行ふ
ロ，必要に應じ日本語及世界各國語を以て佛教事情の通報を行ふ
ハ，外國人の日本觀光に際しては各種の便益を與へ，特にその佛教に關する方面に於て之を爲す
ニ，定時或は臨時に各國語を以て文書の刊行をなす
ホ，その他必要と認めたる事業を行ふ

役　員

第五，本局の事務を處理するため左の役員を置く
イ，局　長　　一　名
ロ，幹　事　　三　名
ハ，評議員　　若干名
局長は本局の事務を總括す
幹事は本局の事務を處理す
評議員は局長の提案に依る重要事務を審議す

第六，評議員は左記の者を以て之に充つ
イ，全日本佛教青年會聯盟理事及主事
ロ，全日本佛教青年會聯盟理事會に於て推薦したる者

第七，局長及幹事は評議員會に於て決定す

第八，役員の任期は二ヶ年とす（但し重任を妨げず）

經　費

第九，本局の經費は左記のものに依て之を支辨す
イ，本局基金の活用
ロ，寄附金
ハ，その他の收入

補　則

第十，本定款に記載せられざる事項は，凡て評議員會に於て協議す

第十一，第一回の役員は全日本佛教青年會聯盟理事會に於て決定す

定價	一部　金　二　十　錢	送料二錢
	一年　金二圓四十錢	送料不要

昭和十年四月廿日第三種郵便物認可
昭和十一年十二月廿八日印刷（毎月一回）
昭和十二年一月一日發行（一日發行）

東京市外吉祥寺337
編輯發行兼印刷人　淺野研眞

東京市牛込區早稻田鶴卷町107
印刷所　康文社印刷所
電話牛込（34）1950番 5049番

東京市神田區一ツ橋二の三
發行所　國際佛教通報局
電話九段（33）4428番
振替東京83015番

昭和十年四月三十日第三種郵便物認可
昭和十一年十二月二十八日印刷納本(每月一回)
昭和十二年一月一日發行(一日發行) 國際佛教通報 第三卷 第一號

Happy New Year

謹賀新年

January 1st. 2503/1937

昭和十二年元旦

The International Buddhist Information Bureau

國際佛教通報局

昭和十年四月三十日第三種郵便物認可 昭和十二年一月二十八日印刷納本 昭和十二年二月一日發行(每月一回一日發行) 第三卷 第二號

The International Buddhist Bulletin

國際佛教通報

第三卷 昭和十二年二月 第二號〔Vol. III. Feb. 2503/1937 No. 2.〕

二月號要目

東京 國際佛教通報局 發行
The International Buddhist Information Bureau
Tokyo, Kanda, Hitotsubashi, II—3
Annual Subscription, ¥2.40 (post free), Single Copies 20 sen (post 2 sen)

Staff of the Bureau

Hon. President	J. Takakusu
President	K. Ohmura
Secretary	S. Takagai
〃	B. Inaba
〃 (in chief)	Ken Assano
Advisers	H. Ui
〃	G. Asakura
〃	R. Hatani
〃	U. Ogiwara
〃	R. Higata
〃	T. Suzuki
〃	S. Suzuki
〃	S. Amakuki
〃	S. Nagai
〃	B. Matsumoto
〃	E. Uno
〃	C. Akamatsu
〃	Z. Ohmori
〃	K. Yabuki
〃	S. Onoh
〃	S. Katoh
〃	M. Anezaki
〃	G. Honda
〃	R. Sekimoto
〃	J. Sahegi
〃	R. Hanada
〃	H. Kohno
〃	R. Takaoka
〃	Z. Kobayashi
〃	S. Yamabe
〃	C. Akanuma
〃	E. Honda
〃	R. Ohmori
〃	E. Kawaguchi
〃	C. Yamakawa
〃	D. Tokiwa
〃	T. Tanimoto
〃	G. Tokiwai
〃	S. Ohtani
〃	E. Ohtani
〃	B. Mizuno
〃	I. Shibata
〃	S. Ando
〃	J. Shimomura
〃	S. Kikuzawa
〃	K. Norisugi
〃	T. Shibata
〃	K. Asano
〃	T. Watanabe
〃	G. Onoh
〃	K. Yanagizawa
〃	M. Shigemitsu
〃	E. Kanakura
〃	S. Tachibana

國際佛教通報局

名譽局長	高楠順次郎
局長	大村桂巖
幹事	鷹谷俊之
同	稻葉文海
同	淺野研眞
顧問（順序不同）	
〃	宇井伯壽
〃	朝倉曉瑞
〃	羽溪了諦
〃	荻原雲來
〃	干潟龍祥
〃	鈴木大拙
〃	鈴木宗忠
〃	天岫接三
〃	長井眞琴
〃	松本文三郎
〃	椎尾辨匡
〃	宇野圓空
〃	赤松智城
〃	大森禪戒
〃	矢吹慶輝
〃	小野清一郎
〃	加藤精神
〃	姉崎正治
〃	本田義英
〃	關本龍門
〃	佐伯定胤
〃	花田凌雲
〃	河野法雲
〃	高岡隆心
〃	小林瑞淨
〃	山邊習學
〃	赤沼智善
〃	本多惠隆
〃	大森亮順
〃	河口慧海
〃	山川智應
〃	常盤大定
〃	谷本　富
〃	常盤井堯猷
〃	大谷尊由
〃	大谷瑩潤
〃	水野梅曉
〃	柴田一能
〃	安藤正純
〃	下村壽一
〃	乘杉嘉壽
〃	芝田徹心
〃	淺野孝之
〃	渡邊哲信
〃	小野玄妙
〃	柳澤　健
〃	重光　葵
〃	金倉圓照
〃	立花俊道

Tales of Buddhist Priests (V)

by **Atsuharu Sakai**

(9) Priest Ryokan

"Ura wo mise
　Omote wo misete
　　Chiru Momiji."

This is the *jisei* or death-bed ode that Priest Ryokan, one of the most famous mendicant priests in Japan, wrote on his death-bed. The ode can be roughly translated:

"Showing one side
　And then the other, alternately,
　　Flutter the maple leaves down."

The variegated authumn leaves are much admired by the Japanese who make trips for their enjoyment in the fall, but at the same time they are suggestive of or associated with sadness in this country, and Priest Ryokan compared his dying spirit to a maple leaf that flutters down by showing both sides unreservedly. Being a religionist, the priest lived a life of asceticism and piety, and he had no secrecy whatever to keep from others in his life, for his life was as simple as a single leaf and no less plain. When Nun Teishin, his faithful

disciple and care-taker, expressed her sorrow in verse for his ebbing life, the dying priest betrayed no grudge but he was as willing to die as a falling maple leaf that leaves its branch at a single puff of wind, for he was fully convinced that he lived and died in the merciful breast of the Lord Buddha.

Priest Ryokan, who was at once ascetic and poetic, was son of Jiroyemon Yamamoto and his wife Keiko, who was daughter of a squire on Sado Island in the Japan Sea, and his childhood name was Eizo, also called Magari. His father was a royalist and made political trips through the country advocating royalty and patriotism. He was good at composing poems, and young Eizo inherited his poetic genius.

Young Eizo was so fond of learning that when he was 14 years old his father put him to school under one Shiyo Sagawa. He studied Japanese and Chinese classics, and he devoted himself to learning by making few friends. Nor did he attend to the affairs of his family at all till he was nicknamed "Day-lantern," meaning that he was of little more use than is a lantern in the daytime.

He avoided company because he noticed most of the people in his village were little read. It was when Eizo was 18 years old that he was determined to be a Buddhist priest, and with the permission of his father he entered the Kosho-ji Temple at Amase, where he became a disciple of Priest Honjo. Eizo taking the tonsure assumed the Buddhist name of Ryokan (literally, Good-generosity) and also Daigu (literally, Great-fool). After staying at the Kosho-ji Temple for four years, Priest Ryokan went to Bittchu Province, where he studied Buddhism under Priest Kokusen of the Entsu-ji Temple.

"It is several springs and autumns since I came to the Entsu-ji Temple," Priest Ryokan writes in verse form. "In this village where there are a thousand houses standing in front of the gate of my temple, I live the secluded life of a Buddhist priest, for I make few friends. When my shubby clothing gets dirty, of which I possess only one, I wash it in a stream; when my food runs low, I go begging

about the streets of the towns near by. I read biographies of great Buddhists, who all tell me that a priest should be content with honest poverty by renouncing the world." And certainly Priest Ryokan lived up to his principle, to the letter, for he had no more clothing than was on his body and laid nothing by during his life of religious devotion.

"When a youngster," he goes on, "I deserted my father in order that I might attain Buddhist enlightenment, but I have had no better success than has a painter who fails to paint even a cat in his attempt to paint a tiger, for I am no better than Eizo born,"

Banjo Kondo, a scholar of Edo (Tokyo) describes his chance visit to Priest Ryokan in the province of Tosa, where the priest lived later in hermitage. He says: "When I was young, I went to the province of Tosa. One day I was caught in a shower towards dark some three Japanese miles from the castle-town. I saw a small cottage, or as it proved, a rickety hermitage about two cho (cho=a quarter of a kilometer) from the highway on my right hand. I went and asked for shelter from the rain. An emaciated pale-looking priest, who was seated alone by a small hearth, greeted me. He had no objection to my staying overnight with him, so long as I did not mind a temple which was too poor to offer me anything to eat or to have a sliding door to protect me from a wind and cold. All I wanted was shelter from the rain and I was glad to stay with him. We sat together by the hearth till late in the night. The priest talked a little at first, but then he kept silent for the rest of the time. He was not having *zazen* (meditation) or sleeping nor did I hear him mutter or repeat the Nembutsu-prayer. He might be an idiot for aught I knew. That night I slept by the hearth and when I woke up in the morning, I saw the priest sleeping by it, with his head resting on his arm.

"It was still drizzling, and I could not leave the hermitage. My host consented to my staying another day, and I was glad that he did. A little after the zodiac time of the snake (10 a.m.) the priest prepared a dough of flour, which he shared with me. All I saw in the hermitage was a small wooden image of the Buddha enshrined on the altar and a book of Chinese classics (荘子) on a small desk. In the book, however, I noticed a Chinese poem written in excellent hand. I am no judge of Chinese poetry, but I was surprised with the skilful calligraphic writing of the poem, which my host must have written. I produced two fans on which I asked him to write some characters. He took up his brush-pen at once and painted Mt. Fuji, over which he dashed off a few beautiful calligraphs.

"We slept again in the same way beside the hearth as we did the night before. On the following morning, the rain cleared up and the sun began to shine. I was again served with the same porridge of flour about the same time as on the previous morning. Before I took his leave, I offered him a few coppers for having stayed two nights. He said that money was no use for him, and he was glad to receive a few tanzaku (stripes of paper on which an ode is to be written) that I offered him instead of the money. This piest, as I later found, was Priest Ryokan of great personality and renown."

Priest Ryokan is known as a man of great personality and religious enlightenment, for he made unusual efforts at self-culture. He wrote ninety-nine "don'ts" with which

he trained himself as a religionist.

Here are a few of his "don'ts" :—

Much talk	Long talk
Fast talk	Meddlesomeness
Talking about own merit	
Easy promising	Exaggeration
Bragging	Quarrel
Flatter	Idle talk
Fault-finding	
Complaint of anything	
Pedantry	Misery
etc.	etc.

Holding another in contempt.

Priest Ryokan lived entirely upon alms that he received during his mendicant pilgrimages. He lay by nothing whatever and literally followed the principle of "sufficient unto the day is the evil thereof." But he used every spare moment in practising calligraphy and in composing Japanese poems of 31 syllables, in which the priest excelled, so that, priest as he was, he is perhaps better known for his calligraphic writings and poems that he composed on every occasion than for his religious learning or priestly virtue. But he was modest and did not abuse his skill in calligraghy. His admirers all prized his writing, but he would not write for them unless he had or he was forced to. Many are stories in which Priest Ryokan was forced to writing some ideograms by his admirers and friends. Oftentimes he was shut up in a room in which he was forced to stay until he wrote some calligraphic characters. But he was more generous with children for whom he was always ready to write or draw something so that at last his admirers asked for his calligraphic writings through their little ones.

A certain rich man, to give an instance, had a number of tree-peomes. One day, during their season, he invited Priest Ryokan to a party for viewing their flowers, After enjoying them, the priest took a flower or two without permission for them. The host said nothing. A short while later, the rich man wanted to have a calligraphic writing of the priest, whom he invited to dinner again. When, however, he saw the priest pluck a flower again, he pretended to be very angry and shut him in a small room where the priest was forced to stay until he wrote something for the host. "Cheating is all right, but force is intolerable" the priest wrote intimating that he was displeased with the way he was treated.

One day Priest Ryokan was basking himself in the sun. He

stripped himself of his coat, the only one he had and, from it he caught some lice, for which his coat was a "nursery." He gave them an exercise on a piece of paper for a while and then he put them all back into his coat. "If these (lice) were singing insects," Priest Ryokan said in an ode of 31 syllables he improvised, "my coat would be the fields of Musashi," for Musashi, in which Tokyo is now situated, was well known for the singing of insects, to which the Japanese listen with great enjoyment.

I cannot close this short article on Priest Ryokan without writing a little on his friendly relations with Nun Teishin (literally, Chaste-minded), his admirer and disciple. She was daughter of a samurai, Okumura by name, of the clan of Nagaoka. She was religious-minded by nature and took the tonsure under Priest Taizen when a young girl. She became his disciple at the age of 29 years, when Priest Ryokan was 70 years old. She was herself a great poetess and on every occasion she composed a poem, which pleased the priest. The first time when she met the priest she expressed her joy in a 31-syllable ode, wondering if she was in a dream from which she might one day wake up. The priest also wrote his reply in verse and said that one might dream a dream in this life of dreams in which one might talk in a dream as a dream might dictate. When Priest Ryokan was critically ill, Nun Teishin stayed all the time at his bed-side and cheered him up by composing odes for his encouragement. Upon his death at the age of 75 years in 1837 Nun Teishin collected his poems in a little book that she called the "Lotus-dews."

When she herself was dying, she improvised the following poem:

"Kuru ni nite
Kaeru ni nitaru
Oki-tsu-Nami
Tachi-i wa Kaze no
Fuku ni makasete"

(The surges on the offing appear as if they were coming in and then as if they were returning; their rises and falls committed to the blowing of the wind.)

Nun Teishin compared changeful human life to a wave that constantly rises and falls under the influence of an unseen power and in this little ode she expresses her willingness to die or come to life as it wills because she also resigned to it. She died in 1872 at the age of 75 years.

Religious Statistics of Siam

(from "*Statistical Year Book of the Kingdom of Siam*," B.E. 2474–75 [1931–33], 17th Number, prepared in the Bureau of General Statistics, published by the Ministry of Economic Affairs, English Edition, III. Population, Table 13 [p. 77] and Table 14 [p. 78]).

I. Population by Religions.

Year B.E. 2472 (1929-30)

Circles	Buddhists	Mohammedans	Christians	Total
Krung Deb........	866,170	46,714	8,725	921,609
Ayudha............	822,592	13,065	4,118	839,775
Prachinburi........	491,899	12,190	4,250	508,339
Chandaburi........	165,841	873	2,912	169,626
Bayab	1,540,062	1,990	7,338	1,549,390
Bisnulok	576,591	123	237	576,951
Udorn	1,055,501	48	9,016	1,064,565
Nogor Svarge......	512,243	483	245	512,971
,, Chaisri	471,424	337	2,781	474,542
,, Rajasima ..	2,817,908	270	4,532	2,822,710
,, Sridharmaraj	808,956	100,027	192	909,175
Rojaburi	571,734	2,784	4,839	579,357
Patani	62,746	272,386	16	335,148
Bhuket	194,759	47,021	261	242,041
Total	**10,958,426**	**498,311**	**49,462**	**11,506,199**

II. Number of Monasteries and Priests (a)

Period B.E. 2473 to 2475 (1930-31 to 1932-33)

Circle	B.E. 2473 (1930-31)		B.E. 2474 (1931-32)		B E. 2475 (1932-33)	
	Monas-teries	Priests	Monas-teries	Priests	Monas-teries	Priests
Krung Deb........	619	12,439	632	12,671	611	13,170
Ayudhya	1,429	17,501	1,448	14,992	1,980	22,427
Prachin............	702	7,880	675	7,928	981	12,057
Chandaburi........	267	3,072	265	2,980	(b) ,,	,,
Bayab	3,104	8,154	3,114	7,901	3,105	7,832
Bisnulok	751	6,672	770	6,867	965	8,025
Udorn	2,080	9,444	2,161	10,325	2,238	10,835
Nagor Svarga......	654	6,236	679	7,123	(c) ,,	,,
,, Chaisri......	469	7,039	470	7,378	(d) ,,	,,
,, Rajasima....	4,786	31,717	4,902	33,725	4,881	33,001
,, Sridharmaraj	944	8,064	956	8,905	1,054	10,478
Rajaburi	584	9,864	595	9,971	1,070	18,063
Patani	87	988	99	1,035	(e) ,,	,,
Bhuket............	182	1,150	186	1,196	190	1,399
Total	**16,658**	**130,240**	**16,952**	**132,997**	**17,075**	**137,287**

(a) From a return made by the Ministry of Public Instruction previously known as the Ministry of Education.
(b) Amalgamated with the Circle Prachin in B.E. 2475.
(c) Amalgamated with the Circle of Ayudhy, with the exception of Changwads Tak and Kambaeng Bejr, which have been transferred to the Circle of Bisnulok in B.E. 2475.
(d) Amalgamated with the Circle of Rajahuri in B.E. 2475.
(e) Amalgamated with the Circle of Nagor Sridharmaraj in B.E. 2475.

What is Buddhism?

By Sohan Shingh

Buddhism lets a man know his ideal. Buddhism is somewhat different from other religions, most of which teach that every man must give obeisance to the creator who exists outside of the earth and that one can never attain on approach with him. Buddhism does not so strongly feature the creator or the god to whom the man prays to be blessed but urges only self-cultivation; for Buddha, Shakyamuni is a historical person who attained this highest perfect knowledge by self-Cultivation.

Buddhism is the teaching which lets a man elevating his ideals, reach Buddhahood and urges all human-kind to attain complete personality. Buddhism is the teaching of peace at any price and of equality in all classes, in all races, and in all the living things in the universe, who is Buddha? Buddha is a source of peaceful life, in a word, when a man reaches the eternal life of peacefulness and benevolence, leaving all his agony, jealousy, conflict, covetousness, anger, fallacy, and this chinging to his life and death.

He attains Buddhahood. Buddha, therefore, can introduce these ideal attributes into our own lives. There is a saying. "The Buddha's earlies life was spent as a mortal when a mortal reaches the highest perfect knowledge, he is a Buddha." The living exeistence itself is the substance of Buddha, and nothing but this. Within every being, however, the substance of Buddha exists, hidden in the darkness of human evil passions, awaiting development. Shakyamuni did justice to all but today Gautama's Country is not free, Buddha has sent Mahatma Gandhi to make India free. Shakyamuni's Hindustan demands full independence today. "Give us liberty or give us death." As long as India is being held in bondage there cannot be prevailed permanent peace in this ambitious world. Without India being free, Asia cannot be free.

India has given to Japan one of the greatest natural talents of Buddhism and now she expects something in its-return.

米國の宗教々育

高木亮範

与へられた題が「米國の宗教々育」といふのであるが，日時と紙數に制限があるので，到底米國に於ける宗教々育の全貌を紹介することも，亦一項目を把へて詳細に亙り說明することも，同時に許されぬことであるから，今は單に近代に於ける米國の宗教々育界に問題になつてゐる項目を羅列するに止めて置かうと思ふ。

先づ米國に於ける宗教々育といつても，新教徒各派の宗教々育，加特力教徒の宗教々育，猶太教徒の宗教々育，また公立學校に於ける宗教々育等を擧げて來ると，各々その立場を異にする處から，隨つてその趣も全然相違のあることが窺はれる。

その中，加特力教徒及びルーテル派の一部で施してゐる宗教々育は，宗教々育上から觀れば最も徹底せるものだといふことが出來る。即ち教區學校 Parish School or Parochial School を中心とする學校組織で，これは彼等教徒はその子女を，一般の公立學校に送らずに，小學校から大學專門學校に至るまで，彼等の經營になる學校に通學させ，宗教的雰圍氣内に在つて普通教育を施す，即ち宗教と普通教育との併行教育を行つてゐて，その教師の殆どは尼僧がこれに當つてゐる。全米加特力教福祉協議會 "The National Catholic Welfare Council" の報告によると，現在米國内の加特力教徒の數は，二〇，〇〇三，七五八（一九二九年調査）で，七，八〇〇教區學校（初等學校）に二，三〇〇，〇〇〇の生徒を有し，中等學校は二，一五八に二三〇，〇〇〇の生徒，專門學校一四〇に四三，〇〇〇の學生，大學二〇に四四，〇〇〇の學生を有し，年と共に學生々徒の數は非常な高率を以つて激增しつゝあるといはれてゐる。加特力教の教育を一層詳細に知りたい人は以下の著書を見られゝばよいと思ふ。

Burns, J. A., "Principles, Origin, and Establishment of the Catholic School System in the United States," New York: Benziger Bros.

McCormick, P. J., "History of Education," Washington. D. C. Catholic Education Press.

Dunney R. J., "The Parish School," New York: The Macmillan Company.

Ryan, J. H., "Catechism of Catholic Education," Washington, D. C.: National Catholic Welfare Council.

Spalding, Archbishop, "Means and Ends of Education," Chicago: Mc Clurg Company.

次には猶太教徒の宗教々育であるが彼等の中，極く少數は加特力教徒と同様に，教區學校に於て普通教育と同時に授けられてゐるのもあるが，その割合は全米猶太人の子供の 〇・〇〇四三にしか當らないし，その學校の數は米國全體で僅か十二校しかないのだから例外として置いても差支へあるまい。その大部分の子女は，一般の生徒と同様に公立學校に通學し，その放課後一時間位の割合で，每日各自の教會に於て更に教育を受けることになつてゐるこの教育は猶太人の傳統的宗教々育を中心として，民族精神及び言語の教育にも力を注いでゐる。恰度，西部沿岸に於ける在留日本人が，第二世の民族教育のために日本語學園を設立して，公立學校の餘暇に教育を施してゐるのと同様の目的である。たゞ在留日本人のは，一般的に眺めて宗教的色彩を極端に拒否しやうとする傾向があるのは第一に彼等の多くが明治時代の教育を受けた儘，社會的思潮の變遷による刺戟を受けることが尠く，今日に於ても依然として教育といふものは宗教と分離して居らねばならぬといふ先入主に支配されてゐる結果と，曾つての排日の猛烈な時代に，それが緩和の一方法として極端な米化を唱えた餘燼が猶ほ存してゐるためとで，努力の割合に民族教育の徹底せぬ憾がある。佛教開教使も多數往つてゐることだから，この猶太人の教育組織を研究し參考として一層の奮勵を希望してゐる者である。

ペンが横道に逸れたが，現在米國に於ける猶太人の人口は，四，二二八，〇〇〇であるといはれてゐる。この中，四，〇七七，〇四二が，八七一の猶太教の組合教會或は組織ある猶太教の團體に屬してゐるといはれてゐるから，在米猶太人の大部分が猶太教に屬してゐると看做しても差支へないわけであるそして八七一の猶太教の團體の中，八五四，即ち九八パーセントは學校を經營して居り，その總數は一，七五四である。その生徒の總數は二四九，四〇九であるといはれてゐる。猶太人の教育を詳細に知らうとする者は，左の著書及び雜誌を參照されたい。

Dushkin, Alexander M., "Jewish Eduction in New York City," New York: Bloch Publishing Company.

Gamoran, Emanuel, "Changing Conceptions in Jewish Education," New York: The Macmillan Company.

"Jewish Education," Magazine. New York: National Council for Jewish Education.

Linfield, Harry S., "The Communal Organization of the Jews in the United States, 19?7," New York: American Jewish Committee.

次に新教徒の宗教々育であるが，私共は普通これを呼んで米國の宗教々育といつてゐるのであるが，これは嚮の加特力教徒及び猶太教徒の教育運動とは，全然別個の途を辿つて發達して來たものである。特に加特力教徒が，その昔，未だ教育が組織的發達をしなかつた時代の形態をその儘持續して，宗教と教育とを同一軌道に歩ませてゐる。それに對して，彼の宗教改革者，即ち新教の祖ともいふべきマルチン，ルーザーは，一方近世初等教育の始祖と崇められてゐるやうに，文藝復興以後の形に現はれた學校組織の主唱者であるところから，觀ようによつては宗教と教育の分離を計畫した最初の人であり，新教徒は積極的にそれが實現に與つて力があつたといふことが出來ると思ふ。隨つて，そこに純粹の意味に於ける宗教々育運動が，新教徒間に興隆した所以が存在するわけである。

處が新教徒の宗教々育運動は決して教會内から，宗教家の手によつて創始されたものではなく，全く教會外の俗人の手による，俗的事業として發達して來たのであるから面白い。新教徒の宗教々育運動の根幹は勿論日曜學校であるが，その日曜學校の先驅といふよりは，その濫觴と看做されてゐるのは今から百五十年程以前に英國はグロセスター市（Gloucester）のロバート，レイクス(Robert Raikes)によつて創設された貧民學校の運動であることは餘りに有名であるが，この運動は何等教會とは關係のないもので，たゞ熱心な信者の手によつて，一種の慈善事業として出發してゐるのである。その影響を受けて，新大陸に開設されたエリオツト（William Elliot）やアスバリイ（Francis Asbury）の運動も，奴隷のための學校で，倶に特殊階級の子弟保護誘導の施設であつた。それが日曜學校といふ名稱の下に，教會内に引入れられて一般に對する宗教々育の機關となり，今日では教會の主要な機能の一となつたのである。されど，その俗人の手によつて經營管理されてゐた傳統的傾向は，極く最近まで持續されてゐた。殊に前世紀の終頃に日曜學校促進のために，凡ゆる方面に亙つて大活躍をなし，今日の大成完備を來す基礎を築いたゼコブス氏（B. F. Jacobs）の如きはシカゴの實業家であつたし，大概の日曜學校の校長は熱心な平信徒がこれに當り，教師も無論さうであつた。それだけ，米國のこの運動は，超教派的によく協調團結して急激な發達をして來たのである。此の種の事業にあつては，宗派的對立は絕對に忌むべきである。

然し乍ら，今日では日曜學校のみが宗教々育の機關でもなければ，青少年のみがその對象ではなくなつて，その範圍が横にも，縱にも驚く程多面に擴充されてゐるから，平信徒の片手間仕事では，到底滿足出來なくなつた。從つて專門の教育を受けた專門家を要するやうになつて來た。今日，米國に於ける宗教々育界の異常な熱心を以つて研究と實施に當つてゐる問題は指導者養成（Leadership Training or Teacher training）といふことである。左にこの問題に關する參考書を二三紹介して見よう。

Barclay, W. C., "Training for Leadership and Teaching." New York: Methodist Book Concern.

McElfresh, Franklin, "The Training of Sunday School Teachers and Officers," New York: Eaton and Mains.

Kearney, Emilie F., "The Teacher Training Class, " New York: Fleming H. Revell Company.

猶ほ今日の宗教々育の指導者には，專門的知識が如何なる程度に必要であるか，またその職責はどの範圍に亙つてゐるか，指導者といつても，今茲に一寸擧げ切らない程多種多様の種別が設けられてゐるが，その種別に一々解說を施してゐるのは，幾つもの著書が出てゐる中，左の加州レドランド大學教授のラフエツテイ博士のが最も適當であらうと思ふ。

Raffety, W. Edward, "Church-School Leadership." New York: Fleming H. Revell Company.

更にその指導者を指導する專門學者の養成も，各大學の大學院に宗教々育科を設けて，多數の教授，講師を置いて，獨立せる一講座をなし，學としてその存在を認めてゐることは，日本あたりの大學では想像もつかない狀態である。ボストン大學なぞでは大學卒業後五ケ年の大學院生活を經て，論文が通過すれば宗教々育博士（Doctor of Religious Education）の學位を授與される規定が設けられてゐる。

されば，この運動の當初に於ては，少數の有給教師を採用して相當の成績を擧げてはゐるが，殆どヴランテアーの教職員によつて永い間繼續されて來たのであつた。然しながら今日では立派なプロフエショナル・ウオーク卽ち職業となつて來たのである。之が基本となつて宗教々育界の凡ゆる部門が非常なる變革進步を來したのである。佛教の宗教々育運動も，學生の遊び仕事であつたり，住職の葬式や法事の片手間仕事である中は，何時たつても理想的發展は望まれないといつてもよからう。佛教の各大學で宗教々育の專門家を養成するやうになるのは何時のことだらう。

曩に，米國に於ける宗教々育運動は現在，横にも縱にも，手の延べられるだけ廣く，その範圍を擴充してゐることを述べたが，先づその縱の方面から眺めるならば，在來の日曜學校は，主に兒童を對象として組織されてゐたのであつた。それが進んで青年に對する教育組織も設けられるに至り，更に發達して，今日では生れ出たその日から教會學校に登錄させるCradle Roll から Adult Department の墓穴に至るまで，人間の一生を通じての教育組織が完備され，猶ほ疾病，不具，その他の事情で教會學校に出席不可能な人々のために家庭科 Home Department も設けられてゐる程完備した實情にある。斯かる組織及び管理上の問題としては，四五年前までは嬰兒期卽ち Cradle Roll を對象とする教會學校の問題が喧しく論じられてゐたが，それも，今日では一段落着いて，今や成人に對する宗教々育の問題が，中心題目として斯界を騒がしてゐる。この問題は在來のバイブルクラスが變革され，それに一般教育界に於ける成人教育の運動に刺戟され，影響されたことも容易に想像がつくのである。左にこれに關する參考書目を擧げれば，

Bovard, W. S., "Adults in the Sunday School," Abingdon.

Darsie, Charles, "Adult Religious Teaching," Bethany.

Lindeman, E. C., "Meaning of Adult Education," New Republic.

Palmer, Leon C., "The Religious Education of Adults," Morehouse.

Raffety, W. E., "Religious Education of Adults," Revell.

Hart, J. K., "Adult Education." Crowell.

Winchester, B. S., "The Church and Adult Education." Smith.

次に同様組織上の問題であるが，これを横に眺めた場合，在來は日曜學校が唯一の宗教々育の機關であつたのが現在の教會に於ける教育的活動は，頗る多角的に發展を來し，休暇を利用せる學校もあり，週間中公立學校と協力の上，一定の時間，特別に宗教々育を授ける週間教會學校，既述の指導者養成機關，その他種々なる青少年のための教育機關たる倶樂部，傳道，禁酒，平和，社會奉仕，保健(娯樂)等に關する諸活動が，整備され，その教育組織は非常なる複雜を極めるに至つたのが現狀である。隨つてこの複雜，煩瑣な組織を合理化せんとする輿論が，一部の識者間に唱えられるやうになつて來た。この運動をIntegration in Religious Education といつてゐる。つまり宗教々育の統制運動である。ローズベルト大統領のＮＲＡの政策以來，社會の凡ゆる分野に於て澎湃として統制運動が起されたが，時代に敏感な宗教々育界に於てもこの時流に乘つてその合理化とか統制とかいふことが叫ばれるやうになつて來たのであらう。これに關してはまだ餘り著書としては現はれてゐないが，參考に左の二種を掲げて置かう。

Coe, G. A., "What is Christian Education ?" Scribner's.

Harper, W. A., "An Integrated Program of Religious Education." Macmillan.

教會内の教育組織が複雜多岐に亙つて來たから，從來の日曜學校といふ名稱も，如上の諸活動との關係上，「日曜教會學校」"The Sunday Church School." と改稱された。そして教會の教育的活動を總稱して教會學校 The Church School と呼んでゐる。この教會學校といふ名稱は，一九一二年に當時ドレーク大學，後にボストン大學の宗教々育科長になつた故アーサーン博士 W. S. Athearn が，"The Church School" なる名著を出版してから，一般にその名稱が流用されるに至つたといはれてゐる。バプテスト教派出版所の宗教々育部書記チャール

マース博士 W.E.Chalmersの著 "The Church and the Church School." に於て，「基督教々育の廣汎な，そして均衡のとれたプログラムに包攝されてゐる學修，教授，保健(娯樂)，奉仕の組織と運行の凡ゆる方面を統一したものが教會學校である。」と定義を下して，左の如くその包攝活動を列擧してゐる。

THE CHURCH SCHOOL
- Sunday School
- Young People's Work
- Teacher-Training
- Missionary Education
- Vacation Schools
- Week-Day Religious Education
- Evangelism & Personal Work
- Stewardship
- Recreation
- Social Service

教會學校の組織，管理に關しては，恐らく百種に餘る多數の著述やパンフレツトが出版されてゐるから，茲に執れが參考書として適當なものであるか擧げるに一寸躊躇せざるを得ないが，手許にあるもので比較的他の書物に多く引用されてゐるものを掲げて參考に資することにしやう。

Archibald, G. H., "The Modern Sunday School," Century.

Bower, W. C., "Religion in the Modern Church," Bethany.

Fergusson. E. M., "Church School Administration," Revell.

Palmer, L. C., "Church School. Organization and Administration," Morehouse.

Cope, H. F., "Organization of the Church School." Doran.

Cunninggim, J. L., & North, E. M., "The Organization and Administration of the Sundy School." Methodist Book.

Stout, J. E., Organization and Administration of Religious Education." Abingdon.

更に「米國の宗教々育」を論ずる場合，教材の發達，教授法，測定學，公立學校に於ける宗教々育等に論及しなければ，全般に亙つて紹介したものとはいはれないのであるが，既に豫定の紙數を可なり超過してゐる上に，締切日もとつくに過ぎてゐることだから，一先づこゝらで擱筆して他日稿を革めることにしよう。以上洵に雜莫なものながら「米國の宗教々育」の一部を紹介した次第である。猶ほ同一の問題を他の角度から眺めたものを「中央佛教」の十一月號と十二月號に，又「教育と宗教」の一月號に拙稿が載つてゐるから參照されたい。(一九三七・一・一八)

資料

中國佛教會章程

第一章 總則

第一條　本會由中華民國全國佛教徒組織之，定名曰中國佛教會。

第二條　本會以團結全國佛教徒，整理教規，宣傳教義，發揚大乘救世精神，利濟羣生，福益社會，爲宗旨。

第三條　本會設會所於首都，爲辦事便利起見，設總辦事處於上海。

第四條　本會於各省及直轄市各縣及普通市，得設分會，省稱中國佛教會某某省佛教會，縣稱中國佛教會某某省某某縣佛教會，（直轄市佛教會，等於省佛教會，普通市佛教會，等於縣佛教會）凡國內名山區域，本會認爲必要時，得設中國佛教會某某山佛教會，其組織等於省佛教會，（以上各項組織通則另訂之。）凡縣市分會，遇緊要事件，得向本會直接行文，但同時須知照該管省佛教會。各分會圖記，均由本會製發。

第五條　本會受中央民訓部直接指導，並受內政部之監督，各省及直轄市並名山分會，受本會及所在地黨該機關之指導監督，縣及普通市分會，受各該省分會及所在地黨政機關之指導監督

第二章 會務

第六條　本會會務如左

一，教規整理與施行。

二，教義之宣傳。

三，黨政之研究。

四，寺廟財產之保護。

五，辦理僧衆教育。

六，提倡生產勞作，但以不違反本教教旨爲範圍。

七，指導佛教寺廟保存法物名勝古蹟。

八，辦理公益慈善事業。

九，設立各種研究所，但以不違反本教教旨爲限。

十，其他應興應革事宜。

第七條　各地叢林，非經本會核准，不得任意傳戒，其核准辦法另訂之。

第三章 會員

第八條　本佛除在家二衆，及歸依三寶護法有力者，均得入會爲會員外，全國僧尼須一律登記入會爲會員，（入會及登記規則另訂之）

第九條　本會會員，分基本，贊助，特別，維持，普通，五種。

第十條　有左列情事之一者，不得爲本會會員，

一，非中國國籍者。

二，違反教者，或破壞本教有顯著之言論及行動者。

三，違反三民主義，有顯著之言論及行動者。

四，受刑事處分尙未期滿，或褫奪公權尙未恢復者。

五，患有神經病者。

六，染有不良嗜好，或破壞清規，及有不法行爲者。

七，未及法定年齡者。

第十一條　會員之義務如左。

一，遵守教規，及本會一切章則暨議決案。

二，精進修持，並教誨徒衆，化導僧俗信徒，及宣揚教義。

三，努力服務本會所舉辦之一切教育慈善公益。

四，遵章繳納會費，及盡力繳納事業費。

第十二條　會員之權利如左。

一，選舉及被選舉權。

二，出家二衆有充任佛教寺廟住持之權，但不遵守前條規定者，得停止之。

三，關於會員間因教務上發生爭議時，得請求本會或分會調解。

四，寺廟或本人有被非法侵害時，得請本會或分會援助。

第十三條　會員證章均由本會製發。

第四章 組織及職權

第十四條　本會以全國佛教徒會員代表大會爲最高機關，閉幕時爲理事會，（選舉代表規則另訂之）

第十五條　全國代表大會之決議案，及理監事選舉結果，於閉會後半月內，呈報中央黨政機關備案，並於會刊公佈之。

第十六條　本會設理事會，由代表大會選舉理事四十九人，候補理事二十四人組織之，並互選正副理事長各一人，常務理事十一人，組織常務理事會。

第十七條　本會理事會，對全國代表大會，負責執行大會議決各案，處理一切會務，督促各分會會務之推進。

第十八條　理事會得分科或分股辦事，（辦事細則另訂之）

第十九條　本會常務理事會，對理事會負責執行議決交辦各案，並處理日當一切會務，正副理事長，均由出家者任之，對內對外代表本會。

第二十條　本會設監事會，由代表大會選舉監事二十三人，候補監事十一人組織之，並互選監事長一人，由出家者任之，監事會對理事會執行會務負監察之責。

第念一條　理事監事，在家者不得過半數。

第念二條　理事監事任期均二年，連選得連任。

第念三條　理事監事出缺時，由候補理監事，分出家在家，各依次遞補。

第念四條　本會於必要時，經理事會之決議，得設特種委員會，或聘請名譽理事長或理事。

第念五條　本會因辦事之必要，經常務理事會之決議，得聘任或雇用辦事員。

第五章 會議

第念六條　本會代表大會，每二年舉行一次，由理事會召集之，但經本會理監事聯席會之決議，或全國省分會三分一以上或縣分會十分一以上之聯合請求，得臨時召集之。

第念七條　本會會員代表大會開會時，除正副理事長爲當然主席外，應由出席代表互推三人至五人爲主席團，主持會議。

第念八條　理事會每四個月舉行一次，監事會每六個月舉行一次，必要時得開理監事聯席會議。

第念九條　常務理事會，每月舉行二次，必要時得開臨時會。

第三十條　理事會主席，由理事長任之，理事長因事不能出席時，由副理事長任之，正副理事長均不能出席時，由常務理事互推一人爲臨時主席。

第卅一條　監事會主席，由監事長任之，監事長因時不能出席時，由監事互推一人爲臨時主席。

第卅二條　理監事聯席會議時，以理事長爲主席，理事長因事不能出席時，由監事長爲主席，監事長不能出席時，由副理事長爲主席，副理事長不能出席時，由理監事互推一人爲臨時主席。

第卅三條　凡會議非有應出席者過半數之出席。不得開議，非有出席者過半數之同意，不能表決，可否同數時，取決於主席。

第六章　經　費

第卅四條　本會辦理一切會務，及各種事業之經費以下列各項收入充之。

（一）　會員會費

甲，基本會員　一次繳納會費國幣一百元。

乙，贊助會員　每年繳納會費國幣十元。

丙，特別會員　每年繳納會費國幣四元。

丁，維持會員　每年繳納會費二元。

戊，普通會員　每年繳納會費國幣五角。

凡寺廟職僧應納維持會員以上之會費。

會員會費收入，除由經徵之縣市分會，以十分之六，留爲辦理會務經費外，應以十分之二，繳送省分會，十分之二，直接交送本會，其由直轄市分會或名山分會經收者，應以十分之四繳送本會。

（二）　補助費

本會辦理事業經費，得依監督寺廟條例第十條，及佛教寺廟興辦慈善公益事業規則之規定，由各分會組織委員會征收之，以二成繳送本會。

（三）　特別捐

於必要時，由理事會之決議，臨時募集之。

第卅五條　本會各項賬目　除由監事隨時查核外，應於代表大會開會時，於理監事外，另推代表三人至五人，組織臨時□□

第七章　附　則

第卅六條　本章程之修改增刪，應由全國代表大會議決修正之。

第卅七條　本章程由全國代表大國通過後，呈請中央黨政機關核准施行。

資　　料

中國佛教會各分會組織通則

第一條　本通則依據中國佛教會章程第四條訂定之。

第二條　凡省與直轄市，及廳與普通市，暨名山區，均得分設佛教會，省稱中國佛教會某某省佛教會，直轄市稱中國佛教會某某市佛教會，縣稱中國佛教會某某省某某縣佛教會，普通市稱中國佛教會某某省某某市佛教會，名山區稱中國佛教會某某山佛教會。

第三條　各分會除受本會直接指導辦理會務外，并受各所在地黨政機關之指導監督。

第四條　各分會會章，須依據本會章程及本通則訂定之。

第五條　各分會之組織程序，除遵照中央修正人民團體組織方案規定外，並依照本通則所定辦理。

第六條　設立分解，直轄市，名山區，普通市，縣，須有佛教徒三十人以上連署發起，推舉代表，呈報本會理事會核准，并呈報當地高級黨政機關備案，方得設立籌備處。

省分會須有本省普通市縣佛教會十個分會以上連署發起，其他組織程序，依照上項辦理。

第七條　各分會籌備處，由發起人推定籌備員，省及直轄市，暨名山區，七人至九人，縣及普通市，五人至七人，并由籌備員互推籌備主任一人，省及直轄市暨名山區，呈報本會，縣及普通市，呈由省會轉報本會，均經本會理事會通過，分別發給籌備證。

第八條　直轄市及名山區分會籌備處，設立後二個月內，應將介紹會員入會志願書及名冊，並應繳本會々費，（依照本會々章第三十四條規定）匯呈本會，經理事會通過後，核發會員證章。

縣市分會，除照前項辦法辦理外，並將會員會費之十分之二，繳送省會。

第九條　各分會籌備完成後，應即定期召開成立大會，省及直轄市名山區，選舉理事十九人至二十五人，候補理事九人至十一人，監事七人至九人，候補監事三人至五人，并將選定之理監事履歷呈報本會，經理事會審定後，分別發給當選證書，普通市及縣選舉理事七人至十一人候補理事三人至五人，監事三人至五人，候補監事一人至二人，呈由省會轉報本會辦理。

第十條　各分會召開成立大會時，省及直轄市暨名山區，呈請本會派員指導，縣及普通市，呈請省會派員指導，并各請所在地黨政機關指導監選。

第十一條　各分會籌備期間之開支，由

發起人籌集之。

第十二條　各分會理事會，互選正副理事長各一人，並互選常務理事，省及直轄市名山區五人至七人普通市及縣三人至五人，各分會監事會，互選監事長一人，以上均分別呈報本會及省會備案。

第十三條　各分會理事，監事常務理事，均由僧俗分任之，但在家者不得過半數。

第十四條　各分會理事長，監事長，由出家者任之。

第十五條　各分會理監事任期均二年，連選得連任。

第十六條　省佛教會代表大會之出席代表，除該會之理監事爲當然代表外，應由各市縣會員大會選舉之，每一市縣佛教會會員人數在五十以上三百以下者，得選代表一人，三百以上六百以下者，得選代表二人，六百人以上者，得選代表三人，但每一市縣佛教會，至多不得過三人。

第十七條　省佛教會代表大會，每二年舉行一次，由省佛教會理事會召集之，必要時得經理監事聯席會議之決議，或全省市縣佛教會四分之一以上之聯合請求，得臨時召集之。

前項代表大會之召集，應於開會前二個月，陳報中國佛教會，請派員指導，並公告之，同時通知本省各市縣佛教會，各佛教會應將出席代表之履歷及提案，於會期前二十天，送達省佛教會。

第十八條　市縣佛教會之會員大會，每年舉行一次，由各該縣佛教會理事會召集之，必要時得經理監事聯席會議之決議，或所屬會員五分一以上之聯名請求，得臨時召集之。

前項會員大會之召集，應於開會一月前，陳報上級佛教會，請派員指導，同時以書面通知各會員。

第十九條　直轄市名山區佛教會之會員大會，准用市縣佛教會會員大會之規定。

第二十條　省代表大會，或市縣會員大會開會時，均須有報到代表或會員過半數之出席，方得開議，其議決案，以出席人數過半數之通過爲有効。

第念一條　省代表大會，或縣會員大會開會時，均應先期陳報所在地黨政機關，請派員指導監督。

第念二條　省代表大會，或市縣會員大會開會時，除正副理事長爲當然主席外，應由出席代表或會員，再互推三人至五人，爲主席團，主持會議。

第念三條　省代表大會，或市縣會員大會之決議案，及理監事選舉結果，應各呈報所在地黨政機關及上級佛教會備案，並公佈之。

第念四條　當選出席中國佛教會　或省佛教會之代表，不得同時代表兩分會，並不得無故推辭或缺席，代表出席之旅費，應由各該佛教會擔負。

第念五條　各分會應用圖記，均由本會刊發之。

第念六條　各分會之職務如左

(一)　辨理本會章程第六條所列各事項

(二)　辨理調查及登記事項

(三)　辨理徵求會員事項

(四)　辨理選舉代表事項

第廿七條　各分會各種會議紀錄，須繕具副本，呈送本會或省會備查，其重要議案，須呈經本會核復後施行。

第廿八條　各分會所收會費，直轄市及名山區，以十分之四解繳本會，縣及普通市，以十分之二解繳本會，另以十分之二送繳省會。

第廿九條　各分會辨理事業費，得依照本會章程第三十四條之規定辨理之。

第三十條　各分會經常費，事業費應于每年年度開始前，及終了後，編造預算及決算書，省及直轄市暨名山區，呈由本會核准，普通市及縣，呈由省會轉報本會核准。

第卅一條　普通市及縣之佛教徒人數較少時，呈由省會轉報本會核准後，得與本省隣縣或數縣合併組織佛教會，稱爲中國佛教會某省某縣某市聯合佛教會，必要時，得於聯合區域內，設分辨事處。

第卅二條　本通則第九條及第十一條所定分解理監事常務理事名額，如因地方特殊情形，須增減時，經本會核准，得酌量增減。

第卅三條　各分會之行動，有違反會章及本通則時，省及直轄市暨名山區，本會得派員指導或改組，縣及普通市，得由省會轉報本會，派員指導或改組之。

第卅四條　省佛教會籌備成立時，該省之本會分辨事處，即日結束。

第卅五條　本通則施行後，其原有之省市縣佛教會，於行文到達之日起，應即照章改組。

第卅六條　本通則如有未盡事宜，得由本會代表大會議決修改之。

第卅七條　本通則由本會代表大會通過，呈請中央黨政機關核准施行。本通則施行日起，前頒之中國佛教會各分會組織通則廢止之。

汎太平洋佛教青年運動

功勞者氏名 （敬稱略 五十音順）

赤澤亦吉	朝倉曉瑞	宮崎匪石	村田龍一
淺野孝之	安藤嶺丸	山田一英	吉田賢龍
泉道雄	岩野眞隆	和田鼎	（以上三十七名）
宇佐美奎賢	小野清一郎		
大村桂巖	大森禪戒		
加藤熊一郎	内田晄融		
木村宗圓	木山十彰		
來馬琢道	佐藤了秀		
柴田一能	杉谷泰山		
其日慶寶	鷹谷俊之		
高楠順次郎	武田豐四郎		
立花廣海	立花俊道		
土屋詮教	中桐確太郎		
中野實範	野村喜一郎		
吉野保	本多惠隆		
松本雲城	三森實言		

表彰狀

貴下ハ夙ニ汎太平洋佛教青年運動隆昌ノ爲メ盡瘁セラレ其ノ功績顯著ナルコトヲ認メ茲ニ記念品一個ヲ贈呈シ其ノ功勞ヲ表彰ス

昭和十一年四月二十五日

汎太平洋佛教
青年會聯盟

日暹佛青の親善

全日本佛青聯盟では昨秋朝日新聞社の訪暹機に託しシヤム對佛青にして左記の如きメツセージを送つた——

×

メツセージ

第二回汎太平洋佛教青年會大會に際し，貴會より多數參加せられたる御好意を回想し，今般，東京朝日新聞社の，日暹親善飛行機鵬型號に託して貴會に深甚の敬意を表し，尙ほ，貴會の御發展を祈り，併せて今後一層の親交を增進せんことを念願す。

昭和十一年十二月五日

全日本佛教青年會聯盟

暹羅國佛教青年會御中

之に對して過般，はるばる同會から返禮のメツセージが到着した。原文は暹羅語で書かれてあるがこれを日本文に飜譯すれば左の如くである。

×

メツセージ

日暹親善增進のための朝日新聞社の飛行機鵬型號に托されたる貴聯盟のメツセージは確に拜受ありがたく御禮申上ます。

我が暹羅佛教青年會は時恰も暹羅國憲法記念日に際會し事務を休んで居りましたため當方より返禮のメツセージを直に同機に托するを得ざりし事を甚だ遺憾に存じてゐる次第であります我が佛教青年會々員一同は昭和九年七月東京に於て開催された第二回汎太平洋佛教青年會大會に當方より參加致しました我が代表に對して御示し下さいました貴聯盟の御芳情を常に追想いたし感謝感激の念に浸つて居ります。

我等は日暹兩國佛教青年會の絕えざる友好を維持發展せしめ行くことを確信致します。併せて我等の最も崇敬する佛陀の慈光によつて貴聯盟が益々隆昌に赴き以て兩者間の親誼がいよ〳〵密接ならんことを希望いたして止みません。

在バンコツク暹羅佛教青年會

佛暦二四七九年（一九三六年）

十二月二十六日

全日本佛教青年會聯盟御中

サ　ラ　ナッタ　ヤ　ム

Saraṇattayaṁ

三　歸　依〔巴利語〕

（1）ブツダム　サラナム　ガツチヤーミ
Buddhaṁ saraṇaṁ gacchāmi,
〔我れ〕佛に　歸依したてまつる，

ダンマム　サラナム　ガツチヤーミ
Dhammaṁ saraṇaṁ gacchāmi,
〔我れ〕法に　歸依したてまつる，

サンガム　サラナム　ガツチヤーミ
Saṅghaṁ saraṇaṁ gacchāmi.
〔我れ〕僧に　歸依したてまつる。

（2）ドチヤン　ピ　ブツダム　サラナム　ガツチヤーミ
Dutiyam pi buddhaṁ saraṇaṁ gacchāmi,
二たび　又〔我れ〕佛に　歸依したてまつる，

ドチヤン　ピ　ダンマム　サラナム　ガツチヤーミ
Dutiyam pi dhammaṁ saraṇaṁ gacchāmi,
二たび　又〔我れ〕法に　歸依したてまつる，

ドチヤン　ピ　サンガム　サラナム　ガツチヤーミ
Dutiyam pi saṅghaṁ saraṇaṁ gacchāmi.
二たび　又〔我れ〕僧に　歸依したてまつる。

（3）タチヤン　ピ　ブツダム　サラナム　ガツチヤーミ
Tatiyam pi buddhaṁ saraṇaṁ gacchāmi,
三たび　又〔我れ〕佛に　歸依したてまつる，

タチヤン　ピ　ダンマム　サラナム　ガツチヤーミ
Tatiyam pi dhammaṁ saraṇaṁ gacchāmi,
三たび　又〔我れ〕法に　歸依したてまつる，

タチヤン　ピ　サンガム　サラナム　ガツチヤーミ
Tatiyam pi saṅghaṁ saraṇaṁ gacchāmi.
三たび　又〔我れ〕僧に　歸依したてまつる。

國際佛教通報局定款

名　稱

第一，本局を國際佛教通報局と稱す

事務所

第二，本局の事務所を全日本佛教青年會聯盟本部に置く

目　的

第三，本局は日本內海及海外に向つて佛教事情の通報をなし，且つ佛教徒相互間の各種便宜を計るを以て目的とす

事　業

第四，本局の目的を達成するため左記の事業を行ふ

イ，日本內地及世界各國より佛教事情に關する質問の通報を行ふ

ロ，必要に應じ日本語及世界各國語を以て佛教事情の通報を行ふ

ハ，外國人の日本觀光に際しては各種の便益を與へ，特にその佛教に關する方面に於て之を爲す

ニ，定時或は隨時に各國語を以て文書の刊行をなす

ホ，その他必要と認めたる事業を行ふ

役　員

第五，本局の事務を處理するため左の役員を置く

イ，局　長　　一　名

ロ，幹　事　　三　名

ハ，評議員　　若干名

局長は本局の事務を總括す

幹事は本局の事務を處理す

評議員は局長の提案に依る重要事務を審議す

第六，評議員は左記の者を以て之に充つ

イ，全日本佛教青年會聯盟理事及主事

ロ，全日本佛教青年會聯盟理事會に於て推薦したる者

第七，局長及幹事は評議員會に於て決定す

第八，役員の任期は二ケ年とす（但し重任を妨げず）

經　費

第九，本局の經費は左記のものに依て之を支辨す

イ，本局基金の活用

ロ，寄附金

ハ，その他の收入

補　則

第十，本定款に記載せられざる事項は，凡て評議員會に於て協議す

第十一，第一回の役員は全日本佛教青年會聯盟理事會に於て決定す

定價	一部　金二十錢	送料二錢
	一年　金二圓四十錢	送料不要

昭和十年四月卅日第三種郵便物認可
昭和十二年一月廿八日印刷（每月一回
昭和十二年二月一日發行　一日發行）

東京市外吉祥寺337
編輯發行兼印刷人　浅野研眞

東京市牛込區早稻田鶴卷町107
印刷所　株式會社康文社印刷所
電話牛込（34）1950番 5049番

東京市神田區一ツ橋二の三
發行所　國際佛教通報局
電話九段（33）4428番
振替東京83015番

昭和十年四月三十日第三種郵便物認可
昭和十二年一月二十八日印刷納本(毎月一回)
昭和十二年二月一日發行(一日發行)　國際佛教通報　第三卷　第二號

昭和十年四月三十日第三種郵便物認可　昭和十二年二月二十五日印刷納本　昭和十二年三月一日發行(毎月一回一日發行)第三卷　第三號

The International Buddhist Bulletin

國際佛教通報

第三卷 昭和十二年三月 第三號 [Vol. III. March. 2503/1937 No. 3.]

三月號要目

東京 國際佛教通報局 發行
The International Buddhist Information Bureau
Tokyo, Kanda, Hitotsubashi, II—3
Annual Subscription, ¥2.40 (post free), Single Copies 20 sen (post 2 sen)

國際佛教通報局

名譽局長	高楠順次郎
局長	大村桂巖
幹事	鷹谷俊之
同	稻葉文海
同	淺野研眞

顧問（順序不同）

〃	宇井伯壽
〃	朝倉曉瑞
〃	羽溪了諦
〃	荻原雲來
〃	干潟龍祥
〃	鈴木大拙
〃	鈴木宗忠
〃	天岫接三
〃	長井眞琴
〃	松本文三郎
〃	椎尾辨匡
〃	宇野圓空
〃	赤松智城
〃	大森禪戒
〃	矢吹慶輝
〃	小野清一郎
〃	加藤精神
〃	姉崎正治
〃	本田義英
〃	門本龍胤
〃	關定雲
〃	佐伯定胤
〃	花田凌雲
〃	河野法雲
〃	高岡隆心
〃	小林瑞淨
〃	山邊習學
〃	赤沼智善
〃	本多惠隆
〃	大森亮順
〃	河口慧海
〃	山川智應
〃	常盤大定
〃	谷本富
〃	常盤井堯猷
〃	大谷尊由
〃	大谷瑩潤
〃	水野梅曉
〃	柴田一能
〃	安藤正純
〃	下村壽一
〃	乘杉嘉壽
〃	芝田徹心
〃	淺野孝之
〃	渡邊哲信
〃	小野玄妙
〃	柳澤健
〃	重光葵
〃	金倉圓照
〃	立花俊道

スワミ僧正の追悼會

第二回汎太平洋佛青大會にインド代表として出席したシュリ・ジナワンサ・スワミ僧正は昨年二月十七日に東大久保の島田アパートで淋しく逝いて速くも一周忌になるが、内田氏によりこの程牛込區河田町月桂寺にスワミ僧正の墓碑が立派に建つたので命日の二月十七日午後一時から内田孝藏、諸岡存、角岡知良、ボース氏等の知友並に佛聯、全聯、汎聯、護國團等が主催になり追悼法要が執行された。（石刷は其墓碑銘）

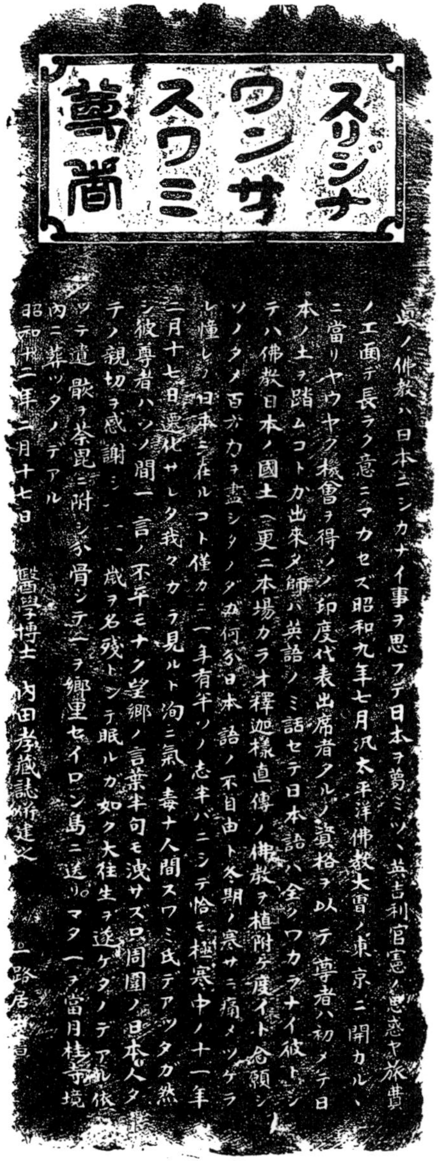

La cérémonie du couronnement au Siam

Nature de la Cérémonie

La cérémonie du couronnement se ramène à deux éléments essentiels :

1°—Le bain rituel et le couronnement proprement dit (Paramarājābhiseka), rite brahmanique avec des altérations d'origine bouddhique ; et 2° la prise de possession de la résidence royale (thalo'ṅ braḥ rājamaṇḍira), purement bouddhique et locale. Les deux parties ne se déroulent pas séparément, mais elles s'entremêlent de façon à former un même ensemble.

Cadre de la cérémonie.—Etant donné que chaque cérémonie est étroitement liée à tel ou tel bâtiment des vieilles résidences royales où se déroule le couronnement, il semble utile de donner quelques renseignements sur la situation de chacun d'eux.

Le groupe de constructions où a lieu le couronnement est désigné par le terme général de Mahā Maṇdira, que rendait peut-être "résidence royale". Il a été construit par Rama Ier et, en fait, il a été la demeure des trois premiers rois de la dynastie. Il comprend trois bâtiments principaux ; le Chakrabarti Bimān, qui est la résidence royale proprement dite et où se trouve chambre à coucherd'apparat ; au nord du Chakrabarti Bimān se trouve la salle Baisāl, sorte de salle des audiences particulières ou salle d'audience intérieure ; au nord de la salle Baisāl, on trouve l'Amarindra, salle des audiences publiques ou salle d'audience extérieure.

Objets et ornements qui servent au Roi au cours de la cérémonie.—Il est bon aussi de donner quelques explications au sujet des diverses pièces qui composent l'appareil royal et qui, au cours de la cérémonie, auront un rôle capital à jouer. En premier lieu, nous avons, naturellement, les couronnes. Le couvre-chef royal varie suivant le degré de solennité de chaque cérémonie particulière. Si on laisse de côte, ce qui va sans dire, les moments où il porte un uniforme militaire (de maréchal ou d'amiral)

le Roi n'aura pas moins de trois couronnes dont il devra se servir, outre les trois chapeaux siamois qu'il portera pour se rendre au lieu de la cérémonie et pour en revenir.

Les trois couronnes sont :

1°—La grande couronne de la victoire avec laquelle le Roi accomplira lui-même le couronnement proprement dit, et qu'il portera aussi à la grande audience et quand il sera promené processionnellement sur le palanquin royal, à la chapelle du Boudha d'Emeraude et de là à la salle Dusit.

2°—La couronne du Kathin que le Roi devait sans doute porter à l'époque ancienne dans la cérémonie solennelle du Kathin (présentation des robes aux religieux par le Roi) et qu'il portera au moment de l'investiture de la reine, quand il recevra en audience les dames de la famille royale et de sa maison ainsi que d'autres de haut rang.

3°—La couronne personnelle du Kathin fabriquée spécialement pour chaque souverain et portée lors des cortèges royaux à travers la ville et sur la rivière.

Après les couronnes vient le grand parasol royal fait de toile blanche à bordure d'or, et composé de neuf étages, ce qui est la maque du pouvoir suprême. L'épée de la victoire, au fourreau richement émaillé est un autre insigne royal de toute première importance, de même que l'eventail et les souliers royaux. L'épée, le parasol l'éventail et les souliers constituent avec la grande couronne les cinq attributs classiques de la royauté. Les autres attributs qui suivent le Roi dans les cérémonies de grand apparat sont le sceptre et les chasse-mouche en poil de queue de yak et en poil de queue d'éléphant.

Parmi les objets personnels au Roi on compte le cordon brahmanique composé de fils, attribut traditionnel de Siva et l'épée personnelle presque toujours portée derrière Sa Majesté, même avant le couronnement, par un chambellan de la maison de Sa Majesté et les "Huit armes de la Souveraineté" qui ferment la marche du cortège royal. Le disque et le trident sont naturellement les attributs respectifs de Vishnu et de Siva.

L'animal et les choses domestiques dont la coutume locale prescrit l'usage lors de la cérémomie d'installation dans une résidence nouvelle sont : un chat (symbole de la vie domestique), une pierre à broyer (symbole de la stabilité), le cornichon (symbole de la fraicheur et par conséquent du bonheur) et les graines de pois et de sésame (prospérité et fertilité).

La cérémonie

Après avoir dûment fait profession de foi, et au temps jugé de bon augure, le Roi est invité par le Grand Prêtre de Śiva à prendre un bain rituel de purification et d'onction, dans un pavillon spécialement construit à cet effet, entre la sale Baisāl et la résidence du Chakrabarti Bimān. L'eau lustrale est un mélange : premièrement, d'eau des cinq principales rivières du Royaume ; deuxièmement, d'eau des quatre étangs de Subarna sanctifiée par un usage constant dans les cérémonies d'état qui comprennement un bain rituel (Mūrdhābhiṣeks) ; troisièmement, d'eau venue des dix-sept cercles consacrée de la façon ci-dessus.

Après ce bain, Sa Majesté se retire pour reparaître ensuite dans la salle Baisāl, en grand costume royal d'ancien temps.

Sur le Trône Octogonal, en bois de ficus, sous le parasol blanc d'apparat, le Roi reçoit de nouvelles ablutions des mains des Brahmanes qui, avec les Pandits de la Cour, représentent les huit régions cardinales du Royaume.

Sa Majesté se rend ensuite accompagué du cortège du trône octogonal à un autre trône dressé dans la partie Ouest de la salle Baisāl, appelé Bhadrapith (le Noble Trône) sous le dais d'un parasol d'apparat lequel, soit dit en passant, n'est pas encore un parasol à neuf étages, mais seulement à sept, le Roi n'étant pas encore pleinement couronné. Pour la même raison, le parasol qui surmonte le trône octogonal, n'a lui aussi que sept étages. Assis sur le Bhadrapith, face à l'Est, le Roi reçoit du grand prêtre de Śiva l'hommage de la cour, ainsi que son nom et ses titres gravés sur une tablette d'or dûment consacrée dans la Chapelle Royale du Bouddha d'Emeraude en même temps que les insignes de la royauté et tous leurs accessoires.

Sa Majesté prononce alors son premier commandement de Roi définitivement oint et couronné.

Cet article ci-dessus est extrait de l'Extrême Asie, Numéro 13, Juillet 1927.

The Tales of Buddhist Priests (VI)

By **A. Sakai**

(10) Priest Yuten

When Priest Jigaku (794–864) visited on a pilgrimage in 808 the province of Musashi, in which Tokyo is now situated, Fudo (Acala) or the god of fire appeared to him in a dream, telling him to enshrine his sacred statue for the benefit of the people of the province. The pious priest carved an image accordingly after the deity he met in the dream. It was an eye-black (meguro) image of Acala, and the place where it was enshrined was named Meguro (literally, eye-black). There are at present five shrines dedicated to the deity Fudo of different eye-colours in Tokyo ; namely,

Meki-Fudo	(eye-yellow)	at Komatsugawa
Meao-Fudo	(eye-blue)	at Setagaya
Meaka-Fudo	(eye-red)	at Hongo
Mejiro-Fudo	(eye-white)	at Koishikawa
Meguro-Fudo	(eye-black)	at Meguro

According to the ancient Chinese idea, by the way, the five colours have the following significances of directions, colours, elements and cardinal virtues :—

	Direction	Season	Element	Virtue
Yellow	center	"doyo"	earth	faith
Blue	east	spring	wood	humanity
Red	south	summer	fire	etiquette
White	west	autumn	metal	justice
Black	north	winter	water	wisdom

"Doyo" means the beginning of the four seasons.

Meguro, which is named after the Meguro Fudo or Eye-black Acala, is a new ward in Tokyo and it is always associated with the Yuten-ji Temple, for which the ward is known. The temple was built in commemoration of Priest Yuten.

Priest Yuten was son of Farmer Zembei, who lived in the province of Iwaki. When a little boy, he was so dull that his disgusted father took him to Edo (Tokyo) in 1645, when Yuten was ten years old, and left him under the care of Priest Dantsu of the Zojo-ji Temple.

"I will take good care of the boy and try to make a worthy priest of him," said Priest Dantsu.

Young Yuten was good for nothing. His head was as "thick as anything," and he had such bad memory that Priest Dantsu found it fruitless to try to teach him a single passage of any sutra. Though the boy was willing to learn anything, every effort on his part to learn the sutra was a failure.

"Say, block head," his fellow-priests would address him in derision, "What have you come all this distance from Iwaki to Edo for? It is a mere waste of money and time."

All sorts of ridicules and derisions were poured upon the dull priest, who bore them with good nature. Yuten on his part was conscious of his weak points and tried hard to overcome them, but to no purpose. He used to get up earlier in the morning than the other young priests and to sit up till late into the night, for he wanted to be something in life.

One day young Yuten appeared before Priest Dantsu when the latter was taking a rest in his own study.

"Reverend Priest," Yuten said crest-fallen.

"What is it? Any harsh treatment again?" asked the chief priest briefly, but kindly.

"They call me a fool and idiot," Yuten went on. "I know I am dull and good-for-nothing. I learn very little for all the efforts I make to learn things. Tell me, Reverend Priest, would it be impossible for me to learn anything or become anything in this life?"

"Success depends upon efforts one makes," Priest Dantsu said kindly, "You need not be discouraged, but study on as hard as you can and you will be a good priest."

"But, Holy Priest, I have poor memory — poorer than anybody else's," Yuten complained. "It is next to impossible to learn a single passage of any sutra. Is there no way of making my memory more retentive?"

"O yes, there is," said Priest Dantsu. "I know something that will help you, if you are in earnest."

"I am in earnest, Holy Priest," Yuten said in real earnest. "I am dying for good memory. I would

kill myself if I could not be anything in this life."

"Well, I will tell you something," Priest Dantsu said, telling the young priest to draw nearer to him. "Well, Yuten," the chief priest went on, "You have bad blood within you. That is what gives you bad memory. You are born dull. Fasting is the only means that will cure you. You repeat the O-Nembutsu-prayer heart and soul with undivided attention, asking for help from on high. Then your blood will be purified and you will have retentive memory."

"Thank you, Holy Priest. I will have fasting," Yuten said.

"But you can take nothing but water during your fasting, which will last not for two or three days, but for three seven-days or twenty-one days. For twenty-one days you would have to live on water and nothing else. You will then feel as if you were fainting. Do you think you can stand all this?"

"I can stand anyting so long as I get retentive memory," Yuten answered resolutely. "I would not care if my arms and legs were to be cut off. May I have fasting, Holy Priest?"

"O yes, you may, Yuten," said Priest Dantsu. "If you are so determined, you may shut yourself in the Fasting-Hall. You can begin it tomorrow."

"Why tomorrow? Must I wait till tomorrow?" asked the impatient young priest.

"You can begin at any time."

"I will begin right now," Yuten said decidedly. "I do not want to wait till tomorrow."

"But fasting is no joke," Priest Dantsu assured. "If you stop it before your time is up, you will incur the displeasure of the Lord Buddha."

"No, I will never give it up before it is over," Yuten said with strong determination.

Young Yuten shut himself in the Fasting-Hall. He sat with closed eyes amid the images of different high priests of the Zojo-ji Temple, repeating the Nembutsu-prayer of "Nam-O-Amitabha! Nam-O-Amitabha!"

The other young priests of the temple laughed at the idea of this simpleton undergoing a fast for twenty-one days, but Priest Dantsu was pleased with his fasting and often sent a young priest to see how Yuten was getting along. On the sixth day of his fasting, the chief priest repaired himself to the

Fasting-Hall. Yuten was repeating the Nembutsu-prayer as hard as he could.

"Yuten," the chief priest called gently.

Yuten opened his eyes and was surprised to see his master-priest.

"Reverend Priest," Yuten said, "I am all right. I can safely go through the 21-day fasting."

"I am glad that you say so," said Priest Dantsu, in encouragement. "The concentration of your mind is all you need now. Fasting is the way to Paradise. Cling to the Lord Buddha and you will be saved."

On the same day, when Yuten was repeating his prayers, half in a trance, he heard a voice calling his name.

"Yuten," it said, "you must come to Narita in the province of Shimosa. Pray the Merciful Fudo and your prayer will be heard."

Yuten called the name of the Lord Buddha and thanked Him for the command.

"You must come right now," the voice went on, "but you must keep silent about your coming to Narita. Have faith in me."

Yuten was lost in tears of gratitude and bowing reverently before the Main Image of the Fasting-Hall, he started at once for Narita. He had little knowledge of the streets of Edo nor had he any idea in which direction Narita lay. It was with great difficulty, therefore, that Yuten found himself on the highway which led to his destination.

He had fasted for six days at the Zojo-ji Temple, taking nothing but water and now he walked a distance of some 30 miles. He almost fell down several times through fatigue, but the kind voice that he heard in the Fasting-Hall always upheld him on the trip, till he tottered on to Narita.

"I have walked all the way from Edo to offer a prayer at the Fudo shrine," Yuten said, when he was brought before Gencho, the chief priest of the Fudo shrine. "I want to shut myself to have a fast in the Fudo shrine."

Yuten told him everything about his own poor memory, the conversation he had with Priest Dantsu of the Zojo-ji Temple, and the voice he heard in the Fasting-Hall, when Priest Gencho, in his admiration for the strong determination of Yuten offered him a meal so that he might begin his fasting on the following day.

"I should incur the displeasure

of the Lord Buddha," Yuten said "if I were to take anything before my time is up. I have had a week's fasting and I want to complete my 21-day fasting here in the Fudo shrine."

Yuten shut himself in the Fasting-Hall of the Fudo shrine, to complete his fast, and went on repeating the Nembutsu-prayer of the Six Words, but he was now too weak to open his eyes, when two days before the expiration of his time he heard another voice.

"Yuten," it called. Yuten turned and saw an old nun who looked as emaciated as himself. "Yuten," she said again, "the Fudo is pleased with your devotion and accepts your prayers. He tells you to go back to your temple at Edo."

"No, Holy Nun," Yuten replied sternly, "I will not leave this Hall before my time expires."

"But the Fudo will overlook your two days," the old nun said.

"But I should incure the displeasure of the Lord Buddha if I were to stop my fasting before my time," Yuten persisted.

"You are too stubborn to be saved," the old nun said, and she disappeared in the air.

Another temptation came to Yuten in the form of an old priest who offered him a cup of gruel one hour before the expiration of his fasting.

"You have done remarkably well," the old priest said to Yuten. "One hour from now and your time is up. Take this gruel, for you must be hungry."

Yuten was now too weak to receive the cup with his hands, and he kept still, repeating his prayers.

"Won't you take this?" the old priest asked him again.

"I would take nothing before my time is up," Yuten said.

"It is all the same as if your time had come," the tempting priest said.

Yuten was too weak to speak any more word and the old priest disappeared in the air.

Finally the Fudo made his august appearance before Yuten, who could hardly repeat his prayers now.

"Yuten, you must swallow one of my swords," the Fudo said, standing majestically before Yuten. "I have two swords: the longer one for wisdom and sagacity and the shorter for wits. Which would you prefer?"

"Give me the longer one," Yuten said in a weak voice.

The Fudo caught Yuten by the breast and forced the longer sword into his mouth, saying: "Yuten, your time has come and your prayers are heard."

At the expiration of Yuten's time of fasting, Priest Gencho came to the Fasting-Hall, where he found Yuten unconscious, blood coming out of his throat, which was broken by the constant repetition of the Nembutsu-prayer. When he came to himself, Yuten felt a new man. Priest Dantsu, of the Zojo-ji Temple, who had suspected that Yuten had given up his fasting, was pleased to hear the story of his patience. Yuten became a noted priest in Japanese Buddhism.

Priest Yuten is well-known for his power, that quieted the troubled spirit of Kasane, one of the most weird ghosts in Japan. There is a stone monument dedicated to her memory, on the compound of the Yuten-ji Temple, where Priest Yuten lies buried. Every time when the play of Kasane is acted on the stage, as it often is, the actors who take part in it offer wreathes to the monument so that their representation may prove a success. The story of Kasane follows:—

Farmer Yoyemon lived at the village of Hanyu in Shimosa Province. He married a wife who brought with her a 6-year-old boy by the name of Suke with her whom she bore by her former husband. Suke had such ugly looks that his step-father was quite disgusted with him, till he told his wife to do away with her son, which she did by pushing him into a rapid river called the Kinu River on Apr. 19, 1612.

In the following year a daughter was born to Yoyemon and his wife, but she was the very image of her dead half-brother, whom her mother had killed. According to records, her skin looked like dried rind of an orange and her face was as black as lacquer. Her name was Orui, but the people of her village called her Kasane (another pronunciation of the same character) possibly meaning "repetition," because she was the living likeness of her dead half-brother.

A Buddhist pilgrim, who happened to come to the village of Hanyu married Orui on account of the small estate that she owned after the death of her parents. But when he saw how ill-natured his wife was, he made up his mind to kill her, and she too was drowned in the same River Kinu on Aug. 11, 1653.

Yoyemon, for the Buddhist assumed the name of his father-in-law after his death, married a second wife, who died immediately after her marriage. His third wife soon followed the second. Yoyemon married six wives besides Orui, who all died without children,

excepting the last one, who bore him a daughter, whose name was O-Kiku. It was this daughter who became mad and said that she was Orui reborn, whom her father had drowned twenty years before. She said also that she had killed all the wives of Yoyemon in order to pay off old scores. Priest Yuten was invited to appease her troubled spirit, and she was cured, O-kiku died on May 3,1730, at the age of 72 years.

On Nov. 23, 1707 when there was a great eruption of Mt. Fuji, Lord Tsunayoshi, the 5th Shogun of Tokugawa dynasty, called Priest Yuten to his Shogunate castle and asked him the significance of the great disaster.

"It is quite an unnatural occurrence that sand, which is found on the ground, should fall from heaven," Priest Yuten said *inter alia* in his explanation, "but no less unnatural it is that beasts, which rank below man, should be elevated above him."

Lord Tsunayoshi was very fond of dogs, and many people were condemned to death because they were not kind to dogs, till he was surnamed "Inu-Kubo" (or "Dog-Shogun), and Priest Yuten hinted that the law should be nullified that condemned man for a bad treatment of dogs. The Shogun appeared displeased with his bold remark, but on the following day he called the priest again to the castle, and admitted his mistake. The law was revised to the great relief of the people of Edo, the Shogunate capital.

Priest Yuten lived at Meguro, where he built a small hermitage, and he died at the age of 83 years in 1718. After his death, his favorite disciple, Priest Yukai, built the Yuten-ji Temple in commemoration of Priest Yuten, under the patronage of the Shogun Tsunayoshi Tokugawa.

The Measles Stone: The Measles Stone is found in front of Priest Yuten's grave on the compound of the Yuten-ji Temple, Meguro. The stone has a hole about 15 inches in diameter, through which a mother is often seen to push her little child three times back and forth, murmuring a prayer, for it is believed that no child that passes through this hole in this way will suffer from a serious case of the measles. According to a priest of the temple, Priest Yuten once had a long argument about religion with a devil till it was convinced of its mistake, so that the people who believe that Priest Yuten subdued the devil bring their children to commit them to his protection against the measles.

Is Buddhism A Religion?

By **Kunitoshi Oka**

Is Buddhism a religion? As to this question, there are various answers. Some of them are negative, and the others are positive. The former hold that Buddhism is a mere ethical doctorines teaching the self-culture, or the philosophical system based on pantheism. The latter, however, hold that Buddhism is a genuine religion to become Buddha or to get to Nirvana the highest Enlightenment.

But to my own opinion, we have an inevitable preliminary problem to decide the question whether Buddhism is a religion or not. That is the theme "What is a religion?" Without the answer for this question, our discussion are all endless dispute.

Then I will clear up the idea of religion-in-general. The problem, however, is also very difficult one to dicide up fully. But we may say safely that Religion is the Human Life having relation with the Holy and Transcendent World. In the world of religion, the belief in Personal God is not always necessary. This fact has been cleared up by the so-called "Theorists of holy idea"; as Durkheim, the French sociologist of religion, Windelband, German philosopher of West Southern School of Germany, and Rudolf Otto, the German philosopher of religion, etc.

According to them, the essential element of religion-in-general is the "Idea of holiness or sacredness." And holiness or sacredness is, at once, the transcendental life, beyond world and irrational consciousness. After all, religion is the absolute and holy human life superior to all other earthly life. Until we come to such a religious life, we can never become happy or peaceful man. Without having such a religious faith, all the wealth even in the world is in vain.

Religion is the highest and final perfection we human can attain.

Here again I will ask myself "Is Buddhism a religion?" But I think and believe, it is no more need to discuss as to the religiosity of Buddhism, since Buddhism has the

above mentioned religious essence common to all religions. Buddhist thoughts are fulled of the idea of holiness or sacredness they theorists of holy idea hold. For examples, the idea of Buddha, the Enlightenment, and the idea of Dhamma are all belong to the world of the Holiness, or Beyondness or the Transcendental life. Thus, theism is no more the only criterion of religiosity.

European people often say that Buddhism is "A rational or scientific religion." Yes, indeed, but it only shows that Buddhism is "More" rational or scientific than the other religions, and nothing more than. Buddhism as a religion, it has some elements that can not be explained by reason or rationality alone. It is not a religion that may be explained up fully by human reason or intellect. Religion will never be inconsistent with reason or intellect, but it is always above these human reason or intellect. Can we explain up the idea of Buddha, Dhamma or the Enlightenment by our reason alone? Nay, never at all.

I have showed the religiosity of Buddhism. In the end, I will discuss on the difference between Christianity and Buddhism as a religion, to help the understanding of Buddhism more perfectly. Christianity and Buddhism are the two great representative religions in the world. But each has its own characteristic feature. Here I will pick up the most important point.

Christianity founded upon the Semitic thought is a sort of Dualism, as God and Man or Heaven and Earth, etc. To divide sharply into the two different categories, here is the characteristic of Christianity. In other word, there are all kinds of dualistic oppositions in Christianity. The relation between the two different categories is Christianity. There is no idea of Oneness or identification, but opposition-idea or relation-idea only. These are the special feature of Semitic Christian thoughts.

Buddhism, however, has a unique characteristic, the thoughts of Oneness or identification of the two different categories. This is the Buddhist Monism or pantheism. Of course, Buddhism starts from dualism, but it is not the final goal nor highest ideal, only the stepping stones to the absolute state of oneness or monistic identification of the two different categories. At the only begining step, Buddhism also has the oposition-relation between the two categories; as Buddha and Sattva (Man), Bodhi and worldly passion, or Nirvana and the life of death and re-birth, etc. But these relation and opposition between the two different categories become Oneness through the Mogsa the absolute Enlightenment or Nirvana.

Thus, the phenomenal world is equal to the real world, Man to Buddha, world-passion to Bodhi, and the Earthly life is equal to Sukhavati the Blessed Land, etc. Such oneness of the two different categories or the monistic identification is the very characteristic in Buddhism.

In Christianity, man is man for ever, never can become God. Because, God is the only one absolute ruler. This is the Semitic Dualism. In Buddhism, man can become Buddha the perfect absolute One, through the Enlightenment. This is the Buddhist monism or pantheism. (to say accurately, this words monism or pantheism are not proper.)

Here I must modify the traditional definition of religion "the relation between man and God" — to "Reliigion is to become God" or to use the Buddhist phrase, "To become Buddha the highest Personality". And so, we can not say that the mere relation between man and God is the religion. To become "The Absolute and Holy One" is the final and highest goal or ideal of all religions. Buddhism teaches us the various ways to this religious world. Here are the branches of Buddhist sect. On these points I will refer to some time or other.

February 15th, 1937.

A Brief Message to Young Shinranists

By **Isao Ito**

I feel convinced that the doctrines of Buddhism — the religion founded by the noble Shakamuni — is from the respective standpoints of philosophy and psychology the most profound of all religions to be found in the world today. But of all Buddhist sects now flourishing in Japan Shin is, as Prof. Reischauer justly claims, the most progressive as well as the most humanitarian sect. It is truly representative of the practical aspect of Buddhism.

Since its establishment in 1224 by Shinran Shonin the history of the sect has now come to cover a period of more than seven hundred years. But a brief glimpse of the fact that many foreigners are unaware of even the name of St. Shinran is enough to make us young Shinranists feel poignantly the necessity of propagating the true spirit of the sect among foreigners and studying profoundly its doctrines.

Of course, the missionary spirit of the Hompa Honganji is well known for its evangelical activities in foreign countries. Among these may be enumerated Hawaii, North America, and so on. We should not, however, feel satisfied with these achievements but should strive to make known the doctrines to those who have not yet grasped them. We (and I mean here the younger students particularly) must consider the best method of carrying out this object. When we look back upon the many learned priests who gave a new impetus to the developement of the Honganji and led it into the position of the most influential denomination we cannot help bearing in mind the following thoughts. The Shin doctrines are not for our countrymen but for our countrymen but for countless others as well.

I am quite sure that Shinran Shonin is awaiting the time when his teachings will find convert among foreigners and gain influence in all parts of the world.

We, the young students, must devote ourselves heart and soul to the study of the Shin doctrines, and at the same time must remember that the Shin sect is not only ours but also the possession of all mankind. I am sure that this is treading in the true foot marks of the Great Leader.

Unless we ourselves put forth our best efforts the doctrines of Shin will perhaps never attain its universal goal. The undefiable spirit of its believers have made it what it is today, and it is up to us to build the church of the future.

And what a joyful panorama will be spread before us when this great church of the future does come into its own!

學國的に海外傳道費を撚出して

佛教外交の一元化

——宗派確執を清算して共同戰線へ——

廣　瀬　了　義

私の過去卅年間の海外旅行で我佛教の浸潤してゐる異境を歴訪しての感想を總括して日本佛教の海外發展策のお答へに代えたい。

先づ最初に日本佛教を外國に移殖する對象から定めてから論を進めねばならぬ。

1. 在外の我同胞に佛教信仰を目標とすれば,
   イ. 第一世に, 祖國愛の强調と佛教々理の宣揚。
   ロ. 第二世に, 市民たるの教養と父祖の地の追懐思慕の情を滿たさせつつ我佛教の特質を宣明。
2. 純然たる外人へ堂々と我佛教の大乘精神を强調して耶蘇教と對立して進展の氣魄を示す運動。

この對象の如何でその手段なり宣傳の方法も自ら異になることは當然であるが,

1. 我佛教の概念なり儀式作法, 習慣などの骨子を平明に要領よく紹介せる圖書を諸外國語に譯して世界各國の大學, 博物館, 圖書館, クラブ, 社交團體, 彼我の大公使館などに配布すること。又一般有志の外人には實費で弘く頒つこと。
2. 宗教映畫・レコードを製作して各國の觀光局, ホテル等と連絡して我佛教の輪廓を周知せしむること。
3. 海外布教師機關を各宗合同事業として起して我外務, 拓務, 文部省などの協力を求め又海外移民會社とも連絡を保ちその實動に權威あらしむること。

等を宗教國策として研究せしめたものである。

次に海外傳道にあたる者の素質の向上を圖ることは最も急務である。

1. 外國語に達者で, 外國の事情にも通じ佛教, 哲學, 法政經濟の學にも明かで, 社會事業スポーツ等にも相當の教養あることを要す。(資格審査)
2. 筋肉運動には自ら進んで從事する言行一致の人で, 場合に依つては農耕を始め自動車の運轉などをも厭はず, 又布教傳道の外に教育者としては, 幼稚園, 小・中・高女生徒の教育, 青年會, 老人居, 勞働者, 留學生, 歐米漫遊の旅行者などにも隨時隨所に會合して親切なる指導者, 相談者たること。
3. 外地にあつては醜き同胞が相鬩ぐ弊風一掃に力めしめ又我海外にあるものの因襲的一切の惡風を矯め我日本精神, 佛教精神に依る美風良俗を培ひ, 惹いては耶蘇教などにも優る佛教々理なり人類愛の體現者として範を示させるだけの力の人を送ること。
4. 自ら好んで外人と交遊して我日本佛教の大乘的見地から外人にも容易に我佛教に歸依し得られる法悦さを體驗せしむるだけの熱意と根氣ある逸材を海外に送ること。
5. 又これら海外派遣の開教師には所屬の宗派は言ふまでもなく各種宗教團體, 報道機關なども學つて聲援し政府筋にても適當に指導し場合によつては之が援助をも惜まざること。

我佛教の戰士を海外に送る機關の完備と適當の人を獲られたならば如何にして, 如何なる地方に我戰士を配置するかが重大問題である。從來の例によると我移民先又は南米あたりは別として大體各地方に日本佛教は行渡つてゐるやうであるが, そのスケジユールは未だ狹隘微力たるを免れない。そこになると耶蘇教徒では外人との密接な關係がついてゐるので大規模に積極的に呼びかけてゐるので, その社會施設なども完璧を期してゐる。近頃我佛教でも寺院・殿堂・學校・病院なども稍形はつきかけたが彼に比しては多分の遜色がある。それには何としても資金の潤澤が必須條件となつてゐる。我佛教の開教師も昨今でこそ各宗本山でも乘氣になつて馬力もかけてゐるが, 我移民の黎明時代には殆んど, 我當局では彼等の存在を顧みられないで, 棄民扱ひをうけ迫害視せられてゐた。又開教師にもイカサマものが跋扈したり又同じ佛教徒でありながら商賣敵として極端, 露骨な醜い排他的行動をみせつけられて移民の信者から愛想をつかされ外人からは佛教そのものの眞價をすら疑はれたことも決して珍しくなかつた。然し開教師でも殉教的な識者もゐて地盤も鞏まり, これから本氣に雄飛しようとすると, 本山なり海外漫遊の所謂宗教家から冥加金を搾取せられるので却つて反感をもたれたものだ。更に近頃となつて急に海外開教師を志願する人々が增したが, ともすれば一獲千金を夢みて渡航する出稼根性で出かけるものが往々あるのは大に警めねばならぬ。

最後に外人から覯られてゐる我佛教はともすれば (1) 教義の深遠幽玄にしてとりつきがたいこと, (2) 小乘的見地から隱遁, 退嬰, 禁欲などの權化のごとき先入があるのが佛教弘通の上に多大の支障があるのである。これらの迷夢を醒まさせ佛教を, もつと現代化せしめ科學的に解譯して研究せしむる端緒を拓いてかからねばならぬ。米國あたりでは滿洲事變後, 日本研究が流行し日本語研究, 日本佛教の歸依者がチラホラ現出しつつある傾向があるのは, 洵に慶しいのであるから, 佛教學の專攻者で英語の達者なものを彼國に遣はすとか, 或は歐米各地の諸大學に日本講座, 東洋講座のあるところとか彼我交換教授のある場合には拔目なく我佛教の資料をこれらに提供して日本文化紹介に必要なエレメントたらしむるとか歐米の各部市の美術館の我佛教に關する陳列品の說明に我佛教思想の要旨を掲げしめその謬れる箇所を訂さしむる事なども一の啓蒙運動である。

從來我佛教徒が歐米人に對しては一部專門家同志を除いては餘り無關心すぎてゐた。今後はもつと我等青年佛徒等が陣頭に立つて歐米先進國に向つて佛教の大旆を翳して行進曲を奏でなくてはならない。(完)

開教師の被選擧權

——外務省令の改廢を要望す——

淺野研眞

一

居留民團法は，明治三十八年三月八日，法律第四十一號として公布されたものであるが，その施行規則たる居留民團法施行規則は，大正十三年十二月七日外務省令第九號として公布されたものである。

而して昭和八年二月四日，並に昭和九年十二月十一日の兩度も改正されてゐるものである。

然るに茲に問題となることは右の省令たる施行細則に於て，開教師が居留民會議員の被選擧權から，除外されてゐることである。

即ち，居留民會議員の被選擧權は，「年齡二十五年以上の男子」に廣く開放されてゐるにも拘らず，「神官，神職，僧侶，其の他の諸宗教師」はその被選擧權を有せざることに規定されてゐる。（第十二條）

實は，かうした條項は，國內法に於ては，所謂普通選擧法の實施以來，中央的にも，地方的にも，既に久しい以前に改廢されてゐるものなのである。

それを昭和八年にも亦昭和九年にも，改正をして居り乍ら，右の條項を存置して居るのは，甚だしく心得ないことである。

故に吾人は，これが即時改廢を要望して止まないものである。これ，この一小論を執筆せる所以に外ならない。

二

尤も今日，組織的な居留民團の存在してゐるのは，天津，上海，漢口などであつて，主として支那に於けるものであるが，これらの地方には，日本の各宗各派の開教師が，それぞれ派遣されて居て，既に永年にわたつて活動してゐるのである。

勿論，その開敎師の中には，いかがはしいやうな者がないでもなからうが，その多くは，高等敎育を受けた有爲の人々である。それは各宗派の開教歷史を記述するまでもなく，大體に於て，之を認めて良いであらう。外務省の寺島前文書課長などもこれを認めてゐられて，吾人の要望を是とせられてゐた。

然し，とかくモダン型の多い外務省官吏諸氏の中には，特に「坊主ぎらひ」の人々も相當にあるらしい。諸宗教師と云つても，その大半は佛敎僧侶であるので，その點が特に目立つのかも知れない。

然し此は「個人」の感情の問題ではなくして，「國家」の政策の問題であることを忘れてはならない。變な私情で國策が誤られてはならない。

歐米諸國が盛んに「治外法權」を振りかざして，キリスト教會の「神聖性」を確保し，それを以つて國力發展のセンターとしたことは，餘りにも著明な事實ではないか？

然るに日本外務省のみは，その「弱腰」政策？に忠ならんとするためでもあるまいのに，何故，何時までも，こんな時代錯誤な條項を存置して置くのだらうか？

とにかく，今からでも決して遲くはないから，此の自縄自縛的な惡條項を直ちに廢止されんことを要望して止まないのである。（完）

スワミ尊者の追憶

醫學博士　內田孝藏

今日はスワミ尊者の一週忌に當り，私は同尊者を思ひ出して實に感慨無量のものがあります。

達磨大師が印度から支那へ來て行き倒れになつた事は誰も知つて居る。然しながら達磨は自分が行き倒れたために所謂印度の佛教を最も根强く支那に植えつけ得た。恰も一粒の種が地に落ちて己れの身を無くした爲め其の植物が幾萬倍といふ程枝も榮えて葉も茂る様に支那の佛教を榮えしめたのであつた。

スリ・デナワンサ・スワミ尊者の我國への渡來と，そして其の最期を考へる時，私は祖師達磨を思ひ合はさないで居られない。達磨大師にしろ，スワミ尊者にしろ，言葉の通じないことと氣候の變り方の甚しいといふ此の二者が彼らを倒れしめた最後の强敵であつたのである。

お釋迦様と其の鄉里を同じうせる尊者は，恐らく，お釋迦様當時の佛敎に最も似通つた宗敎觀念を持つて居たと察せられる。

ところが日本といふ國は色々と變形した佛教を多數の人が信じて居る佛教國である。尊者が其の日本へ，達磨大師の支那行と同じ希望と同じアコガレを胸に抱いて遠くヤツテ來られた事は想像に難くない。然るに其のアコガレは見事に裏切られた。佛敎國としては，僧侶及び信者の質に於ても量に於ても日本が世界第一と，思ひつめて，はるばる渡來した尊者が，其の現實と豫想とのチガイ方の甚だしいのに驚いた事は，恐らく言葉や氣候のチガイに驚いたより以上の驚きであつたらうと思はれる。けれど此の尊者は失望しなかつた。俺は此の國に踏み留まつて何處までも本當の佛教を廣めたい。此の國コソ自らの骨を埋むべき國土であると觀念した。

そうした大決心を尊者に堅からしめた日本ではあつたが，昨年の寒氣は，亦格別であつた。東京は五十幾年か振りの寒さだと云はれる位であつたから，それが尊者にはヒドクコタえたのであつた。一昨年の第一回の冬はドウにか越せたけれども，昨年の第二回の冬のアノ嚴寒には勝てなかつた。周圍の人々が種々手厚い介抱をされたが遂ひに再び立たず，恰度今日から一年前の二月十七日安らかに眠るが如く大往生を遂げられたのである。六十一歲の高齡であつた。彼の健康が抱負に共調しなかつたのである。一面には憫むべき御最期でもあつたのである。

然し尊者當人には更に何ら苦痛を感ずるらしく見えなかつた。その燃ゆるが如き布敎の熱願は常に彼の持物であるタイプライターのキーの音を絶やした事がなかつた。寒いとか辛いとかそんな言葉は一言も彼の口から洩れなかつた。その點は實に敬服の至りである。

然るに右の様な誰もが感ずるトホリ一ペンの感想よりも私だけが特に感じた尊者に對する心持を私はココに述べて置き度いと思ふ。

先づ私は尊者が眞の佛敎家らしく五戒を完全に守り徹して吳れた事に感激したのである。寒い國へ來れば誰しも一パイ飮んで溫まり度いのが人情である。佛教に不飲酒戒のある事をさへ忘れてゐる佛教信者の多い日本の佛教といふものも，確かに尊者を驚かしたものの一つであつたのである。

言葉が通じなかつたとか寒氣がヒドカツタとか，そんな事は實は初めから分り切つて居る。瘦軀鶴の如き此の老人を此土地に長く置けば遂ひには病死を免れぬといふ位の事は醫者でなくても常識を持つた一般の人が見ればわかる事だ。それだからこそ我々は一昨年すでにドレほど尊者に歸國を勸めたか知れなかつたのである。佛靑聯盟からも印度までの郵船會社の船の切符まで買つて上げて，是非お歸りなさいと言つたのであつた。が，歸らうとは言はれなかつた。のみならず，喜んで日本の土になるのだと言ひ通した。强情としか思へぬまでに日本に執着してゐた。我々の方でも，イクラ頑張つても少し寒くなれば我を折つて歸り度いと言ひ出すだらう位に思つて居ると我を折るどころかトウトウ倒れて死ぬまで一言半句も故鄕の事を口にしなかつたのである。斯程まで意志の强い人を今まで見た事がなかつたのである。

それだけに亦，私にとつては此の人間スワミ尊者に對する哀惜の念が人一倍に强いのである。平たく云へば死なれたと言ふよりは寧ろ私が殺した樣に思へてならなかつたのである。といふのは，一昨年，尊者が佛靑大會に出席のため來朝されて，ホテルに滯在して居られた時から，いろいろ御世話をした私として，或る時は私の家へ二ケ月も宿泊して貰つたり，又，當月桂寺さんへ賴んで數ケ月間面倒を見て頂いたりした其の樣な皮相な親切が却つて仇となつて折角の彼の雄圖を可惜挫いたのではなかつたか，と私は自責されてならないのである。イクラ日本が寒いと言つたつて煖房設備もあれば，我々の不充分な御世話以上のモツト溫い心の人々も他にあつたかも知れん。今少し私が徹底した親切をし向ける事が出來たら或は此の老いたる旅人をして斯くの如き悲慘な最期を遂げしめないであつたらうにと私は尊者の臨終を聞いた時どの位，後悔したか知れなかつたのである。

これといふのも要するに私の修業の足りなかつたばかりに斯んな事になつたのであります。事コヽに思ひ至る時今でも私は非常な憂鬱になるのであります。

今日此の一週忌の席上に於て，私は皆さんとは全く異つた左の如き自責の念で一杯であります。尊者が最後に私に無言の裡に訓へて行かれたことは實に偉大な或るものでありました。そして私は，私もいつかは尊者の樣な立派な心境に入り度いと念願する事切なるモノがあります。

宇宙に於ける永劫から永劫に連つてゐる時間と空間とを思ふ時，我々の生涯がホンノ一瞬時であり，我等の生死また語るに足らぬ一小些事に過ぎないのであります　。希くは尊者の死が或るモノを私に訓へた如く幾年か幾十百年か後世の我が日本國土に於て達磨の支那に於けると同樣，永久に朽ちぬ尊い大きいモノを遺して頂ける樣にありたいと，私は潜越乍らシカク望み度いのであります。

昨年の今日，スワミ尊者御臨終に於ける，寧ろ羨ましきまで餘りにも解脫したる態度を想ひ起こし，けふ一週忌を迎へて，思はず愚痴をコボシテ皆樣の御淸聽を煩はしました。

昭和十二年二月十七日

中國佛學會分會組織通則

奉　中國國民黨中央執行委員會民衆訓練部
二十五年十一月七日第四九五〇號批答核准

第一條　各省縣市會員得依據本會會章第十三條之規定設立分會。

第二條　各分會名稱繫以該地地名稱爲中國佛學會某分會。

第三條　各分會會務由本會直接指導外並應受所在地黨政機關之監督指導。

第四條　組織分會應依遵中央修正人民團體組織方案及本通則之規定辨理之

第五條　組織分會手續應依照本通則第一條之規定由發起人報經本會理事會許可並須擬有計劃呈請當地高級黨部轉呈中央民衆訓練部核准方得設立分會籌備處。

第六條　分會籌備處由發起員推定五人至七人爲籌備員報由本會經理事會之通過發給籌備證書。

第七條　設立分會籌備處一月後應將入會人名冊報經本會理事會審查後再定期開成立大會選擧理事五人至七人監事三人至五人。

第八條　分會選出之理監事應將其履歷造送本會經理事會審查後發給當選證

第九條　分會成立及改組時應函請本會派員指導並呈請當地黨政機關指導監選。

第十條　分會理事會互選常務理事三人至五人報本會備查。

第十一條　分會如遇有特別情形者得參照本會會章第十條第十一條規定行之並得於本通則第十條所定理事員額酌爲增減但概須報經本會之認可。

第十二條　分會理監事任期一年連選得連任。

第十三條　分會辨理本會會章第十二條所列及徵求會員各事項。

第十四條　分會會員大會每年至少須開會一次其所議決之重要議案須提交本會複議後辨理之。

第十五條　分會經費依照本會會章第十五條辨理之但如遇特別事故須籌辨特別捐者應由分會提出本會會員大會通過呈請當地高級黨部轉呈中央民衆訓練部核准後方得擧辨之。

第十六條　分會行動有違背會章及本通則者本會得遣派代表指導或改組之。

第十七條　本通則如有未盡事宜由本會理事會議決修改之。

◇スワミ長老の建碑式（二月十七日）◇

中國佛教會災區救護團章程

第一條　本團依據中國佛教會章程第四條第七項規定組織之，故名定曰中國佛教會災區救護團。

第二條　本團以共盡國民義務之旨，實行大乘救世精神，救護各種災難變故爲宗旨。

第三條　本團總部設於中國佛教會總辨事處，所在地設分團，於各縣市分會均稱爲中國佛教會災區救護團某縣或某市分團。

第四條　本團設團長一人由中國佛教會理事長兼任之，各分團各設團長一人，由各該分會理事長兼任之設副團長二人，由各該理事中推選任之。

第五條　本團職務如左・・・・

（一）戰時得請求軍事長官，或戰地司令地官之許可，由本團派救護人員救護受傷兵民。

（二）遇有災變發生時，設立收容所，收容被難災民。

（三）急救受傷兵民。

（四）收殮及掩埋被難兵民無主棺柩。

第六條　本團部設下列各股・・・・

醫務股，凡醫藥診療等事均屬之。

救護股，凡擔架運送急救等事均屬之。

收容股，凡收容災區被難人民等事均屬之。

掩埋股，凡收殮掩理等事均屬之。

文牘股，凡往來文牘編輯保管等事均屬之。

會計股，凡預算決算收支款項等事均屬之。

庶務股，凡本團一切庶務均屬之。

各股辦事細則別訂之。

第七條　本團設總幹事一人，各股視職務之繁簡，各設主任一人，幹事若干人，由團長聘任或雇用之。

第八條　各地如遇災變發生時，得隨時召集各團員組織臨時救辯隊出發救護。（臨時出發救護隊規則別訂之）

第九條　凡年在二十一歲以上，四十五歲以下僧衆，均有爲本團々員之義務以盡國民天職。

第十條　本團々員均應受救護工作各種常識，及關於戰地各種救護動作之訓練。

第十一條　各分團須將團員登記表名冊呈報總團部備核，並應將團員變動或死亡報告表隨時報請總團部查考，其團員登記表，及團員變動報告表，由總團部製發之。

第十二條　本團旗幟以長方形黃地紅佛字爲標幟。

第十三條　本團員服裝平時仍着原有僧衣，訓練及服務時，着圓領短僧衣，一律灰色，各佩臂章，黃地紅色佛字，帽亦黃色頂繡一紅佛字。

第十四條　各分團組織時，須呈報本會暨當地黨政機關備案。

第十五條　本團及分體經費得依照佛教寺廟興辦公益慈善事業規則征收撥用之，如遇重大災變發生，原有經費不敷支用時，得組織募捐隊，臨時募集補充之。

第十六條　本團及各分團經費之收支，每月造具報告表，由中國佛教會審核之，其臨時募集款項，隨時登報公告之。

第十七條　本簡章由中國佛教會理事會通過後，呈請中央黨政機關核准施行。

第十八條　本章程如有應行修改之處，得由本團總部聲敍理由，請中國佛教會決議修改，並呈報中央備案。

中國佛教會災區救護團僧衆訓練班綱要

一，本綱要依據中國佛教會，災區救護團章程第十條訂定之，凡本團々員均應受本綱要所規定編制訓練。

二，各分團成立後，即應舉辦團員登記，照總團部所規定。凡各該縣區僧衆年在二十一歲以上四十五歲以下僧衆。均應報名登記爲團員。

三，各分團々員登記辦理完竣後，應擇相當地點召集各團員編制訓練。

四，各分團僧衆訓練班學科術科如左・・

甲，學科

一，佛教精神講話。

二，生理學及衞生學。

三，藥性常識。

四，日來弗條約及陸地戰例綱要。

五，繃綳帶法。

六，救護法則。

七，軍事常識。

八，毒氣防止法。

乙，術科

一，擔架法。

二，普通初步操法。

三，實習救護動作。

五，訓練班之教練員，得由各縣市分團自行聘請專家擔任之。

六，團員受訓期間，暫定爲三個月，其人數較多之縣（市），得分區或分期舉行。

七，團員受訓之費用由各該寺廟擔負。

八，團員受訓時，不得無故缺課或籍故規避，如有違犯，應由各該團提請當地佛教分會嚴重議處，並呈報中國佛教會備案。（完）

段祺瑞氏追悼會

中日密教研究會の外廓團體たる東亞密教協會では，前者の會長たる段祺瑞氏が去歲十二月二日上海で長逝して去る二月九日は百ケ日忌に相當する。生前同氏は中日密教研究會長として多年兩國民衆の精神的結合と東洋平和のため盡瘁したので同日午後五時から丸の內日本工業俱樂部で政界，財界並に中日密教會員により盛大に追悼會を執行した。當日は各團體より贈られたる花輪，殊に寺內大將，中村前陸軍大臣より供へられた供物は一入參列者の眼をひいた。總裁高岡大僧正の隨喚文，主催者代表正木直彥，許大使，發起人代表岡部子爵の燒香追悼文あり，終つて食堂に入り一同會食，デザートコースに入り正木主催者側代表，高岡總裁，田中前總裁代理，許大使尾崎靜岡支部長，坂西中將，小幡貴院議員，横堀博士，鈴木元天津駐屯軍司令官，水野梅曉，寺西大佐，草鹿古義總務諸氏の各テーブルスピーチあり，いづれも故人の卓見德望並に東洋平和に寄與せる功績を贊稱し，九時三十分散會した。尙は別室にて故人の遺品を展覽した。

サ　ラ　ナッ タ ヤ ム

Saraṇattayaṁ

三 歸 依〔巴利語〕

（1）ブツダム　サラナム　ガツチヤーミ
Buddhaṁ saraṇaṁ gacchāmi,
〔我れ〕佛に　歸依したてまつる，

ダンマム　サラナム　ガツチヤーミ
Dhammaṁ saraṇaṁ gacchāmi,
〔我れ〕法に　歸依したてまつる，

サンガム　サラナム　ガツチヤーミ
Saṅghaṁ saraṇaṁ gacchāmi.
〔我れ〕僧に　歸依したてまつる。

（2）ドチヤン　ピ　ブツダム　サラナム　ガツチヤーミ
Dutiyam pi buddhaṁ saraṇaṁ gacchāmi,
二たび　又〔我れ〕佛に　歸依したてまつる，

ドチヤン　ピ　ダンマム　サラナム　ガツチヤーミ
Dutiyam pi dhammaṁ saraṇaṁ gacchāmi,
二たび　又〔我れ〕法に　歸依したてまつる，

ドチヤン　ピ　サンガム　サラナム　ガツチヤーミ
Dutiyam pi saṅghaṁ saraṇaṁ gacchāmi.
二たび　又〔我れ〕僧に　歸依したてまつる。

（3）タチヤン　ピ　ブツダム　サラナム　ガツチヤーミ
Tatiyam pi buddhaṁ saraṇaṁ gacchāmi,
三たび　又〔我れ〕佛に　歸依したてまつる，

タチヤン　ピ　ダンマム　サラナム　ガツチヤーミ
Tatiyam pi dhammaṁ saraṇaṁ gacchāmi,
三たび　又〔我れ〕法に　歸依したてまつる，

タチヤン　ピ　サンガム　サラナム　ガツチヤーミ
Tatiyam pi saṅghaṁ saraṇaṁ gacchāmi.
三たび　又〔我れ〕僧に　歸依したてまつる。

國際佛教通報局定款

名　稱

第一，本局を國際佛教通報局と稱す

事 務 所

第二，本局の事務所を全日本佛教青年會聯盟本部に置く

目　的

第三，本局は日本內海及海外に向つて佛教事情の通報をなし，且つ佛教徒相互間の各種便宜を計るを以て目的とす

事　業

第四，本局の目的を達成するため左記の事業を行ふ

イ，日本內地及世界各國より佛教事情に關する質問の通報を行ふ

ロ，必要に應じ日本語及世界各國語を以て佛教事情の通報を行ふ

ハ，外國人の日本觀光に際しては各種の便益を與へ，特にその佛教に關する方面に於て之を爲す

ニ，定時或は隨時に各國語を以て文書の刊行をなす

ホ，その他必要と認めたる事業を行ふ

役　員

第五，本局の事務を處理するため左の役員を置く

イ，局　長　　一　名

ロ，幹　事　　三　名

ハ，評議員　　若干名

局長は本局の事務を總括す

幹事は本局の事務を處理す

評議員は局長の提案に依る重要事務を審議す

第六，評議員は左記の者を以て之に充つ

イ，全日本佛教青年會聯盟理事及主事

ロ，全日本佛教青年會聯盟理事會に於て推薦したる者

第七，局長及幹事は評議員會に於て決定す

第八，役員の任期は二ケ年とす（但し重任を妨げず）

經　費

第九，本局の經費は左記のものに依て之を支辨す

イ，本局基金の活用

ロ，寄附金

ハ，その他の收入

補　則

第十，本定款に記載せられざる事項は，凡て評議員會に於て協議す

第十一，第一回の役員は全日本佛教青年會聯盟理事會に於て決定す

定價			
定價	一部	金 二 十 錢	送料二錢
	一年	金二圓四十錢	送料不要

昭和十年四月卅日第三種郵便物認可
昭和十二年二月廿五日印刷（每月一回
昭和十二年三月一日發行　一日發行）

東京市外吉祥寺337
編輯發行兼印刷人　淺野研眞

東京市牛込區早稻田鶴卷町107
印刷所　株式會社東文社印刷所
電話牛込（34）1950番 5049番

東京市神田區一ツ橋二の三
發行所　國際佛教通報局
電話九段（33）4428番
振替東京83015番

昭和十年四月三十日第三種郵便物認可
昭和十二年二月二十五日印刷納本（每月一回
昭和十二年三月一日發行（一日發行） 國際佛教通報 第三卷 第三號

第二回

汎太平洋佛教青年會大會
紀要

THE PROCEEDINGS
of
THE Second
General Conference
of
Pan-Pacific Young Buddhists' Associations

(in Japanese, Chinese and English)

Held at Tokyo & Kyoto, July 18–23, 1934

Price ¥ 3.00

Compiled & Published
by
The Federation of All Y.B. As. of Japan,
Tokio, Kanda, Hitotsubashi, II-3

昭和十年四月三十日第三種郵便物認可 昭和十二年三月二十八日印刷納本 昭和十二年四月一日發行（每月一回一日發行）第三卷 第四號

The International Buddhist Bulletin
國際佛教通報

第三卷 昭和十二年四月 第四號〔Vol. III. March. $\frac{2503}{1937}$ No. 4.〕

四月號要目

東京 國際佛教通報局 發行
The International Buddhist Information Bureau
Tokyo, Kanda, Hitotsubashi, II–3
Annual Subscription, ¥2.40 (post free), Single Copies 20 sen (post 2 sen)

Staff of the Bureau

Hon. President	J. Takakusu
President	K. Ohmura
Secretary	S. Takagai
〃	B. Inaba
〃 (in chief)	Ken Assano

Advisers	H. Ui
〃	G. Asakura
〃	R. Hatani
〃	U. Ogiwara
〃	R. Higata
〃	T. Suzuki
〃	S. Suzuki
〃	S. Amakuki
〃	S. Nagai
〃	B. Matsumoto
〃	E. Uno
〃	C. Akamatsu
〃	Z. Ohmori
〃	K. Yabuki
〃	S. Onoh
〃	S. Katoh
〃	M. Anezaki
〃	G. Honda
〃	R. Sekimoto
〃	J. Sahegi
〃	R. Hanada
〃	H. Kohno
〃	R. Takaoka
〃	Z. Kobayashi
〃	S. Yamabe
〃	C. Akanuma
〃	E. Honda
〃	R. Ohmori
〃	E. Kawaguchi
〃	C. Yamakawa
〃	D. Tokiwa
〃	T. Tanimoto
〃	G. Tokiwai
〃	S. Ohtani
〃	E. Ohtani
〃	B. Mizuno
〃	I. Shibata
〃	S. Ando
〃	J. Shimomura
〃	S. Kikuzawa
〃	K. Norisugi
〃	T. Shibata
〃	K. Asano
〃	T. Watanabe
〃	G. Onoh
〃	K. Yanagizawa
〃	M. Shigemitsu
〃	E. Kanakura
〃	S. Tachibana

國際佛教通報局

名譽局長	高楠順次郎
局長	大村桂巖
幹事	鷹谷俊之
同	稲葉文海
同	淺野研眞

顧問（順序不同）	
〃	宇井伯壽
〃	朝倉曉瑞
〃	羽溪了諦
〃	荻原雲來
〃	干潟龍祥
〃	鈴木大拙
〃	鈴木宗忠
〃	天岫接三
〃	長井眞琴
〃	松本文三郎
〃	椎尾辨匡
〃	宇野圓空
〃	赤松智城
〃	大森禪戒
〃	矢吹慶輝
〃	小野清一郎
〃	加藤精神
〃	姉崎正治
〃	本田義英
〃	關本龍門
〃	佐伯定胤
〃	花田凌雲
〃	河野法雲
〃	高岡隆心
〃	小林瑞淨
〃	山邊習學
〃	赤沼智善
〃	本多惠隆
〃	大森亮順
〃	河口慧海
〃	山川智應
〃	常盤大定
〃	谷本　富
〃	常盤井堯猷
〃	大谷尊由
〃	大谷瑩潤
〃	水野梅曉
〃	柴田一能
〃	安藤正純
〃	下村壽一
〃	乘杉嘉壽
〃	芝田徹心
〃	淺野孝之
〃	渡邊哲信
〃	小野玄妙
〃	柳澤　健
〃	重光　葵
〃	金倉圓照
〃	立花俊道

The Tales of Buddhist Priests (7)

by A. Sakai

(11) Priest Ippen or Yugyo-Shonin

Priest Ippen may be said to be one of the greatest mendicants that Japan has produced in her Buddhism. He lived literally the life of a monk, always moving from place to place without staying anywhere for a long time. but he never begged for food, often going without eating anything for days when he received nothing to eat. Sometimes his asceticism kept him from sleeping on a bed for months on end when no bed was provided for him, nor did he have a bath unless it was offered him. He owned no other clothing than was given him. According to his principle, a Buddhist priest should live on what the Lord Buddha was pleased to give him, and Ippen travelled all through the country on pilgrimages, as his faith dictated him, till he was known by the name of Yugyo-Shonin (literally, Priest Meanderer).

Michihiro Kono, father of Priest Ippen, was a samurai or warrior in the province of Iyo on the isle of Shikoku (literally, four provinces). One night his wife saw in a dream that Bosatsu (Bodhi-sattva) entered her mouth, and she found herself with child. In course of time, in 1239, she was delivered of a son, whose childhood name was Shoju-maru (literally, pine-longevity-boy). This boy grew up to be Priest Ippen, founder of the Ji-shu sect of Buddhism. The name of Ji-shu (時宗), by the way, means the "time sect" as the characters now stand, but originally it meant a sect for the "people of the time," (時衆).

Michihiro, the warrior, was converted into Buddhism by assuming the Buddhist name of Jobutsu (literally, Buddha-like), and our young boy, then twelve years old, began to study Buddhism under him, till he too embraced the same faith at the age of fifteen years. He took the tonsure under Priest Enkyo (literally, Karma-religion)

and he called himself Zuien (literally, Karma-follower). He studied the Tendai sect, to which his master, Priest Enkyo, belonged, though later on he entered the Jodo sect, when he took the Buddhist name of Chishin (literally, Wise-truth).

One of his relatives had two concubines. One day, while they took a nap with their heads resting on a checker-board, their hair turned into two snakes and had a mortal fight against each other, till they had to be separated with a sword. In Japan, by the way, a bride has at her wedding what is called the Tsuno-kakushi (horn-hider) on her hair for hiding the imaginary horns of jealousy, which a woman is traditionally supposed to have. The alleged fight of the two snakes was no doubt based on this traditional saying or popular belief, and our young priest was deeply struck with the horror of human jealousy.

Upon the death in 1275 of his brother, who had succeeded to the family after the death of Jobutsu, his father, a relative of his attempted on the life of young Chishin on account of his small estate for which the former craved. Chishin escaped with a little wound, and his enemy committed suicide. But selfish malignancy on the part of his own kinsman made our religious-minded young man disgusted with the lustful life of this world, and he was now strongly determined to lead a life of devotion to Buddhism.

Our young priest left home on his life-long pilgrimage in 1275. First he visited the Hachiman shrine at Usa in Kyushu, where he confined himself for three circuits of seven days, namely, for twenty-one days, praying for his salvation and the power of helping the people. An oracle dictated him to Mt. Otoko, where he again underwent a self-confinement of twenty-one days, at the end of which he was told in revelation to proceed to Mt. Koya in Kii Province, where he offered a 100-day prayer. On the 15th of the 12th month (December), the last day of his prayer, in the year 1275, the Gongen or God Incarnate of the Lord Buddha appeared to him in the form of an old priest and said: "Because you take pity upon the people, the Nembutsu-prayer is suggested as a means of supreme nature. You go on a pilgrimage through the country by advancing the prayer of the Six Words:

Na-Mu-A-Mi-Da-Butsu (Nam-O-Amitabha), among the people, irrespective of good or bad, believer or non-believer." Priest Chishin was commanded to distribute an amulet of the Six Words among six hundred thousand people for their salvation, and it is said that he invented the way of making fifty or sixty copies of the Six Words at one pressing. The same oracle gave the priest a verse consisting of four lines of seven words each, which roughly translated will mean as follows:—

"The prayer of the Six Words make one permeating law;

The Ten Worlds with proper retributions make one permeating body:

Ten thousand deeds free from worldly thoughts make one permeating sutra:

Such men are the super-best Lotus-flowers."

By these lines it is meant that Six Words permeate the universe and they are the only means of salvation. Subsequently, Priest Chishin founded the Jishu sect and renamed himself Priest Ippen (literally, one permeation) for he now made his mind to "permeate" the country with his footsteps for the salvation of the people.

It was in the same year, 1275, that the Fujisawa-ji Temple was erected at Fujisawa in the province of Sagami, though the temple is now better known by the name of Yugyo-ji Temple.

A Buddhist priest though he was, Priest Ippen was a believer of many Shinto gods whose shrines he visited and he underwent a confinement of prayer and meditation every now and then for a circuit of seven days and nights or longer. He always extended a helping hand to the poor and distressed, telling them to repeat the Nembutsu-prayer, which was the only means of true salvation. It is said that Priest Ippen helped no fewer than 251,724 persons (or 2,500,001,724. according to a certain book) during his long pilgrimages of sixteen years, which covered all the sixty-six provinces of the country. He lived in and for the Lord Buddha, for whose sake he renounced the world and himself, and to him the repetition of the Six Words was all-in-all. All sin was unconditionally atoned for, he would teach, by the repetition of the Nembutsu-prayer. He lived entirely upon alms voluntarily offered, but he never begged for them, for in his belief the Lord

Buddha would feed him in the way pleasing to Him. Indeed he was quite Puritanic in his faith. He was a good talker, but kept reticent on anything but religious. He wrote many poems of thirty-one syllables like many another Buddhist priest, but devotion and faith were the only themes he had for his poetry.

About a month before his death, i. e. on the tenth of the seventh month (July), 1289, Priest Ippen said: "The sacred work of one generation has turned into Nam-Amida-Butsu," meanig that his life was near its end, and he destroyed all the books in his possession by fire. Hence it is a sad fact that we have little literature about the life and deeds of this saintly priest.

Priest Ippen fell ill during his pilgrimage in Awa Province, in 1289, but he would not discontinue his trip, till he came to the Shinko-ji (literally, True-light) Temple at Akashi in Harima Province, where he told his disciples that his return to the Jodo or Elysian land was approaching because his work of salvation was almost over. "The enlightened, like a good warrior," he added" will die without making much ado about dying. They will die with nobody noticing it."

When he was critically ill, one of his disciples asked him what they should do for him after he was gone. "It is a trace that a holy man can leave," Priest Ippen said, "to leave no trace behind. I know not what it means to leave anything behind. The worldly have their hearts set on riches and fiefs; so they commit sin. A Buddhist priest has no longing for riches or a fief; for the only wish that he leaves behind is the salvation the people will have by the Nembutsu-prayer of the Six Words.

Priest Ippen was dying on the 22nd of the eighth month (August) when one Nakatsukasa, a local chief of Hyogo, visited him and said: "If you die today, I cannot be with you at your bedside, as I have to attend to the palanquin of my shrine," "Very well," the dying priest said, calmly, "I will put off my death till tomorrow."

On the morning of the 23rd. Priest Ippen took the cold ablutions and put on a fine robe, and while his disciples were reciting the Amitabha-sutra, he stopped breathing and died, as he predicted before, without anyone noticing it. He was 51 years old (Japanese counting) when he died.

Monument for friends and foes:

In the precincts of the Yugyo-ji Temple there stands an antiquated monument which is now specified as a historic souvenir by the prefectural government of Kanagawa. It is called the Onshin-Byodo-Kuyo-Hi or Foes-and-Friends-equally-fed Monument. It was erected to the memory of those fallen in the battle that Ujinori Uyesugi fought against Mochiuji Ashikaga, the governor of Kamakura., against whom he rose in revolt in 1416. Uyesugi was killed in a desparate fight in which many soldiers were killed on both sides. Priest Son-ei (literally, Grace-venerator), or Priest Yugyo XV, as every resident priest of the temple has the same name of Yugyo, conceived the happy idea of praying equally for friends and foes that fell in the battle, for being a religionist he stood neutral like the Red Cross people, and the monument was erected in 1418.

Lord Oguri and Lady Terute: The Yugyo-ji Temple is always associated with the romantic story of Lord Oguri and Lady Terute, who lie buried in its precints. Their story runs in a nutshell as follows:—

Mitsushige Oguri, lord of Oguri in the province of Hitachi, was falsely accused of rising in revolt against Mochiuji Ashikaga, governor of Kamakura, who sent a troop to attack the castle of Oguri. Oguri escaped, taking ten of his best retainers, but when they came to Fujisawa on their way to Mikawa, they happened to stay overnight in the house of a highwayman, Taro Yokoyama by name, who offered them a poisoned drink. All his retainers were killed, but Oguri was saved by Terute, a maid of noble birth in the service of Yokoyama. His innocence established, Oguri attacked and killed Yokoyama, and then he took Terute to wife. After his death in 1426, Terute built a small hermitage beside his grave on the ground of the Yugyo-ji Temple, where she lived by praying day and night for the happy repose of Oguri till she died in 1440. It is said that because Oguri lost the use of his legs as a result of the poisoned drink, Terute wheeled him around most devotedly in a small cart to offer a prayer for his recovery at different shrines, until he was cured. Their graves at the Yugyo-ji Temple are still visited by many admirers of Lord Oguri (better known by the name of Oguri Hangan or Oguri the Judge) and his devoted wife, Lady Terute.

本願寺派の海外布教に就て

眞宗本願寺派
編譯課主事　宇津木二秀

一

本願寺派海外布教の教線は、東、遠く北米の太平洋沿岸諸洲からユタ、コロラド州まで喰入り、最近はニューヨークに新教會の設立を見て太西洋岸にまで達した。北は樺太、シベリア、滿洲中部に及び、西及南は支那の樞要都市からシンガポール、南洋諸島に延びてゐる。——と言へば南米とあと僅かの地點を除いて、現在日本人が海外に發展してゐる殆んどすべての方面に及んでゐるわけで、たのもしい限りであるが、この茫大な地域に僅々五百にも足らない布教使開教使を點在せしめてゐるに過ぎないのだから、その内容の充實と發展とはまだまだ將來にあると言はねばならぬ。

二

試みにその現勢を最近の統計によつて見ると、

A. 布　哇	
別院、教會、出張所	65
開教使	60
信　徒	100,000
B. 北　米	
別院、教會	37
開教使	61
信　徒	40,000
C. カナダ	
教　會	7
開教使	6
信　徒	6,000
D. 樺　太	
別院、寺院	26
布教使	8
信　徒	24,000
E. シベリア	
教　會	1
布教使	1
信　徒	22
F. 滿洲國	
別院、教會	32
布教使	76
信　徒	51,000
G. 臺　灣	
別院、寺院	39
布教使、教誨師	50
信　徒	4,500
H. 朝　鮮	
別院、寺院、出張所	99
布教使、教誨師	200
信　徒	50,000
I. 支　那	
別院、教會	7
布教使	8
信　徒	20,030
J. 南　洋	
教　會	6
布教使	3
信　徒	4,500

と言ふことになつてゐる。

三

大觀して，布哇，米國，カナダの教線は明治前半の國際的移民が內地の佛教的色彩の濃厚である地方から送られた爲めと，宗主光尊上人が時勢を見るに鋭敏であらせられた爲めに，早くも明治三十一年里見師を布哇に派遣，越えて三十三年薗田西島兩師を北米に派遣せられ，他宗派に先んじたもので，今日に於ては殆んど佛教各派の全部が大小の教線を布いてゐる中に，斷然壓倒的優位を占めてゐるのは當然である。會堂の建築其他の施設の如きも中には百萬金を投じた堂々たる殿堂を有するのみならず，中小學校の經營にては布哇のごときすでに確固たる基礎の上に立てるものあり，從つて，男女靑年團の教化も行屆いた施設を有してゐる。日本人及日系市民十四萬に對し十萬の信徒を有すると言へば略その教勢は察知される筈である。

樺太の布教は布教使の數あまりにも少數なのは解しがたい程で，その發展は主として將來にありと言ひ得る。シベリアは現下の情勢やむを得ないことで，今後も何等かの轉換を見ない限り發展すべくもない。浦鹽の在留邦人僅かに六十餘名と云はれてゐる。

滿洲國の方はその現勢は大體建國以前の成果であつて，今後の發展は國策に順應して大いに期せらるべきで，目下本山當局に於ては滿洲語學院なる新組織の下に堅實な靑年僧の特殊教育と訓練を施して新進出に備へてゐることは注目に値する。

臺灣，朝鮮，支那に於ける教勢は從來他宗派に機先を制せられたかたちもあつたが，近時頓に活氣を呈して來たのは事實で，ことに地方人の教化は次第にその人を得て比較的地味ではあるが着々實蹟をあげかゝつてゐる。勿論その成果はただ將來の事に屬する。

南洋はまだ漸くその緖についたばかりであるが，在留同胞五千六百に對し四千五百までが本派の教團に屬してゐることは，新開ながら目覺しい活動であることは窺知せられるであらう。

四

以上は本願寺海外布教現勢の鳥瞰であるが，茲に現下痛感されてゐる開教の一二の問題に於て考察して見たい。それは主として布哇，北米に關する問題であつて，新興滿洲國についても幾多問題があるべきだが，充分な資料を持ち合さないから差控へる。

米布に關する問題とは，第二世即ち日系市民の教化と白人傳道の問題である。これはすでに久しい以前から識者間に考慮され，ことに大戰後は頻りに論ぜられて來た問題であつて，十數年前に當然今日の如く何等かの施設をなすべき筈のものであつたので，卒直に言へば當事者が怠慢だつたとも云へる性質のものである。

米布に於ける第二世はその環境と教養に於て特異性を有する結果，從來の開教方針では遠く及ばないものがありすでにその缺陷を痛感し，第二世の教化には第二世の開教使を養成するにありとして，數年前より彼地より送られた留學生が內地の中大學に孜々勉學し將來の開教使として活動すべく準備されてゐる。すでに二三名の者は大學の過程を經へて彼地に歸り目覺しく活動してゐるほどで誠にたのもしい事である。ただ將來に於て米布の教團を僅か數年間內地に留學して來た開教使に當然委ね得べきであるか，果してこれ等の開教使が現在の如き組織の下にいつまでも滿足して教化の任に當つてくれるだらうか，或は又彼等がその任務を完全に果してくれるだらうか，など慮るとき，そこに多分に疑問視せざるを得ない問題が橫はつてゐる。

從つて第二世出身の開教使養成だけでなく，從來の如く內地より派遣の開教使にしてよく彼等と協同し得る，又彼等をも指導し得るだけの者を養成するぐらいの施設をなすことが當局としては當然考ふべきことであらねばならぬ。若しこの點に就いて今日何等かの方針を立て得ないとすれば，恐らく十年後には文字通り行き詰るかも知れないと感ずる程である。

更にこの問題を押しすゝめて來れば今後の開教使の待遇方法に言及せなければならないが，これは他日に讓ることゝする。

第二の白人傳道の問題であるが，最近は殊にその氣運が向いて來たことは否めない事實である。それは大戰後の世界的傾向として，精神的に何物かを東亞に求めんとする者が續出して來た爲めでもあらうが，他面米布の教團の今日に至る不斷の努力が報ひられんとする吉兆なりとも言へる。すでにホノルル，桑港，羅府等にはその爲めに特殊機關を設けて努力し居り，相當の成果をあげつゝあり，白人の入門者も多數に及び，又得度までして將來の教團に身を獻げんとする殊勝なものも輩出して來た。

しかしながら，それ等求道者が果して至純な心持のものばかりであらうか又佛教の如何なる點を憧れて入門しつゝあるか，又如何なる種類階級の人物が集つて來るのであるかなどの問題は今日等閑に附すべきでなくして充分に凝視する必要がある。最近本山當局でもこの點に就いて考慮し，何等かの方策を立てられるらしく傳へられるのは至極結構である。

尤も今日は未だ試驗期にあるので，さほどまで立入つて吟味する必要は無からうとも言ひ得るが，これは過去二十年間の事實に徵し又將來を慮る者から言へば，種々の點に於て重大な試練である爲めに吟味を要する事と考へられる。

五

開教に關し人物の養成と共に必要なのは教材である。經典の飜譯，佛教音樂の作製，サービスの制定，教義の說明等々，すでに焦眉の急を告ぐるものさへ多々ある。昨年本山には飜譯課なる一事務所を開いて，この方面に着手し出したが，その實蹟は，數年後で無くては恐らく見られないのでなからうか。

六

今日の世界はすべての點に於て事物を靜的に眺められない時代である。佛教の「無常」の教へが如實に證明せられて，何事も動的に觀察もし，對策を講ずべき時となつた。又，何事も多角形的に處せられねばならない時代である。從つて教團の海外發展も從來無頓着であり得た諸問題を充分に考慮の內に置かなければならない爲めに，一概に論ぜられ，また立策さるべきでない。

以上はたゞ本派海外布教の現勢を一瞥して，愚見の一端を述ぶるに過ぎない。　（一九三七・三・二一）

開教使生活の種々相

在奉天　井上淳念

開教使生活の種々相――わけて我が滿洲國にあつては地域的に全く異つた色彩あり、又各宗夫々の活動がなされて居り、到底、その種々相を充分に述べることは困難であらう。

（一）若さの幼稚

先づ管見するに、概してその生活態は幼稚であり、單純である。それには社會的な原因がある。即ち、該地の我が同胞は概ね所謂出稼ぎ的な生活であり、夫々に產出の地を異にし、宗教或ひは姻戚關係、すべてが疏遠な境遇の中に雜然として相集つたものである。從つて邦人の生活態は時には全く隣接とも沒交渉になりやすく、個々に隔離された小さな幼稚な單純な生活を營むのが常である。その中にある布教使の生活は當然、內地のそれよりは幼稚であり單純であると云はねばならぬ。又布教所、布教使の數も少く開教の歷史は古くも二十數年に過ぎず、今日は漸く開教の地盤が出來上つたに過ぎぬ狀態であれば、傳統的なものを背景とする複雜な非幼稚なその生活の種々相は窺はれぬわけである。多くの開教地視察者は或ひは種々に涉つて批評論難さるるであらうが、私はこの單純さ幼稚さは年齡的なものであり、今後、有爲なる開教使によつて益々發展されることゝ信ずるのである。

（二）社會との孤立

前述の如く、活潑なる社會教化への働き掛けなき布教所にあつては、どうしても社會に孤立となり勝ちである。開教地の市民としても、大半は此處を一時の足留りとして假寓し、轉勤、移住の最も盛んな移動狀態である。從つて布教所との關係は概ね疏遠となり、僅に不幸や年忌等の場合に僧侶を招待或ひは參詣して讀經を乞ふ場合、又は信心深い幾分かの善男善女が時折布教所に出入するといつたのみである。

又、この社會の大部分は青壯年を以て占められ日々の生活に餘りにもあわたゞしく暮してゐる關係上、特殊の者を除いては布教所を顧みない。

一方、開教使も青壯年層向きな近接法を取らず、極めて消極的な舊態已然たる布教に讀經にあくせくして居るので、益々この社會との孤立狀態を著くしてゐる。

而も、此處に在勤する開教使は永久的のものではなく、いつ何時本山命により移動せしめられるかわからぬ狀態にあり、腰の落着かぬ小心翼々たるものさへあるに於てをやであらう。實際、上局に睨まれて己が位置保守のために右顧左眄する樣では、どうして、活潑潮地なる開教への精進行が出來得ようか、願くばせめて半永久的であらしめたい。そして、充分に布教に事業につくして貰ひ度いものである。

社會との孤立、これこそ由々しき社會問題であらう。

（三）二つの型

開教使の生活に二つの型があると思ふ。勿論、嚴密な分類ではなく、斯うした型らしい雰圍氣を感ずるからである。

一は新進氣鋭の士で、働き盛りの青壯年の開教使である。宗教的な情熱にまかせて、社會事業に滿人教化に移民團布教といつた活躍の花々しい生活のそれである。然し、一方やり過ぎなといつた評判非難もある。

二は大小既成布教所におさまつてゐる草分け組のそれである。時には因循姑息でさへある。

この間にあつて多數の在勤青年布教使が、この何れへともつかず希望、煩悶、不滿を抱えてゐる事である。

又、遊擊隊ともいふべき（例へば滿洲靈廟）異色の活動をせんとする開教使もある。

（四）滿僧の提携

最近文教部は宗教行政强化に力を入れる樣になり、奉天市公署にても、宗教團體の統制指導を圖つて宗教工作に努めてゐる。同署社教股では一ヶ年間の工作豫定表を作製したが、其の中には日滿佛教懇談會開催、奉天日滿佛教聯合會結成、宗教專門學校設立計畫、汎太平洋佛教青年大會打合會といつた重要なる項目が擧げられてある。

然し、開教使達の多くは我不關焉たる心もとない態度で、相變らず法事讀經のみにあくせくしてゐるのは遺憾である。

數多くの老大開教使の中に、滿僧と親しく交り、日滿佛教の提携、將來への躍進を語り合ふ者、果して幾許であらう。

況んや、支那語に通達し、滿人教化云々のことは、まこと夢物語り以上の話である。

（五）視察團の酷評に答ふ

假令ひ現在は他處眼にはその生活を相當非難されてゐる從來の開教使でも苟もその熱情を持つて渡滿せる青年時代の開教生活は、ましてその意氣と抱負たるや、到底、今日の浮浪入滿者に伍して漫然と續々渡任する青年開教使の群の及ばぬところであらう。私はその生活を非難排擊するよりは、寧ろ心からなる感謝と慰勞の誠意を以て斯の先輩に對し、よりよき生活へ共に手となり足となつて、盡し度く念願するのである。

よく內地から時折見える曰く何某視察團等々の人々の歸朝談が、中外其の他の紙上に散見せられることであるが其の中に、滿洲の開教使の生活は全く內地の延長以外の何物でもないと酷評せられてある。或ひはその通りであるかも知れぬ。然し、私はそれでは貴方はどういふ季節に渡滿せられたかと反問したい。定つて、春か秋、滿洲といつても內地と氣候の大した差のない良い時候に通り一遍の視察を試みるのであり、酷寒零下何十度に氷雪を犯して視察のあつた事を聞かない。若し結氷期に親しく視察されたなら，二十數年の昔にあらゆる苦勞を嘗めて今日の基礎を築いた功績に對して，心から合掌されるであらう。その本堂は最近族生する高層ビルの間に煤煙に塒れて小さく建つとも，讀經生活にその大部分は費されてゐやうとも，その貧しい境内の一木一草にも先輩の尊い精進行があつた事を銘記すべきである。私は特に滿洲の我が開敎使の生活の種々相を論ずるには先づ其の恩惠を偲び而して溫情を持つて，そのともすれば非難さるべき生活に對する向上改革をすべきであらうと信ずるのである。我が榮えある開敎生活の向上は一に我々青年の徒らなる論難排撃ではなく，あくまで先輩への純情なる助力協力の活動へのそれでなければならぬ。

（六）青年開敎使の名に恥ぢよ

寧ろ，我々後進開敎使は此際よく自省すべき秋である。露滿國境遠い寒烈の移民地にあつて我が本多見，佐々木見の如く，全く眞劍な開敎の第一戰に奮鬪する士はいざ知らず，我々の如く惠まれた都會の布敎所に勤務する者の生活をよくよく三省せねばならない。責は他にあるのではない。同情のない論難の聲に怯え，一犬の虛に和して吠える萬犬のそれであつてはならぬ。

友よ，若き開敎使よ，先づその榮えある名に，恥じざるかを互に見究めよう。基礎は旣に先輩の辛苦によつて成就されつゝあるのである。讀經主義よと他よりの虛の吠えに，已が足許を忘れて或は吠え，或は我不關焉と不感症に陷つてもならない。明日の開敎生活への力強い準備への下座行ともなれ。苟も，現在の生活にし・か・た・の・な・さ・をかこつてゐてはならぬ。

葬式に法事にその腦髓の痺れる思ひもあらう。然し，麻雀や休日の映畫觀賞に鬱さを晴らす生活であつてはならない。その時間があつたら，何故，支那語の勉强をせぬか，城内に滿洲寺院を訪れ，何故，朋友とならないのか。友よ，試みに我が在勤部屋を外から見るもよい。何と，その室氣の煤煙と煙草とに濁れるかを。我々は餘りにも恩寵に慣れ過ぎてゐる。土臺を作つた先輩の其の後の動作を唯見守り，其の出來榮えを嘲笑し，又よちよちあてなく蹤いて行く態たらくではないか。土臺は其の上に立派な建物を築くべきものなのである。バトンは旣に渡された否渡さうにも渡されない後繼走者なのではないか。然し，早晚承けねばならぬのである。私は月に二三回，各宗の諸兄と相會する機會を持つのであるが，餘りにも無氣力な生活の種々相を互に察知して，味氣ない茶菓を喉に通して歸るのである。在勤部屋の我が友よ，君は，開敎に來たのか，滿洲に行つて見ようと來たのか，歸り來つて，ふと語ると「うん，俺は一遍位ゐね，見て置かうと思つて，仲々，ついでがないと來られないからな」「ぢや，何故，さつさと引上げなかつたのだ？」「いや，場合によつてはこつちでもいゝと思つてるんだ」――これでは迷惑するのは門徒であり，本山である。何と功利的な現代靑年の日和見氣分であらう。こんな僥倖心の泥沼に喘ぐ開敎使の生活こそ青年の仇ではないか。

二月二日附の中外紙所載の，大派監督の談話の一節に曰く，

――先づ斷行したいのは盤根錯節に屈せざる溌てば響く若い開敎使を養成する事です。從來の開敎使の再敎育といふ事を考へないではないが，それ等の人々には，それぞれ現在の事務に邁進して貰ひ，新たに精鋭を養ひたいと思ふのです――

嗚呼，なんと，從來の開敎使（我々）は期待されず，現在の事務に邁進せよと，捨てられてゐるのではないだらうか。現在の事務とは現在の生活なのかそれに邁進せよとは，それに耽溺せよとの一大皮肉であり警告であらう。友よ，滿腔の反撥心を以て此の言に報ゆる氣概を持たう。さもなくば我々は居眠りの生活なのだ――唯，玄海灘を越えて來り興安嶺下胡砂吹く滿洲に開敎するてふ名を以て，内地の人々や自己に對して，カムフラージュしてゐるに過ぎぬ。開敎使の生活，それは泡沫の自己滿足であり，內地の人情の煩雜さから逃避しての墮落生活に塒れるのだ。だが，決してさうであつてはならない。友よ，あくまでその名に恥じない生活を打ち建てるべきである。（完）

山西の佛教

道端良秀

實は編輯者の方より,「支那佛教行脚の思出」と云ふ課題を與へられたのであるが，私の支那行脚と言つても大部以前のことであり，今更これを思ひ出して見ても大したこともなし，現在とは多少變化もして居るだらうと思はれるので，私が行脚見聞した，山西省の佛教に就いて，感じたままを，そこはかとなく書き綴つて，この課題の責を塞ぎ度いと思ふ。

(一)

今日山西省と言へば，相當邊鄙な處で，文化の程度も餘程低いやうに思はれて居る。それは政治や文化の中心が南京や上海，或は北平や天津と言つたやうに，海岸近くに集つて，それより遠く距つた地方は，自然諸文化に後れて居るやうに思はれ，事實又後れて居ることは當然のことである。

併し乍ら今過去の歴史を眺め，事實その地を歩んで見ると，この一僻地と思はれて居る山西省は，嘗ては諸文化の中心をなしたところであり，特に佛教文化の隆盛を誇つた地であつたことに氣付かせらるるのである。

先づ誰でも氣の付くことは，現在世界に於いて，佛教遺物上に於ける著明なるものの一つとして數へられて居る山西省の大同の大石佛は，彼の河南の龍門の石佛と共に，支那に於ける二大石窟佛として，有名であるばかりでなく，世界にその類を見ないものであらう。

更にこの二大石佛に次いで，現在尙多くの石佛を有して，在りし昔の隆盛の有樣を物語つて居るものに，大原の近くに在る，天龍山の石佛がある。前者は北魏より隋頃迄の佛教文化の遺物であり，後者は北齊より隋唐時代のものが中心である。

更に又文殊菩薩の淨土として，支那本土は勿論のこと，遠く諸外國に迄喧傳されて，毎年巡禮者引きも切らず，そのために特に普通院なる宿泊處すら建設さるるが如き，靈場五臺山は，實に隋唐宋佛教文化の中心をなして居たものであつた。

一般社會大衆の眞の宗教として，民衆の生命の糧となつたと思はれる，念佛宗は，その根元は實にこの山西省太原の程遠からぬ，汾水の邊りなる玄忠寺であつた。支那淨土教の中心的人物たる曇鸞，道綽，善導は，實にこの一僻村より絕叫せるものであつた。

かく考へ來ると，山西省こそ支那佛教に取つては，最も重要なる地であり支那佛教地理學の上に於いて，重大なる役割を有して居るものと言はねばならぬ。

更に又近時山西省趙城縣に於いて，一古寺廣勝寺より，金代に版行せられたる大藏經の多數を發見せられたることよりして，この山西省の地が，遠く北魏時代より引繼いで，現今に至る迄佛教に取つて最も重要なる位置を占めて居ると云ふことに注意せねばならぬ。

(二)

山西省に於ける佛教の隆興は何と云つても，北魏からである。北魏は初め恒安卽ち今の大同に主都を定めて，南朝宋に對して，北朝の文化を建設したが，後文成帝に至つて南洛陽に都を遷したが，尙舊都恒安は其の文化を維持して居た。

北魏の佛教が如何に急激に發展を遂げたか，堂塔伽藍の建立，佛像の造立などが如何に盛んであつたか，僧尼の數が如何に激增したことか，それらの詳細は彼の『魏書』の『釋老志』によつて知ることが出來るであらうが，寺舍四萬，僧尼數二百萬と言ふに至つてはそれが如何に誇張された數字であるにせよ，當時の佛教隆盛の一般を推察することが出來やう。

これ實に山西省を大體中心とせる佛教と見て差支へないと思ふ。この佛教隆盛の北魏の初期に於いて，僧曇曜によつて開鑿されたのが，彼の大同雲岡の大石窟である。

この雲岡の大石窟は，蜿蜒三十支里に及ぶと文献に記されて居るが，現在は東方の第一窟と稱せられるところより，西方の最後の小さな窟迄は，大體十四五丁位であつたやうに思ふ。東方の四窟はとてもひどく荒れ果てて居たが，流石中央の八窟程は完全であつたが，又それだけ後代の修覆が念入りであつて，中央の六窟七窟目の如きは，實に慘憺たるもので，あくどい赤と靑とに彩色され，道教の神か，佛教の佛か，何れなりやを疑はしむるやうなものすら見受けられたのは，修繕ではなくして，全く改惡である。

その點西方の窟は殆んど雨ざらしになつて居り，窟など半分以上もかけて居て，所謂有名なる露出の大佛もここにあるが，何れも原物そのままの姿にて，實に端麗な氣持ちのいい御姿を拜することが出來て，六朝藝術の眞髓に觸れたやうな，一種の感激を覺へたものであつた。そしてそこに我が推古時代の佛像と一脈の連絡を見出すことの出來たのは，何とも云ひやうのない嬉しさであつた。

當時尙かかる世界的寶物が，馬小屋となつて馬糞の供物が佛前に供へられて居り，物置小屋として無雜作に使用されて，少しも見ることの出來なかつた窟もあつたが，現今は北平より遊覽の爲め便利なる汽車迄出來たと言ふことであるから，さぞかし保存方法も，多少は考慮されて居ることであらうと思はれる。

(三)

五臺山は，大同と太原との中程に在る山で，一名を淸凉山とも云ひ，華嚴と因緣深い關係を持つて居るところであるが，古來より文殊菩薩の淨土として，特に唐宋時代の支那佛教信仰の中心地をなして居たものである。

これは只に支那のみならず，印度西域方面からもこの五臺を慕つて參詣し我が日本からも，興福寺の靈仙三藏，叡山の慈覺大師圓仁を初めとし，寂照，奝然，慧蕚，宗叡，盛算，慧運，成尋等の人々が，この五臺山巡禮の旅に出でたもので，この五臺山の佛教文化こそ，我が日本佛教文化史上に於いて，重大なる役割を演じて居るものであることに注意せねばならぬ。

當時の五臺山の佛教に就いては，圓仁の『入唐求法巡禮行記』並びに，成尋の『參天臺五臺山記』或は又唐の慧祥の『古淸凉傳』宋延一の『廣淸凉傳』宋張商英の『續淸凉傳』等を見れば，詳細にこれを知ることが出來る。

何と言つても唐宋時代に於ける五臺山の信仰はすばらしいもので，年々の國費と云ふものがどれだけこの五臺山の佛事其他に消費されたかを見ても想像出來るものであり，五臺山の七大寺或は十大寺と稱せらるる諸大寺の結構も亦，頗る豪壯華麗なものであつて，金閣寺の屋根瓦の如きは金泥を以てこれを葺き，夕陽映へて山谷明けし，と言ふが如きに至つては，その雄大なる有樣を推考することが出來やう。

文殊の淨土なるが故に，ここに登れば必ず文殊の靈驗を蒙り，得脫することが出來ると信ぜられて，全國よりの巡禮者引きも切らず，その巡禮者の便を計つて，半日行程には普通院なる宿舍を設ける程となつた。

現在荒れ果てて，僅かに塔と，庫裡と半壞の本堂とを殘せる大聖竹林寺は唐代に於いては堂々五臺の七大寺に數へられ，法照禪師の五會流の妙なる念佛の聲は，谷々にこだまして，人々をして隨喜の涙にむせばしたものであつたであらう。

この五會の念佛がやがて，我が慈覺大師圓仁によつて叡山に傳へられ，常行堂の念佛三昧となつて現はれ，我が國に於ける念佛發展の上に大なる貢献をなしたものであつた。

併し現在この五臺山は，全く昔の面影を失ひ，唐宋時代の古き寺塔伽藍は，今はその片鱗をも覗ふことは出來ない。併し乍らその內に於いて涌き出づる泉の如く，五臺山復興の熱意を見出すことが出來た。

大聖竹林寺の如き，已に住持もなき半壞の寺もあるが，すぐその近くに，木の香も新しき龍泉寺の新建築を見ることも出來た。尙諸處に盛んに新しく建造されんとする寺々を見出すことの出來たのは，實に五臺山佛教として喜ばしき限りであつた。

而して不思議に感じたことは，これら諸寺の檀越は多く，山東省より河北省，滿洲にかけてであつたことである。その何故であつたか聞き忘れたが，面白い現象と思はれる。滿洲に多くの信者のあるのは，滿洲の開國傳說と文殊との關係よりして，五臺山信仰となつたものであるかも知れぬ。

現在の五臺山は相當入り雜つて居るやうに思はれる。先づ淸朝時代より急激にラマ僧の入つて來たことで，現在も多くのラマ僧が住居して居るものでその數は普通の僧よりも尙多くを示して居るやうである。

又道教も混肴されて居るやうで，彼の有名な七大寺の隨一と稱せられて居た唐代の金閣寺に參拜した時も，この金閣寺の後の續きには道教の尊像が安置され，道士が十數人も住居して居ると言ふやうな有樣であり，明かに道佛混淆を示して居る一證左であり，更にたしか金閣寺近くの淸凉寺であつたと思ふが，ヒゲの生へた佛像が安置されて居たのは，その最も代表的なものと思はれた。

その他は大體に於いて，ラマと臨濟とのやうに思はれたが，何れにせよ，かかる不純な傾向を有して居たことに今後の佛教に對する理解が注意されねばならぬ。

（四）

支那に於ける淨土教は，普通に慧遠流と，道綽善導流と，慈愍流との三流とされて居るが，その中心は道綽善導流であり，支那淨土教は唐代の道綽善導によつて大成されたものである。それが我が國に來つて，法然の淨土宗の開宗となり，親鸞の眞宗となつて，ここに東洋民族の生命の糧となつたものであるが，このよつて來るところの地は，實に山西省は太原の近く，今の交城縣の西北二十支里に在る石壁山玄忠寺である。

この玄忠寺の地こそは，支那淨土教のみならず，日本淨土教に於いても，等しくその根元地と言はねばならぬ。玄忠寺は曇鸞によつて建立されたものと言はれ，道綽又ここに來りて一生ここを中心として念佛の弘布に努め，附近三縣の七歲以上の人々をして悉く念佛を稱へしむる迄に至らせたること，更に善導この地に來りて道綽の弟子となつて深く淨士の法門を味得し，遂に古今楷定の書たる『觀經疏』を著して念佛教を獨立せしむるに至つた。支那淨士教は正しく彼によつて最高潮に達せるもので，彼等によつて，一般大衆に理解信仰せしむるに至つたものである。

又後の善導と稱せられた，彼の法照禪師も亦，この念佛にゆかり深き晋陽即ち太原に在つて盛んに念佛をすすめここに於いて『五會法文讚』を著すなど，大いに念佛のために力を盡し，更に五臺に入つては，竹林寺に於いて，彼獨特の五念流の念佛を創設して，ここに民衆教化に一新法を與へて，愈々淨土教の隆盛を來したのであつた。

勿論善導も法照も，都長安に出でて活躍したのであつたが，支那淨土教の淵叢地が，この太原を中心とせるものであることに注意して，山西省と淨土教の深き交涉を思ひ出すのである。

（五）

太原は晋陽とも，或は幷州とも稱せられて居たもので，北魏時代に於いても，大同と洛陽の中間に位置して，新舊兩部の文化交通の要路に當つて，重要なる地とされ，又北齊に於いては，この太原の地は北齊の發祥地として後都を鄴に移しても尙別都，或は舊都として，帝都鄴と何ら異なることなき待遇を受け，唐又ここが發祥地として長安，洛陽と共に，この太原の都は北都或は北京と稱せられ，唐の三京と呼ばれて居たものである。

唐代の文化がこれらの都を中心として發展せるもので，その中太原は，五臺山と長安との交通の要路に當り，佛教文化の一中心をなして居たことは，これ又當然と言はねばならぬ。

かくの如く考へ來ると，單なる一僻地の如きこの山西省は，實に中世文化の花を咲かせるところであり，佛教との關係實に深いもので，更に初めに述べたるが如く，近時廣勝寺より，金刻大藏經の發見されたることは，この地方の佛教文化が，唐宋のみならず，永く續いて現在に至つて居るものであることを知ることが出來る。（三月四日）

資料

僧伽救國的史實

第七區專員公署諮議
稽翥青在覺津寺講

今天大醒法師要我到這邊來貢獻一點意見，佛法很深，決不是世俗一般人所能領解的，所謂聖人門前讀孝經，我今天到這裏來好像是這樣的，我現在想講點關於古今和尚救國的史實。

我國有個少林寺，在明朝嘉靖年間，曾經做過一番驚天動地的救國工作，在以前的小說上，說少林寺和尚有如何的神通，近於神話，未免太過一點，而入民國以來各戲院做了一本「火燒紅蓮寺」的戲，又未免把和尚說得太壞了一點。

那時的少林寺和尚，以武藝風聞全國，所以凡是一個少林寺的和尚，他至少總有些拳術，那時日本倭寇，到我中華來作祟擾亂，自宋末經過元朝兩次東征，兩次入寇，由明朝永樂，到嘉請，不但在附近的幾省，就是現在的江浙閩粵一帶也時遭蹂躪所以那時的時局，比現勢還要嚴重，而日本倭寇對我國的侵略，更超過現在的程度，現在不過僅僅東北四省及華北，那時可算處處要受他的搶掠屠殺的，日本人一到中華來，總是拼命的向我國進攻，那時我國人（包括軍人）一見日本人，以爲倭人萬能，馬上就退去，不敢和他對敵，因此，格外增加倭寇來的胆量，所以日本人樂得每年要渡海西來一次，他們進攻的政策，總是先分散人民的力量，使人們見到他要如同對虎一般的畏懼，而後讓他大量的搶掠，結果是讓他們「滿載而歸」。當時正在國難嚴重，人命危若纍卵的時候，少林寺的和尚爲慈悲心所策動，不忍見國家民族如此亂亡，更不忍見無辜的同胞而遭受殘戮，所以馬上就團結起來應官廳之募，走到前綫上和敵人作戰，這時倭寇因爲兵器不健全，而且武藝又不及少林寺和尚高强，結果打了敗仗，所以當時的少林寺和尚，就成爲江浙兩省民衆的救星，把幾百萬的民衆從水深火熱之中救出，把亡種辱國的厄運轉爲太平無事的景象，這眞是一件驚天動地的事，這一件事的史實，現在我把他再仔細講述一下。

嘉靖癸丑年，倭寇突至蘇州松江一帶，人數不過三百人，漢奸土匪和之，官廳起民兵抵抗，人民畏怯，望風而逃，連敗三十七陣，倭氣萬丈，所過之處，搶掠奸淫，焚燒官舍民房，不計其數，有蔡克廉者，擢江人，任松江守官，募僧兵殄滅之，自是以後，我軍多凱旋，倭賊望風逃遁，一反從前之風氣。

六月倭寇至，天圓與指揮朱某迎擊，留僧無極在六團留守，朱指揮以身爲軍官之故提兵先往，爲倭賊所敗，六合孫已被倭攻殺數十人，各地聞風畏懼，是晚僧兵至八團地方，天圓引兵至一團地方，親爲先鋒，月空等排陣於後，倭人以掠得民間裏裏誘之，天圓下令曰····

「有取財物者斬！」月空無極列爲長蛇陣勢，韓都司王守備等繼其後，天圓令各僧以藍靛塗面，倭與交鋒，勇不可當，疑爲神兵，被僧兵殺眞倭數十人，餘衆奔走，墮入坑中者均被長槍刺殺，逃去者入其巢，僧兵圍之，倭首趙大王妻探首出視，一僧持鐵棒躍擊斃之，倭又遁，集羽黨聚於金山，天圓又追及之。湯總兵亦至，相合大攻，悉殲焉。

論僧人武藝，首少林，次伏牛，再次爲五臺，均在中國社會上有出色的成績，因非此範圍以內，姑置不講，總而言之，誰說和尚不能救國，和尚到前綫去救國，雖然似乎犯了學佛的戒條，不過殺一人救萬人。這原是佛教中大乘菩薩行所許可的，所以到了國家危急的時候，和尚也不妨犧牲一切，去爲人類謀和平而參加作戰。

民國二年夏天，黃克强，何海鳴，韓恢，等在南京獨立，張勳馮國璋等去打南京，許多人民苦得不得了，後來守南京的官軍被敗走了，那些道路上滿堆着屍身，城內城外，無論什麼地方，都有死屍給你看到，這時南京某寺有個和尚，率領了許多和尚加入紅十字會去作掩埋工作，經過數十日，才把所有死屍埋盡，這點，雖然沒有什麼可以稱道，不過，因他這一埋，也可以使當地週圍百數十里以內在炎熱天氣免了許多瘟疫傳染，同時也可以表示他有慈悲心，能夠爲國家盡些義務，我認爲和尚能夠作如此工作，才是眞正的慈悲心發現，但是現在的一般和尚，能夠有這樣的嗎，然而也是有的····

「一二八」打仗時，上海做了臨時的戰場，那時的××軍隊實在殘忍極了，用飛機炸彈向我們同胞亂打，被殺死的人，不知其數，把一個有建築的閘北霎時就變成一個人間地獄，試問在這時誰不怕死呢？ 除上前線的勇敢的十九路軍和八十七八十八兩師而外，還有人敢向前去送命嗎？ 這時看到一個弘傘和尚加入紅十字會救護隊，在那槍林彈雨中，毫不畏懼，他奮起精神在性命不可保的時候用大汽車去救出了不少的傷兵和難民這個和尚眞勇敢，我相信像這個和尚的中國一定還有人呢。

現在國難更嚴重了，我們爲國民的應該具怎樣的精神來挽救厄運呢？ 這時和尚也應該負點責任，和尚救民愛國，外國原也很多，當翥青在暹邏時，在那裏住了三年，辦了一個報，對於該國的風俗頗爲知悉，暹人特別信仰佛教，定佛教爲國教，他們的生活，完全要佛化，無論是個什麼人，總得要先做幾個月及或一個月的和尚，他他做和既容易，還俗也容易，同時日常工作也都是佛化，所以那里無論是行政長官，工商學兵，都是一律佛化的，那裏的和尚，什麼都懂得，因此就把整個的暹邏都變爲一個佛教國了。我國政府，現在提倡佛徒應受軍事訓練，可惜佛會同人不大明白政府的好意，曾有過反駁的文字，這些，現在不去討論。

我認爲爲一國之國民，雖不必人人走上前線，但至少總要負點救護和看護的責任，你們都是和尚，雖然不能走進前線去作線，但對於救護的工作總要做些，一般和尚不爲國家盡相當的義務，無怪人家罵他爲寄生蟲，諸位都是學佛有爲的青年，應該認清自己的立場，認清時勢的危險，要本佛教以大慈悲心去實行救國救民的宗旨，在佛教中做一番救國的工作，這是翥青的一點希望。（完）

（上海「佛教日報」民國廿五年十二月念九，三十日號所載）

護國和平會之意義

常惺法師演講

× × ×

本市佛教同仁發起之護國和平會，昨在赫德路覺園，開成立會，並選舉推定會長理事等職各情，曾誌本報，茲復探得該會副理事長常惺法師，當日講演護國和平會之意義，就中國佛教徒對國家觀念應行糾正，及該會組織之不可緩各點，有深切說明，聽衆咸爲動容，爰錄其原文以告！

× × ×

中國佛教徒護國和平會之意義吾人將中國佛教徒與日本佛教徒作一比較，發現一種很大不同點，即日本佛教徒愛國觀念之强盛，往往超過其信仰之宗教，換言之，可以爲國家而變更其信仰，如一二八事件之前夕，日本某僧在大阪宣言，主張對華强硬，是其明證。中國佛教徒國家觀念薄弱，重視佛陀無我無人之主張，往往忽視其國家之利益，如九一八以來，國難嚴重至此，而堅決主張强硬論者，佛徒中尙未多見其人。此實中日佛徒可以互相借鏡，而足資深省者也。平心論之，佛徒爲一國家一民族之利益所囿蔽，而忘失其偉大平等之精神，於其所信仰之教義，固不無遺憾。但在今日之中國佛教徒，實亦未能以此而自詡其偉大。蓋眞正平等無我無人之精神，惟到佛地方能圓滿無缺，在初發心未登地之菩薩，人我界限固自宛然存在，試問當人我界限未忘之今日。吾人身家性命之保障力，非賴國家而何？故中國佛徒之薄視國家，尤其在今日國難嚴重之際，實不能不認爲亟應糾正之病態也。是以吾人今日發起中國佛教徒護國和平會，其最大之意義，即在世界未臻大同以前，國家之界限未經打破，吾人爲求身家安寧法運興隆，實不能不愛護國家，以求佛法有所寄託。但吾人愛護之方法，不以侵略而以和平，使人人知國家之當愛，多方設法以保護之，且不以吾人之愛國，而妨害他人之愛國，則武力無所用，而眞正無我無人之和平方可期，此則吾中國佛教徒護國和平所當特別努力者也。

（上海「佛教日報」二月一日號）

中國佛教徒護國和平會章程

第一章 總則

第一條 本會定名爲中國佛教徒護國和平會。

第二條 本會以聯合國內佛教徒，弘宣我佛慈悲喜捨之教義，實行菩薩利他救苦之願行，維護國家，倡導和平爲宗旨。

第三條 本會會址設於上海，各省市縣得設分會，分會章程另訂之。

第二章 會務

第四條 本會會務如左。

甲 弘揚佛法。乙 研究黨義。丙 救護災區。丁 宣傳和平。戊 舉辦其他利益群衆事業。

第三章 會員

第五條 凡中國佛教徒贊成本會之宗旨者，經本會會員之介紹，理事會審查通過，得爲本會會員。

第六條 會員之義務如左。

甲 每日迴向護國祈禱和平。乙 遵守會章及本會決議案。丙 繳納會費。丁 介紹會員。

第七條 會員之權利如左。

甲 有選舉權被選舉權。乙 免費酌贈本會刊物。

第四章 組織

第八條 本會最高機關爲會員代表大會，閉幕時爲理事會。

第九條 本會設理事會，由會員代表大會，選舉理事五十三人組織之，執行大會議決各案，及一切會務對大會負責。

第十條 理事會互選理事長一人，副理事長二人，常務理事十二人，執行理事會議決各案，並處理日常會務，對理事會負責。

第十一條 正副會長及理事，任期二年，連選得連任。

第十二條 理事會設總幹事一人，由理會選任之，秉承正副會長，理事長，及常務理事之命，辦理經常事宜。

第十三條 理事會設弘法部，救護部，宣傳部，總務部，各部由常務理事選任主任幹事各一人，幹事若干人，分辦各項事務，辦事細則另訂之。

第十四條 理事，總幹事，主任幹事，均義務職，幹事得酌支津貼。

第十五條 本會得由理事會推請海內大德長者居士爲導師，或名譽理事長。

第十六條 本會於必要時，經常務理事會之決議，得設特種委員會。

第五章 會議

第十七條 本會會員大會，每年舉行一次，由理事會召集之。

第十八條 理事會每六個月舉行一次，常務理事會每月舉行一次，均由理事長召集之。

第六章 經費

第十九條 本會經費如左。

甲 會員會費，會員入會時，繳納入會費國幣二角，證章費國幣二角，以後每年繳納會費國幣二角。

乙 特別費，於必要時經理事會之決議，得臨時正式公告募集之。

第二十條 本會經費收支，於每年度終了時，報告或公告之。

第七章 附則

第二十一條 本章程如有未盡事宜，由會員大會議決修正之。

第二十二條 本章程由發起人大會通過後，並呈請黨政機關核准施行。（完）

昭和十年度全聯理事氏名 (順序不同)

大村桂巖	長谷川良信	重永潜	廣橋了次
常光浩然	鷹谷俊之	日種愚道	川口瑞旦
伊藤道機	濱田本悠	渡邊日龍	秦隆眞
淺野研眞	小林良甫	松岡俊三	三森言融
長岡慶信	椎名正雄	鈴木宗忠	粟津勸絲
好村春基	柘植慈想	干潟龍祥	諏訪令海
望月周雄	福井康順	新宅博雄	栗原廣道
竹內道說	坂野榮範	石原堅正	成瀨賢秀
川崎靜子	三尾透關	小林橘川	椎尾調
太田悌藏	小林啓善	眞野耕雲	柴田義勝
久保田政雄	山崎順了	藤井草宣	本多惠隆
須田智嘉子	靜永孝英	和辻覺	利井興隆
岩野きくよ	山邊習學	上山善治	木村宗圓
稻垣眞我	朝倉曉瑞	樋口貫妙	守重哲成
藤井制心	松本雪城	藤谷琢美	多賀義仁
鳥越道眼	渡邊隆勝	朝倉慶友	
本多良明	湖海玄昌		

(以上六十五名)

昭和十一年全聯理事氏名 (順序不同)

大谷瑩潤	伊藤道機	月輪賢龍	富島祥子
淺野研眞	小林良甫	片山久子	本多惠隆
椎名正雄	好村春基	和辻覺	利井興隆
柘植慈想	望月周雄	上山善治	木村宗圓
福井康順	坂野榮範	樋口貫妙	藤谷琢美
川崎靜子	太田悌藏	朝倉慶友	多賀義仁
小林啓善	久保田政雄	增田圓麿	前田信明
須田智嘉子	靜永孝英	眞野耕雲	小松原國乘
稻葉文海	三澤智雄	黒田芳泉	藤井草宣
內山憲堂	竹田智道	水谷源治郎	精園俊介
諸戶素純	東福義雄	大溪賛雄	松岡俊三
福島精巖	島野禎祥	三森言融	大山不二太郎
阪東信子	和田辨瑞	諏訪令海	新宅博雄
山邊習學	稻垣眞我	吉田賢龍	鳴澤寡愆
朝倉曉瑞	藤井制心	久保良英	中川義澄
松本雪城	鳥越道眼	干潟龍祥	栗原廣道
渡邊隆勝	本多良明	石原堅正	堀信元
湖海玄昌	日種愚道	鈴木宗忠	金山活牛
川口瑞旦	渡邊日龍	平等通昭	早石太郎
秦隆眞	阿部現亮		

(以上七十八名)

汎聯ニュース

昭和十二年三月二十三日
全日本佛教青年會聯盟
理事長　大谷瑩潤
國際佛教通報局
局長　大村桂巖
役員各位殿

謹啓　昭和十二年三月二十一日開催の全聯理事會並に國際佛教通報局評議員會に於て協議決定事項は左記の如くに有之候間左樣御承知被下度右御通報申上候也

記

一，第三回汎太平洋佛教青年會大會日本側準備委員會結成の件
〔決議〕　可及的速に準備委員會を結成すること，委員の人選は理事長一任とす

二，汎太平洋佛教青年會聯盟日本側役員選定の件
〔決議〕　理事長一任とす

三，國際佛教通報局の件
イ，規約中改正
〔決議〕　左の如く規約中改正す
規約第五に左の二項を加ふ
イ，名譽局長　一　名
ロ，顧　　問　若干名
從つてイ，ロ，ハ，は夫れ夫れハ，ニ，ホ，と變更す
規約第八を左の如くす
名譽局長及顧問は評議員會に於て推薦す
從つて，第八，九，十，十一は夫れ夫れ第九，十，十一，十二に變更す

備考
右決議中，一，二，に於ける役員及職員の人選は理事長に一任せられたるを以て別通の如く決定し夫々推薦狀を發送仕候

（別紙）　昭和十二年三月二十三日
全日本佛教青年會聯盟
理事長　大谷瑩潤
役員各位殿

謹啓　昭和十二年三月二十一日開催の全聯理事會並に國際佛教通報局評議員會に於て協議の結果，汎太平洋佛教青年會聯盟日本側役員並に第三回汎太平洋佛教青年會大會日本側準備委員の人選を小生に一任せられ候處左記の方法を以て選任致すことに決定仕候間御了承相願度候　　　　敬具

記

一，汎太平洋佛教青年會聯盟日本側役員及び職員の選任方法左の如し
（甲）　役員
（イ）　名譽委員は全聯歴代の理事長を以て之に充つ
（ロ）　中央委員は（1）全聯歴代の主事及（2）國際佛教通報局幹事を以て之に充つ
（ハ）　實行委員は國際佛教通報局幹事を以て之に充つ
（乙）　職員
中央事務局員は全聯事務局員を以て之に充つ

二，第三回汎太平洋佛教青年會大會日本側準備委員會役員及職員の選任方法左の如し
（甲）　役員
（イ）　準備委員長は全聯理事長を以て之に充つ
（ロ）　準備委員は（1）汎太平洋佛靑聯盟委員（常任とす）（2）並に全聯理事を以て之に充つ
（乙）　職員
準備事務局員は全聯事務局員を以て之に充つ　　　以上

國際佛教通報局定款

名　　稱

第一，本局を國際佛教通報局と稱す

事 務 所

第二，本局の事務所を全日本佛教青年會聯盟本部に置く

目　　的

第三，本局は日本內海及海外に向つて佛教事情の通報をなし，且つ佛教徒相互間の各種便宜を計るを以て目的とす

事　　業

第四，本局の目的を達成するため左記の事業を行ふ
イ，日本內地及世界各國より佛教事情に關する質問の通報を行ふ
ロ，必要に應じ日本語及世界各國語を以て佛教事情の通報を行ふ
ハ，外國人の日本觀光に際しては各種の便益を與へ，特にその佛教に關する方面に於て之を爲す
ニ，定時或は隨時に各國語を以て文書の刊行をなす
ホ，その他必要と認めたる事業を行ふ

役　　員

第五，本局の事務を處理するため左の役員を置く
イ，名譽局長
ロ，顧　　問
ハ，局　　長　　一　名
ニ，幹　　事　　三　名
ホ，評 議 員　　若干名
局長は本局の事務を總括す
幹事は本局の事務を處理す
評議員は局長の提案に依る重要事務を審議す

第六，評議員は左記の者を以て之に充つ
イ，全日本佛教青年會聯盟理事及主事
ロ，全日本佛教青年會聯盟理事會に於て推薦したる者

第七，局長及幹事は評議員會に於て決定す

第八，名譽局長及顧問は評議員會に於て推薦す

第九，役員の任期は二ケ年とす（但し重任を妨げず）

經　　費

第十，本局の經費は左記のものに依て之を支辨す
イ，本局基金の活用
ロ，寄附金
ハ，その他の收入

補　　則

第十一，本定款に記載せられざる事項は，凡て評議員會に於て協議す

第十二，第一回の役員は全日本佛教青年會聯盟理事會に於て決定す

定價	一部	金三十錢	送料五厘
	一年	金二圓四十錢	送料不要

昭和十年四月廿日第三種郵便物認可
昭和十二年三月廿八日印刷（毎月一回）
昭和十二年四月一日發行（一日發行）

東京市外吉祥寺337
編輯發行兼印刷人　淺野研眞

東京市牛込區早稲田鶴巻町107
印刷所　株式會社東文社印刷所
電話牛込（34）1950番 5049番

東京市神田區一ツ橋二の三
發行所　國際佛教通報局
電話九段（33）4428番
振替東京83015番

昭和十年四月三十日第三種郵便物認可 昭和十二年三月二十八日印刷納本（毎月一回一日發行）昭和十二年四月一日發行 國際佛教通報 第三卷 第四號

期日 五月一日(土)二日(日)

青年佛徒よ參加せよ！

全日本佛教青年會聯盟

第七回總會

☒參加費（一人金壹圓也）

☒申込期日（四月十日まで）

☒汽車割引（申込次第省線五割引券を送附）

☒申込書（出席申込者は當事務局へ申出られたし）

その他詳細は「出席の栞」を參照されたし。

名古屋市中區南伊勢町一ノ八

全日本佛教青年會聯盟

申込所 臨時事務局

未加盟團體はこの際加盟して出席せられたし

場所＝名古屋市公會堂

昭和十年四月三十日第三種郵便物認可 昭和十二年四月二十八日印刷納本 昭和十二年五月一日發行（毎月一回一日發行）第三卷 第五號

The International Buddhist Bulletin

國際佛教通報

第三卷 昭和十二年五月 第五號 〔Vol. III. May $\frac{2503}{1937}$ No. 5.〕

五月號要目

東京 國際佛教通報局 發行
The International Buddhist Information Bureau
Tokyo, Kanda, Hitotsubashi, II—3
Annual Subscription, ¥2.40 (post free). Single Copies 20 sen (post 2 sen)

國際佛教通報局定款

名　稱

第一，本局を國際佛教通報局と稱す

事務所

第二，本局の事務所を全日本佛教青年會聯盟本部に置く

目　的

第三，本局は日本內地及海外に向つて佛教事情の通報をなし，且つ佛教徒相互間の各種便宜を計るを以て目的とす

事　業

第四．本局の目的を達成するため左記の事業を行ふ

イ，日本內地及世界各國より佛教事情に關する質問の通報を行ふ

ロ，必要に應じ日本語及世界各國語を以て佛教事情の通報を行ふ

ハ，外國人の日本觀光に際しては各種の便益を與へ，特にその佛教に關する方面に於て之を爲す

ニ，定時或は隨時に各國語を以て文書の刊行をなす

ホ，その他必要と認めたる事業を行ふ

役　員

第五，本局の事務を處理するため左の役員を置く

イ，名譽局長　一　名

ロ，顧　問　若干名

ハ，局　長　一　名

ニ，幹　事　三　名

ホ，評議員　若干名

局長は本局の事務を總括す

幹事は本局の事務を處理す

評議員は局長の提案に依る重要事務を審議す

第六，評議員は左記の者を以て之に充つ

イ，全日本佛教青年會聯盟理事及主事

ロ，全日本佛教青年會聯盟理事會に於て推薦したる者

第七，局長及幹事は評議員會に於て決定す

第八，名譽局長及顧問は評議員會に於て推薦す

第九，役員の任期は一ケ年とす（但し重任を妨げず）

經　費

第十，本局の經費は左記のものに依て之を支辨す

イ，本局基金の活用

ロ，寄附金

ハ，その他の收入

補　則

第十一，本定款に記載せられざる事項は，凡て評議員會に於て協議す

第十二，第一回の役員は全日本佛教青年會聯盟理事會に於て決定す

Some Stories of Kannon, the Goddess of Mercy

by **Atsuharau Sakai**

The Senso-ji Temple, Tokyo

On the 18th of the third month (March) in the 36th year (628 A. D.) of the reign of the Empress Suiko (the 34th), Haji-no-Nakatomo, with his two retainers, Hamanari and Naritake of the Hinokuma family, went on a small boat to catch fish in the River Sumida, which now runs through the streets of Tokyo. They had caught many fishes before, but on this particular day no fish were caught, no matter how often they threw their net into the water, and they were about to go home in despair when they fished up in the net something that glittered. What was their surprise when they found it to be a Kannon image of pure gold (1.8 inches tall), which they immediately enshrined in a shrine built on the banks of the River Sumida.

This is the origin of the Senso-ji Temple, which has since been the Mecca for the believers of Kannon, the deity of mercy; and now that over 1,300 years have elapsed since the shrine was erected, it is visited by thousands every day and by hundreds of thousands on special occasions. The Kannon is originally the Indian god, Avalokitesvara, also called the Goddess of Mercy. She is one of the most popular deities in Japan, and there is hardly any village or town in the whole country but has a shrine dedicated to this deity, for she is believed to work miracles for her believers and hear their prayers. And it is a remarkable fact that she has quite a large number of believers in the intelligentzia class of people. At the great earthquake of 1923, for instance, the Senso-ji Temple escaped destruction when all the buildings around the temple were reduced to ashes by fire; standing intact amid all debris reaching for miles around the temple and the people attribute its preservation to the protection of the Goddess Kannon, who is enshrined in it. The priest of the temple will also tell you that it had several miraculous escapes of fire before.

During the era of Kyowa (1801–1804), a farmer who was staying at the Reigan-ji Temple, visited the Senso-ji Temple on one afternoon, when a madman who met him on the street struck at him with a sword. The farmer fell senseless, feeling that he was mortally hurt. When he was brought to life again, however, he had no wound on his body, but it was discovered that the picture of the Goddess Kannon painted on a piece of paper that he carried as an amulet next to his skin under his clothing, was cut through, soaked in blood. It was concluded that the goddess received the sword as a "scape-goat," and saved her devout believer.

Many stories are told about miracles wrought by the Goddess Kannon to save her believers or to answer their prayers. Here is one that the writer heard direct from a nobleman who was saved by the goddess, and who is now a great believer in the deity.

Viscount Vice Admiral Chosei Ogasawara and his Kannon Image

Viscount Vice-Admiral Chosei Ogasawara had a pious mother, who was a great believer in the Kannon. When the viscount, then a young officer on board the H. M. S. "Takachiho," started for the front during the Chino-Japanese war, his mother gave him an image of the Kannon, that had been kept as a family treasure for generations, saying: "You take this holy image of the Kannon with you. Keep it in your own cabin and offer a cup of tea to her at times; and you will be protected."

Though he was not a religious man himself, the young officer, true to his mother's injuction, enshrined the holy image in his own cabin, not so much on account of his devotion to the deity as because, through his sense of filial responsibility, he wanted to set his aged mother at ease. Every now and then, however, when he opened the small niché of the Kannon in his cabin, he was happy, feeling as if his mother were with him on board, for the image seemed always to cheer him up. He could not help bowing before the image

because it always reminded him of his mother.

One night, early in September, 1894, the visconnt saw a great naval operation in a dream. It was a sanguinary one, and his ship received several balls in the battle. He too was hit on the right arm and he was awakened from the dream. On the following morning the young officer wrote a letter to his mother giving a description of the naval battle he saw in the dream, though he made no mention of the piece of a cannon ball that hit him on the right arm.

A little over ten days later the battle of the Yellow Sea took place. Strange to tell, the position of his fleet was exactly the same as he had seen in his dream. It was a severe battle and his ship, which received a few balls, was a scene of veritable carnage after the battle. A cannon ball visited his own cabin destroying anything and everything in it. One of his overcoats, which was hanging on a rack, had 13 holes made by its pieces. But the niché of the Kannon stood safe as it had been left. He opened the door with a kind of reverence and what was his surprise to see that the Kannon lost a few of her right arms (for it was what was called the Senju-Kannon or Thousand-armed Kannon).

Whether this was a coincidence or a miracle, Viscount Ogasawara, who recollected his dream, in which one of his arms was cut off, was seized with gratefulness. He clasped his hands together to worship the image out of unmingled veneration for the first time in his life and "O mother." escaped from his lips unconciously.

"You may call me superstitious," Viscount Ogasawara went on to say "or you may consider this a mere coincidence. But this was what I actually experienced. When, on returning home after the battle, I told the story to my mother, she shed tears of gratitude, and one drop of her tear was enough for me."

The image of the Kannon, that saved the life of Viscount Ogasawara, is to be enshrined within the Big Kannon that is now being erected at Ofuna, near Kamakura.

* * * *
* * *

The Tsubosaka Temple (Translation)

"The Tsubosaka Temple" (or more literally translated "Tsubosaka-miraculous-deed-record") is one of the most popular singing-dramas often represented on the stage in Japan. The story is based on the devotion of O-Sato to her blind husband, Sawaichi, whose sight was restored miraculously by the Goddess Kannon of the Tsubosaka-ji Temple, also called the Minami-Hokke-ji Temple, of Yamato Province, where she offered her prayer.

—— • ——

Whether dream is a life or life a dream, life is little more real than a dream, and yet it becomes real, with its weals and woes, when one lives and realizes it, good or bad.

There lived a blind man, by the name of Sawaichi, in the outskirts of Tosa-Machi, near Tsubosaka, on the Yamato Highway as long and tedious as life drawn long. Born to honesty, he lived as slender a life as a string of his Koto-harp or of his three-stringed Shamisen-harp, by which the blind man earned a living as flickering as the thin smoke rising from his hearth. His wife, O-Sato, in faithful cooperation with her blind husband, picked up odd jobs of mending, washing and starching clothes for her neighbours. Nor was the sound of her fulling the starched clothes less faint than the life they were leading. The song of a bird and the tolling sound of a country bell were sad reminders that brought tears to their eyes and the trickling Imose-Gawa, or the River of Man-and-Wife, was no less suggestive of a sad life.

O-Sato: "Why, what thought made you take out the Shamisen and play on it? You are in good humour today, Mr. Sawaichi."

Sawa: "Well, O-Sato, do I look to be in good humour because I play the Shamisen?"

O-Sato: "Yes. you do."

Sawa: "Nothing farther from it. I feel gloomy almost to distraction. I would sooner die than. . . ."

O-Sato: "You don't say. . . ."

Sawa: "O yes, I feel as gloomy as I would that death might relieve me. Look here, O-Sato. There is something I have long wanted to ask you. Come and take a seat near me. It is nothing important, but it has

always been in my mind, and I have wanted to get it out. Time flies, as they say, like an arrow, and it is three years since we got married. And we had been betrothed from our childhood. We know each other well. Why do you keep anything from your husband? Tell me frankly."

O-Sato: "Why, Mr. Sawaichi, what are you speaking about? Since I married you three years ago, I have not kept anything, even so small as a single dew-drop, secret from you. If anything has displeased you, out with it. Am I not your wife?"

Sawa: "Glad to hear you say so! Out with anything! What can I hold from you? Now, listen, O-Sato. During the past three years of our married life, you have not been at home, even for a single night, after the seventh hour (4 a.m.). I am blind like this, and smallpox has so disfigured my face that I know, and it is reasonable enough, that you hate the sight of me. But if you are in love with any other man, just tell me frankly. I should not have got offended like this, if only you told me so. We are cousins, and when I hear people say that you are pretty, I control myself and am determined not to be jealous of you. Please tell me the truth."

This he said in a clear tone, though he had bitterly to swallow the tears overflowing his sightless eyes, while his wife, too much in torture and agony at these unexpected words, to care either for herself or for life, hugged her husband hard to her breast.

O-Sato: "What is this I hear, O hard-heartedness! Though lowly and unworthy, Mr. Sawaichi, I would not desert my own husband for all the world, or run to any one else. I connot understand how you put so little trust in me—it is too much to be so suspected. The death of my father and mother left me to the care of my uncle, who brought us together. I called you brother —my senior by three years—and we were happy. As ill luck would have it, however, smallpox seized you and deprived you of your sight—an affliction not inherited from your parents. Then on top of that, poverty overtook us. But I cared not a bit about your blindness or our poverty. You are my husband, good or bad, and I shall be your loyal wife till the end of time, even if we suffer the torture of fire and water. What is more, I repaired to the Temple of Kannon, the Goddess of Mercy, of Tsubosaka, and prayed for the restoration of sight to your sightless eyes. When the bell struck the seventh hour at dawn, I slipped out atealthily and struggled up the rugged mountain-paths. Not a single day has passed during these years, but I repeated my supplication before the Goddess Kannon. No response has as yet been returned. What false retribution can this be? Just now I was inwardly accusing the Goddess Kannon of her non-response to my repeated prayer. You took no notice of my faithful love, but instead suspected me to be in love with some one else. Your one word of suspicion put me out of humour. How could I be otherwise?"

Sawaichi was overpowered by the tearful chastity of his wife and his blind eyes also overflowed with tears.

Sawa: "Say no more. It is too much. Since you are wholeheartedly devoted, I would that the Buddha Almighty, who they say restores flowers to a dead tree, might make the dead tree of my blind eyes bloom! Only, I am too sinful—Oh, if even in my future life, I would—no, O-Sato, lead me by the hand and let us go together right now."

Delighted at these words, O-Sato dressed herself lightly and hastily. She handed her husband a slender cane, out of sympathy, and with their courage no less slender but their hope stout, they made their way together to the Temple of Tsubosaka.

When, according to tradition, the Emperor Kammu, the fiftieth Emperor of the Imperial line, had a serious eye-trouble, Priest Kido, of the Tsubosaka Temple, offered a prayer to the Holy Image for a hundred and seven consecutive days, at the end of which time the Emperor was entirely cured of his trouble. The temple is now known all over the country as the Sixth Sacred Place of the West, where prayer is miraculously answered.

Their feet were guided and prompted by the chanting Songs of Praise which happened to be wafted up from below the hill, and Sawaichi and his wife came towards the holy temple.

O-Sato: "Faith is important, Mr. Sawaichi, but sickness is often dependent upon your heart. Your

low spirits will only make you the worse. You are too much dejected to get cured. At such a time you had better divert yourself in cheerfully singing some familiar song."

Sawa: 'You are right. It will only injure my eyes to be in the blues. I will try one for a change. But is there nobody in sight near here? Oh, Fie!

'Whether affiication is merciful
or mercy afflicting,
Oh, my life already despaired
is as evanescent as a dewdrop. . . . .'

Hold! Do not pull me like that. Your sudden pull so scared me that I forget the rest of my song. Ha! ha! ha!"

O-Sato: "Ha! ha!"

Sawaichi and his wife struggled along up the rugged paths encouraged by his cheerful singing, till they came to the main temple of the Goddess Kannon.

O-Sato: "Here we are at last, Mr. Sawaichi. That is the Goddess Kannon over there."

Sawa: "Oh, is this the temple of the merciful Kannon. Oh, most merciful! Namu, O Buddha! Buddha Merciful! Buddha Almighty! Namu, O Buddha! Namu, O Amida! But look here, O-Sato. I have climbed up, as you told me, hoping against hope to be cured. But my eyes seem all beyond recovery, do they not?"

O-Sato: "Nonsense! Do away with your silly talk! Come, Mr. Sawaichi. Faith requires patient devotion. Give yourself up and trust. The merciful Kannon will surely answer our prayer. Let us repeat our prayer, instead of yielding to an idle talk."

This encouragement of his wife put heart into him.

Sawa: "I see that you are right. Then I will stay here fasting for three days and nights. You go home and attend to your work. The three days will decide my fate, whether I get cured or remain uncured."

O-Sato: "Oh, will you? Well said, Mr. Sawaichi. I will go home for a little work and as soon as I am done, I shall hurry back. This is a steep mountain-path. Just a few steps farther up, there is an unfathomable gorge on the right-hand side. You must stay here, without stirring a step further."

Sawa: "Where could I go? I shall have to vie with the Goddess Kannon for patience. Ha! ha!"

His wife smiles, too, and with

her heart lingering behind her, she hurries on her homeward mission, little knowing that this seperation is no more to be trusted in than a lingering frost which now is and then is not.

Sowaichi is left to himself. The desolation of his life is unbearable to him. He breaks down under it and cries.

Sawa: "Oh, it makes me happy to think that my wife has faithfully taken care of me all these years and months. No pressing poverty could induce her to desert me and she has never betrayed a sign of displeasure with me. Instead of getting disgusted with her blind husband, she pays me the greatest attention. What do I repay her? I doubted her faithfulness in turn, and looked at her with all sorts of misgivings. Forgive me, O O-Sato, for my mistrust. If I part from you now, in what life shall I see you again? Alas for me! Take pity upon me!"

Sawaichi falls upon his face moaning, unconcious of all things around him. He lifts his head again.

Sawa: "My wife's constant and devoted prayers of three years have failed to be of any avail. What good will come if I live any longer? The proverb says, 'Retire and there will be two rich men.' (Better seperate from, than be associated, with a person of a different mind; then both will succeed.) My death will be my return to you for your attentions. You live after me, O-Sato, and marry a better husband. There is an unfathomable gorge, you told me, on the right-hand side a little farther up. This is the best place for me to die. If I turn into dust at such a sacred place, I may be saved in the future life. Night has far advanced and while nobody sees me, I will. . . ."

Sawaichi stands up. He quiets his disturbed heart and composes himself. He goes up four or five steps, when he hears the bell of early dawn booming. This is his last speed-up in life, and he gropes his tottering way, in a blind manner, with his cane as his only guide and support. He scrambles up a rock, on one side, where he hears the awe-inspiring stream below. Could it be the voice of the Goddess Kannon, who has come to receive him? "O Namu, Oh Buddha! O Amida!" he cries and and putting aside his cane, he hurls himself headlong down, to

end his miserable life in a miserable way.

Utterly ignorant of this sad event, O-Sato, his wife, hurries back from home. Her steps are quickened somehow or other and she presses on so impatiently that she often stumbles and falls down on this familiar path. She reaches where Sawaichi was and finds him gone.

O-Sato: "Oh, gone. Where can he be? Where has he gone? Mr. Sawa-ichi-i, Mr. Sawa-ichi-i."

She shouts and searches for him. But no voice is heard nor is his shadow even to be seen anywhere. She runs this way and then totters in that, calling the name of her husband. Something startles her in the moonlight shining through the thick branches. It is his cane! She is tempted to look down into the gorge and she seems to see the body of her husband in the moonshine. What should be done? What could she do? Madness seizes her and she runs amuck, writhing. But she has no wings to fly down with. She shouts, but echo is the only reply she gets.

O-Sato: "Oh, heartlessness! Haven't I patiently offered a devoted prayer to the Goddess Kannon all these years and months through all kinds of privations? I minded no hardships, and have never ceased a moment to pray that your sight may be restored to your eyes! What sight do I see today of all days? What will become of me after you are gone? What can I do thus left to myself? What, Oh what can I do? This reminds me now of the song you sang a short time ago. I felt a kind of uneasiness when I heard it, but I little suspected you. You were already prepared for this sad hour of death. I did not notice it. I should not have urged you to come out, if I had known this. Forgive me! Oh, forgive!

"Who can be worse-fated than I am? I am abandoned by my husband, to whom I pledged my troth for the next life as well as this—who, that is not immortal, could ever foresee this long separation? Whether or not earthly hardship is a retribution for a sin committed in a previous life, I can see how my poor husband, who could not see even in this life, wanders from darkness to darkness in his journey to death. Who will guide him in the abode below?"

Thus she soliloquizes in tears, which ceaselessly falling might have increased the depth of the gorge stream of Tsubosaka.

O-Sato: "No, I will say no more. Our destiny was fixed in our previous existence. I shall be resigned. I must hasten on the same journey of death as my husband took, so that I might hand him this cane, his keepsake. Guide me, O Buddha! Namu, O Buddha, guide!"

With these words, O-Sato follows her husband into the gorge and also puts a sad end to the life of a faithful wife.

In the middle of the second month, early at dawn, there flushes a stream of light from the clouds. The sweet voice was heard of a richly dressed and graceful court-lady. She is none other than the Goddess Kannon herself in disguise.

Kannon: "How now, Sawaichi? Listen what I have to say. Your eyes were closed because of your sins committed in the former life. You and your wife are both doomed and are on the verge of death, which may come at any moment. But in appreciation of your wife's devotion to you and the prayer offered from day to day, your lives shall be prolonged. You must be henceforth devoted to the Faith and live a life of pilgrimage visiting the Thirty-Three Sacred Places, in return for the boundless mercy of the Buddha. Do you hear, Sawaichi and O-Sato?"

These words were no sooner said than the graceful person of the goddess disappeared as if blown out, when the bells sounded far and near from below in the air of early dawn and the twilight gradually gave way to day-light. Sawaichi and O-Sato awoke in the gorge which was still dark. They started to their feet.

Sawa: "True! My eyes are opened! Eyes open! Thank goodness! The Goddess Kannon be thanked! Kannon be praised! But who are you?"

O-Sato: "Who am I! Am I not your wife?"

Sawa: "You, my wife? Glad to see you for the first time. Oh, goodness be thanked! But how miraculous! Surely I fell down into the gorge and must have died. I was unconcious when the Goddess Kanon appeared before me and told me everything of my previous existence."

O-Sato: "So was it with me.

I jumped into the gorge after you, but I suffered no bodily injury. Instead, you have your blind eyes opened. This is too good to be more real than a dream. So I see that it was the Goddess Kannon herself that called your name repeatedly and restored you to life. Oh, the Goddess Kannon be thanked and praised! Let us start at once on a pilgrimage."

The sun, shining upon Sawaichi and O-Sato for the first time after their fall, brought to them, like the advent of a new spring, a joy similar to the one felt by a turtle that basks itself on a piece of wood floating on a wide sea. The divine blessing of the Goddess Kannon restored sight to the blind eyes with the happiness of the New Year, and brought to life the man and wife, whose nuptial knot was tied more tightly-so tightly that "no water could leak through it." Oh, how gracious is the Goddess Kannon, to whose merciful revelation everything in life is to be attributed! Sawaichi and his wife offered in the temple the cane they needed no longer and returned their deep-felt thanks to the gods and Buddha with the purity of an early morning. A rock monument was erected in the temple compounds of pebbles as clean, and a pool made of water as clear and pure, as in the Jodo, or the Land of Purity. Oh, how miraculous the Law is in its revelation.

The Kosen-ji Temple and 100 Kannon-images of Kanto

There are many sets of Kannon-images that the pious people visit on their pilgrimages; such as 88 images of the Shikoku Provinces, 33 images of Bando, etc. The modern-minded priest of the Kosen-ji Temple, Tokyo, Junto by name, conceived a happy idea that suits our age of speed. He visited one hundred shrines of the Kannon in Tokyo and its vicinity by spending several years, and he brought a handful of earth from the precincts of each shrine. He buried the earth under the ground in front of the Kannon shirine in his temple grounds. Then he made a lotus-flower of cement over the buried earth, so that one who worships the Kannon of the Kosen-ji Temple can at the same time worship the hundred Kannon images thus represented by a handful earth brought from each shrine; without going through the trouble of visiting a hundred shrines of the Kannon.

Constitution of the Pan-Pacific Federation of Young Buddhist Association

Article 1. Name

The name of this organization shall be the Pan-Pacific Federation of Young Buddhist Associations.

Article 2. Headquarters

The business headquarters of this Federation shall be located at the headquarters of the All Nippon Federation of Young Buddhist Associations, in Tokyo.

Article 3. Membership

The membership of this Federation shall be composed of the Young Buddhists Associations in the countries bordering the Pacific Ocean, and their neighboring countries.

Article 4. Purpose

The object of this federation shall be to unite the Young Buddhists' Associations for the purpose of establishing a system of harmonious co-operation in their efforts to promote the Buddhistic spirit and to strengthen each other by mutual contacts and mutual assistance.

Article 5. Departments

In order to accomplish the said object, the federation shall establish the following departments:

A. Publication Department to publish an official organ.

Article 6. Officers

This federation shall have the following officers:

A. Honorary Advisors.
B. Central Board of Directors.
C. Executive Board composed of Executive Committee and Financial Committee.
D. Central Executive Officers.

Article 7. Duties of Officers

1. Honorary Advisors shall be the advisors of the Federation.
2. Central Board of Directors shall govern the Executive Board.
3. Executive Committee shall supervise the business of the Federation.
4. Financial Committee shall record and transact all financial affairs of the Federation.
5. Central Executive Officers shall transact all business under the supervisson of the Executive Board.

Article 8.

Selection and Terms of Officers

Section 1.

1. Honorary Advisors shall be composed of three members selected from each affiliated country and ten members selected from Nippon.
2. Central Board of Directors shall be composed of two members selected from each affiliated country and five members selected from Nippon.
3. Members of the Excutive Board shall be appointed by the Central Board of Directors.
4. The Executive Board shall appoint the necessary number of men for the Central Executive Office.

Section 2.

Terms of the officers shall be four years, except the Executive Board and the Central Executive Officers which shall be left to the judgement of the Central Board of Directors.

Section 3.

Officers shall be selected at the General Conference of the Federation.

Article 9. Meetings

1. The Federation shall meet once in every four years, and the place of such gathering shall be decided at the previous meeting.
2. Official Boards shall meet when deemed necessary.

Article 10. Finance

Finance of the Federation shall be from the following sources:

1. Membership Fees. (Which shall be set by the Central Board.)
2. Donations.
3. Other incomes.

Article 11.

Admittance and Withdrawal

1. Any Young Buddhist Association which wishes admittance into the Federation shall file an application with the Executive Committee for formal action at a meeting of the Central Board of Directors.
2. Any Young Buddhists Association which wishes to withdraw from the Federation shall state its reason before a meeting of the Central Board of Directors and, with their approval, have its withdrawal formally acknowledged.

Article 12. Amendment

No amendment to this constitution shall be valid unless such amendment shall have been passed up on by the Central Board of Directors' Meeting.

Propositions to the Constitution

1. Publication:

A. This Federation shall issue its Official Organ "Young Buddhists" quarterly or bimonthly.

B. Its object is to carry out the purpose of the Federation.

C. Executive Committee shall supervise the edition.

D. Japanese and English Language shall be used.

2. Financial Plan:

A. Appropriations of the Annual Federation expenses to the affiliated countries shall be:

a.	Nippon	¥ 1,650.00
b.	Hawaii	400.00
c.	America	250.00
d.	Other countries	260.00
		¥ 2,560.00

B. Financial Budget shall be set up by the Executive Board and shall be approved by the Central Board of Directors.

C. Proposed Financial Budget shall be:

a.	Office Expense	¥ 600.00
b.	Salary	600.00
c.	Correspondence	200.00
d.	Publication of Official organ	1,160.00
		¥ 2,560.00

汎太平洋佛教青年會聯盟法規

第一條　名稱　本團體を汎太平洋佛教青年會聯盟（略稱汎聯）と稱す。

第二條　本部　本聯盟の本部を日本東京に置く。

第三條　組織單位　本聯盟は太平洋沿岸諸國及その隣接國、並に世界各國の佛教青年會聯盟を以て組織す。

第四條　目的　本聯盟は各佛教青年團體相互間の連絡及提携を保ち、佛教精神發揚の爲に統一ある協力をなすを以て目的とす。

第五條　部門　本聯盟は前記の目的を達成せんが爲に左の部門を設く。

一、出版部、機關紙の發行。

第六條　役員　本聯盟に左の役員を置く。

A、名譽委員（顧問）
B、中央委員
C、實行委員（財政委員を含む）
D、中央事務局員

第七條　役員の任務

一、名譽委員は本聯盟の顧問たるべし。
二、中央委員會は實行委員會を支配し、これに實務を委任す。
三、實行委員會は本聯盟の事務遂行を管理し指導す。
四、財務委員は本聯盟の會計事務一切を處理す。
五、中央事務局員は實行委員會指導管理のもとに本聯盟一切の事務を處理す。

第八條　役員の選擧及任期

第一項　役員の選擧

一、名譽委員は加入聯盟より若干名を以て組織す。
二、中央委員會は各加入聯盟より二名、日本より若干名を選出せる者を以て組織す
三、實行委員會は中央委員會によりて選出されたるものを以て組織す。
四、實行委員會は中央事務局員を必要に應じて任命す。

第二項　役員の任期

本聯盟の役員の任期は四ケ年とす但し實行委員及中央事務局員の任期は中央委員會によりて決定さるるものとす。

第三項

本聯盟の中央委員は聯盟の總會に於て選定す。

第九條　會合

一、本聯盟は四年に一度大會を開き、その開催地は前回の大會に於て決定さるゝものとす。
二、實行委員會、役員會は必要に應じ適當の場所にて開催することを得。

第十條　會計

本聯盟の經費は左の財源より之をもとむ。

一、會費（中央委員會にて決定す）
二、寄附
三、其の他（出版物等）

第十一條　加入及脫退

一、本聯盟に加入せんとする青年會聯盟は實行委員會に申込み、中央委員會の承認を經て正式加入するものとす。
二、本聯盟を脫退せんとする青年會も亦同樣の手續を經るものとす。

第十二條　本聯盟の規約は中央委員會の承認を經ざれば修正することを得ず　以上

法規に關する細則

一、雜誌出版

A、本聯盟はその目的を遂行する爲年二回以上"Young Buddhists"と稱する機關誌を發行す。
B、實行委員會はその編輯に當る。
C、用語は日英華語の範圍とす。

二、經費の支出

A、本聯盟の經常費を左の割當による年額費にもとむ。

日本	千六百五十圓
布哇	四百圓
北米	二百五十圓
その他	各國より百圓宛

B、經常費の豫算は實行委員會に於て之を立て、中央委員會の承認をうくべし。

C、經常費豫算

一、事務所費	六〇〇・〇〇圓
二、事務主任給	六〇〇・〇〇
三、文通通信費	二〇〇・〇〇
四、出版費	一・一六〇・〇〇
合計	二・五六〇・〇〇

我派の海外布教に就て

臨濟宗妙心寺派
敎學部長　金　仙　宗　諄

我が妙心寺派に於ては，海外布敎と云ふても，まだ北米とかハワイとか云ふ樣な遠方にまでは及んでは ゐない が，近く朝鮮，臺灣，滿洲及支那方面を强いて海外と云ふことが出來るならば，この方面に於ける布敎は，相當に早くから着手してゐる。

先づ朝鮮では，日露戰役の後，古川大航師が先づ朝鮮に渡り，次いで圓山太嶺師渡鮮，最初の布敎監督として京城に臨済寺を創め，法幢を樹てられた。次いで古川大航師京城に妙心寺別院を創設し，後を後藤瑞巖師に讓つて青島に赴かれた。圓山太嶺師後また滿洲に移錫せられた。後藤瑞巖師は大正三年頃京城の妙心寺別院に入り，着々敎線を擴張し，其の間各地に布敎所が次第に設けられ，主任が置かれ，朝鮮全土に亘つて，臨濟の祖風が顯揚せらるるに至つた。後藤布敎監督は，朝鮮總督府を初め，諸官衙の公人なり，又私人なりから，非常な尊信を受け，十數年間朝鮮に於ける敎界の爲めに，貢献する所頗る多かつた。昭和四年，後藤師が內地に歸還せらるるや，華山大義師替つて布敎監督の任に就かれ，後藤師同樣，同地の敎化の爲め大に盡瘁せられつゝある。一昨年朝鮮總督府が,「心田開發」の銘を打つて，朝鮮全土に亘つて，一大精神的淨化運動を起さるるに際して，特に講師を後藤師に委囑せられたのは，同師が在任中の功績の如何を裹書きするものと見てよからう。さて現在の寺院並に布敎所としては，大邱，平壤，釜山，群山，沙里院，南原，大田，興南，杏村，洞山，羅津，裡里等に各一ケ所づつあり，主任及開敎使が相當に布敎上に功果を舉げつつある。

次に臺灣に本派布敎師として渡航された中では，細野南岳師を以て首めとなすが，其の後幾人かの布敎師が續々渡航し，明治四十年前後，兒玉將軍が開基として，梅山玄秀師を拜請して開山となし，臺北圓山に鎭南山臨濟護國禪寺を創設せらるるに到つて，臺灣に於ける布敎上の基礎は茲に漸く鞏固となつた。後臺灣布敎監督は，現任の高林玄寶師に至るまで，幾人か替つてはゐるが，其の間に布敎所も次第に各地に增設せられ，敎線も擴張された。尙臺灣の昔からの寺院は，元來臨濟系統であるが爲め，聯絡寺廟と稱して，漸次妙心寺に付隨するやうになつて來た。本派寺院としては，臨濟寺の外に，花蓮港に東臺寺，高雄に龍泉寺，馬公に妙廣寺，基隆に最勝寺，北投に鐵眞院あり，更に士林，大稻埕，臺北，二水，嘉義，關子嶺，臺南，鹽水，新城，鳳林，岡山，赤崁，旗山，五里林等に各布敎所があり，各主任競つて敎化の實績を舉げつつある。

臺灣には，此等寺院や布敎所の外に，臺北に佛敎專修道場があつて，主として所謂本島人卽ち臺灣土人の僧侶の子弟敎養をなしつつある。この專修道場は，宗門の中等敎育機關であつて，現在の高林布敎監督が熱心に指導の任に當り，數名の敎師これを補佐して，軈て臺灣寺院の住職たるべき，徒弟の基礎的敎育をなしつつある。其の外高雄には，佛敎慈愛院があつて，施藥，施療，感化等の社會救濟事業をなしつつある。これには東海宜誠師が献身的に從事してゐる。因に同師は渡臺以來，已に二十餘年，臺灣語に委しく，能く土語を以て親しく土人に接觸し，實際上の指導誘掖をなしつつ感化を與へ居り，同地に於ける妙心寺派の首動者とも云ふべき人であつて，各方面の尊敬を受けつつある。

次に滿洲では，日露戰役後，細野南岳師，釋佛海師の二人相續いで安東の鎭江山臨濟寺に法幢を樹てられ，特に釋佛海師は最初の南滿洲布敎監督として，大に盡瘁せられたが，後圓山太嶺師が朝鮮から大連に赴き，妙心寺別院を開かれるに至つて，同師釋佛海師に代つて布敎監督の名を襲ひ，其の間次第に布敎所も各地に設けられ，今日では，奉天，撫順，鞍山，錦州，哈爾賓，吉林，克山，山海關，大虎山，洮南，圖們等に，各寺院並に布敎所が出來，主任及開敎使それぞれ布敎に從事しつつある。そして一昨年圓山師病氣の爲め布敎監督を辭せらるるや，山本玄峰師其の後任として就任せられたが，これより先，妙心寺派としては，新興の首都新京に昭和十年に本山で行はれた開創六百年大法會記念の事業として一の別院を新設するの必要を痛感し，新京神泉路に土地を購入し，妙心寺別院を建設しつつあつたが，建築の工事一部竣工するを待つて，山本玄峰師數名の雲衲を隨へてここに錫を留められ，修養道場を開いて信者を接得し，同地に於ける日滿要人の篤き歸依を受けて禪風の舉揚に寧日なき有樣，尙將來に向つては色々計劃もあることとて，大に屬目せられつつある。

終りに支那方面では，嚢に朝鮮の布敎に從事せられつつあつた古川大航師が，朝鮮から青島へ移錫せられ，布敎監督としてここに新たに敎田を開拓せられ，漸く布敎の地盤を固められつつあつたが，大正六年頃內地へ歸還せらるることとなり，今の布敎監督細川禪英師其の後を繼承せられ，盛んに各種の敎化事業を企劃する所あり，特に今年五月からは，東亞禪林を創設し，中學卒業程度の學徒で，將來支那開敎に從事せんとするものの爲めに，三ケ年の課程の敎育を授け，將來支那へ佛敎を弘通すると共に，日支親善の爲め大に貢献せんと焦慮しつつあり。かくて滿洲の別院と相並んで，青島の別院は，名實兼ね備へたものとして，將來を期待せられつつある。支那の布敎所としては，張店及上海に各一ケ所づつある。特に上海の布敎所では，主任伊藤正倜師が，年々內地から替る替る老師を拜請して，信者の爲めに接心會を開き，祖風顯揚に努めつつあり，今年の如きは，杉本全機師を請じて，接心會を開かれたが，丁度此の時杉本師は，一方では臨濟黃檗各派の委囑を受け，上海第二艦隊慰問を初め，支那駐屯の陸海軍將士の慰問をなすべく同地に赴かれ，軍部から盛んな歡迎を受け，謝意を表せられたのであつた。

以上は簡單ながら，現在に於ける，妙心寺派の朝鮮，臺灣，滿洲並に支那方面の布敎の概要である。が勿論一派としては，決してこの現狀を以て滿足してゐるわけではなく，將來は此等の方面にも，又遠く他の海外の方面に向つても，出來得る丈け布敎の上に發展をなしたい希望を有つてゐる。

「汎聯」より「萬聯」へ！

—躍進佛青運動の指標—

浅野研眞

一

いよいよ一九三七年も進み，超非常時局は，今や無條約時代にまで突入したのである。

然し，今更，うろたへたり，騒いだりすることもなからう。況んや怪しげな笛に踊らされてはならないのだ。

無制限的な軍備競爭などは，何んとしても，再反省さるべきものである。敢へて「平和のための固め」を否定しようとするものではないが，國民のお腹がペシヤンコになつてしまつたのでは，如何に立派な武器も役に立つものではないのだ。民福を犠牲にし，民衆課税によつて支辨されるやうな種類の國防費であつたならば，これは餘程考へものだといはねばならない。

吾々は，もつと進歩的な社會政策的稅制の確立を要望せずにはゐられない。特に農村福利と農民生活の向上を眼目としたものを要望するものだ。

然し，その點は今は深入りしないが，要するに「平和のための固め」なるものが，もつと有効に押し進められないものだらうか？

軍備競爭などによつて，所詮共倒れになるの危險を冒してまで，世界各國は狂奔せねばならないものだらうか？

もつと別途な，效果的な方策はないものだらうか？

二

より效果的な方策一私は之を思想工作の方面に於て見出したいのである。

昨年頃から，盛んに「思想國防」といふ用語が流行（？）するやうであるがそしてその鋳造には，實は滿洲で吾々も親しく參加した所のものであつたやうに思ふが，實は飛行機や機關銃などの有形の武器以上に，如何に「思想」が有力な無形の武器であるかは，世人の等しく知るところであらう。

所で，この思想的武器を，最も露骨に，而かも最も有効に逆用（？）してゐるのは，何といつても，ソヴエート・ロシアであらう。そのコミンテルンの強力な組織的宣傳力は，今更多言を要しない所のものであらう。

昨秋，之に對抗して締結された所の，かの日獨防共條約の如きも，實は彼に引きずられたものであつて，實は受身の消極的のものでしかないやうに思へる。

フアツシヨ伊太利は，逆に古典ローマ文化の現代的宣揚運動を起してゐるし，また，ローマ法研究所などを作つて，これだけは何といつても伊太利で

なければ‥‥といはぬ許りの顔をしてゐる。日伊文化交換も近來甚だ盛んのやうではあるが，然し日本からは，どんな「思想」を，どんな「文化」を，代償として提供しようといふのか？

三

廣く智識を世界に求めた明治時代の受身的な文化外交政策の時代は，もうそろそろ脱却されて良い時代ではなからうか？

そろそろ「日本文化」を逆に輸出して，少しは東洋人の世界的地位を高めたいものである。

そのためには，色々な輸出品もあらうが，「思想」としては私は何と云つても，我が「大乘佛教」を第一位に推さなければならないと思ふ。聖德太子以來，この「大乘相應地」に充分に養ひ來られ，日本文化の血となり，肉となり切つてゐる所の，此の「大乘佛教」なる綜合文化こそは，何んと云つても，輸出さるに價ひすべき「思想」であらねばならぬ。

現代印度や南洋地域の原始型の小乘佛教では，プラウドの高い彼ら白人たちの人生觀を納得させることは出來ない。それでは，どこまでも，植民地の宗教として蔑視されるに過ぎない。せいぜいのところ，考古學的乃至土俗學的研究の對象とされるに過ぎないのだ。歐米の佛教學者と云ふのは，皆さうしたカテゴリーの人物なのでしかない。決して佛教を尊信する佛徒ではないのだ？

然し，流石に鼻の高い彼ら白人たちも，敏感なる哲人たちの叫びによつて，「西洋の沒落」を感じ，「光は東方より」と云ふことになつて來た。

ナチス獨逸は，アリアン民族文化として佛教を，そして特に日本型の大乘佛教を進んで執り上げようとしてゐる。革新トルコは，「我等の祖・釋迦」とさへ叫ぶに至つたと云ふ。

此の時，此の期に於て，我等東方の大乘佛徒は，何故，もつと積極的に彼等の要望を滿たさうとはしないのだらうか？何故もつと進んで，彼らの思想的・精神的渇きを醫やさんとしないのだらうか？

極東の香り高き「思想」の贈物——我が日本大乘佛教の輸出こそは，正に今日の大責務なのではないのだらうか？

四

丁度，わが汎聯（汎太平洋佛靑聯盟）の日本側の役員も，ほぼ決定を見るに至つたので，愈よ汎聯の組織的發展となることであらう。

それに全聯（全日本佛靑聯盟）の本年總會は，去る五月一日二日にわたつて，佛都名古屋に於て擧行されたのであるが，丁度本年は名古屋で汎太平洋大博覽會が開催されてゐるので，汎太平洋諸國の佛教徒が，全聯總會にも廣汎に招待されたのである。それらの諸民族のオブザーバーに對して，我々は恥かしくない佛教大會を參觀せしむるに努めたと共に，これを契機として，堅きメンタル・タイを結ぶことを忘れなかつた。

それに明年は，いよいよ第三回汎聯

大會である。開催地に就いては，新興滿洲國に於て開催されることに正式の發表を見ることになつた。この際，我々は區々たる小意見を捨てて，これを機會に新興國建設の文化的意義を，諸民族に知らしむべきであらう。

そして三年後には，いよいよ皇紀二千六百年の佳歳を迎へるのだ。この佳年には，オリンピツク大會を初めとして，諸多の萬國大會が準備されてゐる中に我が全聯關係では，既に昨春の大阪總會の席上で，萬國佛教大會の開催を，逸早く率先して大衆的に決議してゐるのである。

その後，まだ纒つた準備委員會の結成を見てはゐないが，全聯並びに汎聯の諸機關を通して，いよいよ近く具體化することになるであらう。そして我が日本大乘佛教の光被工作の堂々たる步武が運ばれることにならう。

五

題號に示したテーマを說かんがために，私は途方もない廻り道をしてしまつた。しかし，もう，くどくどしく述べ立てることもなくなつてしまつた。

要は，我が日本大乘佛教の世界的進出に，積極的な拍車がかけられねばならない時期であることを痛感して貰ひたいだけである。このことを國策化しても良いではないかと建白したいのである。

幸ひ吾々は，國內的には「全聯」を持ち，汎太平洋的には「汎聯」を持つてゐるのだ。然らば進んで「萬聯」(萬國佛青聯盟）を持たんとすることも，決して無謀なことではあるまい。既にＹＭＣＡなどでは，さうした萬聯を持ち，萬國大會を試みてゐるではないか？

不幸にして，佛教民族は，近代文化に立ち遲れして，白人たちの植民地，乃至は半植民地となつてゐる。そしてメトロポリタンの，母國の，宗教文化に押し縮められてゐるのだ。然し，その白人の母國宗教たるキリスト教の如きにしても，實は植民地宗教の逆輸入による本土征服に出發してゐるではないか？

今こそ吾々は，全東洋人と共に，勇敢に立ち上つて，佛陀の福音を，萬國に傳へ聞かしめねばならない。そして聽て，

萬國の佛徒よ團結せよ！！

と，聲高らかに叫ばねばならない。

かくして初めて眞の「思想國防」の畫龍點睛ともならうといふものである。

また實際，白人の思索體系による佛教イデオロギーの色上げといふこともそれ自體，大きな進步であり，寄與であるだらう。

かくして「汎聯」より「萬聯」へ！このスローガンは「全聯」及び「汎聯」の現段階的指標として，佛徒の等しく念願して止まざる所のものであらねばならぬだらう。

要するに吾々は今や，單にアジヤや，汎太平洋の植民地民族の「お山の大將」的自負を捨離して，母國白人の文化再造の苦惱を救はねばならぬ。そして彼ら白人の自發的參降を期せねばならぬ「行劍」の極致は「無劍」の境地でなければならぬ。軍備の極致は「兵戈無用」の境域に於て見出されなければならぬ。

最後的な國防工作は實に「思想」國防のそれであり，それこそは正に大乘佛教の萬國的光被に存するのである。

かくして「國富民安」の萬國的理想鄉の出現となるであらう。

今や無條約時代の危機に面して，かくて吾々は「萬聯」結成の念願を吐露せずにはゐられないのである。

（完）

佛教和平國際的提議

太　　虛

佛教的和平本質，在諸法——一衆生一世界一事一物以至一原素的各一單位——衆緣生，諸法無自性，諸法無自性諸法衆緣生的理論。——般若——此理論的具體表現，卽是一攝一切攝一的法界，在人羣卽爲『個人是具有協力的和合關係之羣體的分子，社會是具有協力的和合關係之分子的羣體』。由此每一衆生的發心行事，應爲法界衆生的除苦——大悲——成樂——大慈——而動作，方便——每一個人的發心行事，應爲世界人羣的除害成利而動作，以玆和平原則，應用到世界人類，則爲國際和平，應用到國家民族，則爲國內和平。

現今世界人類反和平的鬪爭，則爲階級對立與民族對立的兩大鬪爭，然在中國則旣未形成兩大階級的對立，亦未完成民族國家的統一，遂由國內殘餘封建勢力的軍閥，藉國際之民族鬪爭——如漢奸——與階級鬪爭——如紅匪——的背景，以爲破壞國家民族統一的割據分裂，故猶有消弭內亂以建國家民族統一的需要。

蓋自蘇俄放棄世界革命而建設一國社會主義以來，已將階級鬪爭屈服於民族鬪爭之下，形成民族鬪爭的極端尖銳化時代，此時的中國，設非建成統一的民族國家，則中國民族必爲旁的民族所獨吞或分割，無以自存，故爲救亡圖存而完成統一的民族國家計，對於欲保持封建余勢的內爭，旣非用武力戡平不可，而外來的强鄰侵逼，尤非武力抵抗不爲功，如程滄舫在儒術政治與中國武化一書中所謂：

「我們目前是急切需中國的武化，需要勇於戰，以戰收復失地，同時亦需要辯的外交，爲戰爭後盾，根據這現代的中國武化的新原則，强化一切的組織和活動，政治要絕對的統一，經濟亦須同樣的加以統制，他如敎育以及一般的民衆生活，亦復聯帶的必然的要施以嚴格的軍事化紀律化，强化得像水泥鋼骨一般的結得牢，豎得起，耐得久，靠得住，爲迫於外力壓迫的需要，我們應努力照這樣做，我們應切實做到這樣。」

中國民族爲迫於需要而求建設現代的統一國家安內攘外的武化旣爲必須的工作，故佛教的和平原則，在國內幾無施用之地。

唯是中國現今的內亂旣以國際兩大鬪爭爲背景，則爲消弭內亂的拔本塞源計，端在融解國際兩大對立而建設和平國際，何況在兩大鬪爭一消一長間，階級鬪爭現雖暫屈於民族鬪爭之下，迨民族鬪爭鬆懈後，階級鬪爭必又擡頭，到階級鬪爭敝疲後民族鬪爭又必興起，設非闡明世界人類和平的本然社會眞相，組織和平國際以造成和平的人類世界，俾兩大對立從根本上不復存在，則終起伏於

兩大鬪爭而不獲安定，故建成現代的統一國家，雖有暫圖自存的意義，而未足以言普益世界人類，由此發揮佛教和平原理，以成立佛教和平國際，爲利益國民及世界人類，而作國際的和平建設，實爲現代佛教徒對於人羣應盡之義務，因此應有佛教徒國際和平會之組織。

原來社會——卽人羣——有本然的與構成的二大區別，本然社會卽人類生於是死於是死於是之協力的和合關係羣體，原始的亦終極的卽爲世界，具體而微之初起的則爲家族，擴大而演進則爲國家，由家族擴進爲國家羣體之過程上，則有强族——貴族或武士——的封建，始爲推進家族以成國家羣體之動力，終爲建成民族的統一國家之障礙，故欲建成近代的民族國家，必須剷除封建的殘存，由國家進達爲世界羣體的過程上，則有類似封建的民族國家，亦始爲推進國家以成世界羣體之動力，終爲建成世界的和平社會之障碍，然强族的封建有演進爲聯邦的統一民族國家之一格，故民族國家亦可演進爲聯邦的世界羣體，而佛教的和平國際之運動，亦卽以聯邦世界爲目標。

蓋人類初時生死於家族羣體中，鷄鳴犬吠相聞，至老死不相往來，家族卽等於世界，至進爲封建時代，藉天然的大山巨海爲障隔，自給自足，人民之生死於國家羣體中，國家卽等於世界，在家與國間之强族的封建區域，則等於今之所謂國家，再進爲民族國家時代，則封建區域夷爲中央政府統一下之地方政府，而同時以民族的國與國間衝突或調協之結果，經濟的政治的文化的交相涉入，形成國際間不可離絕的密切關係，遂不得不以聯邦的世界爲趨向，實現人類終極的世界羣體，在聯邦世界中，則今日的民族國家，亦降爲世界聯邦政府統一下之地方政府，無復民族對立的鬪爭，現今全地球交通便利，列强的經濟政治文化皆已形成世界關係，民族鬪爭的結果，無論勝負誰屬，均爲自殺，故函應有國際和平建設，至中國則猶有平內抗外以從半殖民地起爲自主的統一的民族國家的需要。

其以學術或職業，地位，政見，宗敎等等各種關係所集結之團體，則爲人類或出或入於其中之構成社會，雖亦有羣體與分子之協力的和合關係，而可隨宜以出入離合，故異本然之社會，至分裂爲階級對立之組織，尤爲出於本然社會陷入病態之時，失去了全社會協力的和合關係，乃成分立的抗爭，此種抗爭雖或可成爲進化，而亦可成爲退化，且在當時總是成爲社會文化力的分崩與消失，故終以能銷融弭爲上策，由此，對於隱伏在各民族國家間之國際的階級對抗鬪爭，尤有闡明佛教和平本質，建設和平國際之需要。

然此佛教和平國際，應從怎樣的途徑而爲組織，以什麼爲切要的工作吾意當徵集現居東方第一大都市之上海的各國佛教徒重要分子，開發起人會，先成立「佛教和平國際籌備處」發揚佛教和平眞理，應徵集世界各國佛教徒之抱此弘願者，參加發起，俟亞歐美各國佛教徒均重要分子爲發起人後，乃定期召開成立大會，成立佛教和平國際本部，而於有同志佛教徒三十人以上之各國，分設支部，

每年擇於有支部各國輪流開代表大會一次，以議決施行各種建設和平國際工作。

至工作之內容，自應以闡發佛教和平勝義，應用之以爲非暴寡非凌弱非爭覇非侵掠的反戰體理論，以萎打各强橫民族心理上瘋狂的戾氣凶燄，使服淸凉散而平息嗔火，同時，亦實踐布施丼六慶四攝的菩薩方便行，對於防禦或抵制各種掠奪攻戰的設施，予以提倡資助，更廣爲救災濟苦種種慈行，如王一亭居士等新近在上海刱立之佛教黃卍宗會，尤須聯合四衆各國佛教徒，成爲佛教的國際組織，乃能發揮與紅十字會並駕齊驅，或駕而上之的廣大功用，要言之，則本佛法緣生性空眞意義，發宣爲人類和平福音，學習修持種種方便行，以實現大悲大慈普濟普利而已。

於此尤所盼望者，則於佛教敎義上，今不惟漢藏已能交換研究翻譯，而日本，暹羅，錫蘭，緬甸，以及歐美等佛徒，亦已能與中國佛教徒爲個人的或團體的互相往來研習，特猶須速組聯合研究宣傳之機關耳！然尤要者，乃在宣揚佛教和平之眞理，攜手共作各種和平國際之實地行動，從事業上以表現佛教之和平意趣，中日兩國佛教尤有同文之密切連繫，日本昔嘗學習中國之佛教，中國今亦多譯日文之佛學，而在此中日國交衝突緊張之情勢上，中日佛教徒若能從佛教和平精神之感應，廻轉日本對於中國侵略的趨向，俾中國民族有以復興自存，進爲平等和合的眞正親善，同心協力以融解國際的兩大對立鬪爭，爲世界人類的和平幸福而努力，方能發揮佛教對於現代人類的實際功用，日本佛教徒曾誤責余譯骨宣揚抗日，譏爲失去佛教精神，故於此甚望日本佛徒能不失佛教精神，以平等和合來協作國際的佛教和平之運動。

世人又每以政僧譏余，然據孫中山先生之解釋，政卽衆人之事，政治卽管理衆人之事，廣義的管理衆人之事，當無有過於菩薩僧者，亦惟「菩薩僧」乃爲眞正的更無私事而專管理衆人之事一本瑜伽菩薩戒法，其與聲聞僧共者，端在於管理衆人之事，故不同聲聞僧少事少業少希望住，而剴切的表示須多事多業多希望僧住，余固末足爲菩薩僧然志願所在則未嘗一日忘學菩薩僧也。特患未能符政的名實，又何患世人之稱爲政僧，願世之學菩薩學菩薩僧的佛徒，皆驟然興起，以共修此建設和平的國際的菩薩大行。

二六・二・二〇　在上海市佛教會

（上海『佛教日報』二月二十三日所載）

局　報

定款中改正さる

去る四月三十日，名古屋の萬平ホテルに於て開催されたる本局評議員會に於て，

本局定款中第九の"**役員の任期は二ケ年とす**"云々とあるを"**一ケ年**"と改正されたるを以て，念のため玆に報告す。

國際佛教通報局

謹啓　貴聯盟愈々御隆昌奉大賀候
陳者第三回汎太平洋佛教青年會大會は明年夏を以て開催致すべきこと
に相成居候處開催地の決定に就ては第二回大會の決議を以て本聯盟に
一任せられ候に付爾來候補地につき調査交渉を進め來り候處愈々滿洲
國に於て開催することに決定致候間左樣御了承被下度候　敬具

昭和十二年三月二十一日

全日本佛教青年會聯盟

汎太平洋佛教青年會聯盟加盟各位

No. 3, 2 Chome, Hitotsubashidori,
Kanda, Tokyo,
March 21, 1937

Dear Sirs,

We are glad to inform you that the venue of the Third General Conference of the Pan-Pacific Young Buddhists Associations which is due next year has been fixed to Manchukou. You will remember that the task to see to the place of the coming conference was entrusted to us by the last conference. Since then it has been one of the greatest concerns to us to consider the matter and we have at last come to this conclusion.

Yours faithfully,

E. Ohtani

President,

The All Japan Y.M.B.A.

昭和十年四月三十日第三種郵便物認可
昭和十二年四月二十八日印刷納本(毎月一回)
昭和十二年五月一日發行(一日發行) 國際佛教通報 第三卷 第五號

定價	一部 金二十錢	送料五厘
	一年 金二圓四十錢	送料不要

昭和十年四月卅日第三種郵便物認可
昭和十二年四月廿八日印刷(毎月一回)
昭和十二年五月一日發行(一日發行)

東京市外吉祥寺337
編輯發行兼印刷人 淺野研眞

東京市牛込區早稻田鶴卷町107
印刷所 株式會社康文社印刷所
電話牛込(34)1950番 5049番

東京市神田區一ツ橋二の三
發行所 國際佛教通報局
電話九段(33)4428番
振替東京83015番

昭和十年四月三十日第三種郵便物認可 昭和十二年六月二十三日印刷納本 昭和十二年六月二十五日發行(毎月一回一日發行) 第三卷 第六號

The International Buddhist Bulletin

國際佛教通報

第三卷 昭和十二年六月 第六號 〔Vol. III. June $\frac{2503}{1937}$ No. 6.〕

六月 (June)

東京 國際佛教通報局 發行
The International Buddhist Information Bureau
Tokyo, Kanda, Hitotsubashi, II—3
Annual Subscription, ¥2.40 (post free), Single Copies 20 sen (post 2 sen)

サ　ラ　ナッタ　ヤ　ム

Saraṇattayaṁ
三 歸 依〔巴利語〕

(1) ブッダム　サラナム　ガッチヤーミ
Buddhaṁ saraṇaṁ gacchāmi,
〔我れ〕佛に　歸依したてまつる，

ダンマム　サラナム　ガッチヤーミ
Dhammaṁ saraṇaṁ gacchāmi,
〔我れ〕法に　歸依したてまつる，

サンガム　サラナム　ガッチヤーミ
Saṅghaṁ saraṇaṁ gacchāmi.
〔我れ〕僧に　歸依したてまつる。

(2) ドチヤン　ピ　ブッダム　サラナム　ガッチヤーミ
Dutiyam pi buddhaṁ saraṇaṁ gacchāmi,
二たび　又〔我れ〕佛に　歸依したてまつる，

ドチヤン　ピ　ダンマム　サラナム　ガッチヤーミ
Dutiyam pi dhammaṁ saraṇaṁ gacchāmi,
二たび　又〔我れ〕法に　歸依したてまつる，

ドチヤン　ピ　サンガム　サラナム　ガッチヤーミ
Dutiyam pi saṅghaṁ saraṇaṁ gacchāmi.
二たび　又〔我れ〕僧に　歸依したてまつる。

(3) タチヤン　ピ　ブッダム　サラナム　ガッチヤーミ
Tatiyam pi buddhaṁ saraṇaṁ gacchāmi,
三たび　又〔我れ〕佛に　歸依したてまつる，

タチヤン　ピ　ダンマム　サラナム　ガッチヤーミ
Tatiyam pi dhammaṁ saraṇaṁ gacchāmi,
三たび　又〔我れ〕法に　歸依したてまつる，

タチヤン　ピ　サンガム　サラナム　ガッチヤーミ
Tatiyam pi saṅghaṁ saraṇaṁ gacchāmi.
三たび　又〔我れ〕僧に　歸依したてまつる。

The Life of Kōbō-Daishi

By **Zentei Abe**

Introduction

Kōbō-Daishi, the Founder of the Shingon Sect

About 2,500 years ago, Śākyamuni was born in India.(1) Six centuries later Nāgârjuna Bodhisattva (龍猛菩薩) made his appearance in South India.(2) Truly is he called the 'Greatest Saint of the Buddhists,' the 'Greatest Representative of the Mahāyāna School' and the 'Founder of all Buddhism!' At first he studied and practised after the manner of 'heresy' (as Brahmanism now is called by Buddhists) but afterwards studying both Hīnayāna and Mahāyāna Schools, he attained to the 'Great Secret Law,' or Mantras.

The Sūtras of Mahāvairocanâbhisambodhi-sūtra (大日經), Vajraśikhara-sūtra (金剛頂經), and Susiddhi-sūtra (蘇悉地經), on which our 'Shingon' faith is based, came to light through the efforts of this Bodhisattva. He wrote besides the important Śāstras 'Mahāyānaprakaraṇa-Śāstra (釋摩迦衍論), or 'the treatise on the Mahāyāna (Great Vehicle, or Method of attaining enlightenment),' and Bodhicitta-Śāstra (菩提心論), or the 'Śāstra on the heart of Bodhi (or Wisdom),' which are regarded as the most essential to the tenets of the Shingon Sect. Among his disciples, there was one called Nāgabodhi (龍智菩薩), who succeeded to his Teaching and lived an unusually long life. His two disciples, Śubhākarasinha (善無畏三藏 Zen-mui) and Vajrabodhi (金剛智三藏), brought thence the deepest meaning of the doctrine of this Great Secret Law. Reaching China separately, (the one by land and the other by sea), the former, Zen-mui, (who came by the northern land

(1) According to the best modern scholars, Śākyamuni died about B.C. 477.

(2) The Chinese tradition is that Nāgârjuna (Jap. Ryūju) was a disciple of Aśvaghoṣa (Jap. Memyo) and assisted King Kanishka's great Council in Gandhāra, in the Indus regions, when the cannon of the Mahāyāna scriptures was settled and Hīnayāna or Southern Buddhism withdrew forever.

Some Scholars place Nāgârjuna's date A.D. 125 or others after A.D. 160.

route in the 4th year (A.D. 716) of Kaigen in the T'ang Era), translated the Mahāvairocanâbhisambodhi-sūtra (大日經) and gave oral lectures thereon, which were noted down and compiled into a Sūtra by Ichi-gyō-zenji (一行禪師). This is called the Commentary on Dainichikyō in 20 vols., and is considered as the most important book by our sect. It has come to be regarded as the only authority of our faith. Not only Dainichikyō, but Susiddhi-sūtra, are included in Garbhadhātu (胎藏界) School. In these translations of Garbhadhātu School we find a tendency towards the Tendai-sect. In short, Zen-mui represents the thoughts which prevailed in Southern and Western India.

In 720 A.D. Vajrabodhi or Kongōchi-sanzō reached Chang-an by the Sea-route from the South, accompanied by his disciple, Amoghavajra (不空三藏), and translated the Vajraśikhara or Kongōchō-gyo. Also Vajrabodhi translated many others belonging to Vajra-dhātu (金剛界) School. In his works, there is a tendency towards the Kegon-sect. In short, he brought over to China the ideas which were spread over Southern India.

Amoghavajra, or Fukū, who came over to Chōan with his Teacher, returned home after his death, and met Nāgabodhi or Ryūchi and came over again to China. The Emperor Gen-sō (玄宗皇帝) of the T'ang Dynasty was greatly delighted, and ordered him to translate the work called the Yuga-nenjuhō (瑜伽念誦法) or the 'Law of meditating and reciting in the Yoga doctrine.'

Also, he translated many sūtras and is accounted as one of the four great Translators in Chinese Buddhism. Generally speaking, Fukū's belief is founded on the Southern thoughts introduced by Vajrabodhi, and it was through his effort that Chinese Buddihism, which had harmonized with the Northern thoughts introduced by Subhākarasiṁha (Zenmui) became tinged with the colour of the Secret Law.

In this period, Buddhism was exceedingly prosperous in China, it being shortly after Genjyo-sanzō (玄奘三藏), Hiouen-thsang founder of the Hosso-shū, and Genju-daishi (賢首大師), founder of the Kegon-shū, had appeared. In Japan, it flourished in the Nara Epoch, just after the Completion of the Daibutsu Image by Shōmu Tennō, aided by monk Gyōgi Bosatsu. Ganshin, the blind Apostle, arrived from

China.

The chief disciple of Amoghavajra is Keikwa-ācarya (惠果阿闍梨) of Syōryū-ji (青龍寺), in Chang-an (長安). The priest well versed in the Tripiṭaka, taught Kōbō-daishi (弘法大師), the founder of the Shingon sect in Japan.

The Life of Kōbō-Daishi

CHAPTER I

Kōbō-Daishi in His Childhood

Kōbō-daishi was born in Byōbuga-ura (屛風ヶ浦) which is now Zentsuji, Kagawa prefecture, on June 15th in the fifth year of Hōki, 774 A.D. in the reign of the Emperor Kōnin. His father was called Saiki-Yoshimichi (佐伯善通) and his mother Tamayorihime (玉依媛). When seven years old,(3) he climbed a high mountain about 7 miles north-west of his home, where he offered prayer, and made a vow to devote himself to propagate Buddhism and save the people. Then he prayed again that it might be shown him whether the hope he cherished would be realized or not, adding that, if not, he would cut short his life by throwing himself into the depths of the fathomless ravine. According to the traditon, he is said to have thrown himself down the precipice but to have been saved miraculously. The mountain now called Syashin-ga-take (捨身ヶ嶽), it is said, is the very place. An Imperial Messenger once remarked, "This boy is the incarnation of Buddha, not a mere layman."

CHAPTER II

Kōbō-Daishi as a Student

He had an uncle named Atō-no-Ōtari (阿刀大足), who was one of the greatest scholars of that age. At first Daishi studied under him. He was born intelligent and very quick of understanding. The uncle, greatly surprised at the progress the boy made in his studies, suggested to his parents that such a promising lad should not remain in the country, but be sent to the capital. His parents following this advice, prepared for his journey and

(3) At Saikoku-ji (the Shingon temple at Onomichi in Bingo province) a small clay image of Buddha is preserved which the boy Kū-kai (Kōbō) is said to have moulded out of mud when playing with his school-mates.

At the same temple a beautiful image of Yakushi Nyorai — the Good Physician carved by Kōbō-daishi is also preserved. So precious is it accounted that it is only exposed to view once in 50 years.

sent him to Kyōto. In Kyōto he read Chinese classics such as "Shikyo" (詩經), "Ekikyo," (易經), "Syokyō" (書經), etc. with Umazake-no-kiyonari (味酒淨成) and "Syunjū-Sashiden" (春秋左氏傳) with Dr. Okada. With great assiduity he finished his studies and distinguished himself among his fellow students. At nineteen, he wrote an essay called "Sangōshiki" which may be regarded as his Graduation thesis, treating Confucianism, Taoism, and Buddhism from the literary as well as religious points of view. Modern students compare poorly with him both in learning and diction. With the publication of this book, Daishi resolved to devote himself to the studies and practice of Buddhism.

He was initiated into the Priesthood, and was named Mukū (無空). He devoted himself earnestly to the study of Buddhistic works.

CHAPTER III

Visiting the Noted Landscape in Quest of the 'Way'

Kōbō-Daishi regarded the works of Confucius and Laotse as superficial and insipid, and quite unworthy to trust. Being anxious to make a study of Buddhistic lore, he went to Iwabuchi in quest of a Teacher, and found one in the person of Rev. Gonzō (勤操大德), who was one of the greatest priests that the Sanron Sect ever boasted, and looked upon as an avatar of Venus. Daishi was instructed in the Law of Ākāśa-garbha bodhisattva (虛空藏菩薩) by this great priest. The scripture says, "If one repeats secret Mantras a million times over, by this method, one will master the whole Truth of the Universe." Exceedingly encouraged by this remark, Daishi crossed the perilous straits of Naruto, to Awa province, and ascended Tairyū-no-také (大龍の嶽), with the intention of studying this method. In this Mountain a poisonous Dragon lived which every year killed numbers of people in the vicinity.

Regardless of this reptile, Daishi made a seat among the old trees above the precipice and practised asceticism for 100 days. After this, he found his way through several mountains, and proceeding to Tosa Province, at last reached Muroto-no-saki (室戸の岬), where he could enjoy the prospect of the boundless sea in the south. Near a precipice, where the wind whistled through old pine trees and the surge broke

on the shore, he made a hut of brush-wood, in which he dwelt and practised asceticism for another hundred days.

He then made the ascent of Mt. Ashizuri (足摺山), where he saw a huge camphor-tree. The hollow of this tree was haunted by a number of long-nosed goblins (*Tengu*).

When he offered prayer, it is said, a great flame suddenly burst forth and those monsters fled in great perturbation.

In these days, Daishi denied himself almost everything. Even on the coldest winter days, he did not wear more than one unlined garment made of wisteria fibre, whilst in the hottest summer he totally abstained from any kind of cereals. To say nothing of Tosa and Awa Provinces, he travelled over Iyo and Sanuki. So it may be traced back to this journey that, in his later life, Daishi founded the "Eighty-eight temples," and introduced Buddhism into Shikoku. Each pilgrim to these temples feels quite easy throughout his travels in the belief that he has a fellow-pilgrim, Kōbō-daishi, and is always accompanied by him, just as the shadow follows the substance. All this is the result of Daishi's hard journeys.

He then travelled through the San-yo and San-in districts, staying for a while in Harima. Then he made his way to Tōkai-dō, and hearing that Katsura-dani (桂谷) was infested with numerous demons, he proceeded there and, having dispersed those demons, built a temple. The present Syūzen-ji (修善寺) is said to be its site.

He made trips to almost every mountain in the seven provinces of Oh-wu (奥羽). At Mt. Yudono (湯殿山), it is said, he met with the guardian spirit of the mountain. Indeed, these journeys were of no small consequence, for not only did Daishi cultivate the land and diffuse Religion, but he also improved himself in no common measure. We need hardly say that his great literary talent, especially the sublimity of his style, was greatly fostered by his travels among rivers and mountains. It is quite advisable for those who mope and moon in the din and bustle of a city to follow Kōbō Daishi's example and improve themselves in the bold scenery of the highest mountain solitudes.

CHAPTER IV

He Struggles to Grasp the Fundamental Truth of Buddhism

After visiting all the renowned mountains and rivers in Japan, Daishi climbed Mt. Makino-o in Izumi Province and there, in his twentieth year, entered the Priesthood under the guidance of the above mentioned Rev. Gonzō. This monk's posthumous title was 'Dai-sō-jyo.' He was then called Nyo-kū (如空), but afterwards Kyō-kai (敎海). At the age of twenty-two, Daishi received the full ordination (具足戒) and was granted the name of Kūkai (空海) in the Kaidan-in (戒壇院) Tō-dai-ji Nara.

Whilst at Nara, Daishi shut himself up in the Daibutsu-den, and prayed earnestly to all the Buddhas in the Three Worlds, that he might be shown Advaita-dharma (不二の法), which would enable him to grasp the fundamental truth of Buddhism. His prayer was soon answered through a dream in which a man appeared to him who told him that 'the chief of all the Sūtras was Mahāvairocanâhbisambodhi sūtra (Dai-nichi-kyō), and that this was the very sūtra he needed.'

This Kyō might be found under the East Pagoda of the Kumé Temple at Takaichi in Yamato Province. On awaking, Daishi hastened to Kumé and noticing an uncommon-looking place in the central pillar of the Pagoda, which Zen-mui, an Indian savant, is said to have erected when he came over from China. On cutting it open, Daishi found the Dainichi-kyo in seven volumes. He perused the sūtra at once, but failed to clear his doubts, so he resolved to visit China in order to be enlightened.

CHAPTER V

He Goes Over to China for the Further Study of Buddhism

At this juncture Rev. Gonzō came to Daishi's help, and on behalf of his disciple, reported Daishi's desire to the Emperor and begged leave for him to go to China for the further study of Buddhism. The permission was immediately granted to Daishi's great delight, and he prepared for his trip, praying for a safe voyage. Daishi made a vow, and engraved an image of Bhaisajyaguruvaidūrya tathāgata (藥師如來), which is now the principal image of the Kita-in, Ninna-ji in Kyoto. Dedicating himself at the Hachiman Shrine at Usa of Oh-ita Province, he offered also the Prajñāpāramitā-sūtra (般若心經) of one hundred volumes, which he had copied out.

Finally he set sail from Matsu-ura port, Hizen, in July in the 23rd year of En-ryaku, in company with Kadonomaro (葛野麻呂) of

Fujiwara, the Japanese Ambassador to China. When the ship was off the north coast of Formosa, where ths tidal current called 'Kuro-shio' passes, the sky suddenly became threatening, and a heavy storm arose. The ship, stripped of her rudder and masts, was on the verge of sinking into the depths. Daishi then offered prayer to Buddha, and lo! the wind began to abate, and the sea became calm. Thus the ship arrived safely at Fu-chou (福州) in China early in August. Hitherto, the Japanese Embassies to China had landed at Yang-chou (楊州), Su-chou (蘇州), or Ningpō (寧波), these routes being much shorter than the one to Fu-chou. But on this occasion, much against their will, they were blown to the shores of Fu-chou. The Governor of Fu-chou, suspecting them, would not permit them to land.

Although Kadono-maro wrote to the Governor repeatedly, pleading their case and asking leave to land, the latter took no notice of the request. At his wit's end, Kadono-maro begged Daishi to oblige him with a letter to the Governor. Daishi wrote a letter right away without a mistake, and it was sent to the Chinese High Official, who was greatly surprised at its perfect diction and fine penmanship. Then the Governor, regretting his former conduct, at once permitted them to land, and having reported the arrival of the Japanese Embassy to the Court, thirty nine days later gave provisions, and installed them comfortably in thirteen inns which had been built to receive them. About fifty days later an Imperial Messenger came from the capital to inquire after their health. The Ambassador and his suite then went up to Chang-an. When they entered the capital, an imposing ceremony was held. The road they passed along was lined with innumerable spectators. It was towards the close of December in 804 A.D. that they entered Chang-an and by the Emperor's orders were comfortably settled in a place at Sen-nyo-bō (宣揚坊).

CHAPTER VI

Daishi Becomes the Disciple of Keikwa

Fortunately it so happened that Daishi met in Chang-an one of the greatest priests China ever produced, who was no other than the Reverend Kei-kwa of the Syōryū-ji. This venerable monk was the seventh successor to Mahāvairocana, the great founder of the Shingon sect, and a disciple of Amoghavajra of the Daikō-zenji (大興善寺). His Holiness was a great teacher, distinguished both in virtue and learning. When he first saw Daishi he exclaimed "How late you are in coming! I have long waited for you, since I have a wonderful secret to impart to you, and the evening of my life is now setting in. Work your hardest, and master the truths as soon as possible." All present were greatly surprised at this strange remark and wondered what connection existed between the Teacher and the new disciple. During the next months Daishi received secret instruction concerning Ryō-bu, the Two Parts.[5] In the fourth month Kei-kwa gave him the Abhiṣeka, i.e. he consecreted him by sprinkling water on the head (Kwan-jō) as the sign of successorship and said: "The Bhagavat, or Blessed One, gave the Secret Key to the Truth to Vajrasattva, who transmitted it to Nāgârjuna, and so on to myself. Now, because I see you are, indeed, a man well qualified for this learning, I give you the Key to the great secret Doctrine of the Two Parts." Daishi very quickly learned what takes on ordinary man several years of labour. Go-in-shi (呉殷之) in amazement once remarked "He is no common priest, but a Buddha. Though he has mastered the profound truths of the Mahāyāna, he yet appears nothing but a common monk from a small country!"

Amongst Kei-kwa's disciples there was one called Jun-gyō (順曉) who in turn had a disciple called Chinga (珍賀). This last named priest at first felt very jealous of Daishi's success, and spread all kinds of slanders about him, but finally, repenting of his wrong deeds, he apologized for them at Daishi's feet.

Kei-kwa, having transmitted all the occult truths concerning the Shingon sect to Daishi, felt much relieved and bestowed upon his beloved pupil all the Sūtras and other important things. On his death-bed he said to Daishi, "My life in this world is now at an end. These Two Parts contain the most important truths of all the Buddhas, and offer the shortest way to

(5) The Two Parts, that is to say "Taizō-kai" (Garbha-Koṣa-dhātu) and "Kongō-kai" (vajra-dhātu).

Nirvāna. Now that I have given you all these things, I have nothing left to wish for, but that you should succeed, in propagating this Way and delivering welfare to human-kind." So saying, he died on December 15th 805 A.D. (first year Eitei 〔永貞〕, in the T'ang dynasty).

It need hardly be said that all Kei-kwa's disciples, especially Daishi were plunged in deep sorrow. When they proposed to erect a monument to the memory of their Teacher, Daishi wrote the epitaph and a sketch of Keikwa's life in compliance with their request. This shows how highly he was respected as a man of letters even amongst so many distinguished Chinese literary men of the T'ang Era.

CHAPTER VII

DAISHI COMES BACK TO JAPAN IN 806 A.D.

When Daishi informed the Chinese Emperor of his intention to return home, the Emperor was much grieved to part from him, and presenting him with a Rosary[6] made of the boditsi seeds he said with tears in his eyes, "This is my souvenir which, I hope, will ever remind you of me. My intention was that you should stay here and be my teacher. But I hear your Emperor Heijō (平城天皇) is anxiously awaiting your return, so I shall not urge you to stay here." It is heartily desired that those young monks who are Daishi's religious descendants should bear this incident in mind and when abroad, for study or otherwise, should avail themselves of the opportunity to convert some distinguished personages to our Faith and thus prove themselves worthy spiritual sons of Daishi.

When Daishi bade adieu to the Emperor and proceeded to a port in Ming-chou (明州), to embark for home in 806 A.D. (first year of Genna 〔元和〕 in the T'ang Dynasty) many people came to see him off. They were so reluctant to part from him that they clung to his sleeves and would not let him depart. He had to soothe and talk them into reason, before he got on board.

At last the ship weighed anchor, and set sail. When she was on the high seas, a sudden storm arose

(6) The Rosary is peculiar to the Mahāyāna or Northern Buddhism, and is the special emblem of Maitreya (Jap. Miroku).

and the ship was at the mercy of overwhelming waves. His fellow passengers gave themselves up for lost, but Daishi stood composedly and prayed to the image of Aryâcala-vidyā-rāja (不動明王) in Japanese Fudō-myōwō which he carried with him, saying, "After returning home I intend to build a temple and diffuse the Secret Law among the people, so that the glory of the Buddha may be increased, and the country protected from injury. I pray to all the Buddhas soon to deliver us from all the obstacles which lie in our way, and take us home in safety."

Strange to say, the storm which had been furiously raging a moment before suddenly ceased and the sea became calm. All on board were greatly struck by the efficacy of Daishi's prayer. Prior to his departure from China, Kei-kwa had told Daishi that (since he had finished his studies and was about to return to Japan), it would be very advisable for him to carve an image of Fudō-myō-wō and pray for a safe voyage as, most probably, he would be overtaked by a storm, and his life endangered. Following this kind advice, Daishi carved an image of Fudō-myō-ō and got Kei-kwa himself to consecrate it.

This very image which he carried with him on his homeward voyage, is specially called 'Namikiri-fudō' (浪切不動) and is preserved as the *honzon* of the Nan-in (南院) in Kōyasan.

Daishi safely arrived in Tsukushi (筑紫) in October 806 A.D. (the first year of Daidō 大同 in the reign of Emperor Heijō). He was then thirty-three years old. As it was the coldest winter, and snow lay deeply on the ground, he spent the last days of the year in the Kwannon-ji in Tsukushi. The next year he went to Kyōto in compliance with the Imperial wishes. When, through a high official of the Imperial Household, he submitted to the Emperor's personal inspection the list of the Sūtras and Commentaries he had brought over from China, His Majesty highly approved them and was pleased to order Daishi to teach the Doctrine to the people at large.

Soon after, the True Word (Mantra) spread all over Japan and men of all ranks (from the Emperor down to the poorest people), believed in its teachings. At first the high priests of other sects were surprised at the rapidity with which the sect spread, but

their surprise soon gave place to suspicions as to its tenets; hence a Conference to discuss the tenets of the eight sects of Buddhism in Japan was held on March 15th in the first year of Konin (A.D. 810)

In short, all the Laws preached by Śākya-muni are called 'Apparent Doctrine' (Ken-gyō). On the other hand, the 'Hidden Doctrine' is the Law derived from the Dharmakāya (Hossin) or spiritual body of Buddha. It is called 'Secret Doctrine' (Mikkyō). The 'Apparent Doctrine' is that which is adapted to the hearers, but the 'Hidden Doctrine' is the Inner Law understood secretly by Buddha alone. Daishi said, 'The Apparent Doctrine drives away the outer dust, and the Shin-gon, or true Word, opens the treasury, i.e. shows the Inner Truth.

(To be continued)

日滿佛教提携方策

滿洲佛教學院創立委員
　　宗　　空　居士　林　傳　樹

（註三）林傳樹氏は三十年前に日本帝國大學醫學部を聽講したる醫師にして，佛教篤信とともに眞言，天台學に明るく，京都東寺道場に於て覺隨僧正より受法したる眞言居士なり。余が昨年六月チチハルに於て「第一回日滿宗教教化團體懇話會」を開催するや，大に協力贊成し法縁を結び，續いて「滿洲佛教學院創立」の同志として爾來，日滿佛教の流交に水魚の交りを結び目下衣食を節し俱に力勵する勇精の居士なり。殊に同居士は目下滿文「佛教大意」を執筆中である。本文要旨は，余と眞言道場（修法專門）計畫に際し合議の內容を纂寫せるものの一部なり。（半谷範成）

×　×　×

（一）建立不動明王根本道場於新京。以祈禱國基鞏固。及日滿協和不傾不動。由日本眞言阿闍梨主壇。滿洲國之僧侶參贊之。

（二）全國十省省會。舉行仁王護國法會一期。分成三壇。

甲壇　念誦仁王護國經（滿僧諷誦）

乙壇　講授茶羅尼持仁王護國咒

（日僧加行）

丙壇　宣講仁王經咒（佛學精深滿洲居士宣說）

輪流檢大藏行經費各地醵集每省一月。約一年完畢。

以上所求三寶加護之力也。

（三）建立佛學院，教育青年僧侶，以厚學識。

（四）建立修法院補助大德修法，以免供奉欠缺。

（五）各省省會須備全藏經，准流通借閱。

（六）延致高僧居士作（定期，不定期）之講演。以資闡揚。

（七）蒙民信仰喇嘛，喇嘛中亦不少有學識者，民國之後，多失供奉，應再調查補助，以示維繫開發也。

（八）籌設印經機關，印行經典（滿文蒙文）廉價流通。

（九）不良僧尼，勅令還俗。不良善類。冒佛名又。加以取締。

（十）度爲僧侶須有相當學識。再令不准僧人。濫收法侶。

以上皆藉政府人民之力。應求做到者也。

爲政不在多言。在實行若何耳。半谷範成。來問方策于余。聊此管見與之。又日僧尼妻食肉制。此方不敢公然實行。爲護戒律計。此例不開最好。蓋習慣法不可不注意也。吾爲此語。固知得罪時流。爲佛法計。不敢妄語焉。恕之。

創辦『佛教子弟學校』建議書

古　農

佛教爲我國民族之宗教，信仰之者，實佔全民十分之八而强，佛法爲我國民族之文化，薰陶之久，已歷國史四千餘年之半，昔也儒學並興，佛教徒尙可超然物外，今也儒亦不振，民族復興之弘業，佛教徒實已責無旁貸，顧回觀今日國內之佛化，出家者之模範團體，往往以僧格之墮落，不足以副國人之崇仰，近頼諸大德之匡扶，計設佛學院以事教育，稍堪告慰，然須知出家者無不從在家者來，佛教徒在未出家之前，而不能培植其學業，逮已出家之後，從而教育之不特年齡已長，受教之力已薄弱縱使急施補習，勢必分其專學之心，而有事倍功半之失，是故欲復興民族，不得不復興佛化，欲復興佛化，不得不提高僧格，欲提高僧格，捨教育佛教子弟以培其本，濬其源，其道末由。

佛教子弟者，佛教徒之子弟，受佛化家庭之撫育，爲其父兄所期望其同一信仰者也。此等子弟之將來，依信教自由之原則，縱未必盡成其爲佛教徒，然其未能自立，在父兄保護之下，爲父兄者旣已信佛，在家庭之慣習上，當然受一種佛化所薰陶，必不願其子弟有反對之信仰，以妨礙家庭之秩序，此等子弟，設使受不信佛教之師長教訓，易啓其對於家庭佛化之懷疑，而漸成爲一不率教之子弟，爲父兄者之痛心疾首爲何如也。故彼甚嚮教之子弟，必令入彼教會所設之學校，以成其學業，我佛教徒，亦宜同然，故此等子弟之教育，非必廢其普通之學科，而令讀佛書，要在不妨礙其佛化家庭之習性，而於普通學科，爲將來謀生與服務社會所必需者，仍宜應有盡有，至於佛學一科，在中小學，唯課餘隨宜講說，在大學中方設專科，如此則與現在國家學制，不相違悖，苟能創設是項學校，則佛教可由家庭化以達於學校化，再由學校化以達於社會化，至佛教達於社會化，而佛教復興之機，沛然莫之能禦矣。

是故佛教子弟學校之設，直接可以培植在家佛徒間接可以提高出家僧格，睽觀東鄰，號稱佛化普及，佛學昌明者，何莫由斯道也。我國現今佛教居士團體漸臻發達，比之東鄰，猶佛寺也。彼則每寺必設學校以教育其子弟，故能致佛於隆盛，我國居士團體，誠能合力以創辦此等學校，其直接利益，與彼邦同，其間接功德，當超勝於彼國，何以故？彼國出家者少，而我國出家者多，彼國佛教以在家者爲中心，而我國佛教以出家者爲中心也。以是因緣，是項學校，不但我國居士團體宜努力籌設，即僧衆寺院，亦宜協助居士設立之，不寧惟是，我國居士團體能力尙多薄弱，亦可應地聯合信佛教居士之有財力及有教育經驗者，成立佛教子弟學校籌備會，以籌集基金，遵照教育部私立學校規程辦理之，庶幾負責有人而進行有自矣。

農不敏，有見於佛教子弟學校關係之重及創辦之必要，爰備陳理由與方法，以建議於國內各佛教會，各居士團體，及居士之表同情者之前，尙祈發起而實現焉。我國佛教幸甚！　我國民族幸甚！

（中華民國二十六年四月
十一日『佛教日報』所載）

資　料

首都分別實行
僧尼軍事訓練之詳情
出世精神入世事
袈裟卸下換征衫

（南京特訊）本市僧尼實行軍事救護訓練一事，已略誌本報。玆聞訓練總監部派黃瑤爲總教官，並助教二員。已分別舉行，僧部在山西路古林寺門前，尼部在土街口接引庵門前。受訓僧衆，皆着黃色軍服，領章繡紅色『僧訓』二字，袖上佩紅十字以資識別。每日訓練二小時，風雨不停，尼部在上日八時至十時，僧部在每午下二時至四時。最近期內，操基本動作，如立正，稍息，變化隊形及陳中要務等，俟後再教以射擊，等重要戰術及救護常識。參加僧衆，『脫去緇衣換戰袍』，欣欣然有喜色云。

（又訊）中國佛教會南京市分會於日前爲僧尼軍訓事，召集各區寺廟住持代表開會討論一切進行事宜。到會者····光輝，如鏡，嵐川，如愚，悅繹，聞修，用成，隆慧，能忍，萍心，靈壓，大緣，蓮華，昌聖，道惠，能持，玄鐘，春觀，耕壓，廣譯，自明，聖禮，雲錫，水祥，慧光，二空，潤禪，隆法，佛道，大航，圓修，能愚，竺善，愿如，映月，雨花臺永林庵，守慧。主席如愚。紀錄李德宏行禮如儀主席報告····踏山大德····今天召開談話會，特向諸位報告軍訓開始原因。自從去歲五六月間，本城就傳說和尙要受訓練。沒有幾天，下關忽有代表來會報告，以下靜海寺嵐川和尙說，諸位去年約在六月內，第七區敎官孫謀召集我們下關各寺廟住持會議，招呼我們要做制服，以便受訓。我們因爲沒有接到佛教會通知，所以不得不前來報告，召開理監事會討論此事，應如何辦理之後。本會特推代表攜呈向訓練總監部請愿免訓。不料訓練部未曾批准，所有情形前已轉發各寺廟同袍知曉。同時中國佛教會，亦曾請求與本會一樣的批文。故而總會就根據會章第四條組織中國佛教會災區救護團，擬定章程，全國各市縣佛教分會均須組織分團，僧尼皆要受救護看護訓練。其制服式樣，各股辦事人員種種，均皆現定。本會完全遵照總團章程辦理。本來去年冬月間，就要開始訓練。曾經召過幾次會議。結果大家說是臘月黃天，雨雪又多，最好要求緩期，俟等來春開始。到了今年正月底，軍訓會又派員來催，經過一再接洽，不能解決，只好召開第二十二次理監事聯席會議。軍訓會亦曾派員參加。最要緊的就是要本會津貼經費問題，難以解決。據軍訓會王繼志先生說····教官每月薪金一百元，公費一十元，助教三名，每人二十元，號兵十二元，其計一百八十二元，全城僧尼，分爲五區，總共每月需九百一十元。無論如何，要望佛教會方面籌出，送交軍訓會支配。結果，我們沒有答應，只好具呈懇求減少。又未批准。（軍訓會民字第二七五一號指令，本會呈一件爲本會對於教官津貼甚難籌措懇請准予按月由會津貼半數并派員協助收取暨請解釋法規規定教官薪金每月不得超過五十元一案由內開····呈悉，查僧尼訓練應派專門人才擔任教官，薪俸未便減少，至教官薪金，每月不得超過五十元之規定，係以前考乡，現已廢止，另頒有社會軍事訓練新方案，又各寺廟津貼經費仰由該處自行收取，此令！）前幾天我又邀請妙機和尙同去，當面求情。請妙機和尙報告諸位，本星期二陪同理事長到軍訓會先見許科長，後見董委員一再說苦哀求，不容易才答應減少至五百元，每月不得再少分文。至於我們各區訓練救護，看護的用物，還要去買，每月至少總要六百元方可開消出去，所以今天特請諸位前來討論，應該如何籌措。大概無論受訓與否，除八十歲以上，十六歲以下，每人每月要拿出一元來，方纔足數，否則本會就不易交代。務請大家發表意見。共同討論。結果陡門橋觀音閣，東岳廟，曹都巷文昌菴等各當家大師，提出意見，認爲各寺廟住持，個人實在担負不了。最好住持與客師各半，每人每月共同担任一元。其餘不受訓練的人，或年齡已過，或有疾病者，應該由自己負担每月一元。佛教會亦可發給證明書，證明其確有疾病，或年歲已過，並獎勵慨助義務費，庶幾錢不空出。此種亦是大家邀求之一，會議至此，全體均鼓掌讚成，一致通過。遂散會。

（又訊）南京市僧尼救護訓練團，原擬於今日（廿五）在古林寺舉行開學典禮。並舉行謁陵大典，以天雨未克舉行，俟後再行訂期舉行云。（樹百）

調 査 資 料

豐山派海外布教ノ現勢

一，滿　洲

（イ）派遣開教師　五名

內開教師手當ヲ交附セラルヽモノ　二　名

ソノ金額年額　千八百圓也

（ロ）開教所數　二ヶ所（奉天及吉林）

（ハ）新京新寺建立豫定

敷地，武千坪購入濟ミ

寺院本年度中ニ建築着手ノ筈

二，米領ハワイ

開教師一名任命，目下赴任準備中

局　報

定款中改正さる

五月二十三日東京市日比谷松本樓に於て開催されたる本局評議員會に於て定款中次の如く改正せられた。——

第二，'本部'とあるを'事務局'と改む。

第五，ニ，'幹事三名'とあるを，'幹事若干名'

第五，ホ，'評議員'とあるを，'理事'と改む。

以下，'評議員'とあるは何れも，'理事'と改む。

國際佛教通報局

國際佛教通報局定款

名　稱

第一，本局を國際佛教通報局と稱す

事務所

第二，本局の事務所を全日本佛教靑年會聯盟事務局に置く

目　的

第三，本局は日本內地及海外に向つて佛教事情の通報をなし，且つ佛教徒相互間の各種便宜を計るを以て目的とす

事　業

第四，本局の目的を達成するため左記の事業を行ふ

イ，日本內地及世界各國より佛教事情に關する質問の通報を行ふ

ロ，必要に應じ日本語及世界各國語を以て佛教事情の通報を行ふ

ハ，外國人の日本觀光に際しては各種の便益を與へ，特にその佛教に關する方面に於て之を爲す

ニ，定時或は隨時に各國語を以て文書の刊行をなす

ホ，その他必要と認めたる事業を行ふ

役　員

第五，本局の事務を處理するため左の役員を置く

イ，名譽局長　一　名

ロ，顧　問　若干名

ハ，局　長　一　名

ニ，幹　事　若干名

ホ，理　事　若干名

局長は本局の事務を總括す

幹事は本局の事務を處理す

理事は局長の提案に依る重要事務を審議す

第六，理事は左記の者を以て之に充つ

イ，全日本佛教靑年會聯盟理事及主事

ロ，全日本佛教靑年會聯盟理事會に於て推薦したる者

第七，局長及幹事は理事會に於て決定す

第八，名譽局長及顧問は理事會に於て推薦す

第九，役員の任期は一ヶ年とす（但し重任を妨げず）

經　費

第十，本局の經費は左記のものに依て之を支辨す

イ，本局基金の活用

ロ，寄附金

ハ，その他の收入

補　則

第十一，本定款に記載せられざる事項は，凡て理事會に於て協議す

第十二，第一回の役員は全日本佛教靑年會聯盟理事會に於て決定す

定價	一部	金二十錢	送料五厘
	一年	金二圓四十錢	送料不要

昭和十年四月卅日第三種郵便物認可
昭和十二年六月廿三日印刷（每月一回）
昭和十二年六月廿五日發行（一日發行）

東京市外吉祥寺337
編輯發行兼印刷人　淺野研眞

東京市牛込區早稻田鶴卷町107
印刷所　株式會社康文社印刷所
電話牛込(34) 1950番 5049番

東京市神田區一ツ橋二の三
發行所　國際佛教通報局
電話九段(33)4428番
振替東京83015番

昭和十年四月三十日第三種郵便物認可
昭和十二年六月二十三日印刷納本(毎月一回
昭和十二年六月二十五日發行(一日發行) 國際佛教通報 第三卷 第六號

第二回

汎太平洋佛教青年會大會

紀要

THE PROCEEDINGS

of

THE Second

General Conference

of

Pan-Pacific Young Buddhists' Associations

(in Japanese, Chinese and English)

Held at Tokyo & Kyoto, July 18–23, 1934

Price ¥ 3.00

Compiled & Published

by

The Federation of All Y.B. As. of Japan,

Tokio, Kanda, Hitotsubashi, II-3

昭和十年四月三十日第三種郵便物認可 昭和十二年七月二十三日印刷納本 昭和十二年七月二十五日發行（毎月一回一日發行）第三卷 第七號

The International Buddhist Bulletin

國際佛教通報

第三卷 **昭和十二年七月** 第七號 [Vol. III. July $\frac{2503}{1937}$ No. 7.]

七月 (July)

東京 **國際佛教通報局** 發行

The International Buddhist Information Bureau

II–3, Hitotsubashi, Kanda, Tokyo,

Annual Subscription, ¥2.40 (post free). Single Copy 20 sen (post 2 sen)

The Life of Kōbō-Daishi

(II)

By **Zentei Abe**

CHAPTER VIII

He Endeavours to Promote the Weal and Happiness of People

After introducing the Faith into the Imperial Household, Daishi wrote such great works as; 'On Ten Stages of Thought' (十住心論), 'On the Two Doctrines—Hidden and Apparent' (顯密二教論); 'The Key of Sacred Law' (祕鍵); 'On the Profound Meaning of Mantras' (聲字義); 'On the Meaning of Hūm (吽字義); 'On the Meaning of Attainment to the State of Buddhahood' (卽身義) etc., and so completely established the Shingon sect.

Although the Faith had long flourished in China, it was not yet regarded as the highest teaching in Buddhism. Kōbō-Daishi, however, wisely took all Buddhism to illustrate the difference among the sects. There are also two ways of explaining these thoughts.

Meanwhile, the Faith prevailed throughout Japan and all people, high and low, revered Kōbō Daishi with special respect and veneration.

In September, the first year of Kōnin, Prince Taka-oka (高岳親王), son of the Emperor Heijyō, was made the Crown Prince and was soon to succeed to the Throne. But by reason of a slight illness, he abandoned his claim, and became a disciple of Daishi. After entering the priesthood, he was called Prince Shin-nyo (眞如親王). This year Daishi conferred the Abhiṣeka (Kwan-jō), on his disciple Jichié (實慧) at Mt. Takao (高雄) in Kyoto. This was the first Transmission of the Way that was ever made in Japan. After this, many persons anxious to be taught by him gathered in his temple. Among others, Dengyo-Daishi Saichō (傳教大師最澄), founder of the Tendai Sect, received the Kwan-jō of Vajradhātu, or Kongo-kai (*lit.* "Diamond element") at the Jingo-ji (神護寺) Takao, on November 15 in the third year of Konin (812 A.D.) and on December 14, he received the Kwanjō of Garbhadhātu. or Taizōkai (*lit.* "Emblio element"). Thus, Daishi won the Emperor, Court nobles, and the most distinguished priests to his Faith.

CHAPTER IX

Pilgrimage Life of Daishi

With the intention of redeeming the whole nation, Daishi travelled over Japan, dressed like a mendicant friar, and visited all the noted temples and shrines, to pray for the everlasting spread of Buddhism. He first crossed to Shikoku, his birth-place, in the 6th year of Konin (A.D. 815).

He was then forty two years old. It is commonly believed that man meets with some misfortune or other at that age. By way of removing the forth-coming misfortune, he travelled through Shikoku island and founded the Eighty-eight Holy places to crush down the Eight Passions. During his pilgrimage through the island he dispersed the demons in the Zentsu-ji (善通寺) by wonderful strokes of his pen which he made on a tablet. Another time when in a mountainous place in Tosa (土佐), he noticed a rotten wooden bridge, so he taught the people how to build it in a durable style. Up to this present time this bridge is preserved from decay. After he left Shikoku he worked many miracles.

When Kōbō-Daishi visited a village where the peole suffered from scarcity of fuel, he discovered coal, 'burning stones,' and gave it to a man named Gobei-da in Echigo district. At Kusatsu, he saw a poor priest who was in want of oil and taking pity on him, he offered and produced oil out of a rock. This was Kerosene oil, as it is now called.

Now let me ask why he experienced so many hardships, often being even without means of shelter from rain and snow? Was it reason he sought after wealth or fame? Has there ever been one who, so regardless of worldly fame and riches, and so unmindful of himself, was eager to help and promote the welfare of fhe country? Those who pretend to enhance the welfare and happiness of the people whilst, in reality, pursuing their own selfish aims in vanity, consumed with pride, ought to be ashamed to death of themselves.

CHAPTER X

Kōyasan

When Daishi travelled from place to place all over Japan in order to diffuse the Faith and save the people, he always had it in mind to find a suitable place wherein to build a temple. In the early summer of the 7th year of Kōnin (A.D. 817), he found himself in Uchi (宇智) Yamato province (大和國), where he chanced to meet a hunter who, garbed in a suit of blue cloth and armed with bow and arrows, was standing by the roadside with two dogs, one white the other black. He was a stout man, and about eight feet in height. In his appearance there was something noble and different from the usual run of hunters. Daishi accosted him, saying that he had long travelled throughout the land in search of a suitable place to erect a temple, but so far had failed to find one to his mind, and that, probably he, the hunter, having long dwelt among the mountains, would be well aquainted with their topography; and asking him to kindly show him the place if he ever happened to come across such a site.

The hunter replied that to the south there was a high mountain, which had never been trodden by the foot of a man, and on its summit there was a level plain surrounded by high peaks. Purple clouds hung over it by day, and at night a mysterious light appeared. "If you came here to live" the hunter added, "I would help you to build a temble. These dogs are familiar with the way thereto. So you had best take them with you." This saying, the hunter loosed the dogs and quickly disappeared from view.

The place where this event occurred is in the precincts of Inukai-san (犬飼山).[1]

Led by the dogs, Daishi proceeded southward and spent the night at a place across the Kino-kawa (紀ノ川), where in later days stood the temple of Jison-in (慈尊院) dedicated to his mother. The next morning, Daishi trudged along the mountain paths following his two canine guides.

He climbed up the steep and rugged slopes, and was delighted

(1) Curiously "the first hotoke" who brought Mahāyāna to Korea, was led by two dogs when they climbed Kongō-zan (Diamond Mountain) in search of a site for their temple.

to find everything as the hunter had told him.

At length he reached a plain which extended from east to west surrounded by eight high peaks which resembled the petals of a Lotus blossom. This was the very spot for his purpose but, according to the rule of those times, one must petition the authorities to obtain a special piece of land. Therefore, in order to report his purpose to the Mikado, Daishi descended the the mountain, drew up a memorial to the Throne, and presented it together with a map of Mt. Kōya, beseeching his Majesty to grant his request.

His petition being quickly granted, Daishi again climbed the mountain with gladsome heart and, employing many men, caused the forest to be cut down and the ground laid out. To his great joy, when planning the site for a Pagoda, he found a sword, five feet long and eighteen inches broad, buried in the ground, which bore an inscription on both sides. This singular discovery impressed him more than ever with the holiness of the place. Putting the sword into a copper tube, he reburied it with a prayer for the religious purification of the ground.

It was surely no accident that caused him to settle in this holy mountain after his fruitless journeys throughout the whole Empire of Japan. Conquering a steep and trackless wilderness, Daishi laid the foundation of the everlasting prosperity of the Shingon Sect upon the (1)Octagonal peaks of the Lotus.

CHAPTER XI

THE "IROHA-UTA" SYLLABARY

Deeply grieved at the backward state of our country's civilization compared with that of China (whose learning and institutions he had carefully examined and with whose manners and customs he was familiar), Daishi strove to his utmost to introduce culture amongst the people of Japan and thereby enhance their happiness; —here devising ponds to facilitate irrigation, and there spanning bridges across rivers to make communication easier. He took much pains in promoting various industries so as to increase the national welfare.

Believing that civilization had been checked by the general ignorance and illiteracy of the people, he decided to diffuse Education widely among them and thereby increase their knowledge because so far unfortunately, we had no letters of our own. It is true that Chinese literature had been introduced into Japan, in A.D. 285 in the Emperor Ōjin's (應神天皇) reign, when a Korean presented the "one thousand character-ideographs" (千字文) to the Court, but the Chinese characters being very complicated were difficult to be acquired by the masses. Consequently literature was only accessible to the upper ranks of the Japanese people, whilst the populace remained as ignorant and illiterate as ever. Such being the case, Daishi for long endeavoured to work out some simple letters, which should be both easy to learn and applicable to all purposes.

At last, at Taema-ji in Yamato, he invented a set of letters, whose purpose is two-fold. One contains the idea of Nirvāna for human life, and the other (which is very useful, very indispensable for daily use) is the syllabary of Forty-seven Letters, commencing with I "い" Ro "ろ" Ha "は" etc. This has been rendered into English by the Hon Mrs. E. A. Gordon as follows:

"Fragrant flowers are very sweet,
But one day they will fade away:
Who can say 'This World's unchaning'?
Crossing o'er the Mount of Change to-day,
We shall find no dreaming nor illusion,
But Enlightenment!"

Though this set of letters was originally derived from Chinese ideographs possessing the same sounds, Daishi (who was very skilled in the cursive form of Chinese characters) wrote them in the square style which is a very simple form of phonetic letters, so that his syllable is quite easy even for women and children to learn, and is applicable to every use. Unlike the Western alphabets, the forty-seven letters were arranged in the form of a beautiful and expressive song, so as to convey the great truths which Buddha

(1) The Octagon is the symbol of Regeneration, the New Birth of the Soul, which Kwannon confers, as does the Holy spirit in Christianity (see St. John 3. 3–5).

The Lotus is the special characteristic emblem borne by all the manifestations of Buddha in the Mahāyāna teaching.

taught, and that without repeating a single letter. The Hon. Madame Gordon says that the sentiment expressed in the I-Ro-Ha Uta is the same as that of the Nestorian "Hymn of Hosannas" sung at Chang-an in the Syrian churches, namely:

"The Roses and the Lilies and the Blossoms
And the spring-flowers are very lovely
In their appearance—"

Is it not very interesting and encouraging to find that those who are learned in the study of Comparative Religion should affirm that these two hymns are identical in the root of their teaching?

It may further interest our readers to compare the teaching in the I-Ro-Ha Uta with that of the Hebrew and Christian Scriptures, and that given on the replica of the Nestorian Stone which stands just within the entrance to the Oku-no-in in Kōyasan where our Daishi sleeps, awaiting the the coming of Miroku Bosatsu.

Another interpretation of I-Ro-Ha given by "I find no crime in Him" Nakada, a Japanese, is as follows:

I	ro	ha	ni	ho	he	*to**
Chi	ri	nu	ru	wo	wa	*ka*
Yo	ta	re	so	tsu	ne	*na**
Ra	mu	u	wi	no	o	*ku**
Ya	ma	ke	fu	ko	ye	*te**
A	sa	ki	yu	me	mi	*shi**
We	hi	mo	se	*su*		

(*) I think it is quite certain that Daishi must have been present in the syrian Church at Chang-an and heard the Anthem of the Mysteries in which these words occur: "Although He *deserved not to die*, He gave Himself for us that we might be made righteous like Him.

The Mysteries are described as glorious, holy, life-giving and divine, placed on the propitiatory altar united the Coming of our Lord from heaven"—

And just before beginning the above Anthem the priest says:—

"Christ our Lord account your worthy to meet Him with open face. Amen—"

These thoughts are similar to Kōbō himself expressed about the Oku-no-in, Miroku.

The persian rite, or Liturgy of the Nestorians from which they are taken was composed in the first century by Mar Adai and Mar Mari of Edessa in Mesopotamia the holy "Apostles who made disciples of the East."

I found this Liturgy lately in Brightman's "Liturgys Eastern aud Western" pub. at Oxford 1896.

Another curious point and something more than a coincidence is the intentional arrangement of the characters so to read in the irohauta by Kōbō Daishi.

The characters at the end of each line are 'とかなくてしす' 'Toka nakute shisu,' or 'Toka' means 'crime,' 'Nakute' means 'without,' 'Shisu' means 'died.' So, literally it means; 'He died without crime.' [c.f. Isaiah 53. 6-9, 10; Mathew 27. 19, 54 Compare; Mark 14. 15. 18. 38 Joh 19. 4, R. V; I Peter 3. 18, 21-24].

We cannot help admiring the wonderful skill and all-inclusive wisdom of this great benefactor of our Japanese race who, besides this, founded the Sogei-shuchi-in (綜藝種智院)—literally "the Institution of Arts" with the intention of instructing the People in religious morality.

The schools in Japan at that time were all designed for teaching the young nobles, and quite excluded the lower classes; so, with a view to educating the poor people, Daishi founded this Institute to the east of Toji in Kyoto.

How immense. indeed, are his contributions to the civilization of Japan!

CHAPTER XII

"Mishu-Hō"

Not content with carrying out his long cherished desire to establish the Faith on a firm and everlasting basis, and thus enhance the glory of the Buddha and the people's welfare, Daishi also paid great attention to state affairs, and served successively the Emperors Heijō (平城), Saga (嵯峨), Junna (淳和), and Nimmyo (仁明). Taking part in politics as often as duty called, he thereby rendered great and efficient services to those four sovereigns. When in September of the first year of Kōnin (A.D. 810), N. Fujiwara (藤原仲成) and the Maid of Honor, Kusuriko (薬子) excited a rebellion against the Government, Daishi daily proceeded to the Imperial palace at Kyoto and took part in the Conferences at Court, now replying to the questions put by the Throne, now devising strategical schemes until the rebels were put down, and peace restored.

As a true patriot, it was ever foremost in his mind to pray for the boundless glory of the Imperial reign and to establish the Empire in peace, so that often in his writings we find such expressions

---

It is the same idea as in the Greek acrostic whose initial letter read I-Roha-Uta the cryptic name or pass-word "Fish" given to the Messiah by the persecuted Christian—viz.: I Jesus; X Christ; G God's; u Son; s Saviour

as 'Our Country' or 'Our State.' In November, the first year of Jyōwa (承和), in the reign of the Emperor Nimmyo (A.D. 834), Daishi suggested to the Sovereign that he might be allowed to offer a prayer called 'Goshichi-nichi' or 'Mishu-hō' at the palace for the welfare of His Imperial Majesty and the peace of the Empire. This ceremony was to continue for one week, from the 8th of January in each New Year; and the Emperor granted this privilege to Kōbō Daishi. This is still continued in the hands of the Shingon-shū. At present it is oberved in Kyoto at the Tōji monastery.

On the seventh and last day of his Prayer-octave,(1) Daishi proceeded to the Palace and performed the Kwanjō ceremony of sprinkling perfumed water on the Emperor's head.

CHAPTER XIII

WHY WAS TŌJI TEMPLE BUILT?

This Kwanjō baptism is the chief one in Japan. It was first received by Nāgârjuna (the co-founder with Aśvaghosa of Mahāyāna Buddhism) from Vajrasattva (金剛薩埵) in the Iron Tower(2) in South India or, as present scholars say, at Khotan in Central Asia. It was introduced into Japan from Chang-an in China by Daishi. At Chang-an a palace called Choseiden (長生殿), was set apart for the ceremony, which was regularly performed at New Year. In our Japan also, by Daishi's request, an official building called 'Kageyu-shichō' (勘解由司廳) was transformed into 'Shingon-in' (眞言院)—i.e. palace where the Kwanjō ceremony might be performed. It shows how anxious our Emperor was for

(1) Such a line of special prayer is called an "Octave" in the Catholic Church.

(2) The story of Nāgârjuna and this Tower bears a singular resemblance to the Tower described in "The Vision *of the Shepherd*," an allegory written at Rome about the year A.D. 100, which was considered of such importance that it was read for centuries in the Early Christian churches and ranked as Holy Scripture.

The writer, Hermas by name, was granted the Vision after much prayer and fasting. An Aged Lady with a youthful face, who held the Book of Life in her hand, and was robed in a bright garment, showed Hermas the Great Tower which was 'built-upon water," because Life is and shall be saved by water for the Tower was founded by the Word of the Almighty and Honourable Name, into which the Souls of the penitent were baptized.

The exceedingly Old Lady—who seems to resemble Kwannon Sama— is explained to be alternatively "The Holy Spirit and the Church of God."

the country's welfare that he was pleased to adopt this rite and make it a national custom.

Four Empresses became the disciples of Daishi. Kōnin-tennō presented him with the Tōji as a training school for the *mikkyo*, or Secret Doctrine, in A.D. 823, the 14th year of Konin. This hall is called the 'Kyō-Ō-Gokokuji (教王護國寺) literally, "the temple of the Authorized Doctrine for the protection of the Country."

The Imperial Edict then issued says:—

"The temple is for the Propagation of the Secret Doctrine and is a most holy place of Prayer for the security of the land and people against all injury. If the people pay due homage to the Temple, the country will be safe and its inhabitants enjoy peace and prosperity; but if otherwise the Government will go astray and the country be visited by disasters. In fine, the Tōji will rise or fall with the country; for when Tōji is held in high esteem, Japan will prosper, whilst when it is neglected, the country will fall."

Thus Tōji at Kyoto is a most important temple and has the closest connection with the Imperial household; hence its name of 'Kyō-Ō-Gokokuji.' Now then, the ceremony of Kwanjō which was instituted in the first year of Kōnin (A.D. 810) has been kept up in Tōji for over eleven hundred years, interceding for the good health of each Emperor in succession as well as for the everlasting well-being of the Imperial rule. The rite is performed over the robes of the reigning Emperor instead of on his Imperial person.

Besides this, in conformity with the Imperial wishes, Daishi offered prayer more than fifty times for the peace and prosperity of the Japanese Empire. There is none, from the Emperor himself down to the poorest peasant, who has been excluded from the vast favour of Daishi and the grace of the Shingon Sect. The prayer of "Mishu-hō" is, in fact, the foremost amongst the safe-guards of our Empire.

CHAPTER XIV

DAISHI ENTERS INTO REST

In Angust (A.D. 823), the ninth year of Tenchō, in the Emperor Junna's reign, Daishi resigned the post of Daisōdzu (大僧都). Feeling his life drawing to a close, he bequeathed all the other important posts to his disciples, viz. the Tōji to Jichi-ê (實慧); Takao (高雄) to Shin-zei (眞濟); Murō-san (室生山) to Ken-né (堅慧); and the Kōfuku-ji (弘福寺) in Izumi Province, the

Daian-ji (大安寺) at Nara, the Atago-ji (愛宕寺) in Kyoto, and some others, to his different disciples.

Having done this, Daishi himself retired from active life, and with two or three disciples quietly settled down at Koya-san. Several years elapsed, and on December 15th, 834, in the first year of Jōwa, of the Emperor Nimmei, Daishi gathered many disciples together and in earnest soothing tones said:—

"At first I thought I should live till I was a hundred years old and convert all the people, but as you have all grown up, there is no need for my life to be prolonged and I shall therefore enter "Kongō-jyo" the Diamond World (*Vajranirvāṇa*), on the 21st day of next March, leaving my physical self here to protect the Faith from all injury. But you need by no means grieve, for although my physical self will die (or enter into hibernation), my spirit will survive."

Yes,. this point expresses the vast difference between the teaching of absolute Extinction of the Hīnayāna School and the thought of everlasting life of Mahāyāna.

"I will watch over your conduct whether it be right or wrong. Therefore, my Disciples, suffer not yourselves to be idle because of my apparent absence. After my decease, I shall go to Tushita (覩史多)—the Heaven of Joy—and wait on Maitreya (彌勒), but 5,670,000,000 years hence, I shall revisit this world in company with Maitreya Bodhisattva and bear witness to those who have believed the Faith. As for my disciples, during the interval, my soul will daily come and watch over them."

With this Daishi uttered seven vows and told them other important things in detail.

Three months elapsed and on March 15th A.D. 835, second year of Jyōwa, Daishi purified himself and, entering a cleansed room, he sat according to the Rule, and awaited the time of his passing. His disciples gathered around him and prayed, repeating together the Name of Maitreya Bodhisattva.

Then, strange-looking clouds covered the sky, and odours of singular fragrance filled the air. Noticing this, thousands and thousands of clergy and lay-folk climbed the Kōya-san (高野山), and bowing down before Daishi asked for his blessing. As time wore on, Daishi's attitude remained unchanged, and although his breaths became less frequent, his countenance was calm and composed as ever. At last, just as he had predicted, at the hour of dawn—March 21st—he passed away in his sixty-second year to the Heaven of Joy in Miroku's Presence.

鹿野苑に壁畫を畫きて

日本美術院々友　野生司香雪

I.　印度文化の特徴

私はこういふ所でお話するといふことは餘りやつたことがない爲めに，そのお話は皆様には隨分お聞き苦しいことゝ存じますけれども，その邊はどうかお許し願ひたいと存じます。

今晩お話致したいと思ひますことは，印度の佛教の現在と，さうして私の携つてまゐりました壁畫揮毫の次第をお話申し上げたいと存じます。

印度といふ國は一口に言ひますと，宗教に依つて興り而して宗教に依つて亡びた國であるといふ人がありますが，併し私は決してこれは全面的な印度の考察ではなく，一面の觀方であらうと思ひます。それは現代人が科學的に物質文化を生活價値の標準として考へた時は，或はさういふやうな批判が下されるかと思ひますが，全體，印度人は人生を二つの方面を以て考へて居つて，これは獨り印度人に限らず何れの民族にもさうでせうが，その間に自ら印度人には特にさうした考が深いやうに思はれます。それといふのは，一つは物質の世界と，二つは靈魂の世界と斯ういふ風に考へてをります。この二つの世界を程よく調和してゆくといふ事は人間の理想であつて，皆さうあらねばならんと考へてをるのでありますが，決してそれをよく最終まで兩方の調和を保つて勝利を得るといふことは非常に六ケ敷いことであります。そこで印度人の申しますには，「若し民族が國家として發展を望むならば，是非ともその中の物質の世界を追從してゆかなければならない，現在あの歐米人が文化の先進國としてばかり優越の位置にあるといふことは，質にこの物質の世界，即ち物質文化といふものを特に研究していつた結果に外ならない」と申しますのは，これは無論さうであります。併し人が恒久の生命を念願して涅槃といふ不朽の世界を追求せんとしたならば，是非とも物質の世界を離てゝ靈魂の世界につくべきである，と斯ういふ風に彼等は考へてをります。さうして印度人が宗教に依つて興り，而して宗教に依つて亡びるといふことは，要するに，この恒久の生命を追求してゆくといふところに，さういふ事が考へさせられるのではないかと思ふのであります。ですから物質文明を離れて民族としての優越感——恒久の生命を贏ち得ようといふ大なる問題の前には，若し自分の國家が何れの國の殖民地にならうと，さういふ事は大した問題ではない，と斯ういふ考もあるやうで，そこで現代人の得意としてをる分析とか歸納といふ方法は，要するに現象の世界以外の何ものも知ることが出來ない，併し印度人の宗教生活といふものは，その行に依つて現象の奥に潜んでゐる靈的實在を大悟して，その大悟した結果は事物の概念を把捉しようといふやうな考をもつてをるのではないかと考へます。そして，行としての苦行は人間が神と合體する爲には是非とも必要なものである。全體惡といふ行爲が我々の身體にあるといふことは，要するに，我々の物質的要素に宿つてをるのですから，その肉體を苦しめれば苦しめる程靈魂がだんだんと宇宙の實在に一致するものです。つまり宇宙の精靈の働きに依つてだんだん淨化されてゆく。佛教などの言ふ大乘起信論などの思想のそれであらうと存じます。かうして薫習淨化された結果は遂に物質の世界までも支配することが出來るといふのであります。かうした印度人の精神生活，卽ち彼等がとつてゐる日常の宗教的氣分といふものは，縱に三千年の歴史と又横に三億五千の民族に含まれて，その邃く且廣い精神生活といふものゝ縮圖が，今も尙あの聖都ベナレスの町にあるものと考へます。あの町に參りますと，あの大きな榕樹の下で，生れてから一度も刈つたことのない長い髮，而も荒布のやうにもつれもつれて體に垂れ，體は顔から足の先まで牛糞を乾かして燒いたその灰をガンジス河の水で溶きまして，それを體にずつと塗つて，木の下で結伽趺坐して冥想してゐる行者を見ますと，彼等は何時食事をし何時眠るのか，その邊りに生活の什器すら見當らないが，その木の蔭に靜坐してゐる行者の姿は，或時には背に夕日を浴び，又或時は靑白い月の光が瘦せた頬をかすめてゐる。偶々白い長い眉の下から底光りのする瞳を見た時には，何だか今にも雲を破つて出でんとする靈氣が人に迫るやうな氣が致します。こんなやうな景色を我々がぢーと見てをります時には，印度人の宗教生活といふものは今も尙三千年昔の神話時代を想像して止まないのであります。それが宗教の祭といふ一つの儀式になつて現はれましたものを，私は昨年春あの聖ガンジス河と聖ヂヤムナ河とが合流して大ガンジスとなつて印度洋に流れ込む，その合流地點にあるアラハバードに參りました時見ました。時は冬の旱期にありまして，河の水はすつかり涸れて，見渡す限り廣々として際限のない河原にも人を以て埋つてをるのであります。これは玄奘の旅行記である大唐西域記にも出てをりますが，十二年に一度あるお祭で，そこに一のものを供養すれば，千になつて返つてくるといふ言ひ傳へで，玄奘の旅行記にも書いてありますし，今も猶ほ言ひ傳へがあるのであります。そこで朝未明の頃から多くの行者達が行列を整へて，その河の合してゐる所に參りまして沐浴するのであります。その行列が，最初には見上げるやうな大きな象の身體を金色鮮やかに装飾してその上に鞍を置いてをりますが，その鞍には象の装飾に似合はず，裸身の行者，坊さんが何人か乘つてをります。これはやはりその宗派の管長さんとでも申しますか，此處

に乘つてゐる坊さんは偉い坊さんです。さうした象が四頭參りまして，その象の後に續く坊さんがをりますが，全部が全部とは申しませんけれども，その參會者の中約二千程の坊さんはヒンヅー敎のナハガーに屬するもので，一糸纏はずの裸體であります。その裸體の坊さんが威風堂々二列に並んで象の後から續いて何哩かの河を進んで行く，その兩側にはヒンヅー敎の信者が雲の如く群つて之を拜んでをる。我々の習慣から見ますと，さういふ一糸纏はない姿が宗教の行儀作法であるといふのは如何にも奇々怪々たる事實に考へますが，彼等はさうした考は毛頭持たないのであらうと思ひます。或る所に七，八人の女性が並んで，さうして頭髮を解いて前にずうと垂らしてゐる，その髮の上を裸の坊さんが靜かに踏んでゆく。斯ういふやうな景色を目前にした時には，全くこの地上に神の世界を現出してゐるやうな一種の神秘な感に打たれるのであります。こんな樣な摩訶不思議な宗教作法は申すまでもなく，婆羅門敎の流れを汲んだヒンヅー敎と申しますが，又印度敎と言つてもよいものですが，その印度敎の作法であります。その印度敎は婆羅門敎から出たもので，婆羅門敎は西歴紀元前五，六世紀の頃には旣に爛熟の境に至つて，殊に婆羅門敎には四姓の區別，階級的の差別待遇があり，最上階級であり且つ宗教上の實權を持つ婆羅門族と刹帝利といふ王族士族の爲に，毘舍族といふ農民商人工人とか，或はその下に屬するシュードラ（首陀羅）といふ一番下の奴隷階級などは常に差別的の待遇を受け，宗教の爲に救はれるのでなく，宗教の爲に苦しむといふ不思議な現象をみました。

II. 佛教と初轉法輪寺

この時に當つて，あの釋迦牟尼佛が現れて是等の差別を一掃して四海平等，一視同仁の法を說いたのが，只今の佛教であります。これが爲に釋尊の傘下には汲然として集つて，その教は程なく印度大陸に普く弘つたのであります。この教は釋尊の入滅後猶ほ約一千年の間は印度に於て盛であつたやうですが，凡そ西暦五，六世紀頃からだんだん下火となつて，あの十一世紀にマホメツト敎が西から東遷して印度を占領する時に，無慘にも破壞したわけで，それから加速度に衰へ，十三，四世紀頃にはセイロン島を除く印度には地を拂つたと申して差支ない。爾來印度に於きましては佛教は全く暗黑の時代でしたが，こゝに千八百七十年ですか，（少し誤算がありますが）今から約七十年程昔セイロン島に生れたアナガリカ・ダンマパーラー（Anagarika Dhammapāla）といふ人が現れまして，彼は小さい時から早くも佛道に志し，だんだんとその信仰は灼熱して，遂に佛教發祥の印度大陸に佛教を再興しようといふ大なる念願を以て臨んだのであります。さうして彼は世界の隅々までも，佛教のある所以を說いて，日本にも二度ばかり見えたことがあります。その彼の信仰の結晶は遂に佛教三寶完成の聖地であるサールナ

ートの丘に厳として聳え立つ，あの石造の大伽藍ムーラガンダクーチ・ビバーラ（Mūlagandhakūti-vihāra）といふ名前のお寺が出來たのであります。「ムーラ」は初，「ガンダクーチ」は香室，「ビハーラ」は寺で，初の香室の寺と斯う譯すべきですが，私はこれを歴史的意味に於て，初轉法輪寺といひます。この法輪といふのは車であつて，法輪を轉ずるといふことは説法するといふ意味で，法輪は原始時代の印度に於ける武器だつたといふことで，圓い車でありまして，その使ひ方ははつきり知りませんが，昨年シャムに參りました時その使ひ方を大體教はりました。これは話が一寸餘談に移りますが，シャムの銀貨は日本の十錢白銅の如く眞中に孔があいてゐて，その周りに國のやうなものがついてゐます。これは法輪が唸を發して廻つてゐることの現れで，成程佛教國シャムにふさはしいと考へました。その法輪を轉するといふことは，その武器を以て法敵を討ち，以て邪法を拆伏するといふ意味で，先刻平等先生のお話にありましたが，それであります。

III. 初轉法輪寺の壁畫

サールナートの鹿野苑のお寺は始めて說法せられた所であつて，ムーラガンダクーチ・ビバーラといふお寺を歴史的意味に於て斯う譯しました。そのお寺はあの鹿野苑の岡，紺碧の空，雲の峯を背景として聳えてをりますが，其所に釋尊在世八十年の御事蹟を壁畫として遺す爲に，遠く日本にそれを註文してきたのであります。當時文部省に於きましては，私の前任者桐ヶ谷洗鱗氏がこれを擔當することゝなりましたが，同氏は不幸にも病氣に罹つて，今や出發しようといふ時に物故せられたのであります。その爲に私はその後任者として命ぜられることになつて，參りましたのは今から六年前の昭和七年で，その秋渡印したのであります。印度のカルカツタに着きました時，先づこの繪を日本に註文してきた當事者として，先刻申しました佛教再興の偉動者として輝くダンマパーラ尊者をカルカツタの大悟協會（Mahābodhi Society）に訪ねましたところ，尊者は東の國から遙々と來た私を喜び迎へて吳れまして，早くも自分の目的を遂したかの如く喜び，あの眉長き老眼に玉のやうな涙を浮べ，喜びの言葉の數々を傳へるのでありました。その時彼が申しますには，「佛教に依つて養はれたる日本の藝術を佛教發祥の印度に迎へることは何たる奇緣ではないか。これは言ふまでもなく佛の與へられたる尊い因緣である」と彼は懇々と，常ならず長廣舌に語り續けるのでありました。當時尊者は相當重い病氣であつたにも拘らず，その病苦を忘れたかの如く語るのでありました。私達はその瘦せ衰へた病軀を目の前にして長座することを忍びず，再會を約して席を辭しました。

（神奈川縣佛青聯盟「涅槃の夕」講演速記。未完）

日暹佛教協會の成立

去る五月一日午後，名古屋の名刹，日暹寺の大書院に於て，兼ねて計畫中の日暹佛教協會が創立された。

小松原國乘師の司會の下に，緒方宗博師の導師にて巴利語三歸依文を齊唱し，淺野研眞師より經過報告あり，次いで左記各位の祝詞ありて，懇談數刻，紀念撮影などして，和氣藹々裡に此の意義ある會合を閉ぢた。

祝　詞

外務大臣　佐藤　尙武

佛教は東洋に起り，茲に佛誕二千五百年を經て今日の燦然たる文化の隆盛を現前して居ります。そして實に其の間，東洋の諸民族に，汎く其の慈雨を蒙らしめて居ることは，實に多大なるものありと思ひます。元來佛教は印度に初まり，「シャム」，「ビルマ」，支那，日本の諸國に最もよく傳持されてゐるのであります。而して，「シャム」國は佛教を以て國教とする世界唯一の國であります。我が日本も亦，大乘佛教の獨自の發達をして居る國であります。今茲に此兩國間に有志佛教徒に依り，一つの協會の設立されんとするは，時宜に適したるものと思ひます。

想ふに，昨今特に東亞の諸邦の親善を彌が上にも，深かめるの必要を痛感する秋に當り，日暹兩國の間の精神文化に依る提携親善の促進されんとすることは私の衷心より歡びとする處であります。簡單ながら，卑見を陳べて祝詞に代へる次第であります。（以上）

祝　辭

駐日シャム公使

ミトラハム・ラクシヤ

佛教，教育及び文化を通じて，日暹兩國民の握手提携は余の豫て希望せる所にして，此の意味に於て今回本會の成立に對して滿腔の贊意を表するものなり。何卒今後健全なる發達を祈念して止ます。

祝　辭

ピヤ・スリスチカン・バンチョン

日本は大乘佛教の國であり，シャムは小乘佛教の國である。然し同じ佛果に到る點に於ては，何等差異はないのである。

またシャムは材料の原產地であり，日本はそれに加工する工場である。

故にアジアの二大佛教國が，物心兩面に提携親善を圖り，世界平和と人類福利のために努力し，大聖釋尊の大慈悲を全世界に光被せしめねばならぬ。此の意味に於て本會の創立を衷心より喜びとするものである。

日暹佛教協會發會式次第

日時　五月一日午後三時

會場　名古屋覺王山日暹寺

一，開會宣言

一、發會挨拶
一、巴里語三歸依文齋唱
一、經過報告　　一、祝　辭
　外務大臣　暹羅公使　日暹協會長
一、座長推薦　　一、會則審議
一、役員選擧　　一、閉會の辭

以上

追つて同日役員選擧に於て出席者によつてシャム側會長にバンチョン氏，日本側會長に大谷瑩潤氏，副會長に來馬琢道氏が就任され，出席者全部が理事に就任した。

日暹佛教協會々則

第一條　本會ハ日暹佛教協會ト稱シ本部ヲ東京及盤谷ニ置キ時宜ニ應ジテ日暹兩國其他各地ニ支部ヲ設ク
第二條　本會ハ通佛教的立場ニ立チ日暹兩國間ノ親善及福利ノ増進ヲ圖ルヲ以テ目的トス
第三條　本會ノ事業左ノ如シ
　一、日暹間ノ見學旅行，留學等ノ紹介斡旋
　二、日暹關係ノ宗教，學藝及一般文化上ノ諸事項ノ調査研究
　三、會報及圖書ノ出版刊行
　四、研究會，講演會及講習會等ノ開催
　五、其他必要ト認ムル諸事業
第四條　本會ニ顧問，參與及役員ヲ置ク
　一、顧　問　　若干名
　二、參　與　　若干名
　三、會　長　　二　名
　四、副會長　　二　名
　五、理　事　　若干名
　六、評議員　　若干名
第五條　會長ハ日本側暹羅側各一名ヲ理事會ニ於テ推薦ス
　理事ハ評議員ニ於テ互選ス
　評議員ハ總會ニ於テ選擧ス
　顧問參與ハ會長之ヲ推薦ス
第六條　役員ノ任務ハ左ノ如シ
　一、會長ハ會務ヲ總理ス
　二、副會長ハ會長ヲ補佐シ會長故障アルトキハ會務ヲ代行ス三理事ハ會務ヲ執行ス
　四、評議員ハ重要ノ會務ヲ評決ス
第七條　會長理事及評議員ノ任期ハ各四箇年トス，但シ再選ヲ妨ゲズ缺員ヲ生ジ補缺選擧ヲ行ヒタルトキハ前任者ノ殘任期間ヲ以テ任期トス
第八條　本會員ヲ分チテ左ノ四種トス
　一、名譽會員　理事會ノ決議ヲ經テ會長ノ推擧セル者
　二、贊助會員　本會ニ金百圓也以上ヲ醵出セル者
　三、維持會員　本會ノ維持費トシテ年額金六圓也ヲ納付スル者
　四、通常會員　本會々費トシテ年額金參圓ヲ納付スル者
第九條　本會ノ經費ハ會費，寄附金及其他ニヨリ支辨ス
第十條　本會ハ毎年一回定期總會ヲ開キ會務及會計ノ報告ヲ爲シ必要事項ヲ議定ス
第十一條　本會則ハ總會ニ於テ出席會員過半數ノ贊成ヲ得テ之ヲ改正スルコトヲ得

因に主要出席者は左の如くであつた。

ミトラハム・ラクシヤ公使，バンチョン父子，ミス・シヤムことオングゲ・ドアン・プミラツト孃父子，ブン・ルアン・クラボアンラタナ

大谷瑩潤，來馬琢道，小松原國乘，稻葉圓成，藤井草宣，淺野研眞，精園俊介，平等通昭，小櫻秀謙，緒方宗博，神田正法の諸氏。

局　報

謹啓，愈〻御多祥奉大賀候。

陳者昭和十二年五月二十三日開催の本局評議員會に於て御推擧を蒙り，不肖非才をも顧みず本年度の局長に就任仕候間宜敷御願申上候。次に同日の決議により幹事選任を不肖に一任せられ候處下記の如く御選任申上候。次で六月十七日開催の本局幹事會に於て，左記の如く常任幹事を任命致候間何卒宜敷願上候。

幹事　熈谷俊之　常光浩然　稻葉文海
　　　淺野研眞　伊藤道機　好村春基
　　　蜂谷惠晃　坂野榮範　福井康順
　　　藤井草宣　阿部現亮　緒方宗博
　　　川上賢叟　平等通昭　中川議淨諸氏
常任幹事　平等通昭（編輯主任）
　　　小笠原義雄　淺野研眞諸氏

編　輯　後　記

今回長兄淺野研眞氏が編輯主任を辭任されましたので，十七日の幹事會で幹事諸氏の推薦を受け，小生もかういふ雜誌の編輯には興味を持つてゐたので，二十一日常任幹事と編輯主任を受命致しました。宜しく願ひます。

歐米思想界の行づまりと日本文化殊に佛教の認識が高められたことから，日本佛教の研究や關心が高まり，日本への佛教研究の爲の來朝者も日と共に増して參ります。殊に全聯汎聯としては明夏に滿洲大會をひかへ，三年後に世界佛教大會を控へ，既にその準備に立ち遅れの觀もあります。

この秋，國際佛教通報局としては通報機關として宣傳機關として全能力を上げるべきです。不肖，その重任に堪へ得べきものではありませぬ。唯，長老先望の高見を伺ひ，その指導と鞭撻によつて，短を棄て長を取り，分を守つて，本腰に局の運轉と誌の編輯をやつて見たいと思つてゐます。

雜誌の編輯方針としては，長老局長とも打合せ，先望の意見も伺ひ，「通報」の名の如く，日本佛教のニュース（英文）と海外ニュース（和文）を主とし，英文論文を從とし，和文論文は一篇か，又は廢することとします（「青年佛徒」にその任を委ねて）。英文も日本佛教の傳達紹介に努め，日本ニュースは各宗本山大寺のニュース，教界のビッグニュースを中心とし，海外により多く配布したいと思ひます。さし當り八月號は世界教育會議出席外人への「日本佛教紹介」にしたく思つてゐます。私としての本格的な編輯の出來るのは，九月號か十月號でせう。

それよりも局の經營が難關にぶつつかつてゐて，一寸油斷すると雜誌が休刊になる恐れさへあります。發行日の遅れるのも，減頁も，一にその爲です。編輯よりこの方に落處しなくてはならないのは，苦痛です。さし當つて暑中と年賀廣告掲載（五圓づゝ年額十圓）の後援者百名を作りたく希望してゐます。

洛いのに餘り語りすぎました。先任名ヂヤーナリストの後です。「期待」を願ふよりも，指導鞭撻と御後援をお願ひして，擱筆します。（T. B.）

定價	一部	金二十錢　送料五厘
	一年	金二圓四十錢　送料不要

昭和十年四月卅日第三種郵便物認可
昭和十二年七月廿三日印刷（毎月一回）
昭和十二年七月廿五日發行（一日發行）

東京市外吉祥寺337
編輯發行兼印刷人　淺野研眞

東京市牛込區早稻田鶴卷町107
印刷所　株式會社康文社印刷所
電話牛込（34）1950番 5049番

東京市神田區一ツ橋二の三
發行所　國際佛教通報局
電話九段（33）4428番
振替東京83015番

昭和十年四月三十日第三種郵便物認可
昭和十二年七月二十三日印刷納本（毎月一回
昭和十二年七月二十五日發行（一日發行）
國際佛教通報 第三卷 第七號

第二回

汎太平洋佛教青年會大會紀要

THE PROCEEDINGS of THE Second General Conference of Pan-Pacific Young Buddhists' Associations

(in Japanese, Chinese and English)

Held at Tokyo & Kyoto, July 18-23, 1934

Price ¥ 3.00

Compiled & Published by

The Federation of All Y.B. As. of Japan,

Tokio, Kanda, Hitotsubashi, II-3

昭和十年四月三十日第三種郵便物認可 昭和十二年八月十二日印刷納本 昭和十二年八月十五日發行（毎月一回十五日發行）第三卷 第八號

The International Buddhist Bulletin

國際佛教通報

第三卷 昭和十二年八月 第八號 [Vol. III. August $\frac{2503}{1937}$ No. 8.]

八月 (August)

東京 國際佛教通報局 發行

The International Buddhist Information Bureau

II-3, Hitotsubashi, Kanda, Tokyo,

Annual Subscription, ¥2,40 (post free), Single Copy 20 sen (post 2 sen)

The Glimpse of Buddhism in America

By **Mutoku Hayashi**

1. Introduction.

There are considerable numbers of Japanese Buddhist missionaries in California, who are very eager to preach on Loving kindness of 'Sākyamuni; to teach the Doctrine of Buddhism; to have Sunday schools for the young Japanese-Americans. On the otherhand, I know, they are also very eager to collect money to build fine altars and pulpits for their own sect's sake. Yes. they do teach and preach the Gospel of Buddha, but it was always done only for the Japanese people in California.

The attempt of teaching Americans the Noble Path of the Enlightened One has long been neglected,—it was entirely forgotten—by those Japanese Buddhist missionaries. But here is an exception worthy to be remembered. A non-sectarian Buddhist monk, NYOGEN SENZAKI by the name. This is the monk who devoted his thirty years in the teaching of the real significance of Buddha and his doctrines to the decendants of the Pilgrim Fathers, and is still doing his mission. And also he is the man who actually transplanted the seed of Buddhism into the soil of the United States. For thirty years he has been teaching Americans Buddha and his Enlightenment! Day after day, year by year, he did nothing but meditation in a hut with some American Saṅgha. He really did nothing else, for he believes that the meditation is the only and best way to teach and actualize Buddhism to Americans.

Not a single temple was erected by him, nor did he build a tower for the virtues of Saints. Furthermore, it is very strange to say that he never recited even a stanza of Sūtras for the dead for his parishner's sake, because he, in the first place, does not like such ideas and deeds as making money by reciting the Sacred Sūtras, and in the second place, according to the local Japanese expression. "He aint got no parishners at all."

In addition, he has no worldly fame and glory; no family and no money. About this last item, you can bet your last nickel that he seldom has more than a couple of dimes in his purse all the time—one of the very strange phenomena in America.

He hates the propaganda and public anouncement about him and his doings. So little is known his name either among Americans and or Japaneses in California. Nevertheless those who know him well, would never deny that this non-sectarian, hard-boiled monk is the greatest Buddhist ever came to the Golden State from the Land of the Rising Sun.

2. The Speech delivered by Rev. Nyogen Senzaki to the American audience, on the occasion of the Commemoration of Buddha's Birth at the Daishi Mission, Los Angeles, California, April 8th, 1937.

The topic of his speech is "What is Buddhism?" and the highlights of his address is as follows:

Buddhism is a system of thought containing many doctrines. These doctrines were discovered and established by Buddha 'Sākyamuni, some 2500 years ago. Buddha was not an agent of a Supreme Being.

He was a human being, a student of philosophy, a seeker of its ultimate truth. His teachings are, therefore, nothing but human experiences which any one of us can follow, without many difficulties. Buddha said to his followers:

"I am an accomplished one, and all of you are future Buddhas." He was really an accomplished one—one of the teachers who lived a pure, unselfish life and practised what he taught.

One of the Buddhist doctrines which is the easiest to comprehend is the doctrine of Karma. A man gets what he deserves, and nothing more. This is a self-evident fact. If a man has sorrows, it is because he deserves sorrows. If he has joy, it is because he has deserved joy. If he does good deeds, he is accordingly happy. Each pain or joy is provided the exact proportion for his own acts. No Gods or God can increase or decrease what is coming to a man, even though he fears or

worships the supernatural power which he follishly postulates, Most of the people are satisfied, dealing the problem of life with the easy, casual methods. They try to blot off their sins by a hocuspocus of priest-craft. They believe to make a contract with Heaven, to get the happiness of a hereafter, for singing wishy-washy hymns. From the primitive stage of medicine man to the modern days of church organization, the law of causation has been neglected by the majority of selfish men.

Buddhism teaches us that there is nothing haphazard in this life. Everything takes place according to the natural laws. Nothing happens in the world without a cause. The law of cause and effect, thus, eternally works in our life. So-called miracles are as impossible as the reversal of the fixed laws of nature. What seem to be miracles, if examined carefully without any excitement, will be usually attributed to the natural causes.

Every action brings its own results in the material world, in the psychological phenomena, or in social happenings. Badly conducted business will fail sooner or later. Poorly cutltivated field will produce poor crops. The policies of nations may be called very beautiful names, but if the motives and actions are not based on the welfare of mankind, they will never last long. From the kings to the paupers, from the rich men to the poor men, from wise birds to the stupid asses, none can break the law of causation and get away with it.

According to Buddhism, man is responsible for the manner in which he enters upon a stage of life. His Karma dertermines how and in what state he shall be appeared in the next stage of life. It is, therefore, impossible for him to blame chance or circumstance when any misfortune may befall him. Buddhist notion of sin is a condition of a disease of man in his way of development, not yet being advanced enough. Morbidness over it increases the diesease....when a man has good order of his mental and physical condition, he will not have any idea of evil or Sin.

Buddha said: "The world is full of Heavenly persons. They live in a region of calmness and peacefulness." This is the one of the three characteristics of Buddhism.

Another fundamental principle of Buddhism is the doctrine of the continuity of life.

There is no sharp dividing line between this life and the next.

If life begins with the birth, it must end with death. A religion which teaches that life comes forth at birth and thereafter exists eternally is ridiculously illogical. If life is eternal, one can not say, "Here of there life begins." Eternity has no end; and it has also no begining.

The death of body means re-birth, Karma being continued in new bodies through life after life. According to Buddhism, man has no entity to be called soul. He exists as a whole, is all sentient beings, not as individual being. Therefore, a death can not disturb the continuity of universal life.

A true Buddhist does not hanker after his personal immortality. He only endeavors to have a thought or feeling that is worth preserving. He knows that he will come to life as many times as it is necessary to complete the task of the world.

Karma and re-birth are continuous, the one implying the other; and they are inseparable from each other. As sin and suffering bring death, so does death bring re-birth, and to attain Nirvāṇa is to see the fact that there is no birth and no death from the very begining. This is another one of the three characteristics of Buddhism.

The last fundamental principle of Buddhism is that it teaches independence of thought. Buddha originated a religion which actually encourages free thought, instead of forcing the mind within narrow creeds.

His teaching shows clearly the whole reason for sins and throws a new and startling light upon the mistery of life. According to Buddhism, life is no longer baffling riddle, but a wonderful gift which each man may shape as he wishes.

He may ruin his life by wrong doing, or he may make of it a beautiful thing, not perfect yet, but on the way to perfection. Man is master of himself and of his fate.

He himself holds the key to the mystery of life, and veil after veil seperates him fast until he stands face to face with the pure truth. Yet, there is no veil so dark that he can not pierce it.

As soon as he takes upon himself and resposibility for all that has been and all that is to be, he has made the first step towards the Supreme end, for within himself and nowhere else lies the dormant strength, the power, the will by which he may attain perfect wisdom. He has within himself faculties hidden and unguessed potentialities vaster than it is possible to measure, which when develop to their full extent may make him wholly enlightened—even as Buddha himself. There is the last one of the three characteristics of Buddhism.

The three fundamental principles which we have discussed this morning—the recognition of the authentic law of cause and effect, the clear observation of the continuity of thought, a sort of an acid test for a student of teaching. Even though he has read many thousands of Sūtras, or has been ordained by the highest priest of his cathedral, or has donated a million dollars to the Buddhistic movement, if he does not understand thoroughly these three characteristics of Buddhism and he can not practice them in his everyday life, he is not a true Buddhist at all.

3. What are the Japanese Buddhist Missionaries doing in California?

They collect money, build temple, and perform funerals, and there the matter ends. This is what those Japanese Buddhist missionaries are doing in California today. I should say they are doing well, if only erecting temple or reciting Sūtras before altar is Buddhism.

I know they are awfully busy people, collecting money, paying bills, giving lectures, officiating wedding, and going as far as 1,000 miles to Arizona or New Mexico when they were asked to perform funeral. It, however, seems to me that they do the same business as the native Buddhist priests do today or they have been doing for century after century in Japan.

Only remarkable difference lies between the Buddhist missionaries in America and those of Japan, is that the former keep longer hair on their heads, and know how to drive Ford, but the latter keep their heads closely shaven, and are unable to drive even tricycle.

I saw many of the Japanese preachers, clad in American suits, instead of red or yellow robe, walking or driving car in a hurry on the streets of Los Angeles or San Francisco, and I also had chances to look at them teaching sunday school, or making speech on Buddhism in their churches. They seem quite sincere and earnest to their mission. I am quite sure they are really nice people. But there is one thing which I can not understand about them. Why and what for do the headquarters of their sects send missionaries to foreign countries? What is the purpose of sending missionaries to America? Is it simply to make them rnn the same business in America as they previously did in Japan?

It is almost fifty years since the Sacred Followers of Buddha marked the first step in the soil of the Golden State, but during these fifty years of the missionary work in California, little attention seemed to have been paid to the conversion of Americans in to Buddhism. Why? As far as I know these are the key to solve "Why"s:

First: They do not know real SPIRIT of the Mahāyāna Buddhist. And that's all.

Second: They were and have too busy to build their chuches as the best means of securing financial resources, not as the symbol of their Faith. The ideal and spirit of the Trans-Himālayan Buddhists is fortunatley or unfortunately, which every way you care to look at, far beyond their proffesional conscience.

Third: Their linguistic inability. Very few of them could understand English and they never seem to try to study it. Being college graduate, they, of course, read English....read in their own way, without proper care of accent, diction and pronounciation, as if they were reciting Sacred Scriptures.

Fourth: So-called big shots of the headquarters of their sects in Japan, never urgued them to work for Americans. In other words, they paid no heed save how many temples were built and how many Japanese parishners were registered in America.

Teaching Americans Buddhism? Phew! No use. It won't work. This was the dominant and unmovable opinion among them. "Maybe, it's a good idea, but it is not at all practical." they concluded. This has spelled their minds like black magic until they wholly quit the idea.

They undoubtedly might have faced many and never-to-be-forgotten difficulties when they first come to this country, but it might not be as half hard as that which the Spanish Catholic Father Junipero Serra,

Founder of first mission in California, had to experience. In the missionary history of California. there is no greater name than that of Father Serra, who, weak and cripple in body, preached wild American Indians the Gospel of Jesus and finally succeeded in converting them in Christianity.

Today, in New York, Chicago or San Francisco, there is no wild American Indians who shoot and kill strangers. No kayotes and grizzly bears roaming around on the streets of Los Angeles, that suddenly attack and bite Japanese Buddhist priests. No big, bad wolf would scare the Sacred preachers from Japan anymore. Why, then, are they scared of preaching Americans the Noble Path of the Enlightened One?

Before those sissy priests laugh at or ignore of the attempt of the transmission of Buddhism in American soil, as a beautiful, but impractical ideal, they should wash their faces in cold water, and just think of those great Chinese Buddhists who went over to India at the risk of their lives,....and who translated Sanskrit Sūtras into Chinese. Just imagine how tough and deadly it has been to them! Again, think of the great works done by Bodhi Dharma and other Indian monks, who alone came to China as early as 5th century, across the unknown seas and mountains, conquering tremendous difficulties and dangers in order to transmit the teachings of Buddha to China. They were always ready to die for the sake of the Enlightened One at anytime, anywhere. Remember those Buddhists in the past were not sissy, wishy-washy and namby-pamby chickens like the Japanese Buddhist missionaries in California today.

4. How Buddhism was transmitted from Japan to America?

The chief credit and merit in transmitting Buddhism to the United States, must be given to the following four Japanese and an American, namely Soyen Shaku,[1] then the Abbot of Enkakuji Monastery, Daisetsu T. Suzuki, Nyogen Senzaki, Shigetsu Sasaki, and Dr. Dwight Goddard. These five have done mighty good for the spread of Buddhism in general,

1) Soyen Shaku, the former abbot of Enkakuji Monastery, Kamakura.
Daisetsu T. Suzuki, the proffessor of Otani Buddhist College, Kyoto.
Nyogen Senzaki, leader of Buddhist movement, Los Angeles, U.S.
Shigetsu Sasaki, leader of Buddhist movement, New York.

of Zen in particular, among Americans.

In the summer of 1853, there was held in Chicago, the first International Congress of Religion. World-famous religionists from every quarter of the globe gathered together there to exchange ideas and belief on Religion. To join this Congress, Soyen Shaku crossed the Pacific, as one of the representatives of the Mahāyāna Buddhist Association of Japan. While he was staying in America, he met and talked with many of American Buddhist scholars, and published several books on Buddhism. In 1865, he again went to America, invited by Mrs. Alexander Russel, a millionare American woman, and stayed in San Francisco. He taught her Buddhism for a year. This, in the practical sense, is the first time that Buddhism was actually transmitted from Japanese mind to Yankee mind, from a poor Zen monk to a wealthy American lady.

From the scholastic point of view, the most outstanding figure among the five, is Daisetsu Suzuki, author of "Essays on Zen," "The Essence of Zen," "The Studies on Lankāvatāra Sūtra," etc. His books are well known and read among the students of Buddhism in America as well as in Europe. Nearly all the universities and public libraries of American big cities, keep Suzuki's books. Today, his books are "Text" as far as it concerns Zen Buddhism in the world. He wholesaled Buddhism in general to the world, and through his books, Zen, the most highly developed school of Oriental mysticism was first introduced to the elaborated minds of both America and Europe. By his effort, in consequence, the clouds of misunderstanding and prejudice which has hitherto been imposed upon Buddhism, was clearly removed from the eyes of self-conceited White people. It possibly safe to say that he made those conservative English people to give more spaces in explaining the word "Zen" in the pages of Encyclopedia Britanica.

Thus, the seed of Buddhism was sowed on the hotbed of America, and it was carefully cultivated by Nyogen Senzaki, Shigetsu Sasaki and Dwight Goddard, as American co-worker.

鹿野苑に壁畫を畫きて（二）

日本美術院々友　野 生 司 香 雪

IV. 壁畫揮毫の着手

それから後、サンチニケタンに行き、この壁畫に關係ある詩聖ラビンラナート・タゴール（Rabindranath Tagore）を訪ねました。今晩お見えになつてゐるムケルジー（Muckerjee）畫伯の住まはれてをる所に詩聖タゴールは隱棲してをられるのでありますが、其所に翁を訪ねて一應の挨拶をすることに致しました。訪ねますと、翁は快く引見して呉れまして、遠く日本の國から來たその勞を謝し乍ら申しますには、「日本の藝術と印度の藝術はその民族と歴史が異ると同時に、藝術も亦多く異つてゐる。互に異つた藝術の融和を圖ることは至難であるが、今お前がこの印度に佛教の爲に遺さんとする壁畫は印度人に、最も多く觀せんとするものであるが故に、日常培はれた佛教精神に依つて最善を盡して精進して、幸に壁畫が完成して再びお目にかゝる機會がありましたなら‥‥」と言葉を濁して席を去りました。斯ういふやうなことで、未だ壁畫に着手しないうちに多くの期待を持たれ、私はこの重責を負ひベナレス郊外鹿野苑に出發致しました。

ベナレスに到着後間もなく全ての準備を調へ、揮毫に着手致しましたが、そこに思ひ設けん問題が幾つか振りかゝつたのであります。先づその一つは、寺は石造の大伽藍でありますが、その石造の内部には煉瓦を張つて夏季の灼熱を緩和するやうな方法になつてをりますが、その煉瓦の上にコンクリートが塗つてあります。その上に壁畫の下地を畫くのでありますが、寺は大體北から南に向つて建つてをりますが、その寺の長さは約二十間でありまして、横は内部が六間、外部では九間程あります。Aが須彌壇のあるところです。

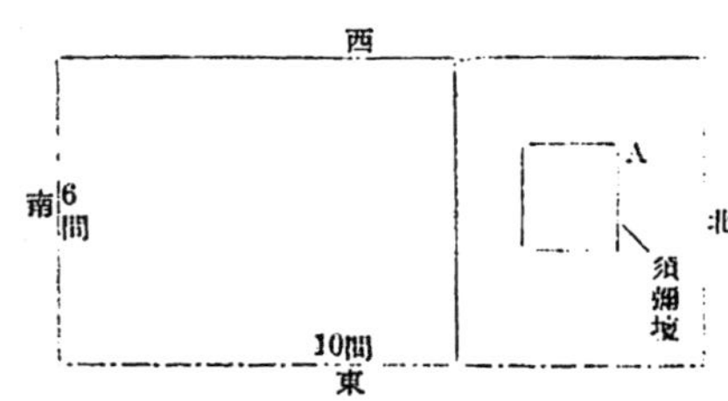

西の方の壁の中心に畫きます畫について、最初私はかういふ事を考へました。それは、自分の健康がどこまで保てるかわからないので、若し途中で健康上に故障が起つて挫折するやうな事があるかも知らぬその折、成るべく大きな畫題を先にして、小さ

い畫題を後に殘して行つたならば，途中で事故が起つても，その大きい畫題だけは遺して置くことが出來ると考へて，一番上に西から東に向けて成道の圖を畫きました。釋尊が佛陀伽耶で西から東に向かれて正覺をとられた爲に，その西の方に畫いて，東に向けるといふのは頗る位置がよいのでありまして，先づ一番佛教史上最も大きな事件であるところの釋尊の悟を開かれて佛になるといふ，その場面を畫きました。

V. 繪具の變色と大小乘の思想的相違

さうしてその繪が出來上りまして約一ヶ月程經つた時，その繪具は色調の濃度が三分の二散逸して了ひました。それといふのは，彼の成道の場面に佛が今や正覺をとられようといふ刹那に惡魔が之を邪魔し，先づ三人の女性に化身して愛慾を以て佛の心を誘惑しようといふことがありますが，その三人の女性は私のアイデアとして色を黄色い女と白い女と黒い女に分け，白い女は言ふまでもなく白色人種を象徴し，黄色い女は黄色人のアジヤ人を象徴し，黒い女は黒坊を現してをり，以て世界の三大民族を色に依つて現さうとしたのであります。黒い女は植物性の藍と燕脂を以て紫色を帶びた黒味を畫きましたところ，その黒坊の顔が一ヶ月經ちますうちにだんだん白くなつて來ました。そこでどうして白くなつたか，植物性の藍と言つて買つたが，まやかしものではないかと思ひましたが，自分で之を分析してみるといふやうな化學的力はないが，幸にその自分の住つてをる所から十哩の所にベナレスの大きな大學がありました。周圍二十哩といふ大きな敷地を有する，內容は別ですが，敷地ですれば世界有數の大學です。それでその大學に行つて，この問題を解決しようと思ひましたが，聞くは一時の恥とは言へ，日本から態々その爲にきてゐる者が纔かにここで一頓挫したといふことを思はれるといふことは忍びないので，よう參りませんでした。そこで仕方なく繪具の材料を一括して日本に送り返して，東北大學に頼んで分析して貰ふことに致しました。ところが不便なことには，郵便がどんなに早く參りましても，二十九日はかゝる，一便遲れゝば三十五，六日はかゝるといふ狀態ですから，ものがきて，直ぐその晩に返事を書いて呉れましても，二ヶ月か，もつとかゝるのであります。手紙がきて之を分析したりして，その結果を知らせて呉れるのでありまして，何でも七十幾日を要してをります。隨分この問題に付きまして焦つてゐる時に，一日も一刻も早く解決したいといふ時に，三ヶ月もかゝらねば解決出來ないといふ事は，氣の短い日本人としては辛かつたのであります。併しそれをやつて次の方法を講ずるより途なく，待つより外ない。ところが，その報告を見ますと，正しく植物性の藍です。するとコンクリートのあくの作用であると思ひまして，このあくを如何にして防止すべきかが問題になつて，又專門家の意見を聽きましたと

ころ，不幸にして適切なる解答がなく，遂に斯ういふやうな事をすればよいか？といふ實に手探り同樣な施設を考へました。之はどうしても專門家の意見にも「これならば」といふ意見が遂にありませんので，それで私は明礬と膠を溶き，鷄卵の黄味を取つて水にうすめ，更にその上にアルミニューームの粉を動物性の膠で溶いてそれを塗つてをき，その上には六回程，最も粗雜な胡粉を塗りまして，胡粉の約五六十倍のホルマリンを塗りまして，さうしてその上に畫を描く，大體畫の下地はさういふことをして描くべく準備をして，後は着々進行して行つたのであります。

然し，今度又起つてきた問題は，皆樣の御承知の通り佛教は印度を中心として北に傳はつた所謂北方佛教と南に傳はる南方佛教，卽ち南の小乘佛教に對し，北の大乘佛教があります，そしてこの兩者は教義に於て著しい差があります。ですから，北方に傳はつた大乘の佛傳を畫きますと，南方の小乘佛教の人には通じないことになります。そこで全體，現在印度に發掘その他に依りまして佛教の盛んであつた當時の遺品として現存するものはどういふものであるかと言ひますと，それは全部が全部ではありませんが，大體に於て大乘系のものが多いのであります。ところがこのお寺に今お守りしてをります坊さん達は南方のセイロン島からきた小乘佛教の坊さんで，それとこのお寺に佛教徒として最も多く參詣するのはセイロン島と，ビルマと，それからシャムの人は極く稀れで，大體セイロンとビルマの小乘の信者ですから，それ等の爲には小乘佛教のものでなければ通じない。その一例を申しますと，釋尊がお生れになる時あの無憂樹の下で降誕されたといふ事は，大乘佛教では三歲の子供と雖も知つてをる事實ですが，南方佛教ではあれは無憂樹でなくて，沙羅双樹になつてをります。丁度今晩の涅槃も沙羅双樹の下となつてをりますが，北方では，涅槃の時は沙羅樹，成道の時は菩提樹，降誕の時は無憂樹と明かになつてをりますが，南方では降誕の時も沙羅樹となつてをります。さういふやうな事實の相違が出て參りまして，印度を中心と申しますが，彼處から出た佛教は北と南に依つて異つてをります。その點に於きまして，私は南の方が本當だとも北の方が本當だとも言はない，皆一つしかないもので，二つに分けるといふことは意味ない，釋尊は一人である，ですからこれは南と北と二つに考へるといふことは抑々間違つてゐる，私はこれを一つに解釋して，自分は南に依つたとか，北に依つたとかといふその考へが旣に間違つたことだと思つてをる，私は之は一つなりといふ心算で，北といふ區別も南といふ區別もなく，一括して臨んだのであります。ですからその結果として，强いて釋迦の事を說明したならば，南と北との混合になつてをるかも知れません。まづさういふやうな南北の大乘と小乘との差から畫題と構圖の上に少からず惱んだことはありました。併し今申し上げます如く，さういふ事は二つあるべきではない，一つなりといふ

解釋の下に進むことにしました。

VI. 涅槃像の揮毫

そこで前申します通りに，最初西に畫きまして，それから南に移り，南から北に向けまして降誕のところを畫きました。それから東から西に向けては涅槃像を畫きました。涅槃は，北が本尊であるから本尊の方に向つて，北頭西面と申しますか，頭北面西と申しますか，佛樣が北枕になつて西向きにお休みになつてをられる畫を畫きました。今晩は涅槃の夕ですから，もう少しこの涅槃像の事を申しますと，涅槃のところを畫きます時に，普通日本にあります涅槃像は坊さんと俗人とが一緒になつてをります。併しこれを私は大體佛の上半身の方には全部坊さんを置いて俗人は置かなかつた，そして王者と雖も俗人は佛の下半身の前に置いて，坊さんは置かなかつた。印度に於きまして坊さんといふものは絶對の位置にあり，假令大臣，大將と雖も坊さんの右に座るといふことは許されない，又坊さんと一緒に座つて事をするといふ事，食事をするといふ事は許されない，坊さんは佛・法・僧三つの中の一つであるから，佛と同じである。ですから，坊さんに對して假令キングが禮拜しても，坊さんは禮を返すといふことはない。それだけ坊さんは尊い，原始佛教の時代からさういふ坊さんに對する絶對の尊敬は嚴として行はれてをりますから，涅槃の構圖の時も上は悉く坊さんにして，下半身に王者はじめ俗人を置きました。これは今までの涅槃像とその構圖に於きまして異つた樣式をとつてをります。それから今一つ，お顏に，私は最初に眼をつぶつた形を畫きました。ところがさういふ形を畫きましてから後，釋尊入寂のあの拘尸那(クシナガ)竭に參りまして，其所に丈六の涅槃像がありますが，その涅槃像は眼を開けてをるのです。パッチリと眼を開けてをります。それから今一つセイロン島の涅槃像も悉く眼を開けてをります。支那及び日本に於て畫いてをる涅槃像は大抵眼をつぶつてをる。この事に付いて或人は，眼を開けてをるのは，入滅せられるといふその入滅の直前であるといふ説明をしてをる人もあります。併し私はその眼をつぶらないで開けてをるといふことは，涅槃といふ事が，入滅一死ぬといふ意味でなく，法身として永遠に滅びない，永遠に生きるといふ意味で，その法身の佛が永遠性であるといふ事を物語るのには，眼を開けてをる方が本當ではないかと思ふのであります。そこで眼をつむつた佛樣の眼を又開けました（笑聲）。最初約一年位は佛樣は眼をおつぶりになつてをりましたが，私の涅槃といふものに對する考へが少し變つて參りますと，佛樣も眼を開けたお姿に變つてきました。

其外澤山の事はありますが，時間もありませんし，既に一時間近くなりましたから，構圖の事に付いて餘り言つてをる暇はありませんが，大體さういふ風な事が涅槃像であります。それと，普通涅槃像は百獸百鳥と申しますか，凡ゆる動物までが來て，この佛の入滅を悲しんでをることが畫かれてありますが，これは大體第八涅槃經にはさういふ事を書いてをりますが，南方佛教には見受けません。私の畫きましたのには多くの動物はこゝに畫いてをりません。只俗人と僧侶との二つのかたまりを畫いてをります。構圖の事は大體それ位にしまして，まあこんなやうなことで繪は着々進みまして，五年目の四月十五日，丁度昨年の四月でありますが，漸くにしてその仕事は曲りなりにも全壁面を埋めることが出來ました。さうして越えて五月十七日にはあのガンジー派の大立物であるパンジット・マラビヤが，この壁畫完成の開眼供養と申しますか，除幕式と申しますか，その式の司祭者となつて，莊嚴なる開眼供養を催すことが出來まして，私はここに長年に亘る宿願を成就することが出來ました。

VII. 壁畫の完成と同胞の應援

最後に一寸附加へて置きたいことは，この仕事は最初約五ヶ月間に完成するといふ計劃の下にあり，豫算もそれだけしかありませんでした。それが何年かに亘りました爲資金の上にも少からざる不自由を來しましたが，幸にして私は惠れたる健康に依りまして，その資金を調達すべく多くの繪を夏の壁畫の畫けない間を利用して澤山畫き，これをシムラ，ボンベイ，コロンボ，マドラス，カルカツタ，國を變へてビルマのラングーン，又シンガポール，シヤムのバンコツクと前後八回展覽會を催して，その都度幾らかの金をポケットに入れては一歩進み，又その金が盡きると次の年別の作品を持つて行つて展覽會をやるといふやうにして，漸く宿願を達しましたが，その展覽會の都度印度の各地に散在する同胞の皆樣が，皆自分の仕事の如く思はれ，若しこの仕事が完成しなければ，自分達の恥であるといふ義俠心を持ちまして，何れの地方の展覽會にも成功しました。ですから，この仕事が恙なく成就したといふ大半は同胞の同情に依るのでありまして，この同胞をかくあらしめたのは，あの佛の廣大無邊の御慈悲の賜と深く合掌するのであります。餘り時間が長くなりましたが，私の申し上げる事はこれだけに致しまして，最後に三寶の爲に合掌させていただきます。（合掌）（神奈川縣聯『涅槃の夕』に於ける講演）

印度だより

三藏阿闍梨ラーフラ・サーンクリトヤーナ

拝啓　貴方の五月三十日附の手紙を嬉しく拜見致しました。それは私が重要な仕事の爲に印度を出發出來なかつたので，上海から轉送されたものでした

貴方の御親切な招待，大變有難く存じます。私はレーリングラードの東洋研究所のチェルバツコイ教授の招待も受けましたので，今の所どこへ行くか判然決めることが出來ません。西藏での梵夾の寫眞が全部成功とは言へないので，この仕事を完成する爲に何時かも一度チベットへ行かうと考へてゐます。若し私がチベットへ行けないのなら，日本へ行く可能性が多い譯です。その場合には，日本に出發する前に貴方にお知らせしませう。私が日本へ行つたら，日本に數年間滯在しようと思つてゐます。私は哲學的論書を數部梵語に還元したく思つてゐますし，又同時に私は數部の佛教論理學の重要な著作を日本語と支那語に譯出するのに日本學者を助けるのに役立つでせうから

1. 因明大疏Pramāṇavārttika（法稱Dharmakīrti著）
2. 因明疏註Pramāṇavārttika-vṛtti（Monorathanandin）
3. 因明疏註Pramāṇavārttika-vṛtti（法稱Dharmakīrti）
4. 因明疏註(Pramāṇavārttika-vṛtti-tikā(Karṇakagomin)
5. 因明疏註 Pramaṇavārttika-Bhāṣya(Prajñā Karagupta)
6. 百五十讃Adhyarddha'sataka（Mātṛceṭa）
7. Vigrahavyavarttanī（龍樹Nāgārjuna）

は印刷中で，一，二，六，七は今年の終には出版になりませう。

瑜伽師地論（Yogācārobhūmi）とヂュナーナシユリ（Jnāna'sri）著のクシャナバンガ（Kṣanabhaṅga）は印刷に附する準備が出來てゐます。最近の西藏旅行中に發見した梵語守本の報告を貴方にお送りします。三部ですが，その內一部を荻原博士に，他を宇井博士に送呈下さい。

父上母上，その他家族の方々に呉々も宜しく申傳へ下さい。敬具

追而，私が西藏に行かなければ，その時は九月に日本へ向けて出發します。

附記。之は印度佛教碩學で先年來朝，我が國際佛教通報局でも歡迎會を開いたことのある羅睺羅（ラーフラ）師の私信であるが，重要な興味あるもの故，採錄した。數回の西藏探險によつて，未見の重要な大乘佛教經典を發見し，之を印刷中とのことで蓋し佛教學界を益すること多大であらう。

海外ニュース

佛陀伽耶回復のセイロンの運動

佛陀伽耶保護聯盟が最近コロンボのウエーラワツテイ，フランシス路三十二に本部を置いて，佛陀伽耶を回復する目的で，發會された。その行事を實行する爲聯盟と協力するやうに全佛教國に有志が參加するやう勸誘狀が發せられた。ガンデイはこの聯盟が發送した印刷物の中で，雄々しくもかう言つてゐる。

『佛陀伽耶が非佛教徒の手にあるは，不合理である。貴方々佛教徒は常日頃何をしてゐるのか。私であるなら，生死の問題である。佛陀伽耶を取り還すのに，生命を献ずるであらう。』

かくして新入會員を得る爲に，ビルマや他の國々で宣傳が開始されやうとして居る。それ故聯盟と協力しようと欲する人々は佛陀伽耶保護聯盟書記と協力して欲しいと望んでゐる。マハンタ（印度教僧正で，佛陀伽耶の法的所有者）に合法的に壓力を加へるものは何でも聯盟に歡迎され，印度教徒で佛教徒に同情を抱いてゐる教養ある人々にも喜ばれよう。マハンタは佛陀伽耶の寺院と附屬の土地に關する時效にかゝはつたやうな權利を主張して，その所有權について少しも道德的な問題を考慮しようとしてゐない。先年ヒンヅーマハーサバ(印度教徒の有力團體)が仲に入つて，ある協定が成立しようとしたのであるが，十一時間も談合した末に拒絕してマハーサバの努力も大菩提協會の努力も無效になつたのである

然し今尚爭鬪は繼續する價値があり印度に於ける教養ある人士の支持によつて，佛教徒がこの最も古い尊むべき聖地を所有するを得るやうになる希望がある。我々はこの聯盟に心からの同情を抱いて高き使命を成功するを欲する。

長阿含の印度語飜譯

大菩提協會の手で，長阿含の印度語譯が最近公刊された。之は三藏を印度語譯する計畫の內，第三回の事業であつた。その書は三五六頁で定價五留比である。主な譯者は日本にも來朝したことのあるシユリ・ラーフラ師で，彼は前二書も印度語譯し，尙うまざる努力をさゝげてゐる譯である。彼の該博な知識と言語學の才能は譯書に至る處に現れてゐる。協會は印度語を用ひる社會がこの出版を繼續するのに助力するを希望してゐるのだが，現今は之等書籍に多少の誤解があり，解し難いとか哲學的にすぎると思はれて，敬遠されてゐるが，一般の讀者に理解し得られる程度のものなので，印度人が流布に努めて，今後の事業を繼續する資力を與へることを切望してゐる、

中國佛教會の日本佛教徒に寄する書

太虛法師の主宰する中國佛教會では北支事變により日支關係が惡化したので，七月十四日午後三時から上海赫德

路總辦事處で緊急理事監事聯合會議を開いて，圓瑛・大悲・常惺・志圓法師等二十餘名出席,「中國佛教會の日本佛教徒に告ぐるの書」を決定，日本佛教團體に發送した。本局に到達したものによれば，佛陀の同體大悲の教義を奉ずる我等佛教徒は國を異にしてゐるが一家の人と同じく，我民族の存亡の秋に當り，日本佛教徒に告げると前提し武力により二千餘年の友誼を破壞し，東亞の和平と世界の和平を破壞せんとする少數の〇〇の發動を制し，四千年の文化と四億の民を助け，世界に著名なる日本佛教學者の獅子吼を現實に移し，大衆の力によつて少數軍國主義の〇〇の危險なる行動を制止せよ，と述べてゐる。表面的には佛教の平和運動とも見られるが，今回の事變は一部日本〇〇の發動でなく，國民の絕對支持を受けてゐるものであり，その點中國佛教會に認識不足があり，太虛法師と蔣介石との關係を考へる時，蔣の反間苦肉の高等政策の現れとも見られてゐる。

國際佛教通報局定款

名稱

第一，本局を國際佛教通報局と稱す

事務所

第二，本局の事務所を全日本佛教青年會聯盟事務局に置く

目的

第三，本局は日本內地及海外に向つて佛教事情の通報をなし，且つ佛教徒相互間の各種便宜を計るを以て目的とす

事業

第四，本局の目的を達成するため左記の事業を行ふ
イ，日本內地及世界各國より佛教事情に關する質問の通報を行ふ
ロ，必要に應じ日本語及世界各國語を以て佛教事情の通報を行ふ
ハ，外國人の日本觀光に際しては各種の便益を與へ，特にその佛教に關する方面に於て之を爲す
ニ，定時或は隨時に各國語を以て文書の刊行をなす
ホ，その他必要と認めたる事業を行ふ

役員

第五，本局の事務を處理するため左の役員を置く
イ，名譽局長　一名
ロ，顧　問　若干名
ハ，局　長　一名
ニ，幹　事　若干名
ホ，理　事　若干名
局長は本局の事務を總括す
幹事は本局の事務を處理す
理事は局長の提案に依る重要事務を審議す

第六，理事は左記の者を以て之に充つ
イ，全日本佛教靑年會聯盟理事及主事
ロ，全日本佛教靑年會聯盟理事會に於て推薦したる者

第七，局長及幹事は理事會に於て決定す

第八，名譽局長及顧問は理事會に於て推薦す

第九，役員の任期は一ケ年とす（但し重任を妨げず）

經費

第十，本局の經費は左記のものに依て之を支辨す
イ，本局基金の活用
ロ，寄附金
ハ，その他の收入

補則

第十一，本定款に記載せられざる事項は，凡て理事會に於て協議す

第十二，第一回の役員は全日本佛教靑年會聯盟理事會に於て決定す

定價			
	一部	金二十錢	送料五厘
	一年	金二圓四十錢	送料不要

昭和十年四月廿日第三種郵便物認可
昭和十二年八月十二日印刷　（每月一回十五日發行）
昭和十二年八月十五日發行

東京市外吉祥寺337
編輯發行兼印刷人　淺野研眞

東京市牛込區早稻田鶴卷町107
印刷所　株式會社康文社印刷所
電話牛込（34）1950番 5049番

東京市神田區一ツ橋二の三
發行所　國際佛教通報局
電話九段（33）4428番
振替東京83015番

昭和十年四月三十日第三種郵便物認可
昭和十二年八月十二日印刷納本（毎月一回
昭和十二年八月十五日發行（十五日發行）　國際佛教通報　第三卷　第八號

第二回

汎太平洋佛教靑年會大會

紀要

THE PROCEEDINGS

of

THE Second

General Conference

of

Pan-Pacific Young Buddhists' Associations

(in Japanese, Chinese and English)

Held at Tokyo & Kyoto, July 18–23, 1934

Price ¥ 3.00

Compiled & Published

by

The Federation of All Y.B. As. of Japan,

Tokio, Kanda, Hitotsubashi, II-3

昭和十年四月三十日第三種郵便物認可　昭和十二年九月十二日印刷納本　昭和十二年九月十五日發行（毎月一回十五日發行）第三卷 第九號

國際佛教通報

第三卷　昭和十二年九月　第九號

The International Buddhist Bulletin

[Vol. III. September $\frac{2503}{1937}$ No. 9.]

The International Buddhist Information Bureau

II—3, Hitotsubashi, Kanda, Tokyo,

Annual Subscription, ¥2.40 (post free), Single Copy 20 sen (post 2 sen)

東京　國際佛教通報局　發行

The International Buddhist Bulletin

A monthly Journal of the International Buddhist Information Bureau founded in memorium of 2nd Pan-Pacific Y. B. A. Conference.

Editor:
Tsūshyō Byodō

Contents

Rules Pertaining to Mangement

1. "The International Buddhist Bulletin" publishes articles dealing with Buddhism in all its aspects and with History, Art, Philosophy, Archaeology and Education of Japan. News of Buddhist activities all over the world is a special feature.
2. All articles, news items, etc. sent for publication are welcomed.
3. All communications about study and tour etc. in Japan are kindly answered in detail.
4. Change of Address must be immediately informed.
5. Subscriptions are payable annually in advance.

Annual Subscription ¥ 2.40	Advertisement rates
(a copy 20 sen)	Cover ¥ .50
copies more than 10 are	Full page ¥ .30
discounted	Half page ¥ .15

All communications should be addressed to — Editor,
The International Buddhist Information Bureau,
II—3, Hitotsubashi, Kanda, Tokio.

Zen, What Does it Mean to Western People? (I)

By Sohaku Ogata.

1. Introductory.

Of those western people who have come to Japan in these latter years for the purpose of studying Zen I have met more than twenty. If I were to include those students who are striving to practice Zen meditation under the guidance of Rev. Senzaki, of Los Angeles, and Rev. Sasaki, of New York, and the members of other Buddhist groups in Europe and America who are trying, though without professional leaders, the practice of Zen meditation, the number would perhaps become quite large. We come to know how much the term "Zen" is becoming popular among westerners, particulary in the intellectual class, when we happen to meet ordinary tourists to this country, or when we take up Buddhist magazines published in the West. A book entitled "The Spirit of Zen" was recently sent out to the public by Mr. Alen W. Watts, the editor of the magazine "Buddhism in England". We learn from this that some interpretation of Zen by a westerner is what is needed now.

Why are they so enthusiastic about Zen; what does it mean to western people? By solving this question we will at the same time know what Zen means to the present time in general. Because the main current of modern thought, both in East and West, is western thought. It will also tell us what the relationship is between Zen and the modern science or intellectual knowledge. Because the western thought is extremely systematic and logical. Moreover, it will perhaps give us an important hint as to the future of the world, because the modern material civilization built up by western thought, has now come to a deadlock of contradiction that is involved in it; and some sort of new theory of life is badly needed. It is often said by westerners, that the sun of glory has set in the West and the light will come again from the East. And Zen is the essence of all eastern philosophies.

As I am no westerner myself, I am afraid I can not interpret as correctly as I should wish to, the western attitude of mind. So all I can do to-day is to give my most personal opinion of what I think may be the chief attraction, that the Zen teaching has for western seekers of Truth.

2. The Western View of Buddhism.

It was about a hundred years ago or so, that western people began to study Buddhism. Since then they have made wonderful progress in their study. The Pāli Text Society, which was fonnded in the year 1881 for the purpose of publishing the ancient documents of Buddhism will complete this work in 1941. The Deutsche Bibliographie des Buddhismus compiled by Lüdwig Held in 1916 mentions more than twenty-five hundred names of books. We shall have an enormous number of books, if we count to-day all the works on Buddhism in various European languages, such as English, French, German, Russian, and Italian and etc. We have learnt, that publications on Buddhist religion in Europe have overhelmingly increased since the Great War came to an end. What is the Western view of Buddhism, then? The Buddhist Lodge of London, being a representative of the progressive movement of Buddhism in England, sent out a book entitled "What Is Buddhism?" in 1929. This book was compiled after a thorough study of one and half years by a group of twenty Buddhists, representing various countries. In the preface, it says: "The recent War proved many things, among them being the failure of Christianity to stand the aoid test of emergency, and the danger of scientific knowledge ahead of national morality.

By the failure of orthodox Science and Religion, Westerners are forced to seek elsewhere for a selution to the problems facing them. Hence the incresing interest in "foreign" religions of every kind, among them Buddhism. The latter's all-pervading influence is due to its being at the same time scientific and religious, in the finest sense of the terms, for it is an aspect of the Wisdom which unites them both. But while

Truth is one it may be presented in many forms, and in compiling a reply to the oft-repeated question — What is Buddhism? — we have prepared an answer from the Western point of view. Even as water may be poured into different coloured bottles, yet remain the same in each, so the Teaching of the All-Enlightened One may be presented in a dozen different ways according to the needs of those to whom it is given.

As Buddhism is part of Truth it is to found in every land, and is the property in some degree of every poet, mystic, and philosopher. Throughout the book, therefore, in quoting other's words as perfectly expressing what wish to say, we have chosen those of Western writers in addition to the Buddhist Scriptures, to the end that we may show how the Dhamma is no alien philosophy but may be found, in fragmentary form, among the thinkers of the West.

In order that our readers may examine these quotations for themselves we append a Bibliography of books from which quotation has been made. As our aim is rather a popular manual than a scholarly treatise we have used the Pāli or Sanscrit form of word, according as one or the other is better known in the West, and make no apologies for inconsistency.

The whole book is in fact a compromise. Compiled by a group composed of many minds, of either sex, both Schools of Buddhism and a dozen nationalities, it is the "common denominater" of many, often conflicting, points of view. Based though it is upon the Thera Vāda point of view, it borrows from the Mahāyāna sufficient of its principles to make once more of the whole the complete philosophy for daily needs which Buddha gave the world. Again, it is, though primarily written for the West, a demonstration to the members of both Buddhist Schools that Truth, as always, is to be fround in the balanced union of the two. It strives to be at once informative and a spur to individual study and experiment, on the one hand giving a comprensive outline of the subject, on the other hand repeating what the Buddha taught his followers, that none can truly teach another — at the best he can but point the Way to self-enlightenment.

If, owing to the exigencies of space, some statements are presented in dogmatic form, it must be realised that Buddhism asks no man to believe, but merely to accept its principles as reasonable hypotheses until experience has shown them to be true.

Part II, which forms the substance of the book, has been arranged in the form of Question and Answer, the Enquirer being, we hope, a representative of the average cultured Westener who genuinely seeks a solution to the problems which the religion of his fathers failed to solve.

The philosophy of Buddhism forms a connected whole and therefore it has proved difficult to resolve it into a reasoned argument, for it has, so to speak, no beginning and no end, but we think that such a form of exposition will appeal to the Western mind.

An intellectual understanding of Buddhism is, however, of little avail, for it must be lived before it can be truly known. Any man is entitled to reject its principles as not appealing to him, but only he who has tested them in daily life is competent to say, and none so testing them has ever said, they are not true.

Although the vast majority of men consider themselves as seekers after Truth, they are but few who welcome it when found. Prejudice, self-interest and mental laziness combine to make the average man prefer his comfortable illusions to the naked truth. Yet some there are who genuinely seek that Wisdom of which each religion and philosophy reflects a part, and will not rest until they find it.

To these strong-minded, fearless few the All-Enlightened One proclaimed the Dhamma of salvation by self-effort, and to such we dedicate this genuine attempt to present the West, in simple form, with the essence of his Teaching."

Again it says in the Teaching Section: "Buddhism teaches the way to perfect goodness and wisdom without a personal God; the highest knowledge without a "revelation"; a moral world-order and just retribution, carried out of necessity by reason of the laws of nature and of our own being; continued existence without a separate "immortal soul"; eternal bliss without a local heaven; the possibility of redemption without a vicarious redeemer, a salvation in which everyone is his own saviour, and which can be obtained in this life and on this earth by the exercise of one's own faculties, without prayers, sacrifices, penances or ceremonies, without ordained priests, without the mediation of saints,

and without Divine Grace."

According to the above mentioned the main interest of western people in Buddhism seems to lie in the fact that the Teaching is rational, and that it emphasises salvation, or rather emancipation, in this life by one's own effort and not by revelation. If it is so, then it is quite natural that Westerners who attempt to get acquainted with the practical side of Buddhism in the Far East come to Zen. For Zen is the only sect of Buddhist teaching in Japan and China that still keeps the lamp of the Dhamma burning and continues the practice of spiritual training as in olden times. However, I know of two Americans, who came to Japan in 1934 and 1936 that were ordained as Shinshū priests. Yet, according to what they have personally told me, they did not care at all for the message of Shinshū, which emphasises the salvation of Amitābhā Buddha after one's death. The reason why they joined Honganji, the headquarter of Shinshū, was, because in America of Buddhist institutions there the branch of Honganji in San Francisco was the best. Besides they were left at liberty to hold whichever Buddhist belief they liked.

3. Zen as the Essence of Oriental Culture.

Among the westerners devoted to the study of the East, generally speaking, Americans are more interested in things artistic while Europeans prefer philosophical inquiry. But they all come to the same conclusion, that one must study Zen in order to realize the East because Zen is the genuine key-note to the eastern mind. In what manner does Zen give the essence of the eastern thought? Let me borrow the exposition of Prof. Suzuki, the best known writer on Zen Philosophy, for the explanation of this subject.

"I said that Zen is mystical. This is inevitable, seeing that Zen is the keynote of Oriental culture; it is what makes the West frequently fail to fathom exactly the depths of the Oriental mind, for mysticism in its very nature defies the analysis of logic, and logic is the most characteristic feature of Western thought. The East is synthetic in its method of reasoning; it does not care so much for the elaboration of particulars as for a comprehensive grasp of the whole, and this intuitively. Therefore, the Eastern mind, if we assume its existence, is necessarily vague and indefinite, and seems not to have an Index which at once reveals the contents to an outsider. The thing is there before our eyes, for it refuses to be ignored; but when we endeavour to grasp it in our own hands in order to examine it more closely or systematically, it eludes and we lose its track. Zen is provokingly evasive. This is not due of course to any conscious or premeditated artifice with which the Eastern mind schemes to shun the scrutiny of others. The unfathomableness is in the very constitution, so to speak, of the Eastern mind. Therefore, to understand the East we must understand mysticism, that is, Zen.

It is to be remembered, however, that there are various types of mysticism, rational and irrational, speculative and occult, sensible and fantastic. When I say that the East is mystical, I do not mean that the East is fantastic, irrational, and altogether impossible to bring within the sphere of intellectual comprehension. What I mean is simply that in the working of the Eastern mind there is something calm, quiet, silent, undisturbable, which appears as if always looking into eternity. This quietude and silence, however, does not point to mere idleness or inactivity. The silence is not that of desert shorn of all vegetation, nor is it that of a corpse for ever gone to sleep and decay. It is the silence of an "eternal abyss" in which all contrasts and conditions are buried; it is the silence of God who, deeply absorbed in contemplation of his works past, present, and future, sits calmly on his throne of absolute oneness and allness. It is the "silence of thunder" obtained in the midst of the flash and uproar of opposing electric currents. This sort of silence pervades all things Oriental. Woe unto those who take it for decadance and death, for they will be overwhelmed by an overwhelming outburst of activity out of the eternal silence. It is in this sense that I speak of the mysticism of Oriental culture. And I can affirm that the cultivation of this kind of mysticism is principally due to the influence of Zen. If Buddhism were to develop in the Far East so as to satisfy the spiritual cravings of its people, it had to grow into Zen. The Indians are mystical, but their mysticism is too speculative, too comtemplative, too complicated, and, moreover, it does not seem to have any real vital

relation with the practical world of particulars in which we are living. The Far-Eastern mysticism on the contrary is direct, practical, and surprisingly simple. This could not develop into anything else but Zen.

All the other Buddhist sects in China as well as in Japan bespeak their Indian origin in an unmistakable manner. For their metaphysical complexity, their longwinding phraseology, their highly abstract reasoning, their penetrating insight into the nature of things, and their comprehensive interpretation of affairs relating to life, are obviously Indian and not at all Chinese or Japanese. This will be recognised at once by all those who are acquainted with Far-Eastern Buddhism. For instance, look at those extremely complex rites as practiced by the Shingon sect, and also at their elaborate systems of "Maṇḍāla" by means of which they try to explain the universe. No Chinese or Japanese mind would have conceived such an intricate net-work of philosophy without being first influenced by Indian thought. Then observe how highly speculative is the philosophy of the Madhyamika, the Tendai, or Kegon. Their abstraction and logical acumen are truly amazing. These facts plainly show that these sects of Far-Eastern Buddhism are at bottom foreign importations.

But when we come to Zen after survey of the general field of Buddhism, we are compelled to acknowledge that its simplicity, its directness, its pragmatic tendency, and its close contrast to the other Buddhist sects. Undoubtedly, the main ideas of Zen are derived from Buddhism, and we cannot but consider it a legitimate development of the latter; but this development has been achieved in order to meet the requirements peculiarly characteristic of the psychology of the Far-Eastern people. The spirit of Buddhism has left its highly metaphysical superstructure in order to become a practical discipline of life. The result is Zen. Therefore, I make bold to say that in Zen are found systematised, or rather crystallised, all the philosophy, religion, and life itself of the Far-Eastern people, especially of the Japanese."

4. The Synthesis of Cultures in East and West and Zen Buddhism.

No thought has ever developed without relation to natural environment in which it was circulated, and to the racial character of people who brought it forth. The reason why eastern thought which originated in India or China is mystical and elusive may be because it sprung from spiritual nations who loved nature and respected the heaven, looming behind the snowy heights of Himālaya ever before their eyes and the mighty rivers of Indus or Ganges. And the reason why western thought is so intellectual and scientific may be due to the systematic and constructive mind of the peoples who were forced to struggle within the crowded and limited area of Europe, which, after all, is but the peninsula of Asia. Shall I sum up the characteristic features of these two currents of thought in East and West? Western thought, I belive, is extremely intellectual and logical. The intellectual reasoning is the action of and stimular for the brain, yet it can hardly be expected to produce happiness or satisfaction. For the intellect of man wants to ask "why" about everything and never stops to inquire. Of all human vanities the most harmful one is intellectual vanity. It frequenently projects unnecessary questions which can never satisfactorily be answered, and yet it rejects the solution of those very questions by means of other than intellectual means.

Lord Buddha once said to His disciples: Suppose here is a man shot at with a poisoned arrow. What should he do? Is he to inquire first who it was who hit him with the poisoned arrow? Should he continue to ask whether he is young or aged? To which caste he belongs? Who is the man who made the arrow? Where did the feather of it come from? If he shonld go on like this, he would die of the poison before he finished his investigation. If he just takes the arrow out of his body, he will soon dispatch the whole matter from his mind.

However, I am not trying to say that intellectuality is all together unnecessay, or that one cannot be at all happy with western thought. What I want to say is, that modern scientific way of life contains a certain a certain disadvantage. To us, it seems that western people too much and exclusively depend upon their intellectual reasoning. Nothing can be better than the proper thing at the proper time. Let me quote a Zen story which tells us something about the attitude of Zen towards intellectuality.

現代支那の佛教事情

早大教授　福　井　康　順

第一　支那現代佛教の特異性

現代の支那佛教事情をお話する前には，どうしても支那の現在の機構を述べるべきであるが，それは先輩に讓つて，こゝには略すこととし，私は支那の現在の狀勢を述べ，殊に，日本に餘り紹介されてゐない，支那現代の思想界が佛教を如何見てゐるかを考へて見たい。

一，支那の現代佛教は日本人に根本的に理解出來ぬものを一，二持つてゐる。支那の寺院では信仰內容が非常に判然してゐないことである。日本では眞宗寺院なら本堂に阿彌陀如來の本尊を飾り，本願寺の末寺で，住職や寺族はその宗派の信仰や教養を持ち，それを喜び，理解してゐる。その他の宗も皆さうである。然し，支那では禪寺に禪僧が住持として入らず，然も本山末寺關係が判然としてゐない。しかも横の聯合もなく，同じ宗の寺の聯絡も組合も協調もない。單獨である。支那にも佛教團體もあるが，例へば中國佛教會は寺院の集りでなく，居士の集りで，尙このやうな傾向が强いのである。第一に寺院に思想的立場がなく，寺院間に連絡と結合がないことで，これは我々が支那佛教を考へるのに，第一に念頭に置かねばならぬ。第二に寺院の住職の任免の標準が判然としてゐない。唐の太宗の建設した憫忠寺は北京にあつて最古であり，戰に死んだ敵味方の靈を慰めたと傳へられてゐる名刹であるが，その住職を何人がどういふ標準で命ずるのか解らず，末寺關係も知られない。唯寺は個人の僧の住所になつてゐるにすぎない。日本では寺院は一定の宗派に屬し，その本尊を有し，その教義を宣布してゐるのであるが，支那の寺院はさうではないのである。ある僧がそこに住み，それらが支那佛教を爲してゐるのである。蔣介石が革命軍を起して北京を占領した時，その憫忠寺に自分の緣故の僧侶を住職に入れ，その僧が又自分の緣故の僧を引いて他の寺院に入れた。張學良が南に入ると元の領內の僧を連れて來て，住職を追ひ出して，その寺に移す。上の爲すこと下之に倣ふで，他の大臣や知事や部將も之を爲すのである。元來支那は中央政府にしても地方官でも，ある地位を得ると，一族と緣故の者でその下の地位を凡て塞ぐ慣であるが，それが佛教寺院にまで及ぶのである。從つて支那の僧には宗派的には何の系統もないのである。從つて太虛が日本に來る時はその團體は彼の一統であつて，名は支那佛教僧侶訪日團であつても，實は太虛の弟子達にすぎない。日本では太虛法師の訪日團を歡迎すれば，佛敎を通じて日華親善が出來るやうに思ふのであるが，その一行を待遇すれば，反太虛派は反感を持つか，無關心になつて仕舞ふ。從つてその人を通じて中國佛敎界は動かせないのである。かういふ點をよく承知して，待遇する必要があるのである。例へば水野梅曉氏がある有力な支那僧と會へば，日支佛敎の提携が出來るやうに思ふが，豈に計らんや，その他の系統の僧は離れて行くのである。支那佛敎は横から見るのと，大分違つてゐるのである。

第二　現代支那の佛敎

一　現代支那の寺院佛敎

支那の寺は佛敎靑年會として呼び掛けるのには絶望である。彼等は日本僧を僧と思つてゐない。戒律を守らぬ故，居士と思つてゐる。且彼等は五千年の古き文化への誇りを心中に持つて，日本文化を輕蔑してゐる。そして支那は戰爭に敗けたとは思つてゐない。上海事變では十九路軍は敗けたが，支那が敗けたのでないと言つてゐる。滿洲事變では張學良は敗けたが，支那は敗けないと言つてゐる。日本へ來て，大寺院を賞めるが，之は外交辭令である。支那には確かに大寺院があつて，五臺山の如きは比叡山延暦寺と高野山金剛峯寺を一にしてもかなはない。五輪の美が實にすさまじい。日本にも東西の本願寺の如き大寺院もあるが，支那では人工の美を尊び，凡て極彩色をなし，素朴を尊ばぬ。老子・莊子は例外であつて，凡て極彩色を木地に施し，日本人は惡どいと思ふが，彼等支那人にはそれが結構なので，白木のものは喜ばれない。私が案內したさる支那僧は何處の寺を見ても感心せず，日光の東照宮を見て，大いに喜んだことがある。支那僧はしかも，日本の寺に住む僧は居士である。戒律を守らず，肉食し，飲酒し，妻子がある。之は僧でない，と思つてゐる。日本人の文化も腹の底まで尊んでゐない。我々としては支那僧でなく，居士に呼びかける方が宜しい。

日本人が語り傳へる支那佛敎は上海北京附近の佛敎のみである。支那に來てゐる日本布敎師の支那佛敎觀であ る。日本僧は在支の日本人にのみ呼びかけて，その日本人から second hand の支那觀を聞いてゐる。在支の日本人にて支那語を知る僧は少く，皆又聞きである譯である。從つて日華佛敎提携には支那の居士に呼びかける外なく，支那現在の佛敎寺院に呼び掛けるのは効果がない。

從つて私はこゝに支那の居士佛敎の現狀を語らう。

二　現代支那の居士佛敎

支那政治經濟界の佛敎への關心。佛敎への關心は支那の政治家實業家の方が日本人より濃厚であつて，佛敎に對する關心が强くて，表面にも現されてゐる。西園寺公や近衞公の日本佛敎に對する關心の如きものではなく，もつと關心が深い。段祺瑞の如きは之であつて，眞言宗に信心であつて，吉井芳純師と親しく，集會の折は精進料理を食ひ，生活も徹底的で，彼の門下で北支那に働く人にその影響を與へてゐる。曹汝霖・高凌蔚が之である。支那では阿闍梨は非常に偉いことになつてゐるが吉井師は阿闍梨と崇められてゐた。所が食事の折牛乳をすゝめられたのだが，飲んでいゝものか解らないので，『腹をこわしてゐるので‥‥』と言つて斷つたら，先方では驚いた。阿闍梨は腹を病ふことなぞはないと思つてゐたからである。吳佩孚も密敎の信者であつて，蔣介石の出る前には吳佩孚が支那を救ふ人とされ，今でも尙力があり，事變がある度に惑星とされてゐる。熱河戰には吳佩孚は暗躍した。その折に魯迅が周作人に會ひ，吳佩孚をかつがうとして殺された。喇嘛宮の羅利宮の大信者で，よく參詣してゐる。また廣濟寺に一信者として大衆の中にまぢつて參拜し，念佛三昧に日を送つてゐると自稱してゐる。段祺瑞も念佛三昧に過してゐると稱してゐる。三年前張學良に柔禁され，毒殺されんとしたことがあつたが，助かり，念佛してゐたが，北京に死んだ。閻錫山も佛敎信者で，政界の惑星で事變毎に出馬するが，こゝにもよく密使が行くのである。趙戴文といふ人は蔣介石の師で閻錫山の顧問であつて，大人物で大仲裁者である。日本で强いて例を擧ぐれば，大隈老公の如き人物である。この人も山西省の佛敎會を作り，會長となり，佛敎振興に努め，唯識學者である。私が山西省旅行中に道の惡い支那の邊村で道がよく修繕されてゐたので，聞くと，趙戴文の七日間の佛寺參籠の爲だと解つた。日支間に戰爭があつても，佛敎の慈悲心によつて提携せしめんとしてゐる位である。戴天仇は監察委員長，日本の大審院檢事總長の如き地位にある人だが，日本と平和ならんとして，他の政客が抗日救國を叫ぶ折に，念佛(經)救國と言つてゐる。王亢生といふ駐日大使館參事官は土耳古大使館から轉任した人であるが，何が日本に來て喜びかと聞くと，寺參りだと言つて，日曜毎に寺に詣るのを樂み，精進料理を食つてゐる。參籠もし，經を讀んでゐる。幾日かは家族から離れ，精進潔齋してゐる。同じく大使の許世英氏も戒律生活を行つてゐる。かういふ具合に著名な政治家で，佛敎の篤信な信者は數多いのである。從つて我々日本佛敎徒はかゝる居士佛敎に働きかけるのが有効であり得策である。

第三　支那思想界の佛敎への關心

支那思想界の佛敎への關心は日本思想界より盛んである。日本の佛敎研究は世界的であるが，日本の思想界の佛敎への關心は極めて少い。然し，支那思想界の佛敎への關心は日本以上である。日本では寺に緣ある人が佛敎に關心を持つのが大部分で，佛敎に注意を拂ふ人は多少に拘らず佛緣のある人である。漢學者は佛敎を侮辱し，國文學者も亦然りである。然し，支那ではさうでなく，大立物は凡て佛敎に關心を持ち，その硏究に沒頭する人もある。今支那學界を茲に區別すると，次の如くである。

一，正統派――之の派は老人に力が

あり，今は亡びつゝある。支那は三千年の社會の底からデモクラシーに動かされつゝあるのである。
二，今文學派――反正統派とでも言ふものである。
三，自由派――新興階級が加つてゐる。
之等の各派の中の巨頭の佛教觀を語らう。

一，正統派

支那では今より二十年前民國六年に北京大學に印度哲學講座が出來，七年に梁漱溟の印度哲學概論が出來た。この人は經濟政策家で，この人の支那改造策は青年の指導精神となつてゐる位に人氣のある人である。溯つて楊文會居士が出て，佛教熱が盛んとなつたのである。

正統派では章炳麟がその代表である。胡適は自由派の代表的な人であるが，然し第一人者は誰かと支那學生に問ふと，章炳麟と答へる。昨年六月七十歳にして死んだ。政治家であつて，李鴻章に愛された學者で兪木越の弟子で，革命三傑と言はれるのは，孫逸仙・胡漢民・章炳麟で，中華民國の名を選んだのはこの人である。革命の戰火の後中頃引退して，蘇州に入り，學問を盛にやつた。支那知識階級の間で，老人には正統派の學者として，若い人には革命の英雄として，尊ばれ，胡適には五十年間の第一の名文家と激賞された傑人である。彼の思想の中心は佛教であつて，唯識論・起信論をよく研究し，著書に『大乘起信論辨』等があり，梵語文法の序文を書いて居り，希臘語・羅典語の知識もある。胡適自らも佛教の知識については章炳麟氏にかなはぬと言つてゐる。支那で『國學』の語は『哲學』の意で，章の案出である。彼が日本人に知られてゐないのは，日本人を蔑視するからである。又梵語の知識を以て因明を論じてゐる。例へば『國故論衡』は荀子の『天論論』の「見」の字を論じてゐる。日本に知られてゐないのは，その知識がない日本の支那研究家に一は難しくて解らぬからである。

二，今文學派

康有爲(一八九八年死)がその代表的な人物で，彼は章炳麟の滅滿興漢に反し，德宗を擁し，クーデターを行はんとし戊戌の變法を行つた。一民間學者であるのに，德宗に會ひ，政體改變を行はんとし，袁世凱の反對で破れ，日本公使館に逃げた。康は大谷光瑞師の如く秀才を集め，教育してゐた。譚嗣同・梁啓超がその弟子で，內譚嗣同は三十歳にて戊戌の役に逃げ損つて殺され，自らも一九〇七年に大連に客死し，梁啓超が殘つた。彼は華嚴唯識の學者で仁學をエーテルで說明し，唯識華嚴の哲學を基礎にして解釋した。非常な雄辯家でもあつた。梁は外交界の大立物となり，政府に世界大戰に參加することをすゝめ，山東問題にて日本と爭ひ，ワシントン會議には外交顧問として大戰の後始末に行き，英米の力を借りて成功して，山東の利權を支那に取り返した。五十六歳にて一九三〇年に死んだが，眉目秀麗，鋭い眼光を持ち，大

乘起信論の研究を出した。「淸代學術概論」は要領がよい。佛教の生住異滅の思想を以て物事を論じてゐる。支那學術は佛教に關心を持つことにより將來に希望が持てるのである。(參照『飮氷處』)。

三，自由派

この代表者は胡適である。彼は中國哲學史上卷によつて令名高く，思想家にて名文家で，日本にも招いたことあり，三面六臂の働きを爲し，今夏も世界教育會議に支那代表として來る筈だつた。昨年胡適は憲兵隊に呼ばれ，何やら取調べられて注意されたやうだつたが，今回の北支事變には仲介に入つたこともある。今年は四十六，七歳で大柄でアメリカ仕込みで，父は臺灣の役人をしてゐたが，日本編入で上海に歸つた。父の五，六番目の妻の子で，父と母とは四十歳も年が違ひ，秀才であつたが，そんなことから不遇であつて，之は小學校を四度も更へたのでも知れる。アメリカ留學の奬學懸賞文に當選し，John Deways に留學した。先秦文學史が論文であつた。アメリカで研學後歸つて，「白話文學」を主張した。之は口語體で文章を書き，漢學文學を棄てよ，といふ主張で，口語でしやべる通りを文章に書寫すのである。之は當時極端なので，老人に蔑視され，ベタ臭い，洋行歸りが何をいふ，と嫌はれた。然し靑年には喜ばれて，後國民政府に認められ，小學校に白話文學が採用された。羅根澤は初め胡適を蔑視したが，中國哲學史上卷が出るに及んで，賞讃した。陳獨秀といふ人は北京大學の文學部長で，河上肇・大杉榮堺枯川を一にした共產主義者であつたが，蔣介石氏に白眼まれ，地下に潜つたが，上海で發見され，殺される所を胡適が命乞ひをして助かつたことがある。胡適は白話文學史を書いたが，之は史的に語られた文學を論じたもので，又「紅樓夢」・「水滸傳」を硏究し，校訂本を作つた。その代表的主著は中國哲學史上卷であるが，之は日本譯も出來てゐる。現在は佛教研究に沒頭してゐる。最近『神會和尙集』を出した。又楞伽經を大谷大學出身の金氏を助手とし，『資校記』として校訂した。雜誌に出した論文をまとめて『胡適文存』を出したが，現在十四卷となつてゐる。『菩提達磨考』もその一である。『牟子理惑論』といふ書も出した。人によつては『胡適何者ぞ，中國哲學史上卷は出たが，未だ中卷下卷は出てゐないではないか』と非難するものもある。胡適は答へて，中國哲學史は佛教の十分な研究なくしては書けない，目下佛教を研究中であつて，研究がまとまつてから，中卷の後漢以後を書くと言つてゐる。事實中國思想史では佛教は重要な役割を占めて居り，胡適の『菩提達磨考』には中國哲學史中卷第一章の題號があるのでも彼に續稿の意志のあることが知られる。弟子羅根澤『古史辨』は中世以後は佛教の入つた哲學史を書かうとしてゐる。東北帝大の竹內義雄教授もかういふものを書かうとされてゐるが，羅根澤のかういふ哲學史は異

類である。我々も支那思想界の努力と熱誠に敗ける恐れがある位である。

變つた所で，支那思想界で「曼珠」の研究が必要がある。この人はヂャナリストとして一流の人で米國や印度へも行つてゐる。レッシッングの研究を出版したこともあり，僧侶であつてかういふ研究をしたのである。至榮があつて，佐藤春夫氏が紹介したことがある。母は日本人であつて，横濱に生れたのであるが，數奇の生活を送つて二十七歳で死んだ。西湖の孫逸仙の隣に葬られた。支那では「死なば西湖の傍」と言つて，西湖は高野山か大谷のやうな所と考へられ，こゝに葬られるのは幸福と考へられ，しかも一介のヂャーナリストであつて，近代支那の神孫逸仙の隣に埋められたのは光榮の至りであるが，しかもそれが國民の獻金によつてである。尊敬された程度が推し知られよう。

これらによつても支那の一般思想界が佛教に如何に關心を持つてゐるかが知られ，之から何か新しい體系を生み出さんとする非常な努力が伺はれ，その眞劍さは日本の思想家や佛教學者より遙かに强いと思はれ，むしろ我々を鞭撻するものがあるやうに感ずるのである。（七月廿五日，第二回全聯指導者講習會に於ける講演筆記。文責在記者）

一，支那事變と中國佛教

今回の支那事變の勃發以來，日本佛教徒は擧つて皇道佛教としての實踐を展開し，外に向つては從軍布教師或は慰問使を派遣し，內にあつては慰問金募集・遺家族救援・追悼法會その他國民精神總動員に參加して，擧國一致の非常時局對處の實を擧げつゝあるが，中國佛教徒は自國の危急存亡に際し，如何なる行動をとつてゐるかは興味あることである。

中國佛教會等が日本佛教徒に訴ふる書を我國各種佛教團體に送つて來たことは既報したが，蘇州の淨土宗の大德印光老法師は『全世界の同胞は觀音の聖號を念ずれば，危を轉じて，安きに爲すを得る。現在殺戮が行はれ，全世界に安樂がないが，皆が觀音を念ずるならば事は息み，太平を享受し得る。よし命を失つても西方に往生出來る』といふ意味の通告を發した。浙江省台州天台縣天台山石梁橋方廣寺では通賢法師等多數の僧侶が聯合して八月二十日から九月四日まで，和平祈禱大會を開催し平和招來の祈禱を行つた。南京江浦縣林春亭居等は江浦縣獅子嶺兜率寺で覺證法師を請じて世界和平法會を勤修した。杭州吳山海會講寺では時局多難救濟の爲毎日一日及十五日に淨土法會及び禮佛法會を勤修し，大乘經論を宣講して，世界和平國土安樂を祈禱し，戰沒將士に回向した。又貴陽にても居士等主催の息災祈禱法會，西安にては超一法師の密法和平禱，嘉興の精嚴寺にて護國息災法會，浦東海會寺では戰死者追悼會が夫々盛大に營まれたとのことである。（上海佛教日報）。

訪　日　所　感

ビルマ　ト　ン・ニ　ョ　ー

私は前世に皆樣とどういふ關係にあつたか存じません。然し，再度日本に來朝して皆樣にお目にかゝり，このやうに和やかな集りを開いて歡迎していただくことは，深い緣のあつてのことと存じます。世間では之を單な偶然な出來事と申すでありませう。然し，我々は之を因緣一佛樣の引き合せと思ひます。私は築地本願寺で催された第二回の汎太平洋佛靑大會の盛大な有樣が目の前にちらつくやうに思ひ出されます。あの折私はビルマでは間際まで誰も行く人がなくて，出發一日前に出席することを決心して乘船して來たやうな次第でした。今回は上海で支那事變の渦中に入つて，スリルな爆彈投下や砲擊の戰禍の體驗を經驗しました。日本と支那とは同じ佛教徒で，近かしく，それが何故戰はねばならないか，私達には疑問です。恐らく，それは食糧の問題から來てゐるでせう。日本は工業國で物產を輸入して，商品を作つて輸出してゐます。それならばビルマは米を產して，時に增產の爲海中に投棄することさへあります。日本は米をビルマから買つて，工業品を輸出すれば，戰爭をしなくてすむと思ひます。

前回の汎太平洋佛靑大會で佛陀伽耶を佛教徒の手に取り戾すことが，議案にかかりましたが，私はその折佛陀伽耶に巡拜してゐないので，參拜してから發言すると，發言を保留しておきました。その佛陀伽耶に昨年初めて巡拜しました。この佛陀伽耶は大地主で金持の印度教徒のマハンク（僧正）の所有になつて居り，僅かにビルマ・セイロンの佛教徒が儀式を行ひ，給仕する力だけを持つてゐるのです。ここの所有權を佛教徒の手に取り戾す議案は印度立法議會に提案され，印度教議員とビルマ佛教徒の代議員の協力があつて，小委員會まで出來たのであります。然し，殘念ながら一九三六年の印度新憲法實施と共に印度本土とビルマは分割されビルマは獨立議會を持ち，議員を印度議會に送らなくなつたので，ビルマ佛教徒代議員の應援がなくなり，この議案も成立の見込がなくなりました。私は巡拜の折生徒一人から一アンナの獻金を持つて佛陀伽耶の寺に獻じたのですが，それはマハンタの手に入りました。私は伽耶の高等法務官に手紙をやつて抗議しましたが，それはパトナの考古局の係りだからその方へ申出よとのことで，その方に手紙を又出しましたが，未だに返事がありません。この聖地は今や買戾す外道がないやうです。

今日皆樣が私達の爲に心からなる歡迎の會をお開き下さり，厚く御禮申上げます。（八月二十六日夜松本樓にて）

國際佛教ニユース

二，ビルマ佛靑ニヨー氏 夫妻歡迎茶話會

第二回汎太平洋佛教靑年會大會にビルマ代表として來朝したトン・ニヨー氏夫妻が今般歐米教育施設視察の途次再度來朝されたので，全日本佛教靑年會聯盟・女子佛教靑年會聯盟主催にて八月二十六日午後七時東京日比谷公園松本樓で歡迎茶話會を開催した。來會者はニヨー夫妻の外大谷理事長福島弘氏來馬琢道師鷹谷俊之氏以下二十餘名で，小數であつたが，和やかな集りで，主賓と同船の滿州鐵道技師ダン氏夫妻も陪席された。小笠原全聯主事司會の下に大谷理事長の挨拶，來馬師の歡迎の辭あり，ニヨー氏の感謝の辭は示唆の多いもので，平等本局主任の通譯あつて，出席者に多大の感銘を與へた。尙同日席上佛陀伽耶奪還問題，日印佛教提携問題なぞも話題に上つた。因みに同夫妻は三十一日午後三時橫濱出帆の郵船樂洋丸にて米國に向け出發された。

三，印度の初轉法輪祭

初轉法輪日（Dhammacakka）即ち佛陀の最初の說法の記念日は日本では未だ行はれてゐないが，印度大菩提協會ではカルカツタ市とベナレス郊外初轉法輪の地鹿野苑今のサールナートで擧行された。カルカツタでは支那總領事 Chen Chang Lok 氏外諸名士の出席あり，同氏は力強き口調で僞善的近代世相を批判し，世を毒するものは言行不一致であるとし，佛陀の說法はかゝるものをすて，正しき生活に入ることであるとし，邪道に向ふ世界の車輪を正しき方向に轉じ，世をよりよくすべきであると演說し，他の人々も所感をのべ，シユリマテイ・ローマ夫人の歌で式を閉ぢた。サールナートにも多數の比丘來賓列席の上，開會され，夜は初轉法輪寺に燈明が献ぜられた。

四，セイロン佛牙寺の大祭

セイロン島キャンデイー市の佛牙寺には佛陀の歯を安置してあるので有名であつて，之は印度本土に長い間轉々として，最後にセイロンのこの寺に安置されるに至つたので，島の最大の寶とされてゐるが，八月には每年この佛牙寺を出て，美しい町を行列で練つて步くことになつてをり，セイロンは愚か各佛教國より多數の佛教徒が參集するのであるが，今年も盛大に行はれ，象が多く加つた奇妙壯麗な行列に，一段と大きな白象に佛牙を入れた黃金の筐が進んだ有樣は世にも壯觀であつた。この佛牙の管理人の地位は極めて重要なものであるが，數ケ月前長年その地位にあつたヌガウエーラ氏(P. B. Nugawela)が死んだので，後任に同じキャンデイの有名な佛教徒ラトワテー氏(T.B.Ratwatte)が選擧された。從來佛牙寺はセイロンで最も富んだ寺であるに限らず，學校も何も建てず，佛教の傳道に役立たないので，新任者の活躍を期待されること多大であらうといふ。

局報

本局第二回目の幹事會が九月九日午後七時より日比谷松本樓で開催された。之より先汎聯中央委員會・全聯常務理事會で本局に對して希望された，十月號を支那事變號とし，正義日本の立場を海外に宣揚する件を付議し，可決，以て政府の精神報國總動員に役立つこととし，その編輯細目は主任と二常任幹事に一任された。尙人事を附議した後財政に關し，本局は第二回汎聯剩餘金より本局に廻附された資金は昨年度に於て費消し盡されたので，今後は月五圓の後援者數名，年額十圓の後援者數十名を作り，且各宗本山大寺のニユースを採錄，海外宣傳を代行して以て若干の補助金を得ることに決定した。

尙長らく本局書記（會計係）として多難なる中を盡力された神田正法師は今回一身上の都合により九月十五日限りにて辭任された。同氏多年の盡力に對し，感謝の意を表す。

編輯後記

本號の緒方宗博師 "Zen, What Does it Mean to Western People?" は多年外人に禪の普及紹介に努められてゐる妙心寺派の同師が今年輕井澤に於て開催された第八回東洋文化夏期大學にて講演された原稿である。日本佛教の海外宣傳の貴重な文献であるが，殘り三頁程は次號に割愛した。この程度の長さのものは一度に掲載しなくては，文意も生らないのであるが，現在の紙面では止むを得ない。在支三年の福井氏の現代支那佛教事情は支那佛教の現狀，思想界の佛教關心を說いて殘すなく，從來一部の所謂支那佛通の傳へる誤れる觀察を是正して餘りある。時節柄，貴重な文献と思ふ。但し何分にも講演筆記故，人名書名に多少誤らなきかと恐れる。

來月號は局報通り，正義日本を海外に宣揚する支那事變號である。多分海外發送用の英文のみとなり，經費の許す限り增頁のスマートなものにしたいと思ふ。今號から感じが暗いといふ意見があつて，表紙の意匠を少し更へて見た。

本誌の内容が英和文混合で，どうもぬえ式存在に思はれてならない。從つて誰に讀ませるのか，目標が判然としないのだ。幹事會でも問題になつたのだが，英文と和文とを分離して，英文は在留外人と海外とのみを目指し，和文は和文のみの號を數回出すとするか，『靑年佛徒』に廻したらいゝと思ふが，一般の御意見如何？　これでは外人には一寸見せられない。或ひは季刊にでもしてもつと有力な充實的なものを出せ，といふ意見もある位である。(T.B.)

定價	一部	金二十錢	送料五厘
	一年	金二圓四拾錢	送料不要

昭和十年四月卅日第三種郵便物認可
昭和十二年九月十二日印刷（每月一回）
昭和十二年九月十五日發行（十五日發行）

東京市外吉祥寺337
編輯發行兼印刷人　淺野研眞

東京市牛込區早稻田鶴卷町107
印刷所　株式會社康文社印刷所
電話牛込（34）1950番 5049番

東京市神田區一ツ橋二の三
發行所　國際佛教通報局
電話九段（33）4428番
振替東京83015番

昭和十年四月三十日第三種郵便物認可　昭和十二年十一月十二日印刷納本　昭和十二年十一月十五日發行（毎月一回十五日發行）第三卷　第十號

國際佛教通報

第三卷　昭和十二年十・十一月　第十號

The International Buddhist Bulletin

[Vol. III. November $\frac{2503}{1937}$ No. 10.]

The International Buddhist Information Bureau
II—3, Hitotsubashi, Kanda, Tokyo,
Annual Subscription, ¥2.60 (with post), Single Copy 20 sen (post 2 sen)

東京　國際佛教通報局　發行

昭和十年四月三十日第三種郵便物認可
昭和十二年九月十二日印刷納本（毎月一回
昭和十二年九月十五日發行　十五日發行）　國際佛教通報　第三卷　第九號

謹告

拜啓　初秋之砌　高堂益々御清榮之段奉賀上候

陳者今回『國際佛教通報』誌上に尊宗教義に關する英文原稿を掲載、且尊宗貴山の重要ニユースを毎號報道致し尊派の海外宣傳機關の職能の一端、貴寺海外紹介の機能の一部をも相果したく、就ては右原稿ニユース等を御寄與・御提供の上、格別の御後援の程懇願申上候

追而來十月號は『支那事變號』特輯と致可、貴宗貴團體の時局活動御報知被成下候は幸甚に奉存候

昭和十二年九月

國際佛教通報局長
大谷瑩潤

各宗本山
大寺名刹　御中
佛教團體

追而御後援に對しては右に相當する部數の「國際佛教通報」を進呈申上げて宜敷候

廣告

一、今回篤志の御方に本局後援の目的を以て、左の如く
一、月額五圓（雜誌刊行書進呈、年賀暑中廣告掲載）
一、年額拾圓（雜誌進呈、年賀・暑中廣告掲載）
の御寄附を御願ひし、本局の經營を御後援願ひたく存じます。局よりは「國際佛教通報」其他刊行書を寄贈申上げ、年二回年賀・暑中の廣告を御掲載申上げることと致します。右に關し局員參堂の折は宜しく御引見の程願上げます。

二、甚だ勝手ながら、誌代前金切れのお方は御拂込み下されば幸甚至極に存じます（後援者寄贈交換を除く）。督促がましく甚だ恐縮ですが、本年度より本局經營は自立自營と相成り、經營上誌代も相當期待すべき事態に相成りました現狀御賢察の上、本局御後援の思召を以て此段切に御送金願上げます。

追而御送金（一年分二圓四十錢）は振替東京八三〇一五番に願ひます。

御送金なき場合は集金郵便又は集金人を差上げますから、その折は宜しく御願申上げます。

昭和十二年九月

東京市神田區一ツ橋二ノ三
國際佛教通報局
電話九段(33)一四二八番
振替東京八三〇一五番

The International Buddhist Bulletin

A monthly Journal of the International Buddhist Information Bureau founded in memorium of 2nd Pan-Pacific Y. B. A. Conference.

Editor:
Tsūshyō Byodō

Contents

Rules Pertaining to Mangement

1. "The International Buddhist Bulletin" publishes articles dealing with Buddhism in all its aspects and with History, Art, Philosophy, Archaeology and Education of Japan. News of Buddhist activities all over the world is a special feature.
2. All articles, news items, etc. sent for publication are welcomed.
3. All communications about study and tour etc. in Japan are kindly answered in detail.
4. Change of Address must be immediately informed.
5. Subscriptions are payable annually in advance.

Annual Subscription ¥ 2.60	Advertisement rates	
(a copy 20 sen. Postage 2 sen)	Cover	¥ .50
copies more than 10 are	Full page	¥ .30
discounted	Half page	¥ .15

All communications should be addressed to — Editor, The International Buddhist Information Bureau, II—3, Hitotsubashi, Kanda, Tokio.

Zen, What Does it Mean to Western People? (II)

By **Sōhaku Ogata**

Ganyo, a learned Buddhist theologist, came to Jyoshu, a famous Zen master in T'ang dynasty, and asked: "Zen teaching emphasises to get rid of every idea of definition. Am I right when I have no idea?" Jyoshu: "Throw away that idea of yours." Ganyo: "I have told you I had no idea. What can I throw away?" Jyoshu: "You are of course free to carry around that useless idea of no idea." Whereupon Ganyo came to the sense of satori.

Eastern thought, on the contrary, is predominately and always associated with action. The fundamental essence of eastern thought is something more than mere intellect, which is called kokoro or shin in Chinese. Kokoro literally means mind, heart, and spirit. Michi or Tao in Chinese is the synonym of hsin the literal meaning of which is way or path. It signifies universal being, at the same time personal or individual existence. To realize unity between this universal being and our individual mind is the main aim of all eastern teaching. Confucius says: "What Heaven has conferred is called 'Nature'; To walk in accordace with this nature is called The Path of Duty; the regulation of this path is called Instruction. The path may not be left for an instant. If it could be left, it would not be the path. Therefore, the superior man does not wait till he sees things, in order to be cautions; nor waits till he hears things, to be apprehensive." (The Doctrine of the Mean.) Therefore, Confucius's Teaching is called Dogaku, (way learning) or Shingaku (mind learning). Eisai, the pioneer Zen master of Japan, says: "Oh, how great the kokoro is." Impossible, to exhaust the hight of the heaven, yet the kokoro reaches beyond the heaven. Impossible, to fathom the depth of the earth, yet the kokoro gets below the earth. Impossible, to pass beyond the light of sun and moon, yet the kokoro reaches further. Impossible, to exhaust the great universes which are as many as the sands of Ganges River, yet the kokoro embraces them all. ....Oh, how great the kokoro is! There is no name for it. And I shall necessarily call it by names such as the first principle, the true form of wisdom, and the wonderful mind of nirvāṇa. Lord Buddha handed it down to Mahāka'syapa calling it "A Special Transmission outside the Scriptures." And this very same teaching Bodhidharma brought to China, from there it afterward reached Japan. It contains all vehicles for enlightenment. This is what is called Zen." To realize this kokoro, that is, to experience the unity of man and God is really the Alpha and Omega of study.

Well, let us look upon the present stage of the world's history. The scientific thought of the West in recent years has created the so called material civilization, and has challenged the whole world. The spiritual civilization which has developed in the East since thousands of years seemed to have been subdued by it. However, look, in what condition are we? What will happen to us to-morrow? What cynicism, that an airoplane, the wonderful child of the twentieth century should attack modern cities, the brothers of its very producers!

So what we are earnestly desiring and longing for is some sort of new civilization, a civilization in which both forces "intellect" and "intuition" will in their manifestation combine and attain "kokoro" to the ultimate well-being of every one and all. Consequently we look to Buddhism, and especially to its form of Zen.

5. The Way to Zen.

Zen is not a religion in the sense that the term is popularly understood; for Zen has no God to worship, no ceremonial rites to observe, no future abode to which the dead are destined, and, last of all, Zen has no soul whose welfare is to be looked after by somebody else and whose immortality is a matter of intense concern with some people. Zen is free from all these dogmatic and "religious" encumbrances. And this irreligion of Zen is what appeals to most western people. So when they find the images of various Buddhas and Bodhisattvas in Zen temples they are quite surprised. They cannot see why they are expected to attend the services in the morning and in the evening while staying in the monasteries. Even when they understand intellectually the inner significance of those images and ceremonial rites, yet their hearts do not

agree with the observance of such monkey business as sūtra-chanting and image-worshipping. They can not reconcile the teachings found in old Zen literature which aims at abolishing all these rites with the practice found in modern Zen temples, and consequently are assailed by sincere doubts. Then, what is the means of attainment to satori, the goal of Zen?

In fact, there is no way to Zen as Mumon says in the Introduction to his book, "Mumonkan", one of the two most important Zen texts: "Buddha mind Zen takes as its essential principle. No gate it takes as its gate. There is really no gate. How one passes through this gateless gate? Some say that whatever enters through a gate is not family treasure." However, here is an interesting story:

Daie was one of the most famous Zen masters under the Sun dynasty. Under him, there was a monk, called Doken, who had been practicing Zen meditation for many years, and yet had not gained satori, the enlightenment. One day he was told to go on an errand to some distant place the journey to which would have taken more than half a year. He became deeply anxious, whether this journey would not prevent him from keeping up his Zen practice. Taking pity on him, Sogen, a brother monk of his, offered to go with him and to do for him whatever he could in order that Doken might be able to continue his meditation on the journey. So the two of them started together on the trip.

One evening, Doken, with a heavy heart, asked the kind brother, "Won't you be so kind to give me some indication as to the attainment to satori?" "I certainly desire to do for you every thing in my power," answered Sogen, "yet there are a few things that I absolutely cannot do, in your stead." "What are they?" "My eating and drinking will mean nothing to you when you are hungry and thirsty. Neither can I go to the latrine for you when you are called by nature." This conversation gave some light to Doken's mind, and he said. "I can never be too thankful to you. Brother, for your kindness of enlightening me." "I am very glad to have finished my job," said Sogen, "Hereafter you can proceed on your journey by yourself." And they departed from one anther, each on his way.

If there is any help or stimulation to be got in Zen study, it would be instruction through personal example. Consequently personal contact with a master is very essential in Zen study. And one's own master should be chosen according to his or her temperament.

On the Buddhism in America

a Letter from American Buddhist Preacher

Goldwater, Shaku Jukō

Gentlemen :—

With much interest do I read each month those articles appearing in your periodical and have from time to time wished to communicate my appreciation, but now that one of the articles has an especially bitter tone, and being selfishly provoked by it : i.e. that lack of understanding within myself, I am taking this opportunity to address you.

Although I have had only a few times been in the presence of the avid writer of the paper in English in your August issue, I could well feel the intensity of his honest and sincere devotion to our great religion Buddhism, and I was better for knowing him this little. Reverend Mutoku Hayashi has however permitted his opinionated ideas too great an unlimited field to permit acceptance by any sane-minded Buddhist.

There can be no doubt that we have in Buddhism many frauds as as any large body must admit it contains of necessity because of its hugeness a certain percentage of incompletely trained leaders. This is most unfortunate. Since I am an American and the charge is against those priests who come to my country and teach Buddhism for those who will accept it, I feel that possibly I may be one of the few people who might answer without offense or personal bias.

The late Bishop Yemo Imamura accepted and promoted with much fine success the activities of Buddhism in English amongst both the Bussei and those Americans who through interest or curiosity later developed a better understanding of this most noble religion. Dr. Enerst H. Hunt taught for many years in the Hawaiian Islands together with his sweet wife Dorothy. It was there over ten years ago I first learned of Buddhism and later became a Buddhist wholeheartedly with happiness

in my heart. From here groups opened up thruout the United States for English-speaking peoples. It is true that even before this, there were scattered attempts to develop a live interest. Mr. A Zorn of California, a Rev. Gruille, a Rev. Kirby, Dr. Dwight Goddard and Mrs. Miriam Salanave are amongst a few names who come to me just now. There were many others, all working with the main purpose of establishing Buddhism here. These peoples worked withwhom they could obtain some cooperation and the only one withwhom they could obtain both cooperation and the necessary freedom to adapt primitive Buddhism into Western conceptuology according to their understandings was the Hongwanji movement. There was one exception to this, and that one was that individual Zen monk Nyogen Senzaki who always offered his assistance to teach and to learn. Since the early beginnings of some thirty years ago, that mark Dr Goddard's pioneering, there have been many Occidentals helped gently with wisdom by various Japanese priests. There have been many Occidentals who have failed as there have been several Japanese priests of too business-like acumen for religious welfare, and these no doubt are the ones to which Reverend Hayashi refers so graphically.

There is no doubt that Nyogen Senzaki has and is still performing a very great service to his fellow creatures and although I fear we are not always so grateful as we should be, Nyogen Senzaki being the great teacher certainly knows gratefulness is not to forthcoming, merely that each must live in accordance to the finest that the teachings he brings to us will permit. This is his greatness.

The constant money-bringingness that is mentioned so much may be admitted with one reservation. I dare presume that because of Reverend Hayashi's constant contact with the suttas that he assumes others too have become staid; this is not actually the case. We in the Hongwanji as well as in most of the Japanese Buddhist sects in America have many Gatherings for different purposes such as Memorial, Weddings, Funereals, etc., and at such times it is often the habit of many who come to leave some money and gifts in appreciation or even in exchange. After all, some people must earn money, some must till the soil, some must weave and some must study the laws by which to wisely govern.

Is it not fair and honourable to exchange amongst all such occupations the fruits of labour? Personally, I have met no priest who was at anytime unwilling to explain any portion of the teachings to any who should be so interested. I do not mean that any priest is so well prepared, I mean that all are willing to do what they can for the eradication of ignorance and the replacement of truth or enlightenment. It does follow that each may have his own interpretation and if this be true, no doubt Reverend Hayashi will not mind my assertion that he has been too ensocopic in making his declaration.

May I say in closing that I hope such fearlessness will be continued by many Japanese Buddhist priests as Reverend Hayashi has exhibited, but that it be better founded before leaving the limited horizon of a personal mind. We Buddhists do need just such honesty and sincere devotion to truth as this leader has shown himself capable of, but in addition and almost more important, is the foundation of "door bases" by which the proper channel for the most good and least harm such power may be used.

next number

(December)

"China Incident"

(Special number)

歐米佛教事情

鷹谷俊之

一 歐米の佛教と日本

國外に於ける佛教の活動狀況を知ることは誠に至難なことであるが，その困難に拘らず尙ほ且つ其の事情を知つて之と連絡し提携して共々に進んで行きたいと思ふのが吾々の人情であるから，日頃の寸暇を割いて私は多少ともこの方面の事情に耳を傾けて來たのである。先年國際佛教通報局の名の下に國の內外に向つて調査事項を記入して貰ふやうに依頼狀を發したが，百數十通の發送に對し回答を得たのは僅か八通に過ぎなかつた事を思ふと，大凡その間の事情を想像することが出來るやうに，人は自分の專門とする方面以外には中々氣が寄らないものである。それに曾て外國に留學して彼地の佛教界の事情に多少とも通じて居つた筈の人も歸朝後自分の專門の範圍內に立て籠つて研究に多忙であるところから年が經つにつれてその事情に疎くなるのである。又國外の佛教團體も或は起り或は消え失せて種々の變化を示して居るので，日本の寺院について吾々が考へて居るやうな常恒性を持つて居ない場合の方が多いのである。例へばドイツのダールケ博士病歿のあとはフローナウの「佛教の家」が經濟的に危機に立つたり，ロンドンに蟠居したダンマパーラ師の大菩提會も，師の歿後ブロードン氏の如き支持者があつて經濟的には大して支障が無くても往年の覇氣を失ふて居るが如きであるから，容易に其の現狀を知悉する譯にはゆかないのである。殊に歐米に於ける佛教は其の地盤が極めて脆弱であつて日本の如く佛教信者と云ふ大衆に立つた佛教ではなく，大學の研究室に於ける佛教研究，國庫補助による佛教研究乃至は特殊の熱心なる求道者の小さな團體の外はセイロンやシヤムあたりからの資金による傳道を意味する佛教團體であるから，その中心人物の喪失は同時にその佛教團體の解消を意味するのである。日本では眞に佛教の爲めになる事であるならば運動であらうと著述であらうと講演であらうと，これを待ち望む大衆を控へて居ることであるから，其事業も甚しく悲境に沈むと云ふことはないのであるし，或る程度の完結を見ることが出來るのである。

斯樣な一應の考慮の上に歐米の佛教を見るにしても，日本に居つて彼地の事情を知り得る場合は著述の涉獵，知友の通信，彼我文化交換の支點等に就いて常にその動きを見るより外はない。この見方は疎雜ではあるが，視野は廣くなる。現に國外に在る者の調査は滯在國に限定されるから，その視野は深いけれども狹いと云ふ難は免れ難いのである。それ故この兩者を常に併用しつつ觀察する必要があることは云ふまでもない。然し近來日本の地に在つて彼地の事情を聞き得る場合が餘程多くなつたのは誠に慶賀すべき事で，これは日本の國力が大に起つて來たことによるのであるが，別しては日本の佛教が重きをなしつつある左證と見ることが出來る。

この一ケ年の間にローマ大學教授トゥチ博士，印度カルカック大學ナリナクシャ・ダット博士及ベルリン大學のエドワルド・シュプランガー博士，ハンガリー東洋美術館長ゾルクン博士等の來朝があり，その他大小數々の白人士が此國の文化特に佛教を求めてやつて來ると云ふ有樣である。前三者はいづれも我國佛教の碩學と數回に亘り佛教研究上の疑義を質し，意見を交換して頗る滿足して歸國した樣子である。尤もシュプランガー博士は日獨文化協會長としてグンデルト博士の跡を襲ひ，一ケ年の任期中は日本に滯在することであるから，同博士の專攻たる歷史哲學の分野にも佛教の見解が從來よりも一段と濃く織り込まれ，取容れられるのでないかと思はれる。これらの來朝者が期せずして「物を持たざる國」からの賓客である點で一致して居るのは偶然の出來事ではないであらう。「物は持たない」が，いづれも新興國の意氣に燃え，より高き理想への憧憬から遙々と吾國へ佛教探求の航海をなし來つたと見てよからう。それは兎も角彼我の交涉が日々と深くなり佛教への理解が漸次高まりつつあることは事實である。

二　歐米に於ける佛教研究

歐米佛教の發端は歐洲人の東洋進出殊にイギリスの印度領有に始まると見ねばならぬ。即ち一七七三年ヘスチングスが印度の初代總督になつた時代を契機として居るかと思はれる。殖民政策の推行にはその國の文化一般の攷究を必要とし，言語・風俗・習慣から文學・宗教・哲學の領域にまで進まねばならなかつた。加ふるにこの必要性は當時西歐に勃興した地上の探求欲と相並んで智識の寶庫を開扉せんとする意欲に訴へられたから，忽ち燎原の火の如くに印度文化の檢討が燃え上つたのである。出先に於ける研究は本國の大學に飛火し，彼此相呼應して益々火の手を上げ，初めは考古的收集の域を脫せなかつたものが發掘・地理・歷史・言語・制度等の綜合的文化の研究に進み，反轉して專門的各部門の研究に移り，英佛獨露和白墺伊米など夫々一騎當千の學者がこれに專注し，その眞面目にして地味な研究は遂によく土語の誤解からパリー語やサンスクリット・西藏語やタムル語などの言語に先ずることを得，その結果佛教の存在を發見し，大小乘教の各經典に於ける思想體系をも見出し，從來西歐の學壇に前例なき思想的寶庫の鍵を得，絢爛の狀を呈した。これが進んでは漢譯經典の涉獵となり，遂には日本佛教の存在

的意義をも理解せんとする域にまで到達したのである。それ故この凡そ二百年が間には印度學研究時代，言語思想の研究時代，佛教研究時代，日本佛教研究時代の四段階の躍進を見せて居るが，その研究態度は飽迄で健實な科學的研究に立つて居ると云ふ點でそれまでの日本に於ける佛學研究とは大分趣を異にしたものであり，その見る角度も從つて多岐であつたから，日本佛教徒に對しても指導的立場にあつたのは當然であつた。日本の佛教徒はこの科學的研究の風を仰いで明治初年以來續々と歐洲に赴いたが，その目的は多く言語と方法論の研究にあつたので，佛教其物に就ての教を仰いだといふよりは佛教の眞諦については寧ろ彼地の學者を啓蒙した點も尠からずあつたと思はれる。それ故言語と方法論との研究を一應終つた日本の佛教學者は歸國の後自國の傳統と資料とを使驅し，屢ば世界的の研究を發表して歐米の學壇を驚かしたのである。斯樣にして日本と歐米の學壇が一先づ平均されて來ると，佛教思想の理解得達の深淺が問題になつて來る。これが現今日本佛教の特に重んぜられる重大な理由である。然しながら泰西の學者がよく困難に耐え，千古の寶庫を開扉して之を吾國にも寄與した功績と恩惠とに對しては充分の敬意を拂はねばならぬであらう。

三　歐米に於ける實踐的佛教

教味得の狀態即ち實踐的佛教は如何であるかと云ふ點を述べて見よう。これは世界大戰後西歐文明沒落の聲と共に漸次擡頭して來たかに見へる。思想的模索が佛教を見出したのである。尤もこれに助緣となつたものは前々からの佛教研究とセイロンやビルマ等南方系佛教徒の歐洲進出であつた。それ故西歐の實踐佛教の大部分が小乘的傾向の强いものであつて，禁欲生活と坐禪とによる心の平靜を得んとするものである。尤も大乘禪の鑽仰者が歐洲にも米大陸にも最近著く增加し來つたことは事實であらうが，それでもまだまだ一般には前者の範圍を出でないのである。歐洲では研究佛教も實踐佛教も共に特殊の人々を除いては小乘佛教の影響を多量に受けて居ることは人の多く指摘するところである。この點アメリカの佛教は一寸趣きを異にして居る。アメリカでは佛教研究の分野に於ても西歐とは遙かに遲れて居たし，其の業績に於ても殊更に見るべきものが少い。從つて西歐の如く小乘佛教の浸潤も亦稀薄であるが，幸ひこの國へは日本から鈴木大拙博士を初め其他の諸師が白人間に喰ひ入つて多年感化を與へて來た關係もあつてか，大乘禪の鑽仰者が大分あるやうである。ドワイト・ゴダード翁の如き特殊の禪鑽仰家が出て居る。總じて云へば此の國は日本と一葦帶水の地であるから，彼我文物の交流は歐洲よりも頻繁である。日本より赴くにしてもアメリカより來るにしても，容易である。京都八幡の圓福寺に外人の專門道場が開設されて居るが，これに投ずる人々にはアメリカの男女が多いと聞く。然しアメリカの佛教が悉く禪

である譯でもなければ上記の少數者がアメリカ佛教を開拓したと云ふ譯でもない。シカゴではマック・ガバーン氏が大學の講壇に立ちつつ，旁々念佛中心の集りを開くと云つて居り，桑港では西本願寺佛教會が中心になつて白人佛教を指導しつつあり，往年ハワイに發詳した白人佛教は＝ューヨークもその種子を卸して居る筈だから，漸次この方面の佛教も立ち上つて來ることと思はれる。八月號の「通報」には「アメリカ佛教の管見」が載せられ，日本佛教開教事情に觸れて劈頭から手非度く共態度の非なることを指摘されて居るやうであるが，これも見解の相異で如何やうにも考へられることであり，又日本佛教のアメリカ移入について特に禪に關係ある五氏のみを擧げられたのも，窮屈過ぎるやうに思はれるが，然し故國を離れ，海外に於て不惜身命の敎化を布いて居られる方々に對しても頭が下るのである。

之を要するに歐米に於ける佛教は研究の佛教は於てもそうであるが，實踐佛教に於ては是非とも日本佛教が指導すべきである。從來の歐米佛教の狀態を以て決して滿足すべきではない。要するに歐米佛教の實踐面に於ては未だ未だ序幕に過ぎない。

國際佛教通報局定款

名　　稱

第一，本局を國際佛教通報局と稱す

事務所

第二，本局の事務所を全日本佛教青年會聯盟事務局に置く

目　　的

第三，本局は日本內地及海外に向つて佛教事情の通報をなし，且つ佛教徒相互間の各種便宜を計るを以て目的とす

事　　業

第四，本局の目的を達成するため左記の事業を行ふ

イ，日本內地及世界各國より佛教事情に關する質問の通報を行ふ

ロ，必要に應じ日本語及世界各國語を以て佛教事情の通報を行ふ

ハ，外國人の日本觀光に際しては各種の便益を與へ，特にその佛教に關する方面に於て之を爲す

ニ，定時或は臨時に各國語を以て文書の刊行をなす

ホ，その他必要と認めたる事業を行ふ

役　　員

第五，本局の事務を處理するため左の役員を置く

イ，名譽局長　　一　名

ロ，顧　問　　若干名

ハ，局　長　　一　名

ニ，幹　事　　若干名

ホ，理　事　　若干名

局長は本局の事務を總括す

幹事は本局の事務を處理す

理事は局長の提案に依る重要事務を審議す

第六，理事は左記の者を以て之に充つ

イ，全日本佛教青年會聯盟理事及主事

ロ，全日本佛教青年會聯盟理事會に於て推薦したる者

第七，局長及幹事は理事會に於て決定す

第八，名譽局長及顧問は理事會に於て推薦す

第九，役員の任期は一ケ年とす（但し重任を妨げず）

經　　費

第十，本局の經費は左記のものに依て之を支辨す

イ，本局基金の活用

ロ，寄附金

ハ，その他の收入

補　　則

第十一，本定款に記載せられざる事項は，凡て理事會に於て協議す

第十二，第一回の役員は全日本佛教青年會聯盟理事會に於て決定す

定價			
	一部	金二十錢	送料五厘
	一年	金二圓四拾錢	送料不要

昭和十年四月卅日第三種郵便物認可
昭和十二年十一月十二日印刷（毎月一回）
昭和十二年十一月十五日發行（十五日發行）

神奈川縣都筑郡新田村新羽2398
編輯發行兼印刷人　平等通昭

東京市牛込區早稻田鶴卷町107
印刷所　株式會社康文社印刷所
電話牛込（34）1950番 5049番

東京市神田區一ツ橋二の三
發行所　國際佛教通報局
電話九段（33）4428番
振替東京83015番

昭和十年四月三十日第三種郵便物認可　昭和十二年十一月十二日印刷納本（每月一回）　昭和十二年十一月十五日發行（十五日發行）

謹告

拝啓　時下清穆之候　高堂益々御清榮之段奉賀上候

陳者今回『國際佛教通報』誌上に尊宗教義に關する英文原稿を掲載、且尊宗貴山の重要ニュースを毎號報道致し尊派の海外宣傳機關の職能の一端、貴寺海外紹介の機能の一部をも相果したく、就ては右原稿・ニュース等を御寄與・御提供の上、格別の御後援の程懇願申上候

追而來十二月號及び二月號は『支那事變號』特輯と致可、貴宗貴團體の時局活動御報知被成下候は幸甚に奉存候

昭和十二年十一月

國際佛教通報局長

大谷瑩潤

各宗本山
大寺名刹
佛教團體
御中

追而御後援に對しては右に相當する部數の「國際佛教通報」を進呈申上げて宜敷候

廣告

一、今回篤志の御方に本局後援の目的を以て、左の如く

一、月額五圓　（雜誌刊行書進呈、年賀暑中廣告掲載）

一、年額拾圓　（雜誌進呈、年賀・暑中廣告掲載）

の御寄附を御願ひし、本局の經營を御後援願ひたく存じます。局よりは「國際佛教通報」其他刊行書を寄贈申上げ、年二回年賀・暑中の廣告を御掲載申上げることと致します。右に關し局員參堂の折は宜しく御引見の程願上げます。

二、甚だ勝手ながら、誌代前金切れのお方は御拂込み下されば幸甚至極に存じます（後援者寄贈交換を除く）。督促がましく甚だ恐縮ですが、本年度より本局經營は自立自營と相成り、經營上誌代も相當期待すべき事態に相成りました現狀御賢察の上、本局御後援の思召を以て此段切に御送金願上げます。

追而御送金（一年分二圓四十錢）は振替東京八三〇一五番に願ひます。

御送金なき場合は集金郵便又は集金人を差上げますから、その折は宜しく御願申上げます。

昭和十二年十一月

東京市神田區一ツ橋二ノ三

國際佛教通報局

電話九段(33)一四二八番
振替東京八三〇一五番

龍谷大学アジア仏教文化研究叢書　刊行の辞

龍谷大学は、寛永十六年（一六三九）に西本願寺の阿弥陀堂北側に創設された「学寮」を淵源とする大学です。その後、明治維新を迎えると学制の改革が行われ、学寮も大教校と名を変え、さらに真宗学庠、大学林、仏教専門学校、仏教大学と名称を変更し、大正十一年（一九二二）に今の「龍谷大学」となりました。

その間、三七〇余年もの長きにわたって仏教の研鑽が進められ、龍谷大学は高い評価を得てまいりました。そして平成二十七年四月、本学の有する最新の研究成果を国内外に発信するとともに仏教研究の国際交流の拠点となるべき新たな機関として、本学に「龍谷大学世界仏教文化研究センター」が設立されました。龍谷大学アジア仏教文化研究センターは、そのような意図のもと設立された世界仏教文化研究センターの傘下にある研究機関です。

世界仏教文化研究センターが設立されるにあたって、その傘下にあるアジア仏教文化研究センターは、文部科学省の推進する「私立大学戦略的研究基盤形成支援事業」に、「日本仏教の通時的・共時的研究―多文化共生社会における課題と展望―」と題する研究プロジェクト（平成二十七年度～平成三十一年度）を申請し、採択されました。

本研究プロジェクトは、龍谷大学が三七〇余年にわたって研鑽し続けてきた日本仏教の成果を踏まえ、これをさらに推進し、日本仏教を世界的視野から通時的共時的にとらえるとともに、日本仏教が直面する諸課題を多文化共生の文脈で学際的に追究し、今後の日本仏教の持つ意義を展望するものです。このような研究のあり方を有機的に進めるため、本研究プロジェクトでは通時的研究グループ（ユニットＡ「日本仏教の形成と展開」、ユニットＢ「近代日本仏教と国際社会」）と共時的研究グループ（ユニットＡ「現代日本仏教の社会性・公益性」、ユニットＢ「多文化共生社会における日本仏教の課題と展望」）の二つに分け、基礎研究等に基づく書籍の刊行や講演会等による研究成果の公開などの諸事業を推進していくことになりました。

このたび刊行される『資料集・戦時下「日本仏教」の国際交流』第Ⅲ期「中国仏教との提携」は、右のような研究プロジェクトの成果の一つであり、第Ⅱ期「南方仏教圏との交流」に次ぐ「龍谷大学アジア仏教文化研究叢書」の第四号となります。今後とも、世界仏教文化研究センターの傘下にあるアジア仏教文化研究センターが、日本仏教をテーマとして国内外に発信する諸成果に、ご期待いただければ幸いです。

平成二十九年九月一日

龍谷大学アジア仏教文化研究センター
センター長　楠　淳證

編者紹介

中西直樹（なかにし　なおき）
1961年生まれ。龍谷大学文学部教授、仏教史学専攻
主要編著
『仏教海外開教史の研究』（不二出版、2012年）
『植民地台湾と日本仏教』（三人社、2016年）
『令知会と明治仏教』（不二出版、2017年）

林　行夫（はやし　ゆきお）
1955年生まれ。龍谷大学文学部教授、文化人類学専攻
主要編著
『＜境域＞の実践宗教—大陸部東南アジア地域と宗教のトポロジー』（京都大学学術出版会、2009年）
『新アジア仏教史04—スリランカ・東南アジア』（佼成出版社、2011年）
『衝突と変奏のジャスティス』（青弓社、2016年）

吉永進一（よしなが　しんいち）
1957年生まれ。舞鶴工業高等専門学校教授、宗教学専攻
主要編著
『Religion and Psychotherapy in Modern Japan』（Routledge、2015年）
『仏教国際ネットワークの源流—海外宣教会(1888年～1893年)の光と影』（三人社、2015年）
『近代仏教スタディーズ』（法藏館、2016年）

大澤広嗣（おおさわ　こうじ）
1976年生まれ。文化庁文化部宗務課専門職、宗教学専攻
主要編著
『戦時下の日本仏教と南方地域』（法藏館、2015年）
『仏教をめぐる日本と東南アジア地域—アジア遊学196—』（勉誠出版、2016年）
「アメリカ施政下の沖縄における宗教制度—琉球政府の施策と行政—」（『武蔵野大学仏教文化研究所紀要』第32号、2016年）

（龍谷大学アジア仏教文化研究叢書4）
編集復刻版　資料集・戦時下「日本仏教」の国際交流
第Ⅲ期　中国仏教との提携
（第6巻・第7巻）

2017年9月1日　第1刷発行
揃定価（本体46,000円＋税）
第6巻 ISBN978-4-8350-7865-6
第Ⅲ期（全2冊 分売不可 セット ISBN978-4-8350-7864-9）

編者　龍谷大学アジア仏教文化研究センター
「戦時下「日本仏教」の国際交流」研究班（G1・UB・S2）
中西直樹（代表）・林行夫・吉永進一・大澤広嗣
発行者　小林淳子
発行所　不二出版
東京都文京区向丘1-2-12
TEL 03（3812）4433
印刷所　富士リプロ
製本所　青木製本
乱丁・落丁はお取り替えいたします。